P9-ANZ-236

The late Bengt Sundkler was the leading authority on African Christian Churches, and he pioneered the study of Independent Churches in Africa. He had a long career as a missionary, in South Africa and in Tanzania, and he became the first Lutheran Bishop of Bukoba in Tanzania, before returning to Sweden as Professor in Church History at the University of Uppsala. Christopher Steed was Bengt Sundkler's research assistant, and he currently teaches African history at the University of Uppsala.

In this magisterial work, Sundkler and Steed review the entire history of the development of Christianity in all regions of the continent. In contrast to the conventional focus on the missionary enterprise, they place the African converts at the centre of the study. African Christians, typically drawn from the margins of the society, reinterpreted the Christian message, proselytized, governed local congregations, and organized Independent Churches. Emphasizing African initiatives in the process of Christianization, Sundkler and Steed argue that its development was shaped by African kings and courts, the history of labour migration, and local experiences. of colonization. This long-awaited book will become the standard reference text on African Christian Churches.

A HISTORY OF THE CHURCH IN AFRICA

BENGT SUNDKLER AND CHRISTOPHER STEED

In honour and memory of Bengt Sundkler, who was the founder of Studia Missionalia Upsaliensia and the editor of its first twenty-seven volumes, *A History of the Church in Africa* is also included in that series.

Cambridge University Press acknowledges with gratitude the generous assistance it has received towards its publication from the Swedish Council for Research in the Humanities and Social Sciences, the Swedish Mission Council, the Faculty of Theology – Leander Foundation for Mission Research, University of Uppsala, the Church of Sweden Mission, the Finnish Missionary Society, and the Swedish International Development Authority (SIDA).

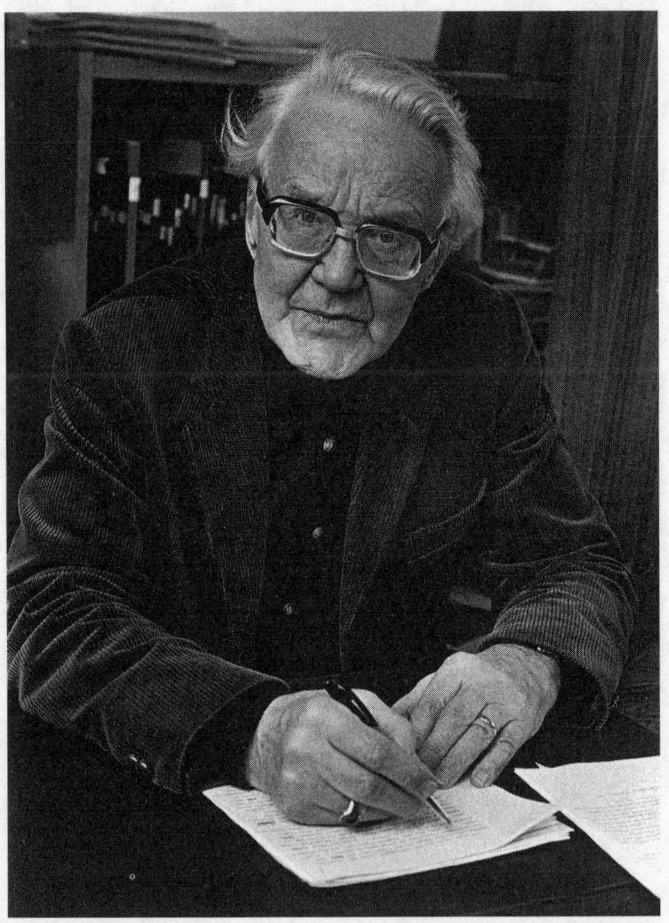

Bengt Sundkler 1909–1995

A HISTORY OF THE CHURCH IN AFRICA

BENGT SUNDKLER

AND

CHRISTOPHER STEED

PUBLISHED BY THE PRESS SYNDICATE OF THE UNIVERSITY OF CAMBRIDGE
The Pitt Building, Trumpington Street, Cambridge CB2 1RP, United Kingdom

CAMBRIDGE UNIVERSITY PRESS
The Edinburgh Building, Cambridge CB2 2RU, United Kingdom
40 West 20th Street, New York, NY 10011–4211, USA
10 Stamford Road, Oakleigh, Melbourne 3166, Australia

First published 2000

Printed in the United Kingdom at the University Press, Cambridge

Typeset in Fournier 11/13 pt. [CE]

A catalogue record for this book is available from the British Library

Library of Congress cataloging in publication data

Sundkler, Bengt, 1909–1995
A history of the Church in Africa / Bengt Sundkler and Christopher Steed.
p. cm.
Includes bibliographical references and index.
ISBN 0 521 58342 X (hardback)
1. Christianity – Africa. 2. Africa – Church history.
I. Steed, Christopher. II. Title.
BR1360.S86 2000
276–dc21 97-15777 CIP

ISBN 0 521 58342 X hardback

CONTENTS

PART III: THE LONG NINETEENTH CENTURY 1787–1919

MAPS

The maps only include place names and ethnic groups referred to in the text.

ACKNOWLEDGEMENTS

We acknowledge with thanks the diligent service provided by the following research libraries: Carolina Rediviva – Uppsala University Library, and the Nordic Africa Institute, also in Uppsala; the Statsbibliotek, Aarhus; and the School of Oriental and African Studies, London. We record our debt to the following mission archives: the Holy Ghost Fathers at Chevilly-Larue, Paris; the White Fathers, and the Capuchin Historical Institute, both in Rome; the Jesuits at Heverlee, Louvain; the Paris Evangelical Missionary Society; the Church Missionary Society, now located at Birmingham University Library; the United Society for the Propagation of the Gospel, kept at Rhodes House Library, Oxford; the London Missionary Society (now the Council for World Mission), and the Methodist Missionary Society, both deposited with the School of Oriental and African Studies, London; Action Partners (formerly the Sudan United Mission), Bawtry, near Doncaster; the American Board, New York. We are very grateful for the financial support received from the Swedish Council for Research in the Humanities and Social Sciences, Stockholm, and the Church of Sweden Mission, Uppsala.

Before his death, Bengt Sundkler had worked for over a decade and a half on researching and writing this African church history. With such a lengthy period of preparation, it was perhaps inevitable that the scholarly apparatus of such a large book became both exceedingly complex and somewhat irregular. Since his passing in 1995, it has been necessary to review the accuracy of and complement the factual material presented, particularly with regard to source references and the system of notation references that Bengt left behind. Although these tasks have to a large extent been satisfactorily accomplished, there is a modicum of such references where it has proved impossible to give adequate source acknowledgement.

In the twenty years over which this book took form, we express our gratitude for the erudite counsel we have received from many scholars and friends around the world, both living and those now of blessed memory. This advice and guidance was particularly appreciated as invariably it was accompanied by an encouragement to us to persevere with writing this history of the Church in Africa, and by a forbearance with our many requests for information. Although many may have forgotten the help they once gave us, we wish to record our indebtedness to the following individuals:

In Australia: D. Dorward and Norman Etherington.

In Belgium: Fr François Bontinck, Fr Omer Degrijse, Fr P. Raymaekers, Fr Auguste Roeykens and Fr Marcel Storme.

In Cameroon: Jean Kotto and Fr Engelbert Mveng.

In Denmark: Johannes Aagaard, Holger Bernt Hansen, Hans Iversen, Lissi Rasmussen and Ane Marie Bak Rasmussen.

In Finland: Juhani Koponen, Henrik Smedjebacka, John Stotesbury and Lloyd Swantz.

In France: George Balandier, Fr Jean Barassin, Fr Paule Brasseur, Henri Brunschwig, Fr Paul Coulon, Catherine Coquery-Vidrovitch, Fr Joseph Cuoq, Joseph Ki-Zerbo, Fr Christian de Mare, Fr Bernard Noël, Françoise Raison-Jourde and François Renault.

In Germany: Heinrich Balz, Bairu Tafla, Hans Jürgen Becken, Peter Beyerhaus, Hans-Werner Gensichen, Erhard Kamphausen, Frieder Ludwig and Theo Sundermeier.

In Ghana: Christian Baeta, (and in France) Francis Bartels, Kwame Bediako and John Pobee.

In Great Britain: Archbishop Donald Arden, Bishop Simon Barrington-Ward, Brian Beck, David Birmingham, John Blacking, Bishop Stanley Booth-Clibborn, Brian Brown, Bishop Leslie Brown, Peter Clarke, Gervase Clarence-Smith, Kenneth Cracknell, Allan Easter, John Fage, W. Frend, Humphrey Fisher, Christopher Fyfe, G. S. P. Freeman-Grenville, Deborah Gaitskell, Paul Gifford, Sidney Groves, P. E. H. Hair, Andrew Hake, John Hargreaves, Adrian Hastings, Archbishop Trevor Huddleston, Cecilia Irvine, Douglas Johnson, (and in Malawi) Bishop Patrick Kalilombe, Rosemary Keen, Elliott Kendall, Martin Legassick, Ian Linden, John Lonsdale, John McCracken, Peter McKenzie, Fergus Macpherson, Shula Marks, Albert Mosley, J. D. Y. Peel, Margaret Peil, Louise Pirouet, Terence Ranger, Andrew Roberts, Andrew Ross, Isaac Schapera, George Shepperson, Fr Aylward Shorter, John Taylor, Jack Thompson, Michael Twaddle, (and in New Zealand) Harold Turner, Werner Ustorf, Andrew Walls, Richard Werbner and Jean Woods.

In Italy and the Vatican City: Teobaldo Filesi, Fr Willi Henkel, Fr René Lamey and Fr Josef Metzler.

In Kenya: Fr John Baur, (and in the United States) David Barrett, James Chege, Agnes Aboum, Jose Chipenda, John Gatu, Bishop David Gitari and Fr Arnold Groll.

In Nigeria: Jacob Ajayi, Emmanuel Ayandele, Fr Emefie Ikenga-Metuh, (and in New Zealand) Elizabeth Isichei, and Godwin Tasie.

In Norway: Sigmund Edland, Torstein Jørgensen, Ludvig Munthe, Olav G. Myklebust and Jarle Simensen.

In Sierra Leone: Edward Fasholé-Luke and Eldred Jones.

In South Africa: William Beinart, Sibusiso Bengu, David Bosch, Nancy Charton, D. Crafford, T. R. H. Davenport, Inus Daneel, Allie Dubb, Donald Cragg, Jeff Guy, Sheila Hindson-Meintjies, Janet Hodgson, J. W. Hofmeyr, Tom Lodge, Anne and Cecil Luck, G. E. van der Merwe, Bishop Stanley Mogoba, Beyers Naudé, Charles van Onselen, Gerhardus Oosthuizen, Jeffrey Peires, John Rees, Gabriel Setiloane, Peter Storey, Archbishop Robert Selby Taylor, Archbishop Desmond Tutu, Martin West, Michael Whisson, Donovan Williams, Francis Wilson and Monica Wilson.

In Sweden: Gustav Arén, Sigbert Axelson, Bishop Rune Backlund, Axel-Ivar Berglund, Jan Bergman, Ingrid Dahlqvist, Karl Eric Ericson, Ezra Gebremedhin, Alf Helgesson, Jan Henningsson, Carl-Johan Hellberg, Stiv Jakobsson, Anita Jacobson Widding, Bishop Jonas Jonson, David Lagergren, Aasulv Lande, Birgitta Larsson, Viveca Halldin Norberg, Björn Ryman, Birgitta Rubenson-Jonson, Samuel Rubenson and Sven Rubenson.

In Switzerland: Hans Debrunner and Paul Jenkins.

In Tanzania: Anza Lema, Wilson Niwagila and Fr Frits Versteijnen.

In the United States: Gerald Anderson, Thomas Beidelman, Henry Bucher, Willy de Craemer, Jean and John Comaroff, Mary Crawford, Donald Crummey, Richard Elphick, James Fernandez, Charles Forman, Dean Gilliland, Rosalind Hackett, Robert Hill, William Hutchison, Noël King, Janet and Wyatt MacGaffey, Phyllis Martin, Birger Pearson, Benjamin Ray, Lamin Sanneh, David Shank, Leonard Thompson, Jan Vansina and Marcia Wright.

In Zimbabwe: Canaan Banana, Ngwabi Bhebe, Ester Gwele, Elleck Mashingaidze, Wilson Nyilika, O. Ramushu and Archdeacon O. Somkence.

We especially wish to thank Aina Abrahamson and Krista Hurty Berglund for typing and revising drafts of the manuscript; Jocelyn Murray for assistance in the early stages of this book; Roland Oliver and Richard Gray for their close concern and encouragement; Jessica Kuper and the Syndics of the Cambridge University Press for their long sufferance with us and their dedication in seeing this book to press; Jenny Oates for her advice and acumen in copy-editing the final manuscript; and Carl Fredrik Hallencreutz and Marja-Liisa Swantz for steadfast support over many years.

ABBREVIATIONS

AACC	All Africa Conference of Churches
ABCFM	American Board of Commissioners for Foreign Missions
ABFMS	American Baptist Foreign Mission Society
AIM	Africa Inland Mission
AME	African Methodist Episcopal Church
AMECEA	Association of Members of Episcopal Conferences of Eastern Africa
AMEZ	African Methodist Episcopal Zion Church
BCMS	Bible Churchmen's Missionary Society
BFBS	British and Foreign Bible Society
BMS	Baptist Missionary Society
CICM	Congregation of the Immaculate Heart of Mercy – the Scheut Fathers
CMML	Christian Missions in Many Lands
CMS	Church Missionary Society
CR	Community of the Resurrection
CSSp	Holy Ghost Fathers (Spiritans)
DRC	Dutch Reformed Church
HGF	Holy Ghost Fathers (Spiritans)
IMC	International Missionary Council
LMS	London Missionary Society
LWF	Lutheran World Federation
MMS	Methodist Missionary Society
OMI	Oblates of Mary Immaculate
OSB	Benedictine Order
PEMS	Paris Evangelical Missionary Society
SACC	South African Council of Churches
SAGM	South Africa General Mission
SIM	Sudan Interior Mission
SJ	Jesuits – Society of Jesus
SMA	Society of African Missions

SPCK	Society for Promoting Christian Knowledge
SPG	Society for the Propagation of the Gospel in Foreign Parts
SUM	Sudan United Mission
SVD	Society of the Divine Word (Societas Verbi Divini)
TEF	Theological Education Fund
UBS	United Bible Societies
UMCA	Universities' Mission to Central Africa
USPG	United Society for the Propagation of the Gospel
WCC	World Council of Churches
WEC	Worldwide Evangelization Crusade
WF	Society of Missionaries of Africa (White Fathers)
WMMS	Wesleyan Methodist Missionary Society

INTRODUCTION

BENGT SUNDKLER

'A bitter pill which the majority of writers on Christianity and missionary activities in Africa should swallow is that they have not been writing African Church History.'[1] This statement by Professors J. F. Ade Ajayi and E. A. Ayandele must serve as an introductory remark to our Church history of Africa. The two Nigerian scholars developed their point by claiming that hitherto Church history had been written 'as if the Christian Church were in Africa, but not of Africa'.[2] It stressed the missionary presence while forgetting or neglecting whatever there was of an African initiative, an African dimension of African Church history. The sort of book which my Nigerian colleagues may have had in mind was not least the detailed and lengthy Mission histories, produced in the pre-Independence period and stamped by this fact. Of necessity this implied a view centred in some Western metropolis and in certain mission societies there. This view of Christianization was to treat it as a Western invasion in sub-Saharan Africa. The continent was mapped out according to mission societies and mission fields.

Confronted with the challenge of Professors Ajayi and Ayandele in the 1970s, I was asked to take on the task of writing a Church history of Africa, covering nearly 2,000 years and an entire continent. How could one attempt this? History, I realized is somehow related to the standpoint and experience of the writer. My own Africa background was largely limited to two Lutheran Churches: one in Zululand and the other in north-west Tanzania, with both of which I encountered situations which seemed to open up more comprehensive perspectives. The Zululand missionary in this case, throwing caution and prudence aside, entered into empathetic contact with what was then termed 'the Sects' or 'Native Separatist Churches' and launched out on a research which was published in 1948 as *Bantu Prophets in South Africa* and as *Zulu Zion* in 1976. The Bukoba experience during the Second World War brought me into contact with an 'orphaned' Church or rather a self-governing Church of immense vitality and liveliness, resulting in two books: *Ung kyrka i Tanganyika* (1948, in Swedish) and *Bara Bukoba: Church and Community in Tanzania* (1974 in Swedish, 1980 in English and 1990 in Swahili). The opportunity to compare these two Churches was useful, more particularly as in 1953 I was part of an IMC (International Missionary Council) Theological Commission and could take this comparison one step further. Through comparison one discovers the distinctive characteristics of each.

In the meantime, the African scene changed as did the writers on Africa: the historical dimension of African reality came to the fore. A new generation of history scholars appeared inspired by Professors Roland Oliver, Richard Gray, Terence Ranger and others. These British history professors did not neglect the Churches as history professors in other countries are wont to; in fact they pioneered both research and interpretation of African Church history. It began with Professor Roland Oliver's *The Missionary Factor in East Africa* (1952). With the 1950s and the 1960s there followed a new period in African history-writing. My work was enriched by relating it to the ongoing international process of African history-writing achieved by this new generation of African and Western scholars. On every point, for every African country and period, I have benefited from these contributions.

My own perspective also changed while serving the Church in Tanzania as a bishop in the early 1960s. I realized the need to re-interpret African religions and church history from a distinct African perspective. At that stage I was encouraged by the advance represented by studies into the history of local African cults, studies inspired by Professor Terence Ranger and others who adopted an historical approach to the study of African religion. A new image of the history of African religion emerges. Instead of the earlier image of a static, immobile religion, to be changed only through the invasion of Western imperialism and its Western faith, we are presented with a dynamic, multifaceted image of local territorial cults undergoing change, sometimes over a period of some 400 years. These cults were exposed to new agencies of change during the nineteenth-century wars and epidemics, which introduced new ecological and economic factors.

However, having recognized the need for a new continent-wide African Church history I had to face a serious question: should such a church history be attempted by a Westerner, an outsider, a European scholar in his shielded study? I see this point almost as clearly as others do. I have tried to place the emerging church, throughout the continent, within African structures such as population movements and resulting refugee groups, within the relentlessly ongoing movement over the savannah, through the forests and along the rivers. As I became aware in Bukoba, the Christian message in the local village was largely transmitted by African initiative, more particularly by groups of young converts looking towards a new fellowship in and beyond village and ethnic community. With all its limitations this book focuses not on Western partners but on African actors.

Although I had some share in African studies with my *Bantu Prophets* and other works, I would like to draw attention to the relationship between the study of Independent churches and that of the mission-related Churches. The more established Western- or mission-related churches have often been relegated out of sight by a hunt for something 'authentically Africa'! Yet it is to the Catholic, Anglican, Lutheran, Methodist, Presbyterian and Baptist etc. Churches that the overwhelming majority of African Christians have belonged and still do. The current depreciation of these 'established' churches is as mistaken as was once the neglect of the 'Independent Churches'. The term 'Independent Church' has in fact now lost some of its glamour, when all churches are in some sense independent. Consider those great numbers – 3,000 or 6,000 – which have exercised their fascination for some time. For South Africa one should perhaps refer to them not as some 3,000 different groups but as *one* charismatic movement with local and personal variations. The Independents are not just another world, peripheral to the real thing. They are actively shaping the *milieu* and expectations in city locations, influencing both Catholic and Protestant, to the extent that an African Catholic archbishop exercising his ministry in a Central African capital, serving also as a healer of the sick (to his great surprise he discovered that his hands could mediate a therapeutic power) was removed from his high office and transferred to Rome.

The role of the individual must be seen as part of vast and fundamental movements and tendencies. Nevertheless, the question could at least be put as to whether it is not a special obligation for church history to emphasize also the role of the individual and the extent to which over-arching trends are modified by the peculiarities of the individual. No other movement in Africa allows the individual African personality to stand out as clearly as does the movement of the Church, yet even here the available biographical and archival material is limited and patchy. Not many archives equal those of the Moravian churches. The two-centuries-old Moravian international rule was that each Christian individual should write or relate his/her life story, as it turned out with significant differences between the life stories of men and women. These biographies were later gathered in Moravian archives and are significant for African Church history.

In places the Church history of Africa is a brief affair; elsewhere it is a matter of 1,900 years of history. The first 1,000 years – in Egypt, Nubia, North Africa and Ethiopia – play a special role in our presentation. Attending the Seventh International Conference of Ethiopian Studies in

Lund, Sweden, 1982, and the Sixth International Conference for Nubian Studies in Uppsala, Sweden, 1986 provided me with the opportunity to discuss matters with specialists in these fields.

What is specific about the history of the church? Is the church anything more than just another kind of sociological construct, informed by its particular ideology; a religious department fashioned by economic forces and social tensions and struggles? The political, social and economic backgrounds are therefore duly emphasized here, but this is not all. This book is a Church history dealing with religious movements, religious institutions and religious personalities. I quote Professor Lamin Sanneh:

> Christianity in Africa has had more than its share of the attention of Western writers, including throngs of social scientists and their disciples, most of whom are interested in everything except the Christian religion. It is as if in our concern to describe the sunlight we concentrate on the shadows, using that derivative relationship as the justification for a reductionist approach.[3]

While as far as possible integrating this church history into the wider frame of African history, my interpretation is basically not just a secular history with the church somehow thrown in, but a church history in its own right. This claim is vindicated more clearly in some parts of the book than in others – in itself an admission that in a work of this kind, conceived and written over a period of twenty years, it was not always easy to retain the same level and tone of interpretation.

If there is a need for a new, overall look at African church history, this does not only stem from the nineteenth- and twentieth-century studies. I must at least hint at the new image of the Donatists (W. Frend), the surprisingly rich new material on the church in Nubia and the great contributions to the study of the sixteenth, seventeenth and eighteenth centuries in the Congo area (Jadin, Bontinck, Rich and Gray etc.). In the nineteenth-century Catholic Church the two great opponents or competitors, Cardinal Lavigerie and Father Duparquet, both stressed their strategies as a 'reprise', a recapture of Catholic positions lost in the Congo and elsewhere in the eighteenth century.

A synchronic comparison between the regions forces itself on the writer dealing with the nineteenth century. The concept of regions might be disputed, for the primary unit is of course the local congregation and the local diocese or church. However, particularly for the nineteenth century, there is a need for this concept of regions. It is suggested that the evangelistic dynamic in the various parts of Africa was sparked by an African equivalent of F. Jackson Turner's 'frontier' idea. The 'line of advance' stretched from

Sierra Leone to Nigeria, Fernando Po and Cameroon in the west, and from the Cape of Good Hope to Zambezi and beyond – sometimes referred to as the 'Church's hinterland'. This 'frontier', and the ever-receding 'regions beyond' are recognized both by the Independent Churches and the mission-related Churches. At the same time we stress the wide chronological discrepancy between the regions. West and South had a lead of half a century – or two to three generations – over the Congo and the East. There is a similar chronological discrepancy *within* the regions: the obvious example is the difference in West Africa between the Coast with its early international and Christian contacts, and later Christian activity far inland.

The concept of a one-volume work may be criticized. But all history is selective, and in this case distinct pedagogical needs determine this selection. In the process of Christianization we can discern a selectivity relating to both communicating parties, Selective Giving and Selective Appropriation.

This book is an unashamedly ecumenical study highlighting Catholic, Orthodox, Protestant and Independent work. Here the book appears at a propitious time. For centuries the two competing confessions, Catholic and Protestant, treated one another with damning silence – plodding along on different sides of the same hill or river, relying on the same vernacular related to the same traditional African religion, dealing with similar daily experiences in the district in hot season and rainy season – yet never meeting. The other party did not or should not exist.

I know of one exception to this rule (see p. 298), a meeting between a Belgian Catholic missionary just arrived in Zaïre, and a British Baptist missionary with long experience from the villages along the River. To their surprise they found themselves as fellow travellers for a day in the same train compartment on the new railway from Boma to Kinshasa (Léopoldville). Fortunately overcoming an initial embarrassment they soon were engaged in a lively and constructive debate on mission evangelistic methods, one of the fundamental problems of Congo missionary policy at the time.

I have had the ambition to attempt an ecumenical history of the Church in Africa. This can mean different things to different people. I take it to mean a book where both Catholics and non-Catholics might find an interpretation of the essential intentions and achievements of their respective churches. An attempt of this nature could only be made now, after Vatican II, the great event of twentieth-century church history. Vatican II gave rise to the possibility of a new order of things, also in Africa. This Church history of mine would love to be a contribution towards a saner order of things. During all these years of work I have been amazed at the persistent generosity which I have met from the Catholic side, from archivists and other scholars in Rome, Paris and Louvain, and from other Catholic scholars in the West as well as in Africa.

The generous opening of Catholic mission archives, after Vatican II, meant a new opportunity. It was an eye-opener to discover that these Catholic archives were in the care of men and women elected at an early age by their respective societies, thus acquiring an excellent command of their task as life-long caretakers of their epistolary treasures. My correspondence over many years with them and their colleagues can now be found in the University Library, Uppsala, Sweden, and can hopefully serve new generations of Church history scholars.

My early International Missionary Council contacts with non-Roman archives and libraries served as an introduction to these rich treasures and I thank them all. Protestant mission archives form the basis of certain parts of this book and it goes without saying, as with the Catholic archival treasures, that only a minor percentage has been consulted, but none the less significant in the interpretation of developments.

The strength of the Protestants was reduced by the fact of their divisiveness. The influence of the International Missionary Council, with its incomparable leader J. H. Oldham and his American counterpart in Zaïre, Dr Emory Ross, held the Protestant forces together. In many African countries Protestants were for decades excluded from whatever there was of the benefits of colonial rule: their share of land for church and school purposes was infinitesimal; administration assistance to their school personnel was imperceptible. Despite this, Protestants developed their own school system, inspiring new generations of youngsters for a new world.

The heart of the matter

Reception of the Gospel is, on the deepest level, an expression of African peoples' 'conscientization', by which they rise to a new awareness, a new conscientiousness kindled by faith in Jesus Christ and his message: 'I have come that they may have life and have it more abundantly' (John 10:10). They could affirm a saving relationship to the Cross, to the Life and Death and Resurrection of Jesus Christ, creating in the hearts of men and women something gloriously new to be claimed and reclaimed in every new generation. Where this did not happen, there was stagnation and a stifling tradition. Where this did happen there was kindled a resolve, through the Church to serve and inspire individuals, groups, nations, and the continent. In the Church, in Christ, was 'a new creation, old things are passed away, behold, all things are become new' (2. Cor. 5:17).

I

THE BEGINNINGS

EGYPT

The Holy Refugees

It was as refugees, according to St Matthew, that the Holy Family came from Bethlehem to Egypt. In later Coptic tradition the pious story has followed the pilgrimage of the Holy Family from the Nile Delta all along the river to Asyut and back again, altogether a period of some three and a half years. Great miracles occurred during the passage. At place after place in a dry land, as the Divine Child stretched out his hand, fresh water wells would spring up and the trees would bow their heads; yes, the very palm tree to which the Mother held her hand during her birth-pangs gave the family shadow from the heat of the sun. (This has a Mediterranean background – *Leto*.) The sick were healed and the dead were raised again. South of Asyut – later to be one of the great centres of the Coptic Church – the Holy Family, having passed ruins of rock-temples and other holy buildings, found refuge in large rock-tombs from the early dynasties of Egyptian history.

This vivid tradition has more to say about the local Church – which has loved to narrate it – than about historical fact. It has been retold by generations and helped to make Egypt a 'holy land', *because* Jesus the Child and Mary, the Mother of God, by their holy presence, had made it so.[1]

The first chapter and the rest of the book

Twentieth-century literature devoted to the first thousand years of Church history of Egypt, Nubia, Ethiopia and North Africa is immense. Finds of sources have added to our understanding of the forces which shaped the spirituality in the Church in those centuries. Archaeological excavations have brought to light invaluable documents and a fascinating world of

Christian art. The UNESCO campaign in the 1960s to save the culture hidden in the sands of Nubia has produced sensational results, and even now, innocent-looking mounds in the sands of the desert may hide buildings, ruins and documents which could change our entire outlook on certain periods of this history.

Scholarly congresses on Coptic Studies, Nubian Studies and Ethiopian Studies gather together scholars from around the world in order to report on and discuss new discoveries of material and perspectives. In view of all this truly impressive richness, the following brief pages attempt a rapid survey based on the volumes published by scholars and experts in this field.

This chapter on the first 1,500 years has a function of its own, related to the book as a whole. This part was written towards the end of the total enterprise. Here as elsewhere, but more so, selection was necessary, and we found *our* selective principle for this first chapter in the great themes which have been worked out for the following centuries. The survey of the first 1,000 years will be related to the general Church history of Africa, with its great themes such as Church and State, Church and indigenous culture, the city and rural population movements, theology and spirituality. Some of these themes, writ large for more recent centuries, will be found as it were, anticipated in those early centuries.

The Jewish Diaspora and the Beginnings of the Church

The first beginnings of the Church's history in the Nile Delta must be understood as closely related to the life of the Jewish Diaspora on the Mediterranean coastline. About the first 100 years of Christian beginnings in the Nile Delta, the fundamental fact of the relationship to, and dependence on, the Jewish community in the city stands out as of primary importance. The Jews represented a highly significant minority in Alexandria with a population of hundreds of thousands. In all of Egypt there were, at the time of Christ, about 1 million Jews, thus representing the largest Jewish community outside Palestine. Two of the five sections of the city into which Alexandria was divided were dominated by the Jews, their synagogues and their culture.

A leading spokesman for the Jewish Diaspora in Alexandria was Philo, philosopher and Bible expositor, international and cosmopolitan Jewish scholar, deeply influenced by Hellenistic culture and concerned with establishing areas of contact and understanding between Hellenism and Judaism. Alongside Philo and his assimilationalist teaching there also appeared the more conservative schools of Jewish thought, less given to allegorical interpretation of the Scripture. It was here in Jewish Alexandria, that the Septuaginta translation of the Hebrew Bible into Greek was created.

In this Jewish world, marked by the Torah and the Prophets, the Sabbath and the feasts, the first Christian groups from Judaea appeared as missionaries, refugees and traders. While at first possibly seeking refuge in the synagogue they were soon prepared to proclaim their astounding and necessarily divisive message, that the Messiah, the Saviour and the Lord had indeed come, in Jesus of Nazareth. Scholars are at present attempting to identify the very place in the city of Alexandria where the first Christians congregated for worship, agape and eucharist, in an area of the Jewish neighbourhood, later known, from the fourth century on, as Boukolou.[2]

A far-reaching generalization can be made at the outset: this religion of the Messiah, proclaimed by Jewish individuals, families and groups, came into Egypt and Africa from the East. It was an Eastern religion, and whatever changes it has since undergone because of its missionary outreach and consequent identification with many cultures, it retains its fundamental consanguinity with its Eastern origins, with Abraham from Ur of the Chaldees, and with those 'homeless wandering Charismatics' who, in the Holy Land, as the disciples of Jesus had been the first to preach the Christian message. 'It was a coincidence for Christianity that it became Westernized' according to Cardinal Jean Daniélou,[3] and the West African scholar E. J. Penoukou adds: 'Likewise it remains a coincidence for the Church in Africa that it received Christianity in a Western form'.[4] Ancient tradition referred to by the learned Eusebius of Caesarea (?265–?340) – 'the Father of Church history writing' – suggests that the see of Alexandria was founded by St Mark the Evangelist, martyred AD 68.

Modern scholarship moves carefully with regard to this Marcan tradition. 'The historicity of this tradition, though unprovable, should not be ruled out ... Indeed the tradition of the preaching of Mark in Alexandria may predate the acceptance of the canonical Gospel of Mark in the Alexandrian Church.'[5] This St Mark tradition has had a resounding echo in modern times. In 1968 the new St Mark's Cathedral was consecrated by Patriarch Cyrillos VI, in the presence of President Nasser, Vice-President Sadat and Haile Selassie I, the Emperor of Ethiopia. On the same occasion the relics of St Mark, seized in 828 by the Venetians, were returned to Egypt by Pope Paul VI in Rome. The relics were thus brought from one cathedral of St Mark to another. (It should be added, perhaps, that another Mediterranean city church – Venice – also counts St Mark as its founder.)

The coastal city and rural inland

For an understanding of the fundamental tensions in Egyptian Church history one has to distinguish between the city of Alexandria and the rest of the country. On the one hand, there was the international Greek-speaking city on the coast with its cosmopolitan culture and Greek Church, turned to the North and to the Mediterranean world – *Alexandria ad Aegyptum* ('Alexandria beside Egypt') – although the city of Alexandria (Rakote in Coptic) also had a Coptic population. On the other, Upper Egypt, the rural region with its emerging Coptic language and culture, monasticism and church, turned away as much as possible from the cosmopolitan world of the bustling city on the coast. Here one was 'Coptic'-speaking, the word being an Arabic form for Egypt. The idea of 'the Egyptian' is a 'fundamental element in this religious community' and emphasizes its heritage from the ancient Egyptians of Pharaonic times.[6] The Coptic language emerged from the second century. The first translations of Bible text were probably made in the third century, or possibly earlier.

From the vantage-point on the coast at Alexandria the spectator could survey the drama of ancient world politics enacted by succeeding regimes and affecting the fate of Egypt and of all Egyptians: the rise and fall of the Pharaohs, to whose political forms and cultural visions the pyramids, temples and ruins bore witness. The Greek era of the Ptolemies followed with its Hellenistic culture, Greek language and Greek pantheon and the intermixture of Egyptian and Greek gods, (particularly the role of the fertility-saviour goddess, Isis).

In the first century before Christ, the Ptolemies were followed by Roman emperors who began to exert their influence with Latin language and culture and with an insatiable demand for and ever-rising taxation of the wheat-lands of Egypt – the granary of Rome. This economic exploitation had been so harsh and sweeping that the narrow strip of arable land along the River Nile could no longer keep up with the demands. The burden of taxation of corn had from then onwards to be carried by North Africa (the present Maghreb). After the fall of Carthage in 146 BC, North Africa was a vanquished country and now had to keep the conqueror supplied by way of annual tribute, while in Egypt, a Roman colony under Mark Antony since 42 BC, impoverished peasants unable to pay their dues fled from their fields into the deserts.

Economic pressure and consequent local rebellions in the Delta led to mounting tensions between Rome and Egypt. In order to ensure obedience the Roman emperors demanded signs – sacrifice at first of a few grains of incense, and later, the handing over of the Holy Scriptures – to prove submission to the Emperor. Those who refused this sacrifice were convicted as Christians and thus disloyal subjects: here was the root of the persecutions against the Christians, the worst of all coming under the Emperor Diocletian, from AD 303–05. The persecutions hit the young Church in Egypt as a traumatic blow, never to be forgotten, forever to be re-enacted in the collective memory of the Church, making the Coptic Church into 'the martyr Church'.

The 'era of the martyrs', inaugurating Coptic Church history, begins with the accession of the dreaded Diocletian as Emperor, AD 284, and the Coptic calendar even today begins not with the Birth of Christ but with AD 284. The actual Diocletian persecution took place in the years 299–304. But in Egypt it lingered on and reached a climax in AD 311–12 under Maximinus. The bishop of Alexandria himself was executed; venerated as Peter Martyr he was the first Egyptian saint, also remembered in the Roman canon of the mass. The greatest tragedy took place in the Thebaid in Upper Egypt: day by day, fifty to a hundred of the 'stubborn peasants', the Coptic Christians were martyred. In Switzerland the Theban Legion, a unit in the Roman army showed the same stubborn resistance under its leader St Maurice and was decimated again and again, to the last man.

The theologians

Alexandria with its Greek and Jewish populations, its learning and international horizons, was the ideal place for theological debate and an acrimonious theological struggle. The Catechetical School, founded in the second century by the Greek theologian Titus Flavius Clemens (?150–?215), otherwise known as Clement of Alexandria, provided a basis for great theological systems. Clement's thought was turned to the heavenly world with the 'Church on High' where 'God's philosophers assembled the Israelites, the pure in heart, in whom there is no guile'.[7] Clement was succeeded in the Catechetical School by Origen (?185–?254), probably the most learned and possibly the most difficult of the theologians of his time. The study of the Bible was his great concern and he produced the *Hexapla*, an enormous volume where the Hebrew text, both in Hebraic and in Greek letters, was placed side by side with four Greek versions of the Scriptures. His allegorical interpretation of scripture follows a tradition going back to Philo and, before, to Alexandrian Judaism.

Various schools of thought soon competed for attention. Gnosticism was a complex religious movement with roots in the Old Testament and claiming to possess certain secret knowledge – '*gnosis*'. Alexandria had these Gnostic systems. Collections of Gnostic manuscripts have been found in the so-called 'Nag Hammadi' texts discovered in 1945 in an old fortress in the desert in Upper Egypt. A young priest named Arius, felt that he could lean on Origen for his own doctrine. In order to extol the person of the Father in the Trinity, to safeguard the unity of God, he made the position of the Word (*Logos*) – the Son – secondary and subordinate. Arius had an uncanny, almost modern gift of propagating his views and ideas. He wrote songs for sailors and millers, for traders and travellers to be sung in the streets and in the harbour. He attracted the masses. All the more St Athanasius, as patriarch, and deeply convinced of the orthodoxy of his position, insisted on the 'consubstantiality' of the Son with the Father. (The term *homousios* was first used by the Gnostics!)

In St Athanasius (?296–373), Bishop of Alexandria 328–73, the Church in Egypt saw its greatest patriarch. Unbending in all his convictions, he had a violent temper and would flog some of his younger priests and imprison or expel bishops. His struggles identified him with the great doctrinal proclamations, the 'creeds', of the Church. Against Arianism and other dangers he safeguarded the great formula about the Trinity which has followed the Church ever since: 'consubstantial (of one being with) the Father . . .' etc. One of the three Ecumenical creeds, the 'Athanasian' (*Quicumque vult*), is named after him. He was himself exiled from his Alexandria see by the Emperor no less than five times, altogether for a period of some twenty years. (In those international times he was once banished, during the years 335–37, to Trier in Germany.) His friend and colleague was the liturgically creative Serapion of Thmuis.

In this book we are not likely to forget that it was St Athanasius, Bishop of Alexandria, who consecrated Frumentius as Bishop of Aksum, thus establishing the links between the Church in Egypt and the Church in Ethiopia which were to last for 1,600 years. For the future of the Church in Egypt it was particularly important that St Athanasius, himself an ascetic, identified with the rising monastic movement: through his influence, hierarchy and monks were to be closely united.

St Athanasius' teachings and ecclesiastical intentions were followed up by St Cyril (380–444) – 'the super-Athanasian',[8] Patriarch of Alexandria 412–44. St Cyril's influence was felt far beyond Alexandria. The Ethiopian Orthodox Church regards him as 'her teacher *par excellence*'. Its most important doctrinal manual, with translations in Ge'ez of St Cyril's main works, bears the name Qerillos (Cyril).[9] This is another indication of the close affinity between the two Churches of Egypt and Ethiopia.

The Desert Fathers and the monks

There were long lines of connection to the Desert Fathers from the earliest generations of the Christian Church in Palestine and in the East generally. Through these first centuries there was a pull from the desert, leading to an opposition movement to ordinary established society and thus altogether different from the Greek world of business, learning and philosophy. One recent interpretation sees the Desert Fathers as a continuation of the Jewish–Palestinian world of travelling preachers and prophets.[10] For generations these men had been looking for radical change, establishing a counter-society of their own with a totally radical way of life, where they could live out their faith in total poverty and withdrawal from ordinary society. They preferred to disappear into the desert mountains for long periods of time. At first it was a question of individuals who, as hermits, withdrew for a life of prayer and meditation finding their abode in a grotto or perhaps an abandoned grave.

In the desert grottoes they found opportunity for prayer, for a life of the Spirit and a realization of the mighty presence of God. The maxims of the Desert Fathers take the reader to a distant, foreign world. St Antony is obviously one of the leaders among the desert hermits but he cannot unreservedly be regarded as the founder of the movement: he built on an older tradition with which he associated himself.

The majority of these desert *abbas* were men of peasant stock, simple men of faith but with unfailing knowledge (by heart) of Bible passages upon which they could feed the spirit. They were distinguished by 'visions, miracles, prediction of events and insight into occurrences in far-away places'.[11] To some of these men, withdrawal to the desert was a reaction against outrages of the State. Torture, persecution, economic exploitation and hunger had combined to exert a horror in the minds of the people, and some of these anachorets became hermits for economic reasons. From the State's point of view the Desert Fathers were nothing but a bunch of objectors to military service and tax-evaders.

St Antony (*c.* 251–356) went into the desert to fight against the demons and to live with God. Renowned for his piety he attracted other men as his disciples. He had to find out 'whether they were Egyptians *or* men of Jerusalem': only to the latter would he give of his time to discuss spiritual matters with them.[12] His life can be studied in valuable primary sources from the late fourth century. Among the best known is *The Life of Saint Antony* by the Patriarch Athanasius, an expression of the veneration that the great church leader and theologian felt for the ascetics in the desert. Later in the history of the Church monks were to write the lives of bishops. In this early Egyptian case, the Bishop and Patriarch wrote the life of the monk, shortly after St Antony's death.

While a distinction between Alexandria and the rest of Egypt has to be made on economic, linguistic and cultural grounds this difference should on the other hand not be over-emphasized. A recent learned study, entitled *The Letters of St Antony* by Dr Samuel Rubenson, shows that at the time of the late third and early fourth centuries – the period of St Antony and his followers – there was in fact 'a much more extensive contact between Alexandria and the towns of Upper Egypt than hitherto supposed'. There was a cultural movement in both directions between city and countryside. Egypt had its share of scholars, philosophers, poets and bibliophiles and was clearly no less literate than the other parts of the Graeco-Roman world. Dr Rubenson makes the point that 'it is unlikely that Christianity was not heard of in the towns of Upper Egypt before the end of the second century'. The literary papyri give a picture of third-century Egyptian Christianity as strongly Biblical and much less Gnostic than has been suggested. In this context St Antony the hermit was deeply influenced by Origen's theology and there he developed his teaching. The spiritual teacher was the father of monasticism, a monastic *abba*.[13]

A somewhat different picture of St Antony and his colleagues is presented in the charming collection of impressions and short maxims of the Desert Fathers, *Apophthegmata*, 'a gallery of monastic icons'.[14] St Athanasius' study cannot be taken at face value. It does, however, give an impression of St Athanasius' own view of a model Christian and of the ascetic in the desert cell. It also shows the monk as having the power to prophesy future events, even if cautious in the use of this gift.

Arsenius (360–440) was different from most of the Egyptian Desert Fathers in that he was a foreigner from Rome where he had held the rank of a Senator and had been tutor to the sons of the Emperor. In 394 he unexpectedly broke with this kind of life and left for Sketis in the Egyptian desert where he remained until his death in 440. While still 'in the palace' he prayed to God: 'Lord, show me the way how I can be saved'. A voice came to him: 'Arsenius, flee from men, then you will be saved'. Later somebody asked him how, with all his education, he could turn for help to illiterate peasants. His answer: 'Indeed I have received both Roman and Greek education, but the alphabet of this peasant I have not yet learned.' Arsenius placed himself under an *abbas*, the dwarf Johannes, and eventually had disciples of his own.

The Pachomian monastic movement

The hermits in their grottoes were followed by a new significant development, the Pachomian monastic movement. As a young soldier, St Pachomius (?290–346) had joined the Christian camp and decided to become a hermit, settling down first with the hermit Palamon and then establishing a community at Tabennesis. He developed his hermitage along creative lines, founding a community of men living together inside the walls of a centre, walls which now could become symbols not of seclusion but of fellowship. St Pachomius gave structure and programme to the movement. There was a rule of life with 194 articles to be strictly followed by the inmates, living in community with colleagues, subordinate to a superior who exercised the spiritual direction of the community.

Each monk had a little cell of his own which could not be locked. They lived together in 'houses', the head being a house-father, and three to four houses forming a group. Each house had to be concerned with its particular handicraft; making mats, weaving linen, or working as fuller or tailor. Three of the houses had more general duties, such as receiving guests or taking care of novices. There were two meals per day. Likewise there were two prayer sessions, early morning and late at night. For the morning session twelve psalms were read, in the evening this number was reduced to six, with prayers and two lessons. The Sunday morning Eucharist was taken by a priest from the community or, if one was not available, a priest from the neighbourhood. This was followed by a catechetical lecture by the *abbas*. In the houses on Wednesdays and Fridays the house-father gave catechetical teaching. In order not to feel sleepy during prayers, the monk had to work his spinning wheel, making thread for his mats; the prayers were thus accompanied by the soft humming of the wheels – perhaps unwittingly soporific. But the monastery was related to the world and, more acutely, within the secular community there were religious devotees: 'the *Koinonia* did not enjoy a monopoly of the evangelical life.'[15]

At the time of St Pachomius' death in 346, there were nine monasteries for men and two convents for women, one of these under the leadership of Pachomius' sister, Mary. The rapid growth of the movement is seen in the fact that at Easter 390, no less than 50,000 monks congregated for the feast. This also explains the rural masses' transition to Christianity in Upper Egypt. The monks were the missionaries of the Church. They were at the same time enthusiastic local leaders of a Coptic national movement about to emerge in the fifth century. They acted as catechists teaching young and old the stories of the Bible and the lives of the martyrs. As the persecutions came to an end in the early years of the fourth century, the monks succeeded the martyrs as the great heroes of folk-piety in the village churches.

After Chalcedon

For Alexandria and Egypt, AD 451 meant the parting of the ways from the West as well as from the Greek Church. Until that time, Alexandria had, as a matter of course, been awarded a leading position in Orthodox Christendom. On behalf of both East and West, Bishop Athanasius had denounced his recalcitrant priest Arius and all his works and thereby played a central role in the post-Nicean period. As Bishop of Alexandria, the authoritarian St Cyril built on solid Athanasian foundations assisted by the enthusiastic support of thousands of monks. Yet, in his effort to suppress the influence of Arius and the related Nestorius, he was to be acclaimed as an authority in the emerging Unionite movement. This taught that in the person of the Incarnate Christ there was but a single, Divine-human nature, thus opposing the Orthodox 'Diophysite' teaching of a Double Nature – Divine and Human – after the Incarnation. The Egyptian monks firmly held to the Unionite position. From AD 452 the Patriarch of Alexandria, representing the Coptic Church, was a Unionite although he has been opposed by a Greek-Orthodox Patriarch till the present day.

After an especially agitated period of doctrinal debate in the West in the period 431–50, the synod of Chalcedon (near Constantinople), a supposedly ecumenical encounter, decided for the 'two natures' and against the Unionite position. Most significantly, its Patriarch, Dioscorus, was deposed. With this fateful decision the Church in Egypt had to orient itself in an altogether new direction. When the state authorities chose Proterius, 'a docile friend of Byzantine imperialism' to replace the deposed Patriarch, the Egyptians immediately chose their own Patriarch in the person of Timothy Aelurus. Unable to remove his imperial rival, the excited crowd of monks and other faithful eventually took their revenge. In 457 they invaded the Baptistery where Proterius was officiating at the Eucharist and slaughtered him, then dragged his body through the streets, burned it and delivered the ashes to the wind.

Very soon the Coptic Church could answer in kind, denouncing Constantinople and the Chalcedonians as 'Diophysites' and 'Melchites' (the Emperor's men), 'running dogs of the imperial regime'. This led to renewed persecutions hitting the Unionite community. On the other hand, this outrage helped to solidify Egyptian nationalism built on the Coptic language and tradition, the Unionite doctrine and enthusiastic monastic leadership.

Fifteen hundred years after Chalcedon, the Pope of Rome, Pius XII, by his encyclical *Sempiternus Rex Christus*, declared that the differences between the Churches were due above all to questions of vocabulary and to the fact that the accusation of Monophysitism was unjustified.

Favour of kings and queens

World politics together with their most personal, even intimate variations, could in certain cases determine the fate of national Churches, such as those of Egypt and Nubia. In Byzantine Constantinople, the ambitious law-giver, Justinian (Emperor 527–65) had, in his youth, shown Unionite sympathies. However, as Emperor he held firmly to that religious policy which was most likely to serve the unification of his vast empire, in this case, the Chalcedonian position. He saw himself as Emperor and priest in one. Church and State were to be totally integrated.

There was, however, an embarrassing hitch: his empress, Theodora (d. 548). A woman of humble background, she had ideas of her own. She was a Unionite at heart and in her political actions as far as she could go. This was to benefit the Unionite Churches in Egypt and in Nubia. Her influence could be seen in the impressive basilicas erected in her time, at her instigation. The lovely wall-paintings, both in Egypt and Nubia, were no doubt drawn after Byzantine models. This, however, could not affect the liturgy, the prayers and the devotions to Mary, Mother of God: which were all Unionite.

'Descendants of the Pharaohs'

On consideration of the fate of the Church in North Africa, submitted to recurrent onslaughts, and leading – albeit slowly – to virtual extinction, one begins to appreciate something of the stamina and adaptability of the Coptic Church in surviving over the centuries. The losses in membership and influence can be comprehended by counting the number of episcopal sees in the Coptic Church: in AD 600 these numbered one hundred, by AD 700 they were reduced to seventy, and by AD 1400 they had been further reduced to forty (and at present, twenty-five bishops and metropolitans in Egypt, two in Sudan and one in Jerusalem).

In the local congregations, however, particularly in Upper Egypt around Asyut, Church life continued, adding its special colour and rhythm to the life of the total community. More than that of any other country in Africa, Egyptian culture represented 'the long duration', to use F. Braudel's term.

Near the River Nile, the Sphinx and the Pharaonic pyramids watched over changes and developments: they had already been there for some 3,000 years when the first Christian preachers arrived in Alexandria. As the Coptic Church emerged, its members took pride in the idea that they were indeed 'descendants of the Pharaohs' and this claim to an ancient origin could, in a critical political situation, be held against even the most powerful invader.

The Copts could assimilate the new without discarding the old. They were inclusive rather than exclusive. This is seen in the fact that old quarries from Pharaonic times were used as Christian grotto-churches, with local settlements lasting for centuries. At Luxor, a pagan temple dedicated to the god Amon was adapted for use by the local congregation. Christian paintings and other symbols were plastered over the ancient pagan symbols, to signify that from now on this was to be a Christian temple. In the case of other pagan temples the Coptic priest and his artisans took wooden boards, placing them over previous pagan reliefs (thereby, incidentally, saving the pagan relief for posterity). Dendera, near Luxor, had in pagan times been a pilgrimage centre to which the sick could turn to be cured. Here a Christian church from about the fifth century was built with pagan mussel-shells also used as symbols in the Christian Church, thus testifying to unhampered survival of symbols. Here also the Egyptian cross took shape in the form of the beginnings of the 'TAU' cross devoted to the Victorious Christ. A century later this cross becomes the Life-Giving Tree, in the form of a cross with leaves.[16]

Some of the pre-Christian temples such as the one in Philae devoted to Isis, the goddess of fertility and salvation, were used for the new Christian religion until about AD 580. From that date, for a period of sixty years (580–640) Christian worship could, without pagan influences, develop its specific forms and expressions.

The Muslim invasion and beyond

By the seventh century the Coptic Church was well established with the Patriarch in Alexandria and bishops and monks and nuns in monasteries and convents. They were leading annual pilgrimages to the tombs of holy martyrs. Then came the Muslim Arab invasion.

Across the Red Sea, southern and northern Arabia had for centuries represented important trading areas. Mecca with its famous black meteorite, the *Ka'ba*, was such a centre. Yathrib (Medina) had three Jewish 'tribes', all concerned with trade and with their religion. Jewish colonies established themselves in various parts of the country and one of the Arab kings accepted Judaism as his religion. Here also the Jewish Diaspora served as a bridge for transition to the Christian faith, in a Nestorian or Monophysite form, together with various Gnostic sects. It is realized of course that prior to Muhammad millions of Arabs had been catechized in the name of Allah the true God, and had learned the prayers, the fasts and the feasts in the schools of the missionaries and monks. At the beginning of the seventh century the majority of the Arabs of Mesopotamia and of Syria were Christians. Traditional Arab religion with its sacrifices and pilgrimages had obviously lost its hold on the people, who were looking for a comprehensive faith.

Muhammad, 570–632, came forward as the prophet of this faith, 'Islam', meaning total surrender [to God]. A successful trader, he had contacts with both Jews and Christians. He felt inspired to withdraw into the mountains near Mecca for meditations. He too was fascinated by the desert mountains, their peace and the presence of God. From about 610 he had a number of visions and auditions realized as the voice of God, given to him by the Archangel Gabriel: he knew that this was indeed the 'religion of Abraham'.

Yet he did not feel accepted at Mecca and in 622 made his *hijra*, or, exile, to Yathrib, later renamed Medina, i.e. 'The City' (of the Prophet). There he found other exiles from Mecca, who became his devoted supporters. The visions and auditions were assembled into a Holy Book, the *Qur'an*. As the three Jewish tribes in Mecca could not accept his prophetic claims he chased them away from the city. Yet, the *Qur'an* always recognized that Jews and Christians were 'People of the Book', who should be treated with a certain degree of toleration.

In 632 the prophet died. Soon his followers went beyond the borders of Arabia with the mottoes: 'Allah Akbar', (God is Greater) and 'Muhammad is His Prophet'. Egypt was a neighbour and an obvious target for this campaign. After a certain number of military attempts the country was won for the Prophet in 641, nine years after Muhammad's death.

The attitude of the Copts towards this invasion was not unique. It was largely similar to that of Unionites in other countries such as Syria and Palestine. Byzantine Constantinople and its imperial regime had long been seen as the enemy, and in these eastern countries the Arabs were at first regarded as a possible ally against the Emperor. The ever-widening abyss to Constantinople and its Chalcedonian faith meant that the Arabs did not meet with any significant opposition, and could establish themselves as rulers of the country. The Arab Muslims also at first allowed free worship, on condition that the People of the Book paid individual head tax, *jizya*.

Over the following centuries, succeeding but different Arab regimes presented the Church with varying degrees of political pressure, resulting at times in conversions to Islam, and other times – i.e. AD 868 to AD 1096 – in the closing of the Christian ranks. Coptic language, art and music flourished. The present city of Cairo was founded in 969 and eventually the Patriarch moved to the new metropolis.

The Copts and the Crusades

Increasingly the Copts were made to feel that they were now a religious minority in a Muslim world. The relationship between Coptic Church and Muslim State depended on variations in Arab regimes, with changes in the caliphates, and on certain local crises. The rulers of the Fatimid caliphate, AD 968–1171, were on the whole tolerant towards both Christians and Jews. Capable Copts were to be seen in high places in the administration, mainly in finance and in the banks. The Copts also had many famous physicians and writers. There were other Arab regimes where the Copts had to suffer serious hardships and heavy taxation, against which they sometimes revolted. Locally, incidents of arson could all too easily be blamed on the Copts and outrageous vengeance was taken: in the period AD 1279–1447 forty-four churches were reported to have been razed to the ground in Cairo alone, and Copts became subject to humiliations and confiscation of every kind.

Dramatic changes on the international scene could expose the Copts to serious pressures. From AD 1100 the Crusades from the West made the Coptic minority suspect. This was particularly so with the Fifth Crusade at the beginning of the thirteenth century. This crusade was no longer directed by kings and knights but by the Pope himself. From the other side of the Mediterranean the ill fortune of this crusade was watched with dismay by St Francis of Assisi. He decided to go himself to Egypt in 1219 to try to establish peace. He was given permission for this by the Cardinal Pelagius and arrived at the scene of warfare in the Damiette branch of the Nile Delta, moving unarmed between the armies in no man's land. The Moslem guards were suspicious at first but soon decided that anyone so simple, so gentle and so dirty must be mad and treated him with the respect due to a man who had been touched by God.[17]

The Sultan al-Kamil, who was also inclined to peace, listened patiently to this surprising intervention. In the long perspective of Church history, St Francis' daring mediation was to inspire Latin missions in Egypt at a much later date in the nineteenth and twentieth centuries.

In the fifteenth century there followed new attempts at contacts between Rome and the Copts. In 1439 Pope Eugenius IV invited Patriarch John XI to the ecumenical Council of Florence and the Patriarch sent the *abbas* of the St Anthony monastery. Later, however, political developments obliterated these attempts. From 1517 Egypt was occupied by the Ottoman Turks, and for a long time contacts between the Copts and the West ceased.

NORTH AFRICA

The Mediterranean over which St Paul sailed to Rome and, perhaps, to Spain, also served as a route for the Christian message to reach North Africa. This Church history will repeatedly emphasize the role of the waters in the propagation of the Gospel: the oceans, the lakes, the rivers. For the first Christian centuries, shipping over the Mediterranean and the Red Sea played a fundamental role. Here was an extensive system of international contact, supplying goods and mediating ideas.

The busy North Coast harbours of Carthage, Hippone, Hadremethum (now Sousse) and others saw foreigners arrive from afar, from Egypt, Greece, Sicily and Rome. From the middle of the second century, Rome could also impose imperial power over North Africa. Sailing ships could cover the distance Carthage–Rome in three to four days. The coastal cities had small Jewish communities with their synagogues and international cultural contacts. The large estates inland, under Roman landowners, had to supply corn by way of tribute to the metropolis. North Africa succeeded Egypt as the granary of Rome and was forced to keep the city inhabitants with the daily ration of wheat. On the estates inland there were Berbers and a Punic population together with large numbers of slaves.

It is not surprising, therefore, that when, towards the end of the second century, a Christian Church on the North Coast can first be identified, it had already reached certain dimensions. One is faced with local congregations of determined men and women prepared to give their lives for the faith. The first historical document of the Church relates to a group of Christians from Scillium in Numidia – at least two of the names seem Berber – who on the 1 August 180 were put to death and became martyrs. Twenty years later Perpetua and Felicitas went to their deaths, thrown to the lions.

Already by the middle of the third century paganism in North Africa saw decay and down-fall – the same period as for Egypt – and simultaneously mass conversion to Christianity occurred. At first, Greek was presumably the Church's language in Africa – even today one can see Greek texts on wall inscriptions and graves – but in the second century there was a definite change to the language of the Imperial power, Latin.

This linguistic innovation was to exert long-range influences, positive and negative, on the Christianization process in the country. The problem was how far could the impoverished masses on the estates and in the harbours identify with the Imperial language and make it their own? If they could not, there was a danger that the rapid Christianization might remain somewhat superficial and that this might show later under the impact of some sudden onslaught from abroad. A comparison with Egypt is revealing. There the Church acquired a national language of its own, Coptic, which became identified with as a symbol of their struggle for autonomy over the language and culture of the Imperialists, the 'Melkite' Greeks in Alexandria. In Northern Africa on the other hand, however much Latin became the proud possession of the intellectuals and the well-to-do, it never attained the same creative, symbolic role as did the Coptic language in Egypt.

Tertullian and Saint Cyprian

Tertullian (*c.* 160–*c.* 220) from Carthage is the first in the line of great theologians in North Africa: a vehement, uncompromising and irrepressible personality with great visions and a dedicated will. Having started as a lawyer and a rhetor he loved words and the play on words, a love which led to his creation of Ecclesiastical Latin. This form of Latin first emerged in North Africa, in and through Tertullian's disturbing writings, demonstrating to much later generations of the Church in Africa what it takes to form, curb and appropriate a language. In Tertullian's case the language emerged from a creative personality, dedicated to proclaiming an overwhelming message, and to reaching out to as many as possible.

There were connections between the two North Africans, Tertullian and St Cyprian (?200–58). Cyprian referred to Tertullian as his 'master'. Cyprian, like Tertullian, had a lawyer's training. When converted both held to a strictly ascetic interpretation of Christianity. Rome had worries with both men, although from different points of view. Tertullian's critical mind ultimately took him over to the Montanist camp. A presbyter himself, he found some bishops difficult to manage and his spirit yearned for a Spirit-dominated religion which the Montanists were supposed to represent. Montanism was 'an explosion of prophetism'.[18] (There are surprising points of similarity between Montanism in the second century and some of the modern ecstatic African prophets and prophetesses in the twentieth century.)

St Cyprian, on the other hand, was involved in a controversy with Bishop Stephen in Rome over the matter of re-baptism of heretics. Here, Cyprian was uncompromising and insisted on re-baptism while Bishop Stephen pleaded for re-admitting heretics by the imposition of hands. There were sharp arguments on both sides and the Bishop in Rome threatened the bishop in Carthage with excommunication. In this struggle of minds Cyprian elaborated his view of episcopacy. While emphasizing the unity of the Catholic Church, with deference to the successor of Peter – his great book was called *On the Unity of the Church* – he was nonetheless determined to uphold the rights of the local bishop and did so to such an extent that he came to be regarded as 'the champion of episcopalism'. These were terrible times for faithful Christian confessors, their existence dominated by the fear of and longing for martyrdom – the 'heavenly crown'. Long before Cyprian was beheaded he had a vivid dream experience. He saw a young man of extraordinary height who brought him to the proconsul's court. The proconsul wrote something on a slab of wood and Cyprian could see his own death sentence. The young man in the dream extended and bent his fingers, one after the other, thereby indicating a respite with the execution of the punishment,[19] but the bishop's dream was followed by stark reality.

Bishop Cyprian's martyrdom

On 14 September 258, Bishop Cyprian was called to appear before the proconsul Galerius Maximus who put to him the following questions:

> 'You are Thascius Cyprian?'
>
> 'Yes, that is me.'
>
> 'You are the leader of these sacrilegious people?'
>
> 'What then?'
>
> 'The holy emperors have ordered that you sacrifice.'
>
> 'No, I won't do that.'
>
> 'Consider it well.'
>
> 'That I have already done. Do what you must.'
>
> 'You have lived in sacrilege and have made yourself the enemy of the gods of Rome. Therefore your blood will be the sanction of the laws ... We direct that Thascius Cyprian be put to death by the sword.'
>
> Cyprian replied: 'Thanks be to God.'

The crowd of Christians cried out: 'Let our heads fall with his!' The executioner arrived and the bishop ordered that this man receive twenty-five pieces of gold. While this was carried out, the faithful spread cloths and towels around the bishop in order to gather the precious blood of the martyr.

Then St Cyprian bound his own eyes. As he could not tie his own hands, the priest Julian, together with a deacon, offered him this service. In that posture Cyprian met death. The martyrdom was enacted by the bishop as a liturgy in which he was, as Christ on the Cross, both victim and priest.

Saint Augustine

St Augustine (354–430) is generally considered the universal genius, the truly Catholic churchman and theologian whose books have been of immense importance for Christian thought throughout the ages and this theology took form in the otherwise little known town of Hippo on the North African coast.

As a young man he was deeply involved in the thought-world of his generation – being a Manichaean for nine years – until he took the step to conversion and Christian baptism in 387. Five years later he found himself – much to his surprise and against his will – ordained and in 394 made bishop in Hippo, to which diocese he was to give thirty-six years of unique leadership and inspiration.

He has interpreted his own life in an autobiography, *Confessions*, in the form of a long prayer to God. It is a deeply personal literary document, intimate at times, with searching self-knowledge – 'a manifesto of the inner world'.[20] These words come from the introduction to *Confessions*: 'You have created us to yourself, and our heart cannot be quieted unless it finds rest in you', *Fecisti nos ad te et inquietum est cor nostrum donec requiescat in te*.

As bishop he had a biblical message to convey. When he found himself suddenly chosen as bishop, he insisted that he take ample time for a retreat so as to read the Bible. He had an extraordinary memory and was able, while preaching, to recall examples and stories from the Old and New Testaments. The Bible was 'the medicine to his soul'.[21] This helped him to formulate his memorable sentences: 'This man who, whenever he says anything, seems to be saying it for the first time.'[22]

He was greatly influenced by his mother, Monica. Dr E. Mashingaidze of Zimbabwe has made an observation of relevance to the Church in Africa: 'It is the mother who encourages her son to accept new ideas.'[23] This was definitely the case with the devout Christian mother of St Augustine (the medieval Church was to call her St Monica). She was from Thagaste in Berber-dominated South Numidia and thus her son the bishop was 'most probably' of mixed Berber background.[24] 'Augustine's Berber descent shows itself in numerous small ways'.[25] It was this heritage, perhaps, which induced Monica to have visions from time to time by which she could advise her son.[26] It was Monica who persuaded him to abandon his Manichaean faith, to which he, as a young man, had adhered.

In his conversion crisis, in 387, St Augustine's Christian mother was his support. She was a truly great woman who had received elementary education and Augustine enjoyed discussions with her, referring to her as a philosopher whose disciple he loved to be. 'She can dismiss a whole philosophical school in a single vulgar word', says Peter Brown, and Professor Ragnar Holte, of Uppsala, writing on 'Monica the Philosopher', says of the dialogue between mother and son: 'There is a most touching and enchanting mutual respect and acknowledgement, or even humility, an ardent wish from either side to be instructed, inspired and elevated by the other's experience and insights.'[27]

As bishop, St Augustine was existentially engaged in the struggle against what he regarded as the three great adversary systems of his generation, Manichaeism, Donatism and Pelagianism. The study of St Paul and of the Bible as a whole made him discover divine grace (*gratia*) as the fundamental power for the religious and moral life of the individual and of the Church. This emphasis on divine grace helped him overcome what he saw as a dangerously and narrowly moralistic tendency in earlier and contemporary theology.

He could try out his thoughts in continuous and daily encounter with the enquiring minds of the young priests in his monastery, and he would generalize and simplify his ideas in weekly sermons to a responsive crowd of people from very different intellectual and theological backgrounds. Add to this something about his complex personality, his freshness and freedom of mind, his immense courage in taking and defending a standpoint – and one has an idea of how he could produce a great and enduring theological message.

St Augustine is the greatest theologian that Africa has produced. Not all theologians are at the same time inspiring preachers and bishops, but St Augustine was. Seated in his cathedral he sometimes preached to as many as 2,000 people, all standing before him as the custom was at the time. 'Augustine bore neither cross nor ring. His figure was slight, his features somewhat sharp, his head shaven. He was usually wrapped in a cloak or *birrus* (probably dark in colour), open in front.' He held his congregation spell-bound and they responded vivaciously to his message. 'This unusual liveliness, presumably a heritage of Berber blood, was fortunately displayed as much in spiritual matters as in the people's outward bearing.'[28] In his sermons in the city basilica he would not forget the poor labouring Berbers. He had seen them working in the fields and heard them sing as they laboured (*maxime jubilant qui in agris*), anticipating humming and hymn-singing of people at work in the fields of Africa some 1,500 years later.

As a Bishop preaching to his congregations, St Augustine was aware of the linguistic problems in the Hippo diocese. Both he and his Donatist opponents recognized there were two languages to worry about, Latin and

Punic, the latter a Semitic language closely related to Hebrew. Because of this affinity of Punic to Hebrew, Augustine used Punic words when he wished to explain biblical words. As a bishop Augustine felt the need of having a clergy skilled in Punic for his diocese. While some of the cultured Latin-speaking class looked down upon Punic as inferior, Augustine insisted on Punic as an honourable part of their native heritage. Even if he did not himself preach in the language and had to use interpreters when necessary, he would, by this reference to Punic words and proverbs, gain the good will of the audience and increase the cheerfulness of the congregation as well as, no doubt, that of his own good humour.[29]

As a preacher St Augustine had none of the pomposity characteristic of some bishops. He had a liveliness which was part of his great communicative charisma. He was the opposite of the pious recluse. He loved to be surrounded by people, the more the merrier, although he felt the burden of his episcopal office. The Bishop's house in Hippo was turned into a monastic chapter and establishment where his young priests were living with their bishop and taught the Bible by him. Sometimes a bad sleeper, he would dictate chapters of his books to his young scribes and co-workers during the night. At least five of these young men trained by Augustine were later to become bishops themselves.[30]

Donatism

As bishop and theologian, St Augustine acted as a polemicist, and from the point of view of North Africa the struggle with the Donatists was of particular importance. While the Catholics were particularly strong in the Romanized cities on the coast, the Donatists dominated the inland plains in Numidia and among the Berber-speaking labourers on the inland estates.

In modern terms one would characterize the Donatists as a 'holiness' movement. According to them the true Church consists of holy members. They felt that they could rely on Tertullian's and Cyprian's authority for their standpoint. Particularly abhorrent in their eyes were the *traditores*, such Catholic bishops who had, in times of persecution, 'handed over' the Holy Scriptures to be burned in order to placate the demands of the pagan state. The Donatists were likely to identify their Catholic adversaries with such *traditores*. In this struggle the Donatists, according to Augustine, represented a 'heresy' and through his long struggle on this front Augustine managed to stamp them with this mark.

African Church history, in later centuries, was to face the fatal power of denominationalism with its notoriously divisive and weakening influence. In the Catholic propaganda of the period, Donatism was seen as an early example of such denominationalism. They were named after Donatus who, in the time of the Great Persecution, 303–05, had become a bishop in North Africa and represented the claims of the holiness tradition in the Church with great vigour. Donatus claimed that his Church was *the* Catholic Church in Africa, 'sanctified by the martyrs and purified from its errors by their leader Donatus.' During the fourth century Donatism experienced rapid growth, not least among the Berber in Numidia, although by about the year 400 they were weakened by inner divisions.

A decisive date in the struggle between Catholics and Donatists was the conference between the two contending parties at Carthage in 411. Each side was represented by no less than 280 bishops, disputing in the large *Thermae* – or baths – in Carthage, under the supposedly impartial presidency of Count Marcellinus, the Emperor's representative. Each side had eighteen special spokesmen – seven speakers and seven deputies, with four invigilators to supervise the drafting of the record. After three days of vehement debate, Marcellinus pronounced sentence in favour of the Catholics, and the Emperor himself was soon to ratify this. The Donatist clergy were to be exiled and dispatched to remote corners of the Empire.

While the Donatist Church must be seen primarily as a religious movement with an urge for holiness, martyrdom and the study of the Bible, their militant arm, the fanatic 'Circumcellions', appear primarily as social revolutionaries. They were determined – by religious fervour and visits to martyrs' graves – to gather strength for a total overthrow of the social and political order. On the big estates near Hippo, Donatist preachers managed to instil on their labouring listeners a deep sense of social injustice. Parallels have been suggested with the Peasants' Revolt of 1381 in England, and the Peasants' Rising of 1524 in Germany.[31] For the purpose of this book on African Church history it is natural to draw the parallel with the Kikuyu rising in the 1950s ('Mau Mau') and the Zimbabwe war of liberation in the 1970s.

Marcellinus' decision was a victory for the Catholic side and for Bishop Augustine himself. That the controversy itself was a tragedy for the Christian cause as a whole was not seen by the conquerors who preferred to expel their adversaries rather than attempting to integrate them as a healthy salt in the body of the Church. It needs to be added, however, that despite his anti-Donatist and anti-Pelagian polemics, St Augustine was led to conceive an infinitely more wide-hearted theology. More particularly, his teaching about grace, according to which faith itself is a gift of God, laid the foundation for a truly Catholic theology. The first life of St Augustine was written by an episcopal colleague of his, Passidius, a comprehensive account of St Augustine's personal development. It is also remarkably balanced when assessing Augustine's contacts with the Donatists. It is an impressive African contribution to African church history.

Arian Vandals

In the year of St Augustine's death, 430, both parties – Catholic and Donatist – were overrun by a more serious adversary, the Arian Vandals who swept through North Africa. In the age of European population movements, a Germanic tribe had begun a southerly move across the map of Europe. They crossed France and Spain, reaching North Africa in 429. On the way they met and accepted Christianity in its Arian, anti-Catholic form. With the capture of Carthage in 439 the Vandals were the masters of North Africa, ruling there for a century. In that period they were to cause terrible destruction of Catholic churches, monasteries and in the personal lives of Church leaders, until in 533, Emperor Julianos of Constantinople managed to reconquer North Africa. The Catholic Church was then given more than a century of respite for reorganization and relatively quiet growth – until the latter part of the seventh century.

The next, and this time definitive, conquest – through Muslim invasion – obliterated most of what there was of a Christian Church. Subject to the Muslim role of *dhimmi* (protected status for religious minorities) both Christians and Jews could subsist for some time in certain areas, although very much on the margins of society and housed in special quarters of the cities. In certain parts of North Africa, islands of Christian influence held out for a long time. In the sands of the country south of Tripoli, archaeologists have found Christian gravestones from 945–1003, and their very local Latin inscriptions (*bixit* for *vixit* and *bitam* for *vitam*) testify to characteristic local influence.

This gallant Berber attempt at writing Latin is perhaps an even more important indication of why there ultimately followed a great difference between the fate of the Church in North Africa and its fate in Egypt. In Egypt the Coptic Church was Coptic, in and through its very own language, proudly possessed, and its means of expression in personal prayer and common worship. In North Africa the Church spoke Latin and the Bible translations were in Latin, a language appropriated for the Church's elite by Tertullian, St Cyprian and St Augustine, but never fully assimilated by the labouring masses on the inland estates.

Thus in a comparatively short period of time the young Church along the North African coastline was overrun by two harsh adversaries – the Arian

Vandals and the Muslim Arabs – and then came the end. This tragic finale has of late been subject to adverse comment directed against the evangelistic inadequacy of the North African Catholic Church, as compared with the missionary drive of the Coptic Church to the east.

The Christian community did not give up without resistance. Towards the end of the 690s the Arabs met with resolute Berber opposition under the prophetess Kahina. The Arab forces under Hassan were repulsed and had to withdraw eastward, but they persevered and soon returned. In 703 Kahina was defeated and slain. Her sons, more pragmatic than their prophetic mother, adopted Islam and from then on Berbers and Arabs made common cause.

Whom to blame?

It has been maintained by one writer that 'the great failure of the African Church was the failure to evangelize' and he suggested that 'the chance to enter Africa from the north was not given again.'[32] Another writer was more specific: 'in the centuries from AD 200 to AD 700 Christianity missed its supreme chance of expansion in the immense land empire from the North African coast to the tenth parallel of Latitude North'.[33]

These reprimands are misplaced. For one thing they do not take into consideration the geography of the area. In the north of the continent geography was infinitely more disadvantageous for evangelization than in Egypt to the east. In the east, two great parallel waterways – the River Nile and the Red Sea – both furthered communication and interchange of ideas, and the Church's missionaries could travel along the water in order to evangelize in the south – Nubia and Ethiopia. These advantages did not obtain in North Africa where beyond the populated zones there stretched the vast impenetrable forests and the deserts.

Of course one might speculate on the linguistic problem: what would have happened if St Augustine and his colleagues had been fluent in the language of the Berbers and thus able to address the Berber-speaking masses and whether this could have changed developments after the onslaught of the Vandals and the final embrace of the Arabs. But somehow these speculations come a little late. History will have to take consolation from von Harnack's version of these matters.

The great historian of the early Church, Adolf von Harnack, in his *Mission und Ausbreitung* (first published in 1915), takes a final look at the fate of the Christian Church in North Africa. He concludes his chapter on North Africa:

> As a Church province, Africa has a timeless endurance in the history of the Church through its three great sons Tertullian, St Cyprian, and St Augustine. It is one of the most paradoxical facts of history that, after St Paul, Christianity received its strongest impulse for further development from the seashore of Tunisia.[34]

NUBIA

The 1,000 years of Nubia's Church history – 450? to 1450? – stand out in the record of the Church in Africa. Consider the drama of its discovery, made only recently in the 1950s and 1960s. For centuries this history had been hidden, until the concerted scientific archaeological efforts of the world community, co-ordinated by UNESCO – with fifty-nine archaeological expeditions to Nubia in the period 1959–1969 – uncovered an extraordinary Christian culture, in ruins, yet sufficiently well-preserved to allow a breathtaking impression of the glorious riches of this ancient Church.

The occasion for this combined effort on the part of archaeologists and engineers arose with the realization that the building of the 'High Dam' between the First and Second Cataracts of the Nile would result in an enormous permanent lake which would submerge and destroy many invaluable monuments. The resulting High Dam Campaign was committed to the 'dismantling, transportation, and reconstruction on higher ground' of ancient temples and other monuments.[35] Certain expeditions, notably the Polish, were in a position to concentrate on the cathedrals of Faras, Abdullah Nirqi and Sonqi, which among other things brought to light 169 Faras wall-paintings of extraordinary beauty and also an anchoret's grotto.

A divided mission

There is an official year for the beginnings of the Christianization of Nubia: AD 543. But perhaps a 100 years before the arrival of the official heralds of the new religion, anonymous witnesses had brought the message into the country. Recent excavations have uncovered a Christian church of unbaked brick from a period well before AD 543, and finds of pottery and oil lamps with the Christian cross and other symbols, also before that date, testify to some Christian activity which 'readily made converts among the poor'. Just as later on, in other parts of the continent religious ideas were carried by anonymous witness. Northern Nubia had been reached by unknown Christians traders, possibly Coptic monks, or Coptic refugees who had arrived along that incomparable way of communication, the River Nile –

bringing with them their objects and with these, ideas and expectations symbolized by these wares.[36]

However, there followed an official imperial initiative which was significant in subsequent development in the country. Emperor Justinian in Constantinople, as much churchman as political ruler, was anxious to preserve the unity of his realm by insisting on the Orthodox faith as formulated by Chalcedon. He could not, however, avoid opposition, particularly as his empress Theodora was an enthusiastic protectress of the Unionite conviction. A Coptic priest named Julian implored Theodora to send missionaries to Nubia and the zealous empress suggested to the Emperor that Julian should be sent. A secret competition between husband and wife ensued, both designing to arrive first with their own special envoy. In this race along the Nile, Theodora won. Julian arrived in 543 thus securing for Coptic Monophysitism the privileged position, while the Emperor's man was initially unsuccessful. Julian spent two years in Nubia and managed to baptize the king and the aristocracy and to constitute in his place the bishop of Philae by the name of Theodore. A former guest house was converted into a church, called by modern archaeologists the 'Rivergate Church', thus using the same method as in Coptic Egypt where former pagan temples or other official buildings could be converted into churches.[37]

The bishop's task was complicated as the country was divided into three kingdoms along the River Nile, with Nobatia in the North – near the Second Cataract of the Nile – followed by the kingdoms of Makouria and Alodia. Around 570, Makouria accepted the Melchite (or Orthodox) faith, while a decade later Alodia turned to Monophysitism (all according to the account given by John of Ephesus, himself a Unionite).[38] Here also the Christian Church presented a divided image.

The impact of Arab rule in Egypt from 641 could not but affect Nubia too, isolating it from ready access to the Mediterranean Christian world. An Arab attack on the country followed in 641, but ten years later the two parties could agree on a remarkable peace treaty which virtually guaranteed Nubian independence and which – with later modifications – was to last for 700 years. The Arabs pledged themselves not to wage war against Nubia while the Nubians promised to deliver annually – later modified to every three years – 360 slaves 'from the finest slaves of your country . . . both male and female'. The Nubians also promised to look after the mosque built in the Christian capital: 'you are not to prevent anyone from worshipping in it . . . and you are to sweep it, keep it lighted and honour it.' The treaty concludes in terms which could be a guide to modern efforts at a dialogue between the two religions: 'Incumbent on you toward us is the utmost observance of the good faith of the Messiah and that of the Disciples and of any of the people of your religion and community whom you reverence. God be the Witness of that between us.'

A royal Church

To a much larger extent than in Egypt, Nubia's Church history was that of its kings, taking on the aspects of a court religion, while the masses were, perhaps, only superficially incorporated into the Church. This gave status to an institution, presumably closely associated with the cosmic powers, and allowed for the planning and building of impressive ecclesiastical monuments and for the commission of artistic work in the cathedrals. Under its Christian kings Nubia, particularly the Nobatia kingdom, saw a rapid economic development with irrigation schemes – some areas had piped water from the River Nile – which benefited agriculture (wheat, barley, millet, and grapes).

The king in Nubia was at the same time a high-ranking priest – the idea of sacred kingship had been transferred to the Church. Some of the kings were remarkable personalities. Merkurios (697–707: 10/30) referred to by sycophantic aristocrats and bishops as 'the new Constantine' gave to Nubia much of its political unity and prosperity. Together with Bishop Paulos he planned and realized the reconstruction of Faras Cathedral and ensured a steady development as far as church buildings were concerned. More than a century later King Georgios I, who ruled for the long period 860–920, was to extend his influence beyond the national borders. With mounting Arab pressure on the Coptic Church in Egypt he seems to have been accepted 'as at least a semi-official protector of the Coptic Patriarch of Alexandria, and thus in some sense responsible for the whole Christian population of Egypt'.[39] Another Nubian king, Georgios II, was approached, during a Church crisis, by the king of Ethiopia to send a canonically consecrated bishop to lead the Ethiopian Church.

There were thus Nubian Christian influences towards the North and the East. Even more surprising is the presumed extension westwards, near Darfur nearly half-way to the Niger, a centre for age long contacts between the Nile and the Niger. At Ain Fara, archaeologists have discovered pottery with typical Christian symbols, a fish and the cross or a dove's head and the cross, all from the tenth century. What once was thought to have been a mosque may have been a church, and the building on the nearby hill-top was built initially as cells for Christian monks.[40]

Faras

Great care was given to the building of churches, from the smaller buildings of unbaked brick in the centre of villages to cathedrals in stone or baked brick, with the cathedral in the capital of Faras as the most prominent. It was built in the seventh century and renewed in 707, the latter a reconstruction under the leadership of Bishop Paulos. This allowed for an artistic activity of surprising wealth, with large mural paintings of biblical and ecclesiastical personalities becoming the inspiration to other ecclesiastical buildings. Many of these splendid paintings may be seen today in the National Museum in Warsaw, the rest in the National Museum in Khartoum. One of the cathedral walls had a list of names of the succession of twenty-seven bishops, a document obviously of immense importance for the reconstruction of the history of the Church and for the dating of the artistic styles of the paintings. The colour-scheme of the wall-paintings shows a chronological development with a scale of colours from the eighth to the twelfth century, with at first violet to red tones and finally dark-brown tones. Of special interest for our history is a picture on the east wall of the Bishop's Hall in the Faras Cathedral. It shows the Madonna and Saint Peter, the bishop's Patron Saint, together with Bishop Petros, the latter with a dark brown face indicating the definitive Africanization of the hierarchy at this time. It is claimed that this picture was made during the lifetime of the bishop who died in 999.

About 926 the Faras cathedral was hit by fire but was later reconstructed. Finally, around 1170, the cathedral dome and the nave vault were destroyed, although for a time the side aisles could still be used for worship. Yet gradually, the sands of the desert with their implacable power surrounded and submerged the cathedral and similar remains and ruins of this Christian culture.[41]

Alodia and Soba

In 580 the ruler of Alodia approached his colleague in Nobatia to ask for missionaries. Dr Jacobielski has pointed out that in Alodia Christianization did not appear through a sudden change but had been prepared by an 'infiltration of Christianity' from the neighbouring country of Aksum. Soba, the southern-most kingdom, takes the Church 400 miles further south into Africa. Soba was converted to Christianity about 580, most probably by traders and monks from Aksum. A cathedral of red brick was built at the capital, the remains of which are currently being excavated. Soba had three churches. The Soba churches seem to have been comparable to Faras and Dongola. It is possible that Soba had adjacent churches with a baptistery between them. To a much larger extent than in Nobatia and Makouria, the Soba churches used timber for the columns of the churches.

The remarkable community of Nubiologist scholars have discussed the similarities and differences between north and south in Nubian Church history. Much of the archaeological material remains to be found and analyzed. Professor William Y. Adams, after writing his authoritative volume *Nubia, Corridor to Africa*, has said: 'the question of cultural differences between the Christian north and south is one that must still be "argued with a shovel".'[42]

Disintegration of a Church

Two forces, from the south and the north, marked the end of Christianity in Nubia. At the beginning of the sixteenth century the Funj people, having accepted Islam, conquered Soba and Alodia from the south. At the same time the Ottomans conquered Egypt and pushed south towards Nobatia. In spite of these military conquests elements of Christian faith survived, particularly near the Third Cataract, and in connexion with certain family rituals. In the eighteenth century the ruler of the Kokka kingdom was still recognized as being Christian.[43]

Why did this Church of Nubia come to an end? For one thing, the faith had not reached deep enough. It was a court religion, the concern of a ruling caste. The people in the countryside had only a superficial understanding of what it was all about. There does not seem to have existed any training of a local clergy. Not only bishops but also priests and deacons were largely foreigners, having been sent there from abroad. Portraits and documents testify to the existence of a Nubian clergy but they were few, too few. Nubia lived for seven centuries in great isolation from the rest of the world – except for its emigrants in Cairo and Jerusalem. The change from an agricultural mode of production to nomadic life took some two to three generations. In the final 'twilight of Christianity' there were strong social influences from Arab nomads, who intermarried into Nubian families.[44]

AKSUM

The waterway of the Nile made possible a rapid expansion of the Church from the Delta and adjoining monastic centres to Upper Egypt and the three kingdoms of Nubia. Similarly the beginnings of the Church in northern

Ethiopia depended on another, parallel waterway, that of the Red Sea, making possible contacts between the Semitic population on the south-western Arabian coast and the northern Cushitic communities in Ethiopia. For at least a 1,000 years before Christ, people had migrated from southern Arabia into northern Ethiopia. The Acts of the Apostles, Chapter 8, has a reference to an Ethiopian eunuch, working with Queen Candace (Qinaquis), of importance for Ethiopian Church history and its relationship to Jerusalem. 'Ethiopian' in this context meaning Meroe, in the modern Sudan. Merchants from Saba on the Arabian coast brought their desirable goods – mats, incense, ceramics – and sometimes decided to settle in the new country.

Place-names often provide important clues to early cultural contacts. In south-western Arabia and in Eritrea and Tigray, certain place-names are almost identical, no doubt brought by Semitic immigrants as they settled on the Ethiopian side of the Red Sea. Linguistic studies, also, indicate these ancient connexions, although an earlier held view of the Ge'ez language as derived from the Sabean is no longer so firmly established; the importance of the Cushitic contributions is becoming increasingly acknowledged. The traditional religion of South Arabia with its moon deity Athtar found its way over the waters to be assimilated with Cushitic pagan beliefs.

The period was one of more mobility and geographical exploits than it is generally given credit for. Meropius, a Christian of Tyre in Syria, went to 'India' and took two young men along, Adesius and Frumentius. On the return voyage they stopped at one of the Eritrean harbours where the crew was intercepted and only the two young men were rescued and taken to King Ella-Amida at Aksum. The king made Adesius his cup-bearer and the gifted Frumentius steward of his fortune. When the king died, Prince Ezana was too young to reign, and the Queen Mother asked the two foreigners to assist her in the administration. Frumentius was now in a position to give special consideration to Christian traders arriving at the court and to provide them with a site on which to build a small Church where he could bring them together for worship. Eventually, Frumentius and his friend were freed to return to Syria and on the way Frumentius visited Patriarch Athanasius in Alexandria. While giving him a vital report on the Church in Aksum, he was able to share with the Patriarch his concern about the need for a bishop from Egypt to guide the emerging Christian movement. For St Athanasius the choice was not difficult. He made Frumentius a bishop and consecrated him sometime between 341 and 346. By this act the ecclesiastical links between the Patriarch in Egypt and the Church in Ethiopia were established – supposedly regulated by Coptic Canons, although very much apocryphal – which lasted for no less than 1,600 years.

One should avoid the simplistic idea, based on Eusebius' *Ecclesiastical History*, that the Christianization of Aksum was achieved solely by these youngsters. The case of Aksum was probably not very different from that in other parts of the Middle East. Christianity spread via the Red Sea as it had done in the Mediterranean: by Christian traders bringing their goods and their witness. The coastal towns and the islands in the Red Sea also provided points of communication for religious gestures and ideas. Frumentius' role was of course decisive, but he could operate in a community which was already beginning to be Christianized.

One can follow the religious change in the country on the coins which King Ezana minted. At first these bore the symbol of the crescent and two stars signifying traditional paganism, but eventually they were replaced by the sign of the cross. The King of Aksum had accepted the new faith, thus following the example of his colleague, Emperor Constantine. In Ezana's time Aksum became distinguished by its unique indigenous art, particularly the impressive high grave-stones, or *stelae*, the largest of them seventy feet high (there was one *stela* 110 feet – 35 metres – high which eventually fell, breaking into pieces). The ornamental patterns of the *stelae* with their depictions of doors, windows and floors indicate that the Aksumites erected multi-storey buildings for themselves in the early centuries of the Christian era. The architectural pattern depicted in these beautiful monuments is repeated in the churches of Tigray as well as in the famous rock-hewn churches of Lalibela. As long as the Semitic influence was dominant in Aksum, its churches were constructed on the mountain-tops, nearer the heavens.

Towards the end of the fifth century, with the arrival of the 'Nine Saints', holy men, most of them of Syrian background, the foundation was assured for the Ethiopian monastic movement in Aksum. 'The Nine' built a number of monasteries and churches, among them Debre Damo in Tigray, the oldest existing church in Ethiopia, established on the site of a traditional pagan shrine. Ethiopian architecture had found its characteristic form. It was of beautiful design, situated on an *amba* – one of the flat-topped hills so common to the Ethiopian landscape. In describing northern Ethiopia, one can write not only of a religious geography but of a religious topography as well. For centuries its high mountain plateaux, falling sharply on all sides, became ideal fortresses and refuges where churches and monasteries were built. Debre Damo is one of the most inaccessible church buildings in the world, to be reached only by hardy sportsmen and, of course, pious Ethiopians. A winding path takes the visitor up a high hill until he stands in front of a vertical cliff. From there one climbs to the actual church with the help of a fifteen-metre cable of plaited copper. The timelessness of early monasticism is almost physically present.

'The Nine', all devoted Unionites, had arrived in Ethiopia at the end of the fifth century as refugees after Chalcedon. Three monks were to become the very backbone of the emerging Church and soon attracted thousands of men and women into their ranks, totally devoted to the Church. They became the carriers of a literary and liturgical movement which gave the young Church its style and its strength, but were also decisive in taking the Christian message to the illiterate masses. They acquired undisputed status and power in the country. The first beginnings of the 'Qêrilos' were now slowly emerging: a theological compilation in Ge'ez of Patristic texts, particularly from St Cyril, which were eventually to become the foundation of Ethiopian theology and faith.

As the churches were built, holy wells with the power to heal all illnesses would miraculously spring up on the spot. It was better not to cross these holy men. If angered they might hit back. Matta Libanos, called 'the apostle of Eritrea', translated the Gospel of St Matthew into Ge'ez, but when leaving Aksum he is believed to have sent a drought to the country lasting for three years. He thus coerced both king and metropolitan to follow his will.

The first two centuries saw the establishment of the foundations of the Church in Aksum, achieved through the determination and devotion of Christian kings and monks. In the sixth century, Aksum had a powerful ruler in Kaleb, 510–58. He came to the military rescue of the battered Christian communities in southern Arabia, and Aksum ruled the Himyarite kingdom in southern Arabia between 520 and 525. With the help of monks Kaleb was able to convert the pagan masses. Placed in the north of the country, with constant contacts with the Syrian church across the Red Sea and having acquiesced to a far-reaching dependence on the Patriarch in Alexandria (later in Cairo), the Church in Aksum presented an image whereby its ecclesiastical experience was an Ethiopian illustration of the universality of the church.

Zagwe and Solomonide Dynasties

However, the glories of Aksum came slowly to an end. The monks took the lead in shifting the centre of Church and State from Aksum in the north to the central highlands. From the eighth century, colonies of faithful Christians began to move south with their Ge'ez language, their liturgy and their Unionite version of Christianity.

In the tenth century there was a revolt led by the Agew chieftainess, Gudit (Judith), followed by a long period of almost fatal weakness of the Christian regime. This was emphasized by the fact that for long decades the Patriarch in Alexandria could not, or would not, send a new bishop or *abun* to be the official head of the Ethiopian Church. In the meantime the coastline was the scene of rising Muslim power. Towards the end of the thirteenth century, Ethiopia was surrounded by Muslim states, and about the year 1300, Islam held sway over half of present-day Ethiopia.

Two dynasties dominated the twelfth and thirteenth centuries: the Zagwe from 1137–1270, and the Solomonides from 1270 – incomparably creative years in Ethiopian religious history. The Zagwe dynasty came to power in a new rebellion of the Agew people in Lasta, the central province. Their most famous king was Lalibela (1190–1225) who built his capital at Roha in the Lasta mountains, later named Lalibela after the king. He was a deeply religious personality, the King-Priest, withdrawing at times for meditation, and an architechtural genius. For three days he had a revelation of the New Jerusalem to be built at Roha. His capital had to surpass ancient Aksum with its Old Testament symbols, such as the Throne of David and the Tables of the Lord. Instead the New Jerusalem was to extol Christ, the New Testament and the Apocrypha. To that end eleven churches were cut out of the red volcanic tuff of the mountain, with an Ethiopian River Jordan in their midst, all inspired by one single vision. These temples, many not visible above ground, were clustered together, and are breath-taking beautiful as well as affording proof of dedication, skill and ingenuity. The Medani-Alem church was the largest and the most beautiful, measuring 33.5 by 23.5 metres. Another sanctuary, Abba Libanos, was built in a grotto.

The siting of the churches changed. They were no longer placed on the high mountains as in Aksum times but, adapting to the local Agew valley population with their river cults and holy wells, the churches were now built close to holy and healing waters. The monks made use of spring waters to Christianize the people. There was a grotto known to have a holy spring: so a church was built inside the grotto. Of course, they brought the Holy Word in that holy language, *Ge'ez* but in doing so they found a spot for the holy building – near flowing waters. This was, in a dry land, a response to a deep-rooted human need for life-giving and healing water. The royal vision and the artisans' craftsmanship transformed the young institution from a Coptic Church into a truly indigenous, Ethiopian Church.

The Solomonides

The Solomonide period developed Ethiopian spirituality at its noblest. The ideological foundation and character of the new kingdom was to be found in its fundamental document: the *Kibre Negest* – Glory of Kings – containing the myth of a sacred link between the Old Testament and Ethiopia. The core of this myth is the legend of the Queen of Sheba – a literary enlargement on certain passages in I Kings 10:1–13: how the Queen visited King Solomon, accepted his faith and bore him a son, Minilik I. When this son had spent some time with his father in Jerusalem, he took the Ark of the Covenant from the Holy City and brought it back with him to Aksum, the new Zion. As important as the Old Testament is to the Hebrews or the Koran to the Arabs, so the *Kibre Negest* is to the Ethiopians. It is 'the most genuine expression of Abyssinian Christianity'. This central myth lies at the root of the national and religious inheritance of a sacred king, people and Church. Ethiopian liturgical and literary life have been inspired by these documents. Every church, with its threefold division, is modelled on the Hebrew Temple and has its *tabot* (altar stone) as its most holy and precious property. At this time, too, the churches were moved onto the hill-tops again, visible from far and wide.

The *Kibre Negest* regards the Zagwe kings as usurpers and relates how all the descendants of the royal house in Aksum were killed: only one boy was saved by the monks and hidden in the monastery. Tekle Haymanot, the outstanding monastic leader – *c.* 1215–1313 – helped this boy to regain royal power. In 1270 he began his rule as Yikunno Amlak, thus restoring the Solomonic dynasty and opening the golden age of Ethiopia. Yikunno Amlak rewarded Tekle Haymanot for his help by awarding to him and the Church one third of state lands as a perpetual feudal benefice. Thus the Ethiopian monk patriarch was able to make his monastery, Debre Libanos, the leading religious centre of the country. The King's bequest was of enormous importance as long as the Church enjoyed the unlimited confidence of the people. When this relationship was questioned, the Church was increasingly to find its land ownership an embarrassment.

Amda Sion (1314–44), one of the most powerful of the Solomonide kings, was successful in his wars against the enemies. His victories led to mass conversion to Christianity and to a period of impressive building of churches and monasteries. His greatest successor was Zar'a Ya'qob (1434–68), 'unquestionably the greatest ruler Ethiopia had seen since Ezana'.[45] He continued his country's military expansion but above all devoted himself to the promotion of church and culture. This king was a religious author who wrote or edited a number of books for the benefit of the Christians. By 'associating the Church more closely with the throne, Zar'a Ya'qob greatly enhanced the mystery and ritual with which the monarchy was imbued and which have become a mark and symbol of Ethiopian sacral kingship.'[46]

The highland of Abyssinia was at the time less isolated than one would expect. From the medieval crusades arose the myth of 'Prester John', and when Ethiopian pilgrims appeared in Cairo, Cyprus and Jerusalem, the Catholic Church desired contact and even union with Prester John's Church. The fifteenth-century Christians saw Islam approach Europe across Asia Minor, and finally capture Constantinople in 1453. The Church through the Council of Florence, meeting from 1439–42 realized the necessity for a united Christendom.

It was during this medieval period in Ethiopia that the rise of the 'Holy Men' occurred. At first, in the province of Shewa, a new militant monastic movement grew, often sharply and courageously critical of royalty and its polygamy. Preparation for life in the great monasteries involved a change in personal identity, with a new garb and a new name. There were three groups of clerics in the Ethiopian church: parish priests, monks and nuns, and *debteras* (men of religious learning). Monasteries provided for the celibate branch of the clergy, and were often the standard-bearers for the various doctrinal parties engaged in internecine arguments. Some of the monasteries helped to fashion the character of the people in their midst, as did the one at Debre Margos, which encouraged the surrounding Orthodox peasantry of Gojjam to sternly resist any foreign influence. Gojjam had thousands of monks and priests, and the adjacent areas of Begemdir and Shewa also proudly claimed a very high number. Women were not encouraged to become nuns until they were over fifty years old and widowed, but many left their families to join an order. Convents usually adjoined a monastery and in Begemdir and Shewa monks and nuns were members of the same religious community. The monks were also the ecclesiastical artists. The monastery acted as an arts school where gifted men would exchange experiences and inspire one another to greater achievements in the beautification of the churches.

In the eyes of the peasant population, the monks had supernatural powers, they could exorcize demonic spirits and were renowned healers. 'Such cures as were achieved resulted not from the holy man's application of a special medical knowledge or training, but rather from his use of religious techniques involving prayer, the cross, the Eucharist, monastic garb and holy water.' This healing power was very efficacious in the monks' missionary activities, reaching out to the unchurched peasant masses. A rumour about a successful healing, together with singing of psalms and sometimes the display of liturgical vestments, demonstrated to everyone the attraction of the monks' religion. After such a demonstration the actual conversion of a particular group or community could be a brief and informal affair, involving profession of faith in the Triune God, baptism and a new name. In the national arena, the services of the holy men were of particular importance in preparation for war: 'predictions and blessings before battle and moral assistance on the battlefield', for which services the king gave them land and booty. From their monasteries the holy men influenced deeply the life of both the nobility and the ordinary peasants.[47]

In these centuries of Zagwe and more particularly, of Solomonide rule, the Church had been given the chance for uniquely significant growth. An indigenous church culture of the highest originality and beauty had been created. Churches and monasteries had, as their richest treasures, paintings and ancient manuscripts of the greatest value. A spiritual heritage had matured to be claimed not only by later generations in Ethiopia, but also by churches throughout Africa and beyond, even to the islands off the American continent. This was as far as the Ethiopian Church had arrived AD 1500, before the advent of Imam Ahmed Ibrahim.

2

MARITIME CONNECTIONS

EXPLORERS OF SEAS AND SOULS

Throughout the Middle Ages the Mediterranean Sea – with Rome, Constantinople and Alexandria – marked the core and, to some extent, the horizon of the Christian Church. In 1453 this perspective suddenly changed. An incredulous Christian world heard that the Muslims had taken Constantinople and that the Hagia Sophia had been turned into a mosque.

No nations were more deeply shaken by this news than Portugal and Spain, themselves only recently freed from Muslim control. They therefore became all the more involved when the Pope called for a new crusade against the enemies of Christianity. The small Portuguese nation – at this time no more than 2 million – was looking for a solution and found it in Prince Henry the Navigator, son of King Joao I, who had the vision and the resolve to find a new passage over the seas.

Gone were the times of using the manpower of oarsmen. Technical advances in ship design were experimented with and worked. Sails, sternpost and compass were the answer, and ever more sophisticated shapes and sizes of sails related to longer and finer forms of 'caravels' and 'galleons'. With the discovery of the potential of sailing ships, there were seemingly no limits to what could be attempted and achieved via the seas.

From the Mediterranean to the Atlantic and Indian Oceans and their peoples, the world outlook changed. Even before Columbus sailed westward, Portuguese ships, often with Genoese sailors, ventured south to Ceuta and to the Canary and Cape Verde islands. In Ceuta they met Arab merchants who knew about West Africa from their trade caravans across the desert. The sailors had already met Africans in Portugal. Black slaves were first acquired from northern Africa as early as the 1440s. With sail-fitted caravels reaching as far as the Upper and Lower Guinea coast, where the off-shore islands of Cape Verde and Sâo Tomé served as embarkation ports, the annual import of slaves to Portugal steadily increased. From 1490–1530 between 300 and 2,000 slaves were brought annually to Lisbon. They

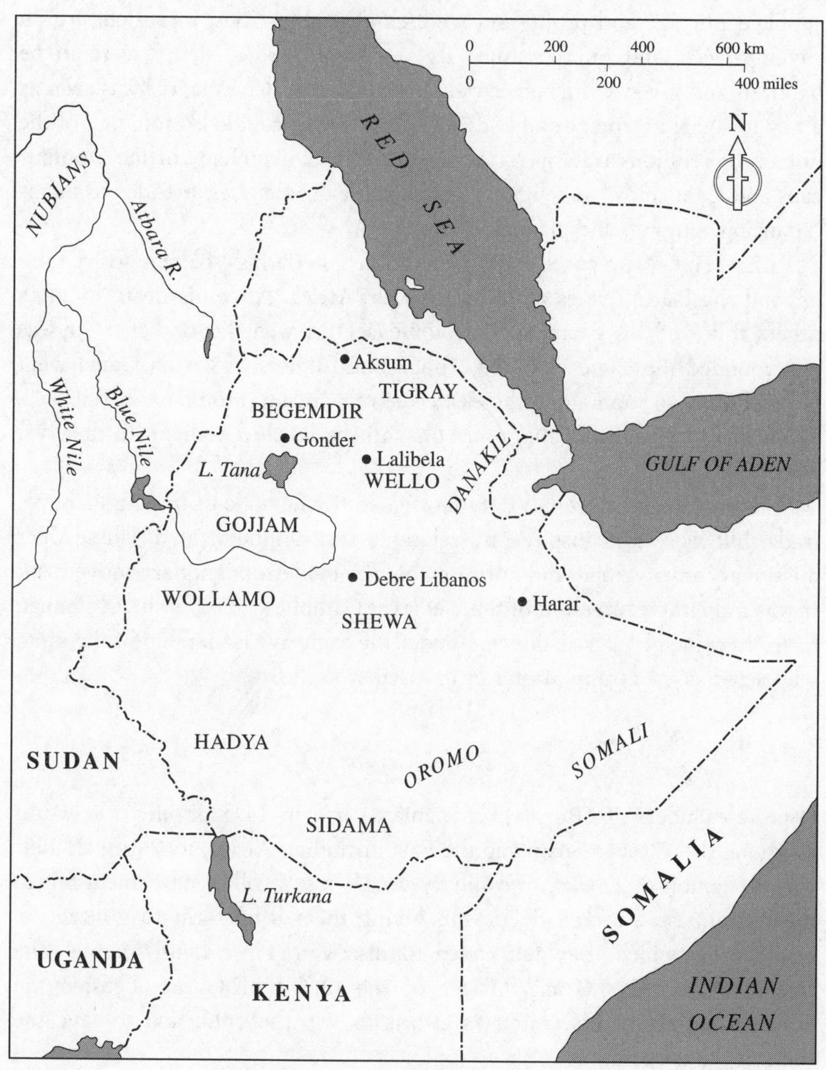

2.1. Ethnic groups and key towns of East Africa.

supplied prestige and profit, and were employed in cities, in agriculture, in royal palaces, and on the ships. By the king's order, slaves were to be baptized and given Christian burial. Conversion to Christianity was seen as a key to social acceptance and advance. The slaves could also join one of the numerous religious fraternities associated with the convents of the Dominicans and Capuchins. At religious festivals, they sometimes attended as bands – dancing, singing, and playing.

Prince Henry prepared new generations of daring seamen to venture beyond the fearful capes along north-west Africa. After his death in 1460, others followed his example. Bartolomeus Diaz went beyond the Guineas and rounded the Cape of Good Hope. The ruthless Vasco da Gama went beyond the Cape and along the east coast of Africa to Mombasa in 1497–98. From there he followed the monsoon until he reached Calicut on the west coast of India.

The Portuguese were not only motivated by the hope of finding lucrative trade, but were also inspired by religious zeal, although at this time their missionary involvement did not resemble the modern missionary movement. It was rather an expression of the medieval Catholic Church in its Lusitanian form. In principle, it was directed under the exclusive leadership of the king, who acted as the Grand Master of the Order of Christ.

Royal Mission

Pope Alexander VI (Borgia), a Spaniard, had in 1493 divided the world assigning the West to Spain and the East, including Africa, to Portugal. This was the famous *padroado*, to ordinary people just a roll of parchment but to the Portuguese a sacred document, giving them legal right to govern the new worlds which they felt called to discover. Their king, Manuel 'the Great', 1495–1521, Grand Master of the Order of Christ, became the director-in-chief of his country's efforts to win the gold, and to save the souls of the dark nations.

For this national–ecclesiastical enterprise the king had at his side a missionary Tribunal, *mesa da conciencia*, consisting of theologians and members from the orders of knighthood. This group was a Portuguese anticipation of Rome's organization almost two centuries later – the Propaganda Fide. Under the personal direction of the king, the Tribunal met twice monthly to settle the numerous matters referred to it. It was an early 'Mission Board', on the threshold between the outgoing Middle Ages and the new era, dedicated to *conquista* in the name of Christ.

This enormous activity and daring exploration – historically speaking comparable only to the exploits of space in our own time – was inspired by a vision of the *zeitgeist* and worldview of the period. Out of this milieu there emerged the special *conquista* idea of Christian mission – a new and unique phenomenon in Church history – and above all, altogether different from any modern concept which was developed in the nineteenth century by Catholic and Protestant mission societies. A Portuguese empire emerged along the coast-lines of Africa and India, and connected with this political conquest there was an idea of Christian conquest, of spiritual crusade and colonization.

It would seem that the *conquista* concept was the invention of the Portuguese Viceroy in Goa, Constantine of Bragansa. It implied establishing trade posts along the coastlines of the oceans and placing chaplains there, along with the traders, to guide them.

Vasco da Gama was on the lookout, he said, for 'pepper and souls'. Pepper and other spices he was to find plentifully to be brought as homage to the king in Lisbon. Souls were a different matter. The special *conquista* task was not so much to preach the Gospel but to induce the foreign peoples to accept Christianity as found and formed in the West. After the barest preparation – learning a pious gesture, 'the Sign of the Cross', and a formula about the Triune God – kings and aristocrats and the masses with the slaves could be incorporated by Baptism into the Christian Church.

WEST AFRICA

In 1458 Diogo Gomez led an expedition to West Africa. In the Gambia he came into contact with a Mandingo chief, Nomimansa, and conversed with him about religious matters. Following a theological dispute between Gomez and a Muslim cleric, Nomimansa expelled the cleric. The chief and others wanted to become Christian, and begged the captain to baptize them, but as he was not a priest he was unable to do this. When Gomez returned to Portugal, he persuaded Prince Henry to send out a priest, the Abbot of Soto de Cassa, to instruct Nomimansa in the Christian faith.

From the fifteenth century, Portuguese societies developed in the Gambia. Settlers married into local families and established small communities, with a church and houses imitating the Portuguese architectural style. A number of churches were built, including one up the Bintang creek called Geregia, a corruption of the Portuguese word for church: *igeresa*. These churches with their communities were served intermittently by visiting priests from the Cape Verde islands (which maintained a staff of twelve friars) or from the convent at Cachau on the Rio Grande, about eighty miles south. But these groups rapidly lost their wealth and prestige, and their Portuguese connections became very tenuous. Some of their descendants emigrated to the Rio Grande, with its Cachau convent, perhaps to preserve their Catholic heritage and their faith.

From 1470 the Portuguese built forts on the 'Gold Coast' (Ghana) at Axim and at Elmina. Dutch, British, French, Germans, and Danes followed. In 1471 Portuguese caravels arrived on the west coast and soon anchored at Mina ('the Mines'), the future Gold Coast. They had brought a few missionaries of the Portuguese Order of Christ. A chapel was erected and the missionaries were prepared to administer daily mass. Preaching and catechization did not seem to be all that necessary for soon there was something more surprising, an apparent miracle. The missionaries had brought along from Portugal wooden statues of the Holy Virgin, and of St Francis and St Anthony of Padua. In the hot and humid climate the face and hands of St Francis changed colour from white to black. The Portuguese governor claimed that the saint was now revealing himself as the patron saint of the Africans.[1]

Before too long there was a mass movement to the baptismal font, sons and wives of chiefs together with a few black nobles. On one occasion the chief of the Efutu people and 1,000 of his men were sprinkled. Yet, having been baptized one had to keep to the faith, as a former female slave, Grace, found to her dismay. She could no longer say the *Ave*. Instead she held that her dead father came during the night to eat small loaves of bread which she had left for him. She was brought to the inquisition judges in Lisbon and was condemned to perpetual captivity in the prison of the Holy Office.[2]

The colonists all brought goods from Europe: muskets, gunpowder, brandy, and trinkets of various kinds. These were exchanged for gold, and later also for people – men and women collected along the River Volta or in the forest belt. The forts were built of stone or wood, surrounded by solid walls and turrets with cannons. Most were sordid places of boredom and whoredom, alcoholism, yellow fever and death, and thus there was much for the chaplains to do. The Danes opened a school for mulatto children in their 'Christianborg' fort, and a soldier was assigned to teach the youngsters from a Danish primer and the Danish hymn book.

One of the first chaplains was Thomas Thompson, 1751–56, sent by the Society for the Propagation of the Gospel. An educated and widely travelled man, he sent four African students to England, hoping to train future leaders. Among them was Philip Quaque, who spent ten years in England, 1756–66. He worked as a schoolmaster and pastor at Cape Coast till his death in 1816. Others also studied abroad and returned to the chaplaincies; J.

Capitein, an African ex-slave trained in Holland, working in the 1740s for the Dutch Reformed Church at Elmina; F. P. Swane, a mulatto with a Ga mother, trained in Copenhagen, becoming catechist and teacher at Christiansborg in the 1740s; and Christian Protten, another mulatto, working with the Moravians first in the West Indies and then at Christiansborg, 1756–69. In 1788 some fifty mulatto and African children from the Windward and Gold Coasts were attending schools in Liverpool.

The coastal forts, symbols of European power, were an altogether closed world, tiny dots on the immense West coast, having no contact with the inland peoples. Until the Europeans arrived, the ocean was a vast forgotten expanse, beyond which some thought the realm of the dead was located.

The British and the French put forts in Whydah, Dahomey, and after 1721 the Portuguese followed their example with a fort, 'Nossa Senhora do Livramento'. The rulers of the place quite possibly did not recognize the ugly irony of the pious name. Far away in Lisbon the king and queen were always prepared to provide for the eternal salvation of their subjects. They sent two priests to the country, and Queen Donna Maria especially commissioned them to convert the African king. They did this with unwavering promptness, informing King Angonglo of the Queen's wish that he be baptized and become a Catholic if he wished to live and die in the true law of God. The king seemed pleased, and declared himself ready to be baptized without delay. The two priests realized the immense potential of the king's readiness – the conversion of the whole population of Dahomey and neighbouring areas – but they had rules to follow, and informed the king that a certain time of catechetical preparation was required. With the assistance of their interpreters, they spent a week translating the Ten Commandments into the local language, looking forward to the great day. Unfortunately, however, they did not proceed fast enough to convey the message of the fifth commandment. The king's brother, to forestall the danger of a royal baptism, poisoned the prospective 'baptisand'.

An individual example of early Catholic missionaries on the West Coast is the life and death of the Spanish Capuchin, Fr Seraphin de Leon, later called 'Senegal's Apostle'. Together with thirteen other Capuchins, he left for Senegal in 1646. Of the fourteen Capuchins, he was eventually the only survivor, a hermit monk in a village on the present-day Sierra Leone coast. He was a remarkable example of Capuchin meditation; to the faithful he became known as one who, in his prayers, was bodily lifted into the air – 'levitation'.[3]

The Christian Gospel came to Africa by ship, over the oceans. However, there is some evidence of daring attempts, characteristically by Franciscans, to bring the message via caravans through the desert. From the beginning of the eighteenth century there are accounts of Franciscans leaving from Tripoli via the Nile and from there finding their way as far as the kingdom of Borno (now in north-eastern Nigeria and adjacent areas of Chad). They were attracted as Professor Richard Gray says, by a 'Christian mirage'.[4] A mirage it remained and we cannot follow this up in detail.

From Sâo Tomé and Príncipe, the nerve centres of Portuguese slave traffic in the Lower Guinea region, the Portuguese could dominate the import of slaves, not only from Kongo but also from the so-called 'slave rivers', including the Benin and Forcados rivers. In characteristic Portuguese manner the slave trade was intertwined with the hope of converting the king, called the Oba, and his population to the Catholic faith. The benefit of conversion was explained to them. Baptism, it was suggested, 'would bring him [the Oba] guns as well as grace'.[5] In providing these advantages the local salesmen were directed by the king in Lisbon who, it seems, attended to every detail himself. In December 1514 he ordered three chasubles for those missionaries who were leaving for Benin: one of the chasubles was of purple satin, with a centre stripe of black damask, another of purple damask with a stripe of green satin, and the third was of camlet with a stripe of Bruges satin. Two albs completed the priestly wardrobe.

This finery could not ensure the attention of the king. The missionaries found that, optimistic rumours to the contrary, the Oba almost invariably managed to avoid foreigners. Father Angel was fortunate however and in receiving him the Oba generously declared that he would build a church for them and provide the missionaries with his own interpreters so that 'they might explain to him the mysteries of their religion'.

All this royal amiability came to an abrupt end in 1665 when the Spanish Capuchins, with astounding audacity, contrived to get a glimpse of some of the mysteries of the Oba's own religion. In the royal palace the Capuchins drifted along in with the noisy crowd, only to find that they were to witness a display of human sacrifices: five men and five animals were to be decapitated on a table with impressively sharp scimitars. When suddenly the foreigners were detected, the master of ceremonies attempted to throw them out, but the Spanish missionaries were not to be that easily dismissed. Fr Felipe de Hijar describes the drama:

> We ... stepped into the middle of the courtyard and begun speaking aloud to the king and the chiefs of the evil they were doing in making such sacrifices, of the state of perdition in which they stood, that the devil whom they served was deceiving them, and so forth.[6]

At that the Oba's men 'rushed furiously upon us and swept us through the courtyard with great violence'.

This attempt was followed by repeated new ventures, until after a change of Oba in 1710, an Italian Capuchin mission was established in Benin city. Fr Celestino d'Aspra gave three years, 1710–1713, to his unpromising task. Nothing is known of his work and with Fr Celestino the Benin mission wound up.[7]

KONGO AND SOYO

In the 1470s Portuguese sailors reached the mouth of the Zaïre River, eager to make *conquista* for their king. In 1497 Vasco da Gama rounded the Cape of Good Hope with a squadron of four caravels and 150 men. They began to explore the East Coast of Africa, from Natal to Malindi. Then, with the aid of monsoon winds, they steered across the Indian Ocean to India, where Goa became the centre of government and church in the Portuguese empire.

During their expansion, the Portuguese dotted both the west and east coastlines of Africa with Portuguese place names: Cape Verde, Mina (the 'Mines', Elmina, the 'Gold Coast'), Sâo Tomé, Algoa – Delagoa (*to* Goa and *from* Goa), Natal, and Mombasa. In all of this the sailors were looking for a face and a king, for Prester John's kingdom, somewhere inside the continent of Africa. Following this lead, the Portuguese were eventually to arrive in Ethiopia.

Beginnings in Zaïre

In 1483 Diogo Cao returned to Portugal, and took along four Kongolese to learn the language of the white man and to serve later as the first interpreters in Kongo. It was on Diogo Cao's second visit in 1491 that evangelization could begin.

The meeting on that coast between canoe and caravel, between traditional ritual with its *nkisi* and Catholic ritual with its crucifix, was one of momentous significance, with almost cosmological overtones. Who were these strange creatures arriving in their enormous vessels, big as whales? They spoke of God, and referred to the world of the ancestors; they obviously hailed from the realm of the departed, for they had the paleness of the dead. In that moment on the seashore of Soyo, two worlds met – or tried to meet – and the encounter opened up opportunities for understanding and misunderstanding, for co-operation and hope, for enslavement and despair.

On board the caravels landing at Soyo – the coastal district of the kingdom of Kongo – were five priests, missionaries of the St Eloi monastery in Lisbon, Portuguese artisans and the Kongolese who had been baptized in Lisbon after catechetical instruction by Father Vicente dos Anjos. This Father had already picked up some of the Kikongo language from his catechumens while still in Lisbon. He was now one of the priests on board. The young Christian Bakongo and this Father thus formed an initial group of communication making understanding between the two worlds to some extent possible.

On Easter Day 1491, the *Mani Soyo* and one of his sons were baptized, in the presence of a crowd of some 25,000 people. The baptism on this occasion could not be followed by the Eucharist for unfortunately the ship with the altar-stones on board was delayed and the altar could not function without these blessed stones placed in the altar. On 3 May 1491 Nzinga Nkuvu, the most important person in the kingdom, was baptized with the name of João together with six leading noble men. To emphasize the significance of this act, Nzinga Nkuvu gave an order that all idols – or 'fetishes' – were to be brought together and burned.

The baptism of these high-ranking figures was accompanied by a psychological phenomenon important in itself but even more so because it was to be re-enacted in future generations, a sign of continuity, of 'the long duration' in the spirituality of the Kongolese people. Two of the men who had been baptized together with the king could report that they had seen identical dreams of a beautiful woman (later identified as the Virgin Mary) who told them that, as baptized, they were now invincible. She urged the king to see to it that his whole kingdom became Christian. But this was not enough. Another miraculous phenomenon was the discovery of a stone in the form of a cross they believed had fallen from heaven. It was carried in procession to the church. The role of dreams as confirmation of a striking spiritual experience can even now be seen throughout the history of the Christian Church, in Kongo and in the rest of Africa.

The baptism of the king was soon followed by that of the queen and of one of the princes, Mvemba Nzinga, baptized Afonso. To the guardians of local tradition this was too much. The energetic thrust of the foreigners inevitably provoked a vehement pagan reaction, and in 1495 the recently baptized noblemen, including young Prince Mvemba Nzinga, fled to the adjacent district of Sundi, while the old king returned to his harem and his ancestors.

This temporary move to Sundi and the return from Sundi a decade later were important. African history includes many such examples of victorious 'returnee', and as one of these, Mvemba Nzinga could use the Sundi experience, when as *Mani Kongo* he set out to lead his kingdom on Christian lines. In the exile at Sundi two Portuguese priests, Goncalve Vas and Rodrigue Anes, accompanied the young prince, becoming his teachers in general Western education and in the Christian faith. When King Nzinga Nkuvu died in 1506, Mvemba Nzinga, strengthened by ten long years of refugee experience, established himself as the new king of Kongo.

The king and his bishop

Mvemba Nzinga is one of the greatest lay Christians in African Church history. Eager as he had been to learn from his Portuguese missionaries at Sundi, he was determined to give the youth educational opportunities. He built a school for 400 boys, and soon a school for girls, led by his sister. Although inclined to his task in the royal traditions of the Kongolese, Mvemba Nzinga was also anxious to lead them in the new ways. Count Pedro Nsaku ne Vunda was appointed to guard the baptismal water; from time immemorial, his clan had guarded the holy water, an interesting example of the continuity of symbols. Destroying the traditional *nkisi* in large bonfires, the king and priests replaced them with another sacred symbol, the crucifix, and the chiefs received crosses for their protection. To the king and his generation, Christianity represented *ngolo* (power), concentrated in these sacred objects.

In 1508 the king of Portugal sent Mvemba Nzinga fifteen missionaries, Canons of St Eloi, most of whom found the climate very difficult. In 1509, the Church in Kongo was brought closer to the church in Portugal and in Rome when Mvemba Nzinga sent his son, Henry, to Lisbon for further studies. During the decade of his father's exile in Sundi, young Henry had been instructed by the two Portuguese priests accompanying the family on their flight. Without doubt Henry spoke Portuguese at this time. In Lisbon he learned Latin, and the king there wrote to the proud father in Kongo that the young man spoke it quite well.

After following his progress for a decade, the Portuguese king, with Papal dispensation, had Henry consecrated as 'suffragan' bishop (officially 'of Utica', in North Africa) at the tender age of twenty-six. No letter or other written statement by the young bishop has survived in the archives of southern Europe. The only record we have of this nature is a signature of 1514. Henry returned to Africa, and his years of ecclesiastical office and activity, however much curtailed by failing health, certainly made an impression. The very fact of the young prince's consecration to the episcopal office must have strengthened the self-assurance of the Kongo Church. The co-operation of father and son, king and bishop, helped considerably to raise the status of the Church at Mbanza Kongo. Bishop Henry died in 1531.

The Portuguese missionaries found a keen promoter of their religious concerns in King Mvemba Nzinga. Occasionally he would preach in the chapel, and thus present the new message more effectively than when it came through interpreters. The king also showed his personal concern for the priests. In 1534, with the help of della Rovere, Nuntius in Lisbon, he wrote to the Pope suggesting modifications of the rule of celibacy. In the letter, the Nuntius referred to the uniate Maronites in Lebanon, suggesting this as a precedent for the priests in Kongo.

Mvemba Nzinga's realm was an independent African kingdom, and at first he corresponded in Portuguese with King Joao of Portugal in terms of brotherly esteem and confidence. Eventually he became deeply disappointed, embittered even, by the Portuguese slaving activities. Toward the end of his reign, four to five thousand slaves were being exported annually. He saw his country being depopulated by devastating shipments of slaves either to mines on the Gold Coast or across the ocean. A constant problem was that of the inexorable rule of *Padroado*: His Holiness had once and for all assigned Africa to the Portuguese – and that was that! When, in 1534, the Kongo Church was placed under the bishopric of Sâo Tomé, established that year, the situation did not improve.

At the time of Mvemba Nzinga's death in 1543, half the population of Kongo had been baptized, some two million people, the result of missionary activity inspired by the king of Kongo, and ultimately directed by that distant authority, the king of Portugal, Grand Master of the Order of Christ. A creative venture was the arrival in 1548 of five Jesuit fathers. They started a 'college' at Sâo Salvador, but were forced by the king's displeasure to leave after five years of devoted work. They moved to Luanda in Angola and established a college which became characterized by their competence and educational ambition.

From Kongo's point of view, the pretensions of *Padroado*, centred on the slave-dealing island of Sâo Tomé with its Portuguese bishop, were a perpetual burden. The Kongolese were therefore relieved when in 1596 Rome evaded *Padroado* by naming Sâo Salvador, formerly Mbanza Kongo, as an episcopal see, with its own bishop. King Alvaro II (1587–1614) could now extend his contacts with the outside world by sending his own ambassador to Rome. But it was a difficult task: the ambassador, on leaving for Rome, was captured by Dutch corsairs, and did not reach the Holy City for four years. On arrival in 1608, he was so exhausted that he died on the day of his scheduled presentation to His Holiness.

Relations with merchants in Luanda and slave dealers of Sâo Tomé made matters untenable. In 1655 a devastating war culminated in the famous battle at Ambuila. The Portuguese army from Angola crushed the Kongo forces and the proud city of Sâo Salvador, with its cathedral and its eight churches, was virtually destroyed, a traumatic blow to the Kongo people. King Antonio I Afonso was beheaded, together with his chaplain and relative, the first black Capuchin, Francisco de Sâo Salvador Roboredo. Civil war and rapid decay followed, and soon there were three contenders for the throne. A turn for the better came with Pedro IV in 1696. He was determined to restore the glory of the capital, Sâo Salvador, but did not succeed until 1709.

The Capuchins in Kongo 1645–1835

The Portuguese authorities insisted that according to their *Padroado* rule only missionaries of Portuguese nationality were acceptable in Kongo. However, King Garcia II (1651–61) had a mind of his own – he was determined to suspend this ecclesiastical monopoly. He was helped by a combination of world political factors offering an opportunity for change. In 1645 Portugal was at war with Spain and Angola was under Dutch occupation. This was when the first non-Portuguese missionaries, all Italian Capuchins could, despite Portuguese protests, slip into the country. Once inside they soon attracted other members of their expanding communities, all prepared to travel in the rural areas, a novelty at the time.

The missionary period in lower Kongo after 1650 was dominated by the Capuchins. Their order in Europe was a rapidly growing reform movement, within the Franciscan family. In the first half century they reached a membership of 3,700 and were soon prepared to send missionaries to the new continents. In 1622 the new Catholic mission organization in Rome, Propaganda Fide, with strong Capuchin representation at the centre, began to plan to send their men to Kongo. This Capuchin mission was in fact the most extensive evangelization effort in Black Africa prior to modern times. From 1645 to 1835 no less than 440 friars were working in Kongo/Angola. The climate was not beneficial. More than half of these men died after only a few years or months in the country, but this did not frighten them, new recruits followed unhesitatingly. These were men who in a time of worldliness and war found strength in meditation and a disciplined prayer life.

Baptizing a people

In the last twenty-eight years of the century, the Capuchins achieved surprising results in terms of numbers of baptisms. Thirty-seven 'preachers' together registered a total of 341,000. Of these, two had each baptized 50,000, one 30,000, another 20,000, four 14,000 each, and eight 10,000 each.[8] How can the large numerical claims of converts be understood? This question must be answered in an historical perspective, relating the situation in its context to both the Latin Christianity of the period and to traditional Kongo culture. There was a tolerant and an inclusive approach to the problem of conversion in Africa. It was made all the more acceptable, as fundamental religious concepts were expressed in Kikongo, all of them related to Kongo cosmology, such as *Nzambi* (God), *nkisi* (holy), and *moyo* (spirit or soul). Usually they followed the example of their ruler. At his baptism a herald would announce what was expected of the crowd, and the masses assembled in the market places would queue up to the baptismal font. Yet there were exceptions. The day after the ruler's baptism at Ngobila, Fr Caltanisetta asked him to have the herald announce that all were to be baptized, but the ruler refused, feeling that each one should be free to decide for him or herself. The energetic Caltanisetta strangely took this to mean that he could begin baptizing everybody 'without distinction'. But he had overstepped his mark.

> As the people did not know the Sacred Baptism, they fled into the bush and it was in vain that we pleaded with them to receive Baptism, by which the sons of the Devil would become Sons of God and inheritors of Holy Paradise. Thus I could not manage to baptize more than 248.[9]

After the ruler's baptism in Nzonzo, 'fetishists' spread the rumour that those who consented to baptism would suffer sudden death. This led to determined opposition to the missionaries' efforts. Rumour could, of course, help too. It promised bliss to those who came forward to 'eat salt', one expression for Baptism. (The Catholic ritual included salt on the tongue.) Preparation for baptism was often left to the Kongolese interpreters. These were married laymen, all from noble families, and some trained in Portugal. They would teach by singing the Biblical or doctrinal sentences to the illiterate groups. Children and youth were the first to adopt the new learning, singing the phrases to the adults at home or in public places.

The first Portuguese Kongo catechism was available in 1556 – the first book ever to be produced in a Bantu language. It was used almost exclusively for slaves imported from Kongo to the plantations of Sâo Tomé. In 1624 Fr Matheus Cardoso's *Christian Doctrine* in Portuguese and Kikongo appeared. The missionaries soon followed Cardoso's method of singing the text of the doctrine in a simple and familiar rhythm. At Sunday worship the people repeated the sacred terminology of the new religion, learning such Latin phrases as 'Ave Maria', 'santissimo sacramento', and 'Salve Regina'. During the 'Antonian heresy' period, Fr Lorenzo da Luca met the self-named St Isabelle, who baptized and gave absolution, using a few powerful words repeated with gusto: 'In nomine Patris, et Filii, et Spiritus Sancti'.

Occasionally the missionary would be able to welcome a 'Prefect' for an inspection tour. Whether in Kongo or in Luanda, the visiting Father would ask the faithful to demonstrate their knowledge about the two fundamental and sacred matters: to make the Sign of the Cross, and to say the names of the Persons in the Trinity. These were obviously regarded as the Christian's 'iron ration': the ritual gesture, and the dogmatic declaration. They were simple, but universally recognizable symbols of the unity and the continuity of Christianity. Preaching in the chapel could refer to them, and they could be used for spiritual insight and meditation. In addition to the Trinity, there was also the Virgin Mother's image, and often the statue of a local saint, preferably St Anthony, the healer from Padua.

Soyo spirituality

During the eighteenth century the Kongo Church slowly but inevitably faded away and in the end only a few sad traces and ruins remained, leaving the impression that it had perhaps throughout been nothing but an illusion, a pious phantasmagoria in the bush and never more than a thin veneer over a groundwork of solid traditional religion. It is therefore all the more significant that a methodological shift of approach to the problem has been suggested and accomplished. The impact of the Christian movement in Kongo 'varied enormously over time and space', between the different districts and from one period to another.

Professor Richard Gray has concentrated his attention, not on the Kingdom of Kongo as such but on one district within the kingdom, Soyo, with its capital Mbanza Soyo and its harbour Mpinda. In focusing the analysis on this one area located just below the Zaïre estuary, soon a dominant power in the kingdom, Gray is in a position to present a surprisingly vivid and convincing picture of Christian devotion and allegiance. Here the Capuchins had an almost unrivalled influence. Moreover they managed to elicit from the king of Portugal an admission that the ruler of Soyo was an independent prince. With the deterioration of the Kongo kingdom as such, Soyo acquired a position of its own and its Church a role of its own.

Two factors combined to achieve this: one, the diplomatic role of the

Capuchins on behalf of Soyo, achieved 'with at least a touch of that skill and charity' which they had clearly demonstrated on a wider scale in contemporaneous Europe; two, the ready response of the elite and the people to the basic ritual design of the Capuchin staff. This was seen in the role of the Christian calendar and the festivals of the Christian year. The ritual on these occasions bound together ruler and subjects in enthusiastic displays of worship and processions. As a matter of course the ruler of Soyo took the lead showing what seemed total devotion. Apart from the ordinary festivals, the Church in Soyo developed two saints' days of special local significance, the feast of St James on 25 July and of St Luke on 10 October, both commemorating not only the witness of these great saints but also of national victories on these dates, all, as Gray has noted, contributing to a 'routinization of piety' at ground level.[10]

Two groups of lay leaders were seen at work supporting ruler and missionaries. One consisted of the interpreters as teachers and catechists, eight or ten in number, men of noble birth, mostly relatives of the ruler, thereby emphasizing the local church's character as a court religion. The second consisted of 'the slaves of the mission', who maintained a hostel and served as medical aids in the hospital; they also accompanied the missionaries on their visitation tours of the district. While others may have harboured fears of certain risks of sorcery in the capital and in the district, these men could afford to be totally fearless, for they were privileged with stronger protection than any sorcery, in the holy medals awarded them by the powerful Capuchins.[11]

Capuchins and the king

It is necessary to quote a few Capuchin missionaries in order to help root out the impression that these Catholics devoted themselves exclusively to wholesale mass baptism, leaving their new converts at that. Nothing gives as vivid a picture of Kongo Church life in the 1690s as the diary of Fr Luca da Caltanisetta, the Sicilian Capuchin. King and nobility were at the centre in his notes: he mentioned the common people only as baptized numbers which are surprisingly high. One day he baptized 254, another day 269, for 1698 he entered a total of 2,373. When visiting Mbemba, he harvested 205 in one day, and remarked that the village was 'inhabited by people who were refugees from Ngonzo because of the wars'. Following Joseph C. Miller's research in the region, it is possible to understand how the village masses turned to the missionary and to baptism. Miller emphasizes the role of the refugees, those coming

> from marginal lands who sought protection and sustenance in those same villages during times of drought. These helpless new arrivals joined war captives in disadvantaged groups of kinless residents constituting a despised lower stratum of society similar to 'slaves' in western societies.[12]

Caltanisetta remembers that there was a daily evening service at Soyo with a 'Litany of Our Lady'.[13] Three times a week this was followed by 'the Discipline' (penitential self-flagellation), and by the Holy Rosary on three other days. Friday morning included also the 'Crown of Five Wounds'. Holy Week was of course the great celebration of the year, when Andrea da Pavia claims that 'all the ceremonies performed in Italy were also followed at Soyo'. On Maundy Thursday they processed with Crucifix, Crown of Thorns, and 'chains' (for flagellation). Holy Saturday had Blessing of Fire, of Water, and Incense with the Paschal Light. The faithful brought a great number of their own calabashes of water to be blessed. 'They then drank that water with great devotion' and each danced home carrying his calabash. At the 'Gloria' in the Mass they beat drums, played instruments, and fired a salvo of guns. The recording missionary admired this display of devoted participation. 'I claim that these African people show more piety than the Europeans.' This Blessing of Water and the carrying home of calabashes was a ceremony recreated three centuries later in Zionist charismatic worship on the Rand and in Swaziland. *Plus ça change* ... ('the more it changes, the more it remains the same thing') is an apt French phrase for these long-term durations, the transfer of new meaning to old symbols. Both early Catholics and modern Zionists displayed the immemorial need for purification and renewal, for Life and Power.

Andrea Pavia was impressed by the people's devotion to their deceased, especially on the 'Great Day of the Dead'. All the participants sang their prayers in Kikongo, and carried 'lights' which lit all the eight churches at Soyo. In surplice and cape the priest led the procession to the tombs where all took part in singing responses. 'The whole night was dedicated to these devotions.' The next morning each came with their baskets of gifts on behalf of the dead. 'We had ten tons of gifts to be distributed afterwards', presumably to the poor.

With the king and nobility, the missionaries had to tread warily. At Nzonzo in 1698, Caltanisetta reported that the local 'duke', Dom Miguel, felt piqued by the Capuchins as they had excommunicated him and 'thereby not shown due respect'. He insisted that they owed him an apology. Caltanisetta was not intimidated for he had Canon Law on his side and informed the duke that 'he had fallen in excommunication No. 15 of the Bull *De coena Domini*', yet if he were to mend his ways, he would be absolved from the punishment.[14] In addition to the king and dukes, the missionary was dependent on the interpreters, who rendered the messages of the monks into the local language. Latin words were mysterious and impressive, but the interpreter's Kikongo brought God's word closer to man's heart. These men were gifted linguists, and soon picked up not only Portuguese but some Latin phrases as well, and could thus serve at Mass. Placed between two cultures, the interpreter became a trusted adviser of the missionary, warning him, when necessary, not to overstep his mark. As the ultimate badge of honour, the interpreter was buried next to the missionary. This was a distinction which made his lay position in the Church particularly attractive: one of merit in his short lifetime, and an assurance of good company for his long dramatic pilgrimage Beyond.

Unfortunately, although the Capuchins came to Kongo with the very best of intentions they had little awareness that the encounter with the Kongolese was delicate, requiring tact, humility, and generosity. Caltanisetta's diary revealed the closed European mind which was so offensive to the African.

> At Mbanza Zolu I sent word to the king to tell the fetishists to stop their dances and these diabolic ceremonies. They replied that they could not stop. Then I said he had to catch them and chain them or else I would come myself and catch them. At that they left ... I beat the heads of two idols one against the other and threw them into the fire. At that, these ignorant people showed their sadness and defiance, and almost in tears with depression they withdrew, not wishing to see their filth being burnt.

The bishop had additional problems. Having moved to Luanda, he found little time for visiting Sâo Salvador: the trip took fifteen days each way. He also complained that he could not find the necessary number and quality of clergy. When the first Capuchins were sent to 'Nigritia' (Africa), the great majority died, only to be followed by succeeding waves of eager colleagues, ready for similar sacrifice. But the toll in Capuchin lives had been heavy. In the nineteenth century West Africa was known as 'the White man's grave', and this expression was no less true of seventeenth-century Kongo. The bishop also felt it almost impossible to train Africans for ordination. There thus remained the special Luanda category of the 'Coloureds' (*métis*). After hasty preparation, some of these were ordained, but not all of them were very devoted.

In the seventeenth century the great Catholic missionaries went to Asia: Matteo Ricci to China, Alexander de Rhodes to Cochin-China, and Roberto de Nobili to India – with their imaginative approach to mandarins and sannyasi. They dealt with 'religione de cultura', having long and venerable traditions and supported theologically by a Propaganda in Rome with its famous 'Instruction' of 1659, the 'Magna Carta' of the Propaganda Fide.[15] Here the Cardinals asked from the missionaries 'intellectual elasticity' and adaptation which 'would imitate the example of Jesus and the Apostle of the nations'.

> Beware of any effort or advice to the peoples devised to make them change their rites, their customs and habits as long as these are not clearly contrary to religion and good custom.[16]

This concerns Asia and the nations and peoples of Asia. What about Africa? What was the difference? Many felt at the time, and others did so during the succeeding centuries, that Africans 'did not have a religion', that their worship, their concerted cry to God was no more than superstition. Africa and its religious quest was at the time too little understood to permit a similar approach from the Africa missionaries, with well-known consequences.

Kimpa Vita – Beatrice of Kongo

This attitude of Westerners left a void in the hearts of men and women, particularly in those who had readily accepted the White man's God and his unassailable truths. It was then that a mere woman, born out of the people, appeared on the scene at Sâo Salvador – Kimpa Vita or Donna Beatrice. Frail and only twenty-one, she had a vision and a message which soon captured the masses and still does so today.

The drama, *Beatrice of Kongo* by Bernard Dadie of the Ivory Coast, was acted by distinguished West African actors when first performed at the *Festival d'Avignon* – the old city of the Popes – in July 1971. It brought home to participants and onlookers alike the depths of feeling in the drama once enacted in real earnest 250 years earlier in old Kongo.

The student of modern charismatic movements in Africa recognizes at once the characteristic features of her personality and her claims. Simon Kimbangu, Isaiah Shembe, William Wade Harris, George Khambule, or sweet old Ma Nku – all belong to the same family. Donna Beatrice appears as a close relative to them all, a revered great-grandmother – although she was still young when burned to death for her alleged crime.

In Beatrice's case, there was a Precursor, an old woman called Maffuta. In 1704 she had a vision of the Madonna who told her that Her Son was saddened because down there on earth, the king was no longer staying at Sâo Salvador, but at Kibangu in Sundi. In her hand she held the proof of her revelation – a stone she had found in the river, in the likeness of the head of

Christ. 'Come down from the mountains', she said, 'and rebuild Sâo Salvador, the capital of kings'.

Soon Donna Beatrice, the young prophetess, appeared. 'Donna' indicates that she was of noble family. In the Kongo villages she was rumoured to be a healer of the sick, like Jesus of old, and was known to give children to barren women. She had a child of her own, given to her in a supernatural manner. Barro, her consort, called 'St John', shared her life but obviously in a somewhat subdued manner. Her initial experience of a near-death was regularly repeated: once a week she would 'die', disappearing in order to speak to God – and then she would rise again. She could foretell the future, and a glorious future at that for Sâo Salvador. The tree-trunks would be changed into gold and silver, and under the stones would be mines with gold, silver, and gems. And there would be quantities of the richest silk and other cloths. This *cargo* theme is of great interest, being rare in African charismatic experience.

Though a woman, Donna Beatrice called herself St Anthony, referring to the great Franciscan saint of Padua, revered by the Capuchins. He had appeared to her in the characteristic brown habit of the monks, and had entered her with his power and soul. With the authority of her extraordinary personality, she, like the Capuchins, ordered the people to burn their *nkisi*, and not only the *nkisi* but also their crucifixes. Her *idée fixe* was to call for the people's return to Sâo Salvador, thus dangerously challenging the authority of the king.

This was too much for the guardians of order in the realm, the King and his Council, and the Capuchin Fathers looking on in horror at this display of blatant heresy. The Council was called together and they condemned Beatrice to death. On 2 July 1706, she and her consort were burned to death at the stake. Many of her disciples, 'Little Anthonys', went about the countryside spreading her message. After the fire, they would with bated breath assure their listeners that the burning place had turned into two deep wells, with a beautiful star appearing in each.

This woman cannot be dismissed as a mere curiosity on the fringe of Kongolese Church history. She had the intuition and courage to intervene during the deep crisis of her nation and her Church. She insisted that it was her Church, too, and that she had a responsibility for it.

An epilogue

To the masses the Christian religion consisted above all in the initiation rite of the new religion, Baptism, and possibly in participating in certain feasts and fasts which still survived as a cultic reality. Increasingly the king was seen as the embodiment of *nkisi*, mediating what the people needed, power, rain and health. He appeared as the head of what must be termed a Christian ancestor cult with its centre in the burial grounds of the kings and with Nzinga Nkuvu – João I – as the traditional hero of the cult.

The nobles had a monopoly on certain prestigious manifestations of Christianity: literacy in Portuguese and membership of the Order of Christ, the Portuguese-inspired Church Order. There are also among the nobles certain pretensions of Christian marriage. The wealthier among nobles could maintain *maestri da igreja* or catechists who looked after chapels, shrines and hospices. Even late in the nineteenth century there were communities of 'Slaves of the Church', descendants of those who had served the missionaries in the old days.

The king of Sâo Salvador, Garcia V, 1803–30 had inherited and kept alive his precious epistolary contacts with the royal court in Lisbon. He would plead with his royal colleague: 'Oh, my brother, king like me', hoping to be given European priests to celebrate his wedding to Queen Isabel. As head of the Order of Christ he also needed a priest to bless the uniforms of the Order with which he invested his dukes and other officials.

When at long last, in 1814, Father Luigi Maria of Assisi did turn up at the court of Sâo Salvador, the king was overjoyed, asking the Pope to make the missionary 'a bishop or a cardinal'. Father Luigi spent eight months in Kongo. In this time he managed to baptize altogether 25,700 people, adults and children, all prepared beforehand by ever-present catechists, and 5,000 for the confessional and the Mass. This was a melancholic numerical decline compared with the situation in the 1780s when a bishop and sixteen fathers on a tour through the Kongo had rebuilt dilapidated churches and baptized 308,000 or when between 1759 and 1774 Cherobino da Savona had succeeded in baptizing 700,000.

Luigi's successor, Father Zenobi Maria of Florence arrived in Luanda in 1816, instructed by the Propaganda Fide to organize and develop the Church in Kongo. He found few things to encourage him. 'I have not found any fruit' of the work done, the danger being that people with great speed were going to Hell.[17] In 1819 Bishop Joao Damasceno found that all were '*sine duce*, *sine luce*, *sine cruce*' (without leader, light or cross).

In the period 1645–1835 no less than 440 Capuchins, the great majority of them Italians, arrived in Kongo. On 7 May 1835 the last of them, Prefect Bernardo da Burgio left Luanda and Africa together with his Kongolese Brother Bernardo de Sâo Salvador. Under new conditions, however, the

Catholics were to return to Kongo at the end of the century. Their claim then that by returning they were making 'a reprise' was not without cause.[18]

ANGOLA

Luanda and beyond

South of Kongo was the vast expanse of the savanna kingdoms, some parts of which came to be known as Angola. When the Jesuits had to abandon their work at Sâo Salvador in the middle of the sixteenth century, they discovered new and promising fields further south on the Atlantic coast. A team of two Jesuit priests and two lay brothers saw that an island off the coast was of strategic importance for colonial conquest combined with evangelization.

In 1575 Luanda became a city, virtually a result of Jesuit foresight and planning. From this place, for two centuries they exercised a vast influence over the future of Angola, particularly in education. At first they carved out big land holdings for their organization, (*donatoria*), and had ambitious dreams of a theocracy in the region. These plans were not to be realized in Angola, although in Paraguay their Jesuit colleagues made a similar attempt somewhat later. At the turn of the century, Luanda had a population of about 40,000 Africans, 6,000 Mulattos, and 4,000 Whites, many of them *degredados* (prison convicts) from Portugal.[19] In this amorphous situation, the Jesuits provided what there was of pulse and structure, concentrating their services in a college and other schools in Luanda. Here they trained an African clergy and a *mestizo* administrative class. They earned the dislike of the colonial leaders by acting as the protectors of the interest of the Africans.

Another woman: Queen Nzinga

The people of Sâo Salvador viewed the Kimbundu highlands, including the dynamic kingdom of Ndongo, with special interest. In contrast to the complicated list of Kongo kings, here was a princess, called Nzinga, 'whose personality dominated the Angolan scene for the next half century'.[20]

Portuguese threats forced the princess and her Kimbundu people to flee east to Matamba. Here this resourceful, powerful woman created a new kingdom, with an elite army which she trained and commanded herself. Together with other kingdoms in the region, Kimbundu and Matamba faced the unrelenting Portuguese slaving expeditions. The princess was adept at politics, and did not hesitate to go to Luanda, to meet the Portuguese governor. She offered peace and trade on her own terms of exchanging ivory for salt and cloth. The royal visit to the emerging coastal city is of special interest for the Church historian. Here, after a year, Nzinga decided to join the Church, a momentous decision of long-term importance for her subjects. Having been welcomed as a princess with proper Portuguese pomp, she was baptized by the Jesuit fathers into the Catholic Church. She was now to be called Donna Ana de Souza, a family name which she shared with her godfather, the Portuguese governor. During her visit to Luanda she may have contacted the Dembos Christians, north-east of Luanda. There most of the chiefs became Christian and at baptism were called *Dom*, and some of them had their own household chaplains.[21]

All these ecclesiastical stratagems, however, did not abate Portuguese slaving incursions into the highlands. Donna Ana then turned from local wars to international power politics. When, in 1641, the Dutch landed in Angola, taking Luanda, she signed a treaty with them, although they were known to be dangerous heretical Protestants. She hoped in this way to end the Portuguese regime in Angola. But the Ndongo and Matamba peoples, hidden in the mountains, had to learn the harsh lesson that international intrigue is a hazardous gamble. In 1648 the Portuguese were again on the scene. Donna Ana, not to be perturbed, accommodated once more, being 're-converted', this time by the aid of new arrivals in the country, the Italian Capuchins. Here it is the changing conditions of the royal elite rather than the reactions of the masses which the historian can follow. One can at best conjecture from later statistical tables the rapidly multiplying effect of an initial royal example for the villagers.

Attempting to make Luanda into a shining model of Christian service, the Portuguese agencies were at the same time engaged in an ever-increasing slave traffic – 8–10,000 exported in an average 'good' year. 'The whole economy of Angola was geared to the slave trade for over 250 years.'[22] The harbour of Luanda became the most flourishing centre for the trade to Brazil, with the exchange of fiery rum, sometimes called 'Demon Rum'. Any qualms that the slave dealers may have felt were assuaged by the thought that prior to leaving the Luanda harbour, the unfortunate slaves were baptized, and their eternal salvation thus guaranteed. Participation in the three annual religious feasts St Sebastian's Day, Corpus Christi, and Assumption Day, further assured this guarantee. In 1760, 200 years of Jesuit service to Angola came to an abrupt end. They were all torn from their college, schools, and charitable institutions – and dismissed.

Pious ideas from Lisbon were eagerly transferred to Luanda. This happened with the Santa Casa da Misericórdia, or under its official name, The Brotherhood of Our Lady, Mother of God, Virgin Mary of Mercy, founded in Lisbon in 1498 and spread throughout the Portuguese-speaking world, to Goa and Nagasaki and particulary to Bahia in Brazil. In 1576 Luanda had its share and the cause was promoted by Bishop Mascaranhas. In 1680 seventy brothers were registered in Luanda. They were known to look after a hospital with 400 sick annually. All this required money, and Luanda of course had the answer to that one: the proceeds from the sale of 500 slaves annually were paid to the Misericórdia. But the Luanda Misericórdia never really caught on, and by 1750 it was 'totally decadent'.[23]

PROTESTANTS AT THE CAPE OF GOOD HOPE

We are concerned here with two distinct African communities, their relationships to the Afrikaner farmers, and their religion. The Khoikhoi were indigenous to the Cape region while the slaves came from abroad.

The Khoikhoi

It is sometimes taken for granted that it was Jan van Riebeck's arrival at the Cape, in 1652, that signified the beginnings of Khoikhoi–European contacts. This was not so, the beginnings of these contacts were much older. Bartholomew Diaz and Vasco da Gama had pioneered the route touching at the Cape on the way to the East and on the return voyage, for occasional and intermittent visits. An increasing number of Portuguese, Dutch, French and British ships followed. Occasionally, a young Khoikhoi would be taken on board ship to Britain, Holland or Indonesia in order to pick up a European language.

With van Riebeck's arrival the Dutch – a group of 126 persons – came as settlers to the Cape, where they built a fort. To the Khoikhoi, van Riebeck became 'a symbol of good will'.[24] The Directors of the East India Company in Holland insisted on principles, and one principle was that the Khoikhoi were free and independent. They were to be paid wages (in the form of rice, bread, tobacco and alcohol) and on a temporary basis only. Even if some whites referred to the Khoikhoi in the same terms as slaves the Khoikhoi still retained much of their freedom, and had their own language and customs.

The young Khoikhoi girl, Eva, surprised the van Riebeck family with her linguistic ability. She became an interpreter. Mrs van Riebeck taught her 'Christianity' in order to become 'the first Christian native of South Africa'.

The two women, the governor's pious wife – a new-comer to Africa – and the young Khoikhoi girl collaborated. She adapted herself to European life and culture to the extent that she could say she had 'a Dutch heart inside her'. She was baptized. She had a sister and Eva taught her sister how to pray to the Lord, 'to which all natives listened with tears in their eyes'.[25] She married a Danish doctor, Peter van Meerhoff, who died less than four years later. It is however difficult to avoid the impression 'that the conversion of [the] Khoikhoi did not rank high on the list of the Cape Church's priorities.'[26]

In 1713 the Khoikhoi community was hit by a devastating smallpox epidemic which drastically reduced the Khoikhoi population from over 200,000 in 1652, to a level that barely escaped annihilation. Towards the end of the eighteenth century tensions between the Dutch farmers and their Khoikhoi and slave servants took on violent forms. In 1788 at Swellendam 200 servants led by millenarian visions 'burnt their Dutch clothes, and killed their white animals, prophesying the end of the world and threatening to kill all whites, after which they would inherit their goods'.[27]

The slaves

The slaves came from abroad, brought for the Dutch farmers on the directions of the Dutch East India Company in Holland. A first lot of slaves were brought in 1657 from Guinea and from Angola while later supplies were mainly from Mozambique and Madagascar as well as from India and Indonesia. In 1793 the European population – men, women and children – at the Cape numbered 14,000 while the slave population was 14,700. One observer commented that, 'having imported slaves every common or ordinary European becomes a gentleman who prefers to be served rather than serve.'[28]

The urge for freedom was ever present in the slave population. In order to obtain 'manumission' or emancipation, a slave should be baptized and know the Dutch language. After being baptized a slave could not be sold. Not only did the masters risk losing their control over Christian slaves but baptism would give the slaves access to Churches and preachers who could reduce their dependence on their 'owners'. The effect was that the number of slaves baptized was minimal. The general rule was that the European farmer never spoke to the slave about religion and only very few slaves were placed in a position to embrace Christianity. One exception was the witness of the Revd M. C. Vos who had spent some time in Europe and there had been influenced by the desire for missions. These few notes refer to the background of what was to become the Cape crisis in the 1830s when slavery, after pressure from British missions, was outlawed.

The Moravians

In the village of Herrnhut, in eastern Germany, the Moravians had built a tightly knit community, a model for similar communities in other parts of the world. They sent missionaries in every direction, to Greenland and Labrador, and to Nicaragua and the Cape. They all went out in faith, with a song in their hearts and on their lips. George Schmidt (1709–85) was one of the early members of the movement, joining the Moravian group in Holland which sent him to the Cape in order to convert the Khoikhoi. In 1737 he arrived in South Africa. He spent only seven years in the country before being evicted as a 'heretic' by the Dutch Reformed *predikants*. Yet, in that short period he managed, against overwhelming odds, to gain a precarious foothold. Half a century later, his Moravian successors could proceed from this hard-won base.

Schmidt acquired a small farm, Baviaanskloof, in the district of Swellendam. It was later called Genadendal, and under that name became known as the model mission station in the country. He met two Khoikhoi men who could communicate with him in the Dutch language, and he soon taught them the 'Three R's' and the Jesus Story. In a year's time he had gathered a group of twenty-eight people on the farm. Together they dug water furrows, planted vineyards and gardens, and sowed fields with tobacco, wheat, barley and oats. Through careful planning, Schmidt managed to buy six oxen and some pigs, and they were given a number of goats. The daily work gave him opportunities for teaching the Gospel. As the wheat was threshed, he told about the seed which must fall into the ground and die. Building a wall, he would explain that the houses must be built on the rock, not shifting sands. The day began and ended with common worship, the evening prayers including a short address based on a Bible text. The group of twenty-eight was soon divided into seven prayer circles according to age and sex, following the example of the Herrnhut 'choirs', or, evangelistic cells. Here was a pattern which, through the related Wesleyan 'classes' was to be of seminal importance for nineteenth-century evangelization in South Africa.

Contacts with headquarters were few and far between. Schmidt was ordained by an official letter dated 27 August 1741, sent by his director, von Zinzendorff in Prussia. The following Sunday, as he rode with a faithful Khoikhoi co-worker, he came to a stream. He decided then and there to baptize his friend, now to be called Joshua:

> Do you believe that the son of God has died on the cross for the sins of all men? Do you believe that you are a damnable man by nature? ... Are you willing through the grace of the blood of the Saviour, neither to shrink from disgrace nor persecution and to profess the Saviour before all the world and to remain faithful to him until death? Do you wish to be baptized?[29]

During the next few weeks another four were baptized, also 'in running water'. In the evenings he would read to them from Zinzendorff's solidly theological 'Berlin Discourses' and often explained major ideas from the Epistle to the Romans. But he met with opposition. As news of these developments reached Cape Town, there were strong objections. This German missionary *uitlander* had not used the prescribed catechism; the Zondereind River, where the baptisms had taken place, was not within his parish, so they were illegal and his five converts must be regarded as not having been baptized. The *predikants* now felt they had a doctrinal weapon to use on this irresponsible German. Schmidt could not even get help from the Governor, who had inspected the Moravian settlement and had been greatly impressed. To the *predikants*, support from the Governor, only a layman in the Church, was not sufficient. Schmidt was placed on a ship and sent back to Europe, never to see his flock again. Before leaving, he handed his Dutch New Testament to Magdalena, one of the converts.

SOUTH-EASTERN AFRICA AND MOMBASA

The Portuguese did not limit their travels and activities to West Africa. Having landed at Mpinda in Soyo, and at Luanda in Angola, their caravels continued south and east. As mentioned at the beginning of this chapter, Vasco de Gama rounded the Cape in 1497 and proceeded along the East Coast of Africa. At the harbours of Sofala, Inhambane, and Quelimane they met Arabs and 'Swahili' in their dhows from the North, also searching for gold and ivory. These were men with long experience of the continent and its trade, and with remarkable knowledge of the river highways and extensive inland routes. In 1505 the Portuguese captured the port of Sofala, using it as stop-over place for connexions with India and its spice markets.

The Portuguese presence along the East African coast, wide-flung in plan and brutal in execution, proved eventually to be singularly futile. In essence, the attempt was a *conquista* variation of medieval crusading exploits, applied in this instance to the Eastern waters. Its purpose was to establish on the rims of the Indian Ocean a 'Portuguese Imperium'.

The study of the economics and political history of this part of Africa is an effective antidote to the popular idea that for centuries people had been happily living here in undisturbed isolation from the rest of the world – until at last the missionary arrived as the agitator. Recent research has shown that, on the contrary, these countries had over the centuries been building up varied and far-reaching contacts with the outside world. The Indian Ocean and the monsoon winds had provided the essential route for travel. Alluvial gold from the reefs and river-beds of Zimbabwe together with copper, pottery, and ivory formed the basis for economic and cultural exchange, as evidenced in cloth from India and objects from as far away as China. 'Large quantities of imported glass beads as well as Chinese, Persian and Syrian china, glass and porcelain, dating back to the fourteenth century have also been recovered in the "Great Enclosure" of Great Zimbabwe.'[30] Rumours of these riches spread far and wide, leading to challenging questions: who was the king of this gold-producing country somewhere inland from the East Coast? Was he perhaps the mysterious 'Prester John' whom the Portuguese had been searching for in vain along the lower reaches of the River Zaïre?

Meeting the empire of Mwene Mutapa

The parallel between *Mani Kongo* and *Mwene Mutapa*, between the King of Kongo and his royal colleague in Zimbabwe is challenging. With little ado, Nzinga Nkuvu of Kongo was baptized only a few weeks after the arrival of the Portuguese missionaries. On the other side of the continent, seventy years later, Gonçalo da Silveira, SJ, was sent to the Emperor *Mwene Mutapa*. It took him about three weeks to persuade and prepare the renowned *Mwene Mutapa* for Holy Baptism. This Jesuit was hand-picked for the purpose, being of a noble family and having spent some time with the Portuguese Viceroy in Goa.

Dom Sebastiao was baptized on 15 January 1561, with his Mother, now Donna Maria, and a number of his courtiers. Around 400 of his subjects followed the royal example. But as rapidly as the royal baptism, came the denouement in pagan reaction. Less than a month after the baptismal jubilations, the *nganga* convinced the King that Gonçalo was a spy and that the baptismal waters were a magic potion which would destroy the recipients. Seven strong men were sent to strangle Gonçalo in his hut.

Like the Arabs before them, the Portuguese were attracted by the prospect of finding gold in the realm of *Mwene Mutapa*, the 'Golden Emperor'. His kingdom became the special sphere of interest for the Dominican monks sent out to strengthen Portuguese rule and Catholic faith. In the Mutapa succession crises of 1628–33, Fr Luis do Espirito Santo put pressure on one of the contenders, Mavura, employing unusual methods for a religious. Through an 'insolently bold' action, he gathered an army of 15,000 men against the competitor's force of 100,000. With 250 Dominican muskets, his troops annihilated the enemy. After the event, he wrote jubilantly to his Provincial in terms revealing the outlook and operations of this generation of Portuguese missionaries.

> With the help of God and by the prayers of our Beloved Lady of the Rosary, our little army was victorious. Our army then proceeded to Zimbabwe, the royal residence, where I built a chapel and placed a crucifix and a statue of the Beloved Lady of the Rosary to whom I dedicated the chapel. I celebrated a Mass of Thanksgiving and then promoted an uncle of the defeated king to be the Lord of the realm. After he had become king I coveted to convert him to our holy faith. I devoted eight months to this daily task until it pleased God to move the king's heart so that he received the holy water of Baptism.[31]

The royal example was followed by the courtiers. Mavura, with the baptismal name of Felippe, reigned for twenty years, not much more than a Portuguese vassal, dependent on Lisbon. He was eager to follow Portuguese ways, and sent one of his sons, Dom Miguel, to Goa. There the young man was received as a novice in the Dominican Order, and eventually gained a Master of Theology and became a teacher in the Theological Faculty in Goa.

At Felippe Mavura's death in 1652, he was succeeded by another son. The identification of religion and politics was again symbolized: the new *Mwene Mutapa*, baptized Domingo, was well-groomed for his high office by a combination of coronation and baptism.

On the presupposition that Papal *Padroado* and Portuguese *Conquista* enterprise had made these regions of Africa theirs, the Portuguese carved out large areas of land for individual Portuguese landlords (*praseiros*). Agriculture demanded great numbers of cheap labourers, preferably slaves.

The East Coast slave trade

Slave trading was an old, brutal business in these parts, which the Portuguese took over from the Arabs. The Church orders had their own slaves, and at least in the beginning felt that their slaves were better off than during their previous days of freedom. There was also a pious distinction about the sale, the same as in Angola: baptized slaves must not be sold to Muslims. At precisely the same period as William Wilberforce raised his prophetic voice in England against the slave trade and slavery in the world, Prelate Fr Amaro de S. Thomas in Mozambique declared that slaves must not be sold to Muslims, for if they were, 'the gates of heaven would be closed to them because then they would be deprived of their chance of being baptized in the hour of death'. A 'Pastoral letter' threatened excommunication to those who sold slaves to pagans or 'Moors', as their Christian faith would be endangered. In the eighteenth century, the slave trade with its rapidly increasing profits became particularly cruel. Fr Francisco M. Bordale wrote in 1835: 'The outrage and horrors in the oppression of the Natives – crimes committed here without punishment – are the causes of the threatening depopulation of the country.'[32]

Dominicans and Jesuits

Two Catholic Orders were at work, Dominicans and Jesuits, including some outstanding personalities. The greatest of them all, St Francis Xavier, SJ, that incomparable *conquistador* of souls, spent six months in Mozambique and on the east coast of Africa in 1541, waiting for the monsoon winds to take him to Goa and South India. The two great Orders were often competing. Because of tensions between them, spheres of interest were created for each, similar to modern Protestant 'comity' agreements. But in the dominant political and economic centres of the country, Mozambique, Sena, and Tete, they shared the work. The Dominicans worked inland, and the Jesuits with the Tonga people along the Zambezi. Both were subject to the direction of the king of Portugal. At first this hierarchical arrangement was mediated through the Governor and the Portuguese Archbishop of Goa. In 1612 Mozambique was released from dependence on far-away Goa, and could regard itself as relatively independent, although still under the king in Lisbon. In the following decades, Goanese merchants continued to play a role through their trading centres along the Mozambique coastline.

The king in Portugal sent his directives to the Governor and the Vicar-General in Mozambique. If the black king was amenable, his brother king in Lisbon could show his pleasure by a personal gift, such as a habit of the Order of Our Lord Jesus Christ. Church and State were inextricably tied together in this *conquista* system. The Portuguese occupied the coastline with its harbours, established forts, and administrative outposts along the rivers.

The *conquista* ideology led to a concentration of pastoral attention to the Portuguese and Goanese elements, and also to the baptism of slaves before they were exported overseas. The people were assimilated into the Church by a hasty method of mass baptism, although officially it should occur only after at least twenty-five days of catechetical preparation. Experience in matters of Church discipline enforced a rule whereby baptism of adults was deferred until their hour of death.

The Jesuits, with their world-wide connexions and experience, borrowed a catechization idea from their colleagues in Goa: a catechism with sung questions and answers. It soon proved to be even more popular with Africans. Catechumens would come singing to church, on their way home, on their way to work. One could hear them singing the answers in their canoes, and mothers could now more easily teach their children the precepts of the Christian faith.[33] A worthwhile task would be to follow up catechetical developments in Jesuit archives with regard to Goa and Sofala.

Searching for Prester John

Wherever the Portuguese landed along the African coast, they looked for a passage leading to 'Prester John', that Christian king somewhere in Africa – or Asia – whom the medieval crusaders had tried to trace and find. As soon as they met the Kongolese, one of the Portuguese captains steered his ship along the Zaïre river, searching for the mysterious king. The rapids and falls on the river soon put a stop to this attempt. On the Mozambique side, the missionaries widened their horizons to the Shire River and Lake Malawi. Here, hopefully, was the highway to Prester John, and the Jesuit Aloysius Mariano was sent to find a way along the coast to Abyssinia.[34]

The Portuguese king and his empire needed gold, slaves, and spices, and it was to acquire these wares that Vasco da Gama, Albuquerque, and others ventured eastward. On the way, they touched at the harbour of Sofala, the golden village; visited Kilwa with its black sheikh and met the Swahili-speaking people at Mombasa and Malindi. At Malindi, da Gama and his men found a number of Indians, with four ships. It was even possible to make personal contacts with them, for one of the Indians spoke Italian: 'India now appeared deliciously close.'[35] It was here that St Francis Xavier dwelt for months, in 1541–42, waiting for a ship to Goa in India.

Fort Jesus at Mombasa

The Portuguese befriended the Malindi population, and with them took Mombasa in 1591. Two years later they put up their fort as a sign of conquest, and as a token of their determination to make this a Catholic stronghold, the station was called 'Fort Jesus', a pious denomination. Francesco da Gama, Vasco da Gama's grandson, placed Augustinian monks as vicars along the Kenyan coast, at Faza, Pata, Lamu and Mombasa. In 1597 Mombasa had a monastery and there were soon 4,000 Christians.

The king of Mombasa acceded to Portuguese requests, and sent his son Yusuf, a boy of seven, to Goa. He returned in 1630, an adult with a new identity: a Christian name, 'Dom Jeronimo Chingulia', and a Portuguese wife. The joy over the convert was short-lived. Already by the following year the young man came into conflict with his Portuguese masters, and on Assumption Day he pushed his dagger into the Portuguese Commandant, reverting to Islam and taking back his name of Yusuf ibn Hasan.

A terrible challenge to the young African Christian community ensued. How deep was their commitment to the faith in Jesus the Christ? A few figures about personal decisions in this utmost crisis represent something of an answer. After centuries of oblivion the complete *processus* of the martyrs was found in Rome, a record of the ecclesiastical inquiry held in Goa, India, during 1632–33, and published in 1980 in Latin and with an English translation by Dr G. S. P. Freeman-Grenville.[36] A total of 250 African and Portuguese were massacred in the town and became martyrs; only four priests and one layman escaped.[37] Another 400 preferred to be sent as slaves to Mecca.

It is vain to speculate on the causes of this military disaster. Climate and incompetence have been blamed. 'The Portuguese, indeed, in their inability to co-operate with either Arab or African were their own greatest enemies.'[38] There were new Portuguese attacks, but the Omani Arabs from Arabia came to the help of their fellow believers, and by 1729 Fort Jesus was definitely in Muslim hands.

Across the Indian Ocean

With the Portuguese presence in the Indian Ocean, the uneasy, ever-changing balance of power in the region had been seriously disrupted. Arabs, Omani Arabs, Indians, Zimba raids from inland, and Oromo raids from the north all threatened the people. With the Portuguese retreat to their stronghold of Goa, the Omani Arabs increasingly dominated the coast until in 1840 – 'a climacteric in the history of the East African coast line' – Said, the Omani ruler, moved from the Arabian peninsula and settled in Zanzibar. This was a date and a decade which would open a new chapter in the Christian approach to East Africa, but this time under very different conditions.[39]

In the meantime other budding colonial powers from the West had emerged on the far-flung islands of the Indian Ocean. The Dutch, touching at Mauritius in 1598, established themselves at Batavia, Java, comparable with Portuguese Goa in India.

The French occupied Reunion in 1638 and with the help of their trading company managed to gain a foothold at Fort-Dauphin in Southern Madagascar. After an initiative from the Propaganda in Rome, the Lazarists began work in 1640. Characteristically the two French Lazarists who arrived that year were accompanied by two Malagasy, which naturally facilitated communication with the people. The seamen from Madagascar had somehow turned up in France and were baptized there. One of the young men was instructed by no less a person than Vincent da Paul, the saintly founder of the Lazarists: 'I use images to instruct him, and it seems that this serves to catch his imagination.' Thus prepared the young man was baptized by the Pope's nuncio.

Illness soon decimated the number of French missionaries, but new recruits followed. For their converts in the island the missionaries managed to found a Christian village, near Fort-Dauphin. They also produced a bilingual catechism – French and Malagash. The importance of catechization was emphasized by a catechetical question whether one could be blessed without following the Catechism, to which there was a very definite answer: 'No, never, because we cannot be good if we do not learn the Catechism.' Then what does one learn in this catechism?: 'All that is necessary to go to Paradise.' There was also information about Purgatory with vivid ideas about the horrors of the place: 'a continuous fire which torments violently'.[40]

ETHIOPIA: REVERSAL AND WELL-NIGH CATASTROPHE

The Muslims and Imam Ahmed Gragn

Islam had a long history in Ethiopia. With Christians in command in the northern highlands, the Muslims pressed forward from the east, especially in the Sidama and eastern Shewa areas. They claimed to have ruled seven Muslim kingdoms, each with a sultan. Even in the Christian highlands, there were a few Muslim colonies, who had to give tribute in gold and silks to their Christian overlords. The province of Hadya even had to annually provide a maiden to be baptized and become a Christian on passing the frontier. The Muslim rule covered a much larger territory than that of the Christians, but while the latter was composed of a comparatively concentrated power in the North, the Muslim areas – only superficially Islamized – were much more divided. Yet the international Muslim fellowship helped their cause. Muslim traders had extensive connexions with Arabia and the Middle East generally, and links with the whole Islamic world through slave-trading and pilgrimages. For long periods the relationship between the two communities maintained an uneasy balance of power, often, however, suddenly disturbed.

Imam Ahmed B. Ibrahim, called Gragn (1506–43), a young warrior from Hubat near Harar, revolted against the humiliating yoke of tribute-giving. He was brought up as a family slave and later liberated, soon establishing himself as a warrior of great promise. He found allies among the Somali and the Danakil. Eventually 5,000 Nubians also came to his rescue. It was rumoured that people had seen visions about the young Ahmed: Was he not the *Imam* of the Last Times? Yes, he was the chosen vessel destined to deliver his people. He stood on the dividing line between the Middle Ages and the New Era, with his Turkish allies providing the modern weapons.

The impact of his army was devastating. There were 3,000 men in full armour, 20,000 with white shields, and a similar number of archers. The 5,000 cavalry had brocade uniforms and blankets covered with gold; their helmets glinted like mirrors. 'Imam Ahmed rejoiced and shed tears of joy.' He bought arms from the Catalans at Zaila, and the Turks provided him with additional muskets and even cannons. He was prepared for a 'holy war'. Muslim women, too, joined the army. 'When their men attacked, they hurled themselves into the battle on their mules, and when the enemy had been routed, they exclaimed: "I took four Christian women", and others "... five or six".'

Latent conflict and hatred between Muslim and Christian flared up in a blaze which laid waste the kingdom. It took Ahmed only twelve short and terrible years to destroy most of the Christian culture built up over hundreds of years. Guns, cannons and lighted torches set fire to the roofs of the churches, and soon everything inside burned: precious books, illuminated manuscripts, vestments, and sacred vessels.

At the famous Debre Libanos, dedicated to the memory of the great St Tekle Haymanot, and one of the glories of the Church, the monks insisted: 'If they burn our church – our pilgrim centre – let them burn us too.' The great majority of them threw themselves into the fire, 'like moths into a lamp'. Monasteries badly damaged or destroyed included Bizen and Abba Satios in Tigray, not far from Massawa; Abba Gerima, some five days from Massawa; and many in the Lake Tana region. At the Hallelujah monastery, the St Mary Church was in ruins. This large centre had held ninety churches under its jurisdiction. All were destroyed. Now only a few hamlets remained.[41]

In the wake of the disaster came rumbles from the south of a vast population movement, that of the Oromo, nicknamed 'Galla'. At first there were sudden and sporadic military thrusts toward the north, increasingly a threat and a challenge to the Christian Church as well as Islam. We will return later to the role of the Oromo.

For the Christian king, Libne Dingil, the Muslim massacre was a terrible blow, and for his people a traumatic shock. Toward the end of his struggle, the king appealed to the European power which had earlier contacted him – the Portuguese. As related already, the Portuguese had been looking for Prester John, the mysterious Christian king, said to be found in the interior of Asia or Africa. Here he was now, Prester John in person, needing their help. In 1540 Libne Dingil died after ruling for thirty-two years. He was succeeded by his son, Galawdewos (1540–59).

In 1541 a Portuguese fleet arrived at Massawa, with 400 men under Christoph da Gama, son of Vasco da Gama. They too had muskets and cannons and finally, in 1543, Ahmed and his men were defeated, with Ahmed killed in battle. Galawdewos faced a devastated country and destroyed churches. The very soul of a proud people, with their great Solomonic dream, was grieved. Many Christians had renounced their faith to become Muslims. When they later returned to their church, a book of penitence, *Mesihafe Qedir*, was produced for them to learn the way back to their Christian faith.

Help in need – indeed too much of it

King and people had been saved at the very last minute, and they felt indebted to their brave Portuguese helpers for military assistance. Over 100 Portuguese soldiers stayed on in the country and formed a settlement of their own in the north. The king and the Church of Portugal sent their own bishop, Andre de Oviedo, presumably to shepherd the Portuguese, but as it transpired, also designed for other matters related to the future of the Church in Ethiopia. The fact that he was a bishop implied a challenge to the Coptic patriarch in Alexandria and his representative in Ethiopia.

Gone were the times of the Council of Florence with its 'ecumenical' vision and concern. This was the period in the Mediterranean of Counter-Reformation and Inquisition, and the Portuguese clergy were part of a narrow system. Coming to Ethiopia, the priests were in for a shocking discovery: Prester John was not the genuine article. In fact, he was a heretic. This obviously had to be put right.

The Portuguese sent four Patriarchs to Ethiopia. The first, in addition to being uneducated, assumed a spurious authority. Before too long he was exiled. The second similarly took for granted that as a Patriarch he had arrived to receive king and Church into the Roman fold. But the Ethiopian King Galawdewos ably defended their ancient connection with the Church of Alexandria. The third, Pero Paez, a Spanish Jesuit, arrived in 1603. He was an outstanding person, a highly cultured churchman, and an eloquent preacher. By his empathy, learning and tact he won everyone to his views and exercised strong influence on King Susinyos. This ruler highly honoured the sacred rites and customs of his people. He arranged for his coronation in 1609 to be held at Aksum, thus renewing the long chain of tradition broken three centuries earlier. He was personally much involved in the ongoing theological debate at the court on the 'two natures' in the person of Christ. Pero Paez convinced him of the error of Unionism. In 1622 the king took the final step of accepting the Roman faith. That same year Paez died. He was succeeded by Afonso Mendez who was consecrated patriarch of a now supposedly Catholic Ethiopia. His appointment soon proved to be an altogether unfortunate choice. Narrow and conceited, he was bent on doing a thorough job: the faithful were to be re-baptized according to the Roman rite; the 'schismatic' deacons, priests and monks were to be re-ordained; and the Ethiopian circumcision ritual and their feasts and fasts had to be abolished.

In a very short time Mendez managed to cause a public uproar and a bitter civil war. Susinyos had to come to the rescue of his people, and published a unique proclamation in 1632:

> Hark ye! Hark ye! We first gave you this faith believing that it was good. But innumerable people have been slain on account of it, Yolyos [Julius], Qeberyal [Gabriel], Takla Giyorgis [George], Sarsa Krestos, and now these peasants. For which reason we restore to you the faith of your forefathers. Let the former clergy return to the churches, let them put in their *tâbots* [altars], let them say their own liturgy. And do ye rejoice.[42]

Which is what they did; the whole nation rejoiced as they had never done before. Susinyos abdicated in favour of his son, Fasiledes. He saw to it that the Jesuits were banished, first to their one remaining centre at Fremona in Tigray and soon from Ethiopia altogether.

The intermezzo with the Portuguese was partly a move by the Ethiopian royalty to invite Western cultural influence. Instead, the anti-foreign reaction resulted in an isolation lasting 200 years. Far to the East, in Japan, and for almost the same length of time, the people experienced a similar kind of isolation. Also there, Lusitanian intrusion, under the guidance of St

Francis Xavier and his fellow Jesuits, led in 1637 to two centuries of hermetic isolation. In the islands of the East and in the highland strongholds of Africa, the Portuguese experience led to strong reactions. In both cases it took two centuries for these traditionalist societies to live down the confrontation with the foreigners. As late as 1770, James Bruce, a Scot and certainly far from being a Roman Catholic sympathizer was suspected at the Gonder court of being a Roman Catholic, possibly contriving to destroy the Ethiopian church.[43]

Two centuries of isolation from the West

In this period of isolation Ethiopia manifested a distinct religious geography. There were wide differences between the highlands, referred to as the 'Christian North' – Eritrea, Tigre and Begemdir – and the southern region, mainly Muslim and pagan. The south also had scattered remnants of an early Christian culture. They had survived the Oromo storm of the sixteenth and seventeenth centuries which swept away most of Christianity and Islam in the area. Also significant was an invasion from the north into the Wollamo province in about 1600. An adventurous squadron of 150 Tigray noblemen and their servants rode on horseback to the southern part of the country and soon transplanted their Christian customs, laws and values. This invasion epitomizes the general tendency of northern influence on the south. According to Professor Eike Haberland, Tigray and Shewa in the north-east and centre, however, remained the models for the southern peoples. Orthodox authority in the south waned at times. Haberland gives the following explanation: the very constitution of the Ethiopian Church made its continuance dependent on the rule of a distant Coptic Patriarch in Alexandria. This Patriarch sent the *abun* (bishop), who alone could ordain priests. When contacts with the north were severed for prolonged periods, the southern priesthood tended to disappear and priestly families soon changed into pagan clans. Mass was performed with difficulty, or not at all. Fasts and feasts survived, although their significance became obscured.

One reason for southern difference from the 'Christian North' was the dominance of its Oromo population, being one of the major peoples of Ethiopia. Nicknamed 'Galla' by their neighbours, they had come as a confederation of tribes in the 1520s to invade Ethiopia from the south. Their story illustrates the familiar theme in African history: that of migration and conquest in the struggle for survival and advance. From the south, they forced their way to two areas in the centre of the country, becoming Christians in the kingdom of Shewa, and Muslims in Wello province. From the latter half of the nineteenth century, Ethiopian Emperors through the Orthodox Church, and Catholic and Protestant missionaries showed concern for the conversion of the Oromo. Their highly complex *gada* (age group) system was an institution of great interest. Its implications for the conversion of the Oromo would provide a fruitful topic for future research.

The tradition of 'wandering capitals' had begun during the Solomonic dynasty, with thousands of tents and huts huddled together to make up a royal camp. Later it became apparent that the country needed a permanent, well-built centre. It was Susinyos' son, Fasiledes, who for various reasons decided to make Gondar the new capital. So it remained for two hundred years. As it was situated north of Lake Tana, midway between Shewa and the coast of Massawa, once established, it enhanced the court's isolation. A number of palaces and beautifully ornamented churches were built there. Some of them were of the finest architectural quality, such as the Abbey Church of St Mary of Qusqwam, reminiscent of the Lalibela churches.[44]

Theological controversies in Gonder

The new capital of Gondar became the centre for sophisticated theological discussion. Contending parties engaged in fierce intellectual battles, quoting their authorities in the Cairo Patriarchate or in the two great Ethiopian schools of the Middle Ages: those of Tekle Haymanot and of Ewostatewos. The original conflict between the 'House of Ewostatewos' and of the 'House of Tekle Haymanot' (centred at Debre Libanos Monastery) during the fourteenth century concerned the Sabbath, lay leadership, and the role of Alexandria.

The ferment caused by the Catholics was an important factor in the continuation of the theological disputes during the reigns of Fasiledes (1632–67) and Yohannes I (1667–82). Both emperors were interested listeners and in each dispute, the final judge. More often than not the losers in such a debate were thrown into prison, there to meditate on their lamentable error. It is characteristic of the times that, at the court, the Ethiopian women also showed a passionate interest in the dogmatic controversies. They were later led by Queen Seble-Wengel who shared the literary and theological taste of her consort, Emperor Yohannes I, and her son, Iyasu (later emperor).[45] The overwhelming majority of the Ethiopian Church was never divided on the issue of Salvation, but only on the understanding of Christ's person.

Rooted in the Christological controversies of the early Church, the disputes were revived by Jesuit teaching on the two natures of Christ, and by Emperor Susinyos' confession of the Catholic faith in 1622. Ethiopians fought to defend the Unionite tenet confessing one unique divine/human nature in Christ, *Tewahido*, brought about by the Incarnation. In the process, however, a new formula evolved and found support in one of the two Ethiopian monastic orders, thus causing a new conflict in the Church.

The followers of Ewostatewos stressed the unction, *qibat*, of the Holy Spirit in uniting the Divine and Human in Christ through this *qibat*, Christ became the Son of God and elevated to divinity. The dominating order of Tekle Haymanot saw in this explanation either subordination of the Son to the Spirit, or a danger of Adoptionism, which taught that Christ was elevated to divinity only at his baptism. The party of Tekle Haymanot argued that Christ was the Son of God by Grace, and that 'his elevation to the quality of a natural son of God was a result of the union of the human nature with the divine.'[46] These 'unionists' were called *Ye-Siga Lij* (Sons of Grace).

There followed several councils of priests, monks, and nobles. The disputes sought chiefly to do justice to the purely human acts of Christ. Gojjam province and the northern areas of Tigray and Eritrea generally supported the *Qibat* formula of the followers of Ewostatewos, while most of the Amhara nobility from the central highlands traditionally endorsed the teachings of the house of Tekle Haymanot. In 1654 Emperor Fasiledes tried to achieve unity by imposing the 'unctionist' (*qibatoch*) formula on the Tekle Haymanot party, but this only led to a rebellion of the 'unionists'. The next emperor, Yohannes I, continued the royal partiality of favouring the 'House of Ewostatewos', and the continuing ecclesiastical dispute gravely weakened the political unity of the kingdom. The accession to the throne of Iyasu I (1682–1706), called 'the Great', led to a period of imposed unity after the new king terminated the theological disputes by coercing the *qibatoch* group to accept the *Ye-Siga Lij* theory.

Peter Heyling and the era of the Judges

Foreign influence could not be altogether avoided. When the new *abun* arrived from Egypt in 1635, he brought a German medical practitioner, Peter Heyling, scholar and lay theologian. His medical skill made him popular, but his real concern was to rejuvenate the Ethiopian Church through translation of the Bible. He helped to translate St John's Gospel (and possibly other books of the New Testament) into Amharic, and published it in booklet form. This was a revolutionary initiative. '*Dawit*', or, the Psalms, and the book of Revelation were known and revered in the sacred language of *Ge'ez*, but meeting the Gospel message in the tongue of the people was something new. In several northern monasteries the theological debate took on a new dimension of reality.

In 1652 Peter Heyling left Ethiopia, and on his way back to the West he was beheaded by a Turkish pasha. Through his Bible translation, his influence lingered on. Ethiopian evangelicals and the Swedish Scholar, Gustav Arén, tentatively suggest that the late nineteenth-century evangelical underground movement within the churches of Begemdir, Gojjam, and Shewa can be traced back to Peter Heyling and his Gospel translations.

The minds at Gonder were occupied not only by intellectual exercises. On the horizon there loomed messianic indications of a warrior martyr, corroborated by millenarian speculations. This concurred with traditions in Ethiopian piety leading back at least to the fifteenth century. It was thought that the name of this messiah, coming to save his people, was most probably Tewodros – the Gift of God. Warlords and emperors appeared, claiming to be the promised Tewodros.

Eventually during the eighteenth century, there was a disintegration of central authority, and the regional nobles (*rases*) took command over their particular areas. This was the time of the *Zamena mesafint* (the era of the Princes or Judges), referring to the parallel experience in ancient Israel in Judges 2:16. The Emperor lost much of his power, so did the *abun*, nominal head of the church. This situation lasted for about a century, until in 1855 a minor chief named Kasa Haylu fought his way to power and proclaimed himself King of Kings Tewodros. The time of the *Zamena mesafint* was at an end.

3

OVERVIEW TO THE NINETEENTH CENTURY

TWO DIVERSE MAPS

A theme

Two quite different maps can be drawn for the nineteenth-century Christianization process in Africa: one explicit, manifest and official; the other – no less important – related to clan and village involved in the cataclysmic changes which overtook African societies.

The first, the official map, covered 'mission fields', consisting of a great number of mission societies and mission stations, Catholic and Protestant, highly visible centres in the African landscape, with church, school, clinic, farm and printing press, together with staff houses. Such centres represented well-defined missionary programmes. From the station there were regular visits to the surrounding population by the Western missionary and/or the African catechists, by foot, on horse back, by ox cart, or by canoe.

In certain cases the mission station was seen as a point of departure for a strategic plan or dream, to reach farther afield. There were to be established so-called 'chains' of mission centres: six of them in a Methodist programme through Transkei designed by William Shaw; a Reformed chain along the south-west Namaqualand coast; or from Natal overland to Ethiopia; or across the continent from Mombasa to Gabon, devised by Johan Ludwig Krapf; or from Gabon to Mombasa, and planned by John Leighton Wilson. David Hinderer, CMS missionary in Yorubaland, Nigeria, was sure of his approach as he wrote in 1852:

> That we are aiming at the Missionary chain through Central Africa is no longer a question ... Two good links we have already towards it – Badagry and Abeokuta and I am sure God will give us ... Ibadan about two days journey NE, as a third. Next to that Ilorin may, by the providence of God, constitute a fourth, and a fifth will bring us to the Niger; and the same number again, if not less, to the Tchad, where we shall soon shake hands with our brethren in the East.[1]

These plans were characteristic expressions of their time, of the European fascinated by the map of Africa, such as it was, as yet unknown and unexplored, to be claimed in the name of Christ.

This missionary map could be analyzed with the material and the methods available, for a conventional mission history. There were the histories of the mission societies and the mission fields, there were the biographies, the hagiographies even, of the Western missionaries concerned: all this had to be compressed into the chapters of a mission history.

Yet, with this approach, producing a history where the Westerner, the foreigner, was the main focus and the African remaining outside the story, was the writer ever to arrive in Africa? As late as the 1960s there were still published ambitious surveys of Churches in certain parts of Africa where the African was – absent. In such cases, fundamental aspects of African history had been missed. One had overlooked population movements and migrations across the continent and their role in the diffusion of the Christian message, and what R.W. July has called 'Revolutionary Africa', meaning the nineteenth century prior to 'colonial Africa'.[2] This takes us to the second and more relevant map of Africa.

In the following pages the reader will meet an emphasis on vast and dramatic changes, in and through the adversities and opportunities, with uprooted refugee – groups and individuals – in 'the spreading chaos of the interior plains',[3] prepared to face and join the new religion. The refugee theme, which is a compelling dimension of this whole book, will provide a significant frame of reference also when we follow developments from the late eighteenth century onwards.

One will meet this theme in the effect of the volcanic outburst of the *mfecane*, initiated in the 1820s in Zululand and Swaziland, striking west into Transvaal, south into Eastern Cape and, above all, north beyond the rivers and along the lakes. Historians of South Africa have of late been drawn into a fierce struggle over the *mfecane* concept, supposedly 'a self-generated internal revolution within northern "Nguni" societies to the west of the Delagoa Bay'.[4] Very fortunately we are not concerned in this book with the *mfecane* concept as such. Our concern is with a series of refugee movements in African societies. Faced with this upheaval, groups and individuals fled wherever they could and in certain cases met with the men and women who conveyed the message of the new religion.

In southern Africa one significant sequel of the *mfecane* was, for our purposes, related to groups forming an early migrant labour movement, from northern Transvaal to the south-east Cape. To a large extent because of generational conflict in their communities, these groups left their villages and moved southward to find work.

In West Africa one meets with returnee movements of liberated slaves, freed from slave ships on the way to the Americas, brought to Freetown and, after no more than a generation, prepared to return to their 'roots' somewhere on the West African coast or in the hinterland. These developments were at least as important for African Church history as any attempt by a missionary society to teach the catechism.

Two aspects have been indicated: the Western missionary approach in and through the 'stations' on the one side and on the other the overarching continental theme of migrations and population movements, leading refugees to a readiness to accept the message. There now remains to attempt a readjustment of the two. At various points of intersection between the two 'maps' or systems, a major transition (or 'conversion' if that term is preferred) takes place from the traditional community to the new fellowship and its faith.

In certain dramatic cases in the first half of the nineteenth century, the foreign missionary was already there to meet and welcome the victims of misfortune and adversity: with the Mfengu in Eastern Cape; with the bewildered survivors of the Transvaal refugee groups; with the early migrant labourers from north of Transvaal daringly moving in little groups over the highveld to Pietermaritzburg, Port Elizabeth or Capetown; and later the enterprising Tonga and Henga along Lake Malawi, meeting in the foreign missionary, his chapel and school, a catalytic influence which was to lift whole populations to a new level; in West Africa meeting the liberated slaves who landed at Freetown and thus bestowing a Christian identity onto individuals who later formed groups of 'returnees'.

Certainly, the mission societies and the missionaries – Catholic and Protestant – will appear on these pages, but with a difference. As far as possible grounded in the history of African communities and structures – more so than in Western denominations – this presentation will emphasize the African initiative, placed on the frontier between faith and faith, carried by young men revolting against what was seen as the pressures of older generations.

Another important – but most often overlooked – aspect of African mobility which we highlight is the fact that the first missionary on his arrival in a village was likely to find a group of young men who had already been influenced by the new message and already been inspired by it to congregate for prayer and hymns picked up on the way. These examples appear so often that we are sometimes tempted – perhaps irresponsibly – to suggest a law:

> That first missionary arriving in a certain African village there to proclaim for the first time the name of Christ – was never first.

Rumour from afar had already done its preparatory work: there were already some young men who by some chance visit outside had been intrigued by the new message and were anxious to acquire that new song, that new name, that new future.

A regional perspective

This study tries to understand the Christianization of modern Africa not primarily in terms of mission societies – whether Catholic or Protestant – but as part of the social reality represented by the different regions. This approach will be carried forward into the twentieth century but is of particular importance for the nineteenth.

From the point of view of Church history, the northern region was dominated by the Churches in Egypt and Ethiopia, while large parts of the map of Africa were vacant and void. Thus only from the end of the nineteenth century did modern missions start in Congo and East Africa. The Catholics knew, however, that they had been there before, in the 'Portuguese period'. They therefore tended to regard their modern missions in Congo and elsewhere as a *reprise*.

Planned mission work was a matter of concern primarily in two of the regions, West Africa and South Africa – together with the island world of the Indian Ocean, reached by British and French ships: Madagascar was at first dominated by British Congregationalists while the other two islands Mauritius and Réunion were served by French Catholics (Holy Ghost Fathers). The latter were to venture towards another island in the Indian Ocean, Zanzibar, which meant, eventually, contact with the East African mainland.

In a survey of the nineteenth-century African missions, Gustav Warneck, the German mission historian, estimated the number of Protestant Christians in Africa in 1910 at one and half million. No less than two thirds of these belonged to South Africa and again a large part of the South African Protestants were to be found in the Western Cape, termed in South Africa as 'Coloureds'. Compared with this concentration in Western Cape there were other parts of the country – Zululand, northern Transvaal and Ovamboland – where mission work had just begun. With a few notable exceptions, nineteenth-century South Africa remained a Protestant country.

From a Church history perspective nineteenth-century West Africa is another world altogether. For three centuries prior to 1800, West Africa had been in economic and cultural contact with the West, from the time of the Portuguese to that of the Danes. Apart from early nineteenth-century efforts in Senegal by the Holy Ghost Fathers, the missions – Catholic and Protestant – focused on the Western coastline from Gambia to Libreville. Certain efforts were made to reach 'inland' but this was largely left for the following century. Certain crucial facts about West African missions of this period give this region its special character.

The Christianized Creole population held a position of its own. Together with African returned freedmen they became the African missionaries for the region seeking their personal 'roots' in the African populations along the coast and further inland. Other groups were formed by the 'Brazilian returnees', freedmen from Brazil who returned to West Africa there to establish Portuguese-speaking, mainly Catholic communities. Ethnic communities such as the Wesleyan Fante on the Gold Coast became a pace-setting Church.

Among the Creoles there was established the Fourah Bay College, 1827, to become for the whole of the West Coast the academic centre, eventually, in 1887, associated with Durham University, in England. The Niger Expedition of 1841–42 sent 145 Europeans and Africans to explore the River Niger, of whom forty died. This casualty proved once and for all that West Africa must be directed – and evangelized – by Africans, an idea already made imperative by the climate. African expectation and Western planning were combined in the consecration of Bishop Crowther. The debate over Crowther's episcopacy was a factor in the emergence of the so-called 'African Churches' in West Africa.

Three categories

Winning the 'nations' for the faith along with individuals was to follow – if it happened at all – by way of certain social categories of people. Naturally it is difficult to generalize for the conditions in the entire continent and the writer, while making these broad generalizations, is aware of some of the exceptions and variations. However, we highlight the following categories: the kings and chiefs; the young men; the slaves and other socially marginalized groups (the women will be a decisive theme for the twentieth century – 'a women's Church').

The kings and Christ

The more the mission directors in Europe knew of Church history, the more they emphasized as precedents the kings and nations of the early Church in the European Middle Ages, as well as the fateful legacy of a Church that had vanished in different parts of Africa – North Africa and the Congo. The less these gentlemen knew of Church history or any history, the less concerned they could be with any prototype of the past, let alone from the Middle Ages. The towering example here is Cardinal Lavigerie who, drawing his inspiration from the examples of the early Church and medieval European Christian kings, sent out his missionaries to the lake-sides of Central Africa to found Christian nations with Christian kings. Some Protestants, too, as we shall see, held similar views, none more determinedly than the Lutheran Ludvig Harms of Hermannsburg, in northern Germany.

If the results of the attempts at winning the kings were meagre, this was not for want of trying. J. S. Moffat, Robert Moffat's son and a good Congregationalist, in a letter to the Directors of the LMS in 1888 emphasized the importance for LMS missionaries to spend sufficient time *enkosini* (at the king's place):

> It ought to be an absolute rule that each one of the missionaries spend three months in each year with the chief [in this case Mzilikazi], not flitting to and fro like a bird which leaves no traces or footsteps. I am certain that this will tell within an appreciable time.

A chapter, subtitled 'The Church at the Kings Way' (page 562) shows how the missionaries in the interlacustrine region had to follow some such ruler for the planning of their work. The king was 'the door' through which one had to pass and there was only one approach by which to get there. Anybody who tried to reach the country in any other way had to suffer for it. On his way to Kampala in 1885, the newly appointed Anglican Bishop Hannington chose another way than the accepted route, over the Lake: he was killed before ever arriving before the king. This can be compared with Coillard's attempt to visit King Lobengula in Zimbabwe. He took the 'wrong' road, was imprisoned briefly at Bulawayo and had to turn back to South Africa, losing nearly ten years in his efforts to establish a new mission field north of the Limpopo. But it was not only a question of a first approach. In Zululand two generations of missionaries tried to win the king with very little to show for it.

On the other hand a few royal converts did appear. For South Africa one notes Kgama of Bamangwato, Kama of the Gqunukwebe and Faku of the Pondo. And one should not forget Sechele of the Kwena, the only African baptized by David Livingstone. Very soon after baptism Sechele was placed under Church discipline but he kept on preaching and studying his New Testament for thirty-eight years until at long last readmitted to the fold.

Sechele's friend Moshoeshoe in Lesotho at least came close to being baptized.

While all this went on, Cardinal Lavigerie in Algiers was involved with the approach to the polygamous King of Buganda, Mutesa. The local Catholic missionary, he insisted, should not have denied outright to the king an access to the Church and its fellowship. Following the example of the early Church, the king should have been informed that he had before him a life-long preparation for Holy Baptism, as a catechumen of the Church and as a friend of the Mission. Accepted as a postulant or a catechumen, he could at the hour of death be baptized *in extremis*.

'Freed people'

The late eighteenth-century struggle for abolition of the slave trade, inspired largely by Anglo-Saxon Quakers and Evangelicals, resulted in 1807 in the [British] Abolition Act prohibiting all British subject from participation in slave trading. Thirty years later, a British Evangelical, Thomas Buxton, initiated a campaign against slavery and *for* 'legitimate trade' – referring mainly to products of palm oil and peanuts. Unfortunately this brilliant formula did not lead to a decline of slavery within Africa. Instead slaves became if anything more important than before, necessary as they were supposed to be for agricultural production, thus leading to a 'slave mode of production'. Although the Atlantic slave trade was coming to an end, the system of domestic slavery was as strong as ever.

In large parts of West Africa slaves had for centuries made up a majority of the population. In Cokwe society, Angola, 80 per cent of the villages were slave villages. Among the Tio and the Bobangi along the Zaïre river, the slaves formed the bulk of the population. At the end of the nineteenth century there were in one settlement 290 slaves and only eight free men.

This being the case on a large scale, one would like to know the numbers of those joining the churches from these social categories. Any generalization must here be built on solid local studies. In any case, the slaves and 'freed peoples' must be seen as part of a general category of marginalized groups, outcasts, aliens and refugees, on the outskirts of society, looking for a new identity and for some security in a world of social and economic destruction. In West Africa the slave trade officially came to an end in the first third of the twentieth century. In East Africa it reached its worst momentum in the 1840s and on his second journey David Livingstone saw terrible signs of 'this open wound'. At this time between 50,000 and 70,000 slaves were reaching the coast every year.[5]

A point of wide application can be safely made, namely that to a large extent it was the aliens, the foreigners, the uprooted, who were among the first to join the Church. They found a solution in the fellowship and concern of the local congregation. The Mfengu in the eastern Cape or in Transvaal belonged to this category. The upper reaches of Natal near the Drakensberg mountains had such 'riff-raff' communities.[6] Not those established in a seemingly solid, ethnic community but the uprooted – individuals and groups – were prepared to join the new fellowship.

There were theological dimensions to these decisions: to oppressed outsiders on the outskirts of society the surprisingly egalitarian message of the Christian hymn in the chapel was supremely attractive. The term *slaves* should be avoided for those groups who became part of the Church, as many thought of themselves as descendants not of slaves but of a *freed* people.

A youth movement

The nineteenth-century church in Africa, both Catholic and Protestant, was a youth movement. This claim can be demonstrated on a number of decisive points, to be corroborated by a theory of generational conflict in many African societies at the time.

The surprising corps of a thousand young boys at the Kabaka's court, Uganda, were perhaps aware of themselves becoming, before too long, *batangole* chiefs in the Buganda kingdom, but less aware perhaps of a fate awaiting some of them as martyrs for their new faith. They were young 'Readers' of a first generation setting an example to young men in the whole kingdom and in the entire interlacustrine region. The 'Christian village' population along the coast of the continent from Senegal in the west via Réunion and Mauritius to Bagamoyo in the east, enabled young couples to build up new Catholic societies in a pagan *milieu*, set apart because of their faith. Gangs of young men, leaving their villages along a wide latitude in the north of Transvaal and Ovambo, going south towards a 'Big Water' to work, were set on acquiring what a young man must have, a gun, and wealth for a future marriage. In the process they found not only a new rifle but also a new religion.

This is not anything unique for African history. It has precedents from earlier times in other parts of the world. The well-known Danish New Testament scholar, Professor Bent Noack, has shown that its roots can be traced to the early Church. The Gospel, he says, with a fine distinction in Danish, *blev hentet, ikke bragt*: i.e., it was, in the first place not brought, by foreigners, but *carried* home by the people themselves. In order to grow the Gospel must not be imposed from the outside but must be planted by those who themselves belong to the situation. In the Middle Ages, in the mission history of Scandinavia well before AD1000, Christianity did not become rooted until the Vikings themselves brought the Gospel home from Christianized Britain and Byzantium. The kings, such as Harald Bleutooth and Olav Tryggvason may have wielded a vast influence but they could do this only because of a sufficient number of people on the spot, in Denmark and Norway, who had met the White Christ, and brought the Gospel with them back home. Thus, it was that the message could spread as rings on the water.[7]

The widespread movement of the young in many parts of the African continent had, initially, some issue of a generational conflict with the old, the elders and the chiefs. Established groups did not need to change. The young on the other hand had nothing to lose and something to gain by moving from the village, leaving because of various frustrations. Young men going away in gangs or groups, struck out and demonstrated the immense mobility occurring in African societies in this period of 'Revolutionary Africa'.

As if these indications of a wide youth movement were not enough, there was set in motion, more particularly in the Congo, not only a youth movement but a children's league of surprising range and proportion. This could happen in a society in disorder and disintegration: everywhere there were children referred to by the Westerners – missionaries and administrators – as 'orphans', until the definition of 'orphan' in a matrilineal society became a legal problem of some significance.

The Catholic Church in Congo – the Protestants were not tempted to follow the lead – had a theory, formed, as they felt, by hard experience: adults in Africa did not respond and could not be won for the faith. The only possible category to aim at was the children. To the Catholics at the time this was part of an international concern, from Mongolia to Congo, and their organization 'Holy Childhood' was founded with this in view. The Jesuits insisted, at least for the troublesome period of 1890–1912, on the formation of what they called 'farm chapels' for children: a Church in Congo had to begin with a generation of children. 'The Church could wait', until these children in their turn were to become adult members of the Holy Church. No prophecy proved more appropriate. The little boys trained by Fr Cleene and others at Boma in 1893 were, in fifteen years time, to become soldiers in the army but soldiers with a difference: they were successful voluntary catechists winning thousands for the faith.

A catechumens' Church

By characterizing the nineteenth-century Church as a 'catechumens' Church' one does of course not suggest that the great majority of converts remained catechumens. The aim of both Catholics and Protestants was to incorporate the individual and the groups, the masses even, into the fellowship of the Church through Holy Baptism. Throughout the century and well into the twentieth century, the overwhelming concern and activity of the local missionary and his African catechists was the daily instruction of catechumens. One cannot emphasize enough the extent to which that mission on the hill, in a more leisurely time than ours, became the orientation point of the masses, ever present in their minds and hearts.

While at first the length of time for catechumens' preparation, both on the Catholic and the Protestant side could be treated with a certain casualness, there was soon an ambition to lay down the law by which a minimum time was determined. On the Catholic side one of the leading missions, while outbidding the others, came to take an uncompromising position to which the others had somehow to relate. The debate continued into the twentieth century and, in the 1930s in Central Africa, attained a certain acrimony. From the outset Cardinal Lavigerie and his White Fathers laid down a rule in unyielding terms: four years, neither more nor less, devoted to the formulae of the faith, to the gestures and the rites.[8]

In principle the Protestant catechumenate was an introduction to the Bible. On the road to the Bible the catechumen was supposed to learn the alphabet and to read, the fundamental idea being that the individual, at least those of the younger generation, would be placed in a position to see for him- or herself what the Word of God said. The teaching included certain select pieces from the stories in Genesis and Exodus together with a synopsis of the Gospels. Certain more established Churches could refer to a Catechism – Martin Luther's or the Westminster Catechism – while other Protestant missions regarded a Catechism with distrust, the idea of such a book smacking of Rome.

However, there were complications. To some missions, with a background in nineteenth-century Holiness Churches, it was felt that an intellectual attainment through the Bible class was not enough. Their missionaries could decide how far the individual had arrived on the road of moral preparedness. One of the towering heroes of the nineteenth-century missionaries was François Coillard of the Paris Evangelical Mission, active in Lesotho and in the Lozi kingdom (south-west Zambia). He felt that he could determine when the individual Lozi had achieved a desired goal of moral perfection. If not, the preparation period had to be extended *ad libitum*, to six years in some cases. In the end the Lozi decided for themselves, worn out by the great man's paternalism, and looked for other available alternatives: the 'AME' (African Methodist Episcopal Church) – at least for a time – or Rome. After fifty years in Bulozi, the Paris Evangelical Mission had gathered at six stations 181 Christians, including 16 per cent under Church discipline.[9]

AFRICAN RELIGIONS

In Africa religion was more than just religion. It was an all-pervasive reality which served to interpret society and give wholeness to the individual's life and the community. The village world and the Spirit world were not two distinct separate realms: there was a continuous communication between the two. Religion was a totality, a comprehensive whole.

Because of this inclusive character none of the usual terms or concepts with which we try to categorize 'religion' has been found satisfactory. One way out is to use the indigenous local term instead. The Baganda speak of *okusanika* – the whole web of beliefs, myths, customs and rituals which go to make up traditional Ganda religion. An old Muganda compared this *okusanika* with the new arrivals, the new *dini*, the book religions of Islam and Christianity coming from outside. '*Okusanika*', he said, 'is our skin, enveloping man and following him from birth until death, wherever he moves. *Dini* is by comparison like a suit of clothes', to be worn, he suggested, for respectability!

A chapter, however brief, on African religion belongs in an African Church history, not just as a background to be conveniently forgotten as the story of evangelization proceeds over the continent. It belongs there as an accompanying echo from the past and, perhaps, as a tempting exit in the future. The early converts, together with Christians of much later generations, could not but feel a relationship with certain forms and expressions of a religious past. We give a personal example, from the Church in Bukoba, Tanzania. One of the finest priests that we met there, E. L., told us that when at twelve years of age he had been baptized and reported this fact to his father, the old man replied: 'Wamala has blessed you' ('Wamala' being one of the 'greater spirits' in local traditional religion). These Christians of that first generation still could well remember the traditional prayers directed to venerated ancestors of the past.

In any case, there is no such thing as '*the* African religion', although there are certainly common traits between various local and regional forms. It is with some of these that we are concerned in this rapid survey. However, by the very fact of speaking of 'traits' or 'factors', we are already artificially isolating certain ideas or phenomena of religion from its lush and fertile soil, from the social and political reality out of which it grew and developed. When claiming that God seemed withdrawn and remote, a *deus otiosus*, forgetful of the fate of the village, the clan and its people, we have maybe already tended to take too Western a view of things, as if the 'High God' concept would cover the essential nature of religion. Yet this was often a matter of perspective. Professor Evans-Pritchard has made the helpful observation for the Nuer that the different aspects, monotheism or polytheism, 'are rather different ways of thinking of the numinous at different levels of experience'.[10]

As Western missionaries made their first contacts with peoples in the west, east and south of the continent, some of them were impressed by this African image of God and attempted to adapt their message to it. The fundamental belief expressed in these concepts of the African God is that of creation and origin. Certain people such as the Dogon of Mali have developed an elaborate cosmogony and can refer to a complex cosmology. This goes for the west as well as the east and the south. The supreme being of the Akan is *Nyame*, of the Yoruba, *Olusun*. More than twenty-five languages in Eastern Africa, from the Lower Zambezi to Lake Victoria, know his name as *Mulungu*. West of these peoples, a group of languages called him *Leza* (or a cognate word). This name is known and used from the Yeye in the northern Kalahari, through the eastern and central districts of Zambia into Zaïre and Tanzania.

In South Africa there were varying traditions for the name of God, but Xhosa and Zulu agree in their use of *uThixo*, an appellation with Khoikhoi background. It took time for this name to become established and recognized. The second half of the nineteenth century saw a lively debate, from a linguistic and theological point of view, on the name of God. The controversial Bishop Colenso insisted that the right names were *uNulunkulu* and *uMvelinqgangi*, 'the Great-Great One' and 'He who was before everything else.'

In Tororo, near the Uganda–Kenya border, the riverine Nilotic people, the Padhola, had the concept of *Jok*, Creator, and of *Were*, a merciful good being. The father placed bread in the hut of the 'God of the courtyard', and as the whole family sat in a circle, he took a piece of bread and mixed it with the liver of a chicken. He then divided the bread into small pieces, throwing them towards the north and the south, the east and the west, and invoking *Were*, he said, 'Take this, eat it, and may you protect us from our enemies.' The

Mankessim shrine in Fanteland, Ghana, was tolerant. It had to be, as it was a centre for a great number of *abosom*, or deities, each with its special priest or priestess. Also among the Akan peoples, the *abosom* would inhabit a natural shrine such as a river, a baobab tree or rock, or take its abode in a man-made shrine, most of them of brass in a room of the priest's own home.[11]

In certain cases there was a preparedness on the part of marginal people or leading men and women to break with the guardians of the ancient cult. There were changes in the new society already prepared in the womb of the old society. Of special interest are a series of so-called 'territorial cults' studied in Zimbabwe, Malawi and Zambia. A territorial cult was 'an institution of spirit veneration which relates to a land area, or territory, rather than to kinship or lineage groupings'.[12] There were different kinds of such cults, whether relating to what is seen as a High God – such as the Mwari cult in Zimbabwe, of which M. L. Daneel has made a penetrating study[13] – or the veneration of divinized human beings. The Mwari cult, beginning as localized worship, has taken on nation-wide significance, having gone through decisive changes.

Another development, particularly in the northern part of Zimbabwe, was the *Mhondoro* cult, where a spirit medium served especially prominent tribal spirits, such as that of *Chaminuka*. It became accepted as the 'Son of Mwari'. There two systems may originally have been seen as different: the important fact is the integrating process whereby they came to be seen as one. New developments took place. Thus a female personality, Kariwara Marumbi, enriched the tradition. She appeared at times of devastating drought. Her songs at Matonjeni changed history: there were five days of continuous heavy rain. The adaptability of the Shona people was also expressed at this time in religious terms. Marumbi's spirit is said to have established direct relationships with Mwari at Matonjeni. In the 1830s the Rozvi kings of the Shona were defeated by the invading Ndebele. But while these military and political changes took place on the surface of history, the cult at Matonjeni continued as before, albeit with its political function weakened.

The claims and commands of Matonjeni were a challenging reality in the lives of many. As of old, people on moon-lit nights went to the Matonjeni cave, bringing their gifts. They took off their shoes and greeted Mwari with the clapping of hands and the shout of his praise names: Mbedzi! Dziva! Shoko! They explained their various petitions about land or chieftainships, or, maybe, fundamental political change. The Voice answered in Ndebele or Rozvi, 'high-pitched as if in a trance': '[African] youngsters . . . have thrown away the African customs . . . I (Mwari) do not want to speak to these Europeanized Africans.'[14] European ways do not 'mend the country'.[15]

In the present century there have been conceptual changes with similar developments in a syncretic, adaptive direction. The new 'Mwari ve Chikristu' and traditional 'Mwari va Matonjeni', it is said, are one, because God is one. 'Jesus was a son of Mwari just as we are all sons of God.' Christ is represented as a great European *Mhondoro*, acting as a mediator at the apex of the ancestral hierarchy.

The M'Bona cult in Malawi and Zimbabwe has been interpreted by Professor M. Schoffeleers.[16] Following careful 'oral history' leading back to the fourteenth century, his studies trace a tradition among the Lundu people according to which a prophet and rainmaker, M'Bona, was innocently killed by the paramount chief. After his death M'Bona revealed himself as a powerful supernatural being to whom also the paramount chief showed his respect. The 'collective trauma' felt by the people over this outrage led to a martyr cult. In this area M'Bona's name is 'familiar to every inhabitant, man or woman, young or old, convert to Christianity or not'.[17] A shrine was erected and sacrifice made. There was a M'Bona pool, the water of which could turn red as a warning of disaster.

The faithful would see parallels between M'Bona and Christ, both providing food, both martyred although innocent. In certain versions of the story M'Bona was born to a virgin and there developed an interaction of the M'Bona cult and Christianity. In 1916 a leading headman told missionary Price at the Chididi Mission that the Christian God was more effective in bringing what a divinity must be able to produce: rain. 'We have no longer faith in M'Bona. Your God can give rain, pray for us or our crops will be ruined.'[18] There are other ways of adaptation: 'M'Bona is now said to be the "Son of God" (*Mwana wa Mulungu*) and the "black Jesus" (*Yesu wakuda*), who is the guardian spirit of all ethnic groups, and not just of the Mang'anja' community.[19]

Prayer is the very heart-beat of religion, also in African religion. Too little is known of traditional African prayer. There is an urgent need for a comprehensive anthology of traditional African prayer from different parts of the continent – edited, we suggest, by an ecumenical team of African scholars. Nothing could more convincingly unveil the life and concern of African religion. Prayer to the divinities is most powerful when accompanied by sacrifice and libations, the latter particularly common in West Africa.

In spite of prayer and sacrifices, illness and ill-fate will befall the individual and the community. The diviner will not hesitate and he will find the self-evident explanation: it has been sent by witchcraft. 'Witch-finding movements' will suddenly appear, accompanied by tragic self-accusations for witchcraft by lonely, isolated or otherwise handicapped persons, not least women. This leads into the depths of African religiosity: it would seem that at present some of the 'Independent Churches' are more ready for dealing with these phenomena than the more polished, established Churches.

Monica Wilson, found parallels in Tanzania.

> Where God was scarcely distinguished from the shades he was thought of as being beneath the earth as they were, but as he is more clearly distinguished he goes up-stairs and dwells above ... In 1935 old [Nyakyusa] men – pagans – spoke of God beneath: young men – pagans – were beginning to speak of him as dwelling above as the Christians did. By 1955 the shift was complete, and to young and old, pagan and Christian alike, God dwelt on high.[20]

Nobody has brought out the dimension of continuity as strongly as Professor Robin Horton. His stimulating article 'African conversion'[21] and subsequent studies,[22] initiated an important international debate on these matters. With his background of brilliant research on the Kalabari of Eastern Nigeria, Horton made the point that with the development, through modern enlargement of 'scale', from a microcosm to a macrocosm, the world religions – Islam and Christianity – were reduced to the role of catalysts, i.e., stimulators and accelerators of changes which 'were in the air anyway'. With this 'thought-experiment', as Horton called his argument, he suggested that 'acceptance of Islam and Christianity was due as much to development of the traditional cosmology in response to other features of the modern situation as it is to the activities of the missionaries.'[23]

From the general view of nineteenth-century African Church history as developed in this book, it would seem that however stimulating this 'thought-experiment' may be and however tempting an overall causal explanation, one should not overlook the role of fundamental changes in social structure, more particularly with regard to population movements. Dr Horton's emphasis on continuity seems not to take sufficient account of the new inspiration from the Biblical message and its appropriation. One question to be raised is whether traditional cosmology and its 'High Gods' did in fact constitute a main attraction of the African religion as experienced both in the village and on a trans-ethnic level, or whether this experience was not rather to be seen as related to other aspects – the ever-present lesser deities, the concern with the ancestors and their fate after death, and threats from powers of evil, witches etc.

An observation in all parts of Africa would seem to be the view of Christianity as not only the way of New Life but also of the New Death. In a *milieu* where death was an ever present threat, the 'New Death' – i.e., the new way of facing the threat and fact of Death – was recognized throughout the continent as something distinctly different. Men and women would appear at the door of the Mission with their question, 'how to die aright?', and there was an answer demonstrated not by an intellectual argument, but by the collective witness of the Christian fellowship in prayer and song, seen as something which no 'traditional' religion could provide out of its own resources, however prophetic.

Writing about the Catholic Church in Uganda, the Revd Dr John Waliggo has emphasized that 'prayers to and for the dead and the baptizing of the dying to assure them of heaven, had a great appeal to the converts'.[24] This was seen as something altogether different from the approach of the old evidence which 'suggests that the impact of Christian eschatology has been widespread and profound'.[25]

In writing this book dealing with a whole continent one is repeatedly reminded of the differences between conditions and cultures in the various parts of Africa. The differences between West, Southern and East Africa are striking, not to mention those between Northern and Sub-Saharan Africa as a whole. This general observation induces a certain caution with regard to attempts at accounting for differences and changes using any single overall formula.

The exclusive use of the word 'conversion' is partly to blame for a certain confusion over this whole issue and we think more especially of the change of religion in a crisis brought about by population movements and similar transitions leading to a corporate decision to leave the old and to accept the new. Also for Africa one needs the advice given by that classical work on *Conversion*, by A. D. Nock, published in 1933. Nock made the distinction between 'conversion' and 'adhesion', the former being the deliberate turning from indifference with a realization that 'a great change was involved, that the old was wrong and the new was right', while the latter, 'adhesion' implies an understanding of the new as a useful supplement to traditional religion. Our understanding of the term is influenced by personal experience on the spot, in Bukoba in north-western Tanzania. There a first generation made their 'transition' to the new, thereby accepting modernity over against an 'uncivilized' past, while a second Protestant generation experienced a Pietistic 'revival' and thus could testify to a 'conversion' in a specific Pietistic sense. Instead of Dr Nock's term 'adhesion' we prefer the term 'transition' over to the new faith and fellowship, followed by the 'conversion' brought by the Revival.

THE WEST AND AFRICA: HUMANITARIANISM AND IMPERIALISM

Compared with the middle of the century, the last quarter of the nineteenth century presented a strikingly different picture. Prior to this period the populations were ruled by, and related to, African kings and chiefs, as well as to acephalous societies of different shapes and cohesion. Missionaries were few and far between but when they did appear they were seen as the permanent representatives of Europe in Africa. The last two to three decades brought revolutionary changes, politically, military and medically.

This was the time of the 'European scramble' for power and for imperial domination. This scramble was not just the result of a sudden stroke of the pen at the Berlin conferences of the Imperial powers. 'There were literally hundreds of European conquests of Africa, not one.'[26] Preceded by a period of 'treaties' whereby enterprising and ruthless explorers and officers made local chiefs place their mark to a treaty, there now followed a first phase of the scramble in the middle of the 1880s, with a second, decisive phase in the latter part of the 1890s which sent shock waves through the populations in the period 1895–1905. A vast change in the military and social climate of Africa ensued.

At the Berlin Congress of 1885, Europe's leading statesmen carved up the African continent into pieces, the bigger the better. In West Africa this could mean that the Wesleyan Minha community found itself cut into two, becoming on the one side of the border French-speaking Togolese and on the other English-speaking Gold-Coasters. The Bakongo, with their strong clan connections, found themselves divided between French, Belgian and Portuguese administrations. Before too long, and particularly in the 1890s, a frightening number of African kings and chiefs were deposed, deported or decapitated. A *pax* on European terms was established.

The change can be seen on the ground, in the villages, with regard to four factors: slaves, guns, rum, and paternalism in high places.

Slavery

Abolitionist attempts at outlawing the slave trade and slavery did not by themselves revolutionize the societies. Expectations of Western abolitionists that the slave trade could be replaced by 'legitimate trade', preferably in the form of palm oil and other agricultural products were not fulfilled until late in the century. In West Africa there were regions where up to two-thirds of the population were slaves; it is thought that 'all Yoruba palm oil exports were produced and transported by slaves until the 1890s'. Local wars and conquests were followed by enslavement.

In the end, however, agricultural exports did provide new alternatives for both masters and slaves: the latter were now in a position to buy land and freedom: an agricultural revolution was under way. However, this turned out differently from what the Westerners had expected. 'It was not the British who made the revolution, it was the slaves. It was a peasant settlement, not a capitalist transition. It provided a pattern ... for much of colonial Africa.' It also paved the way for the evangelization of the masses. The egalitarian message of the Gospel exercised its influence on both groups and individuals.

Firearms

A few figures illustrate the martial situation. By 1880 Buganda had received at least 10,000 guns. By the middle of the 1870s the Zulu had procured 20,000 rifles, just in time to meet the British forces: in 1879 they were able to inflict a crushing defeat on the British at Isandlwana. In Ethiopia, Emperor Yohannes was 'obsessed with guns', and his successor Menelik managed to checkmate the Italian forces at Adwa in 1896.

Yet, 'one has to ask how far it was death rather than the Europeans which really conquered Africa at the turn of the century'.[27] In the 1890s large parts of the local populations died of diseases in Ethiopia, in central Kenya, in Tanganyika, in Belgian Congo, in Angola and in northern Nigeria, culminating in disasters such as sleeping sickness, smallpox etc. Twenty years later these were followed by the devastating scourge of the 'Spanish influenza' throughout the continent. Likewise, the cattle-owning communities in the 1890s suffered terrible losses through rinderpest, from north to south across the continent.

To cap it all the musket and the rifle were followed by the modern Maxim gun assuring the attacker of the upper hand.

> Whatever happens
> we have got
> the Maxim gun
> and they have not

Rum

An unhappy problem was that of 'rum' or alcohol. Travelling along the Ogowe river in 1913, Dr Albert Schweitzer noticed how the villagers were selling their timber to foreign traders and being paid in spirits instead of in cash. Most of the money for the sale of the timber was converted into rum. He also noticed ruins of abandoned homes. A fellow passenger said to him: 'Fifteen years ago these were all flourishing villages', 'Why are they so no longer?' asked Dr Schweitzer. In a low voice the fellow passenger answered: 'l'alcool'. Similar observations could be made elsewhere on the continent at the time. These are corroborated by statistical figures.

In 1890 Cotonou, in Dahomey (the modern republic of Benin), imported over 1 million litres of alcohol in three months. In Belgian Congo in the years 1893 and 1898 respectively, the imports of alcoholic drinks were between 1.4 and 1.7 million litres. In the period 1906–12 the overall imports in French West Africa doubled in volume. In the late 1890s Southern Nigeria imported nearly twelve million litres and this level was maintained in the period 1904–08.

One appreciates the bitterness with which Kenneth Onwuka Dike, the pioneering Nigerian historian, concluded:

> Little of permanent value came to West Africa from the 400 years of trade with Europe. In return for the superior labour force, the palm oil, ivory, timber, gold and other commodities which fed and buttressed the rising industrialization they received the worst type of trade, gin and meretricious articles.[28]

The example set in Africa by White colonialists was in keeping with these facts. Leading export houses of Marseilles, Hamburg, and Liverpool made enormous profits from these sales. Another observation could be made on the spot: too many colonial officials in Africa, of all nationalities, managed to become drunkards and alcoholics.

The missions, more particularly the Protestant ones, were engaged in a relentless war against the curse of drink, both within the Churches and in society at large. A Western teetotal tradition was transferred by the Protestants. Looking at the effects over a century of this campaign one must recognize that the results, limited as they were, were beneficial financially, medically and morally.

Missionary paternalism

Finally there must be a reference to missionary attitudes towards Africans, however difficult it is to generalize on this delicate subject. The period was one when Social Darwinism was making itself felt in society. At this time the missionary in his or her 'field' was, as a matter of course, in charge –

ruling his or her flock about to be incorporated into the Church. There was sometimes a tendency, more so in some cases than in others, towards a paternalistic attitude. This was no doubt meant as an expression of benevolent care and concern and accepted as such by a large majority of African disciples. However, in certain situations the missionaries' paternalistic attitude came to be seen as incipient racialism, comparable to that of the White population at large: such comparisons were made, some times to the detriment of both the missionary and his cause. In certain countries with a large European minority this attitude was more prevalent than in others, and many Africans, among them the Revd M. J. Mokone of Pretoria, the Revd Paul Mushindo of Zambia and the Right Revd Bishop Samuel A. Crowther of Nigeria experienced it in the last decade of the century.

MISSIONARY SOCIETIES

This book deals with the African response to the Christian message and with African initiatives in the conversion of the continent. There is a tendency in the book, perhaps, to neglect Western missionaries, foreigners in the land. Yet, they too, are vital to the story and we include a survey of nineteenth-century Catholic and Protestant missions and missionaries.

Catholic missions

France and the Catholic Church in France became the great missionary factor for a Roman Catholic presence in nineteenth-century Africa. One cannot emphasize this enough. Today, Roman Catholic missionaries in Africa hail from all corners of the world. This was not so in the nineteenth century. Until 1885, what there was of a Catholic mission in Western, Central and Southern Africa was all French (in the North-East, along the Nile, the Italians were appearing).

At the beginning of the nineteenth century, the French Catholic Church did not give occasion for much hope. The dissolution of the Jesuit order in 1773 by the Pope himself, Clement XIV, the French Revolution with its aftermath of religious persecution, anti-clericalism, the bishops' and priests' exodus from France and an overwhelming sense of crisis swept through the cloisters and the colonnades of the ecclesiastical establishment. In this despondency however, were a few shafts of light. A book written by F. R. Chateaubriand, one of the many French aristocrats who had fled to England after 1789, unexpectedly opened people's hearts to a concern for the Church and the cause of the missions. This book, *Génie de Christianisme* (published in 1802), became a rallying cry to the Christian faith. It contained a chapter on 'The Missionaries', a romantic interpretation of what the Church had achieved in distant lands: 'Never did men of learning with their instruments and their plans for higher learning do as much as a poor monk walking along with his rosary and his breviary.'

There was also a shy, small initiative by two Lyon women, mother and daughter Jaricot, destined to become of immense importance for the financial support of missions, 'The Propagation of the Faith', of 1882. It was soon followed by the Bishop of Nancy's similar enterprise. With an eye for needs in China, Bishop de Forbin-Janson started the 'Work of the Sacred Childhood'. Building on regular small donations from the faithful, the two enterprises were to ensure for a century the financial support of missionary 'congregations' which emerged about the middle of the century in France. (A parallel on the Protestant side about the same time – the 1850s – is Basel's *Halbbatzenkollekte*, or, 'half-penny collection', initiated by the Basel financier, Karl Sarasin.)

Daring prophetic voices in the French clergy – Lacordaire, Montalembert, etc. – called the Church to renew awareness of its missionary task in France and beyond. The Catholic orders, not least the Dominicans, found their place anew in French society. A change in the spiritual climate could be sensed in romantic and Ultramontane influences in the Church, with a warmer piety and spirituality. The 'Sacred Heart of Jesus' and that of the Holy Virgin were at the centre. Marian devotions and pilgrimages influenced the concern for missions abroad.

This influence was particularly felt in regions with a long succession of spirituality. There was the diocese of Rennes, in Brittany, with its Celtic background and its tradition of adventurous exploits over the seven seas. And there was Alsace with the dominating influence, over almost half a century (1842–87), of the Bishop of Strasbourg, Mgr André Raess, who greatly contributed to making Alsace 'the classic country of missions' on the Catholic side.

A comparison of leadership structures

In attempting a comparison of the structures and leadership of Catholic and non-Catholic societies or 'congregations' in the nineteenth century, one is struck by a fundamental difference. In the nineteenth century, the modern Catholic mission congregations – the Congrégation du Saint-Esprit, or the Holy Ghost Fathers (the 'Spiritans'), the Société de Notre-Dame d'Afrique or the 'White Fathers', the Oblates of Mary Immaculate, the Society of

African Missions or the 'Lyon Fathers', and the Verona Fathers – were closely tied to the Superior General, whether a Cardinal or an ordinary Father Superior. It was taken for granted that the planning and execution of all work including even minor details, were ultimately in his hands. The Superior General, whether in Paris, Lyon, Algiers or Verona, was a dominating presence in the minds and prayers of the men on the spot in Africa, forming and transforming them.

In the case of non-Roman societies the responsibility of the Director and his co-inspectors was shared with, and sometimes overruled by, a large 'Board of Governors', – the constituted plurality of such a governing body being indeed unthinkable in the Roman Catholic case. It seems therefore advisable to characterize the leaders, whether autocratic or not, and the societies' leading bodies. This is an exercise all the more revealing as these great pioneers outlined the broad strategy and the local policy for the first missionaries, decisive for those who followed them until this very day.

The Holy Ghost Fathers

Upon entering France's missionary scene, François-Marie-Paul Libermann (1802–52), attracts our attention by the intense fire of his devotion to Christ and Mary. Possibly the most creative of Catholic mission leaders of the nineteenth century,[29] his personal development made him the great 'outsider' in the French Church and among its mission leaders. The son of a Jewish rabbi in Alsace who spoke practically no language other than Yiddish and Hebrew until he was twenty, Jacob Libermann – his Jewish name – was eventually led to doubt the faith of his forefathers. In 1826 he converted to Jesus the Christ and was consequently declared dead by his domineering, irate father. Here was a Westerner who in his own body knew what conversion was about and also knew the tradition of the Old Covenant. In Rennes and Paris – in order to practice the 'mystique of poverty' – he identified with seventeenth-century French spirituality in the tradition of the old 'Congregation of the Holy Spirit', founded in 1703 by Poullart des Places. Libermann can be seen as the last in the line of this French spirituality.

Psychological tensions caused by his spiritual struggle made the sickly young man susceptible to epileptic fits and thus, at first, considered unavailable for holy orders. Yet, in 1841 he was ordained priest and accepted as a leader by a group of like-minded devoted young priests including two Creoles, Fr Frédéric Le Vavasseur from Réunion, and Fr Eugène Tisserant from Haiti/Santo Domingo. With his intense Marian piety, Libermann called his group the Congregation of the Sacred Heart of Mary. In 1848, this congregation was amalgamated with the older, more established 'Congregation of the Holy Spirit', which gave the organization its name ('Holy Ghost Fathers', the 'Spiritans', CSSp).

Always sickly, Libermann would say: 'I am crucified personally, wherever I turn I never find anything but cross and suffering'. Mary dominated his thoughts. He devoted his congregation to the Immaculate Heart of Mary because he felt her veneration was particularly important for missionaries labouring in far-away places: 'If they do not give themselves to Mary they will be isolated'. His spirituality created an intense awareness of fellowship with Africa and Africans. He told his missionaries:

> You are not going to Africa in order to establish there Italy or France or any such country. Dispense with Europe, its customs and spirit. Make yourselves Negroes with the Negroes. Then you will understand them as they must be understood. Our holy religion has invariably to be established in the soil.[30]

This to him meant an African clergy with an indigenous hierarchical order. 'Saintliness rather than scholarship' was his watchword as he sent his men to Senegal, the 'two Guineas' and the islands of Reunion and Mauritius.

In the 1850s the Spiritans were a marginal movement, at first largely unnoticed by a French society preoccupied with the mounting tensions which were to culminate in the crises of the 1860s and 1870s. Libermann was followed as leader by the authoritarian Ignace Schwindenhammer, an Alsatian who dominated the scene for three decades, and later by the brilliant Alexander Le Roy. Like other missionary societies, the Spiritans aimed at the 'Inland' of Africa, but well into the twentieth century their fate remained with the difficult task along the West and East Coasts – the great exception being Bishop Augouard's opening on the Oubangi.

For Senegal with its Muslim *milieu* they conceived the idea of 'Christian villages', developed still further on the Indian Ocean islands and among the liberated slaves on the East African coast. These villages expressed the Spiritan policy for half a century until Le Roy, with his personal missionary experience in Tanzania and Gabon, achieved a radical change by placing congregations in proximity to local ethnic communities. Another modification along the road came in the educational field. 'The school in the bush' had seemed just right for Libermann's ideal of 'holiness rather than scholarship'. In the 1940s, the Spiritan educational secretary Fr J. Bouchaud, however, inspired a change to a system more attuned to the demands of modern times.

The Spiritans were fortunate in their missionary bishops: Augouard of Brazzaville and Oubangi, Vogt of Tanzania and Cameroon, Keiling of Angola and Shanahan of East Nigeria. Their greatest missionary was undoubtedly the Blessed Charles Laval of Mauritius. Two missionaries can be seen as representing two different poles of the Spiritan approach to the missionary task, Bishop Carrie of Loango and Fr Charles Duparquet. Placed on the Congo coast in a rapidly changing political situation, Carrie insisted on the virtue of *no* change: 'Change is always regrettable and particularly in Africa. It is disastrous for mission work. We repeat the prohibition of any change in the traditions, usages, regimentations and customs of the mission without our express authorization.'[31]

Not all the missionaries were concerned with *stabilitas loci*, the Benedictine ideal of stability of place and purpose. The most remarkable of the Spiritans, though sometimes difficult to handle, was the omnipresent Charles A. Duparquet, who moved around the continent, West, South and East, with surprising ease and speed. While the usual family background of the missionaries was farming, fishing and craftsmanship, Duparquet's family was of the '*noblesse de robe*'. He was the only son of a rich solicitor's family which lived in Normandy and owned ships in Marseilles; his genes may have induced this ease of mobility!

The White Fathers and Sisters

The difference between Libermann and Lavigerie of the 'White Fathers' could not have been greater. The one was meek and introverted, the other anything but. The archbishop of Algiers – later Cardinal – Charles Martial Allemand Lavigerie was the powerful, enormously active and dominating general of his enterprise. He sent his teams of missionaries to Central Africa working not from Paris or Lyon, but from his episcopal residence in Algiers.

Lavigerie had large perspectives, historically and strategically. Starting his career as a young Church history professor at the Sorbonne, he lectured on the Church Fathers in Egypt and North Africa as well as on the glories of medieval France. History was his *métier*, the shaping of the future his compulsive urge, i.e., how to 'resurrect' history, in African kingdoms under Christian African kings. His secret design, he said, was 'the Eventual Establishment of a Christian Kingdom' in the centre of Equatorial Africa.[32] At first that turned out to be a risky affair. As he sent his first teams of young missionaries across the deserts, he had the disappointment of learning that they were murdered in the attempt. But Lavigerie was not at a loss for ideas. He decided that his missionaries must be accompanied by 'auxiliaries', armed soldiers with swords which he recruited from among the 'Zouaves', the army of the dissolved Papal States (which came to an end with the unification of Italy in 1870). 'Use this sword', was the Cardinal's injunction from the altar, 'for the defence of the work of God, never use it for an unjust cause'. To convert the peoples by converting their kings – and this was of course still in the period of independent African kings – was in the grand tradition of the medieval Church and of Ignatius of Loyola. This was now to be the strategy for winning the nations along the Central African Lakes, regions which had just been 'discovered' – as the Europeans said – by the explorers Speke and Stanley. Finally, one cannot fully understand and appreciate this great leader without reading his personal letters to his missionaries. Here he reveals himself as a tender-hearted spiritual guide of deep personal religious experience.

This Catholic Church about to emerge in Central and West Africa was to Lavigerie necessarily and profoundly connected with the early Church of North Africa. He told his theological teaching staff, who in 1890 were to undertake the task of instructing the future missionaries:

> Teach them and inspire in them a great affection for the Fathers of the Church of Africa . . . So to do is nothing but justice, because we are Africans and because they have left us such great richness. I would like to see the monuments of the Church of Africa interpreted at Carthage.[33]

Words which take on new vitality and meaning in the situation of the Church one century later.

Yet, the general does not win the battle alone, his troops have to win it for him. So it was with the bishops, along with their White Fathers and White Sisters who served the peoples along the 'Kings' Way' in Central Africa. Bishop J. J. Hirth in Buganda and Rwanda and his successor in Buganda, H. Streicher are representative of those Alsace-born sons of farmers who became bishops and founders of great Churches in Africa. All of them were ready as far as possible to make Lavigerie's vision of Christian kingdoms a reality.

Not only did he renew the primatial see of St Cyprian at Carthage by building an impressive basilica; he also had himself nominated by the Pope as 'Primate of Africa' embracing the whole of the continent as Apostolic Delegate to the Sahara and Sudan.

> Algiers is only the open door to a continent of two hundred million souls. It is there, above all, that one has to carry the deed of the Catholic apostolate.

Reading his missionaries' reports on the slave trade in East Africa, he dedicated his later years to a great anti-slavery campaign in the major capitals of Europe, inducing the French government to support the [British] Royal Navy in suppressing the traffic.

The Lyon Mission

Another two French Catholic missions of immense importance for Africa should be mentioned here, one from Lyon, the other from Marseilles. Each of the leaders, both from aristocratic families, had shared in the vicissitudes for the Church of the French Revolution and the Napoleonic period and lived as young exiles away from France for a decade or more. They were thus prepared for fundamental changes in life, the former mission concentrating on West Africa (the 'Two Guineas'), the latter on Natal and Lesotho.

The Lyon mission was formed in 1858 as the bishop – with long experience of mission work in South India – set out with three priests and two brothers to reach Sierra Leone. He was Mgr Melchior de Marion Bresillac. 'To go absolutely as an Apostle, alone or with two companions', was his ideal. A *reprise* of the sixteenth-century Catholic mission in West Africa was their goal. So they went, the six of them. Catastrophe struck. Freetown at this time was hit by a yellow fever epidemic and within two months all six were dead. The Lyon mission had more cruelly to sacrifice large numbers of their personnel. During a period of forty years they lost 393 members through sickness, but they did not give up. Their new director, Augustin Planque proved to be an outstanding leader who was to guide their work for half a century.

Soon after the first group another, international, group was sent, this time to Dahomey with its memories of Portuguese mission attempts in the sixteenth century. On the way to Whydah in Dahomey they stopped over in Freetown where one of their number of three died. In Dahomey they were assigned to a building called 'the residence of the God of the Whites'. Some of the Lyon missionaries were to become experts on Dahomeyan culture, especially Fr Aupiais. 'Avoid Europeanization and discover the rights of the African as human being and discover the values of African culture', was their watchword. In Lagos along the coast they found co-religionists in 'Brazilian returnees', among them Padre Antonio, a Catholic layman who devoted himself to his flock. In 1869 the missionaries started in Porto Novo, and in the 1890s they began work in the Ivory Coast.[34]

The Oblates

The Oblates of Mary Immaculate had as their leader Eugène de Mazenod, representative of a generation of French aristocrat-priests who had been through the aftermath of the French Revolution. Born in 1782 he spent years of exile in Italy from 1797–1802. He lived at the very centre of French Marian spirituality and in 1826 formed a society for Oblates of Mary Immaculate. He had an audience with Pope Leo XII who gave formal approval to the name of the society. De Mazenod took an active part in the preparations of the dogma on the Immaculate Conception in the 1850s. The announcement of the dogma was greeted by de Mazenod, then bishop of Marseilles, 'with a burst of exuberant joy, a sort of vision of the Apocalypse'.

The Bishop could now send out missionaries to other continents, to the United States and Canada, to Asia and in 1851 to Africa, i.e., to Natal and later to Lesotho. The team to Southern Africa was led by Bishop M. J. F. Allard and included Fr Gérard who played a significant role in giving the work its form and enthusiasm. That de Mazenod had a gift of intuition can be seen from the statement he made in a letter to Fr Gérard:

'The moment will come when the merciful grace of God will effect a sort of explosion and your African Church will take shape.' The Marian message informed much of the work.[35]

The Irish

The Catholic presence in nineteenth-century Africa was primarily a French concern and it was French 'congregations' that inspired the Irish Catholics to devote themselves to African missions. The extent and intensity of Irish missionary involvement in twentieth-century Africa makes one take for granted that these characteristics had always been expressed in and by the Catholic Church in Ireland. This was not so. Surprisingly, it has been asserted that up until the closing decades of the nineteenth century, the Irish Catholic Church was 'positively *hostile* to missions'.[36]

The Protestants in Northern Ireland discovered that foreign missions were a British concern and therefore probably a good thing. The Catholics in Ireland knew that foreign missions were French and thus definitely a bad thing – France and all its 'modernism' was suspect and should be avoided. In and through the Church Missionary Society in London, devoted Irish men and women were to give their contribution to the Church in Africa. All the same, two French missionary societies – the Holy Ghost Fathers in Paris and the Society of African Missions in Lyon – managed to infiltrate Ireland in the latter part of the nineteenth century, although for other reasons than missionary: the former as an educational agency – Blackrock College was their great achievement – the latter arriving in Ireland as a language centre for French priests. The Lyon Fathers, moreover, had on their staff an exceptional Swiss, Fr Josef Zimmermann, who worked for a truly indigenous Irish missionary movement in the form of an Irish branch of the Society of African Missions of Lyon. A new generation of young Irishmen undertook their theological studies in Paris. Outstanding among the Spiritans was Joseph Shanahan, who spent nine years in Paris. He was eventually to give forty years to Eastern Nigeria, building an incomparable school system and, as bishop, laying the foundations of vital dioceses in Igbo country.

The Verona Fathers and Sisters

In 1840 the world was informed about the discovery of a navigable waterway 1,000 miles south of Khartoum. The intrepid Turkish sailor Salim Qabudan had succeeded in penetrating the *sudd*, that enormous area of papyrus reeds, and reached beyond it to the African societies living further south, the Shilluk, Nuer, Dinka and others. This was a discovery of enormous importance for the economic and social life of the communities along the River and for the evangelization of these communities with the Christian message.

It did not take the cardinals in Rome long to notice this new opportunity. In 1846 Pope Gregory XVI established the 'Apostolic Vicariate of Central Africa', and the following year, 1847, a first missionary expedition led by the Polish Jesuit Maximilian Ryllo set out from Alexandria to reach Khartoum, then a little town of 15,000, most of whom were slaves. The expedition soon found that they had to contend with a pitiless adversary: the tropical climate. In 1848 Ryllo died, having handed over the leadership of the group of missionaries to Dr Knoblecher, also a Slav. A practical man, Knoblecher managed to sail south with the annual Egyptian trading expedition and could thus contact the extensive communities along the river. They found themselves warmly welcomed by these peoples. But his co-workers were snatched away by death and in 1858 Knoblecher also died.

In 1857, Daniele Comboni had become the leader – a man of vision and visions (in 1864, in St Peter's in Rome he had a vision of his famous 'Plan for the Regeneration of Africa') and of indefatigable energy. He was to lead eight missionary expeditions towards the southern Sudan between 1857 and 1881, each lasting between two and four years. In fact, he aimed to go even further than that: to 'the Central African Lakes' and to 'the Mountains of the Moon'.[37]

In preparation for his third expedition he went to Rome and there was given what he regarded as a divine illumination of his 'Plan'. His problem was: how to defeat that mortal enemy, the dangers of the climate. His method of acclimatization was to establish half-way houses, preferably in Cairo where missionaries and Africans could gradually grow accustomed to a trying climate. He established three 'institutes' for men and women in Cairo. Following his intuition Comboni approached the Vatican Council I, of 1870, and presented his Plan and programme to the Church leaders, and was consecrated bishop. On his way to and from Sudan he contacted some of the great personalities of his time involved with Africa: the explorer and journalist, H. M. Stanley, and F. de Lesseps, the engineer building the Suez Canal in the years 1854–69.

> Daniele Comboni is one of the key figures who have decisively shaped Europe's relationships with Africa. With extraordinary simplicity and perseverance he presented his vision to his contemporaries. As a result he aroused, sustained and directed a growing impulse of active concern and sacrifice ... His achievement is all the more remarkable in that it was accomplished almost single-handed by a young man in his early thirties.[38]

His exploration of southern Sudan brought him into contact with the slave trade in the country. But did not the world know that the slave trade was by now suppressed? Comboni saw for himself and could inform the world. 'The abolition of the slave trade is a dead letter.' Like Cardinal Lavigerie, he insisted on resolute measures to finish this shame of mankind.

Above all he travelled indefatigably in southern Sudan until in 1881 he himself succumbed to the climate and his dramatic, almost romantic life came to an end: 'O Nigritia, o morte!'[39] His Verona Fathers were to carry on the task which he had staked out for them, in Sudan, Egypt and Eritrea, in northern Uganda and Kenya, and in Zaïre. Significant work was done by the Combonian Sisters, 'Pie Madri della Nigrizia', in the countries already mentioned and in Mozambique. We have emphasized the fundamental role of French and Italian initiatives for the nineteenth-century Catholic missions in Africa. These enormous efforts were at the same time international in intent and practical achievement.

Protestant missions

A few Protestant missionaries arriving in Africa were men with experience in the academic or civic world. Among the best-known were J. T. van der

Kemp and John Philip. The former, with a medical degree from Edinburgh had served as a doctor in his home country Holland, while John Philip, a Scot, had been a power-mill manager and, after theological training, Congregational minister at Newbury in Scotland and – for fourteen years – in Aberdeen. The CMS's Alexander Mackay, a Scot and a Free-church man, was twenty-eight years old when he arrived in Uganda and had by then already spent years in Berlin as a railway constructor and engineer. However these were exceptions. The great majority of the new missionaries were surprisingly young. The Scottish Congregationalist Robert Moffat and Berlin's Merensky were both twenty-two, Sweden's J. A. Persson, a Methodist, was only nineteen when he arrived in Mozambique, while Leipzig's Johannes Raum, destined for Kilimanjaro, was accepted as a missionary candidate at the tender age of twelve and sent to a Lutheran Seminary to prepare himself for his task. If, as we hope to show in this book, the Christian movement in nineteenth-century Africa was a *youth movement* – for it was the young and foot-loose who took to the new Christian message – the Western missionaries, too, were young men.

Many of these, on being sent to West Africa, died after a few years, or months, or even days in the trying climate. Others posted in the salubrious climate of South Africa or parts of East Africa could work continuously for forty or fifty years (without furloughs – a latter day invention). Generally the missionaries' social backgrounds mirrored Europe's social conditions at the time. The Moravian missionary recruits, hailing from refugee groups from Bohemia, had been weavers, carpenters and blacksmiths. The young men of Hermannsburg were all Lüneburger farmers.

Mission society organization

The vast number of Protestant societies active in nineteenth-century Africa rules out any attempt to consider each of them separately, so we shall take a synoptic view. The leaders of the Protestant societies – their 'Board of Governors' or 'Committee' – consisted of two categories of men (there were no women members at the time). In the Anglican missions and the Berlin Missionary Society, for instance, the first category consisted of leading civil servants representing lay wisdom. A Lord Justice and other high law officials, a couple of government financial experts together with a General formed a group to themselves. In the Berlin Missionary Society, Lord Justice Göschel served as President of the Society for thirty years. In the Basel Evangelical Missionary Society Karl Sarasin, businessman and canton councillor, was perhaps the greatest layman on any of the Mission Boards in the nineteenth century. The Evangelical Anglican mission, the CMS, also had a leading layman as President of the Society while the High Church societies, the SPG and UMCA, were sure to have an archbishop or bishop as President. The other category consisted of leading clergy, bishops and experienced priests and pastors in Britain, while in the case of continental missions it consisted of prominent preachers and theological professors.

The Executive Committee of the Wesleyan Methodist Missionary Society consisted of President and Secretary plus forty-eight others, the latter being ordained and lay-members in equal proportions, and working committees were appointed for various purposes. This system carried into Africa the model of rule-by-committee which contributed to training in democratic procedure. In these matters the Wesleyan experience in, for instance, Southern Africa, was also bound to influence other Protestant churches.

Selection of missionaries was the most responsible function of a society. The German-speaking societies formed their own seminaries for training. The Berlin Director, J. C. Wallmann, a conservative 'Old Prussian', also found time to lead his seminary, and he and his family took all their meals with the candidates, enabling him to form an opinion of their acceptability for service overseas. Already by 1795, the London Missionary Society had formulated their Rules for the Examination of Missionaries.[40] It provides an understanding of what kind of expectations the Society held for their recruits:

> It is not necessary that every missionary should be a learned man, but he must possess a competent measure of that kind of knowledge which the object of the mission requires.

This 'competent measure' was defined thus: 'Godly men who understand mechanical arts' – and such men would be especially valuable in Africa. Experience showed, however, that this principle of selection had its shortcomings. The LMS's historian added: 'The enormous waste of resources caused by the practical adoption of this view in the early years of the Society's work is an object-lesson for succeeding generations.'

The Moravians

Wherever you dig in Protestant mission history, you strike Moravian foundations. The Moravians, or 'Herrnhuters', were reconstituted as a religious community in 1727 under the creative leadership of Count N. L. von Zinzendorf. No sooner had they constituted themselves as a religious body than they were prepared – in 1732 – to go into the whole world with the 'Great Commission' by way of Danish and Dutch colonial settlements.

This took them to Greenland, the West Indies and, in 1737, to the Cape. The 'Unity', the collective body of the Church at Herrnhut – (situated in eastern Germany) was the missionaries' central authority, administered by a 'Council of Seventeen'.

Mobile and adaptable, the Moravians were able to instil their experiential religion (a 'religion of the heart'), their warm piety and happy musical enthusiasm not only in their own churches in Africa (the Cape and southern and central Tanzania) but also in European Protestantism and English and American Methodism. The congregations were divided into 'choirs', a classical name to denote the singing activity of the Church – an approach bound to appeal to musical Africans. Zinzendorf's successor, A. G. Spangenberg wrote a mission constitution which was to be decisive for emerging Moravian Churches in the Cape, the West Indies and elsewhere. It also served as a model in Africa. At the outset, Spangenberg's constitution represented half a century's world-wide missionary experience of Church discipline problems.

German missionaries for British missions

At first the British societies, the free-church LMS and the Anglican CMS, were to experience difficulties in recruiting British candidates for this utterly unfamiliar life-calling. Both societies were helped by an unexpected but highly rewarding sources from Berlin and Basel. Eighteenth-century Pietistic revivals, particularly with a Moravian background, brought young men to J. Jänicke's seminary in Berlin as well as to the Basel society.

Characteristically, Jänicke's men represented the offspring of foreigners in Berlin, originally hailing from Bohemia. In the years 1800–27 (Jänicke died in 1827) the seminary in Berlin prepared no less than eighty missionaries. Some of these, along with those from Basel, were eventually sent to West and South Africa through the agency of the above-mentioned British societies – an early example of international and interdenominational co-operation, possible in a time well before the confessionalist period from 1850. The CMS in Sierra Leone had its share of the Dürings, Renners, Hartwigs and Nyländers, while in the Cape the LMS missions to the Khoikhoi saw their Albrechts, Sass's and Schmelens. What is more, these young men formed in the ascetic and pietistic *milieu* of Jänicke's seminary were prepared to shoulder any hardship.

What about Basel? It was with a Mission school that the Basel Mission began. This society drew its candidates mainly from the church in Württemberg, Germany, with its remarkable tradition of 'Church Pietism'. The Basel

School training was thorough, extending to five years and including daily studies in Latin, Greek, Hebrew and English on a level comparable to any university instruction at the time. Altogether Basel sent no less than eighty missionaries to the British Church Missionary Society. These were to be given additional English language training at Islington in London, and then dispatched to Asia or Africa. Some of the best-known CMS missionaries in West and East Africa (including Ethiopia) were Basel men, such as Krapf, Rebmann and Gobat. In the 1850s the Anglican society's arrangement with Basel – which had had its problems throughout – came to an end, and the CMS could recruit its men and women from the British Isles.[41]

'On monarchic and aristocratic lines'

The Basel Mission constituency, found mainly in southern Germany and Switzerland, wished to be as closely associated with the Basel Committee as possible, sharing some of the responsibility for missionary work. A suggestion along these lines was suavely expressed thus: 'The leadership of the Basel Missions enterprise is exercised on monarchic and aristocratic lines; which is as it should be.' But they were looking for an associative relationship, even visualized as a 'Missions-Reichstag' (mission parliament), though this was to remain a dream. The Director had, necessarily, to take the lead. Some of these Continental Directors remained for a long time; Josenhans in Basle and Wangemann in Berlin, each for just under thirty years. They knew their fields – Wangemann made two year-long visitations to the South African mission and wrote admirable books about them. He knew the general problems and the details of the situation at least as well as any Superintendent Missionary in the field. (There is a fine tradition among German mission directors of producing important books on the Church in Africa.)[42]

Lüneburger farmers preparing for Africa

Of all continental Protestant leaders, Louis Harms of Hermannsburg, on the North German plains, was the most original. A Lutheran Church leader and mild autocrat, he had a mission strategy the structure of which resembles none as much as that of Cardinal Lavigerie. Louis Harms' ideal was that of the mission of Europe in the Middle Ages when groups of monks, priests and lay brothers went out to found their monasteries in pagan countries, thence to cultivate and Christianize entire nations. He thought of the Anglo-Saxon missionaries of old, settling in Germany, becoming in both spiritual and material matters 'the teachers of our forefathers'. Similarly, Harms sent out – by way of his mission-ship *Candace* – small congregations of missionaries and farmers (referred to as 'colonizers' at the time). The farmers were to attend to the external conditions relating to the self-support of the mission while the missionaries did the spiritual work.

When a first centre had been established, some missionaries would remain put while the others would proceed some two to three miles further in order to establish a new centre and thus eventually permeate the entire nation with Christian influence and knowledge. In this way they felt they could also counteract what they saw as the demoralizing influence of other European groups such as traders, as well as the dissemination of individualistic ideas of conversion. Harms' first plan was to send his men to 'Gallaland' (the land of the Oromo) – well-known at the time through Johann L. Krapf's writings, 'a strong unbroken people similar to the Teutons'.[43]

It was consistent with the particular ethos of this mission that the first young missionaries came from farming backgrounds, almost exclusively from the Lüneburger moors, a geographical provenance which later was much widened. An idea of the theological horizon of these solid youngsters is provided by the list of exam questions at the seminary from 1900, presumably to be transmitted to the Lutheran Churches in Africa later on:

1. The essential difference between the heathen religion and the revealed religion.
2 The most important heresies and abuses of the Roman Church against which Dr Martin Luther struggled.
3. What is according to Biblical teaching the use of the law besides that of the faith?
4. What is a sacrament? Why does the Lutheran Church only accept two sacraments? The relation of Holy Baptism to the Holy Communion.
5. The mission principles which can be derived from St Paul's missionary travels?

Thus apparently well-prepared they boarded the mission-ship *Candace* on their way to Natal, a journey of some months. As this was an eminently religious ship, there were daily services on board for all: 'The ship has been a floating temple'. In January 1854 they sighted Africa for the first time: 'Oh, how moved were our hearts within us. There it was, the land of our destination, and every mouth cried inevitably: "Look, there is Africa".'[44]

With his medieval ideals, Harms was hesitant about whether to allow his missionaries to be married. He was himself unmarried and remained so, 'for the sake of the Kingdom of heaven and of his calling'.[45] But with regard to his young missionaries he wrote to Posselt, Berlin missionary in Natal. Posselt argued for married missionaries and Harms took his advice:

> Had it been a matter of working among the Galla [Oromo], it would have been preferable to send at first only unmarried missionaries. But among the pagan Zulu, where one was to be surrounded by pagans all the time . . . If the missionary has a blessed wife and children about him, then they are his kind little angels capable of making the old sourpuss friendly again.[46]

Bremen Mission

'Legitimate trade and Christianity', said David Livingstone, could have a revolutionary impact on Africa. No mission translated that formula as decisively as the North German Mission in Bremen. The Bremener had formed a peculiar marriage between mission and business. Moving to Bremen in 1850, the large entrepôt town on the River Weser in Lower Saxony, the German mission established contacts with German trading houses, particularly with 'Friedr. M. Vietor and Sons' in Bremen and formed close contacts with other German enterprises connected with the West African 'Slave Coast'. The Vietor family could rightly claim in 1890 that 'in the last thirty years we have been the financiers of the North German Mission'.[47] As a matter of course Mission personnel and property were carried by the company's ships to West Africa. That co-operation could show 'how the mission could help trade and how trade helped the mission'.[48] The Vietor company, ruled by Pietist Reformed and Lutherans, provided Togo and West Africa with commodities excluding 'schnaps, weapons and gunpowder'.[49] Vietor knew that they worked 'for both the expansion of the Kingdom of God and for honest trade'.[50]

The Board of the Bremen Mission consisted of five pastors and six businessmen and was characterized by a Reformed pietism. For nearly four decades, Franz Michael Zahn was the Mission's inspector, a Church leader with a mind of his own. The mission's standpoint, he declared, was 'neither in Wittenberg nor in Geneva nor in Rome but Jerusalem and on the Mount of Olives'.[51]

Venn and Anderson: 'the Three Selves'

A happy co-operation between England and America, between an Evangelical Anglican in London and a Boston Congregationalist, provided Protestant missions with their creative and challenging formula for church building in the Third World: the famous'Three Selves' principle – the self-supporting, self-governing and self-propagating church. One cannot overrate the importance of this concept. Formed in the 1850s, in debate and correspondence between Henry Venn of the Church Missionary Society and Rufus Anderson of the American Board, it was to become the directive idea at all levels of the mission-church relationship – local, regional and international – for more than a century. Often honoured more in word than in deed, it served all the same as the authoritative ideal. Conceived in mission debates first in Hawaii and then in South India, Henry Venn's far-sighted planning brought the idea to early fruition in Nigeria although outside interference eventually caused this to be mismanaged. It can be shown that this formula pushed the Churches in Africa to independence, sometimes with considerable reluctance, well before such independence had been considered, let alone achieved in the political arena.

Henry Venn's name serves to introduce the three Anglican societies, different in churchmanship but united by common allegiance to the Canterbury line of episcopacy and their loyalty to the cause of Africa. Henry Venn's Church Missionary Society represents the Evangelical tradition with its lay President and a relatively lay 'ethos' in the field. This is seen, for instance, in the early role of the Society's engineers and teachers in Uganda and its doctors in Northern Nigeria and Rwanda.

The Anglo-Catholics

The non-Romans in Africa were represented by Protestant missions, large and small, Bible-translating and Bible-expounding, sometimes with little time for such 'extras' as liturgy and church order. It was of immense value, therefore, that a Catholic (although not Roman Catholic) ethos was visible on the Rand, in Southern and Central Africa, on the East African coastline and in some pockets of West Africa. Two societies, the Society for the Propagation of the Gospel (SPG), founded in 1701, and the Universities' Mission to Central Africa (UMCA), founded in 1857 – eventually to be united in 1958 under the name of the United Society for the Propagation of the Gospel (USPG) – directed the work. Episcopal authority and monastic societies gave it its strength. The bishops were mainly from upper-class English society, with Eton and Oxbridge backgrounds, from families which, to a large extent, were prepared to support financially their kin in Africa. St Cyprian and St Augustine of old became the patron saints of the new missions, bestowing their names on highly qualified centres and institutions.

The nineteenth-century Anglican orders for men and women provided valuable mission workers during the new century of rapid social change. The Society of St John the Evangelist – the 'Cowley Fathers' – founded in 1865, and the Community of the Resurrection, founded in 1892, together with the Whitby Sisters are the best-known in Africa; men and women whose devotion and achievements were to mark the quality and outlook of the Anglican contribution in Africa.

Methodists and Baptists

'I look upon the world as my parish' was John Wesley's watchword to his Church. British settlers to the Eastern Cape (South Africa) in the 1820s numbered among them not only a Methodist pastor by the name of William Shaw, a leader of the group, but also a rapidly increasing number of lay preachers of whom some became pastors and missionaries. Soon the Wesleyan Methodists spread from the south to the north, from Port Elizabeth to Elisabethville (now Lubumbashi), where they met with missionaries from the American Methodist Episcopal Church. In West Africa the Methodists likewise were to play a leading role, not least in education. In Southern Africa the *Manyano*, the Methodist women's Church organization, with their evangelistic drive and their colourful uniforms were an excellent inspiration for other denominations.

The arrival on the African coast of British Baptists was heralded by Black 'Returnees' from Jamaica, prepared to serve as missionaries to the continent of their origin – back to their 'roots'. They began work among the liberated slave population in the island of Fernando Po (modern Equatorial Guinea) and later transferred to the Cameroonian coast at Bimbia. In 1848 the first mission leader, Alfred Saker, founded the coastal settlement of Victoria beneath the towering peak of Mount Cameroon, and from here they looked to the inland of the continent.

On 11 August 1877, H. M. Stanley arrived at Boma on the western coast, having concluded his 999 days of exploration along the Lualaba-Zaïre (Congo) river. To Protestants this epic journey gave the signal for missions into Congo and Zaïre. From Cameroon the Baptist missionaries congregated with the aim of reaching the east of the continent by a chain of mission stations. Taking their point of departure from Kongo mission history they contacted the King of Kongo, Dom Pedro, and then ventured inland. The enormous, wide-ranging network of rivers provided the means whereby the Baptists and other denominations could reach African populations in the interior. Using canoes they established links with distant communities and soon mission steamships were also navigating the waters. This led the missionaries to creeks where baptism transformed the mighty Zaïre river and its tributaries into latter-day River Jordans.

George Grenfell, one of the outstanding Cameroon missionaries saw it as his initial task in Zaïre to draw maps of the region. Not always was this pioneering activity popular: 'it was bluntly said that we were a missionary organization and not a branch of the Royal Geographical Society; that our purpose was not to make maps, but to save men.'[52]

In the steps of the ever pioneering Baptists there followed American Presbyterians and Methodists, Pentecostals, the Salvation Army, and the Africa Inland Mission.

The Scots

Perhaps more than any other country Scotland deserves to be referred to as 'a land of missionary concern'. The Evangelical revival laid the foundations for a strong involvement in missions. The 'Disruption' in 1843, through which the Free Church of Scotland was formed and whereby it could leave the Church of Scotland, stimulated the debate on mission involvement in Scotland and overseas, particularly in Aberdeen and Glasgow. Professor John D. Hargreaves interprets the relationship of *Aberdeenshire to Africa*, the title of his book published in 1981, showing the role of north-eastern Scotland in British expansion in general and not least through missions.

In Africa the Scots tended to specialize in certain countries, Malawi, Kenya, Eastern Nigeria and the Cape, building there high-level educational institutions – Livingstonia in Malawi, Lovedale in the Cape, Calabar in Nigeria. It is often overlooked that Scotland also had an 'Independent' tradition, akin to American influence. Both Robert Moffat and David Livingstone followed this and regarded themselves as being 'in the vanguard of contemporary thought, modern pioneers of a new and stronger truth'. Moffat, Livingstone and John Mackenzie went to Africa in the service not of the Scottish mission establishment, but of the Congregationalist London Missionary Society.[53]

The Nordic contribution

Norway, Denmark, Finland and Sweden, although geographically distant from Africa, all had close ties with that continent, in that each Nordic mission society was closely related to some particular country in Africa. The Danes were related to central north-eastern Nigeria (as part of the Sudan United Mission), the Finns to Ovamboland in northern Namibia, where they built a solid 'folk' church. At least one nineteenth-century White missionary to Africa had some personal experience of a type of slavery. Dr Martti Rautanen (1845–1926), one of the Finnish mission leaders to the Ovambo, was born a serf in Inkeri – at that time part of the Russian empire – where serfdom was not abolished until 1861. Thus at an early date Rautanen was prepared to bring the message of liberation to a people in Southern Africa.

The Norwegians were involved in Madagascar and Zululand in South Africa. 'Mission-related Norway knows three maps' it has been said: Norway, Palestine and Madagascar. The Swedish Free Churches were related to Congo and Zaïre, while the Church of Sweden (through the *Fosterlandsstiftelsen*) had old ties with Eritrea and Ethiopia, and later began work in Zululand, Zimbabwe and Tanzania.

The Americans

The American mission leaders, too, acquired the good habit of long life. Rufus Anderson served as a highly imaginative foreign secretary of the American Board for thirty-five years. His personal interest lay with India and the South Seas, but he also devoted himself to African affairs. In the first decades of the nineteenth century it was,

> believed ... impossible to carry Christianity successfully to Africa by other than coloured missionaries whose ancestral heritage and pigmentation made them more acceptable to the native population than the Caucasians.[54]

However, when no Black candidates were forthcoming at the time, the Board, with a view to the climate, turned to the White Southerners instead, believing that they would acclimatize more easily to Africa than the New Englanders. This appeal produced one excellent result in the application of John Leighton Wilson of South Carolina, who was to give distinguished service in both Liberia and Gabon. His only complication was one inherent in the South Carolina social situation: his family had thirty Black slaves, belonging to him 'by marriage'. These, however, Wilson managed to see settled in Liberia. But there were two left with the Wilson family and these 'refused to accept manumission'.[55] The Board had to answer for this impropriety suggesting that Wilson himself was 'morally blameless'.

Most New England missionary candidates at this time came from small towns and villages. In fact, the Board became 'highly suspicious of city-bred candidates'. Therefore, when a young man from the city of Philadelphia presented himself in 1828, it was found that he 'has been brought up with city habits [and] has rather a fashionable air and polished manners'[56] – the young man was rejected. A century later the Board and its views had changed. In the challenging city conditions of South Africa it was such men and women as Dr and Mrs Bridgman and Dr and Mrs Ray Philips of the same American Board, who more than other missionaries were able to adapt themselves to the demands of the situation on the Rand and in Durban.

African–Americans

In the heterogeneous missionary corps to Africa, a refreshing and challenging element was that of the African–American missionaries. Some of them had just come out of slavery – Lott Carey, the first of them, bought his freedom for 850 dollars – and in Congo at that time they were to face rampant slavery, of which they knew much from personal experience. They knew what it was all about. There will be occasion later on to meet with these Black missionaries in Africa. Here we can do no more than sketch their background and the conditions on which they offered their services to the Mission Boards, sometimes without much result. The long and short of it was that only comparatively few Blacks were sent out by ordinary American mission societies. As will be seen in the chapter on the Congo, one American mission in particular – The Southern Presbyterian Church – managed, however, to send a relatively large number of African–Americans to work alongside their White colleagues.

Owing to certain impeding factors at work in recruitment, the Black missionary was somewhat older than his average White colleague on arrival in Africa. During years in a challenging racial situation, the Black recruit would have accumulated a wisdom and empathy which were to be of special value. One must point to the positive experience of men such as William Sheppard with the Southern Presbyterian mission, working among the Kuba on the Kasai, and a number of highly qualified Black women missionaries in the same mission, or Sam Coles working with the Congregationalist American Board for thirty years at Galangue in Central Angola.

The vitality of African–Americans – in the face of repression and racial injustice – was manifested in their specific theological interpretation of their role with regard to Africa and its 'redemption'. The concept was a delicate one, easily misinterpreted, as if one was trying to condone the long terrible past of slavery and segregation. From about 1800, 'Providential Design' was the term used among a group of Quakers and other anti-slavery leaders in the Northern States: 'God, in his inscrutable way, had allowed Africans to be carried off into slavery so that they could be Christianized and civilized and return to uplift their kinsmen in Africa.'[57]

In 1816, the American Colonization Society was founded in close contact with these groups which helped make emigration plans, parallel with the missionary strategy. The Society received funds from White philanthropists and from federal and certain state governments. Its primary object was to help free Blacks to settle in Africa, particularly in Liberia. The Society was active throughout the century and had managed to transport 13,000 African–Americans to Liberia before 1860. In the 1850s, Alexander Crummell who had emigrated to Liberia after finishing his academic studies, developed this same idea referring to

> the wondrous providence of God, by which the sons of Africa by hundreds and by thousands trained, civilized, and enlightened, are coming hither again, bringing large gifts, for Christ and his Church and their heathen kin.[58]

Increasingly these thoughts were combined with Exodus chapters in the Bible and with Ethiopian myths. Even the learned E. W. Blyden, the West Indian who was to become a Liberian official and ambassador, propagated this idea:

> The deportation of the Negro to the New World was as much decreed by an all-wise Providence, as the expatriation of the Pilgrims from Europe ... no indignation ... can prevent us from recognizing the hand of an over-ruling Providence in the deportation of Africans to the Western world.[59]

The Western missionary was of course an individual but he was also seen as a representative personality, representing – whether or not he knew or liked it – Western mores and values. To an even greater extent, the American Black missionary was a representative personality, a fact of which he or she was keenly aware. As they went to Africa and laboured in the field, these missionaries represented the particular approach and gifts of Black America which differed somewhat from those of their White colleagues, as could be seen in the results of their work. Samuel B. Coles at Galangue in Angola – a station exclusively run by American Black missionaries – could say: 'I feel that the record of American Negroes in Galangue will always be a high-water mark in the missionary work in Angola.'[60]

The African–Americans had their own incomparable symbol in Lott Carey, the 'first Black missionary to Africa', born a slave in 1780 on a Virginia plantation. As a boy and young man he laboured in a tobacco warehouse, until he was able to buy his own freedom in 1813. He became a Baptist, naturally, for in the South virtually everybody belonged to that denomination. The local Black Baptist church in Richmond – with a 8,000 membership – provided him with the chance to develop his gifts of oratory and he met the idea of 'Providential Design'. Carey had a colleague, Collin Teague, saddler and harness-maker by trade, whose literary education was limited: 'He can read though he is not a good reader, and he can write so as to make out a letter.'[61] The two men were inspired by the 'Back to Africa movement', organized in the American Colonization Society and implying, in this case, the concept of emigration: the missionary as a settler in the new country.

Carey decided to go: 'I wish to go to a country where I shall be estimated by my merits, not by my complexion; and I feel bound to labor for my suffering race.'[62] Leaving for Africa, Carey did not need to go alone. Together with his friend, Brother Collin, he was accompanied by twenty-six colonists and a number of children – in fact, a Baptist community or 'church' of their own – leaving in 1821 by the *Nautilus* en route to Sierra Leone. He soon moved to the neighbouring new republic of Liberia and worked there for eight years until killed in an accident in 1829.

Lott Carey was a pioneer in more senses than one. He was also typical in that he laboured in Liberia, which was to be the focus of Black missionary work in Africa. In 1897, the Lott Carey Foreign Mission Convention was formed by a number of leading Black Baptist churchmen, 'a plea for our work as Coloured Baptists, apart from the Whites ... Lott Carey is really just beginning to live among the Negro Baptists of the world.'[63]

While the majority of American mission societies were cautious with regard to sending African–American missionaries, there were of course ecclesiastical organizations especially made for Blacks, such as the Home and Foreign Missionary Society of the African Methodist Episcopal Church, the AME. Its role in Southern Africa was important. Yet, its ecumenical significance among the so-called 'Independent' Churches was limited for reasons which the African Churches saw clearly: the AME was foreign, after all, and insufficiently identified with the country's Bantu-speaking Africans. At the outset, in the 1890s, the AME was to spur both fears and hopes in South Africa. It was Bishop Henry McNeal Turner, in Black American terms an 'emigrationist', who tried to send 'skilled and professional Blacks' to settle in South Africa. But, for such plans, this was an unlikely country for such plans. Liberia, on the other hand, was more likely and also received some AME missionaries.

The Southern Presbyterians sent a number of outstanding Black women missionaries to the Kasai. The first and most remarkable of them all was Maria Feiring, daughter of bondservants and freed only in 1865 when slavery was abolished. At thirty-three she began her formal education and at fifty-six she offered her services to the Southern Presbyterians who thought her too old. Undaunted, she sold her house and from the sale of the house she offered to pay all her own expenses. She spent twenty-one years on the Kasai and so did another of her colleagues. They were both outdone by Althea M. Brown who spent thirty-five years in Congo. All these women taught Domestic Science and the Bible and one did linguistic work. All of them had the satisfaction of seeing remarkable results of their labours among the Kuba and the Luba: 'These people are now in the sunshine of the wonderful blessings of God', was how Lillian May Thomas-DeYampert saw her work.[64]

4

NORTH AND NORTH-EASTERN AFRICA

EGYPT

Slowly but surely the once almighty Ottoman empire was crumbling. From Istanbul the Turks had dominated the Muslim world for centuries, from Egypt with its *bey* to Algeria and its *dey*, all in principle with their populations subject to the Sultan in Istanbul.

'The non-Muslims in the countries of Islam' is a good title for a book on Near Eastern Christian Churches, and might well have served as a title for this part of the chapter dealing with the Christian Churches in Egypt.[1] Dr Fattal's formula, focusing on the legal status of religious minorities, emphasizes something fundamental about the role of the Copts in Muslim Egypt: a minority in a staunchly Muslim country. Egypt's population today numbers 50 million, 82 per cent of whom are Muslims; the Copts together with the tiny Greek-Orthodox, Uniate Catholics, Anglicans and other Protestant communities make up only 18 per cent of the total population.

The political scene

The reveille of the nineteenth century in Egypt was sounded by foreigners. Napoleon Bonaparte occupied the country in 1798, although not for long, for in 1801 his troops were defeated by combined British and Turkish forces. However, the French occupation, brief though it was, had a wider significance. The shock of the European occupation of Egypt caused a new consciousness across the Islamic world, including also parts of Islamic sub-Saharan Africa. It had the unforeseen effect of bringing about a Muslim reawakening. This followed not so much, perhaps, as a consequence of Napoleon's ingratiating declaration in favour of Islam – 'the principles of the Qur'an which alone are true and capable of bringing happiness to man' – but rather because of a fundamental change in the Muslim power structure.

For centuries Islam had been on the retreat in the Near East, but Muhammad Ali's take-over marked the beginning of a new Muslim era. The new ruler was not an Egyptian but an Albanian. As such he viewed Egypt's needs and potential from a foreigner's fresh perspective and was prepared to use, for its modernization, the co-operation of any groups and communities which might further his interests. A small agile man with a dark complexion and a reddish beard, he exuded a vibrant energy soon felt throughout the country.

Muhammad Ali (1805–49) founded a dynasty which was to rule Egypt for a century and a half. He introduced a period of modernization and reform – 'the Egyptian renaissance' – and encouraged contacts with cultural and educational interests in the West. A brief list gives an indication of the new pulse brought about by this founder of modern Egypt. Land reforms were initiated in 1809; Egypt annexed Sudan from 1821; a total of more than 300 students were sent for further studies to the West from 1811; the following schools were started: Engineering 1814, Medicine 1827, Languages 1836, Translation 1841; a regular steamship route from Alexandria to London was inaugurated in 1837; in 1836 sixty-seven Muslim primary schools were opened.

In line with these efforts Muhammad Ali entered into contact with the ancient Christian Churches in Cairo. He persuaded the Greek-Orthodox patriarch to move from Alexandria to Cairo in 1846 and appointed educated Copts as financial advisors and ministers of state. He approached the Coptic Patriarch Petros VII (1810–52) and gave the Coptic Church a real chance in the country. The Patriarch responded in kind. It is recalled that when the Pasha's daughter Zuhra had fallen ill – according to tradition 'she suffered from a devil' – the Patriarch sent his Metropolitan John of Minufiah who, like many Coptic patriarchs, bishops and priests, possessed special powers of healing and the art of exorcism. As he prayed over the girl the devil is reported to have come out of her toe in the from of a drop of blood. No wonder that the grateful Pasha accorded to the Coptic community an increased influence in society.

The reforms initiated by Muhammad Ali could not fail to further influence the nation in the times of his immediate successors. Here we are concerned particularly with his grandson Ismail (1863–79). In his time the Suez Canal was opened (1869), a technical and political achievement of immense importance not only for Egypt which thereby came much closer to Ethiopia, East Africa and the East, but also for the communication of ideas and impulses, including the Christian message from Western Europe to East Africa.

Ismail sought to develop Muhammad Ali's conquests in Africa and even made some attempts of his own at empire-building. Egyptian military influence, not least through the efforts of two Englishmen, Samuel Baker and Charles Gordon, extended far beyond Sudan. In the middle of the 1870s it reached close to Lake Victoria, much too close in fact for *Kabaka* Mutesa's well-being. With this threat from the Muslim north Mutesa felt that he had better look elsewhere for allies. Ismail's exertions in this and other respects had one disadvantage, sharply perceived by his financial backers in Europe: in the process Egypt had become heavily and hopelessly in debt, and from 1876 was forced to accept Anglo-French control of her finances. Ismail was later deposed, and from 1882 Egypt was ruled by a British administration with Lord Cromer (Evelyn Baring) as British Agent and Consul-General, 1883–1907.

A reaction to this growing foreign rule came with the Urabi revolt in 1881–2. Ahmed Urabi was an Egyptian army colonel who attempted to win officers, university professors and other educated people for a nationalist programme. His most important ideological co-worker was Muhammad Abduh, rector of the Azhar University and a deeply religious personality influenced by Sufi thought. Abduh gave the nationalist movement its theological foundation. He made bold to proclaim that there was no opposition between science and religion. This meant that Egyptian nationalism while totally loyal to the teachings of Islam could evolve a progressive cultural programme. It also implied the possibility of a generous approach to the Christians. Abduh taught that there were certain Christian trends – Protestantism – which only deviated from Islam in name, not in a deeper sense.

The Copts in the nineteenth century

In Coptic society there have, over the centuries, developed certain class differences, to a large extent following regional variations. The rich and educated families were mainly to be found in cosmopolitan Cairo, while humble artisans constituted the faithful in Upper Egypt together with the impoverished *fellahin* insofar as the latter found their way to the church at all. A number of Copts in Cairo were wealthy bankers, financiers and money-lenders, others were tax-collectors – virtually a Coptic monopoly. A great number were book-keepers. They were even known to have developed a specific Coptic system of book-keeping, another Coptic monopoly in nineteenth-century Egyptian society. If their position in the society was sometimes jeopardized by their minority status, their superior education and knowledge of English and French helped to ensure their economic situation. Generally, they were a competitive group that stressed achievement and status.

This also suggested the need for political caution in times of danger. When, in the times of the British protectorate, Egyptian nationalism took daring forms, the Copts felt excluded and saw this as a solely Muslim concern. For a while the Urabi rebellion led to a distancing between Muslim and Copt. It was not until the end of the First World War that Coptic leaders such as the priest Marcos Sergius openly aligned themselves with the nationalism of the *Wafd* party – speaking of the unity of the Crescent and the Cross – thereby giving a new impetus to Coptic participation in Egyptian political life.

Coptic Church buildings are basilicas with a sanctuary – in fact as a rule three sanctuaries. A special nineteenth-century variation of local church architecture was the 'broad-church', so called because three or more basilicas were placed together under a common copula. This provided space for more altars and was therefore popular with the local priest and his village artisans and builders.[2] On the top of the altar is the ark – a painted box about one foot in width and in height. Behind, there is a wooden screen, at the top of which is to be found a row of icons, and it is claimed that the bones of a particular patron saint of the church are preserved below his icon. This leads to the exuberant effect that the relics of, for instance, St George are claimed in a large number of churches in the Delta, in Cairo and in the Nile Valley.

There were far fewer monasteries in number in the nineteenth century than in the times of the early Church – only nine monasteries with about 300 monks and 100 nuns in five convents. The system in fact sometimes showed alarming signs of disappearing. One heard about the monasteries when there was an occasion for the election of a new Patriarch, who was almost invariably taken from the monasteries. Yet still the asceticism and some great personalities held a wide fascination. There was for instance the healer, Anba Abraham, Bishop of Fayyum (d. 1914). At this time there were also signs that, in the lull, a new lease of life was being given to the monasteries and from the old roots the twentieth century was to see a surprising growth.

The worship of this ancient Church was determined by the rhythm of the Church year. The year was dramatized by a sequence of feasts and fasts, the main fasts being Lent, which gradually extended into a fifty-five day fast (only bread, beans and some sweet oil is permitted); the Christmas fast; that of the Apostles; and that of the Virgin. Each fast was followed by a festival and the Copts observed seven great festivals. In connection with the feast of the Baptism of Christ, in January, the men follow the holy example in the Jordan by plunging into the water. For this purpose some churches use a large tank, but more commonly the rite is performed in the river, provided that holy water from the church has been poured in the river, prior to the plunge. There the priest, having tied on an apron, will also wash the feet of each member of the congregation, a ceremony observed also on Maundy Thursday. The women would as a matter of course veil themselves when outside their houses and also at home when any man was present. Circumcision for boys and girls was abandoned in Cairo but continued in the towns and villages of Upper Egypt. Those who could afford it insisted on making an annual pilgrimage to Jerusalem, particularly after the 1820s when the Copts managed to rebuild certain of their churches in the Holy City.

The Coptic *mulid* – a commemoration service for a saint – was an occasion for intense worship and group experience. Official worship followed the prescribed handbook for these services but Coptic folk-religion has developed the *mulid* by itself. The *mulid* became the time for miraculous manifestations and displays, providing the occasion for mass visitations to the graves in the cemetery, with mass lamentation by the women, sometimes appearing in their hundreds and at their most frenzied; it was also a time for circumcision of newly born boys and their baptism by immersion in a water tank.

Coptic Egypt honours the coming of the Holy Family, and the *mulid* gave a much sought-after occasion for commemoration, a service not seldom related to a forecast of the inundation of the Nile.[3] The displays of the Coptic folk religion provided popular occasions for sharing a fellowship with Muslim neighbours at the village level – there were many more such contacts at this level than has been officially admitted by either side. Along with the official religion expressed in liturgy and catechism, there had over the centuries accumulated a compact heritage of pious folk-religion with *mawâlid* or commemoration services for the Holy Virgin and certain saints, above all St George for purposes of exorcism and healing. More particularly in the rural areas of Upper Egypt, Coptic piety moved in a tense atmosphere of expectation of miracles. The Holy Virgin or St George or some other saint might be reported as having made their blessed apparition, with some strange all-pervading light, a declaration formulated perhaps by some humble layman and immediately shared, and enlarged upon, by the reverential congregation.

This ancient and venerable Church, always referring to St Mark and St George of old and to the sojourn of the Holy Family in their midst – how far did it sense and how far did it meet the challenges of the new times which the nineteenth century brought to the country along the Nile? The question is possibly wrongly and even unjustly put. A millennium of Muslim presence and pressure had necessarily forced the Coptic community to the margins of society, safe in its withdrawn and subdued *dhimmi* position – the Muslim formula for the protection of the people of the Book, Jews and Christians – but no further than that. Quietly and unobtrusively the monasteries and the lowly basilicas melted into the landscape, the plains and the desert dunes, very different from the assertive minaret and the commanding cry of the mueddin's 'Allah illaha . . .'

Muhammad Ali's appointment of Copts to leading posts in his administration was an eloquent indication of the esteem in which the educated Copts were held by the society at large. From the days of Clement and Origen there had been a tradition of learning in the Church in Egypt which was to some extent maintained through the nineteenth century. A contributing factor here was the provision, from the 1820s of printed material to the Coptic Church from the British and Foreign Bible Society and the Anglican CMS. This Coptic influence in high places was continued even into the first decade of the twentieth century.

A measure of the role of the Coptic Church in Egyptian society during the nineteenth century is provided by a comparison of the two leading Patriarchs, Kyril IV and Kyril V. The outstanding personality among nineteenth-century Coptic patriarchs was Kyril IV, 1854–61. Born in Upper Egypt, he joined the monastery of St Antony. Though young, his gifts of intelligence, piety, and drive made his brethren elect him as their abbot. His horizon was widened when, on the invitation of the *abun* of the Church in Ethiopia, he was asked to look into a particular political situation: were the British officers engaged in training Ethiopians in warfare in fact 'missionaries in disguise'?, an investigation which led to the expulsion of these Westerners. On returning home the abbot was elected Patriarch and as such devoted himself to reform in the Coptic Church – 'the Coptic Enlightenment'. The term 'reform' was in fact singularly appropriate. Kyril did something which must be considered very unusual for a Patriarch – it was thought at the time that this had something to do with his early upbringing under the tender care of the CMS missionaries.[4] He led an iconoclastic campaign within the Church forbidding the exposition of Coptic icons in Cairo and Asyut where in consequence some of these precious treasures were burned.

He rebuilt his cathedral in Cairo, built a number of schools and started a college for leading laymen as well as caring for the theological education of priests. He led weekly Bible studies for his priests in Cairo, thereby, it would seem, anticipating the initiative of Patriarch Shenuda in recent times. An indication of his interest in education is the joy with which he arranged for the arrival of a printing press for the Church – the second such contraption in the country – to be welcomed by a procession from the Cairo station to the cathedral. Being absent himself, some critics thought a procession on this occasion too exuberant, but the Patriarch declared that had he been present he would have danced before the machine as King David had danced before the Ark of the Temple: the arrival of an Arabic printing press provided a totally new opportunity for reaching out with the printed word. As a patriarch he was sent to Ethiopia – his second visit – strengthening the bonds with the Ethiopian brethren. His ecumenical benevolence also embraced the Greek Orthodox and Armenian patriarchs in Cairo.

In the few years of his incumbency, Kyril IV managed, through his initiatives and communicative personality, to inspire an interest in Church affairs among the leading laymen. For a brief space of time this ancient Church was moved by something which looked like a claim for democratic participation in the affairs of their own Church. A group of responsible laymen – aware of the fact that in matters of Church reform the state is sometimes more concerned than the Church establishment itself – approached the Khedive Ismail about this matter and the Muslim ruler promptly approved their application. A constitution was worked out giving the Church Assembly power to deal with questions pertaining to 'personal matters' such as marriage, divorce and adoption; the supervision of the Church's budget and finance; its schools together with the Theological Seminary, and benevolent associations on behalf of the poor and underprivileged. Here was an active and devoted group of responsible laymen, proud of their ancient Church and anxious to translate its message into relevant and modern terms.

As will be seen throughout Africa, a Church Constitution does not, of its own accord create life in a Church. In order to function it must be acknowledged and *made* to work – if ignored nothing happens. In 1874, the year the new order was accepted by Government, another Patriarch Kyril, Kyril V, was elected. He was to rule the Church until 1927, a longer period than most heads of Churches. By then he was 103 years old. This Patriarch disliked the idea of lay participation in the affairs of the Church and refused to have anything to do with this new-fangled idea of an Assembly. Decades of disputes between Patriarch and Laity followed. At one time, the Patriarch was exiled for five months, after which he returned unscathed and unchanged. Only in 1927, the year of his demise, did the laymen's party succeed in having the Church Assembly reinstated in its well-defined functions.

Other churches

It was in Muhammad Ali's reign that the CMS Protestants began their work in Cairo. The intention of the Evangelicals was not to engage in missionary activity as such but to try, from inside, to revitalize the ancient Churches. In the view of the CMS in 1829, these Eastern Churches possessed 'within themselves the principle and the means of reformation'.[5]

Characteristically, the Anglican missionaries William Jowett and J. R. T. Lieder commuted between Cairo and Malta. With its Protestant printing press, Malta became a centre for a mass production of Christian literature, mainly Bible translations but also tracts and hymn-books in Arabic, Coptic and other languages, which were widely distributed, particularly in Egypt. The CMS schools for boys and girls founded in Cairo, Asyut and elsewhere influenced the modernization of the Coptic community and hastened the activity of this ancient Church to start its own schools and colleges.

The CMS thereby founded a tradition of attempted identification and thorough study of matters Arab and Copt which, though sometimes weakened because of lack of staff, was maintained until after the First World War. The Review *Orient and Occident*, launched in 1905 and with a circulation of 3,000 – was edited by Douglas Thornton and Temple Gairdner, the latter sometimes referred to by leading Arab critics in Cairo as 'an Arabic poet of genius'. Gairdner also demonstrated that his meeting with Egyptian Islam had challenged his own Christian sociology:

> The brotherhood which Christ brought to earth is infinite and unlimited, *but Christians have limited and particularized it.* The brotherhood of Islam is finite and limited, but such as it is Mohammedans have universalized it.[6]

After a long and chequered history of ever-attempted and ever-frustrated Roman Catholic efforts at a Uniate approach to the Coptic Church, Matta Righet, himself a Uniate Copt from Upper Egypt was consecrated Apostolic Vicar (1788–1821). He began with a church of about 2,500 members in six congregations and with fifteen priests. This body also enjoyed the generous Muhammad Ali's benevolence as seen by the fact that he made Sergius Gali, a Uniate, his Minister of Finance and later Secretary of State. But Righet had to tread warily. Early in the century the Uniates made a couple of efforts at union with the Copts but had to come to the conclusion that those on the other side of the fence were not 'genuine'.[7]

THE MAGHREB

The population of Algeria in 1830 was about three million, divided equally between Arab and Berber groups, including the hardy Kabyl with their distinctive culture in the mountains inland. There was a small but financially powerful Jewish community together with Frenchmen and others. The French invasion in 1830 led to a rapid rise in the numbers of Europeans, 25,000 in 1840 and 350,000 in 1880, half of whom were French. The colonial annexation led to a number of local risings and rebellions, and the French administration had great difficulties in managing the situation. A French bishop was placed at Algiers with explicit instructions to direct his spiritual nurture towards the expatriates, leaving the Muslims in peace. In 1867, Charles Lavigerie, after a few years as a bishop in Nancy, was appointed Archbishop of Algiers with two suffragan bishops at his side. This appointment changed the ecclesiastical picture overnight.

The French Archbishop and French Governor-General immediately became sworn enemies over the fundamental question of whether to allow Christian missionary activity among the Muslim population. As responsible administrator General Macmahon (later president of France) was anxious to keep the peace in the country and therefore insisted that the bishop's activities be limited to the Europeans, not interfering with the Muslim population. Lavigerie maintained that he must be allowed to exercise an 'apostolate of charity' among the indigenous population on behalf of almost 2,000 orphans, who landed at the door of the Mission as a result of the 1868 famine, and the Kabyls.

His visit to the Kabyls provided him with an opportunity to give his version of Church history (and incidentally also allows a glimpse of his approach to those whom he wanted to win): 'We the French and you are of the same blood', he told his listeners.

> Both the French and you descend from the Romans and the French are now Christians as you were once. Look at me. I am a Christian bishop. Once upon a time there were in North Africa five hundred bishops like me and they were all Kabyls, and the whole of your people were Christians. But then the Arabs came and killed your bishops and priests and made your forefathers Muslims by force. Do you know that?[8]

This was only the beginning. Algiers, Lavigerie declared, was the door opened by Providence to the whole continent of Africa.

The Archbishop could not be repressed. Hundreds of orphans were gathered in two communities, referred to as 'Christian villages', with schools and a hospital, and soon no less than six schools and a clinic were built in the Kabyl mountains. On his own suggestion to the Pope he was made 'Apostolic Delegate to the Sahara and the Sudan'. In this role he formed, in 1868, what was to become the incomparable tool of his strategic wisdom and will, the Société de Notre-Dame d'Afrique, generally known as the 'White Fathers' who numbered 300 within ten years. Rapidly rising numbers of young devoted men came as recruits from French dioceses – and soon from abroad – to be trained in France, Malta, and above all at the Maison Carée in Algiers and later near Carthage in Tunisia. In 1885, forty-five novices received the White habit, and the following year there were fifty-four students at the 'scolasticat', the Seminary. In a breathtaking outreach Lavigerie, who had been made a Cardinal in 1882, established his mission in Jerusalem – the Church of St Anne with twelve missionaries, in Tunisia, two outposts in the Algerian Sahara, a college in Malta, and above all, he planned and realized the spiritual take-over of the East and Central African kingdoms.

At his episcopal centre in the far north Lavigerie kept himself surprisingly well-informed about all the latest developments in East and Central Africa. He studied books and articles by Speke, Livingstone and Stanley, and could from these refer his missionaries to details in the East and Central African landscape. This study of African geography was undertaken with one object in mind: to draw the outline but also a detailed map of the future ecclesiastical province of the White Fathers.

Carthage, in Tunisia, was an ideal place from which to scan the whole of the African map. For one thing, Carthage had history on its side. Here Cyprian had served as a bishop and here he had laid down his life as a martyr. Lavigerie was to revive his role in modern times. In the 1880s, more than ever before or after, Europeans were fascinated by the outline of Africa. They felt that, potentially, they owned that large expanse with its lakes, rivers, countries and peoples, and that they were to be the masters thereof. This was therefore a period of grand strategic surveys of the continent.

Far south, at the Cape of Good Hope, a young Englishman placed himself in front of a map of Africa and with an impetuous gesture measured the continent from the South to the far North, exclaiming: 'All that red, that's my dream'. At that time red stood for the British empire and Cecil Rhodes knew that he had the resource to translate his dream into reality – Gold. In the far north, at Carthage, the French archbishop was surveying that vast unknown expanse of the continent. His vision had been predicted for him by a French pope – Leo IX, in 1054 – 800 years earlier:

> Next to the pope in Rome the Bishop of Carthage is the first archbishop and the greatest metropolitan of *tota Africa*, the whole of Africa and cannot leave that privilege to any other bishop in the whole of Africa . . . until Carthage rises again in glory

Lavigerie was going to have that formula inscribed in bold letters on the walls of the new Cathedral of Carthage, being built at about that time. He knew that he had the resource to translate the vision into reality – God.

He did this with incomparable determination and never hesitated to push aside any competitor who was likely to question his claims. These were months and weeks and days pregnant with far-reaching plans for Central Africa. Conferences in Berlin, 1874, and in Brussels, 1876, drew the broad outlines on the map. On 11 August 1877, H. M. Stanley, after his 999 days of exploration from coast to coast, arrived in Boma at the mouth of the River Congo/Zaïre. A new chapter began, which also involved clashes of interest and competition between mission organizations, not only between Catholic and Protestant – that was taken for granted – but, perhaps more acutely, between different Catholic mission societies. Lavigerie, as a comparative newcomer on the scene, was anxious to have the richest plum.

The Holy Ghost Fathers of Paris, after decades on the West African coast, were at this time preparing to move far inland into Congo to the Kasai river and beyond. Bishop Daniele Comboni of Verona and his Verona Fathers had made immense sacrifices in terms of human life with a view to ultimately reaching Lake Victoria; in 1877 Comboni himself even planned a journey to Bunyoro and Buganda. At the same time Fr Planque of Lyon suggested that he, too, have a word: his Lyon mission were preparing to undertake a mission 'to the Mountains of the Moon'. And, of course, one must not forget King Leopold of the Belgians and his programme.

In the meantime at the Maison Carée in Algiers, Lavigerie studied maps and explorers' reports and early in 1878, produced a lengthy 'Secret Memorandum', to be presented to the Pope in Rome. At that time there occurred a change of incumbency in the Holy See: Pius IX died to be succeeded by Leo XIII. No matter, Lavigerie found his way to the relevant authorities in Rome and had his grand plan completely accepted by the new pope. It was the most ambitious project ever conceived in the modern history of African missions. It included four vicariates, two vicariates for the interlacustrine region and two for the Congo, the latter covering more than six million square kilometres reaching towards Stanley Pool (near Kinshasa) and embracing most of the territory which however, some six years later, was transferred to the Belgian Scheut Fathers. There will be occasion to return to these matters later.

One can compare Lavigerie's strategy with that of the foreign mission Churches – Catholic and Protestant – working in Egypt. Their goal in Egypt was *reunion* with Rome or, in the case of the Anglicans, *renewal* from inside the ancient Church. For Lavigerie, it was rather a question of '*reprise*', of the restoration of the Church of St Cyprian in North Africa supplemented by a new and immensely ambitious programme for Central and East Africa: Christian kingdoms under African Christian rulers.

Charles de Foucauld

The limitless horizons of the Maghreb and the Sahara could thus inspire a French cardinal to great plans for the whole continent. Another French priest, closely related to the White Fathers – residing in utter poverty in the desert – also claims our attention.

A scion of high French aristocracy, Charles de Foucauld – 1858–1916 – army officer in the French imperial army in Algiers and explorer in Morocco, was converted to Christ as he approached the rector of St Augustin in Paris and this priest told him: 'Kneel and confess your sins'. From this moment Charles de Foucauld was a different person

He joined the Trappists, living in three different monasteries and practised some time with the Franciscans. Finally he was to build a small mud-hut at Tamanrasset in the Sahara where he was to spend the last eleven years of his life. There he lived as a hermit, not very different, it would seem, from St Antony of old: reading, praying and meditating. Eventually he received Papal dispensation to celebrate the Eucharist alone, without being assisted by a helper.

He took a lively interest in the local language and published works on Tuareg grammar. He translated the Four Gospels into Tuareg, not yet published. He completed the manuscript for a four-volume Tuareg–French dictionary, published in 1951 by Andre Basset. A certain number of other texts by his hand have been prepared for publication.[9]

In the end, in 1916, this defenceless monk in the Sahara desert was murdered in his little mud hut by a band of Tuareg and Sanusi ruffians. He had lived a saint's life and he died a martyr's death, giving thereby an example and inspiration to his Little Brothers of Jesus and his Little Sisters of the Sacred Heart of Jesus. Communities of the 300 Brothers and 1,400 Sisters are at work today in many parts of the world including Tamanrasset and elsewhere in Africa.[10]

SUDAN

The Setting

The Nile flows through the Sudan, acting as a central nerve system for the country. This mighty river links together the Arabized Muslims of the northern Sudanese desert and the Nilotic societies of the papyrus swamps (the *sudd*) and grasslands in the deep south of the country. The fundamental divide in the Muslim north was between sedentary, essentially riverine, societies and the nomadic groups whose grazing areas were generally away from the river.

Southern Sudanese societies were likewise divided into two categories although they were much more closely intertwined. The pastoral nomadic Dinka and Nuer peoples felt a common antipathy towards neighbouring societies of cultivators. The Shilluk, inhabiting part of the bank of the White Nile, were the most politically centralized of the southern societies, a situation that no doubt stemmed from their settled agricultural economy in which fishing was of great significance. Further to the south along the White Nile dwelt the Bari, numerically the strongest group in the area. To the south-west, the region later known as the Bahr el-Ghazal, the population was highly mixed due to the settling of incoming groups of Sudanic-speaking peoples from the west. Located to the south of these groups, on the Nile-Congo watershed were the powerful Azande who, although dispersed, were organized and linked together by their Avongara chiefs. In the early nineteenth century the two worlds of the northern and southern Sudan were vastly different, having little or no contact with each other.

Egyptian exploration

In 1821 Muhammad Ali Pasha, the Ottoman imperial Viceroy of Egypt, conquered the northern Sudan by destroying the remnants of the Funj sultanate. Turco-Egyptian rule lasted until 1881 when the *mahdiyyah* swept through Sudan, driving out foreigners and imposing a vigorous Islamic theocracy state run by the Sudanese. The Mahdist state continued until 1898 when it was overthrown by Anglo-Egyptian forces, who then ruled Sudan as condominium until its independence in 1956.

The 'Turkiyya' period from 1821 exposed Sudan to the modernizing ideas of Egypt's potentate Muhammad Ali leading to European commercial interest in the unknown territories. The northern Sudanese riverine societies accepted this new foreign administration and their nominal status as part of the Ottoman empire. With the founding of Khartoum in 1825 as the administrative and commercial capital, a small Christian community was established in Sudan. This Christian group was composed of Egyptian Copts, sent to Sudan by the Viceroy to administer the fiscal department of his new domain.

Muhammad Ali's main purpose in acquiring northern Sudan was to search for new sources of wealth with which to finance his ambitious plans to modernize Egypt. After unsuccessful gold prospecting in the north-east, he turned his attention to the south of the country. In 1839 an expedition left Khartoum to explore the southern waterways and the mysterious interior. This government expedition broke through the barrier of the *sudd* and finally arrived at a place called Gondokoro, 1,000 miles south of Khartoum.

Although the Viceroy had initiated this unique penetration of the south, for political and economic reasons he was unable to capitalize on this initial exploration. 'Egypt's incapacity became Europe's opportunity and European interest and activity in the southern Sudan rapidly developed.'[11] The 1840s and 1850s saw a growing European presence in the south, in the form of commercial enterprise and Roman Catholic missionary activity.

The Austrian Mission

A Catholic church and school was established in Khartoum in 1842 by a missionary refugee from Ethiopia, Fr Luigi Montuori. Although Montuori left Khartoum in 1845, the attention of the Propaganda Fide in Rome had already been drawn to Sudan in 1844. The Vicariate Apostolic of Central Africa was created in 1846 and Fr Ryllo, a Polish Jesuit, arrived in 1848 as Pro-Vicar in Khartoum. Unfortunately Ryllo died within a few months of being in the country. He was succeeded by a Slovene, Dr Ignaz Knoblecher, who re-established the school and chapel in Khartoum. The hope of the mission was to convert pagan societies rather than Muslim northerners, and with this aim in mind Knoblecher and two other missionaries, Fathers Angelo Vinco and Pedemonte, turned southward. They joined a government White Nile trading expedition and in January 1850 reached Gondokoro in the far south of the country. The pioneering fathers found their efforts hindered by their association with the Turco-Egyptian authorities and by their reliance on Khartoum-based European traders for transport. 'The journey revealed to Knoblecher the absolute necessity of asserting the independence of the mission.'[12]

The problems of mission autonomy and organizational independence were partially solved in 1850–51 by the determined initiative of Knoblecher.

A subject of the Austro-Hungarian empire, Knoblecher travelled to Vienna and founded a society, 'Der Marien-Verein zur Beförderung der katholischen Mission in Central Africa', to financially support the Mission. Whilst in Vienna he gained an audience with Emperor Franz Josef I, who promised protection for the Catholics by establishing an Austrian Consular-Agency in Khartoum. The Emperor also assisted the Mission by obtaining from the Sublime Porte 'a *firman* which granted the mission to Central Africa the rights and privileges which Catholic missions enjoyed throughout the provinces of the Ottoman Empire.'[13] Thus Austria, through royal patronage, became involved in the international missionary enterprise. With finances assured Knoblecher left Vienna for Rome where he successfully pleaded with Pope Pius IX to revoke a recent edict abolishing the Vicariate of Central Africa.

The new Viceroy of Egypt, Abbas Hilmi I (1848–54), welcomed the Pro-Vicar in Cairo and ordered for him a good iron *dhahabiya* (Nile sailing boat) 'for a moderate price' from his own dockyards as a sign of his goodwill towards the Catholic mission. By acquiring this vessel, christened as the 'Stella Matutina' by Knoblecher, the mission's evangelistic potential in the south increased dramatically.

In 1851 Fr Angelo Vinco founded a mission station in Bari country at Gondokoro. He became friends with Nyigilo, a brother of the local Bari rain-chief. The Catholic fathers mistakenly attributed much traditional prestige to Nyigilo, whom they regarded as a powerful Bari chief. For his part Nyigilo grew rich as the local agent of European traders. During a famine of 1859 he was hunted by Bari youths and killed. This episode illustrates the difficulties the missionaries had in identifying genuine leaders in the multiplicity of traditional authority in societies composed of segmentary lineages. The penetration of Europeans into the region has led Professor Richard Gray to conclude that for 'missionaries and traders, the history of their subsequent contact with the south is one of almost unrelieved tragedy.'[14]

As the Catholics established their mission station at Gondokoro other problems arose, namely, over land rights and the Bari perception of the role of the missionaries in their midst. In 1852 Vinco was forced to abandon the incipient mission when the Bari expected the missionaries to aid them in a conflict with the neighbouring Lokoiya. In 1853 Knoblecher, Vinco and three other co-workers arrived in Gondokoro to found a permanent station. When the Mission sought to purchase land a dispute arose, for Bari law recognized only the 'transfer of movables'. This quarrel over land, together with the fact that the Mission reserved to itself sparse provisions convinced the Bari that the missionaries were 'mean and hard-hearted' – an attitude that was hardly conducive to successful evangelism.[15]

Having restarted the Gondokoro mission, Knoblecher returned to Khartoum to gather supplies and skilled workers, only to learn that two of the three missionaries in the south had died; the third, Fr Mozgam, had moved 150 miles north of Gondokoro to found a station called Holy Cross, among the Cic Dinka fisher-folk. Knoblecher returned to the south with nine fresh recruits and they worked tirelessly to build a chapel, school and a defensive wall around the station. The Pro-Vicar translated prayers and hymns into Bari while another missionary, Fr Ueberbacher, also applied himself to the local language, writing extracts of the Gospels and a brief Bible history in Bari.[16]

When European traders attacked the area Knoblecher sided with the Bari people and, after ordering the crew of his own boat not to fire, the Pro-Vicar turned his mission station into a field hospital for the Bari. 'Several chiefs, impressed by the peaceful attitude of the missionaries, came to Knoblecher after the fight to ask the missionaries to settle among them.'[17] More recruits arrived from Europe in 1856 to assist the stations at Gondokoro and Holy Cross but the appalling missionary deathrate brought about a crisis of confidence in the Mission and a reduction of Austrian financial support.

Mgr Knoblecher set out for Europe to confer with the Propaganda Fide and to raise funds but by this time his health was failing, due to fatigue and fever. While journeying north through Egypt he met a group of missionaries from Veron, led by Fr Beltrame and including Frs Oliboni and Daniele Comboni, and urged them to head for the Holy Cross and Gondokoro stations in the far south of Sudan. Knoblecher reached Italy but died in Naples in 1858, aged only thirty-eight. His conviction and indefatigability in the face of overwhelming adversity should bestow on Knoblecher a rare position in the inceptive annals of Christian contact with the people of southern Sudan.

At Gondokoro Christian influence was compromised by the propinquity of European traders and their Muslim northern Sudanese servants. The southern peoples were extremely suspicious of the ultimate intentions of these foreign intruders. No doubt the missionaries were regarded with greater puzzlement as they brought no goods for sale and their relative poverty contrasted with the apparent affluence of traders and commercial agents. The Mission's quandary was one of identification and differentiation. The missionaries needed to establish a distinctive Christian presence that would distinguish them in the eyes of local African communities from the other group of foreigners – the merchants – who were rapidly establishing trading settlements in the south.

The Catholics relied on northern Sudanese Muslims as servants, helpers and as crew for the Mission's boat. Likewise, the traders also employed northerners but in much greater numbers. Many southern Sudanese saw a resemblance between the mission station and the early commercial trading post; the construction of houses behind a defensive stockade, which protected a small group of Europeans, was common to both kinds of alien settlement. One missionary, Fr Morlang, commented that it was not surprising that the Bari 'do not know how to distinguish clearly between our house and the traders establishment.'[18]

Inter-tribal rivalries prevented the missionaries from reaching societies inland away from the main rivers. No such constraint affected the traders, who used force and violence in their ambition to extend the trading frontier. It was impossible for the European missionaries to counterbalance and distance themselves from the display of foreign commercial drive and armed strength. With scant resources and their manpower constantly depleted by disease and death, the Catholics stood little chance of ameliorating the increasing suffering caused by exploitative trade. The prospect of nurturing Catholic communities and the anticipation of steadfast Christian villages could only remain a distant vision.

The first Verona and Franciscan Missions

The Verona expedition reached Holy Cross in 1858 and also established contact with Gondokoro; they found both stations in a parlous condition with no prospect of recovery. The Verona Fathers had arrived in the south at a time when slaves were ominously replacing ivory as the most profitable 'commodity'. Although in 1855 Knoblecher had freed some children enslaved by Khartoum traders, from about 1858 slave trading began to rival ivory as the dominant export. Eighty trading boats left Khartoum in 1859 and many of the merchants sought enrichment through slavery. The Verona Mission was immediately confronted with the destructiveness of the slave trade and their helplessness was compounded by illness and death among their numbers.

Fr Oliboni, one of the Mission's leaders, became ill soon after arriving in the south. On his death-bed, he encouraged his co-workers: 'Even though only one of you should remain, let not his confidence fail, nor let him withdraw.'[19] Many of this new group died, contributing to the twenty-two deaths in the Vicariate between 1851–58, – more than half of the recruits sent out by the Church had died. This led to the abandonment in 1859 of the pioneering stations at Gondokoro and Holy Cross on the White Nile, and effectively the end of an era. At Gondokoro the Bari people appeared indifferent to the fate of the station, while at Holy Cross the *Cic* Dinka wept when the missionaries left:

> If you abandon us, who will defend us from the Danagla armed men, when they come to take away our children? You have helped our poor and cared for our sick; who will console and cure us?[20]

In fact Fr Morlang returned to Holy Cross in December 1860 and persevered in maintaining a station there until 1863.

In 1861 the Propaganda Fide entrusted the Vicariate to the Franciscans and by the following year the Order had fifty-nine recruits in Sudan. Most of these were at Kaka on the White Nile, a large Shilluk village. However, Kaka was a discouraging location for the start of a new mission as it was a prominent southern slave market and collecting place for the transport of slaves to Khartoum. It has been estimated 'that by 1860 an average of 2,000 slaves were sold at Kaka each year.'[21] The Franciscans, too, were gravely affected by illness and death, and within three months, from January to April 1862, a further twenty-two missionaries had died. Appalled by their extreme losses and persecuted by the slave traders, the few survivors abandoned the mission and returned home.

The first Catholic attempts to establish a mission in Sudan were an imaginative and dramatic outreach to the African societies on the White Nile – in one of the remotest interior regions of the continent. 'At that time, when Christian missions were restricted to the mere fringe of pagan Africa, this represented a unique attempt at penetration.'[22] The immense waterway of the Nile was of decisive importance in facilitating the creation of a mission in southern Sudan. Unfortunately, this waterborne mobility also allowed other outsiders into the south, whose activities adversely affected the Catholic mission as well as proving disastrous for the peoples of the region. The destructive nature of this commercial enterprise obstructed the growth of the Vicariate and the radiation of Christian influence.

Daniele Comboni and the second Verona Mission

Daniele Comboni had accompanied the abortive Franciscan mission to Sudan in 1858 and was thus well-informed about the hazards and frustrations facing missionary work in the country. A man of far-reaching vision, he published in 1864 a 'plan' for the 'regeneration of Africa through Africans', and this blueprint was later to inspire Catholic enterprise throughout the continent. Instead of relying on Europeans, he proposed to establish training colleges where African Christians could prepared for evangelistic work in the interior of the continent. He also laid great stress on African women's participation and initiative in the growth of a vibrant Catholic Church in Africa. Resembling Knoblecher in his ingenuity, Comboni travelled the length and breadth of Europe in search of financial subscriptions and his energetic commitment led him to write over 1,340 letters in just the first four months of 1871.

In 1865 Comboni returned to Sudan with three Sudanese Catholics, two lay brothers and Fr Bonaventura, who had been baptized by Mgr Knoblecher in 1851; all three had been educated at the Institute for African Negroes in Naples. In his drive to expand opportunities for the instruction of African Catholics, Comboni opened two institutes in Cairo for both African men and women in 1867. As well as these two educational centres on African soil, Comboni also inaugurated two similar colleges at Verona. By 1871 eighteen out of fifty-four young women receiving tuition in Cairo joined Comboni's group travelling back to Khartoum.

Comboni's attention was now turned west, to Kordofan and the Nuba Hills, rather than to the southern White Nile region. For the present he had abandoned the south in favour of a switch to the western part of the country:

> During the first period of the Vicariate the Africans of the White Nile were found to have been corrupted by the traders ... I therefore thought it best to avail myself of the inland routes and establish a mission between the White Nile and the Niger. It seem to me that these inland regions were in less danger of corruption.[23]

Although Rome had been badly shaken by the earlier experience of the Vicariate centred on the White Nile, Comboni's initiative restored confidence in the Mission; he was elected Pro-Vicar in 1872 when Propaganda Fide gave the direction of the Vicariate to the Verona-based 'Institute for African Mission'.

Strengthened by the arrival of new recruits in 1872 and 1875, Comboni established mission stations in Kordofan province at El Obeid and at Dilling in the Nuba mountains. The Catholics believed that the provincial capital of El Obeid would prove auspicious for their evangelistic energies and they built a successful mission settlement which included a school for technical training. Over 150 apprentices were trained at the school and the Mission also opened a library and a dispensary. Fr Rosignoli described the church at El Obeid:

> It was a very beautiful church: it measured thirty by ten by fifteen metres and the windows were of stained glass. The Christians in the town contributed £E.654 towards the cost and the Africans of the Mission, led by their teachers, gave their work free.[24]

An adventurous and innovative agricultural mission station was built at Mulbas eleven miles south-east of El Obeid. Homesteads were constructed for each of the thirty families who lived at the station, the area of which encompassed more than 300 square kilometres. The settlement at Dilling was not so successful as the Mission unwillingly became involved in a dispute between the local Nuba people and the Turco-Egyptian provincial governor; the missionaries were forced to withdraw and close the station between 1875 and 1877. While at Dilling, some of the Verona Fathers learnt the Nuba language and compiled a grammar and vocabulary handbook.

Comboni's sensitivity to African culture was derived from his earlier White Nile experience which had led him to conclude that mission work required the participation of trained African Christians. However, he was not inclined to accept rapid expansion as the solution; instead, he concentrated on winning the confidence of local African communities. In this way, the partnership of European missionaries and their African co-workers could abate the very real suspicion that the Mission encountered.

Comboni returned to Europe and was consecrated Bishop and Vicar Apostolic of the Central African mission in 1877. The following year he returned to Sudan leading a party of fourteen, which included the first African sisters trained at the Verona Institute. However, they arrived back in a country which was facing a time of near catastrophe after a succession of famines, floods and pestilence. The Kordofan mission stations were overcrowded with destitute families. Comboni later wrote:

> I myself witnessed the extreme poverty of very many locations where whole villages reduced by famine lived on grass, wild seeds and even on the dung of animals. It is impossible to put into words the great privations endured by the missionaries and the sisters.[25]

Like Knoblecher, Bishop Comboni was eventually overcome by exhaustion and ill-health as well as weakened by grief over the death of so many of his missionary co-workers. He died in Khartoum in October 1881, just after the first rumblings of the Mahdist revolution.

As the activities of European traders had contributed to the collapse of the White Nile Catholic mission stations, so Sudanese resentment against the growing foreign political and economic domination grew to angry opposition which, in its turn, destroyed the Verona Fathers' work in

Kordofan. This antagonism towards White men (both Egyptian and European) and their foreign ways led to a political and religious explosion in 1881 known as the *mahdiyyah*, a militant assertion of Islamic fundamentalism determined to extinguish all alien influence in its drive to create an Islamic theocracy.

When Muhammad Ahmad al-Mahdi rallied his faithful in Kordofan, the Verona missionaries at El Obeid and Dilling were among the first Europeans to be captured by Mahdist forces. At least fifteen missionaries were taken to Khartoum and kept there as enforced guests of the Mahdist state. Ten years later, in 1891, some of those missionaries managed to escape from Khartoum.

Although most of Sudan was under Mahdist control, which extinguished all Christian mission work, the east coast – with its port of Suakin – remained in Egyptian hands. A Catholic school was opened at Suakin in 1885 and a church built in 1893, which kept alive the Catholic commitment to Sudan. Fr Daniel Deng Farim Sorur, the first of the Dinka people to be ordained, taught at the school in Suakin for four years from 1885. He embodied Comboni's plan to give African Christians a genuine responsibility in missionary work. Liberated from slavery by Comboni, he went to the Catholic school in Khartoum and later proceeded to Verona and Rome to complete his theological education. After teaching in Suakin, Fr Daniel Sorur accompanied Fr Geyer (the first Catholic Bishop of Sudan during the Condominium period) on a European fund-raising tour for the Central African Vicariate. Never in robust health, he died near Cairo in 1899.

Two other Dinka Christians deserve to be mentioned. Caterina Zenab was one of a group of Dinka who accompanied Fr Comboni north to Khartoum in 1860. Baptized in Egypt the same year, she assisted the Verona Fathers in translating Biblical texts into Dinka. After further studies in Verona, she returned to Khartoum in 1873 'where Comboni described her as *una gran missionaria abilissima* (a highly skilled missionary)'.[26] During the years of the *mahdiyyah*, when Christian influence was all but eradicated, Caterina Zenab continued to live in Khartoum. Dr Douglas Johnson has written that her 'entire career as an evangelist was spent in Cairo, Khartoum and Omdurman, all cities with sizeable slave and ex-slave communities – the population of Khartoum was about two-thirds slave in 1883.'[27] Many of the slaves of Khartoum and Omdurman were Dinka and it was these, her own people, that Caterina Zenab particularly sought to evangelize. In the historical sources for the African Church, men tend to be given more prominence than women as the first Christians and pioneer evangelists.

However, it can be said that Caterina Zenab was perhaps the first Christian Dinka evangelist. She died in 1921.

Another early Dinka Christian was Salim Wilson, born Atobhil Macar Kathish. As a boy he was enslaved by Arab raiders in 1876 but later liberated in 1879 by the Egyptian army. He then met two Anglican missionaries returning from Uganda and accompanied them to Britain in 1881. Baptized the following year, he went to school and later attended an English missionary training college. His evangelistic enthusiasm led him to join three separate missionary expeditions: to Palestine in 1883, to Congo in 1887–88, and in 1893 to Tripoli in Libya. It was in the coastal town of Tripoli that he met a group of slaves from his own Dinka people. 'It was his great desire to return to the Sudan to bring the gospel to the Dinka but, aside from his brief encounter with Dinka slaves in Tripoli, this never took place.'[28] Instead, he became known as 'the Black Evangelist of the North' of England, living in the Yorkshire towns of Wakefield and Barnsley. For a time he worked in London for the YMCA and for many years he addressed CMS meetings throughout Britain. He was ardent in his work as an evangelist, 'at one time holding a bishop's licence as a lay reader in the diocese of Wakefield'.[29] Salim Wilson can be seen as one of the first Africans who – in modern times – directed his evangelistic energy towards Europe: today, this Christian witness from Africa to Europe is sometimes called the mission in return, or the 'Mission to the North' movement.

The Mahdist state of Sudan lasted until its defeat in 1898. After the defeat of the Mahdist state in 1898, Sudan was jointly governed as an Anglo-Egyptian Condominium, until political independence in 1956. Although a condominium, Sudan was in effect ruled by the British, who sought to minimize Egyptian influence. The new rulers were faced with governing an enormous country, where north and south were completely different worlds.

Northern Sudan 1898–1920

The north of the country had certain common attributes: an Arabized culture, a belief in Islam, and various links with Egypt. Both in the towns and in some rural areas, a tradition of Islamic education and literacy in Arabic was part of the heritage of the northern Sudanese. The new colonial masters were faced by the ever-present threat of renascent Mahdism and during the period up to 1920 there were numerous uprisings by Mahdists and other Muslim millennialists. This fear prompted the colonial government to severely circumscribe the position of Christian missions in northern Sudan.

The Verona Fathers returned to Sudan in 1899, followed later in the year by the Anglicans. American Presbyterians from Cairo arrived in 1900. The effective ruler of Egypt, Lord Cromer, and the new Governor-General of Sudan, Sir Reginald Wingate, were both adamantly opposed to any Christian evangelization in Muslim-dominated northern Sudan. Cromer's directive to the newly arrived Christian missions was 'Go South, go to Fashoda'. The Verona Fathers accepted this constraint on evangelism in the north, welcoming an opportunity to renew the work of Knoblecher and Comboni in the south. However, the American Presbyterians and the Anglican CMS wished to stay in the north. Both these missions envisaged their work in Khartoum and Omdurman as an extension of their activities in Egypt. Realizing that opportunities in the north were severely limited, the Americans moved to southern Sudan in 1902; the Anglicans reluctantly followed in 1906 although they only commenced work in 1908. In 1885 the CMS had launched the 'Gordon Memorial Mission' with the expressed desire of working among the Muslims of northern Sudan, and they were particularly disappointed at being forbidden to establish churches among the northern Sudanese.

The colonial government did, however, allow all three missions to develop non-evangelistic work among Muslims, namely, medical and educational work in Khartoum and Omdurman. Already by 1900 the Verona Sisters had opened two schools for girls in the two cities. Although the Catholics began building a cathedral in Khartoum in 1908, nearly all the congregation were Europeans or Levantines following various Catholic eastern rites. Apart from this pastoral care and educational work in the north, the Catholics, under Bishop Geyer, concentrated their resources and efforts on the peoples of southern Sudan.

The Anglicans, on the other hand, tried to develop a more substantial presence in Khartoum and Omdurman. Archdeacon Llewellyn Gwynne (later Bishop) was the leading personality in the growth of the Anglican Church in Sudan. Arriving in the country in 1899 and forbidden – by government order – from working among Muslims, Gwynne concentrated his early efforts on caring for the local Egyptian Coptic community. However, the CMS relinquished this pastoral work when a Coptic bishop arrived in Khartoum in 1900. Gwynne became Bishop of Khartoum (a suffraganship under the see of Jerusalem) in 1908 and initiated the building of a cathedral in the city. Consecrated in 1912, the red and yellow sandstone cathedral was built 'with a ground plan in the form of a Latin cross' and 'attempted with fair success to combine Gothic and Byzantine features'.[30] This ecumenical design was to herald, from the 1920s, an Anglican-initiated ecumenism among the Christian denominations in the Sudan.

In the large urban metropolis of Khartoum and Omdurman, the Anglicans concentrated on medical and educational work. A CMS hospital was established in 1912 in the old Mahdist capital of Omdurman under Dr Edmund Lloyd, who remained its superintendent for over twenty years. By 1920 the annual number of patients had reached 13,500. Dr Trimingham later commented that a feature of Anglican hospital care 'has been the training of Sudanese men and women nurses, and a highly-trained Muslim staff has been produced, sustained in their service by common daily worship.'[31] The Anglicans also ran in Omdurman a leper colony and a home for the needy old and blind.

Anglican educational work in the north was concentrated on the running of girls' schools. By 1902 the CMS already had a Coptic community school for girls in Khartoum. Subsequently, three more girls' schools were opened: in 1905 at Omdurman, in 1908 at Atbara, and in 1912 at Wad Medani on the Blue Nile. To begin with most girls came from Egyptian Copt and Greek Orthodox families – further evidence of the close collaboration between members of both the Eastern and Western Christian traditions.

As the language in the CMS schools was normally Arabic, this soon attracted a majority of girls from Sudanese Muslim families. Although, from 1906, government regulations exempted Muslim pupils from religious education at these mission schools, 'they all provided an education with a Christian foundation and outlook' and these schools 'came to be accepted by both the administration and the local population as useful contributors to education and pioneers of girls' education.'[32] Elsewhere in Africa during the early years of the twentieth century, educational provision for girls hardly existed, so it is surprising to discover that girls' schools were such a hallmark of mission work in northern Sudan. It is also remarkable as an example of the co-operation and trust that existed between missionaries and those Muslim families that sent their daughters to Christian schools.

An informal agreement was later agreed between the CMS and the American Presbyterians over the division of educational provision in northern Sudan. Anglicans were to develop girls' education while the Presbyterians would provide education for boys. In the north the American Presbyterians were linked to Egyptian members of the Evangelical (*Injili*) Church of Egypt. Other Egyptian Christians laid the foundations in 1904 for a Coptic cathedral in Khartoum and a number of schools were opened. The other group representing Eastern Christianity in Khartoum before 1920 was the Hellenic community. A Greek Orthodox church opened in Khartoum in 1910 and other Greek-speaking churches were later opened at Atbara, Gederof, Medani, Port Sudan and El Obeid. In

1918 the Greek Patriarch of Alexandria created in Sudan the 'Holy Metropolis of Nubia'.

Southern Sudan 1900–1920

Anglo-Egyptian authority in the vast area of the southern half of the country was extremely tenuous. The process of establishing colonial authority over a myriad of peoples living in diverse societies was long and arduous. Southern resistance to alien rule, especially by the Dinka and the Nuer, continued well into the 1920s and this led to many punitive colonial military expeditions which sought to 'pacify' the fiercely independent peoples of the south. For the first twenty years of colonial rule after 1900, the government's presence consisted of a handful of administrators living in isolated military outposts. Another alien group in the south was made up of northern Sudanese itinerant traders who attached themselves to provincial centres and military forts. The third group of foreigners in the south were to be the Catholic and Protestant missionaries.

The Catholic Verona Fathers and Sisters under Bishop Geyer arrived in the south in 1903, first reopening a mission among the Shilluk people of Upper Nile province, and then travelling west to the government garrison town of Wau in the Bahr el-Ghazal region. In this remote western province

> it was a great surprise to the missionaries to be greeted by a Christian woman who shouted: 'Ana Margherita!' (I am Margherita!). She was Margherita Cassina, a woman of the Golo tribe who had been baptized at Khartoum in 1880 at the age of thirty years.[33]

The Verona group encountered setbacks at Wau and the surrounding area, not least the death of six missionaries from illness during the first years. Bishop Geyer decided not to concentrate Catholic energies at Wau as the town 'was too "cosmopolitan", and too subject to Muslim influence from the large population of troops and officials stationed there'.[34] Instead, Bishop Geyer moved northwest to the N'Dogo-Gola people to establish a new mission. Their powerful Chief Kayango supported this Catholic initiative and soon a church and school were built by his people at the village bearing his name.

The American Presbyterians arrived in the south in 1902, beginning work in Upper Nile province among the Shilluk at Doleib Hill on the east bank of the Sobat river. The Presbyterians opened a school in 1903 and their medical skills soon attracted people from a wide area. In 1912 they started a mission among the Nuer further up the Sobat at the military post at Nasir, near to the Ethiopian border, opening a school in 1917. Presbyterian ingenuity at these two stations was characterized by an emphasis on craft, agriculture and 'industrial' work, rather than on literacy and school work. The American leader of the mission, Revd J. Kelly Giffen, believed that practical agricultural and trading skills were as important as traditional religious instruction. The Sandersons have commented that this approach 'implied concentration, rather than dispersal, of missionary effort', and that after 1910 the Presbyterians became a somewhat isolated community, 'their energies increasingly concentrated on the management of an economically self-supporting "model farm" tilled by their Shilluk clients.'[35]

The Anglicans arrived in the south after the Catholics and Presbyterians and began effective work in 1908 at Malek in Equatoria province. They initially focused their efforts on the Dinka people, holding reading classes and this resulted in the first Dinka baptisms in 1917. In 1913 the Anglicans opened a mission in the west at Yambio amongst the Azande in Bahr el-Ghazal province. Many Anglicans felt that their missions in southern Sudan should be administratively separated from Anglican work in Egypt and northern Sudan and, instead, linked to the CMS in Uganda. Up until 1935 many Bugandan teachers from Uganda were employed by the CMS in southern Sudan as teachers and catechists, but ultimately this policy was not viewed as a success, primarily because of language difficulties.

The precarious and uncertain situation in the south induced the colonial government to exercise a strict control over the activities of Christian missions. In 1905 a code of official missionary regulations was issued which, apart from limiting the amount of land owned by the Churches and prohibiting commercial activities by them, divided the southern provinces into denominational spheres. The ban on trade cut off an important source of revenue for the Churches, which were already strapped for financial resources to adequately respond to the challenge and potential of Church growth in this vast territory.

The division of the south into mission spheres was particularly galling for the Catholics as they had responded with alacrity to the opportunity of re-establishing themselves in the south. Led by the indefatigable Bishop Geyer, who reached, by boat or on foot, every corner of the south, the Catholics in 1911 wished to expand their work in Azande country, but this area had been declared part of the 'Anglican sphere', although the CMS had not yet opened a mission in the area. The Verona Fathers also wished to rebuild the old Catholic mission at Gondokoro, the first Catholic station in the south founded by Vinco and Knoblecher in the 1850s.

The re-establishment of a Christian presence after 1900 in the south was an arduous process, as both Catholics and Protestants were inhibited by government regulations. They also faced an initially sullen response from many southern peoples, who saw the Churches as part of the new alien authority that sought to impose its arrival through taxes, labour demands, and punitive expeditions by northern Sudanese and Egyptian Muslim soldiers. By 1920 these original hardships faced by the missions had been overcome and the first hesitant beginnings of a movement towards Christianity could be seen.

ETHIOPIA

Introduction

The significance of the Church in nineteenth-century Ethiopia is different from the role of the Church in the rest of Africa at that time. In Africa south of the Sahara, the Churches and their schools were welcomed as heralds of a new day and an enhanced future. In contrast, the ancient Ethiopian church survived into the modern age as a Keeper of Sacred Tradition and as the central legend of Ethiopia, with its Solomonic 'mythical charter', for both Church and nation.

To an outsider, nineteenth-century Ethiopian Church history might seem a period of unchanging timelessness. The ancient liturgy in barely understood Ge'ez, the Church year with its holy days, the immense number of clergy with their place in a feudal society: all emphasized an impression of immovable stability. Yet regional differences point to factors in Church and society which were working for change. The *debteras* spread throughout the country – religious scholars who wielded considerable influence due to their literacy skills – were often receptive to new ideas. In addition to being scribes, they were the dancers and choristers of the Church services. One *debtera*, Aleqa Gebre Hanna, introduced a new style of liturgical dance, 'inspired by the lateral movement of the waves at Lake Tana and of the bamboo reeds in the breeze at its shore'.[36] Although his innovation met with opposition from the traditionally minded clerics of Gonder, he succeeded in implanting this dance in the liturgical traditions of the Church. Tigray, with Habte Sellassie leading the clergy, was somewhat open to modern ideas and innovations. Both Tigray and Eritrea were more 'democratic', less hierarchical and without the strong noble rule found in the central provinces.

Only the barest allusions can be made here to the infinite beauty and richness of the Orthodox worship, whether it was enacted in the splendour of St Giorgiss (George's) Church or in a remote hillside village temple. The liturgical framework was set by the rhythm of the Church year, with its many movable and permanent feasts related to Christ, Mary, and the Saints; and by the constant rule of fasts. There were 250 fast days, of which 180 were obligatory!

The round rectangular Ethiopian church building had its tripartite divisions according to the model of the Temple in Jerusalem: i) the forecourt, *kene mahlet* or the Holy Place, where the cantors sing the hymns; ii) the *keddest* or *hekhal*, or main hall, in the middle where the congregation receives holy communion; and iii) the inner sanctum for the clergy, the *makdas* or the Most Holy, containing the most sacred object of any church, the *tabot*, the Ark of the Covenant – a small tablet of wood or stone – which rests upon the altar, *menbir*, in an Ethiopian church.[37] In fact it is the *tabot* and not the church building which is consecrated and gives sanctity to the church in which it is placed.[38] Close to the church was 'Bethlehem', a sacred small building where the wafers were prepared for the Eucharist by the faithful women of the congregation. Although women were somewhat neglected in this highly patriarchal, ecclesiastical system, they knew that this most holy duty was theirs. From beginning to end, man's life was enveloped by the holy rites of the Church. The new-born child passed through three consecutive rites, performed as one: baptism, circumcision and confirmation. The Eucharist was the central rite with its twenty 'anaphora' prayers, allowing for variation and diversity. Weddings and funerals were, as a matter of course, related to the Church. The clergy, rich in colour, rhythm and singing, both in jubilation and in wailing, treated the liturgical dances with solemn joy and authority.

The role of the saints was striking, including traits which connect Ethiopian village piety with similar tendencies in other parts of Africa. Johann L. Krapf relates how he left the Shewan mountain village of Amad-Washa and descended 3,000 feet to the valley below. When he came across a well, he was told that it was a holy well, which long ago had sprung up at a prayer from a famous saint. But one had to be careful: one should not drink the water at inappropriate times, for then a fierce snake hiding in the well would appear to punish anybody who would desecrate the well and profane the commands of the Saint. There must be some secret subterranean stream linking the well in Shewa with similar holy pools in Swaziland or Zululand! There, today's charismatic prophet descends into the waters, chasing away any lurking snakes with his cross.

From the reign of the Rases to the accession of Tewodros

In the first half of the nineteenth century Ethiopia experienced political division and fragmentation. Ethiopians have called these decades of chaos the 'Era of the Judges', or, the 'Era of the Princes', a reference to Old Testament times when there was no king in Israel (Judges 2:16). The power of the Emperor at Gonder had come to a lamentable end, and the vacuum was filled by many loosely connected, regional mini-states. Each was under its own *ras* who tried to assert his autonomy and exercise control over the Emperor at Gonder.

There were also constant attempts to rejuvenate the cohesion formerly existing in the Highlands, although these met with little success. Sebagadis of Tigray tried to form a coalition with the Christian rulers of Gojjam, Lasta, and Simien, but he failed and was eventually killed after a battle.[39] Wibe of Simien now found himself in 'a pivotal position' and dominated the Christian North for two decades.[40] However, his plan to unite the Christian provinces against the mainly Muslim Oromo clan, Yejju, came to nothing at Debre Tabor in 1842. From their province of Begemdir, the Yejju Oromo controlled the Christian Solomonic dynasty during most of the 'Era of the Judges', 1770–1855. Some individual Yejju took traditional Abyssinian titles and became Christian, but most of them remained Muslim and tried to 'assert their influence and accelerate the pace of Islamization'.[41] This was bound to produce tensions between the Orthodox Church and the State and in the 1840s both Begemdir and Shewa were placed under ban for several years.

In these tumultuous political conditions of the first half of the nineteenth century, the various theological disputes were given a new lease of life. With the same conviction as their predecessors from the middle of the seventeenth century onwards, the monks in the 'Era of the Judges', and during the reigns of Tewodros and Yohannes IV, disputed among themselves concerning the nature of Christ, and the relations of the Holy Ghost and of the Virgin Mary to these interpretations.

The traditional doctrine was known as *Tewahedo* (Union) which, however, by the early nineteenth century had been eclipsed by other theological convictions. Each province of the kingdom tended to support different doctrinal positions. Gojjam and parts of northern Tigray held firm to the *Qibat* (Unction) formula, while the rest of the Tigrinna-speaking area, including Hamasen espoused a modified view of the *Qibat* party. Under strong religious leadership, Begemdir province managed to expel their opponents, and maintained the *Ye-Siga Lij* (Son of Grace) theory during the

'Era of the Judges'. In Shewa province, the Debre Libanos monastery upheld the *Sost Lidet* (Three Births) teaching, a doctrine they had formulated in the late eighteenth century. This new doctrine of *Sost Lidet* was in fact very close to their old position of adherence to the *Ye-Siga Lij* view. In short, by the middle of the nineteenth century, the *Sost Lidet* was being espoused in opposition to the *Hulat Lidet* (Two Births) belief of *Tewahedo* orthodoxy. These fierce controversies followed the pattern of doctrinal disputes in any Church. With moderation discredited, total fanaticism became the measure of faithfulness in upholding faith in Christ, Son of God and Saviour of men. The struggle was aggravated by Ethiopian dependence on Alexandria and its Coptic Patriarch. It was only in 1878, after Emperor Yohannes IV summoned the Boru-Meda Council, that these theological divisions were resolved, when the monks of Debre Libanos were forced to relinquish their dogma and accept the Two Births *Tawahedo* doctrine.

To the modern Western observer these dogmatic conflicts may seem esoteric, but they helped to sharpen wits and to form intellectual concepts. Contemporaneous parallels in North American and Scandinavian nineteenth-century revivals come to mind concerning the interpretation of fundamental theological issues. The disputes were also similar to differences of opinion in other parts of Africa on such matters as baptism in a river as against sprinkling over a font; Saturday as the Sabbath versus Sunday; and varying views on Mary, the Mother of God. Opinions were neat little labels to distinguish one competing group from another. Sometimes they became more than labels, even a mighty fortress. As such, the dogmatic labels, in Tigray, or Begemdir, or any other Ethiopian province, became objects in a political power struggle between local *rases* (nobles), or between the Emperor and *ras*. These hair-splitting doctrinal clashes were intimately related to the political development of Ethiopia and accelerated 'the triumph of provincialism'.[42] They also helped facilitate the spread of Islam.

The prolonged disputes confused ordinary people, who instead perceived a simplicity and power in Islam that was absent from Christianity. Other problems, such as neglect of church buildings and long absences of parish priests over wide areas, often produced 'a feeling of religious insecurity'.[43] By the 1820s the Habab, Mensa, and Marya peoples along the Red Sea littoral had abandoned Christianity for Islam. It was in this period of the 'Judges', in a bitterly divided Ethiopia, that the first Western missionaries arrived: the Protestants Gobat and Krapf and their co-workers, and the Catholic De Jacobis and other Lazarists.

Foreign missionaries

In comparison with the established Orthodox Church, with its 1,500 years of sacred history and majority support, the nineteenth-century efforts of Catholic and Protestant missions were marginal, although significant for those concerned. A few Western missionaries were active mainly in the far north and the deep south of Ethiopia. Around the middle of the century, six of these men were outstanding with their strategic visions and aspirations. Four of them were with the Evangelical missions: Gobat, Krapf, Stern and Flad; two were with the Catholics: De Jacobis and Massaja. To Gobat and Krapf, Ethiopia was only part of a much wider world. For Samuel Gobat, his panorama also included Egypt, and after only a few years in Ethiopia, he became Bishop in Jerusalem. Johann Ludwig Krapf, on his travels with the intention of reaching the Oromo in the far south of Ethiopia, eventually came instead to Zanzibar, Mombasa and Mount Kenya. These places opened up for him a continent-wide horizon, stretching from Zanzibar in the east to the mouth of the river Congo in the west. His dream of a 'chain' of mission stations across the continent became an infectious concept which intrigued many nineteenth-century missionaries. This idea was inspired by the Chrischona vision of a chain of twelve mission stations along the Nile extending to Ethiopia.

Martin Flad represented a longer historical perspective. He went to the 'Falashas', the Ethiopian Jews, and emphasized among the Evangelicals the age-long tradition of fellowship with the people of the Old Covenant. Flad's going to the Falasha is an example of the special conditions of Ethiopia. He was ordained and therefore not allowed by *Abuna* Selama and Emperor Tewodros to work among the Orthodox. In 1860 Flad was joined by H. A. Stern, a converted Jew ordained like Flad, and thus, like him permitted to work among the Falashas on the express condition that converts to the Christian faith were to be baptized into the Ethiopian Church. The zealous Stern managed to become embroiled with the Emperor – and his two servants were beaten to death on the Emperor's orders, while Stern himself was taken to Gonder to be looked after by his colleague Flad. The number of baptized Falashas in 1881 was estimated at some 800 – in 1922 the number had risen to 2,000. These converts represented an influential nucleus in their community. More important in the long-run was the interest these activities evoked in World Jewry, who were later inspired to attempt to incorporate the Falasha into the Jewish world community.[44]

Gobat

The concern which the CMS had shown for Bible distribution in Egypt to renew the Coptic Church, applied also to their plans for Ethiopia. The Society's strategy was to inspire a biblical renewal from within the Ethiopian Orthodox Church. Arriving in 1830, Gobat, a French-speaking Swiss in CMS service, distributed Bible portions and tracts. 'If I had a thousand copies, I could distribute them advantageously.' He also established a dialogue with priests and monks in the heartlands of the country, in Tigray and at the capital, Gonder, in Begemdir.

Although Gobat showed great sympathy with Orthodox views – faithful to his Reformation principles – he challenged some of the Ethiopian teachings on the Virgin Mary, the Saints, the Scriptures, and the rule of fasts. He even formulated a plan for a reformation of the Orthodox Church, including theological education of the clergy, the appointment of Ethiopians as bishops, the spread of literacy and the use of Scriptures in the vernacular.[45] Gobat was able to make suggestions in a way that appealed to his counterparts in dialogue. Many were prepared to see his point, and he won over a number of northern rulers as well as the *Ichege* Filpos. Some of his Orthodox partners were so impressed by his teaching and personality that they were eager for him to be their *abun*. His effort at identification made him dress, eat, and live like an Ethiopian. He furthered what he regarded as Ethiopian interests.

Together with a generation of his contemporary missionaries, Catholic as well as Protestant, he planned a 'Christian colony' where the young candidates might be 'removed from the manifold ... difficulties to which they would else be exposed everywhere except in the missionary houses'.[46] This was of course a reversal of the idea of a renewal of the Orthodox Church from within! Suffering from poor health, Gobat's active term of service was a brief five years. During his final period in the country he was confined to bed. When he later became a bishop in Jerusalem in 1846, he took a special interest in the Ethiopian pilgrims.

Krapf and the Oromo

Whereas Gobat worked in the Ethiopian heartland, Krapf, who had been expelled from Tigray, was preoccupied with a peripheral area, focusing his plans on the pagan Oromo, referred to by Ethiopians and foreigners alike as the 'Galla'. In his approach to the Orthodox Church at the centre of the country in terms of location and significance, Krapf had experienced special difficulties. Invited to participate in the Eucharist, Krapf the Pietist, declined 'because they had mixed up so many things with the Communion which do not agree with the Scriptures, and because by doing so a unity was to be expressed between us and them which did not exist.'[47]

The Oromo in the south were a different proposition: a people where Krapf and his co-worker, C. W. Isenberg, felt they could form the beginnings of a Christian community. They regarded the Oromo as the key to the evangelization of Africa. Krapf soon saw the Oromo not as the 'periphery' but as the 'centre', a potential army of devoted Bible-inspired evangelists to what he regarded as the 'Centre of Africa' – pagan Africa. There was an alluring historical dimension to this vision of his. He compared the role of the Oromo to that of Catholic Germany in medieval Europe. He thought that they could become for Africa what Germany was for Europe.

A gifted linguist, in 1840 Krapf attempted to lay the foundations of this Oromo mission by publishing together with C. W. Isenberg, *An imperfect outline of the elements of the Galla language*.[48] More important were his translations of the Gospels. But Krapf was to be frustrated in his attempts to work with the Oromo. Anxious to keep French-supported Catholic missionaries out, he sought British political influence. He even went so far as to suggest, in a blunt colonialist formula: 'the British must become the guardians of Abyssinia whatever measures must be applied whether they are of a forceable or a peaceful nature.'[49] His attitude led to a refusal by the Ethiopian government to allow his re-entry to the country.[50] Not discouraged, however, he moved instead to Zanzibar and Mombasa on the East African Coast, intending to contact the Oromo people from the south, in 'his celebrated search for an Evangelical El Dorado'.[51] We shall meet Johann L. Krapf again in East Africa.

The Bible in Amharic

One of the most fruitful accomplishments in nineteenth-century missions in Africa was that of an otherwise unknown Ethiopian monk named Abraham, and referred to as 'Abu Rumi'. While on a pilgrimage to Jerusalem, he visited Egypt. There he struck up a friendship with the French Vice-Consul in Cairo, who encouraged him to translate the Bible into Amharic. The two men worked together for ten years and finally Abu Rumi completed his task, with 9,539 small octavo pages in Amharic, with the New Testament published in 1829 and the entire Bible in 1840. He used as his sources an Arabic version, and scripts in Hebrew and Syriac, together with Ge'ez.

Ludwig Krapf published an improved edition of this Amharic Bible in the 1870s. It became the very key to Protestant mission work in the nineteenth century. Missionaries distributed the Bible in their evangelical effort to reform the Orthodox Church from within. In certain northern monasteries, the printed Amharic Bible caused both distrust and fear, as well as great expectations. Here indeed was a 'revolution prepared in the womb of the established society', to use Karl Marx's expressive metaphor.

Once the Bible in Amharic circulated along the caravan routes traversing the country, there was no way of checking its influence. Copies turned up in the most unlikely places, such as at Tseazega in the north. There, in the 1860s, a deacon found a copy in a niche in the wall of the Giorgiss church. Nobody knew how the book had been planted there. The message of the book led to a very lively discussion among the Tseazega clergy. One must try to realize something of the spiritual revolution experienced by individuals and groups in such a situation. Parallels came to mind from churches in the West, less eloquent perhaps and yet significant, of new Bible translations leading to remarkable fresh discoveries of the reality of the Biblical message. How much more that experience must have been felt by those people in Tseazega and in similar places as the Ge'ez Bible was replaced by Abu Rumi's version. The clergy at Tseazega had indeed treasured the Scriptures for many centuries, and could intone 'Dawit' and other texts, as a refuge for the soul and as a fortress of authority and holiness. But Abu Rumi's Amharic Bible vividly conveyed the Scriptural message, and made the words and concepts live in the heart and function in a new way.

De Jacobis has a vision

The Catholics were represented in Ethiopia by two outstanding Italians: Lazarist De Jacobis, working in the Orthodox north; and G. Massaja, the Capuchin, aiming at the Oromo in the south. Both demonstrated 'creative flexibility' in their work.[52] The Catholic Church has shown an appreciation of these two missionaries: De Jacobis was canonized in 1978 and is now referred to as St De Jacobis, and Massaja was made a Cardinal.

There were two factors involved in the Catholic advance after their arrival in 1838. One was the unsettling confusion in the Ethiopian Church resulting from the dogmatic factions. There was general frustration among the clergy who desired a regime of order and authority and were thus prepared to yield to the pull of Rome. The second factor was that in the doctrinal struggle, the Catholics were able to align themselves with two of the factions, *Sost Lidet* and *Qibat*, which seemed close to the Roman position.

The Catholics developed a creative role in two fields: indigenization, a radical will towards identification demonstrated so memorably by De Jacobis; and the formation of an Ethiopian clergy. Ethiopians have written about De Jacobis' life, particularly his faithful disciple, Fr Tekle Haymanot, who wrote a biography in Italian in 1915. People remembered De Jacobis' apostolic humility, as he walked across the mountainous Ethiopian country and through their villages, like any itinerant *Memhir* (teacher). He shared the life of his pupils, eating working and laughing with them. De Jacobis, who adopted Ethiopia as his fatherland, also accepted the liturgy in Ge'ez as the beloved expression of his personal prayer and praise. When Bishop Massaja consecrated De Jacobis as a bishop in 1849, the act was kept secret for three years for reasons of security. De Jacobis' vision and dream was for a reunion between the Ethiopian Church and Rome.

Wibe, the ruler of Tigray had an international outlook and a wish to strengthen his position in the Church. He suggested in 1840 that a commission be sent to Alexandria with the aim of bringing back a bishop. The country had been without an *abun* for many years. Wibe asked De Jacobis to accompany the Orthodox commission, and the Italian Lazarist accepted the invitation. In an optimistic mood, he even said that it was not an *abun* in the traditional sense that Ethiopia needed, but a Coptic Catholic bishop from the Uniate Church of Egypt. 'To his great fortune, this hasty notion was ignored.'[53] When the commission reached Alexandria, De Jacobis was disappointed in the *abun* chosen: the Patriarch decided to dispatch *Abuna* Selama, who sympathized with the Protestants.

After visiting Jerusalem with the commission, De Jacobis took some of the group to Rome. One of these was Kabte Sillase, supervisor of the clergy in Tigray. These experiences transformed him into a relative modernizer, sympathetic to De Jacobis' example. There were some who joined the Church of Rome, among them Tekle Haymanot and Gebre Mikael. The former converted as a boy of fifteen, the latter after the 1840 visit to Rome. With the change of political regimes in 1855, official pressure against Rome became more effective, instigated by both Emperor Tewodros and *Abuna* Selama. Among others, Gebre Mikael was unbending in torture, and died in the process.

De Jacobis' example and teaching not only appealed to individuals but also found corporate support in the Gunda Gunde monastery. This was an independent reaction on their part, born of a very long, local tradition of critical awareness.[54] Their interest is difficult to understand without realizing the unique power of communication exuded by this Italian monk in Ethiopian garb. Bubbling with enthusiasm over ancient liturgical manuscripts and traditions, he shared in the Ge'ez worship and in the social life of clergy and pious Tigray peasants. In the very north, on the eastern rim of the Akele Guzay plateau, an emerging Catholic Church was established in eight parishes, with twenty priests and several thousand Christians. A Ge'ez liturgy common to both Catholic and Orthodox had unanticipated effects, and 'the parishes ... seem scarcely to have noticed their transition from Orthodoxy to Catholicism.'[55]

Tewodros and the Church

It is against the background of political weakness and frustration that one can understand the immense appeal of Tewodros, King of Kings of Ethiopia, 1855–68. Here at last was the miraculous saviour of his people, emerging from a lowly background – 'God created me and lifted me out of the dust' – but rapidly rising to glory and power. For this ruler nothing seemed impossible: 'He is supposed to have planned to capture no less a city than Jerusalem and to marry no less a woman than Queen Victoria.'[56] In choosing the name Tewodros, this daring rebel said that he was fulfilling a prophecy of 'Fikkare Iyesus' that Christ would bring a man called Tewodros to kingship after a long period of disorder. The very name symbolized that he was introducing a new era of justice and peace, bringing to an end the times of corruption and lawlessness. 'Out of dust' he may have come, but his success soon made it relevant to incorporate his parentage with the Solomonic dynasty. After ten years in power, he added 'the Son of David and of Solomon' to his official titles.

The doctrinal divisions in the Orthodox Church were keenly felt by Tewodros, and especially by *Abuna* Selama, the highest ecclesiastical authority in the land, as his own authority in the Church appeared jeopardized. Tewodros therefore, summoned all the clergy of Gonder to assemble at Ambá Chárá. He commanded them to uphold the faith of Alexandria which had been bequeathed to them from previous ages, from the time of Marqos the Evangelist down to the *Abuna* Selama. 'He declared a proclamation with the sound of a horn, saying so.'[57] The Council at Ambá Chárá was instrumental in strengthening the authority of the bishop, and ecclesiastical peace was restored, at least for the time being.

The relationship of the Christian rulers in Ethiopia to their Muslim minorities was similar, albeit in reverse, to the Christian Coptic community living in predominantly Islamic Egypt, governed by Muslims. The Coptic

Patriarch residing in Alexandria appeared to wield an influence over the Ethiopian Church, as he alone chose its bishop, the *abun*. Christian–Muslim relations within Ethiopia, and the country's suspicions of neighbouring Islamic states affected relations between the Church in Ethiopia and the Patriarch in Egypt. Khedive Sa'id of Egypt, wishing to improve conditions between the two countries, persuaded Qerillos IV to undertake an unprecedented journey as Patriarch to Ethiopia.[58] According to Trimingham, Tewodros 'was unable to conceive how a Christian prelate could consent to act as the envoy of a Muslim power.' He thus received Qerillos IV with great wariness in December 1856, even imprisoning him for a few days, and would not allow the Patriarch to return to Egypt until November 1857.

The nineteenth-century *abuns*, the bishops, were foreigners on Ethiopian soil. In spite of their office, they did not substantially affect the life of the Church. In reality, the *ichege* (head of the monastic order of Tekle Haymanot), and the local clergy and monks wielded the real influence within the Church. The *icheges*, appointed from the Debre Libanos monastery in Shewa, ran the temporal affairs of the Church, administering land and property, maintaining discipline, and settling disputes among the clergy.

Because the Church was closely tied to the State, the *abun* was often preoccupied with striking a delicate balance between the various parties and interests. Both the chaos of 'The Era of the Judges' and the strict subservience induced by emperors after 1855, accentuated the difficulties facing the Egyptian foreigners. Qerillos, *abun* from 1815–28, was confronted with the doctrinal controversies raging in Tigray and Gonder as soon as he arrived. Unavoidably, he became deeply entangled, but found himself repudiated by both sides, and met his death in mysterious circumstances.[59]

Abuna Selama, who had a long governance of the Church from 1841–67, was educated at a CMS school in his native Cairo. He retained an obvious – but not unproblematic – personal sympathy for Protestants. His consecration as archbishop in his early twenties caused some astonishment. While his youth was no doubt an advantage for travel in the mountainous countryside, it hindered, at first, the deference to episcopacy that was needed for successful ecclesiastical authority. During the 'Era of the Judges', Selama resorted to stern measures, including an interdict of the central and southern provinces from 1846 to 1854. The Roman Catholics in Ethiopia were aware of his early CMS connections and regarded him with caution. Emperor Tewodros favoured the *Abun*, and if injurious rumours about him were insinuated to the Emperor, he would quote Emperor Constantine of old: 'I hide the faults of my Bishop with my Royal Mantle.' In the end, however, the king and the bishop clashed and Selama was imprisoned for his last three years of his life in the mountain fortress of Meqdela.

Tewodros' astounding energy and enterprise led him to welcome modernization and, to some extent, Westernization. He was prepared to employ Europeans – particularly Protestants – to implement his plans. Bishop Gobat, who had become bishop in Jerusalem but preserved his interest in the Ethiopians, co-operated with Johann L. Krapf at Stuttgart to recruit a group of young Swiss and German artisans from Chrischona, the Pietist centre near Basel, to serve in Ethiopia. Tewodros made it clear that what he required were 'a gunsmith, an architect and a printer', and he specified his wish for 'something which ploughs with a fire-screw' (a steam plough). The first party of Chrischona 'Pilgrims' arrived in 1856 and before long these practical and hard-working young men had gained the Emperor's favour. They remained for twelve years in the service of Tewodros, who appreciated both their work and their company. The king's policy was their integration into Ethiopian society. Two of them, Mayer and Waldmeier, married Ethiopian women; later J. J. Greiner followed their example. These Western pietists were practical and enterprising men who built roads and houses, and repaired muskets. They were devout Lutherans, unordained men who, as a matter of course, participated regularly in Orthodox worship. One of them, Kienzlen, in a debate with the local clergy, maintained that 'the Lutheran doctrine on the Real Presence was identical with that of the Orthodox [Church].'[60] Their relations with the Ethiopian clergy and *Abuna* Selama were, however, not without problems and it was largely the king's favour that protected them.

Bishop Massaja

The second outstanding Catholic was Bishop Massaja. His study of history induced him to undertake a special task in Ethiopia. Like the Lutheran Krapf, he went to reach the Oromo (the 'Galla'). In 1846 the Propaganda Fide Congregation in Rome, as always, well-informed about new opportunities, created a special Vicariate 'to the Galla' for him. This Capuchin perceived his calling as one of being a 'St Francis among the Galla', and formulated his programme as 'the way of Evangelical humanity and Christian charity.'[61] He was a great missionary statesman as well as a medical practitioner. His main aim was not the reunion of the Orthodox and the Catholic Churches, but the conversion of the pagan Oromo. In reality it was not pagans whom he contacted, it was rather nominal Orthodox Christians who venerated the cross, St George and St Michael, but knew little else of the Christian faith. From these people 'an indigenous Church was reconstructed, the Europeans reaping where the medieval Orthodox had sown.' Here the adoption of the ancient Ge'ez language was of little or no value, so he introduced the Latin rite, renewing an approach the Jesuits had begun in the seventeenth century. But he went further. He insisted on Latin, not only in independent Keffa, but also in the ancient heartland of Shewa. He was opposed on this point by his own coadjutor, who advocated 'the absolute abolition of the Latin rite'.[62] However, most of the Capuchins kept the Latin until after Vatican II.

The Bishop was a man of tremendous energy. He claimed to have personally baptized more than 36,000 people, a number reminiscent of Capuchin baptismal statistics from the seventeenth century. Massaja's experience illustrates the political difficulties involved in the Catholic drive to regain a foothold in Ethiopia after 200 years. His first attempt, 1846–50, in close contact with De Jacobis, was limited to Tigray in the north. It ended when he was expelled from Massawa by the Turks. The second period, from 1851–63 in the south, was cut short when he was expelled. The third effort, 1868–79, mainly in Shewa in central Ethiopia, also came to an end, when he was banished on the orders of Emperor Yohannes IV. Returning to Rome, he wrote his memoirs in twelve volumes: *My Years of Mission in High-Ethiopia*, published 1885–95.

Needing large-scale finance quickly, Tewodros sought to tax Church lands, and also to confiscate some Church property and distribute it to farmers who could be taxed. As this would have sharply reduced the numbers of clergy, the Church protested and won the first round of the argument by referring to a traditional code, the *Fitha Negest*, which stipulated the right of the Church to retain its property. Eventually, by 1860, the Emperor acquired Church land in areas where he could enforce his wishes. This seizure aroused much opposition and no doubt contributed to Tewodros' downfall. By alienating the Church he lost his most important ally in his quest for national reunification. Before long, the authority of King Tewodros and that of *Abuna* Selama came to an end. In trying to establish contacts with the Western powers, Tewodros was concerned that his country should be accepted on equal terms. It was on this issue that he fought his last battle at Magdala against British troops in 1868. Defeated, the Emperor shot himself.

Yohannes IV and the Church

Four years later, on the ruins of Tewodros' empire, Kasa of Tigray became King of Kings and crowned himself Emperor with the name Yohannes IV,

1872–89. Only now could the Emperor afford a coronation worthy of his office and of tradition. The unity of Church and State became manifest in a sacred celebration, the likes of which had not been seen 250 years. The ceremony was led by a procession of 3,000 Ethiopian priests. The King wore a robe of silk with gold thread, covered by a white cotton garment which left only the King's crown and eyes visible.

Yohannes IV felt keenly the frustrations of a divided Church, and resolved to terminate the doctrinal controversies. In this attempt, he attacked the *Ye-Siga Lij* (Son of Grace) and *Sost Lidet* (Three Births) parties. He summoned its leaders to meet with him and his advisers at the Council of Boru-Meda in 1878. The scene of the Council was magnificent, reminding one of Constantine at Nicea, or of Charlemagne in his circle of theological advisers, vindicating the full divinity of Christ against lurking ideas of crypto-Arianism. In the centre of the arena at Boru-Meda were the Emperor Yohannes and King Menelik of Shewa, seated on thrones. The chiefs and the Emperor's learned theologians sat to the right, with the *Ye-Siga Lij* and the *Sost Lidet* monks from the Debre Libanos monastery on the left. The entire group was surrounded by sections of the Imperial army, a living wall bristling with spears and guns. The warriors eagerly followed the learned debate. It was time for the Supreme Judge to speak, the Elect of God, King of Kings, King of Zion of Ethiopia:

> It is said that without the body, the soul cannot live. Therefore we have first achieved the reconciliation of the Empire and arranged its affairs. From now on, we are going to turn to the matters of faith. The faith, it is said, is the foundation, all the rest is transient and perishable.

Then turning to those who maintain that Christ is the 'Son of Grace', he said: 'Well, go at it, discuss.'

Ichege Tewofilos came down from his seat and standing on the right, cried: 'Discuss with me!' Before the two kings who acted as judges, the *ichege* began to question the 'Son of Grace' and the 'Three Births' monks. After many days of sharp debate, the *ichege*, speaking to the monk Habte Weld, concluded:

> Because thou addest a Third Birth [of Christ] to the two other Births and because thou has taught this error, thou must be punished, together with all thy co-religionists.

Habte Weld stammered and was not able to reply. Several of his party however, ventured to raise certain questions, but were rebuked: 'You have been convinced by your own words, it is useless now to put (any more) questions.' The time had arrived for the definitive proclamation:

> The one who embraces the belief of the 'Son of Grace' (*Ye-Siga Lij*) party must be punished. Then the multitude praised God who in the hearts of the two kings had renewed the friendship which once obtained between the brothers Abreha and Asheba, and which allowed this assembly to publish the Faith of Alexandria and which confounds the heretics. Alexandria is gladdened and its children's hearts are full of joy. So be it!

The reference to royal reconciliation must have pleased King Menelik. He had been known for his strong sympathies for the 'Three Births' party, but wisely changed his view.[63]

At the conclusion of the Boru-Meda Council, the indomitable Emperor was now bent on enforcing his decision. He announced ultimata, with varying time limits for the conversion of different groups. A faithful son of his Orthodox Church, Yohannes wished to convert the Muslims and pagans of his domains. The Christian heretics were allotted two years in which to conform, the Muslims three years and the pagans five. Perhaps this can be seen as a kind of imperial mission! The Emperor met with determined resistance from some of the Christian heretics. To show the consequences of disobedience, he punished some of the recalcitrant monks by having their tongues torn out. This served as a warning to other errant souls, and peace was presumably restored. The conversion ultimata had success with some important Muslim Oromo chiefs. Imam Muhammad Ali and Imam Abba Watta, from Wello province, were baptized and took Christian names. Although this policy probably did not affect itinerant traders, other Muslims unable to abandon their faith left areas controlled by Yohannis. Nevertheless, within two years, by 1880, over 50,000 Muslims and 500,000 pagan Oromo had embraced Christianity.

Yohannes tackled the Church's recurrent problem of dependency on just one bishop by persuading Alexandria to send four bishops. This enabled him to dispatch one bishop to each of his potential rivals, while retaining his ultimate command of the Church. The Emperor thus provided Ethiopia with the beginnings of a diocesan structure and hierarchy. Powerful agents ensured that the Emperor's commands were obeyed. Church and State co-operated. From the 1870s on, the Church's expansion was intimately linked with the enlargement of the Ethiopian state, accomplished through the state's garrison towns, known as *ketema*. These *ketema* became centres for the diffusion of national culture, including Orthodox Christianity. Every garrison had its own church and clergy. The south-western region of the country became the main focus of this expansion. In Wellega the pagan Oromo converted in large numbers under the influence of their noble families. In the Keffa, Welayta, and Gurage areas, which retained remnants of past Christian culture, people readily responded to signals from the Orthodox centres.[64]

Yohannes was the first Ethiopian ruler to experience the full impact of nineteenth-century imperialism. He defeated Egyptian troops in 1875–76; ten years later, however, he was unable to forestall the Italians from occupying Massawa, a port on the Red Sea coast. Regarding both Islam and foreign missions as threats to political and religious unity, he expelled the Catholic Cardinal Massaja from his domains.[65] Yohannes utilized the growing unity between Church and State in his attack on the troublesome Sudanese Mahdists but, in the battle of Qallabat in 1880, he was mortally wounded. The enforced conversion which he had demanded was contrary to the Ethiopian tradition of religious tolerance, so with his death full religious freedom was restored to the Muslims.

Menelik and the Church

Yohannes seemed a fanatic, at least to those who differed from his views. His successor, Menelik II, 1889–1913, was much more conciliatory. He defeated the Italians at Adowa in 1896, a great military victory which reverberated through the whole African continent with an unmistakable message of African potential. *Abuna* Matewos, who anointed Menelik as Emperor, utilized the political influence of his ecclesiastical office to a great extent. He accompanied the Emperor on military campaigns, and was present at the battle of Adowa in 1896. The Emperor used him as his envoy to Europe, and in 1902 he visited 'Holy Russia'. By collaborating with the Ethiopian nobility, the *abun* became heavily involved in domestic politics at a time when Menelik sought to expand and consolidate the Ethiopian state.

The Church also entered the struggle at Adowa, enhancing the courage and skill of the Emperor and his officers and soldiers. An Ethiopian chronicler tells the story:

> Abuna Matewos, taking the *tabot* (the Ark of the Covenant) of Mary and accompanied by the clergy and monks began to give thanks to heaven and to sing hymns ... in honour of St George ... The Ethiopian monks who had followed the expedition were very numerous. They were wearing yellow cloaks, tunics of skin and turbans with palm leaves. They spent the whole day there, some near to the King of Kings, others near Queen Tayot, others in the midst of the combatants, exhorting the soldiers and encouraging everyone to fight. Nevertheless we believe that it was God who saved us.[66]

Menelik was a progressive ruler, interested in innovation and commerce, and welcoming Western technicians, traders and missionaries. He took an important administrative initiative when he established a capital by building Addis Ababa. He sent his friend, Ras Makonnen to Italy and England. Later this envoy arranged for his own son Tafari Makonnen, born in 1892, to receive Western education. This training served the young prince well, when as Ras Tafari, later Emperor Haile Selassie, he became ruler of the country, 1916–74.

Evangelical activity

Two circumstances fashioned further growth of the nascent northern Evangelical movement: first, missionary involvement with a Bible study group in Hamasen; and second, a relatively new freedom for non-Orthodox activity bestowed by the Italian colonial regime. In 1866, Evangelical missionaries of the Church of Sweden arrived at Massawa with the aim of winning the Oromo for Christianity. They were as determined as their CMS predecessors to invigorate a 'Renewal and a Reform' within the Orthodox Church. They felt free to baptize Oromo pagans, and their first convert, Nesib Onesimus, baptized on Easter Day 1872, became one of the great Evangelical leaders, especially as a Bible translator. However, these Lutherans never countenanced the re-baptism of any Orthodox Christians who turned to them.

Thus initiated, the movement grew. On the first Sunday in Advent, 1872, Onesimus and three students of Orthodox background were admitted to Holy Communion according to the Swedish rite. They felt the great significance of this act: 'both the Evangelical Church of Eritrea and the Evangelical Church Mekane Yesus derive their origin from it.'[67]

The Swedish Mission established itself in and around Massawa and the missionaries made contact with the Orthodox clergy inland at Hamasen. The Bible in the vernacular – Abu Rumi's early Amharic version revised by Krapf in the 1870s, and a Tigrinna collection of Bible portions edited in 1866 – presented an enormous challenge to many priests in the north, especially those at St Giyorgio's Church at Tseazega. They acquired several Amharic and Tigrinna New Testaments and other Bible portions, and sustained an emerging Bible study movement within the Orthodox Church itself. The Swedish missionary, P. E. Lager, never failed to attend the morning service in St Giyorgio's Church, and forged friendships with some of the priests. Haile-Ab Tesfai, younger brother of the head priest, took a particular interest in the Biblical meditations, and became one of the devoted Ethiopian leaders of the Bible study movement. He felt he had received a special revelation from God through a series of dreams, and later insisted that he had these dream experiences before the arrival of the Evangelical mission.

> I saw in my dream how I pulled down the first church of Tseazega and then built a new church. This was fulfilled when the light of the Gospel was revealed to me.[68]

It was not only that vernacular translations allowed the message to be understood, but also that its quintessence – 'no salvation but through faith in Christ' – had an address to the individual reader. This sometimes met with imperial suspicion, for instance from Governor Gebru Wubet of Hamasen, who 'was determined to uphold ancient traditions and discourage further interest in the vernacular Scriptures'.[69] In 1875, a group of thirty-three priests and 120 followers were forced to flee from Hamasen into what was then Egyptian territory on the coast. Their Tseazega villages were looted, and the Bible readers had to seek refuge at the coastal stations of the Evangelical mission. When the Italians established the colony of Eritrea in 1890, the Hamasen refugees felt that the new regime provided greater stability than had previously existed. The missionaries bringing the refugees to a local congregation called Bethel shared this view.

After a decade and a half of enforced exile, these refugees returned to their home villages in the Hamasen highlands. They re-established contacts with relatives and friends, and commenced preaching and distributing Scripture portions. One of these refugees, Yishaq Hemmed referred to his dreams. He had seen a luminous figure bidding him to load his camels and proceed north. He was convinced that this was indeed Christ, calling him to return to Habab, his home village, as his messenger.[70]

The returnees felt that their study of the Gospel had now reached a new level of understanding. Until this time they had followed the Amharic translation, but now they had a hymn-book and catechism in their very own language of Tigrinna, and from the 1890s, the Gospel in their mother tongue as well. Karl Winquist was responsible for these translations. He was a doctor-preacher, who was also a Bible translator, a combination often found in nineteenth-century Protestant mission history in Africa.

The small group travelling from Hamasen to the coast and returning home is an example of the theme of 'refugees' and 'returnees' often found in this study. The Protestant Bethel congregation on the coast grew from 67 in 1889 to 187 ten years later, and over 600 after another decade. The five little hinterland congregations, in and around Geleb and Mensa, totalled 277 members in 1911, all young people of whom the majority were from Muslim homes, with a few from Orthodox families.[71]

It has been suggested that Protestants in Ethiopia failed 'to utilize indigenous Christianity'.[72] The contribution of such leaders as Onesimus, and the corporate achievement of the young groups of Bible readers, both in the north and in the south, would seem to modify this view. Still taking part in Orthodox Sunday worship, these students were involved in common Biblical witness. What they received from the Protestant school and clinic gave them a new conviction which eventually found expression in a Church of their own.

The pagan Oromo had overrun much of Ethiopia, and although their home was in the south, they could be found in most regions of the country. Onesimus however, came from Wellega, and was a liberated slave. Together with a linguistically gifted young Oromo woman, Aster Ganno, he worked on the translation of the Bible into the Oromo language. In 1893, they produced the New Testament in Oromo, and by 1899 they had translated the whole Bible. Onesimus then returned from Asmara in Eritrea to his home in Wellega, and devoted himself to Bible instruction in that area. He felt that there had arisen a strong affinity between the Evangelical Christians in the North, and their brethren in Wellega. An Evangelical Conference at Neqemte in Wellega in 1907 recognized that the Protestant Church was at work in seven places in the south. A foundation had been laid for an Evangelical movement of surprising extent and depth.

The incipient Evangelical movement acquired an important orientation point when, in 1904, the Swede Karl Cederqvist came to the new capital Addis Ababa to serve there for sixteen years. He started a boys' school with instruction in English and Amharic, built a church with services in Amharic and could give medical attention. This became dramatically urgent when Ethiopia was hit by the 'Spanish influenza'. Cederqvist went unfailingly from house to house until he was himself afflicted and died in 1919. Encouraged by the young Ras Tafari, he paved the way for Western missions in the capital and he helped the missionary outreach to the Oromo population in the western part of the country. He was the forerunner of a number of Swedes engaged by Ras Tafari as his advisers for administration and medical services, such as Dr Johannes Kolmodin and Dr Fride Hylander.

5

WESTERN AFRICA

SENEGAMBIA

Ma-Ba, the Grand Marabout of Senegal about 1840, was determined to 'impose Islam on all the infidels in the kingdoms of Senegambia'. In order to achieve his goal he was prepared to use various means, even supporting the claims of Lat-Dyor, the syncretistic *Damel* (King) of Cayor, the most important kingdom between Dakar and St Louis, the European forts and outposts of the coasts. In comparison with the pressures of Muslim power, the Catholic presence appeared extremely limited. The French missionaries spoke of Senegal or Senegambia but, in fact, they were hardly concerned with much more than the two island towns of St Louis and Gorée, with some 6,000 inhabitants altogether, of whom three-quarters were captives and slaves.

The Catholic faith in these parts of West Africa had to a large measure been integrated with the French colonial presence. After the vicissitudes of revolution and wars, the French were at last able to repossess Gorée in 1817. Wolof and Oualo chiefs were willing to consider French trade, and Colonel Julien Schmaltz the first French governor, built a French port at Dagans. Problems associated with European colonial personnel made the French presence ineffective. In the years 1843–48, no less than eight governors succeeded one another at Gorée! The colonial chaplains, legal representatives of the European's religion, fared little better. Some of them were complacent, playing the supposedly sophisticated role of the worldly chaplain. One of them, at least, had the guts to react, although possibly he went rather far: angry at the miserable religious and moral situation, Abbé Tayrasse placed the town of St Louis under interdict and returned to France – a surprising decision with the punishment in this case lasting almost two years.

Since the beginning of the modern missionary period there have been a great number of Roman Catholic organizations, from almost all Western countries, involved in the founding of the Catholic Church in West Africa.

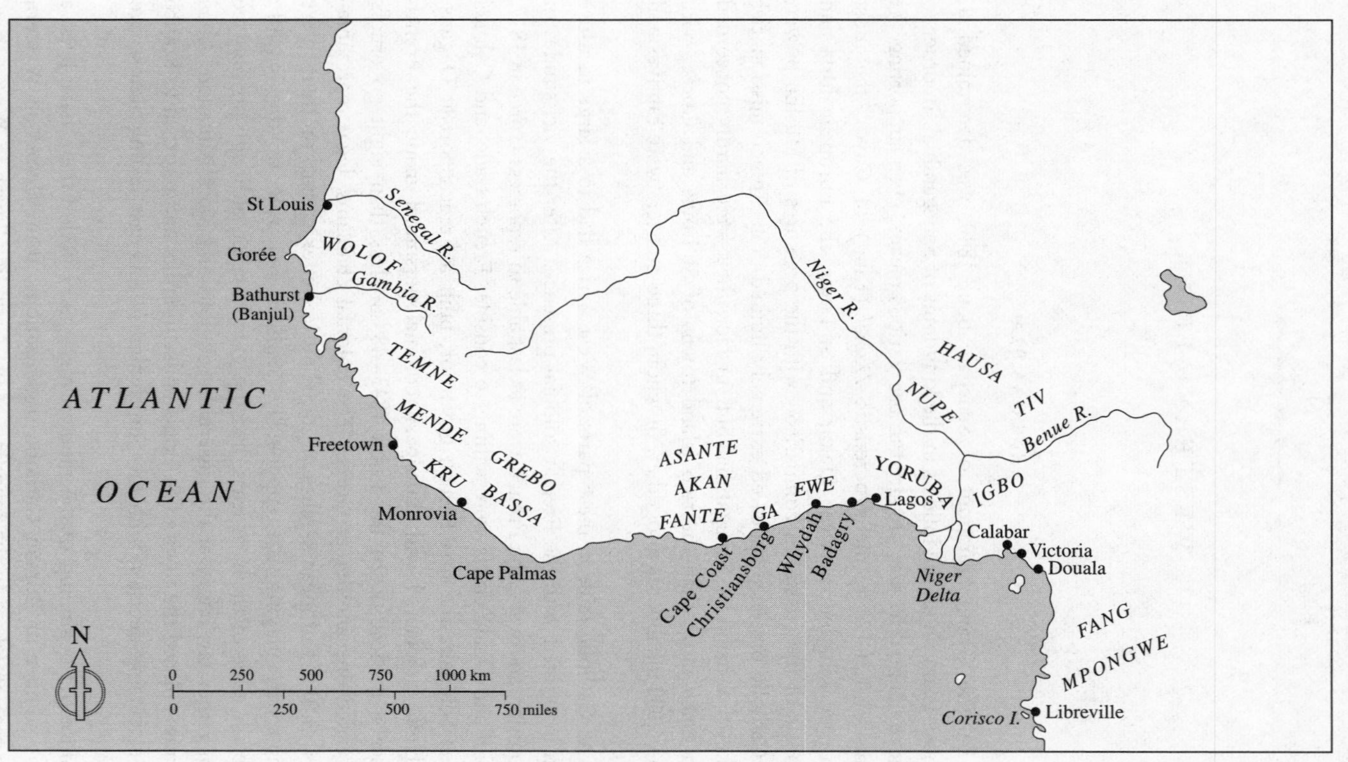

5.1. Ethnic groups and coastal towns of West Africa.

However, the fundamental role of one French society must be stressed, that of the pioneering, the Holy Ghost Fathers of Paris. It should be noted that this Society was formed in the 1840s as a sign of the French Catholic reconstruction, following what, from the point of view of the Catholic Church, appeared as the utter turmoil of the French Revolution.

A few fortuitous contacts with Black theological students from the French colonial islands as well as some other contacts with the situation in West Africa led Francis Libermann to conceive his strategies for an *Oeuvre des Noirs*, which was to develop into a grand plan for the Christianization of what was then called 'the Two Guineas', and what is now the western African coastline from Senegal to Angola. Libermann's mission was to be the pioneering advance force of Catholic missions not only in West Africa, but also in the West Central African coastal region from Cameroon to Congo, and, via the Islands in the Indian Ocean, in East Africa.

The French Catholic initiatives were taken through the co-operation of two remarkable personalities: a devoted nun (the King of France, Louis Philippe, applied to her the highest praise he could think of: 'Madame Javouhey – that's a man'), and by a converted Jew, Francis Libermann. Their programmes and contributions, being of fundamental importance for the beginnings of Catholic missions on the West Coast, need to be, however briefly, outlined here. The Venerable Mother Anne-Marie Javouhey (d. 1851) was a pioneer of modern Catholic missionary work, and founded the Congregation of St Joseph of Cluny in 1807. Ten years later she sent her nuns to the island of Réunion, and in 1819 to Senegal to take charge of the hospitals of St Louis and Gorée. They were the first sisters in Africa south of the Sahara, a significant presage of one of the most important features in the modern missionary enterprise, the role of Missionary Sisters.

When the Sisters arrived in Senegal, they found St Louis under interdict and the Sisters went for twenty months without Mass and Sacraments. This gave Mother Javouhey the idea of herself founding a society of priests who would bring Christian civilization to Africa and form an indigenous clergy. Thus, in 1822, she went to Africa. In St Louis she met a new Apostolic Prefect, P. Baradere, already working along the same lines. However, he laid down such severe requirements for the European missionaries that he did not find anybody willing to co-operate. (He insisted that the missionary must go bare-footed, wearing only a loin-cloth, live on an African diet and sleep on a mat.) He concluded that Africans should be evangelized by Africans and for this purpose he planned a Seminary, but the authorities of St Louis had no sympathy with such a plan and it was rejected by the French community in Senegal.

Mother Javouhey was more realistic. She started a settlement at Dagana, forty miles up the Senegal River, where Africans were to learn modern agriculture. She remained convinced that civilization must go together with Christianity in the conversion of Africa. Her views were confirmed after she journeyed to Gambia and Sierra Leone, whither she had been called by the English Governor to reorganize the hospitals of Banjul (then called Bathurst) and Freetown. The Banjul hospital was at once taken over by her sisters, while she herself looked after the Freetown clinic until she contracted yellow fever from which she only recovered through the devout care of her sole companion, a liberated African slave girl.

Called back by the urgent requests of her spiritual daughters, she returned to Europe in 1824. She demanded that African children, selected by her sisters, should be brought to France to be educated by priests or teachers in her congregation's house. In 1825 the first eleven children arrived. The second part of her plan was to establish a missionary congregation of African and French priests, to be called 'Brothers of St Joseph'. Thus she also received French boys into her Seminary and invited French priests to join the Congregation. By 1833, its nucleus seemed to be secured: she had six priests and two deacons, while six Africans were already studying philosophy and another group prepared themselves to become lay brothers who would teach handicrafts.

In the meantime Mother Javouhey spent five years in French Guyana and became so much distressed by the condition of the African slaves that she prepared her society of priests and brothers to work in all French colonies. Three at least finished their studies in the seminary of the Holy Ghost Fathers and were ordained priests in 1840. Shortly afterwards they returned to Africa and worked in Gorée and St Louis. One of them, Jean Pierre Moussa, was Black, the other two, David Boilat and Asene Fridoil, mulattoes. On their return to Africa in 1842 they duly reported to their official superior, the Prefect from whom however, they derived little encouragement. Abbé Maynard, a member of the 'Clergé Colonial' regarded himself as above all a French colonial official, and ignored his Black colleagues. Fr Fridoil perished in a shipwreck and Fr Moussa, expelled by the French administration went to Haiti. It was a very unfortunate outcome for this early experiment, all the more in view of the preponderance of overseas staff in the Catholic Church in Senegal. Only Boilat survived. And 'survived' is the word. He served as a priest for fifty years until his death in 1901, at the age of eighty-eight.

Two Creole priests from outside the continent, the one from Réunion, the other from Haiti, and one French missionary priest from Madagascar contacted Libermann on their arrival in Paris. Frédéric Le Vavasseur from Réunion had been deeply influenced by the Seminary of the Holy Ghost; Eugéne Tisserant (1814–46) came from Haiti, and Abbé Dalmond from Madagascar asked Libermann to send missionaries to his country. Through the accounts of all three, Libermann received a compelling impression of the lot of the Black man.

The Irish–American bishop Edward Barron was another contact. There was, at the time, a lively interest in Liberia on the part of the American Churches, including the Catholics. Barron was sent there and made Prefect Apostolic of the 'Two Guineas'. For this task he wanted workers: 'He had a country, but no missionaries.' A visit to Libermann in Paris was fruitful, and Barron was able to go to Cape Palmas in 1841 with a small expedition of six co-workers. Five months later, five of them had died, and Barron had moved on to Gabon.

Libermann and Africa

The Propaganda in Rome encouraged Libermann to transform his *Oeuvre des Noirs* into a society to be called 'The Society of the Immaculate Heart of Mary'. Its basic ideal was to go to the poorest. In practice, it should be at the service of the whole Black race and should aim at forming both an African clergy and an African civilization. But the Africans with whom Libermann was principally concerned were those in the French colonies of the islands: Réunion, Haiti and Madagascar, who whether liberated from slavery or not, had been abandoned and left to their own fate. Libermann was deeply alarmed that there were such people 'neglected, forgotten and forsaken in the Church of God'. In order to help them effectively, his congregation, he decided, should be free from any obligation to the government, dependent only on Rome.

Libermann never visited his beloved Africa, but developed his vision of the Church's work there in a series of letters, which included two 'Mémoires' of 1840 and 1846 and 'a Charter of Missions for Africa', to his friend and patron, the Cardinal Prefect of the Propaganda in Rome, J. Ph. Fransoni. Through Fransoni Libermann had the ear of the great missionary Pope, Gregory XVI (1831–46).

Libermann's missionary strategy had two main aims: to propagate the Gospel and to establish ecclesiastical administrative structures. The Gospel had to be demonstrated in a spirit of poverty and humility.

Libermann thus had his society of devotees, some of whom had already been dispatched as missionaries to Africa or Haiti, but the Society lacked official recognition by the French authorities and would thus find it difficult to establish its missions in the French dependencies. Libermann had, however, certain contacts with the Seminary of the Holy Spirit, an establishment founded in 1703 which also enjoyed official status conferred after the Revolution by royal ordinance in 1816 and with the task of recruiting clergy for the French colonies. In 1848 the two – Libermann's Society of the Immaculate Heart of Mary and the Seminary of the Holy Spirit – were merged, using the name of the older partner and with Libermann as the Superior.

The period seemed ripe for formulating great missionary principles. At exactly the same time – 1850–51 – when on the Protestant side Henry Venn in London and Rufus Anderson in Boston, United States, drew the outlines of the grand strategy of Protestant missions, in Paris Francis Libermann laid down his rules for Catholic missions. 'Implant our holy religion by beginning the construction of the stable edifice of a canonically established Church.' Hence he insisted on a carefully deliberated planning for the future: 'The ten souls you save by a hurried and ill-conceived step, by a measure which produces an immediate good result, may perhaps mean the loss of more than a hundred thousand.' The *conditio sine qua non* for an indigenous Church was to 'form a native clergy rooted in the country, a native hierarchy'.

The first means through which to achieve this end was the missionary's personal holiness, strengthened by community life. 'The people of Africa will not be converted by the work of clever and capable missionaries but through the holiness and sacrifices of their priests.' Libermann's spiritual doctrine included a new asceticism: constant renunciation of one's own will while seeking the direction of the Holy Spirit – the 'Little Way' later popularized by St Teresa of Lisieux. This 'asceticism of the little' brought him soon into opposition with his two colleagues, but Libermann quickly resolved this problem by sending them to the mission fields they longed for: Le Vavasseur to Réunion and Tisserant to Haiti. Even before this, another companion, Father Jacques Laval, had left for Mauritius and became a great friend to the liberated Africans on that island.

The second means was national detachment and missionary adaptation:

> Divest yourselves of Europe, its customs and mentality. Become Negroes with the Negroes, and you will judge them as they ought to be judged. Become Negroes with the Negroes, to train them as they should be trained, not in the European fashion but retaining what is proper to them . . . The people must never consider you as a political agent of the French Government, but should see in you only the priest of the Almighty.

The third means was to bring religion and civilization together:

> Our faith will never acquire a stable form among these peoples nor will the nascent Churches ever have a secure future without the aid of a civilization, one that is based on science and work, in addition to religion . . .

The whole of the West African coast became Libermann's concern. He could refer to the experience of those who had come to Paris for his advice and leadership. To Libermann and his generation, the 'Two Guineas' meant the whole of West Africa, from Senegal (or 'High Guinea'), to Angola (the final point of 'Lower Guinea').[1] However, to Libermann the expression the 'Two Guineas' took on a mystical significance as 'a land of redemption': the Black race had unjustly had to suffer immense hardship and Libermann's missionaries were sent to redress this. Planning the 'Two Guineas' he subdivided the region into five administrations, with the Vicar Apostolic presiding at Dakar.

Libermann had his strategy of the bishoprics in Africa officially accepted by both Rome and Paris: a Papal Bull of 1850 constituted them, and it was 'received in France by the President of the Republic, Prince Louis Napoleon Bonaparte'. Libermann insisted that 'bishoprics were more necessary in the colonies than in France; a strong authority is needed – that is what the clergy has lacked hitherto.'[2]

The first bishop on the West Coast

No bishop ever came to Africa, in modern times, with nobler intentions or more real qualifications than Mgr Benoit Truffet (1812–47), although his term of service could be no more than a promising beginning. He shared the fate of most missionaries coming out to West Africa at the time. In early May he arrived in Senegal – 'I have taken possession of my African vicariate Saturday the 8th of May' He died on 23 November of the same year, 1847. He was French, and yet not French. He would in fact not allow the French language to be taught to his young African students. Latin – 'the language of the Pope', his students said – and Wolof, their own mother tongue, were the only languages permitted. Although of course French-speaking himself, he was determined not to be confused with the French for Truffet himself was from Savoy, now in the south of France but at that time part of the Kingdom of Sardinia. An Ultramontanist, he vigorously disliked what he regarded as a liberal, anti-clerical and sometimes Gallicanist Church. He disliked the French influence in Senegal and not only the French. The Europeans as a whole were, according to him, 'the scourge of the African coastline'.

But he was no less critical of the missionaries. 'The missionary has a terrible tendency to be at the same time Pope and King, in spite of the purity and zeal of his orthodoxy.'[3] A harsh disciplinarian, Truffet maintained that the missionaries must conform as much as possible to African conditions. He forbade them to eat meat and bread or to take European medicines. Wolof food and medicines were there to be used. In political matters, Bishop Truffet's stand was no less definite. 'The missionaries must never express political opinions, neither among themselves, nor before the people of the world.'[4] That also went for the slave trade; this should not be discussed by the missionaries who, on the other hand, must know that the slave trade as such 'was a monstrous crime'.

In the West he had met the belief that Westernization was a necessary preparation for Christianization. That this idea was mistaken was shown by the situation in Dakar – then only a little village – and Gorée. The people had been exposed to French influence for 200 years, yet there was not one single indigenous Christian. 'The only things which they have received from Europe was' he felt, 'the love of money, the use of the gun, tobacco and alcohol'.[5] Libermann's thesis was that Africa had to be converted by Africans and that was also Truffet's view. To that end he started a school intended as a seminary for an African clergy. Numbers were limited, not more than seven.

> They are docile and pious. I have divided their workday into exercises of piety, the study of Latin and Wolof, handicrafts which they practise in the shade in the hot afternoon, and agriculture at 5–7 in the evening. Each has got his own garden. The students become in succession sacristans, acolytes, etc.[6]

His Wolof teacher helped him to make a faithful translation into Wolof of The Lord's Prayer, the Ave Maria, the Creed and the Ten Commandments.

Truffet's key objectives have been summarized thus: 'schools, cultivation, the training of native clergy, the training of catechists who would be tonsured, receive minor orders, and not be held to celibacy.' But he was, after all, the bishop of the *Two* Guineas; therefore he sent one of his co-workers to Gabon with a special order to establish from the outset as much uniformity as possible in the work of the mission. This was by way of reconnoitring; Truffet himself was preparing to visit Gabon and the whole of the West Coast when death cut short his plans.

Very little is known of Truffet's contacts with the African population. He stuck to his principles in everything, and he is significant because in the short time granted to him he maintained the vision which he shared with Rome and Libermann: he was charged, he knew, not only to form Christians in West Africa, but to establish and constitute the Churches 'which will soon be strong by their union in the great Catholic family'.

Catholics and Protestants on the Senegambian coast

Truffet represented the tendency towards asceticism and mysticism in the 'Holy Ghost' spirituality. Aloÿs Kobès who took over in 1848 and who, at twenty-eight, was the youngest bishop in Christendom, worked according to the double programme of evangelization and development. He built up a French staff which soon had twenty-two priests, thirteen brothers and twelve sisters. He managed to found Christian villages along the coast, including Ngabozil, where the Church had been given lands, with schools, workshops and a seminary. A model village was built, a Christian community and an emerging cotton industry. He transformed the old Lebu village of Dakar into a place which was to become the first city of Senegal. In avoiding the Muslim inland he concentrated on the preponderantly 'animist' districts of Sine-Saloum and Casamance.[7]

In the countryside surrounding the mission members of the Serere community settled down in five villages. Most of them had fled from an oppressive chief and put themselves under the protection of the missionaries. Their communities grew into Christian villages, and the Gospel also spread into neighbouring places, such as Joal and Mbour. But for the rest, the whole region between the rivers Senegal and Gambia remained almost untouched.

A second Christian area was of Portuguese heritage: the strip between the rivers Gambia and Casamance with the centres of Banjul (Bathurst) and Ziguinchor. It was mostly populated by the Diola people, having an admixture of Portuguese blood. At Banjul the mission of St Mary of Gambia had already been founded in 1848, but the Islamic surroundings hindered further expansion. On the other hand, along the Casamance, where missions followed the French takeover from the Portuguese, a respectable Christian community slowly developed.

The increasing Muslim influence was a factor of which both Church and State had to take account. In particular this applied to the new French governor Louis L. C. Faidherbe who had spent his apprentice years in the administration in Algiers and realized that for political reasons the interests of Islam were a high priority. He did so to an extent which caused churchmen anxiety but which obviously was to have a wide influence on future French administration in West Africa. This did not hinder him from occasionally vindicating the rights of the Christian community. On one occasion Father Duret had decided to suppress the year's celebration of the Corpus Christi procession arguing that in a strongly Muslim *milieu* such a brilliant procession was nothing but a vain show. However, the governor as a good Frenchman was not prepared to leave out a good effect and wrote: 'It is faint-heartedness – to use not a stronger expression – not to celebrate the Feast of Corpus Christi, before Heaven and a population subject to France.'[8]

Kobès was concentrating on his two island congregations, St Louis and Gorée. In 1854 he could report that already seventy-five missionaries, cleric and lay, had arrived on the West Coast; of these twenty-four had died and seventeen had retired for health reasons. Fifteen stations had been founded but eight of them had had to be abandoned for lack of personnel. Kobès discovered that the Sisters of the Immaculate Conception – who already numbered more than twenty – seemed to have found the secret of survival: they 'used to take a little sulphate of quinine, recommended by good doctors'.

Senegambia, as the region of present-day Senegal and Gambia was called, had its missionary headquarters at Dakar. In 1850 it was transferred to Ngazobil, sixty miles south along the coast, where there were vast lands to support all the works of the missions which were successively started: the residences of the Fathers and the Sisters; the schools, minor and major seminaries; a foundation of African sisters (1858) and another of African brothers.

St Louis was soon to receive its first Protestant messengers. In about 1825 a Catholic teacher from a Jansenist background had made efforts to liberate slaves in St Louis. On a furlough in France he was converted to Protestantism and as such returned to Senegal. This was enough for the Government to deem him raving mad, so he was repatriated to France. However, some decades later, in 1862, the country had a Protestant governor, Jaureguiberry, who actively furthered the interests of the Protestant pioneers. The Paris Evangelical Missionary Society sent out a team of three men in 1867 and as good Protestants they soon turned to the translation of the Gospel of St Matthew into Wolof. Of special significance was the fact that they could place an African co-worker, by the name of Taylor, at Gorée. He was a Sierra Leonian of Yoruba parentage, a liberated African from Abeokuta and had studied at Fourah Bay College and become a trader in Gambia and Gorée. The Paris Mission placed him as a preacher in Gorée. Later he was sent to Paris, studied theology there, and was ordained in 1873, becoming at the same time a naturalized Frenchman. Taylor belonged in St Louis and stayed there, preaching in the Bambara language, caring for freed slaves and his little flock of Bambara and Wolof Protestants; solitary, yet solidly carrying on, left to his own devices, yet building up a Christian community.

SIERRA LEONE

A unique factor in West African Protestant history was the modern settlement of two countries to be named Sierra Leone and Liberia, by Black immigrants from the Americas. The 'returnees' who arrived in Sierra Leone from 1787 to 1800, were later numerically overtaken by large numbers of Africans from the Lower Guinea Coast, freed by British men-of-war from ships transporting them to plantation slavery.

The Black settlers

Along the coast the Europeans had built forts and established trading settlements. From the north there had been Muslim pressures, with memories of a *jihad* in 1725. Ethnic communities such as the Temne and the Mende now reluctantly accepted the foreigners. In 1787 the first Black settlers arrived at Freetown and were received by the Temne sub-chief, King Tom. It was he, not the Temne leader Naimbana, who took part in the negotiations. The allocation of land to the newcomers led to conflicts and an attack by the Temne on the British fort. As so often happened in Africa, the settlers regarded themselves as owners of the land. To the Temne, land could only be ceded for temporary use. The formation in 1790 of the 'Sierra Leone Company', aimed at opening a market for British manufactures, led to an administration which became the embryo of British authority, formalized into a Crown Colony in 1808. Returnees came back not only to Sierra Leone, but also to Nigeria, from the West Indies and from Brazil. Those from Brazil were Roman Catholics; those from other areas were mainly Protestant.

Most of the former slaves who came to Sierra Leone were already Christian, with their own Church leaders and preachers. The first contingent of about 400 came via England. Many of them were former sailors or plantation slaves. Five years later fifteen ships came from Nova Scotia with 1,200 ex-slaves. They had gathered in Nova Scotia from many parts of North America and the West Indies. On board, 'captains' had been elected from among the religious leaders of the emigrants. These 'captains' maintained discipline and represented the union of chief and pastor, a combination encountered later in the history of the Church, both in Sierra

Leone and in the continent as a whole. These returnees were already English-speaking, and linked to a Protestant Church, Methodist or Baptist. When one of the groups arrived at Freetown, they marched with their preachers from the shore towards the forest, carrying the Holy Bible and singing:

Awake! And sing the song
Of Moses and the Lamb,
Wake! Every heart and every tongue
To praise the Saviour's name.[9]

Meanwhile the settlement continued to expand with the arrival of the Maroons from the mountainous interior of Jamaica, again via Nova Scotia.

The settlers came as members of Churches, and were to meet new influences in the unfamiliar African environment. One Methodist leader, Moses Wilkinson, who was both blind and lame, was a fervent and emotional preacher. Another Nova Scotian, Joseph Jewett, a devoted evangelist, went beyond the settler community of returnees to the 'liberated Africans'. In this outreach, the Methodists were aided by their incomparable 'class system', developed by John Wesley and his disciples as a flexible instrument for evangelization. It proved to be singularly adaptable to mission situations in Africa. The local congregation was built on a cell system of 'classes', twelve members in each class. There, instruction, inspiration, and interpretation could take place, providing valuable experience for future leaders. Although originating with the Methodists, the system was soon adopted by other Churches in Sierra Leone, including the Anglicans.

The message and organization of the Baptists was not very different from that of the Methodists. Like them, the influence of their original *milieu* in Georgia or Virginia in the United States had been modified in Nova Scotia. Both groups had to be self-sufficient, having no financial support from overseas. The first small chapel the Baptists used after disembarking had a ship's sail for a roof. Their leader, David George, born in Virginia to parents enslaved from Africa, had fled as a refugee to Nova Scotia. He had established a warm relationship with John Clarkson, the British officer who led the fleet carrying the returnees from Nova Scotia to Freetown. Perhaps because of this influence, the Baptist settlers were considered particularly loyal to the administration.

The leaders in the settler Churches were self-supporting, many earning money piloting ships into Freetown harbour. The settler women, who had fought for their rights on American plantations and guided their families during the migration to Nova Scotia, were a tough and independent group. Some, such as Mary Perth, were recognized as Church leaders. She had formed her own congregation while a slave in Norfolk, Virginia. In Freetown she emerged as a leader with keen economic sense and deep religious fervour. In Nova Scotia, women had preached and testified as the Spirit led them. In Freetown, Amilia Buxton started a congregation in her home.

The various British nonconformist missionary societies did not begin to take an interest in Sierra Leone until the turn of the century. When they finally sent missionaries, these were not very welcome. The settler preachers were happy with their own methods and organizations, and were not looking for outside help or interference. Congregations were expected to attend daily services at five in the morning. Their worship tended to be emotional: free prayers sometimes became ecstatic; jumping and rhythmic hand-clapping passed into dancing; and Wesleyan hymns adapted to African tunes.

Death was an ever present reality in that climate. Black men as well as White succumbed to fevers of various kinds, and in the 1820s there was a serious outbreak of yellow fever. Young children were particularly susceptible to diseases such as smallpox, measles, dysentery. Mothers who feared for the lives of their children would turn at such times of crisis to any possible source of help and support. Sacrifices to ancestral spirits, drumming, and dancing provided feelings of solidarity with neighbours.

Britain and the Slave Trade Act of 1807

In 1807 Britain made the slave trade illegal for her own subjects. Nationals of other countries continued the practice, however, and some British subjects did so illegally, or under what amounted to 'flags of convenience'. In 1808 as many as 80,000 slaves were shipped from West African ports. Britain tried to enforce the provisions of the Act by the use of the 'British Preventive Squadron' – naval vessels which patrolled the coast to intercept and capture slave ships. These ships were escorted to Freetown, where their human cargoes were released and placed in townships under mission supervision. These were the 'liberated Africans', and from about 1810 their arrival radically changed the population in the Sierra Leone colony. In 1808 only eighty such arrived, but soon there were about 2,000 a year. Between 1814 and 1824 nearly 13,000 slaves were landed, and by 1834 some 60,000 had been liberated. The majority were Yoruba and Igbo from Nigeria, but there were people from as far away as Cameroon, Congo, Zaïre and Angola.

> Abandoned by their own gods, who had failed to protect them in their homeland, they came up from the hold of the slave ships, like Jonah from the whale, cut off from their old life, ready to be re-born into a new.[10]

They soon became financially independent, with strong memories of their homelands. Eventually, from 1839 onwards they began to realize the dream of returning to their homes by forming syndicates.

While the period prior to 1820 was dominated by the returnee settlers, that of 1820 to 1850 received its special character from the newcomer, the liberated African. At first he was treated as a 'Johnny-come-lately', but was soon able to establish himself in the new situation. This rapid rise of the liberated African community is one of the most convincing examples of what this book claims was the classic theme in the Christianization of Africa: the uprooted group, transferred into a new environment, prepared to be lifted by the Church's spiritual, educational, and practical fellowship and programme.

Economic and educational advance in the Sierra Leone society provided opportunities for the newcomers. The timber trade and export were of particular importance. At Regent, one of the liberated African villages, names were listed of fifty masons, forty carpenters, and thirty sawyers. Groundnuts were exported to France, where groundnut oil was used to lubricate the new French trains a trade which was improved after the practical Wesleyan missionary, Thomas Reader, imported an improved press in 1849.[11]

Anglican work

Anglican work in Freetown predated that of other missions, for from the beginning of the settlements, Anglican chaplains had been sent to them. But mission work did not really begin until the German pastor, Gustav Nyländer, arrived in 1806. He served as chaplain with the Church Missionary Society. He was not impressed with the Europeans he was appointed to serve: 'half-educated young officials, disreputable soldiers, passing sailors, and retired slave traders'. And so he moved beyond the colony borders, to begin work among Africans. In 1810 Wesleyan Methodists decided to send missionaries to Sierra Leone again; they had experienced discouraging efforts in the 1790s. With the arrival of the many liberated Africans, it was necessary to staff the missions in their townships. The CMS sent out increasing numbers of missionaries, still largely German. In 1816 a CMS representative, commissioned to study the situation 'on the spot', made recommendations. He was Edward Bickersteth, a prominent evangelical layman, a solicitor who was ordained just before leaving Britain. He confirmed the fact that the task was not so much among the settlers, as among the liberated Africans coming into the colony in ever-growing numbers. He stressed evangelism – proclamation of the Gospel to local groups and to individuals – as the missionary priority: 'This is your first, your great task; everything else must be subordinate to this.'[12]

Bickersteth's visit and report was one key to successful Anglican work in this period. A second was the co-operation of Sir Charles MacCarthy, governor from 1816–24 and a staunch Roman Catholic who established villages for the liberated Africans. From 1817 the colony was organized into parishes, each with a minister and a schoolmaster. By 1823 there were thirteen such parishes, containing 5,530 persons.[13] There was a 'Congo Town' for the Congolese and Zaïreans, and a 'Portuguese Town' for the Angolans. William Johnson, a German working with CMS, was in charge of the largest village, Regent Town. An 1819 report on Regent indicates surprising achievements:

> The Town itself is laid out with regularity; nineteen streets are formed, ... a large stone Church, ... a Government House, a Parsonage House, a Hospital, School Houses, Store Houses, a Bridge of several arches, some Native dwellings, and other buildings, all of stone ... all are farmers; gardens, fenced in, are attached to every dwelling ... many of them ... exercise various trades: fifty of them are masons and bricklayers: forty, carpenters; thirty, sawyers; thirty, shingle-makers; twenty, tailors; four, blacksmiths; and two, butchers.[14]

Funds came from the government; CMS provided personnel for supervisory staff. The missionary as superintendent of a village was responsible not only to his society but also to the colonial government; he was almost a colonial official. This arrangement, however, ended in 1824.

During MacCarthy's governorship, he took a very close personal interest in what was going on. He reported on what he observed:

> Bells, clocks and weathercocks were ordered from England for church towers, forges for village blacksmiths, scales and weights for village markets. Quill-pens and copy-books, prayer books and arithmetic books were ordered for the schools ... gowns and petticoats, trousers and braces – buttons too, with needles, thread and thimbles, ... nothing was forgotten.[15]

Sometimes, for the missionary, the governor's interest went too far. He attempted to dictate the duration of the catechumenate, and 'wanted recaptives baptized as soon as they began adopting European ways'.[16] When Johnson, the German Pietist, insisted that they must show signs of a change of heart, the impetuous Catholic governor threatened to complain to the

Archbishop of Canterbury. But in this battle of wills, the stubborn Hanoverian won; the governor gave in reluctantly, calling Johnson and the missionary society 'a bunch of fanatics'.

The missionary staff

In assessing the achievement of the few CMS missionaries in Sierra Leone during the first half of the nineteenth century, one must take into account the dreadful mortality rate. Knowledge of this did not help in recruiting replacements, but surprisingly, new recruits continued to appear. And when not many ordained men in Britain offered themselves as missionaries, the Anglican Church Missionary Society turned to German Lutherans. This was the time of interdenominational co-operation prior to the Anglo-Catholic movement. In many cases the pastors proved to be excellent men, and sturdy too. Three of the first German missionaries in CMS employ served respectively nineteen, seventeen, and eleven years.

William Johnson, the missionary who defied Governor MacCarthy, had come from Hanover to London when he heard of the need in Sierra Leone, and volunteered. In Sierra Leone he found that he needed all his qualities of enterprise and imagination when faced with the growing number of destitute liberated Africans. And the flock of Africans came to believe that the young German had special powers – his word seemed to influence people physically. On one occasion so-called backsliders, rebuked by him, 'were temporarily paralysed and had to be carried out of church'.[17] Describing himself as 'a bird in a cage', Johnson was anxious to reach out beyond the colony to what he called 'the interior of Africa'. In 1819 he went with an African co-worker, William Tamba, into remote parts of the Sierra Leone hinterland. Johnson gave seven years of service before he, too, succumbed to the climate.

Some of the early German missionaries – Renner, Nyländer, Wenzel – married returnee immigrants from Nova Scotia, and this strengthened their contacts with the settler community. When Renner was posted to Freetown, the villagers wanted his wife to stay behind to look after them. But all were not content. It soon became clear in Sierra Leone that the social differences between settlers and liberated Africans were increasing. In the Rawson Methodist Church, a settler preacher could speak from the 'Big Pulpit', but a liberated African only from the reading desk. None of the latter was ordained by the Nova Scotian evangelist, Joseph Jewett. He was all for winning the liberated Africans, but thought that once won, they should be kept at arm's length.

Anthony O'Connor, a leading liberated African, noted his religious and even mystic feelings in a journal. He had come from Dahomey in December 1811, and his conversion fitted the Wesleyan pattern of a sudden change. A deeply respected leader, O'Connor and his flock felt slighted by Jewett and his settler congregation, and in 1844 Jewett saw almost all his liberated African members leave, some 2,000, with forty-three preachers. O'Connor formed these into a new Church, the West African Wesleyan Society, which had the triumph of building a large stone church holding 800 people.[18]

Under similar pressures, liberated Africans in the Countess of Huntingdon's Connection – another Methodist group – left their Church and formed the Spa Fields, or 'Free Grace' Church. The Baptists had similar problems; their dynamic leaders among the settlers, David George and Hector Peters, could not hold the liberated Africans. These liberated groups were mainly Igbo, led by an Igbo preacher, William Jenkins. Even in a foreign land, these people were enterprising, and soon became prosperous traders. The Church they founded, the Igbo Baptist Church, was 'the only Sierra Leone Church to bear a recaptive national name'. Most of these new Churches also started their own schools.[19]

The development of educational facilities was particularly important. In the beginning, especially from 1815–27, there was close co-operation between CMS and the government. After that, the missionary societies had to develop their private institutions. By 1840 there were eighteen CMS elementary schools, and fourteen Methodist. In 1845 the CMS founded a grammar school for boys, and in 1849 a similar one for girls. The headmaster of the grammar school was an English missionary, and the parents demanded that the curriculum should be as close as possible to the English ideal. It included Mathematics, Greek, Biblical and English history, Geography, Music, and Latin.[20]

Even a grammar school was not enough. At an early date the missions began to provide for the training of teachers and pastors, since the supply of European missionary staff would be insufficient for the expanding Churches. The CMS had started a 'Christian Institution' in 1816, and in 1827 this was reconstituted as Fourah Bay College. For at least half a century this was the centre of higher learning for the whole of the West Coast, especially for the emerging Nigerian elite. Initially the staff consisted of hard-working missionaries, the best known at this time being Sigismund Koelle, a German in CMS employ. He taught Greek, Hebrew, and Arabic, and is specifically remembered for his massive *Polyglotta Africana* (1854). It included vocabularies and linguistic specimens from 200 African languages and dialects, which he had recorded from liberated Africans in Sierra Leone. The areas represented ranged from Senegal to Mozambique! In 1876 Fourah Bay was affiliated with the University of Durham, England, for the purpose of academic degrees. The Methodists founded their own 'Educational and Theological Institution', known as the 'King Tom Institution'.

Liberated Africans and the return to Nigeria

In the new country, the innate African propensity for community and fellowship found new expressions. The people formed companies founded on the basis of common origin and fate. A 'Big Company' comprised those who had been landed from the same ship; a 'Little Company' consisted of those who came from the same area and spoke the same language – Yoruba, Nupe, Kongo, etc. The companies were ordered in ranks with a King, a Queen, Governor, Judge, and so on. They acted, among other functions, as mutual help and burial societies. Some were able to start savings groups by pooling resources to buy a house, or to buy at auction one of the impounded slave ships mentioned previously.

To these liberated Africans, Sierra Leone was not the end. They were looking beyond its borders. William Davis and William Tamba – who had explored with William Johnson – sailed with J. B. Cates, a British teacher, along the coast as far as Ghana.[21]

In 1837 two Hausa, emancipated in Trinidad, arrived in Freetown on their way home via the port of Badagry. These enterprising liberated Africans soon established a 'passenger service' for 'emigrants', from Fourah Bay along the coast to Badagry. The fare was twelve dollars, but the passenger had to provide his own food. From Badagry the passengers walked inland to Abeokuta. Numbers are hard to verify, but one estimate is that in three years more than 500 people thus found their way back into Yorubaland and even further inland.[22]

In 1839 a group of twenty-three Yoruba traders in Freetown, led by Thomas Will, handed a petition to the Governor, asking that Queen Victoria should establish a colony at Badagry and send missionaries and returning liberated Africans to preach the gospel and abolish the slave trade.[23] These men asking for help saw the vision, but they were too much a part of the Freetown establishment to go themselves. There were others, however, less entrenched in the life of Freetown, who slipped away. Early in 1840 two groups, of fourteen and twenty, left to make their way home.

Egba emigrants, European traders, and missionaries all used Badagry as a stepping stone into the interior. 'Badagry became the first mission station in Nigeria.'[24] Others followed the example of the early emigrants. Within a few years hundreds returned to the very areas from whence they had once been taken as slaves. They were prosperous traders, anxious to share their Christian faith with long-lost relatives and other members of their own ethnic communities. Muslims also returned, just as anxious as the Christians to establish their own communities in Lagos, Badagry, and further inland.

Freetown

Tensions between settlers and liberated Africans were an unfortunate handicap to the life of the Sierra Leone Churches in the first part of the nineteenth century. However, as the economic and educational status of the liberated Africans in Freetown rose, the two communities became increasingly assimilated. Together, they formed a group known in the 1870s as 'the Krio' or 'the Creole', meaning 'Settlers and Liberated Africans and their descendants'.[25] With their schools and their Churches, and their sometimes successful trade, these Krios developed a unique culture in Freetown and the Colony. The sociological role of their Creole language, 'Krio' must be underlined. Its origins are debatable, but scholars agree that it has basic Portuguese structures, and that Jamaican Creole was brought into Sierra Leone with the Maroons around 1800. Whatever its historical roots, the language has played a fundamental role in moulding together groups of great initial linguistic diversity; it has replaced fear and hostility with a sense of common identity and unity. This 'in-feeling' of the Krio-speakers at the centre, also accentuated their distance from the 'outsiders' in the periphery, in this case the inland communities and their African languages.[26] There emerged new tensions, this time between the Krios and the 'Natives' in the interior of the Protectorate. In the 1890s, these tensions exploded into a tragic conflict, in connection with the Hut Tax War. Several missionaries and many Krios, including pastors, were killed by the Temne and the Mende.

Freetown was commonly referred to as 'a city of churches and mosques', or 'a Christian city'. Nothing could be more uplifting than an Anglican service in St George's Cathedral, or in any of its other nine Anglican churches. They were all strictly bound to the order of the Common Prayer Book and its psalms and hymns. Sankey's songs and the Methodist order of worship used the same respectful tone in any of the twenty Wesleyan buildings, such as the Wesley Chapel on Trelawney Street, or the Buxton Memorial Chapel on Charles Street. In both of these leading churches, the congregation was dressed in the latest fashions: the ladies arrived in crinoline and high-heeled boots (their sisters in Monrovia insisted on wearing long white gloves for Sunday morning service); the gentlemen came in their Sunday best, often straight from London's West End tailors. Canon Beaver outdid them all by wearing a top hat – he had ten of them. Christian worship had acquired all the forms and norms of Evangelical orderliness.

The services outside the chapel walls lent themselves to greater freedom and to lively creativity. Young James Johnson, an Anglican, had a brilliant career before him, later becoming bishop in Nigeria. The young priest could not understand why Christian worship in West Africa should have to be bound by rules and disciplines from a far-off country. He fretted at the bonds and bridles of European services. In 1872 he wrote to the Governor of the colony:

> we see around us nothing that we can call our own in the true sense of the term; nothing that shows an independent native capability – excepting this infant Native Pastorate institution ... Whilst we value our connexion with England and use the services of valuable European Bishops, I say that the use of the services of a native prelate and our own Liturgy and Canons is a mere question of time.[27]

The Methodists had their 'love feasts' and 'band feasts', where the women moved as if dancing. As they jogged along with abandon, they invented extemporaneous hymns and 'shouts'. In the streets, the self-styled Preacher 'Anger' Coker presented his messages, introduced or concluded by the personalized song 'Brother Coker go to Heaven, Allelu-Alleluia'. Weddings and burials were grand occasions for display and for honourable competition. For the well-to-do there were wedding dresses from London and hearses 'with rich plumes' when families could afford them.

One of the many prominent Methodist citizens in the Colony was the well-known barrister, Sir Samuel Lewis. This successful layman steered the course of the Wesleyan congregations with great authority. In Church matters, he made use of the stern manners of the Pastor, Benjamin Tregaskis, an Englishman with long experience from the West Indies. Tregaskis had found that things went well only if he was allowed to decide. His interpretation of the Old Testament was coloured by his own attitudes: 'Noah escaped drowning by having the building of the ark entirely in his own hands.'[28] The Wesleyan congregations included some of the 'upper crust' of the educated elite found along the whole West African coast. These and other Churches served as community centres for public gatherings, where the Church life set the tone, with its tea-meetings, missionary appeals, and the laying of foundation stones. With their built-in Wesleyan 'class' system, the Freetown congregations served as training grounds for leadership, democratic procedures and legal skills.

'Far more than England, Sierra Leone was a "nation of shopkeepers".'[29] Christian traders were actively involved in Church affairs. They would also compete in the pious games of testing their Bible knowledge, a 'sport' also enjoyed by their Ghanaian colleagues at Cape Coast or Akropong.[30]

A determined step in the Henry Venn tradition had been taken by the Anglicans in 1861 with the creation of a 'Native Pastorate Church' which included certain local parishes near Freetown. Financially it was still supported by grants from both the CMS and the colonial government. New parishes were added, but in 1876 the Church lost its privileged position when the government withdrew its grant. The bishop, however, was still appointed by the Crown, with his salary paid by the colony. When an ordinance was passed allowing the Native Pastorate Church to hold property, the other Churches reacted with alarm. They did not understand that the ordinance was designed to weaken the privileged 'state-church' relationship of the Anglican Church, not strengthen it. This incident emphasized the precarious position of the Anglican Church in any colony. Any 'Establishment' pretensions could no longer be upheld, however regularly Governor Cardew read the lesson in St George's Cathedral, or however frequently the Anglicans referred to themselves as the 'Queen's Church'. Strong countervailing forces were at work, some of them centred in Methodist laymen, led by Sir Samuel Lewis.

The Anglicans had other worries, similar to the problems Wesleyans experienced with their rule of a five-year rotation for pastors' appointments. In 1887, Bishop Ingham and his Church Council declared that he had the power to move priests from one parish to another, although he was willing to use a longer limit of twenty years in the same parish. He advised the Revd Moses Taylor to move from the Waterloo parish where he had served for full twenty years. When Moses Taylor was unwilling to comply, the Bishop withdrew the priest's licence. Taylor suspected what had prompted these extraordinary measures. Bishop Ingham had introduced all kinds of new ideas: a Church constitution, a Church Council, reliance on lay treasurers, and the vote of mere laymen in affairs of Holy Church. Taylor claimed that the Bishop was nothing but a 'laymen's bishop' who sided with an opposition group in the Waterloo congregation, trying to get rid of a faithful pastor. The priest then took legal advice from the Methodist Freetown barrister, Sir Samuel Lewis, and appealed to the Archbishop of Canterbury under the Letters Patent of 1852, which had constituted the Bishopric. Eventually a reply from Canterbury's legal advisors suggested that the priest was in his full right to appeal. To avoid a lawsuit, the Bishop restored the licence.

Maintaining order in the Church did not end there. To enforce discipline, in 1890 Bishop Ingham drew up a revised series of Articles of Agreement, and asked his clergy to sign. Moses Taylor again refused. This time his hand was strengthened by four equally stubborn colleagues, including the Revd G. J. Macaulay of the Kissy parish. He was a dreaded controversialist, who often wrote fiery letters to the press. A split emerged, between a 'Bishop's party' and the 'Five Pastors' party'. The struggle was not settled until 1897, when the Diocese received a new bishop, Taylor Smith. There was fighting between the two groups, with some local poets even producing songs for the street:

> 'Macaulay go go
> Let us watch and pray
> And labour till the Bishop come.'[31]

No doubt one of the main causes of opposition to the Bishop, in this case, was that he was a European. The Krios had already proved that they could manage their own Church affairs when allowed to do so. Bishop Crowther, the most noble product of the Sierra Leone Church, had been bishop for twenty-five years on the Niger. In Sierra Leone, however, the Anglican bishops were White all through the nineteenth century and up until 1944. The 'Five Pastors' and others were strongly aware that Freetown had produced its own generations of self-reliant Krio clergy and laymen. The disturbances in the Freetown Churches at this time were undoubtedly the result of tensions felt in the Krio community, and an expression of the uncertainty as to the position of Krios in Church and State.

Other issues also led to controversies. At the Anglican Church Conference in 1888, T. J. Sawyerr, the bookseller, went so far as to suggest that the Church would be better rooted in African soil if it modified its rule of monogamy for converts. The debate that followed showed that the problem was not a purely theoretical one. One speaker said rather pointedly that change of the rule would 'make us all honest men'.[32] But Church authorities did not countenance such appeals, and Sawyerr was forced to resign from his position on the Church Finance Committee.

Very few places in Africa at this time have provided as rewarding material as Freetown for a study of religious organization as a basis for the process of social stratification. Education was indispensable in this process, and the Churches were the only agency capable of furnishing that tool.

> The CMS had a core membership of rising citizens. So the Anglican Church grew in wealth and importance. In it the social climber was also able to make the necessary contacts, while his membership of it in turn enhanced his own social position.[33]

Members of educated and prosperous Krio prestige groups were the ones appointed to available senior Government posts during the 1870s and 1880s. They received strong backing from the Anglican and Methodist Churches. They had outdone their competitors and reached the highest jobs available in this stratified society. It was indeed the period of Krio domination in Sierra Leone society.

At the end of the nineteenth century a marked change took place. With more effective medical remedies, and better living conditions, more European civil servants were posted to the West Coast. Another factor threatened the dominant position of the Krio community in Sierra Leone and Lagos. Racist anti-Krio propaganda by Sir Richard Burton exercised its influence in government circles on the West Coast. It was also, strangely, supported by the teaching of Edward Blyden, a West Indian and a great Pan-Negro patriot. He served Liberia and Sierra Leone as educator and publicist, but his concern for what he called the 'Pure Negro' was only matched by his aversion to mulattos and Krios. His criticism strengthened the hand of Governor Cardew in Freetown, whose appointments policy turned against the educated Krios. While in 1892 the Krios had eighteen out of forty senior government posts, by the time the number of posts had risen to ninety-two, the Krios held only fifteen, five of which were soon abolished.[34]

This adverse change formed a background to Church developments along the Coast, particularly in Bishop Crowther's Niger Diocese. From the 1850s the Sierra Leone influence in Southern Nigeria was accelerated by a new economic factor, the forming of the African Steamship Company in 1852, with its sudden 'electric effect' on coastal trade.[35] The number of firms in the West African trade rose from just a few to almost 200 by 1856. This rise resulted in a dramatic increase of Sierra Leone mission activity in Nigerian evangelization. Macgregor Laird, the Director of the new company, was convinced of the importance of African participation in trade, development, and evangelization. As a faithful Evangelical layman, he maintained personal contacts with the CMS during the few years at his disposal. He promoted Christian Krio participation in his own enterprise, and promptly brought Sierra Leone preachers to Nigeria aboard his ships.

Figures quoted by Dr P. E. H. Hair suggest the extent of this outreach. Between 1843 and 1899, the CMS in West Africa was served by 112 'native clergy', of whom at least 100 were born in West Africa, with seventy of those from Sierra Leone. After 1870 some of these African clergy were born in Yorubaland. Fifty per cent of the 112 had been trained at Fourah Bay College, and eleven of them had received academic degrees. Many of the others, including some of Bishop Crowther's clergy on the Niger, had only an elementary education. A large number were employed by the CMS as catechists or teachers. These figures include the CMS efforts. A fair number of the Fourah Bay students became pastors or catechists in other missions. The Sierra Leone pastors also went to other countries: Rio Pongas, Gambia, Dahomey, Fernando Po, and Cameroon. Dr Hair expressed the significant role of the Sierra Leone Church in the general West African setting: 'Thus on an average one Anglican clergyman per annum was produced by a community of never more than 30,000 persons, only a small proportion of which was literate. This is surely a record in Anglican history.'[36]

Women traders and Christianity

In West African history the link between trade and Islam has been well established. Hausa men with their long white flowing gowns and other West African Muslims travelled throughout the region, conspicuous both as traders and for their religious faith. Christianity, on the other hand, has always been linked to the Church congregation and especially to the school. The catechist, paid a stipend by the Christian mission, has been seen as the main proponent of the new faith. While literacy and the school have been thought of as the hallmarks of Christianity in Africa, the role of commerce and business in religion has often been seen as characteristic of Islam in Africa. It comes as a surprise to discover how closely trade and Christianity are linked in West Africa, not by men – as with Islam in the region – but by devoted Christian women. With Church hierarchies of catechists and teachers, pastors and bishops, African women might be thought of as having little chance of being more than faithful, passive, attendees at Christian services. Happily however, the opposite was in fact the case. West African women used their traditions of trade and business to reaffirm and expand their Christian faith.

In many West African societies, unlike those in Eastern Africa, it was women who frequently traded and established businesses, while men were often the farmers. There were, and are, exceptions. Today, one sees many women in the fields, men in the market. Trading has often been an important women's activity, with the market place the centre of communication of ideas and information. The incoming Christian faith during the nineteenth century was also able to profit from the activities of market women. When market women became Christians the Church not only profited in monetary terms, but also gained from a novel approach to evangelization. Christian market women throughout the towns and growing cities of West Africa faithfully used their marketing skills, their mobility and contacts to expand their faith to others. Old traditions were now used for new opportunities of religious expression and identification. Religious innovation was in this case epitomized by these energetic women traders.

It was Krio women, primarily in Sierra Leone, who established the links between the Church and commerce. In the modern history of Christianity in West Africa, Krio society and its contacts along the entire coast stand preeminent in propagating, identifying and experimenting with the Christian message. During the nineteenth century various grandiose and ambitious schemes were tried to expand local commerce by introducing some of the benefits of industrial Europe. Christian missionaries identified with these attempts at developing local industry and commerce. Palm oil, cotton and groundnuts were valuable, and cocoa and coffee became important towards the end of the century. It was at the more modest level of local trade that the unexpected link with Christianity was established.

Krio women traders, firstly in Freetown, then throughout the rest of Sierra Leone and later in most of the cities and towns along the West Coast, expanded their trade and their religion. In the nineteenth century, being a Sierra Leonean was often taken to imply being a trader and a member of one of the two world religions, Christianity and Islam. Most Krios and most of the women traders from the colony were Christian. In Sierra Leone Krio women traders were in the ascendancy during the nineteenth century. By the 1870s Krio society was at the height of its economic power but after 1900 the societies of the protectorate increasingly eclipsed the Krios in terms of political influence, while Lebanese and European companies became dominant economically. Later on, when they could no longer dominate the local commercial world, the Krios reidentified themselves with the professions such as teaching, the law and medicine.

At Freetown on the coast and in the interior, Krio women traders were a bridge between African and Western culture. They organized themselves into trading associations, secret societies and Christian (sometimes Muslim) Churches. For much of the nineteenth century, when these women went up country to trade in the interior, they were in danger, not knowing if their goods might be plundered and they themselves kidnapped. At other times they succeeded in forging good relations with the chiefs and the peoples of the hinterland. Most of these women were Christian and their religious faith was an important part of their identity. In the towns and in the hinterland they were recognizable in their print dresses and their Madras headscarves. More links existed between the Krios and the indigenous population than has currently been thought, and this was in part due to the activities of these women traders. The 'ward system' was a feature of Freetown life, whereby Krio families fostered children from the hinterland communities, taking them into their own homes in the colony and introducing them to Western education and Christianity.

Expanding economic opportunities led to increased economic independence for women. Freetown's Big Market was completed in 1860 and remained a centre for women traders until the 1950s. The Big Market was only for successful traders and there was great competition for the stalls. Every day

> at 6.00 a.m. when the market opened, the women would gather to sing a hymn, hear a psalm and pray together. At the closing of the market those women who remained until 6.00 p.m. prayed together once more ... This display of religious piety demonstrated to all observers the importance of Christianity in the lives of the Big Market traders.[37]

The leader of this religious devotion was the trader Mami Kakabra, also called Mami Pray. She led the Christian fellowship in the market until her death in 1923, and she was also the mother of one of Sierra Leone's best-known Christian pastors, the Revd M. J. C. Cole.

The Big Market was a centre of religious communication and training. The Churches and the mission schools tended to be organized and controlled by men, as pastors, catechists and school teachers. The market gave Christian women the opportunity to complement this more formal side of Christian life by allowing them to develop, as a group, their own sense of religious solidarity. Equally important was the role of the market in providing religious training for the young. Apprentices, the young girls who helped their mothers and aunts, saw devotion to the Church as expressed by the market traders. Faith in Christ appeared an indivisible part of being a successful trader. The profits of these market women were mainly used to educate their children, often at Church schools, and even sometimes to pay for university education abroad in Britain and America.

One of the most prominent women traders was Abigail Jones, who had been brought up by a Methodist missionary family at the 'Female Educational Institution' in Freetown. She served her business apprenticeship under her paternal aunts, inherited the business, and later became so powerful that she could trade with European and American shipping firms. Abigail Jones' business paid for the education of her children as doctors, civil servants and as clergy, and one of her sons, Percy John Jones, became a bishop in the Anglican Church.

Other women traders moved up and down the coast, from Banjul in the Gambia to Calabar in Nigeria, and to be a Christian was an integral part of their identity as they could feel at home in the Churches in other coastal towns. These women were part of a wider West African Christian world. Bure Charlotte Palmer (born 1892), of Yoruba and Igbo descent, was an apprentice trader who married in 1915 and two years later moved to Gambia with her husband. She started trading in Banjul (then called Bathurst) and joined the local Church there, while developing commercial links between Gambia and Sierra Leone. On the death of her husband in 1935 she returned to Freetown and resumed her participation at the Buxton Memorial Chapel (founded 1854) in the city. By 1937 her business was no longer profitable as Lebanese and European firms were squeezing out the Krio women. She then lived on teaching sewing and other classes at the Buxton Memorial School until she retired, renowned for her Christian piety and an honoured member of the Methodist Church.

LIBERIA

Thirty years after Sierra Leone received its Black settlers from America, Liberia also welcomed emigrants from the States. There were early contacts between missions in the two African countries; initially American Episcopalians received the help of Black interpreters from the CMS missionaries in Sierra Leone. After some pioneering efforts in the 1820s, various groups of Black settlers arrived, and in 1838 the total population of American origin approached 2,300. The situation into which they came was similar to that of the Sierra Leone settlers, except that local African attitudes were definitely more hostile. There was also a marked tension between the coastal peoples and those living further inland. The former were determined that any benefit which the missions might bring should remain at the coast.

The American missionary societies which managed to survive the difficulties of the climate and establish themselves on the coast included the American Episcopal Church, the Presbyterians and the African Episcopal Zion Methodist. All of these began organized work in the 1830s. A medical doctor with the Protestant Episcopalians, Thomas Savage, showed how children could be approached with the Gospel when adults were difficult to reach.

In 1847 the Republic of Liberia was founded, an event important also for the Churches. The Afro-American settlers in Monrovia, the capital, maintained a belief in their special role as citizens of West Africa's only free country, 'Liberia'. They saw themselves as representing civilization: 'we, the civilized' against the benighted 'natives', unspecified numbers of 'tribal' communities along the coast and in the as yet unmapped interior. Yet it was among these coast 'natives' that an interesting advance took place among the Kru, the closely related Grebo, and the Bassa.

The catalytic factor for this development was the American Protestant Episcopal Church, with its remarkable list of bishops: John Payne, 1851–71; followed by J. G. Auer, a former German (Basel) missionary from Ghana; and S. D. Ferguson, the first Black bishop in this Church, 1884–1914. In Ferguson's time, the mission centres multiplied to over a hundred. The number of priests grew from ten to twenty-six, and schools from nine to twenty-five. By 1914 the Church claimed 11,000 members. Payne and Auer laid the foundations for a substantial literature in the Grebo language. Auer's hymn-book and other literary achievements helped to strengthen the solidarity of the Grebo community. A young Grebo nationalist, confirmed by Bishop Ferguson, received considerable inspiration from those writings. He was William Wade Harris, who emerged in 1910 as the incomparable 'prophet' on the West Coast.

Related to the Grebo were the Kru, renowned fisherman and seamen. They were accustomed to contacts with foreigners, speaking their own brand of English – 'a highly conservative form of English-derived pidgin'.[38] Mary Kingsley met some Kru who exclaimed 'Help us, we are Englishmen'. An unusual 'peoples' movement' among the Kru took the form of collective Christianization of whole families and total villages. This movement stopped as suddenly and as inexplicably as it began.[39]

A vigorous illustration of Western power was provided by the Liberian incumbency of Bishop William Taylor. He was 'the Bishop of Africa', whose enormous efforts also in Angola and South Africa will be recorded later. Taylor gave twelve boisterous years to Liberia, 1884–96. He took with him twenty-three Black pastors and women teachers from the Southern United States and founded twenty new mission stations as well as several boarding schools in various ethnic communities. 'Self-support' was his missionary principle, apparent perhaps more in the Bishop's manifestos than in any corresponding grassroots practice. His successor, Bishop Hartzell, found that most of these ambitious beginnings had not, in fact, been successful. On the other hand, Hartzell succeded in making substantial contributions to higher education in Liberia, including the College of West Africa in Monrovia.

IVORY COAST

The first attempt at a Catholic mission on the Ivory Coast had been abortive, and hardly conducive to a repetition. In 1895, the French Governor Binger took the initiative of addressing a letter to Planque in Lyon, inviting the mission to the Ivory Coast. He promised that the administration would assist them in every way. The Mission did not hesitate and undertook an enormous effort of recruitment. By 1900, 200 missionaries had already been sent out.

At first the activities were concentrated on practical tasks. The French administrator at Grand Bassam summed up what he saw by repeating in his annual reports the handy phrase: 'The Fathers are making bricks'. But even a mighty French administrator 'knoweth only in part'. They were, of course, accomplishing much more. The new buildings attracted increasing numbers of young catechumens, tended by young French missionary Fathers. Many of these Fathers died in the yellow fever epidemics of 1899, and 1902–03.

Contacts between Governor Binger and the mission were at first so satisfactory that the mission appeared as 'a kind of ectoplasm of the administration'.[40] However, this happy co-operation could not last. In 1905 pressure from the anti-clerical Metropolis led to a crisis.

Mission and administration had a common problem: how to counteract the nefarious influence of the 'fetishes' on the coast. The Catholic missionaries were hesitant on the subject, not wanting to be regarded as destroyers of African culture. But Governor Angoulvant felt that he had had enough, and in 1912 he decided that he had to take a firm stand. 'The fetishes are the greatest obstacle to our political action.' But how to counteract this influence? The White missionaries and administrators studied, debated and planned. This was obviously one of those strange African secrets which could not be opened with Western instruments. However, in 1913 a total stranger, an African wanderer in a white garment with a six-foot-long bamboo cross, passed the Cavalla River from Liberia into the Ivory Coast. He was William Wade Harris, the great Grebo prophet. He had had a revelation from God, and he knew what to do with fetishes.

The Prophet Harris

In one of his visions, the prophet William Wade Harris of Liberia (*c.*1865–1929), contemplated how Christ had sent prophets to the four corners of the world. He was not sure of their number – was it nine, ten or twelve? – but about the number of prophets for Africa he felt assured. They were four and he, Harris, was the greatest among them. Among the African prophets, Harris was the traveller, the restless itinerant explorer. Travel was in his blood; he referred to himself as a 'Kru-boy'. As a 'Kru-boy' he had to be prepared at any time to join whatever ship happened to pass by and set off along the coast wherever the vessel took him. Harris tells us that as a young man he went twice to Lagos and twice as far as Gabon.

The 'Trance-Visitation' of 1910, when the Archangel Gabriel visited Harris, was the decisive event in his life, but he did not receive it unprepared. Before that, he had had long periods of Christian experience. Between the ages of twelve and eighteen, he was a foster child in the home of a Grebo Methodist pastor, his maternal uncle. During these years he received his basic education – he learned to read and write both Grebo and English. (In 1915 an Irish Catholic missionary met him and referred to his 'perfect English'.) In that home he met people who revered the Bible, read it and knew it. Here he was also baptized, Christianized and converted. Here he began to preach.

In 1888, at the age of twenty-three, he was confirmed by the bishop of the Episcopal Church in Liberia. His involvement between 1888 and 1909 widened his horizon theologically, ideologically and politically. Theologically, the Episcopal Church made him a school teacher and Bible teacher from 1892 until 1908. Ideologically, in this period he came into contact with ideas of the complicated and sometimes obscure nationalist E. W. Blyden, and with the American millennialist, Charles T. Russell's 'Watch-tower' message. Politically, as a Grebo, he was intensely aware of his community's opposition to the African-American settlers in Monrovia, who had become the ruling power in the land. He became increasingly involved in a rebellion against the Liberian state, levelling sharp criticism at the Black colonists and their inability to govern the country.

While the Black American settlers were concerned with Monrovia, the capital, most of the White American missionaries worked among the Grebo population. Two outstanding nineteenth-century Protestant missionaries, John Leighton Wilson and Bishop John G. Auer (a Swiss) had given remarkable service to the Grebo, also sharing critical views of the African-American settlers' treatment of the Grebo. Harris took the lead in a Grebo rising against the Republic of Liberia and was thrown into jail. Here he had a visit from a distinguished nightly guest, the Archangel Gabriel. We quote from Dr Shank's account of this unique event in the jail:

> Sometime before June of 1910, Harris the fetisher was awakened at night and in bed – during a trance – was called by God (of the Bible) through the visitation of the Archangel Gabriel who appeared to him spiritually as a man – strange visitant – in a great wave of light . . . He was told that he was in heaven, and that God was going to anoint him prophet, like Daniel . . . He was to give up Western style clothing and shoes; a white toga-like dress, 'shown to him by God' replaced his other clothes . . . The three-fold visitation

> concluded with a triune anointing by God: he was tapped three times on the head and the spirit descended upon his head, feeling and sounding like a jet of water ... He was given a promise of great power, in contrast to the powerlessness of the fetishes.[41]

He was thus called to be a prophet and that was how he from now introduced himself: 'I am a prophet. I am Harris, Harris, the Prophet of God'. But there was no place for him in his own country. So Harris turned abroad and crossed the frontier into the French colony of the Ivory Coast in 1913.

In seventeen months the Black prophet in his white garb, his Bible and his cross reached out to 200,000 people in the Ivory Coast and Ghana. His converts during this time numbered about 100,000. With his booming voice he proclaimed his message. 'He was a born orator, speaking in an abrupt and harsh language.' He began with the fundamentals: 'God is all powerful, so you must burn your fetishes and love one another. Bring me your idols so that I can burn them in the fire. Thereupon I am going to baptize you.' With these few words he apparently gave the solution to the ever-recurrent problem of witches and fetisheers and swept away traditional spirits. When asked what would happen to the sick and how they could make medicine, he answered now, using pidgin English: 'If you believe God, all by nutting, everything be fit do you.'[42]

His teaching included strict observance of the Sabbath and prohibition of adultery while regarding polygamy as an institution needing reform rather than abolition. The message was sharp as a sword: Just as the fetisheers had ruled by terror, the new God could bring death or illness to those who disobeyed him. And that will come by fire. Fire from heaven will descend on you, was a constant theme.[43]

Then there was time for baptism. He carried about with him a little bowl or white dish with water, prayed over the water and baptized with the sign of the cross, in the name of the Father and the Son and the Holy Spirit. With all those masses pressing on for the sacrament, he could sometimes resort to the use of a sudden downpour from heaven and bless them all in the name of the Triune God. That book which he carried had all the answers. He preferred to quote from the New Testament, especially its apocalyptic passages but he was also very much at home with the Old Testament, particularly Daniel and Ezekiel as well as Exodus (on 'the prophet Moses'). In his hands that big volume, in English, became a living book with a compelling message about Jesus Christ.

About himself in relation to Christ he said: 'I am the watchman' (Ezek. 33) 'the last prophet. I am Elijah. I will judge and have a throne. I am the carpet on which Christ wipes his feet', and he referred to himself as the 'Carrier of Christ, the horse of Christ'. Along with the Bible he was also known to carry Bunyan's *Pilgrim's Progress*, that eternal companion of Anglo-Saxon spirituality, written by another, yet earlier, prison graduate.[44]

But he had to press on and move to the next town or major village where already people were waiting in keen anticipation for the prophet's appearance. So he placed twelve 'apostles' in each congregation to represent him. Often these were clerks from European merchant firms. Some of these clerks 'had a decisive influence on the movement which developed out of Harris's visit'.[45] In Ebonou, one such clerk was 'Jaques Boga Sako, who interpreted for the Prophets, became a mainstay of the church as it developed there', writing a fascinating account of the impression that Harris made.[46]

The year was 1914, and Africa was lit up by the apocalyptic flames of a world war. Early in 1915 the French colonial administration – nervous about that vast and possibly uncontrollable movement in the population called forth by the prophet Harris – promptly expelled him from the Ivory Coast. He returned to his own country Liberia where he stayed until his death in 1929.

To the utterly weak Western missions in the Ivory Coast at the time, the Harris movement had come as a complete surprise. To the Roman Catholic missionaries Harris was no more than a misled Protestant, but they soon became aware that their Church had grown dramatically, undoubtedly because of Harris. The numbers had risen from 400 in 1914, to 2,000 in 1917, and baptisms from about eighty annually to 6,700 in 1915 and in subsequent years.

Between 1923–24 the British Methodists set out from their mission centres in Ghana and, to some extent, in Benin (Dahomey), to establish contacts with Fante Methodists working in the Ivory Coast. The mission representative, Revd William J. Platt, found, to his surprise and delight, thousands of Harris Christians all claiming to be good Methodists as Harris himself had supposedly been. Never before nor after did an African missionary face such a challenging task as the one provided by the Harris mass movement. Contacts were now made with the prophet himself in Liberia. In a message to the congregations in the Ivory Coast, Harris declared:

> All the men, women and children who were called and baptised by me must enter the Wesleyan Methodist Church ... No one must enter [join] the Roman Catholic Church if he wishes to be faithful to me. Mr Platt, the Director of our Methodist Church, is appointed by me as my successor to the Head of the churches which I founded.[47]

The situation thus seemed immensely promising – but it had its problems. The gifted young foreign missionary following his Western rules and regulations attempted to enforce monogamy and to introduce a system of self-support, tithing through so-called 'tickets'. These were new and obviously European ideas. In 1928 an opposition group, under the leadership of John Ahui – the chief's son and leader of the Church choir – resolutely went to consult the prophet himself in Liberia. They returned with what they referred to as 'the last will and testament' of the Prophet, signed by Harris, to the effect that 'we do no pay anything for our religion. Here in Liberia we receive baptism and confirmation free', and there was a sufficiently large-hearted formula on family matters: 'If you marry two women, that is awkward, but do it if you cannot do otherwise ... If you can marry ten women, do it, but follow the rules of God.'

Here were elements of a conflict between two contending parties. Only the wisdom of a Solomon could possibly solve it. Dr Sheila Walker provided this wisdom in her summing up of 'the Prophet's true intentions':

> The two mandates actually delegated to each man the task for which he was most suited. Harris's own experience had already proven that an African could convince Africans to make a radical religious change more easily than a foreign missionary could ever hope to do. The missionaries, however, were better prepared to teach the contents of the Bible'.[48]

GHANA

Today nearly half of Ghana's people, in the central and southern regions of the country, are Akan. In the nineteenth century, despite sharing a common language and many cultural features, constant rivalries hindered unity. Two of the most powerful sections of the Akan were the Asante in the inland forest area and on the coast the Fante, who had contacted European merchants and soldiers as early as the sixteenth century. Another strong group were the Ewe in the eastern part. The Ga, less than 10 per cent of the population, probably came from farther east. They founded a series of small townships along the coast, including Accra.

The Ga and the Ewe were patrilineal; the Fante, Asante and other Akan peoples were matrilineal. In the development of the various Churches in the nineteenth century, these differing social structures became influential. Hostility extended between the small kingdoms and chiefdoms of Akan, with the growth of the Asante a special threat. In 1824 they defeated the British, but years later they were themselves defeated by a coalition of some Fante and the British. The Fante were much involved in trade as middlemen, and so were more accessible to the early efforts of missionaries. This created more peaceful conditions, allowing the entry of outsiders coming, in this case not for trade, but for the Gospel.

Trade routes and evangelists

Throughout the southern part of what is now Ghana, there was a complex system of 'great roads' connecting Asante with the coast, four southern and four northern. These 'channels for the flow of trade' and 'for the flow of authority'[49] also became channels for the Gospel. Cape Coast was an early trading centre. In 1760 there were no less than twenty-six trading settlements along the Ghanaian coastline. Up until 1807 the chief commodity had been gold and to some extent slaves. Abolition meant that other goods had to be found, and trade in ivory, cotton, indigo, palm oil and timber developed. The British Company of Merchants, under their governor who lived in the British fort at Cape Coast, aimed at encouraging trade.

At the forts and trading posts there were often chaplains who conducted services and ran schools. Mulattoes and Africans, as well as Western employees, attended the services. At least some of these were baptized. One of the first chaplains was Thomas Thompson, 1751–56, sent by the Society for the Propagation of the Gospel. An educated and widely travelled man, he sent four African students to England, hoping to train future leaders. Among them was Philip Quaque, who spent ten years in England, 1756–66. He worked as a schoolmaster and pastor at Cape Coast till his death in 1816. Others also studied abroad and returned to the chaplaincies: J. Capitein, an African ex-slave trained in Holland, working in the 1740s for the Dutch Reformed Church at Elmina; F. P. Swane, a mulatto with a Ga mother, trained in Copenhagen, becoming catechist and teacher at Christiansborg in the 1740s; and Christian Protten, another mulatto, working with the Moravians first in the West Indies and then at Christiansborg, 1756–69. In 1788 about fifty mulatto and African children from the Windward and Gold Coasts were attending schools in Liverpool.

Some of the young mulattoes and Africans were educated in the school started by Philip Quaque at Cape Coast, which continued after his death under the patronage of the British governor in Freetown, Sir Charles MacCarthy. In the 1820s some of the students at Cape Coast formed a 'Bible Band', which later became the foundation of the Ghana Methodist Church. By 1830 their leader was an African former student, Joseph Smith.[50]

A second group emerged under the leadership of William De Graft, another African. The differences of opinion between the two groups stimulated their search for truth. Although without the leadership of a clergyman for much of the time, they were encouraged first by MacCarthy and then by George Maclean, the governor representing the Council of Merchants. He exemplified the common concern of missions and government at that time: 'mission and government alike stressed the evangelical purpose of the schools.'[51] He arranged for the Society for Promoting Christian Knowledge (SPCK) to give the Bible-devotees Bibles, New Testaments, psalters, and prayer books, all in English. Francis Bartels has described something of the life of the group. On Sundays they would come together in one of their homes often before sunrise. They read Psalms and prayers from the Book of Common Prayer.

> A portion of scripture was then read by the most competent person present and explained in the Fante language, after which they concluded their service by singing part of another psalm and used another prayer from the liturgy. At 11 a.m. they attended divine service in the [Cape Coast] Castle, and at 3 p.m. they again had a service conducted in the same manner as that held early in the morning. During the week a school was held every morning at seven o'clock.[52]

On New Year's Day 1835, a Methodist missionary, J. R. Dunwell, arrived and was welcomed by the Bible Band of thirteen young men. As he preached, he became aware that this was the first sermon they had ever heard.[53] More accurately, it was the first *European* service they had listened to, for they had been preaching the Word to one another for many years. With this long period of preparation events moved fast. After only three months fifty people had received Methodist membership cards, and were meeting for baptismal instruction, for services, and for *agape* feasts. But Dunwell died only six months after his arrival.

His successor, G. Wrigley, died after one year. But the members of the Bible Band continued the work. Some of them, as Fante traders, were already carrying the Gospel further afield to the markets and camping places along the trade routes inland – Christian equivalents of the Hausa traders who carried the Muslim message. A new venture by the missionaries was a school for girls, taught by an African schoolmistress, Elizabeth Waldron. Now girls could also become *sukul-fo* (people of the school). African leadership emerged naturally from the Methodist group.

There was John Sam, a lively evangelist, and William De Graft, the early leader in the Bible Band who became a pioneer missionary to Nigeria. This was after Thomas Birch Freeman arrived, the first Methodist missionary to survive long enough to consolidate the work. He was son of an African father and an English mother, and trained as a gardener and a botanist.

English-born and speaking only English, he came to the coast in 1838. He found Christians in small groups all along the coastal settlements, and soon built up the work. Not learning Fante, he always used an interpreter. He soon contacted chiefs and kings, visiting the redoubtable King of Asante in 1839 and again in 1841. On his way to Asante, he spent some time with the Chief at Fomena, where he used the leaf of a banyan tree to introduce to the chief and his leading men the concept of God as creator. In Fomena he found some of the Fante traders, who acted as a choir when he spoke. He recorded the reaction of the crowd:

> The deepest attention was paid to the great and awful truths ... every minute almost did they utter a hearty *Eou* – 'Yes' – by way of giving their assent ... Corintchie [Chief of Fomena] and his Captains said it was a 'good palaver' ... they said they should like to hear more of them; and especially what *Yancumpon* – God – liked and what He disliked.[54]

At King Kwaku Dua's court in Kumasi, Freeman was faced with the problems of slavery and human sacrifice and challenged the king about these matters. He also used diplomatic tactics in his contacts with the king. After a visit to England in 1841–42, he brought back a sensational gift – an English carriage. Getting it to the coast by ship was one thing, but it took 340 men to get it through the forest to Kumasi. The king graciously accepted it, sending in return a gold pipe for the members of the Methodist Missionary Committee in London. In 1844 human sacrifice was made illegal in the south of Ghana. But it was only after the defeat of the Asante in 1874 and the annexation of their territory in 1896 that this practice could be stamped out there.

Practical aspects of the new education soon appeared with the teaching and use of carpentry and bricklaying. First used in building chapels, such skills were soon copied for private houses, as a prosperous and educated Fante elite began to emerge. They used English, adopted Western dress and ways, and were known as 'Cape Coast Scholars'.[55] Freeman also pioneered in agriculture, building a model farm at Beulah, founded in 1850, and at other similar centres throughout Fante country. Seeds were provided for local farmers, and new crops were introduced: coffee, cinnamon, mangoes, ginger, olives, and grapes.

Traditional religion and the first generation Christians

Conflict arose between the traditional community and the new believers over the 'Talking God' at the sacred grove of Mankessim, centre of the Fante territorial cult. Here was found the oracle, Nanaam, where spirits of the ancestors resided. The traditional priests used the oracle to extend their power and it was said that they also used it to spy. A Methodist member Kwaasiar Ate, a hunter, settled near the sacred grove where other new Christians soon joined him. Eventually a junior priest of the cult of Nanaam, Edwumadzi, also joined, and the group felt strong enough to challenge the cult at its centre. Ate shot a deer in the sacred grove, and Edwumadzi cut some wood there. The chief at Mankessim, hitherto friendly to the Christians, had to intervene. He arrived with his people, flogged the Christians and imprisoned them. He burned their newly built houses and destroyed their farms. The case was taken to the British administrator, Cruikshank, who settled the matter with a wisdom worthy of Solomon. The Christians were to pay the king £200 'as compensation for the insults offered to them through their fetish', and the chief was to pay the Christians the value of their property, £56, together with a fine of £40 to the British administration for contempt of law.

However, the result was the extension of the Church. Some of the traditional priests deserted their cult, and the chief himself decided to support the mission. At a baptismal service more than 200 people attended. This was an important breakthrough, and led later to the linking of the Church with Fante nationalism. Such a development had been prepared for during the decades when the new elite had been educated in Methodist schools and had gained personal leadership experience in Methodist classes and councils. The first president of the Fante Confederation was a Methodist layman and businessman, R. J. Ghartey.[56] The Confederation itself, although short-lived, was a precursor of a nationalist movement at Mankessim, the centre of traditional Fante values and culture, but its leaders were mainly Methodist laymen. Ghartey later became King Ghartey IV of Winneba in 1872. Like his colleagues, he acquired his training in public speaking through his participation in the Methodist Church. Another leader who combined religious and political fervour was Dr Africanus Horton, who came to Ghana from Sierra Leone. The African merging of religion and politics parallels the role of the Methodist Church in the political developments of Victorian England.

Fante Methodists

Church services were still held in English, and English hymns were sung in the chapels, but the sermon was translated into Fante. Of special importance were the improvised Fante lyrics sung to Fante tunes. In the Church, an early tendency to emotional revival continued. Frederick France (1824–85), a member of Freeman's first class in Accra, testified: 'In 1846 I received the justifying grace of God. I rejoiced in God my Saviour and felt that all slavish fear was gone and that the blood of Christ had cleansed me from my past sins.'[57] France served in almost every capacity in the Church, and finally became an 'assistant missionary'. In 1856 at a Cape Coast revival 'sobs and prayers were heard in all parts of the chapel', while at Accra men would 'weep tears of adoring gratitude and rejoicing in God, their saviour'.[58]

Another emphasis stemming from English Methodist piety was the introduction of the temperance movement. Ghartey had met this cause when on a visit to England in 1861, and became a radical propagandist for it. Members of his Temperance Society at Anomabo were called *Akonomnsu* (water drinkers), and the Society was almost an alternative Church. With African leadership in political and social spheres, as well as in the strictly religious, the Fante Methodist Church was in effect a people's movement. But in the eyes of Akan traditionalists, Freeman and Africans like Ghartey represented the White Man's world.

The Bible and the plough – the Basel Mission

While the Methodists served in the Fante area, the Basel missionaries went to the Ga and Twi peoples. The differences between the Wesleyan Fante and the Basel Christian communities stand out very clearly. The Fante lived along the coast and its urban centres. They were largely enterprising traders, always ready for a deal and always on the move to inland areas. They used the same resourcefulness in their work with the Church. The Methodist missions in Ghana grew through the evangelistic drive of individuals. Basel-related communities, on the other hand, were based on the land. Their first four missionaries arrived in Christiansborg at the end of 1828; all four had died before the end of 1831. Three more came early in 1832, but two died within months. Only one, Andreas Riis, survived. In 1835 he moved from Accra to Akropong to begin permanent work outside the coastal towns. His move dissociated the mission from the possibly worldly *milieu* of the towns, and built the Church in an agricultural environment. This rural foundation allowed the mission to play a dominant role in raising the standard of agriculture and in introducing new crops. Later, from 1857, the Basel agricultural station at Akropong successfully experimented with cocoa seeds. From these modest beginnings, cocoa was subsequently to underpin the economic revolution that occurred in Ghana during the early twentieth century. The Basel mission insisted on using the vernacular. They dealt also with a patrilineal and somewhat conservative society, where the father's decision – or the grandfather's – was often crucial in deciding whether a young man would go to school.[59]

The Fante Wesleyans had created a people's movement. Often their expatriate staff numbered no more than three. The Swiss-based Basel Mission to the Twi had more Europeans than any other group in Africa at this time.[60] Between 1840 and 1873 some eighty Basel missionaries, including three women, went to the Gold Coast. In many cases they faced the ravages of tropical illness and an early death. Only one man out of nine survived from those sent out by Basel from 1828–39; only Freeman survived of the seven Methodists sent from 1835–39. Incidentally, Freeman always slept under a mosquito net, although he did not relate mosquitoes with malarial fever. The West Coast indeed seemed to be the White Man's grave; the Niger Expedition in 1841 confirmed this.

Missionaries from Jamaica and Basel

As the Basel Mission wrestled with the health problem, it became apparent that it was necessary to recruit African staff. They sent an expedition led by Riis to Jamaica, which enlisted twenty-five men, women, and children – six West Indian families and three bachelors. They were settled at Akropong, but the experiment was not an unqualified success. So during the 1850s, German and Swiss missionaries continued to come. Included in their number were men of outstanding quality: linguists such as Revd Simon Süss and Revd J. G. Christaller for the Twi language, and Revd Johannes Zimmermann for the Ga. They maintained an ambitious primary school system, using the vernacular; taught English and Greek in the middle schools; and continued with these languages, adding Hebrew, in the Seminary. A hard-working people welcomed their uncompromising academic standards, which helped to set similar standards for education in other parts of the country. Though they set the pace in evangelism, the Methodists seemed far behind in education, a lag caused largely by staff shortage. Eventually they too contributed to raising the educational standards. While the Basel syllabus might seem one-sided, it did include practical agricultural training and far-sighted technical and mercantile enterprises. 'The Bible and the plough' was also here the motto of the times – the plough, the axe, and the scythe. Such aids could reach out into the countryside, helping to transform the economy of the people. In 1855, Hermann Rottman laid the foundation of the Basel Mission Trading Company, by far the greatest Protestant trade enterprise in Africa.

Trends in the Christian community

From the Basel Mission reports sent to their headquarters in the 1860s and 1870s, one can discern trends in the Christian communities, showing what kind of people had become believers. By this time the Mission had been in Ghana for more than thirty years. It had a number of boarding schools and a seminary for training catechists at Akropong. In addition to catechists, it had a few ordained African ministers.

What about the members of the Twi establishment? Are there any parallels to the success of Methodism among the Fante elite? Chiefs and elders of Ga and Twi societies found it advantageous to send one or more of their sons to the mission school. Education might be helpful in contacts with representatives of the European powers in the land, or it might be useful for secretarial assistance. Thus a member of the Akropong royal family, Owusu Akyem, sent his son to school, his brother sent two sons. Owusu's son was soon baptized and received the name of David Asante. He was the first of many promising young men sent to Basel for further theological training. After five years abroad he returned in 1862 and was ordained in 1864, the same year that Samuel Ajayi Crowther was consecrated bishop. Even though David Asante was officially accepted as equal to the missionaries, and widely respected, he was not allowed to participate in the missionaries' field conference. His influence was felt in high places, and individuals of rank asked him for baptism. There was still opposition on the part of chiefs who thought that to allow their retainers to become Christian would undermine their whole position. Chief Kwasi Amoako of Kibi said: 'Must I let my horn-blowers, my drummers, my pipers, my sword-bearers and executioners, my hammock-carriers become Christians? If I do, then I can no longer carry out my ceremonies. Whoever has an obligation to serve me will never be allowed to become a Christian.'[61]

Another group of people, not part of the establishment, were attracted to the Christian faith. These were mobile, unattached young men, who had not achieved any position in society and were looking for new openings. Some attended school, and some took up work in the missionaries' homes as well. Most of the converts at Akropong came in this way. Sometimes orphans were sent by relatives to the mission. Despite the appreciation of opportunities that mission education would give them, people were uncertain of baptism and often there was opposition to it.

At Christiansborg, as at Cape Coast among the Methodists, another group produced many Christians: the mulattos. Some of them, educated in the Basel Mission schools, became outstanding teachers and leaders. One such was Carl Reindorf; another was Karl Quist, who knew Greek and Hebrew as well as German and English and, of course, several African languages. Many of the men and women asking for baptism were, or had been, slaves, and felt themselves outcasts on the fringes of society. Becoming a Christian perhaps did not free them, but it gave them assurance of their own worth, and a place in a caring community. One elderly ex-slave died shortly after his baptism. The missionary recorded his words before death: 'In case the Lord calls me by this sickness I go in peace and joy, for I had lived almost my whole life as a slave and a heathen, but now the Lord has in his mercy received me among his children . . .'

There was opposition from masters when their slaves or pawns asked for baptism, and sometimes the missionaries took the issue to the Chief's court. Usually, however, they appealed directly to the master concerned, promising him that his pawn 'would serve him even better after baptism'. One missionary reported that a rich elder had found this to be true. 'When he discovered that freed Christian servants worked more industriously than they had as heathen slaves, he allowed every slave of his to become a Christian if he wished.' A large number of people pawned into slavery had incurred this status for debts contracted by relatives even before the pawn's birth. Often the debts were to the 'fetish priest'. This led to disillusionment with the officials of traditional religion, and inclined some toward Christianity, seen as a more compassionate religion.

Christian villages

Akropong and Aburi were two centres founded by the Basel Mission in the 1840s, and from there the work expanded to the whole of the Akwapim state. On the coast, Christiansborg and Abokobi became stepping stones for evangelism among the Ga peoples. At each station the personality of the missionary in charge, especially when he remained for a long period, was important in shaping and giving a specific character to the place. The Basel mission structure aimed at an ideal of Christian villages, called 'Salem'. (Freeman started such a village at the farm, Beulah, but for Methodists this was an exception.) The separate Christian village was not in fact as alien to Akan society as one might suppose. Johannes Zimmermann, the remarkable missionary who, perhaps more than others strove to become an African to Africans, founded two villages, one at Odumse and the other at Abokobi.

The first village, at Odumse, consisted of 600 people, mainly Chief Oronkor Azu's wives, children, slaves, and relatives. The chief had invited his friend Zimmermann to settle there; he was one of those chiefs who had become sceptical about fetish priests and would not let any reside in his area. He greeted the arrival of the missionary with great expectation and handed over several young boys, including three of his sons, to be educated by the missionaries. In this case, a real friendship grew between missionary and chief. Oronkor even had a stool made for Zimmermann to use in his frequent visits to the Chief's court. Zimmermann hoped that the Chief would eventually allow himself to be baptized, but social obligations were too great for him to take such a definite step.

Zimmermann became so identified with the people that, in cases of illness, he consulted the African 'nature doctors', as he called them. In 1860 the Basel Mission central committee, after much discussion with the missionaries on the field, decided to free all house-slaves whose masters were members of the mission. Zimmermann voted against this measure. He took the patriarchal conservative view that slaves in Ghana were well-treated and regarded as members of the master's household. When introducing 'divine law' in Africa, the missionaries must derive this law not from Church tradition in Europe, he suggested, but exclusively from the Bible. The traditional social order in Ghana was closer to family law in old Israel than to Western traditions and was therefore preferable to European ideals.

The second village Zimmermann started, at Abokobi, was a new Christian village, not rooted in the traditional community. Zimmermann, a Pietist farmer's son, was greatly influenced by his own background in the southern German community of Korntal. His intention was to found an African Korntal. The well-laid-out village plan included chapel, school, and staff houses in the centre, with thirty houses belonging to the Christian families along five footpaths leading from the centre. An African village 'father' was in charge of the organization of the place, and a Church Council including two missionaries supervised the whole project. Every morning and evening singing was heard from the chapel.

A most interesting village was that at Zantse, established by a prince, Frederick Dowuna, who had been brought up and baptized in Denmark. Though later in life his standing in the Church came into some question, he turned to a greatly respected venture: founding this Christian village as a refuge for runaway slaves and other outlaws.[62] In many instances, the Basel Mission came to be looked upon as a shelter and refuge for people in trouble.

Conversions

Christianity among Africans at this time was not, as it is sometimes assumed, an immobile entity. It experienced its changes and crises. The methods of conversion varied greatly. In some cases there was a collective decision by groups of people to join the Church. Such was the case at Oyarifa, near Abokobi, where whole families joined. By 1875 the congregation had nearly 100 members. Similarly at Larteh, whole families as well as groups of young boys and girls joined, thus forming solid Christian communities in the towns of Akwapim, and in Ga bush country.

In other cases individuals came to the Church, often after great internal struggles. Some followed other members of their families to the Churches; others were attracted by the new teaching on death. For some it was a tension between old and new beliefs – at times revealed through a dream. Zimmermann records the story of a priest named Owu, the medium of the tutelary spirit and an outstanding personality. He heard street preaching near Abokobi and was deeply touched. Coming home from the funeral of a relative in 1857, he lay down half awake and felt as if covered by a cloud. Then someone gripped his head and said 'Listen! You have been the devil's servant; you will be my servant; if not, you will be punished.' Then the cloud dissolved and he became ill. Next morning he had a dazzling vision of an angel. 'Your Lord calls you, rise!' He saw his own body being eaten by worms, so that only the skeleton was left. He was asked, 'Where are you going?' and angels told him to take courage. He then had a vision of the house of God, and the Lord surrounded by angels in white. The Lord said, 'I send you back; tell your friends what you have seen.' He went back, accompanied by seven angels who poured water over his house, and he heard wonderful music. Scales fell from his eyes and he saw again. The priest's friends thought he was ill, as he began to pray, and wanted to give him medicine. But he refused and went to Pastor Zimmermann in Christiansborg to ask for baptism. He took the name of Paulo Mohenu, and became a well-known evangelist. His vision, given here in some detail, is representative of similar nineteenth-century dream experiences. These conversion crises were repeated, from Abeokuta in Nigeria, to Babanango in Natal.

Asante

The fate and future of the Asante kingdom was the greatest preoccupation in Ghanaian internal politics in the last quarter of the century. Up until this time, the Gold *Coast* was just that – a coastline with its old forts and shallow harbours offering launching points for Western traders, a few British administrators, and some missionaries. Also along the coast were opportunities for the enterprising Fante traders. But Asante pressures from the interior were an ever-present challenge to the coastal communities. An attempt to resolve the issue was made when British troops attacked the kingdom in 1873–74. The British proclamation of a protectorate over the coast in 1874 implied a complete social revolution, affecting the whole of Fante society: domestic slavery was abolished. This also influenced the growth and social composition of the Churches.

Even though the British had the upper hand, *Pax Britannica* was far from certain. The young king, Agyeman Prempe, was determined to maintain his kingdom's independence, but a renewed British attack on the city of Kumasi in 1896 led to the final annexation of the Asante kingdom in 1901. Prempe was taken as prisoner to the Seychelles, one of many kings and chiefs throughout the continent to suffer such a fate in the heyday of empire. When Asante was annexed to the colony, the country now consisted of three separate but related parts: the Gold Coast Colony, Asante, and the Northern Territories.

Hausa traders coming from the north-east had found that traditional Asante 'fetish' allegiance opposed Islam and certain of its ritual expressions. With the new political situation, the Hausa often received a warm welcome from British administrators, who saw Islam as the religion of the Black Man. The *zongo*s (quarters for Muslim strangers) sometimes outgrew the towns to which they were attached. A dramatic incident was the conversion of a Methodist catechist in Cape Coast to Islam. Ben Sam had listened to the message of a leading Muslim Hausa. These ideas were transposed into a vivid dream, which bade him and his flock join the faith of the Prophet. Another whole group joined Islam for a time when the financial demands of ambitious Methodists became too insistent. The 'conversion' did not last, however; these wavering seekers made an appeal to their Methodist ex-brethren: 'give us back our names, ... on my sick-bed I have no hope of heaven.'[63]

Two Christian communities still dominated the ecclesiastic scene, the Methodist Fante and the Basel-related Twi and Ga. They retained and reproduced their earlier characteristics. The Basel Mission still had a generous supply of missionaries – in 1892 twenty-two men and eleven women on the Akwapim ridge, some with twenty-eight years of experience in Ghana. A Methodist policy statement from London in 1888 announced the intention 'to reduce gradually the staff of European missionaries on the West Coast'. This was at a time when, for various reasons, some missions in Europe appeared to have lost confidence in African leadership and were replacing Africans with Europeans. Progress in medicine gave Europeans a better chance of survival. Also, in the 1890s an insidious Social Darwinism led some to believe that standards could be maintained only by expatriates. From the very beginning, however, the Methodist Church in Ghana had had strong African leadership and was determined to carry on this tradition. At this time they had only four expatriate missionaries, none of whom had lived in the country for more than four years. There was a staff of fifteen African pastors and eighteen catechists, together with teacher-evangelists in the communities. Often they were the only literate persons in their area, for well into the twentieth century the Methodist Church had to admit that 75 per cent of its adult members were unable to read.[64] In its urban centres on the coast, however, the Methodists placed special emphasis on schools and education. The towns had stirrings of nationalism. The first years of the twentieth century brought news of the victory of Japan over Russia, a fact reported and debated in Ghana newspapers run by Methodist Fante.

The Basel missionaries on the inland ridges were closer to the traditional rulers; some in fact nearer than they expected. Fritz Ramseyer was taken prisoner by Asante troops and with his young family was held captive for over four years, 1869–74. In his diary he recorded that he used the enforced experience in royal Kumasi to good advantage, preaching in the streets 'without anybody daring to answer'. He was assured that the king wished to have a missionary in the place, 'because he knows and believes that it is a blessing to have such people of God to pray for him and his people'.[65]

Chiefs as Christians

A great issue in Ghana society at the time was whether chiefs could be Christians – and whether Christians could be chiefs. The King of Asante, the *Asantahene*, was the keeper of the 'Golden Stool' and the highest power in the land. There were about twenty subdistricts in Asante, all under chiefs with varying degrees of influence, but all owing allegiance to the *Asantehene*. Some communities approached leading Christians, asking them to take on the chieftaincy, with the understanding that they would not perform traditional rites. When Chief Asunafo in Akim became a Christian, his people were anxious for him to continue his authority as chief. Later, with the policy of indirect rule, the colonial government would not accept such a compromise. It insisted on the hard choice proclaimed in the Christian gospel – either Caesar or God, either 'Stool' or Christ. As time passed, and educational opportunities for chiefs increased, they were able to make adjustments.

To the young Church in Asante it was natural to look to royalty and their kinsmen for leadership. The great precedent was David Asante whose father was a member of the royal family at Akropong and had been a friend of Andreas Riis, one of the first Basel missionaries. In the Church, David Asante worked closely with Theophil Opoku, son of the chief linguist of Akropong, another indication of the interesting ties among the Asante elite. David Asante was placed as pastor at Kibi, the centre of the powerful Akim kingdom, and at first had a real influence over the ruler, Amoako Ata. They differed, however, over the domestic slavery issue, and the friendship between king and pastor gave way to bitter reaction from the King: 'I cannot kill you because of the English laws, but I shall trouble you till you leave, and if that does not help, I shall tie you like a pig and have you transported over the frontiers of Akim.'[66]

Expatriates and Africans

The Basel-related Church in Ghana was dominated by expatriates more than many other Churches. These great Swiss and German missionary personalities – Christaller, Süss, Buck, Zimmermann, Ramseyer and others – were of unusually high calibre, and long-lived as well. This expatriate prominence resulted sometimes in 'the Mission's failure to build up a group of efficient and loyal local agents in proportion to the number of missionaries present'. This was possibly one cause of the rather modest evangelistic expansion.[67]

Despite the presence of many Western missionaries, some Africans took a strong leadership role. Samson K. Boateng of Bompata is one example. Bompata was originally only a small unimportant hamlet. In 1877 the people of Dwaben had rebelled against the Golden Stool. Being in danger, they left their home to take shelter at Bompata, which was under a powerful chief. Even there, they were open to sudden attack, so Nana Kwabena Atta, having heard of the Basel strangers, sent an invitation to them. Their presence might act as protection against Asante aggression – not an unusual reason in Africa for seeking a missionary.

Ramseyer responded to the invitation, and sent a catechist, Philip Kwabi, who was later replaced by Samson Boateng. The latter had a pleasing personality and the added advantage of being related to some of the prominent Dwaben people. The chief and elders at Bompata gave him a piece of land and were so co-operative that until he had won his first five converts, he actually stayed in the house of the *abosomfo* (traditional priest). Such men often showed a certain professional solidarity with Christian pastors and catechists. Boateng, ordained in 1898, stayed at Bompata for sixteen years, long enough to establish himself as one of its leaders. He saw a progressive and well-ordered Christian community emerge. To a large extent the first congregation at Bompata consisted of 'ex-slaves and dissident royals'. A group of twenty-five newcomers in 1896 – fourteen men and eleven women – originated from twelve different places. The proportion of slaves was hard to ascertain, since reference to slave origin was a serious offence, and a chief could even be 'de-stooled' for mentioning it. But the proportion of slaves and 'pawns' was no doubt considerable. The Christian congregations also formed a breeding ground for discontented young men in the community who later led the opposition against the chiefs.[68]

It was Boateng who brought the first cocoa pods to Bompata; he also introduced oranges and other exotic fruits, and goats. When a school and a chapel were built, the pastor and the teacher represented such progress and security that in the Yaa Asantewaa rebellion of 1900, the chief and people of Bompata remained on the side of the British. The administration strengthened the chief's power by giving him authority to try civil and criminal court cases according to British or customary law.

Refugee members

A puritanical spirit characterized the Christian community life. Drumming and dancing were forbidden and the traditional puberty rites for adolescent girls were replaced by Church confirmation, 'amid great rejoicing, hymn-singing and reciting of Biblical passages'. One example of the refugee category of Christian converts was Ankoma of West Akim. One of several people seeking refuge from the oppression of a pagan priest, he was baptized in 1889, becoming the only Christian in his community. He began to visit villages, preaching, reading from his New Testament, and singing hymns. As a result, eight people were prepared for baptism and soon a catechist was placed there. Groups formed in other places including Oda, the chief's town. The zeal of a former houseboy of missionary Philip Buss caused so many people to take interest that finally the Mission was called to establish a Church in the community. Two traders from Gomoa heard the preaching at Cape Coast and asked for a teacher. In three years time, no less than fifty new centres had grown up as a result of that request.[69]

The turmoil of war in 1874 drove the people at Juaben to become refugees. When they asked for asylum within the Gold Coast colony, the Basel missionary Buhl advised the government to have them settled at Akim. There the Methodists worked with them and Koforidua became 'the capital of refugees'. It grew into a vigorous community and the original shack used for preaching, dedicated in 1886, was replaced in four years by a proper chapel. Missionary Karl Buck had encouraging results in Akim. At Kibi, where David Asante had been active, he found a congregation of 150 members. Within three years he opened seven out-stations and had baptized more than 500, mainly slaves, converted by their own fellows, men who had been instructed by the missionary. By giving advice on a variety of new cash crops, such as yams and coconuts, Buck helped considerably in raising the socio-economic level of the whole community. Clean and comfortable Christian villages soon developed.[70]

Cocoa and Christianity

Various social and economic developments also had an effect on the Churches. The rubber boom – wild rubber in the Buem and Adele forests further north – led members of the Church to follow their people. A big northward drive of the Church was thus set in motion.[71] Another development was the introduction of cocoa by the Basel Mission. This changed the face of Ghana. In one generation, after 1911, Ghana became the world's leading producer of cocoa and thus relatively rich. Because of this monoculture it was at the same time tied to a shifting world economy. The Basel Mission Trading Company, which had started with palm kernels and cotton, had a large share in the introduction of cocoa, and found a new and growing area of activity.

There were, however, less desirable results. The Ghana Churches and the Christians became very dependent on cocoa for their economic support. A leading theme in sermons was the danger of worshipping cocoa as a god. In 1914 the Basel Mission report stated that 'about 2,000 Akwapim Christians live on their cocoa plantations. Several of them have not taken part in Church services for years.' The large migrant worker population involved in cocoa farming – Northeners and Ewe – led in some cases to depopulation of areas and a breakdown of Church life. The pastor from Date, near Akropong, reported such a situation: only sixty old men and women were left there.[72] Monogamy was also threatened, as men found it advantageous to keep several wives as supervisors on their many plantations. These problems connected with the interest in cocoa caused even some pastors and teachers to be placed under discipline. Sometimes the Mission Trading Company would employ such a man for a few years; when he later made amends according to Church rules, he could rejoin the Church service. While the clash between economic interests and Church laws posed a severe problem it did show that Church and mission were closely involved in the lives of the people.

The relation of the Christian minority to the majority community could sometimes be tense. At Labadi the missionary encouraged the Christians to go fishing on Thursday, a shocking affront to the traditionalists, for Thursday was a sacred day when fishing was taboo. The situation was not much improved by interference from the Governor, who insisted that the Christians had the right to fish on Thursdays, and placed pagan protesters in prison. Reaction was modified by an outbreak of smallpox soon afterwards, which induced a number of people to join the Church.

Schools and High schools

Both Methodist and Basel missions were strong supporters of schools. Far into the twentieth century no other agency took any real interest in African education. Herbert T. Ussher, the British Governor, did have a sudden spasm of educational ambition in 1904; he drew up a scheme to include 'the rudiments of Latin and Greek, Euclid's Geometry, Botany, Mineralogy and Music'. But as Bartels comments, 'needless to say, nothing came of these ambitious proposals.'[73] Increasingly the Methodists concentrated their efforts on their High Schools. The Headmaster of the Mfantsipim High School in Cape Coast remarked, with a good deal of self-assurance, 'I want to raise up a generation of men in the Mfantispim School who will be brave enough to face the problems of their own continent, practically and unselfishly.'[74] But it was precisely on this score that the Fante leaders met the most demanding challenge of this period. These ambitious leaders in Church and school had a serious clash with the European missionary, Dennis Kemp.

Kemp had worked for nine years in Ghana, and could have said, with the Apostle Paul, that he had laboured more abundantly than all. He had taken a personal interest in the well-being and future of young Fante, and had admitted the twenty most promising to his technical boarding school, 'Standfast Hall'. Among them was J. Kwegyir Aggrey, later the great educationalist. Kemp wore himself out, but as has been said by a great Fante schoolman, he worked *for* the people, rather than *with* them. His programme had an emphasis on industrial training, but his reasons were not acceptable in the Ghana of his time. The Negro, he claimed, was not built to be on an intellectual level, with the White race; he was '1500 years behind England'. This triggered a conflict with the emerging Fante nationalists of the twentieth century.[75]

One of the Church leaders involved was Andrew William Parker (1849–1912), who led the case against Kemp. Parker emerged as the very embodiment of Ghana Methodism. He became Superintendent Minister of

Cape Coast, and together with the brilliant British linguist missionary W. M. Cannell, translated the New Testament and Wesley's hymns. These men who did the translating were inspired by Sampson, an Anglican, who already in the nineteenth century had recognized signs of Fante culture. Andrew Parker was also a powerful preacher and an authoritative speaker. he was a Ghanaian nationalist at a time when that was dangerous, and as the newspaper, *Gold Coast Nation*, said of him after his death, 'He was ambitious for Church and State.'

Asante – resistance and acceptance 1896–1920

Methodist and Basel missionaries arrived soon after the 1896 British occupation, but the Yaa Asantewaa rebellion of 1900 soon destroyed these tentative beginnings. Work was renewed after the Gold Coast government had re-established its authority, and in these early years both the Basel Mission and the Methodists enjoyed active government support. By 1908 the situation had become more encouraging, with the two Churches together claiming 2,680 members, although most of these were 'southerners'. For most of the first two decades of the twentieth century, Church congregations in Asante were primarily composed of southern Akan (especially Fante and Akwapim) and Ewe from the Gold Coast Colony. During this period most Asante were, for a variety of reasons, opposed to Christianity. One of the enduring difficulties was the relationship of the Asante convert to chiefly authority and to rites and obligations, seen as an integral part of traditional Asante loyalty. In 1912 the government and Churches agreed on certain guidelines on the obligations of converts to Asante authority: (i) a Christian should not 'be obliged to swear back an oath'; (ii) Christians should be bound to 'render customary service to his Chief' but not be forced 'to perform any fetish rite'; (iii) efforts 'should be made to draw a distinction between fetish and purely ceremonial services'; (iv) Christians were to be free on Sundays.[76]

Anglican varieties

Since the Church of England was an Established Church, one would have expected its agents to insist on a similarly close relationship between Church and State in the old Gold Coast colony. But surprisingly, the beginnings of the Anglican Church in Ghana were in African lay hands. The Anglicans had been in Ghana during the eighteenth century. When missionaries of the Society for the Propagation of the Gospel (SPG) finally arrived in 1901, they found four already existing Anglican congregations. One had been started by the African legal and commercial elite, and another was formed around a small group of Yoruba immigrants from Nigeria. After 1905, the Anglicans expanded in four different areas, in each case through African efforts.

The first, in Western Ghana, resulted from the Prophet Harris movement. It was led by a mulatto prophet, John Swatson, who dressed like Harris, wearing a long white robe and carrying a wooden cross. Swatson was anxious to bring his people into the Anglican fold, and around 1915 a large number were accepted by the Diocese of Accra. The second expansion occurred through the immigrant Yoruba. They moved to the Ghana gold mines as firewood cutters. Taking their faith with them, they established thriving congregations. E. D. Martinson, the Ghanaian catechist who later became a priest, found their leaders to be impressive, prophet-like figures. He respected their evangelical fervour and limited himself to providing the sacraments.

A third group developed near Kumasi. Here in rural Asante members of the royal family started an Anglican school, which received support from 'stool' (chieftaincy) funds. The fourth dimension of Anglican expansion was more heterogeneous and indicated the growing geographical scope of the Ghana Church. It included many different groups. Some were secessions from other missions; some were formed at new railway sidings, mining centres, and large cocoa farms. School-educated people from the coastal towns, or Sierra Leoneans engaged in commercial activities, would gather into groups, eventually seeking connection with the Anglican episcopal authority in Accra.

The Archdeacon of Lagos, in 1904 an Englishman N. T. Hamlyn – was consecrated as Assistant Bishop for the Gold Coast, becoming Bishop of Accra in 1909. Coming from Lagos, he was of the Low Church evangelical tradition, but in 1913 he was succeeded by an SPG missionary and Anglo-Catholic, M. S. O'Rourke. Through him and his successor, J. O. Aglionby, a colourful liturgy was introduced, and a concern for the formation of African priests was felt. The two first such priests were ordained in 1916. An interesting sidelight to the story of the Anglican Church in Ghana is the fact that the *Asantehene* Prempe played a role in its emergence. In the Seychelles where he was banished, he became a convert to Christianity. When in 1925 he was allowed to return for the Prince of Wales' *durbar*, he stood on the platform, 'a quiet figure in black coat and top hat', known to the audience to be a regular worshipper at church.[77]

TOGO

Togo is a small territory with a coastline of not more than fifty miles, and a hinterland extending some 350 miles inland. The Bremen Mission established contacts with Togo in about the middle of the nineteenth century. This mission had already been in touch with the gifted Ewe population for thirty-seven years and in 1884 the German annexed Togo as one of its colonies. Lomé on the coast became the capital, a railway was built from Lomé running inland to Palime. The Bremen inspector, Franz Michael Zahn, never visited the field but he followed developments – both big and small – with keen interest. Among the Togo missionaries one name at least must be mentioned, that of Jacob Spieth, a brilliant linguist and Bible translator. He was helped for twenty years in his linguistic work by L. Rudolph Mallet, a redeemed slave. In Bremen the mission inspector Zahn, a gifted theologian and administrator, was a conservative person who was not prepared to make haste, as he would say, with the ordination of Africans. The missionaries in the West African field were very impressed by their African assistant, Rudolf Mallet, and wished to have him ordained. The mission inspector in Bremen voted against, ruling that Mallet's ordination was 'unnecessary and impossible'.

In this case, however, the missionaries in Togo would not take 'no' for an answer. Missionary Louis Birkmaier decided that reality in Africa looked somewhat different from what it appeared 'at home behind the writing desk' and, together with a couple of other missionaries, Birkmaier ordained Mallet, against the ruling of the mission inspector in Bremen. We may conjecture that this decision against the inspector was unique in African Church history of this period![78]

Thanks to a far-seeing initiative in the field of theological education Togo was soon to have a large number of pastors. This time F. M. Zahn was for the idea, training them in Württemberg in southern Germany. Inspector Zahn was inspired by Bishop Crowther's example, and hoped that Togo would produce similar Church leaders. At Ochsenbach 1884–87 and at Westheim 1870–1900, nineteen young men attended a three-year training course, comprising folk school training and music (organ, violin, harm and singing). As a finishing touch, the African students were taught printing and book-binding. Among these men we mention Solomo Mallet, son of Rudolf Mallet, and Robert Baëta, father of Professor Christian Baëta. Eight of the nineteen were later ordained as pastors in the Togo Church. The Bremen missionaries served until 1916 when the world war made their presence there unwanted.[79]

In 1875, as a German colony, Togo received a German-speaking Catholic mission, that of 'Steyl', the German Fathers of the Divine Word (Societas Verbi Divini). The German mission historian, J. Schmidlin, called this society 'the first and greatest German mission'.[80] Earlier on, Steyl's main field was East Africa, but Catholic Togo was later to play an important role in their missionary activities.

BENIN (DAHOMEY)

During this period in the history of Dahomey, King Ghezo ruled supreme (1818–58), with no competition from the Oyo empire further east. Oyo had stumbled along to its demise. More important than the King's awe-inspiring troops of Amazons, was his economic grasp on the society. Palm oil proved to be so profitable, that it soon outpaced even the slave trade. Some of the 'returned Brazilians', ex-slaves who had established themselves at Whydah, were examples of how fortunes could be made. Among them, Chacha Felix de Souza was the most prominent, as well as fabulously rich.

It seemed wise for King Ghezo to conclude an economic and friendship pact with France. The mercantile house of Régis of Marseilles, having important interests in Dahomey, supported the idea of the pact. They were also in favour of Catholic missionaries. In the pact, France was 'most-favoured nation'; it was worded to protect both the palm oil trade and the lives of French missionaries. In Lyon, a new mission for Africa had just been founded by Mgr De Marion Brésillac (1813–59). Contacts with the Régis company encouraged him to go to Dahomey but Bishop Kobès of the Holy Ghost Fathers persuaded him to work in Sierra Leone instead. Brésillac went with five fathers, landing in Sierra Leone on 24 Ma 1859. The adventure turned into a catastrophe – within six weeks they were all dead of yellow fever.

The Lyon Mission (the Society of African Missions) was now taken over by one of the most outstanding French mission leaders of the century, Augustin Planque. For fifty years he formed its policy and furthered its Dahomey enterprise. In 1861 three young missionaries, one French, one Italian and one Spanish, went to Dahomey. When they stopped in Sierra Leone on the way, the French missionary was struck down by yellow fever. Borghero, the Italian, became the leader, and the two missionaries landed at Whydah, the island harbour dominating the entrance to Dahomey. King Ghezo had died and was succeeded by King Glele (1858–89). He took the missionary for an ambassador of Napoleon III, even though the Italian protested the mistake.

Whydah was a town with a reputed population of 20,000, including some 300 Christians, who were half-cast descendants of Portuguese settlers and liberated slaves from Brazil. The old Portuguese fort had been deserted since 1825, but twice a year an African priest from San Tomé still came to look after the faithful. Just before the arrival of the missionaries, he had tried to carry away the statues and the cross of the fort's chapel. The *yevogan* of Whydah, who governed the coastal area in the name of the King, was so scandalized at this attempt to run off with the 'fetishes of the White man', that the priest was saved from death only by the intervention of the Portuguese. The two missionaries were permitted to stay in the fort, and soon were venerated as powerful White men. The fort's chapel became known as 'the residence of the God of the Whites'. Here the missionaries provided a refuge for the handful of 'Brazilians' whom they found. The chapel had a certain prestige among the community at large. Occasionally, the Dahomeans paid a visit, carrying their calabashes with palm oil, to be burned as a sacrifice. But in 1863, Shango – the god of thunder – spoke mightily. Lightning struck the residence of the God of the Whites, and the missionaries were asked to pay a fine to pacify the fetishes. When Borghero refused he was duly thrown into prison – for half an hour – to see if he would relent. A suitable gift to King Glele fixed the problem just in time.

The veneration of the fetishes, the 'ju-ju' or 'voodoo' as the Dahomeans called them, was – and still is – the main religious practice. At Whydah there was – and still is – a special sanctuary for voodoo-snakes which were permitted to creep along the roads. The ritual murders at Abomey were seldom sacrifices to the spirits, but rather part of the ancestor cult. Wives, courtiers, and slaves had to accompany the deceased king into the other world, so that he would be honourably received by his ancestors. To celebrate a victory in war, there was also the sacrifice of slaves. But Borghero did not despair of the chances of conversion. 'Do we want to make limits to God's grace?' ... 'What gives us confidence is the certain hope of being able to establish, quite soon, an African clergy.'[81]

After only three months Borghero had over 100 children in his catechism classes, and would easily get another 100 as soon as he had enough classrooms. Out of those 200 'there would be twenty who could be chosen for priesthood'; thus, he concluded, 'we might have some priests in ten or twelve years.' In reality, it took five times longer – the mission's first priest was ordained in 1920.

When Borghero was invited to visit the royal court at Abomey, he accepted the king's invitation, but only on the condition that fetishes would be absent, and human sacrifices would not be made during his reception.

King Glele received him with great honours. No doubt, like his father, he was hoping for some profit from relations with a Frenchman. The missionary was welcomed with a Catholic procession, led by people carrying the images of Christ and Our Lady. The few Christians accompanied the priest in white and black cassocks, singing hymns and the fetishes along the road were either removed or covered. The King's men had composed a special song of welcome, celebrating the priestly man 'who comes to teach us the secret of the way to heaven'.[82] But the only concession King Glele gave was permission for the missionary to evangelize the extra-tribal society. The only tangible profit of this visit was that the King appointed Borghero '*Cabocere*' (head) of the extra-tribal people in his kingdom, thus authorizing him to move everywhere without the permission of the sub-chiefs.

Borghero used this permission for further exploratory tours. He went to Porto Novo, Lagos, and Abeokuta, all east of Dahomey; and to Accra, Cape Coast, and Cape Palmas to the west. At Cape Palmas he met the President of Liberia, who promised his support for a Catholic mission to be established eventually in his country. But Borghero was only able to found outposts in the immediate neighbourhood, with one further mission at Porto Novo in 1864. There, and at Lagos, were communities of Catholic 'returnees' from Brazil, called *Amaro*. They were now in Borghero's care. Because Lagos had such a good catechist, for the time being a visiting priest seemed sufficient. This layman catechist, 'Padre Antonio' from San Tomé, was educated in a Brazilian monastery, and went to Lagos to be a missionary among his former companions. He built a chapel for them, held services and catechism classes, baptized the children, blessed the marriages, visited the sick, and buried the dead. He examined Fr Borghero at the priest's first visit, asking him to say the rosary as a sign of Catholic orthodoxy. To Brother Antonio's satisfaction, the Father managed to do so.

Borghero's whole Christian community of some 3,000 members, spread between Whydah and Lagos, was an extra-tribal society. His Christians were black, but they were regarded as foreigners by the indigenous population. The bulk of them were ex-slaves from Brazil; others were adult slaves, converted in the country; and some were children, liberated from slavery by the missionaries. The children were their hope in the school; at least a score of them became catechists – the only real building-stone of the indigenous Church so categorically demanded by Brésillac, the society's founder. On two occasions a dozen of such children were sent to Spain for further training; a few of them returned as craftsmen, but none became a priest. Borghero was convinced that Nigeria and Ghana might prove less difficult to evangelize than Dahomey, and he suggested that the latter be abandoned as a mission.

NIGERIA

Western Nigeria

Sierra Leone took the great initiative for evangelization along the West African coast. The Sierra Leonean 'returnees' to Nigeria and a number of Europeans, mostly British and German, became the effective missionaries to Western and Eastern Nigeria. As nothing else could, the fate of the 'Niger Expedition' of 1841 dramatized the need for Africans as missionaries in West Africa.

Certain developments in Britain during this period had important repercussions for the Christianization of West Africa. Thomas Fowell Buxton, an evangelical reformer, continued the cause of William Wilberforce and Granville Sharp by working for the abolition of West Indian slavery in 1833–34. He proposed a plan for 'the extinction of the slave trade and the civilization of Africa' in his book *The African slave trade and its remedy*, published in 1839. The 'true remedy', rising out of Africa itself, was for 'the Bible and the plough [to] regenerate Africa ... Let missionaries and schoolmasters, the plough and the spade, go together.'[83]

The 'Niger Expedition' of 1841, with 150 Europeans and Africans, was well equipped to translate these ideas into practical action. Members included two Sierra Leonean representatives of the Church: J. F. Schön, German missionary and linguist; and Samuel Ajayi Crowther, African catechist of Yoruba birth. Simon Jonas, a dynamic Igbo who, like Crowther, was a Sierra Leonean 'liberated African', served as interpreter. The Expedition was one of the spectacular failures in the history of European penetration of Africa. Among the 145 Europeans, 130 contracted fever, and 40 died. This had long-term consequences for the Church in West Africa: it seemed finally to prove that Europeans were unfit for the West African climate. Training African personnel appeared to be the obvious answer. Consequently, in the 1840s, Fourah Bay College, where Crowther was teaching, took on even greater importance for Sierra Leone and for service in other countries of West Africa.

An incident during the Niger Expedition was a harbinger of things to come. The group had reached the Igbo town of Aboh, and Crowther preached before the ruler, Obi Ossai, who expressed keen interest. When Simon Jonas translated the Beatitudes into Igbo, the king was visibly impressed by the intellectual achievement of one of his own people. He told the eloquent Jonas, 'You must stop with me; you must teach me and my people. The white people can go up the river without you; they may leave you here until they return, or until other people come.'[84]

Shortly after the disaster of the Niger Expedition, the first attempt to establish Church contact with Abeokuta took place. The Methodist leader in Ghana, Thomas Birch Freeman, reached Badagry in September 1842, and from there sent a message to Chief Sodeke in Abeokuta. The King courteously replied, assuring a welcome, and sent an escort with horses for the missionaries. In December of the same year, Freeman and his companion, William De Graft, arrived in Abeokuta and visited Sodeke. They found him anxious to develop whatever contacts the missionaries could make. He felt that they could conceivably provide support against the military threat from the Muslims in the north and from Dahomey to the west. The ten days at the court were spent in meetings with the king, and with Sierra Leone 'emigrants', many of whom were eager to share the Biblical message. The key relevance of this early attempt to preach Christianity in Abeokuta is that it was made by Africans. Before 1841 this had occurred in an unofficial way through emigrants from Sierra Leone; now, after 1842, these African missionaries were in a position to adopt an African approach to their work. The Freeman–De Graft mission in 1841–42 was followed in 1845 by the arrival of Samuel Ajayi Crowther.

Freeman had left De Graft as the Church representative at Badagry on the coast. Before leaving Badagry, however, Freeman had met Henry Townsend, an Anglican missionary who had recently been sent by the CMS from Sierra Leone. Freeman, the Methodist, and Townsend, the Anglican, celebrated Christmas together, thereby prefiguring a co-operation which their two British-based Churches developed in the following years. After a first visit to Abeokuta, Townsend returned in 1845, this time accompanied by a German colleague in CMS employ, C. A. Gollmer, and by Samuel Ajayi Crowther.

Crowther and the Yoruba missions

Samuel Ajayi Crowther (1806–92) is one of the greatest and most lovable personalities in nineteenth-century African Church history. His life epitomizes the drama of West African history. Born at Osogun, a town of the Oyo (Yoruba) Empire, he was captured in 1821 during an attack on his community. He was sold to a European slave trader, but was liberated by a British naval anti-slave-trade patrol, and subsequently taken to Sierra Leone in 1822, and was baptized in 1825. He was brought to England in 1826 and returned to Sierra Leone the following year, to become one of the first students at Fourah Bay College. As a member of the ill-fated Niger Expedition of 1841, the young teacher came into the limelight of international attention. He again visited England, this time to study, and was ordained there in 1843. Returning to Nigeria in 1845, he worked first at Badagry on the coast, and later proceeded inland to Abeokuta, where he was stationed until 1855.

When Crowther and Townsend reached Abeokuta in 1845, it was an Egba town of probably 50,000. Perhaps two to three thousand of these were Sierra Leonean 'returnees'. Crowther at once began to preach his message; he felt on home ground. Every morning he gathered crowds of between one and two hundred or more under a tree between two markets, preaching in Yoruba. The Egba took the lead in welcoming the Christian preachers, both White and Black, and the city of Abeokuta was soon known as a Christian centre, setting the pace of Christianization for the other Yoruba towns. The role of the Saro (Sierra Leone returnees) was important in spreading the Gospel to their own people, but another indigenous factor played a much more surprising role in the response of the first generation to the Christian faith. This was a prediction by Ifa, the most prestigious of local oracles, connected with the cult of the Orunmila deity. In his studies of Christian conversion in West Africa, Dr Robin Horton has suggested prediction as one of its main causes. Ifa and the beginnings of Christianity in Abeokuta provide one of the most convincing examples. Traditional Yoruba communities always knew that they could rely on Ifa for help in most situations: sickness and health, war and peace, love and hatred. Their confidence in the oracle was strong around 1830, when Dahomean forces threatened their country, and a few years later when the possible arrival of Christian preachers posed another problem. Sodeke and his people decided that they must consult Ifa as to whether they should admit the missionaries or not. The answer was wholly positive. So it was that the missionaries were given an enthusiastic welcome, and were greeted with the highest expectations – whether for the right or the wrong reason must at this point be left as an open question![85]

Although the religious influence of the missionaries was limited, their political impact steadily increased. Abeokuta was surrounded by enemies, their most dangerous adversary being King Gezo of Dahomey. He was a former vassal of Oyo, who coveted much of Egbaland. In 1851 he advanced with an army of ten to fifteen thousand well-armed warriors, both men and women! Abeokuta would easily have been his prey, but the missionaries organized the defence, and the British government sent some aid. The crushing defeat of Gezo was a double triumph for Christianity: at the missionaries' intervention it was agreed to exchange prisoners of war, and the victory was in many quarters attributed to the help of the Christian God. As in many other cases in nineteenth-century Africa, the apparent support of the Christian God in war was contributory to the success of evangelization. The persecution of Christians declined markedly in Abeokuta, and many Yoruba chiefs asked to receive missionaries. Between 1852 and 1857, Christian missions came to the leading towns of Ibadan, Ijaye, Oyo, Ilesha, and Ogbomosho.[86] In addition to the CMS, there were also American Baptists with their famous pioneer, Thomas J. Bowen. Henry Townsend already dreamed of a Christian Yoruba state, united under the leadership of Abeokuta, the city which missionaries hailed as the 'Sunrise within the tropics'.

After Sodeke (d. 1845) the missionaries were intent on establishing contacts with the new rulers of the land, and viewed with satisfaction the attempts by the chiefs in Abeokuta to communicate with Queen Victoria. In 1848 Townsend left for a visit to England, and the chiefs entrusted him with their letters to London. They took for granted that the work of the Christian missionaries was primarily ordered by the Christian Queen. The Queen responded by dispatching two Bibles, one in Arabic and the other in English. Albert, the Prince Consort, emphasized the practical side of the missions by sending a steel corn-mill. When Crowther handed over the gifts to the Egba chiefs, he chose a Bible passage relevant for the occasion. In other contexts of African preaching, Moses the Liberator was the great prototype. On this special day, Crowther preferred not to strike revolutionary overtones: 'I spoke on the prosperous reigns of the kings who pleased God – David, Jehoshaphat, Hezekiah, Josiah. After this, the mill was fixed; some Indian corn . . . was put into the funnel before them, and to their great astonishment came out in fine flour merely by turning the handle of the machine.' The Gospel and the Plough were the *leitmotif* of the missionary work, offered alike to both pastors and princes. Prince Albert's steel corn-mill appears to have precipitated other innovations, such as modern methods of cotton production. Toward the end of the 1850s, Venn reported in London that 'There are now two hundred to three hundred gins at work in Abeokuta, and five or six presses, chiefly in the hands of natives. Cotton is flowing to England in a stream widening every day, and Abeokuta is rising rapidly in every branch of commerce.'[87] The evangelical theme for the time was surely 'Christianity and Commerce'.

Despite these helpful missionary endeavours, a serious persecution of the Christians in Abeokuta incidentally occurred in 1849, and drastic measures were taken to force their return to the traditional gods. Several Christians were put in stocks and exposed to the elements for five days. Women were whipped and put in shackles, and had their heads shaved to remove the effects of the baptism. Crowther knew that the *babalawo* (Ifa diviners) had treated the Muslim minority similarly several times. Now it was especially the Christian hostility to traditional rites which provoked the wrath of the guardians of tradition. Some of the catechumens and converts lapsed, and were struck off the Church rolls. The Sierra Leone returnees, whose speech and dress differed from that of the local people, were regarded as belonging to a separate social group. Therefore, although Christian, they were not molested.

Being from Sierra Leone, Crowther could express himself uninhibitedly against the local religion, but generally speaking, was remarkably tolerant. He had good friends among the chiefs, meeting them with characteristic African generosity. He also had personal acquaintances among the traditional priests, especially the *babalawo*, and appreciated the sincere spirituality of some of them.

Crowther was the pioneer; as the local work became established, others were engaged to take over from him, and he was able to transfer his attentions elsewhere. Among his colleagues, the two noteworthy CMS Western missionaries, Henry Townsend and David Hinderer pursued common concerns, but with divergent strategies and plans.

Townsend, an energetic schoolmaster, became leader at Abeokuta in 1846. He identified himself with the town, where he was resident nearly continuously for the next twenty years. Others might have far-ranging visions of reaching into the interior of Africa. To Townsend, Abeokuta was the world. Crowther had established initial contacts with the chiefs there, and Townsend took full advantage of this opportunity. 'He had the advantage of bringing the realism of a politician to reinforce the idealism of the missionary.'[88] He served as secretary to the Alake, the titular head of the Egba, for over ten years, and was even reputed to have been admitted to the Ogboni, a Yoruba secret society.

The remarkable couple, the German David Hinderer and his English wife Anna, were assigned to Ibadan, the largest of the Yoruba towns and the most formidable military power of the nineteenth century. Hinderer's approach differed from Townsend's strategy of concentration. He looked to the horizons. The 'chain' concept fascinated him, from Badagry and Ibadan to Lake Chad, 'where we shall shake hands with our brethren in the East', (and he meant East Africa!). This dream was an audacious reaction, perhaps, to an altogether intractable reality. Ibadan was involved in an almost continuous series of wars from the 1850s to the 1880s. For a five-year period the Hinderers were confined to the town and the mission compound, but lived all the more closely with the local catechists. At this time, Ibadan had three small congregations, with some 200 converts, of whom one third were communicants.[89]

Measuring spiritual growth is almost impossible, but this prayer of an Egba Christian woman reveals a warm, confident faith. It is the outpouring of the heart in the midst of the dangers of war, when Dahomean troops threatened Abeokuta in 1863, just as the ancient Assyrians had threatened Jerusalem:

> O Lord, lift up thine arm; and ... deliver us from the cruel Dahomeans ... We trust in Thee, O Lord our God ... Thou didst deliver Thy people Israel from the Land of Pharaoh, and hast overthrown his army. Thou didst deliver Hezekiah and his people from the hand of Sennacherib, who blasphemed Thy holy name. Do also remember ... Thy Church, remember Thy servants, remember our children. O Lord God, deliver us for Thy dear Son's sake. Amen.[90]

Already some of the great heroes of Israel's history had been incorporated as ideals, and Jesus as Redeemer. King Hezekiah of antiquity, and his unequal struggle against Sennacherib, became an analogous theme in Abeokutan piety. A century later, the Cherubim and Seraphim Church performed a 'Native Air Cantata' entitled 'Hezekiah Oba Juda' for the Jubilee of the current reigning Alake.[91]

In 1857 Crowther moved his sphere of activity from Yoruba to the Niger country, and it was there that he eventually became a bishop. He was the outstanding representative of the Sierra Leone tradition in the Nigerian Church, insisting on the need for close co-operation with Freetown and Fourah Bay College. Like Freeman of Ghana, he was not regarded as a faultless administrator. His strength lay rather in his trustworthiness and in his strategic purpose, developing the concepts and ideals of his fatherly friend, Henry Venn, the CMS Secretary in London. Crowther was an Anglican Church leader with a pragmatic approach and a generous attitude to African culture. He was an evangelical Bible-oriented Christian, continually involved in translating the Old and New Testament into Yoruba and Igbo. His assistants in translation were local catechists and Sierra Leone pastors, with help from expatriate missionaries such as the Hinderers in Ibadan.

A measure of the political influence of the Sierra Leone emigrants was the Abeokuta *ifole* ('house-breaking') disorder of 1867. Some missionaries, notably Townsend, found it difficult to submit to an African bishop, and the Sierra Leoneans reacted strongly to this attitude. Their leader in Abeokuta was George W. Johnson, a Sierra Leone tailor who had come to Lagos in 1863. He became involved in a controversy between Lagos, with its British consul, and Abeokuta. In order to foster Egba interests, he founded the 'Egba United Board of Management', which rapidly influenced the people of Abeokuta. Its position was consolidated by attributing the town's problems to the small European group, mainly the expatriate missionaries, who became the scapegoats.

In 1867 a complicated political situation culminated in the expulsion of the White missionaries. For more than a decade, Europeans were excluded from the interior and confined to the coast. The effect on the nascent Church was characteristic of the whole development of the Church in West Africa. During this period, all Church work in the interior of Yorubaland, as well as on the Niger, was under African leadership, led by the African bishop. It became 'a remarkable period of training in self-government.'[92] At this same time, the home constituencies of the missions in Britain, France and the United States were affected by a severe world economic recession, with a resultant sharp reduction in the supply of missionaries. All these events emphasized the role of the African staff, in this case almost exclusively from Sierra Leone, and enforced a healthy self-support of the Church.

The Crowther crisis during the 1880s had brought the CMS in Nigeria to the edge of a precipice. This conflict between on the one side Crowther and his African clergy, and on the other, a new breed of young and zealous European missionaries is discussed further in the part of the chapter on Eastern Nigeria (pp. 244). A far-sighted vision of the earlier nineteenth-century African church leaders had been utterly rejected; instead the new mood in the 1880s was influenced by the rise of an ahistorical anthropology and a reliance on the principles of Social Darwinism. Europeans came to believe in their own inherent superiority. As a result the missions, in a reversal of policy, relegated their African members to subordinate positions. Impassioned African lay groups saw the only solution to this setback in a definitive break with the White mission, and in the creation of a genuinely African Church for West Africa.

The controversy on the Niger was widely noticed and deeply felt by Western-educated African society. With the consecration by the Archbishop of Canterbury in 1864 of Samuel Ajayi Crowther as bishop, Henry Venn in London had initiated the most far-sighted strategic Church appointment in nineteenth-century Africa. Its abrogation in 1891 was tragic. The educated laity in Lagos followed the drama with intense involvement, and their anxiety was not confined to Nigeria, but echoed along the length of the West African coast. The acrimonious developments seemed to herald a new and bitter era of tension between White and Black, and also between a self-important clergy and an increasingly race-conscious laity.

For a while expectations among the Anglican laity were concentrated on an alternative African episcopal candidate, James Johnson. He was put under pressure to take the lead in establishing an independent African movement – a 'Church of West Africa'. At that very moment, in 1891, Lagos had an electrifying visit from E. W. Blyden, the 'Pan-African Patriot', voluble and vivacious propagandist, and recently hopeful presidential candidate in Monrovia, Liberia. Invited to speak on 'The Return of the Exiles and the West African Church', Blyden did not fail the audience's expectations. Foreigners and their alien structures and programmes, he argued, must no longer be allowed to dominate the Church in West Africa. The Church should be free, independent, and African.

James Johnson joined a committee to draw up the constitution of the new Church. Yet, the final step was not taken, at least not by him. 'Johnson came to the brink and refused to jump.'[93] A number of factors influenced Johnson's decision; Blyden's political eloquence and the Lagos laymen's pressure could not prevail upon him. Johnson was too much of an Anglican and a theologian, and too closely tied to an English-Anglican ethos for him to abandon his Church. Not that he was rewarded by his superiors for this virtuous attitude. On the contrary, when, after Crowther's death, it was taken for granted that he would be the successor, a troika of one English bishop and two African assistant bishops were chosen instead of 'Holy Johnson'. He was not made an assistant bishop until 1900.

When it was finally realized that Johnson was not going to lead the masses into a separate West African Church, a group of nine Lagos laymen decided, independently, to establish 'The United Native African Church'.[94] Significantly, this was a lay initiative, with no response from the clergy. In spite of its ambitious name, the 'Native African Church' did not prove sufficiently attractive for it to include great numbers. The 'mission churches came through the crisis without a schism to disturb them.'[95]

The Baptist mission had also been through dramatic trials. At the time of the Abeokuta *ifole* of 1867, they had to leave town, with the American missionaries returning to America. An African solution was found: two African-American pastors from South Carolina, J. L. Vaughan, who had emigrated first to Liberia in 1847 and then moved to Ogbomosho; and J. M. Harden, with Liberian experience and a Sierra Leonean wife, kept the Baptist congregations in Ogbomosho and Lagos alive. Soon the Revd Moses Ladejo Stone emerged as the most promising Nigerian Baptist leader. In 1875 a White American, W. J. David, took over the administration with the best of intentions: 'Africa must be evangelized by Africans', was his motto. Yet it was taken for granted that the work must be under White supervision. The Lagos Baptists reacted against this last point and, in 1888, the Lagos congregation was rent asunder. The vast majority of members formed a 'Native Baptist Church', while a minority stayed with the American mission. The split widened under David's successor, who arranged a Baptist variety of the 'purges' so common at the time. The Baptist group was not slow in referring to the Crowther–Brooke crisis (see pp. 244–46) within the Anglican communion. In the Baptist case, the schism lasted about twenty years, until in 1914 the fellowship with the American mission was re-established.

The Methodists were exposed to similar problems, but once again proved the elasticity of their remarkable organization. Disciplinary cases of ministers were handled with considerable discretion, and open conflicts were avoided until the time the energetic British G. O. Griffin became chairman. He too undertook a purge, but with a difference: he dismissed fifteen ministers, seven White and eight Black, and claimed that with a drastically reduced staff, his Church was doing better than ever. This was only a dress-rehearsal, though, for a wider purge in 1917, when sixty-five ministers were removed from the Church roll, after admitting that they were guilty of polygamy.[96] Having been expelled, they formed their own Church, the 'United African Methodist Church'.

Professor James Webster has emphasized that the evangelism of the African Churches was stimulated by the initiative of individuals. The Agege plantations in southern Egbaland were an example of the production and sale of cocoa and groundnuts by new Nigerian and Ghanaian entrepreneurs. There, Chief J. K. Coker was the enterprising and inspiring leader when commercial cocoa farming emerged. Coker's financial skill and active leadership played an important role in the growth of the independent African Churches. Cocoa farming provided financial assistance for the self-support of the established Methodist, Anglican, and Baptist Churches. The 'migrant labour' factor was at work here. From the Agege plantations the African Church spread, as farm labourers returned to their homes, 'bringing cocoa culture and Christianity'.[97]

Up to this time denominational loyalty of individual members had been taken for granted, but the appeal of the African Church set in motion a spiritual pilgrimage by some persons who hurried from altar to altar. An interesting character was David Brown Vincent, alias Mojola Agbebi (1860–1917). His parents were of different ethnic communities, the father a Yoruba and the mother a Sierra Leonean descended from an Igbo family. Born and growing up in Sierra Leone, he later referred to a childhood dream: he saw an angel rescuing him from being clubbed to death by the Devil. He was soon transferred to south-west Nigeria as an evangelist. His contacts with the CMS were brief (1878–80), followed by an even shorter period with the Roman Catholics and the American Baptists. In 1888 he joined the Native Baptist Church, the first independent African Church in Nigeria. With disconcerting ease he graced other Baptist Churches with his membership and potential leadership. He had accumulated ample personal experience when he was elected in 1903 as President of the African Baptist Union of West Africa, which he founded. Mojola Agbebi pioneered the transfer from European dress and names to African clothes and personal names. He was an early fighter for Nigerian nationalism. He preached what he called the 'Christianity of the Bible', different, as he insisted, from 'European Christianity'.[98]

During the First World War a prophet appeared from among the Kalabari people, in the person of Garrick Sokari Braide, a new Elijah, out of the hidden masses of the Delta bush villages. He loved his God and his Church, and spent the nights in contemplation in front of the altar of the Anglican chapel. He was instrumental in launching a religious movement of thousands. He sought recognition and appeared before James Johnson, the Anglican African assistant bishop, but he was pushed aside and thrown into jail; he died soon afterwards. For the Anglican Church these events were a series of crises. Yet the Anglican dioceses survived, scathed and scorched perhaps, but nonetheless vigorous, looking to the future. The prestige in West Africa of the world-wide Anglican Communion, its worship, and its Church order, was immense.

Further north at Ogbomosho, the American Baptists experienced such resistant African tradition that they temporarily had to withdraw. The clash was over funerals, an issue which was felt to be of central importance. Barike, the first convert, opposed the chiefs, elders and the rest of the community by suggesting that Yoruba custom concerning funerals should be changed. He went so far as to insist that the dead should no longer be buried in a compound but 'in the bush' (the church graveyard). This discussion was similar to Crowther's experience in Abeokuta, and to countless other instances throughout Africa of first-generation Christians campaigning over the manner of funerals. The revolutionary Christian idea challenged the very foundations of traditional religion, for it was in the house that the propitious presence of ancestors was most assured. To be buried beyond the limits, was to jeopardize and make impossible that spiritual communion. In the Ogbomosho case in 1879, the outcome was deeply felt: all Christians were expelled from the town.[99]

The Christianization of the various Yoruba peoples cannot be summed up in a single formula; a variety of factors were at work. In Abeokuta, the CMS built on their early advance among the Egba. Their British missionary superintendent, J. B. Wood (d.1897) was surprisingly influential in the area, and was supported by 'the uncrowned king of the Egba', Ogundipe. Although not a member of the Church, he had pro-Christian sympathies. The co-operation between these two men resulted in convincing social and civic consequences of corporate Christianity. Through Christian initiative, the Egba received a Court of Redemption in 1881 with funds for redeeming slaves; a Protestant Relief Committee; a Divorce Court in 1886 which sidestepped the Native courts for Protestant divorce cases; and an Abeokutan Patriotic Association through which Christians could voice public opinion. Wood strove to appease Egba feelings: emulating Townsend, he was initiated into the Ogboni secret society.

In Abeokuta the Christian community was at first a 'foreign legion' but, as it grew into a central group in Egba politics, it paved the way – with its obvious British sympathies – for an eventual British annexation in 1914. Some of the Egba chiefs had long foreseen this trend, and reacted by listening to French overtures, but to no avail. In 1891 they had to give in to British pressures.[100]

Two other cases illustrate Church development among the Yoruba: the Ijebu story, a robust reminder of political and military realities involved in the imperialist scramble for power; and the Ekiti example, one of many places where young ex-slaves, converted elsewhere, brought the new message of liberation and salvation back to their own communities. In the first case, the influence was enforced by conquest and from outside; in the latter, it grew from the humblest of grass roots. In both, results were dramatic and astonishingly rich.

The Ijebu were prosperous traders, operating as middlemen between the interior and the coast. Conservative in outlook and apprehensive of British imperialistic designs, they were determined to keep the Whites, including the missionaries, away from their country. The British Governor at Lagos, Sir Guilbert Carter, was particularly irritated with the Ijebu and referred to them as 'heathens of the worst uncompromising description'. He was determined to bring them into subjection. He found a pretext for this, and during a confrontation in 1892, the Ijebu army was routed. The Ijebu had firmly believed in their old gods, and were genuinely surprised to find their trust misplaced. Remarkably soon, they were ready to make a radical change by accepting missionaries and schools. For the Ijebu, May 1892 was the beginning of a new world. The old order of the Ijebu collapsed and the new was enthusiastically embraced. For the Ijebu this 'educational renaissance' was the vital issue enabling them 'to assert their influence in the politics and trade of the new protectorate, and sixty years later in the new Nigeria ... For good or ill, they continue to nourish that sense of political and spiritual identity which binds the Ijebu everywhere.'[101]

The Ijebu Church – served by the CMS, the Methodists, Baptists, and the Catholic 'African Missions' (Lyon) – soon emerged as the most promising in all Yorubaland. Results were comparable to those in Igbo country to the east. Several factors created that success: first, was the formation of an all-Black Anglican staff in the Ijebu district, under an African assistant bishop, James Johnson, who was himself an Ijebu; second, the CMS emphasis on education was highly appreciated by the ambitious Ijebu; third, was the notion that the Anglicans represented the true religion of the conquerors – the 'Queen's Church': the Anglican mission had moved in immediately after the conquest.[102]

The Methodist effort, under White leadership, showed only modest results, a local comparison which of course cannot be generalized. At the turn of the century, there were over 7,000 Ijebu adherents. All the missions were eager to put the Ijebu to work as voluntary evangelists, a strategy that proved highly successful in the dynamic population.

Two Christian Ekiti ex-slaves exemplified the widespread domestic slavery in Nigeria. The Sierra Leone 'liberated slaves' came partly from the many Yoruba shipped away as slaves from Lagos and Badagry. Some of the slaves, however, products of the inter-Yoruba wars, had been left nearer home and sold to Ibadan, Abeokuta, and other Yoruba states. During their captivity, they met the Christian faith and were converted. There were two examples of 'these barely literate ex-slave torchbearers of Christianity in their fatherland'.[103] One was Babamuboni, who was purchased at Ibadan by a Christian pastor, Daniel Olubi. He stayed as a slave for fifteen years before he redeemed himself. In his daily contacts with his master, he became familiar with the Christian doctrine and worship. He desired to bring this faith to his own people, and realized this intent in 1894. The other case mentioned by Ayandele was that of Samuel Laseinde. Together with members of his family, he had been taken prisoner at Ibadan and sold to the Iwo community. Later he was resold to Ibadan, and finally to a *Shango* devotee at Abeokuta. A missionary redeemed him from this slave-status, and placed him with an Ibadan pastor who taught him the skill of reading, and the tenets of Christianity. Similar to Babamuboni, the young convert wished to go back to the home community; Laseinde returned as a farmer and became a volunteer evangelist. The kind of chain reaction which the witness of these two brought about in Ekiti society must await local research.

Lagos

The *ifole* crisis of 1867 precipitated another change in Yoruba Church development. Until that time, Abeokuta and Ibadan in the interior of Yoruba country had been the centres of evangelization. With the *ifole* barricade in Egbaland, the emerging coastal island city of Lagos assumed a new and leading role for the Churches. This was not without previous preparation. In the early 1850s, King Akitoye was able to take power by means of British naval and military support and with the encouragement of the CMS and its missionary Gollmer. As recompense, the Anglicans were given five pieces of land. At about the same time, the Methodists arrived in Lagos, and immediately realized the city's potential. In 1859 an important group of 130 Brazilian returnees arrived in Lagos, and more than 1,200 in 1872. The Sierra Leoneans in Lagos at that time numbered about 1,500. The Brazilians established a community known as 'Portuguese town' in the centre of the island. They were Catholic, and Portuguese-speaking, sophisticated and rich middlemen in trade and building enterprises. Their Catholic cathedral built in 1881 attracted attention. 'The new Lagos was made up essentially of the Christian villages of the different missions joined together.'[104]

The Lagos Churches put great emphasis on their educational programmes. T. B. Macaulay was an imaginative Anglican leader in this field. He rose to prominence in Abeokuta, was ordained in 1854, and married Crowther's daughter. In 1859 he was transferred to Lagos. The emerging Lagos elite preferred to send their children for education to Fourah Bay in Sierra Leone, or to England. Crowther's six children had all been educated in England. But Macaulay, supported by his father-in-law, started the CMS grammar school in Lagos. It was an expression of the Anglican community's concern for education, and of the exciting role the Christian elite played in the cultural life of the city. Out of the first twenty-five boys in the school, twenty-two came from families whose fathers were merchants or traders, while the remaining three had fathers who were a clergyman, a scripture reader and a carpenter. The Anglican secondary school had a prestige value which no other mission in Lagos could afford to disregard. Eventually, similar schools followed: those run by the Methodists in 1879, by the Catholics in 1881, and by the Baptists in 1883.[105] The opening of secondary schools and Churches provided a great social event in the community.

Lagos was 'regarded as "the port of Abeokuta" and it was on that town that missionary hopes centred for a Christian commonwealth in Africa.'[106] With the traders and the missionaries came the repatriates: the Sierra Leoneans were arriving with almost every mail-boat, the Saro as the Sierra Leonean returnees were called, and the Amaro as the immigrants from Brazil and Cuba were called, of Yoruba origin. 'They brought with them artisan skills and have left their monument in the classical building and baroque plasterwork still to be seen in Lagos.'[107]

Eastern Nigeria

In the first half of the nineteenth century, the Niger Delta and the Eastern coast had the notorious reputation of being the greatest slave trading area in West Africa. The Delta contained several autonomous city states, such as Old Calabar, Brass, Bonny, and Okrika. Migrating from north and west to the Delta islands, people had formed settlements interconnected by a lively communication system. Their fleets of canoes on the navigable waterways provided the ideal means of contact for the exchange of goods – and of ideas.

For a time, the slave trade dominated Eastern Nigeria's relations with the wider world. From 1827–34 more than 200,000 slaves were exported from Bonny and Calabar to the Americas. By 1842 the slave trade was prohibited and activities were geared to legitimate trade, mainly the export of palm oil. However, the problem of an immense domestic slave population remained. In Bonny, the slaves, mostly Igbos, performed all the manual work for the small minority who were freemen. The slaves were an essential part of the 'Houses', the basic structure of the Ijaw community, each House consisting of chief, freemen and slaves. The lowest position in society was summed up in the declaration: 'Slaves be nothing'.[108]

Overpopulated Igboland, to the north, exercised constant population pressure on the coastal islands. Another influence from the north was the famous oracle of the Aros. This 'Aro Chukwu', a religious centre feared by many in Eastern Nigeria, spread a reign of terror over the enormous slave population in the Delta area. A slave knew that to be 'sent to Chukwu' was a fatal journey. Many slaves brought there disappeared. The oracle was the abode of the supreme deity: *Tshuku ab yama* (God lives here), a god who was reputed to need ever-increasing supplies of slaves for human sacrifice, usually connected with funeral immolations. Now it is thought that human sacrifices at the oracle were in fact rare, and that the slaves brought to Aro were instead resold into slavery and exported along secret routes. The

Chukwu oracle developed into an important pilgrimage and trading centre, having regular contacts with slave markets in the Delta.[109]

Even more striking than the active trade throughout the coastal area and the interior, were the international connections with this region. People in Ode-Itsekiri, a capital in the western Delta, had a collective memory of contacts with the Portuguese and the Catholics before 1800. These included sending an Itsekiri prince to Portugal for instruction in sacerdotal duties. The Itsekiri claims of superiority over their neighbouring Urhobo stem from pride in these dealings with Europeans.[110]

Calabar

Missionary work developed in Calabar before it came to some of the other city states. As early as 1839 the Black Christians in Jamaica felt a responsibility toward their brethren in Nigeria. It is interesting that this was the same year the Liberated Slaves from Fourah Bay in Sierra Leone prepared to go to Lagos. There may well have been trans-Atlantic links between these initiatives. In 1841 the West Indians came upon Buxton's book, *The African slave trade and its remedy*, which suggested that 'from among ... the peasantry of the West Indies ... there may arise a body of men who will return to the land of their fathers carrying divine truth ... into the heart of Africa.'[111] This vision of a return from Jamaica to 'their roots' had a stirring effect on the young Church in Jamaica. In 1842 two Scottish missionaries from the West Indies, visiting Liverpool, met British skippers well conversant with Calabar and its needs.

The British Presbyterian missionary in Jamaica, Hope Waddell, and seven West Indian colleagues, decided to offer their services to West Africa.[112] In 1846 the missionary party which arrived in Calabar included Waddell; Samuel Edgerly, printer and catechist; Andrew Chisholm, a mulatto carpenter; and Edward Miller, a Black teacher. They did not come unexpected. In Calabar, King Eyo II of Creek Town had developed contacts with Europe, spoke some English, and was eager for his people to receive Western education. His royal colleague in Duke Town, Eyamba, joined him in an enthusiastic welcome for the missionaries. He thought they would give excellent instruction in the production of coffee, cotton and sugar.[113]

Eyo II co-operated as an interpreter for Waddell, whose time was often spent at the court. The missionary had high hopes that the king would take the first steps to join the Church. Eyo showed a keen interest in the Bible and readily destroyed his many idols. He agreed with the Presbyterians on the sacredness of the Lord's Day, and abolished Sunday markets within his kingdom. He forbade twin exposure, led reform against human sacrifice, and in 1851 put an end to immolation of slaves at funerals. He was a total abstainer, and encouraged school work. However, there was a limit to his sympathies – the stumbling block was that an African king could not follow the missionaries' teaching on polygamy.

The relationship between King Eyo II and the missionaries at Calabar, especially Waddell, can be compared to that between Muslims and the traditional rulers in the northern savannas. King Eyo's dilemma was how to be sympathetic to the missionaries and still retain his Efik peoples' support by upholding traditional beliefs and the related economic structures. Nair writes that 'although King Eyo threw open his compound to the missionaries, acted as their interpreter, and consented to their social reforms when he thought them warranted and acceptable to his countrymen ... he never permitted the missionaries to consolidate their position.'[114] To do this would have incurred the hostility of his older and more conservative followers. His determination to control the nature and pace of change involved Eyo in a series of crises in his relations with the missionaries. Admired by them until he refused to be converted, or to give up polygamy, after 1851 he was caricatured in mission circles as a 'licentious despot'. This was a turning point in the history of the mission; previously Waddell had relied heavily on the king for almost everything.

This story of Eyo II is interesting in a number of ways. First it shows that when the mission felt it was sufficiently independent or able to rely on British support, the missionaries could apply more pressure on the traditional rulers. They could urge their erstwhile patrons to accept Christian mores, especially to discard polygamy. It is also an example of a rulers' dilemma in dealing with missionaries. Even though he might want to accept aspects of Christianity and to abolish some community customs, he was forced to balance the Church against the conservative elements in Efik society; he had to placate both groups. The third issue of interest concerns slavery. The Jamaican missionaries and 'back to their roots' people were a threat to a social structure which they did not fully understand; and the liberated slaves from Sierra Leone were the embodiment of the missionaries' policies.

Waddell and his colleagues from the West Indies had brought along strange bundles of paper which apparently could speak. The Bible had a message of surprising relevance to the circumstances of the slaves. Soon after his arrival, Waddell gave the chiefs a series of 'Sabbath Preaching', emphasizing the need for better treatment of their slaves. The Bible taught, he explained, that the slaves should be treated with justice: 'They are our fellow creatures and have heads and hearts, feelings and passions, like ourselves, and must have justice with mercy, or the land ... cannot be safe.'[115]

These ideas took root, and were one element in the complex of anger, passion and hope which soon led to several slave revolts throughout Calabar: 1851 in Duke Town, 1861 in Creek Town and elsewhere. The aim of these uprisings was not particularly radical, in fact it was strangely modest. The slaves resisted arbitrary treatment by freemen, especially concerning funeral sacrifices where slaves had been the victims of wholesale immolation. But this was as far as the enslaved masses would go. 'Having improved their position within the existing social and political system, it became their interest to uphold it. They did not seek freedom from their slave status.'[116]

From 1849 a British consul was stationed on the island of Fernando Po. The presence of this 'diplomatic representative among sovereign states' was increasingly felt on the mainland. In most cases his advice, when it concerned Christian missions, furthered their cause.[117]

These were the beginnings. The Gospel message had begun to penetrate and to show its relevance to the vast numbers of underprivileged who were becoming the cadres of the Church. The missions became the basis for communities growing up independent of the customs and control of the traditional Efik society at Calabar. The stations gathered round them people who had been given away as presents, twin babies rescued from the bush, and refugees from Efik justice who sought the protection of the missions. The missionaries also wanted formally to emancipate their Efik household members, and from 1855 the British consul began granting them emancipation papers. This encouraged slaves to escape to the mission stations, a development which jeopardized the authority of the traditional rulers. This hastened a conflict between Efik rulers and British power, and a rush of demands by the slaves for British protection. Dr Latham writes that

> The Mission's impact on Efik society was felt in procuring British protection for the refugee slaves, who became members of their households. It was seen by leading slaves in Efik society that the British protection and emancipation did remove the onerous demands which their masters might make ... British protection became a shield behind which the oppressed slaves in Calabar could shelter.[118]

The same was true of another group under British security, the free Africans from other parts of the coast. A more comprehensive term for these foreigners, who were to constitute a considerable part of both the Catholic and Protestant congregations, was the 'Coasters'. They included not only Sierra Leoneans, but also people from Lagos, Dahomey, Gabon, and

Cameroon. It is reported that at Calabar no less than 100 of these 'Coasters' would participate in the Roman Catholic mass on Sunday mornings.[119] In 1853, the Revd I. Jones, a representative of the CMS in Sierra Leone, visited Calabar, and obtained King Eyo's word that he would welcome liberated slaves from that locality. After 1854 many of them settled in Calabar. They chose to live on mission ground, and soon engaged in trade. Although Efik leaders wanted these 'trading' Sierra Leoneans to leave, the British Consul prevented their eviction, 'thereby establishing that, while not British subjects, they were to receive British protection ... Moreover, these free Africans were another group resident in Calabar for whom the British government owned responsibility, and therefore represented an extension of British influence into Calabar affairs.'[120] The role that the mission played with these groups is clear; but also illuminating is the way the mission used official British support and power to sustain itself and its mission-related Africans.

The missionaries turned to more expedient pursuits. Waddell tried his hand at writing Christian books in the Efik language. His colleague, Hugh Goldie, a great linguist, completed the Efik translation of the New Testament in 1862, and six years later the Old Testament also was available in Efik. Together with Ga and Twi in Ghana, Efik thus became one of the very early West African languages to have the full Bible. Energetic mission efforts in routing out traditional religious customs was sometimes less successful and definitely less popular. One missionary's mistake was Edgerly's breaking of the Ekpe drum at the Town Hall. There was a tendency to confuse 'rudeness to people, rulers and gods alike, with courageous zeal'.[121]

Church membership was at first very low, and growth was inhibited by the stern catechumen policy of the Presbyterian mission. Waddell believed that only rigid selection of the first converts would insure the proper 'tone and character' of their cause. His attitude represented a general puritan trend at the time in Presbyterian and Reformed missions throughout the continent. Waddell wrote: 'The first principles of religion must be first taught, though they may in themselves be inoperative to produce conversion; and the law must be preached till it is at last understood, though it should be preached for years without making converts.'[122]

Brass

The Crowther family influenced developments in Brass. Samuel Crowther arrived there as soon as he moved to eastern Nigeria in 1857. During his occasional visits in the 1860s, he found the people and even a traditional priest interested, but the reigning king opposed the new message. It was only after a new king, Ockiya, was installed that the situation became more favourable. The new regime encouraged Christianity and Crowther was able to reach an agreement about schools with the king and seven of his chiefs. Ockiya received baptism on his deathbed, and was succeeded by a Christian chief who personally assisted Church and school.

Although the number of Christians was initially small, Brass was soon regarded as a 'predominantly Christian state'.[123] Lack of staff limited the growth of the mission. The two Sierra Leone teachers recruited by Crowther could not communicate the message sufficiently because of linguistic problems, and none of the West African leaders was native to the place. The quality and level of Christian instruction was limited, using only the Lord's prayer, the Creed, and certain passages of Holy Scripture memorized from a set of '100 Texts'. The real Christian influence was exerted through the personal teaching and fellowship of the local catechist. With rapidly rising Church membership in the 1880s, Brass was for a time regarded as 'the jewel of the Niger', but the lustre abated dramatically in the 1890s, the time of the 'Delta Pastorate'.

Crowther and the Igbo

In 1857 when Crowther moved from Yoruba country to Igboland surrounding the Niger River, the political situation on the Niger was highly disturbed. Most of the city states along the river and in the Delta were at war with one another. The arrival of missionaries and traders seemed to offer advantages, and consequently competition ensued between the states for their favours. There had been previous contacts with the Igbo people; a number of Liberated Africans in Sierra Leone were Igbo. The enterprise differed from Crowther's involvement in Yoruba country, as his staff this time were all Sierra Leonean or local. The headquarters of the mission was transferred to Onitsha on the Niger, which seemed to Crowther to be 'the high road to the heart of the Igbo nation'.[124] It was indeed strategically chosen, on the frontier between the semi-Islamized north and the pagan south. Crowther, however, found it necessary to live most of the time in Lagos for up to eight or nine months of the year and could only devote a third of each year to visitations among the Niger congregations – a fact which was later to be held against him.

Crowther was assisted at Onitsha by an impressive colleague, the Revd John Christopher Taylor. He also was a Sierra Leonean, but of Igbo background, and similar to Crowther in Yorubaland, had come home to his roots. Unlike Crowther, on his arrival he was unable to preach in his mother tongue, but after a year he could preach without an interpreter. 'The psychological effect was magical.'[125] As with Crowther, Taylor's personality commanded the respect of rulers and commoners alike. He was outspoken in his opposition to certain aspects of Igbo tradition: he refused to adopt the 'humiliating posture' of bowing the head to the ground in the presence of rulers; he fought against twin exposure; and preached uncompromisingly against the idols. He had the satisfaction of welcoming into the fold a number of prominent young men who brought their 'jujus', in a bag. One of these said, 'I am tired of these sticks. The word of God now enters my heart; once I was foolish.'[126] Taylor's co-worker, the Revd Langley, preached with such fervour that he even appeared in the dreams of the faithful, calling on them to escape from the wrath of God.[127]

The first converts were not impressive in the eyes of established society – slaves, widows, and a variety of other social outcasts. When over forty people had been baptized in 1862, Taylor and his Igbo staff were already looking forward to a definite advance in their evangelising efforts, but these high hopes were frustrated by the upheavals of wars.[128] Polygamy proved to be an intractable problem here also, leading to 'back-sliding'.

The Sierra Leoneans were practised at forming 'mutual-aid' societies and encouraged the Igbo faithful to organize the 'Christian Relief Company'. Designed to stimulate the growth of a self-sustaining community, the Company helped the Christian groups to win the confidence of their rulers by volunteering to assist them in difficult situations.[129]

While Crowther constantly sought to retain amicable relations with the rulers, his strategy was to situate each of his Niger mission stations at a careful distance from the pagan community. Invariably, education was his chief method of evangelization. By emphasizing the importance of schools, he knew that he could win the good-will of rulers and elders, the majority of whom were already anxious to promote Western education, partly for its prestige value. Although he stressed the modernizing effects of Church education, he was keen to place as pastors his 'native agents' – men with somewhat limited educational attainments. His Niger staff members were middle-aged men, 'barely literate in English and the vernacular, farmers, carpenters, mechanics, masons, court messengers', all Sierra Leoneans like himself.[130] He was convinced that these men of solid Christian character would fraternize with the chiefs, who would look to them 'as equals in years but superior in knowledge'.[131] Such men could achieve greater success than more academically educated pastors, who might become alienated from the community.

This relationship would also ensure a tolerant attitude to local custom. 'Christianity', he insisted, 'does not undertake to destroy national assimilation.'[132] Thus he encouraged any attempt to adapt Christian hymns to native tunes. Crowther's attitude to traditional African religion has been analyzed with great sensitivity by Dr P. R. McKenzie, who called it 'life-participation dialogue', making the crucial point that Crowther's capacity for inter-religious encounter should be seen as 'a Yoruba, a Nigerian, a West African trait'. Crowther was often conciliatory and full of human understanding. He said, 'With the heathen population we have mostly and chiefly to do. Them you must not censure as ignorant, stupid and foolish idolators; your dealings with them must be that of sympathy and love, as you would deal with the blind who errs out of the way.'[133] An Ifa priest once told him, 'Softly you must go with us or you will spoil the whole matter; stretch the bow too much and it will break.'[134] In Sierra Leone, Bishop Weeks had denied baptism to owners of household slaves; Crowther, quoting Acts 15, held that this was too rigorous. He also pleaded that women in polygamous households should not be denied baptism.

The African bishop: challenges and response

In 1864 Crowther became bishop. This appointment was one of the most far-sighted ecclesiastical decisions in African Church history. At a time when the Church on the West Coast of Africa had barely come into existence, this African pastor was consecrated a bishop. Sierra Leone had introduced episcopacy into the region in 1852, but it was an illustration of the climatic hardships of the time that the first three bishops of Sierra Leone all died within a period of seven years.[135] These men were, however, all European – the first African bishop of Sierra Leone was not appointed until 1944!

Crowther's appointment was initiated by Henry Venn, the CMS secretary in London. In 1851 Venn had begun to formulate a theory of the 'Three Selves' – a self-supporting, self-governing, self-propagating Church – and developed his idea of a 'Native Church' under episcopal leadership. In Crowther he found the right man to translate his great vision into practical reality. At first Crowther was unwilling to accept the offer to become bishop, but eventually assented to his fatherly friend's urgent personal appeal. 'Samuel Ajayi, my son, will you deny me my last wish asked of you before I die?'[136]

The frontiers of Anglican dioceses during this period, just as of Roman Catholic bishoprics, tended to be drawn on a generous scale, and Crowther's diocese was no exception. The original licence referred to 'the countries of

Western Africa from the Equator to Senegal'. In reality, his episcopate proved to be a much more limited area. His far-flung territory of 'Western Africa' included problems of communications even within the diocese. For travelling to maintain contact with pastors and their congregations, Crowther depended on the good-will of the West Africa Company and the captains of its steamers. In 1878 the Mission acquired its own steamer, called the *Henry Venn*, but as this was also used for commerce, its existence compounded the tension between company and mission. In this irritated atmosphere, rumours were circulated about the quality of the 'native agents' in the mission. The 1880s saw a change in European attitudes to Africans. Ideas of 'Social Darwinism' both in the West and in West Africa, expressed doubts as to African capabilities. In 1881 a CMS commission issued a damaging report on the situation in the diocese. Toward the end of the decade, a new set of CMS missionaries arrived on the Niger. They were very zealous, and quite prepared to pronounce disparaging judgements on the African Church. While patronizingly appreciative of Crowther personally – 'a charming old man, really guileless and humble',[137] they questioned the African bishop's authority, and were highly critical of Crowther's family and the local pastors. A mission committee suspended a number of the pastors, including the bishop's son, Archdeacon Dandeson Crowther. 'It was unlikely that they would have gone so far if Crowther had been a European.'[138] The old Bishop may have been very 'charming and humble', but in response to this insensitive treatment, he announced his resignation, and died soon after, on 1 January 1892.

There are a considerable number of explanations to the Crowther crisis. A changed outlook and new policies on the part of the CMS secretariat in London led to a tighter control of the African Church from the British headquarters. This, it is sometimes claimed, was an expression of a European racism, from 'overzealous racist white missionaries'.[139] Not so, others retort; it was not racism, but a new puritanism awakened by the English Keswick movement, a revivalist view represented by a generation of young dedicated English missionaries, all aflame for what they thought was the kingdom of God. Bishop Crowther's 'native agents' have been the object of special inquiries from other scholars. It has been claimed that they were not really 'natives' at all, but imported Sierra Leoneans far from home, who found it hard to adjust, and in certain cases were not as satisfactory as might have been expected.[140]

With conflicting interpretations of an incident which will not easily be laid to rest, one is tempted to add still another aspect, supplementary to those already outlined. It is a consideration of the theology or ecclesiology on the part of the missionaries most feverishly involved. Wilmot Brooke, born in 1865, studied medicine in London from 1883–87. While still a student, he joined expeditions to Algeria in 1884 and to the Upper Congo (in order to reach the 'Central Sudan') in 1887. In 1889 he prepared for an independent mission to Lokoja on the Niger, but later in the same year formulated plans for a 'Sudan Mission', under CMS auspices. It was this self-sufficient young man who was to scrutinize old Bishop Crowther's efforts. Another missionary with a similar outlook was J. A. Robinson, a Cambridge scholar, appointed at the age of twenty-nine as secretary of the Niger Mission in 1887. He was sure that the Negro race showed almost no signs of 'ruling' power, and he referred to Crowther's work as a 'nominal episcopacy'.[141]

The attitudes of these young men were not unique in the Protestant world of Africa prior to 1914. There were other zealots besides Brooke and Robinson who desired to pull up the young shoots from the soil in order to check whether they had begun to grow aright. Western actors in the drama insisted on the dictates of the Spirit, but overlooked the fact that a Church, on whatever foundations it starts, and however it develops, lives in a tension between 'Institution' and 'Spirit'. Even the most 'spiritual' organization necessarily develops its institutional frame, even though organization must be, to some extent, informed by the Spirit through the Word and Sacraments administered there. Brooke and Robinson came straight from universities and from Keswick influences, and were sure that they represented the Spirit. In the name of the Spirit, they were prepared to eradicate what had been growing. Such was Keswick's authority at the time, that sufficient resistance against this particular gust of wind could not be mobilized, and serious harm was done to the work in West Africa.

Bonny

The missionaries in Bonny and the other city states were mainly Africans; almost without exception they were from Sierra Leone and were under the direction of Bishop Crowther. The Bishop visited Bonny only very occasionally, but his youngest son, Dandeson, later Archdeacon, served as parson in Bonny from 1871–98. Nearly all the new Church members were slaves, but it must be understood that almost the total population consisted of slaves, ruled by a king and his chiefs.

The Christian message of liberation and hope made the converts less submissive. They refused to take part in the traditional worship of their particular House, and having learned to respect the Sabbath commandment, they would not work on Sundays. For their disobedience, the converts were chained, flogged and in some cases even put to death. Joshua Hart was one example. When he persisted in attending Sunday worship, and refused to eat the local sacrifices, he was tied hand and foot and thrown overboard; a paddle blow on the head completed the murder of this martyr for his faith in 1875. Sometimes freemen were similarly treated. Isaiah Bara and Jonathan Apiape were chained and kept in the bush for a year. The traditional priests appealed to them to abjure, but the answer was unmistakable: 'Jesus Christ has put a padlock on my heart and taken the key to heaven.'[142]

A few kings from the Delta area went to Britain, returning as baptized members of Queen Victoria's Church. King William Pebble of Bonny had once taken refuge in England and was baptized there in 1856. His successor from 1867, George Pebble I, after spending a number of years in England, was a comparatively Anglicized, modernizing monarch and a defender of the Christian cause. He incurred rabid opposition from a dangerous competitor when he challenged the traditional religious power of Bonny by a daring decision. In the local religion, the iguana lizard was revered with special awe: anyone killing an iguana, even by accident, had to die. On Easter Day 1867, George Pebble I declared that the iguana was no longer to be regarded as a sacred animal in the Bonny kingdom, and this was dramatized by a great ritual act.[143]

The king's antagonist was Jaja, a shrewd and able ex-slave who had become the Head of the House that once had bought him. He had risen to the position of high priest at the local temple, and feared that any foreign influence would eventually destroy the independence of the city states. Several chiefs had signed a petition requesting the services of the missionaries in gaining access to Western education for their children. Jaja refused to sign. Moving with his household to an adjacent island, he founded the city state of Opobo in 1870, and was soon regarded as the most powerful ruler in the Bight of Benin. He was secure and his community could rely on his awesome *juju*, 'our religion to which we must keep'. Within less than two decades, however, he was one of the vast number of African rulers throughout the continent who became victims of imperialism. He was accused – quite unjustly – by the British Consul on the Niger, Harry Johnson, who said that Jaja planned 'selling his country to France'.[144]

Okrika

Okrika was another of the city states in the Niger Delta. The first few decades of its Church history convincingly illustrate the decisive role of the

African initiative in the process of Christianization. A trader named Atorudibo introduced the new religion to his people. Frequent trade visits brought him into contact with Christianity and he was soon converted. When he discarded some of the cult objects of his traditional beliefs, he was taken to court and fined. Gaining the support of two chiefs and some Christian immigrants from other city states, he persisted in his new religion, but he had to tread warily. The dominating commercial interests of mighty Bonny were an ever-present threat to the little Okrika Christian community, which had to give guarantees to the ambitious African Christians in Bonny that the mission work would not jeopardize existing trade relations.

The Crowther family, especially Archdeacon D. C. Crowther, supported the Okrika congregation by occasional visits. The Archdeacon introduced the art of brick-making to the people, an activity appropriate for Okrika with its clay soil. This combination of evangelization and industrial enterprise was characteristic of the beginnings of Christianity in the Delta.

For decades the CMS had been reaching out to the Igbo-speaking population. Bishop Crowther's 'agents' from Sierra Leone had been at work from the strategic centre of Onitsha, where there was a congregation of about 400. Along the Niger river there were a few other Anglican groups, such as at Obosi, pioneered by Onitsha Christians. The congregations were placed at or near the river. 'Even by 1900 the farthest outstation was not more than fifteen miles from its banks.'[145] Important as these centres were, away from the Niger very considerable numbers of the Igbo had not heard the Christian message. These congregations on the river stood out markedly from the rest of the local people. The preachers were all from Sierra Leone, and so were the leading laymen – teachers and clerks – who were sometimes joined by individuals and families from a local slave population and were thus foreigners to the area. There were also efforts to reach the Igbo from the south, using the Delta congregations as a springboard to advance inland.

Catholic beginnings

For thirty years, the CMS Anglicans had dominated the Lower Niger, with their Protestant primary schools and their keen involvement in the translation of the Bible into various local languages. In 1885 when two French Catholic missions arrived on the Niger, all this seemed jeopardized. Fr Carlo Zappa of the Society of African Missions (of Lyon) took up his position at Lokoja, and the Holy Ghost Fathers, coming from Gabon, settled at Onitsha, where they received a piece of land from Bishop Crowther. 'I acquired this land for God's cause – take it', was the good

African bishop's generous remark. Townsend, the CMS missionary, not to be outdone in this ecumenical exercise, gave the Holy Ghost Fathers the use of the CMS motorboat in the harbour of Brass.[146]

A certain rivalry had developed on the Niger between British and French interests. As the United African Company (later the Royal Niger Company) met competition from French firms, the economic tussle was viewed as part of a wider political struggle for power. When the two French missions came to the Niger in 1885, on the invitation of French trading companies, rumours about French machinations were revived. In Bishop Crowther's time, close contacts developed between the Missions and the Royal Niger Company. It was widely observed that the spokesmen in both cases – the Anglican catechist or pastor and the company official – were probably from Sierra Leone. With increasing opposition to the company, the local Anglican leadership had to share some of the odium.

Even though at first Crowther generously helped the Catholic newcomers, a vigorous and occasionally unfortunate competition between Catholics and Protestants for influence in society developed throughout Igboland. The CMS were indisputably first in the field, and had valued contacts with the traditional community. But the Igbo people were no longer exclusively concerned with a glorious past, and now anticipated their need to adapt to change. They wished to contribute to the shaping of their own future. The rivalry between the missions became, above all, a struggle over the schools. Education was the decisive route by which the younger generations entered the Church.

The missions were not the only force engaged in the struggle. The colonial government was involved in shaping its own school programme and educational code, providing for the teaching of English in all schools. The government would also give grants-in-aid to schools according to examination results and it abolished obligatory religious instruction for pupils.

The confrontation between the two missions at Onitsha sharpened the issues and forced them to define their educational programmes. Their stances would thus indicate their differing perspectives and mould the future toward which the two Christian communities were heading.

The CMS challenged Government policy. In 1890 the CMS secretary, F. N. Eden, expressed the Society's standpoint which remained representative for a considerable time: 'The teaching in the mission schools would be of the simplest kind – the chief aim of which being to teach the children in the vernacular, so that they may be able to study their Bible when translated for them in the mother tongue.'[147] With this view, the CMS enunciated a widely-held Protestant attitude – a concern for the language of the people. This stance was implemented by the translation and study of the Bible in the vernacular, but at the same time it represented a social concern: the school should not be elitist and thus a divisive factor in the social body. Eden's colleague, Henry Townsend, said: 'I don't want a youth confined by intellectual culture till he becomes an individual of superior caste and must carry with him wherever he goes the comforts and show of civilized life.'[148] Protestants in Igboland therefore developed a system of elementary or bush schools, where the youngsters spent several years learning to read and write and to understand and appreciate certain passages of the Bible.

There was much in this Protestant pleading for simplicity and for the vernacular to which the Roman Catholics would under ordinary circumstances have given their consent. The CMS argument seemed to be taken straight out of Father Libermann's own book 'Africa will be saved by saints and not by scholars'. Both the new French missions were at first wary of schools, coming to Africa with a distinct aversion to their home country's 'lay schools' which were accused of causing havoc and disaster in an increasingly agnostic population. In West Africa, schools and colleges had, it seemed, an unmistakable secularizing flavour, the kind of thing that Evangelical Anglicans and Wesleyans did so well and so eagerly, but which obviously did not bring people into the Kingdom, at least not automatically. Father Zappa, who moved from his first location at Lokoja to Asaba, concurred with this view: 'I have always thought that the school method involves a misunderstanding of our mission which is simply an apostolic affair.'[149]

One of the Spiritans, Father Lejeune, challenged this view. He thought that in Eastern Nigeria schools should be not only tools of evangelism, but also means of bringing the Catholic Church to the fore in African society. He met determined opposition from his pious colleagues when he argued for higher education for the Igbo, although they reluctantly consented to a Catholic high school in Onitsha in 1901. Broken in health, he was repatriated to France. His vision of advanced schooling for the Igbo might have been neglected had it not been for another Holy Ghost Father, from Ireland, who carried the baton much further. Bishop J. P. Shanahan (1871–1943) knew the French well, having completed his education at the Spiritan mother house in Paris from 1883–97. In 1902 he came to Nigeria. Installed at Onitsha, he soon recognized material for 'fully-fledged missionaries' in some of his Igbo pupils: Patrick Okolo, Charles Ndaguba, Willie Onucukwe, and Paul Anekwe.

Shanahan used the traditional Catholic three-pronged evangelistic approach: orphanages for slaves and outcasts; Christian villages; and elementary schools, which he regarded at the same time as anti-slavery instruments. Until 1908 he employed the time-honoured missionary method, in eastern Nigeria, of following the main rivers and their tributaries. From Onitsha he branched out, crossing Igboland with untiring energy and resolve. For the trips along the Niger and its connecting rivers, he used two boats, named *Leo XIII* and *Diata-Diata* ('Hurry on').

In 1908 the Government road system had been sufficiently developed to allow the intrepid missionary to reach into the vast wooded hinterland. Shanahan discovered that the school was the most suited agency for an approach to the ambitious mind and soul of the Igbo. The results were not slow in coming. From 1906–12 the missions opened over forty new schools, and initiated an energetic teacher-training programme. Its success was shown in 1912 when fifty new teachers graduated. Catholic school statistics rose rapidly: 1906, 2,000 pupils; 1915, 13,000; 1918, 22,000; and 1921, 41,000. From its inception, the Onitsha Catholic high school launched a modern programme of industrial education, and such subjects as elementary algebra, geometry, book-keeping, and foreign languages. Some missions raised objections to receiving Government grants because of the accompanying clause about religious neutrality. However, this restriction mattered little to Shanahan, who felt that the local chapel and catechumenate would provide the necessary religious knowledge and direction. Under his inspiring leadership, the schools and the local catechists launched an Igbo mass movement which continued to expand. The only impediment was the lack of staff. During a visit to Ireland in 1913, Shanahan appealed for additional missionaries. Although he received few immediate results, his efforts eventually led to the involvement of the Irish Black Rock College in Igbo higher education.

Owerri

The breakthrough in the form of an astonishing movement, both Catholic and Protestant, took place in Owerri, a district dominated only a few years before by the Aro Chukwu oracle. Very soon after the destruction of that centre, people seemed ready to move as a body in the Christian way. When the British Acting High Commissioner invited the Anglican Bishop Tugwell to begin work in the area, the CMS missionary decided that the mission should not be located in the administrative centre, to avoid confusion with the colonial government. The Anglicans started instead at Egbu, a few miles away from Owerri. Seven years later, when the Holy Ghost mission arrived, the Catholics similarly placed their headquarters at an equivalent distance from the British administrative centre. The CMS were fortunate in choosing Archdeacon Thomas Dennis for their Owerri mission. He became one of the outstanding British missionaries in West Africa, a first-rate scholar, and a man who could say with confidence about himself: 'I [have] set my face Africa-wards.'[150]

Government and commercial clerks and other wage-earners in the Owerri district had until now been men from Bonny and other Delta towns, or from Onitsha to the north. Soon Owerri people were eager to see their own young men trained at one of the mission schools to take over these administrative jobs. The hunger for education in Owerri was deeply felt. In 1905 the Government began a primary school of its own for the sons of chiefs, emphasizing the English language, which it proved to be highly attractive. In 1907–09 the CMS created a small Christian colony at their Mission, consisting of boys looking for a school who were prepared to join the Church. The school produced an unusually rapid growth of the CMS community between 1905–14. Archdeacon Dennis' sister made notable contributions in running both night and day schools.

In the modern Church history of African, the rapid mass movement that surged in Igboland between 1900–20 was unique. Until this time Church advance was slow and cumbersome, and statistics in 1900 told their cautious story. The Catholic Society of African Missions (SMA) (Lyon) reported 446 members, and the Holy Ghost Fathers 1,332. Professor Elizabeth Isichei has analyzed these returns. Of the SMA 446, all but eighty were baptized *in articulo mortis*; of these eighty, thirty were Royal Niger Company employees, leaving fifty local Catholics as fruits of fifteen years' missionary efforts! If the Holy Ghost Mission activity was similar, a statistical calculation would perhaps leave a figure of 150–200 local adherents. For the Protestants, the CMS stations were until 1900 concentrated in only a few places, and consequently did not reach more than 1 per cent of the population.

It is against these hesitant beginnings that the explosive advance in the first twenty years of the twentieth century stand out as even more striking. What were the causes of this surprising growth? The temptation is to reduce the explanation to just one exclusive factor. The truth was probably much more complex.

Until 1900 Igboland had been a singularly closed society, tightly held together by strong traditional forces which kept out most external influences. The British administration, established in 1901 as the Southern Nigeria Protectorate, concluded that in order to control Igboland, the Aro Chukwu oracle had to be erased from the map. The expedition which obliterated the sacred place in 1901–02 caused a violent shaking of the foundations of Igbo society, a traumatic shock to thousands of families and individuals who fled and became refugees. Fifteen thousand fled to the Catholic centres of Aguleri and Nsugbe.[151] In the next few years 'secondary resistance movements' tried to maintain Igbo independence, but the onslaught by the British on the traditional institutions and shrines had been a devastating blow. In western Igboland the *Ekumeku* secret society was similarly singled out for military attacks, which again enforced compliance with the dictates of the colonial power.

With the imposition of British rule from 1900, the position of the missions changed dramatically, to a great extent due to the co-operation between the colonial administration and the missions, both Catholic and Protestant. It did not take long for the Igbo to discover that membership in one of the Churches served as a shield against forced labour and other forms of oppression.[152] They thus hastened to the missions asking for schools to be started in the various localities. The combination of chapel and school was of critical importance for the Christianization of Igboland. A rapidly increasing emphasis on the need for qualified teaching in English became 'almost an obsession'.[153] A reference to Igbo psychology will clarify this urge. Nigerian scholars themselves have pointed to 'an impulse to change'[154] which was embedded in the dynamic nature of their society, and to their inherent striving towards 'success goals'.[155] There was also the revolutionary effect of the colonial government's opening of a densely populated countryside, until now comparatively isolated. New roads criss-crossed the country rapidly, and catechists and teachers on bicycles could now reach distant outposts and connect them with central mission stations.

Apart from these general socio-political factors and the improved communications, the fundamental religious question remains: Why did tens of thousands of men, women and children lose their confidence in the Aro Chukwu and other oracles, in their famous *Ekumeku* and other associations, and decide to abandon them and turn to the White Christ and His Church? A few of the all too rare expressions by Igbo individuals themselves, referring to their conversion to the Christian fellowship may serve to provide some answers. Such responses are at least as valuable as even the most ingenious speculations by others about the religious experience of these Africans.

Northern Nigeria and the Middle Belt

Northern Nigeria was dominated by Islam. The Hausa North was predominantly Muslim, consolidated during the nineteenth century by the great scholar, Uthman dan Fodio (d.1817), who led the 1804 *jihad* in Hausaland. This *jihad* resulted in the rule of some fifty Fulbe emirs over the Hausa population. The six most important emirates, including Sokoto, Kano, Katsina and Zaria, each contained more than one million subjects. All the emirates owed allegiance to the caliph who resided in Sokoto.

A *jihad* was primarily a purification movement to reform a society which had manifested outward forms of Islam, but not its genuine pious spirit and theocratic laws. The *jihad* in Hausaland provided a successful example for other Muslims to emulate, for example, further west where al-Hajj Umar led the most notable *jihad* of the middle of the nineteenth century. Half the Hausa population was Islamized toward the century's end, and sixty years later, at the end of colonial rule, about 80 per cent were Muslim. Islamic law and order were introduced and maintained by a multi-pronged approach: the power of the emirs, the scholarship of the clerics, the fellowship of the Sufi Brotherhoods and the ever-present missionary zeal of teachers and merchants. For all this Muslim dominance, however, it must be remembered that the 'Middle Belt' had large non-Muslim populations, and even if 'the fetishes trembled' under Muslim pressure, the pagan communities there had managed to resist this influence.[156]

Early in the nineteenth century the emirs had occasional contacts with Christians. The British explorer, Hugh Clapperton, visited the caliph in Sokoto in 1824. Learning that the visitors were Christian, the caliph 'asked "whether we were Nestorians or Socinians." ... I bluntly replied', said Clapperton, 'we were called Protestants. "What are Protestants?" says he.'[157] Bishop Crowther was always tactful and generous in his dealing with the Nupe emirs. Later, the Emir of Kano was faced with a more importunate contact with the same 'new' religion. One of his *mallams* (Muslim teachers), Ibrahim, had visited Cairo and had acquired a copy of the New Testament in Arabic. Reading about Jesus, he was led to believe in His Second Coming and informed the emir of this. This was dangerous heresy, and Ibrahim was duly executed in the Kano market. Before his death, however, he had gathered a group of followers and had urged them to flee. They established their small community on the borders of the Kano emirate and formed the kingdom of Ningi. Just before the First World War, they moved to Gimi near Zaria where a Christian community of about 120 came together. In this precarious situation it was Africans who took the initiative in forming a new religious settlement. A West Indian pastor, W. A. Thompson, became their advisor for a time, involving them in developing a sugar industry. They then sought contact with Dr Walter Miller, the Church Missionary Society's medical evangelist. They became convinced that Isa (Jesus) was 'the Spirit of God' with power over life and death. Their religious life together took on an intensity of its own. In the worship there was open confession of sins before the whole community, in terms which remind one of revival movements elsewhere on the continent. 'The Christianity of the Church Missionary Society was clearly answering needs that had not been fulfilled by the sect's old religion . . . ' Here were men 'who could hold a Qur'an in one hand and a Bible in the other, and understand them both with a deep piety and scholarship.' Before long, however, the adults were reduced by a sleeping-sickness epidemic.[158]

A few years after the turn of the century, British forces under the High Commissioner, Sir Frederick Lugard, who had previous experience of political developments in Uganda, conquered the emirates, one after another, and the Protectorate of Northern Nigeria was established in 1900. Lugard was aware of how tenuous this victory was. With only a handful of European personnel, and for other reasons, he had to tread carefully so as not to irritate the emirs, nor to unleash the enormous latent Muslim power in the North. He applied a colonial political system of 'Indirect Rule': the Protectorate was to be administered – in principle – by the emirs themselves. British experience in India had formed this imperial concept. Its classic application was in Northern Nigeria. It was later applied in some other colonial territories and became of far-reaching importance as a political framework for the Christian Church in British colonial Africa.

Military conquest and colonial rule facilitated the extension of modern transport. There were economic and religious links with North Africa, and some people had daring plans in the 1890s to extend a railway from Southern Nigeria to Lake Chad and beyond – to Egypt.[159] These ideas were doomed to remain exciting visions, but the two Nigerian railways dramatically changed and modernized the lives of the people. A line from Lagos in 1896 reached Kano in 1911 and a line from Port Harcourt to Kaduna, via Enugu and Jos, was begun in 1913 and completed in 1926.

With the British Protectorate in the north, the missions concentrated their efforts on the Fulani (Fulbe) emirs and their Hausa people and on the 'Middle Belt', with its predominantly pagan communities. General Gordon's death in Khartoum in 1885, and the creation of a Mahdist state between 1881 and 1898 shook the Christian West. The missions tried to meet the challenge by a bold response: a defence line of mission stations across Africa. The CMS 'Sudan Party', with its controversial leaders – G.W. Brooke and J. A. Robinson – responded quickly. Brooke's death in 1892 and Robinson's in 1891 put an end to their dreams. Lugard, as High Commissioner, insisted that he and his administration would not interfere with Islam. He could not allow Christian missions the normal freedoms they were accustomed to elsewhere. He was less doctrinaire, though, than some of his successors, a number of whom were decidedly anti-missionary. Several British and French administrators shared a negative attitude to missions: Islam was the religion of the African, and any efforts to change his faith were wrong.

In working with the missions, Lugard had to deal with Dr Walter Miller (1872–1952), an outstanding Anglican medical missionary. This evangelical Northern Irish layman was a prominent Hausa linguist and Bible translator. With him should be mentioned: Dr Andrew Stirritt of the Sudan Interior Mission, an uncompromising and dedicated Christian layman, linguist and Bible teacher; and Dr L. Bronnum, the Scandinavian initiator of the Danish branch of the Sudan United Mission in Numan in the East, a medical practitioner like Miller.

In an earlier generation, Sir Thomas Buxton had preached 'the Bible and the plough'. Dr Miller modernized the idea and referred to 'two means, Christianity and education'. He wished to found schools for *mallams* and for the sons of chiefs, an approach well attuned to the High Commissioner's programme of Indirect Rule. Lugard admired the impetuous Christian doctor, even if Miller's activities often threatened the uneasy equilibrium between Muslims and Christians, which Lugard was anxious to maintain. Miller enthusiastically worked out a detailed syllabus for his school using the Hausa language and by 1907 was able to recruit fifteen boys. Eight of those attended classes, but of the eight only two showed a genuine interest in their lessons. In 1908 Miller had acceded to the government's policy that religious education was not to be permitted in the schools. But his own Scripture translations were the only Hausa reading material available at this time: the Gospels of St John and St Mark, the First Epistle of John and other stories from the New Testament. Soon several of the emirs objected to the school and it was forced to close. An alternative education programme was later arranged, this time by Hanns Vischer (1876–1945), the famous British educator and administrator and a former CMS missionary.[160]

In 1914, as the result of imperial conquest, the three regions of the country – Lagos Colony and Protectorate, the Southern Protectorate and the North – were brought together into the single colony of Nigeria. After the First World War, as educated Yoruba and Igbo found employment in the British administration, Christian congregations developed in the Muslim north. Their schools and churches in the *sabon garis* ('new towns') of the northern towns assured a significant Christian presence until the civil war period (1967–70).

Although the new colonial government of Northern Nigeria abolished slavery and enslavement in 1901, a large number of people – mainly children – continued to be victims of enslavement in the period 1900–20. Many of them, once liberated, were too young to know where they had come from, and if they were returned there was always the danger that they would be exposed to the same fate again. The colonial administration decided to found Freed Slaves Homes and in 1908 the Sudan United Mission became responsible for these foundations, which existed for over twenty years and were only closed in 1925. Some of the youngsters were sent to other missions to be looked after and to receive an education: in 1905, nineteen children were assigned to the Catholics at Onitsha and, in 1908, seventeen were sent to the Presbyterian Church at Calabar. In total about 5,000 children and adults came under the shelter of the Freed Slaves' Homes and they 'became one of the channels for spreading western ideas and influence which were of great importance in the emergence of Northern Nigeria into the twentieth century.'[161]

The Middle Belt

The seemingly irresistible southward move of Islam in Nigeria and throughout West Africa was, in the years prior to the First World War, seen as the challenge to Christian missions, whether Catholic or Protestant. Could it be contained perhaps by a chain of missions across the continent? As already indicated, ideas of mission 'chains' across the continent – East to West and reverse – were a well-known strategic concept with mission leaders at the time. The flamboyant German missionary Karl Kumm planned such a chain from Lokoja on the Niger to the Nile and Ethiopia, in order to counter Islam, and he trekked along this axis himself. Here was a more aggressive variety of a common strategic idea.

The Sudan Interior Mission had started work among the Nupe in 1901. The Nupe emirates with their main towns of Bida and Katcha, had a distinct culture of their own, ruled by Fulbe emirs. In 1897 a military force commanded by Goldie had placed the region under British control. Traditional culture and the Muslim Koranic schools had created a 'Black Byzantium', a social system of rank, class and hierarchy. This *milieu* served to emphasize 'the meaning of Nupe life', an aspiration to move upward socially by age-status and merit.[162] The CMS representative, T. E. Alvarez, a 'lay bishop' who devoted many years to the work, shaped Christian schools so that they contributed to this social system. The Canadian Mennonite, A. W. Banfield, a linguist, translated the New Testament into the Nupe language in 1916. The strict social control and the Islamic education hindered the Christian cause, particularly as the main educational work of the Christian mission was in the hands of expatriates.

The Tiv were by far the most populous group in the Middle Belt, numbering about one million at that time. Traditionally, Tiv 'Big Men' relied on their powerful *mbatsav* (witchcraft societies), and were not greatly concerned with the imposition by the British of such new administrative measures as direct taxation. Tiv farmers at this time found a market in the sale of benniseed.

An invitation from Karl Kumm and the Sudan United Mission to the missions in South Africa led the Dutch Reformed Church to begin work among the Tiv in 1911. After the Boer War this South African Church had experienced a 'revival', and young people responded to Kumm's appeal. They had a staff of about twenty, including a medical lady doctor, M. L. du Toit at the Mkar Hospital. These solid Reformed missionaries plodded along, building seven mission stations across the land, without seeing any noticeable impact of their efforts for decades.

Not until 1917 were the first four Tiv baptized, and by 1936 the total of the baptized community was only thirty-one. In conformity with their cultural philosophy, the Boer missionaries maintained that the only language medium permissible for Church and school was the local Tiv. English and the Hausa language were to be avoided. Hausa, the missionaries thought, was too much influenced by Muslim thinking.

To a greater degree than other missions, the Dutch Reformed stressed the Bible and the Sabbath observance. Recorded experiences of individual Tiv Christians in this Northern Nigerian area reveal a Book-relatedness similar to the intense Muslim veneration for their Holy Book, the Qu'ran. The Tiv Church was slow in reaching a 'take-off', but the gradual growth over decades was the preparation for an indigenous Bible School 'awakening' of surprising strength at the end of the thirties.[163]

The Church approached the village head of Salatu in Tiv country and suggested that he send his children to their new school. He thought it expedient to oblige, but sent the son whom he could most easily do without – Akiga, a handicapped boy having only one eye and a damaged foot. He would do as the missionary's houseboy! It happened, however, that little Akiga saw more clearly than most of his contemporaries with two eyes. In five months' time he could write a letter in very neat hand-writing. He became the first Tiv convert, the first Tiv evangelist and the author of a history about his people – *Akiga's Story*.[164] He edited a Tiv newspaper and was councillor to the Tiv delegation at a Northern Nigerian constitutional conference in London.

The Protestant effort among the Tiv was thus, at first, a link in a northbound mission chain. The beginnings of the Catholic work among the Tiv and neighbouring communities were related to the Irish Spiritan mission among the Igbo in south-east Nigeria. From there, German Spiritans came to the Benue region and the Tiv in the 1930s. While the Protestants had started east of Tiv country, the Catholics set out from the west, and following Bishop Shanahan's example, rapidly started schools in the villages, with an emphasis on the English language and thus with a different approach from the school policy of the particular Protestant missionaries at the time. This was the beginning of a missionary move into Tivland, often in the teeth of the population's distrust. It was to take some time – about two decades – until a change was to come, but when it came, it was to be all the more convincing.

CAMEROON

The coastline of Cameroon and Gabon, with its many islands and inlets, provided opportunities for encounters between Africans and foreigners and between old traditions and new ideas. Around the middle of the century Cameroon was hardly more than a few harbours, with small coastal communities under mutually competing chiefs, often referred to as 'kings'. The same picture applied to Gabon. Beyond the coast stretched the immense, impenetrable world of tropical forest. Cameroon had at the time some 140 different tribal groups, each with its own language; the corresponding number for Gabon was forty. There was very little communication between these communities.

Springboard to the coast

The first years of Christian endeavour show surprising parallels for both Cameroon and Gabon, especially in regard to the role of Africans in evangelization. On the Cameroon coast a mere handful of missionaries from Britain and the United States co-operated with Jamaican preachers, teachers, and artisans – all Baptist. In Gabon, missionaries worked with Creoles from Liberia. For Cameroon, Fernando Po, the island in Benin Bay, became the springboard. This island was ideal for communication between cultures, and emerged as a small Christian community. After centuries of Portuguese and Spanish influence, British forces occupied Fernando Po for a brief period, from 1827 to 1834. The British built Clarence, a port to which foreigners were invited. One hundred and fifty Sierra Leonean settlers and labourers arrived, giving the town of Clarence 'its early Creole character'.[165] To these were soon added about 1,000 'liberated Africans' – freed slaves; a group of outcast Bubi from the interior of the island; and a dynamic group of Kru sawyers from the West African coast. British officers and traders formed an upper class. Palm oil and timber were the dominant trades. For the labourers, it was a harsh world, with conditions not very different from those of a slave camp.

In 1841 the Baptist Missionary Society of London placed two missionaries on the island, and for a decade the Baptist influence controlled the cultural and economic affairs. In 1844 nearly forty Jamaicans arrived on the island. These and the Sierra Leone 'Saros' set the tone in the community, producing 'a Creole elite, Baptist in religion, Victorian in culture'.[166] Conversion brought with it both a new culture and a new way of life, demonstrated by respectable Christian gentlemen who divided their attention between their palm oil or timber business and the chapel. Some of the settlers became highly successful traders who, in their free time, acted as influential deacons in the Baptist Church. The town of Clarence was marked by Baptist devotion and piety. This influence did not last. The local Baptist attempt at control of souls and society alienated self-respecting businessmen, and the elite turned away from the Church. The political climate was ever changing. Now the Spanish claimed their ancient rights, and expelled the British Baptists. In 1858 the Spanish effectively occupied the island.

To the mainland

The missionaries then turned to the mainland, to Douala and 'Victoria'. For a generation the Church in Clarence had been a Christian microcosm. Now the mission moved to larger concerns. Alfred Saker, one of the Baptists at Clarence gave twenty-seven years to Douala. This English engineer-missionary was the prototype of Protestant activity in Africa. His combination of engineering, Bible translation and exposition influenced many. He founded and shaped the Victoria community on the coast. Although he did not found Douala, he shaped it, both architecturally and culturally. Douala and Victoria, where he taught brick-making, changed their whole appearance with attractive buildings and busy streets. He had of course to proceed via encounters with the chiefs, such as they were. Those at Douala received the first sermons as 'good palaver', but Chief Bell declared that he must not be *too* much disturbed: 'God make me live, God make me die. But me wish God would let me just alone. No make me die at all – but live here just as we are in this world for ever.'[167]

Black preachers

Among Saker's West Indian Baptist preachers in Douala was Joseph Merrick, an outstanding linguist. Because of his light colouring (he had a White grandfather) and his Western dress, he was called 'White man' by the local inhabitants. He was soon ready to publish the first school book in the Douala language. Being an experienced printer he was able to print it himself. His service in Cameroon lasted only four years, from 1844 until his death in 1848, but in this short time he made such an impression that he has been called 'the founder of Christianity in Cameroon'.[168]

On Merrick's death, Joseph Jackson Fuller, a genial humorous preacher, took charge of the Bimbia congregation. He was also from the West Indies where he had worked as a mason. He had participated in the Jamaican struggle for the abolition of slavery, when the thoughts of many had gone to Africa. His message to those in Bimbia was so convincing that a village chief together with a group of nobles came to him, throwing down their 'fetishes' and exclaiming 'Now we will try yours!'[169] George Nkwe, coming from the Bamileke people in the north, was kidnapped as a child and sold as a slave. He eventually became the property of King Akwa. This meant that even as a Christian and an ordained pastor, he had to pay part of his small salary to his 'owner' who in principle still had the right to sell him. This status no doubt gave added pathos and relevance to the Christian pastor's message on liberation. Both Fuller and Nkwe were ordained by Saker, the former in 1859, the latter in 1866.

T. H. Johnson was Saker's first convert at Clarence and 'the first African pastor of the Bethel Church in Cameroons Town (now Douala) on the mainland'.[170] In 1855 Saker ordained him and asked him to lead the 'Bethel' congregation in Douala, which at this time had fifty members. The Douala were sharply divided during this period, thus providing the Baptist pastor much experience as pacifier and councillor. Another West Indian in the mission was Richardson, a huge and friendly Black pastor. The king of Bakundu welcomed him eagerly, as he had already had a foresight of his coming in a dream. The people, however, had an initial distrust which did not die down, even though they regarded Richardson as a mighty prophet.

From Douala George Grenfell, English Baptist and Saker's successor, acquired his initial knowledge of Africa, from 1874–79. There he formulated his strategy for winning the 'inland', important later on, not so much for Cameroon as for Congo. He did not have the same patience with the Douala as Saker did, although his marriage to a West Indian lady demonstrated a willingness to identify with the people. He felt that the European influence on the pidgin-speaking city people had been less than salutary, and that the future of the mission lay 'inland'. He explored the area south of Douala, among the Basa, making an attempt to combine mission and geographical discovery. Later, on a much wider scale, this combination characterized his distinguished contribution to Zaïrean Church history.

Douala's outreach

Douala and the newly founded Christian centres nearby have been somewhat under-rated in subsequent history. Just as the Douala for many years had middlemen who traded with the inland people the Christian influence of the city congregations was far-reaching. The following cases are just two of many which could be cited.

The very first preacher to the Fumban was a Bamum slave who had been sold to Douala. Having accepted Christianity there, he returned to his Fumban village with his message of liberation. Similarly, one of the first evangelical preachers in far away Luanda in Angola had been sold to some 'Master' in Douala. He too found the Christian faith there. The Baptist message and Saker's influence in Douala had distant repercussions, carried to various places by young men who had come under his influence and that of his West Indian co-workers. Later these men returned to their home communities with two added skills: they spoke 'English' – or rather some form of pidgin – and they could read a strange book called 'Matthew' or 'John' to their amazed fellows. These men reflect for Cameroon also, the role of the 'West Indian returnees' or the 'Brazilian returnees' to the same extent as has been pointed out for West Africa, from Ghana, Togo and Nigeria.

Southern Cameroon

The American Presbyterians, well-established in Gabon through John Leighton Wilson, his colleagues and successors, found a new task in the south of Cameroon – a development of their Gabon work. There they met the Bulu people, who proved to be part of the Fang. These came to the Gabon coast via the Catholic mission in the Yaoundé region – still on their westward drive toward the ocean. The Basel missionaries had spread over wide areas through comparatively small centres. The American Presbyterians used a different method; they built a few, highly-developed centres, including educational, industrial, and medical institutions. The best known was Elat, destined to become for a time the largest Presbyterian centre in the world. From the beginning, they emphasized African leadership, and aimed to make the 'Three Selves' programme a cornerstone of the Church's growth.

A new regime and a new theme

The future of Cameroon was decided at the conference table in Berlin in 1885. Under Bismarck's iron fist the country was handed over to Germany, and remained its colony until 1916. 1885 was the high moment of European imperialism. Cameroon experienced its impact more than most African countries. The German Governor J. von Puttkamer saw the African country as one large business concern. It was 'ownerless land' – the term used at the time – and as such just waiting for the imperialist power to claim it as 'crown land'. Puttkamer was finally recalled to Berlin as a result of criticism against his regime.

Cameroon proved to be an immense and a rich country, with many varied ethnic communities and languages. In the south was the tropical forest region and in the north the savannas and the mountain areas. Migration movements had run their dramatic course through the forests and along the rivers, or were still in progress. Ivory and rubber were the chief products, together with palm oil, cotton and cocoa. The imperial power abolished slavery in the country, in principle. But forced labour, apparently more acceptable, followed in its place. The Europeans, including most missionaries of different confessions, were determined to 'teach the natives to work'. There was systematic so-called 'development' attempts of some regions: Bulu, Grassfields, Yaoundé, Wute, and the north. Hans Dominik, a lieutenant who was urging young people at Yaoundé to join the mission schools, was known for his energetic methods.

At first the foreigners' attention was centred on Douala, with its harbour, and the adjacent country on the coast. The inland was left uncharted and unknown. From the 1880s this was to change radically. A new theme, the supposed superiority of inland peoples over coastal middlemen, dominated the strategy in all fields of activity. This theme concerned not only Cameroon but the whole of West Africa, and was shared by many very different personalities, both Black and White: the West African nationalist Edward Blyden; Her Majesty's local representative, Sir Harry Johnston; the Baptist preacher, George Grenfell; the Irish Bishop Shanahan; and the American Presbyterian, Adolf Good. Inland, they hoped to find great untapped natural resources, as well as hitherto undeveloped human resources.

The midget state of Victoria, with its English-speaking Baptist congregation, was virtually a British enclave. Together with some of the Douala 'kings', it appealed to Queen Victoria to be placed under British protection. When the country was to be turned over to the Germans, they wanted to avoid a transfer, especially as the German authorities insisted that the school language would be first Douala, and later on, German. The Basel Mission, charged with taking over Protestant interests there, believed in forming 'Christian villages', and was anxious to defend the rights of Victoria, Buea, and similar Baptist centres. With the German take-over, the Baptist position was threatened, closely related as it was to Anglo-Saxon interests. The very name of the colony, 'Victoria', had become politically offensive. In 1884 a brief anti-German rebellion by the Douala people was followed by a German bombardment of several Baptist centres.

The 'Native Baptists'

Unavoidable tension also developed between Basel and the Baptists. It had nothing to do with Infant versus Believers' baptism. In fact, the Baptist pastor Joshua Dibundu brought his new-born twins to the Lutheran font for baptism. The real cause of tension was an apparent threat to the congregational administration. During the time of Saker, a strong tradition of lay initiative and leadership had been fostered – the very life nerve of this young Church. Certain irregularities had been allowed, and the newly arrived Basel missionaries were quick to point these out. Here was a parallel to the controversy on the Niger only a few hundred miles away, between Bishop Crowther's 'native agents' and some perfectionist Keswick propagandists.

A cultural factor in the dispute was the language issue: the 'Native Baptists' were English-speaking, or so they insisted, and they resented the superimposition of another European language on their cherished schools. The outcome of the struggle was the 'Native Baptist Church'. Pastor Joshua Dibundu and his people declared themselves independent, and left the Bethel centre to which they had been closely related for a generation. This forged another link in the chain of 'African Churches', laid out all along the West coast at this time. Pastor Dibundu was sufficiently Baptist to orient himself to politically acceptable Baptist groups in Europe. In 1891 when German Baptists entered Douala, he co-operated for about six years, and then broke with them. The Native Baptist Church was once more on its own. The European mission, again disappointed with a troublesome coast, looked with nostalgia to the more promising inland. The (British) Baptist Missionary Society had earlier bowed out of Cameroon – Grenfell and

Comber had already moved to Congo – and was succeeded by the German Baptist mission.

Colonial disputes

A bitter struggle followed between the government and the Basel Mission. Military action against defenceless villages took place, and in 1898 the leading Basel missionary, Bizer, protested: he denied the Government's 'right to sell a whole population to capitalists and speculators. May the Lord God ... bring to naught the evil being planned by the enemies of His Kingdom' Bizer concluded.[171] His protests did not go far. The Government's juggernaut rolled along, and masses of labourers were commandeered from the north and from Yaoundé, the latter already under strong Catholic influence. The two German-speaking missions, the Basel Protestant and the Catholic Pallottine, responded differently to this practice. The Catholics adapted rapidly to an unavoidable situation, and established themselves among the labouring masses, which were increasingly drawn from the hard-working Ewondo area in Yaoundé. Thus their leading men were placed as supervisors. During the day they acted as 'captains' of work, and in the evening as catechists. For good behaviour, the Company gave the Catholics a strong, well-built church at Victoria. The Basel missionaries had difficulties in achieving a foothold at Victoria, to some extent for linguistic reasons. They did not like the pidgin 'English' spoken there, and insisted on using the Douala language. This diminished their chances of contact with the polyglot labour force.

A youth movement

In Abo country near Douala and the Wuori river, a high-spirited youth movement emerged, 'the God's boys movement'. This was a central Cameroon variant of a fundamental theme in nineteenth-century Christianization of Africa: a determined group of young men rallying together as an aggressive revival movement, in this case under the fearless initiative and leadership of a devoted son of the Chief Kotto. It was an entirely African movement carried on for most of the time without the knowledge or support of the Basel missionaries. These young Christian men were modernizers determined to break with their pagan past, so they rejected the powerful Losango secret societies and established their own chapels, schools and catechetical centres.[172]

With the coming of the new colonial power, Cameroon was changed.

Douala, Victoria, and other coastal communities with a shifting, cosmopolitan population, lost much of their former attraction. Government, trade, and missions moved inland.

Northern Cameroon

In the north, both at Bali and at Fumban, the new faith made a bid to function as a court religion, under the protection of the African king or chief. In this respect, it was similar to Islam and its close contacts to emirs and Laminos. At Bali, the Basel Mission started in 1903, with Chief Fonyonga the welcoming host. A solid friendship grew between the chief and the German missionary, F. Ernst. Fonyonga assured the European newcomers that he could solve any of their problems: 'Softy, softy, me be strong too much.'[173] He arranged for the missionaries to preach in the royal court, and required Sunday attendance at Church services by the traditional elite: his wives, the nobles and his officers. When the school opened, to set a good example he volunteered to sit in as a student himself. Five years later the first group of thirty-two boys were baptized and the missionary felt that he witnessed the birth of a Christian congregation.

Fumban, with Njoya, one of the most interesting Cameroonian kings, presented a challenging religious situation. Was Fumban to turn Muslim or Christian? The balance was evenly poised and the issue in no way settled. Hausa traders brought Islam from the north, and two Lagos Christian trade employees brought their faith from the west. The latter could be seen and heard, going through the streets preaching and singing. They were joined by an old slave who had once been sold to Douala, and then had managed to return home. In the foreign city, he had found the Christian faith, and was now anxious to witness about it at home.[174]

The king seemed to lean toward Islam, but his concern for education made him change that posture for a time, on condition that the Christians would adopt his interpretation of the faith. He was very eager for schools, as he had invented a highly interesting alphabet of his own. Like Fonyonga at Bali, he sat down with the students, to learn for himself the magical new signs of wisdom. He also sent his sons to the mission school. Soon close to fifty schools were built in his kingdom.

King 'Book'

Cameroon welcomed the missions, not so much because of their religious message, but because of their schools. They were all 'asking for book'. On the coast, admittedly, educational development had a slow start, and on the slopes of the Cameroon Mountain the plantations were a hindrance. They even required children for their heavy work, defeating the government's own school programme; pupils could not with any regularity attend the classes. Yet, in the first years of the new century, conditions changed rapidly. A widening network of roads opened up the country, prompting the parents to send their young to the schools. The chiefs, too, made great personal efforts to encourage the children's attendance. Competition between Protestant and Catholic also quickened development of education prior to the War. In 1910 there were 11,000 pupils, and three years later, 22,000.

In 1910 state control of schools was introduced, leading to higher standards. The schoolhouse in the village was bigger than the other huts, but of the same material: in the forest region, walls and roof of palm-leaf mats; in the Grassland, walls of clay with a grass roof. All were built by the local community. If the chief insisted and sent a sufficient number of workers, such a building could be ready in a day or two. Rich congregations built their schools of stone, with an iron roof. The building served at the same time as the local chapel; it contained an *ambo* (pulpit), a table, but rarely a blackboard. The children were seated on long wooden poles, each one shared by many in a row. Slates, or pieces of slate, were the privilege of only a few. During a writing lesson, the pieces would be passed from child to child until each had a chance. They shared the one and only primer copy in the same way.

In these circumstances, the functioning of the school depended on the teacher. He was selected from the best students at the central boarding school located at the mission headquarters. Having large classes, the teacher enlisted the brightest pupils as 'monitors', under his direction. The subjects taught were the 'Four R's', including Religion. In 1888, Th. Christaller, son of the Ghana missionary and linguist, produced a primer in the Douala and German languages. It included spelling exercises and brief reading texts on Man, the Family, the Cat, Maize, and Iron. It ended with three pages of religious knowledge: the Creed, the Ten Commandments, the 23rd Psalm, and the Lord's Prayer. There were no illustrations. By 1910 the quality of reading material for the higher classes had improved considerably. The 250-page textbook had a nature section, one on geography, and an extensive one of 130 pages on history. This was a world history in brief, but except for Egypt, no African country was mentioned in this sweeping survey.

Most of these schools were for boys. Inland the number of girls was 10 per cent or less. The Sakhbayeme district in 1913 had 6,600 pupils, of whom *one* was a girl! On the coast, however, the girls had better educational opportunities; Douala had its first girls' school in 1898. Again the versatile King Njoya's Fumban was an exception. The role of high-ranking women in the court chapel was considerable, beginning with the Queen Mother, Njapndunke. She was instrumental in seeing to it that the royal chapel, holding 600 was full for every Sunday service. At Christmas 1909, eighty young people were baptized, including twenty-eight of King Njoya's concubines and princesses.

Islam or Christianity

King Njoya had good relations with Martin Göhring, the German missionary, who was careful not to break with traditional culture. For his efforts, the missionary received the honorary title of *Nkomnchunchut* (dignitary of the palace) and could move at liberty in the royal court. He needed all his versatility to keep up with the even more versatile sovereign, who continuously attempted to form a harmonious mixture of his view of the best in the two new religions. The king even tried his hand at hymnology, perhaps the only Church-going ruler in nineteenth-century Africa to do so. He expressed in the following example a strictly three-tiered universe, consisting of God, king, and commoners.

> In heaven is God
> and Nzoya rules as chief
> His people incessantly
> do give him obedience
> Jesus, God-Father blesses the world.

Like many of his royal colleagues in other parts of Africa, King Njoya took special interest in the holy day of the week, seen by him also as a social institution of importance. Here the Basel missionary suggested reform: the Bamum eight-day week was reduced to seven days, to avoid market days falling on Sunday from time to time.

With the World War, the missionary influence was cut short, and Göhring was interned. Within a year, Njoya, now with the title of Sultan, issued an order introducing Islam and forbidding the preaching of Christianity. In this new political situation, evangelization had to follow other channels. It could no longer be a privileged court religion, but was rather attuned to the faith of those first witnesses to Fumban – a returned slave and two trade employees.

Yaoundé, the Fang and the Pallottines

The Fang migration is one of the most startling population movements through Central Africa in recent centuries. Originating as a small aristocratic minority in Sudan, these people – several thousand in number – had moved from the north-east to the south-west, seeking a dimly conceived goal beyond the Great Waters. Crossing the river Sanaga, they proceeded, as we have seen, toward Southern Cameroon and Gabon, at last reaching the Atlantic coast about the middle of the nineteenth century. They had moved along in small groups of a few hundred, putting up their temporary villages for ten to fifteen years, only to decide to pull up stakes and obey once again that inner urge to move on and beyond, always in the same general direction toward the setting sun. On their migrations, their ears were attuned to the mysterious message of the dense tropical forest and the secret dialogue between the dark powers below and the parrots in the highest sunlit branches above, between the 'belowness' and the 'aboveness'.[175]

As they hastened along, the Fang were driven by supernatural powers much stronger than their individual or collective selves and by the irresistible aspirations of their corporate myth. Its fulfilment would be found on the other side, beyond the Waters. On the march across Central Africa, select members of the group were entrusted with a special duty. As the children of Israel had once carried their Ark, these carried their most sacred belongings, the *Ngi*, the bones of their dead. They were thus reminded of their ultimate fate. After death, the Fang would travel into the realm of the Departed, there to be transformed, becoming white like the Departed. On that voyage they would receive untold riches, exchanging their present misery for glorious abundance. Immensely resourceful, they forced their way through the lands of others. As they moved into what is now Gabon, they met Whites whom they felt they had already encountered in their myth. But these Whites were going in the opposite direction, trying to penetrate 'the Interior' of Africa. This encounter reminded the Fang of their innermost secret.

The Fang soon became known as robust porters for caravans going inland from the coast. In this way thousands of them made their first contacts with the Whites and with the Church. Soon they formed colonies among the coastal plantation workers in Victoria. In 1896 the German station commander at Yaoundé, H. Dominik, sent the first group of chiefs' sons to the Catholic school at Kribi on the coast. It was characteristic of the expanding Fang that soon half that school was filled with their boys. The first baptisms took place in 1897. In 1899 twenty-five boys and a few girls, all baptized, returned to Yaoundé, the boys as expert sawyers and brick-makers. They were eager to transmit to their own villages the new technical and religious message they had received.

The Yaoundé centre

Having returned home, they took a leading part in the Christianization of Yaoundé-Minlaaba. The first Catholic Fathers, the German Pallottines, did not arrive until 1901. Here, as in so many other places in Africa, the first missionaries were preceded, indeed anticipated, by the concerted efforts of young converts. One of these was Atangana-Ntsama, the son of a chief. At the age of fourteen he was one of those sent by Dominik to the school at Kribi. He was baptized there and given the name of Karl Atangana. By baptizing Prince Karl Atangana 'the Pallottine missionaries made in the eyes of the population Christianity into an indigenous religion'. This is the Revd Dr Engelbert Mveng's estimation of the importance of that baptism.[176] Atangana came back home to a career open to Fang talents. He was first a government interpreter, then a judge, and finally a supreme chief in Yaoundé. As a chief, he spent a year in Germany, including a visit to Rome. He helped to modernize his area and was regarded by other chiefs as an example of how to combine Christianity with high political office. There were, no doubt, others of similar calibre in that first group of youngsters at Kribi.

It was as a young school boy that Karl Atangana became a Christian. Those who were already chiefs and well-known leaders of their people found it harder to join the Church, with its disciplinary requirements. This was the case with Esomba-Mentunu in the Minlaaba district. He had to press the missionaries for teachers and a school. When Apostolic Vicar Vieter came to Minlaaba, the chief asked if, as a pagan, he would be allowed to kneel at the roadside to show his respect and to invite in that humble way the blessing of the bishop. This was permitted, and the report has it that 'surely the episcopal blessing called down upon the pagan chief the blessing of God'. After the opening of the school, Esomba joined the catechetical class and was baptized just before the German missionaries were taken away to be interned during the First World War. Chief Mme-Ela, also in the Yaoundé area, expressed his interest in tangible terms: 'Two things my heart has always longed for, a gun and a school'. He dismissed all his wives except the first one and together with her joined the catechetical class, anxious to learn to read and to acquire the language of the German colonial masters. After two years of training the couple were baptized.

Among the leaders was the highly intelligent Wute chief, Mwemba. Like the Fang, the related Wute originated from the Sudan. Mwemba, living along the caravan road to the north, had constant contacts with passing Europeans, who wanted to put up their tents in his hospitable village. The chief told the missionary who prepared him for baptism: 'I have always thought that somebody must surely come to tell us something more specific about God and what happens to man after death.'[177] His note of expectation is reminiscent of the communal myth of his own and related peoples. At his baptism he chose the name of Peter, aware that the name had first been carried by another prominent Christian.

These African leaders became devoted co-workers of the Pallottine Fathers and Brother Tenhaf. The latter was one of those truly amazing German lay brothers who planned and organized the practical work on a rapidly growing Catholic mission station. In Germany, this was the time of *Gross-Wirtschaft* and *Gross-Unternehmen*, and Brother Tenhaf imparted that kind of spirit to the Yaoundé bush. He had some 200 workers labouring for him. Already the road system throughout the region required constant care on the part of the local congregation. The seven roads through the tropical forest area had been laid out with bridges and ditches by Dominik, but Tenhaf and his staff developed the system. The roads were important, for soon the Pallottine Fathers acquired German bicycles for themselves and for the catechists. Rapid Church growth was facilitated by this modern means of communication. The missionary in the centre and the catechists in the outlying villages kept in touch in a way made possible and inevitable by their common Church interest.[178]

Catechists and catechumens

In 1906 the Cameroon Synod stipulated minimum requirements for the catechumenate: knowledge of the Lord's Prayer, the Ave Maria, the Creed – all by heart – and certain acts of faith, hope, charity and repentance. A rapidly growing group of catechists was emerging. In 1908 the first catechists' school opened with thirty-three candidates. By 1913 more than 100 catechists were at work in the district, with about 12,000 catechumens and 20,000 baptized. Some of these catechists, trained by the Pallottine Fathers and the Christian chiefs, became the first African leaders of the Yaoundé Church. As such they were called on to direct the work in the latter years of the First World War, when the German missionaries were taken away.

Sometimes because of personal ambition, a chief insisted that he alone should enjoy the privilege of a school. Then the missionary needed to exercise both tact and firmness to carry through his own educational programme. In 1905 the first outstation had a school; in 1912 there were already twenty-two, and in 1915, forty-nine such schools. There were 5,700 pupils by 1913, and in 1914 almost 8,000. In the beginning there was a tendency to admit to baptism the children of pagan parents. Some Fang fathers would proudly line up half a dozen of their children for baptism. The pagan mother would come to the Sunday service, but might not find space in the packed little church. After the service she could bring her baptized baby into the holy house, make the sign of the cross with holy water, and then happily walk back home: 'Heilige Einfalt' ('Holy simplicity'), the Catholic historian remarks, showing something of the split mind of a modern Catholic Westerner.[179] The Pallottine missionaries felt that, not being hampered by any Protestant competition, they could encourage a baptismal practice otherwise regarded as not commendable. They baptized children of pagan parents without compunction, for were they not assured that these would later be instructed in Catholic schools? The father's mark on a declaration assured that the child would be brought up in the Christian faith. For the girls, the declaration had an additional clause: they could not be married to any but Catholic men.

In 1913, 5,600 were baptized in Yaoundé, bringing the total to 17,600 for the area; the number of catechumens was 6,580. In the space of one generation, 1903–33, 98 per cent of the Fang population in that Yaoundé region were brought into the Catholic Church. This tremendous response was not one long line coming to the baptismal font, but all had a background of corporate expectation. The Church, through its Western and African staff, its teaching and sacraments, was able to meet many of these aspirations. The baptized members would impress upon their neighbours the necessity to receive baptism. A recalcitrant old man lying near the hearth would be reminded of his unavoidable fate by a glowing coal placed on his arm: 'There you see. You cannot endure even this little pain without yelling. In hell you will be more tormented than that, and for the whole of eternity.'[180]

The new movement was not without its adversaries. Pagan resistance centred in the *So* ritual – the initiation rites – and worked through secret societies, but soon the Christian advance proved irresistible. The chief at Minlaaba led the way. As the missionary arrived, the chief declared that he was prepared to give up his hill residence and move down into the valley, in order to give the foreigners the higher ground which they regarded as an advantage.

There is no mistaking the energy which the German Pallottines inspired in the catechumens. The hundreds of labourers in the fields, on building projects, or in other enterprises, were all expected to attend evening catechism classes at the end of a day's work. On Sundays and saints' days, the Church centre in Yaoundé was as lively as any great pilgrim centre in southern Europe. The crowd would wind their way from all directions up the mountain, some coming as far as fifteen kilometres. Long queues of faithful lined up for confession from six to nine in the morning, although most had already fulfilled that duty the day before. The Cameroonian vicariate recorded 131,711 confessions in just one year, 1913. Of these, 90,000 were in the Yaoundé district alone, with 90,000 communions. These are but bare figures, however they represent the stirring of conscience in the first generation Catholics.[181]

GABON

The decades around the middle of the nineteenth century in Gabon saw remarkable developments in the population. On the coast the Mpongwe controlled the trade to the interior and established themselves as 'a trading aristocracy of the Gabon estuary'.[182] They welcomed foreign influence and had close, not to say intimate, contacts with particularly the French navy and traders, while at the time being open to British and American trading and cultural interests. This Mpongwe superiority was, however, threatened by a disturbing arrival of increasing groups of Fang, coming from the north. They were of the same Fang who had, by their migration from the north of Cameroon, provided the sociological foundation for a mass conversion near Yaoundé and further south in Cameroon. Now their irresistible drive towards the waters of the ocean was about to reach its fulfilment. The American Protestant missionary, R. H. Nassau, active on the Gabon coast in 1861, met with one of these Fang arriving after years of migration. He put to the White missionary a question which was indeed strange but which was formulated out of the secret depths of dynamic Fang mythology. 'One man ... quietly and unobtrusively but very steadily was gazing at me. After a while he mustered courage and addressed me: "Are you not my brother – my brother who died at such a time, and went to the White Man's land?"'[183] They reacted in a similar fashion when they met other Whites farther north, on the Cameroon coast and in Yaoundé and Minlaaba. Events in Gabon were from now on largely determined by the pressures and aspirations of the dynamic Fang.

J. L. Wilson and western Africa

From the 1840s the Western foreigners arrived: traders from many countries overseas, sailors from France and the missionaries – Catholic and Protestant – all coming at about the same boisterous time. Not the Mpongwe as such, but the Agekaza clan among the Mpongwe, settled in the Gabon estuary, prepared to receive these White visitors. When in 1843 the French built Fort Aumale they found that American Protestant missionaries had already preceded them by one year. Liberia had for a time been the focus of American missionary interest in Africa but two Liberia missionaries, the Reverends John Leighton Wilson and Benjamin Griswold decided to explore possibilities in Gabon. Dr Henry H. Bucher has suggested that Wilson, coming from South Carolina, brought ideas from the American Revolution – the 'Spirit of 1776' – to mid-nineteenth-century Western Africa.[184] He did this in opposition to early French colonial designs on Gabon, which did not make him popular with the French regime. This American was in principle and practice an anti-colonialist, and set the pattern for the American missionary presence in Central Africa. Wilson was anxious to insure for the African true freedom in and through the Church. He wrote a notable study of the region, *Western Africa: Its History, Condition, and Prospects*, published in 1856.

Wilson later commuted between Liberia and Gabon, thus establishing an American parallel to the simultaneous Anglican Church connection between Sierra Leone and Nigeria. Interestingly, the Catholic leader Jean-Rémi Bessieux arrived in Gabon along the same route – Liberia-Gabon – as Wilson had done two years earlier.[185]

The two American missionaries came on an American ship and it was Captain Lawlin, an old West Coast hand, who in 1842 introduced the missionaries to King Glass and his Mpongwe village, thus giving them an opportunity to explain their programme in terms of evangelization and education. The king and his people found the Americans interesting enough but to them even more interesting was a Black companion whom the missionaries had brought, a Liberian pupil from the mission school at Cape Palmas, Liberia. This young African read from the pages of a bundle of papers, a 'book', an achievement which duly impressed the Agekaza audience. In a surprisingly short time Wilson produced a few booklets in the Mpongwe language including that most important *Hymns in Gaboon*, and brought the manuscript to the printing press in Liberia whence he returned with the printed books and six former Liberian pupils, all as literate as the first envoy. They were to assist in establishing a number of schools.

Alliances were made with Chief Glass and others of his colleagues, and the mission could build its own headquarters at Baraka.

Wilson was much attracted to the newly-arrived Fang. They came to the coast from inland, 'altogether the finest race he had seen in Africa'. He was always eager to look beyond the horizon, and was convinced that there was a close linguistic and social kinship between the peoples in Gabon and those on the East Coast of the continent, from Durban to Zanzibar. He was also anxious that the Mission devote itself to the Fang before they 'shall have come under any of these injurious influences which pervade the sea coast'.

The Protestant leaders on the coast, Saker in Cameroon and Wilson in Gabon, worked happily through Black assistants, who from one point of view were foreigners, but who showed real affinity with the local situation. Saker in the Douala region relied on Jamaicans who had shared with him an initial experience in Fernando Po. To Gabon, Wilson brought his helpers from Liberia. For the missions in Gabon, these were times of small beginnings. Wilson's initial optimism proved to be premature. The Protestants in the area were now represented by two societies. In 1850 American Presbyterians settled on Corisco Island, a southern parallel to the role of Fernando Po in the Baptist work further north. The Corisco venture had more converts, but here also the rigid standards in regard to drink and similar vices, were not popular. 'The fact is, our converts need to be converted over again pretty often', was William Walker's contention. Those who joined the Protestant Church were at first mostly non-Mpongwe and thus foreigners, or slaves, following a pattern common in other places. Women kept quite aloof from the catechism class. It took twenty years of Protestant preaching before the first female convert was registered.[186]

The Catholics

The Spiritans also came to this part of West Africa. After dramatic and tragic adventures in Liberia, Fr Jean Rémy Bessieux moved to Gabon 1844 as the only survivor – his five companions died just weeks or days after their arrival in Liberia. (It took one full year until the Mission in Paris was told that he *had* survived.) On his way to Gabon, Bessieux had found on the island of Principe an eighty-year old African priest, Father Jose, a link with an earlier period of Catholic missions. In 1848 Bessieux was made Apostolic Vicar, or Bishop, of Gabon.

Bessieux discovered the inveterate attitude of the Mpongwe freemen to the problem of work, namely that any such exercise should be avoided and handled only by slaves and women and such like. Bessieux by his own example suggested an alternative approach. After early mass he would walk into the forest and the fields with a hoe over his shoulder to cultivate the ground. Obviously he enjoyed this exertion and the results in that tropical climate were not long in waiting. Soon the Bishop would go out into the Mpongwe villages baptizing the dying and also the newborn children. He was also active linguistically and two years after his arrival produced a Mpongwe grammar and a Catechism, together with a first translation of the Gospels.

Of special importance was Bessieux's friendship with King Denis Rapontyombo. With his 100 wives and 300 slaves he found it difficult at first to join the Church, but showed a positive interest in the work. His son Felix was baptized and became a devoted catechist. After Bessieux's death, the king himself was soon moribund and ready to receive baptism *in extremis*, administered to him by his son, the catechist, who now succeeded him as king.

The first catechists were of the Mpongwe community. When sent to Fang villages, at first very reluctant to receive the new message, the catechist was in certain cases in real danger. One Fang chief warned the catechist: 'When you pour water over the head of the children, you are killing them. Get away!' Soon thereafter, the young catechist was found dead.

The arrival in 1849 of the 'Blue Sisters' (The Immaculate Conception of Castres), was of great importance for the evangelization among Mpongwe and Fang women and girls. A theological seminary was founded in 1856. It met at first with great difficulties. Thirty years after the foundation, the Father in charge wrote: 'This poor seminary has been reshaped ten times. Nothing has come of it, at least not for the priesthood ... But Rome wants an African clergy, and Rome is always right.' In 1899 the first priest was ordained and when in 1919 another three acceded to the priesthood, there was one Fang, Jean Abame, among them. In 1911 the first two African sisters, postulants, began their training.

A new task soon occurred to the bishop, in the foundation of Libreville, the name of which suggested that the place was meant to be a Gabonese equivalent to Freetown in Sierra Leone. A slave-ship with forty-six slaves from among the Vili of Congo was seized and brought to the shore. The Government of Senegal – having the authority over the 'Two Guineas' – ordered that a village, Libreville, be built for them and it was to be 'both Christian and French'. The construction of this village and of the neighbouring Catholic mission – 'Sainte Marie' – went side by side, the latter including a hospital and a school and related enterprises. The new village was laid out with thirteen streets and with houses and gardens and a chapel.

The Bishop expected the liberated community to be incorporated into the Church after a brief period of catechetical instruction. He took an early initiative to that end in arranging for a mass wedding. In October 1849 fifteen couples were joined by him in Holy Matrimony and each were given house and garden. The Catholic bishop insisted on another precept from the Protestant model in Freetown, Sierra Leone and Cape Coast, Ghana: the inhabitants must keep the Sabbath.

The Libreville project was definitely a more limited enterprise than the Freetown counterpart. In 1849 it had fifty-two inhabitants and in 1853 seventy, but it developed its community life with a challenging atmosphere of rewarding hard work and thus contrasting to the life of the Mpongwe neighbours. Taking a longer view of developments, the project did not altogether live up to the missionaries' expectations but its inhabitants were undoubtedly to play an active role in the life of the country.[187]

In the tropical climate Bessieux developed the unusual and enviable virtue of staying alive for decades – 1842–76 – and spending altogether thirty-four years in Africa. At the time of his death, his Gabon diocese counted between 2,000 to 3,000 Christians. Bessieux nurtured good relations with Paris, and with France as a whole, with political consequences. When France in its political distress in 1871 was inclined to give up Gabon as too expensive, it was Bessieux who insisted that the country remain within the French sphere of interest. His political role for Gabon was thus a parallel to the role of the Basel missionaries Sass and Ramseyer for Ghana 1874–96 and to that of the CMS for Uganda in 1892.

Along the coast, Portuguese and French traders had for centuries established their 'factories' and Capuchin missionaries had formed their congregations. Very succinctly this Portuguese influence could be defined as follows. Their influence at this time was not limited to what is now Angola, but influenced cultures and structures all along the coast. It has already been pointed out that it could be discerned on the Dahomeyan coast (today, mostly in the Republic of Benin). Along the Congo coast this influence was strengthened by actual Portuguese political claims to certain coastal pockets such as Loango and Landana and trade influence through the various Portuguese centres. The Portuguese presence was fundamentally buttressed by Padroado pretensions demonstrated on occasion. Portuguese phrases were current all along the coast among the Mpongwe and Kongo and Teke, giving to the coasters' conversation a certain taste of modernization and international contacts.

6

WEST-CENTRAL AFRICA

INTRODUCTION

The pre-colonial setting

Adzindzali, people of the river, was the name for the ethnic communities along the Congo waterway. They considered this a name of honour – they were fishermen and proud of it. In their dugout canoes they would move over vast waters along the main river and up and down the many Congo tributaries bringing their catch to the markets, to Likuba or Ntsei or Mushei, centres used over many generations for the exchange of commodities. For 'the environment of these people which made them fishermen also made them traders'.[1] The Bobangi brought their smoked fish, slaves, pottery and iron implements to a Tio market. They formed their relationship with the Tio to the extent of establishing blood-brotherhood between their chiefs or 'great men', thus widening the horizons of each of these two communities. 'Sharing the waters with non-Tio made them [the Bobangi] more sophisticated and gave them a much broader outlook than that of most of the landlocked agriculturalists.'[2]

Sometimes the Bobangi canoes would take them much further down the river to Kinshasa (soon to be referred to as 'Stanley Pool'), or up the river towards the Falls. Together with other Congo communities they came to be regarded as 'middlemen'. For generations they were confronted with the ideas and ambitions of foreigners: to the west, Portuguese, Dutch, French; to the east the Arabs. Portuguese was the trade language of the western coast.

In the last quarter of the century, the Congo was suddenly and forcibly shaken by Western imperialist powers into dramatic change but it is important to realize that long before the River was 'discovered' by Stanley, lively economic and social exchange had developed between the various communities. Many were already 'societies in flux', with wide differences in degree, the extent of which depended on communication with the outside world.

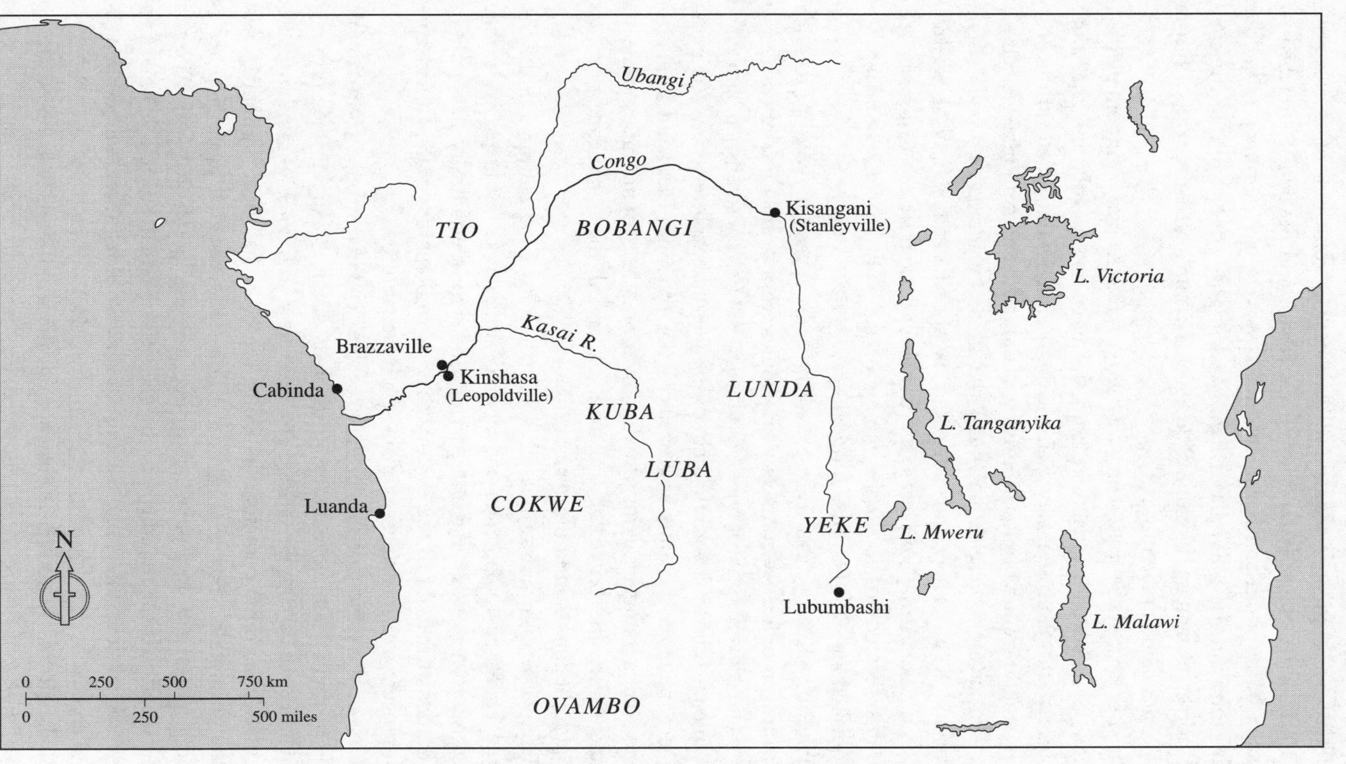

6.1. Ethnic groups and key towns of West-central Africa.

There were great ecological differences in this part of Africa. The equatorial forest lined both sides of the River, and beyond it stretched the savanna in the south and north. In the forest zone, isolated peoples huddled under the immense umbrella of lianas and mighty trees, while in the south and north, expanding kingdoms developed complicated networks of communication and competition.

In the west there was what was left of the Kongo kingdom with its capital, San Salvador, spanning both the north of Angola and the south-western parts of present-day Zaïre/Congo. But in the nineteenth century other kingdoms had obviously greater claims to fame and influence. On the southern savanna were to be found the great kingdoms of Lunda, Luba-Kasai and Kuba. The Lunda kingdom expanded steadily until about 1850, but then began to fall to pieces. Its capital was taken by the Cokwe in 1887 and this seemed to be the beginning of the end: in 1909 the king was vanquished and Belgian rule enforced.

The Luba-Kasai – later to be called the Luba – had moved towards wider horizons through early contacts with peoples from Angola, mainly dealers in ivory and slaves. One of them, Mukenga Kalamba, established himself as supreme chief in 1885 with the help of the German explorer, von Wissmann. These populations became divided about this time into Luba and Lulua, the former being refugees living on the lands of other communities while the Lulua, under the powerful Kalamba, expanded their influence not least through the importation of firearms.

The peoples on the savanna all lived mainly from agriculture. In the case of the energetic Luba, their endangered situation as refugees made them receptive to new ways and alternatives, and with the radically new political conditions at the end of the century they were prepared to align themselves with powers which seemed to promise a better future.

Also in the region of the kingdoms were scattered groups from Angola, some of them claiming membership in the Catholic Church. They provided something of a fragile bridge to the new religious community. For centuries the ethnic communities along the coast had been in contact with White foreigners. For a long time there had existed a great number of trading posts and harbours, providing meeting points between Western traders and African middlemen. In 1875 the French Spiritan, Duparquet, knew of no less than 120 trading 'factories' along the Gabon–Congo–Angola coast.[3]

Shaba (formerly known as Katanga) in the south-east, well-known today as an industrial centre, was renowned for its commercial enterprise more than a century ago. The Hemba, Anza, Sanga and others had formed wealthy communities, having developed copper mines, salt extraction, fisheries and weaving. In the 1850s, Msiri – a Nyamwezi trader from western Tanzania – settled in upper Katanga and founded the Yeke (Garenganze) kingdom, with an aristocracy dominating the local people. The Yeke, with their wider horizons, introduced new commercial ideas which they had assimilated along the trade routes from Zanzibar to Angola.[4]

The slave trade was not a new phenomenon in Congo; it had a long and terrible history, with Portuguese traffic in humans dominating the entire coastal region for centuries. Slave caravans moved steadily along the coast from San Salvador to Luanda in the south, and to Cabinda further north. An estimated thirteen million people were exported from the Congo. In the eastern part of the country, the Arabs exercised constant pressure on the communities, culminating in the exploits of Tippu Tib, the fearsome slave-dealer. The extent of the situation is sharply brought out by two statements. Vansina says: 'Trade, mainly the slave trade, began in 1500 and increased in volume and intensity throughout the centuries. It was the one great continuing event in Central African history until 1900.'[5] MacGaffey, writing on the lower Congo, has indicated the enormous scope and psychological depth of the problem: 'There is probably no one who is not tacitly considered to be a slave by a fair number of his neighbours ... History indicates that most peoples are slaves ... On the other hand hardly anyone accepts this evaluation of his status.'[6]

The slave trade was aggravated by far-reaching domestic slavery. As the Catholic missionaries began their work in the Kasai area near Luluabourg, they discovered that 'every free man owns slaves'.[7] An observer from the 1860s mentions three causes of the extensive slave trade: drought and famine; a judicial system using enslavement as punishment for even minor offences; and a widespread belief in witchcraft, which required the removal of 'witches' from society, in this case by selling them into slavery. As ivory became scarce, communities in search of money resorted to selling people. Vast areas were left looted and destroyed. Boys and girls were sold for a pittance, or orphaned and abandoned without refuge or protection. The missions, particularly the Catholic ones, devoted themselves to the care of these unfortunates, and founded 'colonies' or schools, in co-operation with the Independent Congo State. To the litany of lament and misery must be added the fact that sickness and epidemics were rampant. Smallpox was a killer in the 1890s, but the never-ending ravages of sleeping sickness destroyed three quarters of Congo society from 1880–1920. The Angel of Death held sway!

The imperialist invasion

Against the background of mighty Congo, its peoples and problems, two men stand out in nineteenth-century Congo history: Stanley the explorer, and Leopold, King of the Belgians. After 999 days of forcing his way through forests and along rushing rapids, H. M. Stanley broke through to Boma in 1877. He had crossed the continent from east to west and had shown the mostly navigable Congo to be 'God's highway into the interior of Africa'. He now gave another five years, 1879–84, to establishing the new Independent State of Congo, especially its communications by river and road from Boma to Stanley Pool (next to the capital city of Kinshasa, previously called Leopoldville) and on to Stanleyville (today, the city of Kisangani) and the Stanley Falls. In this book the missionary idea of a 'chain' across the continent from Bagamoyo to Boma is emphasized. Stanley was aware of this perspective: he developed a plan which would, as he said, 'allow the East and the West Coasts to shake hands'.[8]

During the last quarter of the century, the Congo was forcibly shaken by Western imperialist powers. In the 'scramble for Africa', the wily King Leopold called the 1876 congress at Brussels simply a 'geographical conference'. Among its concerns was a crusade against the iniquitous slave trade of Central Africa, a very laudable goal. As a result of the conference an organization was formed, the International African Association, with national committees in the various European countries, in reality a screen behind which more extensive plans could be designed.

In the same period another young explorer, a Frenchman, Savorgnan de Brazza, was making his way from the Atlantic coast through Gabon towards the country of the fear-inspiring Teke, well-known in these parts for their two products, manioc and slaves, and for their great and incomparable king, Makoko. Brazza – 'a man possessed who stops short of nothing and who does not regard anything as alien to his fiery ambition' (*rien d'étranger à sa passion*[9]) – in 1880 managed the unexpected: to establish friendly relationships with King Makoko. He had arrived, he said, representing the French Committee of the International African Association and hoped to find a central place for Europeans to do business and establish contacts with the Africans. He was given a corner on the Congo River, later called Brazzaville. In order to settle the troubles, he asked the king to sign a treaty, which was done there and then.

For the young officer and the French cause this was a resounding victory, the reverberations of which were anxiously registered at the royal palace in Brussels. Leopold urged Stanley on, to see to it that this French threat was averted. Stanley took his time, but he too, obviously, could speak to African kings and chiefs: in 1884 he was able to send Leopold a bag with 400 treaties assented to by 2,000 chiefs.[10]

Several years later, in 1884–85, Leopold was prepared to take the matter of the Congo to the Berlin Conference of European States. This meeting drew the new harsh frontier lines across the map of the African continent. The king referred the decision on his problem of the Congo to the European powers. They unanimously insisted on religious freedom for the missions:

> Christian missionaries shall be the objects of special protection. Freedom of conscience and religious toleration are expressly guaranteed to the natives, no less than to subjects and to foreigners. The free and public exercise of all forms of Divine worship, and the right to build edifices for religious purposes, and to organize religious Missions belonging to all creeds shall not be limited or fettered in any way whatsoever.[11]

These were solemn words. The king had referred his problem of the future of the Congo to the decision of the European States and they unanimously insisted on religious freedom for the missions, whether 'foreigners' – whatever that word was to mean in *that* connection – or not.

King Leopold, 'red rubber' and the missions

The royal contacts with prominent Anglo-Saxon Protestants caused some anxiety in the French-speaking Catholic world. At first, in fact until the end of the 1880s, Belgian Catholics were therefore reluctant to involve themselves in their king's Congo enterprise. The voluble spokesman for international French-speaking Catholic interests in Europe at the time, Cardinal Lavigerie, was particularly anxious about the Protestant influence. He had felt uneasy about the personnel at the king's first conference at Brussels, in 1876, seeing it as a largely Protestant and Freemason conspiracy, this in his view constituting an iniquitous threat to the religious life of the Congo.

Conversely, these same factors made it all the more easy, at first, for some of the Protestant pioneers to associate with the interests of the Independent State. This was particularly true of the English Baptist missionary, George Grenfell.

The beginnings of Christian missions in the Congo, with initial trials and cautious advance, were closely related to the political situation and indeed, to the imperialist take-over of the country by the King of the Belgians. This is emphasized here in that the main outline follows the political history:

a) 'Prelude to Conquest', until 1885; b) 'Church Developments in Congo', 1885–1908; c) 'Church and Mission', 1908–21. The dates are approximate and symbolic so that '1885' stands for the introduction of power politics by European rulers, while the final date, '1921', indicates the appearance of Simon Kimbangu, the African prophet.

Leopold's apparent humanitarian ideology impressed the 1884–85 Berlin Conference participants, and smoothed the way for the proclamation in that same year of the foundation of the 'Independent State of Congo', with King Leopold the Sovereign. Gradually he asserted his authority. No other area was so completely identified with its royal ruler in Europe as this vast land on the equator. In 1906 he could claim: 'My rights over the Congo are to be shared with none, they are the fruits of my own struggles and expenditure ... [I have] the absolute ownership uncontested of the Congo and its riches.'

The State soon revealed its ultimate goal: the gathering of as much rubber as possible, to be exported to markets in the West. Plunder and exploitation followed and led to the 'Congo Scandal'. In 1903, after severe and increasing protests about conditions in the Congo, Leopold appointed his own Commission of Enquiry. To his dismay, their report of 1905 confirmed what the critics had said. In 1908 the King relinquished control and handed over 'his' Congo to the government of Belgium.

No sooner had the European States consented to Leopold's plans – insofar as these were known – than he announced the economic principle upon which the whole system would rest: all 'vacant' or unclaimed lands belonged to the State. (No one explained how the Congolese could claim their own land.) Large 'domains' or concessions of land were given to Belgian financial companies. In 1892 a decree reserved half the area of Congo for exclusive exploitation by the State. In addition, in 1896, Leopold annexed another 'domain of the Crown', near Lake Leopold II, specifically for the king's own property. Now followed the exportation of rubber to markets in the West, which became increasingly dependent on this supply. Belgian administrators enforced, by brutal methods, the bringing of rubber from the forests. Failure to deliver led to horrendous methods of punishment meted out under the supervision of individual local administrators and officers. Mutilation of bodies was not uncommon, even involving the cutting off of right hands as punishment for shortage in the rubber-collecting baskets. This policy of exploiting the forests by the collected efforts of the companies continued unabated throughout the 1890s, culminating in the first years of the new century. 'The Congolese system was too viciously wasteful ... even to use the term exploitation. It was no more than a prolonged raid for plunder.'[12]

One of King Leopold's stated aims in 1885 was to stop slavery and the slave trade. The people in the Lower Congo were now to conclude that the alternative offered by the rubber scandal was not much better. The porterage system decreed in 1889 was a new kind of forced labour. Men were requisitioned as porters and in gangs were compelled to carry heavy loads between the coast and Stanley Pool, on the Belgian side, and between Loango and Brazzaville on the French side. Pressure on the workers was exercised by capturing their women as hostages. Recruiting became extremely unpopular and whole districts fled into the forests and starved. Large areas were depleted and deserted, with vital food-producing fields of millet destroyed.

On the French side of the Congo River, in French Equatorial Africa, the tragedy is less well known, but was fully as brutal. The French historian Catherine Coquery-Vidrovitch in her study of Congo 1898–1930 – the time of the great concessionary companies – has with uncompromising candour described affairs in French Congo. Officials did not shy from any means of coercion. Failure to bring the coveted rubber from the forests would lead to burning of villages or to large-scale massacres. Many preferred to flee towards Leopold's Congo and were 'eager at any cost to avoid contacts with any White'.[13]

Not all missionaries were in a position to know what was going on, at a time when communications were at best hazardous. The fierce drama was mainly staged on the Upper Congo and on the Kasai. There were missionaries who were almost daily witnesses of the exploitation of land and people. Protestant missionaries of great personal courage brought the Congo scandal to the knowledge of the outside world. A few names must be mentioned: Charles Banks, Englishman, of the Congo Balolo mission, E. E. V. Sjöblom, a Swede, working with the American Baptists, both on the Upper Congo, and W. M. Morrison of the American Presbyterian Mission in southern Kasai.[14] The Protestant missionaries were able to provide material for a great campaign launched with uncompromising efficiency by the British journalist, E. D. Morel and the Congo Reform Association organized by Morel and the Belgian socialist, Vandevelde.

The extent of the problem was known to the Belgians, for some of the fast-growing Catholic stations in the forest region, for instance Wombali, became refuges for vast numbers of people fleeing there for their lives. If these Belgian Catholics made any protests, however, their complaints were considerably muted.

Some Protestants had from the outset become to such an extent identified with the original anti-slavery policy of the king that they did not seem prepared to discover the real nature of the 'red rubber' scandal. George

Grenfell of the BMS was a case in point. In 1893 he declared that the Leopold regime was 'exceptionally friendly' *viz*. 'particularly friendly', and it was to take another decade before he changed his attitude.

Even as late as 1900 Grenfell's colleague, Holman Bentley, could state: 'The general organization of the government is very good'. He was thinking then of the fact that the government had 'crushed the Arab slavers' in the eastern part of the state, and he represented Protestant opinion throughout in praising the regime for its efforts to come to terms with the problem of the import and sale of alcohol. He may have remembered that in 1899 Leopold had called a conference in Brussels on this subject. He went on to say: 'Happily the relations between our mission and the Government have been very cordial ... By the General Act of Berlin (1885) liberty of worship was guaranteed to all, and this has been faithfully carried out by the state.'[15] Both Grenfell and Holman Bentley were men with a fine record in the advancement of their work in the Congo. Yet these quotations serve as a reminder of the need for a sense of priorities.

The 'Congo Scandal' and the Protestant campaign cannot be overlooked in this Church history. It is very much part of it, although, for the sake of brevity, one can only recognize the stark facts. The whole campaign had certain far-reaching consequences for Church history: on the Catholic side, there followed a tightening of the ties between the Belgian State and the Catholic Church. The struggle over the 'Congo atrocities' was followed by Liberal and Socialist attacks in Belgium on Belgian Jesuit mission policy, leading to a more exclusive emphasis on Congo as Catholic.

In 1906, Leopold's Congo concluded a convention with the Vatican assuring the Catholics of vast areas of land – 100 to 200 hectares of arable land – in full ownership. It was the Catholic schools which were the primary issue here. At the first Congo Conference of Catholic Heads of Mission, in 1907, Fr Cambier of the Kasai mentioned that the Independent State had regretted 'and with good reason, the inferiority of our schools in comparison with those of the Protestants'.[16] The conference decided that each religious order must have its own Central Schools. The great educational effort on the part of the Catholics found its starting point here.[17]

For the Protestants, the bitter struggle had tangible consequences. Throughout the contest Leopold's men had insinuated that the campaign was part of an imperialist design on Congo from the Anglo-Saxon countries and that the Protestant missionaries, 'the foreigners', were the advance guard to this end. From this time onwards the Protestants were to find it increasingly difficult to get sites for their schools and other centres.[18]

Communications

Church history in the Congo basin would be incomplete without mentioning the development of modern means of communication, the railways and the river steamers. Both Catholic and Protestant missionaries were anxious to use the railway. Correspondence in the latter part of the nineteenth century contains constant references to the progress of rail construction along the river, and the necessity of establishing the new mission centres close to the sidings.[19] The railway between Matadi and Kinshasa on the Belgian side was completed in 1899; on the French side of the River, a road system was followed by a railway project, the so-called 'Congo-Ocean', launched in 1921 and completed in 1934. While this situation could often lead to denominational competition across the ecclesiastical frontiers, a train compartment on the new Matadi–Kinshasa line was also fortunately able to serve as a meeting-place for a constructive and generous ecumenical encounter, as will be seen presently.

THE CATHOLICS

A reprise

The Catholics had, as always, history on their side. To the Catholics the meeting with Congo was a return to old, half-forgotten places. *Reprise* was their term for it in French. They had been there before, both centuries ago and more recently. From 1870, Landana – in present-day Cabinda – became the strategic smithy for the forging of Spiritan plans for the coast. There were three leaders: A. M. H. Carrie (d. 1904), a prudent, orderly man of great perseverance and Vicar Apostolic of Loango from 1886; Philippe-Prosper Augouard, Bishop of the Catholic Church in French Equatorial Africa; and the ubiquitous C. V. Aubert-Duparquet, man of vision and sudden, surprising initiatives. It was these French Spiritans who more than others represented this Catholic theme of *reprise*, and among them none with more zeal and imagination than Duparquet.

In 1855, at twenty-five years of age, he had been sent to Dakar and from there was posted to the coast of Gabon. A rich man's son, he always managed somehow to be more mobile than any of his brethren – more mobile, in fact, than any other Catholic missionary in the whole of nineteenth-century Africa. (He later moved with the same optimism through the sands of Namibia, or towards the lakes of East Africa, and this not in the modern period of air travel, but in the 1870s!) The nineteenth-century missionary was necessarily conditioned by the fundamental facts of geography: oceans, harbours, lakes, rivers and used them all for his evangelizing purposes.

Duparquet felt that his Order did not grasp the potential of the situation in the Congo – and said so. His criticism was regarded as intolerable in a young man, and he was repatriated to Europe, gravely ill, in June 1857. This gave him a chance, in the Paris libraries, to deepen his knowledge of the early mission to Congo in the seventeenth and eighteenth centuries. After a number of surprising twists and turns in his ecclesiastical career, the Propaganda Fide in Rome accepted his proposal to make the Congo a 'prefecture' and young Duparquet himself was made the Vice Prefect. In that capacity he went to Landana, north of the Congo estuary on the Congo coast. When these first missionaries arrived at Landana, they found an economic and social situation strikingly influenced by international contacts with Brazil and Portugal and ruled by three leading families, nominally Catholic. For generations these had made their fortune through slave trading with Brazil, followed toward the end of the century by lucrative palm oil exports. This coastal population, similar to the Kru of Liberia, were mobile, enterprising, and away from home for long periods of time. Sons of the wealthy families went to Brazil and Portugal for their education. Contacts with these people made it comparatively easy for the French missionaries to start their work.[20]

Duparquet initially faced hostility, through the tiresome fact of a drought which here as elsewhere was the missionary's fault, until a torrential shower saved the situation – and Duparquet. In the meantime Duparquet and Carrie trained catechists and prepared catechumens. In 1874, 160 children were baptized.

The Spiritan strategy at Landana was conceived according to its historical, pedagogical and missiological aspects. Their *reprise* had to be approached with utmost tact and diplomacy, in view of Portuguese monopolistic claims to Catholic work in the area. From Landana, Duparquet, Carrie and others explored what was left of Catholic remains on the Congo coast, particularly at two places: Chief Nemlao's centre north of the Congo estuary, and St Anthony, south of the River. They made exciting discoveries which were published in *Les Missions Catholiques*, 1877–81. They were aware that they followed up the work of Proyart and others who had been there 200 years earlier. They felt a continuity with the Catholic past. Near Banana they visited King Nemlao whose people consisted of an immigrant, once Christian colony of people from Soyo further south. They had abandoned Soyo because of an inter-tribal war and as they moved north they brought along their sacred objects, such as three copper crucifixes received from their forefathers. The king told the missionary that he had been baptized and had received the name of Don Pedro. He took his guest into a little church which had an altar and the crucifixes.

St Antony, from the point of view of the Church, had been abandoned for at least half a century, possibly much longer, but some people claimed to have met Fr Seraphin, the last Capuchin missionary. The local king, Dom Pantaleon, had also known the Capuchins. On public occasions the king would take the crucifix in both his hands and give the blessing to the people. He now asked the missionary to baptize him.

A group apart, here and at neighbouring Pinda, was the so-called 'people of the Church'. Their forefathers had once been 'the slaves of the monastery', but had established themselves as an independent, introspective community. Dom Pantaleon did not like them. He said, 'the Church people were not good' – but he had to respect them, for in times of drought they were, after all, a resource group for they would walk in procession through the village carrying the statue of our Lord, which was obviously effective.

Many of the once holy rites and gestures were remembered and dramatized. For Lent the statues were veiled. When the unofficial reader knelt at the altar steps to take some equivalent of a mass he was flanked by two assistants, one on each side. He knew when to change the place of the missal on the altar. On the altar there were six candelabra in black wood and on either side of the altar a big statue, almost natural size, one of the Holy Virgin and the other of St Antony of Padua. There were censers and the remains of a kind of transparent resin for the incense. The congregation knelt and placed their hands together in the gesture of pious prayer. A church bell was still sounded. The missionary was inspired by its sound to exclaim: 'Of the Christian people who have seen thee, and of the apostles who have evangelized these nations, nothing remains. Only thy voice has never been muted and it reminds us of a glorious past.'[21]

It was all there, in its echoes of magnificence and its pathetic decay, the bones of what once had been throbbing jubilant life. Now the dead bones were crying out under those mighty trees for renewal, for life. The discovery of these remnants was a constant challenge to the Landana group to see the Congo Church rise again. To the joy of the St Antony congregation, the missionary was able to place a catechist in their midst, baptize 130 children, and start a school.[22] With his charming optimism Duparquet was even prepared to attach to these discoveries a missiological theory of his own: 'One can in fact much easier preserve in the Catholic faith these Christian populations than convert non-believers to Christianity.

It is more appropriate to maintain the already existing Christian communities than to allow them to perish.'[23]

Landana

At Landana the mission work was concentrated on the children. The early missionaries there reasoned that as the adult generations could not be reached, the children were the only hope for evangelization. As a disciple of Libermann, Duparquet hoped to make some of these youngsters into priests, for according to Libermann's precept, 'Africa must be converted through Africans'. 'Sacred Childhood', an international Catholic programme to care for children in the 'Third World', had originated in France, and now inspired the mission activities on the Congo coast. The educational strategy of Catholic missions, both south and north of the Congo River, at least until well after 1900, followed the organization of this international group.

Bishop Carrie wrote, in French, the 'Code of the Children's work in the diocese of French Congo' (1890).[24] It conveys the tone of order and discipline which permeated the Catholic schools at Landana and in the Congo as a whole. This was to mirror the Divine Order. The code laid down the different categories of children: 'It is in the order of Divine Providence which has thus differentiated human society that we direct each of our children to the particular status to which God calls him/her and according to the rank into which He had made him to be born.' The school had to observe the differences between the children: a few Whites, comparatively numerous mulattoes and the Blacks. These Blacks were children of African kings and princes, destined to become propagators of religion and 'instruments of salvation' for their respective peoples. Others were children of ordinary freemen, or the ransomed children of slaves. Carrie's code, with its accepted discrimination between categories of children, is disturbing to the modern reader. A minority of them later to become leaders would automatically receive better education and even better food. Carrie, a farmer's son from near Lyon, was stamped by his own hierarchical system, the structure of which he also discerned in traditional African society.

Duparquet started a Theological Seminary at Landana in 1875. It began optimistically with a single student, a young mulatto, Louis de Gourlet. As Duparquet often went to other parts of Africa, Carrie took over as director in 1878, with two recruits, Louis Lutete, son of a chief, and Charles Maonde. In 1887 the Seminary was transferred from Landana to Loango, Carrie's headquarters. By 1900 there were thirteen students. However, the climate was bad and illness and death caused havoc. In one decade there were a total of eleven rectors of the Seminary. The report for 1912 states that the Seminary in its thirty-five years had changed directors twenty-four times! In 1892 the first three priests were ordained. Fortunately, Charles Maonde, one of the first ordained, acted as sub-director throughout the period. He was pious and zealous, and exercised a strong influence on the younger seminarians.

Duparquet fully realized the potential of Boma as a base for missionary operations, 'a great population centre with frequent communications with Europe, with Landana [and Gabon], the Interior and especially with San Salvador and the centre of Congo. Here one can easily ransom young slaves.'[25] It was Duparquet's colleague, Carrie, who was to establish the Catholic centre at Boma in 1880.

Moving inland

After Stanley's arrival at Boma in 1877, it was only a matter of time before the Spiritans advanced inland – to the Kasai valley which for years had been their goal. Duparquet had repeatedly underlined their claims to this valley, 'so beautiful as to ravish the eyes of the angels, this ancient and beautiful mission which has been confided to us'. Duparquet insisted that it was the Spiritans alone who should care for the entire region from the northern bank of the Congo River to the Kasai valley.

Carrie sent Augouard on reconnoitring tours to Stanley Pool, the wide swelling of the River close to Kinshasa and Brazzaville. In 1885 Augouard proceeded with 165 porters along the River, and reached the Kasai junction, Kwamouth. The German explorer, von Wissmann, had just journeyed along the Kasai to reach the same junction and had reported immense opportunities for the evangelization of the Lulua and the Luba. On 5 August 1885, Augouard confided to his diary:

> This discovery offers new horizons to geography and allows us to know a magnificent valley hitherto unknown. For us [the Spiritans] in particular it has great importance because for a long time it is to this beautiful river that we have desired to proceed and to try to communicate with the fellow members of our order in Cimbebasie.[26]

His horizon included more than the thousand miles of the Kasai River; it extended to 'Cimbebasie', the present coastline of southern Angola.

Augouard also urged the occupation of the Kasai region, to forestall the threatening Protestant presence. 'The error advances with its Bibles and its gold.' In April 1886 he reported the founding of his new mission station, 'St

Paul of the Kasai'. Only two months later, he was told that it must be closed.[27] Augouard wrote to his mother in a moment of bewilderment that he was 'the wandering Jew of the good God'. He withdrew to the northern, 'French', side of the River. On the coast, Carrie had to give up his promising stations: Landana, Boma and St Antony. King Leopold's Independent State was hereafter to be independent for Belgians only.

Establishing the mission north of the River

When Augouard withdrew north of the River after the Spiritan setback on the southern side, his first attempt to establish himself among the underpopulated Teke was unsuccessful. The solid Teke, old possessors of the land, exhibited stubborn resistance and aversion to new ideas. The neighbouring Lali at Linzolo, new Kongo migrants infiltrating into Teke lands, were more accommodating. G. Sautter, the geographer, characterized the Lali as 'at once assimilative and creative'. These traits again illustrate the migration theme repeatedly emphasized in this book – the openness to new ideas and new faiths found in uprooted peoples. Augouard started his first mission at Linzolo west of Brazzaville. The Catholic Church was now firmly planted in the Congo region of the French Equatorial Africa. The Lali had come into the old Teke country right at the beginning of the French colonization process. Unfortunately, the French Spiritans under Augouard seemed to be a religious accompaniment to the French colonial conquest.

Although Augouard was a great French patriot, he soon realized that Brazza and the French administration were anti-clerical, causing the contacts between the two men to become strained. One cause of this tension was Brazza's interest in establishing Muslim schools in the Sangha district, importing Arab teachers from Algiers. He was convinced that a pro-Islam policy was good for French interests, but Bishop Augouard could not agree. There were other interesting influences at work. The large Brazza exploration expedition included a group of ten African Christians from Gabon whom Augouard had known in their home country. In their quiet way, they witnessed to their faith: never missing morning and evening prayers and regularly touching their rosaries to receive strength for the road. Brazza himself vouched for their good influence on the whole expedition.

Problems of population pressures and movements varied, from underpopulated districts such as the Teke, to other areas such as the Mbochi, who proudly boasted that their Kanguini was 'the biggest village in the world'.[28] Rapid results could not be expected at first. Augouard subscribed to the Landana theory that in the first generation, only children could be won for the faith. In 1895 he reported that the Linzolo group of Christians numbered seventeen children, including some who were ransomed. A Christian village, 'St Isadore', had four Christian families and there twelve children had been baptized *in extremis*. Along the rivers were other such villages: Lekety, Sante Radegonda, each under a Christian chief. The outstanding catechist Anthony Ongondi served this area for thirty years.

The number of converts was thus limited and almost exclusively to boys, lodged in dormitories. A resulting problem was the lack of girl converts, but one missionary found a novel solution – he decided to buy or ransom girls. In May 1905, he acquired eight girls for 328 francs, forty-one francs 'by the piece'. Bishop Augouard was reported to be somewhat unenthusiastic about this unconventional solution, but he did not interfere.

The work began with these rather unpromising results, but Augouard and his men, joined in 1892 by some sisters, showed unrelenting perseverance. They developed stations along the Alima and Ubangi Rivers, using Augouard's steamer *Leo XIII*, succeeded by the *Diata-diata*, and *Pius X*. These travels made it possible for Augouard to publish a detailed map of the Ubangi River, *De Liranga á St Paul des-Rapides*, 1906–07. Times were harsh, particularly in the Ubangi region. As Fr Allaire set up his portable altar for mass in the forest glade, the Bondjo stared at the ritual in utter amazement. The Teke in the Alima region were more welcoming; there the missionaries were able to make visits in the villages and attempt to approach the adults.

Relations between the French administration and the Catholic mission were a cause for concern. Occasional administrators tried to accommodate the missionaries. One even imprisoned certain Teke who had been guilty of disrespect to the missionary, but conflicts with the government were unavoidable. Some of the problems were caused by the posting of catechists in certain areas; Christian villages and their relation to neighbouring traditional villages; marriage difficulties; and problems of private schools. French administrators interfered in the schools by insisting on French as the language to be used, with the option of Lingala, the Lower Congo *lingua franca*. When in 1917 Fr Prat produced three books in the Mbochi language – a catechism, prayer book and a grammar – the administration ordered the volumes to be destroyed.

In his youth, Bishop Augouard had served as a *zouave* (papal soldier) in the 1870–71 war. As bishop, he retained much of the army discipline and authority. He was Vicar Apostolic of Ubangi in 1890–1921. At the time of his death in 1921, his province comprised 13,700 Catholics, 12,000 catechumens, 100 catechists, with 6,000 children in the schools. The French staff included twenty-two Fathers, ten lay brothers, and ten sisters.[29] A gradual shift in the Congolese population occurred. The dominance of the old die-hard generations gave way to increasing participation by the younger generations, resulting in large-scale change in the role of the missions.[30]

Catholic rivalry

Certain aspects of Congo mission history are sometimes considered an uneven tug-of-war between the privileged Catholics and the barely-tolerated Protestants. Such was, of course, the position in the early decades of the twentieth century, but the 1880s and 1890s presented a different drama. Two strong Catholic missions had claims in the Congo: the Spiritans or Holy Ghost Fathers, and the White Fathers, but both reluctantly had to retreat from their positions. The reason was simple enough: they were of the wrong nationality – French, not Belgian. None was more solidly entrenched in the Congo than Cardinal Lavigerie and the White Fathers. In 1879 he presented his 'Secret Memorandum' to the Pope, who accepted it *in toto*. *In toto* is the phrase, for it was a sweeping line across the map of Africa. The Cardinal had reserved Central Africa for himself: two large territories around the Lakes, and another two including most of the two Congos, eastwards down to Kinshasa. He placed his first two missionaries at Kwamouth on the River. The 'hurricane of a Cardinal' – as some of the competing Catholic orders called him – swept aside the paper plans of the other Catholic organizations. The Spiritans, with good reason, regarded themselves as the pioneers in Congo and felt unjustly edged out. They wrote sad, sometimes frantic letters to Rome and Belgium, but the Cardinal in Algiers was not to be confounded. Ever voluble and expansive, he was generous enough to permit elbow-room to the Spiritans. He wrote in 1881 to the Propaganda: 'If thus the Spiritans wish to establish themselves on any tributaries of the Congo, as they appear to do, nothing will hinder them, they are welcome.'[31]

This gesture did not impress the one who really mattered and decided who was to settle in Congo. At home Leopold had become increasingly irritated by the Cardinal's claims. As Lavigerie began to sense the royal displeasure, he suggested that the White Fathers in the Congo should consist of an exclusively Belgian group of men, though they would be responsible to the head of the order, the Cardinal in Algiers. This arrangement would surely guarantee the national character of their enterprise. A fascinating hide-and-seek between King and Cardinal followed, the former devious and cautious at first, the latter increasingly feeling the ground slipping from under his feet. Then came 1884–85 and the Berlin

Conference, and the King knew that *he* at least was on solid ground. Now that the imperial powers had agreed to the Independent Congo State, the declaration about religious and national tolerance could conveniently be forgotten. The King could openly make his long-planned decree that Catholics in the Congo must be 'national', i.e. Belgian, and the Cardinal's men must start packing. The Spiritans too were French, and thus also had to leave. They did this only very reluctantly. Lavigerie's White Fathers could take some consolation in that now they could concentrate with all the more determination on their great work, 'Between the Lakes', from Uganda to Zambia. White Fathers of Belgian nationality were later to return to eastern Congo and develop highly successful work there.

Initial Catholic methods

This book has claimed that nineteenth-century mission in all of Africa was a youth movement. For Congo this statement needs to be more precise. There, especially with the Catholics, it was at first a children's movement. The Catholic Church became engaged in a crusade on behalf of Congo's endangered and enslaved children. This was both an adaptation to a chaotic social situation and the result of thorough strategic deliberations. This children's crusade was part of a wider international programme for the liberation and care for the children in the 'Third World', an expression of the movement of the 'Sacred Childhood'. The Scheut Fathers from Brussels had been entrusted with the responsibility for the Catholic involvement in China, and they were particularly apt for a work of this kind. The Scheut Fathers under Theophile Verbiest had laboured among the orphaned children of China and Mongolia. Taking over the Congo responsibility from the French Spiritans, they were prepared to continue in Africa the work begun in China: to save the children, but now in the Congo. This was also an admission that the programme for the adults had to be postponed. In essence, it also reflected a certain pessimism with regard to the adult Congolese that for the time being the adults could not be expected to be reached with the new message. The Church, however, could wait for the next generation. The Church had time.

A government law of 'guardianship' was promulgated by which government declared itself to be guardian of all orphaned children and ready to take care of them, using for this purpose the good offices of such philanthropic and religious voluntary organizations as were willing to devote themselves to the task. Catholic and Protestant policy differed in this matter.[32] The former accepted the challenge of the law, the latter, except at

Bolenge, did not see it as their task to act as guardians to these children, but rather to save individual souls. In his book on the Redemptorists, Kratz says that this arrangement sometimes led to a 'hunt for children', causing Africans to call the missionaries 'thieves of children'. What was more difficult was that the missionaries did not at first understand the workings of a matrilineal society: 'To us a child is an orphan when it no longer has a father or mother. In Congo an orphan is a child who no longer has mother nor mother's brother, even if it has its own father.'[33]

Leopold's Independent State started 'school colonies' to care for the enormous numbers of orphaned children. The first was in Boma. Belgian non-commissioned officers together with Catholic Scheut Fathers were to train ransomed slaves and orphans as soldiers, tailors, carpenters and masons. Exhibiting the close co-operation between Church and State, one-fifth of those trained at the school were assigned to the Church. The school was fortunate in its first director, Father N. De Cleene, and soon had over 250 children. The daily timetable at the Boma school included three periods of military exercise, three of the 'four R's' including religion, and three of practical work. Fifteen years later, 1,000 miles from Boma, the school colony bore fruit. This example will illustrate the rapid development of the early Catholic work in the Congo, and the role of group dynamics fired by individual Christian concern.

Soldiers as catechumens

In 1907 two Scheut Fathers were given special permission to visit the state post at Inongo. This was a place in the rubber-producing area which was, for political reasons, regarded as a particularly sensitive spot and therefore unknown to any Catholic missionary. To their surprise, they discovered in the large soldiers' camp three impressive catechetical classes. One had 200 catechumens – soldiers, their wives and older children – learning the faith, in Lingala, from Sergeant Mikoti Evariste, a former Boma student from the 1890s. His Christian training at Boma had made him a fervent volunteer catechist, spending his free-time hammering in the elements of the faith. Henri Bokelo, trained by the Jesuits at Wombali, taught a class of 400. Twenty minutes away from the military camp, Mbotikari Henri and Isatote Joseph, also former students from Wombali, taught a third catechumens' class of 1,000! The image of Congolese corporals as voluntary catechists – after having emerged from the chaotic life of slavery – may perhaps suggest a certain affinity in the minds of these young men between the two codes of the new way of life: army regulation and the Church's catechism.

The 'farm chapels'

Faced with the challenge of the multitudes of orphans, the Jesuits, who had been in the Kwango area since 1893 and were inspired by their great leader Emile van Hencxthoven, introduced a peculiar form of mission colony referred to as 'farm chapel'. These centres were established near one or more ordinary Congolese villages but not identified with these. The centre comprised a chapel, various houses for the staff, and students' buildings for practical activities and for the cattle. There were in principle three catechists at each farm chapel selected from among the most gifted of the young generation. They would give instruction in the neighbouring villages in the morning and to the farm chapel children in the afternoon. On Saturdays the catechists would assemble at the central station, Kisantu or Wombali, both large and growing centres. Hencxthoven believed in teaching his young pupils the virtue of work and they were trained in agriculture and crafts. The children lived under efficient control in the farm chapel. After a certain number of years and after marriage, young couples established themselves as Christian colonies in the district. Again, their centres were established at a certain distance from neighbouring pagan villages. While thus supposedly free from unwanted influences they were, on the other hand, expected to act as nuclei of catechetical influence among the traditional villages. Under the energetic and eminently practical Hencxthoven's direction the centres had large dairy and agricultural farms with rice, maize, peanuts and potatoes.

The Jesuits expanded this system to such a degree that in 1900 there were 134 farm chapels in their field with 3,800 children; in 1902 this had increased to 250 farm chapels with 5,000 children. The efficiency of the Jesuit work also had negative repercussions. Van Hencxthoven's farm chapels became the object of fierce opposition both from the local Congolese population – who had the impression that their children were being 'stolen' from them – and from various political, mainly anti-Jesuit, interests in Belgium who attacked the farm chapels as 'a new Paraguay'. (During the seventeenth century and for most of the eighteenth, the Jesuits virtually ran Paraguay, controlling large tracts of land on their estates. The farm chapels were seen by the Jesuits' critics as a way of becoming landlords and having feudal relations with the local population, thus creating a Prince-Bishop/feudal rule.) The Belgian Labour leader, Van der Velde, took a passionate interest in the fate of the Congolese masses and concentrated his attack largely on the methods of the farm chapels. From about 1910, the system was modified, as it was felt that the method isolated the children too much from their own *milieu*, and the name was changed to 'school chapels'.

A change of method

The Belgian Redemptorists – comparative late-comers, arriving in 1899 – followed the method which their colleagues in the other orders on the Lower Congo had established, particularly that of the Jesuit farm chapels. They had been called to Congo for a special task: pastoral care among the railway workers – White and Black – along the new line from Matadi to Stanley Pool. On arrival they were informed that it was simply out of the question to attempt to win adults. Yet, the spiritual work among the railway workers showed the Redemptorists that adult Congolese had been underrated as candidates for the new faith. In the period 1899–1903 their railway chapels registered no less than 280 adults baptized, together with 330 children. This was an eye-opener. It was discovered that whenever an individual was lifted out and uprooted from his tribal *milieu*, and therefore mobile, he was more likely, together with his new group, to accept a new religious alternative, in this case Christian allegiance.

In 1903 the Redemptorists had a new Superior General, A. Simplaere, who had arrived in the Congo in 1900. In a situation where it was taken for granted that there must be no contact whatsoever between Catholics and Protestants it so happened that one day Fr Simplaere found that he shared his railway compartment with a Protestant missionary, the well-known Baptist, Holman Bentley. They could not but discuss what to them seemed the most important of all themes, namely, their respective mission methods. Bentley expressed his reservations about the farm chapels and recommended instead the training of responsible adult Congolese catechists, the very basis for Protestant work. Fr M. Kratz's writing on the Redemptorists in the Belgian Congo has shown the remarkable change which followed the ecumenical exchange of views in that railway compartment. The Catholics now had catechists in the midst of the villages with schools serving at the same time as chapels. An advantage with the hierarchical Church system represented by Simplaere was that once the man in charge had been convinced of the necessity for change, it had also to be accepted by the other missionaries, his subordinates.

A catechists' school at Tumba soon provided workers for the new parishes. The school proceeded on two different lines, one lower, one higher, the latter also providing such sophisticated wisdom as French and arithmetic. In the beginning the preponderance of students from the Upper Congo was felt to be a problem. At this time the congregations regarded their young catechists from far away as foreigners. This difficulty was eventually overcome so that, in 1909, only 5 per cent of the students at the Tumba Catechists' school hailed from Upper Congo. The local congre-

Table 6.1. *Percentage of different ages of people admitted to baptism in 1902 and 1920*

	0–5 years	6–15 years	adults	*in articulo mortis*	unspecified
1902	10.0%	16.8%	49.0%	20.0%	4.2%
1920	35.6%	28.4%	24.7%	8.1%	3.2%

gation at Kionzo, near Matadi, rejoiced in the services of their catechist, Jean Baptiste Matezwa. Born in 1885, he was baptized in 1900 and was placed at Kionzo as a catechist in 1903. He was still holding the same office in the same place in 1965, after more than six decades.

Another problem the Catholics met in their catechetical programme was how long to provide training prior to baptism. When the Tumba missionary announced that those admitted to his class in August were to be baptized at Christmas the same year, the Vicar Apostolic objected, demanding one full year's instruction, a period which, as a matter of course was later extended. At the outset there were large numbers of baptisms *in articulo mortis*. Table 6.1 compares the returns for 1902 and 1920 for the different ages of people admitted to baptism. These figures are fairly representative of any young African Church in its first two decades, apart from the particularly Catholic category of baptisms *in articulo mortis*.

Going south

In the Luba language area, combined political and ecclesiastical interests urged the Scheut missionaries to establish their work in the south of the country. King Leopold needed them as a trusted Belgian screen against possible Portuguese inroads from the south, and they would counteract what was seen as the threat of a rapid Protestant invasion. To the Westerner, southern Kasai was then a forlorn outpost in pagan Africa.

Yet when Fr Emeri Cambier of the Scheut Fathers arrived, moving along the Kasai River, 'from hippopotamus to hippopotamus', he discovered a Christian African community ready to assist him – a corroboration, it would seem, of a fundamental thesis of this book: the Western missionary arriving at any place in Africa always found that he had been preceded by some group of African Christians.

These were the Bimbadi, a group of Angolans who, hired by the German explorer, Wissmann, six years earlier, had arrived in southern Kasai and who for various reasons had decided to stay on in Luba country. Here they all were: Pedro, Feliciano, Sebastao, Johannes, etc. The exact number of these Bimbadi is not known, neither do we know whether they comprised Angolan families or consisted of Angolan men who later took Luba wives. In 1887 they were known to have spoken to the local community of their faith which resulted in the locals throwing their fetishes into the Lulua River and beginning to 'believe in God, punish misdeeds and demand by hook or by crook to be baptized'.[34]

What is important in this context is that the Catholic missionary, when he finally arrived in 1891, found a group of Christianized Africans ready to be his helpers and interpreters – interpreters in more than one sense. They were foreigners in a foreign land, an isolated small group of enterprising young men with a smattering of the new religion, its Latin phrases and its gestures. They had a great influence over the Bena Lulua chief Kalamba, but were also prepared to defend the White missionaries in the Lulua de Nkonko rebellion of 18 July 1895. They were an altogether impressive little beach-head of the new religion on the banks of the Kasai. It must be taken for granted that Fr Cambier served as a chaplain to these Catholic co-religionists. Cambier's method was original and differed from any other attempted by Catholic or Protestant. Thus he did not agree to the conventional individual missionary tours in the district, insisting that such things were so much waste of time and he actually forbade, at least as long as he could, his younger colleagues to try.

When Cambier came to this area, he found a political situation of extreme delicacy: war between the mighty Chief Mukenge Kalamba and his 10,000 warriors, and the emerging Belgian administration at Luluaborg. This was the same chief who, in 1887, had told the Belgian officer, De Macar, that he wanted to be baptized together with his people. The situation had changed since then and Cambier had to tread warily. He tried a 'pre-evangelism' approach. With only his crucifix and his ocarina, he marched nine hours through the forest, followed by one of the Angolan Bimbadi as interpreter, two porters and a boy. Eventually he came upon the first guards near the chief's place. He pulled out his ocarina and played.

> A little boy arrives immediately, creeping through the bushes and another follows him, then ten, and twenty, then the women and the men ... The sudden appearance of Kalamba absolutely magnetized me. [They started their palaver] ... I could not be sorry over the result. After two hours of discussion, the old chief thanked me with tears in his eyes, and promised to rebuild his old village next to the Mission, and with the Government he was from now on to have nothing but amicable relations.[35]

In retrospect the story takes on more sinister overtones than the enthusiastic missionary could have noticed at the time. Unfortunately, the chief was not the only African who thus equated the interests of the two European powers – State and Church. However, this encounter with Mukenge Kalamba gave Cambier enormous authority in the area.

Fr Cambier's Kasai method differed, as already noted, from that in the other Scheut and Jesuit districts. In Kasai, great numbers of liberated slaves came to the mission, most of whom were adults. From the beginning the Kasai communities were Christian villages, 'Reductions' as the Catholics would say, thinking of the Jesuits' Paraguay. The life of the inhabitants was founded on common work and Christian discipline. The adults married according to their own customs and adopted liberated children. Regular religious instruction began only after two years and at first was not aimed at baptism. After this period the catechumenate would follow. This final preparation was limited to those who expressed a wish for baptism of their own free will.

The missionary residences became centres of Christian influence over the local population, who increasingly placed their villages next to the mission. Thereby Cambier's goal was reached: an unforced Christian *milieu* where new converts could take root. To expand the work, some Christian families were sent to start independent centres of their own in new districts. Each group was to form a nucleus of expansion, a 'chrétienté', and each of these had about twenty-five families. They built a simple shed where the people met for instruction by a resident catechist. He was supervised by a missionary who visited the centre three times a week. Cambier fixed the catechetical period at three years. These local congregations were about one hour's walk from the mission, in various directions. The Cambier system, when functioning according to plan, formed a Christian fellowship separated from, yet in the middle of, pagan villages. The chiefs and the local administration could offer the mission thousands of liberated slaves, or these came of their own accord to the station. Thus the statistics for Merode had the following numbers of fresh arrivals, the majority being adults.

1894: 500	1898: 458
1895: 300	1899: 883
1896: 800	1900: 907
1897: 500	

Schools were built for the boys, while the girls were sent to boarding schools run by Belgian sisters.

The Bimbadi from Angola were not the only foreigners in these groups.

There were at first very few local Bena Lulua among them and the Christian congregations consisted of foreigners from all parts of southern and eastern Congo: Kete, refugee Luba, Tetela, Bena Kanyoka and others. The local Luba looked at this invasion with a sceptical eye. The Scheut mission in Lower Congo had similar problems: here the new converts were as a rule from Upper Congo and the missionaries came to be called 'the Fathers of people from on high'.[36]

THE PROTESTANTS AND THE RIVERS

San Salvador

At first the base of Baptist work in the Congo was San Salvador in northern Angola. This was in accordance with the wishes of the Mission's benefactor, R. Arthington, a puritan industrialist in England. In presenting to the Baptist Missionary Society a cheque for £1,000 for the Congo work, he requested the evangelization of Congo with special attention to the 'King of Congo' at San Salvador. So the Baptist missionaries, led by Pastor W. M. Bentley, together with a number of African co-workers, arrived at San Salvador in 1878, and were duly received by Dom Pedro V, *Ntotela*, *Ntinu Nekongo*. The king was gratified that the missionary team included two medically trained men, Comber and Crudgington. Once again medical services helped to open the door for the mission. A recent crusade against fetishes at Luanda may also have helped to prepare the way for the Protestant *entrée* into the north of Angola.

The king, although officially a Catholic, attended the Protestant services and took Pastor Bentley with him on royal visits to the country villages. The evangelical message in the king's presence was possibly modified in the presentation by the voluble interpreter, Misilina. This young boy, once a slave from Luanda, had lived in Cameroon, 'seen the world', and had mastered Duala pidgin. Now he was a returnee to Luanda in Angola. At one point the king seemed so absorbed by the interpreter's version that Bentley asked Misilina what he was saying, reminding him to keep to the subject. 'All right, massa, I was only telling him about de bishop ... him very bad man too much, massa.' Bentley continues: 'I said that I was not talking about the Bishop of Loanda [Luanda], he [Misilina] should interpret my words and not give his own matter.' Afterwards, Misilina explained: 'Yes, massa ... de Bishop of Loanda ... very wicked, too much ... when he died the devil came up under his bed and carried him right away. We all saw it, massa ... like fire.'[37] It so happened that when a prominent inhabitant of

Luanda died, the firing of a rocket apprised the cannon boats and the forts to fly flags at half-mast. This custom had been dramatically misinterpreted.

It was not surprising that the local padres, although personally quite friendly to the visitors, should warn the king against the Protestants. They advised him not to attend their services, as their men did not 'have God's palaver'.[38] As time went on, royal attendance at Protestant services became less frequent. The Baptist mission continued to grow, and in 1887 a chapel for 500 people was built. Twelve years later this had to be replaced by a bigger edifice, holding 1,000. At this time average attendance was 800. A boarding school also contributed to the foundation of a steady Baptist presence at San Salvador and in northern Angola.

Anglo-Saxon Protestants preparing 'chains' for liberation

While the initial Catholic idea of a *reprise* was necessarily related to the Lower Congo, the Protestant dream of a 'chain' across Africa, along the River Congo, was turned to the interior from the outset. Ludwig Krapf, then at Mombasa, thought of an Apostles' Road from Coast to Coast. Arthington, inspired by Livingstone, was prepared to finance such a transcontinental chain and he was in a hurry. It was a matter of apocalyptic haste 'to preach and press on', preparing for the return of the Lord. The role of the River for the rapid evangelization of Congo cannot be overemphasized. Along navigable waterways, for thousands of miles, the missionaries could now move to most parts of the country. No other region of Africa was opened up as dramatically and suddenly to missionary influence as that of the Congo River basin; and no society responded as readily to the great opportunity as the Baptist Missionary Society, using the Congo River as their highway.

In 1884, ten mission stations 100 miles apart were planned – on the map – and eventually placed along the River, from Lukolela near Kinshasa, to Yakusu near Kisangani. From Yakusu the missionary could, with some imagination, look beyond the forests to Aruwimi on the Ugandan border. It was there that the CMS missionary, A. B. Lloyd, had forced his way through – coming from the east! The continent-wide chain was accomplished at last. The June 1899 *Church Missionary Intelligencer* draws the conclusion: 'The chain of Missions which Krapf dreamt about and predicted now actually exists. The links need subdividing and strengthening, it is true.' The planning in London and the achievement in the field in Africa had now been synchronized. For years the general secretaries of the CMS at 6, Salisbury Square, London, and of the BMS at 19 Furnival Street, London, had goaded one another to accomplish some day the impossible but ever attractive dream. Now it was reality – or at least so it seemed to the faithful.

The vision of a 'chain' of mission stations boldly spanning the Congo and the continent was too good an idea to be left solely to the BMS. The apocalyptically inspired Albert Simpson of New York formed a group eventually to be called the Christian and Missionary Alliance, anxious to send his missionaries across the map, before the Coming of Christ. Unfortunately his geography was not quite as strong as his faith. As late as 1896 – when, after all, there were charts and maps to be had to guide him – he announced a plan for an evangelistic movement from Matadi on the west coast to Lake Tanganyika, but through the south of the Congo State, thus cutting across the lines of river communication. Dr Ruth Slade rightly calls it 'a singularly impracticable plan'.[39]

Bishop William Taylor – American Methodist 'Bishop for Africa' since 1884 – with characteristic energy and self-assurance was, in 1885, prepared to turn to the Congo and 'to drive a chain of stations a thousand miles into the interior'. Beginning at Luanda in Angola with a party of fifty men, women and children and soon with another twenty, he pressed on and on, only to be beaten by the climate and lack of solid preparation. If Grenfell the realist classed this enterprise a 'regular Jules Verne affair', it only remains to be said that the 'eighty days' of the famous Jules Verne were here turned into years of tragedy of which nothing much came, at least not in the Congo.[40]

The chain might thus start in Matadi or in Luanda. It could of course just as well be drawn instead from the other, eastern side. One might, like Krapf of old, begin in Kenya and aim at Congo, which is what the Africa Inland Mission did. Via Mwanza in Tanzania they continued towards the frontier of Congo and in 1912 crossed that frontier settling down to work near Lake Albert.

The Baptist entrée

Among Protestant missionaries, George Grenfell's role is particularly important in establishing Baptist work. In retrospect he was to make the interesting observation: 'We commenced our work on the Congo when the country was yet unappropriated, when in fact it was more British than Belgian' – although, as a matter of course, he goes on to say, 'but circumstances have changed'.[41] A parallel can be drawn between his brief period in the Cameroon and his many years in the Congo (1879–1906). He did not especially like the coastal, pidgin-speaking Douala population and much preferred the exploring thrusts in his little steamer, *Helen Saker*, which took him inland into the country along rivers and lakes. This prefigured what he was to attempt and achieve in the Congo. There too he opposed the mission policy of concentrating on the Lower Congo and the coastal population – wherein he differed from his colleague, H. Bentley – and instead made his advance into the interior.

It was this British Baptist who followed up Stanley's discoveries by his own seven exploratory expeditions into the tributaries of the Congo River, to the north and south. Thereby Grenfell demonstrated the navigability of the network of the Congo basin, discoveries of immediate and immense importance for the founding of missions over the entire country. His explorations were summed up in a chart of the Congo River, 1887, from Stanley Pool (Kinshasa) to Stanley Falls together with the great tributaries. This remarkable volume was published in 1887 by the Royal Geographical Society in London.[42]

On his tours along the Congo in the mission steamer, Grenfell was accompanied not only by his second wife, a West Indian whom he had married in Cameroon, but also by at least six young school boys who acted as interpreters and middlemen. The more promising among these were sometimes taken to Britain with a missionary family on furlough. There these young men were given a year's special training. Grenfell's geographical expeditions greatly impressed King Leopold. The king trusted the English Baptist to such an extent that he appointed him to lead the politically sensitive Lunda frontier expedition of 1891–92, with its delicate negotiations with the Portuguese. To the colonial administrators on either side of the River as much as to the African populations hardly anything did as much to dramatize the powerful missionary role as the arrival of the steamers, the BMS *Peace* and Livingstone Inland's *Henry Read*, both from 1884, and the Spiritans' *Pius X* from 1886.

It was thanks to Arthington's generosity and personal involvement in the cause that the BMS had acquired the *Peace*. The very shape of the BMS field, stretching for 1,000 miles along the river as it did, made it imperative to have such vessels. Built in Manchester, its construction provides the perfect illustration of a Victorian combination of Anglo-Saxon missions and British industrial enterprise. For the purpose of being carried by porters from the coast to Stanley Pool the steamer was built in sections, in order to be all the more easily carried overland. George Grenfell himself supervised the reassembling of the parts at the Stanley Pool. Less than ten years later the mission received a new vessel, *Goodwill*, which was longer than the first steamer. This time the reconstruction was carried out entirely by African artisans, and the mission engineer, Bungudi, son of a chief from the Kinshasa area, was in charge. He had spent a year in Britain studying the mechanics of the vessel.[43]

Similar vessels were acquired by other missions, hence the previously mentioned *Henry Read* and the Congo-Balolo mission with their vessel, *The Pioneer*.[44] The French Spiritans had the same idea and in 1886 bought a whaler from France. Taken apart in France and carried in that form by porters from Gabon to Brazzaville, it was reconstructed under the supervision of Augouard. He called the boat *Leo XIII*. A later vessel, built in 1908, was named *Pius X*. Augouard and his co-workers could now travel far inland along the Ubangi and other tributaries of the Congo. They made very considerable scientific observations and two volumes of an atlas of navigation were published. The Catholic vessels became 'ambulatory churches' on the rivers.[45] As he took the early mass at the altar of *Pius X*, Augouard could meditate: 'What a consolation it is to think that the blood of Our Saviour is being shed along our great rivers and thus does sanctify these waters, once witnesses to so many crimes and robberies.'[46]

The guiding principle for Protestant strategy was to find sufficiently concentrated centres of population to allow for a growing Church. A young Swedish Baptist, Arvid Svärd, on arriving in Congo (in 1920) was told by a colleague: 'Do not adopt any tribe which is not worth a whole Bible translation'.[47] The connection between choice of geographical area and the chances for a 'whole' Bible translation – to include both the Old and the New Testament – must be viewed as a particularly Protestant consideration, at least it would not seem to be a typically Catholic suggestion. The Baptist Missionary Society met with this problem more than once, with the many different local languages along the immense stretch of the river. This was why Grenfell preferred Upper to Lower Congo. He was thinking 'in regional, rather than in strictly local terms. It seemed to him futile to concentrate staff on the lower river, when the population of centres like Bolobo, Lukolela, Bangala and Upoto was ten times denser than that of the cataract region.'[48]

Holman Bentley, the Baptist Missionary Society pioneer in Lower Congo and San Salvador, quotes an example of group influence. Selulundini, from near the Wathen station, was an individual with an unmistakable communal character as a Christian chief.

> 'He professed conversion and desired baptism . . . [After baptism] Selulundini is an earnest Christian man and his influence for good is very great. A good number have made profession of faith in Christ from among his people; his town can no longer be regarded as a heathen town, though only a portion of his people can be regarded as Christian converts.'[49]

In his work, Bentley often took walking tours lasting ten days or more. He had been invited by one or more chiefs and was sure to find special response in such villages as had already sent boys to the mission school and were thus to some extent linked to the missionary. Indispensable for the evangelistic tour was the missionary's medicine box. One can hardly overestimate the role of the medical work by these pastors. It provided an *entrée* into the district that not even the most eloquent sermon could. The missionary was often referred to as the 'doctor' as well as the pastor.[50] Mrs Bentley taught the alphabet class in the villages, promoting an enormous literacy campaign in that part of Africa. Bentley and his wife went out as members of a team, and were supported by some of their school boys serving as choir, as interpreters and as an illustration of the mission's work. When Bentley brought along his co-worker Nlemvo, 'some men have so learned to admire Nlemvo (my literary assistant) that they have brought nephews, relatives or slaves to be trained, that they may become like him.'[51]

However, the occasional excursion by the White missionary, important though it seemed at the time, was less effective than the efforts of African Church teams. Six young men and two women 'had united to form the Christian Church at Wathen', near Selulundini's area. The Baptist teaching placed a solemn responsibility on the little group. As soon as a congregation was formed, the members automatically felt duty bound to carry the Gospel message to neighbouring villages. It was out of groups like these that the Protestant catechist emerged, the vital actor and factor in the evangelization of the Congo. A great step forward was taken when the Protestant missions founded a catechetical school for the Lower Congo at Kimpese.

Somewhat reluctantly Bentley and the others realized that some kind of Church constitution was needed. At Wathen a set of fourteen 'Rules' was drawn up. Among them the following:

4. A Christian having two or more wives, to whom he was married during the time of his ignorance, may join the Church but he is not eligible for Church office.
5. Any member of the Church who having a wife shall marry another shall be expelled from the Church.
8. A Christian may not buy another person; this one form of buying alone is expected – that of buying a slave-woman to be one's wife.
9. A Christian may not sell anyone, not even his own relations.

Protestant missions being primarily Baptist meant that both individual and community took a definitive stand for Christ, with a sharpened sense of personal commitment and responsibility for the outreach of the Gospel. As

Protestants they were also concerned with Bible translation, Bible study and widespread literacy enabling people to study the Word. Protestants in Congo also represented a prophetic protest against social injustice and were called upon to make that protest, with varying degrees of response to the challenge.

Going inland

'Inland' to Protestants in Congo had Chinese associations. Just as Hudson Taylor had created his China Inland Mission with an apocalyptic 'faith-mission' programme for China, so Congo was now to have its version of the same thing. It was organized by a group of English Free Church businessmen and pastors, among whom Grattan Guinness, a colourful British evangelist, was the best known. It was called the 'Livingstone *Inland* Mission', implying a definite mission programme and strategy. 'Livingstone' – the name which Stanley had at first given to the River – in this context meant Zaïre/Congo.

The geography of Zaïre/Congo slowed the exuberant plans of the Guinness group, and the mission found it difficult to move much farther than the Falls. However in the first seven years, fifty missionaries went out and nine stations were founded on the Lower Congo. Among these, Matadi, Mbanza Manteke, and Mukimbungu are well-known. The work was soon handed over to the American Baptist Foreign Missions Society. With their long experience from other fields in India, Burma and China, they formed a concentrated field on the Lower Congo, as a frame for the building of an African Church. The change-over to the new mission was facilitated by the fact that most of the Livingstone Inland missionaries were Baptists. After some years, however, the Guinness group took a fresh interest in the Congo. The 'Inland' programme attracted them and they felt a particular responsibility to reach far inland, preferably to near the curve of the main river. Here the network of tributaries to the north and south of the Congo became their area. It was called the Congo-Balolo mission after the leading people in the region.

In her indispensable study of English-speaking missions in the Congo Independent State, Dr Ruth Slade has said that Catholics were concerned with the group, but the Protestants with the individual.[52] Yet Protestant history too, from Henry Richards at Mbanza Manteke in 1886 to Simon Kimbangu at Nkaba in 1921, emphasizes group response to the new message, particularly in its charismatic expressions. Only recently has the role of the remarkable missionary, Henry Richards, of the Livingstone

Inland Mission (1851–1928) been studied, by the anthropologist Dr Wyatt MacGaffey.

In 1886, Richards was at the centre of a sudden outburst of religious enthusiasm referred to by him as 'The Pentecost on the Congo'. This took place at Mbanza Manteke in the Lower Congo. MacGaffey has set the movement in its socio-political context: 'The background to these developments was the final collapse of the power of chiefs' in the Lower Congo.[53] In this state of collapse the masses were looking for health and security.' Richards' first convert was Lutete, a magician who had been accused of witchcraft in Ndemba (his home village) and took refuge with the missionary accompanied by his wife.[54] Under Richards' influence he asked for baptism. Richards, the first European to appear in the district, was seen as a *ngunza*, a prophet. He had certain physical characteristics which made him different from others: he was left-handed, and a hunting accident had left him blind in one eye. Such 'symbols of other-worldly connections ... may have strengthened the respect in which he was held'.[55] He is also remembered by the elder inhabitants as a healer, as having eradicated witchcraft and as controlling the weather.[56] MacGaffey concludes: 'The Pentecost of the Congo, like other movements associated with the establishment of effective missionary and colonial control in the Lower Congo, was a messianic capitulation to a new regime that promised order.'[57]

Something of a theologian, Richards discovered that for the first six years he had preached the Law:

> At first I went to work the wrong way. My first idea was to teach the heathen the folly of idolatry and superstition, the nature of God, about His will as expressed in the law, about duty and morality and such things, as well as about Christ, His word, His miracles and parables, His death and resurrection. But I found it all no use. At the end of six years I had not a convert.
>
> Then in bitterness of spirit I prayed and searched the Scriptures, and noted what the apostles did, and began to follow their example ... They preached Christ and Him crucified. They kept to the one point, and Christ Himself bade them do so. They were to proclaim repentance and remission of sins through Him. Not a hundred things. One thing – Christ and Him crucified.
>
> When I preached *that*, day by day and week by week, then I speedily saw a glorious change! Then I felt clothed with power, and that it was the Spirit of God who spoke through me.[58]

One day his Congolese listeners challenged him on what precisely *he* did about the New Testament command 'to give to every man that asks of you' (Matt. 5.42). He decided to do just that, to give away all of his belongings. Soon however, the people responded by returning these same goods and now asking for baptism. At Mbanza Manteke 600 converts joined the congregation in a broad mass movement. The point to be stressed in this 'Pentecost' is the mass aspect of the movement. Richards himself did not attempt to instigate a group action. On the contrary, he felt 'the danger of mass movements. The people think that if *one* is converted *all* must be.'[59]

Richards distinguished between Revival and admission to baptism: sixteen months after the 'Pentecost' had begun, Richards had baptized only 200 of the faithful. When he reported to New York, Murdoch, the General Secretary at headquarters, encouraged him to be much bolder, to follow the example of the apostles and baptize those who had been willing 'to profess Christ before men'.[60] The Baptist missionary tried to counter this tendency, but found that African group solidarity was too strong for him. Such group solidarity was emphasized again later when in 1894 'its impulse sprang from below' in the Congo Balolo mission.[61] The best-known spontaneous movement around an African evangelist was that of the prophet Simon Kimbangu in 1921. There will be occasion to return to this movement.

Young Luba becoming evangelists

Coming to southern Kasai, the American Presbyterians were to find that they had entered a perfect laboratory of missiological approach. Faced with many small population groups, they had to decide where to begin. The choice was important, for if everything went well, the initial converts would become evangelists to their neighbours.[62] The first two missionaries, S. N. Lapsley and W. H. Sheppard, considered the Kete 'the people most likely to be converted'. The Kete had welcomed the foreigners, helped them build houses and had made them feel at home. They were not interested, however, in the Gospel of the Americans. They had a noble religion of their own and saw no reason why they should change. Sheppard soon opted for the Kuba. In his view, their apparent superiority over their neighbours could be traced to early cultural contacts with Egypt. Sheppard had studied three years at the Tuscaloosa Institute in Alabama where Egyptian origins of African aesthetic culture had been discussed. One of his professors at the Institute, Dr E. Talliferro Wharton, provided the clue: the beetle or scarab design in their carvings, the form of their wooden figurines, and some of their mythological ideas were all 'pale reflections of Egyptian civilization'.

In Sheppard's case an extraordinary element of transmigration endeared him to the Kuba. Greatly daring, he went to the king's court, followed by only nine African volunteers. One of the king's sons recognized the African-American missionary as a long-lost relative. Together with the king and his council, it was decided that Sheppard was in fact none other than Bope Makabe, his father's predecessor on the throne, now returned to earth in the person of Sheppard. The missionary was given a generous welcome by king and people, but he soon learned that his supposed noble ancestry was a disadvantage. It could even be fatal, for after the king's death, each succeeding Kuba monarch would regard him as a potentially dangerous rival. During his twenty years in Congo Sheppard persisted in being faithful to the Kuba and they to a lesser degree to him. The Kuba were fully satisfied with their belief in Chembe, the Creator, and would not be moved by Sheppard's stories.

George Grenfell acted as unofficial adviser to Protestant arrivals in their choice of mission fields, a role assigned to him because of his long experience in Africa and his personal contacts with the Belgian administration. Because of his standing with King Leopold and with the Protestants, Grenfell held an important position in the missionary community, comparable to that of John Philip in the Cape at the beginning of the century.[63] Daring and enterprising, Grenfell nevertheless represented a measured, rational approach and sometimes had to remind his colleagues 'that wings of faith are not the ordained means of crossing continents'.[64] He advised the American Presbyterians to explore possibilities in southern Kasai and suggested that they begin work there in 1890. In the Kasai region, William M. Morrison, the American Presbyterian, played much the same role of unofficial adviser as Grenfell. They both preceded the particular elected Protestant advisers – Emory Ross, Coxill and Öhrneman – who later on, in the early twentieth century, were to assume increasing ecumenical and administrative responsibilities.

A social revolution decided events for the American Presbyterians. They turned to the Luba. But there were different kinds of Luba. Here again one comes across the fundamentally important aspect, repeatedly underlined in this book, of the refugee factor in the Christianization of Africa. The traditional Luba, further south in the heartland of the Lubilashi River Valley, seemed unresponsive. But W. M. Morrison located certain Luba refugee groups forced away from home territory by wars. The British explorer, M. Hilton-Simpson, referred to them as a 'grab-bag of peoples' inhabiting some Kasai centres. Morrison chose these Luba as his field and his colleagues agreed. The great success of the American Presbyterians' Luba work proved the validity of the refugee hypothesis and is amply corroborated by observations in other parts of the African continent.

The historian looking at the total missionary situation in Africa is impressed by a dimension of fortuitous chance, almost fate, involved when a particular mission makes the decision to approach a particular ethnic community. It could prove to be a negative, unfortunate decision, or it could prove to be a positive choice. In the case of the co-operation between the highly mobile and enterprising Luba and the American Presbyterians one is inclined to regard the choice as particularly fortuitous. The pioneers were a couple of Americans from the southern United States, one a White, S. Lapsley, who, however, died after only two years in the field, and the Virginia African-American William Sheppard. Southern Kasai presented a picture of a great number of ethnic communities, but when W. M. Morrison arrived in the Kasai, he insisted on the advantage of concentrating on one big community and thus on a single language. He was able to point to the disadvantages, seen in other parts of the Congo, spreading out over a large number of different language groups – the British Baptist Missionary Society being a case in point.

In the first decade of the century the Presbyterian missionaries were to come across situations in the villages where itinerant Luba who had met the Christian faith in far-off places had, on their own initiative, started local groups of singing and learning believers. (The Luba people would seem to be an especially rewarding place for the study of oral and epistolary traditions relating to these first pioneering African evangelists.) This was the case with a certain man called Muteba, a Luba who had seen the world or at least moved around on the Zaïre/Congo-Angola border enough to have picked up a few fascinating Jesus stories and some of the strange new songs being intoned – presumably – at the camp-fire in the evenings. This was enough for him to act, calling his friends to worship. When at long last the first missionaries did arrive in the area, in 1912, they found an emerging Church with six churches in four villages where regular services were celebrated, thus once again vindicating a common theme for the nineteenth-century Christianization of Africa.[65]

Luebo became the first headquarters of the Presbyterian mission, with special emphasis on agricultural training for which the Hampton Institute, Virginia, seemed to be a stimulating model. Luebo can be seen as typical of a certain phase of mission-related development in Central Africa. On one side of the Lulua River the original trading post, placed on a slave trading route to Angola, had become in turn a government 'state post' and a district headquarters and from the beginning of the 1890s the Roman Catholic mission, directed by Fr Cambier, worked there. On the other side of the river the Protestants built their settlement. The strategic position made the place attractive. At first the Kuta population dominated and the mission work was conducted in the Kuta language – not very successfully from the missionaries' point of view. However, growing numbers of young Luba were redeemed from the slave traders, and the missionaries placed them into boys' and girls' houses. Here were the first catechumens who, before long, became the first leaders of the Christian community at Luebo.

Numbers of Luba migrated to the mission station taking advantage of opportunities for education and medical care. They were attracted by that happy singing resounding from those little thatched church buildings. These Luba migrants became the nucleus of growing population and made it imperative for the mission and its leader, Morrison, to switch from the Kuba to the Luba language for preaching, teaching and book production – a step which soon proved to be of far-reaching importance.

A mission village was established around church, schools with boarding houses, hospital and printing press. Streets were laid out in neat squares, each house being provided with an adjacent fenced-in garden. Planting of fruit trees and garden crops was encouraged. Many ethnic communities in addition to the Luba and Kuba now moved in, to be placed in neighbouring proximity on their own streets. In this way Luebo found itself with a population of about 20,000, one of the largest agglomerations of people in Central Zaïre/Congo. In life-style it was very much a village, the people going out to the nearby forest and springs for wood and water and to cultivate their fields of manioc and corn. The big market was the centre for trade and small cottage industries. All this humming activity had the congregation as its inspiring and directive centre, with six large churches, an extended school system and other forms of teaching and training. In 1904 there were already forty out stations within a four-mile radius. Agricultural training in Luebo took much of its inspiration from the Hampton Institute, Virginia. Then an important decision affecting missions throughout Central Africa was taken at government headquarters in Boma on the Atlantic coast, which was to prove fateful for Luebo. The railway passed it by, and in the end, in 1946, the mission made the inevitable move to the modern city of Luluabourg.

William M. Morrison was a highly gifted linguist and made remarkable contributions to Bible translation. Early on he produced 'Paraphrases of the Scriptures' a small handy volume combining stories and parables from the Old and New Testaments, and this first effort was received with great interest by the emerging congregations.[66] It was also the American Presbyterians who had the personal resources to produce a series of commentaries in the local chiLuba language for each of the books in the Bible. This was the result of the combined effort of two devoted missionary colleagues, J. W. Allen and C. L. Crane. This library of commentaries in an African language has remained unique in the history of the Church in Africa, another indication of the quality of this particular work.[67]

Laying the foundations of the Church, the intention was to adapt it to local structures. The first draft of what later was to be known as the Book of Church Order (1931) made the *Mpungilu*, or Church Council, the central administrative body. It included two missionaries, three African pastors and three African elders from each of the larger stations, together with one pastor and two elders from each of the smaller stations. The *Mpungilu* met annually.

W. M. Morrison was one of the great leaders of the Presbyterian Church in the Congo. With the help of a rapidly increasing band of Luba catechists and teachers, this Church grew to be the strongest Protestant Church in the Congo. In 1918 its 17,000 converts represented 35 per cent of all Protestants in the Congo. A literate and witnessing laity was the secret of this growth, as well as a school system which in 1908 had 17,500 students in day school and 32,000 in Sunday School. Active organizations included a 'prayer band' formed in 1899, and a Women's Missionary Society. The Kasai mission steamer, *SS Lapsley*, named for the first Presbyterian missionary in the Congo, carried catechists to villages along the river banks. In 1907 five African 'elders' and six deacons began work and after theological schools were founded in 1913, the first three African pastors were ordained in 1916.

The Methodists

In 1911 Bishop W. R. Lambuth of the Methodist Episcopal Church (South) consulted Morrison on the choice of a field. On Morrison's advice Bishop Lambuth decided to go to the Batetela. It is misleading, however, to imagine this exploration among the warlike Batetela as a Western one-man show. The Luebo mission could provide no less than twenty African evangelists – apparently all young men, none over twenty – to accompany the bishop to Chief Wembo-Nyama's headquarters. This proved to be particularly helpful for when the dreaded Tetela chief glanced at his visitors he discovered among them a long-lost friend from his youth and this personal relationship made it all the more easy to accommodate the new-comers. The chief's generous welcome to the American bishop brings to mind similar encounters between chief and missionary in other parts of Central and Southern Africa.

Again, for an understanding of the evangelistic break through among the Batetela, and more generally, for the whole of the nineteenth-century situation in Africa, it is instructive to notice that when these twenty young Luba catechists found themselves in a foreign country, they did not immediately retreat to their home country. They were Luba and thus very adaptable. The group stayed on for years with the pagan Batetela. The evangelization at grass-roots was thus not so much something performed by an individual American bishop, struggling to acquire some of the rudiments of the language, but rather by this group of eager Luba catechists, fully aware from past experience of the demands and opportunities of their own primary evangelistic situation.

The numerous non-Roman Protestant societies in other regions of Africa represented a wide variety of churchmanship, from Anglo-Catholics and German Lutherans to American Congregationalists and Canadian Pentecostals. In the Belgian Congo there was – with only a few exceptions – one particular type of Church allegiance: varieties of Anglo-Saxon Baptists, including Pentecostals. There were some non-Baptist exceptions to this rule: southern Kasai had Presbyterians and Methodists from the southern States of America.[68] In the Lower Congo the Swedish missionaries were likewise not Baptists but 'Missionsförbundet', Congregationalists – but, being Swedes, they adapted themselves to the given situation and followed Baptist practice in Congo, while faithfully sticking to their old ways in their home country. The Swedes worked among the Kongo on both sides of the River, and later among the Lali. They had begun in co-operation with the Livingstone Inland Mission in 1881. It was still possible to negotiate with African leaders for the privilege of founding a mission and an agreement was signed. The formula used on the occasion may have borrowed something of its *cachet* from similar documents signed by Stanley or Brazza:

> We, Makayi, Nsinki Kibundu and Mukayi Mukuta Ntokos, Kings of Kibunzi, and our peoples wish that the Mukimbungu missionaries, of the Swedish Mission Covenant, settle with us and teach us and our peoples.
>
> We award them the right to build wherever they please on the hill south-east of the town Kibunzi.
>
> As a matter of course they have full right to use forests, water, roads and land for plantations in our district in the same way as we do …
>
> Signed by the marks of the three dignitaries and K. J. Pettersson.

The Swedish missionaries later transferred their work to the northern, 'French' side. There they were involved with the Dondo, Teke, Kuta and Bongo communities and started a number of stations. Dr Efraim Andersson's study of the 'Churches at the grass-roots' gives valuable insight into later problems of the Church and its growth. 'Slow and reasoned conversions thus formed the majority [of the conversions] during the first decade.'[69]

The Bakongo had reasons both for and against the new religion. The Dondo believed the White men were deceased people who had come back to earth. They may have been bad men, harmful to the community. Others thought the missionaries were 'sorcerers who had come in order to eat the people'. On the other hand, the Dondo appreciated the missionaries' role as medicine men and healers. There was also strong dream activity, which often indicated very definitely that a certain person had to be converted. So the Dondo wavered at first, uncertain which way to turn.

This period of 'slow and reasoned conversions' during the decade prior to 1920 was preceded and followed by two extraordinary mass movements: the 'Pentecost on the Congo' in 1886, and Simon Kimbangu's messianic movement in the early 1920s. MacGaffey has emphasized the lasting importance of the 1886 experience. There was something of a collective memory of this Pentecost on the Congo, expressed in the immense awakening of the masses from 1921. Was it perhaps a measure of the Western missionary control at the time – in terms of prohibitions against polygamy, palm-wine and certain magical practices – that there came another temper into the villages and the congregations in those blank years 'between the times'?

The chance character of some Protestant occupation of parts of Africa is illustrated in the case of the beginnings in Shaba by a couple of Plymouth Brethren missionaries. F. S. Arnot, a Scot, came to Africa inspired by Livingstone's example, and felt inclined to go to 'Garenganze', as Shaba was then known. Arriving in 1886, he established good contacts with King Msiri, the trader from Tanzania who settled in Upper Katanga in the 1850s. Arnot's contacts were his reward for endless attention to the king's whims and fancies. Occasionally he acted as the king's secretary, and Msiri referred to the missionaries as 'my Whites'. When the king was killed in a skirmish with Belgian troops in 1891, the political situation changed radically. Katanga at last became part of the Independent State of Congo.

Arnot spent only a brief period in Katanga. His best-known successor, Dan Crawford, stayed much longer, trying to make the highly individualistic Brethren programme a reality in Central Africa. His mission station near Lufoi River became the refuge of numerous vulnerable people. He took them on an Exodus, to build a new self-contained mission village, Luanza, north of Lake Mweru. His manifesto decreed that 'All tribal differences must be forgotten'; those participating must do so 'as a new and unified group going forward into a new life'. He was directing these people, and at the same time felt that he himself was 'Thinking Black' – the pretentious title of his autobiographical book of 1912.[70] An organization was later built on Brethren principles. It was called the Garenganze Evangelical Mission.

In these circumstances it was fortunate that in 1907 an American Methodist couple, John Springer (later bishop) and his wife started their work in Katanga. King Mwata-Yamvo's Lunda people were interested in his invitation. A nephew of the king, Kayeka, had been captured as a slave and eventually been liberated. When freed he settled at the Kagamba mission and was converted there. The Springers settled at Mwata-Yamvo capital and the king asked them to send him medical doctors. In 1914 Dr Arthur Piper started work and began to build a hospital in the Lunda capital. Even more important in the long-run was the start at Lubumbashi (then named Elizabethville). Methodist work there had been launched in 1914 by a group of devoted African laymen who had met Christianity. The first missionary came to the emerging city in 1917. Before too long no less than 75,000 members were registered in the Methodist Church at Lubumbashi.

ANGOLA

Walter Rodney's angry book with its challenging title, '*How Europe underdeveloped Africa*', addressed itself to all of Africa during the colonial period.[71] However, there does not seem to be any region where his *J'accuse* is as pertinent as in the case of Angola – along with Mozambique. Officially, Angola was subject to Portuguese rule for nearly 500 years. Yet, René Pélissier has vigorously argued, Angola was not in effect colonized until the beginning of the twentieth century.[72] It was the harbours on the coast which the Portuguese reached, while the *sertao*, the inland with its complex assortment of competing ethnic communities, was not subdued until about 1900. The local inland communities were in a state of ever-threatening revolt. For the period 1848–78 Pélissier has counted at least thirty-five military operations and in the following half century more than 150 such operations.

Angola was regarded as an inexhaustible reservoir of Black labour from which Portuguese slave traders and their *mestico* assistants could export their human merchandise across the Atlantic. Officially, slave trade was forbidden by Portugal in 1836, but both Angolan and Brazilian slave dealers effectively resisted this decree. Forty years later, when the trade should have come to a definite end, it still continued and did not indeed cease until the First World War. Decades of forced labour followed. Government authorities and private companies used all available means to exploit the land and the workers on the land. The revolution of 1910 in Portugal replaced the old royal house with a republic and shook the regime in Angola. The new governor, Norton de Matos, tried to liquidate the system of forced labour, but with limited results. The Protestant Churches with their ambitious literary programmes were seriously affected by de Matos' Decree 77 of 1921 prohibiting the publication of vernaculars except as parallel texts (so-called *diglot*) to the Portuguese.

The Catholics

In 1835 the last Capuchin monk left Angola, and thus, a two-century tradition of Capuchin service in 'Kongo' came to an end. For what was left of a Catholic Church a period of almost total abandonment followed. There was no bishop in Luanda until 1849, and up to 1914 a succession of ten bishops followed, representing the Portuguese State Church's influence over the Angolan Church. The first of these, Dom Joachim Moreira Reis, welcomed David Livingstone generously to Luanda. Various men in high places, including the African king in San Salvador, appealed unsuccessfully to Portugal for more missionaries from the 'home country'. As late as the 1870s one could see the Portuguese bishop seated in a marble chair on the wharf of Luanda baptizing unfortunate captives about to be pushed onto ships for Brazil: the religious act was to ensure the eternal salvation of the souls. The act demonstrated only too eloquently the official Church's involvement. Having said this, one must at the same time refer to the Catholic Church fully supporting Cardinal Lavigerie's international anti-slavery campaign.

However help was coming, not from official Portuguese sources, but from a non-Portuguese – and thus 'foreign' – organization: the Holy Ghost Fathers of Paris. From the 1850s they had wended their way along the West African coast and had arrived at the mouth of the River Congo. A thrust south along the Angolan coast followed, with a remarkable man leading. Charles Duparquet, French Holy Ghost Father was one of the most imaginative missionaries of his time. He proved to be a nineteenth-century missionary with a twentieth-century pace and mind intent on winning Angola, Namibia and a few other countries for the Catholic Church. In 1866 he reconnoitred the possibilities for a Catholic mission in the south, at Mossamedes. But from the beginning he met with difficulties. At any display of missionary interest from other Catholic countries, the Portuguese in Luanda and Lisbon would automatically rattle their *Padroado* pretensions: this was their country and nobody else's. Was Duparquet Portuguese? No, he was a 'foreigner' – perhaps even a French spy. Never at a loss for an idea, Duparquet at once made up a brilliant plan to overcome these chauvinistic suspicions and went to Portugal, where he managed to found a mission seminary for the training of Portuguese members of the Holy Ghost Congregation.

In the next few years he proceeded as far as Cape Town, making that his base for exploring Namibia which he crossed in an ox-waggon. He then went on to Zanzibar for two years, exploring with his French co-religionists the potential for a Catholic mission in the Central African Lake region, just discovered by Speke and Burton.

In Duparquet's footsteps, new generations of his Congregation came to Angola: in the period 1866–1940, 284 Holy Ghost Fathers arrived in Angola; seventy-one of them Portuguese, while 213 – mainly French – were classified as 'foreigners'. In the last third of the century, twenty-four priests from Goa provided a reinforcement for the number of Catholic clergy – with venerable associations with the long history of the Portuguese colonial Church. These men represented Portuguese culture and theology, but with an understanding of the special problems found in a colonial situation. In 1881, again on Duparquet's indefatigable initiative, another reinforcement was forthcoming: the arrival of numbers of sisters as teachers and medical personnel – above all, those of the St Joseph of Cluny. One need not emphasize the importance of these devoted women missionaries.

The French Fathers, mostly Alsatian, once having arrived on the scene were long-lived and hard-working. A few examples must suffice here. Fr Ernest Lecomte spent forty-six years on the evangelization of Angola, mainly in the southern region. He founded stations at Bailungo and Bihe – both centres of ethnic communities – Caconda, Catoco, Massaca and Cuanhama. He had a daring plan: to establish a chain of missions right across Angola to the Zambezi River. He was, however, not Portuguese but French and thus a foreigner and was made to remember this unfortunate fact. He defended himself in terms which showed his good-will: 'The nationality of this or that missionary does not mean that the mission itself is not Portuguese. All the Holy Ghost missionaries established in Portuguese territory are Portuguese ... for, with government subsidies they carry out the duty of the Portuguese before Europe and before all humanity: the civilization of its colonies.'[73] Lecomte was fascinated by Bantu languages, feeling that they were 'extremely rich and subtle, capable of expressing such theological complexities as the Trinity with remarkable economy and force.'[74] His other absorbing interest was organizing schools, especially for heirs of chiefs. Some of these young men would soon turn up as the first catechists in the area.

Lacomte's colleague, Camille Laagel, worked at Caconda giving a life service of fifty-three years. He was called 'the White Sorcerer', because of his imaginative use of local plants for his medical exploits, forever praising the Creator for having provided a bounty of curative plants in 'the great Botanical Garden of the Bush', and all for free, 'without ever sending me a bill'. Working with his young African colleague, Abbé Pedro Luis, he reached out to thousands of patients who sought their help for all kinds of ailments, including blindness. On his death, a colleague of his said: 'There is a great need for missionaries of Pére [sic] Laagel's sort: not too much a philosopher, not too modern, but capable of walking on his feet, riding a bicycle or a donkey.' The list of Alsatian missionaries must of course also include the name of Louis Keiling at Caconda, with forty-two years in Angola, (d. 1937). He was virtually the bishop in the southern region among the dynamic Ovimbundu, but being a non-Portuguese he was appointed 'Apostolic Prefect', by the bishop in Luanda. His book in Portuguese, *Quarente anos de Africa* '(Forty Years in Angola'), gives an unpretentious close-up of the Church situation at grass-roots.[75]

Keiling had an eye for the strategic potential of modern means of communication, such as they were in Angola in those days. He kept informed of the planning of the Benguela Railway (started 1903) and placed the new mission stations along the line. The neighbouring Protestant Congregationalists shared the same concern and plan for their stations – another indication of the role of railways in the evangelization of Africa. Some of the southern communities such as the Ngangela were harassed by raids from the powerful Ovambo which induced them to seek refuge with the Fathers and be incorporated into their 'Christian villages'. When Keiling took over the administration and the episcopal responsibility in the south, there were 12,000 Christians. When he died in 1937 there were 262,437, thus indicating a mass movement situation similar in extent and growth to that of Keiling's Spiritan colleagues further north: Bishop Vogt in Cameroon and Bishop Shanahan in Eastern Nigeria.

The Protestants

It is one of the surprises of Angolan Church history that in this compactly Portuguese and Catholic colony, the Protestants – non-Portuguese 'foreigners' – at best, second class citizens, should have gathered such a large part of the Christian community. Late arrivals on the scene, they could, by the end of the colonial period, count no less than 20 per cent of the total Christian community. To this must be added another consideration, no less surprising: while reaching the masses at the grass-roots, they were also obviously ministering to what there was of an intellectual elite. This seems to be borne out by the fact that in 1974, when three political parties were contending for power, their leaders – Holden, Neto, Savimbi – were all sons or grandsons of Protestant pastors and catechists.

Among the 1,000 ordained Protestant missionaries in Africa at this time, the great majority were solid Bible expositors and some were fiery revivalists. However, none was as flamboyant a preacher or as grandiose a planner as William Taylor, the American Methodist bishop who landed in Luanda in 1885. He had had varied experiences as a preacher in different parts of the world. Now it was Central Africa's turn. Elected as 'Bishop for Africa', in 1884, Taylor wanted to establish a chain of mission stations across the continent, from the Atlantic to the Indian Ocean. The key to success was the principle of self-support managed by the 'Transit and Building Fund Society, of Bishop Taylor's Self-Support Mission'. So they set out, the Bishop and forty young volunteers – to be followed after a year by another twenty – all kindled with a vision and with the excessively energetic Westerner's happy conviction that nothing could stop them. After a year they claimed to have organized six stations inland from Luanda, among the Umbundu and were headed for Congo and beyond.

However, contrary to these overheated expectations, Mother Africa did not respond very positively to an approach of this kind. On the whole the Bishop's campaign was a tragic failure and soon only ruins remained. Fortunately the Methodist Episcopal Church in the USA was prepared to take over the task. From 1897 onwards, under Bishop Joseph Hartzell – a balanced leader – the work was reorganized on solid foundations. At the end of the century only eight missionaries were left, but the number rose to thirty in the 1950s.

High quality schools in Luanda and Quessua catered to the young generation and the Methodist 'class' system permeated the parish organization.[76] An example of the role of Angolan leadership is provided by the work of Agostinho P. Neto, assistant pastor in Luanda 1931–38 and later, First Minister in the Dembos area.

The Congregationalists in the Ovimbundu highlands, inland from Lobito, held a central position – in more than one sense. Having arrived in 1880, the mission (comprising the 'American Board' and Canadian Congregationalists) established personal contacts with the local chiefs. The Catholics could fall back on their Portuguese government, while the Protestant missionaries cultivated contacts with the traditional African authorities. It was characteristic that somewhat later the entire body of Protestant pastors in the area were related to royal clans, thereby assuring *entrée* into the life of the ethnic community. In a difficult and sometimes threatening situation a highly competent group of American and Canadian missionaries – among whom must be mentioned the Revd Currie, G. M. Childs and J. T. Tucker – together with African colleagues built up a dynamic Congregational Church, with headquarters at Dondi. An ambitiously planned school system comprised a secondary school, called the Currie Institute at Dondi and the Means School for girls' education. At Dondi there was also a printing press. The personal libraries of Angolan pastors soon testified to the educational concern and intellectual horizons of the leaders of the Church, which was verified (by B.Sr.) during a personal visit in 1953.

7

SOUTHERN AFRICA

INTRODUCTION

The theme of the 'frontiers' pervades nineteenth-century southern Africa, including the history of the Church, providing its peculiar dynamic and drama. In the nineteenth century in the United States the frontier was a movement westwards, across the continent. In southern Africa there was a corresponding movement northwards, from the Cape over the high veld, beyond the great rivers, to the 'interior of Africa'. The 'Great Trek' from the Cape towards the north is the classical illustration of this move: that exodus of sturdy Boers, supposedly a 'Chosen People', struggling along from the rich wheat, wine and cattle farms in the south, over the veld and the mountains, beyond the Orange, the Vaal and the Drakensberg. A second movement north was less far-reaching but no less dramatic and demanding for the individuals and groups concerned. It consisted of the 'Coloured' population, sporadically withdrawing from the Cape towards the Orange and Vaal rivers. It resulted in the formation of a Christian Griqua republic which provided a key to the process and patterns of Christianization of some of the leading Bantu-speaking peoples.

Even more dramatic and far-reaching was the cataclysmic refugee movement, beginning in Natal and speeding along with irresistible force annihilating everything in its way, affecting everybody, hurrying over the subcontinent until at long last it spent its force just short of Lake Victoria. As a result groups would flee into some neighbouring or far-off community, there to submit as clients to the chief. Such refugee groups would, we suggest, be particularly prone to welcoming the new religious message. This argument presents a sharp challenge to European notions about African life and Christian missions in the nineteenth century, their unshakable belief that African societies were static, 'changing, if at all, with infinite slowness and needing the impact of outside influences to break out of the ossified shell of countless years of tradition.'[1]

These three movements had special significance – positively and

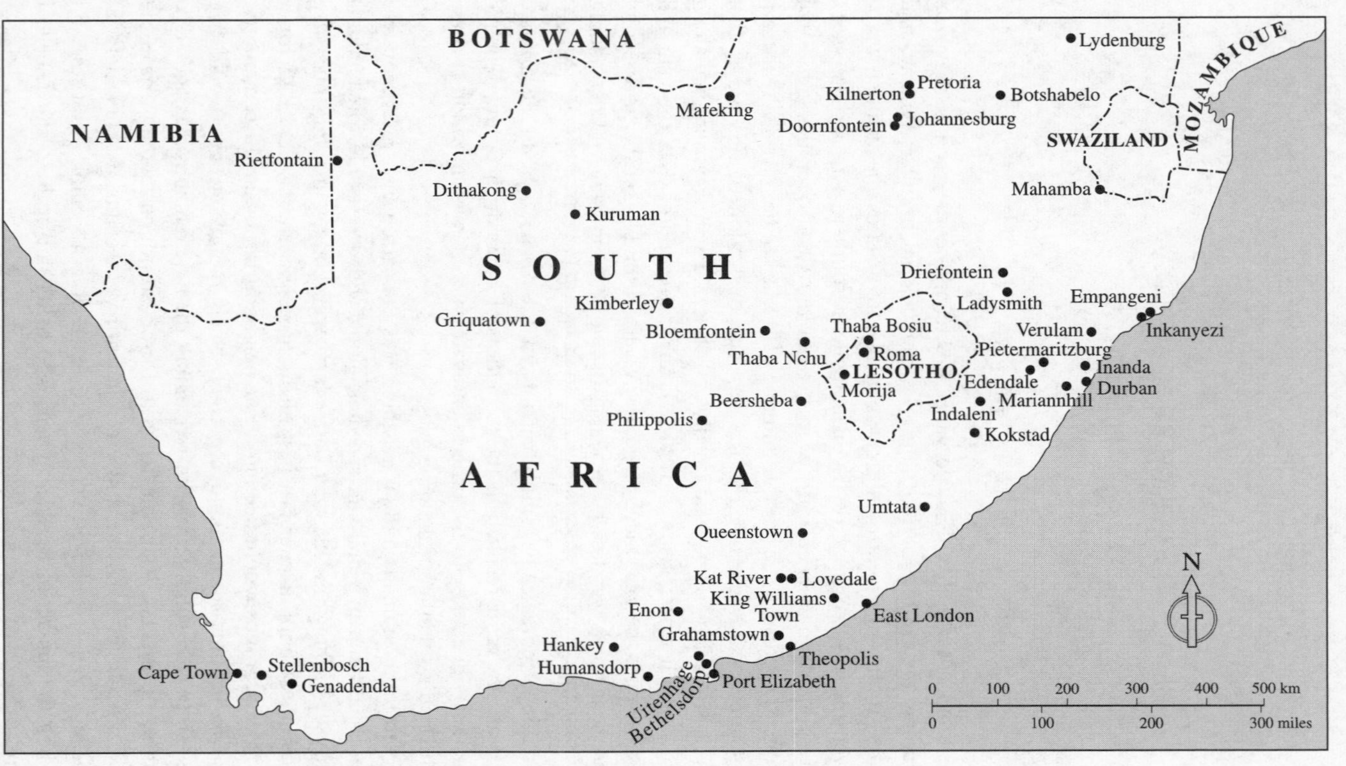

7.1 Key towns and centres of South Africa.

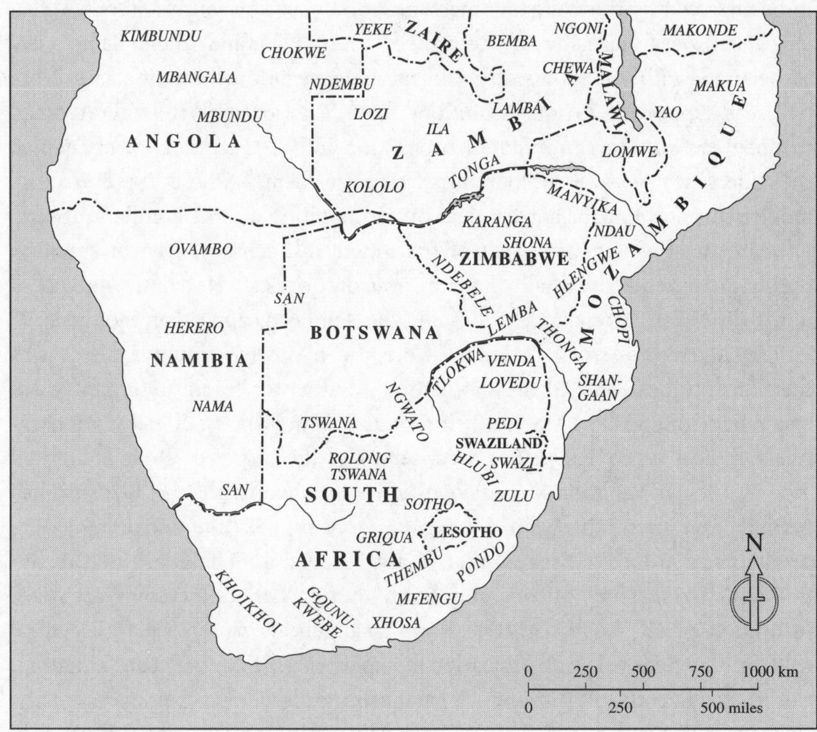

7.2. Ethnic groups of Southern Africa.

negatively – for the history of the Church. From one point of view the Great Trek of the Boers was an expression of a bitter protest against John Philip and the egalitarian policy of the London Missionary Society. The refugee upheaval made African chiefs prone to look for such defence – 'a shield' – as the missionary presence might provide. During that frightful process, uprooted African refugees met Christian messengers. As corporate groups they became prepared to accept the missionaries' leadership and the security of the mission stations – in the Eastern Cape, on the Orange Free State high veld, in Botswana, along the Zambezi and Lake Malawi. The Gospel was seen as help for the encounter on the frontier of life and death. In one generation endangered and battered groups emerged as a new elite, eager carriers of the new message to those who had not yet heard it.

The withdrawal to the north of the members of the emerging Coloured community represented the protest of a disappointed marginal element soon to be attracted by the Christian message, for a very special reason. They had left the Boers' farms and Reformed Church behind them. The new association with the politically radical Congregational missionaries from overseas supporting Griqua ambitions for a Transorangia Republic seemed to open the way to the fuller incorporation into a Christian society which the Boers were never prepared to give to them.[2] These three frontier movements account for a great deal of the mobility and the conflict of South African society in the first half of the nineteenth century. In that situation the missionaries arrived, all of them 'nonconformists'. Not until the end of the 1840s did the Roman Catholics and the Anglicans appear on the scene.

The Moravians from Germany were the pioneers, giving a lead, with their 'institutions' – or Christian villages – and with a tradition of hard work and much song. The LMS English Congregationalists, politically comparatively radical, soon established themselves as the target of Boer contempt. The Wesleyan Methodists coming in large numbers with 'the 1820 English Settlers' and attempting as a mission to serve both White and Black, were protagonists of local African initiative and leadership. The Glasgow Presbyterians aimed not only at education but higher education, including the finest institution of all, Lovedale. The Paris Evangelicals were to play a central role in the national and educational experience of an African kingdom, Lesotho, while the Berlin and Hermannsburg Lutherans, beginning in the Cape and in Natal respectively, made their most significant contribution in Transvaal and Botswana.

The foreigners had to approach the community via the chiefs. After an initial period of mistrust the chiefs accepted the service of the missionaries, not consenting to be baptized themselves – only Chiefs Khama and Sechele in Botswana and Chief Kama among the Gqunukwebe Xhosa were baptized in that first generation. In the eyes of the chiefs the missionary represented desirable power: political power necessary for contacts with the European government, on government's terms; military power as certain Tswana communities as early as 1823 experienced rescue which helped a rumour to be formed: 'any community having accepted a missionary in their midst could not be defeated in war'. The missionary, it seemed, was bound to have cosmological influence with the Almighty, Giver or Withholder of Rain. Then again the missionary would direct the digging of water furrows as help against drought and the missionary could help with the first plough. He had power over words. The power of the word was something with deep traditional roots and was, with the arrival of the missionary, to acquire new meaning. The missionary might also have power over disease. His medicines proved that he was a new kind of medicine-man. Eventually the missionary would establish his 'mission station'. Here new structures of the new religion were already beginning to appear: the chapel and the catechismal class, the school, the printing press and the dormitory for school children from afar, all with potential for a formative influence on the young generation.

Already there was a tendency towards certain regimentation and enforcement of rules and 'Church discipline', with the iron law of monogamy, rules reluctantly or submissively appropriated. Rules about the length of the catechumenate were eventually determined as a result of experience. In the midst of all this regimentation there appeared, from the very beginning prophetic personalities, the greatest of them Ntsikana of the Xhosa. He was to demonstrate that even the briefest contact with missionary preaching could inspire a religious and indeed Christian message of great power, to be interpreted then and much later as a religious and national rallying cry for nearly two centuries. With intuitive creativity, Ntsikana grasped the very core of the Christian message of the sacrifice of Christ and interpreted this in terms of his own Xhosa tradition in a way which his people could accept. His means of communication was the basic language of awe and reverence, but with an added acquired dialect of radical Christian experience. Perhaps there were elsewhere in the ethnic communities other personalities where the creative urge had been awakened by the inspiring Christian song and the Gospel story but there was no opportunity to give to this experience expression and form. Regimentation in the name of the Gospel was only too prone to dominate in the most intimate of personal relationships, that of the faith.

The chaos and turmoil of the refugee situation had unexpected effects on the Christianization process. Young men from the north of the country went as Early Migrant Labour south and east, to the eastern Cape and Natal, to work for a year or two, in order to be able to buy that which every young man should have: a rifle. In the process they found – in the Wesleyan 'class' at Pietermaritzburg or Port Elizabeth, or in the Congregational group in Cape Town – that their years abroad gave them not only a new rifle but also a new religion. In their case this was not a terminal experience but a challenge to carry the message to others. On their return to their villages in the north they would soon gather young men of their own age-group around them; a 'conventicle' of faithful was formed long before the first missionary arrived in the place. Some individual or group of young people had already in various ways and by diverse experiences heard some part of the Jesus story, and had begun to prepare themselves for this new religious experience.

In this highly mobile social situation there was a steady ebb and flow between the south and the north, and between the west and the centre of the high veld, with a give-and-take of experiences – miracles, healings, dreams – which were to stimulate the exchange of ideas among recent converts. This must be seen and interpreted not primarily as a result of individual missionary efforts from local mission stations but as part of the total move and turmoil of South African society. In the midst of the volcanic refugee upheaval or on the southern coast, certain mission centres would become as it were seismological listening posts for this exchange of experience and expectation.

CAPE OF GOOD HOPE?

The Cape community in the 1790s seemed self-contained and proud of its isolation, but changes on the international scene would suddenly affect the situation. In 1795 the British took control – more definitely from 1806 – and the Dutch Company rule was at an end. For the next 100 years, the fate of the Cape and of southern Africa was largely determined by British rule, political ideas, economic pressures and cultural and religious values. The growing European population spread from its settlements around Cape Town into the surrounding countryside, developing stock-raising, wheat-growing and viticulture. This type of economic development demanded constant territorial expansion of settlers and became the root cause of much of the violence occurring throughout the Colony's history.[3]

Before the English take-over, the Dutch Reformed Church was the State Church, its *predikanten* (preachers) appointed by the Dutch Company in Amsterdam. By 1795 it consisted of seven congregations in and around Cape Town and also Graaf-Reinet. As early as the 1780s there had been a stirring of missionary spirit among the Boers. Helperus Van Lier and Michiel Vos were the pioneers of Dutch Reformed mission work, and were well aware of liberal European attitudes. They challenged the consciences of some Whites to consider the need for evangelization of the Khoi even if the idea was slow to take root.

At the local level the stern and rugged heads of the Boer community were automatically also leading members of the Church Council, and functioned as elders and deacons with unchallenged authority. On the farms, the Coloured servants, humbly seated on the floor, took part in daily evening worship with the Boer family. The patriarchal head of the household would read a sermon, followed by a prayer, from Conrad Mel's or Johannes Haverman's prayer books. On Sunday mornings the same audience would be treated to a massive sermon. A few Khoi received instruction, but little was done by the Dutch settlers to Christianize their Coloured servants.[4]

The congregational and social centre of the Church's life was the *Nagmaal* (Holy Communion) held in the local Church four times a year. On these occasions, Boer families came in their ox-wagons from isolated farmsteads to encampments. There they would spend four to seven days taking part in Church services and tending to business and social affairs. In 1829 it was agreed at a synod that all members of the congregation could receive Holy Communion regardless of colour, but this decision was more neglected than followed. The number of Coloureds and Blacks admitted was negligible. Participation of the Coloureds in chapel worship was increasingly discouraged. Separation was effectively practised and in 1857 the Church Synod, using a pious phrase, resolved that 'for the sake of Christ's cause and owing to the weakness of some', separate worship must be the rule. (This state of affairs led to the founding of the first separate Church for the Coloureds in 1881 – the Dutch Reformed Mission Church.)

In the Boer community, Andrew Murray (1828–1917) was one of the outstanding preachers. He did his theological training in Europe, where he came under the influence of the Evangelical revival. He founded a Missionary Institute for lay workers in the Church at Wellington and was internationally known through his many books on spirituality. When Boer students attended Christian conferences in various parts of the world, they would be identified as coming from 'the South Africa of Andrew Murray'.[5] Murray's influence resulted in a 'revival' in the Church about 1860. It was in this context that the first step was finally taken toward mission activity. It was characteristic, however, that the Church had to search abroad for its first missionaries McKidd, a Scot, and Gonin, a Swiss.

These missionary efforts met with hard and uncomprehending opposition from the majority of the Boer Church members, all of them farmers in daily contact with African labourers. In establishing their new republics of Transvaal and Orange Free State, the Voortrekkers maintained that there could be 'no equality in the Church and State between White and Black'. This attitude was to permeate South Africa during both the rural world that predominated in the nineteenth century and the increasingly urban environment of the twentieth century. After McKidd's early death, a young Afrikaner, Stephanus Hofmeyer (d. 1905), became one of the great pioneers of missions in Southern Africa, extending the work from Northern Transvaal to Zimbabwe.

After the British take-over, a few military and colonial chaplains on short-term appointments tried to fill the role of State Church in the Cape. At first their congregation was limited, consisting mainly of civil servants and soldiers. Even more brief were the visits paid by Anglican bishops and priests on their way to India or Australia. They would spend some time at the Cape, ministering to their English brothers and sisters in the faith. The Anglican Church was virtually non-existent in South Africa prior to the arrival of its first Bishop of Cape Town, Robert Gray, in 1848. Similarly, the Roman Catholic Church was largely absent until 1838, when the first Catholic bishop came. These observations are made here in order to emphasize the almost exclusively 'free Church' character of the missionary effort in South Africa during the first four decades of the nineteenth century. A century later, the Catholic and Anglo-Catholic communities dominated much of the scene.

The Khoi-Coloureds

Earlier interpretations of Church beginnings in the Cape do not bring to light the considerable difference between the work among the 'Coloureds' in the south-west of the Cape and that among the Bantu-speaking Africans further east. Nor do they clearly explain that, in the first third of the century, work was almost exclusively directed towards the Khoi-Coloureds. It is important to bring into proper focus the key role of the Coloured Christian groups, particularly the 'Griquas', as intermediary agents in the evangelization of Bantu-speaking communities.

Organizing the story from the point of view of ethnic communities rather than from that of missionary societies provides a more realistic picture of the situation. The Khoi-Coloured communities were increasingly alienated from White society at the Cape. However, they were to play an essential role as a bridge for the evangelization of some of the Bantu-speaking peoples. It is impossible to estimate what proportion of the Khoi were influenced to any extent by contacts with the Christian message. Any such contacts may have had the effect of sharpening awareness of social injustice, inducing groups of Khoi to move from the harsh conditions of life and labour on Boer wheat fields and vineyards to the Moravian 'institutions' and towards the sparsely populated territory north of the Colony. In the wilderness to the north they were determined to establish a more acceptable future of their own. It was there, in search of better conditions, that they wished to live out the new message. The population described as 'Coloured', comprised a variety of communities; Khoi, Oorlams, 'Basters', and Griqua. They lived mostly as nomads at a number of wells, water holes and rivers, north-west, north and east of the Cape.

The Moravians

The initial missionary attempt during the years 1737–43, by George Schmidt had been a failure, or so it seemed. It is the sequel that is most impressive. For when Moravian missionaries after fifty long years returned to Genadendal, they made a remarkable discovery which convinced them how strong the conviction was in that first group of Christians at Genadendal. During all those fifty years the Khoi converts had come together regularly, preferably under the pear tree Schmidt had planted years before, reading the New Testament and praying.[6] The faith was transferred to the next generation, parents teaching their children not only to read, but also to believe. They all kept waiting, sure that the end of the world was approaching, the great event Schmidt had spoken of. When new Moravians arrived on Christmas Eve in 1792, they were told that some Khoikhoi had foreseen their coming in dreams. Lena, the last survivor of Schmidt's converts, unwrapped her New Testament from its sheepskin cover – his parting gift to her fifty years earlier. No longer able to read because of failing eyesight, she asked a young woman to read aloud the story of the Wise Men from the East.

Here was this group of Christians, the first in their ethnic community, despised by the mighty Whites on the surrounding prosperous vineyards because of their unspeakable claim to be believers just like the Whites! They had been baptized, but by someone who was not even legally authorized to administer the sacrament. Deprived of their missionary, they had not surrendered, for they had caught a vision and had been awakened to a new dimension of life. Remarkably, they had received this inspiration not after generations of study, but during only a few years of fellowship with the missionary and his Book.

By 1792 a greater religious tolerance by the Dutch East India Company allowed the Moravians to return to the Cape and to continue the work Schmidt had been forced to leave. Genadendal had seniority over the other centres. At Genadendal provision was made for building a mill, a smithy and a shop to supplement the 230 huts which served as living quarters; a garden and vineyard were also planted. In 1810 the Moravians opened a similar station at Mamre, some thirty miles north of Cape Town and, by 1814 700 had been confirmed. Ten years later, after expanding north, they also established an 'institution' farther east at Enon, north of Port Elizabeth. Here, as at Genadendal and the other stations, the Coloureds comprised the majority of the members. An 'institution' of this period had certain features in common with the later 'Christian village' in other parts of Africa. The mission acquired fairly extensive lands on behalf of the Christian community. The Moravian 'institution' was laid out according to a definite plan in which chapel and school occupied the central position. Availability of water was all important, so institutions were built along rivers or watercourses, or around a spring.

In each case a certain number of Genadendal families were brought to the new place, thus constituting a nucleus of 'reliable families' – as the phrase was – including building masons with which to establish the new congregation and providing a pattern for other missions. Square, thatched, stone houses were constructed and placed along a street with two parallel rows of plots. The stone house and to a certain degree also the ordered placing along the streets were to become a characteristic feature of mission communities in the Cape, just as much as the European dress for the individual converts. The whole place was strictly organized according to a patriarchal rule. The importance of practical work was emphasized and the individual community member received some regular income for the work and could sell to neighbouring farms or to Cape Town his or her produce from the smithy, the mill or from mat making. The days of the week had their religious rhythm and content.[7]

The Moravians were universally renowned for their schools, of which their Cape schools provided good examples. A rare initiative was the infant school. At Genadendal 144 infants between three and six years received alphabet and numbers teaching, together with Bible stories and prayers. The missionary prepared rhymed lessons for these classes, later published in book form. What was more, this provided teaching opportunities for an early form of teacher training at Genadendal. The institution relied on indigenous leadership. The Khoi 'captains' of the place held great authority, with a baton as symbol of office. It is characteristic of the atmosphere of the place that one of the regulations read: 'The missionaries derive their authority from the congregation.'

Most of the missionaries were from Prussia. Many of them had a wide international experience having served for periods of six years or more in other Moravian fields. They were hard-working, enterprising – and patriarchal, qualities which they shared with most missionaries at the time. But as Germans they also had the additional virtue of being highly musical. The hymns and the congregational singing were a great help in attracting people to the chapel. The hymns were Western and pietistic and not set to indigenous tunes, but the Khoi men and women loved them. Certain evenings every week were set aside for hymn singing – together with the German missionaries, not apart from them – followed by singing in the homes. After a year, there were 100 members at Genadendal, with 200 regular attendants.

In Bishop H. P. Hallbeck, a Swede, the Moravians had a leader of outstanding ability. With the help of his German colleagues he had made Genadendal into the leading mission 'institution' of its time. It was often contrasted with the London Missionary Society's supposedly mismanaged Bethelsdorp. Hallbeck attached special importance to the training of Coloured 'assistants', among whom the teacher, Hezechiel Pfeiffer, excelled. He was the first Khoi to be named 'acolyte' or 'Church helper', the first step in the Moravian ministry. More than twenty years later, in 1862, there was a debate as to whether another Coloured leader, Joseph Hardenburg, should be ordained. At the Elders' Conference at Herrnhut, Germany suggested that this be done. But the superintendent in the field, J. F. Kühn, insisted that it would be 'premature' to do so. Unfortunately, this was not the last time that the 'men on the spot' proved to be more cautious than their superiors in the northern hemisphere.[8]

The London Missionary Society

Two personalities dominate the London Missionary Society's work among the Khoi-Coloureds. Both were already middle-aged with a vast experience of life and thus very different from the ordinary medley of youngsters in the missionary ranks at this time. One was a Scot, John Philip, the other a Dutch army officer with a medical degree from Edinburgh, Johannes T. van der Kemp. The former was an organizer and fearless strategist of the total mission endeavour; the latter, while a doctor and an academic, was all the same a romanticist and mystic, but above all intent on identifying with his Khoi congregation.

Throughout the early nineteenth century, the LMS shaped missionary endeavour by its 'independent' policy which stimulated indigenous responsibility and activity. It also developed effective political connections with leading Liberal Evangelical circles in Britain. In this part of Africa, the Society and its superintendent, John Philip, played a role similar to that of the Church Missionary Society in West Africa for Sierra Leone and Nigeria. This African Church history makes the point of the *catalytic* role of the missionary in Africa. This was exactly LMS's role in South Africa. The LMS, through those first decades, set the pace for South African missions and took important initiatives. Its influence was not to be a lasting one however, as its 'independent' policy resulted in its early withdrawal from its labours in the Cape.

John Philip, the Scot, came to South Africa in 1819. Never, strictly speaking, a missionary, he was rather a mission administrator and minister to a congregation of White settlers in Cape Town. He represented *par excellence* the missionary statesman 'on the spot', and carried out his duties by informing the London headquarters of developments. It was Philip who invited the first (European) Continental mission societies to direct their resources to South Africa. He suggested Namibia to the Rhenish Mission; Lesotho to the French Evangelicals; and Natal to the American Board of Boston. He felt that the White settlers' insatiable demand for land and labour could only be detrimental to the rights of the Khoi in Western Cape and of the Xhosa in the east. In 1828, the Cape Government promulgated 'Ordinance 50', 'for improving the Conditions of Hottentots and other Free persons of Colour'.[9] This measure allowed the Khoi the right to give or withhold their labour on the same terms as the White colonists.

In 1833, Parliament in London passed the Act of Abolition of Slavery in the British Empire, and this emancipation took effect during 1838–40 at the Cape. This was a 'major revolution in the legal system of the Cape Colony.'[10] One should perhaps not ascribe to John Philip the exclusive merit for this revolution. Yet to the Boer farmers, mainly from the eastern part of the Colony, it was the outlandish British missionary who more than anybody else had contrived this fundamental social and political change. They reacted by their exodus from the Cape towards the north – 'the Great Trek'. The Boers harboured bitter feelings against Philip whom they regarded as the missionary politician who interfered in affairs which were none of his concern. In their exodus myth, the missionary was the meddling adversary.

Philip achieved much on behalf of the Khoi through his efforts to have their legal status clarified. He sought to give them the means to improve their economic condition through education at the mission 'institutions'. The LMS continued to encourage ventures leading to self-sufficiency, such as timber cutting at Bethelsdorp and Theopolis, and at the new station at Kat River. Of even greater significance were Philip's efforts to form a Christian Coloured state – Griqualand – in 'Transorangia', the region beyond the Orange River. He envisaged this state, to be developed later by William Anderson, as a theocracy under the rule of Christian Griqua chiefs. Through such a political entity, the missions would reach out towards the Bantu-speaking peoples – to the east and the north.

In the Eastern Cape, the beginnings were intimately linked with another of the epoch's great missionaries, Johannes Theodore Van der Kemp, the Dutchman. He had hoped to evangelize the Bantu-speaking peoples in the

Western Cape, but this attempt was hindered by an endemic state of warfare in that area. Consequently his stay among the Xhosa was limited to little more than a year, 1800–01, although in this brief time he managed to establish his reputation among the Xhosa as a healer and a competent rain-maker. He now founded the Bethelsdorp 'institution' near Port Elizabeth. After a family tragedy in Holland had cast a blight upon his life, he underwent a deep personal conversion. He became strongly influenced by the Moravians and was instrumental in forming the Netherlands Missionary Society in 1797. It is not surprising that when he arrived in Cape Town in 1799 he paid a visit to his Moravian friends at Genadendal.[11]

It became clear to Van der Kemp that he should set up an 'institution' for the hundreds of refugees and Coloured farm labourers. And he planned to do this along the lines of the Moravian Genadendal. From the beginning, the project at Bethelsdorp aroused intense opposition from the Boers. They thoroughly disliked John Philip, but Van der Kemp also managed to antagonize the government administrators in Cape Town. They accused him of making no effort to clothe the Coloureds and of not encouraging them in the habits of industry, thrift, cleanliness and subservience to the White ruling class. There is, however, no evidence that he was against improving the material conditions of his Coloured congregation. He aimed to give them a good education and was for several years, involved in a bitter dispute with Governor Janssens concerning the teaching of literacy to Coloured people.[12] The fact that Van der Kemp married a young Malagasy woman and, following his example, James Read – Van der Kemp's successor at Bethelsdorp – married a Khoi woman, did not endear them to Boer opinion.

Bethelsdorp's first decade was one of sickly growth. It lay on poor soil and lacked sufficient water supply. The straw hovels, erected as temporary shelter, were not replaced by more permanent dwellings, for the people expected transfer to a more promising site. Improvement and expansion were delayed because most of the able-bodied men were intermittently away, working on Boer farms. The growth of a Christian community was also difficult here. Education in the faith was sporadic, with students often absent and missionaries often ill; catechumens underwent a long period of instruction; baptism was often delayed, due as much to scruple on the convert's part as to the missionary's hesitation. By 1808 the baptized inhabitants of Bethelsdorp numbered eighty-four adults and sixty-eight children. From 1806 both deacons and deaconesses were chosen from the Coloured converts, and these became involved in decisions of Church discipline. Khoi Christians from Bethelsdorp served as interpreters when missionary pioneers began work at Kat River, Griquatown, Theopolis and

Kuruman. By 1814 these African Christians working on the new mission areas were called 'assistant missionaries' and were paid from LMS funds. At Bethelsdorp, Van der Kemp taught all the baptism classes, for both adults and children. He wrote a short catechism in Gona, a Khoi language, for those who did not understand Dutch.[13]

An offshoot from Bethelsdorp was Kat River, founded in 1816, not far from Grahamstown. The leader, James Williams, a pious London artisan and member of the Bethelsdorp community left for Kat River in 1816. He was accompanied by his family, his interpreter with his Khoi wife and six experienced Christian Khoi families, all of whom were to form together the nucleus of a new enterprise. Bethelsdorp thus hived them off to become the corporate expression of its evangelistic intent. At first the population at Kat River consisted of 900 Coloured immigrants; by the middle of the century this number had increased to 6,000. Such increase was partly due to the arrival of new groups, such as the Mfengu – whom we shall meet presently – who added both to the community's strength and to its internal problems.[14] Community life at Kat River followed the Bethelsdorp model. A congregational characteristic was the emphasis on abstinence from alcohol in that it was thought necessary to counteract the Khoi's purported inclination to drunkenness. Temperance Societies, inspired by ideas from overseas, were formed in the area.[15]

Politically, the situation at Kat River was much more complicated. At Bethelsdorp Van der Kemp had insisted that he be free to act as he wished, and he said so to Governor and other authorities in unmistakable terms. His Bethelsdorp community would never comply with government regulations or intentions. The Kat River mission, on the other hand, was seen by the Government as a buffer against any Khoi or Xhosa disobedience, and Missionary Williams was invited to serve on condition that he kept the government informed of any untoward movement in the Coloured population. For that very reason, James Read was unacceptable as leader of the new community at Kat River. With his Khoi wife and a son referred to as 'a Coloured man' they might represent 'a spirit of disloyalty'! Williams, simple-minded and hard-working – he worked himself to an early death – was one in a long line of nineteenth-century South Africa missionaries who, with all their devotion, believed in missionary patriarchy. However, just as for twentieth-century South Africa there will be cause to state 'Liberalism is not enough', so for the nineteenth century it must be insisted 'Patriarchy was not enough'.

The Griqua

Two LMS missionaries established themselves to the north: William Edwards on the Kuruman River and William Anderson at Rietfontain, north of the Orange River. These outposts, which were not very successful, were nevertheless important as stepping stones used by missionaries going northwards to work among the Griqua and the Tswana-speaking peoples. Anderson remained among the Coloured people for thirty-three years, mainly on the Orange River. Initially he accompanied various Khoi nomads on their wanderings. When he managed to bring them together, they founded a new settlement that became 'Griquatown', centre of the rapidly emerging Griqua state. Anderson can be credited with rooting the Christian community firmly. He taught the former nomads to sow crops and to build houses of stone. With his help, they built a school, where he taught the 'Three R's'.

The Griquas were a minority group among the Coloured, a marginal community which had been slowly but firmly pushed away from the rich and influential centres in the south. From only 850 in 1800, they increased to 3,000 by 1823 and to 4,800 by 1842.[16] Most of them were descendants of Boer frontiersmen and Khoi women. Many of them began to wander northwards, making their own exodus and 'trek' in search of land. At first the Griqua state was no more than a mobile frontier within which various Coloured groups came together under missionary guidance to form a political confederation. They were governed by Coloured 'captains' such as Adam Kok I and his family, Barend Barends, Hendrick Hendricks, and Andries Waterboer. Eventually Griqua centres developed, such as Griquatown and Philippolis. The latter was mainly populated by Khoi who had moved away from Kat River. In the early nineteenth century the Griqua acted as middlemen in the ivory trade between the Tswana further north and the Europeans. Their economic position was considerably improved for a brief period around the middle of the century with the growth of wool farming. They found it extremely profitable to sell the wool in the Colony.[17]

Well before the arrival of the first foreign missionaries, some of the Griquas had become Christian. The early 1800s saw experimentation in establishing Church order on the farms, and criteria for acceptance or rejection of baptismal candidates. Anderson welcomed six new candidates, five men and one woman – Heva Barend. This was obviously a man's world, for the missionary was 'not so well satisfied [with her] as with the rest, but on account of her repeated requests and nothing appearing against her moral conduct we could not reject her'.[18]

The Church took root among the Griqua and played a central role in their lives. It gave them cohesion in times of crisis and danger. John Philip wholeheartedly encouraged the social and religious endeavours of this Christian community during its earliest periods. Even though he normally had very good relations with this group, his task often required considerable diplomacy. They had an acute sense of their own independence, and their relative prosperity made them sensitive to any hints of missionary paternalism. It was not Philip who appointed the Griqua chiefs but, rather, the Griqua chiefs who appointed the missionaries. In the years 1825–50 seven missionaries were posted to Philippolis; the Griqua ordered six of these to leave, sometimes at short notice.[19] They were selective as to the kind of missionary they wanted. Their ideal of a missionary was one of 'strict piety, an impressive preacher, and one who can go about the whole neighbourhood to preach'.[20] Even before 1820 some of the leading men in the Griqua community were elected magistrates and deacons. Earlier than any comparable group of congregations in South Africa, the Griqua achieved ecclesiastical self-sufficiency, the ideal propagated in the London Mission's international programme as being the only sound foundation for Church life.[21]

Griqua initiatives towards territorial expansion were hampered by outside forces and by 'progressive demoralization' from within.[22] The Church shared in the tragic loss of influence and power. The extent to which the Griqua communities resented the steady encroachment upon their lands was dramatically illustrated by their alliance with the Xhosa against the Cape Government during the 1850 war, known as the Kat River Rebellion. The uprising was soon crushed by government troops, who thus put an end to the Kat River enterprise. For the Church, this tragedy was especially poignant, since it had been deeply involved in the vision and the reality of Kat River and Griqualand.

The missionaries saw a bitter irony in the situation. They had inspired the Coloureds with ideals of Christian community life and economic progress. At the same time, the interest in the lands beyond the Colony's northern frontier aroused in the Cape by Philip and others, was a major factor which contributed to the unleashing of that decisive Boer exodus which smothered the fragile Coloured enterprises. In the South African society, these Coloureds were definitely marginal. From there they had to make their second exodus, the trek in 1861–62 of 2,000 Griquas from Griquatown south-east to Kokstad, a distance of about 400 miles. The Church may well have been one of the major centripetal forces that kept the community together during the troubled era immediately after this trek, as the Church deacons maintained regular worship in the *laager*. Insofar as it could without buildings and without a minister, the Church flourished as was to be expected from a strongly congregational community.[23] During their vicissitudes, the Griqua formulated a prayer to express the depths of their need:

> Lord, save thy people.
> Lord, we are lost unless Thou savest us.
> Lord, this is no work for children.
> It is not enough to send thy Son.
> Lord, Thou must come Thyself.[24]

Together with the Mfengu community, the Griqua constitute a most important example from this period of a corporate Christian movement, acting as a trajectory for new religious ideas to other peoples. Three examples will suffice. First, in 1823 they responded to Robert Moffat's plea for help for his beleaguered Thlaping, a Tswana community. The Griqua success in warding off a threatening attack from a northern enemy opened the door to long-term Christian influence in Botswana. Second, a Griqua hunter gave a glowing report in 1833 to the Sotho king, Moshoeshoe. This news of White teachers with a message of peace paved the way for the Paris missionaries to Lesotho. Third, the Griqua chief Adam Kok helped the Berlin Lutherans to establish themselves among the Koranna people. Kok offered the Germans a generous gift: a big farm. How big? 'As far as you can ride on a horse two hours in each direction.' This measure was later reduced to one hour, but even so, the Bethany mission farm, in the southern part of present Orange Free State, was of ample size. The missionary Rodloff rode his Arab stallion as fast as he could, in an attempt to claim as much land as possible for a good cause. The Koranna population on the farm, eventually replaced by Bantu-speaking Tswana, formed a lively congregation under two Coloured leaders, Richard Miles and Adam Oppermann, both effective preachers.[25]

Beginnings in Namibia

About the same time as Anderson developed the work at Griquatown, other missionaries went to the Nama and similar communities further west. H. Schmelen, a German working for the LMS, played a fundamental role in Namaqualand. As soon as he arrived in South Africa in 1811, he devoted himself to the Nama, who were part of the Khoi. He moved with these itinerant communities for fifteen years, riding by ox from one water hole to another over the immense desert wastes, eventually settling beyond the

Orange River near the west coast. After proving that he was able to share their life, Schmelen further identified with these people by marrying a Nama. Three of his LMS colleagues also married Khoi women.

With his wife's help, Schmelen translated the four Gospels into the Nama language. His pioneering life among these people encouraged further work among the Bantu-speaking peoples of Great Namaqualand. In 1804 the Albrecht brothers were welcomed by 'Captein' Kagap, one of the many Nama chiefs. In making their lengthy treks from *kraal* to *kraal* through the barren landscape, the missionaries had little time for catechetical preparations. The report which they sent to their LMS superiors in London conveys an impression of the first attempts at reaching out to the nomad population:

> On the 16th of April nine of the Great Namaquas were assembled (three men and six women) and seven of the Bastards who had been thus instructed. After the ceremony of baptism they took the Sacrament with three other members who had been baptized many years ago ... After this we invited all those who had taken the Sacrament to dine with us ... John ... could not help shedding tears and joyfully cried: 'Oh what great things does God to me who am a great sinner!'[26]

Wesleyan presence in Namaqualand was, for the most part, confined to that of Barnabas Shaw frcm 1816 onwards. A chance encounter with a Nama chief led him to establish a mission station near the Kamiesberg range. It was called Leliefontein and remained his base for a decade. Shaw's introduction of the plough changed the economic basis of the Nama.

The work started in these parts by the LMS and by the Wesleyan Methodists, was soon followed by the Rhenish Society from Germany, arriving in South Africa in 1829. They followed much the same pattern as their predecessors in establishing mission 'institutions' for Coloureds in the Colony, including Stellenbosch and Wuppertal. From there, they went to the Nama in the west. In 1842 they extended their work beyond the Orange River, thanks to vigorous new missionaries, Hugo Hahn, a dynamic Baltic German, and Hans Christian Knudsen, a Norwegian.[27] Their piety was punctuated by lively expressions of apocalyptic yearning. Hahn felt that mission stations did not reach far enough in influencing society at large, and were in fact 'altogether useless institutes'. Believing that Christianity and civilization went hand in hand, he founded a trading company, with headquarters at Otjimbingwe. He developed the export of hides, planting of tobacco, fisheries on the coast and opened a market with great success as well as introduced the plough in northern Namaqualand.[28]

The Rhenish strategy foreshadowed the idea of a 'chain' of mission stations reaching into the 'interior' of Africa, with the Herero being the goal of the northward drive. With this long-term aim in mind, the missionaries tried to make contact with both Nama and Herero chiefs. Relations between those two communities were usually hostile. The Herero owned innumerable heads of cattle and the Nama, under their Captein Jonkers, would attack and take as many cattle as possible. It was not always easy for the Rhenish to be neutral in this long, drawn-out struggle. The Marxist historian, Heinrich Loth with his favourite concept of an Oorlam (Nama) state, ready in the 1860s to take over the command of Namibia, has meticulously gathered archival material to prove the missionaries' bias against the Nama-Oorlam and for the Herero.[29] A peace treaty between the Nama and the Herero was finally concluded in 1870, mainly through the efforts of Hugo Hahn and his colleagues. This settlement had far-reaching consequences, for only now could a determined missionary approach be made to the Herero. It also paved the way for the Finnish mission to the Ovambo. Hahn made repeated expeditions to Ovamboland and in 1866 finally achieved results. The Ovambo chief knew Hahn's reputation as the 'great wizard' of the Herero and was prepared to send his son for education at Otjimbingwe.[30]

Spirituality on the frontier

Denominational surveys and statistical figures cannot convey an adequate understanding of the inner life of any religious group. It is difficult to capture the life of the Spirit. A few indications must suffice for an understanding of the inner, spiritual developments among these groups of Coloured Christians. Also among them, the encounter between the preacher and his listeners was a process of selective giving and selective response and assimilation.

The three missions – the Moravians, the LMS and the Wesleyans – were at one in their zeal in enforcing the observation of 'the Sabbath'. Sometimes, however, there could arise certain inter-Church tensions over this matter. Evans, a newly arrived Congregational missionary from Britain, was disappointed in both the Moravians' Genadendal and Van der Kemp's Bethelsdorp when informed that sewing was permitted on the Sabbath, in places which in other respects, he thought, were recognizably Christian. His colleagues made up for this weakness by making the Lord's Day a most busy occasion with a very full Sunday School programme. Bethelsdorp had twenty Sunday School teachers, half of whom were women. At the related mission centre of Theopolis the Sunday School consisted of 450 pupils, 250 adults and 200 children and twelve teachers. They met for one and a half hour before the worship service in the morning and then for the same length of time in the afternoon.[31]

In the case of the Moravian 'institutions' the fundamental role of hymn-singing in the Dutch language prevailed. During two to three years of a so-called revival at Bethelsdorp, 1814–16, the place was dominated by extended hymn-singing sessions, again, in Dutch. The Khoi knew the language and took a pride in it, although of course it was not their own language of the heart. The Khoi congregation at worship involved much individual and group participation through 'conversation meetings' and 'experience meetings'. At these times, catechumens received instruction on baptism, or comments were made on the Sunday sermon, or a dream would be related in a dramatic way. When John Campbell, the LMS Secretary in London, visited Bethelsdorp in 1815, he reported an *agape* service – a love feast. Presumably, this was the result of contacts with the Moravians. It was followed every Sunday by a celebration of the Lord's Supper.[32]

The first chapters of Genesis – on the Creation, the Fall, the Flood, anticipations of the message of the Last Judgment – attracted keen attention. While many consider the Flood to be a Mesopotamian legend, the Namaqua, taught by the intrepid LMS missionary Schmelen, did not think so. They knew that although the Deluge had swept away the whole of mankind, one man had been saved from the destruction. This man and his family had come to Namaqualand.[33] Many of the first generation Khoi Christians seem to have experienced dreams relating to Judgment Day. Several people told them to James Read and his German colleague, Messer, as they journeyed along the southern coast in 1814. One, a servant girl at a Boer farm – Martha Jantjes – was frightened by a dream and was crying so she could hardly speak. In her dream, she stood by the Church at Bethelsdorp and suddenly heard a noise in the air and a cry: 'There comes Christ to judgment'. At that moment, all the believers 'received wings and flew to the Church'. Although she tried to follow she could not move from her spot. Then she saw a cloud stretched from heaven down to earth, with Christ seated upon it. All those who flew to the Church then drew nearer to Christ upon the cloud. Martha had related this dream to others who had advised her to heed its message, because, 'God used such means sometimes' to bring sinners to him. They indicated that Christ was saying 'Martha, if you remain so indifferent then it will go with you as you saw in your dream'. But the Khoi could express themselves even more dramatically, according to Messer:

> A woman came into mine house and appeared to be quite wild, fell down to the ground, pulled off her clothes, cried out, 'Ah! Ah! I burn, I burn, Hell fire is near to me. Hitherto I could not believe in Jesus Christ but today I am obliged to believe or else I must perish for ever and ever.'[34]

Certain symbols, such as blood and wounds were particularly disturbing to the Moravian Khoi. A young woman named Allet visited Messer. 'She said, "I long for baptism, but – the table, the table", said she. "What table?" said he. "The Lord's table. To partake of the blood of Christ". "Blood is not drunk there, but wine." "I know, I know, I know!" she cried much that he could converse no more with her. Three days later she was baptized.'[35] The Moravian historian writes:

> The efforts of the missionaries centred around the impression of the Cross of the Saviour on the heart of their flock ... A little boy, when asked to state his faith, took off his *kaross* [cloak of animal skins with the hair on] and pointing to his side, head and feet, said: 'Those the Saviour has suffered for me.' When the moon was red one evening another child was also instantly reminded of the Saviour's side wounds, and a man dreamt that he saw a stream of blood pouring forth from the moon.[36]

Significantly, the moon played an important part in the traditional religion of the pagan Khoi. A possible continuation of old Khoi ritual practices were the Christian prayer meetings held in the open air at the time of the full moon.

A very dramatic response to the preaching of the missionaries was the conversion of the redoubtable Jager Afrikaner, a Khoi chief who was terrorizing the whole countryside. He explained that a dream was the decisive factor in his conversion. Elements of this dream keep recurring through the years and even today, in both mission-related and Independent Churches.

> The chief found himself at the base of a steep mountain ... On the left was a fiery furnace, and smoke mingled with lightning ... a sight which made his whole frame tremble ... He attempted to ascend ... He cast his eyes upwards beyond the burning gulf and saw a person stand on a green mount, on which the sun appeared to shine with peculiar brilliancy. Shielding the side of his face with his hand ... he at last reached the long desired spot ... When asked about his interpretation of the dream, Jager Afrikaner replied, 'The path is the narrow road leading from destruction to safety, from hell to heaven ... Thank God I have passed.'[37]

The tearful, highly emotional nature of this Coloured piety is striking and it may have been heightened at this time through contacts with the German Moravians. LMS reports mention approvingly the streams of tears that would flow from these pious Christians. In 1805 Van der Kemp notices how during Brother Read's preaching his voice was drowned by the crying of the people.[38] Messer relates how at one service the voice of the missionary was 'drowned by the cries of the people; most of the communicants wept bitterly at the Lord's Table'. In 1816 Schmelen notes how powerfully the Word of God seemed to fall upon his audience, 'The greatest part of my hearers were drowned in tears, others were unable either to sit or stand'.[39] Again, Schmelen says that all his San Bushmen congregation, men, women and children, would retire into the field to pray after the service, 'which I never saw before'.[40] The Anglican Bishop Robert Gray was aware of the same acoustic effect during the services: the Khoi Christians 'wept aloud'.[41] The crying of the Khoi would become particularly intense when they went out into the bushes to pray after a service, so that 'all the fields were covered with praying people'.[42]

When James Read went north to Lattakoo (Kuruman), he had occasion to preach to a congregation of both Coloureds and Tswana. He observed the same emotional tension that he had witnessed further south.

> Our interpreter was so much affected that he could not proceed, upon which his wife undertook the part of interpreter for him, but in the prayer she also was unable to refrain from weeping ... The Bootchuanas knew not what to make of this proceeding particularly as they consider it disgraceful for a person to weep.[43]

Fortunately for the latter, they were introduced to Christianity by the dour Scot, Robert Moffat. At first Moffat was sceptical of the Coloured piety, 'manifested by redundancy of tears'. But he later changed his opinion after witnessing a revival at Kuruman in 1829.[44]

SOUTHERN NGUNI

The Nguni

There was a marked difference in social structure between the Nguni peoples on the east coast – from Xhosa to Zulu and Swazi – and the Sotho on the high veld. The Nguni society consisted of homesteads or 'villages', thinly spread over vast areas of hills and valleys. These communities were held together as chiefdoms under independent chiefs, and varied greatly in size from 1,000 to 35,000. The Sotho, by contrast, lived mostly in large settlements or 'towns'. The need for sufficient water and for defence caused this concentration of population. This difference of structure led to different opportunities for the transmission of a new religious message and new social institutions. The southern Nguni are sometimes referred to as 'the Xhosa'.

In reality, this is an inclusive term for many Xhosa-speaking peoples: Thembu, Mpondo, Mpondomise, Bhaca, Bomvana and Mfengu.

From the late eighteenth century onwards there was increasing pressure on the Xhosa tribesmen's lands by European farmers. All attempts to find agreement proved ineffective and from 1779 almost endemic warfare raged for nearly eighty years. Depending on what is termed 'war' or 'raiding exploits', there were six or nine frontier wars, including those of 1818–19, 1834–35, 1846–47 and 1850–51. They increased and deepened Xhosa bitterness against the White rulers and made any missionary attempt all the more difficult. The religion of the Whites might be good enough for slaves and women, on the margin of society, but not for able-bodied Xhosa or Thembu warriors. Reaction to Europeans culminated in the nation's suicidal 'cattle-killing' tragedy of 1856–57. A young Xhosa girl, niece of Mhlakaza the diviner and councillor of Chief Sarili, had a vision of the ancestors bringing their rich and fat cattle to the Xhosa's relief: 'They would have an abundance of cattle at a coming resurrection; those now in their possession were to be destroyed'. To crown it all, the 'Europeans would be swept into the sea.'[45] The girl's visions 'have been echoed again and again', especially in some of the most dramatic incidents in the history of the Independent Church movement.[46] The millenarian delusion of 1857 led to the death and destruction of an able and proud nation. Some 30,000 Xhosa were forced to seek work with White farmers. At least 150,000 cattle were destroyed. Thousands of people died as a result of famine. The population of the 'Ciskei' was reduced from over 100,000 to 37,000! Xhosa reactions to Western evangelization must be understood in the light of this history of colonial wars, tragedy and catastrophe.

J. T. Van der Kemp, LMS missionary to the Khoi, aimed at reaching beyond them to the Nguni. In 1800 he managed to get a precarious foothold in the Xhosa country of Chief Ngqika, not far from present-day Fort Hare. Because the political situation was highly unsettled, Ngqika would not allow the White preacher an opportunity to influence his people. But some local Khoi, marginal and dispensable, offered a point of contact. Among them the missionary was at liberty to work. Van der Kemp gathered a little flock of five women and thirteen children, teaching them the elements of the Christian faith. After fifteen months, however, Van der Kemp was forced to leave and eventually settled, as we have seen, at Bethelsdorp. How did he communicate in that short period with his Xhosa-speaking listeners? On this highly mobile frontier anything could, and did, happen. A notorious 'frontier' man, Coenraad de Buys, a Boer outlaw who had fled in 1798 to Chief Ngqika's area, became a capable interpreter.[47]

In spite of his brief stay, Van der Kemp made a lasting impression on Chief Ngqika and some of his people. Much later, the Chief expressed regret that they had not heeded the missionary's advice when he was with them. Several Xhosa, through the years, went beyond the frontier to Bethelsdorp, there becoming Van der Kemp's disciples. Three outstanding Xhosa, later to emerge as leading charismatic personalities, were influenced by Van der Kemp. Jan Tzatzoe, son and heir of the Ntinde chief, stayed almost nine years with the first group to join Van der Kemp. He learned Dutch, the 'Three R's', and carpentry and became not only a successful preacher but also an incomparable interpreter – possibly the most important evangelistic function between two cultures 'on the frontier'. Nxele and Ntsikana had similar backgrounds in Xhosa culture, yet were significantly different in their interpretation of Biblical stories and Christian symbols.

Nxele's father had followed Van der Kemp when the latter was forced to leave Chief Ngqika's realm. The family was influenced by the new faith and eventually the son began to preach: His religious message, with its shreds of Biblical references, included an emphasis on the Resurrection. His remarkable prophetic addresses may have contained echoes from Van der Kemp's message with its occasional eighteenth-century geological and ecological speculations. Nxele spoke of the Creation, the Fall of Man and the Deluge – which event he proved by telling of shells which had been found on the tops of the highest mountains. He said that God would come again, not with water, but with fire. He told of *Taay* (Khoi name for Jesus Christ) who was crowned with thorns. He said that *Dali* (God) first sent Jankanna (Dr Van der Kemp) to them, but that they would not listen. When he left them, *Dali* had now raised up a raw Kaffir to warn them, and had also sent Jankanna's son (identified with J. Read).[48] Nxele told Read about his conversion:

> A large fire was presented before him and persons got hold of him to throw him into it, but then Taay came and delivered him. I asked him to tell the particulars of what he knew of Christ but he said he could not do this now for he should burst into tears.[49]

Nxele announced the General Resurrection of the Dead, to take place right there at Gompo on the coast, near East London. The masses assembled and did their ablutions in the early morning, in preparation for this unusual event to occur at sunrise. Nothing happened, however, but this did not diminish Nxele's influence. In Xhosa culture many years later millennial ideas were to take on nation-wide significance in the 'cattle-killing delusion'. Later he drifted away from Christian associations and emphasized his role as diviner, using traditional red ochre and dance. His political stand in the conflict between competing Xhosa chiefs and the British Government caused him to attack Grahamstown in 1819. This manoeuvre led to his downfall.

Ntsikana (?1770–1821) was son of a sub-chief of the Ngqika tribe. The circumstances of his birth impressed on him, at an early age, the seriousness of life: his mother had been accused of witchcraft, an all too common calamity in tribal life throughout all Africa at the time. She had to flee for her life back to her own family. It was here that Ntsikana was born. As a youth, he heard three missionaries preach: Van der Kemp, James Read, and J. J. Williams.

Ntsikana made his own public appearance when the eastern frontier was closed. Yet it was through him that the 'door of the Gospel' later opened to the Xhosa. It began with a vision one morning in 1815. Next to his favourite ox, Hulushe, he saw a brilliant heavenly object shining in the morning sun with the colours of the rainbow. The same evening, he was summoned to a dance, being considered the best dancer in the area. Three times he was about to enter the movement, but each time there roared a storm from heaven, forcing him to hold back and to leave the dance. On the way home he went into the river, washing the red ochre from his body. Now he had a message: 'This thing which has entered me, it says: "Let there be prayer; Let every thing bow the knee".'[50] His message, in contrast to that of Nxele, was Prayer, Penance and Conversion from Sin and total submission to the will of God. Both men emphasized purification and ablutions, and the centrality of the Resurrection, a concept which had 'the greatest impact as it filled a gap in Xhosa belief'.[51] Ntsikana also warned against prostitution, stealing and witchcraft, and advised following the White teachers as soon as they came into the country.[52]

The way in which Ntsikana conveyed his teaching was infinitely winsome. He was probably illiterate, his congregation most definitely so and there were no books. But Ntsikana had something else: a message. He conveyed his message in the classic African way of communication: in song. He composed four hymns; or perhaps it would be more correct to say that four hymns 'entered' him. They became the central part of his order of worship. As he led a service, he wore his prestigious cloak of leopard skin, and 'in due course this garment acquired mystical associations.'[53] At dawn he would stand in front of his hut, chanting 'Ntsikana's Bell', calling people to worship:

Sele! *sele*!
Ahom, *ahom*, *ahom*!
Zani kuv! *Izwe le Nkozi*! (Come hearken, come hearken the Word of the Lord!)
Ahom, *ahom*, *ahom*, *ahom*, *ahom*![54]

After the singing of three more stanzas of 'The Bell', Ntsikana would enter his hut followed by his flock. Then he sang his second hymn, about '*Dalibom* – the Life-Creator', probably accompanied by traditional dancing:

1. *He! Nankok' u Dalibom; Wases'kolweni.*
2. *He! Nankok' u Dalibom; Os'bizesihleli.*
3. *He! Nankok' u Dalibom; Wasinga pezulu.*
1. See! There stands the Life-Creator: He of the School.
2. See! There stands the Life-Creator: Who calls us to rise
3. See! There stands the Life-Creator: He has ascended![55]

Ntsikana's 'Great Hymn', was later to become something of a national anthem of the Xhosa:

Ulo Tixo omkulu, ngosezulwini
He, is the Great God, Who is in heaven;
Thou art Thou, Shield of truth.
Thou art Thou, Stronghold of truth.
Thou art Thou, Thicket of truth.
Thou art Thou who dwellest in the highest.
He, Who created life (below), created (life) above.
That Creator who created, created heaven,
This maker of the stars, and the Pleiades.
A star flashed forth, it was telling us.
The Maker of the blind, does he not make them of purpose?
The trumpet sounded, it is calling us.
As for his chase, He hunteth for souls.
He, Who amalgamates flocks rejecting each other.
He the Leader, Who has led us
Thou art the great Mantle for us to put on
Those hands of Thine, they are wounded.
Those feet of Thine, they are wounded.
Thy blood, why is it streaming?
Thy blood, it was shed for us.
This great price, have we called for?
This home of Thine, have we called for it?[56]

This hymn was created in the style of traditional Xhosa *isibongo*, a praise-poem with a series of praise-names of God. 'It carries with it the authority of past religious tradition and this authority is carried over to the new meaning.'[57] The music too is pure Xhosa, with a low and plaintive Xhosa air, exceedingly moving. J. K. Bokwe, the Xhosa scholar, writes that 'the weird music of the "Great Hymn" gravely and deliberately led by Ntsikana never fails to move [the old Christians] to tears even to this day.'[58]

Ntsikana's achievement illustrates Xhosa initiative and creativity. Van der Kemp's message and his personal fellowship had been catalytic, but very soon this foreign idiom was translated into the Xhosa language and adapted to Xhosa concepts and visions. The new religion had not yet been reduced to the pages of a catechism or the paces of an intellectual exercise. To Ntsikana and his people, as it had been with Van der Kemp, religion was a matter not of intellect and the paragraphs of a catechism, but of vision and intuition, of song and movement. In Ntsikana and his hymns, the early Xhosa image of God is drawn in strong colours. He obviously identified the Creator God with the God of his fathers and was touched by the Suffering Hero whose blood was shed for the Xhosa. He expressed this faith with an immediacy of feeling and identification that did not appear again for a hundred years, until Isaiah Shembe, the Zulu, produced his *Izihlabelo* – Book of Songs.

The first attempts at evangelization among the southern Nguni – the 'Xhosa' – can be seen in two stages. First, in spite of constant wars and rumours of war between White and Black on the East Cape frontier, some Xhosa did respond positively to what they understood of the new message. The experiences of Ntsikana, the great charismatic personality, were to be a model for later generations among the Xhosa. Second, from the 1820s, the arrival on the eastern front of the 4,000 British settlers, including a number of young Wesleyan 'local preachers' inaugurated a new situation. These men were to face three special evangelistic opportunities. There was, first, the meeting with a marginal community on the periphery of Xhosa society, the Gqunukwebe. Prior to the coming of the English settlers, members of this community had already sought contact with the missionaries at Van der Kemp's Bethelsdorp. Chief Chunywa's family, whom we shall meet later, were Gqunukwebe and therefore the majority of Xhosa regarded them as different and marginal. Chunywa entrusted two of his sons to the Bethelsdorp missionaries and in 1816 the LMS missionaries Read and Williams made a special visit to Chunywa's son, Kobus Congo. These details are emphasized to show that the Gqunukwebe were open to a Christian influence quite early, and their interest was to be strengthened when William Shaw and his Wesleyan colleagues began their work.

Second, there was in the area the effect of the *mfecane* from the north, leading to the Christianization of the Mfengu community. Again one is confronted with a marginal group – of refugees this time – which at the outset were regarded as alien and for that reason prepared to respond positively to the missionaries' invitation. Third, and finally, there was the Wesleyan 'class' system functioning as carrier of the Christian message on the East Cape coast. New generations of Early Migrant Labour arrived at the harbours and other centres of modern activity. Coming from South Africa's far north they now had their first contacts with the Christian message. The Xhosa population as a whole remained unresponsive to the missionary message until the tragic effects of the national catastrophe in the 1850s were beginning to be felt. Nonetheless, on these three important points there was a breakthrough for evangelizing efforts. Predominantly the Wesleyans – and soon also Scottish Presbyterians – were in a position to benefit from these approaches.

British missions among the Xhosa

From 1820 Eastern Cape took on an unmistakably British character, with thousands of young settlers arriving at Algoa Bay. This move was to make the Cape into a British colony, with settlers on the 'eastern frontier' providing a defence line against the Xhosa. Their arrival also brought liberal ideas in political and social matters and a strong Nonconformist flavour in religion. For a whole generation it was taken for granted that South Africa was a non-conformist country. The significance of the arrival of these young Methodist preachers was immense: they initiated a sequence of Methodist missions and influence throughout the subcontinent, from Port Elizabeth to Elizabethville (today, Lubumbashi) in Zaïre/Congo.

Among the young British newcomers in the 1820s, mainly artisans and farmers, there were a number of Wesleyan lay preachers, who developed into a team of missionaries, led by the Revd William Shaw. He had been ordained just before leaving England, and served as chaplain to the group. The rapidly expanding programme also found staff among several new missionaries sent out from Britain. One was John Ayliffe, who later brought the Gospel to the Mfengu. There were linguists in the group: W. B. Boyce, who discovered what he called the 'euphonic concord' of the Bantu noun and published the first Xhosa grammar; and J. W. Appleyard, who translated the New Testament into Xhosa in 1846 and the whole Bible in 1859. These were great achievements by gifted and devoted men.

Fired by the idea that there was 'not a single missionary between him in Eastern Cape and the Red Sea', William Shaw conceived the plan of establishing a 'chain' of mission stations along the southern coast as far as Natal.[59] In the 1820s six mission stations were founded, all named after

Wesleyan leaders in Britain. They formed a 'chain' some 200 miles long, from Wesleyville where Shaw worked, to Buntingville among the Mpondo in the east. Such a 'chain of missions' became a well-known concept of missionary strategy in Africa. H. P. Hallbeck of the Moravian Brethren began a promising chain in 1828, with the foundation of Shiloh, 100 miles north of Wesleyville. The Wesleyan stations were placed close to each other and close to the centre of a local Xhosa chief. The missionaries would often act as 'Court Chaplains', even though the chiefs usually had no intention of becoming Christian themselves.

It was not only the Wesleyans who made useful contacts with the chiefs. In 1837, Chief Gasela welcomed Berlin's missionary, Döhne, with the assurance that he would 'honour him not as a friend and a brother but as a father'. His readiness, though, went not much farther than these polite phrases. His rain doctors were too powerful for him.[60]

On a less spiritual level, the missionaries finding that the financial support from the home country was less than satisfactory had to fall back on a barter economy with a supply of European goods. Arriving in the Cape they 'brought Bibles in their right hands and beads and buttons in their left ... to encourage conversion, as payment for services and as presents for African leaders'.[61] William Shaw explained that beads were as good a medium of exchange as gold or silver or paper money. Missionaries sent detailed descriptions of what was needed: 'small black and white beads or dark blue'. In some places the demand was for 'sky blue, dark blue, white, black and red, but they must not be transparent'.[62] Shaw needed no less than half a ton of beads for his district. Custom made it necessary to give presents to chiefs. At his request Chief Ngqika received 'beads, buttons, knives, tinder boxes, a looking glass, two handkerchiefs, trinkets and brass wire.' Soon beads became part of the Church service, provided for the Church collection.[63]

Very soon Shaw and his colleagues contacted a special group among the Xhosa; the Gqunukwebe. The Gqunukwebe were related to the Rarabe Xhosa of Ciskei. In the eighteenth century, however, they inter-married with the Khoi 'to such an extent that they lost their separate identity', and from that time on, they treasured a tribal myth interpreting their unique origin and history. Chief Pato's and Chief Kama's Gqunukwebe regarded themselves as a community apart, with certain racial characteristics and a mythical charter of their own. The Gqunukwebe were 'marginal' and just as with the Mfengu, their very marginality made their political, social and religious responses different from that of ordinary Xhosa.

When William Shaw first approached this community in 1823, Chief Pato and his brothers told him that they thought of his presence in their midst as a *bescherm bosch* – a bush of defence, from wind and rain. Shaw's mission was given land immediately adjacent to the chief's residence. In 1824, on a visit to Grahamstown, Shaw brought Kama, the youngest of the princely brothers, with him. The young man was highly impressed by what seemed to him mighty church buildings and also by the religious services. He shed 'floods of tears'. A year later he was baptized.[64] His brothers, after their initial display of co-operation, were alienated from the missionary cause, identifying it with the interests of the conquering Whites. They eventually lost whatever land they had possessed and Pato was forced to meditate on his misfortunes on Robben Island. But Kama remained a faithful supporter of the Church. He felt that his status as a Christian chief made him part of the world of the Whites, and he aligned himself with it. In the wars of 1835, 1846 and 1850, he fought on the British side, and kept away from the suicidal national 'cattle-delusion' in 1856–57. He served as a Christian chief for fifty-two years and gave his name to one of the mission stations, Kamastone near Queenstown. His son, William Shaw Kama, followed the Puritan way, first as a Methodist minister and, after his father's death, as a chief functioning at the same time as Methodist class leader and preacher.[65] We also note here that the most common name in South Africa for God, *Thixo*, is not a Bantu term, but derives from the Khoi language. It must be surmised that it was the Gqunukwebe Wesleyans who made the word acceptable to the Bantu-speaking peoples.

The Mfengu

Another separate group within the Xhosa area was the Mfengu. The *mfecane* turmoil had driven certain Zulus to seek refuge south of Natal among the Xhosa, where proud Zulu men had to attach themselves as clients of Xhosa chiefs. Turned into destitute aliens far from their grazing and hunting grounds, they were given a name of derision, 'Fingo' or 'Mfengu'. Outside pressures forged them into a solid unit, looking for a new future. They did so in ways affecting not only the welfare of their community, but also the Church history of southern Africa. The Mfengu story is the classic example of what is called in this book 'the refugee factor' in the Christianization of African peoples. The Mfengu were an ethnic group whose very existence was endangered by *mfecane*. They saw themselves pushed into the margin of Zulu society and beyond and, in this calamity, turned to Christianity.

As the Mfengu hastened south into the Gcaleka Xhosa country, concentrations soon gathered at or near Wesleyan missions. J. Ayliffe, one of the 1820 settlers, an artisan by training, devoted himself to the Mfengu for over thirty years. He opened day schools for the children and night classes for adults. In the frontier wars the Mfengu did not hesitate to side with the British. When the defeated Xhosa had to evacuate their lands in 1835, the Governor awarded these areas at Peddie and Tsitsikamma to their Mfengu competitors. Ayliffe, as another Moses, led nearly 17,000 Mfengu and their 22,000 head of cattle to Peddie. There they settled, about half of them registered as professed Christians. A smaller number moved on to Tsitsikamma. At Peddie, at Tsitsikamma, and at the Presbyterian Burnshill the Mfengu made good use of improved cultivation techniques: water furrows, spades, ploughs and manuring. The Mfengu communities, although run by different missions, were recognized as models of what a Nguni Christian community could be. The Moravian missionaries at Tsitsikamma refused to tolerate the custom of bride wealth. Despite the advantages for the long-term spread of Christianity represented by these communities, there were also drawbacks. The Mfengu were regarded as traitors by the Xhosa for their acceptance of the Christian faith and the White men's culture. Christianity was to a large extent identified with the Mfengu ways. At Peddie, they were constantly exposed to attacks from Xhosa tribes.

While the Wesleyans were the most involved with the Mfengu, the other missions too could claim an active response from these people. The LMS had Mfengu members at Peddie, at Hankey and elsewhere. The Presbyterian missionary, James Laing, played a role similar to that of Ayliffe at both Lovedale and Burnshill. From the 1850s, the Anglicans, too, began to register Mfengu communities. At Grahamstown, Bishop Armstrong, in co-operation with Governor Grey, set aside land and found necessary funds and staff for St Matthew's Institution. It became the principal Anglican training school for Africans in the Ciskei, with strong Mfengu membership. Soon the enterprising and adaptable Mfengu moved on to the new emerging urban centres. At Grahamstown they organized a 'Fingo Village' where Africans could own land; they travelled to Port Elizabeth where they made relatively good money as surf labourers in the harbour and established themselves as leaders in the Black urban community. They went to Humansdorp, and finally to Cape Town, where the Ndabeni Location became the home of a well-known Mfengu concentration. These centres were highly significant for the emerging Church. In them there were now Christian families and groups. New generations of ambitious Christian Mfengu were to embody Christian congregational life and education with ever-rising expectations of some degree of identification with the White Christian community. At the end of the century they were even prepared to transplant their Christian group life much further afield, when 1,000 of them moved – by train – to Bulawayo in Zimbabwe. It must be added that the scene was, after all, South Africa and that therefore, towards the end of the century some of the most vocal Mfengu wrote bitterly about 'the mounting anguish of a subject people ... of laws that oppress the black man alone ... of the imprisonment of our ministers of religion, their being arrested by the police while carrying out their duties as to the Word of the Lord'.[66]

Above all, the Mfengu story, like that of the Christianization of the Griqua, is an antidote to the prevailing idea of an exclusively individualistic transition to Christianity in Africa, as claimed by both missionary and Marxist historians. The Griqua and the Mfengu are eloquent southern examples of a *corporate* transition, a *group* movement to the Christian Church. A similar situation took place among refugee Hlubi groups, who like Mfengu had fled from the chaos of *mfecane*. The gifted Moravian missionary Heinrich Meyer and catechist Samuel Mazwi had succeeded in calling the Hlubi out from their hiding places in the grottoes of the southern Sotho mountains. These refugees were inspired to form active, self-reliant congregations. The Hlubi Chief Zibi insisted on receiving only Moravians in his country.[67]

Pondoland

Further east the Mpondo people – Xhosa-speaking – under their supreme chief Faku applied for a Methodist missionary to reside in their midst. Thomas Jenkins was to serve them for a period of more than thirty years working as Faku's amanuensis for the chief's contacts with the British authorities. Chief and community regarded him as an indispensable model of a European helper. Jenkins' successor was told by the chief to learn from Jenkins in all things: 'that I must say exactly as he says, and do exactly as he does'.[68]

The Mpondo chief himself was not prepared to consider the new message and the missionary had for his evangelistic activities to confine himself to the neighbourhood of the mission station. The few converts on the station were as a rule a 'ragtag collection of tribeless people'.[69] There were very few Mpondo among them. In the early years of the twentieth century the Mpondo chief Victor Poto and his mother joined the Methodist Church and functioned as highly esteemed local preachers.[70]

Two natural allies

The Christianization of these marginal groups, whether Gqunukwebe or Mfengu or Hlubi or Pondo, was fostered by the two natural allies of the missionaries: rain making and the Sabbath. The real measure of a missionary's usefulness was: could he bring rain? The Xhosa expected from the missionary not so much theoretical answers to academic questions, as a solution to their elemental ecological needs. That meant rain. The missionary was opposed to the traditional rain makers and therefore should surely be obliged to provide his own alternative. In the presence of Chief Pato, 1,000 of his men, and 'a considerable body of women', William Shaw was challenged by the rain maker, Gqindiwa, in a high-level debate. The Methodist missionary suggested an alternative: to set aside a whole day for fasting and prayer. Large numbers of people assembled to hear him, including the principal chiefs. Sermons and prayers followed – and rain fell! 'The clouds were rolling up from the direction of great Southern Ocean' and heavy showers poured down. That was in fact too much of a good thing. After two or three days, they asked the missionary to tell his God that they had had enough, acknowledging that this was truly 'God's Rain'. The achievement of a missionary's life and message had to be measured, at this level, in terms of his manifest favour with the Almighty.

It was thus that a mass response to the missionary's story was eventually obtained. The chief might announce 'a formal renunciation of traditional rain-makers by coming to the mission station to pray for rain'. The laborious memorizing of the Ten Commandments in the catechumens' class and the 'Three R's' at the day-school were all very well – but this was the 'real stuff'.[71] The refreshing effect of 'God's Rain' was supplemented by the missionary's water furrow and the plough. Several of the '1820 settlers', acting as local Wesleyan preachers, established themselves also as shopkeepers up-country. They had an interest of their own in helping to promote the use of ploughs. It was all part of the puritan Gospel of work, a way of life required also at the colleges. At Lovedale, under the Scot, James Stewart, all the students were obliged to toil in 'daily manual labour'. 'They are engaged in making roads, cutting water-courses, constructing dams, or at work in the fields and gardens about the place . . . Christianity and idleness are not compatible.'[72]

The Sabbath

All the British missionaries were anxious to convey to Africans the idea of observing the Sabbath. This was apparent during the course of William Shaw's activity in the 1820s, and that of another Wesleyan, William Shepstone, a decade later. In 1833, Shepstone secured a written statement from the Gqunukwebe chiefs that both they and their people would henceforth observe the Sabbath. He managed to transmit the idea of the Sabbath in an imaginative way. In the absence of church bells he and Chief Pato had the inspiration to raise white flags throughout the Gqunukwebe territory every Sunday morning, to announce its arrival.[73] Dugmore, the hymn translator, said that in 1845 Wesleyan services were held three times on Sunday, with the Sunday School also playing a vital role. He obviously had an eye for the concurrence of Gospel and trade, saying that all were 'cleanly and respectably clothed in British manufacture'.[74]

As they had done elsewhere, the Moravians built up their congregations from 'choirs', and the Methodists from 'classes'. Both types formed valuable sociological groupings for worship and education and for the communicative effect of the congregational life. For Wesleyan worship, H. H. Dugmore's contributions to the Xhosa hymn-book were of outstanding value – at least looking at hymn production from a European point of view. His songs were enthusiastically sung by generations of good Xhosa singers. Yet Ntsikana's great and original genius for creating hymns – in real Xhosa – could not but challenge all White hymn translation and expose it as only second-best.

The Anglicans

The Anglicans were comparatively late arrivals in South Africa. The first Anglican bishop of Cape Town, Robert Gray, came in 1848, and served his diocese until his death in 1872. He was a far-seeing strategist and laid solid foundations. It became clear to him that the Anglican Church must formulate its own missionary programme as soon as possible. In 1853 new bishoprics were inaugurated; Grahamstown and Natal. The former included the sensitive area of Transkei, which received independent status as a bishopric in 1873. Both Gray and the new bishop of Grahamstown, J. Armstrong, liked the idea of a 'chain' of mission stations. Gray was also impressed by the comprehensive nature of the Moravian 'institutions', providing instruction in trade, agriculture and medicine, in addition to preaching the Gospel. But his ideal was mission villages, endowed with land that might eventually be owned by Africans, rather than 'institutions'.[75]

Bishop Gray also strongly favoured the concept of elite training. Zonnebloem College in Cape Town, founded in 1858, was expressly intended 'for the sons of Native chiefs', with the first classes being held in the Bishop's own house.[76] Here Governor Sir George Grey and Bishop Robert Gray supported one another. The former occasionally brought sons of leading Xhosa chiefs to the school, and soon the horizon was widened to include sons of Zulu and Sotho chiefs. In 1860 a similar Anglican school opened at Grahamstown, although here the emphasis was more on industrial training. Bishop Gray was supported by the succeeding British Governor, the flamboyant Sir Harry Smith. When the indefatigable Bishop found himself before a gathering of thirty Xhosa chiefs at King William's Town, he received strong support from Sir Harry. The Governor explained to the chiefs

> that the great Father of the Christians – the Lord Bishop – the Chief Minister in this land, of the Church and religion of the Queen, who was appointed to teach him and all in this land the way to Heaven and to whom all the Christians looked up to as their great chief (*Inkosi Inkulu*) in religion, had ridden ninety miles ... to be present at the meeting.

Bishop Gray was aware that his Church was a new and dynamic factor in a hitherto exclusively Reformed and 'Nonconformist' South Africa. He represented the Episcopal Church, which was also the Queen's Church, and he made high claims for his organization because of its prestigious connections. He assumed that the 'Non-conformists' had been eagerly waiting for an opportunity to be incorporated into '*the Church*'. The convenient word to denote the Anglican Community in both Xhosa and Zulu languages was *iChurch* or *iShesh*. Gray went about the country, collecting other Church congregations, having been told that their members were former Anglicans who had joined these Churches when they could not find Anglican services. It was soon reported that the Anglicans were 'happily absorbing all the English religionists whatever may have been their former profession'.[77] Very little concrete is known about the worship life of Churches in the area at this time. As one would expect, it was precisely this aspect of worship which was emphasized by the Anglicans when they began to make their presence felt. On one of his first diocesan tours, Bishop Gray found one mission where 'the same room was used both for school and chapel'. This arrangement was common to all the other Churches, and remained so at the 'outstations' far into the twentieth century. Gray felt, however, that this was 'a very unfortunate and improper arrangement'. In order to teach the Africans the reverence of God 'we should be careful to distinguish God's house and make them feel the sacredness thereof.'[78]

After 1856–57, great numbers of Xhosa, survivors of the tragic cattle-killing catastrophe, came to the mission stations as refugees and beggars. An imaginative response to these needy was offered by the Anglican group at St Mark's Reserve. Here the missionary, H. T. Waters, organized relief work to alleviate the suffering and the Reserve 'became a very city of refuge for the outcast and homeless of every class'. Soon, 1,300 Africans were living at the station and the Church experienced (1858) what the enthusiastic Waters called 'a revival'. It was a haven especially for Xhosa women accused of being witches and of poisoning people.[79] Here, as in Zululand, the mission provided a sanctuary for such cases – *ukweqa*, 'to jump' [the wall] – was the term used. After this, the predominance of women in the Churches became more marked. The class of people joining in the aftermath of Xhosa wars and of the *mfecane* further north, displayed a similar pattern in all of South Africa at this time.

The schools and the 'night schools'

The missions in the Eastern Cape initiated an impressive educational advance. In Eastern Cape today there is still a dividing line between 'red' (the ochre-smeared traditionalists) and 'school' (the educated modernists). *School* was and is the Xhosa term for Christians and for good reason. Schools were the most obvious and useful contribution made by Protestant missions to this Xhosa society. Mission schools also played a role in other parts of southern Africa at this time, but this was pre-eminently so among the southern Nguni. The results were to be seen and heard in the leading intellectual families, the Sogas and the Jabavus, of the period. The elementary school and its teachers introduced new technical achievements which had been brought by the Whites. The introduction of the plough at Wesleyville caused great excitement and the anticipation of a social revolution in their midst. One of the chiefs said: 'This thing that the White have brought into the country is as good as ten wives.'[80]

The Wesleyan activity, through 'class' meetings and evening schools, had an impact far beyond their own local congregations. Among the growing numbers of students in their little night schools, were some who had come from afar, from northern Transvaal and beyond. They were seeking work in the Port Elizabeth harbour, or in Uitenhage or with other communal or private enterprises in the Eastern Cape centres. They arrived in gangs from the north and spent a year or more in the Cape. Before returning to their villages in the north they met the Christian religion. In many cases they became dedicated preachers, some already baptized, some not. There will be occasion to return to these Early Migrant Labourers as the story reaches the northern Sotho communities.

The centres of higher learning were instrumental in forming a numerically limited, highly educated class, an elite. Some of the missionaries among the Xhosa, Hlubi and particularly the Mfengu, had precisely this aim in mind. William Shaw's generation of missions did not use the term 'elite', but liked the concept, emphasizing that ambitious schools were designed for the sons of chiefs. The Watson Institution outside Grahamstown was 'established for the purpose of training young men for School Masters and Native Assistant Missionaries', with a view to creating 'a selected class of natives thereon'. These should be instructed in the 'Three R's' and the Bible, and thus equipped could go forth 'to announce to their own countrymen the glad tidings of the Gospel of Jesus Christ.'[81] The Christianized chief as agent of evangelization was an ideal not only of Cardinal Lavigerie and his White Fathers for missions in Central Africa, but also for nonconformist British preachers in the Cape.

Among the southern Nguni, great educational institutions were founded: Lovedale, on Presbyterian initiative in 1841; Healdtown, a Wesleyan Methodist centre, in 1857; and Blythswood, the Mfengu's special centre, in 1877. The college for training teachers at Lovedale provided one of the most significant opportunities for African Christians and for the formation of an educated elite among them. It was built on the site of an earlier Presbyterian mission station, opened in 1824, which had been destroyed during the Xhosa wars. Lovedale's first class of students included eleven Africans and nine Europeans, of whom seven were sons of missionaries. Its first principal was William Govan, who insisted that the college should be open to all races, that 'Blacks and Whites should meet in the same classes and dine in the same hall.' This principle was upheld for more than half a century, until social contact between the races at school was forbidden.[82] The Scottish staff at Lovedale had the admirable habit of surviving for decades. Govan was principal for thirty years, his successor James Stewart about forty years, and their colleague James Weir fifty-six years! This gave stability and continuity to the work. As early as 1878 Stewart proposed that Lovedale be developed into an African university – 'Christian in spirit, aims and teaching'.[83] Lovedale was influential also in the evolving cultural awareness of the Mfengu, whose ambition was to establish their own educational centre, 'a child of Lovedale'. After raising £4,500, a remarkable financial sacrifice on their part, they realized their dream with Blythswood Missionary Institute.

Tiyo Soga

The schools in Xhosa communities were encouraging centres of support for the Christian missions. The life of Tiyo Soga is an outstanding example of this. Coming from the family of a chief's councillor in traditional Xhosa society, he became the leading spokesman for his generation of the Christian vision for his people.

When William Govan of Lovedale returned to his native Scotland for a visit in 1846, he took with him a Xhosa student, Tiyo Soga (d. 1871). This gifted young man stayed for about a decade in Scotland where he completed his theological studies. He was baptized and ordained there – the first Black South African to be ordained – and he married a Scot. When he returned to his homeland, he found his people writhing in the aftermath of the cattle-killing tragedy of 1856–57. This national calamity made him all the more determined to devote his energies to the reconstruction of Xhosa society on Christian foundations.[84]

Tiyo Soga is significant from many points of view. First, it was claimed in his time and echoed on countless occasions in South Africa after him, that Africans needed generations and centuries to attain 'civilization' and a real understanding of the Christian message. His record refutes this argument. After his return to South Africa in 1857, Soga preached to a British congregation in Grahamstown which included the Lieutenant-Governor and his staff. Highly impressed, His Excellency asked the staff why none of his military chaplains could preach as well as this African pastor, and received the reassuring answer: 'Your Excellency, the sermon is a borrowed one!' 'Oh, indeed', replied the Governor, 'then that makes all the difference in the world.'[85] The idea that any African preacher and Soga in particular, would resort to cribbing his message from somebody else needs no comment here. Second, more than any other African, he represents the great Lovedale tradition in South African Church history, for it was at this school that untold African intellectuals and spiritual leaders were trained. Born near the Chumie Presbyterian mission, Soga was one of the first Africans to attend Lovedale. He was later a highly respected member of the team that worked on the revised translation of the Xhosa New Testament. Third, Tiyo Soga is also significant because he is one of the few African Christians in nineteenth-century South Africa whose personality we can know to any considerable extent. The generous extracts from his 'Journal' in John A. Chalmers' book, introduce the reader to a pastor deeply aware of the Christian struggle. He wrote in 1863:

> I cannot tell what keeps me from God and Christ ... Should I be a spotless salt before I come to Thee to be saved? I know and feel that I cannot save my soul, do what I will but why then not believe in a salvation wrought out for me by the mercy of God ... Preached fluently and with apparent interest from Matthew 1:21. In recording this, I behold my shame and folly ... I have to complain of one grand defect in my character – irresolution ... I have to lament my deadness and hardness of heart ... O God, by Thy Spirit move me, and Thou shall have the entire glory. Lord look upon my soul ...[86]

Fourth and finally, as the son of Chief Sandile's trusted councillor, Soga had an effective knowledge of the Xhosa language and culture. This enabled him to create beautiful Xhosa hymns, reminding one of the infinite potential of the African in society and in the Church, if only given an opportunity.[87]

The William Taylor revival

In comparison with the adaptable Mfengu and the Gqunukwebe, traditional Xhosa communities were largely hostile to the missionaries' advances. Bishop William Taylor, a dynamic representative of the Methodist Episcopal Church of America, came to the Xhosa in 1866. He found them utterly dejected, deceived in their tragic and massive acceptance of a 'special millennium'; beaten by the British and forced from their lands and reduced to starvation by their own credulity. In a seemingly hopeless situation, they were primed for Taylor's message of hope. His interpretation of the Bible viewed the world in a post-millennial, though optimistic perspective. He invited his listeners to look for 'the mellow light of millennial glory reposing on the tops of the mountains.'[88] His preaching stimulated a 'revivalist' type of response from the Xhosa, on a scale never seen before among the Bantu-speaking peoples. They gave vent to ecstatic emotionalism, found previously only among the Khoi. Whites and Blacks alike were roused by the challenge of his message and surrendered to it by their hundreds. Along the coast, from Cape Town to Durban, from one Wesleyan Methodist chapel to another, the revivalist campaign went marching on triumphantly.

The most dramatic breakthrough occurred only a few weeks after the beginning of the talks near King William's Town. It was there that Charles Pamla joined Taylor's team. In discovering Pamla, whose abilities qualified him as the ideal interpreter, Taylor gave new impetus to the call for African leadership in the Churches. This young preacher, one of four preparing to be 'received on trial' [ordained], may have come from Natal, since Taylor referred to him as a 'Zulu'. The way in which he conveyed Taylor's thoughts to the audience drew attention to an aspect almost overlooked until then: the central importance of the interpreter in the Church's work. The Taylor 'revival' was a turning point for the rapidly growing cadre of Wesleyan local preachers. Charles Pamla showed what an African pastor could do if given the opportunity.

NORTHERN NGUNI

The Zulu

Cape Nguni and Sotho chiefs thought it a matter of prestige to have their own 'court chaplain' and certain Tswana chiefs discovered what was called 'a mystical logic' in connection with the missionary: it was claimed that no ethnic community which had a missionary in its midst had ever lost a war. An impression of amiable peacefulness and friendly benevolence is thus conveyed. But Zulu royalty were different. The Zulu had never lost a war and considered themselves invincible. They were proud men and their followers displayed a decidedly negative reaction to the missionary's invitation: 'I am the King's man'. It was true that from 1837–38 King Dingane used Francis Owen, a Church Missionary Society missionary, to write documents to Piet Retief on the King's behalf, during that most dramatic period of nineteenth-century South Africa, when the Voorbrekkers sought to enter Zululand and were then massacred on Matiwane's Hill – later avenged in December 1838 at the Battle of Blood River. Dingane also showed deference to the Sabbath law. However, apart from those concessions, Dingane would have nothing to do with missionaries. He had been warned by his African interpreter from the Cape Colony, Jacob Sembite, that the Whites were only after his land. Dingane's brother and successor, Mpande, was more accommodating to the missionaries and several won his favour with varying degrees of success.[89]

The Zulu-speaking region was divided into two different political spheres: the Zulu kingdom north of the river Tugela, ruled by Shaka's successors: Dingane 1828–40, Mpande 1840–73, Cetshwayo 1872–84 and Dinuzulu 1884–1934, and Natal, the emerging British colony, formed in 1843 with a European population of Britons and Boers, an overspill into Natal of some 100,000 Africans with experience of *mfecane* horrors and, from 1860 onwards an imported Asian labour population. A pressing problem was that of administering the African population in the colony. Sir Theophilus Shepstone – himself the son of one of the Cape Wesleyan missionaries from the 1820's – became Secretary for Native Affairs, the first in a long series of civil servants in South Africa who were sons of missionaries. He dominated the Natal Commission of African affairs. 'Locations' or 'reserves' became the formula for areas of African settlement, with headmen and chiefs functioning at the side of European magistrates: an early expression of what later, in British West and East Africa, was to be known as 'Indirect Rule'.

A measure of the British Government's recognition of missionary expertise is illustrated by the composition of the Natal Native Commission of 1846–47. Two American Board missionaries, Adams and Lindley, were called to serve on the commission to lay the foundations of a Natal 'locations' system. Their plan, later modified, by 1864 included 42 'locations' with a total of two million acres and twenty-one 'mission reserves' totalling about 175,000 acres.[90] The mission reserves varied in size from 5,500 to 13,000 acres. At the time it seemed to offer a positive solution for landless Africans, particularly as the practical Americans introduced a great number of ploughs. This also implied a social revolution here: traditional division of labour between men and women was changed. Ploughs were drawn by oxen – and these had to be handled by men. At times it did, however, cause tensions between missions and African tenants. The American Board in particular with its mission reserve at Inanda, north of Durban, increasingly felt its role as landlords to be an embarrassing problem.

The American Board

Founded in Boston in 1810, the American Board of Commissioners for Foreign Missions at first sent its missionaries to Asia and the Near East. In 1834 the Board sent a team of outstanding missionaries to Natal including Newton Adams, Aladin Grout and Daniel Lindley. They were to transfer into Natal a daring missionary strategy, propounded by the great Boston planner, Rufus Anderson and after him by Nathaniel Clark. Their hope was to convert the whole Zulu nation in one generation.[91] The Congregationalist American Board functioned as a pioneering catalytic body in Natal, similar to the Congregational LMS in the Cape and in Imerina country, Madagascar.

Grout was delegated by his colleagues to visit King Mpande. The king welcomed him and invited him to build a station anywhere he liked. Grout began the Inkanyezi mission near the Zulu capital of Empangeni. The people soon found that he had a special powerful gifts. He could bring rain – and they discovered the secret: one Sunday he appeared in a long black coat and sure enough, it rained! But the king soon lost patience with the White man, and Grout found it advisable to retire to Natal. The situation was so tense that in 1843 the Boston mission authorities decided to recall their men, although they reversed the order not long afterwards, concentrating on Natal and leaving Zululand to others. While African Church work in Natal had hardly begun prior to 1850, the American Board's Inanda station established a Church structure of its own as early as 1849. It was constituted according to Congregational principles and had nine charter members, including their American pastor, Daniel Lindley. Dalida Dube, widow of a chief, was a trusted member, an early representative of the strong feminine strand in the Zulu Church. Her son, James Dube, was a well-known preacher, and her grandson, the Revd Dr John L. Dube, was an internationally respected educator.

Lindley's Boston Congregational background was reflected in one of his statements: 'We persuade men to become Christians, but none to join the Church'. In 1864 the first General Meeting of its members from various stations took place at Inanda. This *Isikhumbuzelo*, with 400 delegates attending, was an example of Rufus Anderson's (and Henry Venn's) formula, 'Self-governing, self-supporting, and self-propagating Church'. This goal grew even more radical when Nathaniel Clark, Anderson's successor, stated that the missionaries had no authority over the native Churches.[92] Of course this declaration was not readily acceptable to the men in the field. The Boston Congregationalists were fifty years ahead of their colleagues in Natal on this issue. But it was a policy which made the American mission more open to 'Ethiopian' pressures than any other mission in Natal. The first part of the 1860s was a boom period in Natal, with the cultivation of sugar a great factor in the economy. Asian labourers came from India to work in the sugar industry. Some educated Africans, particularly those connected with the progressive American Board, became comparatively wealthy sugar farmers. Ira Adams Nembula was faced with a choice between his sugar mill and the invitation to be ordained as a Congregational minister – and he chose sugar. The economy of the colony soared, until 1865, when slump and depression hit, a painful illustration of the dependence of local prices on the world economy.

Schreuder and the Norwegians

In 1845 a forthright young Norwegian Lutheran, H. P. S. Schreuder – who in 1866 was consecrated bishop – made his first visit to King Mpande.[93] His approach was blunt: he brought, he said, a message from the King of Kings and the Lord of Lords. A people which accepted this message would live happily in the land. A people which obstinately rejected such an invitation must perish. 'If they persisted, they would be torn from their land, and it would be given to others'.[94] Four years later Schreuder returned to Mpande. The king had been hit by an attack of gout and one of his sub-chiefs suggested that they call on Schreuder and his medicine pots for help. The missionary came and after ten days of treatment, the pain subsided. Now the king was anxious to have the missionary stay as close to him as possible, in case the royal ailment would return. Schreuder's strategy aimed at succeeding where the Americans had failed, by converting an entire independent African nation. Whereas the Americans had at first turned from Zululand to Natal, Schreuder insisted on going straight into the lion's den.[95]

The most original attempt on Schreuder's side was his *kholwa–konza* (Christian loyalty to the king) concept characteristically related to his approach to the Zulu *nation* as such. Schreuder's concern was with the role of the Christian converts within the Zulu society. They must not be seen as standing outside Zulu society but as part of it, accepted as the king's subjects on a par with other Zulu citizens. They should do any job ordered by the king, even participating in war, thus being soldiers in famous Zulu regiments, when commanded by the king to do so. This was to aim very far, but Mpande and Cetshwayo would not hear of it. Their fear was that such a Christian group might turn out to be a hotbed of opposition. Zulu men and soldiers could not become Christian believers – and that was that. Schreuder's next move, in 1869, was to suggest that his Zulu converts form a deputation to the king with the bishop as a partner. This time Cetshwayo, to their satisfaction, seemed to be more open to their suggestion. A compromise was arrived at according to which Christian Zulu could be used for ploughing and for building modern houses, but in that kind of world any compromise produced its own difficulties. This happened at Empangeni. Daniel, the leading Christian in the place followed the *konza* (regimental royal service) line and did so to such a degree that he increasingly became part of the king's guard. The result was that the Empangeni congregation followed him and in 1872 the missionary found himself left alone on the station – 'a missionary without a congregation'.

Throughout all the vicissitudes of civil war within the Zulu royal house itself Schreuder showed persistent loyalty to the national Zulu authority. However, in the end even he was to find this standpoint untenable. Twenty years of frustration led him to change sides to a 'more humane form of government'. This unfortunately meant war against the Zulu king, and the Anglo–Zulu war of 1879 meant the end: Cetshwayo was captured and in 1879 taken as prisoner to Cape Town. Zululand was divided into thirteen chieftaincies. Later, after the rebellion of 1906, Dinuzulu was sent to St Helena. The change of sides against Zulu power was typical of the great majority of the missionaries, the only die-hard being the Anglican Bishop Colenso in Pietermaritzburg, who remained loyal to Zulu power until the end, against his own British government, as he also did later on with regard to Langilibalele's Hlubi. In the case of the Xhosa in the Cape the self-inflicted catastrophe of 1856 meant the end of open resistance and substantially improved opportunities for presenting the Christian message. Twenty years later it was the Zulu's turn. With Cetshwayo and Dinuzulu both deported and the country divided into numerous small units, Zulu resistance was also broken by harsh measures. Here too an opportunity was now presented for the message of the Prince of Peace, although the message of salvation and new life was to be formulated and lived out in an imperialist age.

Zululand and Natal

Resistance to the White man's religion was stubborn and unyielding, directed by king, medicine men and witch-finders. These latter suggested that the missionary prepared harmful medicines used in making good and noble Zulu into converts. The missionary himself was surely an *umthakathi*, a witch. Any sign that a young man wished to follow his teachings was cruelly punished. The mission station soon served as a refuge, and young girls faced with enforced marriage to some old polygamist would seek sanctuary there. In the southern parts of Zululand, girls would cross the Tugela River, hoping to find freedom and a new future on the other side.

There were a number of complex causes for Zulu attitudes to evangelism. Norman Etherington has disclaimed the 'one-cause' explanation suggesting that 'if only chiefdom or "witchdoctors" or bride price or polygyny could be outlawed, resistance would crumble. But evidence provided by the missionaries themselves refutes each of these explanations.'[96]

Visible results of the evangelistic work in Zululand were discouragingly slow to appear. It took fourteen years before the Norwegians could baptize their first convert. Only social outsiders, despised by the rest of Zulu society, could consider turning to Christianity with impunity. The first ones to accept the new faith were 'marginal' people of various kinds: Sotho refugees on a Boer farm near the Berlin Emaus station, or four *Oorlamse* (Coloured families) at Hermannsburg.[97] Etherington has shown the strikingly alien origin of the first converts. He claims that 46 per cent came from other political units than the area of a particular mission station. 'The Methodist group included the highest percentage of aliens, 70 per cent and the American group the lowest, 31 per cent.'[98] Regular evangelistic visits in Zululand to the *kraals* by the missionary were out of the question. Instead, potential converts were sought among labourers building the new mission stations, as at Hermannsburg.

Two German missions: Hermannsburg and Berlin

The Hermannsburg Lutherans arriving in Durban included ordained missionaries together with devoted Christian farmers, according to the Hermannsburg programme of forming 'Christian colonies'. Berlin and Hermannsburg Lutherans arrived in Natal in 1854. By 1861 the latter had built up a community of about ninety Christians (of whom sixty-two were White). Each of these Germans had his own practical skill to contribute to the common task: there were tailors, shoemakers, carpenters, joiners, masons, cartwrights and one miller. By 1861 they had already built twenty houses of varying sizes. There was also a church, measuring forty by twenty-six feet, with a 'confessional' room. The Berliners had a flexible and enterprising leader in Carl Posselt. He took his own initiatives. 'Despite admonitions from Berlin to convert whole tribes rather than individuals, Posselt gathered converts when and where he could find them ... By making land and security available to all comers, the small Berlin contingent in Natal made more converts before 1880 than did the elaborately equipped Americans.'[99] In 1860 the Germans had already founded twenty-four mission stations, eight in Natal, six in northern and four in southern Zululand, together with six stations among the Tswana; and altogether had 282 baptized Christians.

Allison and the Methodists

One can never sufficiently emphasize the role of the *mfecane* upheaval for the conditions of missions in this area. To their surprise the Zulu found increasing numbers of young foreigners coming from the north into southern Natal. Among these, the Methodist missionary James Allison's Swazi and Zulu Christians composed the largest and most powerful group entering the Zulu-speaking area. To follow Allison in his varied activities after his arrival with the 1820 settlers, one must draw a bold perimeter across the whole of turbulent South Africa. He began by starting a hat factory in Namaqualand! Then in the Transorangia High Veld at Ficksburg 1832–42, he experienced the *mfecane* upheaval and he enlisted some who went with him to Swaziland and southern Natal. Of these, some were Swazi or Hlubi, all the more eager to bring the Gospel to their home areas.

Allison had to learn patience in his pastoral career. With the virtue of patience, he could appreciate all the more the privilege which had come to him and his listeners of sharing in the transforming spiritual revival at Imparani, Transvaal, from about 1838. This awakening, involving

Mantatees, Hlubi and some fugitive Swazi who became Allison's devoted supporters and voluntary preachers was born out of a search for order and a future in a world of chaos and despair, and was to have far-reaching effects. William Shaw, the Wesleyan strategist, realized Allison's worth and suggested in 1844 that he be sent to Swaziland. After an initial visit in 1844, Allison moved in 1845 from his station near Thaba Nchu in Orange Free State to Mahamba, southern Swaziland. He took with him about thirty people, including four teachers, some with a Swazi background. Very soon the Christian influence at Mahamba was so strong that the Swazi king suspected political intrigue. By 1846, Allison and his emerging Christian refugee community of 450 had to flee for their lives, moving from Swaziland to Indaleni in southern Natal. The majority of the refugees were as yet traditionalists in religion, but included sixty baptized and ten 'on trial'.

A methodological point should be emphasized here. In Allison's case we deal with a missionary whose endeavours can be followed in some detail, as the result of admirable research.[100] The extant handbook often gives the erroneous impression that it concerned some individual missionary daringly striking out on his own. Allison's movements from Orange Free State to Swaziland to Natal exemplify the vital point which must again be emphasized – the spread of the Gospel due to the effort of *groups* of people, already influenced by Christianity and as a group prepared to carry it to others.

Allison's Methodist group arrived in southern Natal at the time of an expanding economy, with a need for African labour in railway construction and on sugar plantations. Labour gangs as well as individuals from Transvaal or further afield found their way to Pietermaritzburg and Allison's Indaleni. Allison was a resourceful Methodist with a remarkable gift for making contacts with all Africans, not only with the Zulu. Dr Sheila Hindson's research has uncovered certain salient facts about this refugee 'family' of Allison's. Job Khambule, a Hlubi, had been with the missionary since the Orange Free State days. So had the Swazi brothers, Daniel and Ezra Msimang. They were part of the nucleus of leaders forming a Christian household at Indaleni, near the present-day town of Richmond.

In his report to the Lieutenant-Governor of Natal, Allison speaks of his 'household' at Indaleni:

> I have, your Honour, a village, built after the manner of Europeans by the natives under my pastoral care. I have also a Christian Church there, consisting of 103 members. I have 23 native youths residing in my family, to whom I devote my special attention, giving them daily instruction in religion,

> the arts [he refers to the training of artisans], agriculture etc. Mrs. Allison conducts a girls' school of industry, consisting of 32 native girls, who are taught with a view to their becoming suitable wives to the youths above named.

The missionary was not only a pastor and teacher but a 'father'. A few years later, when the group left Indaleni for Edendale near Pietermaritzburg, the ethos of the community changed from a 'household' to a 'school', with a less family-centred atmosphere.

Allison's move from Indaleni was related to the Wesleyan Methodist iron law that after five years of service, a minister should expect transfer to some other congregation in the 'district'. This arrangement may have had its wholesome effects but the number of crises in connection with its implementation – not least with regard to African ministers in other parts of the continent – shows that it could also have its less desirable consequences. Allison refused the Synod's order to move and, for other reasons of principle also, left the Wesleyan Methodists. (Later, in 1867, he joined the Presbyterian Church.) When Allison eventually left Indaleni, his congregation decided to go with him, and bought Edendale, a farm near Pietermaritzburg. There 100 families, with about 450 people, bought their own individual allotments. The Wesleyan Methodist village with its square houses and artisan workshops resembled a British village. Here the community was an indication of the role of primary education for the Christian congregation. Just as among the southern Nguni, the Zulu *isikole* was generally used as the word for 'Church' in Natal and Zululand. The ever-resourceful Allison organized night schools for Africans at Pietermaritzburg. They were also to play an astonishing role for labourers coming from Venda and elsewhere in northern Transvaal in search of work.

During Natal's economic crisis of 1865, the Africans blamed individual ownership of farms for their sudden financial plight. In 1867–70 about thirty-five Edendale families decided to move again, buying a farm of their own, Driefontein near Ladysmith, for £1,000. It was soon enlarged by the purchase of other adjacent farms, in the end comprising 36,000 acres, altogether bought for £9,000. The families insisted that sale of individual plots was to be prohibited. Economic factors were thus mixed with religious considerations for the move to Driefontein. Land had suddenly – and tragically – become the one great need for the Zulu and Allison was a good adviser on this vital point.[101] In time, some African farmers became relatively wealthy cattle-dealers and, as Driefontein was advantageously placed on the main route between Natal and the High Veld, some took up a profitable occupation as wagon-carriers. More than any other settlement of this kind in nineteenth-century southern Africa, Driefontein was crucial in liberating both individual and corporate initiative. This assuredly was the result of the sense of responsibility which the Wesleyan organization developed in its local preachers. The chapel, its Wesleyan religious life, and its educational ambitions were the community's pulse. A number of the farmers were also local preachers and some were eventually ordained. Among the leaders were Job Khambule, the Hlubi convert from Allison's early days on the High Veld; Johannes Khumalo, one of the headmen at Edendale who became the Christian chief at Driefontein; and Daniel Msimang, the gifted and fiery Swazi preacher. After Allison's death, Msimang returned to his home at Mahamba in Swaziland, the centre of Swazi Methodism.

In Daniel Msimang, the Swazi met a new kind of African. Here was a Swazi with a new identity, wide experience, with Christian education through challenging experiences at Imparene, Pietermaritzburg and Driefontein and with the skills of an enterprising Wesleyan organizer and devoted preacher. He had played a great part in the penetration of Christianity into the life of Zulu-speaking Natal. Not only the Swazi and Zulu listened to him. Boer farmers, who had just begun working the good soil of Swaziland, also came to hear his sermons at Mahamba. Msimang and his colleagues were influenced by the William Taylor movement. But the 'new wave of life' in the Wesleyan Methodist Church from about 1874, *Unzondelelo*, was a genuinely African spiritual break-through. In consequence, the leaders at Driefontein insisted on an African ministry. Msimang conceived the character of the new movement:

> We heard the cries of those who want to be saved. From every side came the testimony ... We felt that we ought to send people to them that their sins might be taken away ... The Ministers asked us if we wanted a Native training institution. Our reply was, 'We know nothing about an institution. We have a wound in our hearts. What can we do to help our people to the Gospel?'[102]

At the outset, the missionaries had their apprehensions about the possible separatist tendencies of the *Unzondelelo*. In 1878, however, the movement received the approval of the Church authorities.

The Driefontein story provides an eloquent illustration of the importance of the refugee and the early migrant labour factors in the Christianization of Africa. The Swazi refugee group of 450 established itself as a modernizing elite, inspired by Wesleyan piety; and Allison's night schools were a lighthouse for labourers who came as foreigners from the north of

Transvaal. Above all this is a story of African initiative and enterprise. The great contribution of Allison and of his co-workers was the education of future African churchmen from a very wide catchment area. Something in Allison's personality and message had a catalytic effect on his co-workers and listeners.[103]

It was in these progressive parishes – Congregationalists on the coast and the Wesleyan Methodists up-country at Driefontein that the idea of 'exemption' became an increasing concern. Under Shepstone's direction, a law of 1864 allowed Africans exemption from Native Law, but only on certain conditions and with infinite restrictions. Such Africans, and only substantial property-holders were envisaged, were to be treated 'for some, but by no means all, purposes as Europeans'.[104] After thirty-nine years, only three Africans in Natal and Zululand possessed exemption to such an extent that they could vote! It was obviously an alluring carrot held before ambitious Blacks, but remained a chimera.

Bishop Colenso

The most astonishing and challenging chapter in the history of the Anglican church in southern Africa was that of John William Colenso, Bishop of Natal from 1853 until his death in 1883. He was probably the most controversial Anglican clergyman of his generation. Though an enterprising and imaginative administrator, he still found time for writing; his literary endeavours represent an enormous output. His studies on the Pentateuch, amounting to seven large volumes (altogether about 3,000 pages) caused a sensation similar to the stir caused in the 1960s by Bishop Robinson's *Honest to God*. Inspired by writings of German scholars, Colenso began to have doubts about the literal infallibility of the Bible. His research became more critical through contact with Zulu Christians. William Ngidi, a catechist assisting him with translation of the Bible into Zulu, asked astonished questions about Noah's Ark. He wondered whether the Ark, with those relatively limited measurements, could really have contained so many animals.[105]

Colenso's discussions with Ngidi are an example of the rewarding 'give and take' of a first-generation missionary's relation with his interpreter, a factor often overlooked. Largely as a result of these conversations, Colenso adopted a 'liberal' view of the Old Testament books. He expressed a similarly controversial view on Atonement in his commentary on Romans. Bishop Gray in Cape Town went so far as to issue a sentence of excommunication against Colenso. However, the Privy Council in London, to which Colenso appealed, ruled that in South Africa, where the Anglican

Church was not an established institution, the Bishop of Cape Town had no legal authority over the Bishop in Natal.

Bishop Colenso's mission strategy was to concentrate his limited staff at his headquarters at Ekukhanyeni near Pietermaritzburg. He operated from there, but seemed to be on the move all the time: among Zulu royalty, British government officials and the ordinary people. Among the Africans, Colenso was respected for his skill as a Zulu linguist and his sympathetic understanding of Zulu culture. He wanted Zulu traditions to be preserved as much as possible. His view contrasted sharply and refreshingly with that of his colleague, Bishop Armstrong of Grahamstown. Both men were appointed to their episcopal tasks in South Africa in 1853. Armstrong thought he knew that Africans 'are without God, true or false. They have no worship whatever.'[106] When translating the Bible, Colenso searched for a genuinely Zulu name for God; he eventually discarded the Khoi word *uThixo* in favour of *uNkhulukhulu*. His strategy of evangelism was the familiar one of starting with the Zulu chiefs, then through them reaching their people. That was why, similar to his great opponent Bishop Gray of Cape Town, he began a school for the sons of chiefs.

Colenso's policies on matters of Church discipline were as controversial as his exegetical views. He maintained that it was right for polygamists to be baptized, knowing that on this difficult issue he was supported by at least some of the Moravian missionaries. Towards the end of his career, he defended without hesitation African interests in two legal cases involving the Zulu Paramount Chief, Cetshwayo and the Hlubi Chief Langilibalele. Like his Wesleyan Methodist neighbour Allison, at Pietermaritzburg, he helped Zulus buy fertile land.[107] He was the first of many Anglican bishops to take a resolute stand on behalf of oppressed Africans. The Colenso era was a painful process, not only for his own diocese of Natal, but also for Bishop Gray and the emerging Anglican province as a whole. The first Lambeth conference of Anglican bishops, 1867, was called together in order to consider the Church's attitude to 'the Colenso affair'. Yet, with the benefit of hindsight, this struggle can be seen to have helped to define the distinct profile of the Anglican province. While pursuing Colenso's fight for social and political justice, they insisted on a Catholic ethos in matters of Church life and polity.[108]

Catholics on the move

Brief reference must be made here to the Catholic beginnings among the Zulu. In 1852 the French order of the Oblates of Mary Immaculate arrived in Natal, exploring the possibilities. The Oblates seemed to have failed in Natal. After years of vain attempts to reach the Zulu, they decided to leave an unpromising field, to the great disappointment of their mission director, Bishop de Mazenod in Marseilles. They turned instead to Lesotho to find there all the more remarkable results.

In the meantime, however, something altogether unforeseen happened on the Natal coast, the beginnings of what later became of great consequence for the heritage of the Catholic Church in Zululand. This provides another telling illustration of what has become the thesis of this book: the role of African initiative, a development brought out recently by an article by Professor G. C. Oosthuizen.[109] He refers to 'Zanzibaris', called thus but in fact being Makua and comparable communities from northern Mozambique, enslaved on the coast and brought in chains on board slaveships, liberated in Zanzibari waters by British warships, and then taken to Natal. (At the same time there were other Makua sold as slaves to buyers on the eastern shore of Madagascar.)

In the present state of research it is not possible to know the exact numbers of these 'Zanzibaris'. In Natal they gathered in two communities on the outskirts of the rapidly growing seaport of Durban. They found a leader in one of their own crowd, with a Portuguese name, Saturnino do Vallo. He had been instructed in the 'Three R's' by a Portuguese farmer and was able to act as a voluntary catechist. On Sundays the 'Zanzibaris' would row across the bay to mass in Durban. There was an atmosphere of freedom in these two communities, in the festivities celebrated at St Xavier: mass with joyful processions, the excitement of boat trips across the bay with banners unfurled and after religious services pleasant informal picnics. Here they were in the 1870s and 1880s, a cluster of uprooted people far away from their own home communities and all the more prepared to respond expectantly to an invitation to join a new community with its religious assurances. They were in a singularly good position to act as stepping stones of evangelistic contacts to recalcitrant Zulu society.

Zulu hopes shattered

On the way from the Boer War to the First World War one meets with ominous dates in South African history: the Zulu Rebellion of 1906 and the Natives Land Act of 1913. The Zulu Rebellion is a complex story with Mission converts fighting on both sides of the revolt, on that of the Government and on that of the rebels. The story has been analyzed and interpreted in a rich study by Professor Shula Marks.[110] Altogether some

3,000 Africans and thirty Europeans were killed in the conflict, related to the introduction of a new Poll Tax and other administrative measures.

The Zulu Rebellion is significant also as a measure of European attitudes to African Christians. The Governor of Natal took the lead in attributing the conflict to the Christian *kolwa*: 'the *kolwa* as *kolwas* were behind the rebellion', he proclaimed with gubernatorial pomposity. Especially frightening were European speculations on the supposed role of the 'Independents'. 'The Ethiopian scare' was particularly inflammable in the Natal province. The fact is that the preachers accompanying the rebels into the field were preaching and praying to Almighty God on behalf of the troops. One of the great chiefs in southern Natal, Messeni Qwabe, was accompanied by a 'black-hatted, white-chokered figure with a prayer book in his hands which roused particularly angry emotions' amongst the Whites.[111] Although this preacher has remained anonymous, we make a bold but, we think, informed guess about his identity, so close to Messeni Qwabe: he was none other than the prophet Isaiah Shembe himself.[112]

The great and tragic drama from the point of all Africans, but more particularly from that of the Christian African elite, was in those years related to *land*, the precious land which they, enterprising African communities, had developed by concerted efforts. Wesleyan Methodist Driefontein was one such community. The other were the sugar-producing farms on the coast, worked by American Board Congregationalists at Groutville, Verulam and elsewhere. In the long run the Natives Land Act of 1913 made all these efforts in vain, doomed to becoming 'Black Spots in White Areas' and 'particularly in the midlands, peasants became serfs'.[113]

LESOTHO

From Zululand to Lesotho: the difference in the roles of the respective paramount kings could hardly have been greater. They represented 'two diametrically different types of states': Shaka 'ruled by fear', Moshoeshoe 'by consent'. The attitudes of the two rulers to the challenge of the new religion were also different. To the Zulu king the issue was not worthy of the attention of his full-blooded warriors. The Sotho leader, in contrast, showed keen interest.[114] A central role in encouraging the spread of Christianity in the country was played by Moshoeshoe the gatherer and leader of the Sotho people for many decades of the nineteenth century. In his youth he had been influenced by one of the most attractive personalities of traditional Sotho society, Mohlomi, a visionary, doctor, diviner and rain maker. About 1824, after being attacked by the Tlokwa from the north,

Moshoeshoe moved his headquarters to Thaba Boisu, an inaccessible mountain refuge. His precarious position made him interested in reports he heard of White foreigners who might come to his aid. A favourable impression was made on him by a Christian Griqua hunter, Adam Krotz, who told the king about services which the strangers had rendered the Griqua. Consequently, Moshoeshoe sent Sotho messengers with gifts of cattle to the missionaries at Griquatown and Philippolis to persuade them to visit him.[115]

At Philippolis news of the Sotho deputation reached three young missionaries of the Paris Evangelical Mission who had recently arrived in South Africa: Thomas Arbousset, Eugène Casalis and Constant Gosselin. These new arrivals were the product of a French Protestant revival movement. Their mission to the Sotho began auspiciously with a warm greeting from Moshoeshoe – forty-seven years old at the time – when they arrived at Thaba Boisu in 1833. An important fact for the understanding of Christian beginnings in any African locality and which will be seen in even sharper relief when approaching conditions among the northern Sotho, can be noted in the case of the Southern Sotho. These first missionaries arriving in 1833 were not the first Christians to appear among the Sotho. There were in fact two different categories of Sotho Christians who had already been influenced by the new religion when abroad, far from home.

Casalis noticed that the first Sotho Christians had already come into contact with Christianity 'as servants in the Colony [of the Cape]'. These young men may or may not have been baptized in the Cape Colony, but on their return they informed clan brothers and tribesmen at large of the new religion.[116] There was also a gathered Christian Sotho community, Sotho returnees from abroad, who settled within the borders of Moshoeshoe's country and they formed the nucleus of the new mission station where they were settled, Beersheba. Here again one sees the Griqua influence. In 1833 Moshoeshoe asked the Griqua chief, Andries Waterboer, placed at Griquatown, that Sotho refugees – dispersed through the *mfecane* – should be allowed to return peacefully to their home country. Moffat estimated their number at 100, of whom thirty-three were Church members and he realized the implication: 'This measure cannot fail of being an important acquisition to the French missionaries as nearly all of them were able to read in their own languages.'[117]

The French missionaries' activity in Lesotho can be divided into a first period of initial influence (1833–48), a brief period of pagan reaction (1848–54), and finally a period of long-term steady growth (1854–1900). Any success the missionaries enjoyed was very much a consequence of their relationship with the king. Eugène Casalis became the king's close friend and adviser. 'In African terms, Casalis was a royal councillor with special qualifications; in European terms, he was the secretary for foreign affairs.' There developed between the king and Casalis a friendship which reminds one of some of the other well-known relationships in African mission history, that of the Ndebele's Mzilikazi with Robert Moffat and of the Bemba's Mwamba with Bishop Dupont of the White Fathers. When Casalis returned to Paris, Moshoeshoe thanked him in glowing terms: 'Oh Casalis, you are my teacher, my father, my mother ... You are a true MoSotho.'[118] Hence, thanks to royal patronage, the missionaries were allowed to start their work. Only a few days after their arrival, they were granted a site for a mission station called Morija. Moshoeshoe was greatly interested in the foreigners' teaching and preaching. He regularly attended religious services, adding his own comments at the end of a sermon and recommending its message to the congregation.[119]

Significantly, it was the Old Testament which most attracted the king's interest. In 1837 he was heard by one of the missionaries to pray publicly to Jehovah, asking him to forgive him his sins and to convert him and his wives, his children and mother and all his people. Moshoeshoe repeated this public request in 1841. Even though the king himself did not become a Christian, he allowed his second son, Molapo, to be educated and baptized.[120] The first Church decade in Lesotho was closely linked with royalty and with people of high rank. It was an elitist movement. At the first baptism, at Christmas 1839, four of Moshoeshoe's sons with wives were baptized as well as several other of his sons, his uncle Libe, leading councillors and the three most senior of his surviving wives. Some of the conversions during these first years were dramatic; that of Tsiame, one of Moshoeshoe's half-brothers, provides an example. Although he received instruction at Morija, having been influenced by a local Christian revival he used his new knowledge to oppose the Church at every opportunity. One day, however, he appeared at a service pale and shaking. He declared in a loud voice that his previous behaviour had only been a front to hide his true feelings and that he now felt bound to follow the divine call.[121] Even in Church, royalty had to be treated differently from ordinary folks. Moshoeshoe's senior surviving wife, in a delirium caused by measles, threw herself to her death over a cliff and her own Fokeng clan claimed the right to bury her with traditional rites, including the parade of 1,000 cattle to honour the deceased. But Moshoeshoe called Casalis and persuaded him to give her a Christian burial, in the Christian cemetery. The king added that, although not a convert himself, he wanted to be buried according to Christian rites.[122]

The missionaries endeared themselves to Moshoeshoe above all by introducing instruments of modern agricultural technology into Lesotho society and by building mission stations. The mission stations fitted well with the king's strategic ideas for the extension of his own territorial authority. Besides Morija, two further stations were established to the south-west on the Caledon River at Bethulie (1833) and Beersheba (1835). They formed barriers against the incursions of Griqua raiders from the west. The station built at Mekoatling in the north-west in 1837 could be seen as a protection against Moshoeshoe's old enemy, the Tlokoa. Refugees from displaced Tswana and Sotho communities congregated around the stations. By 1847 a total of nine stations had been built. The new missions on the edges of Moshoeshoe's territory were well-endowed with ploughs, wagons and stone houses as proofs of the effects of civilization; in this respect they served as models for the rest of the Sotho community. They were, however, more than centres for modernising influences. They were a refuge for harassed and endangered people. In the first hymns produced by their Pietistic French missionaries the Sotho found expressions for their new faith. No idea was more popular than that of the Church – and the mission station – as a 'hiding place', a haven of refuge:

Seforo ke se fumane
I have found a haven
A place of constant hiding.[123]

Prophets and prophetesses were a significant accompaniment to the psychological crisis to which the new faith would sometimes lead. Ana Maketha Mantsupa, niece of Mohlomi and thus well known to Moshoeshoe himself, received revelations well before the arrival of the missionaries. She was a seer in Moshoeshoe's realm, bringing rain, prophesying future events, joining the Evangelical mission and living in a cave where, as a matter of course, a spring with living water would be found, the place nowadays having become a pilgrimage centre for devout Anglicans. The Xhosa prophet Mlageni, acclaimed with the words; 'He cometh, he cometh, Mlageni, our King', was particularly popular at Beersheba. But in the end he did not manage to push out the French missionary Rolland. The majority of the Evangelical Christians at Beersheba referred to themselves as 'Rolland's people', *Ma-Rullane*, and an old member of the congregation proclaimed his happy anticipation of things to come: 'Soon I shall appear before God where they are all assembled: Abraham, Isaac and Samuel Rolland.'

Royal reform and popular recession

The first fifteen years in Lesotho were a propitious period for the French missionaries. By 1848 there was a Sotho congregation of some 2,000 members. In addition, there were 1,000 catechumens and 600 young people who attended schools at the mission stations.[124] Despite this apparent progress during these early years, the hold of these dedicated revivalist missionaries on Sotho society was limited. 'Each mission station was an island in an African ocean.'[125] The influence of the missionaries derived almost entirely from Moshoeshoe's goodwill towards them. As a result of their teaching, the king was moved to introduce four fundamental reforms in the years 1839–43, which expressed his selective attitude to the new religion. First, there was a widely noticed modification of traditional burial rites; second, circumcision rites were abolished; third, the king decided to divorce his additional wives after his senior wife had been baptized; finally, he repudiated the killing of witches. These reforms affected highly sensitive areas of traditional Sotho religion and immediately became a focal point for popular opposition. While these reforms were directed towards traditional society, he also took decidedly modernizing initiatives, particularly with regard to alcohol. He was himself a total abstainer and promulgated a law against the introduction and sale of spirits.[126]

Moshoeshoe did not hesitate to support the missionaries in various ways but would not consider being baptized himself. In 1848 he learned that his Kwena colleague in Botswana, Sechele, had asked for baptism. Moshoeshoe strongly advised against this, and sent a generous gift of ten head of cattle, two horses and some guns, promising Sechele an unlimited supply of guns if he refrained from carrying through this decision. Moshoeshoe wrote to David Livingstone:

> I have my kingdom as well as He [God], and people would laugh at me if I believed and put myself under the power of another. Tell Sechele that.[127]

To these reforms there was sullen resistance among the local district chiefs. The village doctors and witch-finders had reasons of their own to lead an underground movement against the new religion. They had been informed that the missionaries at their communion services in Church were eating human flesh. It was *they*, the White foreigners, who were in fact the sorcerers and who must be resisted on that account. A reaction was secretly gathering and a series of factors and circumstances combined to challenge the new faith.

In France the 'February Revolution' of 1848 adversely affected the financial situation of the Paris Mission, active in Lesotho. Sekonyela of the Tlokwa launched an attack on the kingdom's north-western frontier and Moshoeshoe felt that he had to repay this uninvited attention in kind. As he gathered his people, including the Christians, for his war expedition, the French missionaries advised their faithful against this martial adventure. They even placed recalcitrants under Church discipline. This seemed to the king a blatant case of White disloyalty to Sotho national interest. Thus, after 1848, Christianity was associated with cowardice and disloyalty and in fact the wars and their effects played a decisive role in the religious reaction in the years 1848–54.

A further setback for the Sotho, and one which worked psychologically against the influence of the French missionaries, was the peace settlement made in 1849. In 1833, the Rolong Tswana, with the Griqua captain, B. Barend and the Wesleyan missionaries Archbell and Edwards, had trekked east, from Platberg to Thaba Nchu, the possession of which the Sotho thereupon claimed as belonging exclusively to them. English Methodists pitted themselves against French Reformed, each party representing his particular African chief's interests. The final settlement, in 1849, implied that Lesotho suffered a considerable loss of land and it was under duress that Moshoeshoe was forced to accept this loss. In the end, Moshoeshoe, now a clever pragmatist, decided in 1869 to place Lesotho under British protection. In 1884 Basutoland became a Crown Colony under Imperial control with a British Resident.

In the first two decades of contact with the missionaries it seemed as if the whole of the Sotho nation would become Christian, but there was a sudden change. In 1848 Molapo, Moshoeshoe's son and 'the missionaries' most important convert', abandoned Christianity.[128] This was the signal for a general disenchantment with the missionaries and their teaching, not least on the part of the Christian sub-chiefs and Christian youth. The war situation forced the king to resort to traditional ceremonies, such as purification rites inspired by the *ngaka*, the traditional priests.[129] Lesotho was soon affected by the message of the Xhosa prophet, Mlangeni, who declared that Africans must no longer follow the precepts of the Whites but instead return to their own traditional heritage and wisdom. Moshoeshoe himself was impressed. He enlarged his harem and, reinstating initiation schools, put his trust once again in those ceremonial sacrifices which would strengthen Sotho tradition.[130]

By 1852 most members of the royal house had left the Church.[131] Ordinary converts had to endure increasing hostility from the traditional powers and the missionaries had to face what to them appeared to be provocative behaviour, punctuated by traditional dances. Once again polygamy and circumcision were openly recognized as the true expressions of Sotho identity. The pagan reaction led to a serious reduction of Church membership. Only in 1857 did this membership reattain about the same number – about 1,860 members – as a decade earlier, in a population of about 80,000. This was mainly due to the arrival of three new French missionaries in 1857, who were to influence the growth of the Church considerably: François Coillard, Adolphe Mabille and Eugène Casalis, a doctor and the pioneer's son. After a steady growth in the following years, Church membership was about 3,500 in 1874 although it remained a tiny proportion of the total population of some 137,000.[132] This figure was reached in spite of competition from other denominations. The Catholics arrived on the scene in 1862 and the Anglicans in 1876.

As Moshoeshoe's reign approached its end, the king remained keenly interested in religious matters and not least in the doctrinal rivalry between Catholics and Protestants. At the same time he consulted his own diviners for advice on political and medical matters. For the Church his reign had been dramatic, full of high expectations as well as bitter disappointments. One thing had been proved: the strategy of converting the Sotho nation from the top had failed. Even in the beginning it had only been partly successful. It was under new conditions that the work had to be carried on in a new period.[133]

The Protestants at the Hermon mission station had an experience of a local breakaway in 1872, the very first in Southern Africa. After quarrels over Church administration, a local group left the Church to manage on its own – only to be reconciled after a while. Zulu resistance and Sotho openness to the new religion were also experienced by Roman Catholic missionaries. As already mentioned, the French Oblates of Mary Immaculate had arrived in Natal in 1852. After ten years of hard work and apparent failure, they abandoned the Zulu field and turned to Lesotho where Moshoeshoe gave them permission to found a mission, soon to be called Roma.

Roma in Lesotho

Lesotho was known at the time as a country particularly influenced by Protestantism and the Catholic bishop might well have felt uneasy in making this approach. There were other African rulers – Kgama of the Ngwato, Lewanika of the Lozi and others – who were so identified with their 'own' Church as not to allow competing Churches to enter their country, but Moshoeshoe was different. He welcomed the Catholics and as he did so he was looking forward to witnessing a series of – to him – fascinating religious debates between representatives of the two contending parties. He obviously enjoyed an argument and felt that the religious discussion enlarged his own horizon. About the same time, in 1863, the king similarly expressed his interest in receiving Anglican missionaries for his people. It was not until 1875, however, that these plans could be realized.[134] In Moshoeshoe the Catholic missionaries, Oblates of Mary Immaculate, met an African ruler intrigued by, but above all interested in, the additional Christian alternative and the theological arguments used by both sides of the great divide. The French bishop and his co-workers informed the king that the Protestant faith could not possibly be the true religion of Christ as it had been founded not by the apostles but 1,500 years after the event. They emphasized Sotho cultural values: thus the hierarchical structure of the Catholic Church was in fact, they suggested, similar to that of Moshoeshoe's kingdom. Unlike the Protestants, they were prepared to permit *bohali* (the transfer of bride-wealth cattle). The Catholic liturgy appealed to the king, as did the social work of the nuns, particularly in times of national disaster.

To some Sotho the Reformed preaching service may have appeared as somewhat austere, exposed as they were now to a fascinating display of Catholic liturgy in all its glory, colour and movement inspired by Fr Gérard, OMI, a charismatic personality (d. 1914). He was beatified on the occasion of the visit of Pope John Paul II to Lesotho in September 1988. Fr Gérard's diary records the first solemn baptism:

> At long last the day had come foretold in all eternity, when the Lord was to reveal His love and show His mercy upon the poor Sotho. A procession led by a Procession Cross was followed by two boys from the 'Sotho College', sons of Chief Sekonyane. Then followed, in rows of two, the smaller children all carrying flags and led by the hands of the sisters. Next came older children with palms. There followed the Queen with one of her daughters and then some of the catechumens wearing the robes of penance followed by more children in white, with flags. Then came seven catechumens to be baptized. These were followed by Moshoeshoe himself leaning on one of his sons and lastly, the Bishop in cope and mitre and his crook. As the procession entered the chapel, the rite of the Baptism followed. Holy water was poured on the heads of the catechumens, the moment which the Angels had awaited so keenly for, they were now to have new brothers and sisters in God.[135]

At the village level Fr Gérard tried to build a strong Catholic community spirit. The traditional Sotho way of salutation was now baptized. One greeted one's fellow men with the words: '*Jesus Christ be praised*' and the response: '*And Mary Immaculate likewise*'.[136] Stiffer methods of public penance were introduced. An offender had his crucifix, given at baptism, taken away from him and could not expect to be saluted in the same way as Christians in good standing. Tensions within and between the Churches could not be avoided and were in fact accentuated. Moshoeshoe's niece, Helena, wife of Chief Sekonyane, had joined the Catholics and been baptized after a two-month catechumenate – a short period but she was, after all, a royal person. Fascinated as she was by the liturgical displays of the worship she was nonetheless disappointed with Fr Gérard when he failed to send a permanent priest to reside in her own village. Neither had he managed to prevent an outbreak of typhoid fever – so Helena returned to the Protestant fold. A younger generation revolted too: school pupils discarded their crucifixes, rosaries and medals and Fr Gérard had to organize a Corpus Christi procession through the village streets to assuage the insubordinates.

From the mountains of Lesotho the Oblates could, under their new and inspiring bishop, Charles C. Jolivet (1875–1903), plan further expansion of their work, to Bloemfontein, to Namibia in 1892, and to Transkei. In 1863, inspired by what he saw of Catholic work, the king stated: 'Though I am still only a pagan, I am Christian at heart.' As the end approached, the two competing Churches intensified their efforts to win the king for their side. The Protestant missionary, Théophile Jousse, in reading St John, chapter 14 pleaded: 'Son of Mohachane, a throne is prepared for you in heaven; believe in Jesus, the Saviour of the world, and you will be saved.'[137] The king asked Jousse to inform his old missionary friends Casalis and Arbousset that 'he was now a believer'. Representatives of the two confessions competed for the favours of the dying king and the Protestants in 1870 had set the date for the king's baptism. That very morning, however, the king 'died as he had lived, in two worlds'.[138] The heroic age of Moshoeshoe was at an end. Under the 'Sons of Moshoeshoe' there was often strife and jealousy tending to weaken the nation at a time when the population rose markedly, from 70,000 in 1850 to 320,000 in 1907.

While for a first generation the Paris Evangelical Mission had enjoyed a virtual monopoly, there were now two competitors: the Roman Catholics and the Anglicans. Numerically the Protestants continued to be by far the most influential until the First World War. In 1907 they counted 25,000 while the Roman Catholics, Anglicans and an Ethiopian group together had 6,000. One notes that the Christian influence as a whole was concentrated in the centre and the south of the country, while the north remained a traditional stronghold. The influence of the Paris mission could be seen throughout the country and far beyond, as Dr Judy Kimble has shown in a critical appreciation of the Church's role for labour migration in Lesotho, 1870–85:

> The establishment of a growing number of mission stations with virtually autonomous control over the surrounding areas of land provided an environment conducive to the two significant processes: an 'automization of households' and a weakening of the links between chiefs and their converted followers.[139]

Here again was a variation on the theme of the Gospel and the plough, the latter a labour-saving device which induced ambitious converts to venture beyond the borders.

After a setback in the 1850s, the Protestant recovery was largely due to the initiative and leadership of Adolphe Mabille (in Lesotho from 1859 to his death in 1894). In accordance with Reformed tradition the authority of the Synod was emphasized. The first synod was called by Mabille in 1872 and the first Sotho pastor, Carlisle Motebang, ordained in 1891. Six years later the missionaries' conference gave away to the Assembly (or *seboka*) where missionaries and Sotho leaders together could tackle their common ecclesiastical problems.[140]

THE PEDI DRAMA

The Pedi story embodies a combination of three factors. First, a central enigmatic personality, King Sekhukhune, who was both attracted – and then repulsed – by the strange new White religion; second, early African initiative and selfless Christian devotion; and, third, an outstanding missionary personality with a fine touch (at least comparatively speaking) which, however, was not sufficient to ward off a cruel crisis.

The first few years of Pedi Church history elucidate in sharp relief an important theme in the South African development: the extent to which the spread of Christianity depended on local African initiative. The way in which the Christian message was brought to the Pedi is particularly interesting because the ground for its more formal teaching was prepared by certain Pedi themselves, even though they had not yet been baptized. However, this theme is not confined to the Pedi. It will be brought out in the following pages also with regard to other peoples in the north – Venda, Lovedu and others. The wanderings of these early migrant labourers coming from the north were noticed further south. François Coillard in Lesotho made a special reference to them in the introduction to his book on the beginnings of the Church in Zambia. The period in question is the 1860s, possibly even earlier.[141]

Early Migrant Labour and the new faith

When the first missionary arrived in the Pedi mountains in 1862, he found a group of young men who already had experienced the wider world. Andries Moloi had spent nine years in the Cape Colony and knew Dutch well. He had mastered brick-laying and could serve as a 'captain' of the building team. He became a useful interpreter to the missionaries. Padishe the gunsmith was another young man with a wide horizon. He had travelled widely and picked up his prestigious art. He was a pagan and determined so to remain so. But down south he had learned a number of Bible stories and loved to tell these to young men in the village. They were later to find out that his rendering of the Bible stories was not always reliable, but at least he knew the one about Joseph and his brothers in the Holy Land and in Egypt, which he told to great effect. Blind Katedi was one of his listeners; from that time he was fascinated by the name Joseph. 'When missionaries come to baptize me, that will be the name which I shall hope to be given.'[142] Sewushane, too, became Padishe's disciple. He was of a renowned family, but his father had been put to death after being accused of being a *moloi*, a wizard. Sewushane was, however, consoled by Padishe's teaching. One day he met a visiting English tinker who stayed some time in Pedi country, making powder for the King's guns. This White man did not work on Sunday. 'Sunday is God's day', he said. 'Do not work on that day, until missionaries come and teach you about it.'

Seven of these young Africans in all had been far away as workers and had had some contact with the Christian Church. While five of them soon forgot about their impressions, two, Jan Mafadi (also known as Masadi) and Jacob Mantladi, were anxious to keep and develop what they had learned. Mafadi, in fact, had already been baptized in the foreign country and carried home with him a volume, the Pentateuch in Xhosa and his baptismal certificate, a valuable piece of paper with his own name inscribed on it, which he always carried with him in a metal container. They returned home together, over the high veld, walking for an unknown number of weeks, keeping account of the time: a notch in their walking staffs for every day and a bigger score for every seventh day reminded them of the sacred time division of the new faith. Both received revelations in their dreams. Mafadi had encountered the Church in Uitenhage, near Port Elizabeth, and his dreams about the Fire and the Last Judgement made him recall the teaching which he had heard there. Mantladi, who had worked in a hospital in the Colony, had dreams of a more practical kind, a warning never to drink beer, a warning he would convey to his own people at home. The time in Port Elizabeth had given him a personal sacred word from which to receive strength: 'I live, I am the Lord'.[143] He had to ask the missionary how it happens that when a believer hears the Word of God, his heart keeps on bubbling as if simmering milk.

These young men witnessed about their faith. They preached under a big tree and welcomed hundreds to their services. A spiritual movement was about to begin in the Pedi people, kindled by men like these, only one of them as yet baptized. Later, Sewushane made notes of their message.

> They said, Repent ye, but if you don't repent, God will make a rain of fire to strike you down as with Sodom and Gomorrah. At the judgement, the Son of Man will make the division between sheep and goats. If you do not believe, God will punish you. He will beat you with His stick.[144]

From Mafadi and Mantladi, Sewushane learned 'all the letters' and a prayer. He had heard that when you read the Word of God, you must seek God so that you may see him. 'When you have seen him, you must be baptized by a missionary; if you are not baptized, you will go crazy.' Mantladi retorted that these were lies. 'I believed his words and they made my heart be at peace.'[145] Soon Sewushane himself began to teach others. He knew that Jesus Christ would be coming from the East, from the Rising of the Sun, and that every person on earth was going to see Him. The group around Sewushane and Mantladi felt called to carry the message further: 'The Lord God gave us an overwhelmingly great assurance.' The unusual concepts and ideas which Sewushane expressed were enough for him to be accused before the king: he was misleading the people. However, Sewushane spoke boldly to old King Sekwati of the new faith and had the satisfaction of hearing him declare: 'For a long time I have been dreaming myself and I see missionaries in my dreams. Let them come and I will treat them as I have treated the Boers',[146] thereby stressing that he was known to have handled the Boers with great wisdom.

Another example from Pedi-related communities was Mathabata, a young member of Chief Pahlala's community in Sekhukhune's country. Travelling via Pietermaritzburg where he came into contact with James Allison's Methodist settlement at Indaleni, he was baptized, taking the name Samuel. Allison had promised to pay him a visit but died before he could do so, leaving Samuel alone. His chief would have nothing to do with his preaching. 'Who is Jesus? I never heard of him before ... I am the chief of this country.' The Christian propaganda had to take the form of an underground movement.

After the chief's death, his widow granted Samuel Mathabata permission to put up a combined church and school building. Samuel, who at Allison's Indaleni had seen the importance of education, sent two of his local men to Lesotho for training. In the meantime his community increased in numbers. He had them baptized by the Dutch Reformed missionary Hofmeyer at Goedgedacht, but insisted that they remain Wesleyan Methodists, just like his teacher Allison.[147]

Dinkwanyane, Sekwati's son and Sekhukhune's half-brother was one of the many who were influenced by Mantladi. His status in the society made him particularly important, also in the group of religious seekers. He decided to discard amulets, beer and dances and learned to read and pray.[148] Dinkwanyane and the others were thus well prepared when one day in 1862 the call was heard in the capital, 'The missionary has arrived'.

A missionary arrives

Alexander Merensky of the Lutheran Berlin Mission – twenty-four years of age – first made an abortive attempt to work in Swaziland and later among the Kopa near Lydenburg, until at the beginning of 1862 he turned to Sekwati's Pediland. Old King Sekwati received him well. Missionaries had proved useful elsewhere. The pattern of the missionaries' usefulness in the *mfecane* turmoil was well established. The Sotho paramount Moshoeshoe's contacts with the French Protestants, the Tswana paramount's contacts with the English Wesleyan Methodists at Thaba Nchu and above all Robert Moffat's remarkable fellowship with Mzilikazi himself were well-known. Now the turn had come for the Pedi. The missionaries might serve the paramount as secretaries and function as pass officers. The Boer farmers in the Lydenburg district insisted that Africans who left Pedi country looking for work or for other reasons should carry a pass, hence there was a steady demand for such papers to be produced by the missionaries.[149] Even more important was the medical service which Merensky could offer. Here he was helped by Mantladi with his earlier experience in a Cape hospital. All the while the missionaries gathered the secret followers and new catechumens to Church services.

The German missionary gave the group a resumé of his message. He concentrated on the great Biblical personalities, the Patriarchs, Moses and the others, until the coming of the Son of God. The listeners were exhorted to give up witchcraft and clan oaths. 'We seldom dared to engage in any polemics against the pagan practices. For that we would have needed far deeper knowledge than we possessed.'[150] As for polygamy Merensky suggested that this was a problem to be left aside for the time being and one which would eventually take care of itself. Soon after the missionary's arrival there was a major crisis in the country. King Sekwati died. The consequent ceremonies were felt to pose a problem. Should catechumens follow African custom and have their heads shaved as a sign of mourning? Here, this was a question of conscience. Some of Merensky's helpers may have been led to oppose African tradition in the Cape Colony. The wise Merensky came to their assistance.

> As this custom was also regarded by them as a testimony of suffering and sympathy, we advised them not to expose themselves to any danger for its own sake and not to embitter the pagans unnecessarily.[151]

Sekhukhune succeeded as the new paramount king and at first contacts between him and the missionary were friendly. When there was an epidemic of fever, Merensky was called in. 'Livingstone's medicine' brought healing.[152] After consulting his own experts during a drought, Sekhukhune turned to the missionary. The missionary obviously had something of a prophetic influence over the cosmic bodies in the heavens: he could predict precisely an eclipse of the moon. The king himself, who knew that the clever Whites could foretell such happenings, told his men round the campfire, 'today the women will tremble and tell one another that the word of the missionary was right.'[153] Very soon, some months after the missionary's arrival, the first group of catechumens was baptized. According to Merensky, through their serious devotion they had proved that they were now prepared for the sacrament. The reasons why the paramountcy of Sekhukhune 'provided the bulk of the early converts' were complex. The death of the old paramount Sekwati had caused a vast crisis in the realm: 'It was in this atmosphere of change and latent and manifest strife at the capital that the Christian group grew and this probably contributed to its initial successes and its ultimate failure.' There were 'two broad categories [of the first converts], clients of the paramount and royal wives'.[154]

The clientele of the missionary

Clients in this case were mostly refugees and other poor and kinless individuals dependent on the paramount. One of these, Martin Sewushane, was later to become a leader in the Christian group. He had fled to Sekwati's court after his father's death and because his guardian and his uncle had been killed for 'practising witchcraft.' The large number of royal wives differed among themselves as far as rank and status were concerned. However, they all depended on the paramount and could not, as a matter of course, undergo any change in their status, least of all through baptism, without reference to and permission from the paramount. The best-known of these wives was Tlakale, who after a secret baptism performed by the missionary Merensky, was later to marry Martin Sewushane. It is noticeable that some of these people were in a double sense foreigners and foot-loose people in Pedi society. They had come into the society as refugees, from some other society and from the aftermath of *mfecane*; then, from Pedi country they moved south in order to work for money. It is conjectured here that these men were particularly prone to look for the security and opportunity offered by the new religion.

At first Sekhukhune was receptive to the new ideas. In his selective attitude towards Christianity, however, he was largely typical of Southern African chiefs at this time. He felt it was wise to keep the Sabbath, but was definitely not prepared to repudiate all his wives except one.[155] His only wish would be for the missionaries to live close to him, as 'his eyes'. Sekhukhune's attitude encouraged a number of people, including many related to the chief's house, to ask for baptism. The Christian community grew rapidly; by 1863 there were already 200–300 'visitors' and 115 catechumens. The group felt particularly strengthened because of the baptism of Sekhukhume's half-brother John Dinkwanyane, a son of Sekwati.

Royal dreams

Sekhukhune's attack, when it came, was probably not so much a sudden reversal of attitude as rather the flaring up of some long smouldering suspicion and mistrust. In his kind of world dreams and visions played an important role, which possibly also had some significance in the political sphere. However personal relationships with his family and closest relatives, not least half-brothers were also important factors in making decisions. At the right time all these considerations could sway the great man in favour of a positive attitude to Christianity; but only for a while, since a very different attitude could follow given a change of circumstances. One royal dream in particular was widely discussed in the *kraals* and possibly in the king's council. Sekhukhune had been involved in an attack on a neighbouring people and was greatly impressed by the fact that the followers of the new religion had on this occasion joined his army. Jan Mafadi was among those killed during the attack. Sekhukhune was affected by this example of the Christian's loyalty to his king. Having gone to sleep he suddenly woke up feeling that somebody was there. It was Jan Mafadi, the deceased Christian soldier who looked sternly at him, 'without saying a word'. The king asked: 'Mafadi, from where do you come?' But there was no answer. 'What do you want? Have you come down with rain from heaven?' Again no answer. The king had to rush out of his house and sit down on a stone, but as he returned to his bed and lay down, Mafadi was there once more. Sekhukhune was shaking all over and again had to rush out. The following morning he sent word to the missionaries asking what the dream meant and whether anything that he had done was sinful according to the Word of God.[156]

However there also were factors working in another direction. Insofar as the new teaching affected leading members of the royal house, it seemed to threaten the king's own position. No doubt Sekhukhune was particularly aware of the potential threat posed to him by the baptism of his half-brother, John Dinkwanyane, since the latter might be tempted to use his standing among his fellow-Christians to foment an opposition force. A related matter angered the king beyond measure: towards the end of 1863, after rather less than two years of missionary activity, Sekhukhune discovered that his favourite wife, Tlakale, had been secretly baptized with the name of Mary Magdalene. Merensky, cautious and ever-mindful of the possible consequences, had suggested that the ceremony be postponed so that he could discuss it with the king, but the woman had insisted on receiving the rite. 'How could I withhold the water in such a case?', he was to ask later.[157]

Crisis and flight

As a result of this incident, Sekhukhune suddenly changed his attitude. After summoning what he called a 'blood council', he dramatically accused the missionaries of robbing him of his country. 'You missionaries are liars. You have stolen my people and want to make yourselves kings.' A prolonged drought was obviously caused by the Christian 'witches'.[158] Though the missionaries were accused, it was the Pedi Christians who were punished. The baptized and the catechumens were called upon to give an answer to the question: 'Do you throw it (i.e., the faith) away?' If the answer was in the affirmative, the reply was: 'Then Sekhukhune's heart is quieted.' If no such answer was forthcoming, the person was clubbed to death. A blood bath followed in which Dinkwanyane, as one of those born to rule, was left untouched. Two days later a general exodus took place, during the night, and some 170 adults and sixty children left Sekhukhune's territory.

Merensky managed to negotiate the purchase of a large farm of about 40,000 acres, and it was there that the congregation gathered, soon numbering

1,000 members. In 1892 it increased to 2,750, consisting of two different ethnic communities, Bapedi and Bakoba, settled in two sections of the centre. This was to be 'the Place of Refuge', Botshabelo. 'Until now we had refrained from allowing our Christians to leave the conditions in which they lived among the pagans', Merensky noted.[159] A constant theme in nineteenth-century African Church history writing was that of two alternatives, the Christian congregation being related to traditional society – supposedly affording added opportunities for evangelization – or forming a secluded 'Christian village' shielding the converts from what was referred to as the temptations and dangers of a pagan culture. Under their missionary the Pedi Christians had tried the former but now felt obliged to settle for the latter alternative and did so in a most determined fashion.

A place of refuge and a split

Botshabelo, 'the Place of Refuge', became a mighty fortress built 'on the summit of a high knoll'. Walls fifteen feet high and two feet thick, pierced with loop-holes and built of iron-stone, enclosed a central compound. There were flank defences and a turret over the entrance which gave a clear view of the surrounding country. The village itself had stores and workshops, a mill and wagon building and repair works, catering to the needs of both the Boer and the African population and emphasizing the virtues of work. For a time the school was the largest in the Transvaal. Merensky's *Platzordnung* was the law of the community: later it was to become the model for the Berlin Mission stations in Tanzania (soon to be German East Africa). The village, however, presented the missionaries with problems of its own, albeit of a familiar kind. Pedi 'national feeling' reasserted itself under Dinkwanyane's leadership in connection with his stand against new labour laws introduced by the Boers (the Contract Law).

Dinkwanyane refused to allow his followers to adopt 'Western' social customs advocated by the missionaries. Thus he was opposed to any changes in traditional hair styles: as a sign of mourning Pedi women normally shaved their heads.

In the end Johannes Dinkwanyane, Church elder and son of the Pedi paramount, could no longer stand the patriarchal control of the missionaries. In 1873 he abandoned the mission station, taking more than 300 Christians with him. Eventually they settled at a place called Mafolofolo, a virtually inaccessible mountain fortress. They wanted land of their own and a life of their own, held together by their Christian worship in the big church which they built for themselves in the centre of the fortress. The small community attracted people from Botshabelo but also deserters, the so-called *inboekse-linge* from neighbouring Boer farms, i.e. youngsters captured in the *mfecane* turmoil and kept as indentured labour or domestic servants, virtually as serfs. To these young people Mafolofolo, in its brief three- to four-year history served as a path into the Christian community.

Johannes Dinkwanyane saw to it that the life and ritual which they had known at Botshabelo were upheld in the Mafolofolo congregation. He was the preacher, a teacher took care of the school children, 'and dying children and catechumens were baptized.'[160] Even the missionaries acknowledged that the group's continuing commitment to Lutheran Church order was never in doubt and they expressed this negatively: 'nobody performed Holy Communion'. But the group felt this as a serious shortcoming and Johannes Dinkwanyane went so far as to appeal to the mission to send them a missionary, since an ordained pastor was needed for Holy Communion. The missionaries refused. Firmness on their part, it was thought, would induce the people to come back to the Botshabelo fellowship. All in all, the group at Mofolofolo under Johannes Dinkwanyane was a fascinating example of an early 'Ethiopian' Utopia in the Transvaal rural area, determined to carry on as a Christian community on terms which they understood. They were not allowed to continue for long. The Pedi country was caught up in the brutal power politics of the Transvaal Republic and of British Imperial designs. In a military attack in 1876, Johannes Dinkwanyane was killed and the Mafolofolo Christian community shattered.

From Pedi to Pretoria

There was a far-reaching sequel to this endeavour in the Transvaal mountains. Fifteen years after Dinkwanyane's death, a Wesleyan preacher was placed as a pastor in the African congregation in Pretoria. He was a Pedi, possibly with connections with early Pedi migrant labourers and the mobile Pedi Church. In Pretoria he soon found that he could not accept the conditions under which he was supposed to exist and work and he decided to form a Church of his own, called the 'Ethiopian Church of South Africa'. His name was M. M. Mokone, and he was to become the father of the 'Ethiopian' movement in Southern Africa.[161]

EARLY MIGRANT LABOUR FROM THE NORTH

Northern Transvaal seemed an isolated world hidden among its high mountains, dominated by its conservative old men – and women, for the famous Lovedu Rain-Queen was one of them – frightened of outside forces, White and Black. The Venda seemed a particularly conservative people. Venda reaction to learning something from foreigners was totally negative. 'No plough, no square house, no ox waggon and no waggon road were allowed in the country.' In 1867 the Venda pitted their military power against that of the Boers and were delighted to see the defeated Whites withdraw.[162] However the isolation was about to be modified, already a number of young people were slipping through the net, going south for work. As will be seen on the following pages it was these 'Early Migrant Labourers' who were to return to their home mountains with the Gospel long before any Western missionary had come to their villages.

Going south was part of a northern youth revolt. It may have been related to intervals in circumcision lodges. In a culture where the distance between the generations was very wide, one might refer to a 'generation gap'. One express reason for the decision to leave home was given by all these young men: to find work in order buy a rifle. This was necessary for hunting, providing an important source of meat but also for a more general reason: a man must have a musket, a symbol of his manhood and his maturity and thus acquire a standing in the community. So they left. Dr N. J. van Warmelo writes:

> Common reasons for going far away were accusations of witchcraft, rivalry in the family over inheritance and succession, getting girls into trouble and fear of the consequences, and just young men's boredom with life at home.[163]

There is a problem involved. The written tradition most often refers to one particular person having left the community, eventually to return. In fact it was always a case of a group or a gang which left. As Mohashwa from Mamabolo in Lovedu went south he did so with a whole group of young men: 'We are rifle-seekers from Lovedu country', they said. When he eventually returned it was as a leader of a virtual youth commando – Sotho, Pedi, Venda, Lovedu and others – all on their way to the mountains in the north.[164] At home Mohashwa was able to report that he had finally got to Kimberley. He and his friends must thus have been among the very first in the Kimberley mines.

The northern Transvaal communities with whose representatives we are concerned here are, besides the Pedi, the Venda and Lovedu. The list could easily be extended to include northern ethnic communities further west and east such as the Ovambo in the west and the 'Shangaan' in the east. As one tries to follow them on their daring exploits, one finds that most of them headed for Pietermaritzburg. In the 1850s and 1860s, Natal experienced a boom. Labour was needed for the sugar industry, for transport and other activities. This is where these northerners met James Allison, the Wesleyan missionary at Edendale outside Pietermaritzburg. His night schools and his Methodist singing and worship offered a transforming experience. Here it was that David Funzane, a Venda, was baptized later to return as an itinerant preacher in the northern areas, highly respected even by his chief at Tshakhuma. Khashane, a Lovedu, reached Port Elizabeth, having on the way made his appearance at Moshoeshoe's court in Lesotho.

Port Elizabeth, and more particularly the harbour, was a busy place in need of labour from the north. Both in Allison's Edendale and in Port Elizabeth there were the new experiences of social fellowship, education and religious inspiration awaiting these people, in the form of the Wesleyan Methodist night school and the Wesleyan Methodist 'class', devised to welcome and influence the visitors from afar. Kamela Raphela from Mamabolo in Lovedu went further – he reached Cape Town and was welcomed by the 'Independents' (LMS) who taught him to read. There was also Mashaba, a Thonga from Mozambique who, having been converted in 1875 at Port Elizabeth, was given an opportunity to continue his studies at the Lovedale college – the highest educational institution at the time – and was thus well prepared when he returned to Maputo ten years later.

What was it in the new message that captured their imagination? The extant material provides only occasional reference to this question. The inevitability of Judgement Day seems to have been a major consideration. This message stuck 'in the throat' as the Sotho say. The theme in all these cases is the same; groups of young men looking for a job in order to buy the best that money could give, a musket of one's own, a new rifle, and in the process finding a new religion. Then the triumphant return home: the people of the village congregated to welcome their intrepid young men, who lifted their new guns to shoot and thus to punctuate their travel story. However in the evening they would gather their contemporaries and show them their greatest treasure: a book, a Gospel of St Matthew or perhaps even a New Testament, which they could read from. Something very great had happened to these young men: the rifle and the Book testified to it. They were now new men, they had acquired a new identity and a new name, as well as the secrets of the White man's power – his firearm and his written word.

So far these northern villagers were without missionaries, left to their own devices. One can not but marvel at the way in which a spiritual fire had been ignited in their hearts and minds and sustained there. The possession of a Gospel book – in Xhosa or in Sotho – was the foundation of their gathering. In their night school in Pietermaritzburg or Port Elizabeth they had learned how to spell and bring together letters and words and they could now, in their home village, demonstrate their wonderful new art. In the Wesleyan Methodist chapel and night school they had been inspired to pray aloud and lead other in prayer. What was this if not a little conventicle?

Venda conventicles

One of Allison's converts, Johannes Motsheni, eventually welcomed Lutheran missionaries to his Venda village. He became their active co-worker, bringing along such people as he had approached and influenced while still on his own in the village. The few converts consisted of the missionaries' servants from neighbouring peoples and of Motsheni's wife and his mother. However the administration of the sacrament of baptism had an evangelistic effect and three Venda became catechumens. One man turned up bringing with him his three sons for baptism, including young twins. The appearance of the latter was the result of a highly dramatic decision, for age-old custom held that twins must be killed. The Venda king, Tshivase, told the missionary the reason why they must be killed: 'But, Sir, they are unclean'. In this case, as in a thousand others, the parents' love, particularly that of the mothers, revolted against tradition and the new religion provided a solution, of life and hope.[165]

Then there were the Wesleyan hymns and the meditations on the miracle of the Book and the art of reading. The Berlin missionary, Beuster, surprised at finding the group of believers in Venda country, noticed that they had earlier formed what he called 'a kind of conventicle',[166] thus using for this early Venda religious group a classic Pietist term, in vogue at the same time in nineteenth-century Germany and Sweden. These young Venda preachers, some not yet baptized themselves, were also able to adapt the message to a captivating myth from their own ethnic treasure of stories: a myth about a king who long ago had decided to leave his people in order to discover the place where the rivers flowed into the ocean. Before leaving he shot three arrows into a high tree as a sign that he would return. The return of the gracious king became one of the inspiring myths of expectation among the Venda and, later, a theme in sermons of missionaries and African evangelists.[167]

One Andreas from Venda who was baptized 'in the [Cape] Colony', settled as an evangelist at Shewase. Allison's Indaleni had appeared as a welcoming place for the migrants and some Venda were among them. They were baptized by Allison and after some time found their way back home.

One of the best known Venda evangelists baptized in Natal was David Funzane. As assistant to missionary Schwellnus he served as an itinerant preacher in the northern areas, highly respected by Chief Madsebandela of Tshakome. In fact, as will be seen later, he was to take the Gospel further, across the Limpopo into 'the regions beyond'. The majority of this little group of Venda Christians, including a chief, Totane, soon threw off their Christian allegiance, however. When the first Berlin missionaries, Beuster and Stech, arrived these men preferred to remain anonymous.[168]

Ars moriendi – *Venda Version*

The Church of the Middle Ages had its *ars moriendi*, the art of dying. The nineteenth-century Church in Africa did indeed develop such an art – although in their case it never occurred to those involved that it was a question of an art, but rather that of utter trust in God who was about to provide Green Pastures for his beloved Children Over There, on the other side. Many of these men and women had initially joined the Church with the express hope of learning 'how to die well' and there are beautiful examples of how this became the experience of people in the last few days of their lives.

Rachel was wife of Isaiah Rauwbaas, himself son of a Lunda sub-chief. She fell victim to a small-pox epidemic and knew she was dying. A letter which her husband wrote to the missionary after her death tells the story – incidentally, and even in this necessarily abridged version of the letter, it gives an impression of the personal bonds between an evangelist and his wife:

> She said to me, 'Father, lift me up', for she did not manage to sit up. As I held her up, she said, 'I want to lie down', and she groaned heavily. I saw that her spirit was weak. I placed her down and prayed, and as I concluded my prayer I noticed that she was dying. She said, 'Holy, Holy, Holy is Jehovah Zabaoth, all lands are full of Thy glory. Amen, Amen, Amen.' Together with two old women I knelt and we remained kneeling. She said, 'I see a man coming from the Rising of the Sun, a very white man in shining cloths coming to me and calling me, standing by my head.' She said, 'Another man appeared, very black, and he told me: "You say you pray to God. Let Him save you then from your severe pains".' Then she said, 'I have no time to rest for there are people who call for me.' I asked, 'Who are they?' She said: 'Here they are, surrounding me.' And I asked, 'What kind of people?' And she said, 'They are shining, they call for me to leave.' Then I put her down. On May 27 as she lay down she sang the hymn, *Wie schöne*

Schöflein sind es, die dort im Himmel. At sunset she called for the children and said to Mochadila: 'Stay at home and help your sister to look after her children.' Now we cried and so did the children. She said, 'Go and sleep in peace, do not be afraid. I will not pass away today. You will see me tomorrow.' On the third day as the cattle had been turned out to grass, I took the hymn-book and read hymn No. 111, *Jesus my Assurance*. Then I took the New Testament and read Acts II and prayed. We were together with her until afternoon. Later I opened the Book and read Hebrews 12:5 and we prayed again. Then I read Psalm 143 and prayed. Then she said, 'Now God has saved me from the bonds of death and from the power of darkness. I leave you in peace. Even if I cannot drink more water, there is nothing which makes me afraid. Amen, Amen, Amen. So be it.'[169]

Lovedu pioneers

The Lovedu were strongly affected by what now happened in their midst. At Port Elizabeth, Khashane had been told by a compatriot of his that the Bible was inspired: 'You cannot return to your country without the word of God.' Eventually he came to a Berlin missionary in King William's Town and was baptized there. For some time the missionary used him as an elementary school teacher. But Khashane was soon peparing to return home with a precious possession, a New Testament. The initial group of catechumens round Khashane consisted of his sister and, characteristically, a few foreigners who had moved to Lovedu country. They managed to establish a Christian village of their own. In 1878, two Lutheran missionaries, Knothe and Reuter, visited Lovedu and established contact with them.

The new movement triggered opposition. It was suggested that it represented a dangerous rival to the chief's authority. An untimely drought – and in the country of the Rain-Queen! – made people suspicious. The drought was attributed to a single cause: the new religion. On Good Friday 1884 Modubeng, the Christian village, was attacked by a great number of angry Lovedu. Khashane was shot dead outside his little church, the first martyr of the young Lovedu Church. The village was burned and destroyed and the survivors had to leave Lovedu country. Three years later, Queen Modjadji graciously allowed the Christian group to resettle in her country, but soon persecution of the Christians flared up again and only in the 1890s did circumstances become more favourable for the young congregations.[170] The time even came when Queen Modjadji abandoned her faith in the gods of her ancestors, adjusting herself to the new conditions so far as to forbid, in 1923, the killing of twins and urging her followers instead to trust the Christian God.[171]

An excessive display of religious activity was not popular. This ultimately became Mashaba's experience as he returned from Lovedale to Maputo (then named Lourenço Marques) in 1885. Working for eight years on his own, he built a chapel and a day school around which he collected a Christian community of 200. Four local preachers and one class leader assisted the intrepid evangelist. It was hardly surprising that the Portuguese authorities arrested him and sent him to a slave camp on the Cape Verde Islands for six years.

The missionaries

In order to emphasize the highly significant role of individual and corporate African initiative in the Christianization process, there has perhaps been a tendency on the preceding pages to play down the role of Western missionary strategy and organization. The balance needs to be redressed now, even if only briefly. The young returnees tended to regard their activities back home in the north as to some extent intermediary, preparing for the arrival of a White missionary, James Allison or others. The dominant mission in the north was that of the Berlin Lutherans with a continuous mission field including a number of ethnic communities. Alexander Merensky had led his mission to Transvaal and Pedi, a younger generation of missionaries moved further north. In 1878 A. Knothe founded Mphome in an area occupied by Boer farms. He bought up adjacent farms and established a large tract of property of about 30,000 acres. The outcome of the work in the ethnic communities was still highly uncertain and examples of harassment of Christian converts were numerous. The mission farm under the rule of the missionary by contrast offered a chance for a more planned and peaceful development.

At Mphome, Knothe built a school for evangelists; from there a network of outstations and preaching places was gradually extended to meet the needs of the local population and also from there the imaginative Knothe led a pilgrimage of the converts as far as the Tlokwa district to celebrate the Church's harvest festival. In the *kraals* along the wayside the faithful would preach, pray and sing. This pilgrimage seemed a genuinely African corporate expression of intense religious life. Some of the Berlin Lutherans, like their Hermannsburg colleagues, aimed at a genuine African folk Christianity. One thinks of such comparable features as that of the 'Big Meeting' of the Kuruman Tswana Church and its evangelistic pilgrimage which might sometimes last for weeks.[172] Later, some of the Independent

Churches, such as Shembe's Nazaretha and Lekganyane's Zion were to develop pilgrimages on a grand scale.

Knothe translated the New Testament into Sotho and created a hymnbook, all part of a spiritual activity suddenly cut short by his death in 1895 and by the circumstances connected with his decease. It was Knothe who led his mission into Lovedu country where he placed the indefatigable Fritz Reuter who was to give three decades, 1872–1901, of continuous and concentrated work to this area. The Medingen mission developed into a wide-reaching cultural centre and a growing 'Christian village' was established. In 1885 the Berliners were sufficiently daring to ordain two Black pastors, Timothy Sello and Martin Sewushane. However times were changing: only five years later Sewushane followed the example of the complex Berlin missionary Johannes Winter and the Botshabelo chief, Seth Kchelema, in establishing an Independent national organization, the Bapedi Lutheran Church. This defection by one of their first African pastors, seems to have caused the Mission to react with utmost caution in providing theological training to other Africans, and another twenty years were to pass by until the next set of African pastors were ordained.

Another Continental mission in the north was that of the Swiss Reformed. Their beginnings were related to the French Protestant mission in Lesotho and to Thonga groups in Mozambique. Deliberate and prudent, the thoughtful Swiss were not to be rushed, whether in the case of baptism of catechumens or of the ordination of Africans. The first ordination of a Thonga pastor occurred in 1909 to be followed in 1920 – after the First World War – by the ordination of a group of four Black pastors. The hospital at Elim and the Teacher Training School at Lemana were important centres (founded in 1899 and 1906 respectively). The Dutch Reformed mission from the Cape had placed Stephanus Hofmeyr (1905) in the north. His work was carried on after his death by his son-in-law, J. W. Daneel. While all the missions in these areas were soon looking beyond the Limpopo, towards an opportunity for founding mission work in what was soon to be called Rhodesia, this was particularly the case with Hofmeyr. The conversion of the Coloured clan, Buys, was important in this context. They served as an effective route for carrying the Christian message to the peoples beyond the river, and the Buys clan can be compared with the Griqua further south. The Wesleyans and Anglicans in the northern Transvaal mainly consisted of groups which grew up spontaneously as a result of contacts with the rapidly expanding Christian communities on the coast. Such groups were largely gathered together by the efforts of migrant labourers and received supervision and encouragement through the occasional visits of the Wesleyan pastor, Owen Watkins, or the Anglican, Canon E. Farmer. Watkins, in particular, regarded the whole of the Transvaal as his parish. A process of interaction between mission-related local congregations and African initiative characterized Wesleyan Church life in the last decade of the century.

ON THE RAND 1880–1919

Promise but no fulfilment

Mining and urbanization changed the face of Africa, but nowhere as radically as in South Africa. Geared to 'the two slow centuries of the ox-wagon',[173] the country had led an exclusively agricultural existence on its extensive White farms and in the 'Native reserves'. The diamonds of Kimberley and the gold of the Rand transformed all aspects of life for the different sectors of the population. Church conditions shared in the drastic changes. At the quiet old mission stations, the missionary was a patriarch, ruling over the congregation, its schools, its farm, and sometimes a medical clinic. Suddenly the powerful magnet of the mines pulled everything away from that peaceful isolation, exposing groups and individuals to a totally new way of life. Prior to 1914 the labour force on the Rand had reached 325,000. Of these, 285,000 were African mine workers from as far away as Mozambique and Malawi. These migratory men, after six to eighteen months on the Rand, returned to their home villages, influenced by what they had heard and seen during their sojourn in the Golden City. The whole subcontinent was dominated politically by mounting imperialist designs and clashing interests of British, Boer, Germans and even Portuguese. African kings and chiefs were deported to St Helena or Robben Island, or were in other ways intimidated and humiliated. The Boer–British conflict, caused ultimately by economic interests, exploded in the Boer War, 1899–1902. Fought to a bitter end, it left in its train subjugation and destruction. It took the Boers exactly half a century to recover.

The latter part of the century seemingly brought promise of opportunity for Black Christian communities, particularly in the Cape. Their faith had proved its strength by lifting generations of down-trodden refugees, via Church and school, to a potential elite position in society. However the difference in atmosphere and opportunity between the Cape and the rest of South Africa must be emphasized. In the Cape, the African Christian communities at first grew in a Liberal *milieu* of expectation, very different from that of Transvaal and Orange Free State. The establishment of the Christian Church, its schools and its values had consequences for the individual's personal status in the community. The Cape Constitution of 1853 developed out of the mission-inspired legislation of the 1820s and 1830s. It held that Africans, as anyone else, were entitled to register as voters and to stand for election to the Lower House. African voters 'of the new strata created by the colonial society, ministers of religion, school teachers and others' played an important part in many electoral divisions of the Cape Colony from 1884–1910. Coloureds and Africans in the Cape felt that in comparison with the rest of the country, they were a privileged group.[174] Two leading African newspapers in the Cape, J. T. Jabavu's *Imvo* and A. K. Soga's *Izwi la Bantu*, supported competing political groups: General Botha's South African Party and General Jameson's pro-Imperial Progress Party. With varying degrees of conviction these newspapers upheld the rights of the African Christian elite.

In 1894, as Prime Minister of the Cape, Cecil Rhodes introduced the Glen Grey Act. Part of its objective was to encourage individual land tenure and to establish a system of local councils. Eight thousand allotments were provided for individual Africans. These measures furthered the aspirations of the Christian elite, but another provision enforced a tax of ten shillings on every African male in the reserves who was not employed by a White person. This became part of the machinery which forced the masses of Africans to the mines and the cities. The growing migrant labour system undermined the whole social fabric of African life. African writers, 'in a mounting anguish', saw privileges already acquired being snatched away. In the Cape, Boer and Briton differed increasingly over African policy. The African elite felt obliged to favour their friends, the British. That great best-seller among the Cape Christians, *The Pilgrim's Progress*, translated into Xhosa by Tiyo Soga, had been modernized, so that it related to the practical political problems of the day:

> Why should a pass be forced upon people who have demonstrated in every way that they are loyal British subjects ... For we are equals under Queen Victoria.[175]

Yet – could they be sure that this was enough? The great Xhosa poet, Samuel Mqhayi, nurtured in Christian culture and in the tradition of Cape Liberalism, published a poem during the Boer War where each stanza has a refrain: 'We are Britons'. Although convinced that a British victory was the working out of a Divine Purpose, he felt that the British were forgetting their 'children' in Africa.

You gave us Truth: denied us Truth
You gave us *ubantu* [human dignity]: denied us *ubantu*
You gave us light: we live in darkness
Benighted at Noon-day, we grope in the dark.

A similar development to that in 'liberal' Cape took place in Natal. The Sogas and Jabavus of the Cape had their counterparts in Natal in the *kolwa*, active Christians related to the Wesleyan, the Congregational (American Board) and the Anglican Churches. John Kumalo, head of an Anglican *kolwa* group, represented their attitudes. He regarded Bishop Colenso as his guide and felt that he belonged to 'the root Church', having Episcopal Succession. 'Natives should be inside, not outside, the Christian community', he said with a non-sentimental view of Christianization. Aware of the elite position of his group, he complained, 'We belong neither to the Europeans nor to the Natives. We are a people apart and without proper laws, torn between high promise and threatening deception.' He was mainly concerned about the consequences of the Act of Exemption from Native Law of 1864. In spite of being an 'Exempted Person', Kumalo felt that he was treated 'like any other ordinary native'. It was even worse when Sir Theophilus Shepstone addressed the *kolwa* in terms identical to those he used in speaking to traditionals: 'You too should *bonga* your own *amadlozi*' (praise your ancestral spirits). Kumalo felt that Shepstone 'was inimical to the highest interests of the native people.'[176]

Any illusions regarding the two White communities which Kumalo and his generation of educated Africans may have held were firmly crushed when Boer and Briton were 'reconciled' in 1910. The Blacks were the losers, especially with one outcome of the White union: the Natives Land Act of 1913. The Act came as a traumatic blow, and can be regarded as the foundation of the policy of apartheid, depriving Blacks of their right to purchase and own land. 'As from 1913 we knew one thing: there is no God with the White man.'[177]

Something else was happening at the beginning of the century, in 'happy sunny South Africa'. John Kumalo, the Anglican layman told the Native Commissioner, Mr James Stuart about it: 'Some European clergymen when they meet John in private, will shake hands effusively with John, but when they meet him in a public place, as in the street, they do not do so'. This kind of thing soon was given a sociological term, 'segregation' (a forerunner of apartheid) and when this seeped into the Churches it became the 'lie in the soul'.[178]

The catalyst and the African agent

The World Missionary Conference at Edinburgh in 1910 stimulated a general review of the mission situation throughout the world. In South Africa the missions had gathered for survey and counsel. In 1911 two volumes appeared by Dutch Reformed missiologists, both with an international and ecumenical outlook: the comprehensive *A History of Christian Missions in South Africa*, by J. du Plessis, and the challenging *Studies in the Evangelization of South Africa*, by G. B. A. Gerdener. Their statistics compared the Protestant situation in South Africa with that of Africa as a whole. The total number of Evangelical Christians in the whole continent was estimated to be one and one-half million (or, if including 'adherents', two million), but 60 per cent of these were in South Africa. The great majority of these again were the Coloured population in the Cape. Du Plessis listed 813 principal mission stations and drew the arithmetical conclusion that 'there are 9,600 natives for every station manned by a European Missionary in South Africa'. His younger colleague, Gerdener, went a step further: 'In South Africa every ordained missionary has some 13,000 natives to evangelize', yet with certain differences in the various parts of the country. 'The problem is one of dynamics, as well as mathematics.'

These learned men and most of their contemporaries, however, overlooked one fundamental fact. As evidenced by Gerdener's argument, he considered the European missionary the sole evangelist. He and others were blind to the fact that it was largely Africans who evangelized other Africans. The nineteenth-century missionary on his station, after leading the morning worship in the village chapel and taking his district tour on horseback, functioned as the *catalyst*. He instructed and enabled a team of Africans, who then evangelized other Africans. Stephanus Hofmeyr, of the Dutch Reformed Church at Goedgedacht in the far north of Transvaal, did just that. He prepared parties of Africans who crossed the Limpopo to evangelize in Zimbabwe. Canon Farmer in Pretoria, making his rounds through the Transvaal high veld, discovered hundreds of Africans who, after their transforming spiritual experience on the Rand, became missionaries to their fellowmen.

The great concern of the General Missionary conferences from 1904 into the 1920s, was that of missionary 'comity', how to demarcate spheres of work in order to avoid 'over-lapping' between the missions. However, in spite of long decades of debate, the missions failed to agree. South-eastern South Africa, in Pondoland, Natal and Zululand, had one of the highest concentrations of missions, with nine different societies at work already in

1880.[179] Ultimately, the government, through provisions with regard to the Native trust lands, laid down from 1929 a three-mile-radius rule 'between schools of different denominations', increased to five miles in 1933.[180] The object of the rule was to prevent denominational rivalry in the African reserves. The older well-established missions profited from this rule, but some late-comers encountered great difficulties.

Kimberley and the Rand

The period 1884 to 1914–19 was a time of immense strain and change in South Africa, particularly on the Rand and for the African on the Rand. A number of factors ultimately related to the quest for religious fellowship can be mentioned: the development of the mines; the rapidly increasing roads and rail system, leading to general mobility and preparedness for change; the Boer War; the Zulu Rebellion of 1906; the Boer–Briton Union in 1910 and the related exclusion of the African from the land, through the Natives Land Act of 1913; the First World War. The Rand in this period was a man's world, with the African woman thus far remaining in the villages and there was dramatic intensification of a disease–health syndrome with a desperate search for health. All these factors – and probably many more – taken together underline the role of the Rand for the dissemination of the new religious message to every part of the country and to southern Africa and beyond and this on a scale and with an intensity which would have been unthinkable at the sheltered little mission stations in the so-called Reserves, the Ekuthulenis and the Botshabelos (meaning respectively a 'Place of Peace' and a 'Place of Refuge'.)

At the Mines: Kimberley

The Kimberley diamonds, within a few years, turned the bush into a city. Whites and Blacks gathered from all over the high veld and beyond. The evangelizing effect of earlier migrant labour has been emphasized: men going from Pedi country and southern Mozambique to Durban and the East Cape harbours. A similar long-term evangelization effect took place with Kimberley. The diamond mines were the goal of enterprising Africans from all of South Africa. Wesleyan transport men from Durban, Pietermaritzburg and Ladysmith made regular long and relatively well-paid visits to Kimberley. One can assume that these ambitious laymen contacted their fellow Wesleyans at Kimberley and at Beaconsfield, the latter being a suburb of Kimberley which soon emerged as a centre for Wesleyan, Independent

African and Afro-American Church activity. Very soon no African community in the country was immune to the pull of the mines and none less so than the Cape Mfengu and the Natal *kolwa*, always open to new experiences and opportunities.

The mining industry built chapels for the benefit of the workers in nearly every Kimberley compound. The missions appreciated this 'generosity'.[181] Because of labour control measures, Kimberley enforced a 'closed compound' system. Up to 10,000 men, from twenty-five ethnic communities, were housed within high walls in prison-like conditions, not allowed to leave until the end of their work contract. During the first decades, conditions underground were extremely risky and precautions unsatisfactory. Accidents and deaths were frequent, from flooding and from collapse of rock. Disease, too, took its toll. The 'closed compound' added the annoyance of not allowing friends of a deceased man to follow their comrade to pay him the last homage. Only the *moruthi* (the pastor) was allowed to follow the hand-cart carrying the coffin on its route from the mine – 'the Big Hole' – to that other hole, the grave. Even in these inhuman conditions, the Christian funeral made a difference. While pagans were buried in *mabitha a dimpya* (the grave for the dogs), the missionary at the grave-side with his words, the hymns and the prayers, represented some kind of humane influence.

The Wesleyans had been in this part of the country ever since the unsettling days of the *mfecane*. They did not hesitate to grasp the new opportunity. Pastor B. Impey and James Calvert, in felicitous Wesleyan fashion, organized voluntary local preachers from among the Christian labourers and eventually, in 1886, erected an impressive Wesley Chapel. The Lutheran mission at neighbouring Pniel was well placed to enter the work at Kimberley. The Berlin missionary, stationed at Pniel from 1888–1922, could follow and to some extent influence the Church work at Kimberley. The Anglican community at Kimberley was fortunate to have as its leader J. T. Darragh, a temperamental Irish Anglo-Catholic, later posted to Johannesburg.

At the Mines: the Rand

In the pre-1914 settlements, society was *not* defined in social or ethnic terms. The multi-racial population included a mixture of Afrikaners, Africans, Russian Jews, Coloureds, Asians (Indians and Chinese). It is significant that as the Full Gospel Church of God began its activities on the Rand between 1909–10, though it mainly aimed at Blacks and Coloureds, their services in

Vrededorp and Sophiatown were attracting large numbers of Europeans.[182] It can be surmised that these were 'poor Whites' living in the townships. Sophiatown, founded in 1897; Western Native Township; and Alexandra were examples of townships where Africans could at this time still build their houses with freehold rights. For the fortunate elite who lived in attractive Sophiatown, the value of their place could be increased by hiring out a number of stands or shacks on the site. In 1896 only 8.7 per cent of the population were African women, the majority of them being Christian members of the enterprising Mfengu community from the Cape. During the decade from 1911–1921, the number of African women in Johannesburg increased 180 per cent, from 4,400 to 12,000.[183]

On the Rand, the Africans were housed in townships and compounds. The compounds were of two kinds: mine compounds, with large unattractive barracks in the immediate vicinity of the mines, and municipal and private-industry compounds, housing Africans employed by various city departments or by emerging industry. A whole series of townships spread in a big arc from Doornfontein to Sophiatown.[184] Migrant labour formed the link between the 'reserves' and the Rand. In the process, migrant labour conditions were to be the major problem for African Church life, a continuing threat to Christian home and family life. This must be borne in mind as we approach the life of the Churches, both in the cities and on the 'reserves' or 'homelands'.

Overcrowding, slum conditions and epidemics followed, culminating in the 'Spanish influenza' of 1918–19. To the Black masses, the 'influenza' was a traumatic experience. It also vastly affected the grass-roots level of the Church. A surprisingly large number of hefty African labourers, laid low by the epidemic and brought to death's door, felt that they had 'died' and 'been with Jesus'. There He had told them to return to this troubled earth as His special envoys and prophets. Dramatic examples are those of Prophet George Khambule of Telezini, Zululand, and Eliyasi Vilakathi of Jerico, Swaziland.

The Wesleyan Methodists

The Wesleyan Methodist movement had started in Eastern Cape. The enormous evangelistic impetus initiated by William Shaw and his colleagues had launched a thrust which was to carry their Church from Port Elizabeth to Elizabethville. On the way, however, they were going to meet with problems, none of which was bigger than the clash between Owen Watkins and Mangena Mokone. With their previous work in Transvaal and the Orange Free State, the Wesleyans were in a privileged position to meet the new opportunity on the Rand. 'The special genius of the Methodist Church' asserted itself, 'as a number of voluntary lay preachers offered to take the lead in the mine compounds and in the emerging townships.'[185] In 1891 the Wesleyan district chairman, Owen Watkins, recorded for Transvaal twenty-two missionaries and 237 local preachers, the latter active lay volunteers, both Black and White. There was a unique readiness on the part of Church authorities to let the African co-workers go the whole way from local preacher to the full ministry, without too much ecclesiastical hesitation. The Taylor revival in the 1860s, with Charles Pamla and his colleagues, had shown the way.

The Methodists were fortunate in their staff, particularly with the appointment in 1895 of the Revd William Hudson to plan and direct the evangelistic work. Hudson had more than thirty years' Church experience in Britain before he took over leadership on the Rand at the age of fifty-nine. He produced a large strategical plan for 'The Johannesburg Wesleyan Methodist Extension Fund', to build fourteen new churches at a total cost of £50,000. In the central area of the Rand, five 'prestige' buildings were erected, with a number of smaller chapels on the East Rand and the West Rand. In less than four years, twenty church buildings were constructed and the Albert Street church was extended to accommodate 1,000 people. The ordained staff grew from three in 1894 to twelve in 1899, not counting the ever-expanding army of voluntary local preachers placed in every conceivable corner. Most important were the compound teams, or 'Mission Bands'. Two local preachers together with a band of young Christian men would go into compounds as a team.

> They made their entrance singing, shouting, and moving to the rhythm of their song and went round the compound inviting the men to their services. There were extemporaneous prayers and the sermon was interrupted by interjections and bursts of song when the preacher made a telling point.

At this time there were about fifty local preachers on the Rand with their accompanying bands. They reached up to 3,500 men every Sunday.

Two devices developed in the Wesleyan Methodist Church on the Rand became models for other Churches throughout southern Africa in following generations. From their Church in Britain, Hudson and his co-workers brought the 'Quarterly Plan', appearing four times a year, indicating the placing for each Sunday of a large number of preachers. On this chart, the ordained were recognizable by their initials, the unordained by a number. This practical arrangement could direct and guide more than 100 different preachers and chapels. The other device, which was entirely African, was that of 'Multiple Interpretation'. Because of the extensive nature of the Methodist enterprise in South Africa, including many ethnic communities, the Wesleyans differed from most agencies at the time: the others 'followed' their people from Zululand or Pondoland or Vendaland and concentrated on their special language group. Wesleyan preachers on the Rand faced the need for many different Bantu languages and adapted themselves to the linguistic challenge in good African fashion. Together with the preacher stood the interpreters to his right and left, each prepared to carry the message in his own specific language with much the same gusto as the preacher himself. The role of interpreter had been emphasized in the Wesleyan Methodist tradition by the sudden appearance, during the 1866 Revival, of Charles Pamla, now the Revd Charles Pamla. (He retired in 1913 at the age of seventy-nine, stating that he had been a minister for forty-seven years; he died in 1917.) For many young Africans, the function of interpreter became an entry into the Methodist ministry.

The Healdtown Institute in the Cape had for decades been the great Methodist educational centre. In 1884 Methodist work in the Transvaal received its own centre at Kilnerton, near Pretoria. It included teacher training and a theological school and, by 1907, also admitted girls. Kilnerton became the incomparable nursery of the Wesleyan Methodist Church in the northern part of the country. Owen Watkins, already mentioned as chairman of the district, was particularly impressed by Mangena Manke Mokone, one of his staff at Kilnerton. The young pastor hailed from the Pedi people which, in an earlier period, had provided enterprising young migrant labourers, men who later returned home as devoted evangelists. Mokone wished to further a similar devotion at Kilnerton. Posted from there to the city of Pretoria, he faced a challenging crisis which became decisive – and divisive – for Protestant work in all of Africa. In the city there was a glaring divide between him and his White colleagues. He was regarded by the Whites as just another Kaffir, with a much lower salary than the White pastor. This difference in pay had not appeared so acute in the country, where the African could supplement his meagre income by farming. In Pretoria, the European lived in a fine house in the city centre, while Mokone lodged in what he called 'a stable', in Waterberg and later in Makapanstad. His living conditions induced bitter reflections on his status as an African and as a pastor.

In 1892 the Revd Mokone decided to leave the Wesleyan Methodist fellowship and form his own group, the Ethiopian Church. Although three or four previous breakaways of Independent Churches in rural Lesotho and Transkei had occurred, Mokone's step can claim priority as the *origo* of the 'Ethiopian' movement in South Africa, because of the historically and

Table 7.1. *Membership figures for the Methodist Church, Transvaal district, 1830–1913*

	1830	*1902*	*1913*
English missionaries	2	24	51
African ministers	–	17	36
Local preachers	5	527	2,091
Local churches	3	145	440
Other preaching places	5	215	761
Fully accredited members	78	9,300	21,300
Members on probation	321	3,500	8,300
Adherents	700	42,000	92,000

sociologically important connection between South African Independents and urbanization. We shall return to Mokone later.[186] The role of 'Pretoria' in the thought-world of African Independent Church leaders was of vital significance. Here Paul Kruger, President of the Transvaal Republic, awarded Mokone and his Ethiopian Church much sought-after 'recognition'. Whether this was ever expressed in an official document is less important than the almost mythical awe which the Ethiopian Church and its colleagues held for this purportedly generous reward.

From 1900 a few Wesleyan preachers found their way into some 'Ethiopian' Churches, but most preferred to continue their work within the framework of the mission-related Church. The statistics shown in Table 7.1 for the Methodist Church, Transvaal district, in this period indicates healthy growth.

However Chairman Owen Watkins was already looking farther afield, from the Rand and beyond, towards Zambia. With Isaac Shimmins, he crossed the Limpopo and 'took possession of the regions beyond in the name of Christ and Methodism'. On their journey north they were accompanied by experienced African evangelists, including David M. Ramushu, and established new centres in what became the Rhodesias (today, Zimbabwe and Zambia).

Church women prior to 1920

In the nineteenth century the Church had largely been a youth movement. In the twentieth century it became largely a women's movement. The official date for the foundation of the Wesleyan Methodist 'Manyano' in South Africa is 1907. In that year women held a convention, elected a president and drafted a 'constitution'. Methodist and Congregational beginnings, however, go back to a series of collective experiences. They included the Natal Wesleyan *Unzondelelo* and the Durban Congregational *Isililo* among the second and third generations of Christian women in nineteenth-century Natal, Swaziland, Botswana and the entire range of 'Independents'. There were similar developments among Anglican women in the eastern Cape. An Englishwoman started the Anglican prayer movement in 1908, as the Women's Help Society. The Congregational *Isililo* officially began in Natal in 1912. Its name, meaning 'The Wailing Group', was carried to the Rand. One Western lady advisor, without much success, suggested the more refined 'Women's Welfare Group of the American Board', but *Isililo* was retained as more relevant.

Inspiration for Methodist women on the Rand came from Natal. At Edendale, Natal, Mrs S. Gqosho, a minister's wife, participated in a women's convention and was inspired to try something similar for the Rand. With a group of six friends, she started weekly prayer meetings 'for their families, for their common unity, and for their sins'. On the Rand, it was natural to pray also for their men in the mines, 'that God should hold the mine pillars so as not to fall on the husbands and sons and thus kill them prematurely'. Mrs Gqosho, a person with drive and initiative, held 'revivals' in various places. She may have been a little too forceful; she was not popular as a leader and after 1910 the organization elected a White president instead. That practice continued until 1937, an expression of pragmatism and adaptability. At that time it still seemed prestigious to have as president the wife of the White Church president. It was also practical. The increasingly popular annual conventions, with hundreds of participants from the whole country, demanded arrangements for railway concessions. Women would fill five or more carriages, singing, swinging and praying. An application to 'The General Manager, Railways and Harbours' was more likely to be successful if signed by 'Mrs Burnet' or Mrs Allshorn', than if signed by 'Mrs Hlabangane'. Dr Deborah Gaitskell, historian of the Manyano movement, suggests that many women regarded the minister's wife as ordained. She was not an ordinary lay woman, but had, through her husband's position and her own leading role, acquired a certain status.[187]

The early Manyano movement was involved with 'Revival', rather than with social concerns. It was essentially a prayer movement by and for African women and their families. The kind of Christianity from which the movement emerged was one of pietistic Western revivalism, contrasting strongly with the later activist, social gospel. The Manyano uniform was important. The unvarying Wesleyan colour scheme of black–red–white provided endless themes for speakers at the great annual conventions: the blackness of sin, purification through 'the Blood', the whiteness of holiness. Congregational women, with black skirts and white blouses, added pink ribbons to their blouses for a splash of colour. Anglicans wore white jackets. The uniforms may have differed, as well as their ecclesiastical background, but the spirituality of these conventions had a remarkable common character. Other groups followed the initiative of the three leading missions. They each had their own Bantu name, e.g., '*abasizikazi*' (women helpers), their own distinctive uniform and even a characteristic ethos where ethnic culture permitted. The role of these groups for their respective Churches was fundamental, especially for communication between villages in the 'Reserves' and the urban congregations on the Rand.

These movements originated from common experiences at sickbeds and funerals and from contemplation of the hardships of life and the nearness of death. From Pretoria, Manyano women would set off by donkey cart for an all-night prayer meeting in a village, perhaps some twenty-five miles away. The emotional style corresponded, to some degree, with certain traditional funeral customs. The revivalist message encouraged mourning in the hearers; women would bewail and confess their sins and then publicly commit themselves to a fresh spiritual start. They prayed particularly for their young girls, exposed to the temptations of the city. Their repentance and pledge were 'a new element in African religious behaviour'.[188] Another variation was that of the Congregationalists at Umtwalume in Natal. There a family, joined by other Christian women, would – during some modern personal crisis – go out in the fields and pray all night. This practice was similar to the phenomenon a century earlier of archaic Khoi prayer experience.

One component in the role of music and singing was the fact that each member of this sisterhood of women appropriated for herself 'her own hymn'. An Anglican woman said:

> Before you stand up and preach, you would sing your hymn so that it is known that your hymn is on page so and so. If you are sick then we come to your home singing your hymn ... Oh yes, we have got our hymns with us, they are known.[189]

So strong was the women's movement, that a disturbing question arose. Should women, too, be allowed to preach? Mrs Rosalind Kumalo, a Primitive Methodist, was a born orator of exceptional energy. With the Methodist Church union in 1932, her little chapel was dismantled and she was eased out of the Nancefield church, because her Methodist pastor and others 'did not favour women orators, who outpassed them in influence'. A sly remedy was to allow a Manyano woman to preach, without placing her name on the 'Quarterly Preachers' Plan'.

One of the most impressive examples of Christian women's involvement in local political affairs was that of the resistance to passes in Bloemfontein just before the First World War. In the nineteenth century, the *mfecane* had stranded clusters of Africans far from their original homes, among them the Rolong Tswana. They had settled at Thaba Nchu in the wilderness, in present-day Orange Free State. Served by Wesleyan missionaries, they became increasingly strong Christian communities, where the school and the Wesleyan cell system of the 'class' formed a new society with its own ethos and witness.

The Wesleyan organization stressed a concept abhorrent to the dominant White population in the Orange Free State – social advancement for the Africans. To the Boers, these Blacks on the farms and in the emerging small towns of the high veld, were just Kaffirs. They were born to be domestic servants and farm labourers and should remain so. To the Africans, the Boers, with all their preaching and prayer, were part of an oppressive system of exploitation and repulsion. In 1900 the Orange Free State was the only territory in the country requiring women to carry passes. The ensuing struggle, which broke out in several places, was concentrated in Bloemfontein, the capital of the state and its rail and economic centre. Historically, Thaba Nchu had been the magnet for the Tswana, fleeing from the onslaughts of the *mfecane*. With individual land tenure and good educational facilities connected with Cape high schools, both Wesleyan and Anglican communities had prospered in Thaba Nchu in the closing years of the nineteenth century. However, a serious leadership feud in Rolong ranks induced some of the Black elite to move to Bloemfontein. In 1903 the alarmed Mayor felt that the Blacks threatened to become competitors of the White men: 'We have native Carpenters, Shoemakers, Bricklayers, Surveyors, and Contractors who in their turn employ other natives to work for them.' This attitude recognized the social and educational achievements of the missions at Thaba Nchu.

In 1913 the explosion came in three main centres of the Orange Free State. Hundreds of women marched on the police stations, all demanding an end to the pass laws. Georgine Taaibosch, a twenty-four-year-old active Church and Manyano member, led the women in Bloemfontein. Greta Phillips, another prominent Church woman, was struck by a police truncheon. In Winburg, twenty-three-year-old Ruth Pululu, an assistant schoolmistress, was found guilty of being without a pass. In no case did the riots lead to relaxation of the pass laws, but they had another important effect. By their solidarity and concerted action, these devoted, praying women proved to themselves and to others that their Christian conviction must be expressed in a fight for freedom, for themselves and for their society. These young Wesleyan women in Bloemfontein, Thaba Nchu, Winburg and Jagersfontein, demonstrated the transforming power of the Gospel. The White policemen, the mayors and the enraged town councillors knew what these black women were and must remain: Kaffir girls. The women knew they had come much further. In the chapel, they had listened to the Gospel liberation theme and had proclaimed it in Manyano meetings and to the primary school classes. It had lifted them to a new consciousness, a new awareness of dignity and purpose.

The Thaba Nchu protest, a landmark in women's resistance, was no isolated phenomenon. In 1922, less than a decade later, a women's boycott of European stores followed. Its inspiration was similar to that in Thaba Nchu. It occurred just south of Lesotho in the Herschel district, which had a strong Hlubi population. The issue was a protest against high sales prices in the European stores at the same time as local produce prices were low. The leaders of the boycott were Manyano women from the two leading Churches in the district, Methodists in Herschel and Anglicans in Qumbu. The local Magistrate, devoid of sociological understanding, misinterpreted the situation. He said in his report that the boycott was not justified, as it was led by 'wealthier and well-dressed' converts and that 'therefore the cry of poverty was not genuine'. The new Christian ethos however, with its strong educational ambitions, had developed a new awareness, with new needs and higher expenses. The Anglican women complained that 'the churches and the schools are dead'; they could not afford the school clothes, and so their children could not attend the schools. Three to four hundred women approached the Magistrate's office in a concerted protest. The Manyano had provided both an answer to isolation and a channel for their independence.

The Anglicans

Canon Farmer of Pretoria provides a clue to much Anglican African Church work prior to the Boer War:

> In 1894 there were 50 Native men working hard for the Church. I found that I had to register in the church books thousands who had been converted by these men each year. Baptisms of Catechumens taught by them exceeded 500. I was also surprised to find that these Natives had built for themselves, without any prompting or assistance, rough buildings for churches, with holes for windows and reeds for doors. They were often ornamented inside

> with crude ornamentation in coloured earth and on the wall at the end would be drawn a huge cross in colourful pigment. One of these evangelists is Jacob Dabani. He lived evangelically, never went back to his cattle and possessions but walked from village to village preaching wherever he had opportunity. He had no home of his own ever. He called his converts his children. His influence was marvellous.[190]

Certain aspects of Anglican strategy, programme and ecclesiological claims made the presence of these pioneers increasingly felt, both in the rural areas and in the emerging cities. The awareness of being an Anglican 'province' was emphasized through the metropolitan position of the Bishop of Cape Town, whose status was raised to that of Archbishop in 1897. It was also promoted by a series of provincial missionary conferences, the first of which was held in 1892.

The most significant episcopal appointment was that of Henry Callaway as Bishop of St John's in the Transkei, 1873–86. He was a medical doctor who had once been a member of the Society of Friends. Unlike many of the other Anglican bishops in South Africa at the time, who were appointed to Africa from some parish in Britain, Callaway had, prior to his consecration, experienced two decades of parish work in southern Natal. His Zulu parish, Springvale, showed great strength.[191] The ordination as deacons, in 1871, of Umpengula Mbanda and William Ngcwensa, both of whom had been taught theology by Callaway, indicated that this far-sighted European priest was aiming at African leadership. Callaway and his team of African and European fellow-workers gave to their diocese that particular Anglo-Catholic character which was to be a model for later generations. At first, St John's was an entirely rural diocese, but Bishop Callaway eventually made Umtata into the centre of the diocese. This was one of the many places in Africa where the cathedral constituted the nucleus of a future city – the capital city of the Transkei. From 1877, St John's Theological College and Teacher Training School at Umtata provided much needed educational training.

The Mfengu congregation at St Mark's station, founded by H. Waters, formed the centre of a new diocese, with Callaway as its bishop. The Mfengu made up the dynamic element of the diocese, just as they did in the somewhat older diocese of Grahamstown. A new church at Esikobeni, consisting of a colony of Mfengu emigrants from St Mark's parish, likewise bore the mark of the Christian Mfengu.[192] The Revd J. Xaba was in charge of the African work there, but he also held monthly services for the English community in the district. In 1877, the Revd Peter Masiza (later Canon) was the first African priest to be ordained in South Africa.

Certain local movements in Natal and Zululand were northern parallels to the dynamic Mfengu element in the southern Anglican dioceses. In the north, there were group movements under African leaders, rather than individual conversions. While response to evangelism of the Zulu in Zululand was largely and stubbornly negative, that of the refugee Sotho group of the Hlubi was one of acceptance. On his deathbed, Chief Hlubi's father, Mbunda, advised his son 'to lie down like a faithful dog at the feet of the Great White Queen'.[193] The Queen's own Church was also known as '*the* Church' and the Hlubi encouraged the work of the Anglican mission, under Archdeacon Charles Johnson. Towards the end, Mbunda himself was baptized, with his wife and four of his children. A Zulu priest, the Revd Titus Mtembu, was Johnson's invaluable go-between in forming the Hlubi congregation, which soon grew to several hundred people.[194]

The collective response of a total group was clearly illustrated by the parallel movement of the neighbouring Hlati. Again it was that sturdy English ex-farmer turned Archdeacon, Charles Johnson, who was instrumental in reaping that harvest – about 2,000 souls in all – for his Church. The personal development of the African leader, Charles Hlati, reveals aspects of the mobile situation in eastern Transvaal at the turn of the century. He was baptized in the Wesleyan Methodist Church and began to preach on Boer farms in eastern Transvaal. As a servant of the Dutch Reformed Church, he in turn baptized the converts, soon more than 1,000 of them. Hlati was known as the 'head native evangelist'. After a personal conflict with the Dutch Reformed minister, Hlati and his followers built a chapel of their own. It was on a Boer farm, since there were then no other lands available in that part of the country, but the farmer refused them the use of their chapel. Despite such adversity, they carried on, worshipping in their mud hovels and singing from a Wesleyan hymn-book in the Xhosa language. In the circumstances, the Hlati group revolted against what they felt as discrimination from the Dutch Reformed Church. After contacts with Charles Johnson, the Anglican Archdeacon, Hlati asked his followers if they were prepared to join the Anglican Church and receive the sacraments there. *Siyavuma* ('we agree') boomed the collective response. An important foundation was thereby laid for the extension of the Anglican Church in northern Natal.[195]

With only few variations, the Free Church men in the city – Wesleyan Methodists, Congregationalists, and Baptists – represented a special Anglo-American churchmanship. Darragh and his co-workers, full of veneration for the medieval Church of Ireland with its colour and drama, on the other hand, emphasized ritual in an unmistakable way. In the Boer War, the Boers found the Anglicans particularly obnoxious for representing the 'Queen's Church'. However this term still appealed to Anglicans, whether White or Black, long after the good old Queen had died. J. T. Darragh had come to the Rand and to central Johannesburg from Kimberley. In 1887, Bishop William Carter came to Pretoria (Johannesburg was still part of the Pretoria Diocese) from Zululand, where he had gained his episcopal experience during a ten-year period.

Bishop Carter's creative innovation was of far-reaching importance. Perhaps only the 1950s were to show *how* far-reaching his initiative was. He invited to the Rand the Fathers of the Community of the Resurrection and the Wantage Sisters. These highly visible monks and nuns changed the ethos of the Anglican community. Bishop Carter expounded what he called a Catholic theology. He 'deprecated the dividing of interests into camps and disliked the term "Native Church" as in a way dividing the Body of Christ.'[196] He found a response among the African clergy. The Revd Mtobi held that 'the Church should move on Catholic and not on national or racial lines.' These statements from 1905 were an early proclamation of a message which was increasingly heard during the following decades. Carter was a great organizer. With Fr Francis Hill, CR, in charge of the school system and with the Bishop's backing, the schools multiplied from fifteen to forty-four, with about 10,000 pupils. In 1914 the Fathers of the Community of the Resurrection moved to a new centre, at Rosettenville, then just outside the city boundaries. In the following decades it became the widely acknowledged educational and theological centre for Blacks. St John's high school provided for White youth. The Revd A. W. B. Watson provided an Evangelical counterweight to these 'Catholic' tendencies for the diocese. Having been cured from some ailment through 'Faith Healing', he made this approach his very own. He did not shun 'Brother Lake' and other American Pentecostal preachers of the Apostolic Mission and invited them to lay hands on the sick in his congregation. He was obviously a very serious-minded gentleman: in order to buy an organ, his congregation arranged a Fair in Jeppe Park, with such merriment as dance. The following Sunday, Wilson told his flock that during the time of the Fair, he had prostrated himself before the altar, reciting the Seven Penitential Psalms.

Members and voluntary preachers among the Anglicans on the Rand came not only from within South African borders, but increasingly from beyond, from as far as Malawi and East Africa. In some cases, they had been baptized in the Anglican Church there. One example was John George Phillips, born at Likoma, the island headquarters of the Universities' Mission to Central Africa (UMCA) in Lake Malawi. When baptized, he was given the name of the local Anglican missionary. After 1904, he participated in the contract labour transport from Malawi to the Rand. He sometimes preached to his young colleagues and was a devoted Anglican both at home and in South Africa. Like so many other labouring colleagues in the mines, he developed chest trouble and turned to anyone who promised help, in this case the Zionists. He eventually became 'General Overseer of Native work' and Bishop in the 'Christian Catholic Apostolic Church in Zion'. In his obituary, his daughter, somewhat ambitiously, stated that he had been 'educated at the headquarters of the Universities' Mission [Oxford and Cambridge] of Central Africa'.

'Following our people'

Other organizations which were exclusively mission agencies all decided to 'follow' their own people to the mines and the city: the American Board, the German, Swiss, Swedish and French Societies. In the years prior to the Boer War, the American Board missionary was H. D. Goodenough, an ambitious organizer who found the situation in Doornfontein, Johannesburg, lacking in order and Church polity. He felt that the local Zulu congregation was not structured enough to be recognized as a Church. Individuals would turn up with a letter claiming Church membership, but the missionary did not consider them qualified to vote or to hold office. Goodenough concluded that the Doornfontein chapel was not a Church, but rather an 'Endeavour Society', similar to such societies back home in Massachusetts. Resolutely, he announced this to his incredulous flock – houseboys, rickshaw-pullers, miners and clerks – who on Sundays were proud to belong to the Congregational Church in Doornfontein. He claimed that they did not belong to a Church, but merely to an 'Endeavour Society'. The violent reaction was a Johannesburg parallel to the occurrence a few years earlier in Nigeria, regarding the venerable Bishop Crowther and his diocese. (In Nigeria a group of new and zealous missionaries had undermined the African leadership of the Anglican Church on the Niger, and this was a major factor in the creation of various African Independent Churches, all unconstrained by European control.)

A similar event happened somewhat later among Congregationalists in northern Zambia. The result of Western conceit was the same in all these cases: dismay, frustration and alienation. The meeting in the Doornfontein chapel, Johannesburg, was only the beginning. Later some of the most devoted members of the congregation staged a determined walk-out. In 1917 they formed their own African Congregational Church, under Pastor

Gardiner Mvuyana, with headquarters almost next door to their former Doornfontein chapel.

The Dutch Reformed

The Dutch Reformed mission also became part of the multi-denominational campaign in the Johannesburg compounds. It was led by a missionary with experience in Zimbabwe, P. H. A. Fouche, who had spent thirty-six years (1906–42) in the compounds. Soon he engaged sixteen African evangelists from many different language areas as assistants. To a large extent, his work explains the vast Dutch Reformed outreach in the communities of southern Africa. Immediately after the Boer War, an Evangelical revival occurred in the Dutch Reformed Church, under the influence of young Boer soldiers, returning ex-prisoners of war. It was similar to Andrew Murray's Revival movement of the 1860s. The later movement led to a new involvement in foreign missions, beyond the borders of South Africa: in Zimbabwe, Malawi and among the Tiv people of Nigeria. However with a few exceptions, little changed in the attitude of Boer farmers to the Black and the Coloured Christians on their own farms.

Nonconformists on the Rand

The Christian cause in Johannesburg was not only represented by 'established' Churches. South Africa at this time was still a frontier society, with Johannesburg very much a frontier town. In this kind of world, the quest of both Black and White found other expressions for their faith than those of the Book of Common Prayer and John Wesley's sermons. The overwhelming concern for both Black and White was that of health. Andrew Murray the younger, the very pillar of the Dutch Reformed Church in this period, faced this problem when a personal health problem led him to rely on 'Divine Healing', as propagated by Dr Stockmayer in Hauptwal, Switzerland and Dr Boardman in London. Murray's books made him an international authority on the subject. He was sought out by P. L. Le Roux, missionary in eastern Transvaal, as well as by other rugged preachers who looked to him as their spiritual authority.

Johannes Büchler came as a Congregational school teacher from Cape and Kimberley to Johannesburg in 1889. The Infant Baptism issue led him to abandon the Congregational Church and to found one of his own, called 'Zion Church', with services in West End Hall. In 1898 he opened a 'Divine Healing Home' for Europeans at Jeppe's Town, Johannesburg. For a few years he received his inspiration from J. A. Dowie in Chicago, who ran a 'Zion' centre and published a magazine, *Leaves of Healing*. When Büchler went to Chicago to see for himself, the meeting with Dowie repelled him and he returned to the Rand.

Büchler felt that he had a 'psychic' gift: when he prayed for the sick, White or Black, miraculous healing resulted. Edgar Mahon, born in Maseru, Lesotho, had started his adult life as a Salvation Army officer, after a Standard IV education. He too had a health problem and, as Büchler prayed for him, he was healed. This was too much for the Salvation Army. Mahon was dismissed and started a Zion Church of his own. Subsequent Mahon generations transferred to a Baptist Church with strong emphasis on Bible study. They were active in Black compounds and townships and among Europeans who wanted a Christian community with a healing fellowship.

Another gallant individual was Albert Weir Baker, ex-solicitor from Natal. Having been deeply influenced by a British revival movement, he decided in 1895 to devote himself to a Holiness mission in the Johannesburg compounds. He too sought contact with Andrew Murray, and with the interdenominational 'South African General Mission', of which Andrew Murray was the President for some time. Baker's 'South African Compound Mission' was essentially a one-man show of surprisingly wide outreach. His magazine, *Africa's Golden Harvest*, encouraged 'the promotion of Scriptural, Holiness and Missionary Enterprise'. He established a network of contacts in Mozambique. Regularly visiting compounds, hospital clinics and prisons, he inspired increasing numbers of African workers. Being converted on the Rand, they then prepared to spread the 'Holiness' message to their home communities in the far north. The appeal was narrowly Evangelical. Conversions in the compounds were accompanied by ceremonial renunciation of amulets, or of that modern abomination, the snuffbox. Baker's interdenominational enterprise reached far beyond southern Africa, even to western Kenya.[197] The efforts of Büchler, Baker, Mahon and Le Roux were far-reaching. They may have seemed strange to some of the more established Churches in the City, but these men had faced the working masses with the appeal of the Bible and of their Master.

There is a Johannesburg parallel to the 'Early Migrant Labour' evangelization of the 1850s and 1860s, which first helped to bring the Gospel to communities in northern Transvaal and beyond. Johannesburg was seen by many missionaries as a den of iniquity, and J. X. Merriman, a Prime Minister of the Cape, referred to the Golden City as 'the university of crime'. What is often overlooked is that the opportunities grasped by men such as A. W. Baker and some of the missionaries and African pastors from the established Churches had a vast evangelistic influence. To these people, Johannesburg was not only a 'University of Crime' but a 'Seminary of Faith' as well. Barely literate as the labourers may have been, they felt it was their sacred task to transmit the new message to their own people. Anonymous as they were, their influence as evangelists was nonetheless strikingly effective.

The Lutherans

In spite of much rapid urbanization, South Africa was still largely rural, for the majority of both White and Black. The Church had problems both in certain rural areas of the Cape and Natal and in Transvaal, where the missions were exposed to the impact of the mines. After the First World War, the Hermannsburg Lutherans emerged as the biggest single Church in western Transvaal. The compact Kwena–Tswana area on the western Rand formed an especially strong Christian community and became thoroughly influenced by the Lutheran folk-Church. There was an unmistakable affinity between the Boer farmers and the German farmers staffing the Hermannsburg mission. However most Boer authorities in Pretoria were adverse to missionary activity and individual Boer farmers often made harsh demands on the African labour force. They effectively thwarted attempts to send children to school. The Hermannsburg mission often referred to 'the yoke of the Boers'.

The German missionaries soon made plans to buy farms for the emerging Tswana congregations. Fortunately, they were experienced in financial deals. Hebron Mission, north of Pretoria, was an example. It was paid for with contributions from cattle sold by the hard-working Tswana peasants and from the wages of Johannesburg labourers. In this way they bought 'farms which only a few years earlier had been occupied by Boer farmers free of charge'.[198] There was mutual understanding and respect between these paternalistic German farmer-missionaries and the Tswana peasants. Even though a close co-operation existed between Tswana chief and German missionary, there were some dramatic conflicts. One involved the choice of placing a church on the mission farm *or* on the chief's land. At Bethany in 1891–92, it would never have been possible to erect their impressive temple without the sincere understanding that existed between Chief Jacobus More and missionary W. Behrens. Upon the chief's orders, the people collected £2,000 for the church and over 100 labourers were put to work. In most cases, however, the German missionaries were in command. They preferred to stay where they were posted, often forty years or more at the same station, many without any furlough! Several were succeeded by their sons, thus establishing solid Lutheran dynasties.

A mass movement occurred at the turn of the century. Being baptized had now become fashionable. The two sacraments of baptism and Holy Communion (with confirmation) continued to play a fundamental role in the school system and Church discipline. At the beginning of the year, names of all children eligible to attend school were announced from the pulpit, according to the baptismal register. Six or seven years later, confirmation came as the climax to school life. On the mission farm, every aspect of daily life was ordered according to the rules of the Church: morning and evening worship in the chapel, ploughing, sowing, harvesting, marketing. The missionary and his wife, with the help of the Church elders, managed everything from harvest festivals to wedding cakes as well as school equipment. But there were changes. During the first twenty years (1870–90) of the Hermannsburg Mission, the catechumens had been recruited almost exclusively from the younger age groups. In the last decade of the century, it was mainly older women who attended the catechumen classes. The rural Tswana congregation was a self-contained world, with its own leaders and laws, but the wider world was beckoning. The diamond mines at Kimberley, though exercising their fascination, were fortunately far away. In Bethany, at least, Behrens managed to keep most of his flock at home. The Rand gold fields were another matter, for they lay just next door and soon their lure was felt even in the most shielded Lutheran congregation.

There was to follow a rapprochement by the Hermannsburg missionaries – according to Fritz Hasselhorn, *Bauernmission in Südafrika* (1988) – to Afrikaner ideals and attitudes, not least under the influence of Germany of the 1930s. But on the other side there was in some of these men and women a keen realization of the need for a struggle for justice and equality. This was given an uncompromising expression by Wolfram Kistnaer in his *Outside the camp* (1990).

Strange 'English' ideas of worship appeared: 'tea meetings, concerts, religious entertainment and merriment.'[199] New educational ambitions led beyond the elementary school, making for conflicts between conservative Church elders and modernizing school teachers. The whole system was really shaken in 1907 when at Bethany, of all places, the revered missionary's son, W. Behrens Junior, took his stand with the African teachers and demanded 'higher education', government grants for the schools and higher salaries for the teachers. He took the progressive element of the congregation with him and left.

Some chiefs decided to become Christian in the face of determined opposition from their own people, while others stayed with the traditionalists. For each Tswana people the new religion presented itself as a great drama, compounded by tragedy or benevolence. It involved shifting relations between the paramount chief and his relatives, and its outcome differed. As one considers these dramas, one must remember the equally serious resolve on *both* sides: one, a determination to preserve established order and traditional values and the other, a desire to create a new future for the people, in the name of the almost unknown Lord and Saviour.

The Moravians

Land questions between the Mission as legal owner and African Christians as tenants at times caused tragic conflicts. The State had awarded to the Moravian Silo mission, near Queenstown at the Cape, an area of 8,100 hectares for Coloureds and Africans. The understanding was that while the land itself belonged to the Mission, the buildings and the proceeds from gardens and fields belonged to the tenants. The Coloured congregation, however, thought that Government had given the land to the residents and that the Mission had unlawfully claimed the land. There followed a tragic lawsuit, resulting in the eviction of sixteen families. The legal question over 'mission land' in this and other cases was a serious concern. In 1909 Parliament passed a Mission Stations Act, intending to solve the problem, but it was only a temporary measure, preparing for the final showdown of segregational legislation in the 1913 Natives Land Act. In view of the aforementioned dispute, it was not surprising that this quiet backwater station of Silo should witness the appearance of Enoch Mgijima in 1921. He was a prophet who would shake the whole country out of its complacency. A latter-day John the Baptist, he came to baptize his people not as the Whites did, but in the running water of a stream, a 'Jordan'.[200]

The Catholics

Catholic achievement in Africa and elsewhere has involved excellent planning, long-range strategy and resolute perseverance in adverse circumstances. In Protestant South Africa, however, early Catholic effort appeared strangely tentative, almost as if seeking its way by a hit-or-miss method. When the Oblates of Mary Immaculate were called to the country in 1850, they were told to devote themselves to the Blacks. Scattered Catholic efforts until then had been concerned only with Roman Catholic family groups of European descent. When the Oblates went to Natal to convert the Zulu, they found, as others had before them, that the great Zulu nation were a singularly unresponsive people. In 1862, after a decade of fruitless struggle, they decided to leave the Zulu and turn to a more promising field, the Sotho. Subsequent development showed them to have been far-sighted.

In 1882 Fr Francis Pfanner, an Austrian Trappist – 'a singular personality, of slight build, with red hair and a flowing red beard' – arrived in the harbour of Port Elizabeth, accompanied by fifty Austrian fellow-Trappists.[201] After another year, there were eighty, all prepared to devote themselves to their solemn Trappist calling. By concentrated prayer and meditation they would change the life of South African Blacks. Bishop Ricards, Vicar Apostolic of Port Elizabeth, directed them to a barren place a few miles inland, and for a few years the new-comers tried to make this unpromising task work. Before long they had had enough and in 1884 moved north, not far from Durban. Here they founded Mariannhill, eventually one of the most fruitful missions in South Africa. Father Francis inspired his monks to expand in every direction. From 1885–90 new recruits from Austria and elsewhere arrived in great numbers and many new mission stations were planted in Natal and Zululand.

With all this display of extraordinary activity, an anxious question necessarily presented itself: Was this really in accordance with Trappist rule and ideal? Visitors were sent out from Europe to inspect and in 1892 Abbot Francis Pfanner was suspended. He withdrew from Mariannhill and retired to a tiny out-station. The first six weeks of his voluntary exile he spent in constructing, with a hoe, a knife, and a crowbar, a 'Way of the Cross': 177 steps on the side of a giant mountain, leading up to the summit. New visitations followed at Mariannhill and the Trappists insisted that 'they were doing a greater work for the honour of God by converting the Bantu to Christianity than by adhering to the traditional rules of silent monasticism.'[202] In 1914 the Religious Society was reconstituted with the name of 'The Missionaries of Mariannhill'. They had come to Africa to transform it, but found that they were themselves changed. Africa had a hidden power to change individuals and groups who came to the continent.

The Mariannhill community was shaken by another internal crisis, *intra muros*, caused not by hardship, but by a generous excess of energy and ideas. Father Willebald Wanger (1872–1943) became more and more dissatisfied with the Catechism used in teaching. It was that of Pius X, the authoritative text recommended in a hundred different languages throughout the continent. The Zulu translation had infelicitous Latin terms which the Zulu linguist found objectionable: *igrasia* for grace, *ivirigo* for virgin. Father Wanger, brilliant, stubborn and authoritarian, set out to create his own catechism, assisted by Zulu experts: catechists Mathias Maphalala and Yitus Khathi and Maria Zulu, member of the royal family. Their volume, published in an edition of 10,000 in 1912, had 534 pages and 923 questions. Only a few copies were sold. The size of the undertaking was only a minor problem. Wanger wanted real Zulu and thus many of his terms were found to be more than daring, with the result that there was a storm of protest. In 1920 Wanger returned to Germany, where in 1943 he was executed by the Nazis.[203]

Ethiopian Church Fathers

African Independent Churches as a specifically South African phenomenon show certain southern African characteristics, different from those of other regions of the continent. Compared with western and eastern Africa, southern Africa was dominated by a White minority. This dominance was experienced not only politically and economically, but was felt in the Church as well. The 'colour bar' between White and Black was increasingly accepted by the dominant White section of the population; something to be tolerated and indeed sometimes enforced even in the Churches. The Coloured were the first to experience the problem at the beginning of the nineteenth century. They had expected acceptance and found rejection and alienation and lived with the consequences, embarking on treks to the north, into Namaland, Griqualand and East Griqualand. In the last decade of the nineteenth century, certain African Christian communities, particularly in the emerging slum townships on the Rand, to their surprise and dismay experienced a similar kind of rejection – and they embarked on a spiritual trek along the pathways to 'Ethiopia' and 'Zion'. Not that the European's supercilious attitude was necessarily more pronounced in southern Africa than it was further north, but the unfortunate combination of this with segregation in southern African society was bound to have a devastating effect.

No doubt there appeared earlier sporadic conflicts in some rural areas. We mention Nehemiah Tile's resignation in 1882 from the Wesleyan Methodist Church and his founding of the Thembu Church in 1884. However, it was on the Rand that the trouble started in real earnest. Mangena M. Mokone expressed the programme of his breakaway Church in its very name, 'the Ethiopian Mission'. In his Wesleyan Methodist Church, Mokone had been far from being a marginal person. He was even made head of the new Kilnerton Institute, but all to no avail. Something was amiss. In fourteen points Mokone declared why he could not continue in a mission-related Church. Salary, housing, means of communication, passport problems, and so on, were enumerated, but the intangibles were just as important: 'No African pastor is respected by the White brethren ... The White pastors do not even know the members of their own congregations. They always build their own houses one or two miles away from their parish. The separation shows that we cannot be brothers.'[204]

These statements must be seen against a broader historical background to be fully understood. In nineteenth-century South Africa, the African Church developed in rural areas. Indeed, a patriarchal spirit flourished in the rural congregations – 'patriarchal' in a literal sense of the word. The local African evangelist had in many cases grown up with, and was part, of the missionary's household. Thus, if the missionary and his wife were referred to as 'father and mother', this was often to be understood in a specific sense. In the rural congregation there was a close and almost daily personal contact between the missionary and his local co-workers. The city, on the other hand, imposed totally different living conditions, particularly affecting the atmosphere of such a sensitive social group as the religious congregation. Mokone included a special paragraph about this in his declaration. He highlighted the fact that in the city the missionary chose to live apart from his African congregation: 'one or two miles away'. Very soon this distance was to increase and before too long, missionaries were to appear on the Rand who were not quite sure of the personal names of their African, so-called, co-workers (B.Sr. has come across such cases).

The very name of Mokone's new Church had a programmatic significance. It appeared in the Bible. Mokone referred to Ps.68:31, 'Ethiopia shall soon stretch out her hands unto God' – this was a promise for the evangelization of Africa. It meant the self-government of the African Church under African leaders.

Among Mokone's colleagues were some of those destined to play a leading part in the future of the Ethiopian movement, such as Khanyane Napo, S. J. Brander, Jonas Goduka (Tile's successor) and James M. Dwane. Outstanding among them was J. M. Dwane, a Gaika of a chief's clan. Like Tile and Mokone, he was an ordained Wesleyan Methodist minister (b. 1848, ordained 1881). A gifted speaker, he was sent to England from 1894–95 to represent his Church and solicit financial support for the work. On his return to South Africa, he quarrelled with his mission authorities about the use of this money and left the Mission Church. In 1896 he joined Mokone and Brander and, with his ability and forceful personality, at once became a leader in the new movement.

Through different sources, both Mokone and Dwane had heard of the

African Methodist Episcopal Church founded in the United States in 1816. Dwane was chosen to go to America in order to obtain affiliation with this Church. The mobility of this local leader, going to Western Europe and the United States should be emphasized. On his return to South Africa, he tried to persuade all the Ethiopian leaders to follow him into the AME fold. Together with Khanyane Napo and Mokone, he approached the government of the Transvaal for formal recognition of the Church. This was granted. Dwane's ambitions took him further. He asked Cecil Rhodes for the right to extend his Church to Rhodesia and the Zambezi and he planned to collect funds to visit King Menelik of Abyssinia in order to extend his work to the Sudan and Egypt. In 1898 the AME bishop, H. M. Turner, paid a five-week visit to South Africa. In this short time the Black bishop was accorded a triumphant welcome by the Ethiopians. Turner ordained sixty-five ministers, consecrated Dwane as assistant bishop and bought a site for a future centre for higher learning in Queenstown. In 1898–99, Dwane once again went to America. He was not content with being only an assistant bishop, a position which emphasized the inferior status of the African Church as compared with the Black American Church.

On his return to South Africa Dwane took an extraordinary step. His contacts with the [Anglican] Church of the Province convinced him that the African Methodist Episcopal Church 'could not hand on Episcopal orders because they had never received them'. The outcome of Dwane's deliberations with the Anglicans was the formation in 1900 of the 'Order of Ethiopia' as part of the Church of the Province. On the part of the bishops of the Province this step must be recognized as an act of statesmanship. Dwane was eventually ordained a deacon and was later Provincial of the Order for some years. The majority of Ethiopians, however, did not follow Dwane. The mainstream of the Ethiopian movement found new channels and other independent groups sprang up during and after the troubled years of the Boer War. In 1908 the membership of the Order was only some 3,500. Dwane died in 1915 and was succeeded by another Provincial. Not attracting the broad masses, the Order of Ethiopia was mainly limited to one ethnic community, the Xhosa. However, as an attempt on the part of a leading Church at that time to tackle the Ethiopian problem in a spirit of understanding, it has remained unique in the history of South Africa.

Simultaneously with the departure of Dwane from the Ethiopian Church, American Blacks demonstrated the importance of the American connections with the African Methodist Episcopal Church by sending one of their ablest men, L. J. Coppin, to South Africa as their first resident bishop. Black American missionaries were, however, almost as much foreigners in the eyes of the Ethiopians as the White missionaries. Therefore, a similar opposition was levelled against the AME as against the White missions.

Another important development was that of the African Presbyterian Church founded in 1891 by P. J. Mzimba of the United Free Church of Scotland. Like Dwane, Mzimba was widely travelled, having visited the Churches in Scotland and the United States. His position as a respected pastor of the Presbyterian congregation at Lovedale made his secession the more serious. Two-thirds of this congregation followed him. The fact that Mzimba – himself a Mfengu – carried only Mfengu with him, whereas the Xhosa portion of the Presbyterian Church was unmoved, throws significant light on secessionism in general: like Tile's Thembu Church, Mzimba's organization was not only Ethiopian, but tribal.

'Ethiopians' we classify as independent Bantu-speaking Churches which have seceded from White mission-related Churches chiefly on racial grounds, or, other Bantu-speaking Churches seceding from these 'Ethiopian' leaders. The meaning of the term 'Ethiopian' seems to oscillate between two interpretations:

(a) A general reference to the programme, 'Africa for Africans', with a corresponding aversion to White domination. 'Ethiopia' in the Bible gave antiquity to the claim of the African Church and was thought to sanction of this claim.
(b) The word 'Ethiopian' can be more specific, referring to a particular African country under an African Christian king – Abyssinia or Ethiopia. The Abyssinia-ideology of the Ethiopians, shared also by most Zionists, is in essence an attempt to give to the independent Church an ancient apostolic charter, linking their Church with the Bible and with a Christian African kingship. The 'mythical charter' of the apostolic secession from the Ethiopian Church in Abyssinia does 'Christianize' this pattern.

The peculiar expressions of charismatic or *Zionist* faith are: healing, speaking in tongues, purification rites and various taboos. There are numerous local and individual variations among Zionist groups. However, on careful analysis, Zionists show an amazing uniformity, caused no doubt, by certain fundamental needs and aspirations amongst the broader masses. While thus recognizing a considerable latitude between various Zionist groups – numbering 2,000–3,000 – one could argue that they together form *one* common African charismatic movement, with local and individual variations and names. Whereas the Ethiopian mythology projects longings for a Christian African nation under the 'Lion of Judah, King of Kings', the

Zionist mythical charter focuses their thoughts on the holy land itself. The Constitution of 'the Zion Christian Church' defines the 'Basis' of their faith and organization: 'The name of the Church shall be designated the Zion Christian Church. But ye are come unto Mount Zion, City of the Living God, heavenly Jerusalem, innumerable company of Angels. Heb.12:22.'

The denomination 'in Zion', *eZiyoni*, has a technical meaning. With this name the prophet defines his organization as a New Testament Church which in detail carries out the religious programme supposedly developed by a central figure in the Zionists' Bible, John the Baptist. Thereby, the prophet links his baptisms with that apostolic succession which flows from Jordan, the River of life. 'Zionists', *amaZioni*, is the term used by these leaders themselves and therefore it is used as a comprehensive term in a book by BSr, *Bantu Prophets in South Africa*, 1948. We could just as well have referred to them as 'Charismatics', in order thereby to include some Churches with characteristic common features but which should not be classified as 'Zionists' and which would not themselves be referred to as such. We think particularly of Isaiah Shembe's *amaNazaretha* where features of the relationship to the Leader, of worship and of hymnology differ from those of the Zionists.[205]

THE TSWANA

The Tswana, to the north of Cape Colony, were hunters, herdsmen and cultivators. There were also skilled craftsmen, congregated in large villages. In 1801 a settlement such as Dithakong near Kuruman had 3,000 dwellings with almost 15,000 inhabitants. These compact Tswana settlements were potentially more suited for evangelization than the more scattered Nguni and itinerant Coloured refugees. Three problems, however, made the mission work difficult at times. In the first place, the permanence of Tswana settlements was entirely dependent on the availability of water. If the local spring dried up, the whole community was forced to move and any missionary would be obliged to follow them. Second, the entire area was dominated in the 1820s and 1830s by the ever-threatening *mfecane*. The Zulu onslaught on their neighbours caused war and utter devastation, life was chaotic and the prospects for peace very bleak. People were continuously on the move in search of shelter, subsistence and some form of security. In some cases, whole communities were annihilated. Third, any possibility of missionary activity depended on the local king or chief whose attitude was dominant in Tswana society.

When the first missionaries arrived, southern Sotho, northern Pedi and northern Venda had all existed for decades in mountain caves, ever anxiously on the lookout for devastating attack by Zulu armies or other enemies. Sotho chiefs established almost invincible mountain fortresses: Moshoeshoe's Thaba Bosiu, Moroka's Thaba Nchu, and Sekhukhune's Piring. Their Tswana colleagues on the high veld to the west could not resort to that kind of defence. The arrangement of the Tswana villages constituted both strategic advantage and fatal weakness. The terrible consecutive years of drought in the 1820s and early 1830s reduced the strength of the people. They became very dependent on skilled rain-makers, sometimes the chief or a rain doctor, at times someone brought in from outside. The failure of traditional incantations to bring the expected rain might have persuaded certain Tswana chiefs that the new message of the White men might be helpful.

The Tswana chiefs welcomed the missionary as a potential ally, one who could secure military protection against enemies or provide useful communication with the Cape government. However a chief was not always in a welcoming mood. If a member of his family showed excessive interest in the missionary's message, the chief could suspect his kinsman of using the new teaching to form his own following within the community, potentially in opposition to the chief's leadership. Also, the chief could not ignore the powerful spokesmen of Tswana religion, the traditional priests and diviners. Although he could initially overrule their protests at the Christian presence, he could not always prevent the recurrence of 'pagan reactions' in opposition to the missionaries. The co-operation of chief and missionary were vital to the spread of the Gospel. The chief's personality, his openness to foreign influences and new ideas both for his own and his people's advantage, were important factors. Likewise, the quality of the missionary pioneers must be emphasized. They include Moffat and Livingstone, Merensky and Casalis. Remarkable personal friendships grew up between chiefs and missionaries. But the missionaries were not alone in their endeavours. In several cases they were preceded or accompanied by Christian Griquas who came among the Tswana as interpreters and preachers. Mention must again be made of the anonymous Africans who went south-west from lands troubled by the *mfecane*, to Cape Colony and the coast and later returned with the Christian message to their native lands.

The Griqua in the south formed a path to the Tswana further north. When hunting for ivory, they had told the Tswana of the missionaries, English teachers, who had assisted them in various ways. A recommendation from the Griqua leader, Adam Kok, prepared the Tlaping Chief Mothibi to receive the White missionaries. In 1816 the Chief told the LMS Secretary,

John Campbell, to send teachers and promised that he would 'be a father to them'.[206] The missionaries discovered, however, that even though they might be enthusiastically welcomed by the chief, the people's attitude was still hostile. The Tswana insisted that 'a chief is chief by the grace of the people' and Mothibi had to modify his enthusiasm for the missionaries. Another more experienced missionary, James Read, arrived in Mothibi's village accompanied by Khoi Christians from Griquatown, Bethelsdorp and Kat River. He suggested to Mothibi that 'the good people beyond the Great Waters' had sent generous tokens of friendship from the Christian mission which might be handed over to him if the Tlaping were co-operative. This encounter paved the way for Robert Moffat.

After a few years' apprenticeship, first on a Stellenbosch farm, where he learned Dutch, and then among the Griqua, Moffat arrived among the Tswana in 1821 and gave half a century of solid and faithful work there. He made Kuruman into an oasis in the desert. A visitor wrote:

> Everyone is struck with the beauty of Kuruman, although the site cannot boast of any natural charms. All we see is the result of well-directed labour. A street of about a quarter of a mile in length is lined on one side by the missionary gardens, enclosed with substantial walls, and teeming with fruit and vegetables of every description . . . On the opposite side of the street, is a spacious chapel, calculated to hold more than 500 people. It is built of stone, with a missionary dwelling-house on either side . . . and a trader's dwelling-house and store at the western end . . . At the back of the missionary premises there are store and school rooms, workshops, etc., with a smithy in front. Behind the chapel is a printing office, in which native compositors were setting type for the new editions of Mr Moffat's bible. Thousands of Sechuana books have been well printed and as neatly bound in this establishment.[207]

Moffat built a congregation at Kuruman in 1824 through his catechetical classes and schools, where he instructed the future teachers and catechists.[208] From 1857 he devoted himself to the translation of the Tswana Bible. He was dependent on his African assistants in his work. One was his interpreter, 'William the Griqua, the only individual through whom I could speak freely to his people on the things of God'.[209] No missionary acquired a more remarkable reputation of being the friend of the chiefs – 'even the toughest of them' – than Robert Moffat. Two incidents during the first decade of his missionary activity illustrate themes recurring later in the century: first, the growing belief among Africans that a community with its own missionary could not be defeated in war; and second, the tendency toward emotional 'revivals' among newly established Christian groups.

In 1823, Mothibi's Tlaping were suddenly attacked by the Tlokwa. Moffat secured the help of Griqua chiefs and their troops, commanded by Chief Christian Waterboer. The Griqua's guns ensured victory, despite the numerical superiority of the attackers. The Tlaping now regarded the missionary in a much more favourable light. After the victory of 23 June 1823, Tswana scattered far beyond the territory of the Tlaping were inclined to believe in a Christian missionary's indispensability for military purposes. A year later, the Seleka Rolong were attacked and defeated by the Tlokwa. The Wesleyan missionary, Samuel Broadbent, was active among them, but he happened to be away on the day of the attack. Significantly, Sekunelo, the Seleka chief, later claimed that the missionary's presence would have spared them the onslaught.

Griqua influence also affected Moffat's mission in a deeply spiritual way during his early years among the Tswana. In his wanderings before 1821, he was greatly intrigued by the emotional character of the Griqua and Khoi spiritual life. Some of those who went with him to the Tswana, continued to give way to outbursts of tearful enthusiasm. Moffat felt these experiences were rather embarrassing for the Tswana who came to his tiny congregation at Kuruman. In Tswana society men should not weep after they had reached the time of their circumcision. Therefore, the sudden emotional 'revival' among the small group of Tswana Christians in 1829 was very surprising, especially to Moffat.

> We were taken by surprise. We had so long been accustomed to indifference, that we felt unprepared to look on a scene which perfectly overwhelmed our minds. Our little chapel became a Bochim, a place of weeping ... although it was impossible to keep either order or silence, a deep impression of the Divine presence was felt. They sang till late hour and before morning dawned, they would assemble again at some house for worship, before going to labour.[210]

Moffat's most surprising achievement was his friendship with the Ndebele chief, Mzilikazi, a feared warlord. This friendship was one of the great Black–White relationships in Africa. During the 1820s, Mzilikazi conquered lands and peoples stretching far to the north of the Tswana territories, into the southern part of present Zimbabwe. His military presence there was the greatest single obstacle to the extension of missionary work into northern Botswana and to the Shona people beyond. Moffat's activity at Kuruman aroused Mzilikazi's curiosity and, in 1829, he sent two sub-chiefs to contact the missionary. They insisted that Moffat return with them. The first meeting between Moffat and Mzilikazi, at a place near present-day Pretoria, illustrates the paradoxically strong influence which Moffat's personality exerted on the Griqua and on African chiefs. The initial understanding between missionary and chief was reinforced by Moffat's three subsequent visits to Mzilikazi in 1835, 1854 and 1857. Theirs was much more than just a political alliance. Mzilikazi told Moffat: 'You are my only friend.'[211] Even if the chief probably never considered becoming Christian, his friendship with Moffat gave status in Tswana society to the missionary and his message. Moffat of Kuruman became aware almost unintentionally of a way to the north which could lead to new fields of endeavour. This was through his contact with Mzilikazi.

Moffat was the very embodiment of the 'man on the spot'. Like other missionaries – in his own time and later – he had to put up with a visiting mission director who had strategical visions of how to win the continent of Africa. In 1820, a London director, John Campbell, visited the Hurutse people in Botswana and immediately saw them as the leaping off point for bigger things: they would open the way to 'communication with the Portuguese on the East Coast and from there to the LMS work in Madagascar'. Moffat, the stern Scot, dismissed such speculations as 'building so many castles in the air'. He preferred the hut on the ground.[212]

Livingstone shared with Moffat the same Scottish background of the 'godly poor'. As a boy of ten he began his strenuous working life in a factory, first as piecer and later as spinner at the Blantyre Cotton Mills, with a workday of twelve and a half hours, six days a week. From 8 to 10 pm he learned to read and write and soon was able to learn Latin at the same evening school. Both Moffat and Livingstone were missionaries of the LMS, a Congregationalist society, but their paths of religious development – while definitely Protestant – were not identical. Moffat was 'cradled in Presbyterianism, warmed by his Methodist experience'.[213] Livingstone, while a Scot of the Scots, was far from being a Presbyterian member of the Kirk or the Free Church of Scotland. His father had joined a local 'independent' group in northern Scotland, with a liberal, optimistic theology – very different from dour 'Kirk' beliefs. This gave a glow and a remarkable strength to the son's thirteen years in the factory and to his university years, 1836–40, at Glasgow and in London where he studied medicine and theology. He took a medical degree as Licentiate of the Faculty of Physicians and Surgeons, Glasgow, and was ordained a missionary at the Albion Street chapel in London.

Livingstone's international interest at first focused on China and he hoped to be sent there, but this was changed to 'South Africa', particularly as he had met Robert Moffat who visited London on a furlough. On this visit he also attended a meeting of 'The Society for the Extinction of the Slave Trade and for the Civilization of Africa'. It was here that he heard Thomas

F. Buxton on 'Commerce and Christianity' as the alternative to slavery and the slave trade in Africa. This was his preparation for the mission field in southern Africa when he arrived there in 1841 in order to go to Moffat's Kuruman station, where he began his twelve years of missionary apprenticeship in Botswana. Moffat and Livingstone had many things in common, apart from both being Scots. At Kuruman, they developed a common dislike of the Boers, a feeling reciprocated by the Boer farmers who abhorred LMS missionaries. But several personality differences characterized the two men. Whereas Moffat was content to remain stationary for decades at Kuruman, Livingstone's restless nature forever drove him towards new horizons. Livingstone immediately caught the vision of a 'missionary road', leading northward from Kuruman into the interior of Botswana and beyond – part of a long-term missionary thrust to the 'Regions Beyond'. If Moffat, the missionary, was the 'man on the spot', Livingstone, the explorer, represented the thrust towards the ever-receding 'frontier'. From Kuruman, he very soon established contacts with Tswana communities to the North, reaching as far as Lake Ngami in 1849. On three journeys during his first eight years in Africa, he preached to the Kgatla, the Kwena and the Ngwato.

Moffat and Livingstone differed also in their respective approaches to controversial aspects of African culture. Although he lived for many decades among the Tswana, Moffat never gave them credit for religious ideas and would slightingly refer to 'the national atheism of the Kaffirs'.[214] Livingstone regarded this attitude as a mistake. He thought that deep religious feelings had been expressed among the Tswana from time immemorial.[215] Moffat considered initiation rites to be dangerous customs to be completely avoided by Christian converts; Livingstone felt they were more an expression of national citizenship, a civil act rather than a religious observance. Livingstone was even prepared to view the complicated problem of polygamy with an open mind. His attitude to the encounter between traditional religion and the Christian message was characterized by a refreshing optimism.

Another fundamental point on which the two were at variance was the role of African Church workers. Moffat never really believed that Africans were competent to evangelize, independent of European missionaries. Livingstone, on the contrary, stressed the importance of the African agency in evangelism. He referred to groups of refugees from the African interior who, having heard the message, induced others to listen to it. From this and similar observations, Livingstone drew daring conclusions:

> The interior of Africa – What is the great obstacle to its evangelization? To this subject we invite attention, for on it depends the welfare of a continent

> ... We submit, that the system of fostering our 'proteges' by perpetual supplies from Europe, is unfair to the heathen who have not yet heard the name of Jesus ... The Missionary Society, so long as the present system is kept up, is virtually a go-cart to them, and until it is abolished the full energy of Christian men will never be developed ... Time seems an essential element in African success. No European ought to go where a native Church is already formed. There ought to be an entirely onward movement of the missionary corps in Africa. We want the missionaries to take their place in the missionary field ... the whole of the Colonial and Griqua missions ought immediately to be abandoned ... We have great confidence in the essential vigour of Christianity. It blooms in imperishable youth wherever it is untrammelled by the wisdom of men. Sow the seed, and it never dies. The Divine Spirit will see to it.[216]

Although Moffat remained at Kuruman for nearly five decades after establishing his permanent base there in 1824, he also reached out to Tswana groups farther north and east. Accompanied by Griqua assistants, he visited the Ngwaketse in 1824 and entered into a discussion with Chief Makaba on the resurrection of the dead. Makaba, thinking of the thousands he had slain in war, insisted that the dead must not be allowed to rise. It was characteristic of Moffat that, while continuing to maintain his contacts with the Ngwaketse over many years, he did so from distant Kuruman, preferring to entrust the spiritual care of the Ngwaketse to African catechists. When the LMS finally sent James Good, a resident missionary, to the Ngwaketse in 1865 he was thus able to build on foundations prepared by African catechists. Good had at first worked at Griquatown. When it was no longer of sufficient importance to be maintained as an independent station, he suggested that he be posted to the Ngwaketse area, since a number of Griqua had moved there. He discovered that there already existed, prior to his arrival, a Christian community which had been started in 1848 by the African catechists Sebube and Thlomelang, both attached to the LMS. On his arrival Good was welcomed by Chief Gaseitswe and the two became close friends, their relationship being reminiscent of that between Mzilikazi and Moffat. Church services were held at the chief's court. The chief also considered the missionary useful for diplomatic contacts.[217]

The concentration in this account on Tswana chiefs and their religious attitudes must not lead to the conclusion that the first Tswana converts were members of royal chiefs' families. The first school, it is true, was often organized for the chief's sons, as in the case of the German Lutheran, Heinrich Christoph Schulenburg's school among the Ngwato. This was a common feature in Africa at the time. But the first baptized were often simple folk, marginal people and refugees. At Kuruman the first convert in 1820 was a young blind woman; a lay missionary, Hamilton, had been her spiritual guide. The next two converts were from the Hurutse tribe, refugees to Kuruman from one of the *mfecane* raids. These converts were domestics in Moffat's household, a situation characteristic of the early missionaries throughout the continent. The Tshidi Rolong presented a great exception from this general rule: Chief Montshiwa's half-brother Molema was the first royal convert to Christianity. It was Molema – 'the Apostle of the Molopo River' – who introduced Methodism to the high-veld, helping to establish the two main important foci for the early Church, Mafikeng and Thaba Nchu.[218]

In the enormously disintegrated situation in the whole region in the early years, 1850s–60s, one cannot expect to find solid well-measured information on individual Tswana converts; at best one gathers straws in the wind. Three of them are quoted here for what they are worth: one a preacher, the second a prophet, the third a teacher and administrator, all active in the 1860s. They had been refugees, when they were converted. David Mogata, a Kwena, had been converted by a Wesleyan preacher among the Tswana in the south and then found his way back to his northern home territory. According to Wilhelm Behrens, a German Lutheran, Mogata preached 'in almost all the great towns of the Tswana', including areas west of present-day Pretoria. The second, possibly came from the Seleka Rolong. When he fled as a refugee from the political upheaval, he was caught by Tlokwa troops and stayed with them for several years. During his period of captivity he saw visions, not an unusual phenomenon during that time of deprivation. In the first he foresaw that a large army of Africans from the north would destroy the Tlokwa, which did in fact happen; in his second vision, copper-coloured people with guns and horses joined these attackers – possibly a reference to the Griqua, whose help Moffat enlisted. In his final vision, he saw a large crowd of people, among them men dressed in black clothes who came as men of peace. The third, a young Tswana, met an LMS missionary somewhere 'in the interior', accompanied him to Cape Town, and was educated there. He was baptized and took the name of the missionary, Richard Miles. This custom of naming the convert was much less usual at this time in southern Africa than it was in West Africa. As Richard Miles he was appointed teacher at the Griqua centre of Philippolis and was later transferred by the government as superintendent of the local population at the Berlin Mission's Bethany station, an important halfway-house between Griqualand and Lesotho, with Koranna, some Griqua and soon a strong body of Tswana. It thus became a centre for the communication of new religious ideas to migrants who passed through on their way south, or on their return to home areas.

Chief and missionary

Three main factors dominated the relationship between Tswana chiefs and missionaries: the attitude of the chief's family, the problem of traditional religion and the question of the chief's role in the Christian Church of his community. The chief's attitude to Christianity was complicated by the fact that other males in his family might choose to become Christian. After Christoph H. Schulenburg baptized Ngwato Chief Sekgoma's sons, Kgama and Kgamane, they refused to participate in a ritual concerned with preparations for defence against Mzilikazi's troops. The ensuing tension between the chief and his sons culminated in a civil war in 1866.[219] The cordial relations between Montshiwa, chief of the Tshidi Rolong, and his young Christian half-brother showed that differences among tribal leaders could be resolved amicably by a wise chief and a loyal family. A major study has been devoted to the Tshidi Rolong. With her book, *Body of Powers, Spirit of Resistance, the Culture and History of a South African People* (1985), Dr Jean Comaroff has given an interpretation of the 'Event History', structure and culture of the Tshidi community to the present, which turns out to be a penetrating and absorbing analysis of the Methodist Church in the area.

> While the majority initially resisted the mission along with the chief, a minority resisted the chief along with the mission. Although these local rulers were indeed opposed to formal conversion, the increasingly global threat of (political) subjugation caused them to embrace the evangelists as political allies to a greater extent than they might otherwise have wished or deemed prudent. The vision of the missionaries was mediated in complex ways by their field experience and by South African political conditions.[220]

Chief Sechele of the Kwena decided to be baptized when he was nearly forty. His decision was no sudden whim, either on his part or on that of David Livingstone, the missionary concerned. In our age of assertive scholars, one writer has not a shadow of a doubt that Sechele became a Christian 'more by military considerations than by religious motives'.[221] Others, just as scholarly, suggest that 'what had tilted the balance for him in favour of Christianity will never be known ... it was little short of miraculous that he decided to take the plunge.'[222] In 1842, when Livingstone first visited the chief, Sechele's only child was seriously ill. Livingstone applied his medicines to good effect, one of many cases in African Church history when medical assistance served as a catalyst. Three years later, Livingstone went to live among the Kwena and visited the chief daily. Sechele felt challenged by the White man's command of letters and it took him only two days to learn how to make sense of the alphabet. By 1847, he could read the New Testament. Soon he also asked the missionary to take evening prayers in the Chief's House.[223] Finally, he was prepared to show his acceptance of the new faith in two ways: he gave up rain-making and *bogwera*, the local initiation rites; and, like Israel's kings of old, aimed to build a worthy house for God.[224]

The chief's interest in the new message paved the way for commoners and refugees to follow his example. Whereas sub-chiefs and medicine-men were horrified by his inclination to Christianity, people of marginal status in Kwena society were ready to respond. Khosilintse, the chief's brother, suggested in an excited speech of 1854 that, more than others, it was the refugees in their midst who had accepted the message. 'Did those tribes, the remnants of which have fled to Sechele, reject the Gospel?' The answer to this rhetorical question was, 'No.' The 'refugee factor' was at work also among the Kwena.[225]

From 1847 Sechele began to insist on being baptized. But both chief and missionary were confronted by the law of the Church, which involved the renunciation of polygamy on the chief's part. Admittedly, Livingstone, while officially loyal to the Church's ruling, was not happy about its moralistic rigidity.[226] At first Sechele only expressed his regret that the missionary had not arrived 'before he married so many'.[227] But the intractable law had to be obeyed, and Sechele had five wives, 'decidedly the most amiable females in the town, our best scholars, too', in Livingstone's estimation.[228] The chief had to contend with determined opposition concerning his baptism, both from his own people and from his royal colleague in distant Lesotho, Moshoeshoe, who strongly advised against taking this step. Yet Sechele felt that he had to go the whole way. He dismissed four of his five wives, and on 8 August 1848 was baptized by David Livingstone. To his people this was a calamity. One old man, obviously considering the possible cosmic consequences of the chief's act, told Livingstone, 'You might have delayed till we got rain'. Less than a year later, one of the dismissed wives, Molokon, was found to be pregnant and only Sechele could have been the father. Stern Protestant Church discipline dealt with cases of this kind. Livingstone expected that the chief would be excluded from the fellowship of Holy Communion for two or three years, but the period was extended to four decades and the Chief of the Kwena was not reinstated in the Church until 1889.

'Communicant member' or not, Sechele continued preaching in his chapel for decades and was the whole time an interested Bible student. He related Bible study to his personal problem, being amazed 'how few, few good kings there were in those days'. In 1854 he mentioned that the mighty kings of old, David and Solomon, had countless wives and concubines and still remained men after God's own heart.[229] Moffat had a standard answer in such disputes: the Old Testament was 'abrogated under the new dispensation'. However this argument, while possibly good theology, did not satisfy the chief, who had been told that he was reading the very word of God. Moffat did his best to prevent the chief from preaching, but Sechele could not accept this: 'I am a believer and I have studied the word of God and I must not preach? I *can* pray and how is it that I cannot preach as well as pray? Andries Waterboer preached and why not I?'[230] This outburst had racial overtones: Waterboer was a Griqua (a Coloured) chief. Was he therefore closer to the Europeans than an African was? The situation was aggravated when Khosilintse, the chief's brother, took up the challenge in 1854. Thanks to Robert Moffat's notes, this eloquent plea, 'the deep tones of a stricken soul', has come down to us. It is one of the earliest verbalized protest of the African's feeling of discomfort in the Church and in the 'Christian civilization'.

> Is it because we have not white skins that we are to be destroyed like *libatana* [beasts of prey] ? Why do the English assist the Boers [and] ... supply them with ammunition when they know the Boers? ... Are we only to obey the word of God because we are black? Are white people not to obey the word of God because they are white? ... I speak the truth. My words are not the words of a Boer. They are mine, I, Khosilintse. You know they are the words of truth.[231]

The idea of founding his own Church did not yet present itself as a viable alternative to the chief. But in 1857, Sechele accomplished what to him must have seemed the next best thing. He went into the lion's den and approached the president of the Boer Republic of Transvaal, Pretorius, asking him for missionaries from some other society. Thus it was that the Hermannsburg Lutherans, recent arrivals in South Africa, were directed to the Kwena and from them to the Ngwato. Sechele was greatly encouraged by one of the missionaries, Heinrich Schroder, and through these Germans had a new lease of life as a preacher. The Ngwato King Sekgoma later approached Sechele to get missionaries for his people. Schapera has pointed out that 'Tswana rulers tended to permit only one denomination access to their domains.'[232]

In 1858, Christoph H. Schulenburg began work at the Ngwato capital,

Shosong, a decisive step for the Church among the northern Tswana. An LMS expedition to the north, with special interest in the Kololo on the Zambezi, came to nought in 1860. This became 'in many respects a fateful year for the northern Tswana chiefdoms'. As it seemed impossible then to carry out the trans-Limpopo plans, the mission decided to concentrate its efforts on the Northern Tswana, especially the Ngwato.[233] In Sechele's Church one could see in embryo most of the problems which dominated the South African Church in its later development. Sechele's keen interest in literacy and study, his sensitivity to the spiritual dimension, and his homiletical activity made him an outstanding example of the first generation Christianized chief. The Church's intractable attitude towards polygamy made it impossible for him to be fully accepted, either by the local Church or the local missionaries. He was the only African baptized by Livingstone, who supported him through the years.

The Ngwato

'Monare, Sir, you don't know what you say. The Word of God is far from me. When I think of entering the Word of God, I can compare it to nothing except going out to the plain and meeting single-handed all the forces of the Matabele.' The young missionary John Mackenzie, pleaded with Sekgoma, chief of the Ngwato, that he join the Church, but the chief rejected the proposal in the strongest terms possible. He had tried to get missionaries for his people, anxious not to be outdistanced by his neighbours, the Kwena and the Kgatla who had European missionaries. But the LMS did not seem interested and Sekgoma felt he had to turn to Pretoria for help, together with his royal colleague, Sechele. As a result, Hermannsburg sent their German missionary Schulenberg to Shoshong. The first year he baptized nine Ngwato converts, among them two of Sekgoma's sons, Kgama and Kgamane. That was a step of great importance for the whole future of the Church, as well as for all the people of Botswana.

Kgama, as African ruler at Shoshong, was a determined Puritan and, as such, was resolved to weave his Christian conviction into the social and political fabric of his nation. He laid down the Biblical law for all his subjects. Some of his views on religious matters developed in relation to the preaching of the leading missionaries at his court. One of these was John Mackenzie, the prominent LMS missionary. His sermons would start 'at the beginning narrating the Creation and the Fall'. He would then tell of the life, death and resurrection of Jesus Christ, and later the inevitability of Judgement Day, emphasizing the Ten Commandments. These reminders were balanced by evangelical declarations of love and forgiveness. One would surmise that most first-generation missionaries, whether Congregationalist or Lutheran or whatever, followed this pattern in their homiletical efforts.[234]

Professor I. Schapera has studied the Tswana chiefs as 'Tribal Innovators'. None of them was as determined and uncompromising an innovator as Kgama of the Ngwato, from 1875 until his death in 1923. Among his people, traditional customs abandoned included rain-making in 1872, circumcision rites in 1876, infanticide, bride-wealth, nocturnal dances, polygamy and the levirate. An even more controversial innovation was the prohibition of beer and liquor in 1879. Opposition was so strong that it was repealed in 1895, although Kgama carried on the struggle against drinking until his dying day. In place of the old customs a new set of rules was introduced. Schapera has defined the deeper significance of these changes: 'All the new church services were essentially tribal rites ... Tswana chiefs adopted Christianity as a tribal religion.' This was enforced at a time when the number of Tswana Christians was still very small indeed. Some time before 1880, chief and missionary attempted to introduce universal observance of the Sabbath. The new Christian order brought some unmistakable beneficial effects. Already in 1878, a visitor found that four-fifths of the men were learning to read.[235]

While anxious to establish and maintain Christianity and modern civilization, Kgama was keenly opposed to any move which would jeopardize his authority or that of the Ngwato nation. The dismissal of J. D. Hepburn of the LMS was a spectacular example of the chief's power. Hepburn had been the chief's secretary, interpreter and diplomatic messenger for many years. When, in 1889, Kgama and his people decided to move their capital from Shoshong to Palapye for ecological reasons, a new mission station and church had to be built. The chief suggested that he order Ngwato regiments to assist, without payment. Hepburn, believing in economic self-support, recommended that the king and every Church member should contribute for the construction of the new temple. A tug-of-war between chief and missionary ensued. The king found the demands exorbitant. He felt that the missionary was trying to undermine his position and decided to move the Church meetings to his own Council. Other issues were also at stake. Could the missionary send evangelists to neighbouring people without first consulting Kgama and obtaining his permission? With a keen sense of the political consequences of such action, involving the powerful Ndebele to the north, Kgama reacted strongly against one of the missionary's initiatives. Hepburn had to leave Ngwato country in 1891.

His successor, W. C. Willoughby, an outstanding LMS missionary, accompanied Kgama and two other Tswana chiefs on a political mission to London in 1895. At first Kgama supported Willoughby, but later abandoned him, when the chief felt that Willoughby was trying to give Tswana land to the Whites. Kgama tried scrupulously to defend African authority and the cohesion of his African nation. The chief eventually controlled the decision in any major Church issue. Christianity became a state religion – a paradoxical development from the standpoint of congregational history in English society, but perfectly logical from the point of view of the chief and his people (and incidentally in central Madagascar too). Any dissensions with individual LMS missionaries did not in any way impair Kgama's loyalty to the LMS. His negative attitude to the 'Ethiopians' in Botswana differed from that of his royal colleague Lewanika of Barotseland, or of the neighbouring Ngwaketse. They and their chief, Bathoen, whose brother was an African Methodist Episcopal pastor, expressed sympathy with the 'Ethiopians' until 1930, when they turned against the movement. Kgama understood the potential threat to his own position to be greater from the Independent African Church than from any mission-related organization. He remained loyal to the LMS.

When, in 1912, the LMS missionary Edward Lloyd reported to his board in London, 'we live very much as in the days of Constantine', he showed that even if he knew a few things about Kgama, he did not perhaps know the times of Constantine as well. The Ngwato chief, placed on the sharp ridge between old and new, between Black and White, may have had his foibles, but he was definitely more benign and reasonable than the Emperor of old. One thing, admittedly, the two rulers had in common: the idea of a Sign in which to conquer. We have had to limit ourselves to the chiefs. What about those at the grass roots and their conversion to the new religion? A statement by Professor Setiloane would seem to be particularly relevant to the Tswana situation but has its significance for the other regions too:

> Christianity makes much about life-together and relationships between persons and peoples ... All this teaching derived and based on the teaching of the Old Testament prophets about the care of the widow and the orphan corroborates in many ways the underlying principles of African views. It is my sincere belief that this is the soft spot that opened the open door for the Christian missionaries to win the people to accept their teaching – because they were in fact verbalising values, truisms and concerns which were right at the base and root of their understanding of being.[236]

NAMIBIA

Our story of early Church activities at the scattered water holes of Namibia was followed up to the Nama–Herero Agreement of 1870, but this agreement did not secure more than an uneasy truce. The 1880s saw new tensions between the two peoples. The influence of the Nama Christian minority was soon strong enough to ensure that the community as a whole would turn to the Christian way. They were guided by their Chief Hendrik Witbois (d. 1905), an ecstatic visionary, with occasional revelations from God, directing him and his submissive people to attack the Herero. Under their paramount chief Kamaherero, the latter had hardly been touched by Christianity, although the Rhenish Mission had planned a net of stations in the area. Mission efforts met with determined resistance from Kamaherero, who felt that the mission would weaken his own authority and strengthen the power of the local chiefs. The Rhenish missionaries under C. H. Hahn followed a centralization policy of their own with an emphasis on the Otjimbingwe station, a 'mission colony', a centre for energetic mercantile, artisan and industrial activities.

To the Herero, the colonial period meant utter devastation. Toward the end of the century they numbered 100,000, a proud and dominant people with enormous cattle herds. Then, in 1896, the Rinderpest destroyed the cattle, their national pride. Increasingly, they were pressured by the Europeans, losing lands to the Whites, and being the victims of economic deception. Eventually, wanton killing of Africans set off the tragic Herero War of 1904. To the surprise of the Whites the Nama also took part in the Rebellion. The utterly tragic outcome was nothing but ethnocide. After the war many of the surviving Herero and Nama died in concentrations camps. Participation in the war by the African Christians reflected their degree of dependence on the Whites. Among the Herero, almost all of them were involved; in Namaland, on the other hand, many of the Christians did not take part.

Towards the end of the century, rather ineffective efforts had been made to train evangelists and teachers. According to Lothar Engel, the missionaries had little confidence in the administrative and economic leadership of the Africans. It was taken for granted that only the White missionary could ensure a steady growth. An 'Ethiopian' influence could not be discounted in the 1904 conflict. When the local war was followed by an even worse disaster, the First World War, the Herero Christians decided to form an Independent Church of their own.

Ovambo

Shifting frontier conditions between Portuguese Angola and the south-west caused some of the Ombandju people in Angola to flee from the Portuguese regime, and to settle as refugees among the Ombulantu over the border. Here again, developments in the Ovambo–Kavango Church reflect similar patterns of approach established here to those followed among the peoples of northern Transvaal and Cape Province. The Ombulantu, a traditional priestly tribe and politically dominant, strongly resisted the new message. The refugee Ombandju, on the other hand, were definitely more open to the Gospel than their powerful neighbours; they felt they had crossed the border in order to become Christians. They joined the Finnish Lutheran Mission Church, not as individuals but as families.

Amboland, tucked away in the far north of the country, was on the periphery of present-day Namibia. From there, toward the end of the nineteenth century, many young men walked across the vast Etosha plain to seek employment with the German immigrants. Crossing this desert-like stretch took five or six days. While working in the south, the Ambo were exposed to new influences, including the Christian message as presented by the Rhenish mission. By 1910 there were about 8,000 of these migrant Ambo labourers at a time when Amboland itself had only 2,000 Christians.[237] Ambo men would gather every evening in classes preparing for baptism and were later baptized by Rhenish missionaries. Others after returning home, received further catechetical instruction in their Ambo congregations, creating 'a mission situation at both ends of the journey'. The same theme was repeated in other, untouched Ambo communities. As late as 1926, the Finnish missionary Emil Närhi explored evangelistic opportunities among the Ungkwangali in the far east of the country, convinced that he was the very first to approach this people with the Gospel. Instead, he found a congregation of nineteen men who had already discovered the Christian message while working in the mines far in the far south and had been baptized there. Returning home, they had gathered and instructed others, waiting for a 'White Teacher' to come one day with the blessed water. It was a long wait, and some were about to give up hope when Närhi arrived. He baptized a community of twenty-one who had been taught by their fellow tribesmen. Two years later the Kuringkuru station was founded, with a Finnish missionary in charge.

The beginnings of the mission work with the Ambo had been very strenuous, but then, of course, Finns seemed made for such challenges. In 1870 eight young Finnish missionaries planned stations at three different centres where they were generously received by the local rulers. King Mweshipandeka of Okwanyama allowed the foreigners to teach only him, not any of his subjects. After two years, the work was abandoned in these three centres, but twenty-five years later, the Finns repeated their attempt. In Zululand, missionary H. P. S. Schreuder had cared for the Zulu king's gout. Similarly, in Olukonda, Amboland, missionaries Skoglund and Reijonen ingratiated themselves by attending to royal feet. Skoglund writes that he first tried homoeopathic methods. When these did not work, he turned to the 'Schrattenholz healing method' which gave instant relief. Reijonen washed the wounds with *lapis infernalis* and sulphur. The king was intrigued by the missionary's books, and asked him to consult those printed papers of his to find out if the illness was caused by witchcraft, or if it was sent by God.

The famine of 1877–79 and the mission's resulting relief work somewhat tempered Ambo resistance. The highly stratified Ambo society was not strange to the pioneer Finnish missionary, Martti Rautanen. He had personal experience of such social divisions. Born a serf (in Russian-dominated Inkeri in Finland) and thus possibly unique among nineteenth-century Western missionaries to Africa, this sturdy Finn was an example of the liberating effect of the Gospel. He became missionary in charge and the chief translator of the New Testament into Oshindonga, 1903, and of the whole Bible, 1927. There was a widespread hunger to read the Holy Book and the production of Christian books laid the foundation for Ambo literacy. Rautanen was to play a subtle political game on behalf of the Ndonga communities in the north of the country. Were they to join the Herero against the commonly detested European power or not? Dr Martti Eirola has shown how Rautanen advised King Kambonde and his brother Chief Nehale against what appeared as military recklessness.[238] Rautanen was as decided an anti-imperialist as any of the Ndonga chiefs but the spectacle of the Herero ethnocide was a warning for the Ndonga to heed. The arrival in 1909 of a Finnish doctor, Selma Rainio, highlighted the medical dimension of the mission's work, and encouraged the advancement of women.[239]

The Catholics

The hot and sandy Namib was definitely a Protestant area – although some Lutherans working in the Rhenish and Finnish Missions at times found the Reformed ethos on doctrine and liturgy hard to accept. Despite government pressures to the contrary, the Catholics managed to find their way to Okavango and to get a foothold there. Once again that ubiquitous and irrepressible Spiritan, Charles Duparquet surfaced, now leading an expedition of ox-wagons from the Cape through the sands of Damaraland and Amboland. To him these explorations in Namibia were interludes between his forays into West Africa, Congo and East Africa. His Ambo initiative was part of a strategic plan of a *reprise*, a resumption of former Catholic influence in southern Angola. In 1884, he founded a mission station in Amboland, but tragically, the two missionaries whom he sent were murdered the following year. In 1888 Namaqualand became a Catholic prefecture and, after only ten years, the Church registered 5,000 members.

When Namibia became a German colony, the one place not yet claimed by Protestant missions was along the Okavango River. Here the Oblates of Mary Immaculate from Germany arrived in 1896, after strenuous efforts and tragic loss of life. In the rest of Namibia, tensions between Catholics and Protestants intensified during the colonial period. From afar in Rome, the Cardinals followed developments as closely as the intermittent reports from the field allowed. They tried to understand the problems of adaptation to the foreign *milieu*. The man on the spot, Apostolic Vicar Leonard, suggested, in 1887, that the Africans should gain indulgences connected with the rosary prayer even if they were saying such prayers not in Latin, but in their mother tongue. The College of Cardinals graciously decided that in this case, no special 'Indult' was needed.[240]

8

SOUTH-CENTRAL AFRICA AND THE INDIAN OCEAN

THE WAY NORTH TO ZIMBABWE

The way north into Zimbabwe

The nineteenth-century history of South Africa is characterized by a series of north-bound movements. Economic, political and ethnic factors all played a part in these 'treks'. Going from the south toward the 'Interior of Africa', they were also involved with missionary expansion to the Transvaal, to Limpopo and beyond. Even the waggon track from Kuruman, via Shoshong, to Bulawayo and Zimbabwe was called 'the Missionaries' Road'. The name could indeed have been 'The Scottish Missionaries Road', for it was largely thanks to the remarkable combination of three Scots – Robert Moffat, David Livingstone and John MacKenzie – that the 'road' was planned and maintained. Moffat made his four visits to Mzilikazi along that road, culminating in his journey of 1858 to the court at Bulawayo. On that last visit, the chief gave the LMS land for a station at Inyati, north of Bulawayo. In 1872 another transfer of land resulted in a second LMS station at Hope Fountain. The Missionaries' Road was the official approach to the north for White hunters, explorers, tradesmen and missionaries. Mzilikazi and his successor, Lobengula, expected any foreigners penetrating into their northern country to enter exclusively by that route. The chief could thus rest assured that he controlled any traffic into or out of his land.

But there were other roads to the north. In the 1870s and 1880s, for establishing initial evangelistic contacts with the communities in Zimbabwe, an eastern route was most frequently used. It had particular significance, because of the role of African evangelistic initiative by both individuals and smaller groups. Dr E. K. Mashingaidze has called the approaches from the east the outreach of 'the forgotten African frontiersmen'.[1] The Dutch, Paris, Berlin and Swiss (Vaudoise) missions organized no less than twenty-one expeditions to Zimbabwe from 1869 to 1890. Except for four instances, these expeditions were exclusively African and the African preachers stayed for lengthy periods on their northern frontier. It was the initiatives, sacrifice, Christian conviction, moral courage and physical endurance of Sotho, Venda and Eurafrican evangelists that sustained the evangelist fervour in Zimbabwe over two decades before the colonization of the country in 1890.[2]

Lesotho was the starting point for three expeditions. Two other mission centres, the Dutch Reformed Goedgedacht and the Berlin Lutheran centre Tshakoma in Vendaland, each witnessed the departure of eight expeditions. Stephen Hofmeyr, at Goedgedacht in the Soutpansbergen, was the pastor of a relatively large Coloured community. The sturdy Boer missionary knew the country well. His pastoral concern dealt at first with the offspring of the Afrikaans farmer, Conrad de Buys and his numerous African wives. They formed something of a Eurafrican tribe of their own. From Goedgedacht, the first groups set off in 1869 on combined preaching and hunting expeditions to Chief Zimuto's area north of Limpopo. Hofmeyr became involved in equipping and instructing seven expeditions from 1872–87, mostly with members of the Buys clan as leaders: Andreas, Gabriel and Simon. Sometimes they were accompanied by Lesotho evangelists. There was a parallel between the Buys clan experience and the Griqua outreach; once again a marginal Coloured Christian group served as 'trajectory' for a religious outreach, encouraged in this case by a Dutch Reformed Church (DRC) missionary. These Buys contacts continued until 1883, when Gabriel, the intrepid preacher, was killed and the expeditions abruptly stopped.

The unobtrusive approach of the African expeditions proved to be very effective in the pre-colonial period prior to 1890. Lobengula regarded the Venda as his friends, and was therefore prepared to tolerate their visits, but only if they followed his rules. This was abundantly clear with the combined DRC–Lesotho expedition of 1877, led by the French missionary, François Coillard. His intention was to extend French mission work from the Lesotho Church to the Shona. When he was peremptorily summoned to Lobengula's court and at long last admitted into the king's presence, he was harshly scolded for two crimes. First, he had taken the wrong road into the country. Foreigners must approach via Ngwato country, not by the forbidden eastern route. Second, the Sotho people had betrayed Langilibalele, the Nguni chief, and were therefore Lobengula's personal enemies. Coillard and his party finally had to retreat along 'the Missionaries' Road', back to Botswana. There they contacted the helpful Kgama and made plans for another missionary advance among the Lozi in present-day Zambia.

Three other African expeditions proceeded from the Tshakoma Lutheran centre in the years 1883–88. The Tshakoma mission station in Vendaland was strategically placed on the route followed by Shona workers to and from the Kimberley diamond mines. The Berlin missionaries, Schwellnus and Knothe, had made occasional visits to Zimbabwe. Schwellnus had trained African evangelists going north, at the Mphome Evangelists' school in Venda country. Johannes Madima and a colleague, Samuel were two of his students. Madima made five different expeditions to Zimbabwe, assisted by varying numbers of Africans. In 1888, Knothe brought a group of twelve Venda Christians whom he left behind in Zimbabwe. Three chiefs, Matibe, Mposi and Nyamhondo, were very responsive to their message. The African preachers would gather chiefs and their men for Bible study and even had the satisfaction of seeing the local rain doctor join a Bible class for four eventful days.

Knothe was an extraordinary missionary, with a deep concern for interpreting the Bible message in African terms. Like the Sotho evangelist Asser before him, he knew the great *Soro-rezhou* myth, common to Sotho, Venda, and Karanga. *Soro-rezhou*, (the Elephant's Head) was a royal or messianic myth about an African king in the past who had been martyred. At Chief Madongororo's village, Knothe suggested that in offering gifts on behalf of their ancestors, his listeners were in fact expressing their longing for something greater, for someone else, for Jesus the Christ. They were 'a people in waiting'.[3] Some Chivase people in northern Transvaal had relatives who were members of the same small but highly significant Lemba community. Generations earlier, they had left Chivase and had settled in Shona country, subjugated by the Ndebele. When evangelist Johannes Madima and his team went north, his assistant Samuel asked to be sent to Chief Mposi's area of Myenye in modern Belingwe District. The chief insisted that Samuel stay with him. This was not European mission strategy, but a unique African missionary approach, built on clan connections. The two men, the local chief and the foreign catechist, were related, both being Lemba.

Moses, one of the Christians at Tshakoma, knew that he hailed from Karanga country, at a place called Mabatshene. He went there from time to time for his cattle business and told his Tshakoma congregation and the missionary of his experiences. Here again, in the African approach to evangelism, clan connections were more important than the lines on the White man's map. One of the Lutheran evangelists, David Funzane, educated and baptized in Natal, became a well-known Church leader in Venda country. The teaching which he had received from the English Methodist Allison at Indaleni and from the German Lutherans in northern Transvaal, was sending out long shoots. Funzane volunteered to go to the

Shona and spent some time in the Bikita area. On his trip north, he was met at Tshakoma by a patrol of twenty-five Shona migrant workers who had just returned from the diamond mines in Kimberley. They were some of the pioneers, returning home with a Christian message. Funzane could at least learn from them about their home country. The Berlin missionary, Schwellnus, saw to it that the African expeditions did not lack their fair provisions of friendly gifts for chiefs and commoners: 'white and coloured bedspreads, cloth, pearls and brass-ware'.[4] On their arrival in this northern territory, the African evangelists found the Karanga living in grottoes, just as the Sotho and the Pedi had done before them, to escape ever-threatening enemies. They were startled to see the cross tattooed on the chests of some Karanga, and surmised this to be, perhaps, a survival from the Portuguese missionary epoch.

Colonial conquest

The political picture of the whole region changed radically in 1889: Lobengula accepted protection from the Chartered Company; in the same year the British declared a protectorate over the Shire highlands, concluding their take-over of Malawi (Nyasaland); in Barotseland Lewanika signed a concession giving the Company mineral rights throughout his kingdom and in 1891 the British Government recognized the Company's protectorate over Barotseland. In 1890, Rhodes 'Pioneer Column', 200-strong, invaded Mashonaland and hoisted the British flag at Fort Salisbury (later, as the capital city of Zimbabwe, to be renamed Harare). Two wars followed, the Matebele War in 1893, and the Shona and Ndebele rebellions in 1896. Lobengula had one day asked LMS missionary Helm, 'Did you ever see a chameleon catch a fly? The chameleon gets behind the fly and remains motionless for some time, then . . . darts his tongue and the fly disappears. England is the chameleon and I am that fly.' His melancholy prophecy was fulfilled. Total military defeat was a brutal reminder that the people were now subject to the Whites, their chiefs without real power, their kings vanquished – Lobengula dying 'of a broken heart'. Destitute and embittered the peoples of Zimbabwe tried to adjust to a new situation, which was even more aggravated in those lean years by droughts and by the dreaded Rinderpest.[5]

Some scholars have felt that the majority of Mwari cult leaders helped to inspire the rebellions by traditional religious sanctions and pressures. One significant exception was the cult shrine in the south-west, near Mangwe. Leaders there refused to follow suit, and advised the people to stay away from the uprising. They informed the Whites, including the missionaries, of the imminent danger. Attitudes to missions throughout the rebellion and its aftermath were strangely ambivalent. The Kaguvi medium sent one of his daughters to the Catholic school at Chishawasha and was baptized *in extremis* just before being hanged for his supposed crimes, in 1898.

The missionaries were torn between loyalties in opposite directions. In the Matebele War of 1893, Bishop Knight-Bruce, with an Anglican's territorial view of a diocese, hoped that some kind of neutrality was possible: 'I went as the Bishop of the country in which the war took place and not as the chaplain to any force. Both the combatants, the Matebele and the British South African Company's troops, were my people and the fighting was all in my diocese.'

It must be added that the long-term effect of these *chimurengas* – uprisings – was an underground movement which simmered intermittently until it flared up in the war for independence in the 1970s.

In Zambia, the political take-over of the country by the Chartered Company did not need to take the form of military aggression and war. Faced with the modern possibilities of the 'scramble for Africa', Lewanika and the Lozi, unlike their neighbours, adjusted to the situation. The Chartered Company moved cautiously, but with determination and soon had fairly strong command of the country. During these operations, the real seat of power, even over Zambia, was still in Zimbabwe.[6]

In all of Africa, an initial problem for the missions was how to secure a foothold over a piece of land, in order to build a chapel, a school, a clinic and a few staff houses. The answer was not always forthcoming. Often the missionary had to wait with much patience for months or years for a reply from an African chief or a European administrator. Only then could organized work begin. However, in the early 1890s, this was not a vexing question in Zimbabwe. All incoming missionaries, without exception, became at once the beneficiaries of Cecil Rhodes' 'generosity' and of that of his men. For each of the 200 'pioneers', who became the White settlers of Rhodesia, the Chartered Company set aside 3,000 acres. The missions, after all, could not be treated less generously. An early breakfast with Cecil Rhodes in the field near Fort Salisbury or at Groote Schuur in Capetown, or a talk with Rhodes' lieutenant, Dr Jameson, could mean an immediate land grant of thousands of acres. Bishop Knight-Bruce of the Anglicans was assured the 'right to 3,000 acres of land where ever we place a mission'.[7] Sir Sidney Sheppard introduced Knight-Bruce to Lobengula 'as Head of all the clergy of the English Church to which the Great Queen belongs' – an echo of a similar formula used half a century earlier by Governor Sir Harry Smith, introducing Bishop Gray of Cape Town to a group of Xhosa chiefs.

In his first visit to Mashonaland in 1888, Knight-Bruce had contacted thirty chiefs; now, for four months in 1891, he walked 1,300 miles, visiting forty-five chiefs, and establishing mission stations. His South African Coloured assistant, Frank, followed him and planted white crosses as beacons. In spite of the rapid take-over, the bishop pondered the moral problems of land occupation. In his journal he wrote:

> The whole question of land is a difficult one. I consider that the land which the natives of this country actually inhabit belongs to them ... we found them in possession ... But they only occupy a very small part of the country and it is a question how far land which they have never occupied belongs to them. I have never conceded that [Lobengula] has any moral right to [Mashonaland]. The Mashona, the people of the country who inhabited it before the Matebele came, welcome us.[8]

The Anglicans were not the only ones to receive special treatment. The Roman Catholics already had their stake in the country and got the biggest share. These were brief moments of enormous liberality. In those early 1890s, others appearing on the scene – Wesleyan Methodists, Dutch Reformed, American Board, Salvation Army – were allocated up to tens of thousands of acres of land. It became much more difficult for later arrivals, in the twentieth century. If land grants were to be decisive for the success of the Gospel, the outlook for the Kingdom in Rhodesia seemed firmly assured. The missions followed different strategies in the first decade. Some of them – Catholic, Dutch Reformed, Methodist, Episcopal and American Board – concentrated on their big centres. The Anglicans and the Wesleyan Methodists established 'chains' of stations, the approach of William Shaw among the Xhosa and another Methodist, Isaac Shimmin. Bishop Bruce-Knight and his successor, William Gaul, also found the idea irresistible. At the turn of the century, the missionaries, by this rapid rate of land acquisition, had taken over one third of a million acres in Zimbabwe.

The large farms afforded opportunities for ambitious experiments in Christian sociology. The Jesuits at Chishawasha, 'by far the most splendid mission station in Mashonaland', offered a prime example. Visitors felt that they saw developing in the African countryside modern equivalents of the Paraguay Reductions.[9] At Chishawasha, 'Christian villages' or *kraals* were formed under strict Jesuit regime, all with characteristic Jesuit names: Loyola, Xavier, Montserrato, Manresa (just as the Wesleyans called their central station 'Epworth', after John Wesley's home). In 1906 there were twenty of these villages, with almost 1,600 inhabitants, half of whom were baptized. Training was directed towards practical and industrial work. The Governor of the country, Lord Grey, saw Chisawasha as the model for education in all of Zimbabwe. 'Grey's plan, in fact, was a revolutionary one in its context: nothing less than a government attempt to emulate the Chishawasha approach and to take the lead in the transformation of Shona society through education.'[10] There was a definite policy of 'partial segregation' to keep the Catholic flock on the farms, 'uncontaminated by the vices and gross superstitions always rampant among the natives in this country'.[11]

Zimbabwe and Zambia (then known as the Rhodesias) were for most purposes an extension of South Africa at this time. Similarly, the Church north of the Limpopo was an extension of the churches south of that river. It was part of that 'Hinterland' to which Rhodes and his generation referred. Most of the missionaries came from South Africa. Bishop Knight-Bruce was transferred from Bloemfontein to Mashonaland, and his successor, Gaul, was formerly Archdeacon of Kimberley. Fr Barthelemy, who planned the Catholic occupation in the 1890s, came from St Aidan's in South Africa. The LMS Congregationalists in Matebeleland were closely related to the older work in Cape Province.

These African evangelists from the south were strangers in a new country. Although they preached in the local tongue and identified with Zimbabwean society, they were foreigners with an accent of their own and with a loyalty also to their own clan and mother Church. Some of them insisted that they needed holidays 'back home' just as much as their European colleagues. Some could remain up north for only a few years; others suffered from the unwonted climate and had to be invalided home. Of the eleven Wesleyan catechists who came from South Africa to Zimbabwe, only three, including the leader Josiah Ramushu, made Rhodesia their home. Ramushu and colleagues from other Churches founded new ecclesiastical dynasties, which supplied both ordained and lay leadership in the Churches of Zimbabwe and Zambia.

Mfengu immigrants

In addition to individual catechists from South Africa placed as preachers and teachers in Zimbabwe, one of the most significant Christian group movements in African Church history was the organized trek of 500 Mfengu families, labourers and farmers from the Cape to Bulawayo. It is difficult to determine how large a percentage of these were Christians when they started out on their exodus to the north – some informants have put it at less than 50 per cent. The Mfengu community were to a large extent Christianized by this time. Wesleyans, Anglicans and Presbyterians were well represented among them.

In the Cape, the Mfengu were known for tight social cohesion, intense clan and family loyalty, educational ambition and, in many cases, outstanding personal Christian conviction. Left to themselves as a small emerging elite in a new country, these characteristics became even stronger than in the mother country. Their exodus took place about the turn of the century, but it was heralded in the early 1890s by individuals who, like Joshua's men of old, had gone 'to search out the country' (Num. 13). Gqweni Hlazo had come to Zimbabwe 'as a Pioneer' (W. M. Nyilika's phrase): he had arrived with the Pioneer Column of 1890. Moses Mfazi was another well-known Mfengu Methodist who started catechetical and school work near Bulawayo in the 1890s. Perhaps these early comers informed their friends back home in the Cape of the opportunities up north and an ambitious emigration programme was set in motion. The first group arrived in Bulawayo in 1899 and a second the following year. A third group was planned for 1902, but the intensification of the Boer War made this impossible. Mfengu Christians of different congregations strengthened the ties between the Churches in South Africa and Rhodesia, between the Cape and the Bulawayo region.

Near Bulawayo, the Mfengu were given the Ntabazinduna area and a 'Fingo Location' was established at Bembesi, some miles distant. This was similar to the Cape, where Grahamstown had its 'Fingo Location'. The colony of Tembu immigrants, also from the Cape, settled at Gwaai River. They quickly built their own chapel and a school and began to reach out to neighbouring villages and mines, Selukwe, Gwelo and others. The Mfengu congregations represented a dynamic factor for Christian outreach in the southern part of the country. The large Mfengu Methodist congregation experienced, more than others, an 'Ethiopian' pull from the African Episcopal Church very soon after their arrival.[12]

The Presbyterians were considerably strengthened by the contribution of one man, John Boyana Radasi.[13] He and Josiah Ramushu, the Methodist, were among the leading African Christians in the first generation Church. Radasi, a Mfengu, was member of a South African team of young musicians. He spent some time in America and was converted there, then leaving to study theology in Scotland as Tiyo Soga and other South Africans had done before him. After his ordination, he was assigned to work in Zimbabwe, on behalf of the Free Church of Scotland, arriving in 1904. He held his first meetings in the Hlazo home – it was the local Mfengu community which provided his base. Hlazo, the African 'Pioneer', was now a railway employee and thus could help direct the itinerant pastor's travel plans.

In 1905 Radasi opened a school at Ingwenya, where most of his pupils were Mfengu. Somewhat later he had the satisfaction of seeing his school registered. Radasi's son who, like his father, received his theological education in Scotland, later returned to Ingwenya as a pastor. The Radasi family all promoted school work; their hospitable home gave unofficial boarding to needy children. Radasi's service as a preacher in the Ntabazinduna district spread the work also among the Ndebele people. His efforts to extend his evangelism into western Mashonaland were, however, nullified by discriminatory administrative regulations. Was he not a Black man, possibly with dangerous Ethiopian – and therefore revolutionary – ideas? The Native Passes Consolidation Ordinance of 1913 was an attempt to create law and order of a kind in the country. Radasi gave twenty years of solid service to his Presbyterian Church and the African peoples. He died in 1924.

The Anglicans at St Ninian and St Bede's in the Fingo Location, encouraged by Bishop Gaul, and the Methodists at the Selukwe gold mine and reserve, were all part of the same enterprising Mfengu-inspired evangelism.[14]

At Epworth, Gwelo, Tebekwe and elsewhere, a specific Protestant and indeed Wesleyan Methodist, characteristic appeared – the African group initiative, inspired by the Methodist idea of the local 'class' or community. In the harsh social climate of Zimbabwe, that dedicated small local Christian group, close to the soil and the living conditions of men and women, proved to be an immensely adaptable tool. On their arrival from the Cape, the Mfengu community had 'its due portion of class-leaders and local preachers', prepared to go out in teams into the neighbourhood. The liberating singing of Wesleyan hymns also caught on here. To his pleasant surprise, the missionary would find when he came that African Churches had sprung up, with a chapel, all quite independent of any outside initiative. These had developed at Gwelo and Tebekwe, in the new mine centres and along the railway line.[15]

The new Zimbabwean mission centres exerted their influence also on people in Zambia. One example was Methodist Epworth and its contacts, through the missionary John White, with Luano Valley, 200 miles north of the Zambezi. Chikala,[16] son of a Zambian chief, had come to one of the Zimbabwean mines, and had there gone to the Methodist chapel – a Zimbabwe–Zambia replica of a pattern developed earlier on with Pedi–Venda coming to Port Elizabeth. When he returned home, his father died and Chikala was raised to the position of chief. He walked the 350 miles through Zambia and the north of Zimbabwe to Epworth. He told the missionary that he could not convince his people that Jesus was alive. If only they could see a picture of him, they would believe. White replied that the purity of Chikala's life would be a better testimony to Jesus than any picture. The Wesleyan invasion of Zambia 'owed little to the missionary zeal of the European and much to the perseverance and determination of one African Christian.'[17] When the missionary visited the young chief's place two months later, he found that the chief had been killed by an elephant. But the new leader, an older man, was just as eager for a teacher to stay in their midst.[18]

The example of John White and his colleague Josiah Ramushu and many other preachers was influential. There were dramatic conversions among the people at Epworth. Chirembe, the herbalist and also a chief, was at first a strong opponent of the new message, but was converted in 1899. According to the law of the Church, he had to part with all but one of his five wives and he complied. His eldest son, Jonas Chirembe Chihota, became a zealous preacher.[19]

DAVID LIVINGSTONE

Before considering David Livingstone's trans-continental expedition of 1853–56 it must be underlined that his was not the first attempt to cross the continent. Two Africans, most probably Ovimbundu traders, Petro Joao Baptista and Amaro José had done the crossing half a century earlier, during the years 1806–14. In his book *Portuguese Africa*, James Duffy shows that the two Africans were *pombeiros* (agents of Portuguese merchants) from Angola.[20] A Portuguese merchant from Cassange in Angola sent them on their way. Joao Baptista kept a chronological journal of their adventures and observations as they trekked along via Lake Mweru and to Tete in Mozambique. In his *Missionary Travels* Livingstone refers to them as 'the trading Blacks' insisting that while they were Africans he was the first European to cross the continent.[21] Just prior to Livingstone's own expedition several Swahili traders from Zanzibar appeared in Benguela, Angola after their overland trek. The Portuguese merchant, Silva Porto, accompanied them as far as Lozi country where he met Livingstone. Porto did not continue but several of his *pombeiros* went with the Swahili across the continent to the southern tip of Lake Malawi and the Rovuma, eventually reaching Mozambique. These attempts provide a perspective on David Livingstone's unique achievement.

As he moved over the high veld, along rivers and through forests and morasses, David Livingstone not only made sharp observations about meteorology, geology, biology, ethnography, the medical situation and geography. His journey across south-central Africa, 1853–56, has been called, 'the greatest single contribution to African geography which has ever been made'. He also formed a grand mission strategy for Africa. He was of course an explorer – indeed, Africa's greatest, though he was primarily a missionary. In a debate, in 1973, Dr P. E. H. Hair expressed this emphasis on Livingstone as a missionary in these words:

> If the modern world persists in not taking missionaries seriously – saying either, that he was a great man and therefore cannot have been a missionary, or else that he was a missionary and therefore not a great man – it will never come to an understanding of him. If we slice him up to get from him what we today want from him, we will not get the true Livingstone.[22]

Meeting the Lunda in 1854, Livingstone was sustained by what he saw as a Grand Design: 'we are forwarding that great movement which God is carrying on for the renovation of the world. We are parts of [the] machinery he employs . . . fellow-workers, co-operators with God'.[23]

Working with Robert Moffat in Botswana he had envisaged a strategy very different from Moffat's Kuruman-centred approach. When the two first met, Moffat had told him of 'the smoke of a thousand villages where no missionary had been.' That was the horizon at which the young Livingstone aimed. Robert and Mary Moffat entreated him to be 'permanently settled'. But he insisted on another aspect: 'I would never build on another man's foundation. I shall preach the Gospel beyond every other man's line of things.' The map of Central Africa – until then uncharted and unknown – haunted him. The idea of the great rivers as God-given highways, as means of communication for the evangelization of Africa, forced itself upon him. At that time, missionaries saw the Nile and the Niger in this perspective; for Livingstone the Zambezi and its confluents took on this role. To his dismay, Livingstone found that enormous waterfalls made his idea of a Zambezi 'highway' for trade and communication of ideas non-practicable. To Europeans the sight of the mighty flowing Zambezi River was a great surprise. Professor Gregory gives the background:

> The Kalahari had [until then] been regarded as part of a vast desert, which was believed to occupy the whole interior of Southern Africa, and had been called the Southern Sahara . . . Livingstone's discovery that southern tropical Africa was watered by large rivers, contained many great lakes, and a fertile soil . . . and that its inhabitants were keen traders, expert agriculturists, and skilled craftsmen, was a discovery as momentous as it was unexpected.[24]

In the Kololo, Livingstone had found his strategic community, seen by him as peculiarly prepared to carry the Gospel to other peoples in Central Africa. He shared this vision – of particular African communities as carriers of the Gospel – with certain contemporary missionaries. To Ludwig Krapf it was, first, the Oromo (or 'Galla') and then the Kamba of Kenya who seemed particularly endowed to take the Gospel to both neighbouring and distant peoples. In southern Zaïre, the Luba, and further west the dynamic Fang seemed predestined for a task of this nature and magnitude. Livingstone's Kololo were a population fragment from the Sotho of South Africa who, in the turmoil of the *mfecane* had been driven away as refugees and had established themselves at Linyanti on the Zambezi. Just as Robert Moffat enjoyed a special relationship with Mzilikazi's Ndebele, so Livingstone managed to establish close contacts with the Kololo. They were willing to take him in their canoes both in a westerly and an easterly direction – without the Kololo he could not have carried through with these expeditions. He saw himself as someone who opened the way for others and, similarly, the Kololo community could be expected to bring other peoples into the Christian family. In the end, when the hitherto subdued Lozi almost annihilated their masters, only a handful of Kololo were left. Nevertheless, it could be argued that the few who did survive did indeed form a bridge over to the new Malawi with its emphasis on 'legitimate trade' and Christianity – Livingstone's formula for Central Africa.

At a time when foreigners were inclined to condemn African religions and culture, Livingstone showed a remarkable understanding of this dimension of African life. He held that 'Christianity does not give any licence for assaulting the civil institutions of man', and this included such institutions as most often would bring the African convert under Church discipline. He held the conviction that 'Jesus came not to judge'. He may have had his limitations in listening to other Europeans but with Africans he was always prepared to listen, in order to understand. Coming to the Lunda near Zambezi, he wrote – and one notes the infinite concern and empathy in his phrases:

> They seem to possess a more vivid conviction of their relation to the Unseen world than any of the Southern tribes. In the deep dark forests near their villages we always met with idols and places of prayer ... Here in the still darkness of the forest night the worshipper – either male or female – comes alone and prays to the gods (Barimo) or spirits of departed relatives and when an answer to the petition seems granted, meal or other food is sprinkled on the spot as a thanks offering.[25]

The three expeditions

The Trans-Continental Expedition 1853–56

In November 1853, Livingstone, heading west, left Linyanti, the Kololo centre,with an expedition of only twenty-seven men (and earning a salary of £100 a year). In May 1854 he arrived at Loanda. In September 1854 he began his return journey to the east coast, reaching Linyanti in September 1855. He discovered the Victoria Falls in November 1855 and reached the east coast at Quelimane in May 1856.

Livingstone then spent two years in Britain where in 1857 he published his *Missionary Travels*, appealed to the Universities for missionaries, resigned from the LMS and was appointed 'Her Majesty's Consul at Quelimane for Explorations in East and Central Africa'.

The Zambezi–Nyasa Expedition 1858–64

Faced with the Cabora Basa Falls in Zambezi, Livingstone had reluctantly to recognize that Zambezi was not altogether the 'God's Highway' he had envisaged. After bringing some of his Kololo back to Linyanti he saw the Shire River and the Lake Nyasa.

Inspired by Livingstone's appeal to the universities, the Universities' Mission to Central Africa (UMCA) was formed in 1858 and its first missionaries, including Bishop Charles F. MacKenzie, arrived on the east coast. Almost immediately, that first attempt ended in disaster. Bishop MacKenzie died, as did Mary, Livingstone's wife, (she was Moffat's daughter). The Zambezi expedition came to an end, and the new Anglo-Catholic bishop, Tozer, decided – against Livingstone's angry protests – to move from Lake Malawi to the island in the ocean, Zanzibar. A longer perspective does however present a more positive conclusion: only two years after Livingstone's death, the Free Church of Scotland and the Church of Scotland started work in Malawi and in 1879 the UMCA re-entered Malawi. Nyasaland (Malawi) did not fall into Cecil Rhodes' grasp but became a British Protectorate. Taken together these developments can be regarded as a fulfilment of Livingstone's programme of 'Christianity and Civilization', showing his impact on the Protestant and Catholic missionary occupation of East and Central Africa.

The East Africa Expedition 1866–73 (Searching for the sources of the Nile and engagement in the struggle against the Arab slave trade.)

Before setting out on the East Africa expedition, Livingstone sailed his ship, Lady Nyasa, over to Bombay where he employed for his service, among others, several 'Bombay Christians' (also referred to as the 'Nassick Boys'): Susi and Chuma, to whom Jacob Wainwright and others were added later.

His scientific concern was now to determine what was the *Caput Nili*, the source of the Nile. He held firmly to an hypothesis that the source of the Nile was not to be found in Lake Victoria, nor in Lake Albert, but in the region south-west of Lake Tanganyika, being convinced that Lualaba was the Nile. The argument seems strange now when we know much better than Livingstone. But the issue in itself was an indication of how uncertain the geographical foundations of the map of Africa had remained until that time. The final proof of the Lualaba–Congo (Zaïre) alternative was provided by H. M. Stanley's expedition in 1875–77 ('Stanley's 999 Days').

It was during the course of this search that he came across the Arab slave trade. After what he had seen in South Africa of Boer outrages against Africans it was, for a time, the Portuguese slave trade through Angola which scandalized him. However in the end, the Arabs' callous disregard for African life and the Arab slave trade in Eastern Africa, focused on Zanzibar and Kilwa, with ramifications as far as Manyema in the Congo, shocked him and made him refer to it as 'the open wound'. On 3 November 1871, a surprising contact with the Western world came to Livingstone. H. M. Stanley, of New York, entered Ujiji at the Lake and asked his question, 'Dr Livingstone, I presume?' The two men were now given four months of fellowship and travel together before Stanley left and Livingstone's lonely journey – together with his sixty African friends, the porters – continued through the swamps until the end.

Journey's end

On 1 May 1873, at Chief Chitambo's village near Lake Bangwelo, David Livingstone died. What now followed was remarkable. Susi and Chuma decided to carry the body to the coast so that it could be brought by ship to David Livingstone's home country. But how to do that? The two men took command of the group and Jacob Wainwright read the burial service from the Common Prayer Book. The heart and the viscera of the dead man were removed, placed in one of Dr Livingstone's tin boxes and buried under a large tree.

Susi and Chuma thought of all those communities over whose land they had to pass – and the angry protests: a dead body brought ill-fortune. Very careful preparations were necessary. The body was dried in the sun for a fortnight and embalmed with salt and brandy. The limbs were drawn up to shorten the package and make it look like a bale. It was then wrapped in calico and the whole of it encased in sailcloth. Finally they tarred the whole bundle to make sure that it was watertight.

Thus they were ready to carry their load. It took them five months to reach Tabora and another four months from Tabora to the coast. At last they came to Bagamoyo on the Indian Ocean and headed for the church. With infinite care they put down their burden on the porch, and Chuma uttered those two sublime words, 'Mwili wa Daudi' – David's body.

ZAMBIA: THE LOZI, THE KING AND THE MISSIONARY

The Lozi

Barotseland, or Bulozi, in western Zambia was a highly complex political structure at the end of the nineteenth century. In the period 1840–64 the country was invaded by the Kololo, a Sotho off-shoot from the *mfecane* upheaval. The Kololo community was very much Livingstone's concern with regard to his own travels to the west and east over the continent and for the beginnings of missions in Malawi. In Barotseland their Sotho language proved a help for the mission: from the start Sotho literature such as Bibles and Bible portions could be used. Coming from Lesotho, the French missionary François Coillard, being an accomplished Sotho linguist, could begin at once using the Sotho language. Coillard was also an experienced photographer; his skill in this connection has been studied in great detail.[26] A fascinating study on a wide ecumenical basis could and should be made of 'the nineteenth-century Africa missionaries as daguerreotypists and photographers'.

The 'Lozi' nation consisted of about twenty different communities among which the Lozi, the 'Borena', were in definite command while the others as vassals were more or less subject to the Lozi king and his military power. Dr W. G. Clarence-Smith has pointed to the majority of slaves in the population, perhaps three-quarters of the total. They had to put up with sheer exploitation and preferred to vanish in order to make their living as migrant labourers, harsh enough as a form of existence but vastly preferable to slavery. The whole social structure while complex was also highly centralized, a fact which, incidentally, was to affect the work of the missions.

Connections with South African missions

For the missions in Zimbabwe their early connections with Churches in South Africa have been emphasized in this book. The same perspective applies to the situation in southern and western Zambia. The evangelical mission in Barotseland was an extension of the Paris mission in Lesotho. Similarly, Methodist beginnings among the Ila-speaking peoples were initiated by John Smith of Aliwal North in the Cape together with a group of no less than seven evangelists from Lesotho. Smith's son, E. W. Smith, was one of the leading missionaries and anthropologists of his generation. The Baptists working among the Lamba received their staff, White and Black, from Baptist congregations in South Africa; one of them was C. D. Doke, the well-known expert in Bantu languages. The Jesuits under Henri Depelchin set out from South Africa aiming at the lands north of the Zambezi, experiencing at first failure and disaster to be followed by recovery. (For the north and north-east of Zambia at this time it is equally true that the staff – Roman Catholic, Anglo-Catholic and Protestant – were related to missions to the north and east, in Tanzania and Malawi.)

Church beginnings in Zambia illustrate the fact that missions to an African community ideally needed to find an auspicious time and place of entry. Both the Paris mission to the Lozi and the Methodists going to the Ila-speaking peoples were to discover that they could not have struck a worse moment. Coillard unwittingly walked right into a bitter conflict over the Lozi throne and had to leave the country. When he repeated the attempt seven years later, he once again entered a very unstable situation and the French missionary appeared to side with a competitor of the king. Only the good offices of the trader Westbeech made it possible for him to be accepted by the king at that time. The 'Primitive' Methodists were also unlucky. At the time King Lewanika was desperate about the signing of concessions to the British South African Company and in the crisis all foreigners were an irritant. The Methodists had to wait for more than four years until they could begin to settle down to their task.

As the Jesuits were turned away from Zambia they may have discovered that they too should have been more careful about the approach to the country. Coming from the south they naturally contacted the Tonga people living immediately north of Zambezi and were welcomed by three local headmen and then by Chief Mwemba, not realizing that the King of the Lozi insisted on his supremacy over the Tonga and that to him Mwemba was a mere underling. Lewanika felt offended by what to him appeared as a slight. Just as Coillard on approaching the Matebele in 1876 and Bishop Hannington on his way to Buganda in 1885, the Jesuits were made to feel that they had used the wrong 'gate'.[27] As a matter of course Coillard had brought along from the Sotho Church African co-workers, convinced that Africa must be evangelized by Africans. Two Sotho evangelists were his mainstay, the one, Aaron, 'active, energetic and animated but also sensitive and quick-tempered'; the other, Levi, 'better educated than Aaron, what he does, he does well, but he has not much enterprise.'[28] Their two wives were different: Levi's wife was 'young and has little experience'; Aaron's wife Ma Ruthi 'has grown up in our house [with the Coillards in Lesotho]. She has the soul of a missionary ... she never loses an opportunity of speaking about the Saviour to the heathen that she meets.'[29]

Mission beginnings

The beginnings were small. The first catechumens class of 1887 had two students and characteristically they were members of the missionary's household, evangelist Aaron's wife, Ruth, thus a foreigner in Bulozi, and a serf boy Nguana Ngombe. Of the latter Coillard says 'He is more than a good servant to us, he is as a son.' On his evangelistic visits to the district Nguana Ngombe served as an interpreter from the Sotho language which Coillard used. To everybody's surprise Nguana Ngombe rose in the Church service to declare that he had now become a believer, thanks, as he said, to the teaching of Aaron and Coillard. The challenging situation of the converts is reflected in his words:

> Are you going to say, 'Look at Nguana Ngombe: he wants to be a White man!' How can I become a White man when I was born Black? God is not the God of the Whites only ... I am the first ... Shall I be the only one? You my fathers and mothers, and you my *thaka* [age-class], will you not come with us?[30]

Nguana Ngombe's baptism followed two and a half years later. The king himself had been invited, although he could of course not attend, for it concerned just a serf. However the young man was able to verbalize what had happened in his life. A few words from a little speech he gave on the occasion deserve to be quoted: he spoke for possibly thousands of comparable young men throughout the subcontinent, all with a similar ambition and similar experience:

> When I took service with the missionary, a gun was the object of all my desires. When I had got it I thought myself the happiest man in the world. A gun! *My* gun! ... I used to get up in the night to make sure that I really possessed it. I was always admiring it. But now I know the Lord Jesus, it is he who has taken possession of all my thoughts and all my love and I almost forget that I have a gun.[31]

In 1894 Coillard opened a Bible school with four pupils 'whom I clothe and feed and who manage my domestic work, such as it is. They are my children as well as my pupils.' Coillard took his students along on his evangelistic visits. They had obviously assimilated a hell-and-fire message adapted from the New Testament's view of social differences in the world:

> I made our young men speak, and one of them, a Moshukulumbwe [Ila-speaking], who promises to become a 'son of thunder', closed with these words, uttered in passionate accents: 'I tremble for you; you are lost, *lost*, as I myself was. Be converted to God or you will perish hopelessly. I who am, as you say, nothing but a dog or a slave, a nothing, know then that slaves – yes, your slaves – have already outstripped you and if you do not take care you will find the door shut ... make yourselves little, quite little before God.'[32]

The king and the new religion

King Lewanika took a real interest in the activities of the missionary and often attended Church services, hoping to hear his favourite hymn, *Litaba tse gu imelang*, the Lozi rendering of 'What a friend we have in Jesus'. But in spite of Coillard's hopes he would not himself become a convert and he could do without some of the more lofty expressions of the new religion: 'What have I to do with the Gospel and their God?', he would exclaim, in 1892, in a particularly candid moment. 'Had we not got gods before their arrival? What *I* want is ... especially missionaries who build big workshops and teach us all the trades of the White men: carpenters, blacksmiths, armourers, masons and so on. That's what I want ... we laugh at all the rest.'[33] (It should be added that the king this time felt that he had insulted Coillard and subsequently visited him to explain that he had been harassed with anxieties.)

The educational and modernizing aspects of the mission attracted Lewanika. He needed good schools for his children and for those of the nobility. He was to lay the foundations of a modern Barotse elite and the mission met him half way in seeing this promotion of an elite as one of its functions. The first mission school at any particular place in Africa was often built for sons of chiefs. This was eminently the case in King Lewanika's realm. Already

F. S. Arnot, a Plymouth Brethren missionary who worked at the Lozi capital 1882–84, started a school on these terms and Coillard with his two Sotho teacher-evangelists carried on from there. The king himself set a good example: learning to write most zealously and in his turn teaching his wives and servants so that there was quite a literacy movement at the capital. The young princes would come along to class, it being taken for granted that they were accompanied by 'a suite of slaves suitable to their rank'.[34] Soon Litia, the king's son, a bright young man of sixteen, joined the school, boarding with the missionary. He was destined to become Lewanika's successor as King Yeta III. No sooner had he picked up the 'three R's' than the king planned to send him abroad for higher studies, to Botswana or Lesotho. To the other students Litia's school attendance was a matter of prestige. When he left for higher studies, there was a tendency for numbers to drop.

The one aspect of the new religious order of things which seemed easy to assimilate was the introduction of the Day of Rest. Even for his military campaigns Lewanika would observe the Holy Day. Two of Coillard's young students were taken along in the field to pray, sing hymns and preach to the troops. Coillard thought he saw signs of enlightenment; alleged sorcerers were no longer burnt nor did witchdoctors have to submit to a poison ordeal. Lewanika may even have half-considered becoming a Christian himself but an old headmen found the new ideas singularly trying and warned the king that they were not going to have a Christian for a king. Lewanika had to anticipate a possible revolution over this issue and, autocrat though he was, accommodated, prepared always to achieve as neat a balance of power as possible.

At grass-roots level in the congregations one tried to accommodate old and new. Not all the missionaries were as aware of this as was Adolphe Jalla at Sesheke. His report from 1901 makes the point: 'Our people are essentially eclectic in their beliefs. In cases of difficulty they turn to whomever is at hand, African doctors or missionaries with equal trust.' But things changed. 'No longer is it the period when they offered as sacrifice for rain three oxen, two for the ancestors and one to Jesus Christ.' On one particular occasion of drought, chiefs and rain doctors turned to the missionary – here as in other parts of southern Africa. More than 300 people assembled in the chapel. Two pagan chiefs together with Litia, the crown prince, offered prayers – and to be sure, the following day the first clouds were already beginning to assemble in the sky in order to pour out their beneficial contents on to a thirsty ground. In the next few days there were good rains, 'in order to gladden our hearts and strengthen our faith ... God has responded to our prayers, and made our joy perfect.'[35]

Signs of social change

The Church services, whether conducted by missionary or African evangelist were, for the first decisive years, selective as far as the composition of the participants was concerned. The king, insisting on law and order also in religion, ruled that women could not be allowed to enter the house of God together with men. They must sit outside, near the windows, 'and we men will fill the church'. King and missionary at Lealuyi often used to argue and here was an issue where they differed strongly, but this missionary had enough authority to hold his ground. He saw to it that the women were allowed inside and also were given honourable places in the church. For the individuals concerned it was hard at first to know how to behave: 'The poor ladies looked at each other with stupefaction, then at me entreatingly while the King roared with laughter ... At last they did [sit down]. The victory was won.'

But even the guardians of traditional religion might, in ways not easily anticipated, be hit by the new faith. Siwi was guardian, interpreter and priest of the regional cult of Moramboa at Lirundu, one of the most sacred places in the country. As the trusted servant of his king he had to follow his sovereign as much as possible, thus also when visiting Coillard's or Aaron's church services from time to time. Images and ideas from these occasions could invade the subconscious. One night Siwi had a dream: in his hut he saw two open books and one big light. Overcome by joy he began singing one of the popular hymns and as he woke up he was still singing. When he came to his senses he redoubled his efforts to resist the religion of the Whites, but in the end felt constrained to speak out in the Church service declaring that something fundamental had happened in his life: 'It is me, Siwi, *ngomboti* at Lirundu. You know me. I am a man whose mouth is full of lies and curses. I have strangled and killed people ... Today I want to become a new man.'[36]

King and missionary

The relationship between king and missionary was decisive for what there was of modernization in the country. Once accepted by the king, the missionary was in a central position to exercise a far-reaching influence throughout the country. In spite of hearty quarrels at times with the king, Coillard did in many respects hold such a position. More than any other Protestant missionary in the nineteenth century, for almost twenty years Coillard extended this influence from the nerve centre of the nation. The king and the missionary shared certain common technical interests as, for instance, in the matter of digging water canals and the idea of a 'trunk canal network. Here Lewanika wished to obtain the maximum profits from Coillard without causing him to feel too disheartened to wish to remain.'[37] When Lewanika, greatly admiring his Tswana colleague, Chief Khama, was looking for British protection under Queen Victoria, thus emulating Khama, he trusted Coillard's diplomatic skill: 'Coillard's role was absolutely central to the success of the exercise'.[38] Coillard was even approached by Cecil Rhodes to ascertain whether he would be prepared to serve as Resident of the Lozi country. This offer the missionary turned down: 'I cannot serve two masters'.

Coillard's objective, in his own words, was 'a real deep and vast awakening of these dear people'. In order to achieve this he insisted on an exclusively Pietistic approach to baptism, supported by his domineering wife, the daughter of a Scottish Baptist. Enormously self-assured, idolized in his home country and home church – referred to as 'pre-eminently the missionary's missionary'[39] – he insisted on his ruling and rules and laws, all in the name of liberation.

He, the European, thought that he could register the pious heartbeat in his converts. In 1892 he started a catechumens' group of ten people consisting of the missionary's servants together with three women from the village, 'for whom we have been praying for more than two years'. They were all placed on the long road to baptism. The catechumens' class had to be preceded by an 'enquirers' class':

> They are our joy. But these conversions cannot give me full satisfaction ... The idea of sin is weak in our Zambezian neophytes. I wish to see sinners knocked down like St Paul on the road to Damascus, anxious souls who cannot withhold a cry of pain: 'what can I do to be saved?'[40]

King Lewanika took a different interest in these religions matters: 'diplomatic, secretarial and technical aid from the Mission, they were all subordinate to the most important commodity which Lewanika sought and obtained – the reinforcement of Lozi self-confidence in the face of white encroachment – which resulted from the ritual location of the Mission below the king', to quote Gwyn Prins' brilliant formula for this unique relationship.[41]

Slow growth

At the time of the First World War, the Church reported ninety-eight communicants and 273 'under Christian instruction' while the staff included ten ordained French and Waldensian pastors and twenty-four African evangelists. Under the influence of school and church and of King Kgama in Botswana, Litia became a believer and was baptized. So was Mokamba, son of a highly placed chief and destined to become Prime Minister for twenty years under both Lewanika and Yeta. Dr Caplan says about Mokamba's religious allegiance that it reflected, as among the Baganda, 'an attitude of receptivity to modern techniques and development'. This was the case with a number of young nobles who were mission school alumni.[42] One must however, not draw the conclusion that this necessarily was to strengthen the influence of the missionaries in public life. In fact the absorption into the centres of power of the new mission-educated elite led to a decline in the actual influence of the missionaries themselves.

It was this receptivity to modern education which to some extent explains Lewanika's attitude to the Ethiopian crisis in 1903. The French missionaries had become used to regarding the religious and educational affairs of the country very much as their monopoly. Thus Coillard felt the shock all the more when realizing that one of his most trusted Sotho co-workers, William Mokalapa, during a visit to his home country and to South Africa, had joined the African Methodist Episcopal Church. Mokalapa held out to the Lozi king and his council the prospects of great advance towards higher education under AME aegis and, as shown by Terence Ranger, this influenced king and council. Soon however, this illusion was dissipated but the whole affair served as a challenge to the Lozi authorities, inducing them to go ahead with founding their own Barotse National School in 1906.

The Lumbu–Ila-speaking peoples

The close contacts between the Lozi realm and the Lumbu–Ila people are also reflected in the beginnings of the Church. Lewanika was anxious to establish Lozi groups among the Lumbu and the Ila in order to safeguard Lozi domination there. Lozi groups, Christianized in their home country, became active missionary agents in co-operation with the Methodist missionaries. Repeatedly in this book it has been noticed how refugee groups served as trajectories of the new faith, but here it was another situation altogether: Christian outposts representing a dominant power. When the first two 'Primitive Methodist' missionaries arrived in the country, they were detained by the Lozi king at his capital for three years; this was the time needed for the Lozi power to establish itself sufficiently in the politically sensitive frontier area as outposts against what was seen as a Ndebele threat from the south.

It took a considerable time among the Ila for the mission to get started, but the seven Sotho evangelists from South Africa were at once ready to begin their catechetical teaching. E. W. Smith's arrival among the Ila in 1902 was an important factor. He was active in building up the stations of Nanzela and Kasenga (the latter from 1909–10), which had been established as Christian villages.[43] He also introduced the Methodist preaching system, enlisting converts as soon as possible. Soon indigenous workers appeared. David Mubitana is known as the most powerful preacher amongst the first generation. He had the characteristically Methodist approach with a message about personal conversion and self-surrender. A study has been made of the social background of the first Christians in this Church. It appears that the Ila themselves at first presented a particularly strong resistance to the new message; of the sixteen converts, only one was Ila, while the remainder belonged to the Lumbu or other communities. Characteristically, most of these 'first fruits' were from marginal categories: slaves, orphaned children or half-caste children brought up by the missionaries. They all formed a community at Nanzela, at first isolated from society as a whole.

MALAWI

Malawi, or Nyasaland as it was called during the time of the British Protectorate, is a strip of land to the west and south of Lake Malawi. It includes several small ethnic communities: in the south, Yao, Sena, Chewa, Lomwe and some Ngoni; in the north, Tonga, Henga-Tumbuka, Ngonde and more Ngoni. The *mfecane* dominated Malawi's nineteenth-century history. *Mfecane* denoted the dread arrival of Ngoni armies from the south, raiding and subduing any peoples having the misfortune to lie on their route. The Ngoni invasion was also fundamentally significant in terms of the *group* reaction to the message of the missionaries.

The southern half of the country was a mobile region with migrations into the area from different directions. There were the Yao in the area of the southern lake shores and the Shire highlands east of the Shire river, who by the middle of the century had settled victoriously (a result of African expansionism), while the Kololo relying on their guns dominated the Shire valley itself. There were also Ngoni (the Maseko–Ngoni), the Chewa and others. Makanjira, the most powerful of the Yao chiefs, offered the toughest opposition to the incoming British Commissioner, Harry H. Johnston. Much later, from about the 1890s to the middle of the 1920s, the Lomwe arrived – refugees from intolerable conditions under the Portuguese in Mozambique. While the Yao resolutely established themselves, the Lomwe approached warily, anxiously, subdued, being unwanted and despised. The established Churches had concerned themselves with the steadfast Manganja and the Yao. What about the Lomwe? In the midst of the colonial era they represented a variation on the nineteenth-century refugee theme, being a down-trodden community, refugees from which both state and church held aloof. This time, European colonialism and expansion spurred their population movement.

Southern Malawi was the home of several ethnic communities. Johnston had announced a protectorate over the country in 1890. His original intention was for Malawi to become part of the area to be administered by Cecil Rhodes' British South Africa Company. Even when, in 1891, the British Government decided that this was not to be, he continued trying to keep this option alive until 1894, thereby greatly alarming the Blantyre missionaries.[44] Johnston would have preferred to settle his account with Makanjira without any interference from his fellow-countrymen, and was embittered by the persistent criticism by the missionaries at Blantyre against his military and tax-collecting activities. Dr Laws and his missionaries further north seemed fully occupied by their catechetical and pedagogical chores, but the Church of Scotland personnel at Blantyre were of a different kind. Their work had been founded in 1876, and for fifteen years they had developed their programme unhampered by any government interference. Anxiously they followed political developments further south on the subcontinent and decided against Cape politics, against Cecil Rhodes and all his works: 'We have here very different antecedents and very different relations.'[45]

Territorial cults

South of the Lake, among the Chewa, the M'Bona territorial cult and the Nyau masked dance society were powerful. The cult attracted people with its ancient myth of a prophet inspired by God but slain by a neighbouring chief. The prophet's memory was kept alive at two shrines near sacred pools. The M'Bona cult managed to assimilate certain Christian traits and a religious dialogue developed between the Christian community and the cult followers. Later, trouble between an English missionary and M'Bona officers ended in embitterment: the European had trespassed on sacred grounds. Rather unexpectedly, two fundamentalist missions came closer to an understanding with the cult. Joseph Booth, founder of the Zambezi Industrial Mission and a preacher connected with Chilembwe, addressed some M'Bona followers in 1894, and two decades later a South African 'General

Mission' representative preached from the very door of one of the shrines. Soon some of the senior headmen felt that Christ rather than M'Bona was likely to provide what people needed: rain.

Since the 1960s penetrating research into the history and nature of these territorial cults has been published. These cults spread throughout southern Malawi, northern Zimbabwe and Zambia, conveying the intensity of traditional religion in the area. What then does all this mean for the Church's history? How far does it aid understanding of the transplantation of the Gospel into this soil? It seems that the questioning and prognostication awakened by the territorial cults produced a preparedness for the religious dimension in the widest sense. In favourable circumstances, on the sides of both the African community and European agency, this phenomenon could lead to an especially strong religious conviction, also with regard to the appropriation of the two revealed religions in the area, Islam and Christianity.

Between the M'Bona cult and the missions there was the semblance of peaceful coexistence. But fierce confrontation with the Nyau dance society often occurred. The society had problems of its own, consisting in an uneasy balance between the Ngoni and the Chewa. The missions involved were mainly the White Fathers and the Dutch Reformed. The Catholics did not hesitate to combat the Nyau society. Catechumens were excommunicated for attending the dances and one of the missionaries slashed Nyau drums placed too close to the chapel. The dance society retorted by making masks of St Peter, St Joseph and the Virgin Mary, holding them up to ridicule, although later these figures were in a way absorbed into the cult. The Nyau also burned some Roman Catholic prayer houses.

The missions

The life and death of David Livingstone inspired at least three missions to begin their work in Malawi. Two were from Scotland: the Church of Scotland and the Free Church of Scotland. The division of Presbyterians in Scotland, caused by their diverging relationships to the state, lasted between 1843 and 1930. The Free Church soon exceeded the Church of Scotland in missionary drive and outreach. But the two were one in their common resolve to honour the example of Livingstone through service to the peoples of Malawi. Only two years after his death, they sent missionaries to that country, the Free Church founding their 'Livingstonia', the collective name for the total Scots mission activity in the north. The Church of Scotland took their position south of the Lake in the Shire Highlands, calling it

'Blantyre', the name of Livingstone's birthplace in Scotland. This later, for some time, became the capital of the colonial protectorate.

The Universities' Mission to Central Africa was the third mission to Malawi inspired by David Livingstone. After efforts involving tragic losses of life, they left the area and headed for Zanzibar. However they kept their original destination in mind all the time and, in 1879, returned to work amongst the Yao. They established headquarters at Likoma, the island in Lake Malawi, moving from the island in the ocean to the island in the Lake!

The Livingstonia outreach

With the Free Church in the north, mission strategy had to be worked out on the spot, considering the shifting conditions from day to day. Most missions coming from Europe and North America started on an island or at a harbour. Thus the Scots at Cape Maclear began at the western shore of Lake Malawi. There was an increasingly Islamized Yao-dominated population. Out of the wide variety of people there, the mission built Christian enclaves, similar to the 'Christian village' idea then practised elsewhere on the continent. Amongst these people were freed slaves, Kololo elites with their Manganja servants and Yao refugees. They were all under close mission control, separated from society at large. Dr James Stewart of Lovedale, who gave many years to planning the work in northern Malawi, brought with him four African evangelists from the Cape, amongst them William Koyi. Being outsiders themselves these men could identify with the foreigners in the area. The outstanding pioneer missionaries to northern Malawi were Dr Robert Laws, head of 'Livingstonia' and one of the great mission strategists of the century; a fellow Scot, Dr W. A. Elmslie, missionary to the Ngoni; and the dynamic Donald Fraser who influenced the Tonga and the Ngoni.

The Tonga revolution

We have emphasized in this book the constant 'mediation effect' in which the Christian message was carried by and through Africans themselves throughout the continent. The new convert did not keep the discovery for individual consumption but took the message to others. We have seen this happening in the outreach of the Cape Africans, placed as preachers far from home. It is appropriate to underline this here, too, because the young Church in Malawi almost immediately began to reach out in every direction inspired by the Gospel. We shall deal mainly with the Tonga and the

Ngoni, with only a brief reference to the Henga–Tumbuka and the Ngonde.

Three years later the mission moved further north to Bandawe. An overwhelming response from the lakeside Tonga resulted in Christian congregations and an educated elite. These formed one of the great pacemaking Churches of nineteenth-century Africa, becoming in the process 'the leading African beneficiaries of the colonial regime'.[46] The 'Christian village' programme at Bandawe was abandoned and replaced by evangelization and schools in the Tonga villages. Numbers were limited. The Tonga number no more than 60,000 in the twentieth century and were even fewer in the 1880s. But the potential of this community was enormous. This was their hour.

Here the refugee theme emerges again, but with a difference. Coming from the south the Ngoni had raided the Tonga as they had all their neighbours – Chewa, Henga, Tumbuka. The ever-exposed Tonga fortified themselves with large stockades. When James Stewart came, the first missionary to contact them, their village headman, Mankhambira, explained that they wanted military help, effective 'medicine' to destroy the Ngoni, and new economic outlets. Needing to change their completely restricted existence within the stockaded villages, they welcomed the mission's employment on a wage basis, and the opening of new vistas. It is generally accepted that the Tonga were spared extermination at the hands of the Ngoni by the arrival of the mission and especially by Dr Laws' personal influence on the Ngoni chief Mbelwa. 'The mission remained the sole representative, if not agent, of Pax Britannica.'[47] The Tonga ambitiously pursued individual and group achievement and modernizing ways. Ngoni invaders had dominated them and now the arrival of the missionaries offered them a chance to establish themselves on their own. The Islamized Yao had been the leading economic community in the area, but it did not take the Tonga long to catch up. The new modern economy invading Central Africa required a migrant labour system and, with support from the Scottish missionaries, the mobile Tonga were eager to respond.

Tonga schools

The breakthrough in Tongaland came through the schools. In 1889 two chiefs were prepared to agree to mission schools being started in their villages and soon other chiefs followed. By 1894 there were eighteen schools in Tongaland with over 1,000 pupils. In 1906 the number of schools had increased to 107 with over 3,000 pupils.[48] Village schools furnished the initial impetus. Very soon Tongaland was the 'scene of extraordinary educational enthusiasm', influencing a whole generation to accept modernization and development.[49] Initial results in terms of baptism and church statistics were not impressive. The hold of traditional Tonga religion was strong and the first converts did not appear until 1889. By 1890, there were only fifty-three communicants in the whole mission, including the Cape Maclear outpost and Ngoniland.[50]

At this time, in spite of limited numbers of Christians, Tonga society was already set on the way to Christianity. In this and many similar instances, there was a certain salient point when an African society was *in principle* won over. Any adding up or converted individuals or 'souls' was not really significant. It was already recognized that the structures of society had been shaken and that assuredly the future belonged to the Christian alternative. This resolute expectation had a quickening effect of its own on the drive for evangelization.

The Overtoun Institution

As a consequence of the exceptional educational response from Tonga, Tumbuka and Ngoni, the Overtoun Institution was opened in Livingstonia in 1894. This school ensured 'the continued pre-eminence of northern Nyasaland in the field of education'.[51] Dr and Mrs Robert Laws and another Scot of the same calibre of excellence, Dr James Henderson, gave their stamp to this centre. Laws, the proverbial austere and taciturn Scot, was both an ordained preacher and a medical practitioner, an outstanding example of the Bible-expounding doctor in Africa who, through his personal authority and competence, was acknowledged as the mission leader. He and his wife served Malawi for fifty-two years. Overtoun had an unashamedly British syllabus, with three years of English language and literature, British and European history, philosophy, psychology, mathematics, ethics and sociology. It is easy to scorn this elitism, but the acquired proficiency in English and in Western Christian values made the Overtounians prominent as African intellectuals. Their education prepared them for the time when Africans would run their own affairs in Church and State. This was more than one generation earlier than in other comparable communities.

From Livingstonia to the Bemba in Zambia

Fundamentally, the missionary role with the Tonga, as with the Ganda, was catalytic. The Livingstonia missionaries released enormous, boundless energies, to be channelled into economic and religious activity. The most remarkable result of the Tonga mass movement was an outreach with the Gospel by devoted African teachers – from the centre to the north, to the south and above all to the west. Colonial frontiers did not hamper this. The western move to the Bemba, in present-day Zambia, had strategic implications. The Bemba were a mobile people and their conversion was likely to aid in winning neighbouring societies in northern Zambia. There was an added urgent denominational note: the Catholics stood at the borders of Bemba country and soon advanced much further.

Protestant Livingstonia sent their best men to Bemba. In 1895, John Afwenge Banda, Chewa evangelist (the father of Dr Hastings Banda, the first president of Malawi) began work at Mwenzo, staying for many years. During the First World War he carried virtually all responsibility for the work there. A decade later, Tonga evangelist David Kaunda (the father of Dr Kenneth Kaunda, the first president of Zambia) followed, building up the Chinsali station and guiding its rapid expansion. Livingstonia also sent African 'agents' to other missions in the region: the South African General Mission, the Dutch Reformed Church, and the LMS. Southern Tanzania also received its share, with six teachers going to Moravian Rungwe and another six to the Berlin Lutherans at Ilembula. 'The seeds sown at the Overtoun Institution were blown all over East and Central Africa.'[52] In 1910, Livingstonia, with twelve ordained missionaries and 1,260 unordained African preachers, teachers and Bible women, had a Christian community of 13,000.[53]

Breakthrough among the Ngoni

Almost as surprising as the Tonga Christian revolution was the breakthrough among the Ngoni. Politically they appeared as conquerors in northern Malawi, but the Tonga renewal challenged them. The Ngoni were themselves refugees and at this time were weakened by internal tensions. A strategic master-stroke, again in terms of the African initiative, promoted the mission's entry into Ngoni society. Dr Laws himself had made a first visit to the Ngoni in September 1876, speaking, he thought, to the Ngoni paramount chief – in reality it was a headman who received him. Therefore, the approach could not be conclusive. Three months later the mission sent William Koyi, the Xhosa evangelist from Lovedale, who managed to meet with the real paramount ruler, Mbelwa. Here was an African leader from the Cape, of Nguni background, speaking the language of the Ngoni chief. Koyi walked warily. He did not begin by emphasizing an impending arrival of

White missionaries, but suggested that the king might need a school for the children. A fortnight later Koyi returned to Mbelwa, this time accompanied by a missionary, the Revd Alexander Riddell. The latter showed him the Bible and explained that 'it was this that made our nation rich and powerful.'

This argument was perhaps less Biblical than the pious Riddell realized, but it gave the chief food for thought. In fact, the Ngoni soon followed the Tonga lead. Koyi was placed in charge of the school, and the children liked their teacher. Chief Mbelwa appreciated the advantage of having schools and missionaries, but only on condition that the Ngoni would have a monopoly. Dr Laws expertly circumvented these overtures, but strongly supported his colleague Elmslie, who went to labour among the Ngoni. Although with the Ngoni he tended to be distant and dour, he was a great pioneer missionary.

Problems arose at first with the schools. In patriarchal Ngoni society it was taken for granted that the new educational privileges were only for those of high rank, but the missionaries insisted on treating all alike. Although the first converts in this area were three sons of a Nsenga diviner whom the Ngoni recognized as slaves, in practice Elmslie regarded rank as of special interest for winning those lower on the scale. 'If we can get teachers of a high "tshibango" [rank], so much the better.'[54] Here in Ngoniland, too, missionary contacts with the ruling sector therefore resulted in 'perpetuating existing privilege rather than of replacing it by a new political order'.[55]

The Ngoni were intent on manipulating the missionaries, whom they found interesting as practitioners within the context of Ngoni religious ideas, rather than as advocates of a new religion. The musically gifted Ngoni adapted their African songs to Christian hymns, producing as many as fifty with a characteristic African rhythm and flavour. In the first years, many were danced to as well as sung. Meteorologically 1885–86 was a critical year. Traditional sacrifices for rain were of no avail and finally the rain stopped completely. The paramount chief and his people then turned to the missionaries, trying them as rain-makers, and lo, miracles happened! There were downpours.

The Donald Fraser revival

Donald Fraser was a remarkable missionary. He was of a later generation than Laws and Elmslie, and had been inspired by Keswick, the English 'Holiness' revival movement. This Keswick connection added an emotional element to Livingstonia's evangelization and contributed to both Tonga and Ngoni religious initiatives. From 1898, Fraser led a series of annual gatherings in Ngoni country for baptism and Holy Communion, with up to 10,000 attending. It was a veritable corporate exodus of a people from the old ways into the Church, an 'African Pentecost'. At first these retreats may well have been interpreted by the masses in terms of their own First Fruit ceremonies. There were interesting parallels between the two celebrations. A closer look at these movements reveals the central role of the urge for purification, expressed in individual and group confession.[56]

This was a new dimension altogether. Here men and women burdened with an overwhelming sense of guilt, would sometimes most dramatically shout out and 'throw up' their past, accepting forgiveness and peace from God and from their neighbours. Donald Fraser as a leader could offer freedom to this 'rushing mighty wind', these 'torrents of prayer' and surprising outbursts of elemental religious conviction, in the name of Jesus the Messiah. Among the Chewa in the south, the Catholic Church practised individual confession and absolution from sin and Satan. The Protestant Africans did not have that recourse and some of the missionaries were much too refined or reserved to allow such outbursts of the Spirit. Fortunately, that was not the case with Donald Fraser. He understood these 'revival' outbursts amongst men, women and children as a means towards individual cleansing.

Fraser formulated one of the memorable phrases of nineteenth-century mission in Africa: wishing to turn the emphasis of teaching 'from the negative prohibitions of Christianity to the glorious fullness of its gifts'. There was a vibrancy and enthusiasm through individual and group experience. A decade later, in 1910, the revivalist campaign of the British preacher Charles Inwood gathered thousands of people. Donald Fraser has tried to convey what happened:

> Mr. Inwood was speaking on the Holy Spirit. At the close of his sermon all was very quiet. He asked for a time of silent prayer, and then called on those who were willing to receive the fullness of the Spirit to rise. No one rose. After a time two or three stood, but evidently with a struggle. Then an elder began to pray, confessing before all the sin of having cherished a spirit of revenge for an evil done him. Then another began to pray, and another and another, till two or three were praying together in a quiet voice, weeping and confessing, each one unconscious of the other. And then suddenly there came the sound of 'a rushing mighty wind'. It was the thrilling sound of two thousand five hundred people praying audibly, no man apparently conscious of the prayer ... We were listening to the same sound as filled that upper room at Pentecost. Not noisy or discordant, it filled us with a great awe. Soon some began to cry out in unrestrainable agony ... I started a hymn.

> None seemed to hear aright in the pervading sound, but each man and woman sang, and sang what was uppermost in his heart. It was overwhelming to look down from the pulpit at the audience singing away, every one with closed eyes, singing what his heart prompted. And for two of three minutes no tune could be discerned but that of a mighty volume of tumbling waters ... and the words of confession to which it is set in our hymn-book.[57]

Something else happened in that *milieu* of freedom, inspiration and creativity. People began to write and compose their own songs, with an African rhythm, clapping hands and dancing to these new tunes.[58] Donald Fraser's wife, a medical doctor (and J. H. Oldham's sister), in her beautiful book about her husband, completes the impression of this religious breakthrough as the missionary moved among that African crowd in 1910:

> Presently one or two began to get excited, but Fraser was already down among them, passing from one to the other, laying a calming hand upon them and getting them to sit down quietly. It had all come suddenly and overwhelmingly upon people who had never before gone through any such kind of religious excitement, their teaching having been all along on the lines of Scottish Presbyterianism. Each had now found a tongue with which to utter this revelation that had come to him.[59]

The Tumbuka–Henga was another northern community which had been shaken by Ngoni attacks. When the first missionaries arrived in 1894, they found people hiding behind waterfalls and living in caves to escape the invaders. Work in this area was slow, with the first converts joining ten years later. But they too were gripped by the wave of enthusiasm and in this case the girls joined the Church.[60] Further north, the Ngonde alone managed to resist the evangelistic outreach. The Arab and Ngoni onslaughts in this area had both been relatively short. The Ngonde, with strong religious traditions and with an authoritative chief, managed to ward off European intrusion and, for the time being, any evangelistic attempts.[61]

Southern Malawi

Northern Malawian Church development was dominated by Livingstonia and its influence, spreading far and wide. The Scottish missionary beginnings at Blantyre were difficult, dramatic and controversial. In this Yao-dominated area, refugee slaves would turn up, seeking shelter at the missionary's house. Small communities were established, a motley group of refugees and individuals from varied backgrounds, including educated Kololo. The mission estates employed them all and at the same time gave them the foundations of an education. In the mission village they were exempted from the traditional chief's control. The missionary staff, often European lay artisans, exercised virtual chiefly authority, taking over the role of magistrate and civil governor. In one instance – the 'Blantyre Atrocities' – 1878, severe disciplinary action led to death. The event was widely publicized and the mission both in Malawi and in Scotland defended its position with difficulty. The injurious effects of 'Social Darwinism' had led to an estrangement between White and Black.

At this time the Blantyre mission was fortunate in receiving a new leader, David Clement Scott, one of the outstanding missionaries of his time (at Blantyre 1881–97, when he left Malawi for Kenya). Scott insisted on the David Livingstone heritage, combining 'Christianity and Commerce', a formula which Scott translated as 'the Gospel and modern culture' which also meant deep respect for African culture. He and his successor, Alexander Hetherwick, insisted on generous opportunities for the African co-workers: 'Africans as co-inheritors of world culture – in African forms' was his educational formula; to make the African 'a conscious member of the Catholic Church of Christ' – his ecclesiastical programme. The Church at Blantyre with Scott as the inspiring architect combined Western and Eastern traditions in a beautiful style of its own, 'not Scottish, nor English, but African'.

The school system was developed, new mission stations were founded in their district. Above all Scott had a gift for encouraging his African co-workers. The most important of these were Joseph Bismark, Harry Matecheta, John Gray Kufa (later hanged by the British as one of Chilembwe's lieutenants) and Harry Mtuwa. Scott gave them all tasks to do in which they had both responsibility and virtual autonomy, apart from infrequent supervisory visits from missionaries. The Government Enquiry into the Chilembwe Rising was later to make much of this as being the root of that Rising. D. C. Scott said:

> People will not believe how much the African is capable of doing until they have tried. Our aim is to teach responsibility and at the proper time to lay it on those who have to bear it. In many ways the time has now come . . . It is a fatal mistake to keep the African in leading strings . . . Africa for the Africans has been our policy from the first.

Just as with Livingstonia, Blantyre was British, insisting on the English language; and Scottish, insisting on higher learning. African culture was emphasized, in conformity with Scott's motto. The boarding school at Blantyre was as prim and proper as any on the continent, but at full moon Scott called all boys and girls to dance on the lawn, the dances were those traditional dances which Scott felt were possible for Christians, the sexually explicit ones being excluded from the school repertoire.

Table 8.1. *Figures for school growth between 1899–1914*

	Schools	Teachers	Pupils
1899	80	80 + 250 (ass't)	7,275
1914	750	1,400	67,000

The Dutch Reformed

The Dutch Reformed mission from South Africa came in 1889 to the Chewa, who lived west of Blantyre and whose villages had been devastated by both Ngoni and Yao. Yet they had survived thanks to their genuinely African ability of seeming to accept political domination, while still keeping intact their traditional life. At first the Dutch mission was advised by the Livingstonia mission and assisted by its African staff. In this Chewa area, the chiefs were welcoming, undoubtedly hoping for political and economic benefits. By 1899 the number of DRC missionaries increased to eighteen at three stations. They met baffling problems affecting the African population including the hut tax and migrant labour. They soon became persistent advocates for the Africans against government policies. The effects of migrant labour roused them to imaginative measures, in the form of home craft and industries, weekly markets, mass literacy campaigns and emphasis on care of the family. They were the only mission in Africa known to introduce its own currency at this time. Money was virtually non-existent, so they invented a coin the size of a penny, punched with two holes and stamped 'MM' (Mwera Mission). This arrangement came to an end in 1909. An impressive African school inspector, Albert Namalambe, a former slave, eventually looked after a rapidly expanding network of schools. Table 8.1 shows statistics which document its astounding rate of growth.

With the Presbyterians in the north and in the south and the South African Dutch Reformed with the Chewa, Malawi seemed set for an exclusively Protestant and Puritan future. But the episcopal order brought by the Roman Catholics and by the Anglicans from Zanzibar added a varied configuration to the ecclesiastical scene.[62]

The Catholics

The Montfort Fathers, with a rural French background, came to a place with a veneer of Ngoni rulers lording over a fairly submissive mass of Chewa. In this part of the country the Ngoni found it beneficial to welcome the mission. The Catholics understood the authoritarianism of the Ngoni more readily than the Chewa system which had more indeterminate authority. Not as scholarly as the White Fathers, the Montfortians accepted without long preparation large numbers of villagers who were not always fully aware of the implications of the new faith. While Protestants emphasized elite-formation, the Catholics looked after catechists' training. A Catholic peasantry emerged.[63] From the turn of the century and well beyond, the southern Malawi area remained fluid. New ethnic groups, such as the Sena and the Lomwe, moved in from Mozambique. Uprooted and disconcerted, these immigrants found a haven in the fellowship and worship of the Church.

Anglo-Catholics

Malawi was a 'lakeland', for the long narrow stretch of water dominated the country. No one managed to exploit this geographical feature with more ingenuity than the Anglo-Catholic Universities' Mission from Zanzibar. In 1861 they stood with Dr Livingstone on the threshold of the Promised Land. Now after many years in Zanzibar, they returned to their first love. In 1885 they settled on the island Likoma, established their headquarters and built their cathedral. From Likoma they moved east, south and west and founded numerous outstations in the Shire highlands and along the eastern sea front, where they began sixty village schools. Teaching staff came first from Kiungani on Zanzibar. At the turn of the century, the arrival of women teachers trained on Zanzibar proved a portent of great things to follow.

The future of women's education, at least on the eastern shore, was tied to that long life-line of educational communication between Mbweni College at Zanzibar and Likoma. A generation of qualified African women – the likes of Mrs Kathleen Mkwarasho, and all products of Mbweni, ushered in the tradition of emphasis on girls' education. Just prior to World War I, this had resulted in the attendance of some 500 girls in the school. At Likoma nearly all the teaching staff consisted of African women teachers, some with government certificates. These young women teachers represented an elite of their own. They were foot-loose African women who had once been brutally torn from their tribal background, but were then given a new lease of life through the Mbweni school. Because of their history of uprootedness, they were all the more anxious to identify with the new sacred tradition in its Christian form.

Bishop Hines, from 1897, directed operations in more than one sense, for he was also a doctor, just as the Presbyterian preachers at Livingstonia on the lake's western shore. In the work at Likoma, everyone depended on lake steamers which were utilized in varied ways. The UMCA was quite probably the only mission in Africa to house its theological seminary for a time on the lake steamer, *Chauncey Maples*. With a length of 127 feet from stem to stern, the steamer had a school room in the deck house with seats for thirty students. After some time, seasickness ravaged the students. They warmly welcomed the day when Malawian Theology could settle down on solid, dry land.

Also from Likoma, enterprising Malawians emigrated to gain new opportunities for themselves. One of them was J. G. Phillips, educated – according to the obituary written by his daughter – in 'the Universities' Mission, Cambridge and Oxford'. With that impressive credential he went as a mine labourer to the Rand, but the same fate befell him as so many of his fellow miners. He became seriously ill and was desperately looking for help. The Zionists were there to help and to pray for him and he felt that he was healed. Thus he was prepared to establish a Church of his own, together with friends. He called it *The Holy Catholic Apostolic Church in Zion*. Soon he found himself to be the bishop of the Church, far away from home yet as a Malawian thoroughly at home with his Church and his episcopal position.

Of even greater importance and with a wider outreach were 'welfare associations' connected with the Presbyterian Livingstonia in northern Malawi, but also influencing northern and southern Zambia. Livingstonia and its central educational institution, Overtoun, educated new generations of enterprising men prepared to change and lead the social life of their communities. With a Standard VI education and as a matter of course English-speaking, they formed their 'associations'. The great majority of the members of these were mission teachers or ordained ministers and government clerks. To some extent they were inspired by Booker T. Washington or by Marcus Garvey in the United States, but above all they worked closely with Dr Laws of Livingstonia. From the outset his concern was to develop self-governing African institutions and he aimed high. He aspired to make Livingstonia into the first University of Central Africa, like his colleague at Lovedale in the Cape, Dr Stewart, another Scot and Presbyterian, who also had the vision of an African University (in 1916 resulting in Fort Hare).

The Chilembwe revolution

A resounding bang in the social and religious life in southern Malawi and in Central Africa was triggered by the Chilembwe revolt in 1915. A British preacher, Joseph Booth, hoping to start work in Malawi, founded the

Zambezi Industrial Mission with support first from American Seventh Day Baptists and later from American Seventh Day Adventists. He met John Chilembwe, a young Yao, and took him along to the United States, 1897–1900 – the first Central African to go to America – and here Chilembwe studied at the Virginia Theological Seminary at Lynchberg where he was awarded the BA and BD degrees. He contacted progressive American Blacks in the emerging Pan-African movement who were prepared to help him realize his ambitious plans for an industrial mission of his own. In 1900 Booth turned to the apocalyptic doctrines of Watch Tower and managed to introduce these teachings in Malawi. Chilembwe, faithful to his Providence Industrial Mission, now separated from Booth and was assisted by the National Baptist Convention with funds and Afro-American missionaries. 'There is not a little of the Booker T. Washington technique about his mission training in these years.' About 1910 he had succeeded in producing 'a well dressed and drilled community'.[64]

In the famine period 1912–14, with harsh treatment of African labourers on the European farms, raised hut taxes and rumours of war, Chilembwe's feelings towards White colonialists and farmers 'passed from those of cool co-operation, through criticism, to bitter anger, hostility and finally conspiracy'.[65] The Chilembwe rising lasted from 23 January to 4 February 1915. Chilembwe realized the desperate plight of his attempt: 'Let us strike a blow and die', was his rallying cry. Two White men were killed – a farm manager and a customs officer – and another, a Catholic priest was severely wounded. Chilembwe himself was killed in the fighting, his headquarters destroyed and some of his colleagues were hanged. For Chilembwe's movement the rising had a symbolic significance, anticipating 'a primary African state' with its own 'National African Church'.[66] Limited as it was in scope, it echoed across the borders into Zambia and even as far as Zimbabwe. The Chilembwe rising thus played an important part as an early portent for African independence. Two reflexions: *1.* It was an utterly marginal agency, that of Joseph Booth's which – as the very first in the country – took a promising young Yao to the United States for theological studies; *2.* The intention of his Providence Industrial Mission was a translation into Africa of perfectly balanced Booker T. Washington ideals. However, the intolerably racist attitudes of neighbouring European estate managers caused John Chilembwe to react with violence ending in death.

Booth's varied message was transmitted by two men. Elliot Kamwana, a promising Tonga student in Livingstonia's Overtoun Institution, was disappointed with the promotion chances among the Presbyterians and therefore turned to Booth in 1907. He was enraptured by the apocalyptic Watch Tower message. New images on the pages of Holy scriptures fascinated him and his listeners: the Four Great Beasts that came up from the sea, Daniel 7:3 – did not the Western missionary arrive over the seas? – or the Woman sitting on a scarlet-coloured Beast, Rev. 17:3, and the end of the established order was imminent; a new world was following where Whites would become slaves of the Blacks. The message attracted thousands. In three months Kamwana baptized 9,126 Tonga, many of them children. Here were the rowdy beginnings of the Watch Tower movement in Central Africa, soon to invade Zambia. Charles Domingo, possibly from Mozambique, was one of the foremost of Livingstonia's students and teachers and spent two years at Lovedale in the Cape. In 1910 he turned to the Seventh Day Baptists and without too much success propagated its message about that Other Day in the week.

MOZAMBIQUE

Portuguese rule in Mozambique at the end of the nineteenth century was largely illusory. Attempts at revolts from the end of the 1870s demonstrated African resistance, but the colonial system ground on as before. Portuguese boats were still carrying off slaves from Mozambique in the 1890s. The Africans fled from the large centres into the periphery, resulting in serious depopulation in the country. A government commission of 1894 described the Africans as 'an inferior race'. Some leading Portuguese took a critical view of conditions. One of the ablest, Captain Joachim d'Albuquerque, composed a long litany of failures in one of his books on Mozambique: 'professors without schools and schools without pupils; missions without missionaries, priests without churches and churches without parishioners; even a medical service without doctors'.[67]

When the Jesuits began work in the Zambezi Delta in 1881, they found the task difficult and at times disastrous. By 1902, thirty-seven of them had died. Occasionally Portuguese Franciscans, Dutch Montfortians and Italian Consolata Fathers volunteered for the Catholic missions in this area. In 1910, the Jesuits were driven out of the country in connection with the Portuguese revolution. Bishop Barroso, to whose life Professor Antonio Brasio had devoted a fascinating work, is a noble example of Portuguese Catholic activity in the area.[68] While inertia seemed a rule for Catholic Mozambique, one should not forget the Steyl Mission, 1911–18, among the Atshwabo and the Makua beginning in Quelimane.[69]

Southern Mozambique

The bridge which the Protestants formed between the mountain community of northern Transvaal and coastal congregations in southern Mozambique illustrates familiar patterns emphasized in this study: the refugee factor, the importance of clan relationships, African participation in evangelism and charismatic forms in the spontaneous growth of African spirituality. Groups of Thonga refugees hurried from their Lower Zambezi plains and from the coast into the mountains further inland to the protecting 'Spelonken' – the caves of Zoutpansberg. Here, as Nguni and thus speaking an incomprehensible tongue, they were unwelcome among the northern Sotho. The powerful Venda regarded them as outcasts and they retaliated in kind. Under the command of a Portuguese adventurer, Judge Joe Albasini, they fought *against* the northern Sotho and *for* the Boer Government. When White missionaries arrived from Lesotho in 1873, the Thonga welcomed them expectantly. The expedition from Lesotho included: two prominent Sotho evangelists, Asser and Eliakim; the French missionary, Mabille; and Paul Berthoud, of the newly-arrived Swiss Reformed Mission, looking for a field of work. The Dutch Reformed missionary, S. Hofmeyer at Goedgedacht directed them to the Thonga, known to him for their positive attitude to the Transvaal Government. After a brief initial visit, the expedition left Asser and Eliakim with the Thonga. They stayed for two years, teaching and preaching to the cave communities. In 1875, when Berthoud and another missionary, E. Creux, joined them, they founded the Elim mission. Several devoted Swiss served this young Church, including the well-known ethnographer, Henri A. Junod.

Eventually contacts were re-established with the related Thonga clans on the coast. One day in 1880, Joseph Mhalamhala, 1850–1935, – one of those 'new men' of the period who had been abroad to Kimberley in order to get money for the bride-price – reported to his congregation in the mountains that he had just returned from a six-month visit to the coast. There he had contacted his clan and had also, baptized in 1878, witnessed about his Christian faith. In 1881 he again made the long and arduous trip to the coast, meeting his chief Magunde, who wished to have 'the Book' taught in his area. Returning to the mountains, Joseph brought along his sister and her husband, who then were converted at Elim and baptized as Lois and Eliachib. On 23 April 1882, Mhalamhala was ordained by the missionary E. Creux, 'evangelist and pastor'. In 1882 Joseph and his wife Adele, with Eliachib and Lois, and together with their helpers launched a daring little expedition, preceded by a flag-bearer, and proceeded to the coast. For five years they were the nucleus of the Protestant Church there. They were cheered and challenged by Berthoud's three-month stay in 1885, but except for this brief inspiration, the coastal Church was directed for half a decade by these young converts. Dr H. A. Junod's statement gives a perspective on what happened:

> Even if the Europeans were supposed to possess the Gospel, it was not they who brought the message to the Blacks in this area; it did not come via the ocean, with the civilization and great ships. It came down from the far and unknown interior, brought by an ignorant Black evangelist.[70]

This interchange and constant contact, between inland and the coast, in the interest of the Gospel, provides one of the great stories of African initiative. Joseph founded a centre called 'Antioch', selecting the name of the very first mission station in the New Testament. From his catechumen class at Elim, he remembered especially one main article of Christian doctrine, that of the Spirit, and the tension between the 'Flesh' and the 'Spirit'. He had a constant message to those who sought his spiritual advice: 'You will see what the Spirit will tell you; do as the Spirit tells you.' He had the gift of creating an extended Christian family feeling, and a new form of greeting appeared. When meeting, people would embrace one another, exclaiming 'Be greeted, you are children of the Lord, Beloved of God.'[71]

Lois and Eliachib founded their centre at Ricatla. Here Lois, the hospitable woman leader, exerted the deepest spiritual influence. It was as a women's church that the young Christian community grew. Ricatla became known as 'the Source' of the Water of Life, and developed further the Joseph Mhalamhala doctrine of the Spirit. In order to be accepted as a convert, one had to see visions. 'What have you seen?' was the initial question to the seeker. Hidden in the secluded world of Ricatla, Eliachib's preaching sometimes had unexpected effects on his listeners. The women would stretch out their hands toward heaven and utter heart-rending cries, some would beat their breasts; others tumbled backward violently. Some of these phenomena would not appear again until during Zionist worship on the Rand, where they would be given unfettered expression.[72]

If a person had not seen any visions, Lois and Eliachib knew that he was still 'in the flesh', not yet 'in the Spirit'. A well-defined ladder of insights had to be followed before the seeker could be assured admission to the fold:

1. To be 'beaten by God', through an accident, an illness, a vision.
2. To shed copious tears in meetings, as violently as possible.
3. To show the glory of the coming of Jesus with the words: 'Believe now'.
4. To testify in meetings about experiences of miracles.[73]

Seeking an explanation for the phenomena of exaltation in the congregation, H. A. Junod connects them with cults of possession.[74] Lois and Eliachib also reached a Tembe village where Jim, a member of the chief's family and an enterprising trader, directed a rapidly growing group of neophytes. That he was not baptized, had three wives and possessed slaves did not seem to matter too much – after all – he was related to the chief!

When the Tsonga Protestants arrived in Lourenço Marques – present-day Maputo – they found that the place was already a Protestant sphere of interest thanks to the services of one of the most remarkable of African voluntary evangelists, possibly the most experienced and widely travelled of these men. Here this dramatic story can be referred to only by way of the briefest of notes. Born in Maputo Country, son of an elephant hunter; himself soon expert in this profitable job; to Durban working in the harbour (porter on the breakwaters) and in the sugar plantations; 1875 to Port Elizabeth and its Wesleyan Methodist chapel, heard the Revd Robert Lamplough preach on an Old Testament prophet called Daniel; at this apocalyptic message the stranger from Maputo 'knelt before the pulpit crying for mercy'. He was baptized, receiving the preacher's own name, Robert. To Lovedale, three years evangelist studies; to Kimberley, becoming a Methodist class leader. In 1885 return to Maputo, 'beginning a great mission of which he was the only baptized member'. In 1888 there had emerged an African catechumens' community of 200 members, at nine outposts, with day schools and some teacher training – Robert Mashaba sharing his experience with his younger friends.

He wrote a letter to the African newspaper in King Williams Town, IMVO, appealing for help in the form of an ordained missionary to come to baptize the community; and attended a Wesleyan Methodist synod in Durban. In 1893 the Revd George Weavind arrived in Maputo and baptized the community. In the same year Robert Mashaba, evangelist and Church founder, was ordained. In 1894 there was an African rebellion in southern Mozambique implicating the cautious paramount chief Gungunyana, who eventually was defeated. Robert Mashaba, Protestant in a Portuguese colony, was accused of being involved in the rising; sentenced to life imprisonment and sent to the Cape Verde islands, on the other side of the continent. Released after six years and returned to southern Africa, though not to Portuguese territory. Served as pastor on the Rand, in Transvaal and, finally, in Swaziland, from where he could gaze over the border into his native land.

Things thus developed rather freely until the missionary Berthoud, with a team of evangelists from Elim, arrived on the coast from 1887–93, and from

1896–1903. Berthoud had the idea that his Reformed group could claim priority in southern Mozambique. A few years earlier, the 1888 London Centenary Conference of Protestant Missions had laid down certain conditions for so-called 'comity' agreements between missions in the field and Berthoud, a rigid person of strict principles – himself placed in an infinitely mobile and changing situation – insisted on his rights of comity over against Wesleyan Methodist strategies and activities. He made strong efforts to organize the young Church along more orthodox lines, including a rule of teetotalism. His medical training was a great asset. In the meantime, Anglicans and Wesleyan Methodists arrived at Lourenzo Marques. In the 1880s, the Portuguese Roman Catholics also became aware of their responsibility toward the rapidly growing African community in the capital and sent two Fathers to the area.

Toward the end of the decade, Mozambique had its terrible share of drought, Rinderpest, famine and epidemics. These universal crises caused a new 'revival' among the Thonga Protestants, both at the caves of Spelonken, Transvaal and on the coast. As in so many other cases throughout Africa, an evangelical medic played a catalytic role in this revival. A Swiss missionary doctor came to Antioch in 1891 and reinforced the work of the Protestants. Because of the doctor's personality and his medicines, King Gungunyana at Mandlakazi at last took a positive view of the Church. In nineteenth-century Africa, the Christianization process often included the search for a new identity. One of the chiefs, Ndjakandjaka at Elim, expressed this search in striking words, as he rose to speak in the congregation:

> It is me, it is me Ndjakandjaka and nobody else. My heart has been caught, my heart has been caught, my heart has been pierced. In the night my heart jumped, jumped, jumped ... today I surrender to God. I come today asking to be taught in the Word of God.

Anglicans in Mozambique

The Portuguese authorities and the Catholic Church were suspicious of all 'foreign work', that is, any work done by non-Portuguese. However there were others who saw the immense opportunities in this particular region: of many languages and constant migrant labour groups, *Shangaan* commuting between Mozambique and the Rand and Kimberley. Bishop W. E. Smyth (Anglican bishop of Lebombo 1893–1912) was the right kind of man for this enormous task, dedicated, inventive and adaptable. He knew that 'from a strictly "Church" point of view conditions were hopelessly irregular and some of our order-loving friends in England were horrified.' But Smyth discovered something that was greater than just horror at the disorder: the creative relationship between the Church in Mozambique and the prayer groups on the Rand, and the African power of initiative and leadership for the building up of the Church of Christ.

At first he had no English priests to help him. So he managed to win for the cause Fr Salfey, an Oromo from Ethiopia who had turned up in Zanzibar and was trained in England. The Bishop went to the Rand to contact Chopi migrant workers there. These Chopi on the Rand decided to send one of their number as Church worker back home, John Matthews. He proved to be the right African lay leader, eventually being ordained. In 1912 there were twelve mission stations in the Chopi district, founded by John Matthews. Before coming to Mozambique Smyth had been working in Zululand. So he took along Zulu assistants for the new diocese: Peter Mkize and Ernest Buthelezi and saw to it that they were given theological training, in England and in Cape Town. The Bishop sent his two African co-workers, Salfey and Matthews, to start work at Inhambane, hundreds of miles north along the coast. The Boer War created new problems but above all new opportunities for the Church in Mozambique. All roads to South Africa were blocked and in two months 40,000 mine workers returned, to be housed somehow by African families: 'these refugees were taken in at kraals all over the district'. When the war was over the Bishop received numbers of letters from Africans, revealing what traditional Africa was looking for and, even more, was listening to, in the new message: 'The men who used to sing have gone away, please send us someone to teach us to sing.'[75]

THE CHURCH IN THE INDIAN OCEAN

Madagascar – perspectives

The Church history of Madagascar during the half century, 1820–70, can be characterized by at least five themes: widening the scope; dominating the island; coastline and inland; an autonomous kingdom and an autonomous Church; and a reformed phase.

Widening the scope

'Le petit continent' was part of a larger whole and appeared as one component, albeit the major component, in a larger island world in the south-western corner of the Indian Ocean, with a constant interchange of goods, people and ideas between the islands. This interchange also affected the Church in the region. For decades Malagasy congregational life was lived away from the main island, as an underground movement, biding its time, in Mauritius and Réunion east of Madagascar and on the smaller islands to the west of the main Island. In fact, the perspective can be seen to be even wider, for it was from Réunion and Mauritius that Catholic Fathers planned and accomplished their approach not only to the '*Le petit continent*', but to East Africa as well, via another island in the Indian Ocean, Zanzibar.

Dominating the island – or at least the centre of it

The infrastructure of Merina national politics was established at the end of the eighteenth century by that great king, Andrianampoinimerina. He dominated the centre of the island, Imerina, by placing his military garrisons at strategic points, thereby, incidentally, preparing the future spread of the new religion as this proved to be an ideology fit for officers and soldiers: military posts on the coast virtually became mission stations. The first half of the century was an entirely Imerina Church history.

Coastline and inland

Christianity came to nineteenth-century Africa as a coastal religion, brought there by ship. It was in the harbours – St Louis, Douala, Port Elizabeth, Mombasa and so on – and along neighbouring coastlines that the first missionaries made contact with those who were to become their first converts. This was not so in Madagascar. The first attempts to work in Tamatave, the port on the east coast, proved disastrous and the missionaries, if they survived, returned to their base on Mauritius. It was in Mauritius – inspired and sustained by the sympathetic British governor Robert Farquahar – that David Jones and his Protestant London Missionary Society (LMS) colleagues were informed about the geopolitical facts of Madagascar: the power centre was found inland, at the recently built capital of Tananarive. In order to win Madagascar one had to start from the centre in the highlands which, incidentally, had a much better climate than on the coast, as well as a dominating population, the Merina (called Hova at the time). Having left Britain in 1817, it was only in October 1820 that David Jones arrived in Tananarive where he met the young king Radama I, son of the founder of the Merina kingdom, Andrianampoinimerina.

An autonomous kingdom and an autonomous Church

Politically Madagascar was, throughout the nineteenth century, an autonomous region, the Imerina kingdom. Threatened from time to time by one of the two imperialist powers, Britain and France, the kingdom nevertheless warded off these threats until, in 1885, the country became a French protectorate, and ten years later the land of Andrianampoinimerina was 'deeply humiliated' by the French invasion. From the point of view of the Church it should be added that if Imerina was an autonomous kingdom, the first Christian community remained, for a period of twenty-five critical and creative years, 1836–61, altogether autonomous. These Christian groups hardly ever saw a foreign missionary, whether Catholic or Protestant, other than in one or two cases, in clandestine disguise.

A Reformed phase

During the first half of the century, 1820–70, Christian influences were largely a Protestant history or, more specifically, Reformed. The first pioneers, Welsh Congregationalists, were school teachers and artisans who saw Bible translation as their first imperative task and opportunity. Their Bible and their hymns – and *The Pilgrim's Progress* – inspired a piety which sustained the groups and individuals 'in afflictions and distresses ... by honour and dishonour ...'

Laying the foundations 1820–35

The handful of LMS missionaries in the 1820s, who numbered less than ten, were mainly artisans – carpenters, blacksmiths, weavers and tanners. In modern terms they would be called 'development workers', concerned as they were with alphabetization and with technical training. This pleased King Radama. Fascinated by Western techniques, the King thought of himself as a 'modernizer'. The missionaries taught him English and established, first a Palace school and then two other schools mainly for the aristocracy. Soon the English language was exchanged for the vernacular when their own Malagasy language was domesticated, written and read in Western letters, which was easier to appropriate, as King Radama found, than the Arabic script. An entire generation of young Imerina aristocracy questioned a traditional religion, where the dead were very much alive and where the ancestors held a highly honoured position.

In 1826 the missionaries imported a printing press and with its help they used to the utmost what proved to be a precious time of grace, in producing an astonishing number of their sacred books. In 1835 some 10,000 New Testaments and 5,000 copies each of Genesis, Isaiah and Proverbs circulated among the faithful, together with copies of that most popular book, *The Pilgrim's Progress*. In 1836 the first intense period of missionary influence came to an abrupt end. By that time some 10,000 to 15,000 people had been given school education. Between 1,000 and 1,500 young men had been trained as artisans by David Griffiths and his colleagues and in May 1831 the baptism of the first twenty-five Malagasy converts was celebrated.

The personal interest and passion of the young missionaries was Bible translation. Hailing from a Church of Bible-readers, they wished to share this fundamental experience of theirs with the Malagasy. They may have had little academic training, but they proved surprisingly competent for the task which they saw as theirs. Prior to going to Madagascar they had already started their translation work in Mauritius. With the consent and support of the young King Radama I, they found a group of twelve talented Malagasy to serve as their linguistic co-workers. The first edition of the Malagasy New Testament appeared in 1830 and the Old Testament in 1835. The bulk of the first edition was distributed 'mainly among soldiers and their officers', who were ex-students of the mission school.[76] As these soldiers declared that they must own a New Testament 'in order to start a school on the coast', one recognizes an irresistible Protestant theme seen throughout the African continent. The message of the Book conveyed a message of salvation available to all, regardless of class and wealth which, in a hierarchical society, was naturally seen as an outrageous claim, liable soon to lead to painful death. On the way to that final demise one could sing hymns. In 1828 the LMS missionaries managed to produce their first hymn-book, which became immensely popular. The ninth edition of the hymn-book, of 1870, had 181 numbers.

The dark years, 1835–61

Those happy spring days of a mission soon came to an end. King Radama I died in 1828 – by his own hand – and was succeeded by his widow, Ranavalona I. While the king had been a 'modernizer' and as such a promoter of mission interests, the queen was eventually to change all this. This did not happen immediately, as the queen was aware of the value of schools and the need for the skills of artisans. But there were other considerations, notably the possible threat to the queen's power and authority. This became an obsession with her. In 1835 she announced the death penalty for anybody who continued to pray to the God of the Christians.

The simultaneous appearance of a millenarian prophet, Rainitsiandavaka, did not make the Christian cause any more popular with the queen and her followers. This man, who insisted that his message was given to him through dreams independent of the Bible, claimed that when Christ returned to earth all slaves would be set free, an alarming prospect for any right-thinking member of the Merina aristocracy. The Queen had any suspect condemned to poison ordeals. In total, including casualties from military campaigns, around 150,000 people lost their lives during the reign of Ranavalona I. By 1857 'an undetermined number of Christians had been speared, smothered, starved or burned to death, poisoned, hurled from cliffs or boiled alive in rice pits.'[77] The number of Christian martyrs was at least 200. It was now, as we shall see presently, that the wider geographical sphere of Malagasy interests – the links with Mauritius, Réunion and Nosy-Bé – was to offer a welcome refuge for the converts. In the 1850s two European missionaries, Fr Finaz, a French Jesuit and the Revd William Ellis, a London congregationalist, made clandestine visits to the island.

In Madagascar itself, hiding places for refugees could be found on some hill or in some valley, far from the inhabited areas of the capital; much the same as on the continent of Africa, a first generation of Christians would meet on hills or in caves and grottoes. Vonizongo, north-west of the capital, was such a place where Christian worship continued in highly dangerous circumstances, until, in 1849, eighteen Vonizongo men were martyred and their wives sold into slavery.

But through it all a certain *modus vivendi* was established between traditionalists and Christians. There were Christian confessors in the queen's own family. This period in the Church as a *religio illicita*, a forbidden cult, was far from being an empty period signifying nothing. Re-interpreting the church history of Madagascar, Pastor Rabary – one of the great preachers of Madagascar and of Africa as a whole – attempted in the first two decades of the twentieth century to understand the conditions of the Church in the terrible years of Ranavalona I. He developed two themes, those of 'the Night' and 'the Inner Exile'. The Night was also the time of Jonah's whale when Jonah was swallowed up for three days, praying to God for salvation from his distress – thus prefiguring the Malagasy Church in colonial Madagascar, praying for deliverance from its yoke. That 'Night' in Queen Ranavalona's reign was a time of startling possession cults in different parts of the island, all ultimately related to the sovereign in Tananarive and revealing the depths of the mentality of the population.

This was, above all, the period when the Congregational Church expressed its newly-won faith, in dreams and visions, in reciting their Bible stories, with each convert having his or her own set of five or six or more Bible passages to be repeated again and again. Faith was also expressed in the hymns, the great theme of which was the pilgrimage to Zion, the heavenly Jerusalem – easily confused with the heavenly Tananarive – and informed by that incomparable collection of wisdom, Bunyan's *The Pilgrim's Progress*. In the very midst of Malagasy society, the people had one man of the purest royal birth, about whose legitimacy there could be no doubt, elect for the purpose of uniting Malgashness and Christianity: Prince Rakotond/Radama, born 1829, son of Queen Ranavalona. What is more, in 1845 he joined what there was of a countervailing Christian movement. In the following year he allowed himself to be secretly baptized, thus taking a step that no other royal could afford to take until 1869: one could read the Bible and sing hymns, but not take that ultimate step of a new Covenant, the Baptism. In this young prince messianic and eschatological expectations of a Bible-reading minority in distress found an orientation point for the pilgrimage through the Night.

The most surprising fact about these first dramatic decades of Malagasy Congregational Church history was the speed with which the faith was appropriated, in the hearts of men and women, and extent to which it withstood – with martyrs' determination – the onslaught on the young converts. The witness and example of the foreign missionaries, soon taken away from their faithful, in no way completely accounted for it. For a quarter of a century, 1835–61, the Church was led exclusively by Malagasy Christians themselves, and was, in spite of all terrible dangers, a growing, 'self-propagating' Church. While in 1835 there had been between 1,000 and 2,000 Christians, by 1861, the year of the death of Queen Ranavalona I, their numbers had risen to between 7,000 and 10,000. After 1861 groups of Christians were discovered in far-off places, particularly in the Betsileo region in the south. Here one meets again the refugee theme in African Church history. Numbers of Christians had fled to Betsileo and found refuge in the forests and the hill towns of this distant region. Malagasy Christians point to the power of the Book; the singing of the hymns, with their unwonted rhythm; the vision of *The Pilgrim's Progress* over the red hills of Madagascar. In the midst of oppression, deprivation and death there developed a peculiar kind of Protestant spirituality fed by the Old Testament prophets, New Testament apocalypse and a constant walk with the author of *The Pilgrim's Progress*.

Inter-islands interlude

The two islands Mauritius and Réunion, as parts of an integrated island world, were of such importance for the efforts to reach Madagascar in the years of Ranavalona I, that it warrants some brief paragraphs on the Church situation in the islands. In both islands the role of the French Holy Ghost Fathers was decisive. The conversion of Réunion's population vividly illustrates the relevance of one of our precepts of the Christianization process: the Gospel must be 'carried home', not brought. Frédéric Le Vavasseur, an eighteen-year-old representative of the Creole population of Réunion, was sent to France in the 1830s to study – where he came under Libermann's influence. He became a fervent Catholic and after twenty years returned to Réunion as a priest, a Holy Ghost Father. He had 'carried home' the message. He arrived just in time for the enormous social revolution there, the liberation of the slave population of 60,000. In the plantations he built chapels and technical schools, as well as a noviciate for his Brothers. He also started a 'congregation' for women, the Daughters of Mary. A total transition of the oppressed followed. In 1850 isolated little Réunion had its own Bishop, by the name of Maupoint. Libermann had insisted: 'A bishop is more necessary in the colonies than in France.'[78]

It is in this context that the Réunion island base was to become of primary importance for the Continent of Africa as a whole. Bishop Maupoint managed – at a time when Church authorities believed that they could make such decisions – to persuade the Holy See to declare the whole of the East African coast, from Cape Delgado to the Equator, to be under the Bishop of Réunion. In 1867 he made a preparatory visit to Zanzibar. In the following year his French (or rather Alsatian) Holy Ghost missionaries moved to Zanzibar from Réunion, followed by six Daughters of Mary – the beginnings of modern Catholic missions in East Africa. In Réunion the Fathers soon found that they had to take care of numbers of Malagasy youth. The Malagasy Catholic refugee community in Réunion was able to keep in constant and clandestine contact with groups on the Madagascar mainland. By the 1840s the Holy Ghost Fathers had already started what they called 'Christian villages' for young people in Senegal. This system was now developed further in Réunion. Little villages were started there for Malagasy boys and girls, with the aim of training them to be future carriers of the Catholic witness back home in Madagascar. But soon the perspective was extended further than that, over the wide waters. The small-scale Malagasy educational experiment on Réunion became the model for the grand Catholic enterprise as they moved to Zanzibar and to Bagamoyo on the East African coast, aiming at the inland of the continent.

Mauritius had a Malagasy community of its own from the time before the nineteenth century and the Christian refugees were able to link up with their own compatriots there. Through the secret comings and goings between Madagascar and Mauritius by individuals and groups, Mauritius became the scene of enthusiastic Christian activity by LMS Congregationalists and SPG Anglicans. The Congregationalist Jean Lebrun kept in touch with his LMS co-religionists in Madagascar. Born in Jersey, in the Channel Islands, he spoke French and English with equal ease, an advantage in Mauritius with its comparatively large French-speaking population in the British colony (since 1810). The CMS were fortunate in their choice of Anglican bishops for Mauritius. Bishop Vincent W. Ryan and Bishop Royston are of special interest in the context of the role of the islands as bases for further missionary outreach. The CMS asked Bishop Ryan to take episcopal supervision of 'the East African Mission': the islands further north, Zanzibar and the Seychelles, seemed easily reachable, by Arab dhow, for episcopal visitations.

Soon a vital Catholic community also emerged in Mauritius. The British island colony in 1841 had an English Benedictine as the Catholic bishop, while the most important missionary was one of Libermann's French disciples – Fr Jacques Désiré Laval (1803–64).[79] With theological and medical training, he arrived in 1841 into the multi-racial, multilingual and multireligious Mauritius. Instead of befriending rich plantation owners, Laval went to the oppressed masses and identified with them as far as housing, food and other conditions of life were concerned. The luminous personal example of the selfless padre attracted tens of thousands. In a population of over 300,000 in 1862, 75,000 were Christians (65,000 Catholics and 10,000 Anglicans) and 236,000 were Muslim, Hindu, or followers of traditional African beliefs.

Fr Laval arrived in Mauritius at a dramatic hour. In 1810 the British had captured the island from the French and in 1839 the new rulers abolished slavery, a decision of immense importance for the 47,000 African slaves. In the process the emancipated Africans – replaced as labourers on the sugar plantations by indentured Indian labour – were, however, worse off than before. In their poverty they gathered in Riviere Noire and other corners of the island. Fr Laval devoted himself totally to their service, speaking their Creole patois and holding special services for them. Fr Laval soon had a number of devoted catechists. He selected them – a great preoccupation with him – with spiritual authority. One of the future catechists, to become his personal co-worker, was recruited by an irresistible appeal: 'Emillion, follow God and follow me.'[80] Soon a mass movement developed and Laval could call upon 'women councillors' among the African population to assist not only with catechization but with visitations to the sick, aged and dying and to the prisoners. 'Self-help' was his programme for his poor parishioners and he gave them thereby a new sense of self-esteem and self-respect. The confessional became a place for private instruction where he could show each individual the Christian way of life. This outstanding Spiritan priest and medical doctor served in Mauritius until his death in 1864. In 1979, the Pope declared Father Laval Blessed.

Other islands off Madagascar also benefited from missionary activity, not least Nosy-Bé to the north-west of Madagascar. Fr Rainbaud, CSSp, introduced plants for mass production, including coffee and revolutionized the economic life of the island. The 30,000 inhabitants on Nosy-Bé came for the most part from Madagascar itself, 'from where they had had to flee and to where they wished to return', as the Jesuit Church historian Boudou expressed the situation, with a formula representative of both Catholics and Protestants in the islands.[81]

Madagascar and the slave trade

Two British legal enactments of 1807 and of 1834 putting a 'final' stop to the slave trade and to slavery were of enormous importance for the whole continent but did not unfortunately lead to the end of the nefarious traffic everywhere. One region easily overlooked in this context was that of the islands of the western Indian Ocean, the French plantation islands and Madagascar. In Madagascar various groups were involved in the traffic: in the north, traders of Arab origin and further south Sakalava chiefs. The latter operated a two-way traffic in slaves: purchasing East African slaves for the interior of the Island and supplying Merina and Betsileo slaves for export from the island. After the Church–State union at the end of the 1860s there emerged a new bureaucracy, some of them members of the imperial court. Gwynn Campbell has shown that for their financial operations, slaves were in demand right up to 1895. After 1885 there also emerged virtual *Betsiriry* 'slave republics', mainly Sakalava, living almost exclusively off the slave trade.[82]

The main source of slaves was to be found on the east coast of Africa, opposite northern Madagascar. By the 1870s and 1880s this region, in Malawi, Zambesia and Mozambique, was virtually depopulated as slaves were transported via a number of small ports across the channel to

Madagascar or to Réunion. Profits were as high as 1,000 per cent. The French imperial take-over, with the military occupation of the island, put a final stop to the traffic. In this part of Madagascar, on the west coast, there was one Church, the Catholic Church, which geographically and socially was in a position to approach these foreign groups.

Unprecedented growth of the Churches, 1861–95

If one can discern a thread of 'continuity' in the dramatic nineteenth-century history of Madagascar – as suggested by Dr Stephen Ellis, a scholar of Malagasy affairs, this would seem to consist in the utter dependence of the aristocracy and the nation as a whole on the will and whim of royalty, particularly that of the two outstanding queens, Ranavalona I and Ranavalona II. In 1861 Ranavalona I's long reign came to an end. Her death was the signal for missionaries to return to the island, or to make a bid to establish themselves there. The alleged messiah, Ramada II, became king and the dream could be translated into reality. But it was a rude kind of reality, for the well-meaning young king – open to ideas and political influences from the West – soon destroyed himself with drink and women. After two years on the throne, in 1863 he was murdered. He was succeeded by Queen Rasoherina, with personal sympathies for the Catholic Church, and like Radama she maintained freedom of religion. After Rasoherina's death in 1868, the succession in 1869 went to Queen Ranavalona II. With her and her husband, the prime minister, a new day dawned for the Churches in Madagascar.

Both Radama II and Rasoherina had, more or less half-heartedly, promoted Christian interests but neither of them could take the ultimate step of allowing themselves to be officially baptized. However, on 21 February 1869, Queen Ranavalona II and her prime ministerial consort were together baptized into the Congregational Church. A great number of factors, interests and threats were at work in this situation, competing with and corroborating each other: family, clan and dynasty interests and tensions, in the highest circles of Andriana royalty and aristocracy; active possession cults in different parts of the country; but also the rapidly rising influence of what was beginning to appear as a Protestant party, including LMS missionaries, in the army, among school 'teachers' and in the slave population. This influence could not be neglected and if so, it could best be dominated if royalty joined its ranks. Apart from these general considerations of a political and sociological kind, there was also the personal attitude and decision of the queen herself. In the midst of all her state duties she may have encountered examples of Christian life which appeared convincing and attractive to her.

The baptism itself – which should be seen in the same light as the solemn coronation of the queen – was carried out in the presence of a distinguished assembly: officers of high rank, judges, chiefs, nobility and the preachers of the Protestant Churches in the city. No foreigner was present, the baptism being celebrated by Pastor Andriambelo, scion of a distinguished family. As they followed the simple yet solemn rite of the Congregational baptism service, the onlookers may have perceived that they were present at the most important moment in Merina nineteenth-century history, with potentially enormous significance for the clans and the individuals. For, in the moment when the queen accepted Christianity, all her subjects had, in principle, to follow. It was a cult favoured by the queen and therefore binding on all. This can be seen in the mission statistics. In 1869 Imerina had 37,000 Christians; by the end of the following year, 1870, their numbers had risen to 250,000. This can be followed most dramatically in the area near the capital Tananarive. In 1862 there were some thirty local Church centres with 6,000 participants including the capital. In 1867 there were ninety-two centres with 100 pastors and numerous preachers. In 1869 there were already 468 congregations, with 158 pastors, 935 preachers and 153,000 faithful, all in a Merina population at the time of some 800,000. The LMS moved into harvest time.

The LMS in the Malagasy landscape

The LMS built on the sociological foundations of the urban culture in the comparatively rich and aristocratic northern half of the island. From the traditional rulers of the past the Church was able to take over 'a very parochial system' and 'the parish proved to be almost tailor-made as a system of Church government'.[83] The Christianization of Imerina was a process caused by fundamental factors in Malagasy sociology 'which owes nothing to Christianity'.[84] The transition was not easy. As the Western-oriented section of the population watched the dawn of a bright new day, the traditionalists experienced the change as a trauma. The sudden Christianization process seemed to deprive a proud people of their grand national traditions. The mentality of the people at this time is illustrated by the *Ramanenjana* possession cult, a wide-spread dancing mania involving tens of thousands of people, soldiers, slaves and others, acting as if carrying the baggage of the Queen Ranavalona I, and expressing their hope of a return of the deceased queen.

With a modern sports jargon one might suggest that a race was set. For it was a race between the missionary societies, where one contender, the LMS, because of its antecedents and its contacts with royalty and the aristocracy, could claim to decide the placing of the other competitors, at least as far as the non-Romans were concerned. The Catholics, of course, had their own arena. The LMS were well set in the capital, Tananarive and among the dominant Merina population. They could move forward from a position of strength as compared with that of the others: (*a*) because of their pioneering initiative in the 1820s; (*b*) because of the traditional Congregationalist connections of the Merina royalty and aristocracy; (*c*) because of the role which William Ellis of the LMS was playing in the 1860s in developing policies drawn up by David Jones and his colleagues in the 1820s.

In the early 1860s three churches were built by the faithful themselves in the poorest quarters of Tananarive, raised in a few months by their own efforts, except for some timber 'for which a small contribution was made by missionary Aswell' (as stated in the minutes). Much more conspicuous were the 'Memorial Churches' raised on the proposal of the LMS missionary William Ellis. Returning to Tananarive, where the Churches were now beginning to function again after the times of persecution, Ellis wished these churches, erected 1869–70, to commemorate the Malagasy martyrs. King Radama II, provided the sites while the British Congregationalists showed their solidarity with their Malagasy brethren by contributing no less than £14,000, collected in a matter of weeks. Dr Françoise Raison-Jourde, in a thorough and beautiful study of the building of Protestant temples 1860–69, has brought out the sacred dimension of these Protestant martyr Churches, which made the city into a religious city. In the same way as in the eighteenth century, when King Andrianampoinimerina had created a sacred geography related to twelve hills near the capital, so now the four Memorial Churches in the capital integrated the martyrs into the heart of Malagasy history and helped to 'make persecution one of the best established chapters in Merina tradition'.[85]

Within the LMS framework emerged two special instruments of evangelization, both of great originality: the 'Palace Church' and the 'Six Monthly Meeting'. The Palace Church, in the capital Tananarive, developed as a Malagasy Independent Church, designed, not indeed from below – as was the rule for Southern African Independents but from the top. It was directed by the queen and the prime minister, as of necessity it had to be in feudal Merina society: the Palace Church was for the elite. Ordinary folk could be members of the White-ruled congregations, while the ruling class, or caste –

cabinet ministers, army commanders and higher civil servants – had a Church of their own, which was easily self-supporting. Leading churchmen who emerged from the pre-1861 underground movement could join this Palace Church rather then be subject to missionary influence. Statistically the Palace Church grew rapidly. In 1870 members numbered only fifty, in 1880, 100, and in 1895 there were 160,000 with 194 pastors. The Palace Church sent out its own emissaries, selected and sent by the queen, to outlying districts. They were picked from among the aristocracy. After five years they were recalled to the capital and given high government posts in acknowledgment of their merits to Church and State.

The Six Monthly Meeting

As an expression of the missionary concern of the Church, there emerged a new, characteristically Malagasy organization. This was designed to send out Malagasy missionaries beyond Imerina's borders, to ethnic communities which at first tended to regard any Merina or Hova Church initiative as oppressive. The Six Monthly Meeting was to constitute a unifying force for the three Reformed groups, the LMS, the Quakers and the Paris Mission (the latter from 1900). From 1875 these Meetings took on considerable proportions and soon became a power in the Church life of the Island. Large sums of money were collected by the Malagasy for financing the missionary work of the Six Monthly Meetings. To their surprise some of the Malagasy missionaries found that in a number of places they had already been preceded by anonymous, voluntary preachers, thus illustrating on the Island a theme which has repeatedly in this book been emphasized for southern Africa.

The Meeting brought together immense crowds for worship. Johannes Johnson, the well-known Norwegian hymn-writer who served as a missionary in Madagascar for fifteen years said: 'Never in my life have I heard songs of praise being intoned with such hearty, powerful joy as when an Independent congregation rises to sing, in Malagasy, [Bishop Heber's] "Holy, Holy, Holy".'

The LMS alone had organized no less than 1,200 local Churches and an equal number of schools. In 1881 the Merina government introduced obligatory school attendance for children between seven and fifteen. The village built their schools and provided the teachers with rice. The educationally ambitious Merina established three high schools, for Theology, Education – the prestigious 'College' – and Medicine.

Other non-Roman Churches

The new-comers among the non-Romans – the Quakers, arriving in 1867, were largely an extension of the LMS work both geographically and theologically – the SPG Anglicans from 1864 and the Norwegian Lutherans from 1866 presented a much sharper profile of ecclesiastical leadership than the soft-line 'independent' LMS. Both were episcopal, for the Norwegians, too, at first had a bishop, H. P. S. Schreuder, residing in Zululand – although, as Protestants sometimes do, this bishop resigned from his connection with the Norwegian Mission Society and formed his own Lutheran Society, which was largely American-supported. The Norwegians nonetheless had other characteristics which made their image in southern Madagascar unmistakable. Only three and a half years after their start in the island, they were prepared to begin a highly ambitious Theological Seminary, under the leadership of Lars Dahle, one of the great Western missionaries on the island. The LMS, who had already attempted pastors training in the 1820s, knew that the sources of faith and life for theological education were largely to be found in Holy Writ, with some pedagogical backing from John Bunyan's *The Pilgrim's Progress*. Lars Dahle, on his side, introduced something which in Reformed Madagascar seemed far from Protestant. Without apology he launched 'Dogmatics', 'Symbolics' and 'Liturgics', and gave his theological students essay themes such as 'What is the right doctrine on the sacrements?' Dahle knew the answer to this one and showed it by a 'Presentation' of Lutheran doctrine, followed by a *Fanoherana*, or 'Refutation', of the positions to the right and the left – the Catholics and the Reformed – while happily, the Lutheran position came out all right.

For their self-appointed task of placing the newcomers in the Malagasy geography, the LMS found the Norwegians difficult and tried to keep them away at least from the main point, the capital. In these circumstances, it was to Vakinankaratra, towards the south, that the Norwegian Lutherans oriented themselves and it was in the southern part of the island that they and their American Lutheran colleagues (of Norwegian background) concentrated their considerable energies. In their mission conferences, the Protestants were soon to refer to a 'Congregationalist North' and a 'Lutheran South'. In Rasolomona the Lutherans found the right man to promote general education. He had passed through the theological seminary with flying colours and had later taught for sometime at a teacher training school. On these merits he was appointed Government School Inspector for Betsileo and through his vast influence became the first Lutheran Malagasy to play a leading role in the history of school and Church. In one year, in 1882, the number of school-children more than trebled from 10,000 to 37,000. This brought about a mighty advance for school and Church, particularly as Rasolomona had the charisma to appeal to both parents and children: a Christian mass movement of surprising outreach followed in the Betsileo area. In the end Rasolomona returned to the Theological Seminary and finished as a pastor in his home district: one of the long line of teachers in Africa who, after a long and honoured life of teaching, agree to be ordained and to serve as pastors.

The Anglicans entered Madagascar supported by an ecclesiastical formula which seemed unmistakable, representing an episcopal Church, the official head of which was a sovereign queen, just as at Tananarive. Here, however, as in so many other cases, Madagascar proved to be a paradox, for the Independents, of all people, had established themselves in the position of being virtually a state church, which disliked bishops. At first there were diplomatic hesitations at Canterbury too – while Bishop Gray in Cape Town energetically promoted an Anglican presence on the island – and in the end Tamatave, the chief port on the east coast offered a base for Anglican activity. Bishop A. K. Cornish, consecrated at Edinburgh, set to work in 1874.

The Catholics

The Catholics appeared as late-comers in this Protestant company. Yet, they had been there before, much earlier in fact. They could regard their entrance on the Malagasy scene as a *reprise*, to some extent to be compared with the Catholic *reprise* in Congo. At the beginning of the seventeenth century Jesuits from Goa had arrived, and a half century later, Lazarists from France had made a daring, though ultimately unsuccessful, attempt in the south of the island. The Protestant domination in the nineteenth century seemed definitely to cold-shoulder the Catholics, but these did not give up. From their island bases all round the 'Petit Continent' they kept on jabbing at the mainland, with surprising mobility, hurrying from one little island to another, by dhow, brig or any other floating keel, trying ever new, clandestine approaches. In his two-volume work on the Jesuits in nineteenth-century Madagascar, Fr Adrien Boudou devotes his first volume, of over 500 pages, to this camouflaged prologue of a mission.[86] The most dramatic attempt was that by Fr Finaz, SJ, arriving in 1855 in disguise, with his mother's maiden name as 'Mr Hervier'. He made the acquaintance of one of the princes – conveniently one who was later to be crowned King

Radama II – and was able, in the greatest secrecy to celebrate the mass on 8 July 1855, the first ever in Tananarive.

The Catholics were to find that they had arrived in a Protestant, even, Reformed country. In fact, until the French colonial conquest at the end of the century, they were kept at arm's length by the elite, both geographically and sociologically. Geographically the Catholics found their base not in the Merina centre but among the coastal populations, through Fr Finaz and his Jesuit colleagues in Betsileo from 1903. Sociologically they were to a large extent excluded from the Merina elite and thus concentrated all the more on the less advanced communities, including the vast slave population. There were eloquent exceptions to this generalization, such as the leading Catholic woman of the century, Victorie Rasoamanarivo (d. 1894), married to a son of the prime minister and a luminous Christian personality. Another solitary example was the first Malagasy Catholic priest, Basilide Rahidy, ordained in 1872 after decades spent on Réunion. Only in 1925 was this priestly example followed by a younger generation, when nine Malagasy priests were ordained. The Cluny Sisters gave their precious service not only in girls' schools but also in devotion to leprosy sufferers.

Catholicism was seen as 'the religion of the French', in a country where the Merina elite were English-speaking as far as an international language was concerned, and the 'France-Hova' wars of 1885 and 1895 came as an embarrassment to the Catholic effort. The position of the Catholics as 'interior emigrants' and as a repressed minority was unmistakable for the nineteenth century. By 1900 the number of Catholics was 90,000 and there was still only one Catholic priest. Only from the 1930s can a very definite change be noticed when they came to represent 'a hidden political resistance' movement.[87]

MADAGASCAR 1895–1920

Malagasy Churches under colonial rule

Towards the end of the nineteenth century the strength of the Merina kingdom was gradually fading. In 1885 a 'phantom protectorate' was created by the French, which proved to be the beginning of the end. The Merina government tried to muster its formidable defenders, 'General Hazo' and 'General Tazo'[88] – the forest and the fever – but in the end, in 1895, French forces occupied the island and Madagascar was declared a French colony. The queen (now Ranavalona III) and the prime minister were exiled to Algiers in North Africa, while other Merina princes and office-bearers were shot without further ado.

It was in the relationship of Church and State and in the tension between Catholic and Protestant that these first years of colonial rule were particularly unhappy. The international rivalry of the period could not but influence relationships in Madagascar too. The famous tug-of-war in 1898 between Britain and France over Fashoda in southern Sudan was re-enacted in Madagascar through a series of local small 'Fashodas', hitting primarily the English-speaking Churches. In autonomous Malagasy society the LMS had enjoyed a position of preference which was now turned against this mission and the non-Romans as a whole. Their English language gave them away: could they be really loyal to the new French rulers? The religious conflict in Madagascar, 1895–1910, was a colonial reflex of the international competition between France and Britain and of the sharp Catholic–Protestant discord in France itself, dominated by the virulent Dreyfus affair and its aftermath. The two first French governors-general set the tone for the following development. Gallieni, governor-general 1896–1905, was intent on the Gallicization of the population. With this in mind he opposed the LMS because it was English and presumably a danger to French interests: 'All my efforts have as objects to destroy that influence.'

In 1905, the year of the separation of Church and State in France, Gallieni was followed as governor-general by Victor Augagneur, inveterate atheist and anti-clerical, fighting against the Christian faith as such. Nobody could have been more thorough in his attack against missions and their programme. He deprecated the idea of a Protestant ministry – 'a disastrous idea ... it is necessary to set oneself absolutely against the constitution of a native ministry.'[89] The YMCA, too, was a dangerous idea to be suppressed. Mission schools were, as a rule, held in church buildings during the week: this was forbidden and 2,000 elementary schools were affected in this way. Of the 900 Lutheran schools with 30,000 students, hardly any could continue. The missions tried Sunday schools instead but were forbidden to teach literacy.

'The land of Andrianampoinimerina is profoundly humiliated', was the instant reaction of the people to the French imperialist conquest. A defeated population in its bewilderment felt it had to turn to the assurances of the past. 'The power of our royal talismans has been destroyed by the prayers from across the seas.' Talismans carefully hidden at the time of the queen's baptism in 1869 were now brought out again, conferring what was felt as power and hope on despondent devotees. A line of nationalistic ancestral religion can be traced from 1869 to 1899.

In 1896 slavery was abolished. Two other population movements accentuated the tremor and turmoil in the nation, in their various ways affecting the conditions and life of the Churches: (*a*), the 'Rising of the Red Shawls', a political revolt 1895–99; (*b*), the Soatanana Pietistic revival.

The 'Red Shawls' rebellion struck in all parts of the country, a violent guerrilla expression of a deeply felt *malaise* in the population. It was primarily a Merina movement (called the 'Red Shawls' because the participants stained their clothes with the holy red earth of Madagascar). The movement was sometimes inextricably merged with Biblical ideas and was therefore likely to be confused by the colonial administration with dangerous Protestant designs. An itinerant preacher appealed to his listeners: 'Shall we always live under these Nebuchadnezzars?'[90] The revolt was sometimes led by lapsed Christians, with millenarianism not far below the surface.[91] The rising was officially vanquished in 1899, but while it lasted, it caused – seen in the short-term – much damage to the Christian cause. With a longer view, the Red Shawls were to provide inspiration for a political revolution half a century later.

The Soatanana Pietistic revival had its break through at the time of the most tense political and social crisis imaginable, June 1895, in the year of the French conquest. On 9 June 1895, the Betsileo farmer Rainisoalambo of Soatanana, gathered his twelve Disciples for the first time. A few months earlier he had a spiritual awakening, important both in itself and also from the wider perspective of the Church in the African continent. Almost all the traits quoted by Rainisoalambo and described – by Malagasy revivalists and missionary writers – as unique can be seen as variations of what Zulu or Shona prophets would affirm somewhat later: a serious illness; a dream with a shining figure bidding the dreamer to throw away his witchcraft tools; the role of the Bible; praying for the sick by laying on of hands with consequent miraculous healing. Two additional components had more specifically Malagasy features: Rainisoalambo had been a soldier and he gathered twelve men as his co-workers, 'The Disciples of the Lord'. His Lutheran affiliation made him use Martin Luther's Small Catechism for his teaching.[92]

This revival was to change hearts and minds and, for a while, to vary the geographical spread of a Christian movement in the island. Hitherto religious movements had moved from the north southwards, from Imerina to Betsileo, to the Sakalava, to Betsimisaraka. The Soatanana revival, by contrast, starting in Betsileo, presented a move northwards. The Soatanana movement became a missionary agency for the Protestant Church, reaching out to every part of the country. It was also ecumenically significant, bridging denominational differences between Protestant groups and doing so not through slow theological debate but through sharing common religious experiences.

Certain outstanding political and social factors in the situation after 1914 must briefly be mentioned. The First World War saw no less than 50,000 Malagasy soldiers leave for France and central Europe. The Christians among them are known to have given excellent Christian witness in a foreign land. Their eventual return home was an inspiration to the Churches. In 1913 the VVS (*vy*, *vato*, *sakelika* – meaning iron, stone and network) secret society, nationalist in ambition, was formed by a group of Malagasy intellectuals which included several Protestant pastors and Catholic priests. In 1915 the VVS was uncovered by the French administration and, because of wartime tensions, thirty-four of its leaders received either a long period of hard labour or actual life sentences, including the Protestant Pasteur Ravelojaona 'who is generally considered [to be] the father of Malagasy nationalism'.[93]

The Reformed Churches

The colonial government's anti-Protestant campaign caused serious and lasting damage to Protestant Church property and to the individual's right of choice of denomination. Professor Jean Bauberot of Paris cites these incidents under the following headings: Protestant temples forcibly transformed into Catholic Church buildings; enforced conversions of Protestants to Catholicism; desertion of Protestant schools.[94]

The LMS, the British Protestant mission, had to climb down from its dominant position, held throughout the nineteenth century. A comparison of the LMS statistics in 1895 and 1911 indicates the reduction in numbers. The LMS area was reduced to approximately half its previous size. The numbers of the LMS Christian community were reduced from 352,000 to 160,000; Church membership from 63,000 to 30,000; the number of ordained pastors from 1,050 to 470; unordained preachers from 6,000 to 2,600; and the number of missionaries from thirty-nine to twenty-four. The mission lost a number of centrally placed and important buildings in the capital, above all the prestigious 'College', taken over by the government for the High Court of Justice.

The extent of political and ecclesiastical provocation experienced by the LMS can be gauged by the fact that throughout the period 1895–1913 it was an open question whether the LMS, with its century-long involvement among the Merina, should withdraw from the island. Leading members of the London Board were convinced that the Society could have 'no permanent place in French territory' and preparations for a withdrawal from certain parts of the work were made. At long last, in 1913, the colonial government issued a Declaration on Public Worship in Madagascar, conceding the basic rights which the Protestant missions had been asking for. In the same year a conference was held by the non-Roman Societies in the island: the LMS, the Paris Evangelical Mission, the Quakers, the SPG, together with the Lutherans (Norwegians and Americans).

If reduced in geographical areas and in civic prestige and numbers, the Reformed Church knew another dimension, of interpretation and of depth, sustained by the Bible, the hymn-book and *The Pilgrim's Progress*. This was brought to the attention of the faithful by a remarkable pastor, preacher and church historian, Revd Rabary (b. 1864), descendent of one of the great families of the realm and pastor of one of the Tananarive 'Mother-Churches'. He uncovered sacred sources and manuscripts and made oral Church history a significant concern and a consolation for the souls of his people. Making his appeal to 'History' he thought of the sites of Malagasy martyrdom in the past and of the Tananarive 'Mother-Churches', which he regarded as, in the deepest sense, mothers of faith and spirituality, becoming to him 'institutes of refuge'.[95]

However the LMS had to look further afield. In British Uganda the French White Fathers had invited their English-speaking Mill Hill brethren; in Cameroon – under French and British colonial rule after having been German – the missions appealed to their French-speaking co-religionists for help, but nowhere did the imperial/national combativeness assume such proportions as in Madagascar, and under the French colonial regime the English-speaking Protestants had to suffer in those first colonial years. French meant Catholic, that was all there was to it. In this situation the harassed English-speaking Congregationalists turned to the Paris Evangelical Missionary Society, that surprising phenomenon: French-speaking Protestant missionaries, and a whole team of them, highly qualified and devoted men and women – speaking real French!

In the immensely difficult and trying Augagneur years the Paris Evangelical mission spoke their French on behalf of all the Protestants before the French administration and had to bear the brunt of opprobrium on behalf of all the Protestants. The two societies, the LMS and the Paris Evangelical Mission, divided the great number of local Merina congregations among themselves, united as they were in the 'Six Monthly Meetings' as a common concern for the Reformed Churches. Some reduction of the LMS's original numerical strength was caused by a few indigenous breakaways of a type well-known from South Africa: a 'Tranozozoro' schism from 1894. This took place in a rapidly changing political and social situation. The French colonial period, 1895–1960, particularly affected the Protestants. Protestant

Independents, heirs of the LMS, had been deprived of that ecclesiastical birthright that they had held throughout the nineteenth century. In the colonial context of the new century they came to be all the more ready to embody a tendency towards 'self-government' – an amiable missiological term constantly used in Church-mission parlance – and, beyond that, towards political opposition and freedom.

The Lutherans

'The Lutheran South' had its centre of gravity among the artistic and emotional Betsileo. Together with their Betsileo colleagues, the Norwegian missionaries and their American cousins, all of Norwegian background, were concerned with building an autonomous Malagasy Church. To this end, in the highly charged colonial atmosphere around 1900, they focused on terms for election of a synod for the Church consisting of both Malagasy and missionaries. The struggle over this issue involved everybody in Betsileo and in Norway and, as it happens, that struggle is still carried on, for even in the 1980s a lively missiological debate was being conducted in Norway as to whether this or that partner to the 1900–1910 debate was right or wrong. At the time, Church and school were badly hampered by the intervention of the new colonial regime and it thus seemed necessary for the Church to emphasize its autonomy.

In 1902 the missionaries, together with a representative houseful of Malagasy leaders, no less than 432, came together for a conference and produced a plan for a Church synod. They thought they had created an ideal balance between self-government and self-support, those fundamental concepts in the Protestant doctrine of the 'Three Selves'. The head of the missionary body was Dr Christian Borchgrevink, medical missionary and ordained pastor, who served forty-three years in Madagascar. For twenty-five of those years he served as chairman of the mission, 1869–1912. He died in 1919 – one of a number of Protestant missionary leaders who were medical doctors.

The Malagasy pastor Hans Rabeony, who had studied theology in Norway, was elected chairman of the synodal committee. It was a great moment in the history of the young Church, full of expectation. There only remained the approval, from Stavanger, of the Board in Norway. This however did not come without embarrassing demands for certain assurances. The General Secretary in Stavanger, L. Dahle, himself a former missionary in Madagascar, insisted that self-government presupposed self-support. With a somewhat doctrinaire dependence on the revered missiological formula, he in fact held the Malagasy Church back for half a century, 'perhaps the darkest chapter in our mission history'.[96] Only such Church districts as managed to balance their budgets could send representatives to the Church conference. With its financial power the mission kept control of the Church. The Antsirabe–Stavanger incident is also of some interest from a more general point of view: here the men on the spot represented a more liberal view, working for Malagasy rights of self-determination, while the mission director in the West embodied a steadying conservative influence. This differed from comparable situations throughout the continent of Africa, where the 'men on the spot' often seemed slow-moving while mission directors in Europe and North America pressed for more daring realizations of the church establishment programme. Dahle may have shied away from the proposal from the local Lutheran leaders in Madagascar because it reminded him too much of the Congregationalist–Independent example on the island, too challenging.

On the west coast of the island, the Norwegian Lutherans found the beginnings of their work among the Sakalava hard going. However, they established their work in the harbours and, with the liberation of slaves from 1896, in some of the Makua communities from East Africa. A far-sighted initiative was taken by R. L. Aas in building the Bethel Christian centre inland from Morondava, with its fine educational and medical institutions. The Lutherans were also aware of certain social and economic factors supporting Christian evangelism, through population movements into the region. The colonial introduction of taxation acted as a spur, necessitating large-scale emigration of inland communities to the western part of the island. Different ethnic groups, Merina, Betsileo, Betsimisaraka and Taisaka, all moved to exploit what were rumoured to be new economic opportunities. Having found a piece of land on the coast they proceeded to plant 'Malagasy beans', yielding much better profits than humble rice, and they did so with sometimes feverish energy. New villages sprouted, most of them formed according to ethnic identities. To a large extent these foot-loose immigrants came from Christian backgrounds in the highlands, who now found in their church the social cement needed to shape adequate communities: the hymn-singing in the fields, the Bible groups in the new homes, women's associations, the Sunday school; all recognizable phenomena when looked at from an international sociological perspective, but here taking on the proportions of a social and spiritual revolution.

In the meantime the Lutherans were reinforcing their solid Church institutions, more especially the Theological Seminary at Ivory. It has already been pointed out that the Norwegians were prepared to start pastors training after only a very few years in the field. From 1920 the Ivory Seminary was run jointly by the Norwegians and the American Lutherans. The International Theological Commission, visiting Madagascar in 1956, decided that Ivory, with about eighty students and a highly competent international staff, was 'the most important of the [Protestant] theological establishments in Madagascar'. Johannes Johnson, the Norwegian missionary, suggested that nineteenth-century Malagasy spirituality was marked more by an emphasis on 'Providence' than on 'Salvation', God's grace being expressed in *fanambinana*, the concept of blessing: long life, many children, good crops, rather than by an emphasis on sin and salvation.

The Catholics

The Catholic profile in Madagascar and the dramatic change of that profile stand out in unmistakable relief. It has been suggested that the Catholic Church in Madagascar was heavily handicapped by its foreignness. This was noticeable in the Latin worship and in a peculiar kind of Catholicism in the nineteenth century which, according to Françoise Raison-Jourde's study, was that of 'the Second [French] Empire'. As late-comers on the scene, the Catholic work was initially confined to farmers and ex-slaves.

From 1895 a political aspect was added to this cultural handicap of foreignness. 'It cannot be denied that the incorporation of Madagascar into the French colonial empire had as a consequence the rapid development of the Catholic Mission in the island.'[97] With this compressed statement an allusion is made to the hand-in-glove association of French administration with Catholic, more precisely Jesuit strategy in Gallieni's time. The Catholic profile until then had been one of a Church struggling to overcome this foreignness and alienness, a Church firmly established by an older generation of culturally uprooted priests, who knew more Latin than Malagasy and the ancient customs. At the same time the Church was welcoming from abroad new orders of priests and nuns, notably French Jesuits, traditionally the cultural spokesmen for the Church, and French Lazarists placed in the southern dioceses, thus returning to that task which, very reluctantly, they had had to relinquish in the 1670s.

9

EAST AFRICA

INTRODUCTION

A myriad of ethnic communities of differing sizes and complexities existed in East Africa during the nineteenth century. For Church history purposes we can distinguish four areas in the region: the Muslim-dominated island of Zanzibar and its coastal hinterland; the inland peoples, many of whom lived in small-scale societies in bush, savanna and hilly country; the nomadic pastoralists, including the Masai; and the hierarchical kingdoms further into the interior of the continent, close to the Victoria and Tanganyika Lakes – 'the Church along the Kings' Way'. This multipartite division facilitates our understanding of the general history of the region during the nineteenth century, and also for its developing religious and Church history map.

Within twenty-five years (1863–88) seven mission societies were established in East Africa. They were all inspired, in different degrees, by the visits and work in the region of two earlier missionaries: Johann Ludvig Krapf and David Livingstone. Krapf travelled extensively in East Africa between the years 1844–53. His vision of a chain of mission stations across Africa, another 'Apostles Street', from Rabai on the Indian Ocean coast to Gabon on the Atlantic, stimulated many Protestant mission boards to think in terms of transcontinental strategies. David Livingstone's entreaties for an African Church were on an entirely different scale. A supreme publicist, he caught the imagination of Europe and this popular interest for mission triggered off a missionary 'scramble' in Eastern and Central Africa. The arrival, from the 1860s onwards, of these seven mission societies to East Africa underlines the importance of the coast and the Indian Ocean for Church history. Christianity came by sea, thus the Churches were as reliant on coastal points of entry in the East as they were in West Africa and elsewhere. Both the Anglicans and Catholics established coastal settlements for liberated and freed slaves in a similar manner to Christian centres along the coastline of West Africa. They came to Uganda (1877–79), in the interior of the continent, by way of Zanzibar and the East African coast. For

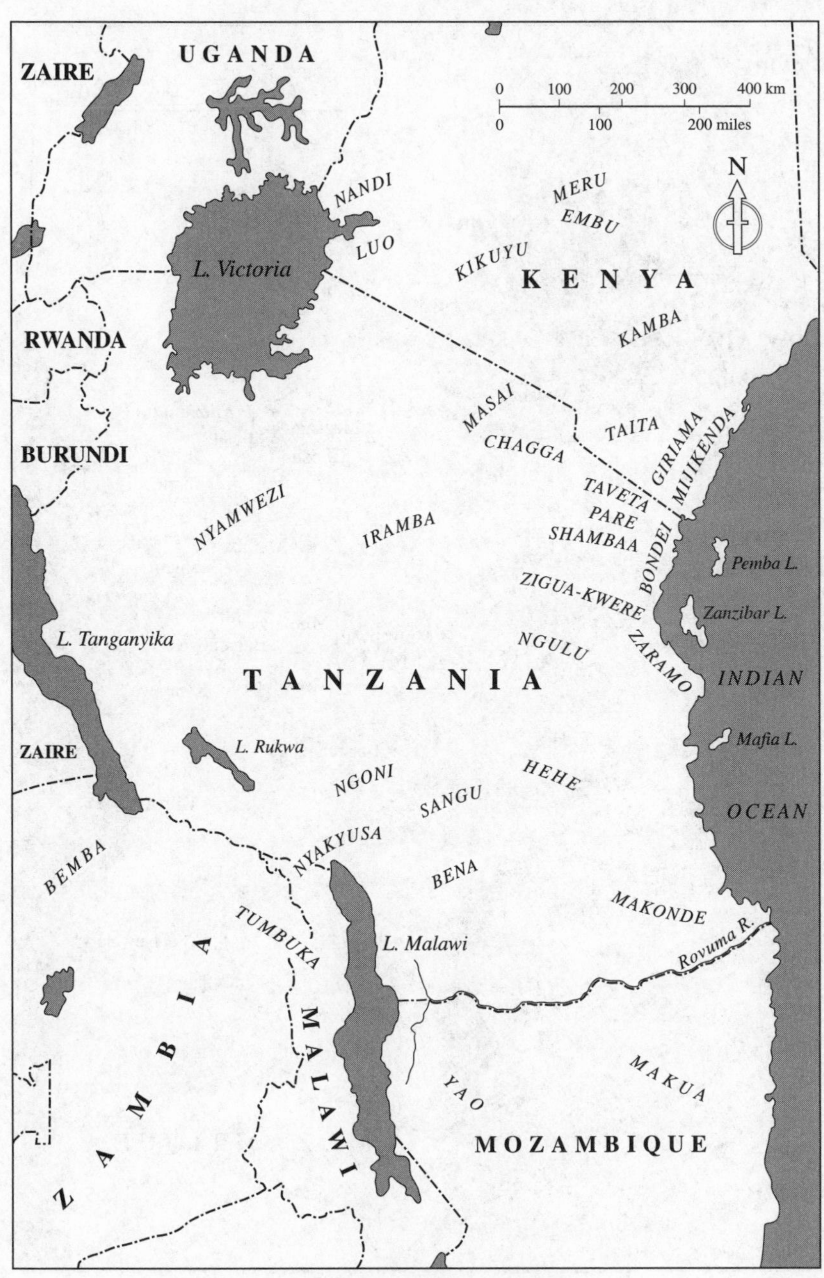

9.1 Ethnic groups of East Africa.

9.2 Key towns and centres in East Africa.

African Church history, Zanzibar and Bagamoyo were crucial as assembly points before the constellation of mission groups could proceed inland. The great desire was to reach the interior of the continent.

'Christianity and commerce' was David Livingstone's rallying cry: to combat the slave trade and to establish 'legitimate' trade. The stability of the East African world during the middle and late nineteenth century was disintegrating under the combined onslaught of new economic and political pressures. During this time East Africa was being assimilated into the world economy, with the main outside influences being Arab and Muslim rather than European and Christian. The intermingling of the Arab–Muslim world with tropical Africa was greatly accelerated during the nineteenth century. A new set of forces emerged linked to the rise of a new Arab–Swahili coastal culture. An international and insatiable craving for ivory and a new internal (also external until the 1870s) demand for slaves led to a widespread destabilization of many traditional societies. Allied to this nefarious trade were the huge numbers of firearms coming into the region (sixteen million guns imported into the continent during the nineteenth century), which precipitated an already precarious situation for many communities. Both the slave and ivory trades were immensely profitable for Arab–Swahili traders: there could be up to 500 per cent price difference between the cost of buying a slave on the western shore of Lake Tanganyika and the selling price in Zanzibar. New centres of power and wealth created by some groups and individuals were thus often founded on the deprivation and loss of liberty suffered by others.

These externally induced pressures were preceded by another, though related, cause of turmoil emanating from the arrival into the region (during the 1840s) of Ngoni warrior bands. Social and political upheaval followed. Military aggression by soldiers organized into age-regiments transformed the southern half of East Africa. Warfare, again often with guns, led to extensive cattle and slave raids over wide areas until the 1890s. Insecurity reigned. Many of these marauding warriors, known as *rugaruga*, served as mercenaries for Arab–Swahili merchants and ambitious local warlords. The combination of warring bands of Ngoni, the constant availability of guns and the surge in demand for ivory and slaves by Arab–Swahili traders, resulted in the pushing back of frontiers of contact. A new unity to the region – linking the coast with the kingdoms in the interior – had been created by violence, rapacity and domination. Many kings and chiefs were overthrown, such as the Shambaa kingdom which split and disintegrated into many rival chiefdoms. Interference by Arab–Swahili traders led to the forging of new and competing alliances, aided by mercenary armed soldiers.

This altered the patterns of wealth acquisition and affected the loyalty of subjects to their chiefs. A new generation of African and sometimes Muslim trader-chiefs forcefully established themselves and created new commercial states. The most famous were Mirambo and Nyunga-Ya-Mawe (both Nyamwezi) and Tippu Tib and Msiri. These warlords, together with the sultanate of Zanzibar, can be seen as part of the local and regional drive to establish power and hegemony over other societies in the area, a momentum that occurred in the two to three decades before the European scramble for Africa.

All these convergent forces were compounded by the compression of time. In West Africa trade and external contact from the coast had started in the fifteenth century, with the Atlantic slave trade reaching its apogee in the eighteenth century. By the nineteenth century new 'legitimate' trade patterns were being created. For East Africa the mercantile impact of the nineteenth century, based on slaves and ivory, was new and more extensive – lasting until the beginning of the twentieth century. This was the situation that greeted the incoming mission societies and their initial groups of African Christians, most of whom had been liberated from slavery.

Although Christianity arrived by ship and mission groups founded their first settlements along the littorals of both West and East Africa, there are distinct contrasts between the Church histories of the two regions. In West Africa external commerce was dominated by Europeans and missionaries were only one group within the White community in the area. Christianity was linked with trade and mobility along the coast: for example, the expansion of the Creoles from Freetown. During the nineteenth century Christianity spread along the coast with many communities and groups embracing this new faith.

In East Africa the situation was quite different. European missionaries were often the sole representatives of European culture and influence. They were thus not perceived, initially, as representing European imperial countries. The coastline was dominated by Islam, under the sway of the Zanzibari sultanate. Europeans and Christian missions were not involved in the East African overland trade, which was, instead, subjugated to the requirements of Arab–Swahili merchants, operating under the ethos of Islam. There was little real Islamic impact inland from the coastal belt, apart from one or two peoples, such as the Yao, who had well-established trading links with the Muslim trading community. In the interior, Arab–Swahili merchants tended to isolate themselves from their surrounding African host communities and often lived in separate Arab-Muslim quarters away from the local community.

Christian mission strategy was particularly concerned with halting the slave trade. The timing was propitious for an extension of Christian enterprise and involvement in the region. With rampant slave and ivory hunting, many societies were breaking up; insecurity and disorder were the characteristics of the era. Individuals and communities lost their established view of life: new identities and social formations were, perforce, sought for. Witchcraft allegations were on the increase, with enslavement a common penalty for those accused as well as their families. No doubt the escalation in witchcraft accusation was linked to the expansion of the market for slaves, adding to the vulnerability of individuals and their families. New designs were needed to combat these developments: a new faith and belief and a new identity were sought in order to liberate oneself from the fear of witchcraft accusations. The Christian message of hope and salvation could help to alleviate these fears. In the southern half of the region the traditional territorial shrines were facing all these new pressures and changes. The rise of new states and chiefs challenged the influence of traditional priests and mediums, and the extending commercial networks enabled a mixing of local cults which thus enlarged the world and religious views of many communities. Many traditional religions became more accessible as they responded to disorder and change: this gave ordinary people greater control over their own religious beliefs. All these changes prepared the way for the incoming Christian faith and facilitated the process of religious change.

Deprived of their group or lineage, individuals and families had no traditional protection against the ever-present threat of slavery. In need of protection, young men became client soldiers to a powerful chief or trader and young women became his wives. The imperatives for seeking a protector and the need for security were ever-present. The Church and the mission station offered an alternative form of protection, with a new identity linked to innovative social formations. A youth revolution, related to generational conflict, was a feature of the changing opportunities and deprivations in the region. The Church provided an alternative.

A feature of nineteenth-century eastern Africa was the appearance of fortified villages created by clusters of people displaced by the violence of the times. The founding of Christian villages was a variation of these new social formations, but with the advantage of not being so prone to attack by raiding bands. Improved communications due to caravan routes and mobility (often forced) resulted in a mingling of cultures. Christian villages facilitated the breakdown of ethnic barriers as they were primarily created by those Africans liberated or ransomed from slavery. This type of distinct village was part of the strategy to combat the slave trade. By the 1890s this need for separate villages had disappeared and the Churches could concentrate on the traditional societies. There was a transition from the idea of the Christian villages to that of creating Christian 'nations'. There were many laudable characteristics of these Christian villages. The stress on literacy, artisanship, agriculture and animal husbandry, together with the solidarity found in the Christian message, gave these new villages a relevance and a purpose in the restructuring and transformation of East African society. The development of Swahili in these communities, assisted by the pioneering linguistics of such missionaries as Bishop Steere and Fr Sacleux, disencumbered the language from its coastal and Muslim associations. The school-educated Christian could feel that Swahili was his own language and that the use of it no longer denoted a Muslim allegiance.

There was perhaps not that much to distinguish this type of formal Christian village from that of the traditional mission station. Often the latter became, inadvertently, the former. In an effort to dislocate the slave trade, mission stations were often placed on caravan routes at strategic places. By design the Churches located themselves in the major entrepôt towns on the main caravan routes: for example, the LMS at Ujiji, the Holy Ghost Fathers at Bagamoyo, and (later) the White Fathers at Tabora. The UMCA opened its Zanzibar cathedral in 1879 on the site of the former slave market.

Caravan routes not only carried trade but disease as well. In Bagamoyo the Spiritans noted outbreaks of smallpox throughout the 1870s and 1880s. This provided a challenge for the mission's rudimentary health facilities and medical expertise. In 1893 the Spiritans baptized over 200 dying Nyamwezi porters, an illustration of the relevance of the new faith in a world often besieged and tormented by the arrival of new and virulent diseases.

Professor Johnson has pertinently observed that mission stations are a 'permanent cultural feature of rural Africa' and that, for many people, not least those in East Africa, they have provided 'a promise of help, of learning, and of a better life'.[1] The weak and helpless mission stations were vitally important as refuges. Dr Iliffe has written that the 'often horrifying autobiographies of women caught up in nineteenth century disorder show an intense desire for security and protection and a preoccupation with the nuclear family which might provide it.'[2] The history of some of these women has been graphically documented by Professor Marcia Wright, who has shown the importance of mission stations as sanctuaries for these uprooted and oppressed women.[3]

Krapf and the first outreach into the interior

Into the island world off the continent, Johann Ludvig Krapf arrived in 1844, a German Lutheran missionary in the employ of the British CMS. The influence of this first pioneer was limited, yet his vision for Africa was far-reaching. Frustrated in his attempts to reach Shoa and the Oromo people in Ethiopia, Krapf went to East Africa, hoping to evangelize Oromo 'Christian remnants' south of Ethiopia. He felt that the conversion of these people would supply the key to the evangelization of eastern Africa. From Lamu, an island north of Mombasa, he hoped to penetrate the promised land of the Oromo – or, 'Galla'. He soon realized that he first had to contact Sultan Said of Zanzibar. Said gave him a generous letter of introduction, recommending 'Dr Krapf, the German, a good man, who desires to convert the world to God. Behave you well toward him and render him services everywhere.'

Krapf spent his first two years on Mombasa island and occasionally journeyed to visit the Mijikenda coastal people. Here he contacted Kamba traders and their 'chief', Kivoi, who was not only an experienced traveller but also a renowned rain-maker. Unwittingly, Krapf, too, acquired this useful label. The day he arrived in Rabai Mpya, about twelve miles from Mombasa, there was a heavy rainstorm. This was acclaimed as the foreign visitor's achievement, and thus a good omen for his work. Just as Krapf believed the Oromo could win the whole of East Africa for Christ, he saw the mobile and enterprising Kamba as the potential missionary agents of Kenya. In Ethiopia Krapf had devoted himself to Bible translation. He now continued this work in Mombasa, beginning by translating parts of the Gospels into Swahili and the Mijikenda languages. He soon welcomed two new missionary colleagues, Germans in CMS service like himself. Johannes Rebmann came in 1846 and Jacob Erhardt, with some medical training, in 1849. After Rebmann's arrival, Krapf moved from Mombasa to Rabai and from this new centre continued translating. He also travelled among inland peoples as one of a party of Kamba traders.

Krapf and his co-workers made contributions in four different areas: geographical exploration, contacts with African chiefs, translation work and the formulation of missionary strategy. From 1847–52 they undertook eight journeys into the interior. Rebmann depended on a helpful Mombasa Arab, Bwana Kheri (or Heri); the Kamba leader, Kivoi, guided Krapf. Rebmann's journey to Chagga country became famous and, at first, was derided. The poor missionary claimed to have seen, on 11 May 1848, a snow-covered mountain on the equator, the summit of Kilimanjaro. W. D. Cooley, one of the geographical experts of the period, spoke pompously for the academic pundits of his generation: 'I deny altogether the existence of snow on Kilimanjaro.' The next year Krapf became the first European to see East Africa's other snow-covered mountain, Mount Kenya. In 1850 Krapf and Erhardt, in a Swahili dhow, followed the coastline south as far as Cape Delgado and the river Rovuma, which bordered on Portuguese dependencies. This was followed by a second, fatal visit to Kamba country in 1851. Krapf's companion, Kivoi, was killed by robbers and the missionary was fortunate to return alive.

In 1848 and in 1852, Krapf's travels took him to visit King Kimweri, 'the Only True Lion' of Usambara. He was impressed by the Usambara monarchy, which had introduced a 'pax Shambala' over neighbouring peoples thereby ensuring, according to Krapf, more civil order and security than in any other country of this coast.[4] Krapf told the king 'the chief doctrines of Scripture, describing the fall of man, and then showing the necessity of the atonement by Jesus Christ, both God and man.'[5] Kimweri was intrigued by the *kitab*, the sacred Book, and consented to the establishment of a mission, which, however, did not materialize until much later. Slightly to the north-west, in Chagga country, Rebmann met Chief Mamkinga of Machame: 'I stretched out my Bible towards him, and told him my only business was with this book, which contained the word of God and which we wished to teach to all nations.'[6] So encouraged was Rebmann by this meeting that he soon returned to Chief Mamkinga, hoping to gain his co-operation in reaching far beyond Kilimanjaro, to the country of the Nyamwezi. This time, however, Mamkinga was less interested and Rebmann had to return one bitter experience richer.

In the linguistic field, particularly with regard to Swahili, Krapf was a pioneer and as such his influence was to prove fundamental. He thought he had found that Swahili was 'spoken, at least understood from the Equator to the Portuguese settlements in Mosambic' and the language thus offered what Krapf always was looking for in peoples and in languages, a key – in this case a linguistic key – to the languages of the interior. He was impressed by the Arabic roots in Swahili, although he was more humble about his proficiency in this language than he was sometimes given credit for: 'a rather imperfect knowledge of the vulgar Arabic which I had acquired in Egypt and on the Red Sea'.[7] He was also knowledgeable about the study and translation of other Bantu languages at the time and referred to Archbell's and Boyce's work in South Africa. His efforts with his local interpreters sometimes revealed problems of communication. They 'would (when consulted on the roots of a Verb or a Noun) stand gaping before me and say "words do neither take root nor bear fruits in our country".'[8] His work on the Gospels into Swahili and on a dictionary of this language and related East African languages was important for Bishop Steere's New Testament translation and this again was to be a basis for translations into other leading East African vernaculars such as George Pilkington's Luganda translation in the 1890s.

The less promising the local missionary work seemed to be in terms of actual conversions the more the missionary's interest was drawn to other horizons. The map of Africa held a mesmeric fascination for nineteenth-century Europe, perhaps because little was known of what lay within the continent's bold outline. Krapf's belief in the Chrischona Institute's 'Apostles' Street' or 'Prophets' Path' inspired him to draw an imaginary line across the continent from Mombasa to West Africa. This map-work led to an ambitious plan for a transcontinental chain of mission stations from east to west. On his return to Europe in 1850, he presented the CMS with such a plan. The opportunity was propitious and the timing excellent. For it was the very next year when the General Secretary of the Society, Henry Venn, first began to formulate his idea of a self-governing, self-propagating and self-regulating Church. It seemed fitting then to widen the perspective far beyond Unyamwezi and the Unknown – even to the West Coast.

The CMS kept faithfully to Krapf's dream. When, in 1899, Bishop Tucker of Uganda visited a Toro outstation across the Semkili River, his missionaries learned that from the other side, from the West Coast, English Baptists had advanced to Yakusu on the Congo, 'within 500 miles of Mengo: in other words, the chain of missions which Krapf dreamt about and predicted now actually exists.'[9] Other missions also became caught up in the fascination of Krapf's continental vision. English Methodists and at least four German missions – Berlin, Hermannsburg, Leipzig and Neukirchen – started work in East Africa. However, Krapf's own colleagues 'on the spot' were much less captivated by the grand design, and so in 1853 Krapf felt he had to return to Europe. There he organized support for Bishop Gobat's 'chain' of mission stations, not on an east–west axis, but an 'Apostles' Street' from north to south, beginning in Egypt. The Alexandria station was to bear St Matthew's name, followed by St Mark at Cairo, St Peter at Aswan, St Thomas at Khartoum and St Paul at Matamma. Only the first two became reality, the others remained a lofty dream.

THE TANZANIAN COAST

The islands along the East African coast formed a vital network of communication and trade, from Lamu in the north to Mauritius and Réunion and the 'little continent' of Madagascar in the south. Arab dhows from Oman dominated these western waters of the Indian Ocean, but there were also occasional French, German and British ships, together with American vessels bringing special white cloth – known locally as *merikani* – from Salem, Massachusetts. In the first half of the nineteenth century, an important political change took place in the off-shore islands. Sayyid Said (d. 1856), the greatest of the Omani sultans, made Zanzibar the undisputed capital of a dynamic economic empire, relegating Mombasa to a position of secondary importance. In the 1850s Zanzibar was strengthened by an active, rapidly growing *banyan* (Indian merchant) community of 5,000 enterprising Asian traders, mainly from Bombay. The entrepôt of Zanzibar provided opportunities for exchange of western and Indian goods for local produce. The island's contribution was primarily cloves and from the interior of the continent salt, iron, ivory – and slaves.

The growing interregional trade between the African hinterland and the harbours of Zanzibar and Mombasa led to the development of routes between the interior and the coast. These trade arteries were pioneered in the eighteenth century by Africans, followed by Arabs from about 1825 and eventually by Europeans. The southern route, linking the inland lakes with the coast, was dominated by the Nyamwezi and to a lesser extent by the traders who gave their name to the 'Gogo Road'. Arab and Swahili traders travelled inland from Bagamoyo, dealing with the Nyamwezi and related peoples. Further north, in central Kenya, the Kamba played a similar role to that of the Nyamwezi for Tanzania. Caravans of up to 500 men would bring iron, ivory and cattle to Kwa Jomvu, a market on the coast near Mombasa. The Kamba held a popular fair there every August. Iron obtainable at the fair was of such high quality that fastidious Arab traders preferred it to 'that of Sweden'.[10] A few Kamba had also been settled for many centuries on the Kenyan coast. They had small trading centres in the territory of the Rabai, originally one of the Nyika communities. The early trade between coast and inland was to have momentous consequences for mission history.

In Zanzibar, a Swahili culture emerged in which townsmen, not rural fishermen, fashioned the way of life. This culture included Arabs and Asians, the slave trade and the role throughout the region of the *wangwana* (Swahili freemen). Being part of an Islam-related civilization, they helped to bring the area together via the arteries of commerce and religion. British diplomatic pressure brought about the abolition of the Zanzibar slave trade in 1873, a date which was also of fundamental importance for Christian missions being the year in which Livingstone died, and when the foundation stone of Christ Church Cathedral was laid on the site of the slave market in

Zanzibar town. Although many Arab slave-owners, particularly in and around Mombasa, reacted violently, Sultan Bargash of Zanzibar did his best to be seen as conforming to the Act. He allowed Bagamoyo to become the coast's premier port, where it soon was a haven for freed slaves, under Roman Catholic supervision. The opening of the Suez Canal in 1869 dramatically initiated a new era in the relationship between East Africa and Europe. Modern influences were to alter the face of the landscape and the faith of the peoples. In Kenya, communities had been hidden behind the impenetrable Masai inland wall. The railway radically changed that situation, reaching Nairobi in 1899, Kisumu on Lake Victoria in 1901 and Kampala in 1931. In Tanzania, a northern railway connected Tanga with Moshi in 1912; a central line from Dar es Salaam to Kigoma was completed in 1914 and to Mwanza in 1928. The railways aided the missions in consolidating their outreach throughout the area. It was the mission-educated generations which, more than others, could use these new opportunities. The railways stimulated export of agricultural produce, but also drew Africa into the embrace of an ever-changing world economy. The final decade of the nineteenth century saw devastating ecological crises, epidemics and almost total Rinderpest. There were also drastic political changes. The imperial take-over led in many cases to the forced flight or brutal annihilation of traditional chiefs.

The Indian Ocean and Zanzibar

The islands of the Indian Ocean formed a natural approach for Christian missionaries in reaching the peoples of East Africa. This self-evident fact has often been overlooked. At this time, first contacts had to be made from the islands in the Indian Ocean; only later, with the opening of the Suez Canal in 1869, were direct links between East Africa, the Mediterranean and Europe possible. Prior to 1869, when plans for the evangelization of East Africa were being made, Zanzibar became the focal point. In the early 1860s three bishops, unknown to each other, planned an approach to Zanzibar and the interior: Bishop Maupoint, a French Catholic in Réunion, the Anglican Bishop Ryan in Mauritius and Bishop Tozer, Anglo-Catholic on Lake Malawi. The three of them planned missions via Zanzibar and from there involved themselves in the establishment of coastal stations, as stepping-stones for work inland.

The drama of African missions at this time – the era of sailing ships – was largely enacted from the islands of the southern Indian Ocean. Mauritius, Madagascar, and Réunion were important centres related to a global missionary strategy. Catholic missions to Zanzibar and the East African coast came initially from the island of Réunion in the southern Indian Ocean. From Réunion and Madagascar the missionaries looked over the vast expanse of the ocean toward the continent of Africa. One of Libermann's closest co-workers, Le Vavasseur, was a Creole from Réunion. He returned to his home island in 1842. In 1848, pious Réunion women formed a congregation of their own, the Daughters of Mary and the following year eight young 'liberated' Creole women were received as members – an eloquent confirmation of the Congregation's resolve not to give in to racial sentiment. In 1857, the bishop of Réunion, A. P. Maupoint, received ecclesiastical jurisdiction over the East African coast, from Cape Delgado to Cape Guardafui. He sent his vicar-general, Joseph Fava, to explore the possibilities on Zanzibar and on the mainland.

In 1860, Fava arrived with three priests on Zanzibar, then notorious for its slave trade. The Fathers did not arrive alone – they were accompanied by six Sisters, the Daughters of Mary, four of whom were Creoles. There has been a tendency in the history of missions to overlook or neglect the presence and activity of these nuns from Réunion. About thirty or forty years of age, they disembarked in their black robes and white bonnets, with their copper crucifixes and their rosaries. They carried with them to Zanzibar their liturgical outline of daily mass and their special medical skill acquired from their vocation as nurses among the slave population in Réunion. It was not long before they were usefully involved with the children of Zanzibar. No doubt, their own racial background made them more acceptable to the particular community where they now worked. Father Fava and the French doctor set up a hospital in the Malagasy quarter of the town. The names of the prominent Fathers who started the mission are well-known. Here are the names of the six Sisters, the first women missionaries in East Africa:

Sr Marie du Sacré Coeur, born Hermance Brunet, 1814
Sr Marie Xavier, born Henriette Boyer de la Giroday, 1822
Sr Marie Héléne, born Clemence Paul, 1824
Sr Marie Antoinette, born Celeste Boyenval, 1824
Sr Marie St Louis, born Elise Laureda, 1836
Sr Marie Etienne, born Antoinette Honsec, 1829

Except for the first two, who probably had received some primary education from their families, the rest were all of 'very modest background' and were all freed from slavery in 1848. They learned to read and write during their noviciate, and received training as nurses in Réunion. The great names of the men such as Fathers Horner, Baur, Sacleux and others, have rightly dominated the history of Catholic beginnings on the East Coast. However, one must not forget the Daughters of Mary – their hands to heal and hearts to feel, with the suffering, the neglected and the downtrodden.[11]

Zanzibar

In the middle of the nineteenth century, Zanzibar had about 150,000 inhabitants, including some 60,000 slaves, most of whom worked on the Arabs' clove plantations. The town's population was growing fast, rising from 25,000 to 70,000 during the 1860s. It was known as 'a typically oriental town'. While this was possibly true of the Stonetown area, where the Sultan, the Arabs and the Asians lived, this expression was less appropriate with reference to the African quarters. Zanzibar had more than forty mosques. There was a connection between Muslim worship and the morphology of town. 'The town is in the first place the site for the great Friday mosque.'[12] Each of the various cultural groups – Arabs, Swahili, Asians, Goanese, Europeans, Malagasy – had its own quarters. The two leading commodities of the Zanzibar market were ivory and slaves, the latter with an annual import during the middle of the nineteenth century of about 25,000.

The Zanzibar slave market was the final African stage in a *via dolorosa* of violence and torture from inland villages to the coast. The effect on the interior was devastating. Men, women and children were torn from their homes and communities, most of them from the south-eastern and western parts of Tanzania. The hunt for humans extended far west, even beyond Lake Tanganyika and Karagwe. A girl or boy, bought far inland for beads or a piece of cloth or a few shillings, would soon be exchanged for cattle or a piece of ivory which could fetch a higher price at the coast. In the meantime, the slave was forced to march farther, in some other slave caravan, if they had not already been bullied to death. At Zanzibar, the price rose for those who had survived the devastating journey to the coast: seven to ten dollars for boys up to ten years, fifteen to thirty dollars for young men aged ten to twenty-one, seventeen to twenty dollars for adult men, and thirty-five dollars or more for adult women. 'East Africa was probably the only part of the world where slavery became markedly more common throughout the nineteenth century.'[13]

Zanzibar had the last open slave market in the world. Bishop Steere remarked: 'there were the rows of men, women and children, sitting and standing, the salesmen and purchasers passing in and out among them, examining them, handling them, chaffering over them, and bandying their filthy jokes about them, and worse scenes still going on in all the huts around.'[14] In 1873 Sir Bartle Frere, British ex-governor of Bombay, was sent to Zanzibar to stop this trade. As already indicated, the export of slaves from the island was officially prohibited that year. David Livingstone, who had seen the terrible devastation of East Africa through the slave trade, referred to it as 'the open sore of the world'. The treaty prohibiting it was signed just one month after his death at Chitambo.

When the Propaganda of Rome established the Apostolic Prefecture of Zanzibar it entrusted this to the Holy Ghost Fathers, or Spiritans, with their experience in West Africa and in Réunion. In 1863 the first members of the Order, all from Alsace, landed in Zanzibar. There were two priests, Fathers Horner and Baur, and two lay brothers. They had cared for some of Réunion's 6,000 slaves and leprosy patients. In Zanzibar they were faced with the familiar problem of slavery; but there was a difference in that the island, with its large slave market, provided them with opportunities for ransoming these unfortunates. The Spiritans soon acquired about 200 slaves, all of them from the African mainland. The Catholic hospital was erected in what was called the 'Malagasy' quarter of the town, a name the priests and nuns could feel at home with. Horner also started three schools, one for Catholics, another for Muslims and a third for Asians. The people built workshops, including a foundry and, with the Sultan's encouragement, began planting coffee, cocoa and cotton. At the Catholic school some students were discovered to have special talent for mathematics and music. Father Baur's brass band learned to play some twenty popular tunes, impressing not only ordinary folk but also His Highness the Sultan himself. Four of the young boys were set apart for seminary training.

Christian centres on the Tanzanian coast

Certain coastal stations acquired special importance for the evangelization of the coast and the interior: Kiungani (Zanzibar), Bagamoyo, Kisarawe and Kurasini (we shall later turn to Freretown near Mombasa). Located amongst a strong Muslim culture, these evangelistic and educational centres persevered in the development of their work and in establishing local roots. They were firmly settled on the coast, thus there was great potential for the beginnings and growth of the Church further inland – Catholic, Anglo-Catholic and Protestant. Through these Christian centres on the coast, 'Swahili' came to mean not only Muslim, but also the school-educated Christian, man or woman.

Anglo-Catholic endeavour

The year 1863, when the Holy Ghost Fathers began work in Zanzibar, also saw the beginnings of the Anglo-Catholic mission there. Having temporarily given up their work in the Shire Highlands of Malawi, the Anglo-Catholics decided to start afresh in Zanzibar under Bishop Tozer. To them Zanzibar was 'the heart of Africa' and with its slave market they felt it was indeed a worthwhile place in which to continue their work. Bishop Tozer was a man of delicate health, and was eventually obliged to make way in 1875 for his assistant, Edward Steere, a man of wide vision whose view of Islam was rare among his generation and particularly valuable in a bishop of Zanzibar. According to his interpretation of Islam, Mohammed 'had really a divine commission to call back the Arabs to the faith of Abraham that they might be so prepared for the faith which is in Christ'.[15] Steere, a Swahili linguist, set a high standard for a succession of Swahili experts among the later UMCA missionaries: Hodgson, Dale, Hellier and Broomfield.

Steere was a pioneering Bible translator. His Swahili version of the New Testament and parts of the Old Testament became the foundation of the Church on the coast. It was also a great reference book for several Bible translations produced in East Africa during the period prior to the First World War. After Tozer's resignation Steere was consecrated bishop in 1874 and at once undertook his Swahili Bible translation. This Anglo-Catholic bishop was convinced that 'our work must all be unsound without a vernacular Bible'.[16] By 1880 the whole of the New Testament was translated and in 1882 he had produced a revised text. He also undertook the translation of central Old Testament books: the Book of Kings, Isaiah. When he died in 1883 he had the corrected proofs of Isaiah on his table. In 1883 the first edition of the complete Swahili New Testament (5,050 copies) was shipped to Zanzibar. One must remember that this Bible translator printed his African text himself and also bound the copies including sewing the copies together. It would be of considerable interest to study the influence of Steere's Swahili translation on a number of other Bible translations beginning with Pilkington's Luganda translation, 1893–97, and other East African translations influenced by and derived from that of Steere.

Steere's churchmanship and that of the UMCA, emphasizing episcopal tradition and eucharistic piety was an alternative to Roman Catholicism in East Africa. He was a priest setting a high example for the religious life of the community and, at Kiungani, caring for varied ethnic backgrounds in the clergy. Steere was looking towards the building of national Churches – 'the Church of the Yao nation', or 'of the Makua nation'. This vision did not fail to inspire the later bishops in southern Tanzania and in Malawi. In 1879 he had the satisfaction of opening the Zanzibar Cathedral, built on the very site of the former slave market. It was consecrated by his successor in 1901.

There were three Anglican settlements in Zanzibar itself. Mkunazini, with Christ Church as their Cathedral, was the headquarters of the mission staff. They later added a hospital, an Industrial Home, and a boys' school. The adjacent Christian village had about 150 people, mostly old adherents of the mission, former pupils and freed slaves. Kiungani, referred to as 'the School of the Prophets', was a training centre for ordinands. As such, it became important for the Anglican dioceses in northern and southern Tanzania, as well as in Malawi. In 1865 nine young boys were baptized in the college's first baptismal ceremony. Some of them were to become well-known leaders: Robert Feruzi, John Swedi, George Farajallah and Frances Mabruki. After another three years they were all confirmed. In 1866 Mabruki had a year of training in England and in 1870 Swedi and Farajallah were ordained as deacons.[17] Mbweni, another Zanzibar settlement, was a Christian village for 250 adult freed slaves and a girls' school. Three Europeans and the African deacon, John Swedi, made up the teaching staff. Dar es Salaam was just next door to Zanzibar and here the Anglicans established the Kichwele Christian village for Wazaramo converts. An African deacon, Denys Seyiti, was in charge.

Catholic initiatives at Bagamoyo

After two years of initial exploration on the mainland, in 1868 Horner and Baur were able to establish a base on the coast at Bagamoyo, north of Dar es Salaam. Bagamoyo was of strategic importance as a point of departure for caravans going inland, an ideal place for the launching of Catholic expeditions to the societies living in the interior of the continent. In Zanzibar the Spiritans had made friendly contacts with the sultan who 'never failed to support the Mission with his lively interest, his steady good-will and overwhelming generosity'.[18] It was in this spirit that the sultan, through his local representative, awarded them a large area at Bagamoyo. Only later did they discover that the occupants of this land, the Zaramo, had first claim to it. The Bagamoyo station grew, as increasing numbers of ransomed slaves swelled the ranks of the community. The presence of these ex-slaves caused the local Zaramo to look down on the Bagamoyo group as inferior. Also, the Zaramo land claims accentuated the isolation of this Christian village, the first in Tanzania. It was an alien institution in the midst of a wider community which eventually became almost entirely Islamized.

The Christian immigrants to the settlement at Bagamoyo cleared land and built houses to welcome a further 200 immigrants. They planted the cross and fired a salute, 'in the name of the Church, the Congregation of the Holy Ghost, and Catholic France.' With its background, the village was of course dependent on the missionaries at first. The Spiritans transferred institutions to Bagamoyo which were by now flourishing in Zanzibar: the orphanage, the agricultural and industrial schools, as well as an elementary school. In 1877 Bagamoyo was already 'a small town', with fifty houses and 300 residents. Twenty years later there were nearly 700 inhabitants. The thriving garden had plants from Réunion, Madagascar and India. Coffee seeds, originally from Réunion, subsequently spread inland, eventually to Kilimanjaro by 1890.

'Prayer and work' was the motto of the settlement where a strict programme of six hours' work in the fields and workshops alternated with catechism, liturgy and singing. After finishing elementary school, youths studied at the seminary and were called Latinists. In 1870 twenty were studying French, Latin, Greek, history, geography and algebra. A noviciate for African sisters was also opened. A relatively large European staff was needed to serve the expanding community. At one point it included five priests, eleven brothers and nine sisters. However, health hazards were always present. Although seven sisters and five brothers, whose average age was only twenty-five died during the first seven years, new recruits regularly arrived from Alsace and Réunion. The missionaries at Bagamoyo included the well-known Father, Charles Sacleux, Swahili linguist, who produced French–Swahili and Swahili–French dictionaries and a Swahili Grammar. Characteristically, he also wrote a book on the 'Lives of the Saints' and several hymns.

The Berlin Mission

Karl Peters, the colonial adventurer who founded the German East Africa Company, Bismarck and their subordinates declared the mainland 'German East Africa', and in May 1887, Germans occupied Dar es Salaam. This coincided with the arrival of two German missions, one Catholic and the other Protestant. There were interesting similarities between the two, as they established themselves both in Dar es Salaam and in the vicinity of the capital. The Protestant, J. J. Greiner, was no newcomer to the African scene, having spent a number of years among the Ethiopian Oromo before proceeding to Dar es Salaam. He had a special concern for the Oromo, like Krapf, with whom he shows striking parallels. Having arrived in Dar es

Salaam in 1887, Greiner soon found active co-workers in Christian laymen from the Near East, Evangelical Syrians and Ethiopians, some of whom had studied at the Scheller Institute in Jerusalem. With these men and women Greiner formed something of a 'Foreign Legion', working among other less fortunate foreigners on the coast. Throughout the continent, it was these foreigners – aliens in strange places – who responded to the Gospel and were the first to be baptized. So it was here with Greiner in his Dar es Salaam or Kisarawe chapels: omnipresent Yao or Tonga from the south, or inland Tanzanians joined the little congregation, while the local Zaramo were at first much more hesitant.

The German Lutheran institute at Kisarawe, inland from Dar es Salaam, began its activity somewhat later. As a missionary in Dar es Salaam, Greiner met with the problem of caring for freed slaves. He needed a centre sufficiently far removed from urban influences to allow quiet development. Kisarawe began its first year in 1893 with sixty students. Greiner had good contacts with the UMCA. Through them he later received both reading material and a trained African teacher, the latter of great importance in giving to the community an example of the potential of those trained at the mission. An elementary school and a middle school with a strong practical emphasis became the centre of the community, which remained rather small. The young teacher candidates received their instruction in the morning, and in the afternoon taught the 'three Rs' to the elementary students.

Greiner had good relations with aging Chief Sanze, who asked for baptism, having been directed to do so in a dream: 'a man in white clothes came to collect me' – a frequent stereotype in African dream activity. Greiner's plans for Kisarawe and his association with the Mission were cut short by the strategy of the German mission leader, Friedrich von Bodelschwingh, who felt that the missionary outlook on the coast was bleak. He decided to abandon the work there in order to create an inland chain of mission stations: Tanga–Usambara–Pare–Kilimanjaro–Lake Victoria. As a result of this plan, most of the Kisarawe students were removed to Lutindi in Usambara in 1896. In protest against this move, Greiner resigned and the staff had to manage what was left of the Kisarawe attempt. The area was further depleted by men leaving to work on the railway. To an extent which Greiner could not have foreseen, the new economic opportunities, the railway and the sisal plantations, gave the Kisarawe Christians chances for witnessing to their new-won faith. The industrial school, particularly its carpentry training, made Kisarawe well-known and supplied a number of foremen from 1905. A considerable number of these foremen became part of Christian groups along the railway-line up to Morogoro and to Tabora.

From the vantage point of the Kisarawe congregation, the two new developments – the move to Usambara and employment on the railways – meant a reduction of local strength. But this was compensated for by a wider outreach of evangelistic activity.

The Benedictines

The Holy Ghost Fathers, or Spiritans and their Western educated African elite were French speaking and, just as in Uganda, the Catholics were referred to as 'the French' and Protestants as 'the English'. But the new Catholic arrivals, the Benedictines, were Germans and spoke the language of the colonial masters. In 1888 these Benedictines began a school among the Zaramo at Pugu, thereby laying the foundations for an educational centre destined to assume importance in the later history of the country. This was a time of serious unrest. During a rebellion led by Bushiri, the mission at Pugu was destroyed, three missionaries were killed and four others taken prisoner. It is not known whether the attackers understood the specific nature of the mission centre. The Benedictines also founded a centre for liberated slaves outside Dar es Salaam, in two Christian villages at Kurasini, for 450 people. The 'Christian village' programme however, showed its inherent weakness. It was, says their historian, too paternalistic and did not give the people sufficient scope for self-expression.[19] By 1904 this particular attempt ended, but by then the foundations had already been laid for what was to prove the Benedictines' highly promising work in the far south of the country. There will be occasion to return to this.

Christian centres on the coast: a conclusion

The five Christian settlements of Kiungani (on Zanzibar), Bagamoyo, Freretown, Kisarawe and Kurasini, were of special significance for East African Church history. They became resource centres and springboards for an advance into the interior. Their disciples confronted complicated situations and were increasingly threatened by Arab economic interests and soon by European imperialism. As they found their way among inland communities and became part of new Christian villages, these Christian coast-men knew that they represented an enlargement of scale and horizon. Some of them had surprisingly broad international backgrounds. The Revd James Chala Salfey, Anglican priest at Magila, was an Ethiopian later to be transferred from East Africa to Lebombo, Mozambique. His colleague, John Swedi, was an ex-Bombay student. Francis Mabruki, of Bombay and

Kiungani, had studied in England for a year. The German missionary in Dar es Salaam in the 1890s had Ethiopian co-workers and Christian Syrians as elders and volunteers. Other Africans had studied in India, on Zanzibar and in Great Britain. These were, admittedly, exceptions, but most of the young people who had 'joined the book' and were readers had come into contact with an international community. The Bagamoyo scholars had to acquire the French language as well as Swahili, even though Sacleux, the French missionary there, was one of the great Swahili experts of his time. Kiungani people moving inland were seen as *Christian* Swahili coast-men, carrying a new culture along with their scanty belongings.

The five centres, including Freretown on the Kenyan coast, were enclaves of Christian converts in a predominantly Muslim *milieu*. They knew the heavy involvement of Arab–Swahili society in slave trading. With Bishop Steere, they felt engaged in a 'race with Islam'. However, as they moved inland, they were to find that the call of the minaret was largely a coastal phenomenon. Islam had, as yet, scarcely gained a foothold inland, and thus there was apparently ample room in the interior for the Christian Book and Christian fellowship.

SOUTHERN TANZANIA

The Universities' Mission to Central Africa

The Anglican drive into the interior from Zanzibar parallels that of the Roman Catholics from Bagamoyo. From Zanzibar the Anglicans moved in two directions, towards Usambara in the north-east and towards Lake Malawi in the south-west. In both of these attempts to reach distant goals they were frustrated, but adjusted to the situation and established what they, at least for the time being, considered to be 'half way-houses'. After Bishop Steere's return from his consecration in 1875, he set out to explore the road to Lake Malawi. Two main factors may have inspired him. A decade and a half earlier his predecessor, Tozer, had abandoned Lake Malawi for the Island (Zanzibar), but had intended to return to the Lake. Steere set out to fulfil this debt of honour. Firstly, he wished to bring the ex-slave returnees back to their homes in the south – mostly Yao or Makua people. Secondly, from his observation point in Zanzibar, he was keenly aware of another major theme which preoccupied the Christian missionaries wherever they moved along the coast: 'It is a race with Islam which shall have the tribes.'[20]

Steere made two expeditions toward Lake Malawi in 1875–76. He chose as his helpers Chuma and Susi, David Livingstone's two companions. In addition to these he took two English missionaries, four 'Kiungani scholars', fifty-five freed slaves and seventy porters under Chuma's expert command.[21] Both at Bagamoyo and at Kiungani most of the young Africans had already received a basic Christian education and an initiation into the Christian way of life. The missionaries wished to carry these newly acquired insights to the new communities. The political situation in southern Tanzania was complex at this time. As Professor Terence Ranger has pointed out: 'the Masasi district and much of the rest of south-eastern Tanzania was a frontier zone into which immigrants from the south' – first Makonde, then Makua, then Yao – 'had been moving during the second half of the nineteenth century.' Around Masasi and Newala there was 'a complex inter-mixture of peoples . . . on the cross-roads of trading and raiding.'[22]

The Bishop's travel notes convey the atmosphere of the journey:

> This beginning of the rains is the spring of the tropical year, the trees are coming into fresh leaf, flowers are everywhere showing themselves. Among the brightest at this time were the gladioli, scarlet, white, lilac, puce, lemon and orange. No one in Yao-land need fear to want flowers about Christmas time.[23]

The Bishop was no doubt anticipating future cathedrals and altars! When the party reached the hill of Masasi, near the present Mozambique border, its weary members suggested they halt there. There were rumours of famine in the areas ahead and the Lake could wait. Having received permission from the local chief, they opened the Masasi mission. From Zanzibar they had carried along Bishop MacKenzie's portable altar and this now became the symbolic centre of the new station. Some of the Yao and Makua chiefs became Steere's friends at Masasi and sent several of their sons to Kiungani, Zanzibar for schooling. This step proved to be providential. When there was a noticeably sullen resistance from most of the local Makua chiefs, 'their suspicion and distrust were returned by the missionaries'.[24] There were even attacks on the new foreign village on the hill. However some of the chiefs' sons with their newly acquired Kiungani education helped to avoid catastrophe.[25]

The Yao chief, Matola I, was interested in the advancement of his people and so, in 1878, he welcomed a new Anglican settlement at Newala, a Yao centre near Masasi. The two Christian villages, Masasi and Newala, were founded by returnees who had experience of both Indian and Zanzibari society. They were now trying to find their 'roots' and trying to live out their new faith around church, school and clinic. Masasi was, to begin with, an enclave of freed slaves who had little contact with the culture of the local people. Later, the groups at Masasi and Newala found themselves under the control of Yao chiefs, among whom Matola I and Matola II showed special interest in the Church as a modernizing agency. The congregations became something of 'a "court" Church rather than a people's Church'[26] and attempts were made to adapt to local culture. This adaptation was both urgent and necessary for communities of foreign origin such as these 'Christian villages' were. Many of the newcomers to both villages found difficulty in adapting to their new life. One of these, the Revd Cecil Majaliwa, had received part of his education at St Augustine's, Canterbury and was ordained a priest in 1901. At Chitanjali he caused a stir by playing a harmonium. But when he came to 'home' territory, he had to relearn Yao, the mother tongue he had lost in Zanzibar. At first he felt isolated among his own people, 'like a cottage in the middle of a forest'. The Chitanjali community had a Christian Yao chief, Barnaba Nakaam, a former student at Kiungani.

The distances from Zanzibar to Masasi and Newala were considerable and it was difficult to maintain contact between Zanzibar and the south. But locally there were strong forces working for the growth of the Church. At Newala the Yao Chief, Matola I, had great ambitions and a broad outlook from years of travel and experience. He co-operated with the Anglicans, encouraging their efforts and often acting as interpreter for their sermons. He sent four of his family to mission schools. The local missionary, Chauncy Maples, later bishop in Malawi, supported Matola I. In 1885 he enrolled as a catechumen in a ceremony attended by a number of other chiefs. The Church's iron rule against polygamy delayed his acceptance for baptism; he was baptized *in extremis* in 1895. Unable to participate fully he compensated by emphasizing the rule of the Sabbath. In religious matters, Chief Matola was assisted by his nephew and Anglican deacon, Daudi Machina, whose daughter married another Anglican priest. In this and numerous other ways, an Anglican elite group emerged, bound together by common family and educational bonds.

In these early years, a relationship of mutual support and sympathy grew between the Church and the House of Matola, a natural union of Church and State. The Anglican missionaries were eager to bolster the chief's position, hoping for a Yao nation and a Yao national Church. Matola I's successor, another nephew, Matola II (d. 1945), had a more chequered career than his uncle. He managed to placate and manipulate both the German and the British colonial masters, but the Church had difficulty in dealing with him.

In the 1890s Vincent Lucas was appointed priest in charge at Masasi, becoming its first bishop in 1926. He was closely involved with the spiritual struggle of the Makua and Yao first generation Christians. When Benedict Njewa, an ordained deacon, accused one of his flock of bigamy, he was threatened with witchcraft. He went to the Government headquarters, took off his cassock and girdle, folded them and asked that they be returned to the Mission. On the spot he became 'insane and violent' and died soon afterward. Lucas met other such instances and tried to help the young converts reconcile the new religion with the old cultural patterns. In 1913 he put forward imaginative proposals for adapting the Yao rites for the dead and the *Jando* (initiation rites). His advocacy of a Christian *Jando* was important since it 'ensured that the need for a man to be at once a Christian and a fully initiated member of his community could be met *within* the Church rather than in revolt against it'.[27] (The Christian *Jando* was their 'confirmation' ceremony, and incorporated several features of the traditional Yao *Jando*.) This was far from being an isolated initiative, carried out only by Lucas. While some colleagues were critical of his daring proposals, many African priests, such as Reuben Namalowe, a Makua commoner, perceived the need for just such a translation of the Christian way of life into terms of the people's ritual experience.

The Maji Maji rebellion

The early colonial period was punctuated by the Maji Maji rebellion of 1905–07, 'an explosion of African hatred of European rule'.[28] It soon developed into a mass movement sweeping all communities and only certain powerful chiefs such as Mlolere of Pogoro could afford to stand aside. The ideology of the movement was religious and millenarian. It was a wildfire kindled by a prophet named Kinjikitile Ngwala, possessed by the Hongo spirit. Hongo was related to one of the country's great territorial shrines near Rufiji. The deity, named Bolero or Kolelo, had the power to give rain and fertility. This time the prophet and his followers provided special *maji* (water-medicine) under oath-taking which gave supernatural power to the adherents. This power would turn European bullets into harmless water and thus make the Maji warriors invincible. Starting near Kilwa, the rebellion spread west and south, with repercussions throughout the whole country. The violence lasted two years, and about 750,000 died during the conflict.

The missions, torn between divided loyalties, were deeply affected by the rebellion. African Christians were faced with an agonizing problem of loyalty. At Lukuledi only six of the 1,250 Christians joined the rebellion, while the rest remained, as the missionaries preferred to say, faithful. The mission stations in the south were fortified by enclosed palisades, to be defended by firearms if need be. At the Berlin station of Jakobi, 2,000 attackers advanced in three waves but were repulsed. One of the Benedictine stations was destroyed and the missionaries forced to flee; at Peramiho one of the fathers and seven African Christians were killed. An unfortunate heavy spirit of submission pervaded most communities in the region. Only the proud Hehe remained as sullen and defiant as ever.

The Benedictines

The German Benedictines, having met with a poor response from the Swahili population along the coast, decided to turn inland. Reconnoitring in 1895 brought them to the Makua, close on the heels of the Anglicans at Masasi, inland from Lindi. They arrived during a period of dangerous tension among the Makua population, caused mainly by Ngoni threats. Knowing that the mission had helped defend the Africans at Masasi against Ngoni raids, the Makua saw the Benedictines as potential allies against this same danger. The German colonial troops had a grudging respect for their military strength. A wise old Makua chief addressed the Benedictine visitors: 'I am old and I have known past and present days. The future belongs to the Whites. Therefore I tell you, my children are free to follow you and to learn the things of the Whites. I shall not hinder them.'[29] A number of chiefs followed Chief Tukutua's lead, sending their children to the mission school and some of the chiefs joined the catechumenate. Audaciously, the Benedictines approached the fearsome Ngoni and surprisingly received a positive response. Father Cassian Spiess became friends with a leading Ngoni, Mputa Gama, son of Zulu, the founder of the Njelu branch of the Ngoni.

Mputa was a man of expanding perspectives and contacts. He was a 'foreigner', born in Malawi, where he had developed links with Scottish missionaries and their schools. Perhaps he hoped the Benedictines would give his people advantages comparable to those provided by the Livingstonia mission. It was this scion of the House of Zulu who gave Peramiho to the Benedictines. Near the eastern shore of Lake Malawi, this mission station was to become one of the most influential in East Africa. Father Cassian won immense good-will from the whole people. He was wise and generous and developed an understanding for the peculiar traditions of Ngoni culture. When he became bishop in 1902 and left Peramiho, his successor was of a different calibre, with more ardour than wisdom. He deliberately destroyed the sacrificial hut of the royal Ngoni family, a sacred place of immeasurable value to the people. In so doing he destroyed much more: for a long time he alienated the Ngoni people from effective contact with the Christian cause. Their participation in the Maji Maji rebellion became directed not only against the colonial regime but also against the mission and its 600 converts.

Defeat in the rebellion and the revenge meted out by the colonial masters broke Ngoni resistance, leaving many of them feeling that the traditional faith was something of the past. This was perhaps why, in the tragic conclusion to the rebellion, many Ngoni chiefs accepted baptism prior to their ultimate fate – execution. Christianity now began to flourish. Converts increased from 484 in 1907 to 4,372 in 1916 and schools from three to sixty during the same period. Not all sons of the executed Ngoni elite became Christian; a minority of them turned to Islam. Many Catholic converts were attracted by the great festivals and the strong fellowship in the local congregations. At Kimo the bishop warned against rapid attachment: 'We dare no longer encourage increased reception of the holy sacraments, for we cannot manage the increase of the work.' The young Ngoni chief, Laurenti Gama, accepted baptism in 1912. There were already African vocations to the Benedictine order at this time and to the priesthood. Paul Holola, a Makua, was for a time, a catechist in the northern Ngoni area and would have become a priest if the Order had seen fit to prepare Africans for priesthood then. As such a decision was deferred, Holola married and carried on as a catechist.

The Berlin and Moravian Missions

Protestant entrance to the southern highlands came from the south via Lake Malawi, rather than from the east coast. Their first missionaries were Germans of South African extraction. The Berlin leader was the experienced Alexander Merensky, while the Moravian leader Theodore Meyer, born on a mission station on the Cape Province frontier, had served as a schoolmaster in Germany. These men came to Tanzania in 1891, shortly after their German imperial administration had seized control of the country. They settled as far as possible from the capital on the coast, perhaps hoping to avoid serious tensions with the German government.

In coming to the Nyakyusa, the missionaries soon found that they had entered a highly religious area where the cults of Kyala and of Mbasi had many devotees. There were sacred groves and streams, alluring grottoes and haunting lagoons, all charged with supernatural powers. The arriving Europeans needed to appreciate the sensitivity of the people to the supernatural dimension of life and of cosmos. A herdsman-priest claimed that the deity whom he represented – Mbasi – had called the White men, meaning the missionaries, into the country. Unfortunately, Theodore Meyer, the gifted Moravian leader, rushed into misrepresenting Mbasi as the Devil, an interpretation perpetuated later in local translations of the New Testament. Possibly an unhurried study of Mbasi, the founding hero, could have produced a fruitful dialogue, rather than discord. On a more positive note, at Ikombe the Berliner missionary, Carl Nauhaus, a man with 'a definite charisma', set up fraternal relations with the priest of the Pali–Kyala cult. Some of the communities in the Rungwe and Safwa areas had 'divine kings' with a mystical aura about them. They were 'priests more than chiefs', and worshipped on behalf of both the spiritual and material well-being of their peoples.[30]

The missionary task was a challenging one. How did they make a start? The answer is that it was not a case of 'starting from scratch'. They were always able to base their initial efforts on earlier experience gained in another, neighbouring field and, through necessity did this using African interpreters and co-workers from that former area. Here they had two Zulu Christians in the group, Nathanael and Africa. (In those days a person was known to the Europeans by his first name alone.) They were to serve as interpreters.[31] In Malawi three Ngoni Christians joined the group. It is not possible to document the extent of evangelistic work handled by Nathanael, Africa and their Ngoni colleagues, but it was probably considerable. Their example and life-style, particularly family life, was in itself attractive. The connections with South Africa tended to predispose these missionaries to certain grand ideas with regard to land matters. They insisted on acquiring extensive areas for their stations. They usually managed to get what they wanted, often against the frustrated protests of the local German administration. The Botshabelo farm example in Transvaal was reproduced in southern Tanzania. During conflicts and widespread rebellions, such as the Maji Maji, the mission was a refuge where endangered groups and individuals could repair.

The irrepressible Ngoni advance from the south of the continent did not finally spend itself until just short of Lake Victoria; then a section of this Ngoni movement turned south-east to settle on the eastern side of Lake Malawi. Wherever the Ngoni appeared, their vibrant thrust necessitated new political alignments in ethnic structures. Yet some of the great communities in southern Tanzania managed to survive without much change. There were the Sangu where women played a leading role in the ritual life of the society. From time to time these communities attacked one another in devastating wars. The Hehe under Mkwawa wiped out a German expedition in 1891, thus acquiring a reputation as the dangerous enemy of the colonizers. The calculating chief, Merere, brought his Sangu to help the Germans in their struggle against Mkwawa. Merensky introduced himself to Merere as 'a doctor who can heal sickness', and became a close friend of the great chief, attending to his personal ailments.[32] In all these power struggles, the subdued Bena had an especially adverse time; the 'Bena of the Rivers' and those in the highlands, were threatened by everybody, pushed and buffeted and were searching for security.

The Bena Christian villages owed much to the corresponding Pedi villages at Botshabelo in the Transvaal, but were also influenced by those on the hillsides of Usambara. Fundamentally, the Christian village was under the command of the missionary, but in practice it was administered by two elders, one man and one woman, later replaced by a Mission *jumbe* (chief or headman). This chief adapted the religious organization to both the traditional system and the colonial government. This formation developed slowly *from* a mission station – with church, school, clinic, missionary's house and a few huts for African labourers and catechumens – *to* a 'Christian village'. The latter grew by division, spreading to adjacent traditional villages in the district. During the 1960s and 1970s, some Christian villages in Bena and Hehe areas were transformed with almost surprising ease into *ujamaa* (self-help and collectivized) villages.[33]

The Christian village was organized according to *mitaa* (house blocks). Houses were built along one side of the village street with fields on the other. At first the layout was devised so that the missionary, after a day's work, could visit and inspect the villages, speaking with each family individually. Law and order were enforced, fines levied and Church discipline exercised, particularly against alcohol and polygamy. Church discipline supported and accentuated the teaching of the Word. It drew a sharp line between the Christian enclosure and the traditional world, a clear border between God's world and that of the spirits. The Christians had taken a stand, affecting above all relationship with their kin. Monica Wilson has expressed the effect of this for the Nyakusa: 'The Christian withdrawal from the pagan rituals implies a partial break with the closed circle of kin, a movement from the nexus of kinship to that of association, from the kinship group to the congregation of believers.'[34] This division was not always easy to maintain. In secret it would be crossed to consult religious specialists, no doubt more often than the missionary would care to know. This traffic continued, as nobody imagined that it was wrong. In spite of the strict discipline, within the walls the faithful were living reasonably contented lives as farmers, carpenters, blacksmiths, teachers and evangelists.

The ex-South African Carl Nauhaus had introduced a set of regulations concerning residence, the so-called *Platzordnung* (local mission by-laws) at Ikombe among the Nyakusa. Ikombe was a Nyasa peninsula where no chief had claimed jurisdiction. Nauhaus used the regulations to maintain order in the settlement and the residents were able to regard their plots as their own.[35] In Bena country, the *Platzordnung* was more strictly introduced than elsewhere. The Lutherans, close to the battles between Merere and Mkwawa, felt that, in a dangerous world, the stockade of the Christian village at Ilembula or Kidugala afforded security.

Under the missionary Priebusch, Ilembula became 'a small chiefdom', with 400 regular attendants at Sunday services.[36] The people appreciated the missionary's medical skills: he vaccinated over 1,200 against smallpox and stressed preventive medicine and hygiene. The whole group gathered each morning in the chapel for Bible exposition, prayer and hymns. They sang with joy both European hymns and genuine African songs. These latter, written by African teachers and elders, readily emerged in the Lutheran Bena and Nyakusa areas. School attendance was compulsory for children. The solidarity of the Christian group, as against the surrounding traditional communities, added strength to the congregation, but had at the same time its poignant human problem. Each individual was very much a part of the clan and continuously faced its age-old obligations. Priebusch, born in 1867, had been a non-commissioned officer in Prussia, and tended to stress military virtues. Law, order and discipline were the rule and he saw to it that they were punctiliously observed; sometimes he emphasized this with the help of the *kiboko*, a whip made of hippopotamus hide. Late-comers for the Sunday worship might feel its sting, as well as Christians who at the death of one of their own clan members would show their mourning, as custom had it, by shaving their hair. Sins such as polygamy led to excommunication from the community. Thus, fairly close to the Christian settlements, melancholy little villages of 'sinners' families' emerged, harbouring memories of past Christian fellowship and also feelings of injustice.

The Moravians established their Christian congregations adjacent to the Berliner Lutherans. They were also Germans, but their policies differed. Approaching from the south, they had been advised by Scottish colleagues in Malawi against the formation of 'Christian villages'. With such a system, the Scots claimed, the missionary would become a '*de facto* chief' and would have constant friction with local authorities. The Moravians in the Rungwe area took this advice. The missionary and the African catechist or deacon came closer to what they liked to call 'the African mind'. This was particularly so with Traugott Bachmann. Beginning as a conventional missionary of his day, after a serious illness he was converted to a new and refreshing understanding of African values.

Very early, too, the Moravians placed full responsibility on African deacons, even taking the step of appointing an equal number of women as deacons in each congregation, two men and two women.[37] The women were inspired by their missionary, Elise Kootz-Kretschmer, 'a woman of enormous talent, prepared through her own background in the Moravian community to look upon souls in an extremely humane and egalitarian way'.[38]

In the Kukwe community, Bachmann worked for the use of African names at baptism and for a genuine local form of confession or 'speaking out' as a preparation for Holy Communion. He was one of the few missionaries prepared to admit polygamists into the Church: 'God does not make the ugly distinction between monogamists and polygamists.' In this concern for a positive approach to African thought-forms, Bachmann was sustained by his mission director in Germany, Bishop Hennig, who understood the importance of social integration of Christian and tribal communities. Bachmann found a devoted co-worker in Ambilishiye, a man closely related to the Nyiha ruling family, who was soon to become the first ordained pastor in the Nyasa Province. The co-operation between Ambilishiye and Bachmann paved the way for an exceptionally imaginative evangelistic approach.

When the Moravians arrived at Rungwe, any dreams which they may have had of an African *folk* Church in a closely knit community were dispelled by harsh reality. The raid-ridden Rift corridor kept supplying them with countless refugees, who were difficult to assimilate. First they had to deal with these groups and their mission stations 'provided a substitute corporate life for them'. The ever-recurring refugee factor was also at work here. A parallel can be seen in the Benedictine approach to the Hehe at Tosamaganga. At first, in their self-assured manner, the Hehe rejected the missionaries' invitation. It was among the *vafugwa*, the servile group among the Hehe, that the Catholic mission found their first believers.[39]

In the nineteenth-century African Church, the school often had a preparatory function for the Christian congregation in its worship and fellowship life. However, the two Evangelical German missions in the south both held a different view. With them, the school 'followed' the congregation and was an adjunct of the Church, helping in the operation of teacher training schools. The product of these training schools was the phenomenon, found in many parts of the continent, of a leader with the dual role of preacher and teacher. Modern pressures eventually replaced the bush school with the middle school, at first mainly devised for the sons of chiefs. It was taken for granted that the class structure of society must also be expressed in recruitment for the school.

NORTHERN TANZANIA

From Bagamoyo the Holy Ghost Fathers proceeded inland in a rhythm of advance and return. This was not a ready-made plan coming out of the missionary's study at Bagamoyo. Instead, it was a highly original strategy which gradually took shape as the first two or three forays suggested a workable approach. It was a local strategy original to Tanzania. The idea of a 'Christian village' was of course a variation on earlier initiatives by the Spiritans along the western coastline of Africa, in Senegal, the Congo and Angola, and also in Réunion. A small reconnaissance team would journey to an inland community. Their first contact with the people of that area would involve negotiating for land and marking out the site for a new Christian village, preferably in the vicinity of the chief's village. After this initial visit, the 'scouting' group would return to Bagamoyo to select a corps of young couples, perhaps twenty to thirty, who would then move to the selected site as founding settlers of the new village. Such new Christian villages were established at Mhonda in 1877, Mandera in 1881, Morogoro in 1882, and Tununguo in 1884. Later the Fathers started similar work in the Kilimanjaro area, by way of the Kenya inland route to Moshi.

The Christian village soon emerged in the bush, close to the traditional one and the chief's residence. The Alsatian Fathers chose their sites with an expert eye for development, close to a rivulet for irrigating the garden. There was a chapel, a house for the missionaries, a store of dried bricks, and twenty small houses, well constructed and insulated, for the Christian families. Each family had goats and sheep, poultry and ducks. There is little information on the social background of the Christian settlers. One should not overemphasize the fact that the groups which built new villages inland were 'ransomed slaves'. These young men and women were not keen to remain bound by historical chains of the past. They saw themselves as modernizing 'Readers', fortified by several years of schooling at Bagamoyo. They were now eager to share their learning with inland peoples. The Bagamoyo settlers spoke French among themselves, and used French for the first generation, until about 1880, when they changed to Swahili.

In 1870 a reconnaissance tour inland was made by Horner and Baur, with the omnipresent Fr Duparquet, 'the Catholic Livingstone'. After active years in West and Southern Africa, he was now spending some time at

Bagamoyo, bent on reaching the 'Central African Lakes'. In 1877 Baur and his party set out for Mhonda, in Ngulu territory, about nine days' journey from Bagamoyo. They followed a similar procedure in 1881, when opening the Mandera station among the Zigua-Kwere, not far from Morogoro. The missionaries turned to the local chief, Kingaru. He was astounded and said to his people: 'Look here, these white people whom I have just seen in a dream during the night, together with the good *Mzee* [the Sultan of Zanzibar]. Did he not tell me to receive them well as I told you already this morning, when I got up. And now, here they are!' The dream, or *déjà vu*, was an important medium of revelation in the African Christianization process, but the Zigua example seems especially interesting. Fortunately for the missionaries, the dream disposed the chief to give his visitors the land they wanted: 'All I have is yours, my house is yours, my land is yours, my people belong to you.' The French missionaries, for reasons of their own, adapting to this level of culture, identified the follower in the dream differently from the chief: 'The two Fathers looked at one another and understood that the "Old Man" was St Joseph, the protector of their safari.'[40] It was seen as a great encouragement when in 1881 the Bishop, Raoul de Courmont, brought to Mandera an utterly sacred object, 'a small part of the Cross upon which had died our Lord Jesus Christ ... That day the people were blessed with this relic.'[41]

Soon a second team was sent from Bagamoyo to put up buildings for the new station, after Chief Kingaru had come all the way to Bagamoyo to guide them to his domain. The mission centre was built in the form of a *boma*, an earthwork fortress, protected by a large ditch and a rampart of earth. Hostile bands of Masai were roaming about, and the new Christian village also functioned as a place of refuge for people whenever the Masai threat seemed imminent. Along the same route taken by the mission team, the Zigua had earlier found their way to the coast, and had become acquainted with new ways of life and ideas. They had met Arabs and coastal Swahili and had discovered that a new religion manifests itself not only in gestures and genuflections but also in elaborate garb and ornamentation. These coastal visitors claimed to be 'civilized' and thus different from those inland, for whom there was a widely used Swahili term, *washenzi*, meaning barbarous or uncivilized.

As the Christian village grew, with its school, dispensary, orphanage and its trades (learned from Bagamoyo-trained carpenters, brick-makers, brick-layers and tailors), the surrounding area discovered that the new people had brought the modern civilized world to their village. Although the new people were part of a patriarchal and centrally directed religious system, they were far from devoid of personal initiative. Neither were they 'terminal receivers'; they expected their new vision, skill and knowledge to be developed for the sake of the surrounding community. Thus they served as a 'trajectory' for new ideas and new social forms. Chief Kingaru's happy exclamation to the missionaries was inevitable: 'You are our coast!' The observation was more significant than was at first realized. The 'coast' was at this time in the eyes of these communities what the 'city' became in the view of the twentieth century: the contact with and springboard to the big world, with its immeasurable riches and its surprising offer of new ideas and opportunities. It was not surprising therefore that many of the local people joined the Christian village. In the course of time, the new religious grouping was to some extent integrated into the surrounding social system.

Kingaru's active co-operation was a great help to the missionaries. He would inform his people about the Sunday services and the meaning of festivals. He would explain the missionaries' teaching, adding comments of his own, such as his elaboration upon the theme of a 'heavenly garden and of a pit below'. With this backing of the chief, the people were soon prepared to follow the basic gestures of the new religion. They made the sign of the cross 'with the seriousness of a Trappist', blessed branches, partook in processions and joined in singing the canticles. For the great church festivals each chief had his people fire a salute. A poignant event was the death of one of the young missionaries, Strebler, at Mandera. When his colleagues buried him, the entire pagan population arrived to follow the strange ritual. The form of worship and the language were entirely alien; and the words and tune from the *Rituale Romanum* were incomprehensible to them:

> *In Paradisum deducant te Angeli*
> *in tuo adventu suscipiant te Martyres*
> *et perducant te in civitatem sanctam Jerusalem.*

Yet the solemn rite had a message of its own, at a more existential level, perhaps more than words could convey: a certain fellowship at a deeper level of human solidarity. Even the participation of humans was not enough! A white wooden cross was erected at the grave and the Zigua noticed that at night, 'the gazelles came there to pray'. The French philosopher, Paul Ricoeur has said: 'Symbol gives rise to thought', and it may well have done so then in the hearts of men and women at Mandera.

The Spiritans were soon prepared to baptize those who indicated their willingness, arguing that 'these people were living in a country where there were Christians already.' Apparently the Bagamoyo nucleus of Christians gave this impression. Preconditions to baptism included settlement in the Christian village and a renouncement of infanticide. At this time the missionaries were fighting this local custom of the fatal exposure of newborn babies. The Zigua believed that children whose upper teeth came before their lower ones were unclean, and should accordingly be killed. In 1881 the missionaries held a big meeting to discuss this issue. Thirty local chiefs attended and a lively debate ensued, but the missionaries did not succeed in inducing the community to break with the custom. There are reasons to believe that this particular stand of the missionaries on a central issue of Zigua custom in this community attracted at least some of the women, especially the mothers, to the Christian faith. It is difficult to decide whether these women were influenced by the women in the Christian village, who had come from another background and were therefore different. 'Ransomed' and trained for some years by the Sisters at Bagamoyo, they were comparatively free from tribal customs and free to take up new tasks such as teaching and nursing.

When the Holy Ghost Fathers evaluated their 'Christian village' policy, they found mixed reactions. From one point of view it had been a great success. By the 1890s there were over fifty such villages in East Africa. Various causes had led people to join these communities. The 1886–87 and 1896 famines forced starving Africans to place themselves under the authority of the mission. In 1888 several Morogoro chiefs formed a confederation led by the Catholic missionary, Father Machon. His Mhonda Christian village had become so influential, that 'one hundred chiefs' acknowledged his suzerainty, accepting him as judge and leader. A colleague of his called him 'the king of the country'.

The 'Christian villages' had their own particular problems. Some of them reported unrest. Their inhabitants chafed under the paternalism and constant control; they demanded greater freedom, as well as payment for their labour. One sharp observer among the French missionaries, Alexander Le Roy, concluded that the church village programme was no more than a Utopia, bound to fail, and that consequently it should be ended. The pioneer Baur sided with him and so did Bishop Allgeyer, who looked toward what he called 'Christian nations' in East Africa, feeling that these would have to be built on other foundations. The alternative, aiming at a closer link with the village 'grass roots', was the use of catechists and the widest possible extension of bush schools.

Yet the difference between the two programmes was not as great as one might suppose. As late as 1912 Munsch, the new bishop in the north, found that the Kilimanjaro catechists consisted largely of 'ex-slaves'.[42] Their training was simple and basic. With 'a good character' and the ability to read and write, a young man was eligible to be an apprentice catechist and might then advance from that position. His task was the winning and training of children for the bush school. The catechist's salary was equivalent to that of an ordinary plantation worker. Priesthood for Africans seemed to be an impossible dream and the root cause of this supposed impossibility must have been 'basic distrust of the African'.[43]

The UMCA in Bondei and the Bethel Mission in Usambara

The UMCA experience in Bondei and the Bethel Lutheran involvement in Usambara were two apparently distinct developments. To the Africans concerned, however, it appeared as a continuous development against a background of successive local conflicts. Professor Feierman has analyzed the political and social situation and has shown how it rapidly became chaotic, with people 'seizing and selling one another ... their merchandise were people.'[44] A number of trading towns emerged, from the coast inward, as far as Gonja in Pare and Chagga country. These towns were centres of exchange not just of commodities, but also of culture and of religion. 'The people of the trading towns learned new religions in much the same way that they learned new languages – one could learn Islam without taking it as seriously as the Shambaa religion of the ancestors.'[45] As an alternative to Islam, some people, particularly women, were attracted to new spirit-possession cults, often a manifestation of prevailing uncertainties and the clash of cultures.

In 1867 a pioneer UMCA missionary, C. A. Alington, arrived in Usambara. He visited the chief of Vugha, just as Krapf had done two decades earlier and similarly received a negative answer. He was not allowed to settle in Usambara, but allotted a location in Bondei country, closer to the coast and the Zanzibar authorities. Alington was assigned to Magila which became the centre of UMCA work. He came with Vincent Mkono, one of the Kiungani senior pupils. He also brought an interpreter, Khatibu, who was Bishop Steere's Swahili tutor. An interesting group of young African churchmen who joined the station helped gain for Magila its outstanding reputation: the Revd James Chala Salfey, the widely-travelled Oromo Anglican priest, eventually posted to Lebombo in Mozambique, accompanied by a Shambaa churchman trained at Kiungani, 'Reader' Petro Limo, nephew of Chief Kimweri; sub-deacon John Swedi, who had studied at Nasik, India; and another sub-deacon, Francis Mabruki, who had studied at Nasik, India, at Kiungani on Zanzibar, and in England for a year.

J. P. Farler, an English priest, was in charge at Magila from 1875 for thirteen eventful years. He won the confidence of the Bondei to such an extent that competing parties vied for his favours. They eventually asked him to be their king. Father Farler thus became a UMCA parallel in East Africa to Father Machon among the Mhonda, White Father Dupont in Bemba country, and Spiritan Father Richard in Gabon. Chief Kibanga was impressed by Farler and offered to send his sons to Farler's school, all sixteen of them, to be educated. In the end there was not room for all of them.[46]

Bondei-Usambara was eventually taken over by German forces, with different areas feeling varying degrees of political pressure. The chiefs in eastern and western Usambara displayed marked differences in their attitudes to European rule. The chief of Vugha, more prestigious than the others, was definitely opposed to any contact with foreigners. When old Kimweri died in 1894, his successor was also unco-operative, as the first Bethel missionaries in the area experienced. They dared to put up their tent, but the king's crier, strutting through the streets, 'in peculiarly drawn-out high notes announced over the big town that any help to the missionaries was forbidden'.[47] The hanging of the chief of Vugha in 1895, for an alleged case of murder, marked a violent end to the resistance to German presence.

In the north-west, on the other hand, Chief Shekinyasi understood the signs of the times and accepted the new conditions. He made a visit to the coast and announced his readiness to receive foreigners. It was to Mlalo in the north-west that Ernst Johanssen and Karl Wohlrab, Bethel missionaries, turned in 1891. They were gifted and competent linguists, but found themselves up against a wall of incomprehension. The Shambaa asked: 'Do you really believe that because of your words and of the stories you tell, anybody here would give up everything which a Shambaa inherits in his heart?'[48] The two missionaries had to wait three years with no signs of a positive response, although a few Shambaa worked for them, living at the mission. These men were exposed to Bible teaching, but did not respond at first. A dramatic rain shower on Easter Day 1894 changed the prospect. Nine boys, aged fourteen to sixteen years, took courage and came to the missionaries for baptism. They met resolute opposition from their elders, but five of the nine persisted. After catechetical training they were baptized on Whitsunday. This allowed for only a short period of preparation, but the missionaries felt they had St Paul's authority on their side. Johanssen's colleague, Rösler, had used the pool below the Ubili waterfall for a baptism service.[49] The UMCA at Magila was reported as using a river for baptizing groups of catechumens. 'Each, as he entered the river, faced west and renounced the devil, and then faced east and confessed the Triune God'.[50] But these daring exceptions were rare. The missionaries were thousands of miles from their European base, but the strength of Western tradition nonetheless prevailed in the baptismal liturgy, and they thus most often resorted to the usual sprinkling method.

Christian villages were a feature of the Shambaa Church. But the ecological conditions of Usambara made the solution more challenging than elsewhere. Three religions faced each other: a traditional village would rest on one of the hills, while a Muslim community faced it along another ridge, and the Christian village occupied a third hill. The Christian settlements were noticeable for their striking square brick houses, and also for their music: the hymn-singing and the Bethel trombones. This arrangement was, however, different from the plan of the first-generation missionaries. Johanssen and Wohlrab were concerned with indigenization. 'It was hard for us to get out of the way of freer development in this wide land and to withdraw to the narrower area around our mission station.'[51] However, the traditional pressures on the first converts were too heavy. It was felt that a Christian life could not be expressed in the thick of traditional ritual. At Mlalo, the first group decided to build near the mission house and formed the nucleus of a village. The Christian villagers vied in keeping their homes tidy and attractive. The leader among them, Shemweta, chose the new name Noah; what could be more logical than calling his village 'Ararati'? Soon another neighbouring settlement was begun and at the consecration of the new houses, six young couples celebrated their wedding. The name of the village had to be 'Cana'!

At the end of the 1890s a serious famine occurred, one which no rain-doctor could master. The newly established Christian villages, spread out along the steep Usambara hills, became refuges for the utterly distressed and dispossessed individuals and families.

It was taken for granted that all villagers should attend daily morning worship in the chapel. The Shambaa are among the great musicians of East Africa, and their choirs sang the chorales and spiritual songs in harmony. The effect of vibrating responses from one hill to another, sometimes on moonlit nights, was unforgettable.

The Chagga and their two missions

The water furrows from the eternal snow of Kibo, running through the eucalyptus forests and banana groves, give to the green slopes of Kilimanjaro their lushness and splendour. Those furrows have also challenged the

Chagga farmers to co-operate. The 'furrow master' was elected by the community, to oversee the equitable sharing of the life-giving water. Although Chagga society appeared homogeneous, by the end of the last century it actually consisted of more than fifty political units. There were constant intrigues between leading chiefs; and the arrival of Europeans only seemed to increase opportunities for the more cunning to manipulate the foreigners, in order to eliminate their competitors and strengthen their own position.[52] The political and linguistic tensions were accentuated by denominational divisions between Catholics and Lutherans, at a time when, tragically, no bridges led from one camp to the other. It was not even simply a Catholic–Protestant controversy. In the 1880s Chief Sina of Kibosho – the 'Napoleon of Kilimanjaro' – hoisted the red flag of the Sultan of Zanzibar on his mountain fortress.

The Chagga had early contacts with Christian missions. Rebmann, Krapf's colleague, had already visited Chaggaland in 1848–49. Chief Rindi, the diplomat among the Chaggas, established good contacts in every direction. He needed assistance from the Europeans with their book learning and their mechanical skills. In 1877, when one of the Freretown lay missionaries of the CMS suggested that the chief might need teachers, Rindi did not hesitate to accept the offer. 'If you want children to teach them, we shall give them to you. And I shall follow you to learn with all my people . . . Meanwhile, send me a Book. Mind you don't forget it.'[53] With the letter he sent gifts: a spear and a dagger, and in return received the Book he was looking for, a Bible – but in Arabic! In 1885 the chief welcomed the CMS to Moshi.

The imperial powers had not yet decided whether Kilimanjaro would be placed north into the British area or south into the German sphere. In 1886 an Anglo-German border commission decided the issue and the CMS missionaries at Moshi found themselves in a German colony. In 1892 they were instructed to leave the country and the Leipzig Lutherans took over. Their first stations during the 1890s were placed at Machame, Mamba and Moshi. The French Spiritans came from Bagamoyo and founded Christian villages between 1891–98 at Kilema, Kibosho, and Rombo. The local political situation was tense, and the German administration established its presence with brutal determination. In 1899 nineteen leading Africans, including Chief Meli of Moshi, were hanged from a tree outside the military station at Moshi. Three other chiefs found it safer to flee over the border to Kenya. Others decided to demonstrate their compliance with the new political and religious authorities.

Land was scarce on the thickly populated mountain and the mission attempt to secure a site was a challenge. When the first Leipzig missionary, G. Althaus, approached the chief and people of Mamba, the Africans responded readily, giving the mission a plot of land on the mountain slopes called Ashira. This seemed generosity on their part, but they were only giving away 'the place of wild animals and corpses', an area where bodies of unmarried youth and barren women were abandoned. The missionary, however, was pleased. Ashira was, as are so many of the Chagga mission stations, a place of singular natural beauty. For the building activities, Althaus received expert help from overseas. Leipzig recruited Tamil artisans from the Lutheran Church in South India, who arrived under the leadership of a Tamil catechist.

There was competition between Catholic and Protestant for the favour of Chagga chiefs. Father Alexander Le Roy, the Spiritan, made an interesting comparison between the strategies of the two church bodies. His view has implications for a much wider area than Chaggaland. Le Roy wrote:

> The Protestant missionary excels by making the Natives mobile (*à les mettre en mouvement*); he makes them into preachers, school teachers and agents of every kind. While the Catholic missionary is mainly concerned – perhaps too much – with the slave, the leper, the sick, the orphan, the Protestant goes straight to the chief and to the young men and to all who have an influence today or who will possess such influence tomorrow. Wherever it exists, Protestantism goes for power.[54]

In fairness, it should be added that Le Roy himself was not above making such a bid for influence with Chagga chiefs. In fact, in this respect he went further than most in that he established blood-brotherhood with Chief Fumban of Kilwa. He relates how on this occasion a 'magician' rattled off a long incantation, followed by responses from the crowd, announcing the most terrible consequences to Le Roy and to the chief in case either of them were to be a traitor to this solemn covenant. Incisions were made in the skin of the two prospective blood-brothers and blood from the wounds of both was smeared into meat which was then eaten by both, three pieces each.[55]

Father Le Roy was a gifted observer of African cultural life and also a generous interpreter of traditional African religion. He claimed that African religion 'is necessarily universal and catholic and does in fact blend with integral Christianity'.[56]

The two contending missions claimed certain areas for their particular Churches, which led to considerable friction. In 1894 the German administrator, Captain Johannes, stepped in and divided the country into separate Catholic and Lutheran regions, with each group agreeing to a strict principle of non-interference in the other's territory. The Catholics could not agree to the zoning suggested, but in the circumstances they felt that their principle had to be waived. In each instance a chief was advised by 'his' particular Catholic or Lutheran missionary, not least when it came to influencing the German administrator. A dramatic development was the case of the Machame chieftainship, until this time a comparatively limited area. Young Chief Shangali, through close co-operation with the Lutheran missionary, E. Miller, and the German administrator, Johannes, managed to extend the borders of his rule considerably, and thus future Lutheran influence was ensured in the western part of the country. Chief Shangali attended school in 1897 and became a faithful Church member. The missionary noted that in a four-year period the Chief had been missing from services on only eight or nine occasions.[57] At Marangu, Chief Marealle was effectively assisted by Fr Blanchard. In his case the chief struck a balance between the two missions and allotted to each one-half of his kingdom. He had one of his sons baptized as a Catholic and another as a Lutheran, while he himself cautiously remained a traditionalist.[58] From 1900 there were two mission schools in Marangu, one Catholic and the other Lutheran, with the recruiting area divided by a rivulet.[59]

Although local power politics played a role in this struggle, differences in personality and temperament, both in the chief and in the missionary, also played their parts. The Kibosho chieftainship, with its proud tradition of power and influence, felt that because their missionary Father Rohmer did not co-operate with their chief, they were given a poor deal. The ecclesiastical division of the country had the effect of a 'fruitful rivalry from which the people benefited'. In some areas this local monopoly favoured a certain social and particularly educational *status quo*. Kibosho and Rombo were Catholic examples and Bruno Gutmann's Old Moshi a Lutheran one.[60] In spite of the example of Chief Shangali and others, resistance to Christian evangelism was strong. In 1907–08 there was a sudden flare-up of paganism, with some Christian elements.[61] By 1910 the pendulum had swung back and Chief Sakwera of Ashira was baptized. Relatively rapid expansion in the number of neophytes followed. At the same time some of the more prosperous Chagga acquired their own version of uncommitted religious neutrality. They had observed and absorbed the attitudes of the growing European population gathered on the fertile slopes of Kilimanjaro.

With varying degrees of conviction, the Leipzig missionaries introduced their programme of an African folk-church. This implied that, as distinct from their Berlin and Bethel colleagues, they would not be party to the formation of Christian villages. The local Lutheran congregation must grow, not apart from, but as an integral part of Chagga society. None stressed this with more determination than Bruno Gutmann, at Mamba from 1902 and at Old Moshi 1910–19. He produced pioneering studies of Chagga law and customs and interpreted the role of the Christian community in terms of an enchanting romanticism, nurtured as much by Wilhelm Wundt's folk-psychology as by meditations on what he liked to call 'the secret of Africa'.[62] However, his studies left most of his colleagues unmoved and tended to make his local congregations less educationally ambitious than the others. However, these congregations may have been all the more attuned to creative art. The life and work of teacher Filipo Njau, Gutmann's pupil and friend – one of the most thoughtful of first-generation Chagga Lutherans – is an impressive illustration of this point.

A short autobiographical sketch of Njau, this central personality in the Chagga Church, can represent a whole generation of these young people, moving from the past into a Christian future. The Moshi mission station was built close to his widowed mother's house. As he came to look at the strange place, a missionary gave him a piece of cloth. 'As I became aware that I had got it for free, I was eager to learn to read.' He moved to the mission, but his elder brothers and his mother insisted that he return home to look after the goats. The nearness to the mission, however, provided chances to continue reading. His elder brother's baptism was a great occasion: Why? 'Because they arranged a feast', in connection with the baptism. When Njau became cook for one of the missionaries, he had opportunities to widen his horizon and see the world: Pare, Usambara, and even Tanga on the coast. In 1911 Bruno Gutmann hired him as a teacher and a mutually enriching fellowship developed. In 1912 he joined the teacher training school staff at Moshi. Gifted and articulate, he had many offers to become plantation overseer or clerk, but he preferred to continue as a teacher-catechist, with less pay but with more satisfaction of another kind. Njau transposed Chagga wisdom and folklore into Christian hymns and interpretations of the Gospel, and wrote a collection of Chagga folk tales in German.[63]

In the absence of 'Christian villages', the first generation missionaries had to work with those Chagga whom they could reach, i.e. the youth. Boarding schools seemed to be the solution, much on the precedent of Leipzig's earlier experience in Tamilnadu, South India. These schools also gave girls and young women a chance. In 1914, out of 100 schools with a total of 8,000 pupils, there were more girls than boys – a rare situation at this time, and one cause for the development of Christian family life in the Chagga Church. Although boarding schools multiplied, Gutmann, the die-hard, would not accept the boarding school system on his station. He shunned it, as he did teacher training and theological schools. All, in his view, were modern devices leading to destructive individualism instead of genuine African values, to be found in clan, neighbourhood and age-class. For both Catholic and Lutheran missions, the school became the most important channel of evangelization, yet neither mission was particularly concerned with developing secular education. The Alsatian Holy Ghost Fathers felt that in Africa the task was not so much education as regeneration, and when the Saxonian Lutherans emphasized the role of books, it spoke not of books interpreting modern life, but rather of the New Testament and the Lutheran Catechism. In the Lutheran missionaries' reports to their mission society there was therefore a certain 'undertone of apology' when the work concentrated on secular education.[64]

The Holy Ghost Fathers at Kibosho and Kilema shared the view of their bishop, Vogt, that the task was not so much to create elites, as to teach the masses. Even though, in accordance with this attitude, no teacher training school had been started prior to 1914, the Catholic village catechist-teacher had a central place in the system. It was taken for granted that adults were unreachable; therefore the masses of tomorrow must be attracted through the children of today. The village catechists were indeed 'the apostles of the new times'. In a very few years, after the First World War, bush schools were to be derided or pitied as 'little nothings'. But so far they were the only bridges to Western culture. In a more determined manner than the other German Protestant missionaries in Tanzania, those from Leipzig adapted themselves to Swahili. From 1906 it was taught in mission schools, and from 1912 it was the medium of instruction in the schools. This resulted in making the gifted Chagga into teachers, clerks and plantation overseers, thus forming the beginnings of a new class.[65]

Meru and Pare

The Lutheran mission made early attempts to evangelize the Meru in the west, the Pare in the south-east, and later the Iramba in the south-west. The very first approach to the Meru in 1896 was tragic. The night after a site had been handed over for a mission station, the two young missionaries were speared to death. Six years later a new, more successful, attempt was made and a chapel and a boarding school were built. H. Fuchs and Paul Rother were Lutheran pioneers in Pare, 1900–16. Rother was accompanied by a devoted and enterprising Chagga teacher, Reuben Moshi, who had been one of the first six in the Moshi teacher training school. That he accepted being sent to distant Pare was in itself an indication of his feeling of evangelistic responsibility. As a rule, the alumni of the school insisted than they be posted as teachers to their own home villages. Such was their horizon and ambition in that first generation. The walk to Gonja in Pare took seven days. There, Reuben Moshi found ample scope for his educational and organizational ability and for his evangelistic drive.

KENYA

The Mombasa coast

The CMS and Freretown

The largest Protestant settlement, created from the wide catchment area of the Indian Ocean, was the one near Mombasa. As West Africa had its Christian returnees from the West Indies and from Brazil, so East Africa too had its returnees, this time from India. Similarly, as for the West Africans the port of call was Freetown, the East African equivalent was Freretown near Mombasa. This enterprise had connections with Mauritius. Bishop Ryan of that island had asked the CMS in 1864 to set up a reception centre for liberated slaves.[66]

This story vividly illustrates the role of the Indian Ocean for communication and exchange. Arab dhows carrying East African slaves to be sold in Arabia, Persia and India, were intercepted by British naval sloops in the Persian Gulf or in British India waters and their human cargo was unloaded in Bombay. The first known transfer took place in 1847 when forty-three girls and twelve boys were released. What was to be done with them in that far-off country? C. W. Isenberg, the CMS missionary in Bombay, took the initiative. Once Krapf's colleague, he had formerly served in Ethiopia and recognized some of the rescued slaves as his 'own' people – some were Oromo! In 1855 a Christian village, Sharanpure, took shape near Nasik, not far from Bombay, with another young CMS missionary, W. S. Price, in charge.

About 200 rescued slaves passed through this Christian centre at Nasik on the west coast of India, learning the 'three Rs' and trades in the institution and government farm at Pachora. Most of them were eventually baptized. Price was convinced that 'some of them would matriculate at Bombay University'.[67] And they were singing! They were, after all, Africans – most of them Christian converts – singing the songs of Zion in a foreign land. This impressed David Livingstone when he visited them in 1865. 'An African composes tunes and has made about twenty-five with songs in his own language – the tongue of Londa.' He was so struck by all the singing that as a dour Scot he felt he had better warn them that 'it was not play they were going to but work.'[68] The school was also treated on that day to a wider ecclesiastical perspective, for they were examined – probably for confirmation – by the bishop of Calcutta. Sir Bartle Frere, then Governor of Bombay, took a lively interest in the school.

They were Africans however, speaking their various East African tongues and eager to return 'home'. In 1864 the first 'Bombay Africans' returned and settled at Rebmann's station at Rabai. Ten years later, some were transferred to the mainland opposite Mombasa. This new community was called Freretown, after Sir Bartle Frere, their protector. The CMS asked Price, who knew these people from India, to form a Christian village with industrial facilities, as a base for an inland advance 'towards Kilimanjaro'. Freretown included two groups of freed slaves: the 'returnees from the East' who with their education and experience became teachers, interpreters and artisans; and the newly liberated from East African waters. Altogether Freretown had about 145 Bombay Africans and over 900 'liberated slaves'. At Rabai, the older and neighbouring station, there were 1,200 former slaves; by 1890 the population had risen to 3,000.[69]

Buxton High School, with room for 100 boarders, opened in 1904. The Catholics began a similar one in 1908, at Mombasa. A Divinity School was opened at Freretown in 1888 with nine candidates, inspired by the Henry Venn tradition aiming at ordination of Africans. George David (d. 1884) and William Jones (d. 1904) were two outstanding Bombay 'returnees'. David, who already spoke many languages, among them English and Hindustani, learned Greek from the missionary William Lamb, and became a candidate for ordination. He was sometimes referred to as the future 'Bishop Crowther of East Africa'. By making a Swahili compendium of basic Bible texts and of Dr Watt's *Simple Catechism*, he made it possible for all to understand both teaching and worship at Freretown. The members could feel that they were indeed 'joining the Book'. David impressed on the newly arrived the being and the omnipresence of God in his formula: *Mungu kila Pahali Yupo*, *juu na hapa* ('God is in every place, above and here'), and patiently persevered with each group, until they could repeat the words without his assistance. 'I am within the mark when I say that he repeated the words at least 300 times. The exercise lasted an hour and a half.'[70] He translated the missionaries' sermons into Swahili and taught the congregation a number of hymns and the Common Prayer liturgy. Because Swahili was a *lingua franca*, it united the people who spoke many local languages in this international centre.[71] Certain cultural patterns indicated the Indian background of the leading group of Africans. At the church services the women would appear 'with a white cloth drawn neatly over the head, as it is worn in India.'[72]

William Jones, trained as a blacksmith in India, also hammered in the great truths of the Gospel. He was ordained a deacon by Bishop Hannington in 1885 and accompanied the bishop on his fatal expedition towards Uganda the same year (see p. 564 this volume). In 1895 Jones became the first African priest in British East Africa. He fearlessly defended the rights of runaway slaves who sought refuge at Rabai after escaping from their Arab masters in Mombasa. Voluble and by nature authoritarian, this African priest was their 'big father', but he felt hampered by his European missionary colleagues and had the temerity to complain about his salary – forty-six rupees per month – the same as a cook in European employ. This kind of comparison, later often made in Africa, was at this time considered undignified for a priest. In 1898 he resigned and immediately received a government job with a salary more than triple his mission pay. In his case, the resignation was not basically due to the question of money but of fellowship and acceptance. Many CMS personnel staged a walk-out in support of Jones, but returned when they received a new leader 'whose paternalism was one of conciliation and who affirmed their respect for the roles of their subordinates'.[73] This leader, arriving in 1900 as the first Anglican bishop of Mombasa and Kenya, was W. G. Peel, a man of vision and understanding.

Unfortunately relations at Freretown between the missionaries and the Eastern returnees were not always harmonious. This problem may be seen as an illustration of a crisis regularly provoked by a change of missionary generations and consequently of a much wider application than that of certain local squabbles at Freretown. The first generation missionaries, William Price and J. A. Lamb, were incomparable 'fathers' of their flock; and Price, who had trained the group in India and had followed them to Mombasa, always appreciated these highly gifted and enterprising Africans. In 1879, however, Price and Lamb left East Africa and a new set of missionaries 'who knew not Joseph' arrived. One of them, J. R. Streeter, applied harsh methods of what he was pleased to call 'education'. Some of his colleagues may have been influenced by Social Darwinism as their contemporaries on the Niger in the Bishop Crowther controversy had been.

Although the Freretown–Rabai complex was to some extent isolated, it did begin to reach further inland. William Jones started the Anglican work in the Taita Hills in Kenya, and contacts were made from Freretown with Mpwapwa and Moshi in Tanzania.

Methodists at Ribe

While the CMS affirmed its involvement in Kenya by participation from the east, from the 'Bombay Africans', the Wesleyan Methodists emphasized their evangelistic work by association from the west, from Sierra Leone. The Methodist missionaries Thomas Wakefield and Charles New arrived in Kenya in 1862, the same time as Krapf left Africa, and inherited Krapf's concern for the 'Galla' or Oromo but concentrated their interest on the Ribe mission, not far from the Mombasa coast. The British Methodist initiative was followed up by the arrival of three Sierra Leone pastors. Their move to the field in Kenya was an imaginative idea on the part of the London headquarters of the mission. It did not however solve all the problems. William Price, with his knowledge of the Kenyan situation, referred to one of the Sierra Leoneans as 'as much a foreigner as a European could be'. The Ribe mission was led by the Revd F. J. Heroe, 1887–90, a product of the Fourah Bay College, Sierra Leone.

Fuladoyo

Another example of Freretown and Ribe influence was the community of fugitive slaves led by (David) Abe Sidi. Here is another illustration of the refugee factor, this time in an East African setting. Abe Sidi had been influenced by the Rebmann centre at Rabai. He formed a Christian community at Fuladoyo, several miles from the coast. This settlement, mainly *watoro* (escaped or fugitive slaves), was composed of many ethnic groups. The indigenous population of the area, the Giriama, with their shifting patterns of cultivation, at this time were known for their effective resistance to both of the new 'Book' religions – Islam and Christianity. Sidi's group, sometimes as many as 500, settled in a neat, well-organized village in the bush and can be seen as a Christian variant of a new type of sociological formation during this period. Fuladoyo appeared as a *kaya* (fortress) with a strong cohesion and an adaptable military defence system. Their Church formed the nucleus of an intense community life.

The Freretown Mission, needing amicable relations with the Arab governor at Mombasa, could not give Fuladoyo the necessary support. An Arab–Swahili attack in 1883 obliterated the community, at least in its Christian form. Abe Sidi was killed, becoming a Christian martyr. The brief existence of the Fuladoyo settlement is a memorable East African example of tough Christian 'backwoodsmen' and of a proto-Independent congregation with intermittent mission connections. It also showed how the apparently unreachable Giriama could choose a Christian way of life.

Fuladoyo was not an isolated phenomenon. There emerged on the coast something of a network of local groups with Christian contacts related to Ribe, Rabai and Freretown. An example of this is the community of Christian enquirers who gathered around Mwaringa of Godoma, who built himself a house in a tree and spent his days reading St Luke's Gospel, 'above ground' to this small group. There were also the so-called 'WaMisheni' who worked as porters but tended to trickle back to Rabai in their declining years.[74]

Kenya inland

The emergence of the Christian Church differed in each of the three East African countries. This difference depended on the extent to which each was in contact with outside influences and whether its internal communications were strengthened or dislocated by such contacts. In Tanzania there was the Arab–Swahili trade route – fundamentally for slaves – from the coast via Tabora to the lakes. This traffic made long-range communications possible in both directions and also fostered an exchange of commodities and ideas between western Tanzania, Uganda and the coast. In Kenya, the Kamba acted as middlemen between the coast and the highlands, but there was less communication and the Muslim communities on the Kenya coast did not achieve the kind of contact made by their brethren in Tanzania further south. The Masai were an effective block to trading networks between the coast and the interior in Kenya.

The railway to Lake Victoria finally 'opened up' Kenya to outside influences. Krapf thought, as we have already pointed out, that the enterprising and mobile Kamba were destined to become the carriers of new ideas to inland peoples. This view attracted eight missionary societies: five German, two British and one American. The commemoration of Krapf's death in 1881 inspired German missions to enter Kenya, and a Bavarian Lutheran mission set out for Africa. However the situation was more difficult than they had anticipated. The climate was trying: six out of nine missionaries sent from 1886–97 were lost because of ill-health or death. Krapf had known the Kamba to be mobile, but the new missionaries found them elusive, and one after the other their mission stations had to be abandoned. This failure was tempered only by the recognition that the remaining missionaries could join the denominationally related Leipzig Mission in Chagga country.

The approach through southern Kenya provided a transit line for traders and missionaries to northern Tanzania. Along this route both French Spiritans and German Lutherans had approached the kings and peoples on the slopes of Kilimanjaro. The Anglicans were ahead of the others, being established on the coast since the days of Krapf and Rebmann. The missionary occupation of Kenya was related to British imperialism and economic enterprise, with a Victorian flavour of Christian evangelism. The Imperial British East Africa Company, formed in 1888, was the key agency in this drama. The company encouraged the Anglican CMS to open stations along the new route to the interior. Hoping for a Kenyan Lovedale, the company invited the Scottish Presbyterian, Dr James Stewart of Lovedale, Cape Province, to work in the area. He had earlier worked as a missionary in southern Malawi. Stewart spent a brief time among the Kamba on the project, but soon returned to the Cape.

With the arrival of British imperial administration, the area between the coast and Nairobi was proclaimed a protectorate in 1895 and Kenya became a crown colony in 1920. The new rulers believed in chiefs as authority for Africans and if a particular African culture had no chiefs, such were provided. As these appointments went against tradition, the appointees were at first unpopular and isolated from the community. Some of the chiefs, however, became competent leaders, with well-deserved respect. Among them, Karuri wa Kakure, chief in northern Kikuyu from 1900, adapted himself to the new situation and was a progressive leader for his people. His recognition of the mission schools and their contribution to the life of the community helped form a positive community response to the schools.

Among the Kenya peoples the Kikuyu were dominant, but the closely related Meru as well as the Embu were important. These highland communities were vital to the trading of the Kamba middlemen. They were all acephalous societies in which power and authority were diffused through a number of constituent parts. A council of elders held the authority in a system which, although patriarchal, had elements of democracy. Land was owned on a family or clan basis rather than communally. Some of the foreigners encountered a strongly religious character in the people, which was often expressed in a high regard for 'seers'. Mugo wa Kibiro, a Kikuyu prophet, predicted the coming of foreigners from the sea, pale-looking creatures who would spit flames of fire and bring other disasters. In the end a saviour would arise in the midst of the people and provide deliverance.[75] Even more impressive and far-seeing were the 'seers' of the Kamba, the famous *athani*, most of them women in trance. Their pronouncements had almost apocalyptic overtones.[76] The Meru consulted Mugwe, the 'failing prophet'.[77] There were similar prophets among the Gusii, the Nandi, the Embu and the Masai.[78] Oginga Odinga has recounted such personalities among the Luo.[79] These traditions indicate an atmosphere of religious expectation which provided a sounding board for a new message.

An American interdenominational group, the Africa Inland Mission (AIM), founded a Kamba station in 1895 and other stations followed. They were seen as part of 'a chain of mission stations' reaching beyond Kenya into Congo. The Catholic Spiritans began work at Kabaa in 1912. Both missions had an uphill task. The Spiritans only baptized their first convert in 1919 and the AIM, after more than twenty-five years, in 1921 reported only 161 baptisms.

The CMS effort among the neighbouring Taveta was more promising. Fearful of the powerful King Mandera of Moshi, the Taveta welcomed the services of the CMS as a means of gaining protection. The first missionary, Alex Stegall, set the tone of the settlement by stressing industrial development together with the puritan Gospel. He introduced new varieties of crops, an irrigation system and brick-making. Here, as in much of Africa, the people first attracted to the mission centres were not so much Taveta locals, as refugees from outside the area. There was, of course, the common pattern in a majority of local congregations throughout Africa; the first mission community tended to consist of displaced Africans, with a foreign dialect and different customs and ideas. If this particular Taveta group developed contacts with the local community, it was thanks to the African pastor, John Mbele. Trained by Stegall, he could interpret the two communities – Christian and traditional – to each other. A crisis occurred, however, in connection with the burial of the pastor's own mother. Taveta burial tradition insists that after a lapse of time the grave should be opened by the dependants, and this was exactly what the pastor, loyal son of a good mother, did. Other Taveta traditions he resoundingly rejected, but when it came to something as close to his heart as the effective burial of his mother, he followed local custom. The congregation was split over this issue, and for a time was shaken. Soon Taveta experienced devastating onslaughts of imperial land-grabbing. Tens of thousands of acres of their land were sold for new sisal plantations at four shillings an acre.

At an early date neighbouring Uganda had an unmistakable modernizing influence on western Kenya. The best known chief in the area, Odera Akango of Gem, had toured Buganda and been impressed by what he saw of mission schools and new agricultural methods. Into this kind of society a number of missions arrived from 1900 onwards. In some African countries the rivers and lakes were the means of communication; in other areas it was traditional land routes. For Kenya, the railway represented this means of communication. This was the signal for an almost unprecedented 'scramble' for missionary occupation. Within ten years nine Protestant and three Catholic missions began in the highlands and in western Kenya, forming the outline of the mission map of the country. Strong denominational competition caused some stations to be founded with the express intention of preventing the 'opponents' from possessing the land.

As with the Taveta, who lost lands to sisal plantations, the Kikuyu's concern was their land. It became increasingly scarce and more valuable because of a rapidly rising population, all in a country where only one third of the total land was arable. The White government awarded not only the settlers but also the missions generous tracts of land, from 3,000 to 6,000 acres for a mission station. While this was helpful for the support of coffee plantations and other missionary enterprises, it was hardly agreeable to the Africans. It was only the first missions who benefited from this largesse, for in 1909 the governor reduced the allocation of land to missions to ten acres, and in the following year to five. But the impression remained: the foreign missions were 'grabbers' of the people's lands. Much of the tough resistance against the missions in the Kenya highlands, at that time and later, was rooted in this fundamental question of land.

The main societies placed their headquarters among the Kikuyu in or near the little railway siding of Nairobi: the Anglicans, the Scottish Presbyterians, the interdenominational Africa Inland Mission and the Holy Ghost Fathers. The United Methodists also came, although they had begun earlier on the coast, at Ribe in 1862. They later moved inland and concentrated on the Meru district, north-east of Mount Kenya. At Kabete, now a suburb of Nairobi, members of the famous Leakey family led the Anglican CMS work, while the theological seminary at Weithaga was run by A. W. McGregor. When the first theological student, Paul Mbatia, enrolled in 1906, his family tried to take him away by force. McGregor calmed them down by threatening to take the matter to Chief Karuri, the influential Kikuyu chief who encouraged the efforts of the missions.

The Anglicans and Presbyterians practised different policies: the former tended to spread out over a large number of Kikuyu stations with a very limited staff for each ('one-missionary stations'), while the Scots placed their fairly large staff in a few main centres. Nairobi, the rapidly growing capital, attracted migrant labour from the Kikuyu as well as from remote communities. The Anglicans were fortunate to have George Burns as their first Nairobi missionary. Having begun his career as a boxer and a policeman, this Australian (originally Irish) Evangelical was also a robust frontier man in his mission work. He was in charge of the work for over a quarter of a century, from 1905 until his retirement in 1932. Hundreds of Kikuyu together with men from other communities attended classes, learned to read and write, and were baptized 'kwa Burnsi'. The first Anglican baptism occurred in 1907 and by 1916 there were regular Sunday congregations of 1,500 in two services, half of whom were Kikuyu while most of the rest came from western Kenya.

Increasing numbers of men from the highlands and western Kenya could now travel by railway to Mombasa. Migrant labourers found a centre in the Anglican Church and night classes at Mombasa. Returning later to their home communities, a number of them became propagators for the new religion. One example of this individual initiative will suffice. Samuel Mukuba was a Kamba refugee from the terrible famine of 1889. He was adopted by a Giriamu family and went as a labourer to Mombasa where eventually he was baptized. Returning home, he immediately built a prayer house and started preaching. His son, David Gitari, was to become the Bishop of Mount Kenya East Diocese and, later, Archbishop.

The French Holy Ghost Fathers soon found a place in Nairobi and the surrounding area. They came to represent the Catholic Church in Protestant Kenya. With their long experience of African missions, they were not surprised when, in 1902, the Italian Consolata Fathers turned up on their premises, presumably to begin an African apprenticeship which would lead them to the ever-enticing 'Galla' in Ethiopia. However, seven years later, in 1909, Rome accorded these Italians the 'Apostolic Vicariate of Kenya'. They had come to stay. The Consolata Fathers followed a policy of rapid occupation by means of hastily constructed mission stations, but they also had a knack of adapting to local customs which other missions might well have envied. Even though the expansive plans of the Holy Ghost Fathers for Kenya were thus partly curtailed, they could derive some satisfaction from the fact that their remaining area included the Kiambu district, destined to become, in the fullness of time, a peculiarly powerful centre. The Catholic presence in Kenya was strengthened and the Catholic image widened by the arrival in 1894 of the English-speaking Mill Hill Fathers to the west of the country.

Jocelyn Murray has shown the important role of Kikuyu and other Kenyan 'agents' from the very beginning of the local Christianization process.[80] Coast Christians or converts from Kamba and Taita communities were brought by the missionary to the Kenya highlands as personal servants, as porters and cooks. These people wered soon employed as volunteer teachers and evangelists. Servants at first, they were taught the 'four R's' and were soon ready to pass on their learning to others. When a missionary was posted to a new station, he would bring along servants and catechists from his former place. Before long these would form a nucleus, conscious of their evangelistic calling and obligations. Along Mount Kenya, the sweet-potato plant (*Ipomsea batatas*) puts out its shoots with its ever recurrent 'runners'. Similarly, the first fine shoots of a Christian fellowship sent out its runners in an on-going process. Within the local community it would as a rule be 'the sons of poorer and less influential men who were the first to show interest [in the Gospel message]. The landless men, the men with few or no cattle, did not need their sons to break land or herd for them,' and could thus permit them to join the catechumens' class. Looking back over the first two decades, 1900–19, one of the CMS veterans, A. W. McGregor, characterized developments in one particular station, Weithaga; there is reason to regard this model as representative of a wider area:

1903–06: Huge congregations of interested folk and novelty seekers.
1906–10: Vigorous persecution of young converts by the traditional community.
1910–17: Quiet, steady development.
1917–19: Beginnings of a great ingathering.[81]

In order to deal with local overlapping and competition between Protestant missions, certain comity rules were introduced, in Kenya a ten-mile radius rule. These regulations applied especially to Church and school conditions in Kikuyu and western Kenya, and demonstrated the need for a closer Church fellowship, possibly a 'united Church'. Plans for a federation leading to a united African Church were discussed and, in 1913 at Kikuyu, the expectation of unity was expressed in a common Holy Communion service for the delegates: Anglicans, Presbyterians, Methodists and Africa Inland Mission. This act of Christian fellowship was the object of a loud attack from the Anglican Bishop of Zanzibar, Frank Weston, and for a long time 'Kikuyu' remained a highly controversial place-name in the debate of 'Faith and Order' problems in Africa and beyond. The matter was a characteristically White European and strictly British affair, and limited at that. The Kenya Churches involved in these negotiations had at this time only a limited number of communicant members and, as a matter of course, Africans were not consulted about the federation question. No African was invited to the negotiations, despite the fact that they were the ones concerned.

10

EAST-CENTRAL AFRICA

THE CHURCH AT THE KINGS' WAY

The 'Lacustrines' – the ethnic communities in western Uganda, along Lake Victoria and Lake Tanganyika – are known because of certain ethnological distinctions between a royal and aristocratic upper class, a minority of some ten per cent of the population and the broad masses of the commoners, the cultivators. Further south, the Fipa and the Bemba fall into the same category. It is realized that the account could profitably have been stretched even further south to the Lozi in south-western Zambia, but there strong links of mission history with southern Africa suggest that this community be treated with the southerners.

Missiologically the entire region is characterized by an exclusive combination of, and competition between, Catholics, the White Fathers and low-church Anglicans (CMS). The exceptions to this pattern are the Congregationalist (LMS) attempt on Lake Tanganyika and further south in Bembaland with, on the Catholic side again the dominating presence of White Fathers, but where the Protestant party consists of Congregationalists and Presbyterians, the latter closely linked with Malawi's 'Livingstonia'.

This structure – with its social tensions and missiological polarities – continued throughout the colonial period, in some places with feudal characteristics or those of a caste society, and together constituting a highly significant framework for the beginnings of a vital Christian Church.

Until about 1950 the ethnological differentiation was explained by a supposedly Hamitic population theory; according to which early invasions had come from somewhere north, Ethiopia or Egypt and the Middle East. But research introduced about 1950 by the Catholic missionary and scholar J. P. Crazzolara has discarded that theory. It is now thought that between 1000 and 1500,[1] there was a gradual influx, rather than sudden overwhelming invasions, of population elements of small numbers of pastoral people, possessing immense herds of long-horned cattle, who eventually became politically dominant in the various countries. A Hinda rule began in

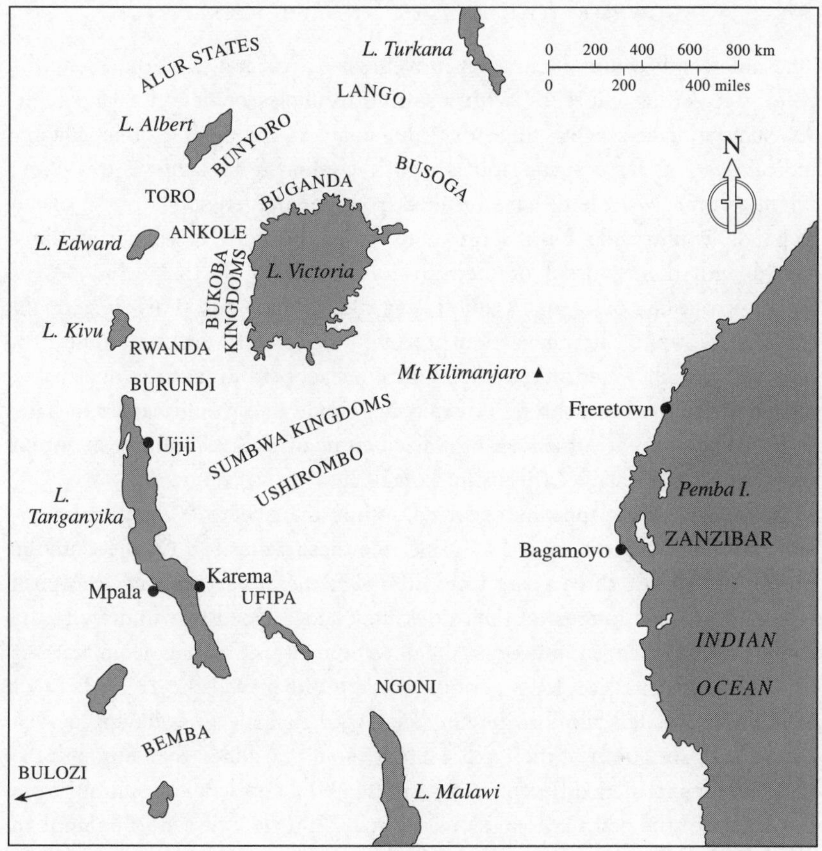

10.1. The kingdoms and key towns and centres in East-Central Africa.

Karagwe and then moved north into Nkore (Ankole). The Hinda in Bunyoro were related to similar population groups in the small Bukoba kingdoms except Karagwe.

All these lacustrine peoples also showed similarities in the religious dimension, with a religious tradition of deities such as Chwezi and Ryangombe serving to maintain and legitimize social differentiation. The social and political pattern manifested large similarities throughout the region in the fundamental role of kingship, sometimes in the form of so-called 'divine' kingship.

BUGANDA, THE *KABAKA* AND THE MISSIONS

The nineteenth-century Christian movement in Africa saw certain remarkable 'pace-setting churches' with inspiring examples of devotion and faith. As such a pace-setting trajectory Buganda is unique and this chapter indicates some factors and forces which combined to achieve this. One might assume this role to have resulted from an energetic penetration of the Buganda countryside by a large number of Western missionaries, duly armed with their Gospel or their rosary and aided by the techniques of British Protestant or French Catholic evangelistic methods. This alone could explain the rapid Christianization process – the clearly visible outline of a national church emerging in only two decades from a tiny nucleus, a martyred few. A breakthrough of this magnitude one would expect to have as its primary agent some well-organized corps of Western whips, intent on incorporating reluctant Africans into the flock.

In fact, the very opposite occurred. While there were Western missionaries at Mutesa's court from 1877, as a rule these were few. Of the Catholic group, for almost three years from 1882–85, there was not one European remaining. In the interest of their flock they had decided to withdraw to the south of Lake Victoria, following the development in Kampala from afar. As for the Anglicans, for long periods of time either Wilson or Mackay or O'Flaherty was left alone at the king's court, their colleagues having moved by canoe to the south of the Lake. Here it should be added that although the two missions in their different ways represented an episcopal tradition, from the arrival of the first CMS missionaries in 1877, it took fifteen years until an Anglican bishop, Alfred Tucker, could take up his post in Buganda, in 1892. Neither of his two episcopal predecessors ever reached Kampala.

The first approach was important. Going to the king, one had to take the right route. Going to Kampala, one had to approach the capital from the south end of Lake Victoria by canoe to the north. Any approach from the east or the north at this time might signify collusion with scheming enemies, Egypt, for instance. When the first Anglican bishop, James Hannington, arrived in 1885 he – as a foreigner – could not perceive these complications and decided to take his party through Busoga (east of the town of Jinja), i.e., the eastern route; it had, seemingly, the advantage of bringing the traveller to his goal faster than by any other approach. But *Kabaka* Mwanga's spies informed their master and he ordered them to have him killed. After a fortnight of dreadful detention, the bishop was speared to death.

The court

In order to understand the peculiar sociological framework in which the decisive evangelistic breakthrough took place, it is necessary to consider both the conditions at the court and the changes that had recently taken place in the power structure of the country's chiefs.

The court on the Rubaga hill, now in present-day Kampala, was part of a vast, sprawling capital extending five to six miles in length and two miles in depth. In the centre within a high palisade of wickerwork was the *kabaka*'s enclosure with 585 houses. These were for the king, his eighty and more wives, his nearly 1,000 concubines and an army of 1,000 servants. This last number included young pages sent by their clans and regarded as potential chiefs. There were also reception halls and an audience room – a vast beehive of a building, on high wooden supports. A recent addition from the 1850s was a mosque, indicative of the king's involvement with Islam.

This court was the very centre of the Buganda universe, thus providing the newly arrived missionaries with their most difficult challenge and, at the same time, their enormous opportunity. The very fabric and organization of this urban court furnished a system of communication emanating from this nucleus, situated within a strictly encompassed central *milieu*.

However in Buganda the very first won for the new faith were those who had special ties to established society, youngsters who as slaves had been ransomed by the missions, to be used by them as retainers or, in the Catholic case, placed in their orphanage. Here we find the first Christian converts, and Christianity also in Buganda was thus initially a slaves' religion, who were regarded by the established local people as 'those bought', *abagule*: some of the Ganda martyrs killed in the anti-Christian purge of 1886, on the order of King Mwanga, were found among the slaves. Some of the free young men who became Christians were incorporated into the local army and accumulated, through plundering expeditions against neighbouring countries, substantial numbers of slaves as their personal property.[2]

Linked to the palace were the households of several officials, the great territorial chiefs, the *bakungu*, highest representatives of the traditional clan system. Over the years there had also arisen a regional administration consisting of *ssaza* (county) chiefs, appointed by the king himself. The authority of the *bakungu* was checked by yet another set of king's appointees: *batangole* (personal representatives of the *kabaka*) chiefs. It was taken for granted that young court pages would in time succeed to such *batangole* posts. To a remarkable extent the system looked after its young, providing opportunities for their advancement.

As a rule, kings in the interlacustrine region insisted that missionaries reside at the royal court, under the immediate control of the king. In this respect Buganda was no exception. This measure, designed to check the foreigners' influence, had the unforeseen effect of aiding the missionaries to reach a large number of people, both at and from the very centre of the kingdom. The missionaries thus had daily contact with a whole generation of young Baganda destined to become chiefs, administrators, teachers and priests. For permission to leave Buganda for the south of Lake Victoria, they had to make a personal appeal to the *kabaka*, and this was on occasion denied. In spite of its possible advantages, the foreigners sometimes felt this court residence rule to be highly limiting. One temperamental Frenchman, Bishop Livinhac, referred to Rubaga as a 'prison'. Having been consecrated in St Cyprian's Chapel at Carthage in 1884, he returned to Uganda and never left Rubaga until his death in 1890. With a quotation from his Latin New Testament, Fr Lourdel likewise complained that he was *in vinculis*.

In the past, the *kabakas* of Buganda had combined the functions of king and high priest. However, about 1800, *kabaka* Ndawula separated the two, thus secularizing his kingship and that of his successors. From then on, the Buganda kings were in principle independent of traditional religion. Without shocking their people or jeopardizing the solidarity of the society, they were free to explore new religious beliefs. The people were able, moreover, to adopt new ideas, so long as these did not conflict with the hierarchical political structure centred in the *kabaka*'s person. In this respect, the kingdom of Buganda was different from neighbouring kingdoms, as Bunyoro or Ankole, where the idea of 'divine kingship' had real force.

Islam in Buganda

A disturbing factor in Buganda politics in the late nineteenth century was the approach of Muslim powers. Egyptian influence was moving southward, drawing both Bunyoro and Buganda into a major world political contest of strength. On behalf of Ishmail, Khedive of Egypt, Samuel Baker, the English explorer, attempted to occupy Bunyoro and in 1874 Emin Pasha reached Mutesa's court. These visits were far from reassuring: 'What do the Turks [their word for Egyptians] want?' was the nervous question.

Another Muslim stronghold was Zanzibar. Arabs from the coast brought both trade and their faith. Mutesa took a lively interest in this religion of the Book. For ten years, 1865–75, he observed Ramadhan, built mosques and followed the Muslim calendar. Islam opened up new horizons to an international world. Further, the Book, although written in a language understood by only a few, brought new knowledge, the rallying cry of the *muezzin* and even a new rhythm of time – the day, the week, the year – giving a new order to life. There was also the all-embracing confession to One God, Allah.

Even though the Muslim challenge was attractive, it repulsed as well, because of its requirement of circumcision. To this Mutesa was uncompromisingly opposed, to be emulated by the other interlacustrine chiefs and peoples. In spite of this drawback, the combination of Islam, Arabic culture and the Swahili language seemed for the time an acceptable option for Buganda. This was indeed one of the hinges of history for this part of the world. The arrival of Western missionaries brought an alternative. Buganda and its neighbours were to face Christianity, Western culture and the linguistic choices which they represented: Luganda and English.

Mutesa concluded that he must not allow the Muslim influence to get the upper hand. The circumcised converts among the chiefs and his court pages appeared to the bewildered king as a potential threat to his own power. In 1875 he suddenly took savage measures to retrieve the situation. Seventy chiefs and pages were burned to death and 1,000 other persons throughout Buganda were killed to complete this terrible purge – a warning of what would befall followers of new religious teachings. This anti-Muslim purge came one decade prior to the anti-Christian purge of 1886.

Before the coming of the missionaries, there were unmistakable signs of a loss of confidence in traditional religion. People were disillusioned with the old gods and were therefore, like the king himself, prepared to turn to one of the two new Book religions. At this time there were several examples of traditional mediums or local chiefs who had premonitions of the coming of a 'white stranger with his little satchel', bringing a new religion.[3]

In 1875, some Westerners appeared at the court, some of them explorers but also other White men, with a Book, but a different Book this time. H. M. Stanley, journalist and explorer and the adopted son of an American lay preacher, was to be forerunner of the missionaries. He was impressed by the character and calibre of the Baganda. As a good Methodist, he saw great evangelistic potential: 'I assure you', he wrote in a famous appeal to the *Daily Telegraph* in London, 'that in one year you will have more converts to Christianity than all other missions united can muster.' This was no empty guess – he spoke and acted as a Protestant lay missionary. For three months he 'laboured diligently' to 'explain the Bible and the Christian religion to the king.' The king had started the process by asking him, 'Now Stanley, tell me and my chiefs what you know of the angels' – a concept common to both competing Book religions. 'Drifting', as he says, 'from mechanics to divinity', Stanley did his best to explain not only angels, but the whole Bible story from Creation to Resurrection.[4]

From Zanzibar, he had brought along an African servant, a UMCA pupil, Dallington Maftaa. This young man became his interpreter and virtually an assistant catechist. Together they prepared a little Swahili book of biblical selections,

> embracing all the principal events from the Creation to the Crucifixion of Christ. St Luke's Gospel was translated entire, as giving a more complete history of the Saviour's life.[5]

Under Stanley's influence, Mutesa called his chiefs together and had them consider the religious alternatives before them. In deliberating with his chiefs, Mutesa emphasized his aversion to circumcision and concluded that if it came to a choice between Holy Books, the Bible was after all the older and therefore better volume. 'As Kintu, our first king, was a long time before me, so Moses was before Mohammed.' And he pleaded with his chiefs: 'Isa – was there ever anybody like him?'

Stanley left Uganda for his geographical explorations further west, leaving young Maftaa alone for two years as an interpreter of the Christian religion at the court. He stayed with *Kabaka* Mutesa for a total of five years. He may have had his weaknesses as an interpreter but he felt a real concern for his responsible task. On 23 April 1876 he wrote to Bishop Steere at Zanzibar. The letter illustrates the role of the African interpreter in a missionary situation:

> My dear Bishop,
> Let thy heart be turned to thy servant, send me Swahili prayers, and send me the big black Bible. I want slates, board, chalk, that I may teach the Waganda the way of God. I been teach them already, but I want you to send me Litala Sundi, that he may help me in the work of God. Oh! my Lord pray for me. Oh! ye boys, pray for me . . .
> Your honour to the Queen, and my honour to you.
> J. Scopion
> alias Darllington Maftaa
> I am translating the Bible to Mutesa, son of Suna, King of Uganda. I was with Henry M. Stanley, together with Robert Firuzi . . . but I being stop in Uganda, translating the Bible.[6]

The missionaries

So impressed was the king by the instruction at the hands of Stanley and Maftaa, that he informed the first CMS missionaries arriving in 1877, that 'he knew to read before (they) came, and knew the Bible'. When they reached

Rubaga, the king showed them his flag – a medley of colours. 'I hoist that flag because I believe in Jesus Christ.' This welcome was a promising beginning for a mission and what followed was to fulfil some of those promises. The principal actors were Alexander Mackay, a Scottish Evangelical and Free Churchman in Anglican service and Lavigerie's White Fathers: Pére Livinhac, bishop from 1884, and Pére Simeon Lourdel, a priest with medical training. In 1894 the White Fathers were joined by the English-speaking Mill Hill Fathers. Their arrival was a strategic move to break the identification of 'Catholic' and 'French'. It is necessary to repeat that the missionaries were most often few in number and absent for long periods of time from Uganda. They were in no position to sweep through the countryside gathering potential converts. What they did through their teaching and example was to exercise a catalytic function. Stanley's optimistic forecast about the potential results of missions in Buganda proved to be singularly accurate. A decade after the arrival of these young foreigners, Buganda was already under Christian leadership, after 'a Christian revolution' or 'counter-revolution', as the case may be. After another decade, in 1900, the 'Uganda Agreement', prepared by the British Special Commissioner and modified by the two English bishops – Anglican and Catholic – set the seal on a largely Christian nation.

If the missionaries were few in number their quality of achievement was the more obvious. Outstanding among the Anglicans was Alexander Mackay. Alexander Mackay (1840–90), the first CMS missionary in Buganda – who was he? Missionaries in those early times were sometimes characterized as pitiable Pietists, dull fellows unable to find any other job and therefore turning to Africa – 'a typical missionary'. In fact Mackay was different from that beloved cliché. He was one of the brightest and most successful young Scottish engineers of his time. He began early. At the age of three he read the New Testament 'with fluency'. At seven his favourite authors were Milton and Gibbon and Robertson's *History of the Discovery of America*. Taking regular walks with his father, the Free Church preacher, he noticed how his father would with his stick demonstrate a proposition of Euclide or trace, on Scottish ground, the course of the river Zambezi, thus inspiring his son to take an interest in that strange 'new' continent, Africa. He achieved maximum marks possible in teacher training in Edinburgh but switched to engineering and went to Berlin to become a locomotive constructor for the German railways, later becoming head of the locomotive department. He also came into contact with the Berlin elite of Christian society and decided 'if the Lord will, to go as an engineering missionary' to Madagascar – the obvious place for a British Congregationalist at that time, so he studied the Malagasy language in Berlin. 'Do not think me mad ... Why should not I go too?' But it so happened that the Anglican CMS appealed for a 'lay superintendent' in East Africa. Mackay offered his services and was accepted.[7]

Mackay, practical engineer, resourceful and enterprising, became the prototype of the Protestant lay missionary, devoting himself to Bible translation and the printing of tracts and gospels. His teaching of the 'four R's' while at the same time being busy with forge and carpentry illustrates an important factor in communication: the forge or the plough, the medicine bag and the scalpel helped to create an atmosphere of empathy and understanding in which a message could be more easily communicated.

Stanley and Maftaa, those earlier laymen, had left traces of their activities in copies of Bible texts. Mackay was 'really astonished to find many copies of this about'. To him and his generation of missionaries literacy was the key to a personal acceptance of biblical revelation. He set up his own printing-press and was soon in a position to translate Scripture portions into Luganda and Swahili. Beginning with a translation of St Matthew's Gospel, this railway engineer on the equator desired to proceed with all speed to the Fourth Gospel. One of his statements gives a glimpse of his theological discernment: 'That rare exposition of the mind of Christ presented by the Fourth Gospel must be in the language as soon as possible so as to convey the deep spiritual truths entirely omitted by St Matthew.' Similarly, instead of the Apostles' Creed, he preferred the Nicene version, 'as the latter is more explicit of the deity of our Lord, and this is the great question just now, as the Mussulmans declare him to be only a prophet.'[8]

At the royal court the missionaries had frequent opportunities to testify to their faith. The ever-vacillating king, faced with competing religious options, developed his own technique of playing one religion against the other. Mackay relates:

> Mtesa began with his usual excuses: 'There are these two religions and which is true?' I left my seat and moving forward on the mat, I knelt on it, and in the most solemn manner I said, 'Oh, Mtesa, my friend, do not always repeat that excuse. When you and I stand before God at the great day of judgement, will you reply to Almighty God that you did not know what to believe because Masudi told you one thing and Mackay told you another? No, you have the New Testament, read there for yourself. God will judge you by that.'[9]

Although seemingly placed on either side of an ideological abyss, the two missions were often faced with similar problems. The issue of polygamy involved not only these two groups, but Muslims as well. The Arabs pointed to the Old Testament prophets. 'They were all polygamists and were yet of God.' The argument interested Mutesa very much. At this time, he was considering becoming a Christian. In September 1879 he approached Mackay and less than a month later, Fr Lourdel. Both, with the same severity, insisted on monogamy, but both preferred to modify their decrees. The Protestant referred to an entirely pragmatic solution, while the Catholic said he must wait for a final decision from the head of his Order, Cardinal Lavigerie at Carthage.

If Mackay's solution was genuine – and nothing in his character would contradict this – he must on this occasion have appeared somewhat naive: 'I said that we in Europe had women servants always in the home, but they were not our wives, and need not be necessarily wives here either ...' Lourdel submitted his question to Lavigerie: 'Was there no way of softening the sharpness of the Church law? Could the King not be allowed to keep just two wives? and [possibly as an echo from the talk with Mackay] keep the wives as his workers?'[10]

To Lavigerie, his ruling was part of his grand strategy for Africa: Central Africa must be Christianized through its kings and chiefs. That had been the case with Europe in the Middle Ages and this was to be the nineteenth-century solution for Africa. But Black kings and princes should not be faced with obligations which they could not fulfil. They must be placed in a category of their own, as 'postulants', and treated according to their station in life. From his studies, Lavigerie had gathered that the Ancient Church recognized not two, but three categories of Christians: catechumens, the baptized and, prior to these, an initial order of 'postulants'. For this tripartite division he knew he had St Augustine on his side.

Lavigerie replied to Lourdel in a series of letters: April and October 1880, February 1881 and, as a last sigh of angry disappointment, in March 1883. Then he exclaims: 'Mtesa is the fortress to be conquered. How I regret that Fr Lourdel did not make him a catechumen when he asked for baptism. What blindness to imagine that such a man would all of a sudden renounce his flocks of women.' Lourdel should generously have informed the *kabaka* that he could indeed become a Christian, but would be placed in a special category of a 'postulant': in making him quite simply to pledge to make his efforts to improve himself, one would promise him that he would be assured baptism in the moment of death. With this reference to the Ancient Church, the Cardinal was without question presenting a most serious challenge to nineteenth-century pietistic missions in Africa, whether Catholic or Protestant.

This correspondence between the missionaries on the spot in Kampala and the Archbishop (later Cardinal) in Algiers shows the importance of the first steps in the mission field and their possible consequences. They should ideally have decided the strategy on the most unmanageable missionary problem in Africa, that of matrimony, and thus the entire future, not least in the competition with Islam.[11]

Before the arrival of the Western missionaries, the Arabs had introduced their challenging distinction between *ushenzi* and *ustaarabu* – barbarism and civilization. The contacts with the Arab traders and recitations from the Qur'an had already stimulated an interest in the written word. Mackay's texts in the people's own language fanned this flame into a passion for books and literacy.

> Sunday, October 19th, 1879.
> All afternoon I have been inundated with visitors, some reading St Matthew's Gospel, and others spelling out their reading-sheets. Yesterday I had four chiefs in at once, and today several also.
> Monday 27th
> All day occupied with readers at various stages. Some I hear in the house, while others I take into the workshop and teach them while I am busy at the vice.
> Thursday 30th
> Took with me to court over a dozen sheets of large alphabets, which we had printed from the types I cut. Mtesa was delighted with them, and distributed them at once among his chiefs and others ... In the afternoon Mtesa had a regular school, having sent for his chiefs, soldiers, etc. ... and those whom we have been teaching.[12]

Mackay the engineer thus devoted himself to literacy and book production and to all manner of practical teaching. From the very beginning he, together with his colleagues, was able to contribute to the development of the country. The Catholic missionaries likewise, together with their catechetical teaching, provided technical instruction. Brother Amans was in turn builder, supervisor of the domestic needs of the mission, gardener – acclimatizing new crops like wheat and rice – mechanic, carpenter and medical orderly. From Zanzibar and Algiers the missionaries brought the first larger mango trees, the first pawpaw trees, orange and lemon trees.[13]

The Readers

The term 'Readers' was used for the groups of young Ganda catechumens which soon spread all over Buganda and from there throughout central Africa in this most successful literacy campaign. These young men were determined to acquire the art of reading in order to know the Holy Book. All the chronicles indicate that these Readers had been taught by other young Baganda at the court. This was a fundamental factor in the process of communication. The catechumen was not a 'terminal receiver', but was expected to carry his discovery further in reaching and winning other subjects and was accepted as a creative actor. Some realization of this expectation must have been at work, activating both individuals and groups.

The first reading book designed for the young, called *Mateka*, had a circulation of tens of thousands. This initial combination of reading and religion made rapid progress among chiefs and commoners at the royal court and from there in ever-widening circles. By the flickering light of fires or torches in their huts at the court, young men – chiefs and pageboys alike – spelled out their texts and jubilantly shared discoveries. The miraculous combination of letters and syllables, whole words and sentences and what was more, in their own language Luganda, grew before their eyes and minds into a knowledge of a sacred history and an understanding of the liberating way of salvation. Mackay, always with a concern for the opportunities of the poor commoners and the downtrodden, reported that he found 'the slaves generally twice as quick as their masters'.[14] In this hierarchical society, the act of acquiring literacy and accepting the Biblical message could not fail to have a certain egalitarian effect.

Was this only an urge for literacy and modernization? No, what happened was something more subtle than that. There was more to it than an intellectual satisfaction at acquiring a new and useful technique. The transition to the Christian faith was made as a response to the search for a new identity: new personality, new name, new community. This longing was emphasized by the reading of these new texts, the recitation and the rhythm of the Psalms, the drama of the parables of Jesus. It was at this level that the Readers felt that they were acquiring a new identity.

Not all was encouraging, however. Tension between Catholic and Protestant missionaries at the court and their emerging little congregations was a persistent problem. Controversial matters – the role of the Bible in Luganda and in the inexperienced hands of ordinary Readers; the place of 'Mary, Mother of God' in prayer and worship; and many other such theological problems took on unsettling importance and often called for divisive decisions. *Kabaka* Mutesa and his councillors realized that the White missionaries were in fact divided and not only on a national basis – they were soon referred to as either 'the English' or 'the French' – but also seemingly with regard to the authority of their faith. As the message was carried from the king's court throughout Buganda and to neighbouring countries by Western missionaries and African catechists, it was done so under the shadow of this seemingly irreconcilable rift.

Conditions in Uganda, as in the whole of Africa, are always more subtle and complicated than they appear to be on the surface. This was also the case with the confessional issue. Even if the clan structure was officially replaced by the king's own *batongole* chiefs, clan connections still remained a very palpable reality. Individuals who had become members of two different churches might be clan brothers, or related in some other way. On certain crucial occasions basic clan connections would assert themselves, cutting across the divisions introduced by the foreigners. On such occasions men would recognize one another, not as Protestants or Catholics or Muslims, but first and foremost as Baganda.

The catechumens

For the new believers, the Word was explained in common daily morning and evening worship at the court. It was corroborated by the Rite of Initiation by Water. It had to be prepared for during years of study and incorporation into the community of catechumens. For both missions there was a time of adjustment regarding the length of the catechumenate in preparation for baptism. Within a year of the Catholics' arrival in 1879, they had baptized nine converts 'and probably a few people in danger of death since then'.[15] In March 1882 the first five Protestant converts were baptized and in April and May of that year two groups of Catholics, eight in all. Lourdel had 'used the advantage of the permission given by Mgr Lavigerie to make some exceptions to the rule of a four-years-catechumenate'. These were only the beginnings. In 1888, after the 1886 martyrdom, each of the two churches already counted about 200 baptized.

In both churches, the corporate aspect of the catechumen class and the baptismal font must be stressed. In their restricted *milieu* at the court, the young pages were anxious to share everything, including their experience of the new religion. It was in this closely encompassed national centre, with hundreds of young boys daily meeting one another in a hot-house setting, that the new religion could be appropriated and interiorized. This was not so much in isolated meditations by the believer, but rather in a *communitas*, an intense group experience involving continuous challenge and response by like-minded young men. It was here that the most searching preparation for initiation through baptism was made, and here that the young converts could together reflect on the identity given to them by the new faith and fellowship and the purifying Water.

This corporate character was soon to expand inland. One example was a village of elephant hunters – a highly prestigious occupation. Two of these hardy men had come into contact with the Catholic pages at Rubaga and carried the good news back to their own people. When the headman of the village then and there declared himself a Christian, 'the whole village' of forty decided to abandon their traditional religion. By 1886 the village had sixty to seventy catechumens. This corporate nature of the emerging Christian groups is also to be seen in the refugee situations in Ankole and at the southern end of Lake Victoria.

In this development, close to great decision-making on behalf of their own nation, these pages could share discoveries of meanings in the parables of Jesus the *Masiya*, or in the precepts and rituals of the Church. They could deepen and refine their spiritual experience. Ham Mukaza, later to become one of the leading chiefs and men of state, expressed his struggle in an early Ganda version of St Paul in Romans VII:

> This war that I have in my heart … is a fight between Mukasa … and Ham … But the new man, Ham, whom God sent to drive out Mukasa, will not allow Mukasa to come back and reign in my body, for God wants to be there by himself.[16]

Three components

One can discern in this transition to the new religion three components. We shall call them Attraction, Reaction and Response.

Attraction

Islam with the Qur'an had prepared the minds for the Book; although written in incomprehensible Arabic, it was perhaps all the more impressive because of this mysterious incomprehensibility. The attraction to that other New Book came in the form of the New Testament in Swahili or through the portions of the Gospels in Luganda translated by Mackay and O'Flaherty and produced at the court on Mackay's printing press.

Only few indications are extant as to what parts of the New Testament were particularly attractive at this time. The young Catholics stressed purgatory and would tease one another on the supposed lack of courage in facing that ordeal at the last. The Protestants here and elsewhere in the region chose passages on the Risk of Life, such as the Five Foolish Virgins who had Lamps Without Oil. Assembled at night in the barely lit hut, they were haunted by its words about the banging, banging, banging on that Ultimate Gate. There were terrifying periods of epidemics menacing the whole of the royal court: 1881, plague; 1882, cholera; 1884, bubonic plague. Great numbers of the inmates of the houses became victims. Young boys, some not yet baptized, would baptize their dying comrades *in extremis* and bury them. In the plague of 1881 eighty Catholic catechumens died, 'only one without baptism'.[17] There was an obvious religious group experience in all this, but at the same time it was discovered that, in that group, the new identity meant an emphasis also on individuality, never before sufficiently discovered.

Reaction

Already before the coming of the missionaries there were signs of disillusionment with the old faith. Mutesa himself wavered all the time between the traditional *lubare* (the traditional hero-god), Allah and the Messiah, between Friday and Sunday and/or both. When sick he would first turn to his traditional *lubare* and his traditional priests and only as a second best resort to Fr Lourdel with his medicines. In this uncertainty and wavering, the young tended to discard their amulets and by this act demonstrated their reaction to the past.

Response

The collective character of the religious group experience at the *kabaka*'s court is striking. It was felt by these young men as an identification with a new life. This soon led to new responsibility, both individually and corporately. In 1884 twelve newly baptized young men were chosen to form a first Anglican *Lukiiko*, or Church Council. They had been selected among those who were already heads of households and groups of pages.

The Namugongo fires

Soon this experience of a new life was tested in the challenge of martyrdom. In the attempt to interpret the Purge of Christians in 1886, this expression of the young men's solidarity in life and death has perhaps not been sufficiently emphasized. The 1880s in Ganda Church history are illuminated by the sharp light of the fires on the Namugongo execution ground. This image has been modified of late, by historical material produced in the form of important chronicles by Baganda participants after the events. These suggest the need for a re-interpretation of the crisis and purge. There are studies by a generation of scholars such as John Rowe, Tom Tuma, Michael Twaddle, John Waliggo and to this list must be added the names of J. F. Faupel, Professor D. A. Low, Bishop John V. Taylor, and Fr J. P. Thoonen.

If *Kabaka* Mutesa had been capricious in religion, alternating between Islam, Catholicism and Protestantism and traditional religion, his young son and successor, Mwanga, was even more fickle. As a prince he had attended Anglican Bible classes and Catholic catechetical instruction. However he was haunted by fears of the dangers both from outside – the threat of Egypt and the German occupation of the East African coast – and inside – the die-hards of traditional religion.

This was followed in 1886 by a purge of Christians in which thirty-two young men were maimed and burned to death at Namugongo, most of the victims being pages at the king's court. While membership of the king's corps of pages was a great honour, life at the court was not without its problems. Mwanga had become addicted to sodomy and tried to use his young pages for this purpose. The immediate cause of the purge was the refusal of these young Christians to comply with the king's desires and what this autocrat took as acts of disobedience. Altogether about 100 people, including non-Christians, were killed throughout the country on this occasion. But the courage and determination of the young Ganda Christians who walked to their death singing *Kila siku tuuslfu* ('Every day we praise Thee') was not in vain. In Uganda, as elsewhere, the 'blood of the martyrs became the seed of the Church'. Existentially these young men knew, to quote T. S. Eliot:

> The only hope, or else despair
> The only hope, or else despair Lies in the choice of pyre or pyre
> To be redeemed from fire by fire.[18]

This attack was not primarily directed against the Church, not an attempt at a holocaust of Christians. The great majority of Christian pages were spared and Mwanga was soon prepared to reinstate leading Christians, whether Catholic of Protestant, as *batangole* chiefs. Tragic though the terrible fires at Namugongo were, they were atypical. Dr John Rowe has studied the Uganda material carefully and summarizes the results in the words: 'Thus, despite the persecution during part of his reign, Mwanga was for his own purposes not anti-Christian, but pro-Christian.'[19]

Aba Masiya and the Ankole refugees

Towards the end of the decade Muslim and Christian chiefs alike became convinced that the basically insecure *kabaka* intended to liquidate them all. They decided to combine forces and, in a series of revolutionary attempts, deposed Mwanga and had him replaced by a Muslim prince. For some time, persecution and revolutionary turmoil made the two Christian factions act together on important matters. Baganda Christian chiefs were currently less concerned with dogmatic niceties than with a basic Christian allegiance: they were *aba Masiya*, the people of Christ, held together by an undifferentiated Christian piety.

This common front was soon tested when the Muslims managed to seize total power in 1888. The Christian leaders, most of them *batangole* chiefs and former pages at the court, had to leave Buganda and found a precarious refuge in neighbouring Ankole. The 'Ankole refugees' were to become a power in the history of Buganda and in the history of its Churches. The role of 'Christian refugees' has often been underlined in this book. The Buganda groups in Ankole, with a total of about 2,000, were 'refugees' with a difference. In Ankole, their position as refugees had made them reflect on and emphasize their identity as Christian readers. They were not destined to remain in the host country, Ankole, but were soon strong enough to fight their way back to Kampala where they seized political power.

One should in fact refer not to one, but to two Christian refugee centres at this time: Ankole *and* the stations at the southern end of Lake Victoria, the Catholic Kamoga and Nyegezi – called Notre Dame of the Exiles – and the Protestant Usambiro. Repeatedly, the missionaries found it necessary, in consideration of the ever-threatening fate of their followers, temporarily to leave Buganda and remain for some time in the south. They were often accompanied by numbers of Baganda faithful, arriving on their perilous flight in their canoes after a voyage on the Lake of at least three weeks. In a foreign land, they found an opportunity for concentrated catechization. To the Baganda refugees this was a broadening experience. Mackay relates how on occasion they were joined in worship by a score of Freretown Christians from the Mombasa coast,[20] who had quite likely accompanied one of the caravans from the coast. Here the Baganda catechumens caught a first glimpse of the universal horizons of the Church. They and their more experienced and widely travelled Freretown colleagues could now meet and be united in common prayer in Swahili. Tradition and background may have been different, yet they were united in a common experience of prayer. Once the Catholic fathers were accompanied by thirty 'redeemed children', soon to be joined by another thirty who came to the exiled community on their own.[21]

Another aspect of the refugee centres was that the two, Ankole and the South End, communicated through requests from the Ankole people for books from the missionaries. Sebwato told Mackay of his basic needs in Ankole:

> I have no book, not even a little one; now, however find me then a book, the New Testament, the Psalms and the Prayer Book; and then also a gun, mine was taken; however, find me another.[22]

The future of Buganda seemed at this moment to lie in the balance – was Islam after all to be victorious? It is difficult to exaggerate the role of this enforced Christian retreat from Buganda to Ankole for a period of about a year. They were on their own, not accompanied by any Catholic or Protestant missionaries, but aware of their potential power.

In the comparative isolation of the refugee situation they had stressed their respective identity as Catholics *or* as Protestants. Returning in 1890 as a Christian force, they were willing at first to forget doctrinal differences. Associated with *Kabaka* Mwanga in order to overcome the Muslims, they successfully established a Christian regime, with the refugees taking over the leading offices in the country. Soon, however, the sense of unity began to disappear and divisions in the realm appeared. The outcome of these considerations was the peculiar Buganda phenomenon of the Christian party, 'an institution conceived in the missionaries' clientage, born of the need for self-defence, and weaned as an exclusive group amid the tribulations of exile'.[23]

What were these divisions? Richard Gray had put the question sharply: 'Did they stem from deeply-held religious convictions or were they, at least in their political manifestations, mainly a label for old lines of patronage and power?'[24] The nature of these conflicts has recently been the object of a series of studies, yet to a large extent the answer to the question was to be found already in 1952, in Roland Oliver's *The Missionary Factor in East Africa*. He pointed out that there were already in the Buganda kingdom some

> who were accustomed to looking outwards, beyond the immediate circle of Bantu states ... [and] who were familiar with the more catholic conception of religion introduced by the Mohammedan traders, some who had developed a capacity for independent thought and a sense of individual responsibility which were fundamental to the Christian scheme of sin and redemption.[25]

This time the question was: Should the country become Catholic or Protestant? In 1892 Captain Lugard and the Imperial British East Africa

Company supported the Protestant cause ('the English'), while the Catholics ('the French') lost the struggle for supremacy. In the settlement, they were given the consolation prize of the Buddu country and certain of the Sese islands in Lake Victoria: a comity arrangement on a grandiose scale was thus enforced. That same year co-operation between Protestant interests and imperial design was again highlighted when the Imperial East Africa Company found itself in a financial crisis. The company had run into a debt of £40,000 and decided to withdraw from Uganda. By special appeal, in only a few days' time, the CMS in London managed to cover part of the needed sum and the missionary society thus 'saved Uganda'.[26] The final imperialist step was taken in 1893 when Uganda was declared a British protectorate.

The Protestant revival

A distinct Evangelical emphasis was introduced by George Pilkington, who had an academic career as a classical scholar. Pilkington, an Irish layman, was able to produce the whole Bible in Luganda in 1897. Using the Swahili version as 'a temporary bridge', he and his gifted Ganda co-workers, Henry Wright Duta and others, together with local teams of men, translated the Old and New Testaments in less than five years! This was not a one-man effort. The role of Bishop Steere's Swahili translation was fundamental as a model. Pilkington as 'the presiding genius of the Luganda Bible' could build on a number of predecessors, Baganda and Britons.[27]

One of the first CMS pioneers, O'Flaherty, made his translation of the Gospels, but his colleagues rejected his attempt: 'Africans had not shared sufficiently in the work'. Alexander Mackay also made efforts at Gospel translation and Henry Duta and Sembera Mackay together with three missionaries (Ashe, Crabtree and Walker) worked on other Bible books. Two Swahili experts among the Baganda, Mika Sematimba and Nuwa Kikwabanga, helped in the translation into Luganda from the Swahili Bible. Pilkington has emphasized that the early homiletical use of these translations of individual Bible books was of peculiar value for the translation work:

> There was none of the ordinary difficulties of searching for words to translate the important terms and phrases of the Gospel; these were not only at hand, but so far stereotyped by extensive use, that any radical changes, had I wished to make them, could hardly have been justifiable.[28]

This translation had already 'been beaten out during many years by the best brains among the Waganda themselves, with the help of Mackay, Ashe, Gordon, Walker and the others who have been here.'[29]

With the Swahili Bible translation already available a necessary tool was provided for a general popular process of linguistic debate in order to find the exact word and the right phrase: 'for years they were thus occupied in hammering out a version on a native anvil'. In its turn, this gave rise to a strong tradition of Bible study and expository preaching. 'There is a kind of oral tradition of interpretation of parables, miracles, etc.'[30] A ripe fruit of this process was a first commentary in Luganda of St Matthew's Gospel by the remarkable Ham Mukasa, 1900, and a surprisingly rich flora of Bible textbooks in Luganda, an explosion of Bible study published in little Luganda volumes, in a few years, but which was not to be repeated later to the same extent.

The result of Pilkington's work was, for half a century, recognized as of incomparable standard. With a rapidly increasing public of 'readers', these teams pressed on with their combined literacy and Bible campaign: 'What we want are books, not thousands, but millions of books.'[31]

In these circumstances, Pilkington, the quintessential Evangelical, was not only a Bible translator, but also a revivalist with a compelling message of 'Salvation' and 'the indwelling of the Spirit'. A product of Keswick piety, he rebelled against what he soon discerned as a tendency to formalism in the Church, a stress on 'outward prosperity' more than 'inward and spiritual grace'. The Pilkington movement introduced increasing numbers of Christians to the need for growth of the inner life, following baptism. 'Oh, for another Pentecost here' – was his concern.[32]

The exciting beginnings of this movement came in 1893. For a certain time Pilkington withdrew in isolation to Kome Island in the Sese archipelago. 'On December 7th, Pilkington returned to Mengo from Kome, and everyone noticed the wonderful change in him. His very face told of the reality of the change.' He claimed that he had 'received by faith the Baptism of the Holy Spirit'.[33]

The African Church saw this 'withdrawal-and-return' as a dramatic presentation of a mysterious spiritual experience, carrying a more compelling message than the usual exercises in the catechism class. (It is tempting to draw a parallel to a contemporary experience, the Mahdi's retreat in 1881 to an island in the Nile: his return from this concentrated retreat was welcomed by the masses as a signal to the Mahdist storm.) The effect was soon felt in the local church. There was public confession of sin by people in high places and low, chiefs and catechists confessing in front of the king and his pages. A rapid building of meeting-houses called 'synagogues' followed, an increase in 1894 alone from twenty to 200. Every Sunday about 20,000 people assembled for worship.[34]

When Buganda's catechists and teachers scattered in the 1890s to neighbouring and far-off places, their message was irradiated by this revival urge. This had long-range influence over time. Forty years later, when the 'Balokole' movement began in Rwanda and Buganda, there was an awareness of its historical roots in the Pilkington Revival. Even his African nickname, 'Bulokozi' (Salvation), connects the Balokole movement with him.

The Establishment

After the terror and chaos of the 1880s, the new decade of the 1890s ushered in the 'Christian era' in Uganda. This was closely tied to the imperial takeover in 1893, providing a new political framework. The Ganda regime at regional and local levels, identical with the new 'Christian parties', flourished under these changed conditions. It established itself as a Christian ruling class, Catholic in Buddu country and Anglican at the centre, Kampala, and the rest of the country. The speed with which this revolutionary transition took place is noteworthy. Readjustments and modifications in Ganda politics from 1893–1914 were manipulated by this powerful Christian class in negotiations with the British administration. An analysis of family connections in this class of modern Buganda takes us back to the dynamic Ankole refugee groups of 1888–89.

Bishop Tucker began ordaining deacons and priests from 1893. In 1901 Anglican clergy already numbered twenty-eight, with all but two having participated at Ankole. Professor D. A. Low has explained that the leading chiefs and the Anglican clergy together formed a homogeneous elite unit of forty-eight. These were to determine Buganda politics on both church and state during the following decades.

Sir Harry Johnston, as 'Special Commissioner', worked out the first draft of what came to be known as the Uganda Agreement of 1900. This was a settlement of political power and land rights between the British government and the chiefs. Through this Agreement, the government ministers and twenty leading chiefs were appointed and given substantial areas of land through the *mailo* system, which was based on the awarding of freehold land, and calculated in square miles. Of these men, only four had not been in Ankole. In fact, by 1900 the important qualification for *ssaza* chieftainship was an active membership in the refugee group a decade earlier.

Initially it seemed to the Buganda chiefs that the imperial power was about to 'eat' their land, and to deprive the *kabaka* of his power and governance. The final settlement, however, made them much more amenable to its acceptance, particularly after fundamental changes in the commissioner's plan through the influence of the two English bishops: the Anglican Tucker and Hanlon of the Catholic 'Mill Hill' mission. On their advice, the size of the substantial land grants set aside for the chiefs was dependent on the status of the individual chief concerned. The agreement was far from being a democratic solution. The chiefs' powers were assured and increased, while the ordinary peasants, the *bakopi*, were relegated to the status of tenants. This meant that a majority of the people would be subjected to an elaborate system of forced labour requirements for certain months of the year. The missions managed to get exemption from *kasanavu* (an obligation of two months' forced labour for state purposes) for all clergy, teachers and church-keepers. Any tenant who did one month's labour for the Church, would thereby be excused from the state labour call. This was a concession for the missions, but at the same time an added burden for local *bakopi*. A task for local research, which cannot be attempted here, would be to discover and interpret what these obligations meant over time for the *bakopi* and their allegiance to the Church.

The *kabaka* lost most by the agreement. As a private person he was of course well provided for, but his absolute power over land and people came to an end. After *Kabaka* Mwanga's exile in 1897, the infant *Kabaka* Daudi Chwa was installed in 1899. Baptized in 1898, he was the first *kabaka* to be a member of the Anglican Church. As he grew up he had to realize that the agreement 'closed the age of absolute monarchy and established the ascendancy of the barons'.[35]

The missions received their share of this agreement bounty. Of the 20,000 square miles in the country, about 100 were made available for them, 'in trust for the native churches'. CMS received fifty-two square miles, the White Fathers thirty-five, and the Mill Hill Fathers nineteen. Bishop Tucker explained that most of the mission lands consisted of lots of 'two to three acres here and there, or four there, just enough to maintain a teacher.' Even so, the three missions gained greatly by this arrangement. In 1914, an additional fifteen square miles were added to the Anglican mission.

Throughout these negotiations, the chiefs kept in constant contact with the bishops. In understanding the role of the Buganda churches with the people, one must consider the powerful effect of the bishops' pleading during these decisive weeks on behalf of Buganda rights. Their support was remembered fifty years later, in another famous political crisis – the deportation of the *kabaka* in 1953. It was taken for granted then that the bishops had also played a political part in that decision, albeit behind the scenes, in what transpired to be a traumatic blow to the nation. The painful realization only slowly dawned that within the colonial framework, the days of the politically powerful bishops had long ago passed. The Uganda Agreement had provided a chance which was not to recur.

The Church Constitution

In the negotiations for the 'Uganda Agreement 1900', a common concern for Bishop Tucker and Archdeacon Walker had been to emphasize the role of the African Church, as distinct from the Mission, in order to have the Church recognized as a distinct body with its own rights and responsibilities. The British Special Commissioner had no sympathy for this argument and ruled out any official recognition of the Church. This was one factor which moved Bishop Tucker to make a first draft of a Church Constitution. For nearly ten years afterwards the bishop and the Western missionaries argued over this proposed constitution.

The realization of the unique character and quality of the Uganda Church had inspired Tucker. As early as 1884, as already pointed out, twelve newly baptized young men were chosen to form the first Anglican *Lukiiko*, or Church Council. The constitution attempted to legalize this council and make it representative for the whole Church. Tucker had ordained the first Buganda clergy in 1893. By 1900, they numbered twenty-one, working with 900 African catechists. They were supported, in more senses than one, both at the regional and the local level by a host of solidly Christian chiefs and sub-chiefs. Here was indeed a remarkable body which in a few years had grown from an endangered and martyred nucleus of witnesses into a nation-embracing institution.

It is an indication of the social climate at the time that the African Church was not invited to the negotiations over the new Church Constitution. When, at the end of 1907, they were at last called on to give their view, they accepted the proposal unanimously. Except for this last-minute gesture, there were no official means by which the Africans could make their own contribution to a document which, basically, was *their* concern.

The debate over the constitution took the best part of a decade. Bishop Tucker's conception was closely related to Henry Venn's vision of the 'Three Selves'. He felt that the mission as an institution was no longer needed, although individual missionaries would be needed in their respective fields of competence, within the Church, but not outside.

The majority of the missionaries, led by Archdeacon Walker, opposed this plan. One should note their concerns. The land question loomed large. With missionaries as full members of the Church they would, it was argued, be co-owners of church land which could easily lead to suspicions from the Ganda population. Secondly, with Western missionaries as full and responsible members of the Church there would be a tendency always to look to the foreigners for decision-making: 'I fear it would prevent the development of independence.'[36] The missionaries should form their own committee outside the African Church and be responsible to the CMS in London. Some labelled the Africans still only 'children' as far as administration and ecclesiastical experience were concerned. This attitude places the debate in the general framework of the period. It was not made more acceptable when one of the leading African clergymen, in an effort to live up to the expectations of the foreigners, agreed that 'the whole position of the Uganda Church at present is that of a child: in age, education, understanding, training and self-support.'[37]

To this was added the usual prejudices known from every other corner of the continent: the African Church had 'not yet' attained 'ripeness'; the education of its leaders was inferior, and one could therefore not expect European workers to be subject to Africans. There were arguments in the debate which must be classified as 'racial' and Bishop Tucker said so! We find the documents later modifying this term to 'colonialist' or 'paternalistic-evolutionary'. Obviously, these were verbal efforts in coming to terms with an unfortunate phase in the Church's development. Financial developments somewhat later were to make the mission realize that its capacity *vis-à-vis* the state was reduced, especially in the educational field. What had once been co-operation was followed by dependence. 'The "Christian revolution" in Uganda was followed by a colonial "counter-revolution".'[38]

The Catholics at Buddu

In the 1880s the Catholics had lost the political initiative. Residing in the district of Buddu, they felt excluded and side-tracked from Kampala. But no matter, they determined to build a kingdom of their own within the boundaries of Buddu, a Catholic kingdom in the heart of Africa. This was their resolve, and this was what they accomplished. Buddu was to grow to become one of the great Catholic areas in Africa. When the first African Catholic bishop in modern times was consecrated in 1939, it was from and for Buddu that he was chosen. Seen in the wider interlacustrine perspective, with its characteristic emphasis on the role of kings and chiefs, the Buddu pattern of a Catholic kingdom seems particularly interesting. Lavigerie himself could hardly have wished for a more literal fulfilment of his dreams.

By the last decade of the nineteenth century there were some 30,000 Ganda Catholics. About two-thirds of these had made the exodus to Buddu. Bishop Jean-Joseph Hirth issued a solemn watchword, encouraging his people to make Buddu a Catholic country before the end of 1892. The missionary in charge of this challenging enterprise was Fr Streicher, later, in 1897, to become the Catholic Bishop of Uganda. A rapidly growing army of catechists helped in the work, the most devoted among them being the Catholic chiefs. With great determination they threw themselves into the task of building the church in Buddu, the blueprint for the construction of which they already possessed, for these chiefs had also been royal pages at Mengo. Thus they saw to it that the mission stations of Villa Maria, Bikira (the Virgin), and others, were to be imitations of the royal capital at Mengo. These became new *twekobas*, royal palaces in a higher key.

An unprecedented burst of evangelistic activity was unleashed. The whole of Buddu seemed like an enormous catechetical centre. Open air classes were held morning and afternoon, alternating with building periods, when catechumens had to carry a prescribed number of bricks per day. Some postulants and catechumens faced a daily six-hour walk to the centre, in hot sun or drenching rain. As they were inevitably late for morning classes, separate instruction was arranged for them. Those catechumens who were also chiefs had special houses built for them. By 1896 no less than 300 such chiefs' houses had been erected at Villa Maria and 200 at Bikira. Other stations had to be content with a trifling fifty each.

The rewards for this activity were plain for all to see. Medals were handed out to the catechumens and then a rosary and another medal when between fifty and 100 bricks had been carried to the building site. Bishop Streicher thought that he had brought a sufficient supply of medals, more than 1,000. In a month these had all been distributed and more were needed.

The amulets of old had to go, for they were of Satan. The medal had another dignity and power altogether. It also helped against headache and fever. In the morning the Catholic husband would open the door of his house and swing medal or rosary in all four directions, praying to the Virgin for blessings over the house, family and fields and for protection against all evil powers. Here were already the beginnings of a widely embracing 'folk'-Catholicism, integrated with patterns of the recent past. The crucifix was an even stronger symbol and of course the local chiefs wore big ones, as large as those of priests. With their recollection of reverential behaviour at the Mengo court, the chiefs would prostrate themselves before the tabernacle as once they had done before the *kabaka*, and they would do so in the middle of the Latin Creed, at *et homo factus est*. If this seemed ritualistic to some visitors, the emphasis on literacy, which had been rather neglected in the first years, helped to balance the impression. Streicher made the ability to read a precondition for baptism.

It has been noted that Cardinal Lavigerie insisted on winning Central Africa through its kings and chief, and pointed to what was felt to be a theologically respectable method. As postulants, these chiefs were already eased over the threshold into the Church. Nobody took the Cardinal's exhortation to heart as definitely as Bishop Hirth, according to his *Directory for the Catechumenate in Northern Nyanza*.[39] Published in French in 1909, this document represents the bishop's policy and experience from the three important areas where he served as a bishop: Bukoba, Uganda and Rwanda. It has, thus, the widest possible relevance for Catholicism in the whole interlacustrine region.

He emphasizes the missionary's duty to win the chiefs: 'never to make them hostile, never to accept but with great prudence bad reports about them from our own people.' They constituted a category of their own as postulants and if they seemed to have approached the Church for 'natural motives', why, God can use all motives in the natural order. When sufficiently numerous, the chiefs should be given special teaching on Sundays about the great verities of the Christian faith: the existence of God, the Bible's teaching on Creation and the Fall of Man and the Promise of the Saviour. They should be taught 'Our Father', and eventually also morning and evening prayers, and the importance of angels. All this education should aim to evoke a desire for baptism, at least in the hour of death, if not before.[40]

Soon however, higher education was introduced. The first Minor Seminary was founded in 1893 and a Major Seminary followed. The first Ugandan priests were ordained in 1913. The first women missionaries, sent from Algiers, arrived in 1899, and the African Daughters of Mary, *Bannabikira*, began in 1903 with a noviciate of twelve novices and numerous 'aspirants'. The foundations of the Church were laid.

OTHER KINGDOMS OF UGANDA

Bunyoro

To the north-west, Bunyoro had always competed with and opposed Buganda. Their antagonism perpetuated a tense situation which has lasted until very recently. The social structure was characterized by the tripartite hierarchy of the Bito kings, the pastoral Hima aristocracy and the Iru commoners, who worked the land.

The king's exclusive authority was sustained by ancient myth and ritual. Mukama Kabalega was imprudent enough to challenge British interests and the 1890s were thick with military campaigns and attacks, ending with the capture of Kabalega and his deportation to the Seychelles in 1899. In the meantime, his son Kitehimbwa was brought to Buganda where he was educated by the CMS. In 1898 the British appointed him to succeed his father, although time was to show that the young king was never fully accepted by his people. The Revd A. B. Fisher and a Ganda evangelist, Tomasi Semfuma, were placed at the royal court to instruct the king and his family. 'Fisher had a greater understanding of and sympathy for the people of Bunyoro than any other CMS missionary.'[41] In 1899 Bishop Tucker visited Bunyoro and on this occasion the king and his sister were baptized. Educational facilities were extended and a notable school was built at Hoima by the CMS.

Nyoro aversion to Buganda and all its works was to hamper Protestant evangelism for quite some time. The CMS was seen as too closely related to Buganda power to be fully acceptable. The language question was to bring Bunyoro close to the neighbouring Toro. It was a help when the Revd A. B. Lloyd introduced Runyoro, rather than Luganda, as the language of instruction in Bunyoro schools. This change caused membership in the catechumen classes to double. But with Lloyd as with Fisher, the Nyoro still felt that they had Ganda preferences. A Nyoro rising in 1906–07 was directed not only against Ganda chiefs, but also against Ganda catechists and pro-Ganda missionaries.

In spite of their rivalry with Buganda, Nyoro chiefs realized in time that they would have to embrace the 'religion of the king'. Of fifty-eight men appointed as chiefs in 1908, 'no less than fifty-two were Christian pupils of the senior [CMS] school at Hoima'.[42]

Lango

The Omukama of Bunyoro was also able to transmit this vision of joining the 'religion of the king' to his north-eastern neighbours, the Langi. They were a different kind of society, 'a stateless society', but with the arrival of the British administration they acquired chiefs in 1912, with Chief Odoro of Kungu as leading personality. There were also here close contacts between chief and catechist, 'to their mutural advantage'. The catechist lived at the *boma*, taught and worshiped at the *boma* and would beat the *boma* drum to call his faithful to worship.[43]

Toro

There are obvious parallels between Toro Church history and that of Bunyoro. There was a similar hierarchy of king, aristocracy and commoners, with the addition, in the Mboga deanery, of Pygmy groups. In the turmoil of succession quarrels within the royal family, young Daudi Kasagama had been brought by his mother to Buganda where, like Kitehimbwa of Bunyoro, he received a Christian education and strong Protestant and anti-Catholic convictions. Appointed King of Toro by Lugard, he furthered Anglican interests as much as he was able, especially when it came to his selection of local chiefs

In 1901 the CMS missionary Fisher travelled round Toro, marking out 165 church sites. The king himself was more pleased than the local owners of the lands, some of whom accused the imported Ganda catechists of deciding to 'eat up' their country. Being something of a modernizer, Kasagama was eager to propagate the value of the strange magic of the mission hospital. He thus allowed himself to be operated on under anaesthetic, 'died', then miraculously recovered.

At first Bishop Tucker was hesitant as to whether the CMS should begin work in Toro country. In the early 1890s, western Uganda was supposed to be Catholic territory. However in 1895 these temporary comity arrangements were partially annulled. The Mengo Church Council (Kampala) with its African majority decided to send catechists to Toro. Some of these had a tendency to concentrate on their own Baganda, strangers in Toro territory. The language of the Church was also a great issue in Toro, and Kasagama joined forces with his royal colleague and fellow Anglican, King Kitehimbwa, in Bunyoro to work for a Toro–Nyoro language. This was part of the attempt to curb the victorious forward march of the Luganda language.

There was often a personal union between chief and catechist. As chief minister for over thirty years to King Kasagama, Nasanieri Mugurusi was no less devoted in serving the interests of his Church. He often spoke of his own personal – and indeed corporate – experience of Anglican baptism. He and his fellow baptizands were lined up on one side of the Mpanga River and were instructed, in the name of the Father and the Son and the Holy Spirit, to pass through the river, to be joined on the other side by the Christians waiting to receive them.

Best known among Ganda preachers and priests in Toro was Apolo Kivebulaya (d. 1933), one of the outstanding Christian witnesses of his generation in the whole of Africa. In her book *African Saint: the Story of Apolo Kivebulaya*, Anne Luck has interpreted his life and witness in vivid and moving terms. His most notable service was among the Pygmies in Mboga, east of Toro and now part of Zaïre. In his youth, after some time as a Muslim, Apolo had become one of the 'Ankole refugees'. There he joined the Protestant group. 'It was then I began to pray from seeing my fellows pray. I learnt to pray before I could read.' As a young catechist he was first posted to Mboga. Through the great hazards and difficulties there, he was characteristically sustained not only by the Word, but also by visions:

> Jesus Christ appeared to me in a dream in the night when I was doubting if I could endure being bound and prodded with spears, and my house being burnt, being beaten every day and reviled and looked at with evil eyes ... When I was thinking about these things I saw Jesus Christ shining like the sun, and He said to me: 'Be of good cheer, I am with you.' I answered and said: 'Who is speaking to me?' He replied the second time saying: 'I am Jesus Christ. Preach to my people. Do not be afraid.' These were the things of my dream and they are quite true. Since that year until now when I preached to the people they turned quickly from their customs and repented.[44]

Decades later Christ again appeared to him,

> in the form of a man [who] stood besides me ... 'Who is speaking to me?' He said: 'I am That I Am; that is my name.' ... Then this man greeted me and I knew him. He was Yohana (John), and so I found an interpreter and I thanked Jesus.[45]

Ankole

In Ankole the Hima pastoral aristocracy comprised about 5 per cent of the population and, like their counterparts in Toro and Bunyoro, they were strongly attached to their mythological Chwezi origins. In 1888 Ankole, as already recounted, had given a temporary home to the prominent Christian refugees from Buganda, Catholics as well as Protestants, whose example exercised an early influence on king and people in the host country. In 1896 the young prince Kahaya became king, with Ganda assistance. Apolo Kagwa, the powerful Ganda prime minister, himself a former 'Ankole refugee', felt some concern for the Christianization of Ankole and sent two Ganda catechists to Kahaya's court. They arrived with the best of intentions, but were soon put out by a regrettable deficiency in Ankole culture. Sad to say, *matoke* (plantain) was not grown in Ankole, and every self-respecting Ganda would understand how bitter this experience must have been! Other Ganda catechists were more adaptable and found the king and prime minister eager students in the catechumens' class. In 1902 they were both baptized, and the king himself, in order to demonstrate his newly won freedom from tradition and old taboos, beat the royal drum – something which only a few years previously would have brought disaster upon the country. Even more surprising was that Kishokye, a royal diviner ranking as one of the king's wives, received catechists at her residence and on her deathbed said she was prepared to give up her diviner's equipment and become a Christian. Her successor became a Reader.

Women in a refugee situation were open to the new religion. Hana Kageya, of a Hima clan and widow of a senior chief in Toro, had fled to Ankole as a refugee. There she worked as a catechist among the secluded and veiled women of the Hima aristocracy. As if there were no limits to her acceptance of strange new things, she was the first person in Ankole to wear glasses.

Ankole society was divided and the Anglicans found that they reached mainly the Hima caste of the population. Of eighteen catechists in one particular sector, sixteen were Hima. Seven of these later became chiefs, and seven went back to their prestigious cattle herds.

The Catholics, on the other hand, turned to the Iru majority. Their work was concentrated in the western part of the country, in Bunyaruguru. The Ganda catechist Yohana Kitanga was the best known of the local leaders of the Catholic Church. He also managed the problematic contacts with the Anglicans with understanding and generosity.

Busoga

Busoga lived in Buganda's shadow, and as Buganda's back door to the East, it was barred to foreigners, who might only enter, if at all, over the Lake from the south. Buganda institutions tended to be dominating models. They were certainly copied, yet with a clandestine or open criticism. This Buganda influence helped to initiate a move towards modernization, accentuated by a new economic factor, cotton. This was, characteristically, a mission-inspired initiative. The 'Uganda Company', formed by wealthy supporters of the CMS in 1904, distributed cotton seed to local chiefs, and in the first year fifty-four bales (400 pounds each) were produced. By 1938 the output had reached 400,000 bales. Cotton brought wealth to a fortunate group of the population, while most of the commoners failed to profit from it.

Busoga did not have a Kabaka of its own and was ruled instead by eight county chiefs. Only from 1906, under colonial administration, did its central council get a permanent President. He became 'the uniting father of the people', and inspired a growing Busoga consciousness. This was a reaction triggered mainly by the combined government/mission policy of sending educated Baganda to run state and church in Busoga.

The British administration and the two missions – the CMS and the Mill Hill Fathers – were preoccupied with what seemed to them a Muslim threat to Busoga. This supposed danger inspired, as a counter-move, co-operation between mission and government. A District Officer might induce a few Muslim chiefs to abandon their faith and join the Church. Candidates for chieftainship took the hint: it was understood that in order to become a chief and to retain the job, one should be an Anglican, like the *kabaka* in Kampala and the king in London. No one could fail to realize the emphasis when, from 1907, a generation of young men were sent to the Anglican Mengo and Budo schools in Buganda, eventually to return with insights and ideals formed at those centres.

In 1907 a Muganda was placed as President of the Chief's Council; six of the other eight principal chiefs were Anglican, the other two 'Traditional' and Muslim. Twasenga, the Muganda President, impressed upon his colleagues that they were not merely government officials but had responsibilities as Christian chiefs as well. They must see to it that subchiefs encouraged school attendance and that local churches were built and maintained. It was recognized in Busoga that Twasenga did more for CMS interests than any African priest. On his inspection tours in the district, he did not regard it as beneath his chiefly dignity to distribute freely to the children hundreds of copies of the *Mateka*, the CMS beginners' booklet.

To the Mill Hill Fathers this intense influence exerted by prestigious *ssaza* chiefs, most of them Protestants, was a challenge. The Fathers at first concentrated their efforts on any dissident subchiefs, in order to acquire a belated foothold. Some of the Catholic *gombolola* (district) chiefs, such as Benefansi Bakaleka, emerged as devoted church leaders, co-ordinately with their local administrative duties. It is a measure of the determination of the Mill Hill Mission that by 1920 they had nearly 1,100 catechists, compared with about half that number for the Anglicans.

While emphasizing the role of chiefs and subchiefs, one must add that only at first was this chiefly involvement a blessing to the Church. From the time of World War I, examples of immorality on the part of Buganda chiefs influenced their Busoga colleagues. This was resented by the local catechists. The 1920s brought strained relationships between chiefs and local church leaders, ordained and non-ordained. This friction was the result of a process of disengagement or of a Uganda version of increasing secularization, imperceptible at first, but soon growing in influence.

The Catholics in northern Uganda

A lack of balance may regrettably appear in the presentation of evangelization among the non-Baganda peoples in Uganda. Louise Pirouet's book, *Black Evangelists*, presents a rich panorama of the initial Anglican work among the Ankole, Toro, Nyoro and others, but there is, unfortunately, no comparable study of the Catholic movement from this particular point of view. However, a local study made in Alur, in the far north-west of Uganda (near Lake Albert), can be used to show that very similar questions and solutions arose within the Catholic sphere. Further work in the archives of the White Fathers in Rome may give substance to what has already been suggested by their archivist, Fr R. Lamey. We may hope that in the future local Catholic research will confirm that such steps were taken at the starting of many local groups throughout Uganda.

There was a combination of congregations related to both the White Fathers and the Verona Fathers, the latter coming from the Sudan into the frontier region between Sudan, Uganda and Zaïre. Two parallel occurrences are at the root of these developments. One, the local chief Okelo had, in a crisis of illness, been baptized *in extremis* by a Nyoro Christian from Hoima, and had recovered. Two, a certain Muganda, Alfred, went to Catholic Buddu to find work. He was baptized there and instructed in the teaching of catechumens. Returning to Alur, he gathered a number of catechumens, passing on all he had to give, including the recitation of 'Our Father' and the rosary.

Chief Okelo, having heard that Alfred had a class of catechumens, told him to request the Catholic bishop in Buddu to send a missionary to baptize these students at the lakeside. The point of this story is much the same as seen throughout this book: the role, particularly in the Catholic Church, of baptisms *in extremis*; the migrant labourer looking somewhere far away for work and finding also the faith; and local African initiative at the furthest shoot of the young plant.

THE LAKE MARGINS: THE EIGHT BUKOBA KINGDOMS

In this book the role of the waters for the evangelization of the continent is repeatedly stressed – the oceans, with the harbours, the rivers, the lakes. Buganda, north of Lake Victoria, dominated this part of the world, its communications, exchange of ideas and models of life. This was so also for the Church. The history of the Church – Catholic and Protestant – in the north-western corner of Tanzania cannot be understood without reference to Lake Victoria and the fleets of canoes plying the northern waters in the early times. (Nobody, in fact, would attempt such a distance on his own; it was always a corporate effort of several canoes.) This geographical position provided excellent opportunities for young Bukoba men eager for new ideas in trade and faith. Of the eight Bukoba kingdoms, it was naturally those in the north – neighbours of Buganda – which were most exposed to Buganda's influence. It was here, in Kiziba and Bugabo, that Bishop Hirth and his White Fathers arrived in 1892, together with a company of about fifty Ganda Christians. It was to Kiziba that the CMS decided to send Anglican evangelists.

Bukoba consisted of eight little kingdoms. Each local king was, by virtue of his office, a sacred personality and the upholder of traditional religion. He was the foremost *embandwa* or diviner and therefore felt the threat from the new religion more acutely than anyone else. King Mukotani of Bugabo expressed this most succinctly when faced with the coming of the first Catholic missionaries in the 1890s: 'If the Whites are allowed to teach everywhere, what will not this new religion do? Will not then even our rivers and forests "believe"? Will our *mishambwa* [sacred trees] escape and not be cut down like ordinary trees?' Rivers and lakes and *mishambwa* used for building Wamala's sacred huts in the banana groves, all these were alive. The king was responsible for protecting this spiritual ecological treasure-house of old, all of which was now threatened by the secularizing foreigners.

Reluctantly and after pressure from the German administration, the kings allowed the Catholic missionaries to build on their land. This permission came only as the result of complicated moves and counter-moves; by the kings, their chiefs and the *abairu* (commoners) on the one hand and by the French missionaries and their resolute body of Ganda catechists on the other, while uncomfortably in the background was the concern of German officialdom. Given such a tension-filled setting, even trivial incidents could spark explosions of displeasure. The king of Kiziba, named Bwuma, borrowed some money from the French Mission and a missionary had the audacity to remind him of his debt! There was an outburst of chiefly wrath and threats. This happened in February 1899, just as the world scene was lit up by a burning diplomatic incident, the Anglo-French quarrel over Fashoda in Sudan, from which the French prudently decided to withdraw. Faced with the chief's anger at being asked to make good his debt, the French missionary drew comfort from what the French foreign minister in Paris had done: 'It was necessary to give up this Fashoda as quickly as possible. That was the price we have to pay for his [the chief's] friendship. Now he is on our side!' The following year, when the king of Kiziba decided to expel all Catholic Baganda catechists from his realm, the German commissioner in Bukoba entered the quarrel. He sent two soldiers to the area and the thirty Ganda catechists returned happily to their villages. In 1901 the German authorities made yet another gesture of benevolence to the mission: the people of the six mission stations were exempted from Government labour requirements.

A Bukoba king was traditionally regarded as omnipotent. However in 1902 when the king of Bugabo expressed his interest in the new religion and his willingness 'to pray', giving his subjects permission to do likewise, he was promptly and effectively restrained by his councillors from such risky extravagance. If you do that, they said, we shall take the royal drum from you and hand it to one of your brothers. Medical help from the mission clinic, educational facilities and personal relationships all worked to attract many to the new religion, but the Christian movement of reading and worship still had to carry on underground. In 1902 Bukoba was visited by a new German administrative officer posted to the district. It was obvious that he took keen and positive interest in the mission's activities and the chiefs found it advisable to take the hint. The local sub-chiefs, more conservative perhaps, still occasionally threatened the clandestine Christian groups: 'What!' they would cry, 'the king does not pray, and yet *you* are praying. You obviously want the Whites to come and eat our country.'

However even powerful Kahigi, King of Kianja, found it better to modify his initial resistance. There was a give-and-take from both parties, king and mission. When a Catholic missionary asked for permission to build on a particular hill, the king refused, but the German administrator interfered, allotting to the mission the hill they had requested and at the same time compensating Kahigi with another piece of ground which, for some reason, the administration claimed as its property. When the mission started building on the Kagondo hill, the king supplied 150 workers. Soon the king asked the mission for assistance in putting up a brick house for his own use. As an expression of gratitude, he sent 1,000 rafters, while at the same time suggesting that he might need a carpenter or two. The mission capped it all by presenting him with twelve well-tailored and ironed robes for his many children.

Church history in Bukoba was also something more than this perhaps fortuitous struggle of power and adaptation. The year 1892 was the time of Catholic arrival in Bukoba. In the same year, the CMS in Buganda decided to send evangelists to their southern neighbours in Bukoba. This initiative was followed by occasional CMS visits later during the decade. The Protestant move, however, was not so much an expression of centralizing

Buganda outreach to the Bukoba periphery, as an exploratory concern of young Baziba to investigate the new religion in prestigious Buganda. In his fresh, first-rate doctoral thesis *From Catacomb to a Self-governing Church*, Wilson B. Niwagila has stressed the local African initiative.[46]

Young Ziba traders, carrying bark-cloth and skins to Buganda, brought back reports of their first contacts with Protestantism. The Bukoba church historian, Dr Wilson Niwagile, has found the remarkable number of five early Bukoba trade expeditions to Buganda, resulting in decisive personal contacts with the Anglican Church in the north. Andrea Kadjerero and Isaiah Kibira were among these young traders who became 'readers' in the foreign country. In Buganda, Andrea was adopted by a well-to-do Ganda farmer and acquired his Ganda family name, Kadjerero. The young generation in Ruzinga Kigarama were attracted by the Ganda example: hunger for education and for progressive ideas. In Buganda they discovered how to build roads and bridges and square stone houses. There they learned the 'three R's' and the use of bandages and pills. Coming back to Kiziba, the first groups of Protestant returnees formed cells of readers. They had to tread warily. The first generation Catholics had to carry on as an underground movement. This applied even more so to the Protestants, opposed by the traditionalists and disliked by the Catholics. A water-level cave at Lake Victoria became a place of refuge for the group around Isaiah Kibira, thus repeating an experience which had been the lot of Christian groups in the south of the continent a generation earlier. Because of his medical dexterity, Kadjerero became known as 'the Doctor'. He managed to demonstrate his versatility in establishing useful friendships not only with his own ruler of Kiziba, but also with the mighty ruler of Kianja, further south. A Protestant group was gathered in the emerging town of Bukoba.

It was here that Pastor Ernst Johanssen of the German Bethel mission arrived in 1907. His first approach to the German administrator for permission to register a Protestant organization was refused on the grounds that one mission was enough for a district the size of Bukoba. However the two Germans – administrator and missionary – met later in Rwanda. This time Johanssen was more successful. He explained that Protestantism in Bukoba was not so much a case of 'starting a mission' as building on foundations already laid by an active African community, eager to have their own pastor. An ordained German missionary was placed at Bukoba in 1910. The CMS in Uganda could now assist by sending Ganda catechists.

RWANDA AND BURUNDI

The Catholics

At both the social and religious levels there were striking similarities between conditions in Rwanda and the Uganda kingdoms of Nyoro, Ankole and to some extent in Buganda. It was tempting, therefore, for the missionaries to apply in Rwanda such strategies as had been successfully developed in Uganda. It soon became apparent, however, that there existed differences, particularly in the political relationships between the sharply divided social strata of the people. Apart from small-scale trade via Bukoba on Lake Victoria, Rwanda had remained comparatively isolated. Such changes as took place in its society toward the end of the century were caused not by innovations from the outside, but rather by ever-recurrent readjustments among the three social groups: royalty, nobility and commoners.

It was well into the 1890s before the king himself had his first contact with Europeans. On this occasion he was particularly impressed by the strange power of literacy, their miraculous means of communication by signs on a piece of paper. Shortly afterwards, in 1897, German forces occupied the country. Three years later, in 1900, Bishop Hirth (having been replaced in Uganda by Bishop Streicher in 1894) and his White Fathers arrived together with a large troop of Ganda catechists, self-assured crusaders 'like a small army on the move'.[47] Hirth, the missionaries and their Ganda catechists managed, through contacts with authorities at different levels, to obtain land for their mission stations.

From the very beginning an agonizing problem was the decidedly negative attitude of the Tutsi. Tutsi chiefs found themselves deprived of their land by mere foreigners. The foreigners were indeed 'eating the land' and Tutsi reacted by refusing to send their children to the schools. Nor was this only a passing whim. Tutsi opposition to Christian missions was to last until after the First World War. The oppressed Hutu responded readily, finding their way to the catechetical centres. Traditionally they had been part of a social system of clientship to their Tutsi masters. Now the mission provided them with an opportunity to break out of this structure. The irony of it was that to a large extent the dependency of the previous generation was now transferred to another master, the White missionary, who could provide protection from political and economic aggression.

The medal was a symbol of this protective function of the mission, and marked the bearer as having taken the first decisive step towards the baptismal font and also into a possibly revolutionary social structure. After only two years, more than 4,500 medals had been distributed. Two years later in 1904, there were 1,500 postulants and more than 200 baptized. As has been observed, Ganda patterns could not always be applied to the Rwanda situation, but on one point at least, these patterns were applied with real success. No sooner were these Hutu baptized than they became instructors of new postulants and catechumens, teaching the prayers and the catechism. The local catechists were the real heroes of the situation, providing the necessary communication between the mission and the villagers. However Bishop Hirth, aiming at perfection from the start, insisted that it was not so much catechists that the Church needed. No less than seventy-seven Rwandans were sent to the theological seminary at Rubya, near Bukoba. But the road to African priesthood was even longer than the route to Rubya. Of the seventy-seven, only three were finally ordained as priests.

The Hutu Church grew rapidly. In 1910 there were seven Catholic mission stations and some 4,500 baptized Christians. Four years later the baptized membership had risen to 13,000! As the Tutsi masters were still holding out, these 13,000 were indeed 'a Hutu Church in a Tutsi State'.[48] However, a few missionaries, in spite of this Hutu preponderance, insisted that Rwanda must be won through the conversion of the Tutsi. They were no doubt aware of Cardinal Lavigerie's precepts. Until the end of the First World War they found little sympathy for their view and received only minimal support from their potential Tutsi friends. But they bided their time: it would soon be their turn.

The Protestants

The German Protestant involvement in Rwanda did not outlast World War I; it remained a temporary effort. Small as it was, it had a quality of its own, because of the personality of its leader, Ernst Johanssen of the Lutheran Bethel (Bielefeld) Mission, whom we met in Bukoba. The Tutsi also did their best to show their contempt for this missionary and his message. Even so, Johanssen was convinced that 'if this tribe [the Tutsi] were won for Christianity, the whole country would be open to the Gospel.' Through his linguistic ability and ethnological insight, he established good contacts in the country. Particularly remarkable was his personal relationship with Mwami Msinga himself.[49]

Johanssen was a German in a German colony who had won the sympathy and friendship of the German Resident, Dr Kandt. He used this advantage in his talks with the king, explaining to him: 'We are Germans and obey our Kaiser who, while not subordinate to any man, does follow the one Lord, whose name is Jesus Christ.' This was much the same kind of approach which missionaries in other colonies applied, although referring, of course, to Queen Empress Victoria or King Leopold. For his visits to the king, Johanssen brought Bible pictures which he explained in his rapidly improving Rwanda, peppered with acquired Rwanda proverbs. He alternated the pictures with models of Western technology, a plough, a steam engine, a windmill and with pictures of steamers and of the airborne Zeppelin. The king wanted to know how it could possibly lift into the air, how far it could fly and whether it was not troubled by showers of rain. These pedagogical efforts eventually emboldened the missionary to ask for permission to build a rest-house at the court. When this request was granted, Johanssen brought catechumens from his Kirinda station to put up a simple building. With some justification and more self-irony, he now referred to himself as 'Chaplain to the King'.

The Protestant group remained limited in size, but had an interesting social composition. Just as Hirth had brought Ganda catechists, so Johanssen brought Shambala helpers from near the coast, where his Bethel mission had been at work since 1891. They served as teachers of the catechumens, as interpreters and in other ways. The first Protestant Hutu congregation at Kirinda was, in fact, a group of boys and girls, about ten to sixteen years of age. They did not form a Christian village but lived on the farms of their parents. Initially two boys and two girls formed the nucleus, but soon their brothers and sisters and other relatives and friends from the neighbourhood were added. The two Shambala families created a home atmosphere for the growing congregation. At Church festivals – Christmas, Easter, Pentecost – the group might expand to twenty or thirty people. Thorough catechetical training was provided, and in August 1911 the baptism of the first class of seven took place. On the same day, as a result of the attractive sacrament of Baptism, a new group of twenty-six catechumens was enlisted.

USHIROMBO

The region south of Lake Victoria had approximately a quarter of a million people in 1890. It was divided into 150 small chiefdoms. The slave route Tabora–Karagwe–Buganda passed through the area. On this route, Ushirombo, because of its trade in ivory and slaves, was the most commercially prosperous of the Sumbwa chiefdoms. In 1890, Ushirombo found itself in the hazardous position characteristic of all little Sumbwa kingdoms at this time: periodically they were harassed by incursions of Ngoni offshoots and fearful *rugaruga* (ruffians). King Ndega had long been troubled by attacks from these neighbours. Ushirombo and other Sumbwa traders visited Buganda, where 'they were unable to resist the general movement [of Christianization] and the majority went to pray'.

In February 1890 four White Fathers arrived: three priests and one lay brother. The missionaries' interest was directed primarily towards the king and the court. Their reports show similarities with the *kabaka*'s court in Kampala: for years the missionaries sat at the king's gate, eagerly snatching moments of contact with the ruler. However, unlike the court at Rubaga, the Ushirombo king had fewer powers of coercion – and he knew it. Lavigerie's admonition to convert the king was more scrupulously followed here than almost anywhere else. A struggle between amulet and medal was enjoined and was fought out at the court week after week. Soon four princes agreed to join the catechumens' class and, after promising to throw away their amulets, were allowed to wear the medal of Mary. In August 1893 the king himself suggested that he get a medal for praying, but as a special exception should be allowed to keep his traditional amulet. He found to his surprise that the missionaries were intransigent: the rule applied to all alike.

The catechumens' movement began to take on sizeable proportions. By December of that year, 400 were enrolled. Two months later, the king himself declared that he was now prepared 'to pray'. He informed his council accordingly and instructed his town crier to proceed through the village, beating the drum, shouting, 'Tomorrow the king is going to pray. Everybody must do likewise – except for the women who, of course, must go to the fields.' Behind the royal scenes an intense power struggle ensued. The king's councillors, possibly encouraged by diviners, could not bring themselves to condone what to them seemed a reckless royal extravagance. But Ushirombo was, as always, ready to adjust to demands of reality and unavoidable facts. As one man, the councillors rose and shouted: 'Well then, we go over to your side, and to God's side. We too are going to pray.' On 6 February 1894, the king and his councillors arrived at the catechumens' shed where they knelt and recited 'Our Father' and 'Hail Mary'. Ndega, king of Ushirombo, was enlisted as a catechumen. On that first day he had two hours' instruction and was 'as attentive as a pious seminarist in a Theology class'.

The Ushirombo case is of interest, indicating some of the rough and ready but corporate methods of persuasion. A central but far from easily settled problem in this kind of history appears: it is all very well to register the transition of a king or chief to the new religion – but how far can one take for granted that commoners were prepared to follow the lead? Here, the decision of the royal councillors was perhaps as important as that of the king himself in preparing the way for a general acceptance of the new religion. The royal example had immediate repercussions. Ushirombo was the point of convergence for a number of neighbouring chiefs and subchiefs and their men, all anxious to follow Ndega's example. When they visited him, he was always ready to display his catechetical erudition. The missionaries felt encouraged by these visits and soon extended their evangelism to the neighbouring chiefs. Coming to King Mpembe of Ulangwa, the missionaries gave medals to the king and a number of his people. King Mugungo of Ugomba and his men also received medals after attending the catechumen class at Ushirombo: 'The king wants all to believe and he insists that his men discard their amulets and put on the medal.' This was obviously a conscientious monarch, for on the way home through the bush he inspected his men and when, to his dismay, he found that some of them did not wear the medal he thundered: 'What, *I* pray but you refuse to do so! You will have to pay me a fine of many lengths of cloth.'

In 1894 King Ndega fell seriously ill and was thought to be dying. He was therefore baptized *in extremis* – a great day in Ushirombo's history. Fortunately he recovered, and it was as a baptized Christian that he now exercised his administrative duties. His four sons in the catechumen class were also baptized. The acceptance of the sacrament did not always bring the expected commitment and Ndega would, on recurrence of illness, resort to the advice of his diviners. The missionaries had to be content with remonstrations against his 'hypocrisy'. The following year, King Ndega finally expired. He had been very weak and was therefore, according to local custom, strangled by his closest subjects. With the royal death the Shirombo population dispersed, it seemed, in all directions, and the mission found instead a response among marginal and foreign elements, mainly slaves captured in war. While on the coast there had been a development from mission-directed Christian villages of ex-slaves to open evangelization in traditional villages, in Ushirombo there now followed a reversal of this sequence. Young couples were placed in a Christian village with houses laid out in streets with mango trees. They became a resource group for the ambitious programme of the mission.

The kingly theme was modified at Ndala, southwest of Ushirombo, for there they had not only a queen, Ntabo, rather than a king, but also a ruling missionary, Fr Mueller, who adopted for himself the chiefly title of 'Mwangolo'. The queen appointed him ruler of part of her chiefdom. He entertained on a scale that matched his ambitions. When giving one of his memorable feasts, as many as ten cows were slaughtered, guns gave resounding salutes, flags fluttered and drums were beaten. Mueller had brought catechists from Ushirombo, but very soon the rapidly growing net of local bush schools produced their own teacher–catechists, eager to strengthen the widespread popular interest in education which was closely linked to the rites of the Church.

LAKE TANGANYIKA AND BAUDOINVILLE

The shores of Lake Tanganyika became related to great international politics. In connection with King Leopold's Brussels conference 1884–85 an 'International African Association' established two stations, Mpala and Karema, on the western and eastern sides respectively of the lake. Soon however the Association abandoned these stations, handing them over to the White Fathers who had just arrived on the scene. The social situation in the area, with slave trading, constant military raids and attacks of every kind, was one of utter chaos. This led Lavigerie to the most original and daring of his missionary measures and concepts, that of an armed protective auxiliary to accompany the regular missionaries. This was part of Lavigerie's grand strategic idea of a 'Christian kingdom' in Central Africa. He found his man for the purpose, a Captain Joubert. Lavigerie sent Joubert for the task of providing an armed protective auxiliary to be regarded as a king-substitute, with a special place and prestige in this group of missionaries, helping to uphold law and justice, thus constituting, alongside ordained priests and the lay Brothers, a third category of his own. Joubert, a solid Breton, had a unique preparation for his task, having served a decade in Pope Pius IX's regiment of Zouaves in Rome and there being promoted to Captain. At the Mpala centre on the lake shore, Captain Joubert established himself as an authority effectively supported by continuous encouragement from the Cardinal in Algiers. Joubert married an African women and had ten children with her.

On the local scene the missionaries devoted themselves to what their colleagues further west in Congo did, ransoming slaves and gathering them into Christian villages, while hundreds and thousands of children were looked after in orphanages, both categories becoming the beginnings of the catechumenate. Another new Lavigerie idea and initiative, the fruits of which could be seen in the Lake Tanganyika region, was that of Maltese-trained medical doctors, including Dr Adrian Attiman who worked at Karema on the west of the Lake. Trained with fifteen others at a medical school in Malta, Attiman arrived in Tanzania in 1889 and came to give a very long period of service indeed, active as a medical man and a catechist until his death in 1956.[50]

It was also from these originally foot-loose social groups that a future priest emerged. Stephen Kaoze, trained in theology by local missionaries for the stipulated extended term of seventeen years and ordained in 1917 as the first African Catholic priest in the Baudoinville diocese and in Belgian Congo. After research into his own ethnographic community, he became an ardent spokesman of Black consciousness. His many years of theological study had an alienating effect on him and in the end – he died in 1951 – he had serious psychological problems.

In order to understand the situation in the area one must remember the ravages of the climate. A number of bishops or vicars apostolic came out to Lake Tanganyika only to die in the very same year of their consecration. Their names tell the same story: Guillet, Coulbois, Charbonnier, Bridoux, Lechaptois, dying after a year or a few months in service. In 1892 Victor Roelens arrived in (Belgian) Upper Congo to become Vicar Apostolic in 1895. He saw Baudoinville, at first a village of some hundreds, grow from groups of orphanages and Christian villages to a central place for Church and State, an illustration of the 'location' of Christian mission stations leading to urbanization in Africa. From initial orphanages and Christian villages a city was to grow.

The method of mission work in this region was to establish schools where children could learn 'to know God and his law'.[51] Strong discipline was enforced. Absence from one class was punished by a morning's unpaid labour at the mission. 'Obstinate absence' resulted in twenty-four hours in prison.[52] Here the school was to give not only education – or whatever there was of it – but also protection: 'to keep the children under the surveillance of a teacher to watch over them better than their parents who do not care'. In 1895 the missions started a catechists' school.[53]

UFIPA

This long procession of kings, chiefs, priests and laymen 'between the Lakes' had to be joined by some women. The Fipa were the people to provide them. The aetiological myth of Fipa kingship presents not men as originators but three women, a mother and her two daughters. So it seemed natural that Christian women were to play a leading role at the beginning of the Fipa Christian story. Near the frontier of Ufipa was Karema, the colonial station built by King Leopold's International African Society on the eastern side of Lake Tanganyika. The corresponding station on the western side was Mpala. In 1886 this society decided to hand over the Karema station to the White Fathers, who promptly contacted King Kapufi of the Fipa. The ceremony of blood-brotherhood between the king and Bishop Charbonnier was a promising start. Kapufi explained to his guest the significance of the solemn rite: 'Now you are King of the Fipa just like me. My country is your country, my people is your people. You can settle with your missionaries wherever you wish. Officers of my court will announce to all subchiefs that they must receive you as myself.'

The Fipa Church grew from a combination of kings and slaves. A decisive step towards the Christianization of the people was taken when in 1899 Kilatu became king. From the outset, he saw to it that mission stations were founded and set an example for his small nation by joining a school class in order to acquire the 'three R's'. As a busy administrator he always carried a catechism on his journeys and studied this book, admonishing his sub-chiefs and village heads to do the same. As a supreme judge his concern was to introduce 'Christian European principles' in the administration of law. After a two-year postulate he was accepted into the catechumenate in a solemn rite, renouncing Satan and all his works and receiving the cross round his neck. Two years later Bishop Adolphe Lechaptois arrived at the court in time for 15 August, the Feast of the Assumption of Virgin Mary's Ascension. He had come to baptize the king, his queen, his two sisters and their husbands. A final week's preparation preceded the great day.

All chiefs and other leading men of the kingdom were present. Unda, abbess of the Black Sisters, once married to a Fipa king, was godmother. The German administration co-operated as one would expect from a colonial power, sending gunpowder for the salute – and the warriors of the king 'made it speak with a loud voice'. The bishop poured water over the heads and the queen cried with tears of joy. After baptism, the king as father of his people handed out gifts to the poor. Kilatu, now Wilhelm Adolf (named after the Kaiser and the Bishop) was already well on the way to being acclaimed the 'First Christian King in Tanganyika'. The effect of this baptism was obvious to all. The old queen mother asked for baptism following the example of her children; in her case the sacrament was administered *in extremis*. In 1910 the royal house of southern Fipa followed suit. The two royal houses, in the north and in the south, had for generations been adversaries, but on this occasion, King Kilatu served as godfather. The royal examples were followed by commoners of all descriptions, at first by the grandfathers and grandmothers, then by chiefs' sons through the School of Princes at Mwazye. 'Almost every village' now had its own mission school. After King Kilatu's death, his sister Johanna Nti, a devout Christian woman, ruled until 1932.

The broad mass of the population existed under very different conditions.

Slave dealers threatened the region on both east and west sides of Lake Tanganyika for decades and the White Fathers, particularly under Bishop Bridoux, had to concentrate much of their energy on the freeing of slaves and the building of a Christian community among them. 'The nascent African Catholic congregations were comprised almost entirely of ransomed slaves'.[54] This phase of the development came to an end however, when in 1893 the Belgian administration expelled the Afro–Arabs from eastern Congo.

THE BEMBA

The encounter between Central African kings and foreign missionaries takes us finally to Bembaland, in the north of present-day Zambia. No meeting between tribal and ecclesiastical authority was as dramatic as the one involving Chitimukulu Mambwa and Bishop Joseph Dupont, at the end of the 1890s. On the surface this was just another occasion when a missionary tried to win a foothold – or large tracts of land – for his society and its activities. Dupont aimed at Bembaland itself. From a temporary foothold he could begin to make his influence felt. He was seen as a great hunter and an effective healer and, as such, caught the king's imagination.

The Frenchman's entry into the royal presence was in splendid style: 'Clothed in white burnous and preceded by four pages bearing a carpet, he cut a much grander figure' than any of his ecclesiastical or administrative competitors.[55] His rapidly expanding influence was felt on another and deeper level, related to the legend of a refugee people. Some 200 years earlier the Bemba had left their original homeland of the Luba (now in southern Zaïre) and trekked as refugees towards the east, finally to settle in present-day Zambia. Their legend has it that as migrants looking for a refuge they had been led by a white magician, in Bemba, *luchele nyanga*, who some say was an unknown Portuguese from Angola. This legendary figure exercised a strong pull on the imagination of the people, not least among the leading clan, that of the chitimukulu, or paramount chief. Joseph Dupont, the French missionary, was just the kind of man who would relate to such a legend. By an extraordinary coincidence he had started his African career in Luba country, the original home of the Bemba – a mighty portent indeed! Larger than life, he was personable and dominating, boisterous, perhaps even arrogant, with a charismatic appeal. As a young seminarian, he had enlisted in the Franco-Prussian War of 1870 and became an expert shot. When embarking on a fortnight's hunting expedition, he would take along some 200 young Bemba and use evening campfires to tell the Gospel story.

At the king's enclosure, he proved to be a much-needed medical authority and, at his own encampment he cared for a refugee population of over 10,000.[56] Suddenly the Bemba nation faced a grave crisis. The old Paramount Chief Mwamba was dying and one could, after his demise, expect a cruel and sanguinary change of regime. However in a surprising climax, the dying chief appointed the bishop, his newly acquired friend, to be his successor, giving him 'the whole of his country with the rights of the soil, all his goods movable and immovable, real and personal'.[57] 'He is the son of Luchele Nyanga', the people shouted their acclamation at the apparent fulfilment of their legend. It is on this level of identification with the most sacred legend of the Bemba that the influence of the missionary must be understood. However much one may feel tempted to minimize the importance of this pronouncement of a dying man, it proved to have far-reaching effects on the role of the Catholic Church in Bembaland.

Dupont apparently took his elevation quite seriously and exercised his new powers for a period of three months. He increasingly felt the mounting irritation of the local British administrators who were competing for authority. Soon another member of the ruling clan was named paramount chief and Dupont could henceforth concentrate on his ecclesiastical task in its more restricted sense. The British South Africa Company granted him a large fief, giving him the right 'to exercise the authority of a native chief over an area of not more than ten miles surrounding and including Chilubula', (Dupont's residence).[58] The Company obviously believed that they had the power to dispense African land! This award of territory became the basis for a rapidly expanding Catholic work in the north.[59]

CONCLUSION

1. What did these missionaries set out to do? In this region – Buganda to Bemba – the White Fathers carried with them Cardinal Lavigerie's vision and tried to translate it into royal reality in Central Africa. Lavigerie held in mind the Church's history in the European Middle Ages, from Constantine onwards: Christian kings making their nations Christian. From his vantage point in Algiers he instructed his missionaries to follow this lofty example. Some Anglo-Catholic leaders on the east coast likewise aimed at winning 'nations', rather than individuals. Other missions in Africa felt that they had to remove their flock from the influence of the chief, gathering the converts into Christian villages. In this region, on 'the Kings' Way', the missionaries insisted that they had to go to the king and stay with the king. In the last decades of the

century the missions' relationship was not yet with Governors and District Commissioners but with African kings and chiefs, who had to be approached with circumspection in the hope of one day seeing the kings as baptized members to the Church.

2. To a degree that had, perhaps, no parallel elsewhere in Africa at the time, the Church in the interlacustrine region exhibited inter-Church communication and mutual social and religious influence which challenged and inspired the Churches. Buganda in the centre set the tone for many of these developments, too much in fact for some, as certain nations insisted that their local culture and language were being threatened by an overpowering neighbour. But this was only the converse of Buganda's actual influence as model for the other communities and Churches by its rapid acceptance of the Western religion, its values and mores.
3. On his visit in Buganda in 1875 H. M. Stanley issued an appeal to the Churches in Europe on behalf of Buganda and its King Mutesa; the Christian vision was spurred on also, it seemed, by a fear of the Muslims getting in there first. From the viewpoint of the Catholic missions – the White Fathers and the Mill Hill Fathers – the approach was seen in terms of Cardinal Lavigerie's vision of building a Christian kingdom in the centre of Africa. King Mutesa and his successor Mwanga did not live up to these high expectations. It was only when David Chwa, at the age of five, was enthroned as *kabaka* that the Anglican Church could nourish a hope of having a Christian king, and kings and chiefs becoming members of the church through baptism. However, in many cases such expectations were not fulfilled. As late as 1903, the Catholic Holy Ghost Fathers, who had hoped that an African Constantine would emerge, were regretting that 'they still had not seen a complete tribe led to the baptismal font by its chief, as had happened formerly in Europe'.[60]

II

CONTINENTAL PANORAMAS

THE COLONIAL STATE

The years 1920 to 1960 are characterized by the transition from a colonial period to that of the Independent African state. Functioning in this context the churches were conditioned, sometimes marked, by this political framework. A few brief paragraphs must here serve to indicate, from the point of view of the churches, this signature of the period.

The British

In the 1920s the British established a relationship between administration and population through the system of Indirect Rule, thus ensuring the continued role of the chief. This system had been conceived by Lord Lugard while working in northern Nigeria with emirs and other prominent chiefs. The British administration was to exert its influence through the chiefs, a system that was kept in force until the 1950s. A country which experienced a prominent application of this system was Tanzania. Both Catholics and Protestants had to adapt themselves to the practice of Indirect Rule while it could work out differently depending on whether the chief was Catholic or Protestant: in principle this denominational difference was not supposed to tell but in practice the priest/pastor or missionary found that a Catholic or Protestant chief would react differently to a request for a school and church site according to his denominational affiliation.

The church in nineteenth-century Africa was dominated by the catechist-teacher. The 1920s saw the gradual parting of the ways between the two: between the church-oriented catechist and the village school teacher with his higher training – often from church-inspired teacher training colleges – and with government-provided 'grants in aid'. In the long-run the teacher began to act as a local or regional centre of opposition, more particularly with regard to a certain patriarchal attitude on the part of the Western missionary. The beginning of the 1920s saw a change in the outlook on education through the ideas of the American-inspired visiting Phelps Stokes Commissions. In this context, the Ghananian educationalist, J. Kwegyir Aggrey for a few years exerted a far-reaching influence on the Protestant school system. Independent Africa was discovered in the school room. Kwame Nkrumah in Ghana, Obafemi Awolowo in Nigeria, Julius Nyerere in Tanzania were discovered as school boys by the missionary on tour in the district, who realized among those boys there was one who must be given a chance in life, by way of the secondary school.

Urbanization was part of the new, twentieth-century migration determined by the mines – the Rand, the Copper Mines in Zambia and Shaba (Zaïre) – and the migration to the plantations in East and West Africa. The result was to be seen in the case of the Rand: the men moved to the mines in their hundreds of thousands, whilst the women remained in the home village guarding the hearth and the family. Here the role of the women in the churches was of fundamental importance: they were the church-goers and they looked after the work of the church and often its worship. The period witnessed positive, though sometimes unsuccessful, attempts by the missions to care for the men in the mines.

Mission strategy presented a problem. Pastor Mabille, scion of a well-known Paris Mission family in Lesotho investigated the situation. In Lesotho every able-bodied man moved to the mines and the Rand. Left in Lesotho were the women, the children and the eleven mission stations; the latter were each looked after by eleven ordained missionaries, while only one ordained man was posted to the Rand. Attitudes are difficult to define but the attitude towards the city by that generation of missionaries can easily be demonstrated: it was one of a slight aversion while one felt at home on the secluded mission station in the countryside.

The French

The French political system in Africa – French West Africa and French Equatorial Africa – developed very differently from that of the British and the Belgians. The French had their chiefs widely diversified: Moorish emirates, Niger sultanates and Cameroon lamidates, and the French devoted at least as much consideration to these dignitaries as in the British case. Inevitably, however, external and internal forces began to exercise their influence. Robert Delavignette sums it up: 'Black Africa was colonized before it was understood, and it was emancipated as soon as Frenchmen thought they understood it.'[1]

World War I brought enormous changes to all of Africa; in the French case these were related to the fortunes and the fate of the Free French. The Brazzaville Conference of 1944, led by General De Gaulle and his co-worker Governor Felix Eboué – a West Indian – outlined the relationship between France and Africa. There was not a single African at the conference but all the same 'the Conference became the subject of a myth, [and] it was the Africans who created this myth'.[2]

TWO WORLD WARS

The First World War

Peace of a sort was what the imperialists thought they had brought to Africa. Certainly, there was forced labour of various kinds and degrees, with consequent protest movements, but any recalcitrant chief could be conveniently deposed, deported or hanged on the nearest miombo tree, thus creating Pax Belgica or Pax Britannica or Pax Germanica. Then there was August 1914 and all this came to an end.

Two World Wars and, in between, an international economic crisis changed the face and fate of the world, Africa included. These were wars between White men 'beyond the Seas', in Europe. Yet Africans in their hundreds of thousands were soon drawn into the universal conflict, as soldiers, carriers and labourers and, in the Second World War, also as drivers, orderlies and armed soldiers. They came upon bewildering situations. One does sympathize with that African patrol in the First World War in southern Cameroon which, facing a hostile patrol led by a German officer, sent back a request for a 'White man to come shoot white man: let black man shoot black man'.

The impact of each of the wars on African peoples was quite different. The First World War, as far as Africa was concerned, was fought on African soil, resulting in the rapid invasion of German colonies into the west and the south, while in the east, German forces under the command of Colonel von Lettow-Vorbeck kept part of the territory until the very last day of the war, 11 November 1918. For the African masses this meant above all requisition of large contingents of African porters, called 'carriers', uprooted from their villages and forced to subsist under terrible conditions. The fighting was uncomfortably close to the local communities, causing untold suffering, famine and deprivation.

In German-speaking East Africa (Tanzania) the fate of African members of English-speaking missions was an ordeal. One example must suffice. Martin Kayamba, born 1891 in Zanzibar, of the Bondei community, was a characteristic representative of the Anglican UMCA literate community. The war of 1914 made him a suspect person, was he not connected with English missionaries? Did he not speak English? He was probably a spy. So he was put into prison with criminals. He observed how Canon Petro Limo, the Anglican priest, and over 100 UMCA African teachers were brutally treated in prison. With his fellow prisoners he was constantly chained. 'It was the road of the Cross ... We were made to run all the way with stones on our heads'.[3] After the war, he represented his country in London, in 1931, over the matter of the proposed East African Federation.

In both Kenya and Tanzania British missionaries took the initiative in forming a 'mission carrier corps' of their own. In Kenya some 2,000 men were led by that redoubtable Scot, Dr Arthur of the Church of Scotland Mission, while in Tanzania another 2,000 men were placed under the command of the Bishop of Zanzibar, Frank Weston. There were casualties in these contingents too, but nothing like those suffered in the government-organized corps. With Bishop Weston it was said that 'the men obeyed every word of his without question ... because of the way the Lord Bishop treated them, as a father and his children'.[4] For his efforts the Bishop was awarded 'the local rank of Major (but never gazetted)'. One must underline the collective experience of these men, in an often dangerous situation.

The war also brought Africans as soldiers and workers to the European theatres of war. The most significant individual African warrior in this First World War was, probably, a young Lari-Congolese soldier, Andre Matswa. He was promoted to sergeant in the fields of Flanders and returning to his home country, he carried great ideas of his own.

Enforced migrations

A few figures convey an impression of the magnitude of the population transfers which came to Africa and to Africans in and through the two World Wars. With regard to the nineteenth century we have underlined the role of aggressive population movements across the continent bringing changes also to the religions, more particularly for the process of Christianization. The first half of the twentieth century saw another kind of momentous exodus through the two wars. In the First World War German East Africa (Tanzania) was one of the theatres of war and the British in other parts of the continent sent African troops there: Kenya and Uganda 22,000, Zaïre 8,400, Zambia 4,100, Malawi 3,180, South Africa 18,000, Sierra Leone 3,500. In total, to conquer German East Africa, Britain deployed over 50,000 African soldiers and used in excess of one million carriers and other labourers. From northern Nigeria 25,000 were sent to Cameroon and from South Africa 35,000 to Namibia. They were far from being mere onlookers. Jan Christian Smuts of South Africa gave those who fought and laboured for the Allies in German East Africa this testimonial: 'It was the *tenga-tenga* [military labour] who won the campaign'.

'Union sacrée' – after all

In 1904, the French Government declared the separation of Church and State. This affected the French colonial dependencies, including French West Africa. The missions, including those of the White Fathers, were harshly dealt with. Expressing themselves carefully, they referred to this as 'a policy of vexations rather than persecutions'. This order of the day marked the whole atmosphere as well as the provision of social services such as schools and hospitals.

Ten years later there was a world war to be fought through to the bitter end. French missionaries fought loyally for the cause of the *patrie*. At the end of 1916 the Vicar Apostolic of the French Sudan (Mali), Alexis Lemaitre, M.Afr., had to be invalided home to France. When his presence became known, the highest political authorities in the country, Georges Clemenceau, the Prime Minister, and Raymond Poincaré, the President of the Republic, sought his advice. They summoned the Bishop to appear before them. Clemenceau received him first asking: 'What is wrong with the Sudanese, tell me?' The Bishop answered: 'How much time can I take, five minutes or one hour?' Clemenceau replied: 'Take two years if you need it.' A few days later President Poincaré likewise called the Bishop. Both had an overwhelming problem: the recruitment of African soldiers. 'My dear Bishop, France needs all its children. You only can organize and direct this campaign, I ask you to take care of it.' The Bishop, a communicative man ever-prepared to establish contacts with friend and foe answered: 'Monsieur le Président de la République, I am your man.'[5]

In Burkina Faso, Bishop Thévenoud had earlier expressed doubts: 'It is better for the White Fathers not to be involved in this business for there is nothing less voluntary than the voluntariness of which one speaks.' Three years later he wrote: 'Our Christians could not stay aside, we consider it well to send them forward.' In co-operation with the newly appointed governor-general of French West Africa, Bishop Lemaître and his co-workers started their recruitment campaign. Many young catechumens joined up 'under the flag', but the population was restless. Amongst certain ethnic groups there were rebellions but these were warded off. The colonial administration admitted that Fr Dubernet's presence was the reason that these rebellions did not spread. Some twenty missionaries were mobilized for hospital service, a considerable percentage of the numbers at the time. Schools were opened and these mission schools could now be subsidized by government grants.[6]

Malagasy and Sotho soldiers in France

From Madagascar, a French colony, 45,000 'voluntary' Malagasy were sent to Europe. The Christians among them gave unforgettable testimonies of Christian dedication. Wherever they were sent, in military camps, on troop transports or in French churches and chapels, they congregated for prayer, hymn singing and Bible study. This hymn-singing became a characteristic mark of the Malagasy soldiers, from France to Hungary and Greece.

The conditions of war, which brought Africans away from the home village to distant parts of the globe, sometimes provided unexpected discoveries of the universal fellowship of the church. The Sotho contingent was sent in 1917 to the fields of Flanders and in October of that year the Paris Evangelical Mission managed to take a group of them for a few days' visit to Paris. They were guided by a young lieutenant with a famous name, Ernest Mabille, who took them to the Eiffel Tower and other sights. He even managed to bring them to see the biggest chief of all, Field Marshall Joffre, and to shake hands with him. Later there were to be periods of contacts between the 'South' and the 'North' in the world. Towards the end of the century there were to follow new ways of contact with African Christians coming as missionaries to the West, 'mission in return', as this was to be called. But in Paris, in October 1917, this was one of the very first occasions. The group also visited the Evangelical Mission and met some of the old missionaries and saw some of the Protestant chapels in the capital. Afterwards one of them, Edwin N'Tlade summed up his impressions: 'At first we did not find any of our co-religionists here in France, and the others [in the armies] mocked us. That reproach made us feeble, we who are but weak men. But now we stand before you.'[7]

With the take-over of German territories by the Allies in the years 1915–18 and the Treaty of Versailles in 1919, the mission map of Africa was drastically changed. For the time being German missions were eliminated from the map of the continent – except for South Africa. German missionaries were interned or repatriated and, as far as possible, replaced by missionaries of other nationalities: British, French, Belgian, American, Swiss and Swedish.[8]

An opportunity lost – and gained

In one of her valuable studies of the church in East Africa, Louise Pirouet wrote a paper in 1970 called 'The First World War – an opportunity missed by the missions'.[9] Missions would complain about the injury that the war brought to the Christian cause, but, she insists, the real injury was a lack of trust on the part of the patriarchal missionary who did not realize the opportunity for the churches' autonomy during and after the war. Bishop Weston of Zanzibar, who saw deeper than most, reminded his missionaries that 'the African and not we are the permanent leaders of the African church'. Too easily missionaries deprived themselves of a chance of understanding what the time signified to the African Church. On the other hand there were also African Churches which indeed, already in and after the first war were given an opportunity to respond. Significant was the extent to which local African pastors and layman shouldered the administrative and evangelistic burden, from Togo to Tanganyika. For the young Churches this appeared as something of a blessing in disguise.

Mussolini's war

On the eve of the Second World War, Africa watched its own ugly dress rehearsal of an impending second conflagration. Italy and the *Duce*, Mussolini, had never forgotten the defeat at Adowa in 1896 and sought revenge and an Empire. The Italian invasion proved to be a serious challenge and threat. The international role of the Vatican and Pope Pius XI, Mussolini's Lateran Treaty of 1929, establishing the Vatican City, had to be paid for. In its journal *Osservatore Romano* the Holy See tried to remain neutral in the Abyssinian conflict. Some of the Italian bishops on the other hand made embarrassing chauvinistic proclamations. The Pope himself was not helped by Archbishop Hinsley's supposedly apologetic statement on his behalf in London, 'What can the poor helpless old man in the Vatican do to prevent this or any other war?'

After nine months of slaughter the Ethiopian war came to an end in 1936 – for the time being. Archbishop Castellani was sent as Apostolic Visitor to Addis Ababa to find out about the spiritual needs of the population. He did so with a piece of home-made theology of his own saluting 'all the heroic soldiers of the Italian army which the world admires but at which heaven has no need to marvel since it is their ally'. Non-Italian Catholic missionaries were replaced by Italian priests. The French bishop Jarousseau, having served as a missionary for fifty years in Ethiopia, was expelled. The

Protestant missionaries were all expelled. The Coptic *abuna* Petros, who refused to submit publicly to the foreign army, was beheaded. The Italian military and ecclesiastical authorities even went so far as to attempt to detach the Church of Ethiopia from its relationship with the See of Alexandria, appointing Anba Abraham as *abuna*. This met with sharp opposition from the Ethiopian Orthodox Church which excommunicated Abraham and the archbishops and bishops appointed by him.

Thousands of young Ethiopian refugees meanwhile found their way south into Kenya, where they were gathered into English-speaking schools arranged by the Swedish lay missionary and teacher Anton Jönsson. When the Italian invasion came to an end in 1941, these educated Ethiopian men were given special preference in the service of the Emperor Haile Selassie, providing their country with an elite of Western-trained men, another illustration of the theme of Christian returnees, which has appeared in other parts of the continent.[10]

The Second World War

At Mbandaka, hidden in the Zaïre forests, it was not always easy to follow the drama on a distant world scene. When at long last the steamer *Theresita* docked at the Bokele outpost, the missionaries of the Sacred Heart with Father G. Hulstaert, the Africanist, came down to the boat calling out, 'Brother Captain, what is the news?' – 'Great news, the war is over.' – 'War? what war?', was the reply. Years back they had learned that Germany had attacked and invaded Poland. After that, no news had come through. This example is probably extreme but it gives an indication of the isolation of certain inland areas in those years, before the widespread use of the radio.[11]

The Second World War took African troops across the globe to distant lands in the West and in Asia: to France and Italy, to India, Burma and Singapore. The distance from the home village to the war of the Whites could sometimes make the significance of the fighting difficult to comprehend. One day in 1941, B.Sr. sat in a hut in Zululand with some tough old Zulu men. They asked me about the progress of the war, and I complied with the latest news. 'Why don't they forgive one another?' (*bathethelelane*), was their question. I tried to show that this was not *that kind* of war – a rapid skirmish with bow and arrow, followed by hearty reconciliation – but something more challenging, not least for Africa and every African.

More than any other country, South Africa experienced a tough African resistance to the war recruitment drive. Was this not a White man's war, which did not concern them. They had not forgotten some of the disasters in the First World War, with vivid memories of *SS Mendi* which went down in 1916, when 615 people lost their lives including a large contingent of South African Blacks.

But if the war brought Africans to distant countries in Europe and Asia it also took them across the map of Africa to the other side of the continent. From South Africa General Smuts sent White and Black troops against Rommel in the North African deserts. The South African racial pattern was carried along into the battle for freedom: Black troops were not allowed to carry firearms but only knobkerries (wooden war clubs). 'In the event of an emergency any European private shall have command of the Non-European personnel irrespective of rank.' From Sophiatown, Johannesburg, Dr A. B. Xuma pleaded: 'African boys are dying in defence of freedom, democracy, Christianity and human decency in South Africa ... South Africa must play the game with the Africans now.'[12]

The virulent changes of the war for Madagascar – Vichy, British, de Gaulle – meant adjustments on the home front, but through it all the Church carried on with its local work. West African troops came to Malagasy villages and Pastor Johanese Rakotovao taught baptism classes to these soldiers, some of whom were eventually baptized in Malagasy Churches. 'The Malagasy pastor did missionary service to foreigners in his own home – because of the war.'[13] A new vision of the universality of the Church could, in the midst of war, be glimpsed.

In the development of African Church history in the twentieth century – the surprisingly rapid growth in Christian community belonging and in educational attainment – came life at the war fronts. In the First World War there were only a few Christians among the Africans who served. In the Second World War 'roughly sixty per cent of the soldiers were nominally Christian'. And to this term 'nominally Christian' must be added the reflection that this kind of war brought challenges where any 'nominal Christianity' could be transformed into glorious Christian witness. 'Besides the missionaries who served as chaplains, a large number of African ministers also played their part in the organization of spiritual work among the troops wherever they went.'[14]

German missions

Once again German missions were particularly hit by the war. An indication of the decline for German Protestant missions is provided by comparing the number of German Protestant ordained pastors: 267 in 1939, but reduced to

120 by 1953. Financially German Protestant missions went through dismal years between the two wars, from a drastic, almost total slump in 1923 and the Depression, through to the anti-mission Hitler years which, from 1933, imposed severe limitations on the transfer of funds overseas to German missions and their staff. This missionary hardship led in 1934 to the creation of the so-called *Devisen* (foreign currency) emergency fund, through which German missions became dependent financially on charitable support from American, British and Scandinavian missionary societies. Then followed World War II and the second elimination of German missions but compared with the first war this second elimination process only affected British territories, as German missions during the 1920s had only been re-admitted to British dependencies. This time the non-Roman missions were much better prepared to meet a world crisis. The International Missionary Council in London and New York and the Lutheran World Federation, with the Augustana Lutheran Mission, was able to assist with personnel and financial help on a generous scale. What was even more significant this time was the fact that the Churches now had a staff of devoted African leaders, ordained and laymen, who could steer the Churches through the crisis and in so doing invigorate the autonomy and self-esteem of the Churches.

In such a peculiarly loaded situation as September 1939, an outstanding individual church leader might manage to secure safe-conduct for his fellow workers. This was the case with Peramiho in southern Tanzania, the German Benedictine centre and the largest in the country with some 100 German missionaries, ordained and lay, men and women. Peramiho also had some German-speaking Swiss, foremost among them the Abbot, Bishop Gallus Steiger, OSB, (in Tanzania since 1906, abbot in 1931, bishop in 1934, died 1966). Bishop Steiger, hard-headed and determined, travelled the hundreds of miles to the capital, Dar es Salaam at the beginning of September 1939, and insisted that Peramiho could take care of its German problem on their own, by placing each German under a local Swiss colleague, thus incidentally ensuring the peaceful development of the southern frontier region of the country. There and then this appeal was accepted *in toto* by the Dar es Salaam mandate administration.

Further west in southern Tanzania a comparable situation developed. The Catholic Prefecture Apostolic of Tukuyu had been confided to the German Province of the White Fathers. The German Prefect Apostolic was forced to resign and all German superiors of missionaries were replaced by other nationalities. Germans were otherwise allowed to remain. In Uganda the (Italian) Comboni missionaries were interned at Katigondo Seminary for the duration of the war and their work was confided to English-speaking White

Fathers.[15] The great majority of the 100 German Protestant missionaries in Tanzania could not, with one or two exceptions, accept the conditions of parole offered by government and were interned or repatriated, creating a dramatically changed situation for the Protestant churches.

On the other side of the continent, in Cameroon, the situation developed in a similar fashion. Some of the German Protestant missionaries were not above a suspicion of Nazi sympathies and all of them, except four Basel and three Baptist missionaries, were interned and taken to Jamaica for the duration of the war. The official instruction implied 'to intern all enemy missionaries except nuns'. In this case this meant that the Catholics 'lost only seven of its missionaries' and only two of their major mission stations were deprived of priests for the time being. In fact, 'the Catholics made great strides during the war'. Right at the beginning of the war, 'the Catholics dared the unthinkable by opening the first secondary school in the country'.[16]

Burma

Burma was far away, but the Burma front seemed insatiable. From all parts of the continent men were sent there. From Bachama, Mbula and Longuda, Nigerian men volunteered. The Christians among them found that they had a protective net of their own, through the contact with the home congregation. Pastor Mathiesen sent a monthly letter to all soldiers from Adamawa. At the front Mallam Habila Aleyideino was the contact man: he kept the men in touch with their folk at home, many of whom could neither read nor write. He visited the camps and brought greetings from the Church at home.[17] In a neighbouring camp some men were from Tanzania. At a particularly dangerous skirmish Amos Lyimo from Moshi, a trained telegraphist, found himself in the trench together with an Englishman, who told his African friend, 'You Amos can pray; you better pray now.'[18]

Preparing for the future

Both wars but more particularly the second, had a broadening effect on the outlook of the peoples of Africa. This applied particularly to the individual soldier or carrier in the armies who had been to Flanders or to Burma and who had, once and for all, exchanged the old village for new visions. The Burma perspective changed the view of things. Before the war the African soldier may have thought of himself as belonging to a clan or a tribe. The war made him a citizen of a country and a continent. The (British) Army

Educational Corps made him part of 'the biggest movement in mass education that Africa had ever seen', making the individual prepared for specialist skills such as those of medical orderly, educational corporal or sergeant, or one of the thousands of lorry drivers.[19]

However, this also concerned the great institutions of the continent, political, economic, social and religious. It quickened the pace of intergroup and international relations and raised sights to larger perspectives. Towards the end and immediately after the war a surprising number of young men – hardly any women yet, but their time was to come – found their way to the West, to Paris and Bordeaux, to London and Manchester and to New York and Harlem. In the 1920s some of them already had established contacts with the Pan-African leaders, with Marcus Garvey and W. E. B. Du Bois. Pan-African responses in the United States and in Britain were formed into important new ventures and organizations: the Council on African Affairs, founded in 1941 with Max Yergan as director, a Black American who had earlier been YMCA secretary in South Africa; the African Student Association founded in 1940 by Dr Karefa Smart of Sierra Leone, influential in those years in the World Christian Federation and for the beginnings of the World Council of Churches; and finally, the African Academy of Arts and Research from 1943 with the Revd Buyabuye Mdodana of South Africa as a member of the executive. These initiatives were all important not least for a young generation of West Africans including Robert Gardiner of Ghana. They were inspired by the Atlantic Charter of 1941, Roosevelt's and Churchill's combined creation, and saw this as an early promise of political freedom as an outcome of the struggle of the war. 'World War II had served to universalize the struggle of oppressed peoples against colonial domination'.[20]

To some extent this trend was represented by the Protestant West Central African Regional conference 'Abundant Life in Changing Africa', in Léopoldville 1946. The role of Emory Ross, the African counterpart of J. H. Oldham, interpreted 'the meaning of the conference', meeting in the middle of Africa immediately after the Second World War. It meant, he said,

> first of all a full awareness of change: the change *in* Africa and the change *for* Africa in the world. In Africa its people are rising, most of them peacefully, some of them belligerently, but nearly all of them rising. To this rising, Christian missions have contributed notably. The Gospel of Jesus Christ when accepted and applied leads and enables men to rise as does nothing else in the world. The broad Christian education which most missions in Africa have given has aided that rising enormously.[21]

TIME AND EXPECTATION IN THE CHURCH

Two closely intertwined concepts determined the conditions of the churches and their planning. These two factors always influenced developments, yet their role, positively and negatively, seemed greater during this period, 1920–60, than ever before or after and affected this African continent more than any other. They were Time and Expectation. 'We have time' was the assured proclamation of the Westerner. Van Bijlsen, one of the radicals of the period, in 1955 projected the future of what was then Belgian Congo. In 1985 that territory was to celebrate the centenary of Belgian rule. It was time in that far-off year, 1985, van Bijlsen suggested, to give the Congolese (soon to be referred to as Zaïreans) their independence. Almost as soon as this startling, and in Belgium highly unpopular, proposal came off the printing presses, Congo had become Zaïre and the revolution was on.

In the Churches the message about Time was largely that it was 'not yet'. Henry Venn's and Rufus Anderson's programme in the 1850s implied African self-government and eventual 'euthanasia' of the missions, but when the question of self-government was brought up in the councils and committees of the Churches, the answer was 'Not Yet'. Not that this view was exclusively a White view. It permeated the African synods as well, enfeebling and debilitating. In 1946, just after the Second World War, the Basel Mission field secretary suggested to the General Synod in Cameroon that the President of the Synod be an African. This was refuted by the majority of the Synod with the assertion that the Time for a transfer of this top position had not yet arrived. However, the Basel Mission persevered and in the General Synod of 1950, the Revd Peter Essoka was elected President. The point about this decision is that in both 1946 and 1950 the initiative for a transfer to African leadership came from the metropolis, in this case Basel. Throughout these decades there has been a tension between the Men in the Metropolis and the Men on the Spot. The former, impressed by Rufus Anderson's and Henry Venn's precepts about the self-governing church, could with the perspective of distance insist on Transfer Now; the latter, having spent a life time in the African field and thinking that they knew their Africans of yesteryear, were sure that a transfer could not happen until some other time.

Another example, this time from Zululand, should be mentioned. The young Swedish missionary at Ceza, Zululand in 1942 – in fact the present writer (B.Sr.) – informed his missionary colleagues that he had been asked to proceed to Tanzania to help out in a situation where in the war all the German Protestant missionaries had been interned. He suggested that he knew of an ideal replacement in the Revd Thomas Luthuli who, in addition to his other qualifications as a pastor, had the advantage of speaking the language, Zulu, as his mother tongue, not laboriously memorized as in the case of the foreign missionary. The reaction of the mission staff was discouraging: 'Was that African ready?' In the end the Revd Luthuli was appointed. Suffice it to say that the transfer to African leadership in this case proved to be highly invigorating, both for the local Zulu congregation and for the Zulu Lutheran Church as a whole.

Time, we say, was intertwined with Expectation and the idea of 'not yet' was another way of implying a lack of Expectation. This lack of expectation has been the most serious deficiency in the Western approach to Africa in this century, as well as in the White missions and their approach to the African church. Expectation is, of course, basically a theological and Biblical term, although nowadays it is most commonly used in economics.[22] The missionaries had built their institutions – schools, hospitals, farm centres and industry – all involving men and money. The Western Men on the Spot could not easily imagine that anybody else could manage these institutions. The administration of the property and the money might be jeopardized by some eccentric transfer to people not prepared for such a move. Certain crises challenged these attitudes. Two World Wars acted as effective pace-setters to the so-called Orphaned Missions, i.e. ex-German missions. Suddenly they were left without their Babas and Mamas, who were now safely interned elsewhere, and the presumed African successors had been given a somewhat limited theological education. Yet, in the crisis the only possible solution was a step forward, in faith and hope and – expectation. The consequent story magnificently verified the rightness of this move, 'a blessing in disguise' for the Churches concerned: in Tanzania, in Cameroon, in Togo and in Ghana.

Some denominations were more daring than others. In nineteenth-century South Africa, the Wesleyan Methodists had taken the lead and pressed on into the new period. They were told by some of their own people and by others that their extravagant boldness had led to numerous 'Ethiopian' breakaways. Yet, taken as a whole, the great number of Wesleyan ministers proved to be a pressure group in the country, leading to a transfer to African structures and inspiring others who were more slow-footed. But then the Wesleyans, an inclusive church with all the communities represented, also had their own problems. The election of a President for the Church in South Africa was one such problem. It took time until the obvious choice, the brilliant educationalist and pastor, Seth Mokitimi, was finally accepted as the President of the whole Church in 1949. This opened the way for many similar decisions in Southern Africa and again, also here, the expectations of the few proved a blessing to the many.

Tradition and continuity

The old traditions had gone and been discarded, together with much of the African traditional religions. What came in their place? Can a new tradition be invented? A few examples may indicate the meaning and depth of the problem. At the Kampala conference of the All Africa Conference of Churches, July 1963, Dr Kofi Busia of Ghana, sociologist, statesman and devoted Wesleyan layman, gave a lecture where he interpreted the yearnings of a continent for a new Christian tradition to give meaning and stability to life. 'As I reflect on the history of the Church in Africa I am struck, I should say, awe-struck by its survival and continuity.'[23] He thought of the price that had had to be paid for transmitting the Gospel: of the seven men and five women from Numidia executed in AD 180 for refusing to abjure their Christian faith, and more recently, of the fifty men and women in Sierra Leone whom the CMS had lost in the years 1804–24. He also recalled his own Methodist home chapel at Cape Coast, Ghana. The pulpit bore a plaque with the inscription which as a young boy he had seen many times: 'The first five missionaries to the Gold Coast lie buried beneath this pulpit.' He read out the names and dates between 1835 and 1837 of those Christian missionaries who had given the sacrifice of their lives.

By the strangest coincidence Pastor Rabary of Tananarive, Madagascar, referred to those very same years of the 1830s, as a sign post for the Christian faith in his country. As a Congregationalist minister in Tananarive in about 1905, he was an heir to the nineteenth-century Christian history in a free African country, which all of a sudden had lost its freedom and its position with a certain social prestige. When, in 1895, the imperialists took over Madagascar, Rabary felt he had to interpret God's guidance in and through the terrible deprivation which this Protestant Church had experienced. In order to do this he referred his listeners to their very own Christian tradition in Madagascar during the fearful years of Queen Ranavalona I, 1835–61, years of persecution and martyrdom. It was a story of persecution and death of hundreds of young Malagasy Christians, in that very place of Tananarive, 'the city of martyrs', and 'the city of light'. His listeners were invited to a Church peregrination of the holy places where topography itself preached: – that sacred ground, those sacred stones – constituting the reliquiae of the martyrs and this, Rabary suggested, was the challenging tradition of which they were all a part.[24]

By definition tradition is part of the Church's history. It cannot be offhandedly invented, in order to fill a void or a lacuna of some kind. Church tradition emerges out of the experience and pathos of a crisis subsequently recognized and appropriated by later generations. In Kampala Catholics and Anglicans could remind their faithful and the Church throughout the world of their own sacred tradition of the Baganda martyrs from the years 1885–86, and its meaning interpreted by the great Western poet:

We only live, only suspire
consumed by either fire or fire.[25]

The need for tradition could take on other forms, made alive in a situation of crisis. In Bukoba, Tanzania, Pastor Andrea Kadjerero (1880–1985) was deeply hurt when, without reference to him or his flock, the fate of his Church was decided over the heads of his African community – in that the little Evangelical Church was, with a stroke of a European pen, handed over to South African Wesleyans, a decision taken in conclave by the Anglican Bishop Willis in Kampala and these South African Methodists. Pastor Andrea set in motion a temporary countermovement lasting three or four years. His initiative has been interpreted as a Tanzanian equivalent of an Independent Church. What actually happened was far from anything of the kind. Kadjerero's opposition concerned the thoughtlessness and hasty decision by two Westerners not conversant with the local situation. Kadjerero insisted on the continuity of that ecclesiastical tradition which had sustained the life of the Bukoba Church, and his provisional opposition was made in order the more to stress this life-long tradition belonging to the community where he had been confirmed, the Anglican Communion. The point about him was his vindication of that ecclesiastical tradition which he knew and loved.

The mission-related Church had top levels of leadership, a formal leadership which as a matter of course lay in the hands of the White foreigner. There was a hierarchical distinction between the Western missionary with his administrative and economic power and influence and the local African staff – pastors, catechists, teachers, elders etc. However, almost unknown to the White man there prevailed all the time an informal leadership, exercised by the local African pastor and by evangelists and catechists. Within that network the African had far-reaching influence, expressed through his personality and message by personal guidance and relationship and by the tenets of Church discipline. With the African takeover, the formal leadership structure was also handed over, defined in a written constitution. With this take-over there also went a change in the hierarchical relationship towards a differentiation between ordained and laity, and between Church administration and a voluntary body.

In the perspective of Time and Expectation one sees how certain factors, some restraining, others pace-setting, affected the transfer in the Churches. An attitude of paternalism on the part of certain Westerners could not but have a restraining effect on the African Church. This was notoriously so in South Africa. There a standard argument over and against the African population could always be relied on. 'We Westerners for our technical achievement and literary culture needed two thousand years [or 300 years, as the case may have been] to arrive at this point in our development, and most likely you Africans will need the same number of years.' So there was no hurry now over the matter of a transfer.

From the standpoint of Africanization the role of the institutions was something of a paradox. In principle the institutions had been the social carriers of new ideas of progress on Western lines. The school system with its apex in a teacher training college or a secondary school did have that function. The hospital with its emerging cadres of African orderlies, nurses and doctors, had a similarly modernizing effect: there the complaint was often that the mission hospital was not modern enough in terms of equipment and medical literature. Through these and other similar Church institutions one entered the modern dimension of society. Yet, when it came to the point, these same institutions often constituted a serious hurdle, heavy and expensive as they were. Both partners in the transfer debate had their doubts as to whether the African Church should really try to carry that extra burden of responsibility.

It is difficult to arrive at a just comparison between Catholics and non-Catholics on this central point, the two systems being so different. The Protestant approach to transfer was part of a long-term process of selection and preferment whereby a certain individual would be brought forward. The Roman Catholic system, ruled from Rome, with its Pope and its Cardinals, implied that an announcement of the name of a priest was made in Rome and the regional and local Church was thus informed that So-and-So had been appointed bishop or whatever the position may have been. It is in this light that the appointment and consecration of Joseph Kiwanuka as Bishop of Masaka, southern Uganda in 1939, was so significant.

After the Second World War it was possible for mission executives to make visitations by air to the 'field'. Nineteenth-century inspection tours had been enormous affairs, lasting months and even years, resulting – in the case of highly competent German mission directors – in large volumes interpreting the *milieu* and growth of the young shoot of a mission. After the Second World War mission executive visits could be brief, sometimes only a matter of days, and to the point, dealing with some specific problem, such as racial relationships, finance etc., and designed to lead to a quickening of the policy and practice of transfer.

An unfailing means towards transfer – on the Protestant side – was found in the constitution of the Church. The work on this Church legislation was surrounded by a great deal of awe, and all levels of a Church – local, regional, national – were involved in its production. Together with the annual debate on the budget the discussion over the refinements of the constitution was an important stage in the on-going process of Church democratization. In certain cases the Church constitution preceded the arrival of a national political constitution by decades. Sometimes a Western Church might even send its mission director from the metropolis to the local Church, to be involved for a couple of years with this one thing, the constitution.[26] While this was a well-meaning gesture it was also an admission that this particular concern was to a large extent a Western problem. When, in a Church meeting in Soweto, Bishop Manas Buthelezi referred to the constitution of the Church, solid old Zulu pastors and elders retorted: 'We were not there. We were nothing' – (when the constitution was made).

In truth a constitution was, most of the time, a variation of a legal Church enactment from some Western country with certain local additions. (One could meditate on what a genuinely African constitution would look like: probably it would contain references to clan and family and to *ubantu*.) At the time it was also realized that the value of the effort must not be overrated. The Revd Colin Morris – Kenneth Kaunda's friend and co-worker – had a greater right than most to pass judgement when in 1964 he said: 'The Church is perpetuated not by the handing down of a constitution or deed but by the living witnesses, the true Apostolic Succession, those in every generation who can claim by experience "Christ is the Lord".'[27]

Nothing discloses the difference between the two confessions – Catholic (including the Anglo-Catholics) and Protestant – as clearly as their attitudes to Tradition. Here Catholics, as a matter of course, had no problem but rather showed a thankful and thoughtful acceptance of Tradition as Foundation of the Faith and the Church related to Rome and the Pope. The Protestants on the other hand had inherited from their Western missionaries a certain reserve and hesitation towards tradition as a possibly fatal competitor, with Holy Scriptures as the only admissible authority. However, the Protestants also searched for their own recovery of Tradition. The historian soon discovers that the Protestants too have sought to vindicate church tradition albeit in other forms, related to the soil and the African experience. The two testaments of the Bible constitute the basis for such a tradition appropriated as the authority of the faith.

In a situation where only very few preachers possess their own concordance, a set of the most important Bible texts is eventually established, referring to the great personalities of the Holy Book: Noah, Abraham, Moses, Hezechiel 37, Daniel 2–5, etc. and in the New Testament texts referring to Jesus the Healer and to that Saul who on the road to Damascus was converted into St Paul. Something of a condensed Bible thus emerges at the local level containing the great salvific truths of the religion. There are even degrees of this textual condensation until, at the far end, one meets that lonely illiterate Zionist preacher in Zululand whom we once knew: while preaching he would call out an instruction to his literate secretary: *uMateu five*, being his point of reference for any homiletical exercise. But apart from this Biblical authority and tradition there are, as the American scholar Dr Jaroslav Pelikan has suggested, 'nonverbal or at any rate non-conceptual elements of tradition', a suggestion which seems to apply particularly well to some of the African Churches. These comprise above all that wealth of Christian truth and conviction contained in the hymn-book and transposed to the individual faithful by easily memorized rhythm.[28]

CHURCH STRATEGIES

The Popes and Africa

The First World War had come to an end and it was time for the Church to consider anew its task in the world and, more particularly, in Africa. A number of factors and forces converged to make the 1920s a peculiarly creative period in Catholic missionary outreach to the African continent. First of all, there was the directive role of the Popes and the Propaganda Fide. The 'Missionary Popes', Benedict XV and Pius XI, responded magnificently to the challenge of the new era. In 1919 Benedict published the encyclical *Maximum Illud*. It emphasized the necessity of propagating the Catholic faith to all and the need for an educated indigenous clergy prepared to take over the leadership of the Churches in their respective countries. Seven years later, Pius XI, the 'Missionary Pope' *par préférence*, issued his *Rerum Ecclesiae* which can be seen as a reinforcement of *Maximum Illud*. Indigenous clergy were to be given precedence while the Western missionary was to take an auxiliary position. While Pius XI emphasized indigenization, he also exhorted 'every religious order to engage in missionary work, with the result that he saw the number of missionaries doubled in his reign'.[29] Theological seminaries were to be erected and indigenous orders for men and women were to be instituted, thus pursuing initiatives taken earlier in the pontificate of Gregory XVI (Pope 1831–46). To reinforce these changes a missiology faculty was established at the Gregorian University in Rome. During Pius XI's papacy the total number of non-Western priests increased from 3,000 to over 7,000 (located mostly in Asia and Latin America). To those who regarded the training of an African clergy as premature and who referred to the encyclical as the Pope's 'pious wish', Pius XI retorted: 'No, it is our will and command.'

The new signals from the Popes were interpreted by the missiologists in the West, a leading figure among them being Father Pierre Charles, S.J., Louvain: 'The indigenous clergy is not just a decoration on the mission building. If it did not exist, the mission itself would not exist. It is an indispensable instrument for making the people worthy of God ... It is the Black Church which will convert Africa: the church of the missionaries is only a transitory stage.'[30] Local leaders on the spot took heed. A case in point was Bishop Vogt in Yaoundé. As a faithful Holy Ghost missionary of his generation he had had his hesitations about the possibility of a highly educated African clergy. But – *Roma locuta*, the Pope had spoken – and the matter was settled – it was as simple as that.

An African clergy 'is Our will and command' according to Pius XI. This papal command was indeed needed for things to change on this issue in Africa. Because of the central role of the Popes in this matter it is referred to here. A danger signal was raised by Fr Augustin Tellkamp, SVD, in his book of 1950, *Die Gefahr der Erstickung für die katholische Weltmission* (The Danger of Suffocation in the Catholic World mission).[31] His argument was that the rapidly rising numbers of faithful together with the millions of catechumens on the one hand and the short supply of priests on the other implied a threat to the healthy growth of the Church.

On the eve of the First World War the Catholic Church in Africa had 7,000,000 baptized together with 1,000,000 catechumens and these figures doubled in the decade 1928–38, while the numbers of African priests was minimal: only 287 for the whole of Africa. To be sure there were some bright spots. The Masaka diocese in Uganda had its first African Catholic priest in 1913 and Tanzania in 1915. Masaka had forty-six African priests under its African bishop from 1939. Near Lake Tanganyika the White Fathers were able to refer to the early ordination of one of the first African priests, Stephen Kaoze (1885–1951), the first in the whole of Zaïre, ordained in 1917. However, these were exceptions. In the great number of dioceses the outlook was bleak indeed.

There was a hopeful intake of young candidates into the junior seminaries, but those who persevered to the end, to ordination as priests, were few. In Bishop Roelens' diocese in Zaïre, out of 200 students only ten persisted. The Bishop meditated on these figures: '"That's very slight" some would say. "That is a very great number", will be said by one who knows them intimately. It was in fact a miracle of grace.'[32] Hard facts were pitted against this miracle of grace. Life in the isolated, restricted world of the seminary could in the long run be a trying experience. After five or six years in a primary school would follow six to seven years in a junior seminary and then eight years in the senior seminary – the latter including three years 'Philosophy' and five years Theology, with one year practical Church work. Throughout this seminary existence the young man was never supposed to visit his family or home village. He had indeed moved over into another kind of existence, with Latin and its firm discipline, and this was only the beginning.

To this initiative for an indigenous clergy was added the concern for a national hierarchy with indigenous bishops, and here again the problem of 'indigenization', a problem which had to wait for Vatican II and beyond. The whole image of the Catholic missionary enterprise was fundamentally changed: from national institutions to the international and universal centre in and from the metropolitan centre in Rome. No longer were missions to be directed from local places in Algiers or Lyon or Marseille or Paris or Mill Hill or Blackrock or Maynooth, but from Rome as the centre. In this perspective the claim raised in African missions for having what was referred to as 'national missions' became increasingly a contradiction in terms. Nobody felt this contradiction as sharply as Pope Pius XI. The Pope had a temper and nothing could arouse that temperament as surely as a reference to 'our national mission'. It took the Belgians about three decades to see this point and to do something about it for the education of 'all' in what was then 'Belgian Congo'. Portugal of course needed more decades until revolutions in Lisbon and in Luanda changed what there had been of a country called Angola.

'The perfect prefect'

The proclamations of the Popes were prepared in co-operation with others. Willem van Rossum (d. 1932), from 1918 the head of the congregation for Propaganda Fide, assisted both Popes. This Dutch Redemptorist was a remarkable mission leader. In this century he inaugurated the role of Dutch churchmen in international Church matters, both on the Catholic and on the non-Roman side. The appointment in 1918 of a Dutchman to the Italian establishment caused some apprehension: 'the whole of Rome caught a fright'. It did not take long, however, for van Rossum's creative power and vision to be acknowledged, and it is probable that his hand can be detected in the two papal encyclicals. Pope Benedict XV referred to him as *il perfetto prefetto*, the perfect prefect. It was natural for van Rossum, as head of the Propaganda, to see to it that this ancient institution acquired a central role, and certain measures to this end were taken. In Lyon, the Society for the Propagation of the Faith – founded in 1822 – had for a century collected and distributed funds for the Church's work overseas. Its place in Lyon had highlighted the decisive role of French missions for the entire nineteenth-century Catholic mission work. In 1922 this Society – despite some French protest – was transferred to Rome, thus emphasizing the one metropolis and placing the great French contribution within an even wider context.

Africa's mission and martyr history was brought to light in Rome when on 6 June 1920, Pope Benedict XV declared beatified twenty-two Bugandan martyrs (to be canonized in 1964) – the first Bantu-speakers in the Catholic calendar of saints. The occasion was memorable: 'For the first time, African drums and African rhythms echoed through the vaults of St Peter.' Pope Benedict spoke of 'the present decisive hour of Africa'. In the new atmosphere of expectation and missionary vision in Rome, Pius XI consecrated six Chinese bishops in 1925 and, perhaps more startling, in that same year the cardinals were considering the appointment of an African bishop for the rapidly growing Church in Uganda. However, there was hesitation, caused by rumours of opposition to such a step on the part of the British administration in Uganda which forced the cardinals to shelve the matter – only to see it revived years later, in 1939.[33]

African cultural values

Africa's visibility in Rome was accentuated in 1925, the 'Jubilee Year', by a great international missionary exhibition. Pius XI was personally involved. Archivist and alpinist, the Pope had invited the famous ethnographer, Father Wilhelm Schmidt, SVD, to Rome in order to prepare a display of ethnographical material on mission work in the field. Father Schmidt gathered around him a highly competent staff which, including Fr Pinard de la Boullaye, SJ, and Fr Briault, CSSp, set to work bringing impressive riches of African art to the Holy City. The role of the monasteries in promoting liturgical arts must be mentioned: St André in Shaba (Katanga); Ndanda in

Tanzania; and the Swiss Bethlehem Fathers in Gwelo, Zimbabwe (Serima centre) have also played a part.

Western missions were often portrayed at the time as having destroyed the cultural values of indigenous peoples, particularly in Africa. The Exhibition eloquently demonstrated that some of the missionaries, not least in Africa, had other designs. An outstanding example was Father Francis Aupiais (1877–1945), active as a 'Lyon' missionary in Benin (Dahomey), 1903–27. In Benin he organized popular festivals – for weddings, Epiphany and in commemoration of St Joan of Arc – and accorded to local customs an honoured place alongside the Catholic rites. More than any other Western missionary in Africa he demonstrated the values of African religion and the potential cultural strength of the young Church. It should be noted that these initiatives were taken as early as the beginning of the century. Fr Aupiais represented a new generation coming to the fore, dramatically present in the 1925 Exhibition and in the following 'Jubilee' exhibition in Rome in 1950.

African bishops and apostolic delegates

An effective bond between Rome and Africa was established through the twentieth-century institution of 'Apostolic Delegates', i.e., papal envoys to the Churches with a supervising function (envoys to States are of course referred to as Nuncios). Beginning in the 1920s Africa saw its first Delegates to South Africa from 1922, Belgian Congo, British East and West Africa from 1930, and French West and Equatorial Africa from 1948.[34] An illustration of the importance of the Delegates can be seen in connection with the introduction of the Legion of Mary into the Church in Africa. In 1936, a young Irish woman, Edel Quinn – sent by her colleagues in Dublin – came to East Africa to make the Legion of Mary an integrated part of the dioceses. On her arrival in Kenya she was introduced to the Apostolic Delegate Antonio Riberi and explained matters to him. He was immediately won for the cause and circulated information about the plan to the whole Anglophone episcopate in Africa. He thus made it possible in a few years for the Legion to secure a foothold throughout eastern, central and southern Africa. In 1944, Edel Quinn died in Nairobi. One point about the introduction of the Legion is the decisive intermediary and recommendatory role of the central agency of an 'Apostolic Delegation'.

However much Pius XI wished to be involved in Africa on behalf of the Catholic Church, he was to find that no Pope was as hemmed in as he, surrounded by a Fascist state. The Italian scene in the 1920s and 1930s was dominated by *Il Duce* (Mussolini) and his imperialistic designs aiming at expiating what was to him a humiliating Italian defeat in 1896. To him Abyssinia took on a symbolic importance. Even more so, in African opinion 'Ethiopia' took on a symbolic role on behalf of the entire African continent. African opinion held that the Pope did not sufficiently indicate that he had perceived this. This then, became a challenge to the Catholic Church throughout the continent, especially on the west coast with its emerging nationalist press, lead particularly by the Nigerian nationalist Dr Azikiwe. The outcome of the Fascist crusade meant that the Roman Catholic Church once again lost its influence and reputation in Ethiopia or at least its foothold in Ethiopia, for the third time – the first and second times being in 1631 and 1879 (Cardinal Massaja).

Van Rossum's successor as Prefect of the Propaganda Fide was P. Fumasoni-Biondi (1933–60). In 1939, he prepared the appointment of the first two African bishops in modern times, Joseph Kiwanuka for Masaka, Uganda, and Ignatius Ramarosandratana for Miarinarivo, Madagascar. These two men, the one for an English-speaking and the other for a French-speaking territory, were associated with the White Fathers and the Jesuits, the two societies which particularly emphasized higher education for the African clergy. Masaka had already a large membership, with no less than 325,000 Catholics, 90,000 catechumens, forty-six African priests, and over 200 African sisters. Bishop Ramarosandratana at the outset had only two Black priests, although his nearby French brother bishop promised to transfer four, and then seven, Malagasy priests from his own diocese.

Pope Pius XI was looking forward to their consecration with keen anticipation: 'I wonder whether the Divine Providence will bestow upon me the joy to consecrate an African bishop in Rome. The Missions in Africa represent today the richest harvest of conversions.'[35] But his hope was not fulfilled – the old missionary Pope died at the beginning of 1939. The consecration, performed by Pius XII, took place on 29 October of that year.

During the time of Fumasoni-Biondi's incumbency, David Mathew was appointed Apostolic Delegate for English-speaking West and East Africa. Consecrated Archbishop of Apamea in Bithynia, and residing in Mombasa between 1946 and 1953, Mathew came to this task with extraordinary gifts as a scholar and a writer. Having previously been the Apostolic Vicar to Ethiopia (1945–46), Mathew was – more than most in the African Church – aware of the imperative demands of the changing times. He perceived what the independence of India in 1947 implied for the rest of the Third World, and for the Church and its meaning for Africa. The dramatic theme of the 1950s was to be a resolute preparation of the African clergy and an African hierarchy.

An unexpected but all the more valuable reinforcement of the Church was provided when at Easter 1957, Pope Pius XII published his encyclical *Fidei Donum*, a message particularly directed to the needs of the Church in Africa and 'its millenarian destiny'. Here the Pope exhorted all the bishops in the West to transfer some of their clergy for service in Africa. The effect was astounding. A great number of 'Fidei-Donum-priests' from various countries in Europe and the United States placed themselves at the disposal of the new African episcopate, effectively helping with humble yet necessary background tasks.

The 1950s saw a fundamental change in canonic law, of immense importance for the Church in Africa and its future. This change meant the ending of traditional *ius commissionis* by which, until then, mission territories had been entrusted to missionary societies. From then on they were commissioned to hierarchies in Africa and were soon, as we shall see, entrusted to African archbishops.

The men of Le Zoute

Both the Catholic metropolis in Rome and the Protestant churchmen meeting at Le Zoute, Belgium, were facing Africa and its opportunities in a new era. Despite their being divided and not on speaking terms, there was in the best of these Africa-oriented churchmen, on both sides of the great divide, a common concern for African culture and African identity. They were, at least officially, anxious to encourage these interests within their Churches.

The idea of a Protestant Africa conference was formed as early as 1919, when peace at last came to Africa and the world. It was raised by a young American, later to become one of the leading missionaries in Africa. At this time he already represented American interests in Belgian Congo, a region where Protestant interests were particularly impeded. Emory Ross's idea was of a 'Mid-Africa' conference to be held in Zaïre. This move proved to be premature – a conference of that international nature was called together forty years later in Kampala in 1963.

The Le Zoute conference of 1926 was called together by the International Missionary Council, with Dr J. H. Oldham as the incomparable secretary. Chairman of the conference was Oldham's brother-in-law, Donald Fraser, with thirty years' experience from Malawi.[36] Another prominent name was that of E. W. Smith, British Methodist from Zambia, representing a new generation of mission scholars with deep understanding of African values, author of a number of important books such as *The Golden Stool* (1926),

Aggrey of Africa: a Study in Black and White (1929) and *African Beliefs and Christian Faith* (1936): books which have profoundly influenced subsequent generations of Africans and missionaries. That same year, 1926, the International Institute of African Languages and Cultures was founded with headquarters in London, with E. W. Smith as one of the leaders. He also edited the Le Zoute volume, entitled *The Christian Mission in Africa*, published in 1926.

The 220 participants at Le Zoute came from every corner of the African continent and the whole spectrum of denominations was represented. Le Zoute became the meeting place for a generation of mission executives, secretaries and scholars, men – there were only a few women among them – with a generous understanding of African religion and culture. The list of delegates reads like a bibliography of writers in the field. There were statesmen, such as Sir Frederick Lugard and the Belgian administrator Louis Franck, as well as scholars and educationalists, including Professor Julius Richter and Professor Dietrich Westermann of Berlin, Raymond Buell of Harvard, and Dr Jesse Jones. Only five were Blacks, including John Dube, the Zulu educationalist from Ohlange, Natal, and the Methodist pastor, Z. R. Mahabane, representing the African National Congress (this was a time when that affiliation could still be officially maintained in South Africa), and Max Yergan, African-American YMCA secretary, active in South Africa.

The conference gave its time to a critical review of missionary education and to the formation of education policy, deprecating the lack of effective supervision of some mission schools and advocating links between African education and the philanthropic traditions of the southern states of the USA. The conference 'adopted or adapted' the Jesse Jones philosophy on the relation of education to the African's cultural inheritance and the place of African languages in the educational programme.

In the long-run, however, it seems that Le Zoute's major achievement was the search for and the formulation of a new approach to African culture and 'African values'. Professor D. Westermann, with long missionary experience in West Africa (in Togo), expressed this latter concern with finesse and authority:

> African community life is for us the mother soil into which the divine seed is to be sown and out of which a Christian society will grow ... If we dig deep enough and try to live permanently in close touch with the African mind, we shall discover more points of contact, new ways of approach will open ... The African, apart from his magical practices, believes in God. He is not a tribal God, but Lord of the universe and the Christian missionary can in most cases introduce himself as ambassador of the God the African knows.[37]

These were far-reaching words which an earlier generation, 'our more puritanic and legalistic predecessors', had not always comprehended.[38] Neither was the reference to 'points of contact' likely to endear itself to the new kind of German-speaking dialectic theology, inspired by Karl Barth, which at the very time propounded its non-compromising message.

Westermann's statement was followed up by the South African Methodist Z. R. Mahabane, although with a variance caused by the segregation practice in his own country: 'The black man still believes that Christianity comes from God, so he still clings to it although his mind is in a state of revolt against Western Christianity.'[39]

The relationship between Christian standards and African religion and custom was discussed by the conference in terms of 'adaptation'. Most notably this was done by the Moravian Bishop P. O. Hennig, ex-missionary:

> Granted that polygamy is a heathen abuse of the divine order of things, we nevertheless maintain that the Christian Mission has no right to treat as illegal conjugal unions contracted by heathen according to the legal standards of their people. We further hold that the Christian Mission has no right to refuse to such, if they believe in Christ, the sacrament of baptism and with it the right of entrance into the Christian Church.[40]

The proposal was discussed but rejected by the majority.

The potential of the task and the perspective for the future were interpreted by that great (and now forgotten) missions scholar, Julius Richter of Berlin: 'Nowhere in the world has the Church such an overwhelming importance as in Africa.'

It goes without saying that this Protestant conference could not aim at unification of the missionary forces represented at the gathering. At least, however, it meant an inspiration through the realization of the fact that the missions, more than ever before, had to take into account the values of the African's past in building Africa's future.

There were important matters which could not be dealt with in a conference of this kind, meeting only for one short week. Oldham, the genius of concentration in all things, focused his attention and that of the conference on modern education and the values of African culture. In comparison with the simultaneous signals from Rome, one notices the absence at Le Zoute of any reference to theological education. There were one or two rapid references to the subject, characteristically by Canon E. F. Spanton, of the UMCA, Zanzibar, with its special concern for priestly training. Oldham was disparaging towards the signs of 'churchianity', to use the term of the time. B.Sr. remembers explaining to him some thirty years later the concern of one of the International Missionary Council (IMC) commissions on the 'Training of the Ministry in Africa', – by Baëta, Bates, Michaéli and Sundkler – claiming a priority for theological education: 'Not less than one-fourth of missionary personnel and effort should be whole-heartedly directed to the training of ministers.'[41] Oldham was not to be won over: 'I could not care less' was his retort. Only in the 1950s was this matter to be of central concern for the IMC and for the Churches in the field.

The Orthodox in East Africa

At long last the Orthodox also appeared on the East African scene, but when they did arrive it happened in a strange roundabout way which did not, at least at first, promise to lead to the desired goal. It began with an enterprising and relatively privileged young Muganda, Reuben Mukasa, known as Spartas, who struck out against what to him seemed an unbearable paternalism on the part of his Anglican missionaries. When he wrote to the Anglican bishop this ecclesiastical worthy answered: 'I have often told you in conversation, my dear boy' etc.

Spartas had studied at Uganda's Eton, the Budu Secondary School and had, like many of his generation during the First World War, joined up with the King's African Rifles. He taught English to Nubian non-commissioned officers. A young man of his calibre could not be easily deterred, particularly as he was aware of the opportunities offered by the 1920s. He corresponded with the Marcus Garvey-led Pan-African movement in the United States, more particularly with Bishop G. A. McGuire of the African Orthodox Church in New York. The bishops in New York suggested that he contact their representative on the African continent, Bishop D. W. Alexander of Beaconsfield, Kimberley, South Africa.

He broke with the Anglican Church – one of the very rare 'Ethiopian' breakaways from the Anglican church in Uganda – and was soon prepared to invite Bishop Alexander to East Africa. This visit took place in 1931–32. Spartas and his friend Basaajjakitalo were ordained priests in the African Orthodox Church. The Orthodox church was thus established in East Africa – or was it? Spartas himself soon had his doubts about the particular succession claimed by Bishop D. W. Alexander. 'There is a real sense in which Spartas has created something greater than himself.'[42] He abandoned his bishop in the south and turned north instead, to the Greek Orthodox Church in East Africa and the Greek Patriarch in Alexandria, whom he visited in 1946.

That same year Alexandria gave formal recognition to the Orthodox

Church in Uganda. Spartas could now send young Baganda for studies to Alexandria and later to Athens. Three of these became medical doctors and a fourth, T. H. Nankyama, pursued theological studies in Athens; he was eventually to become bishop. A Greek metropolitan of East Africa was appointed and Spartas was from now on ecclesiastically related to him. In 1946 the Orthodox Church of Uganda had, officially, 10,000 members, the majority of whom lived in Buganda. In 1958 East Africa became the Irimoppulis archdiocese within the Alexandria Patriarchate. The metropolitan residing in Egypt did from time to time visit his province.

The Orthodox church in Kenya grew even faster than in Uganda. In Kenya the Orthodox were inspired by the visit of Archbishop Makarios of Cyprus, an outstanding and dramatic ecclesiastical and political personality who had an experience which endeared him to the Kenyan masses. In 1956 he was exiled for one year to the Seychelles where he was visited by another well-known 'prison graduate', Jomo Kenyatta and they became great friends. With Kenyatta as President of Kenya, Archbishop Makarios paid an official visit to Kenya in March 1971 when, in a few days, he baptized 5,000.

The Orthodox presence in Africa was hailed with enthusiasm by the whole Orthodox world. The Greek theologian and missiologist, Metropolitan Yannoulatos gave solid theological foundations to the work. A theological seminary was opened in Nairobi with staff members from the Orthodox Church in Greece, Cyprus and Finland.

Orthodoxy is always something more than mere organization or institution and so it is also in East Africa. The essence is the Divine Liturgy, the beauty and sacred mystery communicated by the iconostasis, where the icon conveys to the pious individual a realization of Incarnation. To this are added the solemn movements of the clergy with their sacred books and vessels and the unforgettable music of the choir. Bishop Spartas proved to be a highly gifted liturgiologist. He translated the Orthodox Liturgy of St John Chrysostom into the vernacular, into matchless Luganda.

EDUCATION

The nineteenth-century mission school in Africa was largely an extension of the catechumens' class. To the Ten Commandments, the Parables of Jesus and/or the Ave Maria, were added the 'Three Rs'. The ambitious exceptions to that general rule – whether in West or South Africa – need no emphasis here. What there were of schools in Africa were most often mission schools. The missions held 90 per cent of all village education in their hands. Colonial governments' concerns were: recalcitrant chiefs, threatening revolts, droughts and bad harvests, *not* young people's education. Much of that situation prevailed far into the twentieth century. With the schools came the printed word. C. E. Wilson of the Baptist Missionary Society, London, told a conference at High Leigh in Britain in 1924: 'Almost every word printed in African Native languages is Christian'.

Between 1920 and 1945, however, a fundamental change took place. Schools now became the concern of colonial governments. There was a significant difference between British and French educational policies for Africa. British policy suffered from a certain dichotomy regarding its final objective. It aimed simultaneously at two diametrically opposed goals: to produce an educated elite which would form the core of a native administration; and, in accordance with the overarching British policy of Indirect Rule, to avoid creating an educational elite, which might undermine the authority of the traditional chiefs, the basis of the Native Authority system. The French had no such scruples. Their goal was to create a political and professional high calibre elite that could identify with the French cultural image. In accordance with these ideas, Charles de Gaulle and Governor Eboué at Brazzaville in 1944 insisted on the metropolitan language, French, for the most distant little village school: 'The programme will be conducted for use either in private or public schools.'

These differences particularly affected primary education. At the higher educational levels one should not overemphasize the difference between the British and French policies. In practice, the colonial administration 'concentrated on producing as close a duplicate of Cambridge and Paris as was possible within the African territories.'[43]

In London the matter of mission-directed education rested in Dr Oldham's strong hands. He had a wide net of important contacts in the Colonial Office and in the Ministry of Education, and he persuaded the government to call an expert meeting, on 6 June 1923, which included governors of British territories in Africa. This consultation was 'a turning point in the history of African education'. The principle of co-operation between colonial government and missions was laid down so as to secure permanent and effective machinery for consultation both in the African territories and at the Colonial Office in London.[44]

The British Colonial Office Advisory Committee – on the initiative of Dr J. H. Oldham and the British Missionary Societies – introduced a memorandum emphasizing partnership in education between government and missions. Government supervision was carried out by school inspectors and mission schools were awarded grant-in-aid. In spite of a world economic crisis and World War II, colonial governments made efforts to live up to the mounting expectation held by elite groups as well as by the masses. Government primary schools and 'Native Authority' schools were started under the supervision of government inspectors and before too long there were government secondary schools whetting the appetite for university colleges and academic achievements. There is a certain periodicity in this development. The early 1920s laid the foundations and brought new initiatives while an educational heave in 1944 saw plans for 'Mass Education' of the African communities in the British dependencies and, in the French dependencies, plans for making elite groups French-speaking. (In the French language, as is well known, 'elite' is not a pejorative word which it tends to be in the other European languages spoken in Africa.)

Through a concordat with King Leopold in 1906, the Catholics were entrusted with the responsibility of African education in Zaïre. For the first half of the century education was the exclusive prerogative of the Catholic Church in its supposed capacity of 'national mission'. In spite of incessant pressure the Protestants had to wait until 1948 before they could begin to benefit from government subsidies for their schools. Belgian educational policy, being decidedly patriarchal, concentrated on primary education. Thus, there was a first-level primary school lasting for two years and a secondary level, at schools in urbanized areas, with courses lasting for three years. Ever-increasing numbers of Belgian nuns and teaching brothers devoted themselves to supervising the village education. What there was of higher education was largely provided by way of theological seminaries. Some of the seminarians did not persevere to the end of the Senior Seminary or to ordination and would thus make up the group of the so-called *evolués*, to be compared with the *assimilados* in the Portuguese system.

In the early 1920s, British Africa discussed innovations in African education. The schools in the bush, it was alleged, were only 'little nothings', according to the uncompromising judgement of a visiting international commission, and the textbooks used in those schools were deemed 'absolutely absurd, having no sort of relation to native life'.[45]

The new light came from the United States, more particularly, from Black colleges of industrial education in the southern states. They had an exciting educational tradition from Booker Washington's days at Tuskegee, followed by an eloquent Ghanaian, J. K. Aggrey. Aggrey was to play a creative role in propagating in Africa what was seen as the new idea of Negro education. Dr Thomas Jesse Jones, a Welshman and a believer in Negro industrial education, found a collaborator in Aggrey who helped make Jones' so-called 'Phelps Stokes Commissions' – for West and South Africa in 1920 and East Africa in 1924 – something of a success. Both men were aware that the Tuskegee (and Hampton College) approach had sharp opponents in the African-American world. Two leaders, W. E. B. Du Bois, with his National Association for the Advancement of Colored People (NAACP), and Marcus Garvey with his Universal Negro Improvement Association (UNIA) were opposed to the Tuskegee model, advocating instead Black liberal arts colleges as instruments of African-American protest and advance. Colonial governments were anxious to keep Du Bois and Garvey out of Africa while welcoming the Jesse Jones plan for so-called 'Jeanes Schools', which seemed to promise a more balanced future with an agricultural bias.

The best example of the Jeanes Schools was the one at Kabete in Kenya, with J. W. C. Dougall as principal. Dougall was one of those Scots who gave remarkable leadership to African education in colonial times. Somewhat later, as educational advisor to Protestant missions, he could serve the good cause more widely. Adaptation to African social conditions and community feeling were the watchwords for the Jeanes Schools programme. Over time the Jeanes Schools results were limited, for they did not last beyond the Second World War. But 'the Jeanes Schools Debate' in East Africa and elsewhere helped stimulate an interest in African education and played a role in the formation of the British Colonial Office Advisory Committee on African Education. Its most useful recommendation for the village schools included plans for rural and industrial uplift. However, the essential factor was that the bush schools were now successively supplanted by government-subsidized primary schools.

The nineteenth-century bush school – which largely carried on functioning until World War II – had been a revolutionary factor in village life dispite all its limitations. Yet, it was a frail little thing as far as buildings and pedagogical material were concerned, with its teachers lacking both adequate personal knowledge and teaching skills. However, teacher training colleges were erected which produced a new generation of qualified teachers, a new quality of school facilities and equipment appeared and there was a transformation of scope and academic ambition. Slowly the village school developed into the middle school, while the secondary school was chiefly introduced after the Second World War.

These centres, whether Catholic or Protestant, were all boarding establishments, an aspect easily overlooked. The Christian boarding school – particularly when it had at its centre a chapel of some distinction – gave to young generations certain intangibles, a personal experience of Christian community life and Christian culture, with its own rhythm for the day and the year. Common prayer in chapel, morning and evening, with their ritual and characteristic melodies, Sundays and feast days related to a sacred tradition and the community feeling with its special atmosphere, its *esprit de corps*, its history and its potential gave an introduction to a new world. This experience was, admittedly, the privilege of an elite, but many of these men and women were later in life in positions to transmit something of their experience on a much wider scale, locally, regionally and nationally. Taken as a whole, this boarding school life was probably the greatest contribution the churches made to young Africa in those years.

In fairness, it must be added that others may have taken a different view. F. Yao Boateng, a well-known politician and Presbyterian in Ghana, in an article entitled 'The Catechism and the Rod, Presbyterian Education in Ghana', felt, as the title of his critique suggests, that:

> enforced religious instruction ... is not the way to induct people into the Church ... Today I feel myself a very religious person; however, this is despite the Church, not because of it. The Christian environment provided by my parents [his father was a Presbyterian minister living in the mission area, 'Salem', of the town] has proven much more important than all the mission school experiences combined.[46]

A map of church influence in Africa would be dotted with the names of teacher training colleges and secondary schools, both Catholic and Protestant, initiated and administered by missions with increasingly an African staff. These educational centres with their attractive libraries, that new world of books, oriented minds towards alluring horizons. It would seem invidious to attempt to list the names of these great leading schools. Such a list could not omit the educational centres in South Africa, vitally important for aspiring students coming from as far as Uganda – until it all this came to an end through the ill-famed 1953 Bantu Education Act of South Africa.

There was a drama in African missions in the two decades following the Second World War, in the transition period over to African independence. The chief as a local and regional power was on his way out from the centre of things and was succeeded by the school teacher, now appearing as the key to the future. In the industrialized West the radical leaders had started out as trade union employees. In Africa all of the great political leaders had begun their careers as school teachers. The teacher was the factor of change in the village. Himself influenced by the winds of change and by modern political and cultural ideas, he imparted these to the younger generation. From within the four walls of the village school he reached out to the future of the continent.

The Christian village school teacher built modern Africa. By the inspiration of his school activities and programmes he changed the village community. He was also a local preacher, explaining the visions of the Bible and keeping in contact with the mission in town. As an African he was often musical and led the church choir which gave him power to make or unmake anything of importance in the community.

Inevitably conflicts sometimes appeared between the African teacher and the Western missionary *cum* school inspector, but this was the exception rather than the rule. Much more common was the good co-operation between the two. One example must suffice. Chief Awolowo's autobiography gives a vivid impression of the mutual esteem between the principal of the Wesley College in Western Nigeria, E.G. Nightingale, and the young teacher Awolowo. The missionary principal insisted that the young generation must protect and develop anything that was indigenous: language, culture, style of dress etc. 'Awo' said: 'I think that he was a great pioneer'.[47]

The attitude of the missions to changes in educational policy varied a great deal. There were missions which, by their enlightened planning and performance, pioneered this change. Others hesitated or wavered: was this why missions were in Africa after all? they asked. Was this the right way of spending mission money and employing personnel? Above all, was the African prepared for this kind of thing? Was he not limited to becoming a good artisan or a faithful catechist? One could not be too sure whether the African masses were really prepared for the change – until in the late forties, there was a most remarkable mass movement, with a passion for schools. In this, as in so many other ways, Eastern Nigeria took the lead.

Some missions, both Catholic and Protestant, were inclined to make this educational change because of their background. With their Libermann tradition from the 1850s – 'holiness rather than scholarship' – the Holy Ghost Fathers at first tended to take a conservative stance on education. However, individual experience or group decision could initiate a change. Father J. Bouchaud in the Cameroons, with a leading position in his 'Congregation', convinced his brethren to adopt a radical approach for his own mission, a move destined to influence the whole continent.

In East Africa, Catholics were challenged by Archbishop Arthur Hinsley and his message during a visitation in 1928. His directive to Catholic missions in the east and elsewhere in Africa was uncompromising:

> Collaborate [with government] with all your power; and where it is impossible for you to carry on both the immediate task of evangelization and your educational work, neglect your churches in order to perfect your schools.[48]

His warning was not always heeded. He was, after all, a Briton and in Tanzania at the time almost all Catholic missionaries were non-Britons: being German, French, Dutch, American and, in Kenya, Italian. But criticism of Hinsley's advice did not last for long. The White Fathers in western Tanzania saw the point and acted on it, while the others were later to follow the example, which was to result in flourishing Catholic secondary schools all over the region.

While insisting on the need for higher education, one should not forget that Africa – and not least East Africa – has produced a great number of men and women who, with not much more than elementary school training, have used the opportunities which the work in a mission could provide and educated themselves by strength of their innate gifts and determination. One example among many comes to mind. Enos Benjamin Boru was originally from Tana River on the Kenyan coast. Contacts with a Pietistic German group took him to Somalia where he pioneered and where he met his wife. He contacted a Swedish Lutheran mission there and worked with them. As the work in Somalia came to an end because of political changes in the 1930s, Boru went with the Swedish mission for pioneering work in Mbulu, north-western Tanzania. In the end he was posted to Magomeni, Dar es Salaam. With his fluent English, excellent Swahili and Christian conviction, he made a lasting impression.

The urge for higher education led to a pyramidal structure of education with a wide base and a very narrow peak. Three countries illustrate this trend. In 1938 Zaïre had 725,000 pupils in primary schools and 600 privileged individuals in secondary education. In 1958 1,500,000 received primary education and 18,000 were in secondary institutions. In 1959 Ghana had 483,000 primary school pupils while secondary school students more than doubled in the decade from 6,000 in 1950 to 15,000 in 1959. Uganda in 1950 had 159,000 pupils in primary and 700 students in secondary education; in 1959 these figures had climbed to 993,000 for the primary sector and 3,728 in secondary schools.[49] At a time when most of African education was in mission hands a personal factor could be noticed: the role of the missionary, Catholic or Protestant, in finding in the primary school, that bright young boy or girl to be helped along to new achievements in the secondary school.

The numbers of the privileged who could enter secondary schools being so low, the Catholic seminary – senior or junior – was of the greatest importance. Only a certain percentage of those who entered junior seminary did in actual fact continue to priestly ordination, but for a large number the junior seminary with its extra provision of Latin and Philosophy gave a highly regarded competence for the educational world and for the expanding civil service.

In this period the African teacher was moving away from mission control. No longer could there be the matter-of-course identification of school teacher and local preacher. The work of a school teacher was becoming a calling in its own right, with a new attitude on the part of the teacher to the missionary and all that he represented. There was increasingly a critical attitude to the local missionary. At last the teacher could feel free from the missionary's paternalistic control and/or from the local pastor's or priests's dictates. Others again – and these were the great majority – experienced a new sense of free identification with the Christian endeavour.

The missionary manager

The role of the missionary was also affected. In British dependencies from Zimbabwe to Kenya and Uganda, and in West Africa, the role of the missionary with regard to government subsidized schools passed through a considerable change: the missionary was appointed 'supervisor of schools' with the duty to inspect each local village school four times a year. With perhaps fifty to sixty or more schools in his district, this was a full-time job. The missionary had become virtually a school inspector on the cheap. Some felt this was a good solution, for it helped to pay the salary of the missionary. It implied a closer relationship between mission and educational department. It also imparted a new image of the missionary as a school-man or a school-woman, a school supervisor. That was now what missions were for: to run schools.

The task of managing the church school fell to the African pastor, and an inordinate amount of time and energy was spent on educational matters, welfare, finance, dealing with government etc. In Ghana much of a pastor's time was spent running the schools. Church resources were heavily channelled to running schools and this may, in certain cases, have led to inadequate pastoral care. However, once a Christian community and congregation was established, broader concerns than schooling made themselves felt. Church schools soon were serving a wider community than the local Church.

As numbers of schools increased, so did the body of teachers whose Christian commitment could no longer be assured. Denominational rivalry linked to the power of controlling education resulted in incoherent educational planning. Increasingly, missions and Churches were preoccupied with the strategic problem of whether to direct personnel and money primarily to evangelization or to an ever-more demanding school system. This problem was acutely felt and most courageously faced in Ghana, in its Methodist

Church, where both Western and African leaders were aware of the risks involved in the choice.

L. B. Greaves, Methodist educationalist in Ghana and later distinguished educational advisor to the Protestant missions in East Africa, voiced the Church's concern in an address to the Methodist Church in Accra, in 1949: '"Use the School to build up the Church" is essentially a pioneering slogan', but, he felt, there was now a reverse order of importance, to 'use the Church to build up the School'. He could visualize a Church 'impoverished in money and in spirit by the magnitude of the effort diverted to its schools and a ministry in bondage to its schools and, what is worse, hugging its chains ... "Without my schools I cannot be a Methodist Minister".' This, he felt, was a threat to the life of the Church. 'God must not be put into the margin in deference to the State's neutrality.' He pleaded that it was now for church educationalists to concentrate on teacher training and girls' education.[50]

His younger colleague, Thomas A. Beetham, as Principal of Wesley College, Kumasi, had earlier anticipated Greaves' concern with this warning: 'In striving for universal Christian education we must beware lest we wake up in thirty years' time to the fact that there is no longer a Christian Church to provide it.'[51] Throughout the continent this debate went on. With varying emphases Catholics and Protestants explored ways and means of resolving the problems in their synods or in encounters with government authorities.

Education, with its emphasis on literacy and book-learning, tended to divorce students from society, and especially from productive agricultural work. The growth of literate education could lead to a social conflict between adults and the now powerful young. Education tended to lead to an urban-oriented outlook. Through schooling, the young usurped their place in the society's hierarchy as they mastered the skill and power of reading and writing. The young became mediators between the community and the outside world. This gave them power and prestige. Thus, the elders and traditional authorities were displaced in the new order of things.

In the years before Independence the Christian teacher in the village school was to take on a new role as local leader and interpreter for the emergent African nationalism and thereby to help to lay the foundation of modern Africa. In those areas where Indirect Rule had been the guiding policy during the colonial period, the chief had been the local leader. In the years of transition over to Independent Africa, this role was taken over by the teacher. At a time when certain African countries discovered their political salvation in various kinds of 'socialism', the village teacher could re-interpret that socialism as a modern expression of 'our traditional African system of communal co-operation'.

This also affected the congregation which developed an important role of mediating and resolving new tensions. Although the Christian congregation was a new social form, it was inherently supported by a traditional communal ethos. Thus an important role of the Christian congregation was, firstly, to regularize new social conflicts; secondly, to mitigate and moderate this change in the balance of power within society; and thirdly, to redevelop a new harmony and strength of unity based on a Christian communal identity. The congregation thus ordered an otherwise growing disunity. The role of the clergy as a mediating force should not be overlooked. Societal conflict was ritualized by the forms of Church services and the new congregational organizations and activities – women's societies, youth groups, associations of young men (and women). Church congregational identities of young men's associations ('improvement societies' etc.) were carried over to the towns and helped to reduce some of the destructive effects of such rural–urban mobility.

To what extent did this generation of highly educated teachers become factors for secularization? It is easily claimed that they were indeed such factors and on a continent-wide scale. But while it is easily claimed it is not easily proved. In his own limited fashion the present writer (B.Sr.) has followed the problem, at least in East Africa, ever since, in 1943, the head of the new Makerere Secondary School, Dr Turner, told him that he spent half his time discussing with the students a possible reconciliation of the Creation stories in the Book of Genesis with the new knowledge in modern Biology, a problem which in those parts of East Africa received a special urgency with the discovery in 1959 by Dr Louis and Mary Leakey of *anthropos* australopithecine *Zinjanthaopus boisei* and, within the next two years, of *Homo habilis*. With a certain periodicity of a decade at a time related to the opening of new secondary schools, this same question would arise, in Kenya or in western Tanzania: had the Bible teaching in the village school been misleading and if it was, could one then trust anything else in that Book?

So the questions were formulated by ever new generations in secondary school essays throughout a continent. Yet, largely these new generations were, being African, too healthy to allow themselves to be bogged down in radical doubt or that famous 'secularization'. Very soon – this is our personal impression and there is room for dissidence on this point – these young men and women were pillars of the local congregation, a body which to them was seen as the religious expression of an ineradicable African community.

ISLAM—MUSLIM RESPONSES TO CHRISTIAN EDUCATION

At the dawn of the colonial period, in 1899, Anson Atterbury, an American writer, stated: 'Islam in Africa will be comparatively easy for Christianity to overcome.' This view was shared by many early twentieth-century European observers of Africa, who asserted that 'Islam is nothing without political power'.[52] Writing in 1912 on the newly formed Murid Brotherhood in Senegal, Paul Marty, an authority on West African Islam, thought that this particular Muslim confraternity would not survive the death of its founder, and thus he predicted the Brotherhood's disintegration. Yet, today, the Muridiyya embraces over 500,000 Senegalese Muslims.

Colonial conquest

Writing in the aftermath of European military subjugation of Muslims and Islamic polities in Africa, early European observers could not but think that Islam had been dealt such a blow that it was unlikely to recover. After all, the catalogue of colonial conquest in Muslim areas was impressive. France triumphed over such West African Muslim leaders as Maba, Samori, Momodu-Lamine, and defeated the Tukulor state. Britain crushed Muslim opposition in the Hut Tax War of 1896 in Sierra Leone, and in the battle for the conquest of northern Nigeria, at Burmi in 1903 – where the Caliph of Sokoto made his last stand. In the Sudan the battle of Omdurman in 1898 destroyed the Mahdist State and the death of its *khalifa* the following year appeared to strengthen British control of this once fervent Islamic land. In Uganda, British military intervention in 1892 and the Uganda Agreement of 1900 saw the near submergence of Islam in Buganda, while in Malawi, British force of arms defeated Muslim Yao chiefs between 1891 and 1895.

In East Africa, German military forces destroyed Muslim coastal opposition in Tanganyika, and hanged the main leader of this coastal resistance, Abushiri, in 1889. It would be wrong not to mention Sayyid Muhammad Abdallah Hasan of Somalia, who remained the only major Muslim leader who was undefeated and free of European control. Known better by the derogatory and inexact appellation, the 'Mad Mullah', this religious and intellectual leader succeeded for more than twenty years in maintaining his independence from British and Italian attempts to subdue him. The Sayyid mounted 'a military movement that was both long sustained and successful, perhaps more so than any other movement led by an African Muslim leader of the nineteenth or early twentieth century'.[53] His poetry ranks among the finest of Somali verse and is often an eloquent expression of his determination to remain free. Only with his death, naturally, in 1920 did Somali resistance crumble. 'With him died the hopes of his followers for an independent Somali Muslim state on the traditional model.'[54] Apart from Somalia, there was plenty of evidence to suggest that Muslim power and vitality had been reduced by these resounding onslaughts, and consequently there arose a belief that Christian Europe could contain Islamic influence in Africa. A complementary part of this perspective was the idea that Africa could now be comprehensively evangelized for the Christian message.

The growth of Islam

We can now see that these turn-of-the-century predictions were widely off the mark. Instead, 'in half a century of European colonization Islam progressed more widely and profoundly than in ten centuries of pre-colonial history. In this short space of time it seems probable that the number of Muslims in tropical Africa has at least doubled.'[55] The causes of this expansion and the concomitant relationship between Muslims and Christians, within the colonial framework, will be the main thrust of the rest of this chapter.

It could well be argued that for large parts of Africa, it was the expansion and influence, however pervasive, of Christianity that provided the impetus for African Muslims to adapt and respond to the new colonial era. Christianity was, after all, perceived by many Muslims as representing the underlying fabric of both Western culture and especially the secular civilization, that the colonial rulers were introducing, to whatever degree, to African society. The challenge of Christianity and its attendant cultural characteristics, was met by African Islam in a variety of ways, often after much discussion among Muslim society. Responses to Western education can be appraised as the most important issue in this period facing Muslims.

Colonial administration and response to Islam

Once conquest had been achieved and apprehension of the 'Islamic Peril' reduced, the colonial powers were faced with the problem of reaching an accommodation with their new Muslim subjects. There was little of a well-thought-out colonial policy towards Islam, and consequently the imperial responses were based on expediency in each situation. France discriminated between Islamic groups, supporting those that would facilitate colonial administration and suppressing others that appeared a threat. Britain developed a policy of Indirect Rule in its main Muslim area of West Africa, northern Nigeria, but this system was essentially based on pragmatism. With a ratio of one colonial official to 250,000 northern Nigerians there was little else that Britain could do.

Both European powers were extremely suspicious of the activities of the large number of Muslim teachers, the *marabouts* and *mallams*, especially as many were itinerant and thus their influence could not easily be regulated. Instead, French and British officials developed their administration in Muslim areas in conjunction with established indigenous rulers, such as emirs and leaders of Sufi Brotherhoods or Orders. Islam provided the colonial administration with literate (Arabic) groups, such as clerks, warrant officers and chiefs. Islamic law was recognized and promulgated over wide areas as it was easier to administer than the various local laws and customs. In Tanganyika, the German colonial administration adopted Swahili as its official language and used coastal Muslims as junior officials in governing the mainly non-Muslim peoples of the interior.

Muslim adaptation and Islamic expansion

From the side of African Muslims, there was no co-ordinated Islamic response to colonial occupation. Opposition, initially, was shown by some Muslims in northern Nigeria by resorting to the traditional Islamic response of *hijra*, or withdrawal, by fleeing from European-controlled territory. Other Muslims in West Africa decided on cultural and spiritual *hijra*, i.e., withdrawal from and non-involvement with Europeans, the colonial administration and Western education. Examples of this kind of opposition were the Bamidele movement in Ibadan, southern Nigeria, during the 1930s, and the Hamalliyya movement, founded in 1909 in French West Africa. Most Muslims, however, generally accepted the colonial take-over, and the majority of Muslim leaders co-operated with the authorities, because of which they were duly rewarded through recognition of their traditional position and leadership.

This colonial *modus vivendi* with Islam gave the religion a certain prestige. The appointment of Muslims to colonial bureaucracies and as warrant officers in colonial armies (with imams attached), where the uniforms were Muslim-inspired, all tended to give Islam an elevated status. As a result, there was much prestige and social progress to be gained by converting to Islam, especially for Africans of lower status or class, or for those who lived on peripheral areas, surrounding established Muslim centres. 'What the [Islamic] conquests of the nineteenth century could not do has been accomplished by the social revolution which has taken place through

European occupation.'[56] Trimingham was alluding to the disappearance, at least in West Africa, of a kind of equilibrium that had existed between Islamic societies and non-Muslim peoples. Under European rule, Islam was often given a decisive advantage by colonial acceptance and encouragement of the religion. New opportunities for integration, mobility and the development of urban centres facilitated the expansion of Muslim Africa. Colonial rule brought about a cessation of local hostilities and generally established peaceful conditions for travel, trade and the related Muslim proselytizing activities. The ubiquitous Hausa and Mande (or Dyula) traders of West Africa, ignoring unimportant colonial boundaries, were able to reach and sojourn in areas that had hitherto, for a variety of reasons, been impermeable to Islamization.

Seasonal migrant labour assisted the spread of Islam, as foremen and plantation overseers were often Muslims. Thus migrant workers were influenced by Islam and they in turn carried the new religion back to their homes. This particular kind of Muslim influence is exemplified by the rapid Islamization of Mossi seasonal workers from Upper Volta to the Ivory Coast and Ghana. A similar process occurred in Togo, which before colonial rule had accepted little Muslim influence. Many Tam (or Kotokoli) went to Ghana after the First World War, became Muslims and, on returning home to Togo, extended their new religious affiliation to their families and communities. Old trade routes were the lines of immigration and acculturation. Cattle from the savannas of West Africa went south, while kola nuts from the forested areas went north. Migrants from Hausa and Mossi communities travelled south to Ghanaian towns and established 'strangers' quarters'.

The growth of these strangers quarters, or *zongo*'s as they are known in Ghana, had an even greater impact than seasonal migration on the development and gestation of Islam. The growth of new towns and increased urban opportunities, all engendered by the new colonial economy, led to the development of fairly permanent strangers' quarters. Coming from different areas, the majority of non-Muslim immigrants, such as the Gurma and Grunshi, adopted Islam when they joined the *zongo*. 'Detached from their tribal organization in a foreign country, they found in Islam a new cohesive factor. As Moslems they could attach themselves to the Moslem communities which flourished throughout the Gold Coast.'[57] But these strangers' quarters sometimes experienced difficulties, stemming from ethnic differences. In the Kumasi *zongo* recurring factionalism within the Muslim community led to a dispute (which started in the 1940s and continued until the early 1970s) about the leadership of the *zongo*, and thus over the control of Kumasi's central mosque. Related to this was tension between local Asante Muslims and immigrant believers. In the Muslim *sabon gari* (new town) of Ibadan, Hausa residents maintained a communal cohesiveness that tended to isolate them from the surrounding host society, including local Yoruba Muslims.

An analogous, but reverse religious situation can be seen in the development of Christian 'new towns' or 'strangers' quarters', known by the Hausa name of *sabon gari*, on the outskirts of northern Nigerian cities such as Kano, Katsina, and Zaria. In 1927 there were 5,000 southern Nigerians, mostly Christian mission-trained traders and officials, in the *sabon gari* of Kano. But the differences between Muslim and Christian stranger quarters was most marked. Christian southerners in northern Nigerian *sabon garis* had generally Western education and thus 'Christianity with its emphasis on the new literacy, became the religion of an [Westernized] elite'.[58] Conversely, migrants who joined the Muslim *zongos* in Ghana were poor, illiterate and worked as labourers in the gold mines or in the cocoa plantations.

Western education

The challenge of Western education and the response of Muslims to new educational opportunities is arguably the most important and widespread issue that faced Muslim communities during this period. It was even more of a critical subject with regard to the education of Muslim women. Most Muslim communities had their own traditional system of Qur'anic education which, in pre-colonial times, had seemed a fairly adequate medium for the dissemination of Islamic knowledge. When faced with the development and the possible opportunities for Western education within the developing colonial state, they 'found it impossible to insulate and immunize themselves completely against the new forces'.[59] Muslims could only ignore Western education at their peril, especially in view of the dramatic Christian response to, and development of, modern education.

The main problem for Muslims, quite understandably, was the perceived link between Western education and Christianity. Most schools were run by Christian missions, who expected their pupils to be open to the Christian message. Writing on Malawi, Bone comments: 'Even where Muslims were admitted parents feared, with some justification, that they would lose their children to Christianity and discouraged them from attending.'[60]

In northern Nigeria, with its own scholarly and literate tradition, Western education was not popular and, as a result, there were 'problems when the British tried to "modernize" the society by grafting on to the Islamic traditions an educational system within a more or less Christian context.'[61] As part of the policy of Indirect Rule, Britain had excluded Christian missions from the north and even when the CMS was allowed into Kano emirate in 1929, it was expected to concentrate its activities to the Christian southerners in the *sabon gari*. The result of this lack of Western education meant that out of an 'estimated twelve million people in Northern Nigeria in 1952, only about a quarter of a million had a basic competence in English, while in Kano ... only about 23,000 out of 3 million people were literate in English, and of these 50 per cent were from other parts of Nigeria.'[62]

It was a deliberate policy by France and Britain to exclude Christian missions from strongly Muslim areas and because of this there was little development of Western education. Many colonial administrators thought that an orderly, if slow, development of Islam and its attendant culture, was more suitable than access to modern education and Christianity. British officials in particular often showed great disdain for the 'trousered' Western-educated African and preferred what education there was to be in the vernacular and not in English. In contradistinction, writes Crowder, 'far from trying to control the flow of ideas from the West, the missionaries positively pumped them into West Africa. The pump was the school, the end product an educated elite and a mass of young men with primary education in the three Rs ...'[63]

In south-western Nigeria, Islam and Christianity were well-represented, with both religions increasing their numbers and often having members from the same Yoruba family. Because of the proximity between these two religions in this area, it is not surprising that Muslims were influenced and impressed by the standard of, and the enthusiasm for, Christian modern education. This is perhaps the main reason why Yoruba Muslims have been more responsive and innovative with regard to Western education than most other Muslim societies. The colonial government in Lagos gave a measure of assistance to modern Muslim education but the support was hardly on the scale needed in order to satisfy demand. Instead Yoruba Muslims formed various societies whose task was to provide Muslims with a 'Western education not in conflict with Islamic principles'.[64] The Ansar-ud-Deen Society, founded in 1923, was the most famous of these Muslim educational organizations: by 1960 'the society had about 50,000 members and ran several teacher training colleges, secondary schools and over 200 primary schools'.[65] Concomitant with this expansion and integration of Western and Islamic education was the development in south-western Nigeria of a modern Islamic culture. Abeokuta was the home in 1933 of the first Muslim printing press and by 1952 the town had sixteen Muslim presses.

In Ghana the first group of Fante Muslims, led by Benjamin Sam – an ex-Wesleyan teacher and catechist – opened a Muslim school at Ekrofol on the coast in 1896 which was based on Western education. Unfortunately the school closed in 1908 because of an outbreak of disease in the area. These early attempts by both Ghanaian and Nigeria coastal Muslims illustrates the need felt for a modern expression of Islam. This need was partially fulfilled after Fante and Yoruba Muslims appealed for assistance to the Ahmadiyyah movement in India. The Ahmadis responded by sending their first missionary, Abd-ur-Rahim Nayyar, to West Africa in 1921. Other 'modernist' Muslim groups in southern Nigeria viewed the Ahmadis with suspicion, and consequently their activities attracted a greater following in Ghana.

Outside of coastal West Africa, Muslim Western education was barely developed in the other regions of the continent. Only in the southern tip of the continent was modern Islamic education and thinking developing at this time, among the Cape Coloured Muslim community. Here 'an Arabic-Afrikaans literature of religious instruction soon developed.'[66]

In Malawi, Yao Muslims who comprised 10 per cent of the population (at the present time about 600,000) were unable to gain access to Western education for most of the colonial period – because Christian missions dominated the school system. 'Up to 1926 all western education in Malawi was mission education. It was the practice of some mission schools to educate only pupils of their own denomination, thus excluding professing Muslims.'[67] However, a number of Muslim Yao chiefs asked the colonial administration in 1928 to provide Western education without Christian influence, but apparently with no result.

The 250,000 Muslims who lived in the Maniema region of the Belgian Congo faced a similar problem to that confronting their Yao co-religionists. With education in the hands of Christian missions, 'Muslim children were either excluded from the schools, mainly operated in Maniema by the White Fathers, or suffered strong pressure to convert to Christianity.'[68] In 1948 a Muslim organization financed by the Ismailis was refused permission to establish a Muslim school in Kasongo.

In Uganda, Muslims although constituting 13 per cent of the Buganda people, could not compete with the competitive Protestant and Catholic Buganda groups. 'Nearly all Moslems were relegated to the commoner class by virtue of their landlessness and their separation from Western (largely Christian missionary) influence and education.'[69]

In Tanzania the German colonial administration established schools for coastal Muslims as part of a policy of creating junior officials (known as *jumbes* and *akidas*) who could act as intermediaries between the German administrators and the peoples of the interior. Christian missions objected to the adoption of Swahili as the administrative language and also to the rule of coastal Muslims over non-Islamic areas of the interior. British administration after the First World War reversed this German policy and instead encouraged Christian mission schools to provide junior officials for inland areas.

Perhaps the Muslim Swahili coast of Kenya, with its great centre of Mombasa, provides an acute example of an Islamic society's dilemma over whether or not to accept Western education – this time for Muslim women. Western education began on the coast in the 1930s and was much influenced by the opening of a Muslim girls' school in Zanzibar. In 1933 a boys' school was established in Mombasa, drawing support from many Muslim notables, and this success led to the opening of a girls' school in 1935–36. Sheik Mohamed Abdallah Ghazali founded and maintained these schools, and he might be seen as the innovator of female education among Mombasa's Muslim community.

Preceding the creation of these schools a lively debate took place over the merits of female education and relevant Qur'anic interpretations on this issue. Pressure was increasing for the provision of some kind of modern education for girls and many Muslim families were already hiring Christian mission women, notably from the CMS, to educate their daughters. A Muslim leader, Sheik Al-Amin wrote an notable essay in 1931 on 'our duty towards women', and how female Muslim education offered an example of positive European imitation. Sheik Al-Amin argued:

> we will be aiding our girls to join the mission school, where most students come to read. And those poor people do not know that they have put their children in HELL, for missions do not open schools except to trap Muslims into becoming Christians. To send a child to [mission] school is the worst sort of crime.[70]

In 1938 the colonial administration took over both the girls' and the boys' schools, with the Government Girls' Muslim School having over 100 pupils. Purdah was accepted in the school and instruction was given by European mistresses. Although the school had comparatively few places (rising to 880 pupils in 1962) it exemplified the process of adaptation and response in a conservative Muslim community. Undoubtedly, it was Christian mission girls' schools that were mainly responsible for this change of attitude.

On balance, throughout Africa, Muslims were hindered by their hesitant response to Western education even taking into account the lack of opportunities. This became very serious given the vital importance of education in the development of the modern state in Africa. At grass-roots, Islamic society in Africa was divided in their perception of the relevance and correctness of Western education. Many Muslims, at the village level, opposed modern education, mainly because 'Christian-sponsored Western education was evidently seen as a mirage designed to lure Muslim children from the straight path.'[71] Other opposition stemmed from a refusal to co-operate with colonial rule and its institutions. On the other hand, it is apparent that many Muslims desired Western education, free of Christian influences, but were frustrated by the lack of suitable opportunities. Backwardness in Western education meant Muslims were ill-equipped for involvement in the apparatus of the colonial state and its successor, the modern independent state, and this hindered the appeal of Islam. Islam was increasingly seen as a conservative force in African society, whereas Christianity with its mission schools was viewed as an avenue for advancement and opportunity.

This growth of conservatism as a characteristic of African Islam can be exemplified by its responses to nationalism against colonial rule and from the extent of Muslim participation in nationalist circles. Alienation from Western education of course motivated some Muslims to play an active role in the development of nationalism in some countries, notably Tanzania. Writing about the Tanganyika African Nationalist Union (TANU) in Tanganyika, Dr Iliffe notes that 'Muslim trader-politicians were at first its most characteristic leaders, and use of Swahili gave its ideology many Islamic overtones to balance those which its western-educated leaders derived from Christianity.'[72]

Muslims in other countries, in contrast, were often slow to respond to nationalism, either because of antipathy or through being handicapped in expressing nationalism in Western terms. Trimingham, no doubt with the Muslim elite in mind, wrote: 'In the political sphere, having adjusted themselves to the colonial rulers who accorded them a favoured status, Muslims clung to the status quo, fearing the loss of privileges, and reacted against the brash nationalism of the new men.'[73] However, the heart of the problem of why Islam generally could not transform itself into a force for change was the absence of a comprehensive Muslim system of Western education. Christian education had a near monopoly in the development of the new force of nationalism. 'From the mission schools emerged many of the political leaders of modern West Africa, and from these schools, too, emerged the backbone of their support.'[74]

Islamic diversity in Africa

It would be profoundly wrong to regard Islam as a uniform religion with a constant level of 'orthodoxy' in all areas. The diversity among African Muslims is perhaps most clearly illustrated by the role and types of Sufi mystical orders or brotherhoods which permeate the entire area of Islamic Africa. Many of these orders originated in North Africa and the Middle East and then spread to Tropical Africa were they were generally 'Africanized' and domesticated to suit the needs of a particular area of Muslim Africa. Dr Iliffe writes with regard to Tanganyika that 'Brotherhoods were characteristically "second-stage" organizations deepening the faith of existing Muslims, much like revival movements in Protestant Christianity, although in Tanganyika – again like Christian revivals – they also proselytized among followers of indigenous religions.'[75] Spread by wandering religious teachers, traders and local pilgrims, the colonial powers found it difficult to control the spread of these orders. Colonial policy was consequently based on discriminating between brotherhoods: favouring those that appeared pliant, while suppressing others that seemed subversive.

In East Africa the two main Muslim brotherhoods were the Qadiriyya and the Shadhiliyya. Both arrived on the mainland by 1900 and spread rapidly during German colonial rule, reaching Muslims in Zaïre and Malawi in the 1920s. A characteristic of Sufi brotherhoods throughout Africa was the importance that adherents attached to the regional centre and base of each particular order. These centres of religious activity, such as Bagamoyo for the Qadiriyya and Kilwa for the *shadhiliyya* (both East African coastal towns) drew pilgrims from the entire region. 'As Bagamoyo and Kilwa decayed economically, so their religious importance grew, a tendency accentuated by the mainland's gradual intellectual emancipation from Zanzibar.'[76]

Economic decline was, of course, not a prerequisite for the success of an order's spiritual heart or centre. Just the opposite was the case for the Muridiyya in Senegal and its headquarters at Touba. Founded by Amadu Bamba in 1886, it was viewed with hostility by the French who exiled its leader first to Gabon and later to Mauritania, until 1912. From that year the French administrators altered their perceptions of the Muridiyya, mainly because the Brotherhood showed tremendous economic enterprise in establishing new villages and clearing virgin land for ground nut cash crop production. Apart from assisting the colonial economy, Touba became a focus of economic prosperity as well as developing as a centre of religious prestige. The French administration feted the Muridiyya for its agricultural successes and favoured its leadership with recognition – partly by preferential allocation of land. Although Amadu Bamba died in 1927, his successors followed his policies of keeping followers submissive by stressing the importance of agricultural work as a way of gaining salvation in the next life.

The Muridiyya was a response to European colonialism and it lends itself for comparison with similar movements in Africa. Dr Cruise O'Brien, an authority on the Muridiyya writes:

> The closest comparison with the Mouride position, perhaps, is that of the independent African Christian movements in the Congo basin in the early twentieth century, for there is considerable similarity in the two colonial situations. The Bakongo followers of the prophet Simon Kimbangu gave expression to their tribal feelings in a Christian idiom (as the Wolof Mourides used the idiom of Sufi Islam) ... Kimbangu's slogan 'Obey God, not the administrator' may be compared with Amadu Bamba's early, defiant claim to be the servant of God and obedient only to him.[77]

Defeated by European force, both movements exhibited a degree of hostility to colonial rule that was often expressed through 'an abstention from any other than Utopian assertions of independence'.[78]

Both the Qadiriyya and the Tijaniyya were widespread in West Africa, the latter order having spread from North Africa in the nineteenth century. The Tijaniyya, like many brotherhoods, experienced tensions and schisms, mainly arising from disputes over leadership succession. One such split occurred in 1909, when Shaikh Hamallah founded the radical and antagonistic brotherhood in French West Africa called the Hamalliyya. It was characterized by its hostility to European values and its appeal to poor and deprived groups who saw the order as a means of social emancipation. Tijani leaders felt threatened by the Hamalliyya and sought French support, which led to the suppressing of this movement.

African Muslims and the wider world of Islam

Another division in Tijani circles occurred in the late 1920s, when Ibrahim Niass established his own branch of the order – sometimes known as the Reformed Tijaniyya – with his spiritual centre located at Kaolack in Senegal. Ibrahim Niass can be seen as the single most important personality in twentieth-century West African Islam. Born of a leading religious family, he won a large following across the breadth of West Africa, irrespective of colonial boundaries. In 1937 he performed the pilgrimage to Mecca and met there the Emir of Kano; on his journey back via Morocco and Fez, he seems to have been created Caliph (leader) of the Tijaniyya. Before this event Niass had proclaimed himself 'The Saviour of the Age' in 1930 and attracted fame and followers in many countries, not least in many of the cities of Nigeria. He travelled widely, and on a visit to Ghana in 1952 he was accorded much respect by the country's prime minister, Kwame Nkrumah. Ibrahim Niass, who died in 1975, is probably the West African Muslim luminary who did most to strengthen the ties between West African Islam and the wider Islamic world, at a time when colonial governments were content to keep them apart. As vice-president of the World Muslim Congress as well as being linked to the Muslim World League and the Arab League, his activities 'connected his followers with Muslims in the rest of the world'.[79]

For many African Muslim societies the increased integration with the wider Islamic world, and a heightened awareness of it, occurred in a variety of ways. Much greater numbers of African Muslims performed the pilgrimage, which most times was a spiritually enriching event as Africans met with pilgrims from all corners of the world. They could compare Islamic practice in their own society with that of the Islamic heartland, as well as with that of other countries they had journeyed through. Attachment to a Sufi brotherhood allowed adherents to learn about wider developments from other branches or chapters of the same brotherhood. Colonial rule often increased the awareness of educated Muslims to political and religious developments in the Middle East, and to the involvement of European power in the region. In 1914 the Ottoman Sultan of Turkey called on all Muslims to join a holy war (*jihad*) to fight France, Britain and Russia. During the Second World War Britain circulated among leading Nigerian Muslims a speech by the King of Saudi Arabia expressing his country's and Islam's gratitude for British assistance and protection. Thus the colonial powers used the wider world of Islam to shape Muslim public opinion within Africa.

As the century progressed more African Muslim students studied in the religious centres and universities of North Africa and the Middle East, the most renowned centre being the University of al-Azhar in Cairo. This quest for education by Muslims has parallels with the stream of Africans, mostly Christians, who journeyed to Europe for higher and further education. Colonial governments attempted to control the influx of Islamic ideas, often by screening Arabic and Islamic books and papers. African students studying at the centres of Islamic thought were in touch with all the mainstream Islamic ideas, and often when they returned home they were dismayed by the lack of orthodoxy in African Islam. The Wahhabiyya movement, which stressed puritanism in Islam, was a revival movement brought to West Africa in the 1930s by Africans returning from Mecca. Wahhabis condemned moral laxity, Sufi brotherhoods and Islamic magic as practised by marabouts in West Africa. The Ivory Coast was one of the main centres for Wahhabi activity between the 1930s and the 1950s and it experienced the tensions between these new reformers who wanted an Islam faithful to the Qur'an and the traditional Sufi leaders and *marabouts*.

The challenge that faced these new reformers in their zeal to establish orthodoxy was the substitution of the microcosm of much African Muslim belief for the macrocosm, the idea of a universal religion with a supreme God. Islam in Africa still faces this problem of transition, but in their search for respectability, Muslim scholars and students have to be careful that they do not destroy local diversity, which is the hallmark of a people's religion, and which so intimately links the African Muslim with the soil, the sand and the sky.

12

LOCAL PERSPECTIVES

CATECHISTS AND CATECHUMENS

The catechist

Representative voices bear witness to the role played by catechists in the rapid advance of the Church in this period. 'The village catechist, with his slender qualifications and very modest pay, is the real hero of the Christian situation in Africa.'[1] A revival in southern Cameroon in 1937 resulted in the opening of four Presbyterian catechist schools, with two-year courses. The men trained there formed the backbone of the Church for a whole generation, doing all the pastoral work except the administration of the sacraments. Catechists played a role in another Presbyterian Church, the Mission Philafricaine in southern Angola. There were two kinds of catechists: those with four to six months' training 'but not ordained', and those with three years' training who were 'ordained as evangelists'. In this Church all the pastors came from this latter category, having been catechists and evangelists, with one year's additional pastoral training beyond their evangelist schooling. In the local communities, catechists were still regarded as leaders.

> For twenty-nine days in every month, these communities are looked after by a teacher, who is already fully occupied in running the school, or by a catechist, who may not always have been very well instructed himself. Apart from the small amount of attention that a priest can give on his monthly visits, the entire work of teaching catechumens, confirmation candidates, first communion classes and penitents' classes is done by the teacher or catechist.[2]

In the 1920s and 1930s, most of the village work was still the responsibility of the teacher-catechist. On the great day when the French, Belgian, or British administrator came to inspect, the catechist would be there with his school class, in his capacity as trusted representative of his African group. He was still the big *Massa* of the village. He was in immediate contact with traditional culture, but represented also the decisive thrust of a great religious movement throughout the continent. He was still there in his little wattle-and-daub chapel, although aware that he had eventually become something of an embarrassment, in his position half-way between pastor and voluntary lay helper. This situation is movingly interpreted by Joseph W. Abruquah in his book, *The Catechist*, about his father, a Fante Methodist catechist in Ghana.[3]

In the period between the two world wars, the Protestant catechists in Zaïre performed heavy state-required labour, usually road work. New legal conditions were officially laid down in 1945. Catechists and others employed by the missions, and totally dependent for their living on mission pay, were exempted from such duties. Voluntary helpers, however, who did not work full-time for the mission, undertook such tasks along with their fellow tribesmen.[4] Many Churches had planned for decades to reduce the number of paid catechists and to replace them with ordained pastors *and* voluntary helpers. In 1949, the Protestant Church in the Ivory Coast – the result of the Harris movement – with a Christian community of some 50,000, had three pastors and 160 catechists. The British missionary in charge, determined to reduce the number of catechists drastically and treble the number of pastors, appointed voluntary 'local preachers' instead of salaried catechists. Most Churches in other countries shared the same intent, but did not always translate it into action. With increasing school education, opportunities for advancement and higher pay were more favourable than before. Most new catechists now were therefore those who had failed to enter higher education centres, or those who had proved unsuccessful in examinations. A leading, highly educated pastor in Cameroon was emphatic: 'For the future, the catechists must disappear. Those we get now only destroy the work.' In Protestant churches, the catechist became the object of increasing sharp and persistent criticism from Western missionaries as well as African pastors of Central and West Africa:

> It is degrading for an educated man to go into a rural district and become a catechist ... We must get rid of our group of catechists ... Of our 1,550 catechists some are well-trained, others are a bunch of riff-raff. They are not qualified to take any other work. The name catechist has fallen into disrepute in our country.

The Methodist Church in Ghana has had a special problem with catechists. In principle, Methodist missions rely on a corps of class leaders and local preachers, but this system was never developed in Ghana. Instead, the paid catechist was shepherd for the local congregation. With the catechist's poor salary, most able ones took up more lucrative employment.

> The churches therefore have to fall back on the much poorer, untrained catechist, locally recruited; and he is generally only marking time until he can get into some better sort of employment, or into a training college for teachers. And because through the years we have relied upon the paid agent, there is now no reliable body of class leaders and local preachers to carry the work in the churches. In the towns there are the ministers; it is the villages that suffer.[5]

In their report, *Lay Leadership in West African Churches*, the Methodists stressed that in West Africa, 'we need more ministers far more urgently than we need catechists.'[6]

A Uganda pastor said: 'Very few men stay on as catechists for life. In olden times our catechists used to stay. But the financial situation nowadays makes this difficult.'[7] As a lay reader, a man was to receive seventy shillings per month, but often that sum had to last for three months. Taking a job in the Public Works Department, he would have a guaranteed salary of 150 shillings per month. In Benin, the Methodist missionary reported that 80 per cent of the catechists left for commerce soon after completing their training. In 1951, Cameroonian catechists had progressed so far as to stage a strike. The promotion from Church catechist to garage mechanic was alluring in South Africa and elsewhere. A catechist in Tanzania, a dynamic preacher and fisher of men, became the president of the communal hunt. Why? He 'simply got tired', or as the local Revival group suggested, 'he loved worldly glory and he hoped to curry favour with the Government'.[8] His case is not unique. But there are also hundreds of examples of Christian men who have withstood better pay and higher status in society, to serve their Lord as simple catechists. Catechists were able to keep their particular authority in some local congregations. Few pastors dared to reprimand an evangelist for a mistake, though in some cases the pastors tended to be domineering over the catechists. In Cameroon, a generation ago, a pastor could expect the catechist to work for him in his garden. Where caste distinctions existed between nobility and peasant groups, the priest from the nobility could not eat with catechists of the peasant strata. This would explain a comment by two Mbega catechists in Zaïre, now priests in the Anglican Church. They spoke about Apolo Kivebulaya, the Ganda preacher who became the apostle to the Pygmies: 'Apolo baptized us, and – he took his meals together with us.' Fortunately, a remarkable degree of co-operation emerged between pastor and catechists.[9]

The previous paragraphs have summarized the situation in the Protestant Churches and could as well, almost word for word, be applied to the Catholic Churches. The catechist was originally the actual missionary to his people and the undisputed leader of the congregation gathered around him, his authority based on his personal Christian commitment. With growing educational facilities able young men turned to more lucrative jobs, while the ranks of the catechists were sometimes filled with drop-outs without much moral authority even when they had passed through a catechist training school. Their payment being a constant problem and their performance often a disappointment, the tendency was – especially after Independence – to have the bulk of them replaced by voluntary forces with concentration on a few truly qualified ones.[10]

Two men from the west and the east of the continent will have to represent the immense army of Catholic catechists. Pontian Walakira, of Masaka, Uganda, has recalled what happened in the catechism lessons. The *Bannabikira* (Daughters of Our Lady) Ganda nuns were the teachers.

> We repeated after them, thereby completing the dialogue. The nun, for example, asked: 'Who created all of you and placed you on this earth? Answer: God created us and placed us on the earth. Then all of you answer.' We answered, 'God created all of us and placed us on this earth.' And then, 'Who is God?' And she gave the answer, 'God is all spirit and has no body. All of you repeat.' And then we repeated, 'God is all spirit and has no body.' She asked again, 'Where is God?' and gave the answer, 'God is in Heaven. Now all of your repeat.' And we answered, 'God is in Heaven.' The teacher: 'What is Heaven.' And then she told us, 'Heaven is a pleasant place where good people see, stay and enjoy themselves with God forever. Now you all repeat.' And we repeated what she had said.[11]

Walakira suggests that the students had to stay at the mission for six months for such a course. 'It seemed to be an exercise in memorization rather than in understanding.'

West African catechists cannot be better represented than by Simon Alfred Ki-Zerbo, of Ouagadougou, Burkina Faso. He was baptized in 1900 and took to serving the newly arrived White Fathers as a cook, mason and catechist. In 1916 he had on a particular occasion to defend the missionaries with danger to his own life. He taught his village congregation and prayed with them and baptized thousands of them, children, adults and the dying, especially during epidemics. He also had to act as a village healer. He managed to remove sores by sucking out the sepsis from the infected part with his mouth. When he was 100 years old he was given the rare honour of being taken to Rome, there to be introduced to the Pope who awarded him the insignia of the Order of St Sylvester. What did the visit to Rome mean to him? 'I shall tell [my fellow catechists] that I have had the chance to see Christianity at the source, at its root, that I am even more than ever convinced that I am finding myself on the true road to salvation, the road leading to God.' The old centenarian had a competent guide for his journey to Rome: his son, the world-renowned historian of Africa, Professor Josef Ki-Zerbo.[12]

The catechumenate

Alexander Le Roy, leader of the Spiritans in Paris, had missionary experience in Tanzania and in Gabon, where he was a bishop. He defined the Spiritan attitude to the catechumenate as a dislike for a lengthy period of catechetical preparation: 'The essential thing is to lay the foundations; the future is for the perfecting but there must exist something first in order to be brought to perfection later on.' Le Roy produced a catechism of twenty-five chapters, arranged according to a Trinitarian plan; Creation, Salvation, Sanctification. The great Spiritan bishops: Augouard in Oubangui, Vogt at Yaoundé, Shanahan in eastern Nigeria, and Keiling in Angola, established rules in accordance with Le Roy's principle of a rapid incorporation of the masses into the Church. Even so, they insisted, if possible, on necessary preparation. Augouard knew of missionaries in his diocese who baptized after only two or three months of preparation, but he tried to lay down a rule of eighteen months. He wrote to Le Roy to ask whether this demand was perhaps 'too rigorous'.

At Yaoundé Bishop Vogt found a tradition already established by his predecessors. The German Pallottines had, during the First World War, laid splendid foundations for the catechumenate, with a two-year training of three hours a day. They were served by an ever-growing army of devoted catechists, numbering 225 just prior to the war. Bishop Vogt and his French Spiritans built on these solid foundations, with an enormous catechetical effort in the 1920s and 1930s. By 1936 there were 2,725 catechists. Vogt was always anxious to stress his indebtedness to his German predecessors and their catechists. His co-adjutor, Bishop Griffin, disagreed with the lengthy preparation, and advocated Le Roy's rule: baptize after the shortest time of preparation; a detailed upbuilding could come later. The missionary Pope, Pius XI, agreed. In April 1932 he urged: 'Occupy the country as rapidly as possible. Later on you can deepen your approach. If not, you are apt definitely to lose many a pagan.' A controversial catechetical institution which Vogt took over from the inventive German Pallottines in Yaoundé, was the Sixas, a boarding system for women catechumens about to be married. The candidates stayed at the mission in special halls and took part in a concentrated catechetical course: six months for pagan girls, and one or two months for those already baptized. There was a daily routine of worship, three catechetical lessons, and rather lengthy sessions of manual labour. The Sixas became the target for an entertaining, if somewhat mischievous, novel by the Cameroonian novelist Mongo Beti, *The Poor Christ of Bomba*.[13] The requirement of manual labour, readily misrepresented as forced labour, led to the cessation of the Sixas in 1933.

The Spiritan approach to the catechumenate represented one pole of the diocesan organization. At the other pole was the tightly organized ecclesiastical realm of Lavigerie's White Fathers around the central African Lakes. Their programme required four years of preparation. Every individual had to be a postulant for two years, a catechumen for another two years, and finally a participant in a pre-baptizmal preparation. This iron rule applied not only in the early years of the work; it continued throughout the period. Men, women, and children walked across the hills of Rwanda, Burundi, and Bukoba to reach the mission station. They left their homes in the early morning and returned in the late evening, to be exposed to the catechetical drill of missionary and catechist. During the postulate they learned 'the prayers', the outline of the catechism, and explanations of 'the great truths'. The young, more educable, also studied the 'Three R's'. The longer catechumenate included the Mass and the mysteries of the Rosary, with explanations of the Eucharist, the penitentiary obligations, and the Christian life. Baptism took place during a three-day retreat, a strict programme with two sessions of instruction per day, teaching the use of the Rosary, and also some manual labour at the mission. Three days at the mission followed the Day of Baptism. The Superior explained the Christian life, the customs of the mission and the Sacrament of Confirmation. The White Fathers meant business – and so they do, even today. Lavigerie's orders to his missionaries for a catechumenate of four years have prevailed through the generations. A century later, they are still recognized by his successors as necessary for the building of solid Catholic communities on the equator.

However, criticism of this standpoint came from the leading Catholic missiologist in the first half of the twentieth century, Fr Charles, SJ, of Louvain. In a debate on 'the Catechists as Agents of Conversion', he said that imposing a lengthy catechumenate was equivalent to condemning the missionaries of old, Franz Xavier in the East and the Franciscans in Mexico, as well as the Church which had approved of their action. The length of the catechumenate should depend on local conditions, and should be decided there, under the supreme authority of the Holy See. The reaction in the Congo and in Rwanda and Burundi was vociferous. The six Catholic vicariates around the Lakes insisted on their four-year period. The other twenty settled for two to two and a half years, a stipulation which could be reduced if, for instance, a village was being invaded by heretics; the period could then be cut to ensure a Catholic take-over. In 1932, at the Bishops' synod in Kinshasa, the Vatican was represented by the Papal Delegate, G. Pellapiane. He took the absent Fr Charles to task, speaking 'against certain theories propagated by some missiologists who would prefer to shorten and even to abolish the catechumenate. Such theorists if allowed to influence missionary action would result in generations of bad Christians.'[14]

One would like to know to what extent and at what level an individual catechumen was able to appropriate those strange new concepts of teaching: those mysteries of the Faith, of Trinity and of the Eucharist. One can only speculate on these things. One can try to visualize that village group in Rwanda setting out in the early morning, in the dry or the wet season, heartened by the rhythm of a drum, or singing a newly learned hymn. Perhaps someone might add to the gaiety by telling the story of the bishop in distant Buganda who, when inviting his faithful to prayer, would say *Tusaabe* (meaning 'let us wash ourselves with soap') instead of *Tusabe* – let us pray. There would be ripples of laughter. As for their own language, *they* were the experts, while the foreigner was only a stumbling learner. There would be many in the group: a man who must come to a decision about family affairs – how to settle for only one wife, according to the law of the Church; an old woman who had come to church to be eligible for the right kind of burial; several young men, anxious to break with the authority of older generations and willing to accept the new ways of tomorrow; a young woman whose child had been bewitched and died. One must not forget the group aspect. The impressive statistics of thousands on the move to the baptizmal font is not simply a matter of so many individuals. The figures indicate rather a strong corporate movement, strengthened by clan relationships. They point to people only partly aware of the reasons and forces driving them forward, people who were searching for a new security and strength in this ongoing march into an unknown but attractive future.

PREACHING

The sermon is an integral and fundamental part of Protestant worship. As a rule the worship service consists of a few hymns, prayers and announcements, arranged around the sermon as the central component. If there exists, as it is sometimes claimed, an affinity between Catholic worship and certain forms of traditional African ritual, one could perhaps make out a case for an affinity between Protestant preaching and certain forms of African oratory. To study African preaching adequately would require the collection of sermons from a number of Churches and individual preachers throughout the continent. In this case this has not been possible and one has so far to be satisfied with a few studies and with individual observations over the years and in different countries.[15] An occasional seminar on this theme, held at Makumira Theological College, Tanzania in 1979 – with participants from Mozambique, Namibia and Tanzania – had the significant result that it showed the existence of a vast oral tradition related to different generations of preachers.[16]

Protestant preaching

Homiletical activities in Protestant Africa in the period 1920–60 might be classified under three headings.

The village homily

In a number of Churches throughout the continent the Protestant preacher was left with what was called 'the freedom to choose his text'. A lectionary, with prescribed texts for the Sundays and feast days in the church's year, was sometimes regarded as contrary to certain Protestant principles. Here is not the place to discuss these principle, but only to recognize their effect: in a surprising number of cases they resulted in the preacher – pastor or catechist – offering only a very few texts and one standard sermon. The 'mainline' Protestant Churches on the other hand have found it necessary to follow a lectionary, thereby assuring the preacher and his flock of a wider variety. It was regarded as an important part of the missionary's work – and later, of the African pastor's task – to prepare homiletic instructions on a weekly or quarterly basis. In some cities, as for instance in Douala, it was possible to meet as a group every week for this purpose.

In the ordinary village homily the preacher explained the text, verse by verse. The method seemed to him relevant, as his Gospel text was arranged in verses, not in paragraphs. In Namibia the Ovambo sermon used a variation of this verse-by-verse method, considering only the first verse or verses of the text. The introductory word or words determined the sermon's content, regardless of the text as a whole.[17] Not only Bible quotations but also the rich treasure-house of local proverbs served as points of contact between preacher and congregation. He might begin by intoning the first words of a proverb – a pithy phrase of age-old wisdom: 'The Haya say . . . ' After a brief pause, the listeners in unison would fill in the rest of the well-known saying: *Obaz omuhanda . . .*, *Oguribatwiwa*. 'Many a man asks for the road – and yet he walks in it.' After the service the elders of the parish in certain cases discussed the sermon with the preacher. In Nkongsamba, Cameroon, he might be told, 'Today you deserted from the text'. Less often was the preacher's attention drawn to a certain moralistic note in the sermon, an effect of a general Pietistic heritage. A verbal attack on the new taboos – drink, dance and various forms of polygamy – tended to crowd out much of the Gospel message.

Another means of establishing contact with the group used to be the occasional rhetorical interrogation, 'Am I wrong here', or 'Do I tell a lie now?', answered with an assuring emphatic response by the listeners. With increasing sophistication produced by both theological education and by modern influence, this lively appeal to the crowd seems to be on its way out, regarded as not sufficiently cultured. When it reappeared in Mzee Kenyatta's approach to his political meetings in Kenya, it may have gained new strength. The preaching experience in the chapel even influenced local languages and their forms. Methodists in southern Mozambique told the present writer in 1953 that they had noticed, how through the preacher's homiletic appeal, the reciprocal *ana*-form of the Bantu verb had become much more frequent than it used to be before the arrival of the Gospel.

The village sermon must be appreciated against the background of a live, pulsating *milieu* with its tensions and afflictions, its witches and spirits, its fears and hopes and expectations, its sighs and tears, laughter and jubilation, *and* the Gospel text bringing the Holy Land with its demons and Beelzebub and its healing miracles close to the African village, and in the midst of all, the Christ, Son of God and Saviour of the world. In that *milieu* the sermon was never just an isolated solo performance but a giving and receiving and responding in an electrifying fellowship where those concerned, preacher and listener, were bound together by an overwhelming experience of challenge and renewal. Because this was the reality of the village worship, one cannot easily go along with a mechanical differentiation in African Churches, between supposedly charismatic 'Independency' on the one hand and supposedly stuffy mission-related preachers on the other. In the first half of the twentieth century there appeared throughout the continent those first-generation preachers, with limited training, maybe, but carried by the enchantment of a new discovery of the Word and its transforming power.

The seminary-trained pastors

The seminary-trained pastors in mainline churches represented a dominating group of African preachers. As a rule they had started as teachers in some mission school and had acquired a certain pedagogical concern which they now directed towards their listeners in the church. Later, three or four years of theological education gave a basis for homiletical work. The continuous sermon preparation week after week, for decades, was their personal contribution to what later came to be known as 'African Theology'. This implied both the form of the sermon (a theme, two or three points developing the text, and a final appeal) and the contents (often a typological parallel between the Gospel message and the Old Testament with its People of God). Sometimes the homiletical form could be felt as an encumbrance. 'We are imprisoned by this demand for "order" in the sermon', as one Tanzanian theological student, later to become a bishop, expressed it.

Space does not allow long quotations here from these expositions delivered with characteristic African eloquence, fluency and conviction. (A source book of significant African sermons is very much needed.) Suffice it to say that at a time when the sermon seems to be fading out in certain of the churches in the West, it experiences a renaissance in Africa. It has been the present writer's privilege through the years to listen to outstanding African preachers, more particularly in South Africa and Tanzania but also elsewhere throughout the continent, and it is only with regret that one withstands the temptation to quote from these memorable sermons. The message – if it can at all be summarized in a few strokes of the pen – expressed not so much certain intellectual themes and concepts but rather a dramatic meeting with the great Biblical personalities: Moses the Liberator – 'Let my people go' – and Jesus the Healer and Forgiver of Sins – 'Ephphata', be Opened – and some of the others, Noah with the Ark, Abraham and his son Isaac and David the Anointed King.

A region with special interest in this context is Ethiopia, having three Churches with great homiletical traditions. A comparison between these would provide an impression of the variable homiletical heritage. There are the Evangelical Churches, EECMY (Ethiopian Evangelical Church Mekane Yesus) and the Word of Life Evangelical Church, and the preaching by pastors from these Protestant Churches could be compared with the homiletical heritage of the priests and monks belonging to the massive Ethiopian Orthodox Church. There are both points in common and differences. This task of comparison cannot be made here and we hope that such a study will soon be undertaken.

The basic ritual of the Christian religion, baptism, had in the nineteenth century begun to gather the masses, but at the beginning of the twentieth century, the form of this ritual underwent a fundamental change: in a movement from the font to the River Jordan. The Pietist character of most Protestant missionary spirituality was manifested in sermons about the man

Saul who on the road to Damascus became St Paul, a new man with a new identity and a new name. There emerged in this period throughout the continent an ambitious system of preaching-aids in the various local languages. At the midweek meeting of preachers, the missionary – and later, one of the ordained African pastors – would preach a 'model sermon' or several, for the following month. These homiletic efforts would be more or less faithfully reproduced on the following Sundays by over fifty catechists in a hundred chapels. The Luba Presbyterians in southern Kasai were well-served by two missionaries: Charles L. Crane and J. W. Allen.[18] They produced a series of printed commentaries to *all* the books of the Bible! This unique series has recently been revised and edited by Mary B. Crawford. The new commentary for the fourth Gospel in Luba is more complete than the other volumes, 400 pages in length.

In the case of many of these remarkable preachers there was, in the act of preaching, an ongoing process of African theologizing. One of the greatest preachers we ever listened to was the Revd Michael Mzobe, of Hatting Spruit, Natal – Zulu and Lutheran. His meditation on Easter morning, 1939, resulted in a reconciling of the Old Testament and the New. In his sermon notes in Zulu, which we have before us now, forty-five years after the event, he even defined the relation between the two great beings in the Bible: 'The Bible says' – this is the grand conclusion of the preacher – 'Christ is the *Umvusi ka Adam*, Adam's Resurrector'. This altogether original theological idea, worthy of St Irenaeus of old, solved for him that disquieting query of generations of African Christians: what happened to the Old Ones, to our Ancestors who died without being baptized?[19]

By the middle of the twentieth century certain leading Bible schools had reached out to thousands of preachers with prepared homiletic material. We consider examples from South Africa, Zambia and Ghana. Lovedale Bible School, Cape Province, both carried forward its nineteenth-century evangelical concern and, in a modern social and political context, adapted the message to the situations in southern Africa and beyond its borders. In the 1950s *The Preacher's Help* from Lovedale was published in English, Xhosa, Zulu, Sotho, Tsonga and Kikuyu, as it had been earlier also in Afrikaans, Tswana, Zezuru and Bemba, with its highest monthly circulation in 1947 of almost 5,000 copies; towards the end of the 1950s this had dropped to 2,600.[20] This *Preacher's Help* featured a sermon outline of two pages and some introductory Biblical material. The leader of the Lovedale Bible School – Revd Owen Lloyd – found that the average preacher was not ready to prepare one new sermon a month 'once they have gathered their own personal "gospel" they hawk it round the circuit'.[21]

For Central Africa, the issue has been treated in a valuable study by the late Gerdien Verstraelen-Gilhuis, called *From Dutch Mission Church to Reformed Church in Zambia*. It contains a lively chapter 'Profiles of the first ministers', including the homiletic performance of four pastors.[22] Quotations of some of their significant statements provide a glimpse of the kind of church and place where these Dutch Reformed Mission pastors had to function. Justo Mwale (d. 1955), published two collections of Chewa sermons with the characteristic title, 'To turn into another man'. In spite of his Dutch Reformed connections he referred to the purpose of the African National Congress: 'to prepare a good future in our country for the coming generation'. His namesake Jafeti Mwale (d. 1940), in meditating on the task of a pastor said 'God has blessed his hand to do the work of God'. Petro Phiri (d. 1968), prepared his own private Bible concordance. He insisted there was no difference between White people and Africans, 'A white person is a bricklayer, a black person is a bricklayer. All of them have built one house: the house of God'. Hezekiya Th. Banda spoke out on the race question in the Church: 'The Whites were seeing African ministers as second class ministers, like children'. But 'before God there is no chief. There is no segregation in heaven although there is on earth. We are one in heaven.'

West African sermons, more particularly among the Ghanaian Methodists, were inspired by a certain ambition in their preaching. As a Methodist preacher one could not allow oneself to deliver just any indifferent sermon. There was always a pressure from the ever-expectant audience – and from one's Reverend colleagues – to achieve something out of the ordinary. Consider C. A. Pratt, President of the Methodist Conference of Ghana in the late 1970s. He was a Fante and as an experienced teacher he had a command of the Fante language 'that would be difficult to excel'.[23] Another wizard in Fante preaching was G. R. Acquaah, the first African president of the Methodist Conference in Ghana, whose homiletical achievement was matched by his musical gifts. K. B. Dickson, a scholar and musician was a great communicator and this gave lift and lustre to his delivery. In the Ga language Peter Dagadu, generous ecumenical leader with wide international connections, was known as an impressive preacher. E. A. Sackey was another great name, effective in both English and Fante. Together with his Anglican friend, Bishop Ezra Martinson, he shared a secret: both were Freemasons, and an observer of such things (F. Bartels) has made a point about the two men: 'the source of their gifts of oratory [was] traceable to their roles as chaplains in the craft'.[24] Finally, Paulo Mohenu, the imaginative Presbyterian preacher had an interesting personal background rare in this generation of church leaders: he came from a traditional cult and was converted to Christianity.[25]

Revival messages

Revivals in various regions of the continent – in southern Cameroon, 1937 (Presbyterian), or in East Africa from the 1920s – created their own types of sermon. The basis was to be found in the personal 'testimony' of the revivalist, man or woman, ordained or lay person, emphasizing sin and victory over sin. A theologically informed pastor if influenced by this movement, tended to stay with this approach over years and even decades, assured that he would meet with an enthusiastic response from the group. Invitations from churches in the West and Asia gave these men and women a wide public. Internationally renowned preachers belonged to this movement: the late William Nagenda of Buganda or Bishop Festo Kivengere of southern Buganda, as well as a great army of local preachers throughout the region: teachers, hospital orderlies and businessmen. Increasingly there was a tendency to load the sermon with a number of Bible quotations, indicating chapter and verse, giving the impression of the preacher's Bible knowledge. Also related to this category of African preachers were two great Zulu revivalists. Nicholas Bhengu (d. 1985), a man of vast personal influence and appeal as a preacher. 'He is the Billy Graham of South Africa' was an estimate at the time, to which the present writer used to retort: 'He was more than that, he was the Nicholas Bhengu of South Africa'. For the other, Job Chiliza (d. 1963), head of the African Gospel Church, we may perhaps refer to *Zulu Zion*.[26]

The Protestant Revival involved not only some outstanding individual preachers but engaged an ever-increasing mass of men and women. A significant example was Presbyterian Lolodorf, southern Cameroon, in 1937. 'We had an "*oban*", a slave drive for Christ.' In seven months there were *26,000* professions of faith. This led to a whole series of Bible meetings and, as registered by the meticulous American missionaries, 79 per cent of those who professed in 1937 returned the following year for more Bible study and instruction. The preaching in the chapel came alive as the total congregation was involved with the Bible and the appropriation of its message.

Catholic preaching

For a study of preaching in the Catholic church in Africa during this century, we turn to Siegfried Hertlein's remarkable series of three volumes,

Wege christlicher Verkundigung.[27] His work gives us a deep insight into the life of the Catholic church in all its variations (no monolithic Catholicism here!). Although the title of the work could lead a reader to think that it mainly deals with preaching, in fact this is only so to a limited degree. Along with Fr Hertlein's books one can refer to some of the solid homiletical volumes produced this century in East Africa as sermon preparations. A certain development in homiletical sophistication can be discerned from a Bagamoyo volume of 1917, where the preacher is counselled always to return to and never to forget to warn against certain African customs, such as turning for help to diviners, the wearing of amulets, taboo problems etc. In eastern Zaïre the Alsatian Father Leonhard Massmann published two volumes of sermon collections, and the ever-enterprising Fr Walbert Bühlmann has written a study on African homiletics in *The Word made Flesh*, a collection in Swahili.[28]

A most instructive collection can be found in a series of sermons by Zairian Fathers in the *Revue du Clergé Africain* during the 1940s and 1950s. In the nature of things these printed sermons produced in the French language cannot altogether convey the immediacy of the local vernacular situation. Yet they allow an insight into the kind of popular dogmatic statements which have been made on certain occasions and which without any doubt were meant to meet a real need and to answer real questions among the listeners. There is a little essay on 'the hidden life of our Lord: the young Jesus in his home in Nazareth helping and serving his parents, with the appeal, "You children who listen to me, help your parents as Jesus did" '.[29] There are also speculations on various themes of the Creed such as the phrase 'descended into Hell'. Here the listener is made to understand that there were in fact two different sections of Hell, one for the evil spirits meeting their well-deserved punishment with much unutterable pain, and another section for the righteous spirits: and it was to this that Jesus descended. Here one meets our First Parents, Adam and Eve, and our Father Abraham, and King David, and, why not suppose, some of our own ancestors who lived honest and right-minded lives. All of these were waiting for the Saviour and did not have to suffer as those damned to Hell, for they were possessed by a strong desire to see God, to delight in Him and to come to Heaven. And suddenly the radiant spirit of Jesus was there. Here they are looking to the saints such as the Blessed Mathias Kalemba, the martyr of Uganda crucified by pain, but now in the glory of Heaven.[30]

Preaching in Africa is a theme only very occasionally treated in the literature. The African sermon is the result of the instant, proclaimed with great conviction and then left to the listeners' memories, easily forgotten.

Only an infinitesimal part of these African sermons have survived by way of the printed word. The most dramatic collection of sermons, born out of a collective traumatic experience, are those of Malagasy preachers in Tananarive during the years 1900 to 1920. By good fortune these have found their interpreter in Dr Françoise Raison-Jourde. Her study is no more than thirty pages yet filled with spiritual insight and personal empathy.[31] These sermons relate to the most pathetic social situation for Malagasy Protestantism, after the French imperialist take-over in 1895. It will be recalled that Protestantism, in a Congregational form, had in the 1860s become the state religion on the island, when the queen was baptized. In 1895 the unthinkable happened: Madagascar was brutally deprived of its political independence, and, after another decade, 'free-thinking' atheism was proclaimed. The Protestant Church then withdrew into the catacombs: the 'night' and 'the interior exile' became their mode of survival. It was through the 'night' that pastors Rabary and Ravelojaona by preaching and teaching led their faithful as Moses of old had guided his people from the land of slavery into freedom and light. Dr Raison-Jourde's study is by far the deepest interpretation anywhere in Africa of a collective homiletic and spiritual experience.[32]

THE AMBIGUITY OF HEALING

An incessant struggle against disease and for survival and health has remained a constant theme in modern Africa. The health question is also of central importance for an understanding of the Church's history, both in its mission-related forms and in its 'Independent' manifestations.

Sickness

The piod 1920–60 was inaugurated by a devastating pandemic, the 'Spanish Influenza'. Towards the end of the First World War in August 1918, a sudden explosion of the Influenza ravaged the whole African continent, hurrying along the rivers, the railways, the roads, in the west, the north, in the south, the centre and the east. The drums of death were for ever heard in the land. What could man do? In Lagos a government decree, in order to avoid dangerous gatherings of people, declared the closing of the Churches. Thus Thomas Orimolade, later one of the founders of the Cherubim and Seraphim Society, could all the more fervently bring the masses together and call upon the heavenly powers for help. In the compounds of the Johannesburg mines sturdy workers were at the very same time hit by the scourge. Two of the most impressive of these men, George Khambule and E. Vilakathi, reputedly 'died' at this time, for three days spending this time 'with Jesus', at the end of which they were directed by Jesus to return to the earth there to proclaim the Saviour's message: highly original and colourful religious organizations were the outcome.

The overwhelming impact of the Influenza surpassed the earlier calamities: malaria, blackwater fever, smallpox, sleeping sickness, tuberculosis, plague, typhoid, relapsing fevers and a great many others. Each of these diseases had their own history on the continent, endemic or imported, and they managed to destroy populations in limited or extended areas, but nothing as terrifying as the Influenza. In all, some 2,000,000 people over the whole continent died as victims of this pandemic. To some extent this flare-up marked the end of an era of illnesses. It has been suggested that 'by c.1920–30 the demographic decline experienced by many people was halted and accelerating population growth became the norm.'[33] Still, whole areas could be seen to be in the danger zone. In 1939 A. T. and G. W. Culwick, anthropologists, in a government report referred to the Haya people in north-western Tanzania as 'a dying people'. On this particular point it is of interest to add that in less than two decades a combination of mission hospital services and a deeply felt moral regeneration, a Protestant 'Revival', had turned catastrophe into an auspicious time – at least for a period.

In the 1930s and 1940s the arrival of sulfa medicines and antibiotics heralded a period of rapid population growth: 'Cheap, effective drug therapy, the only hope for the rapid alleviation of mass illness in poor tropical countries, was only possible in the last fifteen or twenty years of colonial rule.'[34]

Western medical services

At the end of the colonial period the whole of Africa had some 450–500 Catholic hospitals and there was a similar number of Protestant hospitals.[35] Each of these institutions, in order to function, had required immense efforts of planning and work in terms of buildings, equipment and medicaments, but above all of personnel: doctors, sisters, nurses, medical assistants. In each case the medical service had begun with a humble dispensary, eventually developing into a fully equipped hospital, sometimes a central hospital. It is not possible to include a list of all the truly notable personnel, Catholic and Protestant, in the hospitals. A few names will have to represent them all – the regional surveys will try to identify men and women in their local institutions – and to this will be added an indication of the particular civic role of some of these doctors. Dr Albert Schweitzer (1875–1965) theologian, physician, musician, Nobel Prize laureate, from that Alsace which has produced many remarkable missionaries for Africa – worked at Lambarene, Gabon. He became a symbolic figure for the entire medical profession in twentieth-century Africa, and his motto 'Veneration for Life' has had an immense appeal.

From East Africa the Protestant medical missionary tradition was upheld by the Anglican CMS in Uganda. Soon after his arrival in 1896 Dr A. R. Cook started what was to become one of the best-known hospitals in East Africa, at Mengo, Kampala. After a fire the hospital was rebuilt on a more ambitious scale. The prime minister of Buganda insisted, 'If God has allowed this our hospital to perish, it is to show us that we must build a bigger and a better one'. Dr Cook was assisted by a brother, also a doctor as highly qualified as himself, and later by a nephew arriving in 1909 with X-ray equipment, not to speak of the impressive and irrepressible Mrs A. R. Cook, herself a registered nurse. For the building activities at Mengo hospital, the Buganda *Lukiiko* contributed as well as the CMS and the Cook family in Britain. The Cooks were part of an Evangelical tradition, according to which a doctor should preach the Kingdom of God and heal the sick, with the insistence that spiritual work was far more important than the relief of physical suffering. Uganda had a need 'for doctors and nurses full of love for the Lord Jesus and keen on winning souls for Him'. Dr A. R. Cook retired from Mengo in 1937 but remained in Uganda, 'a vigorous senior statesman' until his death in 1951.

Moving from Anglican Uganda to Catholic Tanzania, one notices the Ifakara Medical Institute in the centre of the country. It was started in 1921 by Swiss Capuchin sisters and appeared for some time as 'medical help without doctors'.[36] Of great importance was the role of the lady physician Dr Schuster, at first active at Peramiho Benedictine centre, 1936–39 and then from 1943–56 at work in Mahenge district. In 1951 the Ifakara hospital was founded, an expression of co-operation between Swiss Capuchins and the Medical Faculty of the University of Basel. The continuity in staff was another remarkable fact about this Catholic work: for more than twenty-five years the centre had the same priest, the same building brother and the same sisters for maternity work and general hospital work.

After studies in their home countries and in the West, a generation of West African doctors started practising, none more impressive than the Nigerian Sir Francis Akanu Ibiam (born 1906). The Hope Wadell Training Institute at Calabar gave him his first educational opportunities, followed by King's College, Lagos. A government medical officer suggested to him that he devote himself to medicine and his own farming family were ready to assist him financially. In 1936 he qualified as a doctor at St Andrews University, Scotland and at the London School of Tropical Medicine and Hygiene. His wife Eudora Olaynika Sasegbon, a Yoruba teacher, had trained as a nurse in England. They felt at home in the Presbyterian Church, its educational ambitions and its ecumenical horizons. The young couple started their medical career on a missionary's terms, with a salary of £200 per year. During the 1940s and 1950s at Itu and Uburu he proved to be a first class doctor with a strong Christian conviction. He became a leader in the ecumenical concerns of Nigeria and a leading personality in the World Council of Churches and in many other highly prestigious organizations. In 1960 he became Governor of the Eastern Region, Nigeria. If ever one man pioneered the medical profession's role for the progress of Africa, as a factor for change, it was Sir Francis Ibiam. In 1951 he was knighted, thus sharing this British and Commonwealth honour with Sir Albert Cook of Mengo, Uganda, and Sir Clement Clapton Chesterman of Yakusu, Zaïre.

In his ecumenical work Sir Francis Ibiam contacted colleagues in other missions in Nigeria, highly dedicated to their medical work, such as the Sudan United Mission, the Brethren Mission, the CMS, and the Sudan Interior Mission with its immensely important eye hospital in Kano. A remarkable figure was Dr P. W. Barnden at the Vom hospital, near Jos; he was doctor, pastor and engineer in one, and the suspension bridge near Bukuru was his useful creation. On the Catholic side in eastern Nigeria medical services were immeasurably strengthened by the arrival in 1924 of the Sisters of the Holy Rosary, Killeshandra, called to Nigeria by the ever-resourceful Bishop Shanahan, soon to be joined by the Sisters of the Holy Child Jesus and the Medical Missionaries of Mary, the latter from Drogheda, Ireland. A surprising number of well-established and equipped hospitals, leprosy hospitals and maternity clinics sprang up in the bush, with a corresponding number of high standard nursing schools.

These activities in western and eastern Africa were all part of a 'Golden Age of Medical Services' – at least so it appears in hindsight, from a much later period when one could not always be sure that hospitals and medical pharmacies could provide medicines and sterilized dressing material. An indication of a certain change of the times has been shown very sharply by Bernard Hours in his *L'État Sorcier, Santé Publique et Société au Cameroun*.[37]

The Belgian colonial service recognized a category called 'medical assistants'. At the end of the colonial period there were eighty of these in the country, seventy-seven of them Catholic and three Protestant, this despite the fact that the Protestants had already developed highly competent hospitals, such as Kimpese, Yakusu and Luba. De Craemer and Fox offer as an explanation for this disparity the differentiation between the so-called 'national missions' and the so-called 'foreign missions'.[38] About the time of decolonization these men expressed their dissatisfaction with the social position of medical assistants, 'a creature of colonization', already *dépassés*. With Independence they managed to obtain, through the World Health Organization, opportunities for further studies at French and Belgian university medical faculties in order to qualify as doctors. In their communities they functioned as much as indispensable factors for change – just as the teachers and nurses – emphasizing the blessings of sanitation and hygiene and interpreting a scientific explanation of medical problems.

Tradipractitioners and prophets

'Tradipractition' is a recent term of French origin, signifying African medical practitioners operating according to traditional African experience. Many Africans, and by no means only the less educated among them, felt that the Western medical approach was insufficient and limited, for it had overlooked the role of the supernatural world. Western medicine did not see that there were two kinds of illness, the ordinary diseases including Western diseases, and also a whole field of Black illnesses, *ukufa kwabantu* (in Zulu), where the White medicine and approach must fail and where only traditional practices could prevail.

This problem brings us to a point of fundamental importance for it presupposes some understanding of the African world-view, African psychology and anthropology. Here the role of the spirit world is of basic importance, while the Western view was seen as an expression of secularism. There is a non-material world with its divinities and spirits affecting the human being and well-being unknown to the modern Western medical profession. The African *mganga* (in Swahili, medicine man) has built up a whole system (of science) of his own and can rely on a vast experience of special medicinal herbs, the reason why some of these men are known as herbalists. We are thus brought into a spiritual world with its own laws. Victor Turner has noted here that sickness is seen as a sacred calling manifested in the form of a possession. His observation applies to the Ndembu of Zambia but has a much wider application.[39]

It is sometimes taken for granted that this traditional approach belongs to the past and to the peripheral outposts of society. In fact, it flourishes not least in the modern city today and is hopefully resorted to in order to accomplish what a modern Western medicine cannot achieve. It came as a great surprise when in 1974 the Revd Dr Lloyd Swantz recorded that he had interviewed some 700 medicine men in Dar es Salaam and that these men, according to the interviews, treated some 5,000 cases of sorcery *every day*. In the crowded conditions of the city, the patient and his or her family and clan tended to blame certain illnesses on their neighbour, instigated by the neighbour most likely to have promoted the illness by way of sorcery.

The healing prophet

The tradipractitioner with his ancient knowledge and trusted experience is today being supplemented by a new therapeut, as critical of scientific Western methods as the *mganga*, and sure of the supernatural powers of God, transforming and directing man's life. The fast-growing prophet Churches, their messages and practices, at present constitute a serious challenge to the other more or less established Churches in this field of sickness and health. With unshakable faith and conviction they have insisted on a spiritual world rooted in God, beyond science and technique. The therapeutic function of the prophet-healer and his healing community is both widespread and deeply felt. The individual member of the prophet's community when asked why he or she joined this particular group will invariably and persistently answer: 'I was ill. They prayed for me. I am now healed.'

Three brief examples from southern Africa which the present writer has come across from a life-time's experience in this field are no more than variations on a vast theme:

1. The Revd Titus Msibi at Kwaluseni, Swaziland, and pastor of the St John Apostolic Church, looked at his little settlement of huts which served as wards for his patients, some of whom had been staying with him for several months in the hope of healing, and he declared: 'This is not a church: it is a hospital.'
2. In Evaton, on the Rand, the 'Apostolic' founder of Msibi's Church, Ma Nku (Mother Nku) exercised her ministry to an ever-increasing crowd of people. One of them, it was found, was a Lutheran from Pretoria at whose state hospital he had worked as an orderly. Years ago he had been afflicted by rheumatism and felt that through his working at a modern hospital he was in a better position than most to be relieved of his distress. He tried there and elsewhere, but no White doctor could help. At long last he heard of Ma Nku and turned to her. She prayed for him – and he was healed. Thus restored he returned to his old place of work in

the state hospital. Soon however, the old affliction returned and eventually he had to crawl back to Ma Nku at Evaton, who once more prayed for him until the illness was removed. There he stayed for ever, close to the 'Mother'.

3. A most dramatic performance of prophetic healing was that of Johannes Galilee Shembe at Ekuphakameni, near Durban.[40] What gave the prophet's prayer its peculiar power was the application of the father's – Isaiah Shembe – black veil. Johannes Galilee went about in the big hall among this desperate shouting, crying mass of women, from time to time hitting out with the veil, ordering the demons to depart. There may, possibly, have been other connections between prophet and patient. In any case the result was reported as astounding. In all these cases the essential therapeutic factor was the personal relationship between patient and charismatic healer, within a *milieu* of care and concern, continued for weeks and months. The White doctor's rapid round through the ward could not, it seemed, be as effective as this personal encounter.

Blessed water made holy by the prophet's prayer – in a pool or by bottles, thousands of them – is an additional boon. Dr Kofi Appiah-Kubi in his book *Man cures, God heals*, on the Akan peoples of Ghana, adds another 'potential source of healing', and one it would seem that is particularly African: music.[41] The well-known Revd Dr I. K. Prah of the Life and Salvation Church used music to healing effect: 'especially those with mental, emotional or spiritual problems. Barren women, impotent men, the blind, the lame are often healed in such services.'[42] The rhythm and the joy of the drum obviously affected the inner man. One of the most powerful prophets on the West Coast has been Albert Atcho (b.1903) at Bregbo village near Abidjan, a disciple of Harris whose teaching he expanded. The engaging point about Atcho is his claim not only to copy the founder but to develop his doctrine. Harris, Atcho felt, did not sufficiently stress the danger of witchcraft. But Atcho born with the power to fight witchcraft was able to cure such illnesses.

THE INVISIBILITY AND VISIBILITY OF WOMEN

During the period 1920–60 African women were profoundly influenced by the changing economic forces in society. The introduction of a cash economy served to emphasize men's superiority and women's inferior position as obedient minors. The new crops introduced by the needs of a world economy – coffee, tea, cocoa, cotton etc. – were worked by the hands of women on behalf of the men. The money earned had to be set aside for the husband, because the produce from the trees belonged to the husband who had inherited the land and the trees. The woman's position was weakened as economic cultural forces turned against her: 'Oppression has been given a cultural dress'.[43] The Church's role with regard to this development was ambiguous. On the one hand the Church had opened up new opportunities for women through education for girls and through roles for local leadership. On the other hand there operated, in and through the Churches, discriminatory practices upheld by divine authority. The missions, whether Catholic or Protestant, originating in the nineteenth century were largely expressions of a patriarchal society and these attitudes seemed to fit in with an African society in its patriarchal and matriarchal forms.

This decline of women's status has been pointed out by Esther Boserup, *The Condition of Agricultural Growth* (1965) and *Women's Role in Economic Development* (1970), both of which analyze female farming systems as compared with those of men.[44] Boserup maintains that the decline in women's status was related to the transition from hoe to plough in African agriculture. Her argument is relevant to our book, not least because of the extensive role of Western missions introducing ploughs throughout the continent, on a surprisingly large scale. Many studies have been devoted to the Boserup thesis suggesting that not only the women but all Africans in this period lost control over production and thus became more dependent. 'Women are at the bottom of the heap and Boserup is correct that they were ignored by the agricultural services.'[45] It must be added that these tendencies were fortunately counter-balanced by the fact that the majority of the missionaries were women who often worked with women and girls. There was thus an undercurrent not visible on the surface which later was to find expression in women's capacities to assume leadership and bring up a new generation of educated women.

Women did not always take this oppression meekly in their stride. Two of the most dramatic women's revolts in this period happened in areas where the churches were particularly significant. The Aba riots in eastern Nigeria were against taxation proposals. The Bamenda *anlu*, the most violent form of female protest in the Cameroonian grassfields, opposed colonial administrative innovations in agricultural techniques. Social and economic conditions did of course vary greatly over the continent. In Nigeria, some women – such as traders in the markets or teachers managed to make a much higher income than the men; if she was a pastor's wife, 'she keeps him in the ministry', we have been told.

One must not forget that most important category, the African mothers.

In the early history of the African church the martyrs and saints all testified to the role of their Christian mothers in their lives. We now refer to that ordinary devout Christian woman, looking after her home and her family. Her husband might be absent for long periods of time because of migrant labour, while she would look after the children whom she, surprisingly, managed to take through primary school and sometimes to high school and further still. These praiseworthy women were invisible, yet, when surveying the twentieth-century Christian movement, one is impressed by their role in the lives of the new, educated generations. They were the pillars of the parish and cared for the local Church, its worship and its social involvement and they prepared it for the great feast days of the year.

One of them, Navonacle Gerson Marissa, born 1901 and from Lutheran Pare in Tanzania, might represent them all. Her husband died when the youngest of her nine children was a year and a half year old. Mrs Marissa brought up all nine, two of the daughters to become university graduates, and several other children with post-secondary education in other institutions. People gave her the highest accolade that they could think of, 'She is a man.' In her case and in many similar, this achievement was related to the Church and made possible through the solidarity of the Church. In traditional Tanzanian society, daily prayer in the hut was often led by the man. In modern society, the regular daily prayer is said by the mother. Professor M. L. Swantz has written: 'There is no other community where women can emerge as leading personalities as in the Church.'[46]

Not always was this women's influence welcome. There were sometimes complaints of the 'feminization' of the Church, voiced from the Cape to Cameroon and beyond. But nobody could deny that the women were animators of society and the Church, not least in societies seemingly falling to pieces. Anticipating developments in Independent Africa – after 1960 – one meets remarkable examples of women who, having obtained leading positions in government and society, are totally devoted to their Church. An example from Anglo-Catholic Tanzania comes to mind: Mrs Thecla Mchauru, secretary and then president of the country's Women's Union. A generous personality and a devout Church woman nobody could quote the names of her bishops – 'Fr Vincent' or 'Fr Trevor' – with greater affection than she.

The sisters in the African Church

Pope Pius XI's encyclical *Rerum Ecclesiae* of 1926 with its call for men and women's orders provided a great inspiration. In 1925 the number of African sisters as a whole was close to 1,000. This number was doubled in 1933 and quadrupled in 1949, reaching 6,000 in 1960. At Karema in Tanzania the Sisters of Our Lady Queen of Africa had been founded in 1907. In Buganda Bishop Streicher founded the *Bannabikira* community of women, which devoted themselves to teaching catechumens in the fast growing Masaka diocese. In 1919 the African Sisters community had just over 100 members, in 1942 they were 300, and by 1961 they numbered 525. In neighbouring Bukoba, the BaTheresa community showed a similar development. Almost all had come as young girls, after four or six years in primary school, but adult women were also admitted. Thus fifteen teachers in Morogoro (Tanzania) were accepted for this calling. In Rwanda, in Kivu and in Zaïre generally, there was a rapid growth of nuns and their communities. In East Africa the Bishops' Conference of 1936 discussed relating these communities to the government's educational system: admission to the novitiate was to follow only after passing the Government Teacher's Diploma. For this entire period, the nuns generally, African and foreign, must be seen in relation to their immense importance for African women's education. The rapidly rising numbers of Catholic secondary schools for girls are unthinkable without these devoted contributions by nuns. It might be thought that a women's religious community would be the fruit of a relatively long Church history. That this does not need to follow is shown by the rapid development of a religious order among the Mossi women of Burkina Faso. The Catholic Church was established in the country by the White Fathers and started its first little village school in 1902. In 1927 Father Thrévenou became Apostolic Vicar. In twenty-five years no less than 700 catechists were active in the country. The role of African Sisters can be seen in a charming study of a religious community among Mossi women, *Pâques Africaines*, written by Sister Marie Le Roy Ladurie. She shows how a vocation to the religious life came very early in the life of these women; the first thought of becoming a nun was often kindled at Baptism or at the First Communion. One Sister wrote:

> I was eight and after the First Communion, I was overcome by an extraordinary joy. I was not hungry, for I felt too much joy. I said 'I shall be a nun'.

Another wrote:

> At ten at the time of my first communion I decided to be a Sister. I had a great desire to be a priest in order to touch the host. Well, as I could not be a priest, I decided, I shall be a sister and a sacristan so as to be close to the altar.[47]

It is an exception that African Sisters allow themselves a critical view of certain aspects of their community life. One such exception is the article by Sister Ancilla Kupalo of Kenya, 'African Sisters' congregations: realities of the present situation'.[48] Her view includes reflections on developments prior to the independence of Africa. There then existed what she describes as a 'yes-yes mentality', 'taking refuge in the virtue of conformity, confusing it with obedience'. Some African sisters, she suggests, 'became Religious before they became Christians'. Blind obedience was the recommended attitude. The virtue most appreciated was, she suggests, 'childishness'. The sisters were 'given another coating of a foreign way of life, unrealistic sometimes, artificial most of the time'. That such criticism was possible was in itself a sign of a new freedom coming to the fore in independent Africa. This sister's view has not been left unchallenged: an 'all too negative assessment', is Sister Dr Mary Hall's statement.[49]

The manyano

Manyano is the common name for the extensive Protestant prayer movement of dedicated Church women, from Cape Town to Shaba (Katanga) in Zaïre. As has been pointed out, this movement emerged at about the beginning of the twentieth century in Natal and in Cape Province. In the period 1920–60, it proceeded further north over the continent. Originally a Wesleyan Methodist and Congregationalist sorority, it was promoted in all Protestant Churches, with certain local characteristics: the prayer groups meeting on a specific weekday – 'Thursday is *manyano* day' – for prayer, spiritual meditation and common social concerns, particularly with regard to the young; they all donned a common uniform, of various shapes and colours, and this uniform dramatized the visibility of the movement and of the role of women generally in the Church. For that very reason women in certain colonial dependencies decided that a conspicuous uniform must be avoided. In Portuguese Mozambique the local Reformed youth *Patrulha* (scouts) and Women's Fellowship groups shunned any distinctive mark: 'We hide from Government', these women in 1953 confided to the present writer.

These women's group established their own, sometimes very effective solidarity across frontiers: Wesleyan *manyano* from the Cape to Lubumbashi; Anglican Mothers' Unions from the Cape and Johannesburg to Masasi and Kampala; Lutheran prayer women from Durban to Moshi; Congregationalist *manyano* from Durban and Groutville to eastern Zimbabwe; African Methodist Episcopal women from Evaton to Lusaka; East African 'Revival' sororities from Rwanda to Mombasa; and charismatic – 'Zionist' –

ramifications in all directions and across all frontiers. These women's international and inter-tribal outreach may sometimes have been hampered by political boundaries, but their role for the growth of a spiritual climate where ideas of Church union could flourish must be underlined.

The great majority of the *manyano* women were housewives with a primary school education, all of them ambitious on behalf of their children's education. Inevitably there might sometimes arise tensions between the male clergy and the local *manyano* group, but on the whole excellent co-operation prevailed. Not always have these *manyano* women and their achievements been fully appreciated by some of their more highly educated Black sisters. The words of Betty Kaunda, wife of the first President of Zambia, on the occasion of a Mindolo conference in 1970 on Women's Rights in Zambia, need to be quoted in this context: 'The well-educated, the less educated and uneducated women in this country must learn to work together.' She went on to say: 'It has been estimated that 90 per cent of Zambian women over sixteen years of age had two years or less of education.' Mrs Kaunda's concern is not limited to her own country alone.

Women in the Independent Churches

The role of women in such charismatic Independent Churches as were founded and led by women – e.g., Ma Nku at Evaton, Johannesburg, or Alice Lenshina Mulenga at Chinsali, northern Zambia – was particularly marked. If ever the twentieth-century Church was 'a women's movement' this term applied particularly to the Zionist and Apostolic Churches. Here the women, under their charismatic Mother-Prophetesses could expand and develop to the full their own style of life and of worship. Yet any attempt to identify the Independent Church movement as a purely feminist concern is misleading. This can be seen in those lively Independent groups – the male prophet's *communitas* – such as those of David Lion in Maseru or John Masowe in Port Elizabeth and Nairobi. There it was taken for granted that the submissive mass of women strive on behalf of the Leader, and any profits deriving from long hours of labour were, as a matter of course, presented as part of the humble homage to the great men.

Nku of the St John's Apostolic Church was induced – probably by a dream – to appoint two bishops to assist her, but was soon to find that these preferments led to her own ruin. One of these men, Bishop P. Masango, was as leader and healer a simpleton compared with Nku herself, but he managed, parrot-like to copy Ma Nku's gestures and phrases to the extent that he, a Zulu would – in Swaziland! – throw into his sermon formulae in seSoto, obviously borrowed from Ma Nku. The great annual Assemblies had no hesitation at all on this point: the visibility and the spiritual presence were those of the great Prophetess herself while the male bishops remained distinctly marginal straw-men. The movement owed everything to her. But in the Whites' court Bishop Masango managed to show that, officially, he was in charge and thus entitled to rake in the tens of thousands of pounds – the sum total of the happy offerings from the faithful given to her – which in the end were adjudicated to him.

13

NORTH AND NORTH-EASTERN AFRICA

THE MAGHREB

Black Africa's struggle for Independence did, in the main and with certain tragic exceptions, avoid violence and bloodshed. Algeria, on the other hand, had a long and terrible war, 1954–62. When this came to an end with an 'Algerian Algeria', this historical change was due to the leadership of an extraordinary personality, with extraordinary courage and extraordinary determination, Charles de Gaulle. About 800,000 French men and women left Algeria, returning to France, leaving behind some 200,000 Europeans, a figure soon to be reduced to about 25,000.

Since the beginning of the century the Church had obviously been a foreign body consisting almost totally of foreigners. The contacts between an Algerian-dominated majority and a French dominating minority were very much limited. What there was of contacts between the two religious communities could be experienced in the countryside rather than in the cities: only in the countryside, the Cardinal said, one saw those 'simple, easy and human contacts'. The Catholic Sisters – Charles de Foucauld's Little Sisters of Jesus – devoted almost all of their time to Muslim families. In the Catholic schools Muslim and Catholic children were taught together: 'A school open only to Christians would not be a Catholic school', the Cardinal declared.

Appointed to the diocese of Constantine in 1947 – Archbishop in 1954 and Cardinal in 1965 – Léon-Etienne Duval concentrated on problems of poverty and unemployment and the insecurity of life for the proletariat. With regard to the Church his position was without reserve: 'The church in Algeria has chosen not to be foreign, but Algerian.' A certain part of the clergy and of the Sisters (Clarisses) and five out of the six Catholic bishops took Algerian nationality.

One should not disregard the fact that a certain number of students from sub-Saharan Africa found their way to Algerian university centres: some of these students were Catholics in search of higher learning.

In this period, 1920–60, Protestant missionaries were also at work in Algeria and Tunisia: American Methodists, the 'North African Mission' working through hostels, hospitals, Bible study groups, 'a presence and witness but little more'.[1]

It was, as always, important not to be overwhelmed by a short perspective but to retain the long view. Nobody held a longer view than Cardinal Roncalli – later to be Pope John XXIII – when visiting the Maghreb in 1950. He encompassed the three religious communities together, Christians, Muslims and Jews (the latter some 40,000 in Algeria and 60,000 in Tunisia at that time). 'I see them all in the light of Abraham, the great patriarch of believers.'

EGYPT

The years after the First World War in Egypt were a period of unrest, revolts and strikes. Economic conditions were dominated by fluctuations in the price of the main cash crop, cotton. There were sharp economic differences between the 12,500 landlords holding close to 1,000,000 hectares and the 1,500,000 farmers with about half of that acreage. The population was growing rapidly, from about 10 million in 1900 to 15 million in 1937. There was an increase in the numbers migrating to the large cities of Cairo and Alexandria, together with Asyut in the south, the centre of the Copts, forming a largely Christian part of the Muslim-dominated country.

The years 1919–52 were a period of modernization followed by a Socialist revolution under Naguib in 1952 and Nasser in 1954. There was a certain emancipation of women from 1923 – the veil was no longer necessary – and in 1952 there followed women's universal suffrage. More than others, Coptic women were now in a position to benefit from this change: they could function as medical doctors, lawyers, engineers etc.

An organized mass movement, *wafd*, gathered what there was of an early Egyptian nationalism. Here Muslims and Copts were at first united by the common political aspirations, with the watchword 'Egypt for the Egyptians'. For two decades the Copts rallied to the *wafd* programme. Makram Ebeid Pasha, a leading Copt, guided his people: as long as he supported *wafd*, the Copts as a whole followed the programme.

This was a period of remarkable inter-religious toleration. Muslim sheikhs spoke in Coptic churches and Coptic priests addressed Muslims in the mosques. Marcos Sergius, a Coptic priest and a leader of the revolution of 1919 spoke from the pulpit of al-Azhar University pleading for the unity of crescent and cross.[2]

Was this the longed-for hour of concerted Christian missions to the Muslim? John R. Mott, ecumenical leader of Protestant missions, visiting Egypt, thought so. He had asked 'one of the most eminent [Muslim] professors at al-Azhar what gave him the greatest hope for Islam.' The reply was: 'I see no hope; materialism is overwhelming us.' Mott went on to say: 'Moslems can be converted; Moslems have been converted; Moslems are being converted.' He could detect only one complication with regard to his standpoint: 'The Oriental churches are not ready at the present time to co-operate in this vast and urgent undertaking.'[3] Developments during the 1930s dampened these expectations. An increasingly anti-missionary campaign followed. In southern Egypt Christian parents were fined for sending their children to Coptic schools rather than to the compulsory village state schools, with their predominant Qur'anic teaching.

The monasteries

In the meantime Coptic Church life continued very much as it had always done, in the monasteries and in the village churches. Also in this period the great strength of the Coptic Church was the monasteries, a world of their own. A visitor to the Anba Samwel monastery asked Abuna Matta al-Maskin – this hermit who had started as a graduate in pharmacy and worked as a pharmacist until he felt the call to an ascetic's life – whether any of his disciples ever cherished the idea of going on a pilgrimage to Jerusalem in order to visit the Holy Places. The hermit replied:

> Jerusalem the Holy is right here, in and around these caves. For what else is my cave, but the place where my Saviour Christ was born, what else is my cave, but the place where my Saviour Christ was taken to rest, what else is my cave, but the place from where He most gloriously rose again from the dead? Jerusalem is here, right here, and all the spiritual riches of the Holy City are founded in this Wâdî. There is the Holy Sepulchre, and over there is the Mount of Olives, and there, at the well, there is the water of the River Jordan.[4]

There was the old kind of monk and a new kind. At the al-Muharraq monastery they remembered their leader, or *hegoumenos*, who memorized the Bible much in the same way as the Muslims memorize the Qur'an. He could perform miracles, healing the sick and casting out devils where he met them, a charismatic in an ancient church structurally similar to modern charismatics in other parts of the continent. Some of these hermits were more solitary than others. The monastery of Baramus had received an Ethiopian hermit who lived a life of complete isolation for twelve years: 'he had neither spoken nor seen anybody during this time.'[5] This Baramus monastery had been a home for Ethiopians for longer than other monasteries in the Wadi Natrum. In 1920 there were seven of them, in 1959 three.

The as-Surian monastery on the other hand had modernizers. There was Abuna Makarios as-Suriani with an academic background of a law degree from the University of Cairo, an arts degree from the American University in Cairo and a masters degree from Princeton in the United States. For some time, 1944–46, he taught at the Coptic Seminary in Addis Ababa. He helped to bring his Church into the ecumenical movement, representing its interests at the WCC assembly at Evanston in 1954. He thus anticipated a new generation of monks appearing after 1960. In this context it should be added that Makarios was the last of the Patriarchs (1942–45) to be elected from the bench of bishops. After Makarios all the Patriarchs were elected from monks: Yusuf II, 1946–56; Kyrillos VI, 1959–1971; and Shenoudah III, 1971–. Kyrillos had been a recluse living in a deserted windmill for over thirty years. As a patriarch he was reputed to have the spiritual gift of healing and clairvoyance. He encouraged young men to stay for retreat and meditation, and under his influence many of these were to become active workers in the Church.

But a wind of change was sweeping through the monasteries, which were soon feeling a disturbing 'encroachment of the world', in the shape of visitors and tourists. The Shell Oil Company had its share in this disturbance by macadamizing the road to Anba Antunius monastery. The millennia of camel caravans were being replaced by jeeps. For the period 1953–58 one of the monasteries registered no less than 367 foreign visitors of all nationalities arriving by motor vehicle. A cautious warning was issued: 'It is well to remember that there is no gasoline station beyond Ain Sukhnah'. The Cairo magazine *Images* tried to attract visitors: 'An excursion for your weekend: the monasteries at the Red Sea.'

Lay concerns in an ancient world

This isolated hermit world of ancient monasteries in the desert sands was only one side of Coptic reality, although perhaps the most creative. The village and town churches along the Nile were the centres of Coptic life. Here signs of renewal were increasingly to be seen.

Laymen in the Church were greatly frustrated by the seemingly endless rule of Patriarch Kyrillos V who presided, with very little concern for the laity, over the church for fifty-three years until his final demise in 1927. Coptic laymen were to find expressions for their keen involvement in the

Church. Above all there was the 'youth worship' movement or the Sunday school movement. A theologian was the founder and inspiring leader. Habib Girgis, head of the church's Theological Seminary 1919–51, in his youth had a decisive spiritual experience: a voice told him in his heart to place life and soul in the service of theological education and of the church as a whole. He extended his concerns to a comprehensive Sunday school movement reaching out to every parish, town and village in the country. There were of course Sunday school activities in other countries of Africa during this period, all related to the World Sunday School Association, founded in Rome in 1907 (later developed into the World Council of Christian Education), but the Coptic movement had a quality of its own, more genuinely tied to Church and society, perhaps, than in most other countries.

This period also saw the formation of Coptic Welfare associations involved in spiritual, educational and social services of the Church. In Cairo alone there were in 1973 more than 150 such associations initiating schools, orphanages, hospital clinics etc.[6] In the Coptic Church these associations appeared at about the same time as welfare associations were organized by the Protestant Church in Central Africa.

The other Churches

The Catholics were represented both by a Uniate Coptic Church with a patriarch in Alexandria and by Roman Catholic missions, above all the Franciscans, Dominicans and Jesuits. There were also Carmelites, Christian Brothers and others. The Franciscans have continued to uphold to the present day the legacy of the venturesome initiative to visit Egypt, in AD 1219, taken by their founder, St Francis of Assisi. Traditions from the earliest days are honoured by the Church of the Holy Family at Matariya, near Cairo, where the Tree of the Holy Virgin is preserved. There the Family is reputed to have rested on its flight: on the Child's summons the Tree bent down low so that, in the heat of the day, the Holy Mother could enjoy its fruits. The Dominican Institute of Oriental Studies, founded in 1928, was closely related to Fr Lagrange's Biblical School in Jerusalem. An impressive multitude of Catholic sisters, more than thirty 'Congregations', are at work in the educational and medical field, among them over 300 Comboni Sisters, 220 Franciscan Sisters and a great number of Augustine Planque's Missionary Sisters of Our Lady of the Apostles.

Douglas Thornton saw the vision of 'preaching in the market place'. His

Anglican co-workers of the CMS devoted themselves to literacy and book production. Thornton's highly gifted colleague, Canon Temple Gairdner and his co-worker Constance Padwick, produced Christian reading on a surprisingly wide scale and of impressive quality. The (American) Presbyterians established an efficient education system for their church in Upper Egypt. The ecumenical concerns of Lambeth 1920 and of Stockholm 1925 attracted the non-Coptic churches. The Greek Orthodox patriarch of Alexandria, Photios, attended Nathan Soderblom's Stockholm conference. A local 'Fellowship of Unity' gathered together; from the beginning of the 1920s, some of these Churches, with the Anglican Bishop Gwynne as President and the Swedish diplomat Harald Bildt as Secretary.

SUDAN

After the Egyptian revolution in 1919, Britain tried to minimize Egypt's role in the government of Sudan, as well as reduce the Muslim presence in the south of the country. In 1922 the three southern provinces were declared 'closed districts' and northerners were excluded, while southerners were discouraged from travelling to the north. The assassination in Cairo of the governor-general of Sudan, Sir Lee Stack, in 1924, and the revolt by northern Sudanese soldiers in Khartoum, led to the withdrawal from Sudan of the Egyptian army and was later followed by the departure of Egyptian civilian officials. Although the Sudanese government continued its prohibition on Christian evangelization in the Muslim north, the colonial authorities increased their support for the educational and medical work of the Churches in the south.

Northern Sudan

The Catholic presence in Khartoum until the 1950s was generally limited to expatriates with very few northern Sudanese members. During the 1950s a number of Catholics from the south moved to Khartoum and the Church was able to provide a fellowship for these migrants. The Presbyterian Church in the north continued to co-operate with the Anglicans, opening in 1949 a joint church in Omdurman. The withdrawal of Egyptians from the Sudanese administration and the departure of Egyptian traders in 1932 following a financial recession in the Sudan led the Presbyterians to close their churches in Wadi Halfa, Karima, Port Sudan and Atbara. This loss of numbers was later offset by incoming Presbyterians from the Upper Nile, and new churches were opened at El Obeid, Dueim and Shendi.[7] In 1948 the

Coptic Orthodox Church was divided into two dioceses, one for northern Sudan and the other for the south of the country and Uganda. Both archbishops resided in Khartoum.

Anglican work in Sudan continued under Bishop Gwynne who, in 1920, took charge of the newly created diocese of Egypt and Sudan. However, the diocese was divided into two missions, one for Egypt and northern Sudan, and the other for the south of the country. Between the years 1926 and 1935 southern Sudan was brought together with northern Uganda to form the diocese of the Upper Nile; after 1935 southern Sudan was ecclesiastically rejoined with the north of the country. In Khartoum during the 1920s the Anglicans took the lead in establishing ecumenical contacts with other churches. 'Bishop Gwynne was ambitious that the [Anglican] cathedral should be used as a meeting place for all Christian traditions, and from 1924 a unity service was held each year in which representatives of Orthodox and other Eastern Christian Churches regularly took part as well as Presbyterian and Free Church representatives.'[8] Having been in the Sudan since 1900, Bishop Gwynne retired in 1945, and the Sudan was then made a separate Anglican diocese.

Anglican and Presbyterian co-operated in the provision of educational opportunities for Christians and for those Muslim children whose families allowed them to go church schools. The experience of Sitt Faith illustrates the importance and ramifications of girls' education provided by these Protestant churches in Khartoum. Sitt Faith attended the Presbyterian School in Khartoum North and in 1931, after a long struggle, she was baptized a Christian. Although born a Muslim, her mother was a Christian Amhara who had been kidnapped from Ethiopia and taken to Sudan. Sitt Faith's conversion from Islam to Christianity was the talk of Khartoum and needed the approval of a British official and two Muslim judges. She taught in a church boys' school in Omdurman and translated the Bible into colloquial Arabic – which many southerners, unable to read classical Arabic biblical texts, could understand. Between 1951 and her death in 1962 she taught colloquial Arabic and became head of the American Mission Language School, teaching over 100 missionaries Arabic.

In 1933 the Anglicans launched a new mission venture in the area of the Nuba mountains, south-west of Khartoum. Although located in the northern part of the country, the people of the Nuba mountains are not Arab and are mostly non-Muslim, speaking some fifty different languages. The government supported both the CMS and the Sudan United Mission (SUM) initiatives to develop work in the Nuba mountains. The colonial authorities wished 'to introduce the Nuba directly to Western techniques rather than assimilate them to the Arab Sudan, and to foster a distinct Nuba culture under Christian influence offering an alternative goal to Nuba aspiring to a more sophisticated way of life.'[9]

By 1936 the SUM had established three schools including two boarding schools in the Nuba mountains, while the Anglicans also provided intermediate and teacher training instruction. Both missions had to teach Arabic as Coptic teachers were employed in their schools. From the 1940s many young Nuba men migrated to the cities of Khartoum and Omdurman, where they found a welcome in the churches and in Christian associations in the unfamiliar urban surroundings. Although Church growth amongst the Nuba peoples was slow and of a limited extent, the foundations were laid for a later expansion that occurred during the 1960s and 1970s, after independence. While some Nuba became Muslims, other found in Christianity a distinctiveness that reinforced their own identity against the pressures of assimilation into Arab Muslim culture.

Southern Sudan

From 1926 government provided grants to Church schools and in 1928 a Language Conference was held at Rejaf to determine the development of southern education policy. The Sandersons have written that the Rejaf conference was 'the one occasion on which Government officials and missionaries collaborated as equals and colleagues, rather than as supervisors and subordinates'.[10] Apart from deciding to replace Arabic with English as the language of government and communication in the south, the conference also chose six southern 'group' languages for use in schools and for the co-operative production of text-books.

The Sudan Interior Mission (SIM) began work in the country in 1937 after they were expelled from Ethiopia in 1935 by the Italian invaders. They opened stations at Mabaen and Chali in the Blue and Upper Nile provinces and, as their work was primarily among the Dinka people, they took over the work of the SUM at Melut and Paloich. Of a somewhat isolationist perspective and of 'a rigidly fundamentalist faith', the SIM decided in 1944 not to join the Southern Sudan Christian Council, formed by the Anglicans and Presbyterians, on the grounds that the council was 'to prepare the way towards future organic union' of the Protestant churches.[11] The SIM rejected all governmental interference including the sphere system and the prohibition of work among Muslims.

ETHIOPIA

Ethiopia was a vast country with a number of different populations and the Church history of Ethiopia was related to a dominating political and cultural minority, the Amhara. On the other hand there were Christianized populations in Tigre in the north, and the Oromo and others in the south. During the time of Menilik II, 1889–1913, Orthodox priests and monks were directed to approach the pagan populations with a view to have them baptized – without much previous instruction – and thus made members of the Orthodox church. While these tensions had been felt throughout the centuries, they became particularly acute in the period now discussed.

Between the two world wars Ethiopia was dominated by the ugly experience of Mussolini's imperialist aggression against a seemingly defenceless people. The attack in 1935 had been preceded by occasional military threats. Fortunately the country, in its hour of trial, had a great personality at its head, well-known both in his own country and internationally. As 'Ras Tafari', the son of Ras Makonnen, he was regent from 1916 and in 1930 crowned as Emperor. In view of the military situation the Emperor decided in 1936 to take the case of his people to the League of Nations in Geneva. World War II made Britain an ally of Ethiopia against Italy and the military situation was radically changed, but the distress and suffering of the people were still immense. Where could people turn? Smaller and bigger guerilla bands found their way into neighbouring countries, mainly into Sudan and Kenya.

Eritrean and Ethiopian guerillas in Sudan welcomed the Emperor and returned with him to Addis Ababa in 1941. Into Kenya no less than 6,000 refugees, including at least 1,500 young men, managed to cross the southern border to spend some four to five years there until, after the Italian debacle, they were able to return to Harar and Addis Ababa. Their experience in a foreign land illustrates one of the fundamental themes of this African Church history, that of 'refugee' and 'returnee'.

The refugees from Ethiopia found their way to Isiolo in northern Kenya and eventually to Voi in the southern part of the country. In 1938 Anton Jönsson, a Swedish teacher who had served with the 'Bible-True Friends' for two decades in Harar, reached the refugee community in Kenya and was after some time asked by the British administration to act as superintendent of the group. With this he combined the tasks of teacher in the schools and of camp preacher whenever an opportunity presented itself. This teaching kindled an interest in the English language and Western culture as well as Ethiopian and Eritrean history and culture. In 1941 'Mussi [Monsieur]

Anton' followed the Ethiopian community back to Ethiopia and the Emperor welcomed the returnees as potential officials of his administration. Some of these young men were posted as ambassadors to capitals in the West, to Nigeria and to the Near East. Anton Jönsson was assigned to the task of establishing a National Library, opened in 1947 after Jönsson's energetic appeals to libraries in the West.

The Italian crisis 1935–41 and the Emperor's return to his country in 1941 acted as a powerful inspiration for Ethiopian nationalism, affecting also the *abuna*ship of the Ethiopian Orthodox Church. For more than 1,500 years the responsibility for appointing the *abuna* had lain not with Ethiopians but with the Patriarchate in Alexandria and Cairo and the *abuna* had been a foreigner, an Egyptian Copt. Ethiopian self-esteem was to some extent consoled by an arrangement that at the side of the *abuna* there was always an *echege*, an Ethiopian celibate monk nominated by the Emperor to look after legal aspects of the Church. In the debate that followed in the 1940s and 1950s it was ultimately the Emperor's authority that helped the Church to achieve its independence. The Emperor may throughout have had a tendency to be torn between feudalism and modernity, yet when it came to the question of the Ethiopian Church's independence, he was determined and uncompromising.

For more than ten years the discussion went on between Addis Ababa and Alexandria–Cairo. From the conference in 1946 it was reported that 'a very animated discussion [on this subject] arose'. A continuous exchange of ecclesiastical delegations between the two Churches followed through the years until at long last an agreement was reached in 1959, according to which the Ethiopian archbishop acquired the title of Patriarch. Abuna Basileos, born 1891, was elected as the first Patriarch.

Among efforts at modernization and renewal should be mentioned a new translation of the Bible into Amharic and the foundation of the Haile Selassie University at Addis Ababa in 1948.

This Ethiopian Church, constantly looking to the north, tied to Alexandria through long centuries and turned to Jerusalem and its Temple, also knew a hidden village spirituality attuned to religious displays and forms more prevalent further south in Africa. This could be seen in connection with the immensely popular pilgrimages in the countryside around Aksum, Lalibela and other leading monasteries and churches. Here the faithful would approach the holy place carrying torches. Soon the mass of people organized itself into dancing groups with a presenter leading the singing and hand-clapping stimulating the dancers to sing the honour of some saint, while the women accompanied with their shrill *Ililili*. They had joined the pilgrimage in order to obtain healing for some disease, looking for caves and grottoes with wells of water. (In the case of the Yared monastery there was sufficient water to guarantee the running of a factory bottling mineral water!) The visit of the individual was followed by a promise: 'If I am healed I shall bring so and so many wax candles to the church.'

Next to any Ethiopian Church building was a school, from which the passer-by could hear the children recite their lessons: the Psalter of King David and the Gospel of St John were their intellectual and spiritual food.

Apart from pilgrimages there are within the Church innumerable cases of healing from complaints such as spirit possession, performed by priests of the Church. One of them, M. Wolde had managed to heal 1,190,898 people in fourteen years. These refer to ordinary physical complaints but above all to mental illnesses which were induced by 'the Devil' and exorcized by the priest.[12]

The Orthodox Church of Ethiopia thus presented certain elements which looked unmistakably charismatic in terms of healing groups in Southern Africa, with interests close to the people and perhaps a portent of the time in a future when hierarchy, liturgy and charisma could be joined together in a living whole on the African continent.

Throughout the centuries Ethiopian monks had gone to Egypt to live and pray there. The most remarkable example of this spirituality in the twentieth century was Abuna al-Masih al-Habash from Hamasen in Ethiopia. At twenty-five he joined an Egyptian monastery living in a cave beyond the Baramus monastery. Once a week he would receive from the monastery the necessities of life: water and bread.[13]

Foreign Missions after the Italo-Ethiopian War

An important change in the 1940s led to a new status for foreign missions, Catholic and Protestant. For political reasons there had been constant Orthodox suspicion against the foreign missions: 'were they perhaps foreign spies'? In 1944 the Ethiopian government issued a decree according to which the country was to be divided into two parts: 'Ethiopian Church areas', cared for exclusively by the Ethiopian Orthodox Church (except for foreign aid to medical and educational services), *and* predominantly non-Christian, so-called 'open areas' where foreign missions were to be free to work. This was a decision of vast significance and the missionary situation was completely altered – although one must, in a country such as Ethiopia, avoid applying a doctrinaire interpretation of the situation, either before or after 1945: regional, local and personal factors played their role.

A changing world situation affected the recruitment of missionary personnel for south-western Ethiopia. Thus foreign missions withdrawing from Mao's China in 1949, such as the Norwegian Lutheran 'Samband', found their way into the 'open area' of the Oromo.

The decree of 1944 helps to reveal hitherto clandestine developments in the country, particularly among the Oromo in the south. A century earlier Ludvig Krapf, as we have already pointed out, had made the acquaintance of Oromo men and declared that they were to become the great African missionaries to Eastern Africa. In the new situation with a war of aggression against Ethiopia, Oromo preachers developed a creative role in their personal encounter with the Bible and its liberating message in Exodus and the salvific message in the New Testament.

Occasional conferences of the local leaders helped to visualize the form of a united Evangelical Church. Some of the leaders were themselves ex-Orthodox priests and at least Qes Badima Yalew, an authoritative personality in Addis Ababa, tended at first to look to an Orthodox model as an ideal. With their Orthodox background some of the Evangelical preachers knew their sacred hymns of old and could quote them in their sermons.

At least two missions, both with roots in the nineteenth century, tried to hold fast to their bold strategy of the past, to work for the reformation of the Orthodox Church and to do this as far as possible from within the Ethiopian Church. The Anglican Alfred Buxton, with his Bible Churchmen's Missionary Society, with admirable perseverance stuck to this programme. In 1934 he said, 'We desire that all people of Ethiopia should be members of the Orthodox Church. Therefore it is our earnest wish to help this same Orthodox Church ... with the provision of Scriptures.' The Swedish Fosterlandsstiftelsen (Swedish Evangelical Mission) looked to the same noble heritage. The Revd Martin Nordfeldt at Nedjo insisted that his mission accept the rite of Baptism as practised by the Orthodox Church – on this score differing from both the Roman Catholics and the Adventists. In Nedjo, every Sunday morning Nordfeldt took his people with him and joined in Orthodox worship and then later in the day took the same group to his Evangelical church – at least he did so until 1941, when he left for Tanzania and its own particular Lutheran church problems at the time.[14]

Some of these Evangelical preachers were laymen, others were ordained. Daffa Djamma, connected with the Lutheran Hermannsburg mission, was ordained by the German missionary Wassmann on the very day in 1941 when Wassmann himself was expelled from the country. These local groups lived by the Bible insofar as certain texts were published and available in the vernacular.

In the case of the Sudan Interior Mission, certain Bible texts were available in the local language and for the time being these formed the core of their collective Scriptural knowledge. The faithful appropriated the message in that a precentor sang fundamental Bible texts and the congregation answered in chorus with a similar Bible text as a refrain.

But the Evangelical front was not united for long. Infant Baptism became also here a divisive shibboleth and the powerful Sudan Interior Mission with its great number of missionaries – with a Baptist tradition – formed the Word of Life Evangelical Church, while the Lutherans – related to Scandinavian, German and American missions – formed the Evangelical Ethiopian Church Mekane Yesus. In both cases the beginnings were slight, making their subsequent growth all the more remarkable.

The Roman Catholic missions, maintained and sometimes promoted during the Italo-Ethiopian war, found themselves in a ruinous situation after 1941. All their missionaries had to leave the country, their property was registered as 'enemy property' and as such administered by government. At first anti-Roman propaganda was rampant. Here also it was the neglected and forgotten rank of catechists which maintained and developed the work, particularly in Harar.

An improvement in relations between the Roman Catholics and the Ethiopian government came in 1948, related to a change in political positions on the Eritrean question. The government in Addis Ababa wished to see Eritrea return to the Ethiopian empire and the Catholics of Eritrea, apparently, shared this view. This was more than a political move; it also affected the liturgical language of the Catholics. Catholic priests in Tigre, used to the Alexandro-Ethiopian rite, now agreed to work in the south of the country, together with Ethiopian priests using the Latin rite. These priests of the Alexandro-Ethiopian rite went to Bonga, Donga and Sacco and from Addis to Metcho using the same rite. To a large extent the continued practice of the Roman Catholics was due to these men.

Education was another matter that helped the Catholics. In 1945 Government invited Canadian Jesuits to take charge of the Tafari-Makonnen School on condition that in their work they appeared in mufti. Four years later they were also entrusted with the direction of the University College of Addis Ababa. All this paved the way for significant changes towards the end of the 1950s. Diplomatic relations with the Vatican were established in 1957 and a hierarchy according to the Alexandro–Ethiopian rite was instituted. An apostolic Exarchate was created at Addis Ababa in 1951 and in 1961 Addis became the metropole for an ecclesiastical province followed by other similar provinces. French Lazarists directed the seminary: French and Dutch

Capuchins took charge of vicariates at Harar and Jimma. For many years now the White Fathers have been helping to run the Ethiopian uniate seminary at Adigrat, Asmara.

Significant developments took place at the capital, with its cathedral, 'Holy Trinity', and Saint Saviour's served by Maltese Capuchins. At Mendida a monastery with autochthonous Cistercians was established and at Gouala near Adigrat there was now another centre with sacred memories of Blessed da Jacobis. The immense personal devotion of these people was noted as the first Roman Catholic family in the area provided the Catholic church with no less than thirty-six priests, monks and nuns.

In Eritrea, Keren and Asmara were now served by Italian Capuchins, theological training was given by Cistercians while the newly-founded university had as its staff Combonian Sisters. At Asmara the Cistercians sang the Psalms in Ge'ez. The Embatkalla Junior seminary has Eritrean Capuchins as teachers. Well-known service in the Harar region was given by two leprosaria with some 800–900 lepers.[15]

14

WEST AFRICA

FRANCOPHONE WEST AFRICA

The Holy Ghost Fathers arrived first on the coast and established their work along the Atlantic coastline, ever conscious of their concern for the inland to the river Niger bend. But they were not alone. The White Fathers coming from Algeria claimed their rights. They had a reputation for knowing the Sahara, and acquired the preferment of the Propaganda in Rome. They were placed at certain strategic points in the immense, sparsely populated inland.

They were French and were to find that at this particular point in time they had to meet with opposition from the French colonial administration. The mission had great difficulties from the side of the French colonial administration because of the influence in West Africa of the anti-clerical campaign in France 1900–05. These bitter political struggles in France were exported to Africa. Anti-clerical laicization attitudes were carried by the French colonial administration. De Benoist in his rich and valuable book, *Église et Pouvoir Colonial au Soudan Français*,[1] one of the great Church and State volumes on the colonial period, has shown that while in general the attitudes of the administration were unsympathetic and even hostile – administration and mission were involved in a sort of small war, both parties involved in 'a dialogue of the deaf' – there were exceptions attempting human contacts and personal understanding, which on occasion took astonishing forms. When in 1902 the railway had reached Kita, the administrative personnel invited the mission to bless the new arrival, the railway station, the rails and the carriages. One cannot be sure how the local African population on this occasion interpreted the ritual activities of the missionaries but in any case it was a breakthrough in the wall of estrangement.

The Catholic educational effort was criticized: 'In my view, lay education alone can succeed in order to extend French influence.'[2] There was no persecution of the Catholic partner but a hostile attitude, keeping children away from the schools and the catechism, and a general insecurity of the administrative aspect which made Catholic planning and strategy difficult.

The First World War radically changed this situation. In an earlier chapter on the two world wars there was an opportunity to point out how the problems of war and recruitment of African soldiers for the war effort brought the government in Paris and the bishops in West Africa to a common understanding.

The period 1920–60 helped the two parties closer together. From the early 1920s the Catholic Church in Ouagadougou had a new bishop, Johanny Thévenoud. Born in 1878 he arrived in the territory in 1903 and served as a bishop from 1921 until his death in 1949. He was one of the greatest church leaders of his generation, a prince-bishop, with his happy combination of missionary concern and practical social involvement. His successor, Archbishop, later Cardinal, Paul Zoungrana described Thévenoud's contribution in the following words:

> He fought persistently against French anti-clericalism for French culture in his seminary at Pabré, incessantly trying out experiences in handicraft industry and agriculture, attempting to break through the patriarchal Mossi culture by working for the liberation of girls.[3]

Throughout his life, Thévenoud collaborated with the colonial administration or prevailed against it according to the circumstances, with the one great ambition solidly to plant the Church in Burkina Faso. One example: Bishop Thévenoud more than anybody else took the initiative of importing merino sheep into Burkina Faso. If this move later on proved to be fraught with veterinary problems, it also showed the Bishop's far-sightedness. His contacts with the colonial government were on the whole good, but the administrators feared his struggle for the freedom of the young women of the country. He was highly esteemed by his diocese, its priests, sisters and laity, and was in his generation one of the great bishops of Africa.

In the Thévenoud period 254 missionaries arrived in the region (159 priests, 30 brothers and 65 nuns). Of these the Ouagadougou diocese received 65 priests, 13 brothers and 28 nuns. For the apostolic-vicariate of Bamako the figures were 53, 11 and 28; and for the apostolic-prefecture of Bobo-Dioulasso, 41, 6 and 9 respectively.[4]

Burkina Faso

From the beginning of the twentieth century the Christian presence in Ouagadougou has had a powerful impact on the modernization of the city, from being a pre-colonial Mossi town, transformed into a colonial headquarters, and finally becoming the capital of the independent country of

Upper Volta, later renamed Burkina Faso. Arriving in 1901, the White Fathers under Fr Guillame Templier soon established their own 'Saint' quarters in the heart of the city. In 1919 the population of the town was 19,000 but soon after the population rapidly declined, to 10,700 in 1931, only surpassing its former peak in 1948. Increased labour migration, particularly to Ghana, the world-wide economic depression and the abolition of Upper Volta as a separate colony and its amalgamation with the Ivory Coast in 1932, were all factors contributing to the demographic stagnation of Ouagadougou between the world wars. In 1947 the French government recreated the Upper Volta colony and this, combined with economic growth and population migration to the town, increased Ouagadougou's population to some 57,000 in 1960, the year of its independence. From being primarily a Mossi town, Ouagadougou became cosmopolitan in the years after the Second World War.

Ouagadougou has been described as 'a "Christian" town in which the majority of the people are Moslems.'[5] For the first twenty years of the twentieth century the Christian presence was solely served by the Roman Catholic Church, under the White Fathers, and later the White Sisters. The first Protestant group, the Assemblies of God, arrived in 1922–23, and the first large Independent Church, the *Eglise Apostolique de la République Voltaique*, was formally launched in 1958.

The Catholic work in Ouagadougou was ably directed by Fr Joanny Thévenoud, who had arrived in the capital in 1903. By 1920 Thévenoud had developed such a forceful presence that he was appointed a member of the administrative council for the colony. Both the White Fathers and the White Sisters focused on the young generation. In the 1920s the White Sisters started a carpet factory which at one time employed over 230 teenage girls. This vocational education was developed with the aim of creating a nucleus of young Christian women who, married to Christian men, would provide 'the foundation of a developing Church'.[6] The White Fathers opened a junior seminary and in 1927 supported the foundation of the 'Association of Catholic Mossi Men'. In 1942 the first Mossi priests were ordained and one of these, Abbé Yougbare, in 1956 became Bishop of Koupéla 'and the first African bishop in all of French Africa'.[7]

The growing Christian community of Ouagadougou was at first centred around the 'Saint' wards (St Julien, St Léon, St Jean-Baptiste and St Joseph), and many of the converts were employed as clerks and government officials. In these wards over 75 per cent were Catholics, compared with an average of one-third for the whole of Ouagadougou.

Mali

As the headquarters of the colony was transferred to Bamako in 1908, the missionaries had at first to experience political adversities caused by the anticlerical attitudes of the French administration. There was a tendency in official reports to forget or ignore the mission. There was tension not only between administration and mission but also between African chiefs and the mission. Young people were denied permission to attend mass and catechism. Chiefs accused the catechumens before the administration, suggesting that they refused to pay taxes or do appointed labour. Slowly this changed for the better. In 1922 the Catholic mission was given a site for building a cathedral at Bamako. Between the wars, the diocese of Bamako had fifty-three priests, eleven brothers and twenty-eight sisters.

Also here there was a quarrel between administration and mission over the liberty of young women to chose their own husbands. When in 1929 at Tougan the government insisted that engaged young people had to register before their marriage, the missionaries foresaw 'catastrophic consequences' of this action.

During the Second World War an ethnic rising, among the Marka and the Bobo broke out 'in all the villages'.[8] Whether it was a genuinely religious movement, called '*les priants*' – 'those who pray' – or rather a local political rising was vividly discussed at the time. The local administrator made a tour of the district and arrested 400, men, old people and women. The women were freed after one month in jail, the old men after three months, while some men had to spend two years in prison. The people at the grass-roots turned in masses to the catechumenate.

Ivory Coast

The period 1930–60 was to both Catholics and Protestants a time of harvesting the many thousands won for them by Harris. The prophet was a broad-minded leader free to bring some of the converts to the Catholics or the Protestants; denominational schisms were irrelevant to him. Before Harris, the Catholics numbered no more than a few hundred. After Harris their number increased to 8,000 in 1917 and 20,000 in 1922. The Wesleyan Methodist William J. Platt, a missionary in Ghana, had expected to find a few thousand Methodists and was surprised when faced with a 'torrent' of a Methodist movement. He reported on the situation to his mission in London and they responded by sending a handful of missionaries. One of them attempted to reconcile the situation by placing a sign on the church building: 'Protestant Wesleyan Mission, Founder W. Harris'.

As they were wont to do throughout the continent the Wesleyan Methodists built schools. The Dabon school later served as a seminary for the training of evangelists and school teachers. In both groups, Catholic and Protestant, Harrist influence was discernible, helping making them 'Africanized'.

The Harrists

In the new period, after 1930, the Harrists were also a genuinely Ivorian organization, to be found in most of the southern villages. However, there was a certain ethnic dimension to the Harrists' membership in Ivory Coast. To a large extent they were Ebrie, an ethnic group near Abidjan. Of fifty Ebrie villages, only three were *not* Harrist, the rest were all the followers of the Prophet, even to the extent of criticizing Catholics and Protestants for being 'foreign', non-African; their own leader was 'the son of Africa'. When nationalism erupted in the Ivory Coast, the Harrists claimed that Harris had promised that a 'son of Africa' was one day to rule the nation. This Harris prophecy, they suggested, was fulfilled in the person of President Felix Houphouet-Boigny.

However non-Harrists tended to write off the movement as something 'for old men'. It was therefore time to present a new image. In 1955 Harrist leaders met for their first conference, under John Ahui, Harris's successor. Here was the occasion for codifying the doctrine of the Church. A young African medical doctor, Buno Claver had as his concern the modernization of the movement through the 'Union of Harrist Youth of the Ivory Coast'.

A 'First Booklet of Religious Education for the Use of Harrist missions' was published. It contained the theology and ecclesiology of the Christian group movement, with questions and answers:

> Q. What is God like?
> A. No one has ever seen him and no one ever will see God. For this reason one must never worship through a picture or a statue. The sacraments are two: Baptism and Holy Communion. The preacher invites the postulant to kneel to hold the holy cane-cross with his hands. The preacher puts the Holy Book on his head saying: 'This is the book of God: you must obey it'. Then having removed the Holy Book the preacher sprinkles water on the person's head in the name of the Father, the Son, and the Holy Ghost ... Babies may be baptized at their parents request as protection until they are old enough for a definitive baptism.

The Harris commandments are ten. For example, No. V: On Sundays, all work is prohibited (Harris urged his converts to work hard on every day but Sunday); No. X: You will not drink alcohol.

The hierarchy of the Harris Church included several hundred Harrist ministers, among whom thirty were elected by the leader Ahui to become 'ministers with cane'. There are also 'apostles', in charge of the temporal affairs of the church. 'Elders' act as an advisory board to the apostles and the ministers. There are also the guardians who keep order during church services. In 1961 a national central committee was formed subject to the authority of the supreme prophet, John Ahui.

Togo

In 1918–19 the results of the First World War had dramatic consequences for the churches in Togo. In the Catholic Church German priests were replaced by French from Lyon and Paris. French Sisters devoted themselves to education and medical care. Benedictine and Comboni Fathers added to the Catholic strength. An Alsatian, François Ignatius Hummel, with long experience in Ghana came as bishop to Lomé in 1918. In the period 1920–47 five Togolese priests were ordained. A rapid population increase took place in the Lomé region: with the coffee and cocoa boom this region was rich, and this increase was intensified after the Second World War. The Catholic population increased from 92,000 in 1945 to 214,000 in 1960.

The Protestants were assisted by missionaries from Scotland, the USA (Evangelical and Reformed Church) and the Paris Evangelical Missionary Society. To the north of the country, after the Second World War, came the Assemblies of God.

In the north the centre of gravity was found in the Kabre community. Tied to the harsh conditions of landscape and soil – *Steinbauer*, 'stone peasants', Leo Frobenius called them – the Kabre were looking elsewhere for a livelihood. Migrant labour to the south provided the answer and this brought them into contact with the Christian communities on the coast. Going singly or in small groups they thus were in a position to 'fetch' their new religion back to the home villages. Those coming from work in the south constituted the first small nucleus of catechists, resulting in a 'conversion by osmosis' of many hundreds of Kabre, to use the brilliant formula by Robert Cornevin.[9] The Protestant Kabre community comprised one pastor, 3 theological students, 16 catechists and 7 catechist students, 23 teachers, and 300 communicants.

Characteristically the Kabre constituted an important recruiting ground for the Togo army and police (the president Etienne Eyadema who started in the army was himself a Kabre). Here we should add that there is generally a relation between Christianization in Africa, with its pietistic heritage and church discipline, and recruitment for jobs of discipline and order. One thinks of the Tiv in Nigeria or of some of the Balokole groups in Kenya. The subject deserves a comprehensive study.

SIERRA LEONE

Introduction

Twentieth-century Church history of Sierra Leone in many ways offers a marked contrast to its nineteenth-century antecedents, when Freetown and its Krio population initiated the Christian outreach along the West African coast – from Gambia to Cameroon. The significant regional role of the Sierra Leonean Church had declined by the time of the First World War. The remarkably successful Christian contribution by Freetown Krios to other countries in West Africa, such as Ghana and Nigeria, in many ways obviated the continuation of this role. The success of Krio Christians in transplanting the Christian message in other societies along the coast can be seen as naturally leading to a reduction in Freetown's evangelical outreach. However, twentieth-century Christian society in Freetown failed to continue this tradition of outreach to its own 'interior' peoples in the Sierra Leone Protectorate, inland from the Colony at Freetown.

Political and economic change

In 1896 British rule was extended from the Crown Colony of Sierra Leone (which during the nineteenth century meant Freetown and its environs) to include the surrounding inland and coastal societies, when a Protectorate was declared. Large numbers of inland peoples such as the Temne, Limba, Mende, together with the coastal Sherbro and Vai, found themselves under British rule. These and other peoples living in the Protectorate made up over 95 per cent of the total population; the remaining 5 per cent, about 75,000 (of whom about 30,000 were Krio) lived in the Colony, including 35,000 actually in Freetown. Professor Porter has commented that it is 'one of the paradoxes of history that this declaration of the Sierra Leone Protectorate, while uniting the country politically, divided it culturally and ethnically.'[10]

Christian Krio ascendancy was abruptly broken by the Hut Tax War of

1898, which broke out in two separate risings among the Temne in the north and the Mende in the southern half of the Protectorate.

> Nearly a thousand Creoles serving up-country as missionaries and traders were killed, along with a handful of white missionaries. This slaughter, carried out chiefly by Mendes, deepened Creole fears of the 'aborigines', and reinforced their growing estrangement from the tribal societies of Sierra Leone.[11]

Nearly a century of growing, if intermittent, contact between the Krio and many adjacent societies had resulted in suspicion and enmity.

Much of this contact had been established by Krio Christian (and Muslim) women traders, whose religious faith was an indivisible part of their identity. These women had developed the 'ward system', whereby Krio families fostered children from the hinterland societies, taking them into their own homes in the colony and exposing them to Western education and Christianity. However, most of these wards chose not to return to their inland homes and, instead, assimilated into Freetown society by taking Krio names and joining in the vibrant church life. By remaining in the Colony, these individuals could not become much needed cross-cultural communicators between coastal Krio Christian society and the inland peoples, a role that might have ameliorated the growing suspicion between the two.

The years following the Hut Tax War were particularly difficult for Krio society. Unfairly accused, by the British colonial administration of inciting the 1898 rebellions, and viewed with hostility by the inland chiefs and their peoples, Krio society turned inward, preoccupied by its own anxiety and lack of influence. This despondency was heightened by changes in British attitudes towards Krio participation in colonial administration and government. From the time of the creation of the Protectorate, the Krio were excluded from its administration and the 1898 risings 'strengthened the determination of the colonial government to keep the protectorate separate, culturally and administratively, from the colony which by then comprised the whole Freetown peninsula'.[12]

Even when retiring from the colony's own government the Krios found themselves replaced by Europeans, and they 'were deprived of the administrative responsibilities and opportunities for which their education had equipped them'.[13] Professor Fyfe has concluded that the 'Creoles came to realize that a government which moved its servants away bodily, and recruited outsiders to fill senior posts, was becoming utterly estranged from them.'[14]

By the turn of the century, in the new age of mercantile and colonial imperialism, Freetown Krio society faced the prospect of economic eclipse by Lebanese and Syrian traders on the one hand, and by European commercial interests on the other. In 1901 there were forty-one Lebanese in Sierra Leone; by 1911 this number had risen to 266. Within the first two decades, these Levantine traders had effectively replaced the earlier Krio traders in the Protectorate. There was understandably much resentment against these new arrivals. Although a number of Levantines supported the Freetown YMCA, and also contributed 25 per cent of the money given to the Red Cross during the war, the Krio viewed them with suspicion. The Lebanese were accused of introducing and spreading the Spanish influenza epidemic of 1918, during which some 70 per cent of Freetown's population became sick, and over 1,000 died in little over three weeks. Sickness reduced the numbers of those strong enough to farm and this led to a shortage of rice. Hunger, combined with Krio indignation, exploded into anti-Levantine riots in Freetown during July 1919.

> For those Creoles involved, the violence was a spontaneous expression of pent-up frustration discharged against the most convenient scapegoat in Sierra Leone – one which was foreign, numerically vulnerable, and could be held in contempt as somehow 'less civilized'.[15]

This outburst and the ensuing government demands for riot compensation further estranged Krio society from the colonial administration.

In 1924 a new constitution brought closer together the 'provincials' of the Protectorate, the Krios and other inhabitants of the Colony. Krio society now had to contend with the rise, under the system of Indirect Rule, of a provincial elite composed of Temne and Mende paramount chiefs. In 1905 the government had opened a school at Bo for the sons and nominees of the Protectorate chiefs and thus, by the 1930s, a new group of literate traditional chiefs and other educated 'provincials' had come to office and they increasingly challenged the remaining power and influence of Krio society. This unity, forged at the Bo government school, of the leaders of the various Protectorate peoples became significant importance in the contests with the Krios over constitutional advancement during the years 1947–51. 'The two main interests in the Protectorate, the chiefs and the educated men, were being brought closer together in their common antagonism to Creole extremists.'[16] A new constitution was introduced in 1951 which gave political power to Dr Milton Margai's Sierra Leone People's Party (founded the previous year), a predominantly Protectorate party which had electorally defeated the rival Krio party, the National Council of Sierra Leone, led by Dr Bankole-Bright.[17] By 1961, the population of the Protectorate numbered over 2,250,000, compared with about 100,000 for the Colony, of whom around 30,000 were Krios. The prime minister (later Sir) Milton Margai, led the country to independence in 1961.

Church History of the Colony

Church development in the Colony was dominated during the twentieth century, as in the previous century, by the Krio society of Freetown. The two largest churches continued to be the Sierra Leone Church (Anglican), and the Methodist Church.

The (Anglican) Sierra Leone Church

Henry Venn's policy of creating 'self-governing, self-supporting, self-propagating native churches' appeared to be finally realized in 1908 when the CMS formally withdrew from its evangelistic work in the Protectorate and in the hinterland of the Colony. Between 1907–26 there were no CMS missionaries in the Native Pastorate Church, and of the thirty-two CMS staff working in the Sierra Leone Mission between 1910–42, most were teaching at the two CMS grammar schools or at Fourah Bay College. Thus not only the Anglican Church in Freetown, but also Anglican work in the Protectorate, were in the hands of Krio leaders of the Church.

However, the Anglican episcopate of Sierra Leone remained under the control of the CMS in London. In 1898 Ghana and Nigeria had been separated from the Diocese of Sierra Leone, which nevertheless still encompassed an enormous area, all the way up the West Coast to Morocco and also taking in the Canaries! The diocese was able to shed these other obligations when it was reconstituted in 1930, then including only the Colony and Protectorate of Sierra Leone.

It is remarkable that Sierra Leone, the earliest centre of CMS work on the West Coast, was among the last of the West African Anglican churches to gain an African bishop. It was only in 1937 that a Sierra Leonean was raised to the episcopate in their own diocese, when Archdeacon Thomas Sylvester Claudius Johnson was consecrated assistant bishop. Bishop Johnson had previously spent a long and distinguished career in promoting Anglican educational work in Sierra Leone. It is also of interest to note that the second Sierra Leonean assistant bishop, consecrated in 1948, the Rt Revd Percy John Jones, was the son of Abigail Charlotte Powells Jones (d. 1942), one of the greatest Krio women traders. Born in 1868 to a Yoruba liberated slave, Abigail Jones had been brought up by a Methodist missionary. She served her commercial apprenticeship under her paternal aunts, inherited the business, and later used her profits to educate her seven sons as doctors, civil servants and clergy, sending three to England, including Percy who pursued theological studies and was later ordained in 1929. Abigail Jones 'was a legend in her own time. Establishing a reputation as the queen among Big Market traders, she maintained and expanded one of the largest firms ever run by a Krio woman.'[18]

It was not until 1961, a few months after independence, that the Anglican Church gained its first African and its first Sierra Leonean diocesan bishop with the consecration of Moses Scott (d. 1988). Born 1911 in Calabar, eastern Nigeria, Bishop Scott's family illustrate the coastal diaspora of Krios from Freetown. He was educated at Fourah Bay but an eye illness delayed his ordination until 1945. Bishop Scott made notable contributions to the extension of the Anglican Church to the peoples of the Protectorate, serving at Yongoro and Makeni. Later, he was vicar of St Paul's Church at Bo, the central town of Mende country, becoming Archdeacon there in 1958. In 1969 he was appointed Archbishop of West Africa, the first African to hold that post, and retired in 1981.

Anglican educational work in Freetown had a long pedigree of valuable service to the cause of Christian education and evangelical expansion. In 1910 there were thirty-nine Anglican primary schools in the Colony, preparing children for secondary education at the boys' Grammar School (estab. 1845) and at the girls' Annie Walsh Memorial School (estab. 1863). Local church members were disappointed that the CMS – who ran both the secondary schools and Fourah Bay College – had not continued, during the years 1905–20, the policy of appointing Sierra Leonean principals. This can perhaps be related to the problem of 'control and devolution', between mission society and local church. Having relinquished its evangelical work to the local church, the CMS wished to maintain their influence over Church schools and education. After 1920, the leadership of the Grammar School was returned to African educationalists.

Unlike the boys' Grammar School, the Annie Walsh Memorial School for girls remained under CMS missionary principals until the 1960s. During the 1930s girls were beginning to be accepted into Fourah Bay College, and the girls' secondary school provided many of the first women graduates. Krio women have a long history of valuing the importance of education, and one 'of the subsidiary but widespread functions of many [Protestant] women's associations in Freetown is to raise funds for secondary-school scholarships for girls, since all schools in Sierra Leone have fees'.[19]

Fourah Bay College, founded as the 'Christian Institution' in 1816, was the oldest surviving educational and religious training centre along the West

African coast. Its survival, however, was in doubt by the end of the first decade of the twentieth century. That the nature of higher education at Fourah Bay had undergone a qualitative change, also placed it in jeopardy. It was no longer solely an institution for evangelism through just the training of clergy and mission school teachers, as it had also evolved into a centre teaching the humanities, medicine and law. Happily CMS finances were not entirely cut, and Fourah Bay continued until it gained new vigour in 1918, when the Wesleyan Methodist Mission Society 'very wisely decided to make use of the college for training Africans, instead of attempting to set up a separate institution'.[20] Its success during these lean years was in large measure due to the persistence and vision of Revd T. S. Johnson, the future Anglican bishop.

By the 1940s Fourah Bay had developed into a truly national ecumenical educational centre, with support also from the Evangelical United Brethren Church. In 1928 the colonial government established a teacher training course at Fourah Bay, and in 1943 the College absorbed the Methodist Women's teacher training institution. This successful co-operation paved the way for the enormous expansion that took place from 1950, when Fourah Bay became a government institution, and later a full University College in 1959. Bishop T. S. Johnson has written that 'one cannot find words adequate to express the great debt which the country owes to the C.M.S. for having shouldered, almost unaided for over a century, the work at Fourah Bay College.'[21]

In handing over Fourah Bay to the government, the Churches 'made it a condition that the Christian tradition of the College should be maintained'.[22] The fulfillment of this wish cannot be better exemplified than by reference to the life and work of the Revd Canon Harry Sawyer (1909–86). Born in Freetown and educated at Fourah Bay, Harry Sawyer was a member of the College's academic staff for forty years, 1933–73. As chaplain, professor and dean of theology he helped to educate generations of Sierra Leonean and other West African church leaders. Although from a Krio family and sensitively observant to Krio spirituality, he also gained deep insights into Mende linguistics and religiosity. As principal of Fourah Bay and later vice-chancellor of the University of Sierra Leone, he became one of Africa's foremost guardians of intellectual independence and educational high standards.

In Freetown he 'served the Sierra Leone Church faithfully until the end and as long as he could, he assisted in services at St George's Cathedral where he was a Canon'.[23] As a churchman, Harry Sawyer was not only a devout Anglican but an ecumenical figure who was a member of the Faith and Order Commission of the WCC. After retiring from the University of Sierra Leone, he went to teach at Fourah Bay's sister institution, Codrington College in Barbados. 'His vigour, his enthusiasm and his total devotion to the cause of education and religion, made him a household name and almost a legend in his lifetime.'[24]

Women in Freetown Church life

We have already mentioned the importance of the Anglican Annie Walsh Memorial School for girls, and the market women's trading background, as mothers of leading lay and clerical Christians. Most Christian associations are organized and run by women, and they provide necessary avenues for religious leadership and expression, in contradistinction to the male-dominated clerical and formalized Church hierarchies. In 'Freetown society it is important to behave in a religious manner. For women, religious piety is extended through participation in one or more of the women's associations attached to the Church.'[25]

One of the earliest founded twentieth-century women's organizations was The Martha Davies Confidential Benevolent Association. After Jesus Christ had appeared in a dream in 1910 to Mrs Martha Davies, a widow, she founded the association and it soon grew to be one of the most successful (out of about fifty) 'bands' in Freetown. In her vision, Mrs Davies 'received the command to get Christian women together to work sacrificially for increased membership in the Churches in Freetown and for Christian charity to be practiced freely in the community, especially towards the destitute and sick'.[26] Martha Davies died in 1917, and was succeeded by Mother Jane C. Bloomer who 'was instructed in a vision how to compose hymns of praise in Krio and re-arrange regular Church hymns in Krio to fit into the form of composition popularly known as Shouts'.[27]

In the late 1950s the association had 150 full members and about another seventy on trial. Most of these Christian women societies were prayer and hymn-singing groups, with an emphasis on faith healing and 'feeding the soul'. However, these associations did not develop into independent or separatist Churches as happened, for instance, in Nigeria. It 'is a moot point whether this group is a Church in the sense in which we have been using this term, since the majority of its members belong to one or other of the formal denominations, particularly the African Methodist Episcopal. The congregation is composed almost entirely of women from the more modest income groups.'[28]

Adelaide Casely Hayford (1868–1960), the wife of the famous Ghanaian lawyer, was one of the most remarkable Christian daughters of Krio society. Born in 1868 in Freetown she was educated in England and Germany and returned to Sierra Leone with a mission to improve the educational opportunities for girls. Brought up in a Wesleyan Methodist family and married to an Anglican, she never ceased in her attempts to forward her Christian and educational ideals. In 1915 she delivered a lecture at the Freetown Wesley Church on 'The Rights of Women and Christian Marriage', which launched 'a new career, a new image for her in Freetown, not as a daughter or a wife but as a woman in her own right'.[29]

In 1919 she became president of the Young Women's Christian Association and during the following year she became the first educated African woman to visit and travel over much of the United States. With the aim of learning about Black women's education and with the task of raising funds for her envisaged girls' school, she spoke at numerous churches and institutions in America, both White and Black, and she soon gained an impressive reputation. In 1923 Adelaide Casely Hayford launched her most ambitious project: an independent secondary 'Girls' Vocational School' in Freetown. Part of her school's prospectus read: 'Training will be both literary and vocational and above all and underneath all, will be the principles of character building as laid down by the Great Master Builder, Jesus Christ himself.'[30]

On a visit to Britain in 1935 she became interested in the Moral Rearmament Movement (MRA) after meeting the founder, Dr Buchman, at an Oxford Group meeting. On her return to Freetown she launched the movement in Sierra Leone, believing it would lead to a revival in the Churches. 'Her life-long interest in world peace ... and her generally broad but deep religious commitment which went beyond the restrictions of race and country' led Adelaide Casely Hayford to propound MRA as her last public involvement in Sierra Leone.[31]

The 'Provincials' in the Protectorate

The two main peoples in the Protectorate are the Temne in the north and the Mende in the south of the country. The Mende chief was a secular ruler, 'but he possessed no strong religious mystique. The Temne chief, by contrast was invested with a "chief's holiness" at his consecration ... linking him to the ancestors in Futa Jallon.'[32] During the nineteenth and twentieth centuries most of the Temne people have become Muslim, and many of the Temne converts to Christianity have met their new religion while in the process of migrating to Freetown and the Colony and thus not in their own homeland. Earlier nineteenth-century mission work in Temne land was destroyed during the 1898 Hut Tax War, and evangelization only recommenced with the expansion of the railway northwards in 1914. However, most of the Church work in the north during this century has tended to minister to the small groups of Krio traders and civil servants that have established themselves in these northern centres.

The Christian reception among the southern Mende people has been much more encouraging. The United Brethren Church, who started work in 1857, have become during the twentieth century the main Church in the region. However, Krio influence, even in the Protectorate, was also a strong feature of the Church. Between 1912 and 1946 nearly half of the pastors in the Church were Krio. Much energy was spent on the provision of mission school education where none had previously existed. Although the Church had only 4,735 members in 1946, its influence through the mission school was much larger. Two former prime ministers of Sierra Leone, Sir Milton Margai and Dr Siaka Stevens have belonged to the Church.

In the first half of the twentieth century, not more than 5 per cent of the provincial peoples became Christians. The Anglican CMS had withdrawn from Sierra Leone by the beginning of the century and left mission work in the Protectorate to the local Church. The poor results led the CMS to change its policy and it resumed work in the Protectorate in 1942.

The Wesleyan Methodist Mission Society (WMMS) had also withdrawn from the Colony, with local Wesleyans in charge. However, unlike the CMS, the Methodists had retained their involvement in mission work in the interior, particularly among the Mende. As part of this policy, the WMMS had also in place a missionary in Freetown at the Mende-speaking immigrant Church. By the 1930s various tensions had arisen between Church and mission. Although the Freetown Methodist churches were run by Krios, the Chairman and Superintendent was a missionary, with authority over the whole Church, Krio and Mende. In 1937 the Mende Church held its annual meetings separately from the General Synod of the Church, and it was only in 1966 that the missionaries and pastors of the Mende circuits were integrated into the General Synod.

GHANA

Christianity and cocoa underpinned the material and spiritual advance of the Ghanaian people during this period. The revolution in land-use, from forest to cocoa farm, had become widespread by the 1920s. New economic opportunities, through new commodities and enhanced communications, gave to both peasants and chiefs a new rural-based prosperity. This well-being was to be of vital importance for the renewed growth and vitality of village Christianity and the development of rural Ghanaian folk-Churches. Rural wealth and village Christianity assisted Church growth in both coastal and inland towns and cities, both old and new. Urban Church life and growth was based on rural Christianity. Village chapels and primary schools led to large urban Churches and their attached secondary schools.

By 1920, the Church was well-integrated into southern Ghanaian society, with the Wesleyan Methodists and Basel Mission having worked for over eighty years in the Fante and Akwapim societies. The Bremen Mission had worked in Eastern Ghana, amongst the Ewe population since the 1840s. During the 1880s the Catholics started work in the country, with the Anglicans following after 1900. In the years after 1900 and before the First World War, Methodists, Presbyterians (Basel Mission), Anglicans and Catholics had begun work in the middle region of Ghana, in what was known as the Ashanti Crown Colony. However, it was only from 1920 that the Churches began to gain a wide following. In the northern region, in what was known as the Northern Territories Protectorate, the field was very much left to the Catholic White Fathers, until the Protestants seriously started their work in the region after the Second World War.

The First World War had a dramatic effect on the development of Ghanaian Protestant Church life. At the beginning of 1918, both the Basel and Bremen missions had been proscribed and missionaries who were German nationals had been interned. The United Free Church of Scotland Mission, known as the Scottish Mission, arrived from Calabar, eastern Nigeria, under the leadership of the Revd A. W. Wilkie, and this new mission provided limited support for the continuation of the two former German missions. The banishment of these missions led to a real devolution of power and authority to the local Churches in eastern and central Ghana. In 1926 both the Basel and Bremen Missions were allowed to return to Ghana, where they found great changes in local Church development and autonomy.

The Christian Council of Ghana

The Protestant Missionary Conference in 1926 at Le Zoute, Belgium, provided the external stimuli for the creation of the Christian Council of Ghana in 1929, by the Wesleyan Methodists, the Presbyterians (Basel and Scottish missions) Evangelical (Ewe) Presbyterians (Bremen mission), Anglicans (SPG) and the African Methodist Episcopal Zion Church. Co-operation between denominations led to an increase in the co-ordination of Church facilities, and reduced the unnecessary duplication of schools and congregations. In 1937 'the member Churches of the Council made history by organizing the first open-air joint worship to observe the universal week of prayer'.[33] The 1939 earthquake that shook Accra provided another opportunity for ecumenical prayer and support. During the 1940s the question of theological education became central to the Council's deliberations. The Christian Council successfully agitated for a Faculty of Theology at the new University College of the Gold Coast at Legon. In the late 1940s the Council co-ordinated the Christian response to the *Tigare* witchcraft eradication movement that was then sweeping the country. The Council published a pamphlet entitled *Tigare or Christ?*, which was distributed in thousands to churches throughout the country.[34] This action provided a united and strong Christian response to the problem of witchcraft.

During the 1950s, the Christian Council took on new responsibilities under the chairmanship of the Revd Christian Bäeta (Evangelical Presbyterian) and the first full-time general-secretaryship of the Revd Peter Dagadu (Presbyterian *cum* Methodist), who served until 1958. In 1957 the 'Ghana Church Union' movement was launched, and in 1959 the Women's Committee was created to co-ordinate the work of women in the churches. This recognition of the key role that women played in African Christianity was seen by the new general secretary of the Christian Councils the Revd T. A. Osei in 1958, as a 'major decision on a long felt need and a milestone in the progress of the Christian Council'.[35] Also by 1959, the Council had played a key role in the re-establishment of Trinity College, an ecumenical theological training centre, from Kumasi to a site adjacent to the University of Ghana at Legon.

A central personality and pastor in Ghanaian Protestant circles was the Revd Peter Dagadu (1907–60). Peter Dagadu's ecclesiastical career is an example of practical ecumenics both within Ghana and world-wide. Born into a Presbyterian family, Peter Dagadu was educated as a teacher at the Basel Mission training college at Akropong, and later posted to the Presbyterian school at Obawale, transferring after two years to Odumase. His desire was to become a pastor, but under Presbyterian rules and conventions inherited from the Basel Mission, seniority of age and experience was, at that time, of great importance. Peter Dagadu decided to leave the Presbyterian Church in 1934 for the Methodist Church, declaring: 'In the Presbyterian Church you have to grow old before you are ordained. I want to do some useful work before I'm too old for it.'[36] With amicable agreement both the Presbyterian and Methodist Churches agreed to this unusual request and in 1940 Peter Dagadu was ordained a Methodist minister.

After working on the Accra circuit and at Wesley College in Kumasi, Peter Dagadu became general secretary of the Christian Council of Ghana, from 1952–58. He initiated the annual event of Christian Home Weeks, which still continues to be such a distinctive hallmark of Ghanaian ecumenism. In 1955 he organized the important meeting on 'Christianity and African Culture', with 126 participants.[37] A compilation of lectures given to this meeting was published, and it provides a stimulating insight into contemporary Christian responses to ancestor worship, libation, witchcraft, and cultural world views. During the 1950s, he became a member of the Central Committee of the World Council of Churches and was thus able to practise his innate Ghanaian ecumenism on a world stage.

Southern Ghana – the Gold Coast Colony

Methodists

The coastal town of Cape Coast was the premier urban centre of Ghanaian Methodism. From the town, the Church had expanded along the coast, both westward and eastward, and inland to the frontier of the Asante kingdom. After 1896, Fante Methodism reached into Asante itself, to their Twi-speaking Akan neighbours. In 1905 the Synod of the Church had divided the district into an eastern section, comprising Accra, Aburi, Juaben and the Volta region, and a western section which included Cape Coast, Elmina, Sekondi and Methodist work in Asante.

In 1918, the Methodist Church had a national following of nearly 80,000 people in 261 congregations, and was served by 12 missionaries, 42 African pastors and 665 catechists and teachers. There were also 240 schools with nearly 15,000 pupils. Two years before independence, in 1955, Ghanaian Methodism had expanded to embrace a community of 170,000 in 1,227 congregations, ministered to by 56 Ghanaian pastors, 19 missionaries and 3,807 catechists and teachers. By this time, the Church also ran over 780 schools with nearly 110,000 pupils. A comparison of these statistics shows the continuing central importance of Methodism to Ghanaian Christian life and identity.

The turn of the century had witnessed a cultural revival by the predominantly Methodist-educated elite society of Cape Coast. This cultural awareness was very much based on the Methodist Mfantsipim leading secondary school. John Mensah Sarbah and J. Casely-Hayford were leading supporters of Mfantsipim who related the education provided by the school to the wider cultural values of coastal and Fante society. This coastal

Methodist elite was very much at the centre of Ghanaian politics during the 1920s, especially with the creation of the National Congress of British West Africa (NCBWA), a successor to the Cape Coast-based Aborigines' Rights Protection Society (ARPS). One of the ARPS' first secretaries was Dr Kwegyir Aggrey, the most famous Ghanaian educationalist of the 1920s, who came from a Methodist background. Aggrey played a prominent role in the development of Africa education, by his membership of the Phelps-Stokes African Education Commission.

In 1935 the Methodist Church celebrated a centenary of work in Ghana, with processions and services in 767 churches for a following of over 125,000. In 1944 the final and entire translation of the Bible into Fante was completed. However, the problem of literacy remained, with an estimated 75 per cent of Methodist adults unable to read. During 1944 the Church launched a Commission on the Life of the Church, which published its findings in 1948 under the title, *I Will Build My Church*. The report was hailed as 'one of the most penetrating documents that the Church has anywhere received for its study in recent years' and in its 171 pages it covered every facet of Church life and the nature and purpose of Christian ministry.[38]

By 1937, twenty-six out of twenty-nine circuits were under African leadership, and by the early 1940s the local synod had resolved to replace missionaries with Ghanaian Church leaders. By 1949, forty-seven men and twenty-two women had been sponsored by the Church for studies in Britain. In the same year, the Church elected its first Ghanaian chairman, Revd Gaddiel Acquah. After 125 years of association, the Methodist Churst of Ghana became independent from the British Methodist Conference in 1961.

Leading Methodists included the Revds L. B. Greaves and T. A. Beetham – both important missionary educators in the Church, and Dr K. A. Busia, scholar, statesman and a leading lay Methodist.

Presbyterians

After the expulsion of the Basel missionaries and the arrival of the Scottish Mission, the key event was the Synod of the Church in August 1918. A Synod Committee was appointed, composed of eight Ghanaians and three missionaries, which ran the Church between the biannual Synods. Although missionaries retained control of the Central (financial) Fund and educational work, after 1918 'all major decisions were made by Synod and Synod Committee.'[39] In 1926 the name 'The Presbyterian Church of the Gold Coast' was adopted.

The long career and devotion of Revd Nicholas T. Clerk (1862–1961) deserves to be mentioned. Of Jamaican parentage, Revd N. T. Clerk became Synod Clerk to the Church in the difficult days of 1918 following the expulsion of the Basel Mission. His steadfast hand guided the church until he retired in 1933, aged seventy-one years. The second African to be educated in Europe by the Basel mission, he later worked for unity between his own church and the Evangelical (Ewe) Presbyterians, but this was not to be. The Revd N. T. Clerk and his family represent a noble standard of Christian service through the generations. His own father, a teacher, had been the leader of a group of West Indians that came to Ghana to work for the Basle Mission, and N. T. Clerk's own son, Charles Henry Clerk, later became a successful pastor in the Church.

Despite the heritage of educational training facilities at Akropong and Aburi, the Presbyterian Church, for a Protestant mission, was quite late in beginning secondary school education in Ghana. It was only in 1938 that the Presbyterian secondary school for boys opened at Odumase Krobo, with a girls' secondary school opening soon after the Second World War. In 1924 the theological seminary at Abetifi was amalgamated with the teacher training college at Akropong. In 1927 Governor Guggisberg opened a combined newly built college at Akropong, exactly 100 years after the beginning of Basel work in Ghana. Akropong has retained its tradition as a centre of educational excellence and artistic ability; a new Twi Bible was completed in 1960 by Dr C. A. Akrofi, an outstanding linguist.

The Presbyterians embraced a total Christian community in 1918 of 30,000, including 10,000 children, in 196 congregations served by 30 ministers and by 316 teachers in 179 schools. By 1959 the number of Presbyterians had risen to 182,000 (including children), in 686 congregations served by 89 pastors and by 4,300 teachers in 858 schools.

Catholics – Society of African Mission

Catholic work was centred on Cape Coast, where Bishop Ignatius Hummel resided between the years 1906 and 1924. During his time the number of Catholics had expanded to over 40,000. In the far east of the country, in the Keta region, the first Catholic Ghanaian priest, Fr Anastasius Dogli, was ordained in 1922. The Keta region, with 12,000 Catholics and 2,000 children in 36 schools, became a separate diocese in 1923.

The Cathedral of St Francis in Cape Coast was dedicated in 1928, in time for the golden jubilee of modern Catholic work in Ghana. The first two Akan clergy, Revd George Ansah from Elmina and Revd Francis Menyah from Pedu near Cape Coast, were ordained in 1935.

Although Bishop Ernest Hauger, the vicar apostolic between 1925–32, had spent much effort in establishing scores of village primary schools, the Catholics lagged behind the Protestant Churches in creating its own educated elite. For many years Catholics had pressed for a secondary school. Only with the arrival in 1933 of Bishop Porter was the first Catholic secondary school, St Augustine's, opened at Cape Coast in 1935. The first girls' secondary school was only opened in 1946. St John's secondary school at Sekondi was opened in 1952.

Bishop Porter wished to develop public lay responsibility in the church, and to this end he launched two 'open' societies: the Catholic Young Men's Society, and the Women's League. Porter was anxious to circumscribe the influence of the Catholic lay secret societies of the 'Knights'. The 'Knights of Marshall' was a voluntary Catholic secret society, founded in 1925, and named after the lay initiator of modern Catholic work in Ghana, the magistrate Sir James Marshall. Most members were polygamists and thus non-communicants in the Church, and their secrecy was disliked by the clergy. In 1937 the Knights of St John was started at Saltpond, semi-military in organization but stricter than the Knights of Marshall, as they insisted that their members should be communicants and thus not polygamists. Uneasy rivalry has characterized relations between the two orders, with the Johns smaller in number and often with a lower social level than the Marshalls.

In 1943 American SVD Fathers (Society of the Divine Word) took charge of Accra and the central coastal area. In the same year the first Ga, from one of the Accra's leading families, Sam Washington van der Puije, was ordained. The first Catholic bishop of African descent was consecrated in 1953, when Fr Joseph Bowers, an American, became Bishop of Accra. In 1960, Bishop John Kodwo Amissah was the first Ghanaian to become Archbishop of Cape Coast, succeeding Archbishop William Porter who had been Vicar Apostolic of the Gold Coast since 1933 and Archbishop from 1951.

The symbolism of Ethiopia was already well-understood by the Ghanaian urban literate intellectual elite when the Italians invaded the ancient kingdom of Abyssinia in 1936. The outcry in Ghana and the rest of British West Africa against this aggression was soon focused in criticism of Pope Pius XI and the Catholic Church's silence over Italian action against Ethiopia. Much harm was thus done to the Catholic Church in West Africa. Some Catholic missionaries were accused of being fascist spies, and many Africans believed that collections in Churches and missions were financially helping the Italians in Ethiopia. There was a widespread belief that the dictator Mussolini controlled the Vatican. This anti-Catholic feeling was, unfortunately, supported by some individual Protestant missionaries.

At the Cape Coast headquarters of the Catholic Church, young people publicly renounced their membership of the Church. The situation demanded a counter-attack, with priests trying to explain the exact role of the Church in the conflict. The Church formed a number of Catholic societies and youth movements to mobilize its members. Members of the Catholic Women's League and the Gold Coast Catholic Young Men's Society agreed to boycott the radical nationalist press – especially Azikiwe's *African Morning Post*.

The Italian invasion of Ethiopia had a lasting effect on the growing numbers of educated West Africans, especially teachers and clerks. The issue posed a challenge to the Catholic Church and the controversy also affected other Churches. It forced the Catholic Church to enter the realm of politics and nationalism for the first time, and to argue its case and compete for public opinion. This foray into public debate and counter-attack was a foretaste of what would be a commonplace response for all the Churches in the era of mass nationalism after the Second World War and the coming period of decolonization and independence.

Anglicans – Society for the Propagation of the Gospel

The Anglicans re-entered Ghana in 1904 after an absence of eighty years. The railway town of Sekondi was initially chosen to be the centre of Anglican work, with easy rail access to the gold mining towns of Tarkwa and Abosso. In 1916 the first two Ghanaian priests were ordained – the Revd E. D. Martinson and Revd E. F. H. Thomas. Ill-health dogged the growth of the Church and in 1923 Bishop O'Rorke (consecrated 1913) was left with just three Ghanaian clergy. With the appointment of Bishop Aglionby in 1924, the Church established its headquarters in the capital city of Accra. By 1948 the Church had 35,000 members nationally, served by thirty-five clergy.

One of the most impressive achievements of Anglican work in this period was its involvement in educational matters. Adisadel College, the SPG secondary grammar school, was opened at Cape Coast in 1910. By 1933 the college required new buildings but finance was lacking. The boys of the school decided to build the new schools themselves: 'they had heard of the monks who built Buckfast Abbey with their own hands: why should not the school build Adisadel?'[40] Girls' schools were opened at Sekondi and Accra, run by sisters of the Order of the Holy Paraclete. In Asante, as we shall see, Anglicans pioneered theological and girls' education in the region both at Kumasi and Mampong.

In 1949 the Church celebrated the jubilee of Bishop Aglionby's consecration, and in 1951 the Anglican Province of West Africa came into existence.

Central Ghana – Asante

Methodists and Presbyterians

For the Methodists, a dramatic expansion occurred between 1920–23, following the lightening preaching tours by Sampson Oppong in Asante villages and in Kumasi. He arrived in the city 'dressed in a long white gown, carrying a wooden cross and crowned with a garland of flowers'. Apparently, 'Sampson wore a khaki robe when travelling, a black one for preaching, and a white one for relaxing.'[41] A mass movement to Christianity followed in his wake, with the Methodists alone claiming 20,000 converts by 1923.

The Methodist commitment to its work in Asante as central to its expansion throughout the country was underlined when the predominantly Fante synod decided to underwrite the costs of moving its training institution for teachers, catechists and pastors, from Aburi to Kumasi. Wesley College, Kumasi was opened in 1924 by Governor Sir Gordon Guggisberg, who commented that it was one of the most impressive buildings ever erected in the West African inland. The names and high reputations of such missionary educators as L. B. Greaves, S. G. Williamson and T. A. Beetham are intimately linked to the growth and advance of Wesley College.

In 1926 the newly returned Basle missionaries were initially restricted to their former work in Asante. In 1929 Basel missionaries proposed that Asante should be a separate District Church under their guidance and thus separate from the Ghanaian-dominated Synod Committee of the Church. The Synod rejected giving the Basel Mission any special powers in Asante, but it supported the removal of territorial restrictions in 1930 which had been placed on the Basel and Bremen Missions. The advent of the Second World War again led to the internment of most of the Basel Mission staff, placing additional responsibility on Ghanaian and Scottish Presbyterians.

In 1943 the Methodists and Presbyterians opened a joint secondary school in Kumasi, called Prempeh College. This meant that Asante Church members would no longer have to travel outside the region for secondary education. In the same year, the two Churches also co-operated in establishing a theological college, Trinity College, in Kumasi. Trinity College was of far-reaching importance in changing the character of Presbyterian clergy. From 1946 young men specifically trained for the ministry joined the older group of Presbyterian ministers, who had themselves come from a teacher–catechist background.[42] These younger ministers were much more open to Christian accommodation of indigenous forms of culture and belief.

In 1929 the Basel Mission opened a new hospital at Agogo in Asante. This hospital has become perhaps the most important inland medical centre run by a Protestant church, in what is normally a Catholic-dominated medical field.

Catholics: Society of African Missions

Responsibility for Asante was given to the Society of African Missions, which had previously received jurisdiction over work in the Gold Coast Colony. The opening of the railway line in 1903 between Sekondi and Kumasi facilitated Catholic beginnings in Asante. Bishop Klaus (Vicar Apostolic of the Gold Coast 1904–05) took the train to Kumasi in 1905 and at stops on the way, discovered 'that Christians from the Coast who were working in the gold mines had set up Catholic communities.' In Kumasi he found 'a Catholic congregation of about eighty members. It had been established two years earlier by James Cobbina, an Ashanti baptized in Cape Coast.'[43] In 1908 a mission house and chapel were opened on a little hill above the *zongo* with its Muslim trading community. Today, in the heart of the city, the twin spires of St Peter's Cathedral (built 1927–29) stand on the original Catholic mission site, providing an arresting sight in the townscape.

Apart from Kumasi, the other principal Catholic centres were Obuasi, Bekwai, Berekum and Konongo. Kumasi gained its first bishop in 1932, with the creation of the 'Apostolic-Vicariate of Ashanti', to care for the 12,550 Catholics in Asante. Bishop Paulissen, a Dutchman, was met by a great crowd at Kumasi station and after having 'blessed the clergy who had assembled to meet him, Bishop Paulissen went up to speak to the Asantehene and the Queen-Mother. They stood under their great State umbrella waiting to greet him.'[44]

In the Brong–Ahafo region, to the north-west of Kumasi, a hospital was built in 1948 at Berekum, staffed by American medical sisters. Irish members of the Sisters of St Louis took charge of girls' education in the Asante vicariate, opening a secondary school for girls and later a teacher training institution. However, boys' education lagged behind, and a secondary school for boy was only opened in 1952 at Opoku Ware near Kumasi.

The major Catholic event of the 1950s was the creation of the Ecclesiastical Province of the Gold Coast in 1950, and the national Eucharistic Congress of 1951, held in Kumasi. The Papal Legate,

Archbishop Matthew, was greeted by a crowd of 80,000, and he was welcomed in St Peter's Cathedral by Archbishop Porter of Cape Coast and the new Bishop Bronk of Kumasi. Thirty bishops, archbishops and prefects-apostolic took part in the seven days of the Congress, with 200 priests giving Holy Communion to thousands of people. On the last day, from Rome Pope Pius XII directly addressed the Congress over loud-speakers, 'speaking, for the first time in the history of the world, to his African children gathered in Kumasi.'[45]

However, the year 1951 also had an ugly, dramatic aspect in Kumasi. Bishop Paulissen retired in 1951 from the diocese of Kumasi and was succeeded by the Dutchman, Bishop A. van de Bronk. Some Asante members of the Knights of Marshall wanted an Asante priest to become the new bishop, while Fante members of the Knights of St John supported Bishop Bronk. This ethnic divide seriously affected the church in Kumasi with each side accusing the other: 'The fight became rough: the chaplain of [the Knights of] St John was stabbed in the back, the dissidents came with cutlasses to the cathedral, burnt the bishop's throne and broke his staff, and this went on for years, although the group was in a minority.'[46] The first Ghanaian to become Bishop of Kumasi was Fr Joseph Amihere, who was consecrated in 1962. Bishop Amihere had previously been headmaster of St Augustine's secondary school at Cape Coast.

Anglicans: Society for the Propagation of the Gospel

Fante Anglicans in Kumasi had from 1910 received visits from clergy resident in Sekondi. In 1913 the Anglican Church (SPG-sponsored) appointed a mission station in Kumasi with a resident priest. For many years, Archdeacon Morrison looked after Anglican work in Kumasi. He named the first Church after St Cyprian – the African bishop and martyr – and laid the foundations of St Augustine's Theological College. Monks from the Anglican Benedictine Order arrived in 1924 to take charge of the Kumasi parish and to start theological training. These monks, including Dom Martin Collett, Dom Bernard Clements and Dom Gregory Dix, set a high standard of theological education in Kumasi and they established a Benedictine tradition of liturgical worship that has remained to this day.

In 1929 the sisters of the Anglican Order of the Holy Paraclete took charge of girls' education in Asante. They established the convent and secondary school of St Monica's at Mampong, the second seat of Asante royal authority after Kumasi. In the following year, 1930, a teacher training college for women was also established.

A number of Anglican lay associations were established in Kumasi, beginning with the Womens' Guild of St Mary, created in 1924. One of the founder members, Mrs Isabella Acolatse, has written that 'the members then were illiterate but, through the Sunday School classes, they could read and write the vernacular.'[47] Other Anglican women's organizations included the Guild of the Good Shepherd, the Rosary Guild and the Guild of St Anne's.

One of the notable characteristics of Anglican work in Kumasi, is the link between the Church and Asante royalty. The Anglican church of St Anne's became very much the parish church of Asantehene Prempeh II. 'Blessed with favours from the Royal House of Ashanti, the church has the second largest flock in all the Ashanti parishes', after St Cyprian's cathedral.[48]

The beginnings of these close links started in the Seychelles. Asantehene Prempeh I had been seized by the British in 1896 and after incarceration in Sierra Leone, he arrived in the Seychelles in 1900. He remained in exile until 1924, when he triumphantly returned to Kumasi after twenty-eight years. Soon after their arrival, 'Prempeh and some of his followers began to receive religious instructions from some chaplains of the [Anglican] Church Missionary Society.'[49] He was baptized in 1904. In keeping in touch with events in Asante, he also corresponded with Revd Morrison, the Anglican Archdeacon in Kumasi. This correspondence no doubt privately helped influence, behind the public clamour, the government's decision to repatriate Prempeh.

One of his sons in the Seychelles became an Anglican priest, returning to Kumasi in 1930 after theological training in Mauritius.

Prempeh's decision to become a Christian became well-known in Asante, and the example of his conversion assisted Church growth in Kumasi. He strongly supported the evangelization of Asante and 'in his letters to his wives, children, sisters and other relatives in Kumasi, Prempeh urged them all to embrace the Christian religion'.[50] On his return to Kumasi, Prempeh actively joined in the Church life of the city, until his death in 1931. On the day of his funeral great crowds came to mourn, as 'the orderly funeral procession wound its way from Manhyia [the royal palace] to St Cyprian's (Anglican) Church'.[51]

This new and significant tradition of royal favour towards the Churches was later continued by Asantehene, Prempeh II. With the restoration of the Asante Confederacy in 1935, Prempeh II was officially installed as Asantehene:

> The famous and historic Golden Stool was carried to St Cyprian's for Thanksgiving services on behalf of the Asantehene. The Otumfuo [His Majesty Prempeh II] with his chiefs entered the west door in splendour and was received by wardens, clergy and a long procession of altar-servers to his

> stall where, as a king, he was aspersed with holy water and censed during offertory. The Golden Stool incidentally was placed before the Altar of Our Lady.[52]

The once hidden Golden Stool, embodying the soul of the Asante nation, was thus placed under the benevolent protection of the Virgin Mary in an Anglican church!

Northern Ghana – The Northern Territories Protectorate

In the southern two-thirds of the country, Catholics, Methodists and Presbyterians were able to develop a 'national' representation. In the northern third of the country, in the Northern Territories, most Churches were hampered in extending their work because of the colonial government's bias towards regulating Church representation by sphere of interest. It was only during the 1950s that the main Ghanaian Churches felt free to develop their work in the north. The result of this lack of opportunity for missions meant that the Northern Territories became seriously disadvantaged in educational provision when compared with the Gold Coast Colony and even with Asante.

Catholics: White Fathers

In West Africa the Church has generally expanded inland and northwards from the shores of the Atlantic coast to the south. However, the small band of White Fathers came to Ghana southbound, from the savanna town of Ouagadougou. More by accident than by design, this Catholic mission arrived in northern Ghana in 1906 following fears of expulsion from French territory. They established a mission station at Navrongo, close to the border with Upper Volta, but not without difficulties from the British administration. The French Father-Superior was expelled in 1907 and the colonial administration stipulated that all the missionaries should be British subjects and that English was to be the language of educational instruction. By 1912 all the White Fathers were French Canadians (and hence British subjects) under the leadership of Father Morin.

The colonial government's view of the White Fathers developed from early suspicion and hostility to an attitude of tolerance for the Catholic work by the end of the 1930s. In the first years the mission was faced by threats of expulsion, because of British fears that the White Fathers were pro-French and thus subversive; later on, during the 1930s, officials felt that the mission's work encouraged dissent against the newly established Native Authorities of colonial Indirect Rule.

It was pressure from influential British Catholics on the Colonial Office in London that facilitated the establishment of a convent by the White Sisters at Navrongo in 1912. This kind of metropolitan pressure also was of importance in 1929 when the White Fathers, after twenty-four years of little progress in conversion, wanted to expand from Navrongo to adjacent areas. Governor Guggisberg's colonial government in the Gold Coast opposed any expansion by the Catholics in the Northern Territories, and having decided on a policy of mission spheres, the administration awarded the entire north-west region to the Anglicans. However, the Anglicans were not in a position to open a new mission field, and the Colonial Office in London found the idea of mission spheres in northern Ghana inappropriate. The Governor was duly instructed to lift any geographical or citizenship restrictions that had been placed on the White Fathers. Professor Benedict Der has commented that the 'intervention of the Colonial Office was crucial in determining the future development of the White Fathers' mission.'[53]

Entry into the north-western region led within a few years to a mass conversion to Christianity among Dagarti society. This mass movement into the Church caused conflict, however, with local chiefs and colonial administrators. The dramatic incident that caused this movement to Christianity was a worship service at Jirapa in 1932, attended by chiefs and elders, for the praying for rain in the middle of a severe drought. Here as in other parts of Africa, within a few minutes of the Christian service a heavy rainstorm fell on the village, and news of this miraculous event brought people from all around the area to the village church and the White Fathers. 'In whatever light one views the rain incident, there can be no doubt that it provoked a serious reaction against ancestor-worship.'[54]

The growth of the Catholic Church in the north-west coincided with the introduction of Native Authorities under the system of Indirect Rule, and this gave rise to serious disputes with local chiefs over demands for Sunday labour from their subjects. Instead of giving labour service on Sunday, Christian converts were in church and at catechism classes, and in this devotion they were naturally supported by the White Fathers. A number of catechists, for example Porekuu (the father of the future Bishop Dery), attracted large followings on their evangelizing journeys. Many chiefs feared their own power was being usurped by the influence of catechists, and these traditional authorities successfully demanded that the colonial administration support them. As a result, Native Authority policemen tried to stop people from attending church services and a number of catechists were assaulted. It was a testing time for the mission as some 'converts did think that in becoming Christians, they were absolved from obedience to the chiefs.'[55]

The situation deteriorated to the extent that the chief commissioner convened a conference in 1936 between the White Fathers and the traditional authorities, at which they successfully managed to resolve their differences. Freedom of worship was to be guaranteed, chiefs undertook not to hinder Christians or force them to work on Sundays. In return, church members would work on roads during weekdays. The White Fathers had always paid for labour services, and this policy influenced the Native Authorities, who themselves began in 1936 to pay for labour rendered which previously they had demanded for free. The improvement in relations was assisted by the appointment of a new district commissioner (1936–38), H. A. Blair, who supported the building of a number of chapels in four villages; the event of Chief Gana's of Jirapa death in 1938 also reduced the tensions between Church and Chief. Gana had previously obstructed the mission but on his deathbed he was baptized into the Catholic Church.

The Catholics had established a seminary class at Navrongo in 1931, and this led to the creation in 1936 of a small teacher training institution. The White Fathers' aim was to keep their pupils and use them as teachers to help build up the community. The Fathers refused to employ teachers from the Akan south of the country, mainly because of their fear of disruptive influences and the lure of new opportunities in the more developed south of the country.

After 1946, the growth of mission education was controlled by the Native Authorities, who decided where the White Fathers could open schools and whether they would qualify for a grant. These limitations placed on the educational work of the Fathers 'more than any other factor, probably accounts for the retarded educational advancement of northern Ghana'.[56] It was only from 1929 that the Mission first received small grants-in-aid for their schools; this was after they had created a favourable basis for developing education for girls, and also opened a school for boys. Pupils were fed at the mission during the lean months and the schools were vacated when help was most needed on the family farms. Dr Bening writes that this 'facilitated constant comparison between the rigorous home life and the regular supply of food and clothing at school'.[57]

Protestants

Presbyterian work in the north had begun at Yendi in 1912, but came to an end in 1918 with the expulsion of the Basel Mission. In 1936 the Methodists and Presbyterians co-operated in providing a pastor for the Akan diaspora population at Tamale. It was only from 1949 that Protestant evangelization work was able to develop in the Northern Territories, with the opening of mission stations at Tamale (1949), Salaga (1950) and Bolgatanga (1955). Methodists and Presbyterians co-operated closely in the growth of this relatively new mission field.

NIGERIA

For the Church in West Africa, the western region of Nigeria was an area with very distinctive characteristics. Its people were nearly all Yoruba-speaking, with a common cultural and historical tradition. Although there are many sub-groups, such as the Egba–Awori, Ijesha, Oyo and Ekiti, they were all united by language and by a strong Yoruba consciousness. A comparison can be made with the other two regions of the country.

The northern region was dominated by Islam, preserved and enhanced by the colonial policy of Indirect Rule, which to a large extent insulated the northern savannas from the Christian faith.

The eastern region was composed of a number of ethnic groups which generally lived in dispersed clusters of homesteads, detached from the few large towns of the region. This network of communities lent a particular character to Catholic and Protestant work and education. With little or no Islamic influence in the region, one of the main concerns of the Churches was the prevalent belief in tradional religion. The 1952 eastern region census recorded half the population as Christian and the other half adherents of traditional religion. As one might expect, the few larger towns of the region (over 40,000 inhabitants) in the early 1950s were overwhelmingly Christian, but curiously, the census also recorded that all the other sizes of towns were predominantly animist. Another feature of the eastern region was the unfortunate rivalry between Catholics and Protestants, especially in Igbo areas, which sometimes created new social cleavages.

Western Nigeria: An Urbanized Culture Combined with Trade and Agriculture

Perhaps uniquely among African peoples, the Yoruba had a long urban tradition of networks of towns and dense settlements. This urban culture was closely linked to agriculture. Farmers belonged to lineages whose compounds were in the towns and many Yoruba who lived in urban areas worked on the land. Urbanization, migration and a thriving rural economy were all factors that affected the growth of Christianity during this period.

Cocoa farming

Christianity played a significant role in the establishment of cocoa farming, and the new religion was seen to be intimately linked to the achievement of prosperity. Cocoa trees were first planted in Nigeria by the Agege planters in an area near Lagos during the 1890s. Most of these Agege men belonged to the so-called 'African Churches' that emerged at this time. From 1900–20 it is estimated that 10,000 men came from all parts of Yorubaland to labour on the cocoa plantations. The Agege planters supported their African Church teachers and superintendents, who travelled around the region seeking converts as well as recruiting labour for the plantations. Christian influence combined with tangible evidence of material progress had a profound effect on the thousands of men who annually came to work at Agege. They went home to their own communities further inland, armed with knowledge about new crops and a commitment to a new religion. The effects on Yoruba society of the faith and work of the pioneering Agege planters was dramatically seen in the 1920s when cocoa farming became widespread. From 3,857 tons of cocoa ready for export in the period 1910–14, the amount jumped to 27,276 tons in the years 1920–24, and by the late 1930s (1935–39) nearly 100,000 tons of cocoa were being exported.

The example of Christian converts living a healthy and affluent life was a powerful argument for the new faith. Prosperity based on cocoa widened the appeal of the Christian message. Literacy and schooling had traditionally been the avenue for advancement in the Church, but success and wealth, derived from the cocoa boom, allowed many Yoruba families to take a respectable position in local Church life, as well as affording an education for their children. Thus many cocoa farmers, though unschooled themselves, became the 'Big Men' and patrons of their congregations.

The buoyant rural economy of western Nigeria had an interesting effect on Church schools and Christian education. According to the 1952 census there was proportionately a greater literate population in the towns and cities of northern and eastern Nigeria than in the countryside. But the situation was the reverse in the western region. The western regional average was 16.9 per cent but all the towns, including the major cities, had a lower percentage of literates than this. Church schools were thus very popular and very widespread in the cocoa farm villages and, consequently, partly responsible for attracting and retaining a larger proportion of literates in the countryside than in the cities. This situation was probably unique at the time in Africa.

Traders and Christianity

Apart from the migrant farm workers who spread Christianity, itinerant traders were instrumental in introducing the new faith to their home communities. The commercial opportunities in Lagos and along the coast attracted many young men from inland communities. The experience of 'going out' as a trader allowed for personal independence and many in their travels either became Christians or Muslims. Professor Peel has written fascinatingly about young Ijesha cloth traders – the *osomaalo* – and although they at first mostly lacked formal education, their occupation led them to Christianity. This is an interesting parallel to the more widely known role of Muslim traders in West Africa. Peel also incisively notes that although many Ijeshas went to the predominantly Muslim trading centre of Ilorin, in northern Yorubaland, few received their new religion from their customers. Instead, their 'felt cultural superiority would ensure that the form of that religion would come from home, where Christianity was predominant.'[58] The outburst of *osomaalo* trading, with its remarkable population mobility, occurred at certain peak periods, 1910–14, 1920–24 and 1930–34. A number of primary schools were built in Ijeshaland and in 1934 the Ilesha Grammar School was established: 'the popular demand for education grew because of its consequent rewards; and the missions, as purveyors of that education, were rewarded with converts.'[59] The whole story with its continuous rhythm of outward-bound migration and return home – sometimes after an interval of decades – was a purely African phenomenon. For decades no British CMS missionary was settled in the area. Church leadership was provided by an African pastor, the Revd R. S. Oyebode from Ibadan, who spent thirty years in the district, 1896–1927, assisted by catechists and teachers.

Past and future

The eventual transition to a new period after the First World War did not imply a sudden break. Institutional and personal factors underlined continuity with the past. Certain names represented that continuity. Archdeacon Dandeson Crowther, the bishop's son, died in 1938, aged ninety-three, a link with the early years of Nigerian church history. His relative, Herbert Macaulay, great-grandson of Bishop Crowther, prominent layman and outstanding critic of the British govenment, represented a bridge to the future when in 1923 he founded the Nigerian Democratic Party, an inspiration to the modern nationalist movement in the 1940s and 1950s. Among European churchmen, Melville Jones, Bishop of Lagos from 1919, was outstanding. When he retired in 1940 he had served Nigeria for forty-seven years and his wife for fifty years, laying foundations for what was to follow.

Sudden tragic crises followed in the wake of the war. The influenza pandemic of 1918 hit West Africa. In Ghana, 'all churches, schools and other meeting places, closed with little obvious effect'.[60] After the First World War, the influenza epidemic spread throughout Nigeria, affecting up to 80 per cent of the population. In Nigeria the death toll made people turn to 'divine healing' through emerging Independent Churches promising to overcome illness; the Cherubim and Seraphim, the Aladura and similar Independent groups appeared – soon the same bug hit South Africa and resulted in similar ecclesiastical results.

Lagos

Lagos, the capital of the country, was the first city in Nigeria to have a cosmopolitan character. Nineteenth-century antecedents included the Sierra Leonean and the Brazilian returnees, the European community and Yoruba refugees escaping the wars and troubles inland. By the end of the century Lagos had strong, well-rooted Christian and Muslim communities. The development of the port from 1906, and the completion of the railway to Kano (700 miles) in 1912 stimulated commercial life and enticed many thousands of Yoruba and other peoples from the interior as migrants to the city.

In 1901 the population of Lagos was estimated at 42,000; in 1921, it was over 100,000; in 1950, 230,000, and in 1963 the city's inhabitants numbered 665,000. The 1920s saw a slowing in the rate of growth of the city's population: by 1931, it had only increased to 126,000, from 100,000 in 1921. The 1920s was a decade of disaster. Beginning with the influenza pandemic of 1918 and its aftermath, more deaths followed during the 1920s from the outbreak of bubonic plague. Somewhat later in the decade, the world economic depression also reduced the city's prosperity.

The huge increase after 1945 was accounted for by the immigration of Igbos from eastern Nigeria. From the 1940s Lagos received thousands of new immigrants looking for jobs, especially young Nigerians who had been to mission school and who could read and write. After the Second World War the city also accommodated large numbers of ex-servicemen.

Although the population increased nine-fold between 1911 and 1963 a certain level of ethnic homogeneity was maintained, as some 70 per cent of the inhabitants were always Yoruba. The Igbos in Lagos in 1950 accounted for 45 per cent of the non-Yoruba population and they were consistently the largest 'stranger' group, rising from 0.5 per cent of the city's population in 1911 to 15 per cent in 1963. Other groups such as the Edo and Hausa were never more than 5 per cent of the Lagos population. Indeed, the Hausa community declined as a proportion of the city's populaion, from 5 per cent in 1911 to 2 per cent in 1963. It would appear that during this period the northern Muslim community in Lagos had little influence on the growth and character of Islam among Yoruba society.

After the Second World War the religious balance of Lagos shifted in the favour of Christianity. Prior to 1950 there were more Musims (50 per cent of the population) than Christians, who then accounted for 25 per cent of the inhabitants. The overwhelming majority of Muslims have always been Yoruba. The 1963 census recorded the following religious affiliations: 55 per cent Christian; 44 per cent Muslim. The increased Christian representation in Lagos was caused by the influx of easterners, especially Igbos – of which many were Catholics.

Social divisions in Lagos were similar to the other large cities in western Nigeria: the least 'progressive' were Muslims, indigenes and generally the lower classes. By comparison, the socially more progressive groups were Christians, school-educated, and generally middle–upper class. Control of Lagos Town Council generally rested with well-educated Christians: in the period 1950–59, 68 per cent of the the councillors were Christians and 32 per cent Muslim, although after 1945 there were more Muslim Yoruba councillors than Yoruba Christians.

The Churches dominated the educational provision of Lagos; the 1921 census showed that only 10 per cent of the population were able to read and write, while another 20 per cent could partially read. At this time the Anglicans and Methodists ran thirty out of the forty-seven schools in Lagos, and they had more than half of the 9,800 pupils. The Baptists ran one school and the Catholics administered eight – all originally for children of Brazilian returnees. By 1921 the government ran one secondary school in Lagos, King's College, and from 1916 the Churches received some government finance for their church schools. In 1922 the synod of the Anglican Church decided to exclude Muslim children from its schools in Lagos and, although only partially implemented, this helped motivate Yoruba Muslims to create their own Islamic schools. In the early 1920s there were attempts to start Muslim schools based on a modern curriculum; in 1923 the Ansar-ud-Deen

Society was founded to provide a network of Islamic schools. This Islamic initiative was partly linked to the educational policy change in the local Anglican Church.

The new immigrant groups to Lagos tended to concentrate and live together, sometimes in well-defined areas of the city. A long way from home, it was natural that people from the same town, area or region should band together and form clubs and societies. A multitude of associations were created with the aims of providing mutual assistance, support and a common solidarity for those away from home, or to cement new friendships emanating from one's school or job. The Churches gained new converts through these channels as Christians were highly influential in many of these organizations. In addition to these 'immigrant' associations, there were also locally based 'improvement societies', and often their main aim was to improve the quality and increase the quantity of Church education and schooling. For example in Ijesha, in Yorubaland the 'Young Ijesha Improvement Society' was established in 1923 with one of its aims being the foundation of a grammar school in the town.

Church organizations and associations played a major part in the quest for social, moral and spiritual acclimatization. Choirs, bible classes, youth organizations and especially women's associations were all part of the Churches' response to urban life. In Lagos as in other west Nigerian towns, the Anglican congregations followed the *egbe* pattern (modelled on the secular *egbe*, or social clubs). These *egbe* are small associations, based on sex, age and marital status and can be likened to the traditional Yoruba age-sets. A large church with members from different geographical areas would divide their *egbes* along similar lines. These social clubs were also arranged along ethnic lines. A large Catholic church in Lagos, for instance, might have an Egba Men's Association. Within each denomination most towns had at least one church, often the 'mother' church, to which the educated elite would go and be seen to worship.

One difficulty faced by the churches was how to respond to traditional or neo-traditional social and cultural societies, which could often be secretive by nature. This problem exercised the Anglican Church in western Nigeria from 1914 until the time of independence in 1960. The Ogboni was a traditional religious society that was particularly strong among the Egba and the Ijebu. In 1914 some African Christians led by an Anglican clergyman, the Revd Jackson Ogunbiyi, founded the 'Christian Ogboni Society'. Ogunbiyi was influenced by a wide variety of ideas, from the Keswick Convention to English Freemasonry, and this led him to the idea that the Ogboni 'in a Christianized form, would produce a more binding fellowship than the rather loose brotherhood of the normal church congregation'.[61] In 1929 the Anglican Bishop, Melville Jones, dismissed Ogunbiyi, who then started his own Church and continued his Ogboni activities. At the insistence of the Anglican bishops the appellation 'Christian' was dropped from the Society's name and it took the title, the Reformed Ogboni Fraternity (ROF), and opened its membership to non-Christians. The fact remains that the ROF was extremely popular among the Anglican clergy and congregations, and many were secret members. It became a sophisticated inter-urban association and spread to educated Igbo and Hausa groups.

Ibadan

Although Ibadan had a larger population than Lagos, it never reached the same level of diversity of immigrant groups. While the majority of the population of Lagos in 1921 were immigrants, Ibadan had less than 3,000. In the 1931 census Ibadan's population was recorded as 386,000, and twenty years later the religious composition of the city was estimated as 60 per cent Muslim, 32 per cent Christian and 8 per cent traditionalist. The indigenous population was fairly homogenous, largely Muslim, less literate and more oriented to agriculture. The immigrant population, greatly expanded after 1945, was hetrogeneous, mainly Christian, more literate and largely involved in administration and commerce. Ibadan probably has the greatest concentration of Muslims of any town in western Nigeria. For the western region as a whole, it seems that the percentage of Muslims declined as town size decreased – they were strongest in the large cities. Christians were proportionally more numerous and important in the hundreds of smaller towns in the region.

The Catholics made Ibadan the centre of their activities in western Nigeria. Their first mission started in 1894 and they opened a school in the city in 1900. In 1907 they moved their headquarters to Ogunpa, in the centre of the sprawling city. A number of Brazilian returnees moved to Ibadan to assist the mission, but it was only in the 1920s that the Church began to establish itself. From this time the Catholic presence was linked to immigrant members of the Church, who then resided in Ibadan. In 1943 the White Fathers arrived to take charge from the Lyon Fathers (SAM). The Lyon mission had suffered from an acute lack of personnel, with only three priests working full-time in the 1930s and 1940s. A college for preparing boys for the priesthood was started in 1908, but at the beginning met with little success: by the early 1950s this seminary at Oke-Are, on the outskirts of Ibadan had helped train 120 priests, the first being ordained in 1929. A catechist training centre was started at the same station in 1921.

The mother in the dream

It is all very well to register certain trends in the development of the Church in Africa but what about the reaction at the grass-roots, in those generations of young people who joined the school and the chapel? Very little, unfortunately, is known about this. It so happens, however, an interview was undertaken (by B.Sr.) in October 1953, with the Anglican Bishop of Ibadan, Alexander Akinyele. It is quoted here at some length because it has elements of religious experience – the role of the mother, in this case the dead mother; and the role of a decisive dream – which quite possibly are representative on a much wider scale.

Born 1875 Alexander Akinyele was a third-generation Christian and began school in 1885. During the period 1888–93 he lived in an Anglican missionary's house as a school boy and a servant. He must have been a most promising young boy for in 1893 the missionary recommended him to the governor, Sir Gilbert Carter, in Lagos, to become his 'private clerk', an unheard of opportunity for a young man.

> But then in the night I had a dream. I saw my mother who died in 1891, coming to me in a dream. She came to remind me of the promise I had given. The day before I left home in 1888, my mother prayed with me in our home. As I knelt before her she made me promise that I would do only God's work, in His church. She made me promise on my knees, if you please. That was the most wonderful point in my life.
>
> After that I could not sleep the whole night. To become a Governor's clerk was such a great thing. I would so much have loved to go to the Governor. Next morning the missionary saw me crying and asked me what was the matter. So I told him. I had to send a letter to the Governor. Later the Governor patted me on my back saying, 'Of course you must keep your promise to your mother and to God. So you must not come to me.'[62]

If it is claimed here that this experience in 1893 may be representative, it is of course not suggested that every young Christian Yoruba at the time wished to be sent to the British governor, but rather to make the more serious point of showing the role and importance of the Christian mother, not only in Yoruba Christianity but throughout the continent. Here again the conversion experience is brought to a decisive point by a dream. It is our guess – it cannot be more than that – that while in Catholic experience the woman in the dream may take on the features of the Holy Virgin:

Tes Enfants noirs sont de l'heure tardive . . .
Mère du bon conseil,
éclaire-nous, sensibilise-nous . . .
sensibilise-nous à Dieu[63]

in Protestant experience it is the mother who comes, as an intermediary between the searching soul and God.

A Nigerian Pilgrim's Progress

Striking examples of Nigerian writing directly inspired by the Christian faith are the Yoruba-language novels by Daniel Olorunfemi Fagunwa (1903–63). His grandfather was an Ifá priest, but his father converted to Christianity and became 'Father' (of the congregation) of St Luke's Anglican Church at Oke Igbo. His mother, a worshipper of the river goddess Osun, also converted and became 'Mother' of the same Anglican congregation. Daniel Fagunwa briefly attended his local Church school before transferring in 1916 to the Anglican training centre of St Andrew's College, Oyo. In 1929 he decided upon teaching as a career and later became involved in publishing.

A man of strong Christian commitment, his six novels are set in the traditional Yoruba world but are all concerned with preaching Christian ideals. This formula proved successful as each of his books was reprinted no less than ten times. His first, and best-known novel, *Ogboju Ode Ninu Igbo Irunmale* (The forest of a thousand daemons) was published by the CMS, and became a required text in Church schools.[64] A scholar of Nigerian literature, Dr Afolabi Olabimtan writes: 'The belief in magic is strongly attached to religion in the Yoruba tradition and Fagunwa shows how unacceptable this belief is when compared to the Christian belief in a loving God who can be approached without magic or any intermediary.'[65]

He used biblical words, statements and parables in his novels as well as depicting the use of prayer in reaching God. Writing in Yoruba, he was able to have a direct effect on young people. The well-known Nigerian man of letters, Professor Abiola Irele comments that Fagunwa 'responded early to the need for a literature in the vernacular, at a moment when a new cultural consciousness began to emerge out of changing social conditions'.[66] Sometimes called the 'Defoe of Nigerian literature', Daniel Fagunwa can be seen as the father of modern Yoruba creative writing.

Yoruba Church music

Yoruba musical tradition had much to give to the Church's worship, and two names must be mentioned here. In an earlier generation there was the work of the Anglican Canon Josiah Ransome-Kuti, 'the Singing Minister of Nigeria', active in Abeokuta where he started new churches helped largely through his musical talent. He would sing his own compositions such as 'Our God is Impregnable'. The same ability to use Yoruba music and rhythm was shown by the gifted Methodist pastor Ola Oluda, born 1908, probationer 1934 and in 'full connection' 1938. A slight, rapidly moving man he was for ever trying out new tunes on his harmonium. He lived music. Sometimes the gestation period for a new hymn tune to be born could be long. He mentioned to one of the present writers that one particular hymn – 'The God of Abraham praise' – had taken him five years until at last the inspiration was there. He published pamphlets with Christmas carols; for Passion Week; for Easter, for harvest festivals and for weddings, for children and for funerals. He used drums and gourds. His catchy tunes infused freshness into Methodist worship.[67]

Not all foreign missionaries took the trouble to think of the context of the Christian message, but some did. One of these was a young arrival in 1930, by the name of James Welch. For the Vespers he reacted to the barely translated English phrases in the *Benedicte*:

> 'Wai Ifroste ... gbe Sno – Bless ye the Lord.' It seemed silly to me. So I altered it to 'O Ye waving palm trees – Bless ye the Lord.' I got the church leader to sing the different Verses, and then the whole congregation – we were in the open air – sang the chorus to rhythmic dancing, 'Praise Him and magnify Him for ever', at the end of each verse. I can tell you it went with a swing![68]

Aiyetoro

On the Nigerian coast, between the surf and the mangrove swamp, lies Aiyetoro, the town of the Holy Apostles' community. Situated 100 miles east of Lagos, this town built on stilts, with tidal waters beneath it, has created a unique form of religious life and community. Aiyetoro, meaning 'The world is at peace', was founded in 1947 by Ilaje fishermen inspired after 'reading an account of the lives of those fishermen in a work called the New Testament and they decided to follow out the methods advocated as literally as they knew.'[69]

In 1929 a branch of the Cherubim and Seraphim Church was established in the Ilaje area, but during the 1940s tension arose between the congregation and local society over the observance of traditional customs. Led by Philip Eretan, Zacchaeus Lila and Ethiopia Ojagbohun Peter, many Church members decided, in the face of continuing hostility, to break away from their traditional villages in order to form a new community. They arrived on a barren sandbank with nothing but their clothes, a few tools and their faith. Yet within a few years the Apostles community had grown from austerity to great prosperity, with many Anglicans and other Church members joining it. A visitor to the community has remarked that 'the necessity of withdrawal from a hostile world and for the creation of a new community where God's law shall be the guiding force are objectives clearly seen and understood.'[70]

By 1960 the town had about 3,000 inhabitants, all of whom were usefully occupied, including the old, the crippled and the children. The virtue of communal work was an important component of their religious doctrine and faith, and this led to tremendous prosperity for the community and the rapid development of the town. An observer in 1957 wrote that 'there is universally a higher standard of housing than is found anywhere else in Nigeria.'[71] Its fishing fleet expanded to include scores of canoes and a number of mechanized trawlers. Factories and workshops were built in order to make the community self-sufficient in tools, nets, clothing and food. Yet the town also kept abreast of technological change, by buying sewing machines, securing advice on boat building, and installing electric generators.

One of the first buildings erected by the Apostles was a large church. Services were generally held at dawn and lasted two hours before the day's work. In the first years of the community there was little formal worship, as they held the belief that religious devotion was integral to the life and work of the community. The whole tenor of daily communal life with its purposefulness and hard work has led Professor George Shepperson to wonder if the 'intense communal work produced a situation with an implicit doctrinal assumption of "*laborare est orare*"?'[72]

In the late 1960s the Apostles' community experienced tension and division related to changes in generation, social system and ethos. There was a problem of keeping young adults within a rather isolated, quiet and strict community; and the problems were accentuated by new leaders who introduced private ownership. Aiyetoro faced a problem common to all utopias, the succession of leadership from the 'pioneering' group with its own strong close-knit leadership and wide vision, to a new generation in a different world of political independence. For all this, the remarkable achievement of the founders of the Holy Apostles community and their Christian faith cannot be denied.

Eastern Nigeria

For the continued effort at the Christianization of eastern Nigeria two factors stand out: firstly, a rapid mass movement to the Churches; and secondly, an exceptional educational drive leading to a high degree of literacy, an urge for secondary education and its follow-up at a university level. Both factors were carried forward by dynamic ethnic communities.

The chapels and the schools changed the landscape, and there was a vast outreach of east Nigerian influence into the country as a whole: to Lagos the capital and, increasingly, to the Muslim far north where Christian communities from the south settled in the *sabon garis* of the northern cities. As British adminstrators ceded the way to Africans for a number of government posts, reactions from the locals did not fail to appear, sometimes revealing a delicate situation. 'We all have fear of one another ... Some fear the sheer weight of skills and the aggressive drives of other groups.'[73] Before too long this fear was to explode in a tragic civil war.

The Catholics and Bishop Shanahan

The Catholic Church first started their modern work in 1885, led by the French, including Alsatian Holy Ghost Fathers. For political and linguistic reasons the Irish branch of the Spiritans became responsible for much of the congregation's work in British-administered Africa. Father Shanahan arrived with Irish Holy Ghost Fathers in eastern Nigeria in 1905, and he immediately saw the potential of the Church school as a means of establishing a Catholic presence through the region. In this concern for the school, he predated both the Methodists and Anglicans by establishing a whole network of schools, so that by 1920 the Catholics had 559 primary schools with 33,700 pupils. The opportunities for founding schools and churches were endless but a lack of resources hampered an adequate response. In 1920 there were only nineteen priests for 71,500 catechumens and 25,000 baptized. Great reliance was therefore placed on the 900 catechists.

At the time it was thought that this extensive African direction of Church work was without parellel in Irish missionary endeavours. On a visit to Ireland in 1920, after his consecration, Shanahan appealed to the Maynooth College for 'secular' priests to work in Nigeria, and it was agreed that they would serve for terms of five years. Perennially short of staff, Shanahan felt this was a reasonable way of solving his problems, but this agreement was unauthorized by his Order, and the Spiritan Congregation showed its disapprobation of the Bishop's initiative. The Maynooth recruits soon demanded a separate organization and this was granted in 1929, after an unfavourable report on the state of the diocese by the Apostolic Visitor Dr Hinsley, which also led to Shanahan being asked to resign. The Maynooth priests founded their new Order with the name of St Patrick's Missionary Society and they were assigned to the southern part of the now partitioned Vicariate.

Onitsha was the centre of both Catholic and Anglican work in the region. The Catholics concentrated on primary education and did not open their first secondary school – Christ the King, Onitsha – until 1932. Only in the 1940s were the Catholics able to challenge the Protestant supremacy in grammar school education in the eastern region. Throughout the period there was educational rivalry between Catholics and Protestants. This competition – especially amongst the Igbo – continued, and during the 1950s a new generation of Nigerian nationalist politicians exploited these differences. Most of the politicians in the eastern regional government (established in 1951) were Protestants and their educational policy proposals were seen as at least pro-Protestant, if not openly anti-Catholic. As many of the ordinary voters were Catholic, their church soon organized protests and petitions against the regional government's educational policies. A compromise was reached, and by 1960 the government ran 25 per cent of the primary schools, the Catholics 38 per cent, the Anglicans 19 per cent with the remaining 18 per cent shared between the Methodists and the Presbyterians, as well as some secular institutions. With the increase in the number of Catholic secondary schools, a greater number of political and social leaders of the region came from a Catholic background. Traditionally the Catholic Church had disliked its leading men and women to enter politics, preferring them to work inside the Church.

The Federal Association of Catholic Teachers (FACT) was created in 1937 and this meant that the Catholic hierarchy had to accommodate the newly organized influence of mission school teachers – as Protestant Churches had already uncomfortably done. The churches disliked their teachers acting as unionized employees, and in 1940 Catholic school managers (who were often missionaries) complained about the secular demands made by the FACT. It was, of course, the forgotten legions of Church school teachers (many of whom were also catechists), who really extended the Christian message – with its belief in progress through the Church school.

Together with his Irish co-workers – priests and nuns – Bishop Shanahan had laid the foundation of an impressive school system. From the two centres of Onitsha and Owerri the work radiated out. In 1926, after twenty years of Shanahan's leadership, the Catholic Church had grown from 2,000 to 60,000, with 90,000 catechumens. In 1960 these figures had increased to 725,000 with 285 catechumens. There was a total of nearly 3,000 Catholic primary schools, twenty-eight normal schools and thirteen technical schools with a total of 407,000 pupils.

Presbyterians in the East

The Church of Scotland Mission led the way for secondary education in eastern Nigeria, with the opening in 1895 of the Hope Wadell Training Institute at Calabar. It was of far-reaching importance for teacher training in Nigeria. In 1922 out of a total of 370 trained teachers country-wide, over 120 had been trained at the Presbyterian-run Institute in Calabar. It later became a centre for all Protestant pedagogic instruction. Nnamdi Azikiwe, the first President of Nigeria is perhaps its most famous 'old boy', though the Institute's and the Presbyterian Church's most outstanding scion and medical missionary is without doubt Sir Francis Akanu Ibiam.

The Presbyterians took the initiative in developing interdenominational links with other Protestant Churches. They organized a series of Calabar educational conferences in 1904, 1911 and 1917. By 1938 there were joint colleges and training programmes with the Anglicans and Methodists, and this facilitated some rationalization in educational planning. The 1924 Phelps-Stokes Fund team of four on African education included two members with experience from the Presbyterian Institute in Calabar.

The Presbyterians differed from other Churches in their approach to education, as they ran 'all-age' comprehensive schools which were not separated into primary and secondary schools. This policy helped to safeguard a high standard of teaching and, by keeping up their morale and commitment, managed to maintain the stability of teaching staff in Presbyterian schools. Standards were kept in spite of pressure to expand and temptation to stretch resources. This strict approach to Church schools occasionally led to friction between the Presbyterian leaders and the teachers. The Church disliked their teachers comparing themselves with civil servants, and this tendency by school staff led in 1936 to a teachers' strike for more favourable conditions. The newly formed Nigerian Union of Teachers (NUT) – much of whose early leadership had attended the Hope Wadell Training Institute – intervened and, together with the government, forced the Presbyterian Church to increase teachers' salaries. It was only in 1974, after the civil war, that the Presbyterians transferred their educational system to the State.

Christian-inspired Nigerian literature

The expansion of Christian schools, together with the rapid growth of towns and cities in Nigeria, led to the emergence of a large literate public eager to use the new opportunities for reading and writing. The desire for school education was overwhelming. The benefits of literacy were obvious in terms of jobs, status and social participation. The advance in literacy also led to the blossoming of popular literature, often inspired by Christian faith.

Pioneering Christian missionaries were here, as elsewhere, concerned with translating the Bible, catechisms and hymns into African languages. Standardization of dialects and linguistic unification was an essential part of this work. In both western and eastern Nigeria the Anglicans had established a tradition of vernacular literacy that, in fact, was much older than that of literacy in English. In 1854 the Revd Townsend:

> fitted up a printing press and inaugurated a printing school in the mission compound at Abeokuta. In 1859 he founded the *Iwe Irohin* ... which appeared as a Yoruba-language fortnightly ... [and] it was the best organized of the mission papers at the time ... and more importantly, it was the first to be published in an African language.[74]

In eastern Nigeria, as early as 1859 the Revd Taylor, a CMS missionary in Onitsha, had produced the *Isuama Ibo Katkism*, and in 1860 the first Igbo Bible was published. The work of Archdeacon Dennis in devising a 'Union Igbo' should be mentioned.

For the period 1920–60 two different categories of Christian-inspired popular writing can be referred to. The first, which we have already mentioned, are the Yoruba-language novels by Daniel Olorunfemi Fagunwa. Secondly, there is the Onitsha Market literature, from about 1947. This form of popular literature has since spread to other towns in eastern Nigeria and many hundreds, if not thousands, of pamphlets have been published. Most of the authors were educated at Church schools and became enthusiastic propagandists of Christianity. For better-known authors such as Ogali A. Ogali and Okenwa Olisa, 'Christian attitudes and principles provide one of the major inspirations of the pamphlet literature, and the Bible one of the chief literary influences.'[75]

Onitsha's position as a leading Church centre, and thus an educational epicentre, was one of the factors that accounts for this popular pamphleteering. By the late 1940s the town had the largest number of primary and secondary schools in eastern Nigeria – including eight grammar schools. The return of demobilized soldiers after the Second World War was another reason for Onitsha's rise as a publishing centre. With war bonuses to invest, ex-soldiers stimulated the local economy and as many of them had served in Asia they returned with copies of Indian booklets, which served as a model for Onitsha's own market literature.

This market literature showed the ability of authors to attune their writings to the lives of their readers. By relating their stories and advice to the problems and anxieties felt by their readership, the pamphleteers injected a moral dimension into their literature. Professor Obiechina writes: 'The Christian impulse in many of the popular pamphlets is clearly shown in Christian imagery and vocabulary. Temptation, sin, confession, contrition, forgiveness, repentance, and such Christian concepts occur frequently in the writing.'[76]

Northern Nigeria and the Middle Belt

The Middle Belt

In the virtually neglected 'Middle Belt' new and dramatic Church growth followed. The peoples in this area harboured memories of traumatic experiences from nineteenth-century Hausa–Fulani raids – many of their villages were destroyed and the inhabitants carried off into slavery – which made them determine never to accept Islam or Muslim overlords. They looked for security on rocky plateaux and in caves and other mountain retreats. Certain peoples such as the Chibuk managed through their heroism to resist the onslaught and were later held in great esteem by their neighbours.

Into this region the missions, mainly Protestants, came in the twentieth century, cautiously at first but with increasing strength and determination. Grimley reports that in one of the societies it was a leper with relatives in seven different villages who led some of his community to Christ. In the case of the Higi people a blind man played an important role in so doing. There was a preparedness for change and for common, collective change: Ausu preached to his home village but found the response disappointing, whence he told his listeners that he was to move to another village. Then the reply was, 'Don't go. Stay here and we will all become Christians.'[77]

These radical Evangelical missions had their own method for the work: 'Bible Schools'. The concept of a Bible school in this modern form is, perhaps, mainly an American idea but it was found that in Nigeria this approach worked beautifully. In the years 1929–52 the Sudan Interior Mission (SIM) opened no less than eight Bible schools, which produced indigenous workers, pastors and evangelists. These proved to be the key to the future, for it was when these indigenous workers could apply themselves to the work that dramatic results appeared.

A great increase in the number of missionaries followed after the Second World War, coming in two waves. They felt that the region embracing the Middle Belt was the great challenge to Nigerian Christianity. Both the SIM and the Sudan United Mission (SUM) had of course a comparatively long history, from the turn of the century, of missionaries working in the area. But what now followed was a 'revitalization, a recovery of mission,'[78] a 40–75 per cent increase in missionary personnel, with evangelism as their main priority. From about 1960 a second wave appeared, leading to an amazing growth with some 25 per cent annual growth in the 1960s. It is claimed that this would not have happened without 'the reawakening of the missionary work' beginning in 1946. With only small numbers of converts in the scattered communities in 1925, the figures for the two leading mission federations had risen dramatically by 1960. The SIM had about 300,000 with 550 missionaries, and the SUM embraced another 500,000. The missionaries felt that they had a special programme. Hitherto, missions had been too individualistic. Now they had to go for entire communities winning them for Christ. The young missionaries were looking to their missiological authorities for relevant strategies: McGavran's and Vicedom's 'group conversions through chains of families' and to Nevius and to Tippet, and in the Middle Belt region the missiological laboratory, producing, together with the rapid increase in numbers, more victorious charts and diagrams than any other mission on the continent.

Another change could be noticed in the missionary leadership in the region. It has already been pointed out that the pioneering period, around the turn of the century, was dominated by medical laymen acting as Protestant leaders. They were the medical doctors, W. Miller of Zaria, N. H. Brönnum of Numan and others, healers and Bible expositors with an assured personal authority in the group of Western missionaries and among Nigerian co-workers. After the Second World War a new category of Protestant laymen was to take a lead. These were the Christian technicians and engineers, mainly from the United States, practical men capable of attending to any major or minor technical problem arising in the bush, fired with an Evangelical concern for the salvation of Africa and as much Bible expositors as their medical predecessors. Some students of recent developments in Independent Africa love to think that only the arrival in Independent Africa of 'Development Experts' of various kinds has at long last produced the kind of service Africa needs, through doctors and engineers. In fact these people had been there before, although under mission auspices, and not altogether without beneficial results.

Two local examples, including the largest of the ethnic communities, the Tiv, must suffice to illustrate this Christian population movement in the Middle Belt.

The beginnings at Lamurde

The local church at Lamurde (from 1921) did not start – as is conventionally taken for granted – with a foreign missionary under a tree speaking to a flock telling them from his Holy Book about the fundamentals: the Creation, the Fall, the Flood, the Exodus and the Coming of the Messiah. These things were to be told in due course but they were preceded by other events.

In the case of Lamurde, the chief himself, Mbi, had had some contacts along the River Benue which made him positively interested in the new message. The countryside had been overrun by small groups of freed slaves without anywhere to turn. As has already been indicated the new colonial adminstration had started a 'Freed Slaves Home', to be run for the government by the SUM, with expenses paid by government.

This is another example – as late as the 1910s and 1920s – of a phenomenon which we have met on many occasions in this book. The neglected and disregarded groups of freed slaves, of no use or consequence whatsoever, gathered in a mission 'Home' there to meet a new life, healing and help, and a family fellowship – a Reality which the foreigners called 'Christ' – and certainly a nucleus of catechumens and baptised was formed at the Rumaisha Freed Slaves Home on the Benue River.

But it did not stop there. This nucleus was only the beginning of greater things to come from an emerging Christianization movement in this part of Africa. At the rumours of Christian beginnings at Lamurde, young converts at Rumaisha were prepared as groups to move to Lamurde. 'This group of Christians and catechumens provided the Christian community into which the local converts could be accepted as they were being won for Christ.'[79] Rumaisha was also able to send other teams of young people to other outposts, and from there new Christian communities could emerge.

Tiv breakthrough

It has already been pointed out that Christian beginnings among the Tiv were slow and subdued. The Christian movement at first appeared as 'a dormant church', hardly likely to develop. It is all the more instructive to follow the surprising change that inspired and lifted the movement – causing it suddenly to flare up and become a dominant influence in the society.

The introduction of modern communications, particularly the building of the East Nigeria Railway, 1920–23, had, as mentioned earlier, altered the social situation. About 4,000 young men were employed in railway construction and earned relatively large sums of money. The Tiv consumer economy was born. An important result was the abolition in 1927 of exchange marriage and the declaration of bride-price marriage as the only legally acceptable form. Administrators and missionaries co-operated amicably over this change. The older generation of school-educated men came to the fore in Tiv society. The 1930s saw a change in the world of traditional ideas. For five dramatic years, 1934–39, an anti-witchcraft movement, *Inyanibuen*, met with a ground-swell inspired by a non-Tiv named Shiki and concerned with countering the deep-seated tensions in Tiv society. This cult led people to surrender their magical 'fetishes' and to drink a healing potion. As suddenly as the movement hit Tiv society, did it rapidly come to an end in 1939.

In those troubled and excited years there unexpectedly arose a Protestant counter-movement in the villages, taking the form of Bible-study 'schools' which were to become a permanent feature of Protestant Church life. At the root of this extraordinary change of a total society – affecting Catholics and Protestants alike – was a youth revolt against the old die-hards. The young generation was looking for a future-oriented society through Christian education in English, and no longer in their Tiv vernacular as the well-meaning Dutch Reformed missionaries preferred.

Young men – to be found above all in the army and with the police, looking for discipline and progress – were keenly aware of the need for development, particularly in agriculture and literacy. An economic crisis made people look beyond material things.[80] In 1936 Tiv society was hit by a sudden slump of benniseed on the world market when its price was more than halved. At the village level the preachers proclaimed that this was a sign that the Devil tried to 'spoil the land'. The Tiv had a concept of 'mending the law', and it was Christ who had come to 'mend the law', therefore, Tiv law had to be 'healed'. Suddenly an urge for development sparked the appearence of a number of indigenous Tiv Christian songs or hymns set to Tiv music. In their hymns and in their new New Testament (published in 1936), the people discovered a way to reconciliation and redemption.

What was the reaction at the grass-roots level in the village? Isholibo Saai, who may have been representative of his generation in the 1930s, had his answer to this question. What finally made him listen to the new message

> was the fear of death. I remembered the big fire which the preachers spoke about. The Lord will make the earth to perish through fire but those who believe in the Lord Jesus will not perish. These things made me walk in the way in order to escape the fire.[81]

The Pietist view of the faith was stimulated by the reaction to the local Catholic neighbours who appeared to accept beer, dances and similar sinful exercises.

Dr Eugene Rubingh, with his penetrating study of the Church among the Tiv, has made the interesting observation that 'the stance of the Church in this emergent society is complex: it is at once radical and conservative' – radical in that the Church has stood 'in the forefront of the forces of change', yet, the Church is also 'one of the most conservative bodies in Tivland', which has brought along 'the renaissance of tribal self-consciousness'. Declared autonomous in 1957 – and in 1959, member of the federated 'Fellowship of the Churches of Christ in the Sudan' – the 'Tiv Church of Christ' heeded the exhortation of one of the nation's great men: 'No matter how much learning you have, know that you are a Tiv. However, do more than simply be a Tiv; know the affairs of the Tiv, for that is your glory.'[82]

The Dutch Reformed missionaries had laid a firm foundation of self-support in the congregations. They had been warned by the conditions of their own mission in Malawi where, from the beginning, the young Church had been financially supported by the 'Home Church' in the Cape, South Africa. Among the Tiv they were therefore insistent on stimulating a more active Church. A rapid growth could be registered. The number of bush Bible schools in 1936 was 25, in 1941, 214 and by 1961 over 550. Communicants in 1957 numbered 1,800, in 1967, 10,000 and in 1969, over 14,000, while the Sunday attendance in those years respectively was 23,000, 143,000 and 180,000.

Political independence in Nigeria in 1960 made the presence of South Africans unwanted and they left, handing over the work to the Reformed Church of the USA. Tiv Protestants remember the time of the first missionaries with appreciation. There was something in the faithful solidity of these missionaries, in their medical work and in the translation of Holy Scriptures, which survived revolutions.

The Catholic contribution in the whole Benue area was at first made by different nationalities of Holy Ghost Fathers: German, English, Irish and Canadian, while the dioceses are now in the charge of Nigerian bishops and priests. The Bigard Seminary at Enugu, started 1924, and with 450 students at present, has a Nigerian rector and eleven Nigerian professors. This seminary, serving eastern Nigeria as well as the Benue region including the Tiv community, is the biggest theological seminary in Africa. Over 1,040 students have passed through the seminary and over 360 of these have become priests, of whom twelve are bishops.[83]

15

CENTRAL AFRICA

CAMEROON

Politics

In the Church history of modern Africa a few concentrated periods of time seemed in a special way to indicate that the whole religious future of a country lay in the balance. For Buganda – together with the interlacustrine region as a whole – the years 1885–97 were such a period of suspense and re-orientation. The 1920s in Cameroon was another such period of compressed time. Prior to World War I, the beginnings of the Church's life had necessarily been tentative. Tucked away in isolated areas in the tropical forest, it was difficult to foresee what would result from that initial encounter with the Gospel. In the 1920s a Christian mass movement was to provide an overwhelming demonstration of the effect of that encounter.

Southern Cameroon rapidly grew to be a Christian country. In 1961, half the population there was registered as Christian, with 650,000 Catholics and 500,000 Protestants while over 70 per cent of the primary school age children attended school. For the Muslim north, the story was quite different. There, only one-tenth of the population were Christians. Politically, the Versailles Peace Treaty of 1919 made the Cameroon a mandated area under the League of Nations, divided between a western British and an eastern French region. The country's mandated definition served to remind the imperial powers – Britain and France – of the duty to prepare the country for independence. The years after World War II were marked by constant riots and upheavals among the new elite and the impoverished masses. In 1945 and in 1955, riots were particularly vociferous, and metropolitan Paris, with its hands full of the problems of Ho Chi Minh and Dien Bien Phu in Vietnam, was keen to avoid similar developments among 'the highly politicized people of southern Cameroon'.[1]

On economic and social grounds Cameroon communities differed. The cosmopolitan Duala had their international connections and its tradition of a

Protestant – especially recalcitrant Baptist – propensity for independence, while their neighbours were the impoverished Bassa, 'radical, even anarchic and individualistic'. Further east, the Beti agricultural bourgeoisie, near Yaoundé, were much influenced by the Catholic Church. In the south, the highly educated Bulu population had been influenced by American Presbyterians through impressive educational centres ('What is your religion?' – 'I am Merkan'). In the north the remarkably enterprising Bamileke had their relatively rich planters.[2]

For a time the tensions within and between the masses were checked by the imperial powers and by the European companies busy exploiting the mineral and agricultural resources of the country. But following the Second World War, there was a new atmosphere of African political initiative. The influential French Catholic layman, Dr Aujoulat, formed the 'Democratic Block of Cameroon' (BDC), mainly supported by the Ewondo–Beti population with their moral strength and moderate attitude. They were soon eclipsed by Um Nyobe – with an American–Presbyterian mission background – and his 'Union of the Populations of Cameroon' (UPC), formed in 1948. The country's political climate was suddenly highly charged. Was the UPC perhaps Communist and Um Nyobe a West African counterpart to Ho Chi Minh? Nobody could be sure and suspicions and antagonisms were intense until the country became independent in 1960. All these tensions and tendencies could not but influence the ecclesiastical scene in the years 1920–60.

The Protestants

For a Western missionary organization arriving on the Cameroonian scene in 1917 it seemed logical to try with a union scheme to settle the tensions in Duala Protestantism. The Paris Evangelical missionaries managed to combine the three competing Baptist groups, forming 'the United Baptist Churches'. As soon as the agreement had been signed, however, the union began to break up. It had only papered over serious cracks in the new building. Tensions were caused by differing views on Church discipline and personality conflicts, particularly regarding the forceful pastor Adolphe Lotin a Same, a captivating preacher, hymn-writer and Church music composer. From his Duala look-out he cultivated wide international connections with, among others, Marcus Garvey and his Black Star shipping line. To the new missionaries these and other contacts were suspect. Lotin was excluded from the ministry and proceeded to lead a new secession called the Native Baptist Church. For decades both the French administration and the other Baptist Churches were to regard this body as a thorn in the flesh.

Lotin was determined to obtain official recognition for his Church and he fought for legal acceptance with a perseverance reminding one of Ethiopian Churches in South Africa at the time. In his case, as in the South African one, the efforts were without result. Numerically, Lotin's Church was not very impressive: 5,000 members in 1945 with five pastors, and 11,000 in 1948 with sixteen pastors. In 1946 Lotin died and was succeeded by Moses Mathi Mathi who extended his influence geographically and changed the Church's name to the Baptist Cameroonian Church. Surprisingly – presumably because of some change in administrative personnel – he managed to obtain what the group had been struggling for for half a century: official legal recognition, in 1948.

Further north the powerful sultans, including Njoya of Fumban, had shown an interest in the missionaries' concern but in the end opted for Islam. It was most likely two Nigerian clerks and a slave from Douala who introduced the Christian movement in Fumban. It seemed a promising start but with the sultans' declaration for Islam the Church was pushed aside and had to subsist, if at all, as an underground movement.[3]

In the midst of all this the early 1920s saw a sudden landslide of a turning to the Gospel. By his tireless evangelistic tours in the area, the charismatically gifted Duala pastor, Modi Din exerted his influence. On some of these tours the Revd Modi Din could align himself with missionary F. Christol, a teacher at the Ndunge Bible school from 1922 (this school re-opened in 1947: until which time twenty-five pastors were ordained). The two men inspired the growth of a spontaneous movement, of expectation and personal decision-making. The Revd Modi Din reached the whole of the 'Grassfields' in the French as well as the British areas: 'My work consists in advising the Christians and catechumens with joy', he summarized his work. 'I move from village to village. The work proceeds; it has become like the wheel of a bicycle which turns round and round.'[4] In certain respects this movement reminds one of the Harris movement further west, in the Ivory Coast. It did not last long, however. Perhaps this had to do with the attitude of the majority of the missionaries in the area: they were not too sure about the Revd Modi. Did he not move too fast? Had he given a sufficiently long time for the catechumenate? This spiritual breakthrough could not be found in their missiological textbooks and the potential of an awakening was, in the name of 'orthodoxy', to peter out.

With 140 different ethnic communities and numerous mutually incomprehensible major languages in Cameroon the linguistic problem was acute in the religious institution, the church. The Church was in principle – if not always in practice – to transcend these age-old boundaries. The Latin of Catholic worship (prior to Vatican II) was a constant drastic reminder of the claim to universality – the message in catechism and sermon had however to be adapted to local languages and vernaculars.

The Protestants struggled more or less successfully with the problem which in their case was more radically tied to the vernacular as vehicle of a spiritual message, in a period when vernaculars passed through their own rapid change. Since German times, 1884–1916, the international harbour community's language, Duala, had played the role of church language to the Presbyterians. Older Presbyterians in Western Cameroon also insisted on Duala as the language of prayer, song and sermon. This linguistic garb could be seen as a shield against the onslaught of modern influences. The younger generation, anxious to leave German and Duala behind and to make French and English their international languages, felt increasingly estranged from the Church's official policy and thus, inevitably, a chasm grew between the generations over this intractable matter of language. The young strove to appropriate French. When Emmanuel Mounier, the Catholic writer, visited Cameroon in 1947 he was asked by an ambitious school class: 'Why do you so often send out only second rate Frenchmen here and not your best?' This same youthful irritation could at times climb to the highest levels of theological education.[5]

A large linguistic group such as the Bulu in the south could extend its claims and influence over neighbouring ethnic communities so that, for instance, some Basa had to use Bhulu for their theological studies. The language problem could lead to secession from the Church. The Ngumba, a small, tightly knit ethnic enclave of some 15,000 members within the Bhulu area, were not prepared forever to suffer Bhulu superiority over their religious thought-world, in religious instruction, hymns and sermons. 'They did not have the means of learning anything in their own mother tongue, not even to praise God in it.'[6] A vivid local tradition among the Ngumba recalled that in 1898 an American missionary, Robert Oscar, had generously promised that they would in due course get the Bible in their own language, thus applying a well-known Protestant principle of the availability of Holy Scriptures in the mother tongue. They waited in vain however. On Christmas Day 1933, Ngumba leaders met at Bibia and decided to sever their connections with the 'mother Church', in this case the American Presbyterian mission, and to found their own Independent Church with their own worship and pastors. Twelve years later the Mission made a gesture of reconciliation, suggesting the building of Ngumba schools and preaching in Ngumba in certain chapels. The community was split over the issue, some accepting the terms of settlement, others bitterly opposing any Bhulu suggestions. Pastor S. N. Ngally later started a translation of the New Testament and prepared a hymn-book with no less than 440 hymns in the Ngumba language.

The Catholics may have appeared as more conspicuous than the Protestants, yet Cameroon Protestantism, through its community life and social activity, provided striking examples of that initiative and participation which one likes to associate with a peculiarly Protestant ethos, not least in Africa. The Presbyterian mission to the Bulu – a community closely related to the Ewondo of Yaoundé – established solid congregations in the country's south. At first they felt that the growth of the congregations was not promising and they decided to try a different strategy over a period of a decade and abide by the results. Emphasis on African local leadership and the principle of the 'Three Selves' had to be applied. An ambitious school system was introduced – and the response from the Bulu youth was startling. The work was concentrated in a few leading congregations with a network of higher institutions dedicated to educational and medical services. An amazing growth of the Church followed with some 70,000 in total baptized in 1925, 85,000 in 1962, and 200,000 in 1968. The Church at Elat with thousands of keen participants in the Sunday worship held for a time an international record, being then recognized as the largest Presbyterian Church in the world. (It has now supposedly been eclipsed by the South Koreans.)

All this had a stimulating effect on the Bulu population and their Church, forming an active and extrovert rather than a contemplative spirituality. One bright example is that of Joseph Njock Bot, who for thirty-five years served as a teacher, happy, voluble, active. He was one of the thousands of mission school teachers throughout the continent who, parallel with their school activity, were engaged in social and political work. Availing himself of all the higher educational services in the country he developed his leadership skills. The American mission provided international contacts: in 1939, he represented the Church at the Christian youth conference in Amsterdam, Holland. In 1952 he was appointed head chief of his 'Canton Ndok Bea South'. As such he published his 'Canton NBS News', a cyclostyled news sheet with an uncompromising Puritan message indicating what he regarded as the social effects of the Christian Gospel. Alcohol and tobacco were taboos to this African chief: 'any person who drinks alcohol is an enemy of progress in our land'. The chief came forward as an impatient reformer who also wished to abolish the bride price: 'At what price do you wish to sell your daughter?' was his propagandistic formula for combating an ancient custom. The Bulu clans must be seen to function better than hitherto. Clan meetings must be directed to discuss the progress of the country, was his plea – and his command.[7]

The Catholics

The Versailles Peace Treaty of 1919 implied that the German Pallottines were replaced by French Spiritans, and on the Protestant side the Paris Evangelical mission replaced the German-speaking Basle mission. A new mission thus followed up the promising Catholic beginnings at Yaoundé. Bishop François Xavier Vogt was transferred – 'translated', to use the canonical term – from Tanzania to Cameroon, and in this case Tanzania's loss was Cameroon's gain. Vogt in Cameroon was one of that remarkable group of Spiritan bishops in Africa at the time, including Shanahan of Eastern Nigeria, Augouard of Brazzaville and Keiling in Angola. Vogt had the task of leading and stimulating one of the most extensive mass movements in the twentieth century, which he did with outstanding leadership during the years of his Apostolic-Vicariate in Cameroon, between 1922 and 1943.

It is characteristic of Vogt that he credited the Ewondo catechists with the results harvested in that mass movement. In this and in so many other cases he was keen to emphasize the merits of the training given to the catechists by the German Pallottines before the war. There was soon an army of nearly 1,500 catechists directed by an African 'Catechist-Inspectors' elite. Vogt said about them: 'They can manage the most impossible situations and bring light where the missionary might risk losing his Latin ... and his patience.' One of them was Joseph Ayisi, chief catechist and Vogt's advisor in linguistic questions. The older Catechism, based on Pope Pius IX's excessively theological and theoretical booklet, was now replaced by one in Ewondo formulated by Ayisi, in a direct form with brief questions and answers. This catechist could thus lay foundations upon which, under new conditions of freedom and informed creativity, there was to appear in the 1970s an Ewondo catechism which speaks of 'the God of our fathers, the God of Abraham and the God of Jesus'. The decisive role of the Yaoundé catechists and head-catechists in the 1920s imposed itself when it was still thought improbable that African priests would be forthcoming to any appreciable degree. The high academic requirements and the celibacy rule were still regarded as excluding Africans from the ordained priesthood. This was to change soon enough, however. Dr E. Mveng, SJ, has characterized these Ewondo and Bhulu catechists. Pillars of the Church were: the

Mbangue, father and son, both devoted catechists, the latter, one of the leading 'permanent deacons' in Southern Cameroon; Pius Otu at Yaoundé, trained by the Pallottines, who produced the first parts of the Scriptures, the Missal and the Catechism in the Ewondo language; the charismatically talented Pierre Mebe, who founded a Franciscan Third Order at Yaoundé and built a chapel for its members; and the musician, Francoia Eze, who knew his Gregorian Missal by heart.

In Tanzania, Vogt had shared with some of his priests a concern about 'the Bagamoyo method', meaning collecting the young converts in Christian villages. In Cameroon Vogt was to promote and lead a *Volkswanderung*, with a whole population irresistibly on the move to the baptismal font. These people seemed to be teeming out of the tropical forest, walking for two to four days in groups of forty or fifty, led by the catechist. They would queue for days on end at the central stations for the privilege of saying a prescribed confession to a harassed missionary.

In the period 1916–39, the Catholic population in southern Cameroon increased ninefold. By 1939, the Yaoundé Diocese had 208,000 Catholics and 91,000 catechumens with sixty-four priests (all Westerners), twenty-four brothers, fifty-eight sisters and 2,000 catechists. A decade later, the Catholic community had risen to over 1.3 million. Vogt was overcome by a feeling of 'suffocation' because of the enormous masses of catechumens. He incessantly appealed to his superiors in Paris for help. He found the situation impossible and pleaded with the Director in Paris for dramatically increased numbers of French staff:

> You do not give us the means to avoid a catastrophe which is threatening the last few years. Recall me and place somebody else in my place. We have this year baptized more than 10,000 adults, not counting some 1,500 cases of baptisms *in extremis*. This poor diocese suffocates as a result of numbers.

Bishop Vogt of Yaoundé identified with a fast-growing mass movement. Yet, he was defeated by his coadjutor, Bishop R. Griffin and – by Pope Pius XI himself. The issue was whether to consolidate already established congregations – which was originally Vogt's idea – or to press on, occupying ever new groups of the population. The question was referred to the 'Mission Pope' who insisted: 'Occupy the country as fast as possible. Later on you can work in depth.' The bishop's policy in these and related matters placed him at variance with the French governor but, then, Vogt regarded French administrators in any case as his adversaries and as 'hypocrites', as he was wont to say. In view of the much cherished generalization in the West about missionaries as lackeys of the colonial powers, it is interesting to notice this and similar examples at the episcopal level.

The whole system of Catholic and Papal spirituality was brought to bear on the local Ewondo village groups. In 1926, Pope Pius XI had promulgated a 'Jubilee' with 'indulgences': in order to receive remission for special sins, the individual Christian had, on five different days, to visit their church, four times a day, each time praying according to the intentions of the Pope. For each visit to his church the Christian would have to say five Patres (Our Father), five Ave Maria and five Gloria Patri. On certain conditions he could acquire the Jubilee remission twice, once for himself and once for souls in Purgatory. To the Protestant these regulations may seem unfamiliar. Yet, one is left with an impression of the enormous power of a system which could insist on such spiritual exercises and apparently achieve compliance. It would, however, be incorrect to suggest that this Catholic Ewondo spirituality was primarily imposed from above. On the contrary, the village catechist was there to interpret and transform the official message into familiar terms giving it his own emphasis on the experience of Christ and thus meeting the problems of everyday life in the village. Eschatology and the Last Judgement predominated in his teaching and there was an accent on social relations in and through the village congregation and worship: 'The more you have social relations, the more you are a person.'[8]

CONGO—BRAZZAVILLE

While Belgian Congo and Portuguese Angola manifested a close symbiosis between Church and State, in French Congo the situation was entirely different. Here an attitude which the Catholics referred to as 'laicization' was the rule. At both the national and the local level, French administration handled these matters with aloofness, even with a touch of disdain.

The scene and the expectation

In the early 1920s, life began anew in Brazzaville – and so did Death. The 'Spanish Influenza' took a terrible toll. At least forty people a day were buried in the African townships. In 1933 a pneumonia epidemic was fatal to many children. The new city, with a rapidly rising population packed in the houses and hovels, was the scene of both expectation and despair. The catastrophes in the area, added to other factors, stirred religious fascination, inspired especially by rumours from the other side of the River about Simon Kimbangu.

On the French side, André Matswa, an ex-Catholic catechist, had been influenced by Simon Kimbangu, and was hailed by his own Lari community as a Liberator. He was imprisoned and after numerous escapes and subsequent recaptures, died in prison in 1943. But his Lari, including many Catholics and Protestants, looked to him as a potential Returnee, considering him a religious prophet, a Moses or even the Messiah. In the 1960s, this role was exploited by an abbé-politician, Foulbert Youlou, also a Lari. The underlying religious quest and expectation sensed by the masses still reverberated. An adequate interpretation of the Catholic or Protestant *Dibundu* spirituality in Pointe Noire or Brazzaville today, cannot be made without some reference to that *milieu* of anticipation created by these supposedly marginal groups. Brazzaville was alive with messianic rumours and these affected both Catholics and Protestants. To this must be added the role of the railway (from 1921) from Brazzaville to Pointe Noire – the 'Congo–Ocean' – and the port of Pointe Noire which together dramatically stimulated the move of the population from the countryside to the new cities, Brazzaville and Pointe Noire.

In 1940 a West Indian civil servant, Felix Eboué, was made the governor general of French Equatorial Africa. In 1944 Charles de Gaulle, at a conference held in Brazzaville, outlined a constitution for Free France and 'announced a major liberalization of France's relations with its overseas possessions'.[9] These were momentous events which affected every African in Congo–Brazzaville and beyond.

In Bishop Augouard's time, Brazzaville was only a small administrative centre, and the missions considered it not much more than a transit post on the way north, along the Zaïre–Ubangi Rivers. When Augouard died, in 1921, there were 6,000 Africans and some 400 Europeans there. As the settlement on the gentle hills grew, the layout along the Congo River was apparent: a European centre in 'the Plain', between the African towns 'Bacongo' and 'Poto-Poto'. Augouard had built his cathedral on 'Mission Hill' in the European quarter. Although there was presumably plenty of wood in the Congo forests for such a building, for prestige purposes the wood for the church was imported from France. The building was later succeeded by the present Cathedral of St Firmin.

Sudden crises would forcibly remind the ecclesiastical establishment that their influence on the masses was not as assured as they would like to think. On both sides of the River, one could overhear from time to time the signals of the surprising power of the Great Absent, ever present in the thoughts and expectations of the people. In dreams and in visions they looked to the prospective Returnee, coming to them in power and glory. Fundamentally, this was what shook the Catholic diocese in 1933. That year, Linzolo, the oldest mission in the diocese was to celebrate its fifty-years Jubilee. This happy occasion would give bishop Guichard and his missionaries an opportunity to emphasize not only the forward-looking strategy of their work, but also the value of an established Catholic tradition, 'the creation of a worthwhile past'. The whole district with all the chiefs, and the Diocese were expected to take part in this proud celebration. But the programme was boycotted because of the Lari nationalist upsurge against the treatment of their hero, André Matswa. He and his colleagues had collected over 100,000 francs in support of their *Amicale* Association, of which Matswa was President/Founder. Matswa's imprisonment embittered the entire Lari population – Matswa, himself a 'Lari to the bone', was their hero.[10] Similar tensions were felt at the same time in the Protestant church: at Kingoyi the 'ngunzist' (prophet) movement expressed its opposition in anti-missionary songs:

> The superintendents accuse us to the Mission,
> The Mission itself accuses us to the State.[11]

The Spiritans

The Catholics were effectively represented by the French Holy Ghost Fathers. The Bishop of Brazzaville invited teaching Orders and Sisters' Congregations to serve in the educational and medical institutions in the Capital and in Pointe Noire: boarding schools for boys and girls and the College Chaminade, catered to a new generation of educated *evolués*.

After 1919, Congo soldiers were repatriated and could proudly report that they had been baptized while in the army. They felt entitled to *gagner la confesse*, to take their turn in the queue for the confessional in the Cathedral. In 1920, Fr Joseph Bonnefont – called *Maboni* by the Africans – had been transferred from a bush parish to Brazzaville. He formed congregations in Bacongo and Poto-Poto and was sympathetic to his city parishoners, but he was not always impressed by the religious knowledge of the returning soldiers. When some of them were uncertain about the number of Persons in the Godhead, Fr Bonnefont decided that, for the time being, they would not be admitted to Mass, however much they might brandish their baptismal certificate, signed in the Flanders battlefield.

Several new Catholic churches and chapels were built in the townships, including Wenze, where the poorest strata of the population lived. There Fr Hyacinthe placed chapels for worship. The finest architectural achievement was that of the Basilica of St Anne, started in 1943 and completed in 1949. At the end of the First World War, Fr Brottier, a Spiritan, had built the

Cathedral of Dakar as a sign of Franco–African friendship. Now, similarly, after the Second World War, Spiritan missionaries led by Fr Lecomte raised the Basilica to promote Franco–Congolese friendship. The architect, Roger Errel – a Protestant with a keen interest in Gregorian chant – was inspired to use local styles for his design, notably those from the Logone district in Chad. He applied the characteristic ogival shapes to the exterior of the church. When the 'Messe des Piroguirs' – the Canoeist mass – was sung in the large Basilica, the effect was captivating. The original 'African' style of the interior of the building also stimulated later liturgical innovations in the region.

The village chapels and their catechists had initiated these masses into the Christian faith. In the Bacongo township, the Kongo–Lari dominated the social life in the churches. From relative obscurity they were lifted to a new national role, which they accepted with the greatest self-confidence. In his *Sociologie des Brazzaville Noires*, Professor Balandier made a point when referring to an African labourer arriving in the city: 'In fact, the life in the town entails for him as for the majority of town dwellers a *laicisation* of thought which would hardly have been possible in the traditional milieu.'[12] While this observation is pertinent for cities in the West, it cannot automatically be applied to the African city. With their propensity for a mystical and religious dimension, heightened by the André Matswa interlude, the Lari in Bacongo were able to keep their attachment and loyalty to the Church, even in the city.

The Spiritans had founded Christian villages along the Zaïre–Ubangi rivers, which served their purpose of creating Christian communities. These eventually became new towns, such as Bangui and Berberati, with a network of Christian dioceses stretching as far as southern Chad. Also here the mission station was a 'localization factor'. The Apostolic Prefecture of Ubangi–Shari, established in 1909, later became an archdiocese. It developed into a strong Catholic area, despite the existence of various Baptist communities. In this broad web of congregations, the Church stored up for itself a difficult task, with repercussions into the present day. There was an inevitable tension between the southern centre around Brazzaville, with all its educational, medical and other institutions, and the northern periphery – a deprived and exploited area, ready for radical solutions to challenge the south.

The Protestants for self-governemt

The Protestants – Swedish Congregationalists with a Believers' baptism – spanned the River. They started in the 1880s in Lower Congo, on the Belgian side. At the end of World War I they expanded northward from a crowded mission area to the same Kongo people, but on the French side of the River. When the first three converts had been baptized at Madzia, near Brazzaville, the young men came to the missionary's house in the evening and knocked at the door. They asked: 'Tata [Father] give us rules and laws'.[13] Their humble request represented the search by young people over the entire continent. Uprooted from clan and custom, they were looking for new sanctions to guide them through a dangerous world.

Soon, however, the young congregations faced other more overwhelming dimensions of the religious quest. The Prophet movement hit Congo 'as an avalanche'.[14] Dr Ephraim Andersson has analysed the effect of the Kimbangu and the Matswa movements on the growth of the Evangelical Church. The revival within the Evangelical Church was as drastic as any on the continent, but their missionaries approached the matter with empathy and understanding. On 19 January 1947, the movement began at the Ngouedi Theological Seminary. It came from within the Church itself, and from the heart of a theology student, Bwana Kibongi. He was burdened with guilt at having 'despised the word of God', and was also concerned that the whole Seminary, was 'rotting in sin'. 'He ended by crying out in a trance, and expressing the distress he felt in his heart.'[15] In this case, the missionaries did not stand aside, but were themselves challenged and involved – and the Revival was contained within the Church.

Working towards self-government for the Evangelical Church was another theme in the Congregationalist history of the Congo. The Swedish missionaries represented a Free Church, founded in 1878, three years before they started their mission work in Congo. They came from a Sweden dominated by a Lutheran National Church, and they were proud of their Free Church tradition. In Brazzaville, therefore, their fundamental question was how to assist in the formation of a Free Church in Congo – free, that is, from a Western Free Church mission. At the mission, the Swedes were in charge, but uneasily. They were aware of their goal: self-government for the African Church. One of their group, Dr Karl Laman, had pressed for this since 1923. In 1929 their leader, 'Tata' Flodén, about to leave for Sweden, did not want to go without having achieved what the Home Church Board wanted, and what the African Church ought to desire: a Free Church – a self-governing Church. So Flodén wrote a Constitution. This was hastily accepted by the missionaries, and with much more hesitation by the African leaders:

> Having heard that our friends in Europe and our own Whites wish that the leadership for the congregations and God's work shall be handed to us, the people of our country, we do not wish to oppose this ... We are fearful of

> this responsibility. But knowing that God wants it and in the hope that we will not be left alone we wish to try it in the name of the Lord.

Arvid Stenström, representing a later generation of missionaries, has described this 1929 draft of a constitution as 'fuzzy'. Its weakness did not really matter, for the constitution was never put into practice. In the years to follow the question in missionary circles was whether the African Church was sufficiently 'mature'. This was the same hesitation felt in most other missions throughout the continent. In spite of the apparently affirmative answer to that question given by the 1947 Revival, there were still doubts about this 'maturity'. Retorts came from Africans, accusing the missionaries of going back on their promise. Not until the dramatic advent of political independence was the Evangelical Church constituted as an autonomous Free Church. The African leader, Jaspar Kimpolo, sent a generous African greeting to the mission's supporters back 'home' in Sweden: 'Greet them and thank them that we got self-government before we asked for it'. Professor George Balandier, studying the Brazzaville churches at the beginning of the 1950s, found that being a minority the Protestants constituted more coherent and active groupings than the Catholics. [16]

In 1935 another Protestant mission came to Brazzaville, the Salvation Army, at the same time as its Belgian branch started work in Kinshasa. While the Congregationalists had a tendency to keep away from the capital, the Salvation Army officers, faithful to their traditions from the London slums, thrived in cosmopolitan Poto-Poto. Here again the faithful discovered the great resource of the confession. The Flag and the Rope, and that potent red letter, 'S' – seen by many Congolese at the time as standing for *S*imon K – gave symbols to a Protestant community notably lacking in such. These astonishing Means of Grace obviously brought a feeling of purification and new life to the individual and to the masses.

ZAÏRE-CONGO

Zaïre-Congo was an immense country, eighty times the size of Belgium and very sparsely populated. This low population density was further accentuated after 1945 by an increased migration from the villages to the towns and the cities. After the First World War new means of communication were developed in the Congo region: the Belgian airline Sabena began to fly to Kinshasa and Lubumbashi; Air France to Brazzaville, Douala and Pointe Noire; and Transport Portuguese to Luanda. Nevertheless, the Congo region was dominated by one single and central geographical factor: the river Congo–Zaïre and its tributaries. The role of the River, even in this new period, was still vital for communication and for the Churches in their evangelization. The Church canoe, and later the Church motor boat, were ideal for reaching out with the Christian message. The spectacular arrival on the Congo and Ubangi waters of Grenfell's *Peace* and Bishop Augouard's *Leo XIII* in the 1880s and 1890s was not forgotten. These boats were followed by more efficient river craft, constantly in use.

The railway started the great revolution in communications. Early ventures in this field have already been described. By the 1920s, extensions to the Katanga–Shaba region were connected to the Benguela–Lobito route. One of the railways with the most dramatic effect in the region was the Congo–Ocean line, built 1921–34, from Brazzaville via Dolisie to Pointe Noire. The railway transformed the countryside: 4,000 villages were brought into effective contact with the capitals of Brazzaville and Kinshasa and the fast-growing harbour on the Atlantic coast. The railway made it possible for the individual, as well as families and groups, to move from the village to the city. The Kongo–Lari communities were innately mobile and now, with the railway, they could still keep in touch with the lands of their ancestors. One must not, however, forget the enormous cost in human lives which the construction of these railways involved. In the exploitation of forests and lands by the concessionary companies, forced labour was an acceptable solution. Those pressed into service had no voice, not in Belgian Congo, nor in French Congo, nor in the hot cotton fields of Malange in Angola.

The Belgian colonists in the country represented a limited but decisive minority, no more than 7,000 in 1920, reaching a total of 110,000 in 1959 which, it was thought, would assure a permanent Belgian dominance in the territory. In 1955 the Belgian journalist and academic A. A. J. Van Bilsen published a design, according to which Belgium should launch a long-term plan. In 1985 Belgian colonial rule was to celebrate its centenary: Van Bilsen suggested that this would be a propitious year for the Belgians to hand over the country to the Congolese – a suggestion which met with angry protests from the Belgian public. However, only a few months after the publication of this programme, the political situation had changed beyond all recognition.

Kinshasa (Léopoldville)

Léopoldville–Kinshasa did not become the capital of the Belgian Congo until 1930. Up until then, Boma on the coast had been the capital and, in reality, the colony was still administered from Brussels. At first the new role of Léopoldville as the capital brought an influx of people. During the Great Depression of the 1930s, however, 6,000 men were removed back to the villages. The Second World War changed the outlook. Social facilities improved: schools, dispensaries and maternity hospitals. The provision of family allowances for married workers provided another reason for couples to settle in the city, thus establishing an urbanized population, which looked on the city as its home. The population of Kinshasa grew rapidly: 60,000 in 1942; 120,000 in 1947; and 250,000 in 1952. Most were immigrants, coming from Lower Congo or Kwango, with a significant minority of Angolans. The Scheut Society sent some of their priests to learn Portuguese; on their return, they served the Angolans in Kinshasa. Other missions went to the Lower Congo region for the same linguistic reason, and returned to serve immigrants from that area now living in Kinshasa.

The war years in Kinshasa, with Belgium overrun by enemy troops, presented special difficulties and opportunities for the Belgian missionary staff. The Scheut mission were in charge of Kinshasa. It was characteristic of the situation here, as elsewhere, that the 'Provincial' decided not to reside in the emerging city, but at the more familiar Bokoro in the countryside, while the successor, Mgr Georges Six, as vicar apostolic of Kinshasa 1934–52, became a leading figure in the city. An increasing number of nuns' orders arrived to take charge of girls' education and of medical work.

In 1942 the Scheut mission had a staff of 136, including sixteen priests, twenty brothers, five Jesuits working in schools, and ninety-five nuns. Immediately after the war there was a dramatic rise in the numbers of staff, not only in Kinshasa, but throughout the whole country. In 1946 the first three African priests of Kinshasa were ordained, among them the future Cardinal Malula and the future assistant bishop of Kinshasa, Mgr Moke. The emerging class of *évolués* were closely related to the Catholic church.

The Scheut missionaries were the first Catholics to work in Kinshasa, and have remained the most important religious group in the city: of the eighty-eight Catholic priests in Kinshasa in 1955, seventy were Scheut and thirteen Jesuit. When in 1935 Europeans received the right to live in the *cité indigène* (African quarters), new parishes were formed. One such parish was Christ the King, divided into two congregations, each with 36,000 members. In the 1950s it was under the dynamic leadership of Abbé Malula. The parish of St Pierre was larger still, with 80,000. Family and personal care, and educational services, were to a large extent the concern of the sisters. Of the 163 sisters serving in Kinshasa in 1955, fifty-eight worked among the Europeans, and 105 exclusively with the African population. African sisters, Franciscans, cared for the Bandalungwa parish.

For boys' education the Scheut mission had an enthusiastic organizer in 'Tata Raphael' (Fr de la Kethule de Ryhove), who developed the elementary schools into practical middle schools. In 1919, Tata Raphael had founded the Congolese Sports Club. Well before the Second World War football had become the craze of the young, who gathered in teams carrying irresistable names such as 'The Star', 'Union', 'Excelsior' and 'Standard'. The Queen Astrid Stadium and the Sports Park of General Ermens attracted the young of the city.

The formation of voluntary associations increased the sense of belonging in the city. In 1930 the Catholics organized a short-lived association for traders and artisans. The Christian Trade Union movement, inspired by the Federation of Christian Syndicates in Belgium, was a permanent feature. In 1948 a *Mutualité Chrétienne* was founded, with monthly subscriptions and benefits paid for marriage, illness and death. It was a modern adaptation of the traditional *Lemba* healing association in the region.

The *évolués*, who numbered some 10–15,000 in the 1940s and 1950s, became increasingly important. The concept of *évolués* was difficult to define; de Schrevel refers to forty different definitions![17] Generally speaking, the term referred to those with a school education, engaged in professional jobs and more or less alienated from the traditions of the ancestors. Many of those who had studied in the Catholic Junior Seminaries belonged to this group. Not all Catholic seminarists perservered to the end, which was ordination as a priest. The most dramatic example of those who fell by the way was Joseph Kasavubu – later to be the first President of the Republic – who, while in the Senior Seminary, had been showing disturbing signs of a critical mind and was therefore virtually dismissed by his Spiritual Director.[18]

Post-primary schools grew up, with 'Old Boys' associations from these schools expressing their pride of achievement and offering opportunities to discuss new political ideas. Mission-directed study groups for Congolese *évolués* were also very successful. Started by Jesuit missionaries, these associations soon managed on their own, led by men such as Jean Bolikango, the Grand Old Man of Zaïrean-Congolese politics. They became the meeting place for Zaïrean-Congolese *évolués*, and a training arena for future politicians. These groups fostered new leaders, such as the previously mentioned Joseph Kasavubu, and Thomas Kanza, the first Zaïrean-Congolese university graduate.

In 1925 Louvain University in Belgium took an important step. It opened a school for medical assistants at Kisantu, a Jesuit institution. In 1931 this was followed by an agricultural school at the same site. These were the beginnings of what was to become a university which, in 1950, moved to the capital. By 1950 the four major theological seminaries, begun in the 1930s, had produced 154 African priests and, ten years later, 400. The first African bishop was consecrated in 1956, to be followed in 1959 by the establishment of the 'hierarchy of Congo', with six archbishoprics and twenty-six dioceses. The years of rapid Africanization had come – just in time.

The city provided the women of Zaïre-Congo with new opportunities. The life and activities of Kinshasa women have been interpreted in a remarkable and charming book by Suzanne Comhaire-Sylvain, published in 1968, and building on local research of two different periods, 1943–45 and 1965.[19] In 1961 the young, of all ages up to twenty-five years, constituted nearly 63 per cent of the total population of the city, while the female population was as high as 862 for every 1,000 males.

The mission schools, Catholic and Protestant, provided the fundamental educational opportunity. The Catholic primary schools of St Peter and in the city area were directed by the nuns of St Augustine. There were coeducational schools run by the Baptists and the Salvation Army, with some of them strongly emphasizing practical work.

Various girls' and women's associations supplemented the formal school education. Such examples were the Girl Guides, the YWCA and the Catholic Xaveri groups with 60,000 members throughout Zaïre. The Xaveri movement was organized into three groups according to age: the 'Happy Ones' for the seven to ten year-olds, the 'Ardent Ones' for those aged ten to fourteen and the 'Radiant Ones' for those between fifteen and twenty-five. The 'Christian Family Movement' was a Catholic organization, which also admitted members from other creeds. Although few in number, its influence was deep and and pervading. As in other African countries, the Legion of Mary also attracted women in Zaïre-Congo, caring for all classes of women including those that had been less fortunate with regard to school education. It was particularly strong in the 1950s. Another association was delightfully called the 'Society for Promoting Elegance'.

The 'Association of Protestant Women', founded in 1946, had a strong Baptist membership. Madame Marie Mattie, a Baptist nurse, was the President of the Association. In 1946 she was already on her first visit abroad, to a Baptist world conference in Nigeria, while her Catholic counterpart, Madame Nkume, represented Zaïre-Congo at the Catholic conference in Lomé, Togo, in 1949. Some observers at the time liked to see this representation as part of 'a feminine pan-Africanism'.

These first pioneers of international contacts set the tone for a rapidly increasing international mobility among Kinshasa women. The catalogue of visits by women from Kinshasa to the rest of the African continent, to French-speaking Europe and to the United States, provides impressive reading. The generations of women in the family supported one another with regard to the same womanly ambition. When a social science student, related to the Salvation Army, refused to marry because of her young age and the fear of jeopardizing a professional career, her grandmother encouraged her: 'Don't interrupt your studies. Go as far as you ever can. If you don't continue, you will regret it for the rest of your life.'[20] Fathers also were sometimes influenced by the changing perception of women. One Protestant pastor decided not to receive a dowry for his daughter: 'That kind of thing does not exist with us'.[21] The international horizon helped to modify a certain sanctimoniousness which hitherto had passed for proper Christianity. 'As children we were not allowed to wear jewellery or trinkets, but now the missionaries [themselves] wear them. They don't dance yet, but they no longer get angry when they hear of the young generation doing so.'[22]

Lubumbashi (Elizabethville) and Shaba (Katanga)

After the First World War, the city fathers of Lubumbashi took to social engineering, designed to create humane conditions for the rapidly increasing urban population. Until that time, African workers lived in four 'work camps', which were on the outskirts of the European city and belonged to the region's major employers. These camps had notoriously disregarded public health measures. Governor Lippens took office in 1921. He benefited, perhaps surprisingly, from a visit to the Rand mines in South Africa, which motivated him to develop the idea of a modern African city. The old *cité indigène* was destroyed and replaced by a planned, hygenic new city.

Of equal importance was the decision by the mining companies to break with the system of migrant labour, then dominant in southern Africa. They developed a system of stabilized labour whereby African workers were encouraged to stay for long periods of time, together with their families. These policies led to city planning and new residential quarters for Africans. They also affected Church organization. Houses were built of brick, and each block had its own sanitary facilities and water supply. At the time, these provisions were a great advance. In 1929 the city had a population of about 12,000; by 1960 this had risen to 250,000. Most of the mineworkers had been recruited from Zambia, but this supply came to an end during the Depression in the 1930s. From this time, most labour for the copper mines came from the Luba people in the southern part of the country, a group with strong Church connections, both Catholic and Protestant.

Human social engineering had been an objective of colonial administration. The Catholic Church also made this programme its own, with the added Christian concern for human contacts, as well as individual and family care. Rome allotted Lubumbashi to the Benedictines. This pervasive Benedictine influence adversely affected other religious bodies in the area. The Catholic Salesians withdrew to Sakania in the southern part of Shaba. The American Methodists experienced the pressure more heavily than anyone else. They had made a promising start in Lubumbashi in 1917. Under the guidance of Helen Springer, wife of John Springer (Bishop from 1936), girls' education and women's organizations flourished. But with increasing Benedictine domination, English-speaking American Protestants were not wanted in the city. From 1928, the Springers settled instead at Likasi (Jadotville) in another area of the rapidly expanding Shaba (Katanga) Copper Belt.

The Churches, an overview

The Church in Belgian Congo was structured into three tiers: Catholic, Protestant and the Prophet movement. It had parallels in Angola, but both similarities and differences in French Congo. At the top of the pyramid in Belgian Congo was the dominating Roman Catholic Church. Its position was emphasized by King Leopold in the concordat of 1906, and maintained by the Belgian state when it took control from the king in 1908. Church and State in the territory were definitely all-Belgian in character. King Leopold had insisted that Catholic missions should have an exclusively Belgian staff. They were referred to as 'national missions', an ironic term in the African context. Belgian missionaries contributed a vital infusion of service and devotion into the Catholic body of the colony. From 1920 to 1960 nearly 120 new Catholic Orders and Sacred Congregations were posted to old and new stations throughout the country. After 1919, the area also included the densely populated, mandated territories of Rwanda and Burundi. At the time, Belgian Congo was quite depopulated. Being forty-three times the size of Rwanda–Burundi, its population was only two and a half times the size of that of the territories to the east.

The altogether remarkable growth of the Catholic Church in Zaïre can be seen by comparing the situation at the beginning of the 1920s with that of forty years later. In 1920, out of a population of over ten million, there were 655,000 Catholics including 265,000 catechumens. By 1960, the total of Catholics had risen to 5,700,000, including 640,000 catechumens. This rapid increase should be accredited to the army of village catechists: 7,660 with eighty-five women in 1923, 20,000 in 1959, and by 1961 some 163,000 and no less than 2,600 sisters with 910 African sisters. Father van Wing stresses 'the massive participation' of women's orders in their work for girls' education and medical services.[23]

The dominant Catholic position in Belgian Congo was evident in regard to both land grants and educational subsidies. Both policies were developed from the concordat of 1906. A comparison of land grants in 1932 to two Catholic and two Protestant missions is revealing. The Jesuits received 37,000 hectares, and the Scheut Mission 16,000, while the American Baptists were granted only 209 hectares, and the British BMS 226 hectares! In 1942 the Scheut mission was awarded an additional grant of 41,000 hectares of pasture land in Kasai.

Below the Catholics in the three-tiered pyramid were the Protestants. They increased in number from 50,000 in 1908, to 108,000 in 1926, and to almost 1.8 million by 1960, the majority of them Baptists. With a few important exceptions, they followed in the footsteps of the pioneers, George Grenfell and Henry Richards. Officially, they were 'foreign' missions, operating on the periphery of a Catholic colonial society. Seen as outsiders and intruders, they were either scarcely tolerated, or vigorously pushed from a precarious foothold, as in Shaba and the Kasai regions. The Belgians realized that their small European country ruled a very large African colony, and that their precious possession was possibly in danger of being appropriated by other countries with imperialist designs. Protestant missions tended to be suspect representatives of such countries. They lacked the privileges granted to the Catholics, particularly with regard to government support for mission schools. Given these handicaps it is surprising that the Protestants managed to persevere and progress so well.

In the 1920s there were sixteen Protestant societies: nine American, four British, and three 'Continental', including the small Belgian Protestant Church (supposedly a 'national' mission). The largest numbers were related to the Africa Inland Mission and the Adventists. Centrally placed among the Protestant missions were the Disciples of Christ, the American Methodists, the American Presbyterians and a rich assortment of Baptists. From the outset, the Presbyterians had concentrated their work on the southern region of Shaba–Katanga region, but rapid urbanization gave enterprising Presbyterian Luba the opportunity to move to Kinshasa and other cities.

In addition to being a political irritant, Protestant missions also supposedly posed a religious danger to the souls of Africans. Mgr de Clercq referred to 'the Protestant spirit with its indifference to religious teaching and its predilection for arithmetic'. The danger to the souls applied even more to the third group in the three-tiered system: the Prophet movement, an unfortunate offspring, it was held, of the Protestant *libre examen* – the free and unchecked study of the Holy Scriptures. From that dangerous practice of Bible study no good would come – only unwanted questioning and ambition in the African masses. Such a danger must be eradicated. Church and State, together with the mining companies, had tried to do exactly that in 'extirpating'[24] the Kitawala groups from Shaba in the 1920s. Yet even the seemingly complete round-up and imprisonment of Simon Kimbangu and his followers in 1921 did not guarantee total eradication. The Absent Prophet was still very much present in the dreams and expectations of the masses.

The Catholics

By the 1920s a new period dawned for the churches in Zaïre-Congo. Two major innovations occurred: a Protestant 'revolution from below' created by Kimbangu – at least that was how the colonial authorities regarded it – and a Catholic 'reform from above'.

At the beginning of the 1920s the Jesuits had just come through a particularly hard time in the Kwango area, reviled in their home country by radical Belgian politicians for their 'farm-chapel' system in Zaïre-Congo. To this was added the ravages of epidemics in the population. There were times when the Jesuits seriously considered withdrawing from the area.

However, during the that decade new opportunities appeared. Dynamic apostolic vicars – Stanislas de Vos, Sylvan van Hee and Alphonse Verwimp – led the work. In Father Joseph van Wing the Jesuits had an outstanding missionary strategist, perhaps the leading Catholic missionary of his time, in charge of the Kisantu district. Van Wing and his colleagues were deeply concerned about certain adverse effects of the Congo social system. He was keenly aware of the changing times. 'Twenty years ago,' he said, 'the missionaries still believed that they had all the time ahead of them', but there was now a period of 'rapid evolution of African societies'.[25] In the Kisantu area the matriarchal social system had both advantages and disadvantages. One of the defects of the system appeared after the death of a husband when the woman, as a widow, was left without legal protection and her goods were either destroyed or consumed or buried. With regard to marriage, illness or death, there were other such grievances for both old and young.

In discussions with Catholic catechists and other senior Christians and certain pagan chiefs, van Wing managed to work out a modification of traditional custom. He suggested that at the husband's death the widow and her children should inherit the husband's estate. She had to stay on in the husband's village under the custody of her in-laws. Through a series of far-reaching popular assemblies he had his proposals discussed and accepted by the population. In June 1924, 560 heads of Catholic families in the Kisantu region were summoned to a plenary meeting. Point after point in traditional custom and in the new reformed concept was discussed and unanimously approved. Two months later another plenary meeting included pagan chiefs. In 1925, 600 women were called to an information meeting and finally in June 1926, 800 heads of families at Kisantu and 450 at Kimpako were summoned to a final meeting which adopted and confirmed the suggested reform.

This was an entirely different approach to the social problems of the population, broader and deeper than that of the ordinary catechism class, creating a new basis, a *preparatio* for a concerted community move towards the Church. Only a personality of outstanding capacity such as van Wing could achieve this, through active support of catechists and the assent of pagan chiefs. Van Wing was anxious not to destroy but to *modify* local custom. It goes without saying that the fact that Father van Wing was a Belgian, with a high standing with the Belgian administration, helped him in his efforts. The new concept spread to other matrilineal communities and also to certain patrilineal areas where the father exercised an excessive authority. Here also a healthy modification of local custom followed.

The Church in Zaïre-Congo did not spread evenly throughout the land. It varied as far as Church history and Christian experience are concerned. In some parts it has a very long history and in others a very short Catholic tradition. There are districts with fascinating Christian traditions from the sixteenth and seventeenth centuries, and yet in adjacent areas, both Catholic and Protestant communities sprang to life as late as between the two world wars. The best examples of the latter category are, perhaps, the communities between the Rivers Congo-Zaïre and Loyi–Ngiri, founded as the Catholic Libanda Mission by the Scheut Fathers in 1933. The old centres from which the work spread were Catholic Mankanza (then called New Antwerp) and Protestant (represented by the Disciples of Christ) Bolenge. A few lines on developments in this limited area must here represent the Church's role in rural Zaïre-Congo.

From these centres catechists in their canoes reached out to villages along the Ngiri river. Their work illustrates the local history of the Church in this world of the rivers, its vital swarming life of the very first beginnings of a local Church history, with a microcosm of the Church along the entire length of the Congo-Zaïre River and its hundreds of tributaries. The first catechists sent from Catholic Mankanza and from Protestant Bolenge were all foreigners, from other communities, and therefore at first they were met with suspicion by the local population which mostly consisted of liberated slaves and others. A breakthrough in the Ngiri area came, characteristically, with a couple of young local men who had been bold enough to venture as far as Mankanza, where they hoped to find work and money. In the process they found the new religion. They returned to the home area and, knowing the mentality of their own people, they were in a position to introduce and recommend new catechists – a story similar for both Catholics and Protestants.

Catechumen classes were started in the villages and these were visited perhaps twice a year by the missionary from Mankanza or Bolenge: one had to wait for two short periods in the year when the rivers were full, thus making communication by canoe possible. Small Christian communities were formed as young men moved to establish Christian villages at the catechist centres. Catechumens were eager to join, believing that the Christian centres freed them from the obligation of forced labour: the Church centre at Libanda became, here as elsewhere on the continent, a place of refuge. Catechists became chiefs of the Christian village communities. They even visited polygamous households and brought wives from there to be married to others. Leading Catholic catechists, such as Martin Ndomba or Bavon Sempa, were determined adversaries of the Protestant community who were thought to have sent epidemics such as the Spanish Influenza in 1919!

The daily labour by priest and catechist with the preparation of their enormous masses of catechumens corresponded at the village level with the overall strategy and debate at the hierarchcial level. There was a discussion going on in Zaïre-Congo at this time to which we can here only allude. An episcopal conference at Kinshasa (Léopoldville) in 1907 had laid down a general rule of two years as a minimum for the period of catechetical training. This had been confirmed by later episcopal conferences in 1919, 1923 and 1928. Speaking at a later conference in 1932, Bishop Verwimp inserted an humane consideration according to which the individual catechumen could in fact show signs of a 'baptism of desire', a *baptisma flaminis*, prior to the baptism in water, a *baptisma fluminis*. There were obviously differences between different local traditions. At Kisantu the catechumen had to live two years and three months at the mission, receiving two instructions a day, and there were modifications because of family background whether from a pagan or Christian home. (It should be added that the rule of spending months or even years at the mission implied that the catechumen not only received instruction but also had to assist with practical work such as building work on the big mission stations.)

There was also at this time the pressure of the principle laid down by Cardinal Lavigerie, the rule of a four-year catechumenate. The episcopal conference of 1932 established two and a half years as the minimum. On this occasion the Apostolic Delegate Dellapiane took the opportunity of warning against certain missiologists in Europe. He referred obviously to Fr Charles of Louvain who, in a somewhat light-hearted fashion, had questioned the value of overly long periods of instruction for the catechumenate. This position, the Apostolic Delegate suggested, would 'prepare generations of bad Christians' and possibly numerous apostates. The minutes of the meeting go on to say: 'The bishops unanimously approved the declaration of Mgr the Apostolic Delegate.'[26]

Contacts between these peripheral Christian village groups and the Church centres were kept alive particularly during the Christian festivals. Along the rivers one could see the processions of canoes on the way to church, with their choir-singing echoing over the waters. Such a church visit might take three to six days, over a distance of 150–200 kilometres.

The special retreats increasingly became a means for the spiritual life of the congregation, showing once again the immense spiritual care for the individual and the group. The Kikwit diocese can be quoted as an example. In the rural areas the retreat lasted three days and could bring together 250–300 men, exceptionally as many as 500. In the cities the retreats were planned for a week with instruction twice a day. Sometimes there were specialized retreats for men only, for women, youths or catechists. The participants brought their individual breviary and rosary, sleeping mat and food. The programme included early mass and four instructions per day with other spiritual exercises, as well as two hours of practical work per day. In the White Fathers' tradition the retreats were held four times annually, integrated into the Church year. This was particularly so during Lent, the very name for retreat being 'to fast'.

Catholics at Lubumbashi (Elizabethville)

In the east, at Lubumbashi, Bishop Jean Félix de Hemptinne found time for highly practical and civic concerns. This prince of the Church, a son of Belgian aristocracy, lived in Lubumbashi from 1920 until his death in 1957. He became the leading figure in Lubumbashi and Shaba (Katanga) affairs, closely connected with the interests of government and the concessionary companies. He made his cathedral, located in the very centre of the city, into a 'dominant force in local affairs'.[27]

As the Benedictines had done before in history, in the Europe of the Middle Ages, so the Benedictine Bishop de Hemptinne was striving for the Christianization of local society. De Hemptinne's vision for Lubumbashi, and for Shaba as a whole, was the Christianization of society through Catholic schools, through a local welfare policy derived from Catholic inspiration and through Catholic 'associations' to aid and guide the uprooted immigrant. In short, to bridge the gap between the old life in the village, and the new life in the city – between the spirits and the Spirit.

The Bishop's directives were carried out by Fr Gregoire Coussement, 'the single most powerful man in the city'. He organized city clubs and Catholic associations similiar to those in Kinshasa. They were founded on ethnic lines, and under the leadership of well-educated Africans, who had personal connections with powerful chiefs in the home community. The clubs performed 'an important assimilative function for rural Africans, new to the city'.[28] They made it easier for the immigrants to be part of their new surroundings, as well as to maintain contact with the rural community back home.

Jamaa

'Adaptation' was the missiological term of the inter-war years, and the missionary concern – whether Catholic or Protestant – was to adapt the Christian message to the culture of the people. Fr Charles of Louvain went further, speaking of the 'mystique of adaptation'. 'In every missionary activity', he went on to say, 'the *approach*, as the English say, is of capital importance. If you have in your soul that supernatural sympathy then you will at the right moment be able to pronounce the words of life eternal.' In the footsteps of this Belgian Jesuit missiologist, the ordinary missionary in the field made an attempt to translate theological insight into practical action. A whole generation of Catholic and Protestant missionaries took to the mystique and technique of adaptation. They might express their honest ambition by collecting African proverbs, with the aim of introducing their sermons with a pithy local proverb, thereby placing the message in the appropriate context and *milieu*.

All this was good – as far as it went. But did it go far enough? A young Belgian Franciscan friar, Placide Tempels, working among the Luba in southern Shaba, asked himself that question, thereby changing his life and that of many of his Luba friends. Arriving in Shaba in 1933, he was to teach the catechism. This little volume had all the answers, but unfortunately not to the questions which the Luba were asking. Mgr de Hemptinne OSB, knew what to do with African culture: 'One must destroy the pagan in order to construct the Christian.'[29] The young Belgian missionary was not so sure about this approach. He wanted to *know* these people whom he was instructed to patiently catechize. 'What are your thoughts, your aspirations? You are like me and are searching for something.' Then he added: 'I put aside the catechism, my textbook, and I addressed myself in a direct way to [the Luba]'. Much later, his followers were to compare these new insights with the old methods of evangelization: 'In the past they taught us religion the same way that we learned French or algebra. But now, in the *Jamaa*, God has become alive.' Of course it had to be a Franciscan to make that attempt, foot-loose, free, ever-prepared to ask new questions and to see new visions. In this way a deep personal union between Western missionary and Christian Luba was established. A most astonishing movement of Church revival was conceived, the *Jamaa*.

In his exchange with the Africans, Tempels told them:

> In unveiling to me the depth of your human being, you have been 'fathers and mothers' to me, who have helped me to discover for myself the truth of my being. You have given me something. I have drunk and have eaten your words.

He was groping for an understanding of 'Bantu thought' and found it in three fundamental values: 'life, fecundity and vital union'.[30] In 1945 he published an interpretation of these ideas in *Bantu Philosophy*. Upon publication the book was widely acclaimed; later, it was severely criticized by leading authorities in the institutional Church.[31] When Fr Tempels went to Belgium on leave in 1945, he was advised not to return to Shaba.

The 1950s afforded new opportunities for a common search for 'life, fecundity and vital union', with an emphasis on the *bumuntu* (humanity) of Christ and that of the Virgin Mary. As Christ 'was one with Mary and mankind', the Luba Christian family of husband and wife, 'as *baba* and *mama* together as a unified couple', could likewise experience a living encounter with Christ, Mary and the priest.[32] 'By the grace of God, priest and *baba* and *mama* will become ONE.' It was even implied that the divine love between Christ and the Virgin Mary was an incestuous relationship, but exempt from the taboos that apply to ordinary human beings. This profound experience was strengthened by the role of 'prescribed dreams', sought after by participants, whether Luba Christians or European priests. In certain cases the dreamer might be led to vomit the threatening influences of sorcery and thus be purified.

Generally Zaïrean-Congolese Christianity, also in its Catholic form, was expected to give its members the coveted opportunity of higher education. In this as in other aspects, Tempels was different. He abhorred 'intellectualization' and felt that books and schooling were a barrier to the depth experience of life and religion that *Jamaa* represented. *Jamaa* was, of course, not a mass movement. It is estimated that the number of *Jamists* in the three main cities of Shaba was approximately 1,600. But what may have been lacking in quantity was compensated for in a quality of life which ordinary Christian membership did not always provide.[33]

Education

A pragmatic educational programme was part of Belgian colonial policy. The Belgian approach differed from the select elite, assimilationist thinking of the intellectual French. The Belgians were concerned with educating the Congolese masses through a broad long-term strategy, which implied insulating them from outside influences as well as limiting class differences within the literate population. Literacy was taught in the vernacular, with little use of French, and the post-primary curriculum was restricted to technical and vocational education.

At first, financial subsidies to schools were given only to Catholic missions. They alone managed the schools on behalf of the big companies: the Benedictines in Shaba for Union Minere; the Jesuits in Kwango for Lever Brothers; and the Marists in Kivu for the African Great Lakes Railway Company. After almost half a century of protest and proposals, the Protestants achieved a change of colonial policy. This breakthrough was notably achieved by the able leadership of the American missionary, Emory Ross, supported by Dr Oldham of the International Missionary Council. In 1946 the Belgian Government at last decided to support all missions with educational subventions at the same level. An extensive network of mission-directed bush schools spread throughout the country.

Between 40 and 60 per cent of African children were in school. In 1950 over 920,000 children were in educational institutions and, by 1958, the figure was one and half million, including 246,000 girls. In the central mission schools, girls were almost as numerous as boys. But in the traditional countryside, resistance against girls' education was strong, despite the efforts of the many Catholic sisters. What percentage of all these school-children managed to retain literacy throughout life and whether they had access to books for reading, are of course other matters. The whole emphasis in the schools was on lower-primary education: 87 per cent of the children were in primary schools, and it was taken for granted that they would not advance beyond this humble limit. The official colonial expectation as to their educability beyond the primary level was obviously limited.

For most of the period secondary education was neglected by the colonial authorities. In 1948, however, educational reform added a new dimension to schools in the country. It was accepted that an indigenous elite should be created, by establishing academic secondary schools. At its independence, Zaïre-Congo had two main categories of secondary schools, lower and higher, including fifty-eight vocational trade institutions. The total enrolment in 1960 at the secondary level was 29,000.

It should not be overlooked that, in fact, the Catholic Junior seminaries functioned as substitute secondary schools for most of the colonial period. After some years of study, a certain percentage of these seminarians decide that the priesthood was not for them, and either withdrew or were expelled from the seminary, to look for other jobs.

It was a positive surprise when, at the beginning of the 1950s, it was announced that the Catholics planned to found their own university college. Jesuit missionaries and particularly their leading man, Fr van Wing, took the initiative. In 1954 the University of Lovanium was opened near Kinshasa, a private Catholic institution related to the University of Louvain in Belgium.

In 1955 a state university was established at Lubumbashi in the southern mining region of the country. To begin with, Louvanium had seventy-seven African students and ten Europeans. In 1961 there were 350 students, of whom twenty-five were Belgians. Louvanium was a Catholic venture and the Protestants were seeking a solution of their own. At Kisangani (Stanleyville) a beginning on Protestant lines was made.

Political change came more rapidly and more radically than anybody had expected, and, certainly in the field of education, what had been achieved was a variation on the theme of 'too little too late'.

The Protestants

In her *Handbook of Protesant Churches, Missions and Communities 1878–1978*, Cecilia Irvine has with never-failing acumen registered all missionaries coming to Belgian Congo, including the new arrivals after 1920, and all the names of Western missionaries in their ever-changing combinations of moves and endeavours, with individuals from the USA, Great Britain and the Scandinavian countries.[34] Characteristically, no more than one or two African names are on the list, except for nineteen Africans and twenty-two Westerners killed in the 1964 rebellion.

The Kimbangu phenomenon, to which we shall return in a moment, had a muzzling effect on the work of the Baptists in the Lower Congo. They felt that they had to lie low and not speak too loudly, lest they also were taken for a prophet movement, thus running the risk of being banished to some remote corner of the vast country. A hush of decorous formality fell over their worship and fellowship, but the innate Baptist vigour and vitality could not be checked altogether. The most striking example of this was the development at Vanga (Kwango).

Vanga

The success of the American Baptists at Vanga (Kwango) was due to both sound planning from the start and courageous decentralization at a psychologically opportune moment in the development of the district. Dr William Leslie had begun his career in the older Baptist districts near Kinshasa, and when he began work in the new area of Kwango district, he insisted that the new work should be self-supporting from the start. The district comprised a population of about 250,000 in some 420 villages, over an area of about 8,500 square miles – the size of Israel. After a decade, only about 100 had been baptized, but there was gradual growth. About the same time as the mission started, big business reached the district with interests in the palm oil industry.

In 1931–32 Leslie's successor, Lewis Brown, decided to break with the central station idea and to decentralize the work. Prior to this, *all* the members and catechumens had had to make regular monthly trips from their local villages to the central station for worship and instruction. Instead, five new district centres were established under African pastors. It was a Western initiative but with the emphasis on African self-government and leadership. The work made rapid strides. In 1933 the number of baptisms passed 1,000 for the first time in any one year. Motor roads – such as they were – began to be laid about the same time, in order to facilitate the transport of palm nuts and palm oil. Transport thus also became easier for the Churches.

The decentralization programme of the Church was carried through with great determination. The Vanga mission soon had thirty Church centres and 420 catechetical centres in the villages. Each Church centre was under an African pastor, who had studied for two or three years at the Theological

College at Kimpese, following five or six years' training in mission school. Church membership was 26,000, with an additional 3,000 under discipline and about 8,000 catechumens under instruction. A great many schools were opened in the district, and apart from the 11,000 pupils receiving elementary instruction from the catechists in the 420 villages, there was a rapid growth of enrolment to the primary schools in the thirty Church centres. Throughout the period, the local Churches assumed financial responsibility for the schools. Self-support was the very principle of the work. In the ten years between 1945 and 1954 Church contributions in the area increased from 156,000 francs to over 3,300,000 francs. This covered the salaries of all the pastors, catechists and regional school teachers, as well as the buying of all books and supplies for the Churches and schools.

Factors which facilitated growth at Vanga should be noted. Thanks to the palm oil industry in the area, there was not as serious a dispersal of the male population as elsewhere, since the majority could remain in the area. Men comprised some 40 per cent of the active membership of the Vanga Church. Between 1912 and 1955 about 34,000 were baptized there and 26,000 of these remained resident members in good standing throughout the period. The success of the work can be ascribed to the ability of the Vanga Church to retain its graduates. In the decade 1945–55 not a single teacher trained at the Mission School at Kimpese had left the work of the Church, in spite of the attraction of work in the palm oil industry. For many years, all finance had been left in the hands of the African Church itself. Devolution to African leadership was the watchword.

Bolenge

Protestant connections with Bolenge were developed and widened for a number of reasons. As early as the turn of the century the American mission, the Disciples of Christ, had placed a medical doctor there. Herbert Smith, the ordained missionary, was a dynamic and enterprising man who ambitiously started the 'Congo Christian Institute' for the training of teachers and pastors. In 1949, the Bolenge Institute was enlarged and expanded with the help of staff from the Congo Bololo mission, the Covenant Church mission and the Swedish Baptist mission. This provided improved opportunities for Protestant education throughout the country. The motor boat from Bolenge could be taken as far as distant Mondobe, weeks away from the educational centre. Bolenge also had its own profitable sawmill. This mission-related Christian community became a trajectory for industrial activity, a springboard towards the modern world. By 1953 it had become apparent at Bolenge that the catechist had become much more of a real leader in the community than the administration-appointed chief.

In a primarily Catholic country such as Belgian Congo the Protestants had their own problems, not only a lack of privileges, but also due to an innate Protestant insecurity in ecclesiastical matters. The visit to Belgian Congo in 1953 by the IMC Commission on Theological Education – of which the present writer (B.Sr.) was a member – disclosed in certain cases a dissatisfaction common to many African pastors. They were, after all, ordained to be pastors in the Church of Christ, but it was not always clear that their Western colleagues, diffident as they preferred to be about ecclesiastical distinctions, realized the implications of this. It was resented when on the occasion of a local visit from the official Belgian administrator, the Westerner would introduce his colleague with the deprecatory formula: *voici notre catechiste*.[35]

Methodists in Shaba

At Likasi in Shaba (Katanga) Bishop Springer and his wife gave seven years of devoted service. This quintessentially American missionary couple were optimistic and energetic organizers. Helen Springer had been a 23-year-old recruit in Bishop William Taylor's ill-prepared and recklessly adventurous mission to 'West Africa' in the 1890s. Having survived those years of trial and hardship, she married John Springer. Through the continent-wide connections of the Methodist Church, she inspired the people of Shaba with her experience from women's movements further south. A motto of hers was: 'I don't like to hear that word "can't" used in that way: "it *can't* be done". What ought to be done, can be done.'[36]

In this part of Zaïre, around Likasi, the Methodists strengthened the educational system. In the 1940s, they started a seminary for catechists and pastors at Mulungwishi, initiating a long-term programme for the higher training of pastors and laymen. Some of the promising young men were sent to the Methodist training centre at Mutare (then called Umtali) in Zimbabwe or to the United States. One of those young Methodists to achieve later political notoriety in Shaba was Moise Tshombe.

Simon Kimbangu

Harris of Liberia gave less than two years, 1913–15, to what was to become the greatest Christian mass movement on the West Coast. Simon Kimbangu, 1889–1951, born at N'Kamba in the Lower Congo, was to give no more than five months in 1921 to the dramatic beginning of what was to become the biggest Independent Church in Africa, and of these five months only the first two were spent in freedom, while the latter three months were spent underground, until his arrest. The two men shared a common fundamental experience: a vision and revelation of God giving them a command to witness, to preach and to heal.

The colonial authorities arrested Kimbangu together with his twelve apostles, two medalled chiefs and a young prophetess. A military court in October 1921 condemned Kimbangu to 120 lashes and death. King Albert in Brussels commuted this to life imprisonment. Kimbangu spent thirty years in prison on the other side of the vast colony, at Lubumbashi (Elizabethville), far from home, until his death in 1951.

If one needs examples of colonial violence and inhumanity, here is one. For the Congolese, the Belgian colonial administration began badly and sadly. After the vicious years of the 'Congo rubber atrocities', came the sleeping sickness epidemic which reduced the population by half. After the First World War, there was drought and a serious economic crisis. In 1918–19 the continent-wide and world-wide 'Spanish Influenza' also hit the Congolese, and no hospital or medicine – if indeed one could find any – could help. All this caused a malaise in the masses; insecurity and hopelessness.

To Simon Kimbangu his Baptist alignment came naturally: to be a Protestant Christian in the Lower Congo was to be a Baptist. He joined the Baptist Missionary Society where he went to elementary school and was baptized. In view of a much discussed incident in the very last minute of the prophet's life, 12 October 1951, one must stress the fact of his baptism in July 1915 (and in an African river at that), near Ngomba-Lutete.

He served for some time as a teacher in a Baptist mission school, and it is known that he loved to recite the story about young David who miraculously killed the mighty Goliath. With an eye on later developments, one could say that the Protestant Mission was, unwittingly, already fostering the future leaders of the Independence movement.

Sometime later, the entire region was shaken by another epidemic, the Influenza ... 'and behold a pale horse, and his name that sat on him was Death'. The common phenomenon found throughout Africa was the Influenza pandemic of 1918–19, that came, at that very time, to George Khambule in Zululand and Eliyasi Vilakathi in Swaziland. Simon Kimbangu in Congo heard the Voice saying to him: 'I am Christ. My servants are unfaithful. I have chosen you to bear witness before your brethren and to convert them.'[37] But he did not feel prepared to obey the call and resisted for three years.

In April 1921, he visited a family in his home village at N'Kamba. He found the woman of the house suffering and felt constrained to pray for her with the laying on of his hands – and she was healed. It all began there. A *ngunza*, a healing prophet who could deal with afflictions of various kinds had arisen in their midst. The power of rumour took care of the rest. This prophet could heal and even raise from the dead, they said. Healing the blind, he followed the same procedure as that described in St John 9:6. The water used was from a spring at N'Kamba and the spring made N'Kamba a holy place, the new Jerusalem, which it remains today. All this made an enormous impression on the masses. People congregated from near and far. Dr John M. Janzen in his remarkable study, *The Quest for Therapy in Lower Zaïre*, has referred to 'the embeddedness everywhere of symptom and disease language', and Simon Kimbangu was an artist of this linguistic dimension of his own culture, much more so than any Western medical expert at the time could ever be.[38]

Embarassingly little is in fact known about the prophet's message. There were general references to 'the fall of man' and 'the sacrifice of Christ', and injunctions to throw away fetishes and learn to trust in God. There was the conventional ban on polygamy and dancing. During an exciting few weeks at N'Kamba the prophet was known to have sometimes been 'shaking' and speaking in tongues.

Kimbangu was 'relegated' to a prison in Lubumbashi (Elizabethville), totally isolated for his remaining thirty years from family and flock, and with him the first generation of local leaders was placed in custody in other centres. In the 1940s there were some 4–5,000 relegated in four agricultural labour camps in different parts of the country; the Ekafera 'colony' in the Equator province (also known as Coquilhatville Province), organized for particularly 'dangerous' prisoners.[39]

The effect of this procedure was astounding. Those few weeks of revelation by the prophet in 1921 had a far-reaching effect. In spite of the veil of silence in the population there were, in the 1930s and 1940s, recurrent rumours of a possible return of the prophet. Great excitement was caused by the apperance in 1935 of new arrivals in Kinshasa (Léopoldville) by new missionaries in white uniforms and with drums. Sure enough, the uniform displayed the highly potent letter, 'S', obviously a reference to the prophet's first name. The *S*alvation Army from Brussels was given more attention on entering the Belgian Congo than they could ever have expected.

There is a somewhat hazy description of the prophet's last day in the prison hospital. One account has it that a Sister Eudoxie gave the dying man baptism *in articulo mortis*. The traditional explanation is blurred, as we say, by the fact that the prophet's son, Joseph Diangienda (who later became the leader of the Church), arrived a few days later and challenged the highest ecclesiastical leader in the city, Bishop de Hemptinne, about this rumour. 'Monseigneur ne fit que dire mal de mon père, disant qu'il était mort dans de mauvais sentiments.' The 'fact' of a baptism *in extremis* is obviously open to different interpretations, not least because of the embarassment thus displayed.[40]

The faithful had to persevere in their underground movement, with its own secret communication network of a kind where Africans – not least Congolese – were of course much more astute than any colonial supervisors. On a visit to Kinshasa in 1953, B.Sr. happened to buy in the market a small wooden sculpture. On turning it over, he detected on the foot of the piece the two initials 'S.K.', no doubt a greeting to the unknown visitor from the Congolese catacombs.

Through contacts with the Belgian governor-general, the movement in 1958 secured recognition. In 1960 the body of the prophet was exhumed and brought to the 'New Jerusalem' of the Church, at N'Kamba, and placed in a specially built mausoleum. From that moment there followed an impressive growth and consolidation, contemporary with the independence of Zaïre. Under the leadership of Joseph Diangienda, an able staff assured the Church a remarkable administrative strength. A determined readjustment of the movement towards supposed 'orthodoxy' set in, sustained not least by a fascinating interest of this modern prophet movement in the very first origins of the Christian Church in Africa, looking towards Egypt and Ethiopia.[41]

ANGOLA

The favoured position of the Catholic Church continued to be strengthened and finally, in 1940, a concordat and missionary accord was signed by the President in Lisbon, Antonio de Oliveira Salazar. The privileged position of the Catholics as a 'national mission' was formalized while no Protestant mission, as a 'foreign' agency, could be granted 'legal personality'. Government subsidies to the Catholics increased from 200,000 US dollars in 1940 to 1,130,000 in 1960, but there were no government subsidies for Protestant schools or hospitals. The Protestant community was alienated and, at best, tolerated as a second-class community. It is therefore surprising to find that the 1950 census with 1,300,000 Catholics had no less than 560,000 Protestants.

Protestant missions found themselves in a new situation with the promulgation of the Government's 'Decree 77' of 1921. Until that time, these missions had been comparatively free to use Angolan languages for their publications and catechetical teaching, obviously a condition of fundamental importance for Protestant mission work. This now came to an end. The decree prohibited the publication of vernaculars except as parallel texts to the Portuguese language (so-called *diglot*). This raised considerable technical problems in the preparation of books and greatly increased the cost of publication.

The system of forced labour prevailed throughout the period. In an interview a French Holy Ghost Father who had arrived in Angola in 1935 recalled how the system of slavery lasted until the 1930s and how the Catholic mission until 1939 could use prisoners as labourers on their establishments. World War II also aggravated the situation for the Angolan communities. Under terms which remind one of King Leopold's Congo atrocities, Angolan blacks were to bring rubber – fifteen kilograms per person every fortnight, having to walk twenty to thirty kilometres to collect their rubber. In the hot valleys, the cotton workers were herded together under the supervision of the henchmen of private companies. In such circumstances the local mission work, for Protestants and Catholics alike, could only be a tough affair:

> My best catechist could not read and he did his teaching job by reciting the Catechism to the village crowd, all according to the blessed Catechism of Pope Pius IX of the 1850s, with its famous questions and definitions, 'Who is God? . . . ' He could also lead the group in singing. Every Sunday he would bring half of his village to the Catholic mission for exams at the central church – a ten mile walk through the hot valley. The following Sunday the catechist would bring the other half of the village together.[42]

The position of a catechist, utterly poor as he was, was a coveted privilege, eagerly competed for by the young men. As catechists they could avoid being drawn into the forced labour system and had a certain standing in the village.

In a difficult and sometimes threatening situation a highly competent group of American and Canadian missionaries – among whom must be mentioned Revd Currie, G. M. Childs and J. T. Tucker, together with African colleagues, built up a dynamic Congregational Church, with headquarters at Dondi. An ambitiously planned school system comprised a secondary school, called the Currie Institute at Dondi and the Means School for girls' education. At Dondi there was also a printing press. The personal libraries of Angolan pastors soon testified to the educational concern and intellectual horizons of the leaders of the Church (which was verified by B.Sr. during a visit in 1953). Protestant missions in Angola comprised British Baptists, Methodist Episcopal in the Mbundu country near the capital Luanda and American and Canadian Congregationalists in the south among the Ovimbundu.

16

SOUTHERN AFRICA

ZAMBIA

Zambia, or Northern Rhodesia as it was then called, was during the 1920s 'a poverty-stricken backveld Protectorate which only few people could have identified on the map'.[1] The population was entirely rural, many being involved in fishing on the lakes and along the Luapula and the Zambezi. Enterprising pioneers from Malawi, 'black Scots' from the East, became store-keepers in the bush and might sell their commodities on such markets as were springing up in connection with the emerging mines. After the years of Chartered Company rule, a 'Protectorate' was established in 1924, and in the 1920s copper was discovered, upon which the conditions and the outlook of the country was totally changed. Towards the end of the 1920s four large mines were being developed on the Copperbelt and at each of them a town soon emerged, with a small European and a large African population, with Ndola the main commercial centre. By the 1950s, 120,000 Africans and some 38,000 Europeans worked in the mines. Migrant labourers in their tens of thousands came from the rural communities of Zambia and Malawi, all coming for the very first time to a mine and to the city.

The Africans working in the mines were a floating population, staying for about a year or, if married, for nearly two years. The authorities having learned some lessons from the social situation on the Rand, made certain arrangements for the housing of married men and their families, but no plans were made for a permanent Black labour force. Urban communities might become a threat to White domination. The world economic crisis at the beginning of the 1930s also hampered any real attempts at the stabilization of a permanent labour force. It was a strange new world to which to come. In the 1930s silicosis and related diseases were on the increase, and statutory precautions for work in dangerous places were almost non-existent. Zambia could no longer be seen as just another wide open country with isolated communities and churches, hidden from one another in the distant corners of the land. Copper was a factor drawing the economies, the social services, and all other activities into one centre. To a more definite extent than any other country in Africa, one industry dominated everything else. The Churches wished to utilize this new structure for a more effective service in that one central area.

The Copperbelt became the dominant centre not only of finance and enterprise but also increasingly of racial discrimination. The European staff on the mines were to a large extent South African who, as a matter of course, carried the racial patterns of their own society northwards. However, these attitudes were not restricted to the mines alone. Even some mission stations in the sheltered countryside had their share of discrimination. A shocking example – more widely known because of the publication of the autobiography written by the African involved – was that reported by the outstanding Bemba pastor and Bible translator, Paul Bwernbya Mushindo. For forty years he worked daily at the Lubwa mission station together with a Scottish missionary, R. D. MacMinn, whose South African wife strictly followed the social patterns of the south. The two men of God, the one White and the other Black, were concerned with that most sacred missionary task, the interpretation of Holy Writ into the Bemba language and the most ambitious Bible translation enterprise in the country. In African society at large, Mushindo, thanks to his unique ability and personality, was highly regarded, but in all those decades he never entered MacMinn's house during the latter's tenancy. Their co-operation 'lacked lightsomeness and the authentic reciprocity of true friendship'.[2] Mushindo writes: 'MacMinn had a strong colour-bar as regards Africans. He would not share his food with an African Person. No African could use his cup to drink water out of. His wife could not shake an African's hand without gloves on her hands.'[3] Mushindo came to the tragic conclusion that 'there could never be true friendship between a White man and a Black man.'[4]

On the Copperbelt it did not take young converts, from Malawi or from Bemba country, a long time to adapt themselves to this challenging situation. Before the missions moved in with their schools and social centres, there had emerged a spontaneous African Christian movement. To his surprise A. J. Cross, a Baptist missionary active in the adjacent Lamba area, came upon some of these anonymous activities. He was an eye-witness, and wrote in 1929:

> At Ndola ... a self-supporting, self-governing native Church has grown up, and it is daily gaining in strength and experience. A very vigorous evangelistic work is carried on by the Church ... A body of elders governs the Church, these elders arrange the Church's evangelistic programme and the instruction of the converts besides the ordinary services of the Church. In

> the pastoral work they are particularly successful, and one has often been struck with the spiritual sagacity they have displayed in dealing with difficult cases of discipline, or in the restoration of erring members ... Two evangelists are engaged in full-time work entirely at the charges of the Church, otherwise all work ... is done voluntarily in the members' hard-earned leisure. [Thus] also at three or four of the other mines. Natives of widely varying tribes speaking different languages, whose ancestors were once hereditary enemies are making the grand Christian experience of working and worshipping in closest unity and co-operation ... [and] they give objective proof of their oneness in Christ Jesus.[5]

Missions had been active for a considerable time and were now represented by the successors of the Coillards and the Father Duponts. Significant names of leading missionaries were those of J. J. Doke, linguist and Baptist; E. W. Smith, ethnographer, Bible translator and Primitive Methodist; Alston May, bishop – UMCA; Walter Fisher, medical doctor and leader of an active 'Open Brethren' mission in the north-west; and Mabel Shaw, educationalist, Congregationalist and brilliant interpreter of the life of her girls' school at Mbereshi in the north of the country.

In the country as a whole there could fairly easily be established a co-operation between missions in terms of the conventional rules of comity, and this was observed by the non-Romans. The Roman Catholics on the other hand, with their two main societies, the White Fathers and the Jesuits, could not accept this imposition upon their activities.

The Anglican Church in Zambia with its High Church (UMCA) tradition – thus related to Anglicans in Malawi and Zanzibar – was, comparatively, a late-comer to the Zambian field. Other denominations had already established themselves locally and the Anglicans had to find new centres. Over the endless stretches of a sprawling country, Bishop Alston May (bishop 1914, died 1940) asked himself, 'What kind of unity and homogeneity could you find? The clergy and other members of the mission are in many instances known to one another by name alone.' The Bishop had to try to bind his diocese together:

> For twenty-six years he had no home [in order] that every corner of the Protectorate might be his home in turn. He lived in his boxes and was always on tour. In the early days on foot with carriers, later on he used a bicycle and later still, but long before the roads were really fit, he had a succession of commercial motor vans which he spared as little as he spared himself. The van of the moment contained everything he possessed and could possibly want. His clothes, books, vestments, sacred vessels, camp-bed, bath, tent, and cooking utensils ... He was a real Father in God to Black and White alike.[6]

Under the new Bishop R. S. Taylor, the Anglicans ordained eight deacons in 1943. The Wesleyan Methodists sent reinforcements from the south, the most interesting being Pastor D. M. Ramushu. He represented a family where the grandfather, a Wesleyan catechist in Transvaal, had been posted to Zimbabwe, founding an important family of preachers, teachers and other servants of the church. The appointment of the young D. M. Ramushu to Ndola in Zambia was thus a continuation of the line of ecclesiastical family succession in the service of three countries.

The influence of the mission and its entrenched traditions could at times and in places be felt as oppressive. Nowhere was this to be seen as clearly, and as unexpectedly, as in the famous showcase of Coillard's mission to the Lozi. In 1923 the Evangelical Mission Society in Paris felt constrained to enlist the opinion of an external examiner and that year sent one of the finest observers in the Protestant world, Maurice Léenhardt, French missionary (in New Caledonia) and sociologist. His report shows that after forty years of activity and with eight ordained foreign missionaries, the net result was 181 Christians on six mission stations, with 16 per cent of these under discipline. The church was entirely in the hands of the missionaries – 'withers away in the hands of the missionary' – for lack of vision and of a healthy strategy.[7] The question was whether the mission was to leave the field altogether, or to hand over part of it to neighbouring missions, or whether to attempt a change of strategy. Léenhardt had to tread warily – his authority in the Society of that time did not go unchallenged – but his analysis of the situation could only lead to a new start.

On the other side of the country, near the border with Malawi, the South African Dutch Reformed Mission was in control, with their particular ethos of hard work and racial segregation. How did an African church react to such a situation? Fortunately there is a remarkable study of this particular church by the late Gerdien Verstraelen-Gilhuis, *From Dutch Mission Church to Reformed Church in Zambia*, an outstanding study which interprets, sometimes with sensitive innuendo, how, in this missionary-controlled structure, the African propensity for initiative could make itself felt by gallant African pastors and irrepressible African women.[8]

Malawi's influence on Christian Zambia was to be seen not least in the shape of the 'welfare associations', the idea and inspiration of which came from the Livingstonia mission in Malawi and its Overtoun Institution. At the capital town of Livingstone in southern Zambia, at Broken Hill, Ndola, these welfare associations gathered together hundreds of young men. In each case the office bearers were men educated at Livingstonia. Their concerns varied: the creation of a library of their own; starting an African newspaper; a reconsideration of rules about native passes; and arrangements for travel by rail at night, all expressions of a Christian concern for their fellow men. They insisted: 'We were reading our Bible and knew that every human being was the same. Our idea of equality came from the Bible.'[9]

The missions – from the Catholics to the Open Brethren and the Adventists – all had their different approaches to 'the African soul', as they understood it. But no religious group came as close to that 'soul' as that called to life by Alice Lenshina. The illiterate prophetess herself is sometimes interpreted as if her experience was unique. To the student of South African charismatic groups an interesting point about her is the extent to which her fundamental revelation is a variation of that of a number of men and women in both South and West Africa: Her death-and-resurrection experience in 1953, which made her the privileged outsider, had many parallels in South Africa, not least at the time of the 'Spanish influenza' in 1918–19 (G. Khambule, E. Vilakathi, J. Masowe). Her injunction against sorcery and witchcraft, expressed in terms of a woman John the Baptist:

> Shout to the desert, shout
> Leave beer and witchcraft.

Her claim to have been given by Jesus another Bible, the real true one; and her call to the faithful to flee to her Zion:

> You, the mountain of refuge which stands in this world,
> you, the highest mountain . . .
> you who have climbed this mountain
> rejoice, sing.
> You are fortunate, you have found the refuge.

All these characteristics have vivid parallels elsewhere. Of course it was not a matter of 'loan', but what psychological laws were at work in her and the others I cannot say.[10] Her appeal had an electrifying effect. She began in a quiet, almost subdued way and saw to it that soon after her death–resurrection she was baptized in the Presbyterian Church, by her neighbour, the Revd Paul Mushindo, whom we have already met. However, soon her movement spread like wildfire – an apt image. Both Catholics and Presbyterians in the region saw their congregations depleted and before too long the hurricane reached the Copperbelt. The movement lasted some ten years, 1953–64, when it came to a bloody end in the 'Lumpa War' against the army and police of the new state of Zambia.

In spite of its strength Lenshina's movement was geographically and tribally limited. Jehovah's Witnesses, on the other hand, reached out to all the corners of Zambia. The beginnings were to be found in Malawi, but soon it was from southern Rhodesia that the most powerful Witness influence was felt. Again the same factor which we have recognized for the nineteenth- and the twentieth-century spread of religious ideas was at work. 'Labour migrants returning home from the Southern Rhodesia mines carried the Watch Tower teachings across the Zambezi to Northern Rhodesia where by the end of the 1930s nearly every part of the country was familiar with the gospel of the Black millennium.'[11]

It took the mission a comparatively long time to realize the nature of the social evolution and its implications for the Church. In 1936 the Anglicans still felt that all baptisms should be performed 'back home', on the rural mission stations, rather than in the mining township chapel. In the 1920s Dr J. H. Oldham and the International Missionary Council had been concerned with Kenya. They now turned to the Copperbelt by sending a highly competent commission of enquiry to suggest a line of action for the churches. The report, *Modern Industry and the African*, led to the formation of a 'United Missions on the Copperbelt', 1936–55.[12] This was the name for a team of co-operating missionaries, the leadership among whom was taken by Presbyterians, Baptists and Congregationalists. However, the practical concerns of the team, promoting education and social welfare, suggested wider participation and the mission, at least temporarily, comprised everybody from Anglo-Catholic to the Brethren. This also meant a challenge to the missions to send members of their staff, Africans and Westerners, to the emerging Christian communities at the mines. The common concerns of the United Mission helped to stimulate the idea of a United Church for Zambia.

The complicated, long drawn out Church union debate in Zambia can be summed up in a few words. Beginning with a Presbyterian–Reformed union in Malawi in 1924, the process of unification also involved Zambian Congregationalists, Methodists and Lozi Reformed: all combining in the United Church of Zambia in 1965. There were, however, impeding factors at work. The Methodists hesitated for a long time. Here again the British situation played a role: this was the time for Anglican–Methodist union negotiations in Britain and the discussions in Africa could not, it was felt, be allowed to jeopardize the final outcome on *that* front. However, in 1965 Methodists too were able to give their consent to the Plan of Union. Another factor was the spiritual climate of the day. These were the years of intense Church union debate in India and Sri Lanka, leading in 1947 to the formation of the Church of South India. In South India the Anglicans had been the leading partner and most of them were related to the 'Low Church'

CMS. In Zambia, Anglicans were represented by the High Church UMCA, which took a critical view of the South India scheme. This attitude influenced the Anglo–Catholics in Zambia, its Bishop and local leaders, to the extent that while they took an active part in common social services, they did not participate in the union negotiations or in the final United Church. The scope of Zambian union was therefore 'nonconformist'.

Church Union in Malawi and Zambia has been an ongoing process for at least forty years. It has been noted that some churches, for different reasons, kept away from the actual Union process: the Anglo-Catholics, the South African General Mission, the Plymouth Brethren (Christian Mission in Many Lands), the Baptists and the African Reformed Church. There were differences in Church policy: language issues, concerning interpretation of conference 'procedures from English to Bemba and *vice versa*';[13] racial issues: a Dutch Reformed practice, inherited from the so-called 'Mother Church' in South Africa, insisted on separate seating at meals in conference. Malawi and Zambia were both involved and Malawi had a longer Church history and at the time a more determined African participation. While Africans were never effectively represented in the Union negotiations, there was also no Zambian counterpart to Bishop Azariah's leading role in the South Indian church union negotiations.

Until about 1945 the Union proceedings seemed to be geared exclusively towards Bantu-speaking congregations, although they were not represented on the Union committee. After World War II, however, there was a change in the theological climate, under the influence of the ecumenical debate in the West, and this led to an increasing number of participants insisting on a multi-racial Church. On the Copperbelt no less than seven different European Free Church groups had established their own worship patterns, although the total membership in the 1950s was less than 1,440. In each case they represented a highly mobile, white membership, with sometimes limited concern for the ecclesiastical problems involved. One effect of the union negotiations was the stimulus it gave to theological education and the ordination of African pastors. Zambia had lagged behind on this score. In 1925 its eleven non-Roman missions had, with over 1,500 catechists and teachers, only four ordained men, three of whom were Wesleyan Methodists. In 1938 these missions with about 600 catechists had eighteen ordained men, with the Anglicans and the Methodists in the lead: the eighteen also included six ordained Seventh Day Adventist preachers.

With all the evidence of these more or less established ecclesiastical bodies in the territory – Roman Catholic, Anglo-Catholic, Methodists and Presbyterian–Reformed – the sprawling country also made room for less known missions tucked away on the periphery, in the far corners of the land. Two of these missions must be mentioned here.

The Kalene Hill Mission among the Lunda, in the north-west was founded by Dr Walter Fisher and related to the 'Brethren' tradition in Africa. Fisher was close to F. S. Arnot (1858–1914), the famous missionary traveller who had walked through Central Africa, Angola and Shaba (Katanga) and made a great impression wherever he went, and was 'in many respects ... [the] true spiritual successor' of David Livingstone.[14] The Arnot connection led Dr Fisher to begin his work in Angola. In fact, for many years he straddled the frontier regions between Angola and Zambia until he settled in the Kalene Hills in 1906. The region was one of the most isolated, sparsely populated areas of Zambia, but the arrival of the Fisher family – the tightly knit kin aspect has remained a fundamental feature of the Open Brethren mission – initiated a social revolution among the Lunda. Large numbers of Lunda settled near the mission from which they could obtain both traditional and new crops. The neighbouring Ndembu community, exposed to brutal treatment by colonial administrators, fled to the Kalene mission, which thus reproduced the general theme of the mission station as a refuge, in this case, not only for individuals but also for groups of people.

Some of the village chiefs began to pay tribute to the mission as a sign of submission. The mission hospital became a social centre for the population, and today the hospital has 200 beds, with two doctors and other staff, Black and White. Fisher's sons and daughters became devoted members of the mission team, founding orphanages, expanding the agricultural enterprises, doing Bible translation work. Singleton Fisher, an inspired preacher, translated the Bible into Lunda. While the north-west region as such functioned as a labour reservoir for the copper mines – in 1939, 33 per cent of the adult male population at Kasembe were migrant labourers away from the villages – the Brethren community at Kalene, with outposts, offered fine on-the-spot opportunities for agriculture and some home industry.

The Open Brethren's spirituality informed the groups. There was adult baptism by immersion for those who were admitted after the elders had ascertained that true conversion had taken place. After baptism the convert was admitted to the 'Breaking of Bread' services. The elders, as a matter of course not ordained, were the pillars of the congregation. The Bible was and is the centre of common worship while the idea of a Church year was reduced to Christmas, Good Friday and Easter Day, 'but not in a formal way'.[15] Kalene may have appeared as peripheral but the contact centres in the Copperbelt were maintained when one of the Fisher sons became a doctor there. There are in Zambia 400 Open Brethren 'assemblies' with some 9,000 baptized believers. In Zimbabwe there are twenty groups of baptized believers, and in Natal, 2,000 'believers in fellowship'.[16]

Max Weber, the German sociologist, held the view that there is a correlation between the ethic of ascetic Protestantism and capitalism. Some of the Zambian religious groups seem to live up convincingly to Weber's expectations and definitions. The Seventh Day Adventists in southern Zambia illustrate this thesis. In 1903, an Adventist leader, Pastor Anderson, started work at Rusangu in the south, where he obtained 5,000 acres of land for his church. Soon he and his African co-workers showed that they could make full use of the opportunity. The introduction of the plough and draught-oxen revolutionized local farming. This also affected the primary school. Six hours in school were devoted to agriculture, cattle farming and carpentry training: it was 'in every sense an Industrial Mission'.[17] This kind of innovation had been attempted by other missions but without great success. The tight social control and solidarity of this apocalyptic Adventist group – 'Jesus is coming soon' – made it succeed. The emergence of the Copperbelt and its need for cereals gave a fresh boost to African farming and to none more so than to the Adventist congregation.

However, with mounting resources and self-reliance the African group became increasingly critical of missionary control. They decided to leave the Rusangu fellowship and established themselves on a new basis at the Keemba Hills. A measure of their success and the prestige that this gave them was the fact that when, in 1936, the Government introduced maize control quotas (in order to protect White farmers from African competition), the Keemba Hill farmers, 'because of the quality and volume of their maize output, were allowed the unique privilege of participation in the European [grain] pool'.[18]

The planning, co-operation and drive of these men helped them to new success. In 1937, the Northern Rhodesian African Congress was formed in the southern part of the country. Four of the five founding members were Adventists and the group could be counted on to support the rising nationalist movement. They were all lay preachers used to public speaking, a fact which informed their Bible exposition in church and their arguments in the nationalist struggle. Together with the Anglo–Catholic UMCA, in 1949 the Adventists had the highest number of ordained men. Very soon they were individually and collectively involved in the efforts of the African National Congress. Here was a combination of religious inspiration, financial acumen and political vision, which made this African group particularly interesting and impressive.

Among the Zambian Churches the African Methodist Episcopal Church (AME) presents, from certain points of view, the most interesting profile. In the 1950s it emerged as 'virtually the established Church of the Congress Party'.[19] Kenneth Kaunda, the General Secretary of Congress was a local preacher and choir leader at the Lusaka AME Church – he was later to become a member of the United Church of Zambia, whose ecumenical programme was close to his heart. Other prominent Congress leaders also took a leading position in the AME. If the Churches related to European missions seemed to take an unduly long time over the Africanization issue, the AME, by definition, appeared fully Africanized. A statistical survey of 1971 placed the AME as the third in size after the Jehovah's Witnesses and the Roman Catholic Church. The future of the AME seemed fully assured.

Yet, what seemed to be the Church's greatest strength could, in certain circumstances, stand out as its most intriguing weakness, for the AME was also a mission-related Church, only it was related to a Black Church in the United States. For decades, on the Rand, this connection had been felt to be a problem, and it was now increasingly seen as such in Zambia. When the other Churches increased their Africanization programme, the AME, ironically, appeared as a Church with a non-Zambian bishop, appointed by Americans and in certain cases functioning as no more than an *episcopus in absentia*, far from the hustle of the local Zambian situation. Also in Zambia the AME had its own built-in tensions: between a programme of pan-African nationalism and a concern for Zambian nationalism, and between certain community interests, such as between Lozi and Bemba. In 1974 these concerns led to a Zambian break from the AME, in the formation of the African Methodist Independent Church (AMI).[20]

MALAWI

Political preferences

With the *pax Britannica* the future of the 'Protectorate' seemed bright. The capital at Blantyre – then at Zomba, and finally at Lilongwe – governed an enterprising population. Unfortunately early promises in the economic field were not fulfilled. The lack of modern infrastructure, particularly communications, made local efforts generally ineffectual. The situation is summarized in the title of an economic study, 'The making of an imperial slum: Nyasaland and its railways 1895–1935'.[21] Ultimately, it was as migrant labour – to the Copperbelt and the Rand – that the majority of men had to earn money for their families – and the hut tax. 'At least forty-five per cent of adult males were absent from the Mzimba district and sixty per cent from West Nyasa.'[22] From this point we shall now describe developments in Malawi until 1960, and shall later consider these as an integral part of events in the wider region of Central Africa. The idea of a closer union between the British Central African territories had been under discussion by politicians since the 1920s. Under pressure from White settlers in the two Rhodesias, but against emphatic and bitter opposition from emerging African nationalist opinion, the Federation of Rhodesia and Nyasaland was pushed through in 1953. Salisbury (now Harare) became the capital of the new political formation thus emphasizing the leading role of the White-controlled industrial and farming power of Southern Rhodesia, while both Northern Rhodesia and Nyasaland were left behind in many respects, such as educational opportunities.

Change of missionary focus

With the 1920s there was a shift of emphasis on the Malawian Church scene, geographically and denominationally, from the north to the south. Prior to the 1920s in the north, Dr Laws' Livingstonia had been the leading institution symbolising the undisputed dominance of Protestant, or more specifically, Reformed, churchmanship in the country. In this new period the Presbyterian Church's creative evangelistic outreach extended into Zambia and as far as the Rand. In the south a dramatic development took place under Catholic leadership and inspiration. The Lomwe had, as previously mentioned, arrived as refugees, unwanted – except that the mission welcomed them. (A study of Lomwe 'mentality' – of a refugee people made to feel inferior as a second-class community, and anxious to overcome this social handicap – would be worthwhile.) The mission also consisted of late-comers on the scene – the Montfort Fathers arrived in 1901 – and was at first less than popular in the established African and European communities. The combination of refugee community and mission was powerful. The sheer numbers illustrate this point. There was an annual increase of between 2,000 and 3,000 baptized. From zero in the 1920s the membership had in 1970 risen to 180,000 Catholics or 26 per cent of the total population in the district. Dr Ian Linden writes: 'The [Catholic] Church's neophytes were more than three-quarters new arrivals in the area.' The question to Churches in the region was which of them would be mobile enough to meet the needs of these newly arrived groups. Looking at subsequent development, he states: 'Today the [Roman] Catholic Church in the southern region of

Malawi might without exaggeration be called the "*Alomwe*" Church', with a strong Lomwe majority.[23] The development illustrates, once again, a point repeatedly made in this book for the nineteenth century; how a dejected refugee community meeting with a welcoming mission could, by way of chapel and school, walk into a new future.

At first there was considerable African opposition to the education drive. Parents who sent their children to school would find that during the night big stones or wooden poles had been placed at their doors as a warning. Even so, the 'Three R's' combined with singing and church festivals held appeal. There was an affinity between these Montfort Fathers and their flock. The local Church seemed as 'a remarkable replica of the one [which the missionaries] had left behind in Limburg, Quebec or Brittany; it was profoundly conservative and made up largely of peasants.'[24]

Here, as elsewhere in Africa, the visit of Archbishop (later Cardinal) Hinsley meant raising the sights to higher education. In 1942 the Catholics started their secondary school at Zomba; a great challenge as the 'Government assisted schools tended to undermine the foundation of that peasant church.'[25]

Another international visitor bringing inspiration to the local Church was the Irish woman Edel Quinn, founder of the Legion of Mary in Africa who visited Malawi in 1940–41.[26] In 1956 there were no more than eleven branches of the Legion of Mary. But as the Montfort Fathers, an order of 'Teaching Brothers' – under the dynamic leadership of Dr Martin Schoffeleeers, applied themselves to the task, in three years this figure rose to fifty-six.

Livingstonia

Dr Laws' undisputed authority was now called into question and, what is more, by his own people. The charismatic Donald Fraser opposed the elitist emphasis on the Overtoun Institution; he aimed at a mass education rather than intensive education of the few. And W. P. Young, who was to succeed Laws as head of Livingstonia, insisted that the institution was 'making the College here like the Church, a purely European thing quite unrelated to Africa'.[27]

Laws the visionary had been decades ahead of his time. His able colleagues felt that they must serve the needs of the present day, instead of anticipating possible developments. 'The time was not quite ripe yet for such a full development', was the theme repeated here as in so many other African countries. In the transitional period between the wars, the Phelps

Stokes educational philosophy inspired village education for the masses. Yet, very soon the Malawians' clamour for something more than the 'Three R's' and the Catechism – namely, secondary education – was to be heard loudly in the land. It was all a matter of deciding, in the 1920s and 1930s, what time it was in Central Africa. Laws, at least, knew that it was high time.

Transition in Livingstonia

In the 1920s Livingstonia still dominated the educational establishment. The layout of the place with its avenues and brick buildings reminded the visitor of Aberdeen or Edinburgh. There was a 'Madoda Avenue' for the houses of senior Africans and different quarters for Whites and Blacks – not until 1947 was this 'racial zoning' recognized for what it was – and subsequently abandoned. It took another ten years for the staff to meet on first-name terms, all indications of a common atmosphere in Southern Africa. Livingstonia's students were able to find positions in mines and schools in Zambia. 'A Livingstonia leaving-certificate was a passport to continuing privilege.' In Malawi many of them volunteered as Church elders.

However it was not always easy to retain the loyalty and services of the alumni. The Protestant institution had imparted a sense of freedom which in certain cases complicated matters. A widely noticed case was that of Levi Mumba, staff member at Livingstonia for the first years of the century, and a man of initiative who served as Secretary of the North Nyasaland Native Association from 1910–12. He became the first president of the Nyasaland African Congress. Increasingly, he felt restricted by the mission. The salary was too low and there were marriage problems. Taken together these factors made him cut his ties with the institution and, apparently, also with the Church. He thus became, possibly, the earliest Central Africa, example of the intellectual taking an individual stand for independence from the Church.

For the Presbyterian institutions in the educational and medical field one must not forget the evangelistic work at grass-roots level. This also applies to the Reformed Church in the Central Province. The emphasis of this Afrikaner mission was on agriculture; at the same time it was part of the school programme to resist the English language as far as possible. Every African Christian at Mvera and Nkoma was required to have a garden for better farming. The mission played a central role in promoting modern agriculture in the Central Province. The new centre at Nkoma soon became a little town with post office, hospital, nurses' training, teachers' training, theological college, printing office, carpentry workshop and commercial shop.[28]

Attempts at Church union

While Protestant union negotiations are best considered within the framework of the Churches in Central Africa as a whole, there must be some brief reference to developments within Malawi itself. Again the central figure is Dr Laws who as early as 1893 drew the outline of a 'Presbyterian Church of Central Africa'. In 1904 the two Scottish Presbyterian missions formed a common synod for the African congregations, 'the Presbyterian Church of Central Africa'. They invited the South African Dutch Reformed missions in Malawi and Southern Rhodesia to join.

This proved complicated because the two Synods of the Dutch Reformed Church (DRC) had different home mission constituencies in South Africa. The mission in Malawi was related to the Cape Synod, which was co-operative and encouraged the union which took place in 1924. The mission in Southern Rhodesia (where many Malawians went to find work) was related to the Orange Free State Synod, and its general secretary, J. G. Strydom, effectively blocked any union. According to Strydom they were probably theologically 'liberal' when it came to the infallibility of the word of God, the Atonement and – that new scare in South Africa in the 1920s – the idea of evolution. These were the supposedly theological reasons for non-cooperation. There was also a non-theological consideration of tragic significance: the racial factor, with rejection of commensality at synods. With all their claims to possess Biblical orthodoxy, they did not extend this orthodoxy to what in the eyes of the African Christians was fundamental: human fellowship in the name of Jesus Christ. The mission council in Bloemfontein thus issued its *non possumus* in familiar terms: 'The Synod of the Church of the Free State has resolved not to allow their Presbytery in Rhodesia to unite with the Church of Central Africa, Presbyterian . . . they will not unite with another body which does not have a positive Reformed Confession.'

In the local congregations, the pastor, elders and evangelists went about their tasks. A leading personality was the Revd Harry Kambwiri Matecheta, a Yao connected to the Presbyterian mission at Blantyre, who served among the southern Ngoni for forty years. In 1933 he was elected moderator of his Church. He was ably assisted by his wife. Her last words on her deathbed sum up the faith and aspiration of a whole generation of forgotten women in the church with simple eloquence: 'My way is open. I am glad my children are all educated, married and settled. I am not worried. I have done my duty.'

ZIMBABWE

The Two Nations is the discerning title of Richard Gray's book of 1960 on British Central Africa.[29] Not one nation but two, segregated from each other, Black and White. The tiny White minority at the beginning of the 1920s managed to avoid being integrated into a 'greater South Africa'. Yet, the complacent Rhodesian assertion 'This is not South Africa, you know', could not hide the racial discrimination in the country. If it was not South Africa, it was deceptively like it. As the towns and the cities emerged, Blacks were given to understand that they did not really belong to this world of the Whites. They should therefore keep off the pavement and walk in the street.

Political development 1923–79

The political development of the country has been highly dramatic. A brief outline of a few significant facts shows that 'Southern Rhodesia' became a British colony in 1923, with a governor appointed by London and with an assembly and a government elected by Rhodesian settlers. Under the influence of the rising economic power of Northern Rhodesia and its Copperbelt, the White settler minority campaigned for a unity of the 'two Rhodesias' and Nyasaland (Malawi), and this in spite of strong opposition from African opinion in the three countries, especially from Malawi ('Don't sell us for copper').[30] A Federation of Central Africa was forced through in 1953, with its capital in Salisbury (Harare). This was the time of an emerging African nationalism, stimulated not least by the co-operation of the White prime minister, ex-missionary Garfield Todd, but rejected by the powerful White establishment, a situation which led to Todd's resignation.

The African National Congress with Joshua Nkomo as president became the centre of African political ambitions, leading to the detention of a number of ANC men at Gokwe, a hot 'Siberia' in the Zambezi valley. The Whites gathered their forces in a 'Rhodesian Front' while Nkomo organized his own referendum in which 467,189 Africans voted against the White constitution and only 584 for it. The Federation could no longer hold together and in 1964 Southern Rhodesia announced a 'Unilateral Declaration of Independence' – UDI – with Ian D. Smith as prime minister. Against this illegitimate regime African nationalism rose with immense strength, with strikes in the mines, and 'freedom fighters' mobilized both inside and outside the country, and a silent but very effective witness of prison detainees isolated in their cells for longer or shorter periods of time.

The African demand for 'majority rule' led to an agreement in 1978 signed by Abel Muzorewa, Methodist bishop, who had become president of a united ANC in 1974, the Revd Ndabaningi Sithole, Congregationalist pastor, Senator Jeremiah Chirau and Ian D. Smith. This obviously provisional combination was soon overthrown and in 1980 Robert Mugabe was elected prime minster with an overwhelming majority and the Independence of Zimbabwe became a fact.

Land and inequality

The 'structural racism' of the social and political system was brashly demonstrated by the promulgation in 1930–31 of the Land Apportionment Act. This divided up the country and gave 50,000 Whites (a number which later rose to a peak of 250,000) approximately 49 million acres of the best land, while 1 million Blacks (later rising to 6 million) were allowed 29 million acres, much of it useless land in the low veld. When a government native commissioner, P. Nielsen, faced the problem of apathy in the reserves and the radical failure of White rule in 1925, he had to ask himself: 'It is true that we have given them peace, but is that enough?'[31]

Nielsen had overlooked the fact that even in the 1920s there were determined efforts by Africans themselves to remedy the situation. These early political efforts must be seen as forerunners of subsequent large-scale political organizations, led by such men as Joshua Nkomo, Ndabaningi Sithole and others. The early organizations were to some extent inspired by associates from neighbouring countries, both north and south.

The Rhodesian Bantu Voters Association, founded in 1923 by the Zulu Anglican teacher Abraham Twala, was one such body devised to promote African participation in political life. The great propagandist was a woman, Martha Ngano, of the Mfengu community from the Cape, also a teacher, connected to the Apostolic Faith Mission. Being a woman she may at that time have been regarded as an outsider and her Mfengu affiliation no doubt strengthened that impression. However, if these points were handicaps, they simultaneously lent force to her impassioned message. Being an outsider, she was determined to see the rural situation for herself and in public meetings she was soon recognized as a spokeswomen for the rural masses as well as for the Bulawayo membership. Parallel with Twala's association was the Rhodesian Native Association (formed in 1924), whose president, J. S. Mokwile, was a former teacher in the Dutch Reformed Church and the son of a Sotho evangelist. He had studied at the Tiger Kloof Institution in South Africa, and his new organization invariably gave the impression of Christian participation.

The contacts with South Africa for higher education – including theological training – and for work, prior to the Afrikaner political take-over in 1948, deserve to be mentioned. The role of the Mfengu as Black South African settlers in the Bulawayo region corresponded with southern Rhodesian migrant labour to the Rand – and in both directions the Churches were affected. This applies not least to the Independent Churches, their emergence and their widening horizon. They had been exported to Zimbabwe, by men and women baptized in Zionist rivulets near Alexandra or Pimville on the Witwatersrand. The contact with charismatics on the Rand must also be understood in terms of the Rand Zionists' ambition at that time to take advantage of their seemingly unlimited potential in the regions beyond, up north.

Although the vast majority of Africans were employed on European farms, or worked in their own reserves, the mining industries – gold, coal, asbestos – attracted increasing numbers of workers. In 1919 the mine labour force was 30,000, rising to 90,000 in 1937, with the men mostly 'Shangaan' from Mozambique or others from Malawi and all recruited by the Rhodesian Native Labour Bureau. For more than one reason mine work was called *chibaro* by the labourers, meaning 'slave labour' or 'forced labour', and this term is also the title of Professor van Onselen's well-known book on southern Rhodesian mine labour. The wages were kept low: they were constantly adjusted downwards for the years 1912–33. With harsh, inhuman treatment often leading to accidents and illness, there was little in the way of consolation for a poor man's soul, except for the message of the Watch Tower preachers in the compounds, such as this one in Bulawayo in 1923:

> The end of the world is near. Goliath was a very strong man but David, a small man, killed him. This will be the same with us and the White people. You must hold fast for the kingdom is near. This time the White people will come behind us, but they will soon be our servants as they have had good times in this world.[32]

The 1920s in Zimbabwe were dominated by the land question, until in 1930 the small White minority forced through their Land Apportionment Act. This had been met with resolute opposition from missionary circles, and particularly from two men: John White, Methodist and chairman of the Rhodesian missionary conference, and Arthur Shearly Cripps, Anglo-Catholic, poet and visionary.

The mission schools

From the late 1920s the mission primary schools were closely integrated into the government programme. Nowhere in British Africa was this tendency as marked as in Southern Rhodesia. The ordained missionary served as a superintendent of schools supported by government which paid the travel expenses of the missionary's inspection tours. Church interests were provided for in that the ordained superintendent of schools was, at the end of the school inspection, free to call together a Church meeting. With some thirty to forty schools in his district to be inspected regularly four times a year, this meant that the missionary was virtually tied to the government system with links provided by comparatively generous government grants.

There was opposition. The Anglican priest Arthur Shearly Cripps firmly refused to have any truck with the government system. Frank Noble, Methodist and president of the general missionary conference insisted that government take over the village primary schools while the missions keep their secondary schools, and the Lutheran missionary-cum-ethnologist Harald von Sicard, pleaded for a more definite focus on evangelism. The majority of missionaries however went along with the government provisions aware of the economic advantages of the system, but less aware of the fact that the image of the ordained man's *raison d'être* was bound to his school function which was eventually to be challenged by a new generation of African pastors.

Two types of Church

There were two types of mission-related Church. Some were comprehensive in reaching out across the entire country to both Black and White. They were represented by Anglicans, Catholics and Wesleyan Methodists. The other type were geographically limited and concentrated almost entirely on the African population.

With their headquarters and cathedrals newly built during the 1920s in the capital Harare, both Anglican and Catholics gave the impression of being solidly established. The bishops, the Catholic Aston Chichester, a Jesuit, and the Anglican Edward Francis Paget, vindicated this impression. Both were descendants of British aristocracy and represented their Churches in the magnificent manner of the colonial epoch, entirely at home with governors and prime ministers, and in the end they both became archbishops. In line with this Church establishment, the Methodists also built their Holy Trinity Church just behind the parliament buildings, claiming that they too had a share in the development of the Colony with its 'responsible self-government'.

Anglican work in Zimbabwe (then Southern Rhodesia) was largely shaped by the men and women of the Community of the Resurrection, with their centre at St Augustine, Penhalonga. The church at St Augustine, dedicated in 1932, is renowned for its 'Romanesque' architectural style and was constructed by Fr Robert Baker to serve the liturgical usage of the time. It became the centre for theological training, and an African women's community called the Sisters of the Holy Name, had an orphanage, and ran some forty outstations.[33] The art school led by Fr Edward Paterson at Cyrene, near Bulawayo, should be mentioned for its imaginative work. The Sisters of the Resurrection, from Grahamstown in the Cape, extended the Community of the Resurrection's work in the main centres of the country such as Harare, Bulawayo and Rusape.

It is a measure of the transcendental character of the Christian religion that the best-known of the Anglican priests was the least representative of Anglicanism as an institution: Arthur Shearly Cripps – 'God's Irregular', celibate priest and self-forgetting ascetic.[34] At a time when denominationalism was rife, with its claims and counter-claims, it was seen as a beacon in the dark when Cripps the Anglo-Catholic established a life-long friendship with John White, the Wesleyan leader. Their co-operation in the momentous political issues of the day is one of the noble pages of the Church's history in the first half of the twentieth century. Cripps also had close ecclesiastical relations with the Dutch Reformed dominee, A. J. Liebenberg.

At the Anglican Penhalonga the first, and private, initiative was taken to start an African secondary school. This was again due to the vision of the Community of the Resurrection Fathers and their member Fr Alban Winter. He did not receive much encouragement from government circles but managed to find support within his own mission society, the SPG, and the Beit Trust. In 1939 a first batch of six students was admitted to the new secondary school. As a good Englishman Fr Winter aimed at taking the students to a Cambridge School Certificate but owing to war conditions this proved unattainable and they had to settle for a South African Junior Certificate instead.[35]

Barbara Tredgold, Anglican church worker, was personally influenced by Dorothy Maud's Ekutuleni ('House of Peace-Making') fellowship in Sophiatown, Johannesburg, where she served for a few years. In Harare she managed to create a similar community, Runyurano, with White women co-workers and young Africans, all engaged in social service sustained by Anglo-Catholic worship.

A conflict between an ecclesiastical institution and an African charismatic body is related to the Anglican story. In the 1920s Francis Nyabadza, a Shona, became an Anglican catechist. Encouraged by the local missionary he founded a lay guild dedicated to St Francis of Assisi, a community of devoted Anglicans – eventually comprising some 150 men and women. They pledged to participate regularly in daily morning and evening worship and to abstain from smoking and drinking. Nyabadza was soon found to possess gifts of prophecy and healing and a faculty for significant dreams. In such a dream he saw the shape of his future church building, and according to his dream image, an impressive structure was raised with its altar section surprisingly like an iconostasis (and this it would seem, without the dreamer ever having seen an Orthodox Church). To ordinary Anglican Africans these claims seemed preposterous and their antipathy was not lessened when in 1935 the Anglican bishop, Edward F. Paget, generously asked for admission as a member of the guild, proclaiming it to be 'a branch of the Anglican Church'. The bishop went further than that. Nyabadza was given to understand that he was 'authorized and ordained as a priest in this Church'. Later, however, this claim could not be upheld and Francis Nyabadza in 1942 officially withdrew from the Anglican Church, a victim, perhaps, of the struggle in a bishop's heart between personal generosity and Church officialdom. Francis Nyabadza died in 1951 and was succeeded by his son Basil Nyabadza, who was killed by the Rhodesian security forces in 1977. Basil's son, Francis, became the new leader carrying on the work 'by evil report and good report'. He has been sustained not only by his faithful African community but also by the extraordinary backing of liberal European friends of the guild and of Zimbabwe.

Methodists

The Wesleyan Methodists were also 'a nation-wide Church with a double mandate', caring for both Black and White. Their finest time at the national level was, perhaps, the 1920s, under John White's leadership. White (1866–1933) was one of the old timers in the country, having arrived in 1894. He was head of the Waddislove educational centre and chairman of the Methodist district, as well as a translator of the New Testament into Shona; he was also chairman of the Southern Rhodesian Missionary Conference. White's contribution confirmed the traditional impression in southern Africa of the Wesleyan Methodists as an established power in the land. He extended Wesleyan Methodist influence into Zambia and as far as Shaba in the Belgian Copperbelt.

As chairman of the missionary conference he promoted the formation of an African Christian Conference in 1928. This organizational solution was a characteristic concession to the general pervasiveness of southern African segregation. John White may have felt that with the Revd Thomas Samkange, also a Wesleyan Methodist, as chairman of the African conference, close contacts between the two bodies could be established.

The strong educational ambition of the Wesleyans was expressed in the fact that the Revd Matthew Rusike was the first Black person to become a superintendent of schools, approved by the government in 1936. Africanization of the ministry had always been a Wesleyan Methodist concern. It took some time for the chairmanship of the whole Church to be Africanized, but in 1965 the Revd Andrew Ndlela was the first African elected 'chairman of the district'. For Ndlela, acting at a time of political turbulance, the double mandate was a challenging concern. In trying to keep the Black and White sections of the church together he may, at the time, have lost some credibility among the African nationalists.

Village Methodism, at the grass-roots, has been admirably interpreted by Dr Marshall Murphree in his *Christianity and the Shona*. He emphasized the vital role of women in the Methodist Church, in his estimation being 'a women's church' and 'in some ways independent of the Church proper'.[36] The *manyano* movement from South Africa had produced a rich offshoot in a strong Zimbabwean organization, dramatized by annual conventions with up to 5,000 women happily participating in four-day camp meetings.

In Shona society there is an important and mysterious possession cult, called *shawe*, and the Church women were greatly concerned by it. The *shawe* patient, in the Methodist service will be surrounded by her Christian sisters, who 'will place their hands on the subject's head, pray, sing, quote Scripture, place a Bible on her head and command the *shawe* in the name of Christ to leave its victim'.[37] This approach achieved, within the framework of the Methodist Church, an integration with what was felt as the real needs of the people, in terms which otherwise would have taken the patient into the camps of some charismatic Independent group. The men have their 'Fishermen's Guild', dominated by instruments and singing in local tunes, with their leader providing the rhythm and the choir supporting with a powerful manly bass.[38]

Professor Terence Ranger has demonstrated how, through the influence of these Churches in the eastern part of the country – Methodist Episcopal, Anglican and Roman Catholic – and their linguistic work through the decades, a particular 'Manyika' identity developed 'continuing underneath the rise of Shona cultural ethnic awareness and Zimbabwean political nationalism'. The missions thus played a role for 'the invention of ethnicity in Zimbabwe'.[39]

Protestants in the East

The two American missions, the American Board in the Rusape area and the Methodist Episcopal Church at Mutare (then called Umtali), both established themselves in the east of the country. They gave their African constituencies an experience of wide ecumenical contacts and educational opportunities on an international scale. The fate of the Methodist bishop Ralph Dodge, bishop from 1956 brought home to his Church an acute sense of the consequences of a determined political stand. In 1964 he was deported from the country and succeeded by the first African in the series of bishops, Abel Muzorewa. Methodist Muzorewa felt that he had been converted during a 'revival' week and he expressed his experience in terms which were different from those of the first generation preachers: 'On that day of days Christ gave me a spiritual microscope, spectacles and earphone to see and hear for myself what Christ offers.' As a bishop from 1968 he regarded 'the whole gospel for the whole man' as his message. This included a political stand, which led, in 1971, to his election as President of the African National Congress. In his search for majority rule he signed an agreement to that effect in 1978, together with Ndabaningi Sithole, Chief Chirau and Ian D. Smith.

The sphere of activity of the American Board Mission from Boston was geographically concentrated in the Marandellas to the east. This mission, which placed Ray Phillips as social animator on the Rand, now placed E. D. Alvord as agricultural missionary in the rural Marandellas. Alvord, 'a textbook representative of muscular Christianity', was something out of the ordinary.[40] An English aristocrat, the British High Commissioner to South Africa, Lord Harlech, met the American Alvord and was awed by what he saw: 'He was champion wrestler and leader of his college American football team in the Far West. His size in collars is eighteen and a half inches. He has no superfluous fat. He had the largest wrists of any man I have ever seen.'[41] This kind of man was made for Rhodesia and its stony soil.

His achievements in mission work came to the notice of the Chief Native Commissioner, and Alvord was appointed 'Agriculturalist for the Instruction of Natives'. This meant 'the real beginning of the development of the reserves'.[42] At a time of severe controversy over the Land Apportionment Act in the country, the missionary, now a government servant, was able to begin to develop the reserves. He had a staff of four Europeans and eighty-seven Africans to implement his plans for agricultural demonstration work, centralization of the reserves, soil surveys and conservation and irrigation work. 'A programme was at last under way, on a scale unrivalled in colonies to the north, to revolutionize life in the reserves.'[43]

Alvord could not expect to be popular among the Europeans. He 'was shunned and treated as a pariah by the Europeans whenever he went to town'. For one thing the missionary was an American, a trained scientist and was encroaching on 'European' territory. But this White man, in 1928, felt that 'European farmers who could not stand African competition "would do most good for Rhodesia by moving out".'[44]

The Salvation Army drums

In the Mazoe Valley to the north of Harare, all fertile powers seemed to work together for the common good, and this more so than in other comparable areas of the country. The Salvation Army received an allocation of land from Cecil Rhodes for their work, and the *Mhondoro* mediums – after a deep crisis of confidence emanating from the *chimurenga* (uprising) of 1896 – did their best to welcome the foreigners. Major (of the Salvation Army) Frank Bradley had arrived in 1901, served until 1921, and was succeeded by Major Barker. Both were greatly helped by an African Christian pioneer, Major Ben Gwindi, who worked for over sixty years as a mission teacher and became a leading Salvationist officer.

The atmosphere of expectation and co-operation between old and new can best be ascertained by the role of the medium of Gwangwadza at the opening of a church during Major Bradley's time. The medium had been offended at first by not having been informed about the church building plans, but was later placated by a gift of a number of yards of cloth and was thus prepared to attend the opening ceremony – a great occasion in the area. Having entered the church in a possessed state, the medium chose to sit 'right on the Altar'.[45] He listened quietly to the missionary's sermon and was particularly impressed by the reading of the Ten Commandments: 'This is the law of *Musika vanhu* [the Creator] which we also recognize and keep.' The medium's benevolence towards the mission was caused not least by the fact that the mission was seen to take the local traditional religion seriously. This impression was created by the personal attitude of the missionary, who by his way of life witnessed that 'the Black man and the White man were the same and equal'.[46] All this afforded the Salvation Army considerable goodwill in the area. With a few exceptions all the schools were in the Salvation Army's care and direction, a service that increasingly was appreciated.

The traditional *Mhondoro* cult was, after all, concerned with solving the people's worldly problems such as drought and the coming of the rains. As long as these concerns continued to be met, the two religious systems, the traditional and the Christian, were seen as mutually complementary.

The rhythm of the army drum and the liveliness of the army hymns helped to attract, and keep, the people. This showed through in the comparatively impressive statistical returns for the Salvation Army: a Christian community in 1961 of some 60,000, with 280 ordained African officers (and 111 European) and nearly 750 African lay staff.

A general observation on mission involvement

The beginnings of this period, particularly the 1920s saw Pentecostal enthusiasm in some of the mission-related Churches under the impact of Western preachers. Thus Rees Howells, a Welsh preacher and healer, arriving at the South Africa General Mission at Rusitu, was able to testify to great commotion in the name of the Spirit: 'like lightning and thunder the power came down. I had never seen this even in the Welsh Revival.' The Methodist Episcopal Church in the Mutare (Umtali) area experienced a similar awakening. The Anglican Canon Hallward referred to the 'conversion of a district – practically of the people'.[47]

All this was not to be confined to jubilation in the chapel but would reach out as efforts to African development through ploughs and better agriculture. Dr Michael Bourdillon suggests that some correlation between Churches of an evangelical Protestant character seemed to produce members 'significantly more oriented to social and economic development than their neighbours'.[48]

The Roman Catholics

In the first half of the twentieth century it seemed a foregone conclusion that Zimbabwe was a Protestant country, or at least a non-Roman sphere of interest, and that the Catholic presence was bound to be limited, a fact that made the sudden growth of the Catholic Church in the second half of the century all the more surprising. If we place this brief summary of Catholic missions at the end of our list of Western missions, we do so realizing that in an independent Zimbabwe – after 1980 – the sequence in terms of growth and influence of the Catholic Church was going to be altogether different. This can be followed in some detail in the history of two dioceses, Gweru (Gwelo) in the south-central part of the country and Mutare (Umtali) in the east. Within a few years both had risen from humble beginnings to an impressive size and strength, and this in the most harassed period of the country's history.

In the south-central region the Catholics had been a practically unknown quantity when the Propaganda in Rome placed the Swiss Bethlehem Fathers with their bishop Aloysius Haene at Gweru (Gwelo). Born in 1910, Haene had arrived in Zimbabwe in 1940 and was consecrated bishop ten years later. The diocesan staff increased from thirty priests in 1950 to nearly 100, of whom fourteen were Africans, in 1974. There were then also 100 professed African sisters together with the same number of European sisters. They provided the staff for the rapidly growing educational system and for medical services in their hospitals and clinics. The new arrivals amongst the priests devoted themselves to organizing retreats and refresher courses.[49]

In the east, at Mutare (Umtali), Catholic activity began in real earnest in 1957 under Bishop Donal Lamont. Born in 1911, Lamont was an Irish Carmelite who came to Zimbabwe in 1946 and was consecrated bishop in 1957. He had arrived at a time when the Catholic population was led by an English bishop, Aston Chichester. As an Irishman Lamont had his own views on colonialist regimes. As a priest at Mutare he had been joined 'by numbers of other Carmelite priests from Ireland'.[50] Within twenty years, eleven very active mission stations had been created, together with an extensive educational and medical system. All this ran in parallel with the daily pastoral work by priests, catechists and lay co-workers.

Both these young dioceses had begun under European bishops. A difference can be discerned in the political ethos of the two dioceses: the Swiss coming from a neutral country on the European continent, with dignified adaptability in trying circumstances; and the Irish, temperamental and, in the dramatic conditions of the period, unyielding and revolutionary.

One should not believe that Bishop Lamont's standpoint was acceptable to everybody in the White community of the Catholic Church. In June 1974 the Committee of the Chichester Club, a group of Catholic businessmen in Harare appealed 'to His Holiness Pope Paul VI, in the interest of peace, racial harmony and justice in Rhodesia, to forthwith remove Bishop Lamont from this country and from Africa'.[51] In various ways, 'Bishop Lamont's public outburst signalled a new era for the Catholic Church in its relationship with the Rhodesian Government'.[52]

Bishop Lamont's pastoral letter from 1959 onwards and his 'Speeches from the Dock' prior to his being condemned to ten years hard labour (commuted to deportation) made him and his Church the most uncompromising challengers of the colonial period and of Ian Smith's regime.

Throughout Zimbabwe's history the bishops of the Anglican Communion had, as a matter of course, been the official spokesmen for the Christian cause. On Zimbabwe's Independence Day, 19 April, 1980, the new government, under the Catholic Robert Mugabe, entrusted that role to the Catholic Archbishop of Harare, His Grace, the Most Revd Patrick Chakaipa.

To this presentation of the new Catholic contribution must be added that of the Jesuits with their vast farm centre and enterprise at Chishawasha near Harare. The Jesuits were 'old timers' in the country, claiming a century-old history in these parts of southern Africa. As Jesuits they were more conscious, perhaps, than their co-religionists, of the complexity of the Rhodesian situation – at a time when it was still permissible to speak of complexities – and of the double mandate to both White and Black to which the Catholic Church felt a responsibility.

At Chishawasha German Jesuits and Dominican nuns with their strict discipline helped train a class of enterprising African artisans and tradesmen. In 1932 a noviciate for African sisters had been started at Makumbi, near Harare. In a study of the development of religious life in the country, Sister Mary Aquina refers to 375 German Dominican sisters in Zimbabwe in 1975, and eighty-nine in Zambia. To these must be added women's congregations coming from other countries in the West, who also had established houses in Zimbabwe. The Dominicans insisted that the first African women should have academic training. Thus they were posted 'to secondary schools and teacher training institutions before they were accepted for full religious training.'[53]

Leading African priests have related the Christian message to African cultural tradition. The most important is Fr Joseph Kumbirai's contribution in gaining a place for the *kurova guva* ceremony in the Catholic burial rite, perhaps the most far-reaching form of adaptation ('inculturation' in Vatican II terminology) on the African continent. On the anniversary of the burial of any Shona, the *kurova guva* ceremony involved the offering of libation (beer) to the ancestral spirits.[54] Fr Kumbirai explains: 'The proposed burial rite meets the Shona spiritual need with its *kusasukidza* prayers where the dead ancestors are asked by the living to take their child to God. The proposed ritual has ... met with tremendous enthusiasm and applause: "This is what we call praying" ', the faithful exclaim.[55]

It was in their schools that the Catholics could most conspicuously develop these 'incarnation' attempts. In 1968 Catholic teacher training received a new 'Teachers Manual, Grade I', entitled *Our Way to the Father*, by Sister M. Siena. With charm she tackled the haunting problem that had troubled generations of Africans – of all Churches – ever since the arrival of the Christian messengers: what was to happen to their unbaptized ancestors as they faced God in heaven? Her reply:

> *Our good ancestors are in heaven.* We learned that all people on earth are God's children. If they try to please the heavenly Father then, when they die, He will take them to heaven. Because those people tried to be good and please the heavenly Father while they were on earth, God rewarded them by taking them to heaven.

No wonder that there follows a *Children's Response*, to be sung:

> 'Our good ancestors can now see God and are very happy.'[56]

Independent Churches in Zimbabwe

At the beginning of the 1980s, the country had more than 120 Independent denominations.[57] In this history of ours, room cannot be found for more than a handful of them. Dr Harold Turner has pointed out that 'no area of Africa has been better served for serious work [on Independent Churches] than Rhodesia–Zimbabwe.' Pride of place must go to Dr M. L. Daneel's great work on the Independent Churches among the Shona (to be completed in four large volumes, of which three have appeared, 1971–88, and with a remarkable set of photographs taken by the author himself).[58]

The 'Ethiopians'

In the emergence of both types of Church – Ethiopian and Zionist – Zimbabwe became a halfway-house between Malawi to the north-east and South Africa, receiving influences and ideas from both sides. In Zimbabwe there has been a tendency to neglect those Churches of an Ethiopian type, as if they were less significant than the charismatic groups, particularly so as the Ethiopians of Zimbabwe represent a variation of their South African models.

The African Congregational Church was a secession from the American Board Mission in Zimbabwe, and from 1942 it was concentrated primarily in Ndau country. The leader, an ex-evangelist of the Dutch Reformed Mission, Moses Ruwana, had a Standard IV education and an evangelist's training. His ordination through other preachers moved him deeply. His reflection on this occasion of personal preferment and responsibility indicates the strength of emotion and devotion of an African Church leader (expressed in about 1950): 'As I knelt down to receive their benediction, my chest grew so heavy in me, that I thought I would die'.[59] Through Ruwana the Church was able to realize something of its ambition to reach out to the whole country. In the 1960s the Church had about '8,000 members with six ministers and a substantial body of sub-leaders.'[60] It has, as a matter of course, not avoided the fission which has been a concomitant of congregational churchmanship in Southern Africa.

The First Ethiopian Church was another typical product of South African influence, introduced to Zimbabwe by a labour migrant, who returned to his home in about 1910 as a 'bishop'. It soon transpired that this organization was an ideal place for a power struggle and the rise of other ambitious local leaders. Unity was sought when a collection of Independent Church leaders met together and laid hands on Macharutya, the preferred leader, and pronounced, in the consecration words that reminded the participants of the ritual for traditional induction: 'You have come being you . . . I am giving you the name and Church leadership (*ubishopi*).'[61] Ideologically this group felt strengthened, during the dramatic time of the Italo–Ethiopian war of 1935, by their supposed association with the Orthodox Church of Ethiopia, the truly African church, and thus representing true Christianity.[62]

The Charismatics

However, it was through their Zion Churches that the Shona peoples produced their most creative and powerful Independent organizations.

Samuel Mutendi was of Rozvi descent, a fact of special importance for his role in the country, as the Rozvi were regarded as superior to other Shona communities.[63] Mutendi could trace his descent through the royal houses – a good start for any prophet in Zimbabwe or elsewhere. As had many first generation Zionist preachers, he had begun as a member of the Dutch Reformed Mission and served for a while as teacher and preacher in that church. As a migrant labourer he went, as did everybody else, to the Rand. In Pretoria he met Edward Lion from Lesotho, of the Zion Apostolic Faith Mission, and Legkanyane, the two potentially most powerful South African Zionist leaders.

Mutendi was inspired by South African Zion's claim to be the genuine Biblical Church. He could not find the name of the Dutch Reformed in his Bible, but 'Zion Apostolic' was definitely there, both in the Old and the New Testaments. In 1923 Mutendi returned to Zimbabwe, now as an ambassador for Zion. When, in Transvaal in 1925, Legkanyane changed the Church's name to Zion Christian Church, Mutendi followed suit. Gradually, however, the strong relations with South Africa were broken and Mutendi emerged in Zimbabwe as a leader on a national scale. But he had his troubles. Between 1929 and 1961 Mutendi's Zion knew no less than thirteen schisms, but his immense personal authority asserted itself.[64] He could not be shaken. He knew 'that those who have been chosen by God will not go elsewhere'. Yet the embarrassing number of secessions from Mutendi's Church showed, even with him, certain weaknesses. This could not happen with the two great Shona Zion leaders Johane Masowe and Johane Maranke, both among the most interesting charismatic leaders in the whole continent.

Christianity during the nineteenth century was, as we have seen, effectively promoted by the mobility of certain groups in the population. In twentieth-century Africa, with its closed colonial frontiers, this mobility seemed to have come to an end. Missions were confined to their particular spheres of activity according the idea of 'comity', with three- or five-mile radius regulations. The charismatic Independents were different. They were for ever slipping through any net laid out for them. As they moved across the length and breadth of the continent they looked towards another horizon and were scurrying over an altogether different kind of map.

Johane Masowe

Consider Johane Masowe, his calling and his movements over most of Black Africa. In the early 1930s, Shoniwa Moyo, a young Shona with personal experience from three or four mission-related Churches, went through the essential requirements for a prophet: he 'died' and then rose to life again. This happened near Marimba Hill, where he had retired in order to pray and meditate. Coming down from the mountain to his village, he lit seven candles in his hut. There was a radiant correlation between those seven candles in the hut and the Seven Lamps of Fire above. One of the most popular Bible verses with the Prophet himself and his Church was Rev. 4:5, 'and before the throne burn seven torches of fire, which are the seven spirits of God'. He was wearing a white robe and held a Bible and a staff with a crucifix. His fundamental religious experience on the borderline between life and death had transformed him: He was no longer Shoniwa, but Johane Masowe, Johane from the Wilderness, or, in fact, Johane the Baptist. He had an apocalyptic message for the wicked world: the hour of Judgement was at hand.

Here was an African prophet for his African people, and a movement of young people soon gathered around him, the secret Messiah in their midst. More than two decades later B.Sr. visited this group at Korsten, Port Elizabeth, and this was his impression:

> I may have met him, but I do not know. When I asked leave to meet the prophet or the bishop, I was told that he was away. But the very man whom I addressed may very well have been the Messiah, John Masowe or John of the Wilderness. He built a tightly-knit community in an atmosphere of apocalyptic expectation around the Bantu Messiah. Known to his people, he remains unknown to the world at large. Officially the community is ruled by a 'Bishop' but this Person is only a front, a *persona*, a mask, to the wicked world outside. Officially the mask belongs to one Jack Sithole, but this too is a mask because Jack Sithole is really Johane Masowe. Behind the decoy of these masks, hidden in the white-robed mass of thousands of believers, is the real Messiah.[65]

Professor Terence Ranger has shown that by 1938 the Masowe community felt forced away from their communal fields because of the administration's break up of communal lands. This precipitated the community to move to other occupations and other countries.[66] Johane Masowe and his Apostles left their Shona country and moved to Bulawayo to the south. A few years later they slipped over the border into Transvaal. In the years 1943–47 Masowe and his associates explored settlement possibilities along the route from Cape Town to Durban, and at the end of the 1940s the *communitas* settled at Korsten, Port Elizabeth. Under South African conditions they were classified as prohibited aliens, but the Prophet turned to Botswana and managed to obtain from there tax receipts which enabled the community to safely settle at Korsten, working with carpentry for the men and basket-making for the women. All the time, however, the Damocles sword of deportation hung over them and this increased the need for mysterious taciturnity by leader and flock.

They were ordered to leave the Union within six months, and now cherished plans to move to Israel instead. After repeated warnings they were finally deported as a group of no less than 1,880, and in 1963 they headed for Lusaka. They had however, as we have already intimated, their own map of Africa, and accordingly in 1967 they moved to Nairobi. Biblical authority brought them of course, for on their map Nairobi was in the middle of Africa. Isaiah 19:19 declares that 'there shall be an altar to the Lord in the midst of the land of Egypt' and 'Egypt' to them was another word for Africa. In 1969 they moved south to Mozambique but all this time the Prophet Masowe himself was seriously ill, spending his time mostly in Dar es Salaam.

In 1973 the Prophet moved to Ndola in Zambia, where he died. The corpse, in a coffin with a glass top – an arrangement made in order for the Prophet to behold Christ at the Second Coming – was brought to Rusape in

Zimbabwe. There the Prophet was buried in the presence of nearly 17,000 people, while in 1975 the total membership of the Church, in nine African countries including Zaïre-Congo, was generously estimated at half a million.

Johane Maranke

Johane Maranke, too, showed exceptional mobility by reaching out far into Central Africa to Kasai. Of royal descent and with a mission background in the Methodist Episcopal Church, he knew the exact date when a strong divine light and inspiration fell on him: 17 July, 1932. This happened near the Nyengwe mountain and he heard the Voice saying: 'You are John the Baptist, an Apostle. Now go and do my work ... You are blessed, son of Africa.'

Having started out from his Shona country district, he first turned to Transvaal and the Orange Free State, but then went north towards Kananga (Luluabourg) in Zaïre. Here he came in order to hold his *Paseka* (Holy Communion) ceremonies; it was taken for granted that for this holy rite only the Prophet himself would do. In 1964 he had nearly 11,000 followers in Congo (Zaïre) and the following year 10,000 in Malawi, while the Church claimed 50,000 in the Rhodesias (Zambia and Zimbabwe). When he died he left behind thirteen widows, eleven of whom were taken over by the Prophet's son.

These men convey, in sharp relief, the character of the Shona Zion Churches. It was not primarily a Protestant congregation of charismatics, and not just a pastor–preacher bringing his flock for the Sabbath morning worship for some homiletical exercise of a rabble-rousing kind. Rather, it was a *wandering communitas*, an extended family living together, worshipping, healing and working together, bringing the yields of the group's collective labour to the feet of the prophet. They moved together over vast spaces of the map for long periods of time, and shared together fundamental secrets which could not be divulged to the *goyim*, whether Black or White.

MOZAMBIQUE

To the extent that Portugal underdeveloped Mozambique, the African population and more particularly the Protestant groups, an unwanted minority, had to suffer.

A military coup in Lisbon, in 1926, initiated the rule of the 'New State', under Salazar's leadership – and dictatorship – determined to make Portugal and its so-called empire, once more a world power. Salazar could refer to a venerable history; the royal *padroado* of 1454 from half a millennium earlier was given a new role in a modern world. The New State treated the Catholic Church as its close ally. Catholic missionaries of Portugal were placed on the salary lists of the state. In 1940 a concordate was established with the Vatican. Bishop Teodosio Gouveia, consecrated in 1936, was made also a cardinal from 1940–62. 'Portugalization' of the African population was his aim.

New mission centres under Franciscan inspiration were opened, particularly in the north, but their number was not sufficient. The Cardinal took the unprecedented step of looking for non-Portuguese missionaries. Thus Italian Consolata Fathers were placed south of the Save river while from 1946 White Fathers were placed between the Save and the Zambezi rivers.

Solid non-Roman missionaries established themselves at the end of the nineteenth century: Swiss Presbyterians, American Episcopal Methodists and Anglicans (of the SPG) with their Lebombo diocese among the Yao in the north, followed by the African Methodist Episcopal Church. A new generation followed after the First World War of a radical Protestant tendency: International Holiness, Baptists, South Africa General Mission, Free Methodists (USA), Nazarenes, Seventh Day Adventists and various Pentecostal groups from the USA and Canada.

The situation for the Protestants, perpetually resisted and hemmed in by the Portuguese authorities, has been well summed up by Ira Gillet, with reference to his Methodist Episcopal Church:

> 4,575 Christians in 147 villages of our eleven circuits [parishes], beaten down but not dismayed, salute you. Hundreds more, for reasons best known to themselves, are at work on the mines and the plantations and in the sawmills of the Transvaal and Natal. Other hundreds from the same villages, for reasons best known to the government and the colonists, have been caught by day and by night, and sent to work for six months on railroads, roads and private plantations. Many up-land crops have failed partly or entirely due to lack of rain or lack of time to attend to them, or for both of these reasons.
>
> At the same time cloth, nails and the simplest necessities have increased several hundred percent in price.[67]

As pointed out in this quotation, the way to Johannesburg and its mines provided an escape-route from an unbearable and ever threatening situation. The mine in Johannesburg became a way out for these migrant labourers. Remarkably, the mine also provided unforeseen benefits by the 'Protestant compound rooms' with voluntary, informal education. Here these men were given training in the 'Three R's: 'the teachers in such compound classes were only one or two steps ahead of their pupils but remarkable results were reached.'[68] There were two great motives behind this literacy work in the compound. Letter writing home to the family was one such hoped-for skill. The other was the hope of reading one's own New Testament in one's own language. The New Testament in Tshwa was a constant best-seller in the compounds.

SOUTH AFRICA

The political scene until 1948

The Boer War was a great divide for South Africa. Becoming a British dominion in 1910, it was nevertheless a pluralistic country, split between Boer, Briton, African and Asian. For the Boers 'The War' meant one thing only – the Boer War. It was a traumatic experience and it took them half a century until the Nationalist take-over in 1948, to live it down.

Through his actions at Versailles, 1919, General Smuts placed South Africa on the world map. His country was now part of the world and of 'humanity' – a sweeping term highly acceptable at the Versailles conference table, but less so 'back home' at Vereeniging or Volksrust. After years of tension between Herzog and Smuts, the two generals formed a coalition in 1933. Their 'fusion government' suggested the idea of a kind of White unity. The agreement spoke of 'the recognition of the Natives as a permanent portion of the population of South Africa under the Christian Trusteeship of the European Race'. 'Christian Trusteeship', a paternalistic term, was supposed to safeguard African interests. For a majority of English-speaking Whites, including White churchmen, the 1930s and 1940s seemed to be a comparatively 'Liberal' period. Jan Smuts and his Finance Minister, Jan Hofmeyer – financial wizard and faithful Sunday School teacher – were in charge. 'Liberal' was the outlook and formula for common-interest organizations serving mainly African concerns. The Race Relations Institute followed the 'Joint Councils of Europeans and Natives', both under the inspired leadership of J. D. Rheinallt-Jones.

However, the chasm between White and Black was accentuated. In 1936 Cape Africans, in spite of massive Black protest, lost what political rights they had had for a century. In its place a Native Representative Council was formed to represent African interests, but it proved powerless – a 'toy telephone'. Dr Edgar Brookes and J. D. Rheinallt Jones as senators, and Mrs Margaret Ballinger in the House of Assembly spoke for the African – gallant Liberal voices in a far-from-liberal House.

The social scene on the Rand

A series of ominous warnings had followed World War I. In 1919 in Johannesburg, police brutally crushed several disturbances over employment and passes. The 'Labour' Party's unholy alliance with the National Party made possible the formation of an industrial 'Colour Bar'. An armed attack on the 'Israelites' at Bulhoek, Queenstown in May 1921, left 187 fanatic believers dead. There was suddenly mounting discontent with the impossible economic and social conditions in cities from East London to the Rand. Many churchwomen participated in the riots. A disturbing editorial appeared in the *South African Outlook*, December 1921: 'What is the Christian religion for if it is not to succour the helpless?'[69]

In this so-called 'Liberal' period prior to 1948, 'segregation' between White and Black (although not recognized as such) was firmly established in most English-speaking Churches. In the light of post-1948 developments there is a tendency to absolve that earlier period from the evils of racism. That is to take too superficial a view. The walk-out of African leaders from several European Churches into the camp of the 'Independents' provides a strong indication of the African protest. With increasing urbanization came a chilling decrease in personal relationships and human contacts between the races. Segregation denoted a prevailing attitude which, in general, dominated Black–White relationships in both state and community, and deeply affected the Churches – their life and worship – along with the relationships between White missionary, Black pastor and catechist.

Yet there was at this time no legislative act concerning this relationship. There was, instead, a self-imposed reticence in the dominant group of the population towards subordinate Black colleagues. This was, in many Churches also, 'the lie in the soul': on the one hand a pretention and programme in the name of Christ, and on the other hand – in the name of self-preservation and fear – an acceptance of society's segregationalist attitudes and capitalist values. Such policies may at the time have been seen as 'Liberal'. They proved not Liberal enough, however, meaning with this term that the missions with a paternalistic and generally petit-bourgeois outlook on society lacked a compelling awareness of the economic plight of the Blacks and of the social abyss between White and Black, in some of the Churches as well.

For the rapidly swelling African population on the Rand, the Western Urban Areas, including Sophiatown, had their own appeal. There Africans could buy their own plots as freehold, if they had made the purchase before 1923, the year of the Urban Areas Act. Similar privileged areas providing freehold plots included Evaton and Alexandra. The Western Areas housed more than 50,000 Africans, 3,000 Coloureds, 1,500 Indians and nearly 700 Chinese. A sample survey in 1951 showed that three-quarters of the population had lived in the city for more than ten years, and about one-third had been born there.

The Africans in the Western Areas fell into three classes. At the top were the petite bourgeoisie: professional people including medical practitioner Dr A. B. Xuma, once president of the African National Congress, representing a middle-of-the-road African liberal line; with teachers, ministers, clerical workers and traders. The largest group included the working class, with monthly wages from £5 to £16. At the bottom, housed in little tin shacks sublet by the plot owners, were the 'lumpenproletariat': the unemployed and, perhaps, some anti-social gangs. The petite bourgeoisie had bought their plots and built their houses, assured that with a freehold, they could not be evicted. That proved to be a false hope.[70]

In this climate the Christian Council of South Africa was formed. It was linked to the wider international organization, the International Missionary Council (IMC), of 1921. In South Africa the international body was supported by most English-speaking missions, and perhaps surprisingly, by representatives of the Dutch Reformed Church. In 1934, John R. Mott, the IMC chairman, made an extended tour of the country. Two years later the Christian Council was formed. That the leadership of the new council should come from the Dutch Reformed Church was unexpected. The DRC pastor William Nicol became president of the new council and a winsome young pastor, John Murray du Toit (also DRC) became its secretary.

Dutch Reformed leaders of the Christian Council were now in charge, as hosts of the council's affairs. The surprise at the time was such that Dr Abraham Viljoen, later interpreting the situation exclaimed, 'Is it the dawn of the millennium?'[71] Nicol was unperturbed. He saw his promotion in a wide perspective: 'We are but acting in accordance with the spirit of our own time. We are being carried along by the tide of co-operation which rightly belongs to the century.' Unfortunately, after only four years, that 'century' of co-operation came to an abrupt end. The war in Europe made Herzog part ways with Smuts. Nicol left the Christian Council to help found instead a federation of Afrikaans Churches in 1942. He was soon the administrator of Transvaal, another example of the close identification of Church and State with the Afrikaners.

The Boer nationalists in power

In 1948 the Nationalists assumed power under Daniel Malan, a one-time Dutch Reformed pastor. At this point the political scene and social climate in South Africa took on the intensity of a fateful drama. Every new Act and every new year brought challenges and an ever-widening polarization between White and Black. For the African however, there was little difference between the pre-1948 'segregation' policy and the post-1948 'apartheid' regime. Yet, as minister of native affairs and later as prime minister, Verwoerd ushered in an era of brutal power leading to measures affecting the entire fabric of African society.

The legal enactments on African affairs during the 1950s amount to a frighteningly long list, including most importantly (in regard to Church life): the Group Areas Act of 1950, extending residential and occupational segregation; the Bantu Education Act of 1953, whereby mission schools were taken from the hands of missions in order to produce more effectively an education 'for Africans only' (mission schools at various educational levels had for a century been fundamentally important for Africans); and the Native Laws Amendment Act of 1957, which brought apartheid to one of its ugliest consequences – the infringement of religious freedom.

This was articulated in defiance campaigns during the middle of the 1950s throughout the country, especially on the Rand and in the Eastern Cape. 'The age of the social engineers'[72] manifested itself in vast removals of African suburbs and townships on the Rand. The Western Areas, including Sophiatown, were bulldozed down in the face of bitter protests by the African National Congress together with Fr Huddleston and other churchmen. Tens of thousands of people were removed twelve miles from the centre of the city to what is now 'Soweto'. Similarly, the Coloured people in Cape Town were deprived of their 'District Six'.

In this context a question arises: How far had the Christianization process among the Africans gone at this time? One can of course answer this in statistical tables: so many thousands of Christians . . . etc. But to seek out the significance of the Christian way in times of great stress or a vast national crisis, such as the 1950s defiance campaigns, is more relevant.

African political protest in the cities and to some extent in the countryside soon took on sweeping dimensions. This applied especially to the Eastern Cape, with the cities of Port Elizabeth and East London in the lead, where 'a mood of religious fervour infused the resistance.'[73] Here the campaign was accompanied by 'days of prayer' and fasts. The *manyano* women in their colourful uniforms participated and accompanied Congress speeches with hymn-singing. Later, they attended their own nightly Church services with prayers for the success of the political campaign.

By this observation it is not claimed that multi-coloured *manyano* dresses or hymn-singing and prayer groups within the mass of protesting workers would, as such, make the protest movement to some extent religious or Christian. However, it is affirmed that the religious stand, of which, for instance, the women's uniforms and hymns were symbols, helped individuals and groups to a new social awareness not acquired at that time in any other way or form.

One thinks of the sustained Christian witness of the great political leaders such as Dr J. S. Moroka or Chief Albert Luthuli. It is difficult to mention more balanced Christian gentlemen than these two, both having been presidents of the African National Congress, the former from 1948–52 and the latter succeeding his colleague. They were now hounded as dangerous rebels. Luthuli was banned three times, the last time for five years. In 1936, after highly meritorious service at the Adams High Schools where he had worked with the principal, Dr Edgar Brookes, and with Z. K. Matthews, Luthuli was elected chief of his own 'Kolwa' community (Umvoti Mission Reserve). There Luthuli presided over the affairs of some 5,000 people, all living on about 10,000 acres. His political involvement in the ANC cost him his post, for in government eyes he came to be regarded as unfit to continue as chief.

In the midst of these struggles Luthuli, a Nobel Prize laureate, reflected on the function and failure of the Church in South Africa:

> How far do these Churches represent something alien from the Spirit of Christ, a sort of patronizing social service? Do not many Christian ministers talk down to us instead of coming down (if that is the direction) among us, as Christ did and does? ... White paternalist Christianity – as though the whites had invented the Christian faith – estranges my people from Christ ... In South Africa the opportunity is three hundred years old. It will not last forever. The time is running out![74]

From that great Methodist leader, the Revd Seth Mokitimi, came an impassioned warning:

> To Christians whatever their race or clime the issue is fundamental. It is a flagrant denial of all that is implied in the fatherhood of God ... The way of peace and goodwill in South Africa is plain: it is the way of co-operation and not of enforced segregation. May Christians everywhere unite in realizing it before it is too late.[75]

Education in South Africa is a chapter of its own with its own drama and tragedy. The first acts of this drama were particularly good, the final act of

1953, particularly bad. It began under the theme of trusting co-operation between Church and State. At the time of the enforced hand-over, the country had just under 5,000 African schools with about 800,000 pupils, about 18,000 African teachers and 500 English-speaking European teachers. Practically all these schools had been built and run by the Churches. One thinks of the high quality of those educational centres, such as Lovedale with Fort Hare, 'the South African Native College' – which for generations received eager students from most countries south of the equator, thus establishing invaluable contacts beyond the frontiers. Amanzimtoti with Principal Dr Edgar Brookes, Ohlange with Principal Dr John L. Dube, or Healdtown with Principal Seth Mokitimi, were all institutions led by dedicated educationalists.

In the name of apartheid all this had to go. Primary and higher education were taken out of the hands of the missions and taken over by government, i.e. almost exclusively Afrikaner, or Boer, officials and teachers. The effect of this change was for all to see. Instead of education as an instrument for advance and progress, the Africans came to see it as a tool of enforcing docility.

The Churches 1920–60

Any attempt at covering the whole of the missionary activity would be self-defeating in that it would necessitate lifeless enumeration of societies and individuals, names and dates. It is necessary instead to work out in sharp relief the profile of a few dominating churches, the state-related Dutch Reformed Church and, the great opponent of apartheid policy, the Anglicans. To them will be added the Roman Catholics. There must also be room for consideration of a couple of other mission-related churches as well as of the role of the 'Independents'.

The Dutch Reformed Church

There has been a tension within the Dutch Reformed Church itself, which can be followed over the decades, between an Evangelical endeavour at co-operation and a Nationalist urge for polarization. The root of this tension is, we think, to be found in the unsolved influence stemming from the Andrew Murray tradition within the Church. As we have noticed already, this tradition came to the fore when the DRC was already to be involved with the ecumenical 'Christian' Council of South Africa in its very first years. The first secretary of the council, as mentioned before, was himself a scion of the Murray clan. Soon however, this influence was quenched by the nationalist revival from 1938–48 and beyond. It surfaced again in 1953–54 when the DRC attempted to call leaders of all Churches to discuss 'Christian principals in multi-racial South Africa', to quote the title of the conference report. The Evangelical professor at Stellenbosch, B. B. Keet, gave the opening address on that occasion. He felt that 'the time has now arrived for the Church ... to lead the State in the direction of unity. I say, *in the direction of unity* ... Then it may be that a glorious surprise awaits us, and that it will come far sooner than we, with our human calculations, consider possible.'[76]

Throughout the 1950s some of the World Council of Churches' leading men in Geneva – such as the two Dutchmen Dr Visser t'Hooft and Professor Hans Hoekendijk – made their visits and could in good Dutch discuss the fundamental problems of the Church. Again, in 1960, the World Council of Churches sent a highly representative ecumenical delegation to establish contacts. The consultation held at Cottesloe, Johannesburg, included eighteen Black participants with Bishop A. Zulu and Professor Z. K. Matthews. A key phrase in the resolution read (and it is both strange and embarrassing, that this needed to be said):

> No one who believes in Jesus Christ may be excluded from any Church on the grounds of his colour or race. The spiritual unity among all men who are in Christ must find visible expression in acts of common worship and witness.[77]

So far the Evangelical section had managed to make its voice heard. But once again the deep tensions within the Church were brought to the fore. Prime Minister Verwoerd made a pronouncement condemning the stand taken by the DRC delegation, and very soon the erring Cape and Transvaal Synods had to fall into line. Now the ecumenical voice was silenced for a long time.

The rapidly increasing number of mission societies in South Africa had been a concern since the beginning of the century; the forty-three mission societies in 1911 had increased to fifty-eight in 1925, and eighty-five in 1957.[78] In view of this proliferation it seemed logical for the DRC to look beyond the borders instead. Up north, in Zimbabwe, Malawi and Zambia and as far as among the Tiv people in Nigeria, the DRC were actively engaged – but not in South Africa itself, in spite of the fact that Professor Gerdener claimed that the DRC was 'the only really indigenous Missionary Society in South Africa'.[79]

In South Africa the test case was the Transkei. Here the Wesleyans had started as early as 1827 and had covered the whole area with a wide network of strategically placed mission stations, outposts and schools. In 1950 their membership in Transkei was close to a quarter of a million. The Anglicans likewise, with a membership of 110,000 in the Transkei and a lively educational programme, were well established in the area. So were the Presbyterians with their strong membership not least among the Mfengu population. The 'five-mile radius rule' ensured that the societies already established could feel confident about their preserve. In 1951 all this seemed to jeopardize any DRC attempt at being involved in the Transkei. Less than 1 per cent of all Blacks in the Cape were members of the DRC Bantu Church.

At this very time a momentous change was taking place. DRC missiologists refer to it as 'the Great Missionary Revival of 1955–60'. And this awakening directed its energies precisely at the Transkei. Surprisingly, the most important factor in bringing about this change was the publication of a national Commission report in 1955, the so-called Tomlinson Report, for social and economic development of the Bantu Areas.[80] This served as a catalyst for new thinking, planning and attitudes about missions in the Dutch Reformed Church. Professor F. R. Tomlinson, as chairman of the Commission, signed a statement of 3,755 pages, analyzing the conditions of the Blacks in the country. A lay member of the DRC, he also included an analysis of the religious situation. In doing so he placed it within the widest possible context, relating to the African continent as a whole. 'Africa may be roughly divided into three chief Religious regions, namely:- (*a*) a North African Islamic block, (*b*) a Central African Pagan block, and (*c*) a South African Christian block.'[81] This presented a challenge to the South African Churches for the Christianization of all of Africa: 'the centre of gravity of foreign missionary action should be shifted from South Africa to the rest of Africa, so that both South African and Overseas Christiandom [*sic*] can launch a joint and widespread missionary action.'[82]

It is rare for an official report on economic problems, even in South Africa, to include missiological perspectives of such magnitude. The claim to be a Christian country was supported by statistical proof. In 1900, the number of converts among Africans was about one in four; by the 1950s, this ratio had advanced to one in two.[83] However, the continent-wide vision held by the Commission did not preclude a keen interest in the situation at home. Here Tomlinson felt there was need to change an arrangement common to all missions. They were no longer to be hampered by the five-mile radius rule, and the Commission recommended the abolition of that rule. Sites for schools and churches were to be allotted 'in accordance with the merits of each application', always a useful bureaucratic device. This would lead to registration *de novo*, of all Churches, the object being 'to ensure thorough attention to the spiritual needs of the Bantu. Churches and State *must* go into action with closed ranks.'[84]

It was in fact high time to perform a *volte-face*. To the North, from Brazzaville, Accra and Lagos, one already heard the rumblings of volcanic political changes, heralded by India's Independence in 1947. Africa too might change, and this time beyond recognition. One side-effect of this change was the retreat of the Dutch Reformed missions from Central, East and West Africa, from Kenya and Nigeria, achieving a return to the laager, in order better to concentrate its energies on the home front.

An enormous drive of Church development and building activity followed in the Transkei from 1955 – the so-called 'Golden Age' of DRC missions. Growing from eight stations with as many ordained missionaries in 1955, there were in 1960 no less than twenty-five stations (seventeen of them quite new) with twenty-nine ordained missionaries. A theological seminary with excellent staff was opened at Decoligny. The planners realized that there were only thirty-six evangelists in the field, and set out to increase this number, eventually reaching a total of 323. The DRC was obviously well-prepared to meet whatever new developments might arise in the Transkei.

About 1910, there had occurred a Pentecostal breakaway from the DRC, the 'Apostolic Faith Mission'. This group referred to the Dutch Reformed as a 'rich man's Church', but to its own 'Apostolic Faith' as particularly appealing to the Afrikaans-speaking 'Poor Whites' in the city and on farm land. The present membership is 300,000. One would expect this charismatic Church to take a different racial view from the established DRC. However in this kind of society, racial segregation constitutes a fundamental pattern. The Apostolic Faith Mission has largely followed the same racial policy as the Dutch Reformed Church, particularly after the Nationalist Party take-over in 1948.

The Anglicans

More than most the Anglican Diocese of Johannesburg had in this period to bear the brunt of the struggle against the political and social consequences of apartheid. No apology is necessary for including here a few names. There were the bishops, Geoffrey Clayton and Ambrose Reeves, Archdeacon Redvers Rouse, and the splendid company of the Fathers of the Community of the Resurrection, (CR), living and teaching at Rosettenville, Johannesburg, or living and sharing in Sophiatown.[85] Among them were

Fr Raymond Raynes, priest-in-charge of the Sophiatown parish, 1934–44: Fr Trevor Huddleston, priest at the Church of Christ the King in Sophiatown from 1943, outstanding fighter for the cause of the Africans and author of that unforgettable book on Sophiatown, *Naught for Your Comfort*;[86] and Fr Michael Scott, writer of *A Time to Speak*,[87] another dedicated celibate and leader of passive resistance campaigns. Their remarkable co-worker, Dorothy Maud, created important centres for family care, Ekutuleni in Sophiatown and Leseding in Orlando. Fr Blaxall, head of the Home for Blind Africans at Ezenzeleni, was for some time secretary of the Christian Council of South Africa. By evil report and good report, these men and women fought the good fight.

Canon Andreas Rakale was known as a pastor of souls. In the large army of voluntary lay members, the best known of the women was Julia Moselane. Her great concern in the slums of the Western Areas was the retrieval of lapsed Christians. Although she had no formal education, she had strong theological convictions of her own, and was always ready to verbalize them; she was fluent in four African languages. She insisted on the fundamental effect of Holy Baptism: 'Cattle herds have their special mark. Through Baptism you carry the mark of Christ because you have received the sign of the cross on the forehead. You belong to Him and you must return to Him now.' She also explained the role of the priest in confession: 'At confession the priest is nothing. He only transmits the forgiveness and blessing of God. All the priests are just soap in God's hand.' Another Anglican lay member with great influence and outreach, was Harry Madibane, the Anglican principal of St Cyprian's School, Sophiatown, with about 1,000 children.

The city with its White ghettos and Black slums, highlighted a basic problem, illustrating its existence beyond doubt: how does the Church, with its ordained staff of largely rural background, function in the South African city, with its increasing racial stratification? In the rural areas of the nineteenth century, and well into the twentieth, the Western Protestant missionary and his family had identified with the people. Their Ekuthulenis and Botshabelos were pious mission stations in the peaceful isolation of the bush. The missionary was the *baba* and his wife the *mama*. They looked after the needs of their wards, and in meeting with the missionary the flock would refer to themselves as the 'children' looking up to their spiritual parents. By and large this paternalism, in a period when his Western education was scanty and his horizon limited to clan and tribe, was acceptable to the African.

In the city on the other hand, with White and Black living geographically, socially and economically far apart, the Western missionary and his family seemed 'bourgeois' and distant from the people, and thus irrelevant to the harsh conditions of the African. Yet, when the two parties met in common evangelistic activity or conference, the usual roles of paternalism still held. Now, however, these roles had become unacceptable, because the parties shared no effective, trustworthy identification with each other. Here the celibate missionary played a part, whether Anglican or Roman Catholic, whether monk or nun. They all lived and thrived at Sophiatown. They identified with the people and fought to the bitter end for the African community.

The bishops sometimes had to make very unpopular decisions, speaking out for the One Undivided Church. Large sections of White Anglican members feared and detested this seemingly irresponsible radicalism of their bishops. They said so in frequent letters to the press: 'Bishop, remember: 95 per cent of the members of your diocese are against you' (meaning 95 per cent of the White membership of that particular diocese). This did not disturb Bishop Clayton or the others. They were not interested in that kind of arithmetic, but looked for a Catholic solution to the problem. This was their finest hour.

To the list of bishops the name of Bishop William Edward Smyth should be added, who in his retirement (from Lebombo) acted for twelve years as chaplain at Beda Hall, Fort Hare. Dr Z. K. Matthews, in his autobiography, has beautifully interpreted the role of this old man, who was totally identified with the young African elite at Fort Hare.[88]

The Catholics

Nineteenth-century South Africa was a Protestant country and gave every indication of remaining so. The Catholics were late-comers on the scene and, except for in southern Natal (Mariannhill) and Lesotho, were largely unknown to the African masses. The Catholic Church had been 'the object of ridicule and prejudice', as one Catholic historian expressed the situation thus supplying an inverted parallel, we presume, to the view which about that time was offered Protestants in preponderantly Catholic countries on the same continent.[89]

The 1920s saw the beginnings of a vast change. This happened simultaneously with, and as a result of, a move in Rome when the new prefect of the Propaganda, van Rossum, took the lead in mission matters. In 1922, Rome appointed the Dutch Dominican, Bernardus Jordanus Gijlswijk as Apostolic Delegate in South Africa. This proved to be an appointment of great importance. Representing the Holy See, the Apostolic Delegate could co-ordinate international initiatives in terms of religious orders, personnel and funds, as well as guiding local efforts and surveying the scene from his headquarters in Bloemfontein – a centre which under his successor was moved to Pretoria in 1946. He helped to strengthen and extend the position of the Church, particularly in extending the work among the African population. Neither was the fact that he was Dutch lost on the Afrikaans-speaking population: prior to 1948 there was still a certain degree of affinity between South Africa and Holland.

The vast political changes on the mission map of equatorial Africa enforced by Versailles 1919 had significant repercussions for the Church in the south. From Tanganyika, the German Benedictines were directed to Zululand, Alsatian Holy Ghost Fathers transferred to Kroonstad, while from Cameroon the German Pallottines found their way to Oudshoorn and to Queenstown, all supplying a welcome reinforcement of the Church in South Africa. Above all, the Oblates [of Mary Immaculate] who in the nineteenth century had initiated the Catholic advance in South Africa, particularly in Lesotho, were now in a position to move ahead, more especially thanks to their German and Canadian provinces. Before too long, no less than five dioceses – and among the most important: Durban, Bloemfontien, Johannesburg, Kimberly and Maseru (Lesotho) – were under Oblate bishops and half the Catholic population in the country was entrusted to their care.

To complete these statistical comparisons: in 1911, the Catholic Church comprised 24,000 Blacks and 25,000 Whites; by 1980 there were 1,500,000 Blacks and 500,000 Whites. The fact of a tightly organized Church body was emphasized when in 1953 an 'ecclesiastical hierarchy' was established for South Africa with four archdioceses (archbishops in Durban, Capetown, Bloemfontein and Pretoria) and in total twenty-three dioceses. In 1952 there were in the country fifty-seven sisterhoods with 6,000 nuns, and 1,500 priests and 700 brothers.

With all this conspicuous growth, the Catholics at first preferred to tread warily through the minefields of South African politics. Surprisingly, in the Catholic case too, this led at first to supposedly 'normal' solutions in an abnormal world such as establishing in 1947 two racially segregated theological seminaries, one for Whites, the other for Blacks, with a White rector for the Black seminary. In 1975 he was replaced by a Black rector, yet even then integration proved difficult.

In Zululand the Mariannhill Fathers continued their work. Best known throughout the country, and in Africa as a whole, were the initiatives taken by Fr Bernard Huss who formulated a programme for Catholic action in the words: 'better hearts, better heads, better homes'. Prior to Bernard Huss,

Protestant South Africa hardly knew of the Catholic work in the country, on the fringes of society. Fr Bernard Huss placed the Catholic Church on the map of South Africa as he developed his educational programme for Africans. At first he met with sullen distrust from the Zulu and the Sotho (his last ten years he gave to Lesotho, where he died in 1948). Was his programme anything but another fancy of the White man, designed to deceive those whom he claimed to assist?

Very fortunately Huss was in 1915 placed as head of St Francis Teacher Training College at Mariannhill and he reserved for himself the teaching of Religion, Psychology, Music and Agriculture, an unusual combination: only a German could do justice to such a load of work. The principal's heart was *in the land*. In 1913 the Africans had 'lost the land', through the Natives Land Act. Huss lectured on the continued 'Waste of Wealth', the terrible waste through soil erosion, caused by overstocking and thus overgrazing, whereby God's good soil was squandered and sprewed out in the Indian Ocean. A comprehensive programme was set in motion. First he felt he had to see for himself how others had managed a comparable task. He went to the USA, Britain, Ireland and to his own Bavaria, looking for ideas for co-operative movements, People's Banks and agricultural work. In 1927 he formed the 'Catholic African Union', CAU, uncompromisingly challenging the up and coming ICU (the Industrial and Commerical Workers' Union) and its Marxist programme.[90]

These were ideas to be translated into the very soil of Natal and Lesotho. Then there were the oxen: how to use their power to the full, discarding the old-fashioned shoulder-yoke, using instead the head-yoke – all in the name of Jesus the Christ, and all this strengthening Mariannhill and transforming the lives of many. Mariannhill and Fr Huss exercised an inspiring and catalytic influence on young generations in Natal and Zululand. The greatest example of this influence was the role of Dr Benedict Vilakazi, ex-student of Mariannhill, doctor of linguistics at the University of Witwatersrand, compiler, together with Professor C. D. Doke, of the *Zulu–English Dictionary*.[91]

What a German staff could achieve in a surprisingly short time was shown by the Benedictine work at Eshowe. After Versailles 1919 the bishop and his co-workers had been evicted from Tanzania. In their new *milieu* of Zululand they lost no time in building up a congregational and diocesan life of great significance. The missionary staff which in 1924 had counted seven Brothers, twelve Fathers and twenty-one Sisters, had over twenty-five years increased to twenty-eight, thirty-two and fifty-eight respectively. They began with three main stations and after twenty-five years these had increased to twelve, with 140 outposts and sixty-seven schools. The

Benedictine Sisters under Sr Victoria Mandl helped to form an African sisterhood. There the three 'professed' in 1936 had increased in 1972 to eighty-nine. Near Empangeni a pilgrimage centre, Fatima, was founded, and since 1954 annual pilgrimages from the whole diocese to Fatima have become a centre of intense Marian spirituality. This can be compared with Lesotho, which had its own Fatima spirituality, reaching a climax at the Ramabanta Mission with 10,000 taking part in a Midnight Mass with a torchlight procession.

In Lesotho, French, German and Canadian Oblates developed the work. From one main mission station the organization had increased to almost 300 principal and secondary stations, with 120 priests, 60 brothers and 430 nuns – more than half of the latter African. But had the Africanization programme for the staff really taken off? Then in 1952 Lesotho had its first African bishop, Emmanuel Mabathoane, of royal descent, later to be Archbishop of Maseru when in 1961 the kingdom acquired its own 'ecclesiastical hierarchy' distinct from the four provinces in South Africa. University education for Africans seemed an impossible ideal, but the Lesotho Catholics knew what to do about it. The Oblates developed their higher seminary into their own University College of Roma, not far from Maseru.

Other Protestant Churches

The missionaries of the American Board, as a Congregational mission, especially Ray Phillips, placed great emphasis on work in urban areas. While most missionaries at the time were rurally orientated and only occasionally (and then reluctantly) came to the city, Phillips, of Boston, Massachusetts, felt perfectly at home in the city. In Johannesburg he started the Bantu Men's Social Centre. He developed a varied programme, from boxing to poetry and hymn-singing. Sunday in Sophiatown was also punctuated by the rhythm of the Salvation Army drums. After General William Booth's visit to South Africa in 1891, Salvation Army work was particularly strong among the Zulu and in Mashonaland, and increasingly in the African townships on the Rand.

The enterprising Methodists reached out to vast numbers. In the early 1930s in Britain, the three branches of Methodism united: Wesleyan Methodists, United Methodists and Primitive Methodists. This was a great advance for those who held the broader ecumenical view, but it was felt as a threat by some local preachers who had not been consulted and resented this neglect. This happened simultaneously with the world financial crisis, which hit South Africa too, and was felt especially on the Rand. The quarterly

Church fee was raised from two to two and a half shillings. To the British chairman of the District, sixpence seemed a minimal increase, but to many unemployed and impoverished men and women in the slums of Pimville or Alexandra, it meant a sudden crisis.

In Pimville, the Revd J. Mdelwa Hlongwane was the devoted Methodist pastor. In the 1920s he published interesting pamphlets on family and marriage problems. Now, tumultuous Church meetings were held to discuss the Church fee. The British president of the district told me years later: 'I just let them keep on ranting and letting off steam – while I read the latest issue of the Tatler.' In that kind of crisis, such an attitude showed far from adequate leadership. Hlongwane took his flock out of the mission-related Church, and formed his own 'Bantu Methodist Church', which, at first, was satisfied with two shillings per quarter! By the end of the 1940s it was high time for an African Moderator, one closer to the sufferings and the aspirations of the great Black community. From the 1950s, social and political pressures compelled religious organizations, including the *manyano*, to shift from a revivalist emphasis to an expression of social protest. The *Asikweli* ('we will not enter') bus strike in 1953, and the Sharpeville tragedy of 1961 gave new direction to the message of the *manyano*.

The Lutherans had an ambition, to represent a challenging theology in a theology-void country, with its 'two kingdoms' in order to manipulate some kind of co-ordination of Church and State, and with a Bonhoffer-inspired effort at conceiving a 'confessing Church', with its own 'Confessions Africana'. In the 1960s a Lutheran visitor produced a study of *Lutherans in South Africa*.[92] It deplored that the Lutherans were 'not an urban-oriented community' and that their strength was to be found in the rural areas, realizing that in the Transvaal countryside the Lutherans were the dominant Church – a solid tradition dating from the nineteenth century.[93] According to the report these facts seemed to imply weakness. In the longer term, however, when Lutheran dioceses, their African bishops and African rural deans had to face obstreperous Bantustan police, it appeared that this Lutheran tradition, hidden and largely unknown, had a certain pungent strength of its own.

Not that the Lutherans either were exclusively rural-orientated: no African Church in South Africa could afford to be. This was shown more particularly when the first African Lutheran bishop for the Rand was elected: Bishop Manas Buthelezi, son of a faithful evangelist in Zululand, himself an internationally recognized radical theologian and, of course, banned by the South African government for five years prior to his election as a bishop.

The Pentecostals

The tough Afrikaner community proved to be much more susceptible to the Pentecostal message than was sometimes realized. The very 'Mr Pentecost', himself, world traveller for the modern Pentecostal and charismatic movement, Dr David Du Plessis of Los Angeles, was an Afrikaner from South Africa.[94] The Apostolic Faith Community founded in 1915 under the leadership of the Revd P. L. Le Roux, also originator of Black Zion in South Africa, soon grew to a membership of more than 100,000 and double that number 'affiliated', with a charismatic message and experience.

But the greatest Pentecostal surprise and breakthrough was reserved for Natal's Asian community, comprising some 165,000 in 1921 and about half a million in 1960 (by the middle of the 1990s nearly one million). This Asian population gave the impression of being monolithic Hindu and Muslim communities, far from any contacts with the Whites and their Christ. Into this impoverished Asian community there arrived in the 1920s a dynamic British Pentecostal preacher, J. F. Rowlands and his brother who after a few years in Pietermaritzburg founded a 'Bethesda' in Durban in 1931. Bethesda was very soon able to branch out establishing a number of local congregations among Asians in Natal and Zululand, all under Pastor Rowlands' unashamedly patriarchal direction. Rowlands did not spare himself. In one year, 1947, he is known to have preached 568 sermons, at an annual salary of a humble £75. In 1948 the movement claimed that 'no other Church in South Africa and [only] ten in the world, can show such phenomenal progress', settling for 'continuous revival', a programme formulated 'against nominal Church pro-devil' influence.[95]

The poor but infinitely hardworking community kept to their Bible and its salvation message, never embroiled with the pressing political concerns of South Africa: 'We have no room in Bethesda for agitators. We are Pentecostal', was a declaration that could have been made with the same determination by their Afrikaner brethren in the Apostolic Faith Church. Being apolitical in a political world, Pastor Rowlands was all the more insistent on the new opportunities from higher education: 'Keep abreast of the times. Our growing audience are not stopping at Standard VI. We have many, many JCs and Matric worshippers in our congregation.' Strict rules were laid down for the faithful. The qualities expected from those elected to the Church council were uncompromising:

> *Faithfulness to all Church services*. This includes proper meetings (Bethesda or elsewhere), mid-week service, Sunday morning and evening ... [and]

faithfulness in financial support of church. In future, Councillors will not be permitted to handle wines, spirits, liquors . . .[96]

These Pentecostal Asians in Durban may have appeared as an exceptional, wayward group in the world of African Churches. Yet, looking at the movement in a wider perspective one discovers how admirably they fit into the general theme developed in this book. Uprooted from their background in Tamil Nadu or Andhra Pradesh or Gujarat they were brought into a foreign land which made them query their own religious foundations. After some hesitation they were able to permit themselves to be drawn into this warm, happy and healing community. This Pentecostal Church, started, directed and inspired by one man, reached – over half a century – dimensions which stand out by comparison with those of the established churches which attempted to reach the Indian community. In 1970 the Roman Catholic Church registered 14,000, the Anglicans 6,000 and the Wesleyan Methodists 2,500. Bethesda at that time reached 30,000 Asians. There were also a number of other similar Pentecostal groups among them, all interpreted in two highly informative books by Professor G. C. Oosthuizen.[97] The beginnings of this Christian community before and after the Second World War had been difficult. But once the breakthrough had been made, these men and women and children found to their utter surprise a happy home in their refuge under Jesus the Christ.

A multiplicity of African Churches

In a rapidly changing Africa, terminology in various fields is subject to a 'law of obsolescence'. Terms which once seemed useful may after decades prove to be unserviceable. The formula 'African Independent Churches', introduced in a book by B.Sr., published in 1948, seemed adequate at a time when other writers without hesitation referred to them as 'sects' or 'Native Separatist Churches'. But with all of Africa north of the Limpopo Independent and with most of the mission-related Churches Independent as well, one's question is whether there is any reason for using this term 'African Independent Churches'.

South Africa had the most rapid increase of these Churches: in 1918 they numbered seventy-six, in 1932 they had increased to 320, while the estimate now is some 3,000. What is perhaps even more surprising is the number of scholarly studies of these 'Independents'. A bibliography for all of Africa on the subject, published in 1977, by H. W.Turner holds 1,906 titles and since then no doubt several hundred have been added to this bibliographical bounty. It is suggested that these Churches can be divided into two main categories, the 'Ethiopian' Churches and the 'Charismatic' Churches, the latter often referred to in South Africa as 'Zionist'.

Ethiopian Churches

The Ethiopian Churches were a particularly southern African phenomenon. There were definitely certain 'African' Churches in West and East Africa as well, locally referred to as Ethiopian but only in South Africa did this movement take on significant dimensions. Within the Ethiopian movement one can discern two different categories, an African type and an Afro–American variation.

The African type

The breakthrough of an Ethiopian movement took place on the Rand, at the beginning of the 1890s. Mokone's initiative was followed by a number of Wesleyan and Congregationalist pastors. The 'Ethiopian scare' was to be a concern in the missions for half a century between the Boer War and the Second World War.

Soon these men established themselves as leaders on the Rand. Gardiner Mvuyana in Doornfontein, and his successors, leaders of the African Congregational Church; Paul Mabilitsa in Alexandra – a Zionist leader with an Ethiopian frame of mind; J. Mdelwa Hlongwane at Pimville, founder of the Bantu Methodist Church in 1932, and his competitor Ramushu are among the most important examples. For generations the Western missionaries had in their all-White conferences subscribed to the tenets of the 'Three Selves', but now, African pastors asked for the precise date of this alleged transfer to African leaders. The Ethiopian Church movement was an elemental protest against what was seen as delay and even deceit by the missionaries and against a patronizing attitude of the White population in general.

At the same time – it needs to be stated – the great majority of pastors and catechists in mission-related Churches remained loyal and faithful members. They were just as aware of the pressures of the political situation and of personal injustices as the Independents. But in their case other values prevailed, in spite of everything: particularly the idea of participating in a world-wide 'ecumenical' Church body, a value recognized as inalienable and emphasized in their theological training and thinking.

South African governments – whether before or after 1948 – did not, as sometimes happened elsewhere, throw their Independent Church leaders into prison or banish them to some distant periphery. Instead they neglected them and treated the movement as something of a joke. In the hope of acquiring 'government recognition' all the 2–3,000 Churches regularly and worshipfully sent their annual reports to Pretoria. Throughout the period 1900–60 exactly eleven were indeed recognized, and of these only four Churches were recognized *after* the crucial year of 1925 until, in 1965, the government had the good idea of resolutely abolishing this administrative machinery. This strange contact – or lack of such – between the government of the country and the Independents had started promisingly enough, when in the 1890s in a sudden mood of generosity, old President Kruger had awarded recognition to Mokone's Church. Sixty years later this privilege was officially withdrawn from this organization because of alleged political instability. Instead, the government in Pretoria, always recognizing power when it sees it, turned its benevolence to Christian Legkanyane's Zion Church in northern Transvaal.

Particular crises inspired the emergence of different types of Independent Churches. Four events of political concern were especially productive for the Ethiopian protest: the Zulu rebellion of 1906; the Natives Land Act of 1913; the world economic crisis of 1930–33; and Mussolini's invasion of Ethiopia in 1935–36. The Zionists were different. In their case two events of a cosmological and affliction-generating character inspired the forming of their groups; the threatening Halley's comet of 1910, and the devastating 'Spanish Influenza' of 1919.

The Ethiopian Church leaders on the Rand represented a rallying-point for any incipient mass protest against mission establishment but also, in a more general perspective, a political protest against White segregation – later to be called apartheid. In this body there were men regarded by their followers as outstanding leaders and eloquent preachers, with their characteristic Wesleyan or Congregationalist – or in some cases Anglican or Lutheran – emphasis, all united in a common loathing of an unbearable system whereby any young White pastor could be placed over a group of African pastors as director of the work for no other reason than that he was White. He might not know – or even attempt to learn – any of the relevant Bantu languages.

Not only the Rand and Kimberley but also the Eastern Cape has produced powerful leaders and Churches. Mention must at least be made of the dynamic Bishop J. Limba of Port Elizabeth and, above all, of Nicholas Bhengu (1909–85), Zulu preacher – his father was a pastor of the Lutheran mission in Zululand – with headquarters in East London and regional centres in Port Elizabeth, Durban and Johannesburg. A question of classification arises as to how far Bhengu should be termed an 'Independent' Church leader. He established himself on his own and in 1950 founded his 'Back to God Crusade'. For years he was related to the (American and South African) Assemblies of God, a loose association of Pentecostal groups and was, discreetly, sustained by them: particularly with regard to Government recognition this contact was valuable to his movement. He retained his responsibility to appoint staff. Politically he kept a low profile and was therefore, particularly after 1948, disliked by African nationalist leaders. Instead Bhengu, with a determined Pietistic conviction and with his powerful command of the masses, emphasized the social and moral aspects of his teaching: 'We will only be taken to freedom when we have complete faith in God alone.'[98]

African–American

While some of the Ethiopian groups emerged from a local conflict, other Churches of this type were related to a African–American background.

1. The African Methodist Episcopal Church, (AME) had from the 1890s established contacts with the Ethiopian movement in South Africa. The 'AME had an important image-making quality in that its membership included blacks of great stature'.[99]
2. 'The Church of God and Saints of Christ' was another Afro–American Church which caught the imagination of Ethiopian groups and individuals, particularly one Enoch Mgijima. Soon Mgijima was excommunicated by the American leaders of the Church who criticized his message. Cosmological events, more particularly the appearance of Halley's comet in 1910, inspired him. For this and other reasons he felt alienated from the American Church. He founded his own organization, the 'Israelites' as 'Bishop, Prophet and Watch man'. It was under Mgijima that the Church established itself at the Bullhoek location, near Queenstown. This led to a tragic conflict with Government authorities: 117 Israelites were killed on 24 May, 1921, an incident of importance in the history of the Independent Church movement in South Africa. It led to the appointment of a Government commission – all-White, as a matter of course – which in 1925 proposed certain conditions for Government recognition of Independent Churches. An administrative machine was set in motion – if that is the word for this strangely inactive agency – supposedly working in the interests of the Black Churches.
3. For international outreach and vast ecclesiastical pretensions, Daniel

> William Alexander (1883–1970) outdid all the others. Of West Indian and Indonesian ancestry he was, according to South African laws of racial classification, a 'Coloured'. In his youth he joined and then abandoned a number of Churches: at first he was in contact with the Catholics, his mother's Church, and then with the Anglicans. He then turned to the Ethiopian Catholic Church in Zion and to Khanyane Napos's African Church, with some activity on the side for the True Templars. After this oscillating experience an announcement of the African Orthodox Church in the United States caught his eye, a new Black denomination founded in New York in 1921 and headed by the 'primate and archbishop' G. S. McGuire, a West Indian with links to Marcus Garvey's Universal Negro Improvement Association. At first Alexander's contacts with McGuire were through correspondence, but this enabled him when celebrating his first mass as bishop of the new Church to omit the *filioque* clause from the Nicene Creed, in accordance with Orthodox tradition: a new shibboleth had thus been introduced and Bishop Alexander knew that he was unique in South Africa with this ecclesiastical sophistication. Later he also added another Orthodox speciality, the reference to the Apocrypha: in a country of Protestant Bible readers it was a triumph to point out that these Bible readers had omitted a significant part of the Bible.

In 1927 Bishop Alexander proceeded to the United States to be consecrated as Archbishop and Primate of the African Orthodox Church by McGuire and others. He could now claim to derive his episcopacy from the J. R. Vilatte succession and from the Patriarch of Antioch and ultimately, from St Peter of Rome. From that moment nothing could stop him. He consecrated bishops in South Africa and extended his influence to East Africa, a totally new departure, for his role in East Africa was to be even more far-reaching than that in his home country.

The Revd Reuben Spartas of Kampala requested Archbishop Alexander to visit Uganda and in 1932 Alexander ordained Spartas and a relative of his as priests. However Spartas, a cautious man, soon became suspicious of Alexander's alleged Orthodoxy, and turned to the Greek Patriarch of Alexandria, a development which later was to be of dramatic importance in East Africa. Three years later Archbishop Alexander made a second visit to East Africa, this time concerned with the Kikuyu in Kenya. More than any other comparable churchman, this Kimberley archbishop – a newcomer on the scene – inspired the Kikuyu national movement, particularly with regard to the clitoridectomy issue and his influence has been quoted as a factor behind the outbreak of the 'Mau Mau' in the 1960s. In the 1960s Archbishop Alexander fell out with his Black American colleagues and, instead, concentrated on his church headquarters at Beaconsfield, Kimberley. Throughout all vicissitudes he relied on his Apostolic Succession. His successor the Revd Daniel Kanyile, residing at Ritchie, South Africa, was in 1972 made 'Patriarch Mar James II., D.D., D.Theol'.

Charismatics

In South Africa the Whites also had their charismatics. It began with them. About the turn of the century three international charismatic waves swept into the country. There was a Swiss charismatic influence through an apocalyptic Herisau community led by Johannes Buchler and others. Secondly, there was Zion, properly so called, brought to the Rand and western Transvaal and Natal by the emissary of John A. Dowie of Zion City, Chicago. Thirdly, Californian Pentecostalism, mainly from Los Angeles, arrived in 1908, leading to what was to become the Apostolic Faith Mission. The White revivalists – ex-DRC pastor P. L. Le Roux, ex-Salvation Army officer Edgar Mahon, and others – could not but influence the Africans too. Very soon Africans acquired the peculiarities of Zion and Pentecostalism – healing, prophecy, glossolalia etc. – more deftly and heartily than the hidebound Whites, and this was expressed in thousands of Zion and Apostolic churches.

A certain pattern of South African prophetism attracts our interest.

The religious dimension

These men and women had – as they without exception would claim – met God, or, at least, one of His angels, and that encounter set them apart, giving them a conviction of divine direction and of a new identity. This was of course the case with Prophet Harris and the Aladura on the West Coast and with Simon Kimbangu in Zaïre, and it is equally true of the prophets in South Africa. They refer to a date and place when they were confronted with the Almighty and received their Revelation and their irrefutable marching orders. This movement therefore has to be interpreted not only in sociological and psychological terms but with an awareness of the religious dimension as well.

The propensity for ritual

The religious dimension can clearly be seen in the inexhaustible Zion capacity for ritualizing everything; this unconquerable African genius for transforming any tedious Western concept into glorious, joyous rite and rhythm.

The waters of Jordan–Bethesda

The focus of the Zionist Church is the river of Jordan and the pool of Bethesda. One of the prophets referred to his church as a 'Water-Church': the Zion movement is a movement of baptizers. In a world where sin, sickness and death are ever-present destructive forces, purification, baptism and healing in Zion are linked together as the positive, restoring powers. Here the Spirit is experienced. Nowhere can it be as effectively appropriated as through the water of the pool or in the Jordan with its 'living water'. The wicked Whites only knew sprinkling for their baptism, so there was another forceful reason for the Blacks, by contrast, to be purified by 'much water'.

The prophet as healer

'This is not a Church: it is a hospital', one Swazi Zionist leader told us. The patient would stay for weeks and months at the prophet's place, to be prayed for and treated with holy water and other unfailing means, while at the same time insisting that they must not touch medicines. The healing aspect of the charismatic community is fundamental to the whole movement.

Pilgrimage to the Holy Mountain

The term 'Zion' refers to the affinity with Mount Zion of the Bible. Of all the Zionist churches none has managed to realize this ideal as decisively as Legkanyane's Zion Christian Church. At the Church's festivals, especially at Easter time, their headquarters in northern Transvaal, 'Zion City Moria', becomes the pilgrimage centre for thousands of faithful. This Church developed and accentuated tendencies which were to be seen from the beginning of the Zion movement.

The 'Zion' churches and the 'Apostolics' have a similar historical background in the variations of American Pentecostalism from the beginning of the twentieth century, and they have largely developed along similar lines. There are other movements of a more definite 'nativistic' character. The best known of the Zulu prophets, Isaiah Shembe (d. 1935), followed a line entirely his own. He was the most original and, hymnologically, the most creative of the prophets. His fame as a healer extended far and wide. His Nazaretha Church had two centres, Ekuphakameni, near Durban, and the Inhlangakazi mountain, 100 miles inland from Durban. His hymns and those of his son Johannes Galiele Shembe (d. 1967) and of his grandson, Londa

Shembe (shot dead in his home in 1988), show the quality of this intense religious experience.

Shembe's difference from the Zionists is obvious. The focus is not on Jesus Christ but on Jehovah of the old Covenant, seen as a symbol of a religious counter-movement. His hymn no. 154 has the following verse:

> I believe in the Father
> and in the Holy Spirit
> and the communion of saints
> of the amaNazarethea.

These lines are revealing for what they say and for what they leave out. These hymns remind one of the special musical quality of Shembe's hymn tunes – meditative, slow moving and infinitely solemn when sung by the 10,000 faithful, all in white; very different from Zionist shouting.

NAMIBIA

Namibia had been reached by Finnish Lutheran missionaries under the leadership of Martti Rautanen – who had started life as a serf in Russian Inkeri; for fifty years he preached Liberation to the Ambo, until his death in 1927. With characteristic quiet and persevering energy these Finnish missionaries undertook, in this the most forgotten corner of the continent, to lay the foundations of a solid and sound 'folk' Church. They started pastoral training – in 1925 seven were ordained, in 1937 another twelve. Schools and hospitals were built. For the latter, Dr Selma Rainio (1873–1939) was the pioneer of medical work. After the Second World War the Ambo Church received twenty-five new missionaries: they reached their destination by a sailing ship which took more than three months to get there.

For the purpose of this Church history which emphasizes African Christian initiative related to African social structures, it must be underlined that a real advance in the north was achieved through a refugee movement. Ombandju refugee groups from Angola decided to flee from the unbearable Portuguese regime in their country, moving south into Amboland. Here they settled among the Ombulantu population and found that this group was a particularly interesting community, a 'priest tribe' among the Ovambo. To their hosts the Ombandju explained that they had fled across the border in order to line up with a new religion, that of 'Christ' and they were prepared by way of families to accept the new faith. At the Nakayale centre in the north-west, they heard the powerful preacher Zacheus Iihuhwa (ordained in 1925, died in 1976) who devoted himself to these refugees. He knew that the powerful Ovambo community so far resisted the preaching of the Gospel but found that the Ombandju refugees listened with keen anticipation to the Jesus story.

Further east were the Uunkuanjama. At the beginning of the twentieth century German missionaries had started work among them and in 1920 the Finns took over responsibility for this community. In 1926 the Finnish missionary Vilho Närhi explored possibilities among the related Uunkwangali, hitherto obviously without missionary influence. One can imagine his surprise when he found a Christian 'conventicle' in the place (see p. 394). A group of nineteen young men had walked south for work in the mines in central Namibia and there found the Gospel. Returning home they started a small congregation among their own people. They found a leader in the African pastor Noah Shengetu, a man with a characteristic background. He was an ex-diviner who had become a powerful preacher: 'When Noah Shengetu came to a village, all became Christians, except the few who could not stand the sound of the Church bell.'

A parallel development was to be found with those Ambo men who went to the German farms inland from Windhoek. They crossed the Etosha plains – a trying experience of five to six days walking through desert-like conditions – until they reached their goal: they had a religious experience very similar to their brothers in Uunkuanjama.

Remarkably the Ovambo–Kavango Lutheran Church was to a large extent spared the experience of breakaways from the ecclesiastical fold, which happened much more further south among the Nama and the Herero. Namibia in those days may have appeared as an isolated area but all the same the emissaries of Marcus Garvey's Universal Negro Improvement Association reached the country, proclaiming 'Wake up Ethiopia! Wake up Africa!'[100] The Anglican missionary Michael Scott, who radically identified with the position of the Herero, brought their cause to the United Nations in New York.

The German missionaries tried a difficult balancing act between concern for the African population and a conformation with South African 'Native' policy. This showed particularly when government in Pretoria appointed the greatest of their missionaries, H. Vedder, as Senator with responsibility for African affairs, a great honour from the point of view of Pretoria. Herero reaction was sharp: 'He who after all is our father, goes to Government in South Africa.'

The Herero, deeply injured and almost annihilated by their colonial masters at the beginning of the century, hesitated for years until in 1955 they took the definitive step. Hosea Kutako (1870–1970), the son of a chief and member of the Rhenish Mission Church took his people along with him into a new Church and Reinard Ruzo gave it its name – 'Oruuano' (fellowship) – what they had been looking forward to in the mission Church but had not found there. The Nama further south criticized the programme of the Lutheran theological training and instead joined the AME in 1946.

MADAGASCAR

In the 1930s Madagascar – 'le petit continent' – seemed far away from anywhere, 'isolated both geographically and psychologically'.[101] The Second World War changed all this. The new governor-general in 1939, Marcel de Coppet, a member of the French Socialist party and a Protestant, read the writing on the wall and prepared for Madagascar's participation in a war which had to come. In 1939–40, 15,000 Malagasy troops were sent to France. After the French debacle in 1940, the Vichy government ruled Madagascar for two years until British troops took over the island in 1942. In 1943 the British handed Madagascar to the Free French forces and General de Gaulle.

After the war, two Malagasy were elected to the Constituent Assembly of the Fourth French Republic. They were placed in Paris and campaigned there for the autonomy of the country. Also after the war the first political parties emerged, one of them Catholic, another Protestant. The unease and uncertainty of the country exploded in the Madagascar revolt of 1947, at first led by 'fanatical sorcerers who proclaimed that the ancestors wanted the Malagasy to destroy all agents of modern change'.[102] The sacrifices in lives were heavy although the estimates of the losses fluctuate widely, between 10,000 and 90,000. The conflict cut deep into the Malagasy soul: 'it took France thirteen years to deal with the problems posed by the 1947 revolt.'[103] In 1959 Philbert Tsiranana was elected president, friend of de Gaulle and of French culture. Among prominent politicians was the Revd Richard Andriaramanjato, mayor of Tananarive. The Churches prepared for the future in struggling over the past.

The Six Monthly Meeting had been a federative rallying-point for the Reformed missions (LMS, Paris and the Quakers). Hopes were expressed from time to time for this Six-Monthly Meeting to develop into a united Malagasy Protestant Church, but these dreams were not translated into reality. More substance was to be seen in the plans for a united Protestant theological college or seminary. Yet, there again, denominational interests dominated. In 1956 as the International Missionary Council's distinguished Theological Commission visited Madagascar, it found no less than five different Reformed theological seminaries, three of them for the LMS, one each for the Paris Evangelical Mission and the Quakers. All had insufficient and overworked staff, often with disappointing libraries – trustworthy old volumes in English from another century – and while emphasizing Bible knowledge, with hardly any teaching in Christian doctrine. The more deserving students were sent for further studies to theological faculties in France and Britain, being prepared for local and international positions where Malagasy Christian eloquence and vibrant personal convictions were being felt.

In the 1930s and 1940s some new revivals followed in the steps of Soatanana. Two of them were inspired by women, one of whom had an experience similar to that of her Zambian sister in the faith, Alice Lenshina: dying and rising again. Another movement started with a personal break-through of a pagan chief, one night overcome by a Vision and a Voice. After that he was duly baptized and a religious movement followed, referred to as a 'revival'. There was also a group describing itself as a 'Bible Baptist' Church from 1930.

The conflict in 1902 between the Church in the field and a domineering Mission Director over autonomy in the Lutheran Church has been referred to in an earlier chapter (pp. 507–08). It took the church almost half a century to overcome the consequences of this set-back. The change occurred in 1945 with a constructive proposal by the well-known missionary and Church-leader Fridtjov Birkeli, which implied one Malagasy Lutheran Church with its General Synod and its executive Church council, and with the full co-operation of the Norwegian and the American missions.

The Catholics saw a rapid increase in their numbers. The great mass of new converts, particularly on the western coast consisted of liberated slaves, to whom the new dispensation gave an opportunity to form new respectable communities, 'far away from their former masters who remained Protestants'.[104] They and the Catholic farmer parishes on the coasts could be counted on to be firmly pro-French, anxious to keep away from any political extravagances such as the revolt in 1915 and the rebellion in 1947 which, if they were related to the Churches, found a response in other denominations.

Yet, related to the Vatican in Rome the Catholic Church in Madagascar was made aware of the explosive changes on the international political scene. At the end of the 1940s the Cardinals saw the writing on the wall, and for the Eucharistic Congress in Tananarive in 1951, the Pope himself sent a message which could not have been more exciting, almost revolutionary: 'The Church in conforming with the natural law recognizes the freedom of the people to govern themselves.' A great advance was the appointment by the Vatican in 1939 of the first Malagasy bishop, of Miarinarivo. The consecration of Mgr Ignace Ramarosandratana showed the way into the future. Apostolic vicariates were changed into dioceses, and in 1955 there were nine dioceses. In that year the hierarchy was established for a Church with some 1 million baptized. In 1960 Bishop Sartre of Tananarive decided to resign to make way for a Malagasy archbishop, in the person of Archbishop Rakotomalala, later cardinal. In 1960, too, an Apostolic Delegate, for Madagascar and the surrounding islands – Mauritius and Réunion – was appointed. But the limited numbers of Malagasy priests remained a persistent problem. Only in 1950 did the total number of Malagasy priests reach 100, and in 1980 it reached 150, to be shared among a rising number of dioceses.

Of great value for Catholic spirituality was the translation into the national language of Thomas à Kempis' *Imitatio Christi* ('Imitation of Christ'), a Catholic counterpart, perhaps, to the Protestants' immensely popular *Pilgrim's Progress*. A small group of Jesuit Fathers applied themselves to the problem of Church and Malagasy culture, under the leadership of Fr Rahajarizafy, SJ. Anticipating later developments, it needs to be said that the Catholic Church radically faced a central issue of Malagasy culture, the famous 'corpse-turning' custom, *Famadihana*. Here we approach an area cautiously left aside by other missions. On all sides there were Church regulations against this custom, but the rules were not always carefully followed. For the Catholic Church to adapt this custom would more than anything else help officially to obliterate any earlier impression of foreignness, with the continual problem of the nationality of its bishops and more particularly the nationality of its priests. That may have been a consideration in 1987, when Cardinal Razafimaharatra announced that through an official general act, thirty-one missionaries – about equally Malagasy *and* foreign – buried in the years 1956 to 1970, would now undergo the *Famadihana* custom.

17

EASTERN AFRICA

INTRODUCTION

Looking at the continent from the imperial centres of power, East Africa in the 1920s seemed something of a backwater, fifty years behind West Africa. Mission statistics – such as they were at the time – show that in Kenya, Tanzania and Uganda, the Church had only just begun forming its local congregations around 1920. The number of Protestants in the whole area totalled 235,000; Uganda leading with 145,000 while Tanzania and Kenya together – 42,000 and 47,000 respectively – did not begin to approach that figure. On the Tanganyika coast during World War I, Islam increased rapidly and in the Kenya Highlands the arrival of land-grabbing European settlers inevitably made 'the White man's religion' less than attractive. Uganda, however, was a case of its own: Catholics and Protestants, encouraged by a dramatic Church history of preceding decades were assured of a decisive influence in the country, with opportunities for rapid outreach towards the east, the west and the north.

Forty years later, in 1960, the picture had changed altogether. The number of Christians in the region had increased: the Catholics from 600,000 to 5 million and the Protestants from 235,000 to 2,540,000. The increase had taken place primarily in inland communities, firmly making the Churches part of East Africa and its peoples. How had all this happened? The credit must undoubtedly go to the labours of the increasing number of ordained Africans and even more to the local catechists whose plodding yet inspired evangelistic and educational work has often been neglected. Protestant catechists numbered nearly 20,000 for the whole region (Kenya 6,226, Tanzania 7,433 and Uganda 5,850), and there were 13,300 Catholic catechists. The period 1920–60 is one of great change for the East African peoples and their Churches. Two of the underlying themes of this chapter are (*i*), the Churches' response to chiefly power and African culture, and (*ii*), Christian expansion and the growth of urbanization in East Africa.

The chiefs, the Church and African culture

This was the chiefs' heyday in East Africa, especially in Uganda and with regard to the self-assured and powerful chiefs in Tanzania's west and north together with the newly appointed – and therefore less confident – versions nearer the coast. The Churches' role must also be seen in relation to the chiefs. Basically, the system of Indirect Rule depended on the era's scepticism towards the chances of moulding non-Europeans to European culture. 'We must ... not destroy the African atmosphere, the African mind', was the view of Sir Donald Cameron, the new Governor of Tanganyika who arrived in 1925.[1] To him, Africans belonged to 'tribes' and the administration's task was 'to find the chief'. Having identified the chiefs, the European administration, while keeping as far as possible in the background, should educate and supervise the African leaders. The system bolstered the power of the chiefs but managed at the same time to underdevelop the ordinary farmer, dependent as he was on the whims of the chief.

Early urbanization and the Churches

Slowly at first, then rapidly, urbanization became a determinative feature in rural East Africa. World War II marked the difference. The cities and towns also formed the conditions for the Churches as they, with some resistance and much distaste, adjusted themselves to the inevitable.

It is difficult fully to appreciate the differences between the three East African capitals in colonial times. At the risk of some exaggeration one could draw the picture in the following terms, incorporating the position of the Churches. It should be noted that the three capitals had risen as cities after World War I:

Kampala: an African city with an African king (*kabaka*), boasted three cathedrals – one Anglican and two Catholic – situated high on glorious green hills. An emerging university college was supported for its recruitment by prestigious secondary schools (e.g. 'Budo, the Eton of Africa' and Kisubi, the Catholic centre). The British governor and his staff resided at Entebbe on the shores of Lake Victoria. While in the other two capitals the *lingua franca* was Swahili, in Kampala, Luganda and English were used in preference.

Dar es Salaam: an Asian city on the Indian Ocean with Arab, Gujarati and Goanese *dukas* (shops), Sikh artisans and an African proletariat. A Catholic cathedral and a centrally placed Lutheran church were built in German times, the former serving for sixty-three years as the only Catholic parish in the city. The Anglican Collegiate Church of St Alban of 1934 became the prestigious government church with participants 'of all types, from the governor himself downwards'. Prominent secondary schools – Catholic Pugu and Anglican Minaki – trained the future African elite, at a safe distance from the capital. With *uhuru*, after 1961, cadres of well-educated young men and women related to the inland Church communities thronged to the capital, changing the Church scene dramatically.

Nairobi: a European city at the foot of the Kenya highlands, containing townships and slums for African clerks, servants and the proletariat. Churches were built in the city for Whites – chapels in the slums for Africans. Impressive Church-founded high schools outside the city, such as Alliance and Mangu, served as a focus for the ambitions of an African elite.

UGANDA

The kabaka, chiefs and Church in Buganda

In Buganda a non-Roman Church, almost unhampered by Protestant rivalry, dominated the political and social scene for decades by virtue of its remarkable history and the combined forces of governor and bishop, chief and priest. It is a unique story in the history of the Church in Africa.

In London, kings and queens were crowned in a ceremony performed, not by the prime minister, but by the Archbishop of Canterbury. In Kampala, the *kabaka* was likewise crowned in a ceremony full of the richest symbols, not, indeed, by the governor, but by the Anglican bishop, as mandated by the Archbishop of Canterbury. That the family life of respective *kabakas* was to cause the bishop and Church administration problems was another matter, best left to the future on these solemn occasions. At the *kabaka's* side was his prime minister, the *katikiro* – the 'immensely powerful' Sir Apolo Kagwa (knighted 1905) – who held his office for forty years. For this great statesman, his Church affiliation fitted like a hand in a glove. He could daily view the cathedral on Namirembe Hill – completed in 1920 – with great satisfaction, perhaps even with a sense of secret identification. For he knew, along with everybody else, that in those difficult war years when the new cathedral was being built, he had given the lead to the voluntary workforce by appearing early every morning to pick up his load of bricks, place it on his immense head and slowly but surely tread his way up to the top of the hill. Only then was he prepared to proceed to his office and attend to the administrative business of the day.

A succession of Anglican cathedrals – Kampala 1890–1920

1. An enlarged Buganda hut, 'looking in the distance like a huge long haystack', with a thatched roof, resting on poles straight from the forest, set in rows about six feet apart, about forty-five feet high. Blown down in a gale, 1894.
2. Similar quality and style. Taken down in 1901 to avoid the fate of its predecessor.
3. Sun-dried brick building with three pyramidal spires over centre and transepts, thatched roof. Dedicated 1905. Struck by lightning 1910.
4. The plan of this cathedral was not at first meant for Africa, but was an adaptation of a design by the architect Beresford Pite for Liverpool Cathedral. Sandstone and brick, with a tile roof. Built during World War I, adding considerably to the difficulties of construction, it measured 210 feet long and could accommodate a congregation of 3,000. The Uganda Church members raised some £18,000 which in terms of effort was equivalent to the raising of at least £250,000 in an English diocese at that time. The pulpit and the bishop's throne were made by students at the King's School, Budo.[2]

The first generation of powerful pastors had given their particular stamp to the work and influence of the Church. Their prestige was immense in a Church which had developed from a small persecuted group to a national established Church in a few decades. Their rich estates (*mailo*) had been awarded to them as individual family property. Some pastors' sons became rich landowners and respected laymen in Church congregations but most of them never considered taking holy orders.

The traditional political structure in Buganda and adjacent kingdoms consisted of a well-defined hierarchical system of office, from *kabaka* (king) to village headman. Bishop Tucker had adapted the administration of the Church closely to this traditional order. The political and ecclesiastical systems of office corresponded very closely throughout the geography of the land:

kabaka	bishop
saza chief	rural dean
gombolola chief	chief priest
muruka chief	deacon
mutongole chief	first-letter catechist

The African rural dean usually lived near the *saza* residence and had close contact with the chief. 'The rural dean was the religious *saza* chief.' An ordinary priest addressed the dean as *mukama wange* (my king, or, my chief). Because the priest had a lower income and usually less education than the emerging civil servant chief, the priest's influence with the chief tended to depend solely on the churchman's personal qualities.

A fascinating figure in the synod of Ganda clergy was the Revd Apolo Kivebulaya (1864–1933), who preached for decades at Mboga in the tropical rain-forest of eastern Zaïre, with its shy pygmy population who accepted the priest as their spiritual leader. Baptized in 1895, ordained a deacon in 1900 and a priest in 1903, Apolo was one of the most dedicated and attractive servants of the Church. He was a man of visionary dreams, Christ appearing to him shining like the sun and speaking to him: 'I Am That I Am, that is my name.'

In his book, *The Growth of the Church in Buganda*, John V. Taylor has interpreted not only the 'growth' but also what he calls 'the period of disengagement', 1905–55, which includes certain aspects of decline.[3] This latter element came to the fore in continuing missionary control which tended to be 'protective and possessive'. The pyramidal structure of the Church allowed the missionaries, intent on handing over responsibility to the Africans, to do so by 'withdrawing upwards into a higher level in the administrative hierarchy'. At the same time, this necessarily led to a lessening of personal, face-to-face contacts at grass roots level.

The chiefs, who at first had shared responsibility in the Church with the priests – many of them were ordained and had for some time served in evangelistic work – were followed by a younger generation of more highly educated men who were often less committed to the Church's work. The priests who had in the beginning been recruited from the leading clans were followed by a new generation keenly aware that the social position of their ministry was declining and their financial situation, as compared with that of the chiefs and teachers, was deplorable. They were now recruited from a class of 'second-letter catechists'. The old style catechist was passing from the scene, an unlamented exit only because in his village he was so far removed from the centre at Namirembe Hill as to be largely forgotten. Taken together, these facets of a process of 'disengagement' over half a century – reducing the presence and influence of the local level of chief, priest, catechist and missionary – was a serious challenge to the growth of the Church. The bishops felt they had to act, and they acted together, Anglicans and Catholics.

In 1918 the three bishops in Kampala – one Anglican and two Catholic – united in addressing a letter to the British governor on the moral climate in the Protectorate. They referred to the heroic first generation of martyrs, witnesses and devoted Christian chiefs – Anglican and Catholic – who had passed away ceding the place to a generation much greater in size but with perhaps less devotion, much more preoccupied with power, position and the wisdom of this world. Well, government ought to do something about the moral climate – particularly the sanctity of home life. The Christians, they said in a letter,

> have always been taught to connect morality with religion ... The attitude of religious neutrality has been misunderstood as identical with religious indifference and misinterpreted as implying indifference also as to moral character.[4]

The chiefs' morality had increasingly given cause for concern. Government and Church must be seen to co-operate in these matters:

> Without some such cooperation neither the authority of the State, nor the moral influence of the Church, working single-handed, will be able to stem the present current.[5]

In 1906, Bishop Tucker had called on government to treat Uganda as a 'Christian Country', and the idea of Uganda as a Christian nation was born. Government must overcome its neutrality in religious matters and give a lead.[6]

The letter of 1918 was an outstanding document as a sign of an united effort, a rare phenomenon in the Ugandan climate of denominational strife. The Anglicans had to bear the burden of responsibility. With a strong Muslim minority in the north, and with the Catholics increasing rapidly in Buddu as well as in the other kingdoms, the near monopoly of the Anglican position in Church and State seemed a problem. The Uganda Agreement of 1900 had laid down a highly preferential division of the three religious parties: Protestant, Catholic and Muslim. This was strictly adhered to in the following decades. A few figures will suffice. The religious distribution of chieftainships for Toro in 1920 was: forty-seven chiefs for the Protestants, ten for the Catholics, none for the Muslims and two for the Traditionalists. Comparable figures for Bunyoro were eighty-three, twenty-five, six and forty-one; for Ankole, ten, none, one, none; and for Busoga in the east, forty-five, four, four and one.

The governor's reply to the bishops' letter suggested that the bishops had taken too narrow a view while government must represent a broader definition of morality. Government's concern was to civilize rather than Christianize the country. Any disciplinary problems of the Churches with regard to the chiefs' marital and private life was a question between these men and the Church. This was to lead to a dramatic showdown. Thus, on

Christmas Day 1921, the Anglican Bishop Willis, took a step which shook the Ganda people: he had to suspend *kabaka* David Chwa from Holy Communion. Both in Catholic Buddu and in the Anglican areas the matter of the chiefs' polygamy had become a concern. It also had repercussions outside Uganda. For instance, in Bukoba most of the eight chiefs, baptized in the Catholic or Lutheran Church, soon had to be disciplined, becoming something of an embarrassment to the Churches.

In Uganda the situation seemed unchangeable. The two Churches in Buganda had assumed the leadership. In the Kampala–Entebbe area, higher educational centres for men and women were established, including what was to become the Makerere University College. Here was also the renowned Makindye Hospital with which no other clinic in the entire area could be compared. Buganda and the new generation of mission-educated Baganda were thus assured a continuous place of preference, not least since the 1930s brought a new lease of life to the Anglican diocese through the East African Revival. It was significant that for many years the great lay and ordained leaders in that movement were Baganda, such as William Nagenda, a Revivalist preacher on a world scale. However below the surface of seemingly calm Buganda, the rumblings of volcanic movements could soon be heard, in the Churches too, auguring unexpected changes for the Buganda establishment. In the periphery of the vast territory new voices and new languages were heard, inarticulate at first, but soon irresistibly demanding attention.

If the Ugandan Church situation appears less complicated than that of the other two East African territories, it may be attributable to the ever recurrent 'Buganda Syndrome'. This refers to a tendency to limit attention to the central kingdom of Uganda while forgetting some of the urgent problems of those in the so-called 'periphery'. In the circumstances, these brief sketches of the Catholic and Anglican Churches in the period cannot help but deal, in the main, with Buganda.

The Catholics

From 1920 the Catholic Diocese of Masaka, with its strong foundations dating from the days of Bishop Streicher, went from strength to strength. Africanization of local leadership proceeded as fast as the senior seminary produced its priests. The diocese was carried forward by that 'exile mentality'[7] which it had retained ever since its dramatic beginnings in the 1890s. A linguistic factor emphasized the diocese's 'exile' characteristic far into the new century: the White Fathers were French-speaking, whether they came from France, Canada or Holland. The Catholics were still referred to as *BaFransa* in a British protectorate where the Protestants were *BaInglesa*. The other Catholic mission in Uganda, the Mill Hill Fathers, were English-speaking.

Far away from the political centres of Kampala and Entebbe, the Catholics set out to form and build their spiritual kingdom in Buddu, the most developed Catholic diocese not only in Buganda but possibly in the whole of Africa. Marian devotion gave intensity to teaching and worship. A Catholic medal – 'a shield against Satan' – and the rosary carried by Christians in good standing gave distinction to the individual and a feeling of solidarity with the community. The crucifix was an 'elitist symbol'[8] carried in a larger size by chief and catechists. Holy water blessed by the priest helped against illness and could be carried home to the *shamba* in bottles. A vigorous folk Catholicism formed in that pleasant land of Buddu. The catechist was at hand in the village chapel, teaching catechism and the skill of reading. The catechists were numerous. In the 1920s Buddu had 333 of them. They enjoyed local prestige but they were also expendable. At a time when football was introduced to fascinated Ganda masses, Catechist Tito Zebasaja complained: 'A catechist is like a ball, he must go where he is kicked.'

Priests could not be kicked – at least not to the same extent. The first two Baganda priests were ordained in 1913, in the presence of a crowd of 15,000. The training of African priests had at first seemed a most unpromising proposition – particularly as the White Fathers as a matter of course insisted on the same high standards for Africa as elsewhere in the Catholic world. The standards were possibly too high, so several missionaries suggested they be lowered and thus adapted to the level of the people. It was in this crisis, as on so many other occasions, that Bishop Streicher's iron will showed the way: 'To get one indigenous priest is for me more important than converting ten thousand people', he insisted. History proved him right. Less than a decade later the first African was appointed superior of a station in Buddu. After another decade, in 1934, the White missionaries could be withdrawn from their positions as heads of stations and Africans alone placed in charge of the eight stations. Some of the White Fathers' stations were enormous centres, comparable only to the Benedictine Peramiho in southern Tanzania. The Villa Maria station with its forty-nine buildings and twenty-eight priests appeared as a huge Christian village. And in Kampala, in 1925, a new cathedral for 5,000 was built on Rubaga Hill.

This was when the Pope in Rome, Pius XI, considered the establishment of African hierarchies. From Rome's perspective, Masaka – with its fifty-six

African priests in charge of the parishes – seemed the logical place to begin. Thus, in 1939, the Pope announced the appointment of a Ganda priest, Joseph Kiwanuka, a member of the Community of White Fathers, as the Bishop of the Diocese of Masaka. The year 1939 seemed early for an episcopal appointment but for the fact that the Vatican had already in 1926 decided to appoint a Masaka priest as a bishop. There were, however, certain pseudo-political hesitations at the time: it was rumoured in Rome, probably wrongly, that the British adminstration would not accept an African as bishop. After the death of Pius XI, Pius XII consecrated Kiwanuka bishop. One Chinese and one Indian priest were consecrated on the same occasion, an illustration of the universality of the Church. At Masaka, bishop and priests were supported by the sisters. By 1899 the first six White Sisters had arrived in Buganda and ten years later the foundation was laid for an African sisterhood – the *Bannabikira*. In 1925 there were already 160 of them in more than thirty mission stations, only four of these being non-Buganda. The system was complete with its enormous strength and its inherent authoritarian limitation. No Church synod was deemed necessary to be called for the entire period 1923–74.

Catholics in East Africa provided numerous examples of staying power, modern versions of the classic *stabilitas loci* ideal: men and women who gave forty years or more to a local congregation, exerting a spiritual influence of great and lasting strength in a particular place. However there are also examples of an extraordinary personal influence across the length and breadth of two or more territories, changing lives and conditions of new generations. A remarkable example was that of Mother Mary Kevin of Dublin (1875–1958), and her work in Uganda, Kenya and elsewhere.

Having joined the Franciscan Sisters of Mill Hill in Ireland in 1898, when she made her professional vows, Mary Kevin went to Uganda in 1902 with Cardinal Vaughan's Mill Hill Fathers. Her little group of Irish sisters began at Nagalama, thirty miles from the Mill Hill headquarters at Nsambya Hill. The focus of the work was on girls' education and soon also on medical work. The strength of Anglican medical services under Drs Sir Albert and Howard Cook and Lady Cook inspired the training of Catholic medical workers under Dr Evelyn Conolly. Before long a group of girls at the Nsambya Girls School approached Mother Kevin with a view to joining the Franciscan order as nuns. In 1926 fourteen postulants entered the noviciate and donned the Franciscan habit.

In order to enlist highly competent co-workers, Mother Kevin started a noviciate in England. This later moved to the Mount Olivet Convent in Ireland, becoming 'The Congregation of Franciscan Sisters of Ireland', for the training of African teaching nuns. At first, Catholic medical work had to struggle with impediments in canon law but, after many years of effort at all levels of Catholic officialdom, Mother Kevin, together with others, was able to achieve the lifting of the ban on obstetrics, meaning that from then on nuns could also act as midwives. Mother Kevin and her African nuns gave their services to schools including secondary schools, hospitals and leprosaria. A tough senior government official recorded his impression of Mother Kevin:

> She is an amazing woman. The whole department may have decided that she cannot have approval for all her private enterprises. She calls on us. She is perfectly simple, perfectly charming and perfectly inflexible! Invariably she gets what she has come for; invariably she is proved to be right! She is a wonder, a woman totally dedicated to religion, she keeps us all on our secular toes.[9]

In every instance the work was influenced by a Carmelite spirituality dominated by the two Teresas, St Teresa of Avila and St Teresa of Lisieux. With unfailing faith and humour, Mother Kevin would solicit their help: 'She had a life-long friendship with St Teresa of Lisieux.' In 1948, the congregation had over 200 African sisters. Twenty convents were at work in Uganda, four in Kenya and two in South Africa. When Makerere University College was inaugurated in 1948, there were, to everybody's surprise, among the few girls with requisite university entrance qualifications, a number of Mother Kevin's Franciscan Sisters.[10]

The Anglicans

New times had come to Uganda and its Anglican Church. From the 1920s with the rising prestige of government-supported education and of teachers with higher education (increasingly trained at the Makerere University College), there was a drifting apart of Church and school and priest and teacher. The new 'African Teachers' Association' levelled its criticism against the Church. They felt that they represented modern times and the future against that somewhat out-dated institution, the Church. One of the leading Budo-trained teachers told me, 'We old Budonians were trained to think fast and freely', implying that the possibly slow-witted priest was left behind.

In a diocese historically inspired by Henry Venn's fundamental ideas, Africanization could proceed with determination: local congregations and soon rural deaneries were in the hands of African priests. The first African assistant bishop was consecrated in 1949. The problem with the choice of the Revd Aberi Balya was that he was a Toro, not a Ganda, so the appointment was resented by the Ganda. By 1957 the number of assistant bishops had increased to four; in Masaka, Ankole–Kigezi, Toro–Bunyoro and Rwanda–Burundi. In that year they were installed as bishops of their dioceses. At the beginning of the 1920s the African clergy numbered seventy with some 4,000 catechists. In 1960 the number of African clergy had risen to 323 with some 5,310 catechists. In the meantime, however, the majority of European staff had been diverted to educational and medical work and were thus paid by government subsidies. Amongst the European staff, only the bishop, the archdeacon and a couple of men at the theological seminary were engaged in specifically evangelistic work.

The Anglican bishop had at his side at this time three assistant bishops, one European (for Rwanda and Burundi) and two African, Anglican missionaries were few. In his autobiography, Bishop Leslie Brown wrote that in his time in Uganda (1953–65) 'the Catholic missionaries outnumbered the Anglicans by at least ten to one.'[11] The Anglican priest comparing his education with that of the impressive new generation of Catholic priests and their long theological preparation felt that he was not sufficiently prepared for a new era with urbanization, politicization and secularization. This was a complaint which he shared with Protestant colleagues elsewhere on the continent. Yet, in fairness, it must be added that Ugandan theological training should be viewed from a wider perspective. Its theological college, Mukono, had a teaching staff of exceptional quality. It was here that John V. Taylor served as principal, 1945–54, later to be succeeded by the Revd John Poulton. Here, theological training aimed at producing not so much a stiff and heavy uniform as a liberating process, leading the student to the sources in Holy Scriptures and related to the values of religious drama, African art and culture. A special concern was the training of the ordinands' wives. It was felt that the pastor of the flock should be seen as part of a Christian family, providing – ideally – an example of Christian family life. The academic attainment of the new generation of Anglican clergy was not the first priority. Something of an Anglican folk Church was emerging, closer to ordinary people and to the grass-roots than had been possible at the beginning of the century with its near identity then of *saza* chief and priest.

An impression of Africanization in the Uganda Church is provided by the situation in one of the Archdeaconries, Mbale (Busoga). In 1956 the archdeacon himself was an African and had as his co-workers six rural deans, over twenty local priests and over 300 lay readers (three classes) and some 500 assistant lay readers. However, the recruits for these posts showed that the same embarrassing mechanism was at work in Busoga as in some other parts of East Africa: they consisted mainly of young men with a primary education who, having failed to acquire a secondary education, turned to the Church for guidance and work. The bishop and archdeacon were always looking out for men with secondary education, but the salary situation made this attempt less than successful.

The social position of the Anglican priest was strengthened by his leading role in the local educational system. Schools were under the direction of the African clergy, who chaired all education committees, boards of managers and the Archdeaconry Board of Education. For the rest, the priest was 'perpetually settling family troubles'. From the 1930s Anglican Church life in Uganda was deeply influenced by the East African Revival, to which Uganda was more exposed than any other country. Revival cut across the established order of the Church. It also affected the theological college at Mukono. Revival created in the individual Bible student a new awareness of the essential Biblical values and a new thirst for the living waters, sometimes implying a critical attitude to the teaching provided in the seminary. The Principal of Mukono in the 1940s was J. C. Jones. To the ears of the Revivalists it sometimes appeared that their principal nourished doubts with regard to some of the Biblical verities and this devoted Welshman came to be seen by his students as a 'Liberal' theologian, possibly the first example of this type of reaction throughout Central Africa. The reaction from the students was extreme. Just before their concluding exam, the whole final-year class left the college, determined to have no truck with doubt and query in a place that should provide sure and immutable answers. (It should be added that the theological tutor in question returned home to Wales, where he was promptly made Bishop of Bangor.) Eventually, some of the rebels returned to the college to be duly ordained, while the majority preferred to serve as lay witnesses throughout Uganda and East Africa, with a certain critical attitude to the official image of the Church.

It was a *lay* movement: doctors, teachers, builders, carpenters, drivers and home-makers, testified that they had found a new life and came forward as active members of the 'Fellowship' *and* of the Church. The common experience of 'brokenness' and salvation paved the way for a new relationship between White and Black in the Church: the 'Bwana-subordinates' relationship was outmoded and people could now meet naturally on a first name basis. The 'Fellowship' in Kampala and the city's environs pioneered this change on behalf of Uganda as a whole, with repercussions throughout the region. Its impact on the Kigezi region in southern Uganda was, and still is, particularly strong. As a result, a disproportionately large number of Ugandan Anglican clergy come from among the Kiga (of Kigezi).

With all its apparent peacefulness, violence disturbed Uganda in the 1940s, with riots in 1945 and 1949 and the murder in 1945 of the Protestant *Katikiro* (chief minister), Martin Luther Nsibirwa, on the steps of Namirembe Cathedral. There were tendencies to return to traditional Ganda religion. *Kibuuka*, the god of war in earlier times, reappeared in a young Catholic 'priest', Kiganila.[12] The traditionalist tendency was sharply accentuated in connection with a traumatic national event on 30 November, 1953, when the *kabaka* was exiled to Britain by the British Governor. The country was thoroughly shaken. The crisis also revealed how far political developments had diminished the role of the Church in the nation. The Anglican bishop, Leslie Brown, had been on tour in the north of the country but was accused of complicity in the governor's action. In a hastily assembled meeting of rural deans the bishop was able to show that the governor's decision had indeed been taken without his knowledge. In the end the deans were reassured – 'but – you *ought* to have known!' At the time of the 1900 'Agreement' the Anglican Church had represented the 'Establishment', and fifty years later it was hard to accept that the heroes of the glorious past were now no more than shadows.

This was a time of suspense and expectation. A Ugandan politician remarked: 'We are all Johns waiting for a Messiah', an observation which is interesting from at least two points of view.[13] It was, possibly, the first time that a Ugandan politician adapted New Testament categories to a political statement. More specifically, the Messiah in this case did not seem to be far away. The return of the *kabaka* from his London exile after two years made him into a *kabaka yekka*, 'kabaka only', the name soon given to a political party with mainly Protestant members.

In the meantime the Makerere College at Kampala proceeded apace. It was common to all three East African territories and provided a focus for ambition and aspiration for the young. Founded in 1922, it was known as 'Makerere College' until 1963, Makerere University College 1963–70, and finally – after the breakup of the federal University of East Africa – as Makerere University from 1970. From the point of view of the two Churches in Buganda a particular promise was seen in the founding of a religious studies department at the university with Catholic and Anglican chaplains at work among the students. The Makerere chapels provided room for remarkable African religious art by, among others, Elimu Njau.

This Anglican Church on the equator represents so much of the Church history of the entire region that it would seem inevitable to attempt here a brief sketch of its characteristics, past and present. It is episcopal and, since 1960, a province within the Anglican Communion, with its own archbishop but for all that having a strong lay character: evangelical and Low Church to such an extent that the high altar in Namirembe Cathedral is without an altar cross, the objection to that piece of ecclesiastical furniture being that it would be too 'Romish'. The three English bishops after 1920, J. J. Willis, Cyril Stuart and Leslie Brown, each brought their special personal gifts and contributions. Willis, successor to the legendary Tucker, transmitting to a new time the strengths and the claims of the early history of the Church; Cyril Stuart, with infinite patience leading the Church through the trials and upheavals of the Revival; Leslie Brown, an internationally recognized expert on the worship of the Church, with a charismatic gift for the liturgical life of the flock. The first generation of African bishops, such as the Rt Revd Erica Sabiti, largely came from a background of the Hima social class and were devoted leaders of Church and Revival.

The African priest in the local congregation, perhaps with a son or grandson studying at the Budo secondary school, increasingly aware of his own academic limitations in a country adorned with the splendours – and stimulated by the challenges – of its Makerere University, was able to concentrate on his Biblical message of Salvation and New Life. He was part of a Church which, since the 1930, had been largely defined by the East African Revival, preaching and, what is more, practising a faith which in the 1970s was to be tried by torture, persecution and murder, in the 1980s going through the seemingly endless political struggles of the country. Surely for one Church history that is enough.

Northern Uganda: Catholics and Protestants

Northern Uganda, its Nilotic population, its many languages and its culture, is different from the rest of the country. The missions were different too. In the Catholic case, the Verona Fathers from northern Italy had arrived along the Nile. On the Protestant side there were 'African Inland' missionaries, but 'Inlanders' who were part of the Anglican Communion, soon to receive an Anglican archdeacon as organizer of the evangelical work – a European to be succeeded by an African, Hezekia Ajule. Yet, the role of African initiative proved to be similar here to that in other parts of Uganda and Africa. The Alur returnee who brought his Catholic message to his northern home village has already been referred to (p. 593), and there was a brief allusion to this young catechist's contact with the local chief Okelo, illustrating the themes which have been emphasized for other parts of Uganda. The

Protestants were to experience similar things. For six years, the Protestants did not seem to meet with any positive response. Then it all changed. An African from the north, in 1924, found himself as a road labourer in the south. At the camp, he received a new direction in life and set out to bring the Gospel to his own people at Yole, north-west of Arua. The message was thus not propagated by foreigners but 'carried home' by their own people.

The Catholic missionaries made Gulu their centre. In 1923 there were nineteen Verona Fathers, thirteen Verona sisters and six brothers working with some 300 catechists. In the decade 1923–34, the number of staff, Black and White, almost tripled. To this a fresh addition was made – the first American Teaching Brothers of the Sacred Heart – leading to a corresponding rise in the educational system. A remarkable Catholic scholarly achievement must be mentioned: that of Fr Joseph Crazzolara, born 1884. After two years in the Sudan, he arrived in Uganda in 1910. He published important anthropological studies on the Nuer, the Luo, the Acholi and the Lugbara. This learned scholar also wrote the first Catholic catechism in the Acholi language.

Between 1949 and 1969 there was an enormous rise in the numbers of Catholic members. Fifty-five per cent of the total population was now Christian. 'The country had been Christianized in half a century.' The Church in the Northern Province was then divided into four dioceses. There were problems, above all, the rules of Christian marriage, seemingly insoluble as they were. The Fathers had to concur with the statement of Fr Adrian Hastings: 'Modern matrimonial canon law is totally unadapted to our African situation.' The population of those 'regularly married according to the Church laws' was very low. This could lead to congregations of 100 boys and girls and less than ten adults. This had once obtained in the nineteenth century and was now demonstrated anew in this faraway place: the Church as a 'youth movement'.[14]

The Protestants – after that initial experience of the African 'returnee' carrying the Gospel to his home village – saw remarkable changes. The Lugbara women's annual conferences were soon numerous and had to be divided on the basis of separate parishes. These women had known their traditional place in society: subdued and dejected. The Gospel had a surprising message of equality for *all* human beings – and the Lugbara women could raise their heads. The work of African evangelists and their schools and catechetical centres laid the foundations for these changes. At the end of the 1920s, there were sixty primary schools, twelve junior secondary schools and one senior secondary school, together with a teacher training school. The remarkable missionary couple, A. E. and F. M. Vollor, and their African collaborators translated the New Testament into Lugbara in 1936. At once people were seen 'digging for the New Testament', in order to earn the shillings needed to buy it in their own language. Then followed the Alur New Testament and the Alur Bible in 1955, while other languages were studied with a view to preparing new Bible translations.

RWANDA AND BURUNDI

Further west, the Belgian empire had been awarded by Treaty of Versailles a rich plum in the form of Rwanda–Burundi which had been part of German East Africa until 1917. In 1919, Versailles made the country a mandate under the League of Nations and thus not a colony – a distinction which a powerful African king could try to manipulate as far as he dared. In 1921, Bishop Hirth's long rule over the Rwanda–Burundi vicariate came to an end. The following year, Bishop Classe took charge of the Church in Rwanda while J. Gorju, missionary in Uganda since 1895, became bishop in Burundi. As White Fathers they held Cardinal Lavigerie's vision before their eyes: a Catholic kingdom in Central Africa, and Rwanda–Burundi seemed just the place for the realization of this ideal.

However, as it turned out, neither of the African kings in the 1920s were all that promising as potential converts. King Mwamabutsa of Burundi had been enthroned as ruler at the tender age of three. Eventually he married a Christian princess but was never baptized himself and in the end, with the revolutions of the 1960s, he fled the country. His colleague in Rwanda, King Musinga, was known to have been pro-German: a good thing when the Germans were in charge but a bad thing once the Germans were no longer there. He was also known to adhere to the traditional religion. The Belgians kept him on for a decade and then deposed him in 1931 in favour of his more amenable son, the catechumen Rudahigwa, who became *mwami* with the name of Mutare IV. Here at last was the king who could fulfil Lavigerie's dream. In 1943 he was baptized in the presence of fifty Catholic chiefs, with the Belgian governor general as godfather.

The beginning of his reign also marked the beginning of the conversion of the Tutsi. Until World War I the Rwanda Church had been largely a Hutu Church while the Tutsi aristocracy hesitated outside the Church gates. Now a momentous change set in motion a veritable Tutsi tornado. Between 1932 and 1936, the Tutsi virtually tripled Church membership from 81,000 to 233,000. Church government and feudal hierarchy went hand in hand. Tutsi diviners could be seen burning their amulets. Young Tutsi thronged to the catechumen centres and as they filled the school rooms they found Tutsi

Table 17.1. *Roman Catholic Church statistics in Burundi*

Year	Mission stations	Baptized Christians	Catechumens	European priests	African priests
1922	5	14,500	30,000	15	–
1927	10	28,500	44,000	25	–
1935	19	140,000	192,000	49	10
1937	22	253,000	227,000	54	12
1949	34	610,000	240,000	118	29
1957	71	1,200,000	353,000	244	117

teachers eager to raise the intellectual life of the aristocracy. The rumour spread that the king wanted people to make the sign of the cross in greeting him, and chiefs began to serve at Mass. In the late 1930s, parishes were already managed by Rwanda priests. As the whole atmosphere made the Church into an *ecclesia triumphans*, the Christianization movement swept over the green hills. The triumph reached its apex in 1946 when King Mutare IV himself, in a grand ceremony, dedicated his country to Christ the King. The pro-Tutsi Bishop Classe enjoyed an authority comparable only with that of his Benedictine colleague in Lubumbashi (then named Elizabethville), de Hemptinne.

The tension between Tutsi and Hutu in the Church could be smoothed over for a time, but neither really bridged nor healed. Even in the theological seminary the old antagonism, although dressed in Latin, could be felt as humiliating. Tutsi dominance was complete but the Hutu fellow-students were not likely to forget.

In Burundi, Bishop Gorju waited six years, trying to find a new approach. Then, in 1927, he radically changed the whole structure and system of the diocese. The Synodal statutes of 1928/1929 laid down the rules for a new method, with the most far-reaching consequence for missionaries, African priests and catechists, and for every catechumen on the hillside. The results can be seen in black and white (see Table 17.1).

'Away from the station' was the slogan. Instead of bringing the catechumens for four to five days a week to the station and to the missionary, Gorju reversed the whole process. The Church founded a wide net of local centres and catechists were sent out to be responsible for the work there. The focus of the whole work was switched from shepherding the Christian flock to the conversion of the pagans. At the root, there was a difference in theology. Hirth had wanted 'good Christians' who could serve as models of faith and knowledge to the pagans. Gorju was out to win the pagan masses. The six months' final intensive training on the station came to an end. The catechumens were taught in their own villages, and the task of the missionary and the African priest was to control the work of the catechist. Here Gorju was adamant. The control had to be rigorous. 'Even if all the Protestants in the world were after us, I would not concede this point.' Gorju was convinced that the result of the success of the catechists corresponded exactly to the amount of attention the missionary and priest were able to give them.

In Burundi, the evangelization was only to a comparatively limited extent dependent on the conversion of the chiefs, but their particular influence was nonetheless important. By about 1948, thirty-two of the thirty-six *saza* chiefs and 441 of the 536 local chiefs were Roman Catholics. Yet in the Rwanda case there was a disturbing complication which in the long-run could prove to be the kind of temptation to which a Church leader could not allow himself to yield: a tendency perhaps to give prominence to one particular section of the community over others in the same Church, and this on account of its members' supposed superiority in terms of height or length or features or mythical history. Therefore the upshot of the drama could not be triumph pure and simple, but in the midst of triumph, tragedy, and in the midst of victory, vicissitude, as independent Rwanda and Burundi were to experience civil war and ethnocide on a terrible scale.

Both Rwanda and Burundi had a number of 'non-conformist' Protestant missionaries, among them the Seventh Day Adventists, representing a Hutu *culte de contestation* in a predominantly Catholic *milieu*.[15] In 1968, they had reached out to 326 places of regular worship. There were also Free Methodists, Danish Baptists and Swedish Pentecostals, the latter – in Burundi – by far the largest number of Protestant Hutu.

THE EAST AFRICAN REVIVAL

The Protestant revivalist character of the Anglican Church in Uganda was reproduced and intensified by their co-religionists in Rwanda. At first, the Anglican missionaries in Rwanda consisted almost entirely of medical doctors, 'with their Cambridge medical degrees and upper-class backgrounds'.[16] Their evangelical convictions were clear: the Anglican mission was 'to operate on Bible, Protestant and Keswick lines'. Earlier our attention was drawn to the Protestant medical doctors' role as Church leaders in Africa, and the Rwanda experience bears this out. Together with the doctors, there were a few men and women concerned with Bible translation and Bible study. It was in the spiritual fellowship between English doctors and African orderlies in Rwanda that the East African Revival emerged,

Dr J. E. Church being the initiator and leader. One young leader was Kosiya Shalita, a Tutsi from Ankole, later to be consecrated as Anglican Bishop of Ankole. The British missionary staff had a stronger character of family connections than elsewhere. The Revd H. E. Guillebaud with his wife and daughter were the Bible translators.[17]

The Revival changed the climate of Protestant Churches in East Africa. After a first generation in the Churches devoted to catechism drill and grind, they were now in the 1930s unexpectedly hit by a transforming inspiration. Low Church Anglicans (the CMS), Methodists, Presbyterians, Lutherans, they were all radically transformed by this evangelical infusion and brought together in a warm 'Fellowship'.

With its singing, the ever-repeated theme song, *Tukutendereza* (We magnify Thee), its ever-repeated personal testimonies about sin and overcoming sin by total surrender to Christ, the Revival appeared as a genuinely African movement, knitting together as strongly integrated groups, a new clan, that of Christ. Yet, this genuinely African movement borrowed some of its initial inspiration from Europe, from Keswick in England, through British Evangelical medical doctors. It started in Rwanda, or rather in an Anglican, CMS, hospital in Rwanda, with the doctor, J. E. Church. It was in the meeting between Western doctor and African orderly at the hospital, together kneeling before the same Saviour and finding one another in Christ, speaking to one another, for the first time, on first-name terms, that this movement began.

From this geographical point in the bush, in Rwanda, the movement spread to Uganda, to western Tanzania and soon much further afield. Of course, the breakthrough did not happen at once. The first pioneers in each country and region of a country had to encounter embittered resistance, until one day these very opponents came forward in the 'Fellowship' confessing serious sins – theft, whoredom, relying on witchcraft – and were then, under enormous acclamation from the Brethren, welcomed into the Fellowship. At first Kenya and eastern Tanzania insisted that the Revival 'belonged to the West' (*magharibi*) – Rwanda, Uganda and Bukoba (north-western Tanzania) – and should hopefully remain there not disturbing the peace of established and highly respected ecclesiastical bodies. However in unknown and surprising ways the Revival hurried along, winning its adherents in the tens of thousands.

A broader sociological study should be made on the social background of men and women who joined the Revival. There appeared, it seems to us, a new generation of lay people in the Churches no longer satisfied with the self-evident proclamations of pastor and catechist, who were looking for a more radical personal message. There were the teachers, the hospital orderlies and nurses, the building contractors, masons and artisans, the shopkeepers, the housewives.

In Kenya the message was brought forward, above all, by railway men – as we have seen in other chapters of this book, these gentlemen on rails were a factor of the greatest importance for the evangelization of Africa – and by officers and privates from the army and police. These men stood up in the Fellowship of the Church, confessing sins of some size and significance and, sometimes with tears, asking for forgiveness, praying for the new life in Jesus Christ.

The Revivalists, both men and women, were modernizers. The language gave symbolic expression to that need for newness and life. In one's Swahili speech one used great English terms – 'Fellowship', 'Convention' – also in one's regular epistolary contacts all over the East Africa region. A wide ecumenical understanding and co-operation was brought about but an ecumenicity of a special kind. In Central Europe the defenders of the faith asked themselves anxiously 'Should good Lutherans hobnob with Anglicans?' – could there be any links between the two? This fellowship on the equator through the Revival was brought about not by intellectual argument or theological definition or by any 'Faith and Order' declaration but by experiential togetherness. There had been formed here a unity of 'blood-brothers' in Christ, a deeper and much more intense unity than elsewhere.[18]

TANZANIA

Chief and Church in Tanzania

In Tanzania, the chiefs still dominated the local and regional scene though their powers were certainly curbed by the League of Nations Mandate government. On the whole, these mighty men were more dependent on governor and provincial commissioner than they cared for. But from the point of view of the local ethnic community and the religious group it appeared as if the old order was still in force, with seemingly absolute powers vested in the chief.

Already in the German period the king of the Fipa was, as has been mentioned, baptized to be thenceforth known as Wilhelm Adolf Kilatu. The other Fipa princes were instructed at the Mwazye School for princes, and the Catholic Church with the White Fathers was well on the way to winning the entire community. By 1920, 75 per cent of the Fipa were baptized. The picture would however not remain altogether without shadows from the

Church's point of view. The Depression in the 1930s affected the area, and the 'Kamchape' witchcraft eradication movement was a challenge to the Church. Yet, fundamentally, the Catholic influence remained strong as the 'conventional religion' of the region. For the vast majority of the Fipa, Church affairs belonged to Fipa culture, and the White Fathers managed to influence certain sectors of social and economic life. 'Folk Catholicism' was a reality.[19]

In the southern highlands the chiefs at first protested against the introduction of schools: 'The children after instruction became rebellious and maintained that they were under the Mission only, not obeying the Tribal Authority.' This was applied to all forward looking missions in the area impartially, e.g. the Benedictines, Consolata Fathers, UMCA and the Berlin Mission.[20] But there was soon a tendency to start schools for the sons of chiefs. The most ambitious of these was a government endeavour, the Malangali 'tribal school', in southern Tanganyika, mainly serving the Hehe and Sangu communities. W. B. Mumford, the Government School Inspector, used Hehe and Sangu elders as tutors for the students.

Further north in Tanganyika, priests in the Shambala-speaking area belonged to the leading Kilindi clan, thereby providing a connection between priest and chief, typical of the first generation development in the Churches. In northern Tanganyika several chiefs among the Arusha, Meru, Chagga and Pare peoples were Lutheran. Some of these had been teachers or hospital dressers before being elected as chiefs. They were often related by marriage to leading Lutheran pastors, thus giving the pastors relatively easy access to the chief. In Chaggaland, some of the Christian chiefs were highly devoted members of their Lutheran Church. They were anxious to defend its good name in the times of need – 1939 to 1945 and beyond – and keen to enhance its image both nationally and internationally. At the first All African Lutheran Conference at Marangu, the nature of the Christian ministry was discussed on a continental level. The leading Chagga chief, Marealle, suggested that the Lutheran Churches accept episcopacy in their system rather than persevere with their Church presidents and superintendents. His proposal met with an enthusiastic reception and episcopacy was introduced by the local Lutheran dioceses in the period 1960–87. A decade later, a European observer expressed his distaste for this – in his view – untimely proposition, adding with considerable conceit: 'It did not emerge from the Church itself', (*nicht aus dem Raum der Kirche*), as if leading laymen in the Church should not voice any opinions but leave it to pastors and missionaries alone.[21]

In the highly rank-conscious Hima society of Uganda and western

Tanganyika – 'the Kings' Way' – the pastor was continually made aware of his place in relation to the chief. Whether he was allowed to eat or to drink tea with the chief or not was seen as a measure of his social standing. The local congregation would immediately realize his, and thereby their own, status. In Ankole, social differences among the people were also clearly reflected in the Church. From the beginning of the Church's history, the Ankole priests were usually of Hima origin, and the two rural deans belonged to this rank. However, after 1945, most new priests came from the peasant class. Relations between ministers from the two different social levels were sometimes strained. A student from Ankole noticed a Hima rural dean and a peasant-class priest eating together in 1955: 'They had goat's meat and they ate together, this *never* happened before.' The objective truth of this statement is less important than his subjective impression of its exceptional character. The priests and pastors of noble blood realized that their number was rapidly diminishing, but they were convinced that their conciliating influence was needed. When an Anglican assistant bishop in south-western Uganda, coming from the peasant class, dared to challenge the moral standards of the head of his kingdom, priests belonging to the nobility were strongly critical of the Bishop's prophetic outburst.

In the Bukoba area in Tanganyika a similar social revolution occurred, although it was less drastic than that in Ankole. Three of the fifteen Protestant pastors in the 1950s came from noble families, one of them was the rural dean. These three men felt that good contacts with the chief were useful for the Church and gave the pastor added prestige. The chief and his family were given special chairs at the services, while the humble crowd of ordinary Christians sat on grass spread on the floor. With the British take-over from 1919 the chiefs felt a pressure to accept the religion of the colonial power. This could be seen in the Bukoba area with its eight local 'kings'. The new district Commissioner, D. L. Baines, was a determined official who saw to it that young members of chief's clans were sent to Buganda for higher education. He concentrated his educational efforts on the Hima section of the society. Around 1920, five of the eight 'kings' were baptized according to the Anglican rite, this being the 'religion of the king' in Kampala as in Buckingham Palace. The brother of one of these Bukoba rulers, later a teacher, was also sent to Buganda for his training. He writes in his abrupt manner: 'The beginning of the Christian religion in my life: my first missionary [*muhibiri*, 'preacher', is the term he uses], Mr. D. L. Baines, District Commissioner in Bukoba from 1917.'[22]

There was sometimes a tendency for the poor pastor to appear too compliant to his mighty chief. On the other hand, the pastor's Christian conviction might give him courage in a critical situation, as in the following example from Bukoba, Tanzania, 1942.

When it was known that the Lutheran youth group, 'Buhaya's Hope', had widened its membership to include girls, the chiefs in Council were incensed and demanded that the movement be forbidden. They knew what to do with young girls. So they instructed their secretary, Mwami F. X. Lwamigira – at the time the great showpiece of Tanzanian Indirect Rule – to address a letter to the 'Evangelical Mission'. It began with a Luhaya proverb: 'The woman is a sheep, she spends her time in the kitchen and eats there.' For such a creature to participate in meetings with boys was completely improper, and the chiefs asked the Mission to stop such unseemly association.

Pastor Jonathan Karoma was asked to respond to the letter. He was himself definitely not of the chiefly clan but had a hereditary distinction of his own; being the son of an *embandwa* (diviner), when young he had started out on the *embandwa* road until one day a British District Commissioner had him placed in the Protestant school. He was baptized and eventually became a devoted catechist, later to be ordained – a charismatically gifted preacher and totally fearless. Courage was needed at this very time, when there was a rumour in the villages that the German missionaries had been interned, and the 'religion of the Protestants' of which he was a member had been forbidden. Pastor Karoma started his letter in a deferential way:

> My Lords,
>
> We thank you for your letter. You are quoting our proverb: 'The woman is a sheep ... ' Well, in the past women were sheep, but now the light has dawned also for them so that they have become civilized beings, just as we men. What do women do?
>
> Bear children ... Sheepish?
> Rear children ... Sheepish?
> Attend the sick ... Sheepish?
> Plough and cook ... Sheepish?
>
> ... Is this bad? ... But what is really bad is whoredom ... Therefore we have laid down a law that young men and women before being married have to be medically examined ... As I see it, 'The Hope' cannot be dissolved.
>
> Revd Jonathan Karoma,
> Your faithful servant[23]

At the beginning of the 1920s in the south of the country, the German Benedictines were, as Germans, ordered to leave Tanzania but were in 1922 replaced by Swiss members of their order. The two Benedictine abbeys, Peramiho and Ndanda rose to become immensely impressive centres of Church and culture. After the Maji Maji rebellion, ending in the tragic defeat of the Ngoni chiefly elite, the population turned with great determination to Christianity and the Catholic Church. In 1912 the young Ngoni chief Laurenti Gama was baptized, and the number of Christians at Peramiho, almost 500 in 1907, rose to nearly 4,400 in 1916 and to 200,000 in 1968. The number of European priests was regularly high – about eighty – but so was, increasingly, the number of African priests and brothers. In accordance with Benedictine tradition, the place – with its abbey and churches, schools and centres of practical training – resounded with song and music of the highest order. The Revd Stephen Mbunga, OSB, was a creative contributor to African Church music.

A fundamental problem was that of a vernacular. The Germans had introduced Swahili and, looking at the situation in a coastal perspective, the Dar es Salaam government in British times likewise pressed for Swahili. The inland communities in Tanzania, together with Buganda, rejected Swahili; the linguistic connotations of Arab slavery from the nineteenth century were too strong for some of these communities. Muslims on the coast were commonly referred to as 'Swahili'. But if Swahili, what kind of Swahili? From the beginning of the century there was a heated controversy between two schools of linguistic thought: the British – particularly among the UMCA experts on the coast who followed 'Zanzibar Swahili', and the German Lutherans together with other inland missions who set out to 'de-Arabize' and 're-Bantuize' the Swahili of the Bible. The outstanding contribution in the latter camp was that of Karl Roehl of the Bethel Mission, with missionary experience from Usambara and Rwanda. His attractively produced version was a daring attempt welcomed by the inland communities, not least as far as the translation of the New Testament Epistles was concerned. In the inland villages the coastal Swahili of the Pauline Epistles was almost unintelligible to the ordinary reader.

African culture on the coast: Zaramo women

As for the work among women and girls, the inter-war period also saw a highly imaginative initiative – among the Zaramo people near Dar es Salaam – inspired by Anna von Waldow of the Berlin Lutheran Mission. Born 1894, she spent a decade, 1930–40, working with these people. There was a Zaramo tradition of forcing pubescent girls to sit isolated in their respective homes for a period of between two and eight years. This supposedly prepared and matured the girl for marriage. The physical and mental consequences of the practice were such that in 1929 the local congregation on its own, took the initiative to limit the *waana-wali* period to one month only. This was synchronous with early political initiatives taken by the local Zaramo community through 'African Associations'.[24] At this very time Anna von Waldow appeared on the scene. Because of her remarkable personality and educational aptitude she was able to identify with the local situation. She won the confidence of the Christian mothers as well as of the pagan and Muslim communities.

After the shortened *waana-wali* period the girls were now gathered in a common centre to be taught the three R's and agriculture. The method of education was authoritarian but also involved strong democratic elements. The girls chose among themselves, by rotation, an 'elder' for each week in turn. The new education was integrated into Zaramo culture and aimed at education for leadership. Soon it was possible to place the girls as women elders in the congregations, as teachers in schools and members of the Church synod. Developed by Anna von Waldow, this practice became a model for some of the other Lutheran missions in the territory.

Masasi and African culture

Nobody followed the debate on African culture as boldly as the Anglo-Catholic Bishop of Masasi, W. V. Lucas (1883–1945). Fascinated by the nature of liturgical action, Lucas, on his arrival at Masasi as a young priest, took an interest in the boys' initiation as a protracted liturgical process. To the Yao and Makua communities among which he was working, the *lupanda* ritual was a fundamentally important *rite de passage* with circumcision for the young boys in the community. Instead of condemning or ignoring this social institution, Lucas tried to 'Christianize' it. Instead of raising a lupanda tree as in the traditional rite, there was now a wooden cross in the centre of the glade, and rather than calling upon the ancestors one turned to the Saints of Holy Church. At night there was time for drums and dance although the dances were now chosen according to a list approved by the Bishop. Circumcision followed in the forest, performed by an African orderly or doctor. This was followed by a six-week preparation for confirmation – including instruction in the community's code of honour, given by the local chief. Subsequently, individual confession was said (which of course had also been part of the traditional ceremony). The boy's head was shaved, and his old belongings burned and he was dressed in new clothes. On the last Sunday, all met for Thanksgiving Mass in the cathedral and as a finishing act, the priest led the young to the west door where with enormous enthusiasm from the crowd the young, who under the protection of the Church had become men, were returned to their relatives.

In an utterly complex social situation in southern Tanzania, Bishop Lucas found African deacons, teachers and elders who were interested in replacing traditional rites and symbols perceived as intolerable in Christianized ceremonies. He needed this collaboration with African Christian leaders as the European clergy were largely opposed to his initiative. Some of the African deacons were all for it. Their active collaboration in the rites helped them 'to define and increase their prestige'. The Christian *jando* was seen as an acceptance of the new social realities, associated with the passage of boys through the mission school. Not all Africans agreed with the Bishop, however. Some 'progressives' in the diocese felt that the Christianization of the initiation rites tended to retard cultural development:

> It helped to preserve the idea of their importance and necessity at a time when the general crisis of initiation might have resulted in the dwindling away of initiation into the mere act of infant circumcision.[25]

DAR ES SALAAM

Zanzibar and the coastline in the nineteenth century had represented the Churches' focal point, with its leaders the Catholic Vicar Apostolic of Zanguebar and the Anglican Bishop of Zanzibar. While still retaining his old title, the Bishop of Zanzibar moved to the mainland, to Magila, and the Catholic Vicar Apostolic to Dar es Salaam. This was more than just a change of episcopal residences. Dr G. W. Broomfield of the UMCA, a sharp and learned observer with disappointing experiences of Muslim society on the island, exclaimed that a prophet must come to rouse 'the dead consciences of . . . Zanzibar and that such a prophet could only come when called and sent by God.' The mainland seemed more promising.

The mosques dominated Dar es Salaam visually and acoustically. In the inter-war period the capital had a Muslim appearance. Only with Independence in 1961 did this image change substantially as the Christian inland communities sent their young to the city. Asian trade and a harbour facing India gave an impression of enterprise. In 1921, Dar es Salaam had a population of 20,000, in 1950: 72,000, and in 1964: 150,000 including 35,000 Asians, 3,000 Goanese and 4,000 Europeans. The great majority were African labourers; with Independence, there was a cadre of African civil servants.

It took time for the Church to discover the city. The Anglo-Catholics, who had traditional links with Zanzibar and remarkable educational and medical centres on the coast, did not start in Dar es Salaam until 1921. Dar es Salaam, largely with Arab and Asian businessmen, had to await the coming of Independence in 1961 in order, as a Church centre, to assume a centripetal role of welcoming rapidly growing Christian communities from the Churches inland. The emerging city and the towns were also unwelcoming, hostile places to the pastor. A synodical council had posted one of these pastors, from the far west of the country, on a short-term assignment to the capital. He did not like it: 'I now have to *buy* food', he told the present writer, then his bishop, thus summarizing the most unbearable fate a man might have to face.

Coastal plantation and evangelism

Sisal, even more than coffee, cotton or gold, was Tanzania's great money-earner at this time. Between 1923 and 1938 the country's share of sisal on the world market rose from 27 to 36 per cent, the business being run by Asian, Greek, German and to some extent, Swiss and British firms. The sisal was exported to be processed as hemp for the harbours of Western Europe, North America and Britain. It was these sisal plantations which attracted the anonymous labouring masses, where the individuals were simply referred to as *manamba* in Swahili, meaning numbers. They came from the impoverished famine areas of the central provinces and the Ha and Rundi in the west, as well as from the Makonde and Makua communities in Southern Tanzania and Mozambique. Among the masses of sisal workers there arose something of a hierarchy according to ethnic provenance, while women and child workers were to be found at the bottom of the pyramid.[26]

No study has yet been made of any evangelistic activity on these plantations. It so happens that the present writer had close personal contact during World War II with certain foot-loose groups of evangelists prepared in the name of Christ to abandon their ordinary work to be involved for some time with the spiritual well-being of these masses. At the home base they were a highly progressive group of Christian Revivalists among the Ziba in northern Bukoba (west of Lake Victoria), just hit by the East African Revival and soon ready to carry the message further afield. Faithful members of their Lutheran Church, they formed themselves into a body which they – with some forgivable recklessness – referred to as 'Victorious Christianity'. The 'victory' in question consisted in giving up for a long while their own business – farm (*duka*) or fishing canoes – which in the meantime were taken over by their local friends and fellow Revivalists, the latter prepared to replace them later. So they went from the north-west to the coast at the other end of the country, spiritually sustained by their three books, the Swahili Bible and hymn-book together with that remarkable

Protestant lay dogmatics of the period, Dr J. E. Church's *Kila mtu mwanafunzi wa Biblia*, (*Every man a Bible reader*).[27]

Their adventure did not bring them any financial profit but widened their horizon and helped to make them and those now committed to their spiritual care aware of the unity of the Church – a unity transcending tribal and denominational frontiers. Once again, this involvement illustrates the dominant theme of this book: the role of African initiative in the Christianization of Africa. How far and how deeply the listeners in those outdoor Bible meetings received their fervent message – in the light of the pressure lamp – is in itself a task for research. Judging from a thousand similar experiences throughout the continent at the time it cannot have been without impact on the anonymous groups of labourers from afar, themselves uprooted and possibly prepared to seek new direction in life.

Upon mentioning this Lutheran diocese west of Lake Victoria, we must momentarily digress to make a general point about the quality of mission-related Churches. At present there is a romantic tendency in some African history-writing according to which only the so-called Independent Churches are seen as expressions of vitality, while a great number of mission-related Churches, on account of their connections with the West supposedly lack that virtue.

It is time to modify this bias. Sustained contact with the congregational life of the latter category of Churches should give a lasting impression of its essential character. Certain personalities embodied this vitality, such as Jonathan Karoma in Bukoba, 1908–*c.* 1978. Karoma's family background was distinguished in that his father and elder brother were both *embandwa* (diviners). This heritage imbued him with a peculiar affinity with the spiritual depth-dimension of traditional African religion. B.Sr. had the privilege of knowing him well. For eighteen months, 1942–43, B.Sr. followed him daily to every local congregation in the diocese spending two or three weeks in each parish. Daily B.Sr. had occasion to listen to his captivating message. If a charismatic preacher is one who exhibits 'overweights of joy' and conviction together with depth of Christian insight, all marked by humour and utter seriousness, then Jonathan Karoma was a charismatic. Throughout his life he gave the impression of being completely at home in his Lutheran Church. To him, this was indeed a 'place to feel at home', and even if he was an extraordinary personality, he was not alone in thus appreciating his Church: a number of his colleagues would have been prepared to make the same claim for themselves.

By overemphasizing the role of the Independent Churches with their prophets and prophetesses, one does not give full due to generations of dedicated pastors and leaders in the established Protestant Churches. There was never any propensity towards 'Independency' with Karoma. In fact, when for a time an Independent breakaway did occur (through the Revd Sylvester Machumu), Jonathan Karoma was among the sharpest opponents of this deviation, warning against the fatal consequences of division in the body of the Church. There must have been in the African Churches hundreds like him – but their existence and function in the Church has never been recognized.

One thinks of his congregation, Kanyengereko, in Bukoba and his daily contact with men and women in that congregation, his creative dealing with the youth movement begun by him and Evangelist William Bwanuma – a youth movement which saw its task as ministering to the old and destitute. He represented a whole generation of Christian converts throughout the length and breadth of the continent – the builders of the congregation, inspirers and sustainers of life and freedom leading people to new discoveries in the Bible, as a source of wisdom and life – not a divisive but rather a cohesive factor.

The Catholics

The growth of the Catholic Church in Tanzania is exemplified in the personal experience of the most outstanding of its bishops, J. Blomjous of Mwanza, in the western part of the country. 'When I came as a bishop to Mwanza [at the southern end of Lake Victoria] there were 9,000 Christians; when I left in 1965, their number was 200,000, organized in three dioceses.'

In the inter-war period there was a marked difference between west and east in Tanzanian Catholicism: the west directed by the White Fathers in their ambitious educational programme, rapidly rising school system and progressive attitude toward Africanization of the Church; the east with a number of Catholic missions appearing comparatively cautious and conservative with regard to educational policy and Africanization. In this British territory *all* Catholic missionaries, whether in the east or the west, were non-British, with non-British bishops – all wary of British ideas and policies. This became obvious to Bishop Hinsley in 1928 as he made his tour of East Africa with a view to radically raising the educational standards of Catholic schools. Nobody saw this need as clearly as Hinsley, determined as he was to win his Catholic brethren over to a British system of generous collaboration of Church and State in school matters. But Hinsley – the future Cardinal Archbishop of Westminster – did not at first find much positive response in Tanzania.

For most of the period 1920–60 the house of Catholic bishops was divided over this fundamental issue of education. In eastern Tanzania there was a dominant 'Libermann' tradition with its bush-school ideal, supposedly adapted to the needs of the African masses – and just right for the Church's real business which was evangelization and literacy. When in 1947 Bishop David Mathew came as apostolic delegate, he discovered this difference between the two schools of thought among the bishops – and played on it in the episcopal synods. Historian and student of international affairs, Mathew's concern was to 'indigenize' the Church as fast as possible. India, together with the rest of colonial Asia, was becoming Independent: soon it was to be Africa's turn, with enormous consequences for the Church. That meant first of all, the forming of a highly educated – but not bourgeois – clergy and episcopate. These were fundamental directives for the dramatic changes of the 1950s, prior both to political Independence and to Vatican II.

It is not possible to follow in detail the rapid development in the various dioceses. Suffice it to note that in the period 1918–68 the number of Tanzanian Catholics rose from 60,000 to 2,350,000. The strongest Catholic dioceses were those of Moshi, Bukoba, Karema, Songea and Mahenge. While the first two shared a dominant role in their respective communities with comparatively active and influential Protestant Churches, the latter three appeared as almost exclusively Catholic. In 1953 an ecclesiastical hierarchy was established in Tanzania with two Church provinces: Tabora and Dar es Salaam. The diocese of Bukoba, which in 1917 was in a position to ordain the first African priests in the country, in 1952 saw one of its priests, Laurian Rugambwa, become the first African bishop, first of Rutabo and then of Bukoba. He was later to be raised to Cardinal (residing from 1965 in the capital, Dar es Salaam). Characteristically, he came from one of the leading chiefs' clans in Bukoba.

The capital on the coast increasingly demanded the Catholics' attention. In 1945 it was still possible for the Fathers – on their busy motorbikes – to keep in contact with their total membership in Dar es Salaam. The proportion of priest to Church membership was an ideal 1 to 700. But even so, the Fathers felt that they did not make a sufficient impact: 'A sermon, religious instruction to school children and even house visits are not enough', a noble complaint in a situation when others may have felt this was more than enough. The Catholic missionaries were now Swiss Capuchins, with an increasing staff.

What happened in the twentieth century to the nineteenth-century Christian villages inland? The local congregation at Mandera can here represent the story of the Church in the eastern zone. It was founded as one of the very first Christian villages forming inland offshoots from the mother Church at Bagamoyo. Through the decades faithful individuals personified the tradition. When Catechist Mzee Eugene died in 1936 he was remembered as a striking representative of the past. Mission-inspired cotton plantations helped the whole community economically, transforming the countryside and the local economy. In one year, 1938, the mission bought 1 million kilogrammes of cotton for its gin.[28]

In the 1910s the numbers had declined because of the Church's involvement in the war. Disappointed that the missionaries had let their Christians down when drafted to military service by the Germans, many turned to Islam. In 1956, Christians numbered 3,600 and the catechumens sixty-five, while the average Sunday service attendance was 852. For Easter no less than 1,470 'made their Paska' and, what is more, fourteen Mandera youngsters were studying at the Bagamoyo Seminary. In 1955 the first priest born at Mandera, Bartholomeo Mwenguo, was ordained. The day after the ordination he took his first Mass at the altar of his native church. Church bells were sounded, guns were fired and drums beaten, and two cattle given by the Christians were slaughtered to feed the immense crowd. In 1958 a new church was built and consecrated. The catechumenate at Mandera was an intense corporate and individual experience as the neophytes of the Church would spend long periods at the centre.

The two world wars made their distinctive mark on Church development in Tanzania. The coincidence of political settlement after the first war affected the Catholics as well. Most striking perhaps is the case of the Alsatian Bishop Xavier Vogt who had to vacate Morogoro and the British-mandated territory of Tanzania only to be immediately translated to Yaoundé and the French-mandated territory of Cameroon. With Vogt's demise from East Africa, Tanzania's loss was indeed Cameroon's gain. Such was the fate of Alsatians, frontier men on the borderline between supposedly inimical peoples in war-torn Europe.

In the Kilimanjaro area, British authorities were determined to close down a mission of the Spiritans, considered 'German'. As a good Alsatian, Auguste Gommenginger was able however, to produce an official document from 1870 showing that he had then opted for French nationality, thereby ensuring in the new era an undisturbed continuity of Catholic work. Gommenginger was a powerful mission leader at the Catholic Kilimanjaro stations, Kilema and Kibosho. He was an old-timer in the area having arrived in 1890 as the generous benefactor of the people. This was because he had brought the first coffee plants to Kilema from Morogoro (to which it had first been carried from Réunion by that other Alsatian Gommenginger in the Kilimanjaro area, Charles).

The Benedictine centre at Peramiho, near Songea in southern Tanzania, is an altogether astounding creation and undoubtedly the largest and most impressive Christian centre in Africa. When President Nyerere visited the centre in the 1960s he said: 'You have got everything – except a prison.' Founded in 1898, the first beginnings were destroyed by the Maji-Maji uprising, but it was later rebuilt. In 1931 it became an *abbatia nullius*, a Benedictine abbey whose abbot exercised episcopal powers and who was known as bishop. In connection with Peramiho we should of course also mention the all-African monastery at Hanga, founded by Peramiho but directly dependent on the Benedictine St Ottilien monastery in Germany.

Peramiho was dominated by the abbey church, built in a Romanesque style during the Second World War, with another twelve local churches and parishes in the district with some 26,000 Catholics. The abbey had 150 monks, sixty-five of whom were priests, with forty of these working at Peramiho itself and the others employed in the surrounding parishes. One hundred sisters worked and studied at Peramiho, living in three convents. The St Augustine Seminary with about 100 students assisted the Catholic dioceses in southern Tanzania. At the seminary the renowned Father Stephen Mbunga (d. 1972) studied, adapted and produced African Church music. One should think of Peramiho as a place resounding with liturgy and song, both on ordinary days and especially so, of course, on the feast days of the Church. A nurses' training institution had over 100 students and the girls' secondary school educated another 150 students. Medical work was not neglected: the hospital had over 300 beds, which included a special section for TB patients. In addition the abbey managed two leper villages.

The place echoed not only with pious hymns and glorious Church music, but also with the bellowing and grunting of the farm's 500 cattle and 200 pigs, with attached abbatoir and dairy. There was also a seed-bank for sun hemp, a nitrogen-collecting plant for soil improvement, and a hydro-electric power station. To these collective activities can also be added the resounding hammer strokes and the mechanical beats from the many workshops: for building and brick-making, motor vehicle mechanics, plumbing, carpentry and joinery, shoe-making, flour milling and from the printing press. Throughout East Africa Peramiho was known for its publications: two magazines in colour, with production runs of 18,000 copies. A wide range of books and religious posters were also produced.

One could continue to detail the astounding result of so much Christian activity and service until – in a new era of *uhuru* – it seemed too much of a good thing, at least in the eyes of modern politicians and administrators. But then, we have of course already taken the step into another era, critical of the past achievements of big Western-type institutions, and now anxious that services and development should not be concentrated to one locality but instead available to 'all'.

There is another side to the Peramiho story, an evangelistic aspect. Most of the Catholic communities on the Islamic Tanzanian coast were founded by migrant Catholics from the interior of the country, i.e., from Peramiho, another illustration of the role of African initiative in Church history all over the continent. In a possibly hostile environment it was an achievement to encourage one's fellow Christians to remain faithful, to go to Church on Sunday and to bring the newborn to the baptismal font. It was also a request by Peramiho Catholics that led to the foundation of a new parish in Dar es Salaam, a home for Peramiho Christians for their new life in the city.

Anglicans

In the inter-war years, Anglicans, Lutherans, Moravians and Catholics made up the traditional missionary body in Tanzania. The Southern Baptists from the United States, newcomers in the field, had only six missionaries in three centres in the late 1950s; but very soon they numbered nearly eighty missionaries in thirteen centres! The Swedish Pentecostals had started among the Sukuma in the west of the country and ambitiously covered almost the whole country including the capital. On the coast, the Universities' Mission (UMCA) represented the most progressive planning for higher education, culminating in the foundation of the Minaki Secondary School, some twenty miles from Dar es Salaam. Minaki was seen as the modern twentieth-century edition of what Kiungani on Zanzibar had been in the nineteenth century. Under the leadership of Robert and Dr Mary Gibbons, Minaki became a well-known centre, with a good number of pupils from the secondary school going on to the University College at Makerere and with a training programme for medical assistants.

Bishop Frank W. Weston (1871–1924) was the living embodiment of the Anglo-Catholic movement – its theological and liturgical tradition and its social involvement, a 'Prince-Bishop', as the author of his society's history called him. More than anybody else, he gave purpose and direction to his diocese 'of Zanzibar'. The Anglican missionary staff on the Muslim coastline included men and women of remarkable quality. Canon G. W. Broomfield – later General Secretary of the UMCA in London – had close contacts with the government's education department in Dar es Salaam. It did not take department officials long to recognize in him and his colleagues a competence at least as high as any represented in the department itself at this time. These contacts between the Anglican mission on the Tanzanian coast and the government could be seen as a parallel to the contacts between the Mill Hill mission and the education department in Kampala.

Fr Augustine Hellier of the UMCA was entrusted (together with Canon H. Butcher of the CMS, Kenya) with a 'definitive' revision of the Swahili Bible, published in 1952 – an achievement of permanent gain for the Church in East Africa. The Anglican St Alban's Church was built in Dar es Salaam's town centre. Canon John Sepeku, who had served for many years at Magila, was transferred to the city where he became Bishop and eventually Archbishop. Almost as well-known was his brother, Edmund John Sepeku, a layman with charismatic gifts of healing. In the 1960s and 1970s this layman had a noteworthy practice along those lines in the Church.

The Protestant scene in Tanganyika was strengthened by a new Anglican arrival, the Australian branch of the CMS. Assisted by a fresh injection of Australian Low-Church Evangelicals, the Anglicans devoted themselves to the centre of the country: Dodoma and Morogoro, as well as Mwanza in the west. These areas had been somewhat neglected. The Christian communities there took on new importance from the 1930s and 1940s when they came under the sway of the East African Revival. Bishop Omari, a recognized leader in his Diocese of Morogoro and also in the Revival movement, conveyed an uncompromising evangelical message.

The Lutheran case – from African initiative to African leadership

The aftermath of the First World War made a distinctive mark on Church development of the missions in Tanzania. In the Moshi area at the foot of Kilimanjaro, German missionaries were allowed to stay on until 1920. Then they were all repatriated and the young Churches were suddenly left on their own. There followed in that Lutheran Church 'a period of empty mission stations', a two-year testing period of fundamental importance for later growth. Without much preparation, the burden of leadership now fell on the shoulders of African congregations and their young teachers and evangelists – the educated men in these groups. The two years gave the congregations a glimpse of self-government.

The Moshi 'period of empty mission stations' had a parallel in the Evangelical Church in Bukoba, in the west of the country, aggravated by a high-handed transfer of Western missions without reference to the local African Christians. As the German 'Bethel' missionaries were interned in the

First World War, the Anglicans of Uganda in 1917 provided clergy and catechists to their Bukoba neighbour, but in 1924 a shortage of staff forced them to withdraw from Bukoba. Wesleyan Methodists from South Africa then announced their interest in taking over the work and this was duly decided by the two British missions while the African group was placed before a *fait accompli*. The local Haya Church and their forceful leader Andrea Kadjerero objected strongly to this arrangement and held out for four years in opposition to the foreigners, seen by them as intruders. In the end the German Bethel mission was allowed to return to Bukoba. The Wesleyan Methodist incident – it was no more than that – should be seen as an occasion when the local Bukoba Church accentuated its urge for self-government, without in any way establishing an Independent Church.

Chagga leaders in Moshi took the initiative in arranging evangelistic campaigns, some bringing them as far as the Usambara mountains towards the coast. An incidental effect of the time 'on their own' was the increased feeling of affinity among the different ethnic communities within the Church. They had been divided because of linguistic and other barriers up to that time. The sons of two trusted Church leaders of this time later became recognized in Church and State on a nation-wide scale: Bishop Stefano Moshi, head of the Lutheran Church in Tanzania; and Solomon Eliufoo, Minister of Education in Nyerere's first government – an indication of the continuity of influence in and through Christian families. In 1926, when German missionaries were again admitted into Tanzania, a team of highly gifted men representing continuity with the past arrived: Bruno Gutmann, Johannes Raum and Paul Rother.

To those who had experienced the brief period of being on their own in the 1920s, it seemed natural to work for an autonomous African Church. However, it must be remembered that Gutmann, for example, did not understand African Church autonomy in the terms of leadership primarily through an ordained African clergy. He distrusted seminary-trained leaders and advocated instead what he called the 'self-expression of the African congregation'. In 1930 the Rules for an Evangelical Lutheran Church were accepted and the Church was officially constituted. It was taken for granted that the General Assembly promised subordination to the 'Fathers', the Leipzig missionaries. For the Germans, their *Volkskirche* ideal was on the way to being realized.

In 1934, to provide African pastors as leaders to the local congregations, the Church organized a theological course of a little more than one year. After that short period of study twelve teachers were ordained, having received the barest 'iron-ration' of theology. Their principal consoled himself with the Pietist adage that *pectus est quod facit theologum* (it is the heart which makes the theologian). About that same time a solid foundation was laid for the self-support of the Church. The northern area was a coveted terrain for European settlers, and the Leipzig mission was successful in acquiring their portion of the bounty of the land. Very soon the returns on 70,000 coffee trees supplemented the 'Church tax', the annual giving of the Church members.

It seemed providential that the Augustana Lutherans found their way to Tanganyika in the 1920s. As the Australian CMS had gone to the centre of the country, so did the Augustana mission, going to the communities of the Iramba and the Turu. Within a short time they managed to plant stations, schools and hospitals in the area. It was during and after the Second World War, however, that the Augustana mission was to make its outstanding contribution to the Church in Tanganyika. When the Protestant German missionaries were interned and their mission stations classified as 'Enemy Property', the colonial administration entrusted the American Lutherans with the overseeing of those stations. The African Churches, 'Orphaned Missions' in the paternalistic language of the time, responded magnificently to the challenge, in the seven corners of the country.

An umbrella organization, the [Lutheran] Mission Churches' Federation, helped to bring all of them together for common interests, with Dr Richard Reusch as the colourful President of the Federation. At this time, throughout the continent, the Western missionaries tended to control the Churches. During annual Synod sessions, their private deliberations at breakfast contrived to settle, beforehand, the agenda and any decisions to be made. Reusch used other means: during Synods, as President, he held his very early morning conclaves not with missionaries, but with Christian Chagga chiefs. With them he prepared in some detail the business of the day and suggested the lines to be taken. At the Synod meeting, the chiefs would develop their views, thus conveying a happy impression that this was indeed 'the voice of Africa', not to be gainsaid.

As the Church was to be autonomous, it needed a constitution, and the ever-resourceful Reusch complied. Although this constitution paid lip-service to autonomy, there was a paragraph about the superintendent which gave Reusch sweeping power of 'confirmation or rejection of proposals of the General Assembly.' (One must remember that this was wartime, and that Reusch had an eye to the government officials in Dar es Salaam who had to be assured that the African Lutheran Churches were under safe control.) Bruno Gutmann had considered the *Selbstbewegung der Gemeinde* (self-reliance movement of the congregation) as the aim of missions, but

Reusch looked to the Chagga chiefs as the real African leaders for the Churches as well. In the Tanganyika of Indirect Rule, the government in Dar es Salaam appreciated this policy, while several African pastors represented the opposition to this particular missionary.

With the end of the war, a totally new situation obtained. Again an Augustana missionary was in charge, wholly dedicated to the goal of African leadership. Elmer R. Danielson had a wide international perspective. He brought the International Missionary Council (IMC) message from Whitby, Canada, 1947, to Marangu in Tanganyika: 'Pre-eminent importance will be attached to the wishes of the younger Churches affected.' Danielson pressed the issue of immediate transfer to African leadership, sometimes against missionary opinion. He had the attitude and the authority to take up the cudgels against the colonial government for threatened local communities, as in the case of the alienation of Meru land to white farmers, 1950–54. An executive council was elected, and Solomon Nkya's son Eliufoo, became Church secretary and treasurer. Young people of the northern Lutheran Church were now given opportunities to study in the United States, thanks to a Lutheran World Federation scholarship programme.

It was also in the Church of northern Tanganyika, on the lush slopes of Kilimanjaro, that the first continent-wide African Church conference was held, at Marangu in 1955, under the auspices of the Lutheran World Federation. A number of lecturers from other Church traditions also took part, such as William Nagenda, the well-known Anglican Revivalist from Uganda, and Max Warren of the CMS, London. During the late 1950s, the Church was still led by Western presidents, succeeding one another after brief periods at the helm. The time was ripe for change. In 1959, Stefano Moshi was installed as president. He became Bishop in 1960, and thus, leader of the Church *before* the country's independence with a fully Tanzanian Church Council, and then, the incomparable president of the Evangelical Lutheran Church of Tanzania, established in 1963.

In the 1950s, women were trained to be parish workers in the Bible school in Mwika and under their leadership a formidable women's organization was built in the highly enterprising Lutheran communities on the slopes of Kilimanjaro, after men went to seek employment in the cities of East Africa. The women's leadership was enhanced, not least because of the educational opportunities they had within the Church. Both girls and boys attended primary education in equal numbers and the Girls' Middle School and a teacher training college played an important part in the assertion of women's self-identity. The schools also prepared the way for a number of women into secondary school and the university. However, the Church in local congregations also involved a great deal of local leadership by women. Enterprising churchwomen even built a church with their own hands.

KENYA

Land and labour

Land and labour problems formed the political climate for Kenya missions in this period and created a series of crises more intense than in any other country north of the Zambezi. Though these issues can only be briefly mentioned here, they are indeed part of the Church history of the country. African land seemed a no man's land to be appropriated after the war by European settlers – mostly ex-servicemen – and meted out as enormous farms. There were 17,000 Europeans in Kenya in 1931. How to find labour for these plantations? The first post-war governor, General Northey, had a solution. Government officials were instructed 'to exercise any possible lawful influence to induce able-bodied male natives to go into the labour field'.

However, government officials and settlers were not the only Europeans in the country. The missionary forces, recently (1918) brought together in the Alliance of Protestant Missions, reacted as firmly as they dared. A so-called Bishops' Memorandum was published, signed by the two Anglican bishops of Mombasa and Kampala together with the staunch leader of the Presbyterian Church, Dr J. W. Arthur. They claimed that the government's instruction was tantamount to compulsory labour. But these churchmen were also bound to consider the interests of the European settlers and were not prepared to regard compulsion in itself as evil. They could favour some form of it, 'at any rate for work of national importance' as long as certain safeguards were observed. This was the kind of balanced, toothless statement which such organizations find a way to accept.

There were others however who reacted more vehemently, particularly when, in 1921, African women were directed to work on the European coffee plantations. Nobody reacted more resolutely than Harry Thuku, a young Kikuyu telephonist at the Treasury, hailing from the same Kiambu region as his contemporary, Jomo Kenyatta. Since childhood Thuku had had close personal contacts with a missionary society, the Gospel Missionary Society (in 1945 amalgamated with the Presbyterian Mission). Through all the vicissitudes of the political struggle he retained his contacts with the missionaries of his youth, John Henderson and W. P. Knapp. In 1921 Thuku became leader of the East African Association, which operated particularly among the Kikuyu in Nairobi, and was concerned with specific grievances rather than being generally political. While in the 'Reserves' on a recruiting drive, Thuku was arrested (1922), and at a spontaneous protest gathering the nervous police opened fire, killing at least twenty Africans. Thuku was exiled to the north of the Kenyan coast, and was away for nine years. Kikuyu supporters of his at the CMS, Kahuhia, founded another and more explicitly political society, the Kikuyu Central Association (1924) with the support of the missionary Revd Handley Hooper.

In the Kisumu area, near Lake Victoria, another CMS missionary, Archdeacon W. E. Owen, took the lead in opposing government policy. He had had years of missionary experience in Uganda and found the move to Kenya's political climate trying. In 1922 he founded the Kavirondo Taxpayers Welfare Association and envisioned a utopia which nobody else dared to verbalize at this time: 'native states, running their own affairs under the guidance of an efficient Native Affairs Department'. His standpoint of 'active liberalism was laced with paternalism toward Africans', making him at once esteemed and appreciated by most Africans and enormously unpopular with the Europeans in the country, who referred to him as 'Archdemon Owen'.[29] From the racial discrimination on the coffee plantations Owen was looking to the Colonial Office in London.

The Kenya situation alarmed the missionary executive in London, Dr J. H. Oldham but 'he was able and industrious enough to keep abreast of the officials, to counter policy with policy, and often to arrive first with a solution.'[30] His hand was strengthened by the advice of a medical friend with a colonial background from Kenya and Malawi, and with sympathies for the Society of Friends and socialism, Dr Norman Leys, the most radical protagonist of African interests in his generation. Their correspondence over Kenyan affairs has been published by Dr John W. Cell, under the arresting title, *By Kenya Possessed*.[31] Dr Leys' position with regard to the Churches was unrelenting. 'The Church has not *thought out* Christian politics and economics. Thousands of volumes on private morals, none on the larger half of life.' Oldham, by the courage of his thought and action did produce that volume 'on the larger half of life'. His advocacy in high places in London on behalf of African interests in Kenya was remarkable, unrivalled at the time in any of the European capitals of the colonial powers. Oldham's influence largely determined the formula in the British White Paper of 1923: 'Primarily Kenya is an African territory ... The interest of the African natives must be paramount.' Taking into account the enormous competitive economic interests in Kenya of Europeans and Indians, this principle was to be the key to the future – a key seemingly neglected and even mislaid sometimes, but found again to open the lock.

In the last few years of the nineteenth century the Church had found a precarious foothold on the Islam-dominated coast. There was Mombasa with its Anglican cathedral and bishop since 1900. Mombasa also had its very conspicuous Catholic Cathedral of the Holy Spirit. As a harbour and an Arab and Asian trade centre Mombasa provided work for inland migrant labour. The CMS saw this as an opportunity: a medical doctor, R. K. Shepherd – 'a man of incredible energy and great ability' built a couple of hospitals. The Buxton High School catered mostly for Indian boys; it took time until African youngsters could be induced to enter there. In the 1930s, the woman doctor, Alma Downes-Shaw took up hospital work in Mombasa starting out with her 'strong faith, £10 and a bicycle'. Not all missionaries liked her colour-blind social contacts. She saw to it that White and Black members of staff took their meals together: in an increasingly racist Kenya this was not altogether proper.

During the first years of the twentieth century the missions took the train to the Highlands to settle there and sometimes to go further afield to Kisumu and Lake Victoria. For the Churches in Kenya, Mombasa was surrendering its place of preference to Nairobi and the Highlands. There was also Freretown, a monument to evangelical vision and international outlook in the nineteenth century. Freretown had its theological seminary with traditions from the past and with an uncertain future. In 1930 it was moved to Limuru near Nairobi, a move symbolising the new and central role of the capital for the Church too.

During the first third of the twentieth century the Revd George Burns, with his Irish-Australian brogue, *was* the Anglican Church in the city: one worshipped *kwa Burnsi*. Protestant Church-life in Kenya was decidedly evangelical but there were also degrees in evangelicalism, and Burns from Sydney was definitely Low Church. Invited to preach in a Highland chapel, Burns discovered two lighted candles on the altar. These he duly snuffed out with the grumbling remark: 'I can see perfectly well without those'. However, he had a heart for the poor, a category to which almost all of the Nairobi Africans belonged to at the time – and they loved Bwana Burns. They filled his churches and chapels to capacity for Sunday services and the Friday prayer meeting, and they learned to read and write in his night-schools while the newly baptized were given opportunities for witnessing to their faith. What there was of a Burns theology could best be described as millenarian: he was in a hurry to baptize as many Africans as possible 'before the Lord returns'.

The inter-war period brought changes. In 1927 Nairobi had its own Anglican cathedral. The CMS acquired their own hill, a Nairobi counterpart to the Namirembe Hill in Kampala – with a church, schools and community centres. A new, highly competent generation of missionaries arrived in Nairobi, among them Leonard Beecher, later bishop and then archbishop. These men and women had a wider outlook and concern for social problems than their predecessors; yet, placed in the 'White Highlands', they could not but share its responsibilities and its incisive problems. The Presbyterians had their St Andrew's Church where the Revd David Steel was a renowned preacher, in the great Presbyterian tradition. Their solution to the social ills of the country was to suggest slow evolution, as if the Church or anybody else had time – when time was fast running out.

The geography of Kenyan Protestantism presents a very different picture from that of neighbouring Uganda and Tanzania. In Kenya, it was split up into bits and pieces giving it a unique development. How did this come about? General factors leading to this disintegration in Kenya include the political role of the White settler community with government land-policy on the one hand and, on the other, the role of the railway. The latter enabled missionaries of various denominations to found stations and out-stations along this new artery of economic enterprise. Some missionary societies spread their work over the whole country, setting up stations in widely separate areas. Others concentrated on one limited area and language group, others on two areas. The first mission to work in Kenya, the Church Missionary Society, ultimately had work in three areas: the Coast, the Highlands and Nyanza (or Kavirondo). The Church of Scotland Mission confined itself to the Kikuyu and their close kin, the Mwimbi, east of Mount Kenya while the Methodists, also early arrivals, developed work at the Coast and later among the Meru, north-east of Mount Kenya.

One mission possibly more interesting than any other was the widespread Africa Inland Mission. This body regarded itself as an African version of Hudson Taylor's 'China Inland Mission', a revivalist 'faith'-mission with its 'Home Board' in New York. As shown in earlier chapters this group first settled among the mobile and enterprising Kamba, east of present Nairobi, and then spread westwards in Kenya, reaching over 500 preaching places by 1948 and 1,000 by 1968. They also soon spread to western Tanzania and eastern Zaïre. Insisting on what they thought to be their 'doctrinal orthodoxy', they contrasted this with supposedly 'modernistic' tendencies in other missions. The Mission was torn by a series of crises, mainly over the Africanization issue and over the question of 'evangelism *versus* education'. There was also friction between the Kenya missionaries and the General Director, C. F. Hurlburt – directing his Kenya missions from distant Zaïre – and between Hurlburt and his 'Home Board' in Brooklyn, New York. This led to Hurlburt's resignation and induced the New York Board to reorganize the constitution of the Mission so as to secure its own control over the African work.

However, a fundamental tension arose between the numerous White missionaries and the barely submissive staff of Africans (catechists and pastors together with the younger generation and their educational ambitions). Officially, the mission subscribed to the programme of the 'Three Selves': self-supporting, self-governing and self-propagating Churches in Africa. But the African Church viewed the actual situation differently and Kenyans felt that they were not given opportunities for educational advance. They were led to reflect on the fateful aspect of a certain kind of mission coming to an ethnic community. A narrow and educationally limited mission could jeopardize the opportunities of an entire people. Some of the educationally ambitious among the youth joined other Churches such as that run by the Church Missionary Society, while others, insisting on the right of Kamba Christians to be Kamba, in Kamba country, formed their own 'African Brotherhood Church', a well-organized 'Ethiopian' body. Another offshoot of the African Inland Mission was the 'African Christian Churches and Schools', while still others formed the 'Africa Inland Church' (1942). In Tanzania a 'shadow' organization had been founded in 1938 with the name of 'Ecclesia Evangel of Christ', but this left African leaders dissatisfied with the degree of 'independence' envisaged.[32] In Mwanza, Tanzania, the powerful pastor, Jeremiah Kissula, emerged as the leader of the 'African Inland Church', later becoming its bishop.

Along with the three or four leading Protestant missionary societies active in Kenya, a number of smaller organizations were already at work, among them the Gospel Missionary Society, a Baptist group with a background in the Moody Bible Institute, Chicago. They were few in number and comprised two missionary families; the Revd William Knapp and his gifted wife, and a Jamaican medical doctor, John E. Henderson. In 1902 they arrived at hilly Kambui in Kikuyuland, thus coming to an area which, with its dynamic population, was to be of special importance for the history of Kenya in colonial times and later. Harry Thuku, E. N. Wanyoike and Waigonjo wa Ndotono were all Kiambu men whose contacts with this little group of missionaries were strong.

Not all missionary organizations were prepared to encourage real Africanization of the Church, but the Gospel Missionary Society was. Knapp's Gospel Society joined the Presbyterian Church in 1946. Functioning as a close-knit family of mutual help and confidence between missionaries and converts, it gave to ambitious young generations of men and women some of the education they were looking for and a degree of Christian fellowship which more 'established' societies did not always provide. Because of the Church's family aspect – with the Revd E. N. Wanyoike a leader – the young converts accepted the new laws and rules of their Christian community throughout the vicissitudes of Kenyan social history and persisted in maintaining lasting fellowship. Knapp insisted on the converts' abandoning traditional Kikuyu custom, including the ancient burial custom whereby the corpse was simply left in the bush. Instead, the Church's own burial ground near the church became a hallowed place. An indication of the strength of personal relationship between missionary and African pastor is provided by an unfortunate confusion in connection with Revd Knapp's own burial in February 1940. He had himself decided exactly where he and his wife were to be buried: near the church and facing eastward, 'so that I can always "see" people coming into and going out of the church'. As ill luck would have it, there was a mix-up over the burial sites – to Revd Wanyoike a shocking oversight. He saw to it that in July of 1940 the coffin was disinterred and placed in the anticipated area.

A controversy over women

In 'building the African Church' in the 1920s, some of the missions insisted that they must honour 'the values of the African's past'. In colonial Kenya the controversy over female circumcision, more correctly termed clitoridectomy, engaged the passionate attention of Church people. As the issue could easily be interpreted as mainly a matter of respect for African custom in general, it is necessary here to mention technicalities. It was claimed that there were two forms of the operation, a minor one limited to the excision of the clitoris and a major form involving cutting of the labia minora and majora as well. The operation itself was embedded in a symbolic set of rituals. Here was an issue of fundamental importance to the African communities and the stand taken by the different missions for or against the custom was to determine their place in society for decades to come.

The Church of Scotland Mission led the attack on female circumcision and by the early 1920s it was a rule in that mission that baptized Church members undergoing the operation or allowing their daughters to do so were disciplined by suspension from Church membership. It was not surprising that a mission as strongly dominated by medical doctors as that of the Church of Scotland should take such a firm stand against the custom. They knew what it was all about. The Africa Inland Mission soon followed suit. At the Presbyterian station of Tumutumu the issue first became political and led Christians to openly, if reluctantly, break with their Church. The Tumutumu Kirk Session demanded a declaration of loyalty from all baptized Church members on pain of suspension. No compromise was possible and about 200 people, 7 per cent of the Tumutumu congregations, were put under Church discipline. Dr J. W. Arthur's determined and uncompromising stand on the issue at this time was a major factor in the crisis.

The Presbyterian decision to force the issue among its own adherents resulted in disaster, at least temporarily. The agents of the mission at its Kikuyu station in Kiambu district were in 1929 required to declare their loyalty to the Presbyterian position. Twelve out of fifty-three refused to do so and left the mission. Eighteen of fifty Church elders refused to so commit themselves. Fully 90 per cent of the mission's communicants refused to follow the mission's directions. Total Presbyterian school attendance dropped from an average of 728 in 1928 to only eighty-seven a year later, and parents refused to accept as teachers those who had declared their loyalty to the mission on the issue of circumcision. The Africa Inland Mission followed similar policies and experienced similar consequences.

Within the Church Missionary Society communities the controversy was considerably less intense. Here different practices were followed at different local stations. At Kabete, with the Revd Harry Leakey in charge, the policy was one of reluctant accommodation. A carefully worded compromise was issued by Bishop Heywood as a pastoral letter on 1 January 1930, condemning female circumcision but stopping just short of absolutely forbidding the practice on pain of Church discipline. The ambiguity of CMS pronouncements prevented the necessity of choosing between obedience and schism, between what amounted to being a Christian and being a Kikuyu. At Kabare, the Pastorate Committee came to a significant decision: not only would they permit circumcision at puberty but they would conduct it under the auspices of the Church. Two men and two women – all Christians – were chosen as operators for boys and girls respectively. The foundations of Protestant cities in Kenya as expressed in the Alliance of Missionary Societies now seemed threatened. Dr Arthur, from the Presbyterians, replied that a decision along these lines 'would probably burst the Alliance'.

In a second pastoral letter (1931) Bishop Heywood bowed to the dominant body of opinion in the diocese. Female circumcision would no longer be forbidden if it was conducted privately, caused no physical injury and if all associated 'heathen practices' were abandoned. At Kigari however, the local Anglican missionary, John Comely, and his elders unanimously ruled that any communicant allowing female circumcision in his or her family would be stricken from the Church rolls. The response to these decisions represented in Comely's words 'nothing less than a crash'. Out-schools were closed and many teachers left the mission, particularly at the larger centres. Former CMS adherents swelled the ranks of the Salvation Army which had been introduced into Embu in 1928 by migrant labourers returning from Nairobi and other towns. Polygamists and those who left the CMS over female circumcision became members of the Salvation Army. The very success of the CMS in retaining the loyalty of its own potential independents meant that more than any other mission it was forced to confront the consequences of its rivals' failure.

In the short perspective the Western missions in Kenya were thus severely criticized for their lack of understanding of African custom, values, etc. In a somewhat longer perspective however the situation could suddenly change. The fact that on one day in June 1982 fourteen young girls in the Rift Valley area died on account of the custom made an impression on the highest authorities in the land. The President of the Republic outlawed female circumcision and instructed medical authorities and the police to see to it that the order was obeyed.

One outcome of the female circumcision controversy was the formation of a number of 'Independent Schools'. Not a very substantial movement numerically – in 1935 there were no more than thirty-five such schools with some 1,500 children – it had, however, a symbolic value as an expression of Kikuyu opposition to what was seen as racial discrimination and of their struggle for political independence. The majority of these schools formed an association of their own, the so-called KISA, Kenya Independent Schools Association. Two decades later, in the years of the Mau Mau Revolt, the Independent Schools acquired a certain notoriety as one possible source of the political protest. The formation of Independent Schools was also an expression of African fellowship on an international scale. The South African Archbishop D. W. Alexander of the African Orthodox Church visited Kenya twice, in 1929 and 1935, and on both occasions he was in a position to suggest that the Western missionaries' stand on the female circumcision problem was anti-African while he was pro-African and therefore supported traditional custom and the cause of Independent schools.

The Nyanza melting-pot

The Nyanza region has a special significance for African Church history. Two linguistically and historically different ethnic peoples lived – and sometimes clashed – together: the Bantu-speaking Luyia and the Nilotic-speaking Luo. These two societies developed strong fissiparous tendencies, and this was also reflected in the Church life of the region, resulting in many boisterous Church bodies.

Professor Michael Whisson has shown that the young migrant labourers working in Nairobi or Dar es Salaam gained their faith in the cities. On returning to their home village they changed the layout of the village on a central point: where traditionally there had been a men's hut in the centre they now built a chapel, and there these young voluntary preachers, themselves recently baptized, were able to build themselves up on their faith. At Liganua, some eighty miles from Kisumu, Jemsi L. Oganga, who as a young man had joined Canon Burns Bible school in Nairobi, invited his contemporaries to leave their fathers' homesteads and join him near the new church. This new village was 'the greatest single innovation', a Christian village, known as *laini* around the church. They built rectangular houses, conspicuously different from the old-time round huts and they lived 'according to Christian precepts'. They were greatly encouraged in their tremendous initiative by the Anglican Archdeacon Owen and the local pastor, the Revd G. S. Okoth.[33]

The Churches followed the railway as they had done during the nineteenth century in many other countries, for example in Britain, Sweden and the United States. Nairobi grew from and around a railway siding: Kisumu was the end of the line. The possibility of rail connections was the decisive factor in the siting of many mission stations. Nairobi, on the edge of Kikuyu country, became a major centre. Its economic, social and cultural opportunities attracted great numbers of young men from all over the country (the women came later). But the railway did not stop at the noisy siding of Nairobi. With the help of Indian navvies it continued up and over the Rift Valley to Kisumu on Lake Victoria. Later a northern branch continued over the western escarpment to Kampala, Uganda.

A number of new Protestant missions turned their attention to western Kenya. From North America – and unusual for that branch of Christianity – came the Friends' African Mission, to work, primarily, among the Maragoli; this mission resulted in the largest Yearly Meeting of Friends in the world. The Salvation Army also came, and Swedish Lutherans of a strictly conservative variety. The Africa Inland Mission, established in Kambaland, extended its work to Kavirondo. New North American groups included the Church of God (from Anderson, Indiana, USA); the Canadian Pentecostal Assemblies of God; the National Holiness Association; and the Seventh Day Adventists. Western Kenya with Kisumu as the centre increasingly became a home for one particular brand of Protestantism: Fundamentalism. Here

Anglican Evangelicals, Lutheran Confessionalists and of course the Church of God, as well as others, managed to toughen each other along the Fundamentalist road.

It was probably no wonder, given this rich mixture of Churches with lively traditions of singing, using instruments, speaking in tongues and exuberant services, that western Kenya should have become the *origo* – the breeding ground – for charismatic Independent Churches, in Kenya usually called 'Spirit Churches'. It was even to have rather unusual breakaways – from the East African Revival movement and from the Roman Catholic Church. Western Kenya became the home for more Independent Churches than anywhere else in Eastern Africa. From there, with its especially mobile population (Luo men in particular worked for the East African Railways and Harbours Administration) the movement spread via rail and road, but now in reverse, eastwards – using the return ticket, as it were – to Nairobi.

Many of the local Nyanza chiefs were appointed by the colonial government, with the strengths and weaknesses that this implied for their authority. As a rule the chiefs welcomed the missions, while jealous of one another for this new Christian influence and the mission school, an institution which at first – here as elsewhere – was regarded as a 'school for Chiefs' sons'. Dr Lonsdale has drawn a distinction between 'the not unfriendly attitude of the chiefs, recognizing in the missions a further source of power, and the suspicion of the masses'.[34] Having acquired relatively large areas of land on which to farm – about a thousand acres each – the missions provided 'both employment and refuge'. In a real sense 'the missionaries became chiefs', and their hospitality and protection were seen as 'chiefly functions'. The employees and tenants in each case became a nucleus of the first Christian communities.[35] The colonial administration encouraged the chiefs to send their sons to mission schools and there emerged a number of 'lasting Church–chief alliances', particularly among the Luo. Good repute in Church work could help make a person eligible for chieftaincy: thus Paulo Mboya, a Seventh Day Adventist teacher, was finally elected as chief. In 1933 he was the first Kenyan to be ordained pastor in his increasingly important Church.[36]

Among the Tiriki community the Church situation from the beginning had been complicated. Nowhere in East Africa did a chief's attitude play such a dominant role in the lives of an ethnic community as among the Tiriki, part of the Bantu-speaking Luhya of western Kenya. The Tiriki lived in an area of small competing communities in a singularly mobile population. The fundamental social institution among them was their initiation ceremonies, surrounded by total secrecy. In 1902 the American Friends arrived and soon acquired large tracts of land. Tensions arose between the missionaries and the Tiriki concerning circumcision, the symbolic basis for tribal identity and unity. Most missionaries were highly critical of the supposedly immoral initiation camps. What annoyed the Tiriki even more was the fact that the most active response to Christianization came from their neighbours, the Maragoli. While the missionaries found the Tiriki singularly unresponsive, the neighbouring Maragoli people proved all the more eager to learn new things from the foreigners, by working for them. The Tiriki therefore at first decided that the Christian community was composed of a bunch of aliens and refugees, amongst whom there were possibly dangerous witches, and any self-respecting Tiriki would do well to keep away from such company.

In 1924 the Tiriki appointed a new chief, the forceful Amiani. Three years later, in connection with the lively Kaimosi Revival of 1927, the chief converted to the new religion in its Quaker form. This acceptance of the new religion had great consequences for the role of the Church in the area. Not only did the chief retire all his thirty wives, except one, but he took a keen interest in all Church matters both big and small. A new church building was needed and Chief Amiani in a generous mood gave the unheard of sum of a thousand shillings to the construction, a large portion of the total cost. He thus felt he could dictate the form of church and its roof. It was here, however, that the community was divided. The American builder claimed that it was enough with *four* crossbeams for the roof, while Amiani who knew the climate in the area insisted on *six*. A clash of personalities ensued and Amiani left the Friends mission, joining instead the hitherto almost unknown Salvation Army and becoming a devoted propagandist for the Army and its drums. Another positive aspect about the Army was that their commanding officers lived far away from Tiriki and Chief Amiani could rule the Church unhindered by any unwanted inspection.[37]

Amiani was followed by two men who managed to bridge the abyss between pagan and Christian initiation practices: Sagwa, a hereditary initiation chief who to the pagans' dismay joined the Salvation Amy and helped the Tiriki Christians to develop their own initiation ceremony; and Hezron Mushenye, a member of the Friends Mission and elected chief in 1946. He converted the Tiriki to his Christian faith by distancing himself from the Maragoli section, and he established himself as a modern secularized ruler by flaunting the obvious Pietist rules of conduct: he would drink beer (the European bottled variety) and extended his family by two extra wives.[38]

The Christian missionaries to Nyanza arrived from two directions.

Firstly, as already mentioned, a motley group of radical Protestants, mostly American, arrived with the extension of the railway from Mombasa and Nairobi. Secondly, the two established although competing mission societies, the Anglican CMS and the Catholic Mill Hill Fathers, came across Lake Victoria from Buganda. This initial contact with Buganda should cause no surprise. Nyanza was politically part of Uganda until 1921, when the area was transferred to Kenya, and this missionary overspill to Kisumu was part of the remarkable African evangelistic drive from Kampala in all directions: north, east, south-west and, in this case, to the south-east.

The CMS, attempting to gather within one fold both the Luo and Luhya communities, established their centres in the southern part of the Nyanza region. As mentioned above, the Kavirondo area of Nyanza was first evangelized from Uganda. The Nyanza Archdeaconry was only transferred from the Diocese of Uganda to the Diocese of Mombasa in 1921. The first two Archdeacons, J. J. Willis (later bishop in Uganda) and W. E. Owen, had both given long service in Uganda. They expected the same kind of initiative in evangelism which they had seen in Uganda and they found it. Bishop Willis writes:

> With two or three exceptions the entire work of evangelization and education, so far as it has gone, has been the work of native teachers, Kavirondo born. In this matter Kavirondo independence has asserted itself. Trained or half-trained in a Mission school, the convert returns to his native village and is lost to sight. Next time the missionary meets him he is in self-imposed charge of a little congregation of readers, from which in due course a little group of candidates for the catechumenate emerges. So the work grows out much of it in its initial stages is carried on in entire independence of the European.[39]

Willis had previously been the headmaster of the CMS Maseno High School, and this institution was of great importance for the future of the entire region. As soon as these young student disciples of his were baptized they could be sent out as witnesses to their newly-won faith, going out 'two by two' according to St Mark 6:7 and, as Willis insisted, according to the Iona model.

Among the missionaries to East Africa, W. E. Owen has a place of his own. It was generally taken for granted that British, particularly Anglican, missionaries were somehow related to the British administration. This could be through bonds of personal friendship – the same college at Oxford or Cambridge could be a help – or certainly by virtue of a common culture and values. These ties and attachments could militate against allowing themselves to criticize government measures and actions. To a certain extent this role had therefore to be performed by others, as for instance one or two American missionaries, notably the Lutheran Elmer Danielson of Moshi, Tanzania, over the notorious Meru land case. However, in western Kenya a Briton, and an Archdeacon at that, came to be identified with loud and persistent criticism of government policy and action.

Having arrived first in Uganda in 1904 and coming to Nyanza in 1918, Owen became the dominant spokesman for the rights of the African masses. As President of the Kavirondo Taxpayers Welfare Association – a Kenyan counterpart to the Church-inspired social 'associations' in British Central Africa – he never tired of defending African interests. To him it was 'a missionary duty to give publicity to African grievances'. But his churchmanship was his very own and he never felt at home with the East African Revival. He also did not regard it as the Church's task to form an African elite, but rather to aim the Christian message at the masses.

Being so near Uganda (with regular ferries plying from Port Florence, Kisumu, to Port Entebbe, Uganda) the East African Revival movement came early to the Nyanza region. Norman Green, a missionary doctor at Maseno, the large CMS station near Kisumu, was an important early link with Rwanda. Nyanza, as well as being the place from which many 'breakaway' Churches emerged, was also the scene of a much rarer rift, emanating from the Revival movement. An oft-claimed feature of the Revival has been that it did not result in new separatist groups but, here, it did. As early as 1948 a group arose known as *Kuhama* (to move out, to separate). Some Revivalists, mainly Luo, preached that the saved ones should separate themselves, not only from sin, but also from all sinful institutions, including the Church. Later the *Wahamaji* (Separated Ones), also known as *Joremo* (People of the Blood) were opposed by another group, *Johera* (People of Love). After a confusing period of conventions and negotiations, involving the Anglican Church leadership and made more difficult by the considerable distance from Nairobi and the presence on the spot of certain new and inexperienced local missionaries, a complete break came in 1956. The *Joremo*, led by an ordained Anglican, Matthew Ajuoga, formed 'The Church of Christ in Africa', with Ajuoga as bishop. The *Johera*, led by Assistant Bishop (later Archbishop) Festo Olang, remained within the Anglican Church.

A number of causes for this breakaway have been stated, notably by Dr D. B. Barrett who devoted central sections of his well-known *Schism and Renewal in Africa* to the Nyanza Church problem, concluding with the point that 'the entire movement of independency' in Africa was a 'failure in love'.[40] While this highly sentimental conclusion has obvious propaganda value, it must, surely, be supplemented by a consideration of the actual situation. There one finds at the bottom of this crisis an intractable tension between two ethnic societies, the Luhya and the Luo, and this was also felt in the Church.

As the tension between the two communities mounted in the early 1950s, it was decided to make the Luhya Church leader the assistant Anglican bishop of the region. This was complicated by the fact that he was a Luhya priest with a Luo name and educated as a Luo: when it was announced that he was in fact a Luhya he never was accepted by the Luo section of the diocese. One can speculate as to what would have happened had the Anglican authorities attempted to solve, or evade, the problem by yielding to sociological realities, and thus appointed *two* assistant bishops, one for the Luo and the other for the Luhya. It is quite possible that an arrangement of this nature would, at least temporarily, have obviated the crisis, although at an inadmissible price for the Church and a victory for sociological dexterity over theological design. It is possible to regard the Luo–Luhya crisis in 1956 as a preview of other such conflicts in comparable Churches in subsequent decades.

If Nyanza underwent this very considerable Anglican breakaway, it also produced a Roman Catholic separation, taking its cup from the highly active lay movement within the Catholic Church of the area, the Mario Legio (Legion of Mary). An Irish-founded movement, the Mario Legio had grown in Kenya largely through the work of Edel Quinn, a young Irish women sent out as a missionary in 1936. She was already suffering from tuberculosis (TB) when she arrived but she travelled widely within and outside Kenya, and was in Kisumu not long before she died, in Nairobi in 1944.[41] Between 1960–62 a Luo woman named Gaudencia Aoko and her follower, Simeon Ondeto, led an exodus from the Catholic Diocese of Kisii and formed the Church called 'Maria Legio'. The leader – Simeon – became known as the Holy Father, and Roman Catholic forms of liturgy and the use of Latin continued. In that Church one heard 'Gloria!' rather than the more usual 'Hallelujah!' preferred by the Protestant-derived Churches.

To a large extent the proliferation of charismatic groups in Nyanza was the outcome of local African initiative, thus in line with the general theme of this book. Yet, in at least two important cases, one can point to initial Western stimuli. Among the American Friends, one of the first two pioneers, the Revd Chilson, in an address disclosed to his avid listeners, only too prepared to comply, that his Church 'back home' in the United States was indeed a group of 'Shakers'. From there it was only a short step to a dramatic display of these desirable spiritual activities, leading to the Kaimosi

Revival of 1927, one of the great events in Nyanza Church history. Many charismatic groups can be traced back to these lively beginnings.

Similarly, the 'Church of God' at Kima produced offshoots of the same dramatic kind. Kima had interesting beginnings in 1904, started by A. W. Baker of Johannesburg, whose work on the Rand (p. 418) had reached far and wide. Baker sent his daughter, Mabel Baker, to guide the Nyanza work. As long as the mission was under Baker's control, it used for worship the Anglican Book of Common Prayer and Baker was supposed to be 'a friend of Pentecost'. In 1923 the Kima work was taken over by the Church of God from Anderson, Indiana, by their missionaries, the Ludwig couple. Mrs Twyla Ludwig had charismatic revelations. In 1960 she recalled to the present writer how she was hit by the Holy Spirit, 'like oil running down head over body', a story she would repeat to a great number of impressed congregations. She had, according to her son, special powers: 'When she prayed for rain we reached for umbrellas.'[42] Western missionaries of this type were not unknown in the Nyanza region, a fact to remember when trying to explain the emergence of an Independent Church movement in the area.

There is unfortunately no place here to discuss the fascinating Independent Church material which the present writer gathered in Kenya in 1960, invited by the Christian Council of Kenya. But we cannot refrain from mentioning the happy possession of publications by the 'Kenya African Independent Communion Churches of East Africa', with a membership extravagantly pretended to be some '900,000 indigenous Christians'. This Church led by the 'Rt Revd Paul David Kivuli' recognized the Emperor Haile Selassie as the 'protector of the faith'. The Church's most precious possession was:

> a mystical wild cross made of beads and skin symbolizing the light in the darkness, said to have been brought from the south of Ethiopia into this country now known as Kenya before the arrival of the White man's Christian faith in Africa South of Ethiopia ... The Cross represented much in Christianity without a Bible. The priests used the stories of the Cross for the spread of Christianity about AD 1000.[43]

This little home-made myth, in the Church's official communication to the government, is an interesting indication of something serious and important: the need for tradition and history, as old and reverential as possible.[44]

'Mau Mau' and the Churches

A 'state of emergency' was declared in Kenya on 20 October 1952. That date marked the recognition of the anti-colonial revolt generally known as Mau Mau, though that name has never been accepted by the participants.

The 'Emergency' laws and rulings applied primarily to members of the Kikuyu-, Embu- and Meru-speaking peoples situated north and north-east of Nairobi, between and around the Aberdare Range and Mount Kenya. The Kikuyu, Embu and Meru were among the most advanced, in Western terms, of Kenya's inhabitants. From the beginnings of the colonial period they had in general welcomed schools and missions, and profited from their education. But they had also deeply resented the loss of land to White settlers and the fact that the inclusion of adjacent areas in the 'White Highlands' had set limits on their expansion. Many young men found themselves landless and became squatters on White farms. It seems that it was among this displaced (and less well-educated) group that the first oath-taking fellowships emerged. For if Mau Mau was about self-government and the right to self-determination, it was also, and perhaps primarily, about land.

With the introduction of the state of emergency, the African peoples were at one stroke divided, in the eyes of the administration, into 'Mau Mau' and 'loyalists'. All were presumed to be Mau Mau unless they could prove otherwise. When Home Guard Units were set up, men could prove their loyalty by joining up. Membership of Mau Mau came through 'taking the oath' or 'drinking the oath', which committed the participant to solidarity with the rest of the group. So from the beginning, one loyalty was set against another. Men, women and children took the oath, although only a small proportion of those were on active duty with the forest guerillas. But many of the Kikuyu, Embu and Meru recognized a primary loyalty – to the Christian God and his Son, Jesus Christ. The oath involved drinking blood and a promise of willingness to commit violence. Although the Churches to which they belonged were not pacifist, many Christians in their own reading of the New Testament had come to pacifist conclusions. So they posed a threat to the solidarity of the group in the struggle against the colonial regime.

In the Kikuyu, Embu and Meru areas the main mission-related Churches were the Anglicans, Presbyterians and Methodists. All three had been much influenced by the East African Revival movement from the early 1940s. Through local meetings and sometimes country-wide gatherings, it brought together Christians of many Churches. For those who did identify themselves with the Revival there was a breaking down of the wall between Black and White which had sadly affected even Christian missionaries. Strangely, some of the most Evangelical missions, whose emphases would have appeared very close to those of Revival, were neutral or even actively opposed to it. By some it was called 'the Rwanda Heresy'. The reasons are complex. At least one mission-related Church excommunicated members unless they withdrew from the Revival fellowship.

It was out of the 'Revival Brethren' in Central Province that the main opposition to the Oath, and to the violent struggle against colonialism, emerged. A significant number of both men and women who refused to 'drink the oath' were killed on the spot, and so the young Church had its martyrs. Others were cut and beaten and died later of their injuries; many others who were beaten survived. Many ordinary simple men and women went in fear of their lives for several years, and made their homes as refugees around schools and mission stations. And because they (usually) refused to join the colonial Home Guard units and carry arms, they suffered also from violence by government forces. Theirs was a difficult witness. What made it harder was that the basic aims of the freedom fighters in the forests were also those of the Christians. They also wanted to see an end to colonial rule; they were also concerned about land, and political rights, and the apartheid-like discrimination in Kenya. But they were unwilling to use violence to achieve their ends.

Essentially, then, the Kikuyu Churches took a neutral stand during the state of emergency. They refused to join actively (and violently) with either the forest fighters or the administrative forces opposing them. Missionaries of all societies, with very few exceptions, went without firearms, and tried to get justice for Africans who were detained without cause, or mistreated while detained. Undoubtedly many Kikuyu patriots saw the Christians as traitors and stooges of the White men, a reputation which has had to be lived down.

A few individual Christians, and one particular Church, did take an active part in fighting Mau Mau. Before the emergency a split had occurred in the Africa Inland Church in the area south of Murang'a (then named Fort Hall). The breakaway Church was the 'African Christian Church and Schools' (ACC&S). The name suggests what was in fact the main cause of the division, educational policy. With some outstanding young leaders, and having strong connections with Senior Chief Njiiri of Murang'a, ACC&S Christians took up arms on the government side, even to the extent of going on patrol in the Aberdare forests in search of gangs. It is worth noting that ACC&S members who were also active in the Revival did not participate in this.

When Mzee Jomo Kenyatta was released from prison, and then detention, in the early 1960s, Church leaders, including Revival leaders, were quick to welcome him and to pledge their support in building a new Kenya. The Anglican bishop of Murang'a (Fort Hall), the Rt Revd Obadiah Kariuki, had an especially important role here because he and the future president had married two sisters, daughters of Senior Chief Koinange of Kiambu. The bishop was one of Mzee Kenyatta's few visitors during the prison years at Lodwar.

After Independence was granted in 1961, and Mzee Kenyatta had become President, there was remarkably little in the way of revenge killings or even of the ill-feeling which might have been expected after so violent a period which really amounted to a civil war. Undoubtedly the Christian Churches were able to, and did, provide a lead in the work of reconciliation and building a new Kenya.

Mau Mau took the Churches unawares. It highlighted the chasm between a largely bourgeois Church and the real needs of the African population. The ethnic communities with their tribal, economic and educational differences included the problems of the landless Kikuyu who seemed then, and later, without a chance and what was almost as bad, without informed and concerned spokesmen. The Churches just like the emerging political parties cared for and tried to reach the comparatively prosperous.

After Mau Mau, Kenya had somehow to begin anew. It seemed providential that the National Christian Council of Kenya (NCCK) brought in an experienced sociologist, S. A. Morrison (formerly a CMS missionary in Cairo) to assess the situation. The burden of his analysis was that the Church had never taken the city seriously. To overcome this weakness a net of community centres had to be built all over Nairobi, and soon five such centres started their activity: youth work, adult education, women's work, etc. The enormous opportunity was matched by generous ecumenical funding. Janet Lacey of the World Council of Churches had the vision to plan big for a challenging situation and to direct ample sums for the new enterprises. Three expatriate specialists were to show what the Christian Council aimed at: Stanley Booth-Clibborn, later Bishop of Manchester; Andrew Hake, specialist on industrial management and, later, author of the book *African Metropolis: Nairobi's Self-Help City*;[45] and Gordon Mayo, concerned with youth and college students, (soon to be succeeded by Zadok Otieno). Conferences, publications and modern Church magazines helped to make the new Limuru Conference Centre into a lively meeting place for political, social and Church interests. Taken together, these initiatives in the aftermath of Mau Mau anticipated Nairobi's role as the leading ecumenical centre in East Africa. After Mau Mau the Roman Catholic Church saw mass conversions into its fold, due to the vacuum that had been created and to the need for moral rehabilitation.

The local Churches with their Pietistic and rural background sometimes found it difficult to follow the new trend. Their constant answer to all problems was 'Revival', and this sometimes meant a tendency to eschew the obstreperous reality of the city's social life.

18

INTRODUCTION TO INDEPENDENT AFRICA

CHURCH AND STATE IN AFRICA

In 1955 representatives of twenty-nine 'Third World' nations from Asia and Africa met in Bandung, Indonesia. 'We are united by race and religion', the host, President Sukarno announced, somewhat exaggerating his claim. Only two men, although all the more colourful and significant, came from Africa: Nasser of Egypt and Nkrumah from Ghana. In 1941 Nkrumah had returned to Ghana after a decade in the United States and another two years in Britain. While abroad, he studied widely (amongst other things gaining a degree in theology!), observed the racial problems then besetting America and, most significantly of all, launched himself into pan-African and nationalist activity. In Ghana he was now to initiate a 'Positive Action Campaign'. Soon he did more than that, for he became the inspiring conductor of a continent-wide orchestra, drums and all. His impetuous message was broadcast through newly-bought radio-sets in every village throughout the continent and set the tune for an impatient appeal echoed from country to country: not 'Self-Government' but 'Self-Government *Now*'. His vision and action showed that Independence was within reach: a whole new generation of political leaders in Africa could follow the lead and the tune. In 1958 Nkrumah sponsored the first All African Peoples' Conference, held in Accra, and a forerunner of the Organization of African Unity (established in 1963).

The breathless speed with which this enormous political change took place is illustrated by A. A. J. van Bilsen's book and its message. Van Bilsen, a Belgian sociologist and politician, in 1956 published his *Vers l'independence du Congo et du Ruanda-Urundi*. Three decades later, van Bilsen argued, Congo would celebrate its centenary as a Belgian colony, making that year, 1985, the appropriate occasion for handing over independence to 'their' colony. General opinion in Belgium thought van Bilsen's suggestion impossibly premature: 'Van Bilsen became a veritable pariah after publishing his moderate proposals for a thirty year plan'.[1] But what happened? Only a few years after, in 1959, the King of the Belgians visiting Léopoldville/ Kinshasa attended the independence celebrations, and the revolution was in full swing.[2]

The first generation of African political leaders – 'the Founding Fathers' – were men of wide international experience and inspiration: Nkrumah of Ghana, Azikiwe and Awolowo of Nigeria, Senghor of Senegal, Houphouet-Boigny of the Ivory Coast, Dr Hazoume of Benin, all of West Africa, and from East African Kenyatta of Kenya, Nyerere of Tanzania and Dr Banda of Malawi. They had spent long periods in the United States, Britain and France, and were in various ways inspired and influenced by the ideas and visions of pan-African leaders, such as Marcus Garvey, Du Bois, George Padmore and Ras Makonnen. They met these men and their colleagues at pan-African and other conferences, notably the one held in Manchester in 1945. While emphasizing this international dimension of African nationalism, we remember that the nationalist breakthrough was triggered by factors in the local situation. Nearly all these leaders, as well as other national and local politicians, were influenced in their formative years by missionary education, and were products of Church-related educational enterprises. The commitment to Western-type schools by Churches throughout the continent, and the educational efforts of their congregations, were among the factors that led to the creation of a constellation of brilliant leaders, the 'founding fathers' of the African nations.

In colonial times it was rare for an African – except perhaps in the case of a traditional chief – to gain access to the regional commissioner, let alone to the governor. This privilege was reserved for Europeans only. This observation is made in order to underline the change brought about by independence at the personal level. The local teacher now found that he had personal access to, and democratic contacts with, the President, and he was happily aware of the fact that he and the President in many cases shared a similar background as school teachers with common interests and concerns.

One particular aspect of this transfer to African political leadership is often overlooked. The newly elected presidents and prime ministers were sustained by an entire generation of African village teachers, trained in mission schools and teacher training colleges. Involved in the political struggle these teachers supported their leader by carrying his message from the Party's headquarters to the villages and translating it into attractive and concrete terms. Our example is – inevitably – from Tanzania during the 1960s, but is certainly paralleled in many other countries and places. Under the leadership of a local teacher a group would shout the political slogan, to be echoed and amplified in acoustic volume by the crowd, 'Uhuru na

Nyerere', to be followed by 'Uhuru na Eliofoo', the latter a less well-known name but denoting the then Minister of Education (the son of a Chagga catechist) and therefore of great interest to the local school community. Christian teachers from the 1940, and 1950s helped to build the new Africa on the local scene. In due course they themselves became ministers – ministers of state or, as the case might be, ministers of religion.

A popular view in the West and in some African circles after the Second World War held, as one of its most cherished dogmas, that the supposedly close relationship between the colonial government and Western missions implied that when the colonial system finally crumbled, the Church was bound to wither and die with it. Subsequent history has proved this forecast wrong. The colonial system in Africa certainly came to an end, with the rise of autonomous African states. But far from accomplishing its anticipated decay and obliteration, the Church has grown and flourished, sometimes more so than any other institution.

The relationship between Church and State in Africa in this period is much too variegated an affair to be summed up in any one neat formula. In independent Africa the Church was to play a prominent role, sometimes hushed and isolated, other times taking the role of a healthy and disturbing counter-movement. In the West there were other powerful institutions to check and challenge the power of the state: the judiciary, the trade unions, the financial foundations and the companies with an authority and prestige comparable to that of the state. This was not so in the African one-party or military-ruled state. Particularly in the late 1970s and in the 1980s, due to poverty and corruption, there ensued a decay of the state while the military on one hand and the Church on the other stood out as possible alternatives and as countervailing powers in the land.

Looking at events over the thirty-year period after 1960, no churchman was likely to feel triumphant about achievements but they might have reason to say, in all humility, that while various political systems had proven frail and sometimes disastrous, the Churches, existing close to grass-roots level had proven stable and sometimes even strong, at least as far as the statistics of 'Church growth' show.

A common pattern of political development throughout the continent can be discerned. Political independence was obtained in a spirit of *rising expectations*. At first these expectations were inspired by democratic ideals of Western democracy or by some form of socialism, Marxist or otherwise, and allowed for competing parties. However, these plural systems were soon supplanted by either dictatorial military rule or strict one-party structures, which in a number of cases were used to impose the authoritarian idiosyncrasies of the leader. Examples include Nkrumah's self-adulation as the *Osagyefo* (the Saviour) with the slogan 'Seek ye first the political kingdom and all other things shall be given unto you', and Mobutu's 'authenticity' decrees which led to open conflict, lasting for years, between the president and the Catholic cardinal. Finally, and most tragically, there was the degeneration into tyranny and unrestrained terror in the cases of Amin of Uganda, Bokassa of the Central African Republic and Marcias Nguema of Equatorial Guinea. Primates lost their lives along with their clergy and humble followers as was the case in Uganda when Archbishop Luwum was murdered by Amin's henchmen in February 1977 while, a month later, the Archbishop of Brazzaville, Cardinal Biayenda, was slain in the aftermath of yet another *coup d'etat* in Congo.

To a surprising extent these conflicts were related to what we would call 'the syndrome of regionalism' in the structure of modern African politics: a fateful survival from the drawing of political frontiers leading to tensions between ethnic communities. During the colonial period these had somehow remained under control, but after independence they flared up in brutal friction and civil war. The Churches, both Catholic and Protestant were affected by these conflicts. The worst of these developments took place against an international economic slump caused by a drastic rise in oil prices in 1973, adding to the immiseration and indebtedness of some countries. Instead of rising expectations, there now followed a plague of *mounting frustrations*.

During the 1950s Dr Frantz Fanon, the Martinican psychiatrist, articulated his sharp uncompromising criticism against colonial rule in Africa and elsewhere, in *Peau noire, masques blancs*[3] and his *Les Damnés de la terre*.[4] Twenty years after independence, Father J. M. Ela of Cameroon published his *Le cri de l'homme africain*, carrying the same conviction and power.[5] Ela exposed the injustices and tyranny in some independent African countries, showing how there was 'a consolidation of these republics of silence', an extended *gulag* in independent Africa itself. However, as a devoted churchman he turned to the Church for a solution. Could not the Church contribute to the liberation of the African protest and make the Africans free to speak out in their own countries, thus preparing a new society?

Old and new influences on the political scene conditioned the role of the Churches. A number of countries argued for socialism in its various forms – Marxist–Leninism according to Moscow, Cuba or China – and imposed this as the official ideology of their one-party state. A particular nonconformist idea was that of General Achiempong of Ghana who tried out the alluring teaching of an American lady spiritualist.

On the other hand there were the 'politics of affection' related to local ethnicity in politics, language and culture, a tendency which was taken for granted and promoted, even when censored.

Ethnicity took on a large variety of forms. In Congo, Foulbert Youlou, a Lari, was able to successfully claim that he carried Andre Matswa's spirit (another Lari) and even got away with it for a while. At other times ethnicity led to devastating revolts and wars, with repeated ethnocide – such as Rwanda and Burundi, or Sudan. In the south of the continent tensions between White and Black led to drawn out liberation wars – Zimbabwe, Namibia, Mozambique, Angola – while in South Africa it took a dramatic generation to embrace apartheid and then to shed it.

In other countries, notably Zaïre, Mobutu Sese Seko's 'authenticity' petered out into stalemate and a dead end. A country rich in natural resources was thus turned into a lamentable poor land, with only one family, that of the president himself, enriched beyond all measure, while the vast majority of his people became increasingly poor.

A refreshing exception from the general rule of one-party dominance was the way in which Benin managed its transition from Marxism to democracy. With 495 votes the General Council practically elected unanimously the Archbishop-Coadjutor of Cotonou, Isidore de Souza, as chairman of the High Council of the Republic.

At a time when African states lost most of their credibility, the Churches, both Catholic and Protestant, came out as powers of solidarity and strength. Throughout the continent, Catholic bishops proclaimed their social concern and political opposition by way of common Lent encyclicals, to be read from the pulpit in all the Churches of a diocese. In a South Africa still dominated by apartheid the Church, more particularly the Anglicans – through Archbishop Desmond Tutu and others – Methodists and Presbyterians played a decisive role which was eventually to lead to the liberation (after twenty-seven years in prison) of Nelson Mandela and indeed of the country as a whole.

Could the Church provide a lead in the search for 'a Second Liberation'? Hitherto the African state was 'an overloaded state', industrialization was carried out by public rather than private agencies. The state had now become like an albatross around the African neck. The 'starting point must be a committment to people's participation and empowerment and to the principle of accountability'. The Dag Hammarskjöld Foundation conference at Mweya, Uganda in 1990 has this to say:

> The Second Liberation will not come easily or without pain. It will not come without the mobilization of all its soldiers and especially its youth; it will not come about without a determined start.[6]

Table 18.1. *The Churches in Africa: Total growth 1900–2000* (in millions)[7]

	1900	1950	1965	1980	2000
Total population	118	222	306	450	770
Total Christians	4	34	75	146	351
Roman Catholic	1	14	34	71	175
Protestants	1	9	21	45	110
Orthodox-Coptic	2	8	13	17	32
African Independents	0	3	7	13	34

This period of political independence for Africa provides an opportunity to consider the fast statistical growth of the Church in the period seen against the background of the total population. This growth relates also to the rapid urbanization of the continent, a factor which we shall follow up later in this chapter.

This statistical survey reveals two fundamental facts: the slow but determined increase in the first half of the century and the enormously rapid growth towards the end of the century.

The concatenation of two epochal events – the Independence of Africa and the Second Vatican Council (together with the emergence of the non-Roman All Africa Council of Churches) – were to determine the growth, development and problems of the Churches in Africa during this period.

One concern was the rising influence of ethnicity, in high places and elsewhere, related to what Professor Goran Hyden has called 'the politics of affection'.[8] Africanization meant not only a change in the colour of administrators of Church and State: it also implied a determination of the locals to see to it that the new leader to be appointed came from the right place and spoke the right vernacular. The vast problem of ethnicity in the Church, aggravated and embittered in some astonishing cases, can only be hinted at here.

We also allude to one highly laudable effect of clan affinity: the economic solidarity of the educated extended Christian family. In Africa education costs money and secondary education a lot of money, to be found somehow, somewhere. An ordinary African family with some eight or ten children develops its own solution to this disturbing predicament. One or two of the eldest children will have to sacrifice over ten–twelve years, paying (from their salaries as school teachers or hospital orderlies) for the younger ones, the latter always knowing that they are indeed indebted for their higher education – secondary and university – to elder brothers and sisters, or more distant relatives. This whole pattern of economic support by kith and kin is very distinctly African and is referred to here as, to a large extent, it concerns the educated Christian family. There is a theme here for local research on a highly worthwhile subject.

New missionary dimensions

Independent Africa demonstrated new dimensions of Christian missions. The African Churches themselves carried the message of Christ across geographical, tribal and linguistic frontiers to an extent to which we cannot do full justice here. For the Catholics we refer to Ramón Echeverria's examples: a Luo priest at work in a largely Kikuyu parish; Buganda missionaries active in Burkina Faso; Zaïrean sisters founding communities among the Nyamwezi in Tanzania.

The English-speaking Anglican Church of Uganda found its way into French-speaking Shaba (Katanga) in Zaïre. The Lutheran Church in Tanzania, on the initiative of its General Secretary Joel Ngeiyamu, saw to it that the Lutheran message took ecclesiastical form in countries towards the west: in Shaba (Katanga); and in the south: in Malawi and Mozambique. To these examples can be added similar ones in West Africa and Southern Africa. In dealing with the Independent Churches we have referred to an irrepressible proclivity in these groups for slipping through any boundary and thus expanding to new peoples and groups.

However, during this period a new dimension was added, that of 'mission in return', the Church in Africa suddenly showed an evangelistic outreach to those Western Churches which had begun as mission societies in the first place. In the first generations of the nineteenth century the Christian movement was, as we have suggested, a youth movement. Today 'the mission in return' found its irresistible messengers in groups of young Africans, more particularly in musical choirs, who spent periods of time in Western Churches, transforming European Church life as they went.[9]

LIBERATION AND THE COMMUNITY

The struggle of Africa and of Africans for liberation, justice and dignity could not but provoke questions aimed at the international community. Four such issues must, however briefly, be alluded to here: firstly, on Racism and the Christian message; secondly, refugees in Africa; thirdly, the place of the poor in the community and in the Church; and, fourthly, AIDS and the Church.

Racism and the Churches

When the World Council of Churches published its *Programme to Combat Racism* in 1969, the Churches were awakened to a new awareness of what was in fact *the* fundamental problem of the twentieth century. The ecumenical movement had of course encountered the problem before. In 1924 Dr J. H. Oldham, with his incomparable sense for fundamentals, published his *Christianity and the Race Problem*, pointing to the Cross of Christ, 'which in teaching us that all we are and have is God's gift ... cuts away every ground of superiority and pride and makes possible a real brotherhood on the basis of our common relation to God.'[10] The life and death of Dr Martin Luther King (1929–68) and the involvement of the World Council of Churches, then under the direction of Dr Philip Potter, led to this new departure in 1969. Racism as an ecumenical problem, the World Council was saying, was more than a matter of attitudes and practical solutions. It concerned the very nature of the Christian faith.

Professor John Deschner of the United States, member of the Faith and Order Commission, has shown that the race problem was, at the deepest level, a 'Faith and Order' issue of immense importance for an understanding of Baptism, the sacrament of Christian identity, and of Christian *koinonia* in and through Holy Communion. 'Where racism is a problem, can we rightly celebrate the eucharist if our congregation, our ministry and our liturgy do not visibly manifest the power of Christian unity to reconcile the races ... Race is visible: rightly understood that is not the tragedy but the glory of "race".'[11]

It was a far-reaching personal initiative by Bishop Kibira, Bukoba, Tanzania, which prepared the way for a final decision in 1984 by the Lutheran World Federation on the question of 'apartheid and the Churches'. Seven years earlier, in 1977, the Dar es Salaam Assembly of the Lutheran Federation had, in learned theological language, appealed to the White Churches in southern Africa to recognize that the situation in those countries constituted a *status confessionis*; yet this kind of recognition was in fact to lead to endless evasion and procrastination. Bishop Kibira was set on counteracting this by calling a conference of some seventy African Lutheran Church leaders from all over the continent to meet at Harare, Zimbabwe, in order to act as a determined pressure group recommending that the Churches in question be suspended from LWF membership until such time as they publicly and unequivocally rejected apartheid. On the strength of this recommendation, the Budapest Assembly in 1984 decided to suspend the membership of two Lutheran Churches in South Africa, with a view to encouraging those Churches to abandon their policy of apartheid and to move to visible unity with the Lutheran Churches in Southern Africa.[12]

'No Place to Feel at Home' – Refugees once more

Definition and numbers

Independence, yes – but for whom – for which section of the population of a newly independent continent? We have met the refugee problem before and seen it as a fundamental factor in the Christianization process in nineteenth-century Africa. In 'this continent on the move' the refugee factor has been an ever-recurrent phenomenon. To underline this, the very first sentence in this book pointed to the refugee theme for the continent's Church history.

The staggering dimension of the problem after 1960 is seen in the statistics. Of the world's 5 million refugees 50 per cent are Africans in Africa. Yet, for all the millions one is apt to forget that they are the compound sum of suffering of so many individuals and families, or shreds of families, torn from their roots, from their land, from a meaningful existence, forced to flee headlong for refuge elsewhere. In the period 1960–90 this question took on seemingly impossible dimensions. The 'Commission of Ten', a body within the Organization of African Unity (OAU), stated in 1979 that since 1965 the number of refugees in Africa had increased sixty-fold. Who then is a refugee? Two well-known Swedish lawyers, G. Melander and Dr Peter Nobel, in their book, *African Refugees and the Law*, define the concept 'refugee' as a person who:

> owing to well-founded fear of being persecuted for reasons of race, religion, nationality, membership of a particular social group or political opinion, is outside the country of his nationality and is unable or, owing to such fear, is unwilling to avail himself of the protection of that country; or who, not having a nationality and being outside the country of his former habitual residence as a result of such events, is unable or, owing to such fear, is unwilling to return to it.[13]

There is another dimension to the problem which shows that being a refugee is now more difficult than ever. Previously one moved as a refugee across a frontier with a well-founded hope eventually to return to one's village and *shamba*. Now the frontiers are more definite, more excluding, through the techniques of a modern police force. The refugee realizes that he/she crosses that frontier *for ever*, with no hope of ever returning.

The refugee situation in the first decades of independence was defined as 'Living in the Shadow of Death'. More particularly this applied to the ever-changing situation in northern Uganda and southern Sudan and the seemingly hopeless movement for ever to and fro, from Sudan into Ethiopia and Eritrea and from Eritrea and Ethiopia into Sudan. Dr G. Kibreab points out that 'out of Sudan's 527,000 refugees, 389,000 are from Eritrea. This indicates the enormous size of the problem.'[14] This great refugee drama was also played out in North East Africa, in Somalia and Sudan, 'perhaps the major crisis area on the continent'.[15] In Sudan the tensions between a Muslim north and a Christian south were aggravated by the refugee problem until at long last a temporary settlement was reached in 1972, with the assistance of the Protestant All Africa Conference of Churches and its General Secretary Canon Burgess Carr. This peace agreement was, however, not to last and the Sudanese civil war recommenced with a vengeance in the early 1980s. Here we cannot follow the varieties of causes, nor the repatriation and resettlement problems linked with the refugees. We shall indicate only a couple of cases and even these must be strictly selective.

The Hutu and Tutsi

The ethnocide in Rwanda and Burundi started in Rwanda in about 1960. There the Hutu population, coming to the end of their tether with the overlordship of the Tutsi suddenly struck back with arson, cruelty and death on a frightening scale, and the Tutsi were forced to leave their country. They found refuge in neighbouring countries: Zaïre, Burundi, Uganda or Tanzania.

As they arrived in Karagwe on the border of western Tanzania – a dejected company of once impressive Tutsi men, women and children – the local Catholic and Lutheran Churches had to act. We remember the discussion in the synodal council of the Lutheran Diocese of Bukoba. Dean Matia Lutosha rose to speak. He was the grandson of the king of Kianja and thus offspring of a privileged community which, 400 years earlier, had settled in those hills. A solid, confident pastor, he was part of the well-to-do African establishment in the area. There was personal conviction in his words: 'I have always known that we were all, fundamentally, refugees. That is why I appeal to the Diocese and through the council to the Lutheran World Federation on behalf of these our unfortunate brothers and sisters.'

Besides the first necessities – clinics and schools – other amenities were established. The drama in Karagwe has a special historical significance in that it sparked off the world-wide refugee assistance programme of the Lutheran World Federation.[16] This kind of assistance could take place in a country where the president, Dr Julius Nyerere, was ever ready to guide the planning of a nation-wide refugee service. At the conference on refugees held in Arusha, Tanzania, May 1979, Nyerere said:

> African refugees are an African problem. I do not believe that dealing with the problem of 3–4 million people and giving them a chance to rebuild their dignity and their lives is an impossible task for forty-six nations and their 360 million inhabitants.

Later on, it was the Hutu from Burundi who underwent a traumatic experience. They had seen their next of kin tortured, murdered, hacked to death in a fratricidal civil war, with between 50,000 and 100,000 dead and tens of thousands forced to flee to neighbouring Tanzania.

The majority of the Hutu from Burundi coming into Tanzania were Protestants – in the Burundi fashion, which meant they were Pentecostals. At Ulyankulu the first 21,700 refugees were given land. After a flood in 1979 part of the population had to move. Now there are 4,000 in Ulyankulu, nearly 20,000 at Katumba and 6,400 at Mishamo. These people are all hard-working farmers – producing maize and other food crops. The government authorities initially encouraged them to grow tobacco for sale to the national tobacco company, but at this these pious Pentecostals drew the line: smoking is one of the Protestant sins in Africa, and as Pentecostals they must not be party to encouraging such an obnoxious evil. They also established themselves as a co-operative community of their own. There were iron-smiths, taylors, butchers, workers in six electric mills, a bicycle workshop, shops and a restaurant. Twice a week – Wednesday and Saturday – thousands would meet at the market to exchange of goods and services.

The heart of it all is the chapel. One sees them walking along the paths in the area carrying their Kirundi New Testament coming to Church gatherings three times a week, Sunday, Tuesday and Friday evenings. Each of the three local centres – Ulyankulu, Katumba and Mishamo – has its own Church president and have the following numbers of voluntary workers: elders: 7, 21, 12; deacons: 13, 0, 29; evangelists: 66, 157, 63; all at 30, 60 and 33 outposts respectively.

On arrival in the new place they found large numbers of Pentecostal brethren in other parts of the country and established contacts with them, while always retaining a certain distance. They offered some friendly criticism of the locals: their drums were not the right size and shape and they invariably clap hands in church, a custom which Burundi Pentecostals would not recognize. In the camps there emerged something of a twenty- to thirty-year Church history. These people were free to fashion their religious life on their own, perhaps along entirely new lines. But as one tries to understand the dynamics of this development, one finds that almost invariably worship forms, or lack thereof, from back home in Burundi remained the norm and model in the new land too. The faithfulness to their own Pentecostal past is complete. Fundamentally, this is a symbol of the need for identity, in this case an identity through continuity. The Church traditions in distant Burundi may not in themselves have been very ancient, at the most half a century, but they were *their* sacred traditions, not to be questioned or tampered with.

Tied to their own past, they were, however, as a Pentecostal community, singularly prepared to manage the necessary adaptations to a new, enormously challenging situation. Local groups for Bible study and for inspiration and revival, led by a great number of devoted voluntary agents, helped families and individuals to find their way through a dangerous world.

Botswana

A fascinating account of a refugee conversion story is that of the Etcha Hambukushu, a river people of fishermen, hunters and blacksmiths, who for two centuries had lived in southern Angola under harsh Portuguese rule. In 1967 there was war and guerillas entered the villages to fight the Portuguese. Four thousand Hambukushu decided to flee south into north-west Botswana, 'in a traumatic exodus not unlike the flight of the children of Israel from Egypt'.

An Anglican priest, Ronald C. Wynne, worked with them for years, learning their language, telling them the stories of Exodus in the Old Testament and that of the Refugee Child of Bethlehem, and also pioneering adult literacy work. With rare empathy he prepared the people for the decisive step. In the 1970s, after years of wise preparation, they were led as a total group to experience common baptism in the Okavango river. The Eucharist, that common sacred meal, had in this community 'remarkable converting power'.

The Hambukushu story, only alluded to here, is an illustration of what has come to be, in this African Church history, a persistent theme of the nineteenth and to some extent the twentieth centuries, that of the uprooted group looking for security and pushing their roots in new soil.[17]

The Poor

There is inevitably a link between the struggle against racism and the Churche's concern for the poor, the suppression of the very poor by the very rich. In Independent Africa, with dramatically rising urbanization there followed a widening abyss between the rich and the poor, a problem which took on a new urgency for the Church at the end of the twentieth century. The Gospel obviously was addressed to the poor and was concerned with them. How could this concern be expressed in and by the Church in the last decade of the century – and beyond?

Two recent books provide help towards an answer, John Iliffe's *The African Poor: a History*,[18] and *Uprooting Poverty: the South African Challenge* by Francis Wilson and Mamphela Ramphele.[19] Dr Iliffe defines poverty:

> two levels of want have existed in Africa for several centuries. On one level have been the very large numbers – perhaps most Africans at most times – obliged to struggle continuously to preserve themselves and their dependants from physical want. These will be called the poor. On another level have been smaller numbers who have permanently or temporarily failed in that struggle and have fallen into physical want. These will be called the very poor or destitute ... epidemic starvation for all but the rich gave way to endemic undernutrition for the very poor.[20]

Paradoxically the problem can be seen most sharply in South Africa. 'Paradoxically', because South Africa is by far the richest country in Africa with enormous riches hidden in its soil. Yet, that country provided the most glaring cases of inequality. The 'most striking feature of poverty in South Africa is the degree of inequality that exists ... the gulf between grinding poverty and massive wealth.' The economists speak of a *Gini* coefficient for measuring economic inequality, and South Africa measured the highest among the fifty or more countries in the world for which data were available. Poverty in South Africa was pervasive. In 1980 the proportion of people living below the subsistence level was estimated at:

50 per cent for the population as a whole
60.5 per cent for Africans
81 per cent for Africans living in reserves (or 'Homelands')[21]

Vatican II brought to Africa not only rejoicing. The prophets among the priests, particularly in Cameroon, challenged the Church in the name of the poor. There had of course been Western bishops and laymen who had insisted on the Church's duty with regard to the poor: with the greatest vigour perhaps, Bishop J. Blomjous of Mwanza. Among African Church leaders nobody could do this with greater authority of historical and theological understanding than Fr E. Mveng of Yaoundé:

> In Africa poverty is not only a socio-economic phenomenon. It is a human condition in its deepest root which has been destroyed, traumatized,

> impoverished. In Africa, who is poor, and who is not? The triumphalist arrogance to whom the Church is nothing but an enormous machine of oppression reminds us of this fact every day. Therefore we say 'Alleluya', for the Church in Africa for its hour has sounded.[22]

While Fr Mveng teaches at the university and speaks – with great authority – in the academies, his colleague J. M. Ela was to be found in a miserable village in northern Cameroon. Not only Vatican II but also the writings of Fanon inspired him. 'What characterizes the situation is the growth of inequality in independent Africa.'[23] He quotes President Senghor:

> In colonial times one could protest and one had the people on one's side. Today one is colonized and one lies to the people in telling them that they are free. To many Africans there is a lack not only of drinkable water and of a sufficient quantity of animal protein but also of a space of liberty where he can speak 'without tether or censorship'. The Church should liberate the African protest, allowing the African to speak.[24]

Professor Mveng goes even further, and deeper, in his interpretation of poverty in Africa, when he speaks of 'anthropological poverty'.[25] This is not just economic or financial deprivation but a condition where one is impoverished of one's very humanity when one's very human being is being denied.

Health care, AIDS and the Churches

In the last few years Africa has been hit by a plague of terrible proportions. In some cities 40 per cent of the adult population are infected. Statisticians produced their grim forecast: in the year 2015 there could be 70 million cases of the disease in Africa south of the Sahara. More than a quarter of a million children are already orphans: in 2015 the number of orphans could be 16 million. Some 40 per cent of children born to infected mothers could develop the illness and many would die before the age of five. The whole system of medical services was affected as most beds would be required for this pandemic.

*A*cquired *I*mmune *D*eficiency *S*yndrome, commonly known as AIDS (in French SIDA) has become a major concern around the world. The number of people with AIDS or the Human-Immunodeficiency Virus (HIV) is growing rapidly. The first cases were diagnosed in the early 1980s in Europe, USA and Central Africa, and the virus causing the disease was first described in 1983.

In Africa the disease is most widely spread in the western-central, eastern and southern regions of the continent, while the countries north of the

Sahara have, so far, only recorded a few cases. Countries with a high proportion of infected people in the population include Burundi, Rwanda, Uganda, Tanzania, Zambia, Zaïre and Ivory Coast. Here the disease affects men and women in their most active years, as well as infants infected by their mothers already before birth. The disease is mainly spread in the larger cities by migrant workers, with their families in the countryside and prostitutes in the towns. It continues to spread also into rural areas, with the chief routes of transmission via the main roads.

Through their medical work the Churches in Africa soon became involved in AIDS work. Initially the activities focused on patients coming into the health institutions with AIDS symptoms. Technical solutions were sought. However, it soon became clear that the medical/technical part of the problem was not the whole problem. It is as important to deal with the social, psychological and economic consequences.

Here the local congregations have a very important role to play. The hospitals cannot care for patients dying of a disease for which there is as yet no medical cure, so the patients go home to be cared for by their relatives. As AIDS is a sexually transmitted disease, usually both husband and wife are infected and become ill, and are thus dependent on others. Here congregation members as well as staff from the health institutions coming on regular visits play an important role (e.g., the Lutheran Church in north-western Tanzania, the Anglican and Catholic Churches in Uganda, and the Salvation Army in Zambia). As the disease particularly affects young adults, mothers and fathers, many children have been orphaned and many old people have lost the support of their children. These are groups for whom the Church has traditionally taken special responsibility. Pastoral care and education are important activities that are part of the role of the Church, its priests and pastors and catechists, all of whom have a heavy task to fulfil. Much support is needed, much love and acceptance.

The World Council of Churches started a programme to support the member Churches in their AIDS work in 1986, when the First International Consultation was held in Geneva. The consultation called on the member Churches to be involved in pastoral care, social ministry and education to alleviate the consequences of the new disease. A hearing was held in 1987 to bring the issue to the Churches. A booklet called *AIDS and the Church* was published. Also a small manual for health workers mainly in Africa was produced and translated into several local languages in Africa and is widely used both within and outside the Church. A second booklet was published in 1988, this time to guide pastors, teachers and youth-leaders in their educational work. In 1988 the Second International Consultation was held in

Moshi, Tanzania, with special emphasis on the situation in Africa. The report from the consultation, *AIDS and Pastoral Care* offered guidelines for the work of the Churches. In 1989 a workshop was held in Barbados to develop a manual on pastoral care for Church-workers.[26]

AFRICAN CHURCH MUSIC

Only after the 1950s was there a large-scale turn to genuinely African music for the Churches, but this is not to say that such a tendency was not expressed well before that time. A case in point was Ntsikana around 1820 in the Eastern Cape in South Africa. A young Xhosa chief, having heard a few sermons from the LMS missionary van der Kemp, experienced a spiritual awakening and produced four highly original songs with a most central Christian message. Ntsikana's hymns were to initiate a Xhosa tradition and a Xhosa national anthem, inspiring generations of South Africans up to the present day. A century after Ntsikana, Isaiah Shembe of Zululand composed songs for his Nazaretha Church of the greatest originality, totally different from the arduous translations of the Westerners.

A kind of solution for music in the African Churches was for long seen in the 'Tonic Sol-fa' method. Here the founder was John Curwen, a Scottish musician who had never been in Africa but was able, particularly through the Lovedale school in Cape Province, South Africa, to conquer and capture the field for about a century.

An opposition movement against the domination of the Tonic Sol-fa came early, however. Professor Percival Kirby complained that 'the music of the White man was usually a bed of Procrustus for the speech of the Black'. And the South Africa Hugh Tracy was to create an African Music Society from 1947, with a journal from 1954. A certain number of Africans and Western pioneers created African music, among them A. M. Jones, Anglo-Catholic missionary and musician in Zambia. With him we mention the Swedish Church musician Dr Henry Weman who devoted himself to this concern. There was also a Ghanaian school led by Professor Nketia, Revds Amu, Mensah and Gbebo, together with Nigerian composers; outstanding among them were Fela Sowando and Laz. E. N. Ekweume. An increasing discontent with the expressions of African Church music was to be heard at this time not least from the Frenchman, Alain Daniélou, who regarded conventional methods as 'a cultural genocide, a colonialism with most brutal forms of genocide and slavery'.[27]

The 1950s were to see important changes in this field, an awareness of the need for music growing from a national, African context. Joseph Kwele's

'Katanganese Mass' writeen in about 1950 illustrates this tendency together with the 'Missa Luba' by Kamina singers. Fr J. Lenherr worked among the Karanga-speaking communities of the Shona cluster, devoting himself to this concern.

At this time special categories of singers were, sometimes unexpectedly, to produce African Church music of captivating quality and beauty. In Ghana Fante lyrics gave expression to the highest degree of choral improvisation. Here a catechist's scripture reading was followed by the congregation joining in the required chorus. The Anglican Youth Fellowship in Nigeria must be mentioned in this context. There was also the Uganda Foundation for the Blind, and the Leper Settlement at Uzuakoli in Nigeria, led by the Methodist doctor Harcourt Whyte. In Ethiopia the Protestants of the Oromo people have produced African music of great beauty, and the Ethiopian Orthodox Church was concerned with its traditional Church music, the average Church singer training for seven years in order to master the complexities of the Church music.

Outstanding among these was the Lumko Music Department from 1979. This institute gathered more than 1,000 compositions and promoted African musical instruments. This Catholic institute also gathered Zionist Church music. One of the great features of Lumko is its active promotion of African music by modern methods.

19

NORTH AND NORTH-EASTERN AFRICA

THE MAGHREB

The Church's history in the Muslim north – the Maghreb – is of special interest: the precarious existence of a tiny Catholic minority in 'a sea of Islam'. In Independent Africa as a whole, after 1960, the Church has increasingly gained in number and influence. The Muslim north represents the exception to this rule. Here, one should not expect impressive Church statistics or loud and rabble-rousing revival. Instead there is a discreet Christian presence, through prayer and service – where service is at all possible and allowed – and a deep spirituality expressed in devotion and meditation, related to the hidden life of Jesus in Nazareth, our Lady of Africa and 'the saints of Africa'.

The modern Christian history in these countries was determined, and delimited, by the revolutionary upsurge against French colonialism after World War II. In Algeria this led to a bitter civil war during eight long, terrible years, with consequent French surrender and exodus, and Algerian rule under Ben Bella. In Tunisia, after a conflict of much shorter duration, the country's independence was assured under the Paris-trained lawyer and journalist Habib Bourguiba.

While concerned primarily with daily problems in an ever-changing political and social situation, the Church in Algeria and Tunisia was able to derive inspiration from its relation to history. These lands hallowed by the memory of St Cyprian and St Augustine and the other early Christian martyrs appear to the Catholic as emblazoned by sacred history. 'It is a historical fact that long before any French colonization and long before the arrival of the Muslims the Church was an extraordinary factor. St Augustine is an authentic son of this country.'[1]

The relation to history and to Rome gives strength for the task today. Cardinal Léon-Étienne Duval (born 1903, Bishop of Constantine, Algeria, in 1947, Archbishop of Algeria in 1954) could confront any criticism levelled by some of his faithful against him and his cautious policy. On the Feast of St Augustine in 1950, he told his diocese:

> Sometimes my faithful [people] do not understand me and secretly criticize me for mixing into things which are none of my business. One day perhaps, my brethren, you will reproach me for not having spoken sufficiently loudly, for not having warned you and for not having cried out telling you what is your duty. On that day, the stones of this sanctuary will cry out, confirming that the Church did indeed speak out, that Rome has spoken and that the echo of the successor of Peter was heard in this very place.[2]

Because of the Cardinal's outspoken plea for friendship with Muslims he was referred to as the 'Bishop of the Muslims', but he insisted that as a bishop of the country he belonged to all and everybody. If not, he would be the chief of a sect. 'It is by fraternal love that one attains to universality.'[3]

With Algerian independence in 1962 the majority of the Church buildings became state property and were changed into mosques or centres for social work. The vast majority of the non-Arabs left for France while twenty-six Catholic priests took Algerian nationality. The cardinal explained: 'There has been continuity: right from the Algerian war and independence the Church saw itself as serving the total population of the country.'[4]

For some years the Catholic schools were able to carry on as before, but from 1976 these 'private schools' were integrated into the state school system and the Catholic men and women were then engaged in teaching in the state schools and colleges, or in medical work. The Protestants – Open Brethren and North Africa Mission – were involved in giving Bible correspondence courses.

In the inland mountains, during the Algerian war, it was well-known that Catholic priests and nuns had served the sick and bound up the wounded: after independence they could, unhampered, carry on this service and also continue their worship in the chapel, to the discreet ringing of the bell.

The following question was put to the Cardinal in 1984: 'Is the Church just a remainder of colonization or has it a place in Muslim Algeria?' His answer summed up the meaning of the Catholic presence in the Muslim country:

> A leading Muslim answered that question in the following way: 'In this immense ocean of Islam it is good that there are some islets of Christianity.' We are a very small minority compared with the twenty million Algerians, most of them Muslims. But does not this statement of a Muslim affirm the spiritual kinship which unites all those who believe in the true God, Creator of the Universe, Father of the human family.[5]

In Tunisia, too, after independence in 1962, a *modus vivendi* was signed between Rome and the Government of Tunisia. Except for some Church buildings even now used for Christian worship – altogether forty-two 'cult places' – the Church surrendered all other Church property to the Tunisian state, 'definitely and free'. The archbishop, consecrated in Rome in 1965 became a *Prelate nullius*, placed immediately under the Holy See.

The group of White Fathers at Tunis and elsewhere devoted themselves to dialogue with Islam, through two highly significant institutes: the Institute des Belles-Lettres Arabes, with its renowned leader Father Demeersemann W.F., and the GRIC, Groupe des Recherches Islamo-Chrétien, consisting not of official delegates but of private scholars who together study the Qur'an and the Bible. They maintain contacts with the IPEA in Rome, the Institut pour Etudes Arabes, and its review *Islamo-Christiana*.

The heart of the matter is the Eucharist, celebrated in utter simplicity and sincerity in some private room, with a table and a white cloth, and bread and wine – 'where two or three are gathered in My name'.

From his eagle's nest in Algeria in the last century – that period of colonial triumphalism – Cardinal Lavigerie spanned *Tota Africa*, the whole of the continent, looking for ways and means of converting the masses and the millions. His successors in the Maghreb today have a much more limited perspective, even if restriction in this case may imply more of depth. It is suggested that some of their experience might serve vicariously in a future on behalf of *Tota Africa*.

EGYPT

Christians in modern Egypt

In Egypt post-colonial developments can be observed very clearly: nascent Egyptian nationalism, emerging Islamic fundamentalism (the Muslim Brotherhood from 1928 to the present day), and the ensuing period of Arab socialism, up to the present social unrest and increasing confessionalism. Through all this, the Coptic Orthodox Church not only survived social and political upheaval, but persistently defended the place of Christian faith in modern society, perhaps more successfully than any other Church in the Arab World.

The Copts – a minority

Ninety-three per cent of Egypt's Christian population of some 6 million belong to the Coptic Orthodox Church, making it the largest single

Christian Church in the Middle East, and an important member of the World Council of Churches. The Coptic Catholic Church (autocephalous since 1824) is the largest of the smaller Christian communities in Egypt, counting about 250,000 members. There is also a Coptic Evangelical Church – 'The Synod of the Nile' – and a number of European denominations (Anglican, Roman Catholic, Pentecostal, Plymouth Brethren etc.) with chiefly non-Egyptian membership. But how many are the Copts as such? This is an issue of great political consequence. The consistent pattern is that representatives of the (to all intents and purposes) Muslim government admit a figure equal to about 5 per cent of the total population, whereas Copts themselves claim about 10–20 per cent. In real numbers the discrepancy becomes more obvious: today, Egypt has about 60 million inhabitants, growing by more than a million every year. It makes a great difference to public life in Egypt whether there are 2.5, 5 or even 10 million Copts: a minority of such clear distinction and cohesion as the Copts cannot be excluded from parliament, or political, military and other public positions. The conspicuous absence of Copts in public office became uncomfortable for President Sadat in his efforts to re-orientate Egyptian commerce towards the West (the policy of *infitah* initiated in 1976). He tried to amend this during the years preceding the Camp David treaty (1977–79), by appointing a Copt as Foreign Minister, Dr Boutros Boutros-Ghali,[6] and by adding ten Copts to the four elected to the National Assembly. Still, fourteen members of parliament out of 390 is not even 5 per cent . . .

The Copts often claim that Muslim predominance – especially marriage restrictions imposed by the *shari'a* – has continuously reduced their proportion of the total population. However, the Coptic community has participated in the population boom from the 1940s and onwards. Their social status and social life (monogamy, birth control) have, however, retarded their growth compared with the Muslim majority in Egypt.

Urbanization and nationalization

The colonial era introduced new patterns and institutions into Egyptian life that changed its urban environments considerably: motor vehicles, trams and electricity, mail and telegraphic communications, the expansion of white collar occupations, secular schools and universities. Copts of urban middle classes thrived as merchants, lawyers, medical doctors, bankers and state clerks. Many new Church buildings were erected, some in the very heart of Cairo.

The Suez crisis in 1956 was the beginning of the end to an uncritical embrace of Western ideas. Among the ever-growing community of urban Copts the Nasser regime, however, provoked the first wave of emigrants, a devastating brain drain (to the benefit of Britain and the USA) which has since continued as an outlet for unemployed university graduates, devoid of opportunity. Even after 1976, when Soviet friendship was definitely something of the past, the Copts have been enormously over-represented in this emigration flux from Egypt. The Coptic community in the USA and Canada is believed to number more than a million.

Those Copts who belonged to the urban upper class were affected by Nasser's nationalization programme launched in 1961. There were the semi-feudal landlords of the Nile valley, of whom many were Copts, with a traditional concentration in the Asyut region. Nasser's effort at land reform created strong resentment in this rich and influential group, which lingers until this day. This basically conservative opposition found a temporary political structure in the Copt-dominated New Wafd Party.[7]

Liberation and the democratic process

Of vast importance – far beyond the Christian community – is the strong traditional emphasis on education. Until 1940 Coptic schools represented about 60 per cent of all schools in Egypt. Primary education was given by Coptic monks and priests long before it was made obligatory by law. Sadat's first teacher in his Delta village was such a monk. Not least the Catholic branch of the Coptic Church continues to lead the way in modern pedagogy, catering to at least as many Muslim students as Christian in more than one secondary school. In backward rural areas, young Coptic university graduates devote several years of their life to literacy programmes (in the style of Paulo Freire),[8] where Muslim girls are their most rewarding target group, although this programme, known as Rural Diakonia, began as an internal service for poor and isolated Copts.

Coptic nationalism

In Egypt, as in other parts of the Arab world, the nationalist movement was not primarily based on confessional ideologies, but rather on a religiously indifferent concept of a de-colonized, pluralist society, inspired by socialist revolutionary ideas. Thus we find Christian as well as Muslim intellectuals at the forefront of this movement after World War II. The primacy of Nation over Confession in contemporary Egyptian thought has been stressed by Dr

Maurice Assad, one of the Coptic representatives on the Middle East Church Council and the World Council of Churches.

The Copts have played a part in the search for justice and peace in the Middle East. The Church's patriarchs stood firm in supporting the return to Egypt of the Suez Canal Zone, and called for justice for the Palestinians and permanent peace in the Middle East.[9] In 1967, during the third Arab–Israeli war, jubilant masses assembled in the Cathedral of St Mark in Cairo:

> Islamic and Coptic dignitaries jointly hailed the holy duty of defending the country as willed by God and therefore destined to be crowned by victory. These religious–political demonstrations for national solidarity should not be regarded simply as unpremeditated, spontaneous acts produced by the crisis. For several months, Cyril VI (i.e., Anba Kyrillos) had proclaimed the basic identity of goals of the Christian Gospel with the aspirations of the Arab Socialist Society. As in every national crisis, the Copts have stood solidly behind the Government.[10]

Copts and Muslims in Egypt

Several developments have contributed to the more or less continuous deterioration of the Christian position in Egypt:

(i) the conflict between conservative Copts and the Muslim government which boiled down to a personal feud between Pope Shenoudah III and President Sadat;
(ii) the isolation of Egypt from the Arab world following the 'Camp David Agreement' after which Egypt was accused of treason against the Arab and Muslim cause; and
(iii) emerging Muslim fundamentalism in Egypt and Syria, through the Muslim Brotherhood, reinforced by the Khomeini revolution in Iran in 1979.

In a speech in May 1980, Sadat publicly criticized Coptic leadership. The Church leadership had, according to Sadat, engaged in a campaign to 'blacken his name and the name of Egyptian Muslims in an appeal to Christians in the United States and the Vatican'.[11] The speech was followed by a flood of counter-accusations not least focusing on the discrepancy between theory and practice in the Muslim government's religious freedom policy. Although President Sadat had promised in 1972 to grant fifty building permits for churches annually, the actual figure after eight years was a tenth of this. In a new desert suburbia, four mosques had been built, but of the one promised Coptic church there was no more than a cornerstone. President Sadat on the other hand, accused Pope Shenoudah and other leading Copts of planning for an independent Coptic state in the province of Asyut, with its strong concentration of Coptic population, farmers and land-owners. The Asyut university has been the site of the most violent clashes between Copts and Muslims in recent years; many Copts in the southern Nile valley consequently live with their suitcases packed, ready for emigration.

On 5 September 1981 the Sadat regime issued a decree which affected all religious groups in Egypt, resulting in more than 1,500 arrests. The decree had severe implications for the Coptic Church: state recognition was withdrawn from Pope Shenoudah III, who was put under house arrest in the monastery of as-Surian. Eight bishops and sixteen priests were detained. The Copts restrained themselves from violent protests, perhaps chiefly by remembering the bloody riots in Asyut and Cairo in 1979–81. When President Sadat was assassinated on 6 October 1981, many Copts saw God's hand at work. The Church was also struck, however, as the bishop for external relations, Anba Samuel, was killed on the same occasion. The new president, Husni Mubarak, allowed a legal process to determine whether it was correct to depose the Pope Shenoudah. Eventually the Pope was reconciled with the state and returned to office.

The wondrous events of 1968

The disastrous war against Israel in June 1967 marked the end of Nasser's prestige, the defeat being the final blow in a long chain of post-revolutionary disenchantments. It was the Coptic Church that provided Egyptian society with a source of healing and renaissance of national pride. In *The Story of the Copts* Iris Habib al-Masri recalls the year of grace 1968:

> It formed a striking contrast to 1967. For in 1967 the Egyptians experienced one of their worst depressions throughout their long history. To the Copts the depression was double: not only was their homeland defeated in war, but this devastating defeat led to the fall of Jerusalem into the hands of Israel: the Holy Sepulchre and other holy spots became barred to them.[12]

Then, on 2 April, 1968 a series of apparitions of St Mary began in the neighbourhood of her own church in Zaytoun, a suburb of Cairo. The Holy Virgin continued to appear for almost a year. 'Thousands flocked nightly to witness the apparition. Many healing miracles continue to occur to the pilgrims of this famous shrine.'[13] President Nasser himself is known to have gone to Zaytoun in a covered limousine, where he was told directly by the

Virgin to release a Coptic priest, *Abuna* Zakkaria, whom he had ordered arrested for performing miracles and thereby converting many Muslims to the Coptic Church.

A papal committee was set up to examine the apparitions and ensuing miracles; a number of books and learned accounts of the subject exist today, in Arabic as well as in European languages. Iris Habib, one of this century's foremost Coptic Church historians concludes: 'Oftentime she effected surprising cures: not only did the blind see and the lame walk, but even surgical operations were evaded by Her interception. She healed and helped whoever implored Her: Muslims and Copts, Egyptians and foreigners.'[14] These wondrous events partly took the edge off the anti-Christian sentiment that was due to result from a defeat, where the 'Christian West' (mainly the USA) had been instrumental on the side of the adversary. Thus the inauguration of the mighty St Mark's Cathedral in central Cairo (on the occasion of the 1900th anniversary of St Mark's martyrdom) was a joyful celebration where both Copts and Muslims took part. President Nasser and his nearest colleagues (among them Anwar as-Sadat) attended the inaugural feast celebrated by the Pope Anba Kyrillos VI.

The monastic renaissance

Another striking feature is the explosive rebirth of the monastic movement. As recently as only thirty years ago the old monasteries in the Wadi Natroun desert were worn down and scarcely inhabited. But during the 1970s and 1980s the monasteries – fortresses of monotheism through the ages, as they are called by Muslim scholars – experienced an ever-growing influx of young Coptic university students. Some go to spend a year or more for the sake of retreat and spiritual renewal, others remain, passing the probate period and eventually entering monkhood. The diaconal and educational programmes of the monasteries are ambitious, including medical care, agricultural development, irrigation and other activities for the nomad communities of the surrounding desert. External factors may have contributed to this new golden age in monastic history. Exiled Copts (mainly in the USA and Canada) and ecumenical friends, such as the Churches in West Germany, were able to transfer capital to the Coptic Church and its monasteries. Some basic facts of life in modern Egypt may also play a role: growing unemployment, lack of housing and opportunity for young people make it next to impossible for men of the lower middle classes to marry and establish a family before the age of forty. Monastic celibacy is therefore a viable alternative.

A cautious estimate would say that between two and three thousand students visit the monasteries every year, spending at least a couple of months in the desert. The number of regular monks has increased about twenty times since 1970, from about thirty to around 600. A new thrust in theological education and pastoral training had begun in 1875 (with the re-establishment of the Theological University College in Cairo). It was not until 1972, however, that a branch was established in Alexandria, followed by another five branches in 1975–76. In this context the monastic revival can be better understood: it is in the monasteries that the old Coptic language and the teachings of the Desert Fathers can best be appropriated.

The new means of airborne communication have made contacts between Orthodox Egypt and Black Africa more attractive and, perhaps, impelling than ever. Groups and delegations from sub-Saharan Africa discovered new evocative aspects of the life of the Orthodox Church. Bishop Patrick Kalilombe of Malawi, one of the most brilliant observers among Catholic bishops of his generation, came to Cairo and to the desert monasteries. (He knew North Africa well from spending five years with the White Fathers at their centre in Algiers.) He was shown something important in Church life. The supposedly isolated monastery was no longer isolated for it was connected with the church, and crowds coming from the outside world could meet the monks in and around the church. Here was a fundamental pattern: the faithful coming in from the 'world', coming to the church as meeting ground and thus contacting the monastery, 'the power house'.[15]

Copts in exile

An important element in the life of the Copts after the revolution is the exile, especially after 1956, when Nasser declared Islam to be the religion of the state, in spite of heavy protests from the Copts, who had tried to prove themselves as loyal as any other citizens. For various reasons – mainly economic, sometimes religious, Copts have left Egypt and gone into the diaspora in the USA (Los Angeles and St Louis), Canada, Austria, Britain and Germany. Today the number of exiles is no less than 2 million, which means that virtually every Coptic family in Egypt has one or several members abroad. Whenever the situation of indigenous Christians in Egypt has shifted, the Copts in exile (e.g., the American and Canadian Coptic Association, ACA) have voiced vehement complaints and accusations against the Egyptian government, which has sometimes made things worse for those left in Egypt. In exile the Copts have come into contact with other Christian denominations, for example other Orthodox communities with whom they share a similar predicament. Thus the Russian Orthodox Church in Vienna has opened its main Church building for Coptic Mass every Sunday morning: a fine example of how Chalcedon no longer divides. Similarly Syrian and Armenian Orthodox persons can be seen to worship with the Coptic congregation in Stockholm.

In the 1960s the Coptic Orthodox Church officially discovered the Church in Africa in the form of the African Independent Churches in Nairobi and Kinshasa. A Coptic bishop was posted to Nairobi in order to cultivate these contacts. It was suggested that there existed a special link between these partners: they were unmistakably indigenous to the African continent and might have important interests in common. One might even suggest that with some of the African Churches there was emerging a new orientation, no longer to the West – Europe and the USA – but to the North – Egypt and Ethiopia. This orientation North might conceivably become of importance in the new century and millennium approaching.[16]

ETHIOPIA

Haile Selassie's regime in Addis Ababa seemed stable and strong. Internationally it enjoyed high prestige as seen by the fact that the Organization of African Unity (OAU) and the Economic Commission for Africa chose Addis Ababa for their headquarters. Yet, the regime was feudal with enormous differences between a privileged Amhara elite and the great mass of the people; the majority lived in poverty and destitution – with illiteracy widespread – and for some of these years in terrible famine. The feudal landlords, including the Ethiopian Orthodox Church, owned more than 90 per cent of arable land. These factors prepared a hot-bed of defiance and in 1960 there was an attempt to overthrow Haile Selassie and his government. The attempt did not succeed – but it was a portent.

The Orthodox Church

When *Abuna* Basileos passed away in 1970 there followed an election in Addis Ababa and the Electoral College with its 156 members presented a short list of three names with *Abuna* Tewoflos of Harar receiving the highest number of votes. This result was submitted to the emperor who graciously approved of the election and of *Abuna* Tewoflos as the new patriarch of Ethiopia. Tewoflos was a well-known Church leader with an excellent reputation in the ecumenical movement throughout the World Council of Churches and other councils.

Both emperor and patriarch had the ambition to bring their Church into contact with the wider ecclesiastical world. This was seen not least in the Oriental Orthodox Addis Ababa conference of 1965 when the Ethiopian Church acted as host to venerable heads of Churches from Egypt, Syria, Armenia and India. The secretary, Dr Abebe Retta, a leading Ethiopian layman, has suggested that the role of the emperor in taking the initiative for the conference and its successful realization gave the meeting 'a setting similar to that of the ancient Church'.[17]

A theological faculty, integrated into the University in 1961, was first headed by Dr Samuel, theologian of the Syrian Orthodox Church of South India.

Sometimes one of the bishops would realize the missionary duty of the Church and in 1961 gathered a number of his priests to visit the pagans in the south-west in order to have them incorporated into the Church.

The Ethiopian Orthodox Church was a venerable institution with, in 1970, 61,000 priests, 12,000 monks, 57,000 deacons, 31,000 *debteras* (choir leaders) and 827 monasteries, transmitting to new generations sacred words, melodies and gestures of an ancient liturgical past, not to mention the great numbers of nuns. At the village level there emerged, alongside the official liturgy in the Ge'ez language, a popular spirituality close to the ordinary people and the actual social needs both of the individual and their communities. One can see this in a wider perspective when projecting Ethiopia on the map of Africa.

Revolution and repression

In 1974–75 Ethiopia had a 'creeping revolution': the military forces took command and the emperor – the 'Conquering Lion of Judah, Elect of God, Descendent of the Queen of Sheba and King Solomon' – was removed, driven, as it was claimed, 'to a safe place', tantamount to murder. In 1976 the new political leader, Menghistu Haile Mariam, published his 'National Democratic Revolutionary Programme' and in 1977 a fully-fledged Marxist–Leninist revolution was enforced with eager Stalinist and Cuban assistance.

The formula 'Marxist–Leninist' was, for a while, a popular slogan with African leaders in certain parts of the continent. It could be seen as a dashing declaration of modernity and, maybe, reform, a determination of seeing one's country developing and progressing. Menghistu's Ethiopia was different. In his case 'Marxist–Leninist' meant a translation into an African world of the policies, police methods and propaganda of Brezhnev's Moscow.

Eritrea

The colonial past marked Eritrea's modern history and role. Italian culture and language influenced Eritrea from the 1890s. In connection with World War II the British were in command for a few years and after the war Ethiopian sovereignty followed a United Nations Organization decision of 1952 to federate Eritrea with Ethiopia. In 1962 the Ethiopian empire annexed Eritrea. These developments fomented Eritrean nationalism and the beginnings of an Ethiopian–Eritrean war. Great numbers of Eritrean refugees sought a tenuous refuge in the Sudan and prominent Eritreans went into exile. The war between the two countries was bitter, culminating in 1978 with a Soviet-led offensive against the Eritrean liberation forces. The war expanded to become the most devastating on the African continent in the 1980s.

The Falasha

In a book operating with a theme of 'refugees' and 'returnees' it seems inevitable to mention the Falasha, the Black Jews of Ethiopia. This community was located mainly in the Gondar region; they also formed a distinctive social caste in the city of Gondar. For over 2,000 years the Falasha existed as a minority group with their special Jewish traditions, customs and claims.

There were repeated international Jewish attempts to come to their assistance. In 1954 the Jewish Agency established a teacher training college for them in Asmara, the capital of Eritrea. Another attempt was sending twenty-seven boys and girls to Israel, preparing them to become teachers in Falasha village schools, a project which, however, soon came to an end. International Jewish organizations tried to help. In 1973 the Sephardic Chief Rabbi stated that the Falasha belonged to the tribe of Dan and were indeed Jews to be saved from absorption and assimilation. In Gondar the fate of the Falasha became increasingly difficult, with an Ethiopian governor blaming them for crop failures and famine.

After enormous hardships – their houses and synagogues were burned down or taken over, their cattle stolen, their lands expropriated – there was at the end of the 1970s an exodus – 'Operation Moses'. Hoping to get through to Israel certain Falasha groups fled to Sudan from where they hoped to proceed to the 'City of David'. After political manoeuverings airlifts in 1984–85 transported them from Sudan to Israel. There are now some 15,000 Falasha in Israel while for various reasons some 7–8,000 remain in Ethiopia.[18]

Marxist–Leninist Church politics

The Menghistu regime managed to destroy much of what belonged to the Churches, their lands and property, concentrating first on the expatriate Churches as 'foreign interlopers', while leaving the Ethiopian Orthodox Church to be dealt with later. Regarding expropriated Church property, one can mention the 'Radio Voice of the Gospel' – a multi-million dollar radio station – the Mekane Yesus Church office building, the Bible Society's headquarters, headquarters of the Baptist Bible Fellowship, the hospital of the Seventh-day Adventist Hospital, the Mennonite secondary school and Bible Academy; nearly all the 600 Lutheran churches in the Western Synod in Wollega, etc. etc.

However, the attack went further, depriving the Orthodox Church of many of its traditional books and liturgical objects, infiltrating monasteries with *agents-provocateurs* in order to humiliate and subvert the monks. The Patriarch Thewophilos and three other archbishops were arrested, the patriarch now being assumed dead, while the archbishops had to spend six to eight years in prison. Other archbishops were murdered or imprisoned, and fourteen archbishops were dismissed from their posts. A new patriarch named Thacla Haymanoth was appointed, 'a man of humble origin and supposedly a man of the people, an apolitical, submissive and uneducated man who combines rigorous ascetic practices with selfless philanthropism'.[19] Important churches and monasteries were turned into museums. Ecclesiastical objects and works of art were removed for being 'calculated to insult the oppressed masses'.

Special negative interest was shown to the 'new' Churches: Pentecostals, Full Gospel, and Jehovah's Witnesses, alarming to the regime because of their attractiveness to the young and the military. The well-known Lutheran Church leader Gudina Tumsa, general secretary of the Mekane Yesus Church, was arrested in 1979 and is believed to have been murdered.

When the Menghistu regime came to an end in 1991 and Menghistu himself fled the country, it was discovered that through all these trials and vicissitudes the Churches had survived as a vast underground movement, of increasing strength. As the Marxist regime tightened its grip on the Church, whether in the form of the Ethiopian Orthodox Church, or the Protestant or Roman Catholic Churches, it was seen as the refuge to which to turn for help and succour. There had been an astounding increase in membership. The Evangelical Church Mekane Yesus had grown from about 25,000 in the 1940s to 800,000, and the Word of Life Evangelical Church (related to the Sudan Interior Mission) from a few thousand to over 900,000. There had been a tendency for small groups to meet clandestinely for Bible study and prayer. In the Orthodox Church there was a completely new opportunity for lay Leadership.

In the meantime the Eritrean churches – Orthodox, Catholic and Lutheran – continued their work, particularly in educational and medical services. A far-sighted initiative was that taken by Combonian Sisters in founding the University of Eritrea, with the sisters and others forming the teaching staff.

20

WEST AFRICA

FRANCOPHONE WEST AFRICA

The Westerners with their governors and generals have survived in a fashion in African tradition after 1960, objects of sullen scorn: 'at last, it seemed, the land was rid of them, never to return'. There was one exception to this rule: 'N'Gol' was different, N'Gol being the name under which the 'Man of Brazzaville', Charles de Gaulle, was known in Gabon and elsewhere in French-speaking Africa. In Brazzaville in 1944 he had declared 'the right of Africans to run their own affairs', proving thereby that he was a sufficiently great personality to appreciate the potential of modern Africa and of Africans. His name and life were 'a sacred seed which grew remarkably well in African soil'. In French-speaking Africa there developed a de Gaulle legend and myth. In December 1959 at St Louis, Senegal, de Gaulle interpreted his view of the Franco-African community and he did so with overtones which his African listeners, more so perhaps than was the case with politicians from other countries, recognized from the Bible in their chapels: 'Abide with me, for it is towards evening and the day is far spent' (Luke 24). He was thereby laying foundations for a policy 'at the Summit' which, much later in the day, in 1990, could be pursued by François Mitterrand in co-operation with the heads of Francophone African states.

For the following brief sketches on Church–State relations in French-speaking West Africa 1960–90, certain common elements stand out:

1. A north–south syndrome, roughly between the inland Sahelian states and the countries along the coast, is a fundamental feature of the region and is important also for the Churches, in fact, particularly for the Churches. The southern region saw mission-inspired developments in the educational, social and medical fields, advances which did not appear to the same extent in the corresponding northern region with its dominant religion of Islam. In the Independent period 1960–90, ethnic and cultural differences sometimes evolve into serious tension and violence.

2. Varying degrees of relationship to France, both during General de Gaulle's time and later, were manifested, economically, socially and educationally, with different rates of personal accommodation of French politics and culture, sometimes not altogether without a certain mystique of attachment to the French language and culture. We begin with a brilliant example, that of Senegal with President Léopold Sédar Senghor 1960–85.

Countries along the coast

Senegal

The Christian community in Senegal resides mainly in the south among the Serer and Mandingo populations. For centuries the Serer held aloof from the domineering Wolof and Fulani in the north. When these accepted Islam, the Serer had an additional reason for not going along with the northerners, being open instead to the other alternative of an international religion, Christianity. It was here among the hard-working, groundnut-growing Serer population that the Holy Ghost Fathers had established their faithful and it was here that Léopold Sédar Senghor grew up, born 1906, the son of a well-to-do farmer and trader. At school he received a training characteristic of what the French-speaking Holy Ghost Fathers could offer: rigorous training, with the use of the vernacular strictly prohibited. At sixteen he had the calling to the priesthood and for a while entered the Junior Seminary in Dakar. When, later on in life, as President he attended the consecration of an African bishop, he exclaimed, 'I could have stood there'.[1]

A helpful book by Jacques L. Hymans shows how this privileged young man was prepared to accommodate a number of new influences. After studying in West Africa he entered a prestigious school in Paris where his closest friend was a young man by the name of Georges Pompidou, later to become the President of France. Hymans follows the intellectual influences to which Senghor was creatively exposed: Alioune Diop and Aimé Cesaire; Teilhard de Chardin, Emmanuel Mounier, H. Bergson and Charles Péguy. He served in World War II and was taken prisoner by the Germans, as well as realizing his role as a poet – *négritude* and its variants – there 'is not a single poem of Senghor's that does not bear the mark of a hidden divinity'.[2] His French orientation made him look in politics for a French West African Federation and then an 'African road to Socialism', until in 1960 he was elected the President of Senegal, serving this largely Muslim nation until

1985, when he retired. In 1983 President Senghor was elected a member of the French Academy.

As will be recalled (see pp. 173–78) the French-speaking Holy Ghost Fathers were old-timers in Senegal, with a succession of twelve bishops between 1863 and 1955. The last in the succession, the famous Marcel Lefevbre, was made archbishop of Dakar, to be succeeded in 1962 as archbishop by Hyacinthe Thiandoum, later cardinal. The Catholic community of over 300,000 members had six dioceses, with thirteen national priests and seventy expatriate priests. There are over fifty Senegalese sisters and 185 expatriate sisters.

In the south of Senegal the Holy Ghost Fathers had been at work ever since the nineteenth century. The evangelistic work did not seem promising. Fr Juloux sent one of his students George Manga to Diola, still unbaptized. 'He said that when the priests left in the Fourteen War, all the Christians returned to the *ukine* [traditional religion] and left Chritianity ... My first work was to find the Christians.'[3] But things changed. The middle of the 1960s saw a breakthrough to something new. 'The nationalist movement encouraged people to be assertive about their political and even their spiritual needs ... There was increased pride in being African, in doing things in an African way.'[4] Something else occurred in the 1960s. A new order, from Spain this time, arrived: the Pierist Fathers. They became the exclusive order in Esulalu. The new missionaries were well-aware of the nature of peasant religion in their own native Spain and thus prepared to allow room for a meeting and blending of Diola religion and Christian faith. Most people in Esulalu still believed in the power of the *ukine*. 'Rather than seeing this as a sign of Satanic influence, [the Pierist Fathers saw it] "as part of a universal need to find a protection against illnesses, misfortunes etc." Father Miguel talks of the deep religious sensitivity of the Diola and the parallels between Christian and Diola ritual and belief.'[5]

One looks at this encounter in southern Senegal in the perspective of long history, of the *longue durée*, to the experience of Matteo Ricci and Roberto de Nobili of old. Is this perhaps the place where at this time and in the new century there will emerge a Diola Christianity without being too much hampered by critics?[6]

After World War II there was a fresh influx of smaller Protestant missions, mainly from the USA. An original initiative was that taken in 1973 by the Lutheran Church of Ovambo-Kavango in Namibia. The Independent period of course knows of initiatives whereby an African Church sent men and women as missionaries across an adjacent border. The decision of the Ovambo-Kavango was different: going as missionaries to that far-off country in West Africa, two families from Ovambo-Kavango came, a pastor with his wife (a nurse) and a teacher-family specializing in literacy. They proved to be excellent linguists, learning the Serer language. For a variety of reasons, including a tense political situation in Namibia in the 1970s, this Ovambo initiative did not continue but was succeeded by a group of ten Finnish missionaries active in Namibia. In 1985 there was an agreement between the state of Senegal and the Finnish Missionary Society according to which this society was to serve through health care, provision of water, education and alphabetization, in exchange for certain reductions in custom duties and taxes. The same year three Serer pastors were ordained. The Church has eight congregations. There is a Bible school and one of the missionaries, pastor and musical specialist, has worked on a liturgy based on Serer musical foundations.

Guinea

The political independence process had to take into account General de Gaulle's Africanization programme implying co-operation between France and the French-speaking West African countries. The French initiative towards co-operation met with positive acceptance from French-speaking West African countries – with one exception, Guinea (Conakry). Sekou Touré had launched a 'Marxist–Leninist' programme and ninety-five per cent of the population voted against the French proposal. This meant an irreparable break between the two regimes. Visiting Conakry in 1958, de Gaulle felt 'enveloped by the organisation of a totalitarian republic'. He left Guinea 'saying portentously: "Adieu la Guinée!".'[7]

Here the Christian message and fellowship were to be severely tested: a country with some 5 million people of whom at least a million fled as refugees to neighbouring states. While the Catholic Church had some 65,000 adherents, the Protestants (Reformed, Pentecostal, Jehovah's Witnesses) were not far behind. In 1961 the French archbishop was expelled and in 1967 all foreign missionaries, some seventy Catholics altogether, were expelled. At first only a dozen African priests remained, coming from other African countries, some of these were soon ordered to return to their home countries. The African archbishop, Raymond Tchidimbo, with Holy Ghost Fathers' connections and fervent a nationalist at first, largely supported the political regime. This did not help, however. In 1970 he was imprisoned, condemned to hard labour for life, finally to be released in 1978. What does an African archbishop say to his people on such an occasion? Tens of thousands of men, women and children were waiting for him to appear through the prison gate. He said it all in three words: 'Le passe est passé' – the past is past.

Eighteen years after the expulsion of the missionaries some of them returned to the country and to the Church. How had the Catholic community reacted through all these years?

1. *Prayer*: 'Father, when you were still here among us, we did not pray. It was at the time of your departure that we understood the value of prayer. And we have prayed for all these twenty years.'
2. *Perseverance*: As strong pressure was brought to bear against the Church – from the Muslims, from government and its all-powerful 'party'. They persevered, supporting one another in a charity strengthened by the affliction.
3. *Organization*: They formed Christian communities, with parish teams devoted to the training of local leaders, particularly catechists.[8]

Ivory Coast

In Houphouet-Boigny the Ivory Coast had a President who was a wizard in the art of pragmatic rule. After initial bows to Communist ideals he played the French connection to the full, inviting numbers of French advisors for the administration of his country and promoting Ivorian–French co-operation. In Church matters Houphouet-Boigny showed the same versatile and pragmatic virtues although as a matter of course primarily concerned with his own Roman Catholic Church. Also it was to what he believed to be Catholic interests that he raised his most eye-catching ecclesiastic monument, the enormous basilica at his birthplace Yamasoukro. In September 1990 Pope John Paul II visited the country to consecrate this new cathedral in Yamasoukro, a ceremony witnessed by the ageing president together with a congregation of many thousands.

In 1974 a Convention was reached between the State and the Catholic Church over educational matters. The schools and their youth were a concern for both State and Church. The problem of the *déscolarisés*, unemployed school leavers, rapidly became a concern in Abidjan and other West African cities. There was a tradition according to which artisan jobs were only for non-Ivorian Africans, or for women. The Ivorian male youth could manage by taking any kind of 'business' while attempting, through private schools, night schools and other means to attain that elusive diploma.

The Christian Church in the Ivory Coast – whether Catholic, Protestant or Harrist – is still only a minority in a population of strong concentrations of traditional religion and Islam. From a statistical point of view there are great differences between the regions, more marked now than ever before, between the great concentrations of Christians along the coast and the relative paucity of adherents to the faith inland. While Roman Catholic numbers in the Ivory Coast are comparatively limited, the Catholics all the same exercise an influence out of all proportion to their statistical size. This was the effect of new generations of secondary school- and university-trained men and women soon to fill the posts in the state administration. The Catholic school system was sustained by devoted sisters and school teachers.

As a result of this activity of the Religious, there was formed in 1965 a Diocesan Congregation called 'Our Lady of Peace'. This African women's order held its first General Chapter in 1976 and has thirteen 'houses' of which ten are concentrated in the diocese of Abidjan. In 1976 Mother Angelina Aku was elected Superior-General. Since 1960 Archbishop Bernard Yago, born 1916, has guided the Church; his long rule has assured solidity and growth. For West African French-speaking intra-diocesan organizations Abidjan has become a centre on a par with Kinshasa and Nairobi.

In the past there had been a tendency to regard the Harrists as a 'religion of old men' and to abandon it for more prestigious Catholic and Protestant Churches. However, the youth of the Harrist Church changed the course of the movement. This was the period, 1960–90, when a process of institutionalization particularly affected these prophet movements, albeit in different ways and by different means. In Kimbangu's case in Zaïre this proceeded by way of a family conclave, with the three sons of the Prophet functioning as a highly respected team and supported by an able group of administrative assistants. In the case of the Harrist movement a different procedure was at work: here a generation of young men took the lead. In 1972 a first Congress of Young Harrist Intellectuals was held. The chairman was a distinguished medical doctor, Bruno Claver, anxious to modernize and standardize Church practices.[9] Symbolizing the past was the Congress's honorary president, the famous traditional healer Albert Atcho. The great majority of the participants were young men aged between twenty and twenty-five.

Togo

We have referred to the north–south syndrome after Independence: serious tensions between the south and the north in the nation, between an economically and educationally privileged south, with its institutions and opportunities, and a neglected north. One example was Togo, a country where half of the population is known to belong to 'traditional African' communities, and the increase of Muslims has been rapid, now half a million, or 17 per cent of the population; an 'Institute for Muslim–Christian relations' seeks to promote a dialogue.

French-speaking Togo was brought to political Independence in 1957, by politicians from the south, principally by Sylvanus Olympio, hailing from a family of 'Brazilian returnees'. He was prime minister during the years 1956–61 and president from 1961–63. Eventually, in 1967, Olympio was succeeded by a military man from the far north, a Protestant officer in the French colonial army, later known as General Eyadema. As president he managed to nationalize the rich phosphate mines – until then run by a French company – thereby bringing vast wealth to his small country. He was politician enough to win over to his side various influential southern groups, such as the trade unions, thus methodically building up his influence.

However, this was as nothing compared with the 'Sarakawa miracle' of 1974, suggesting the intervention of supernatural powers in African politics. On a flight north his plane crashed, the French pilot and three other passengers were killed while Eyadéma, although injured, survived. Out of the wreck 'the Eyadéma myth' was born. The place of the disaster became a national shrine, with the wreckage still well-preserved to be stared at by ever new groups of pilgrims. Here was the legacy of a perfect 'civil religion' or 'national religion', with its Revelation, sudden and dazzling, its place of worship, its metallic icons, torn and twisted maybe, but manifesting nevertheless extraordinary supernatural powers; faithful devotees and a conquering messiah.

Eyadéma's command of his northern troops and his pragmatic leadership in the south guaranteed his continued domination. The rich phosphate company assured the country's wealth. Among African statesmen-colleagues he chose Mobutu of Zaïre as an ideal. The latter's authenticity campaign could be adapted to Togolese conditions and General Eyadéma's baptismal name Etienne – good enough for the Paris Protestant missionary who once baptized him – was changed to Gnassingbe.

Whatever the preference for the north, Lomé, the capital on the coast, was still the financial centre. This showed particularly with the 'Revendeuses' of Lomé, the women resellers specializing in multicoloured textiles, making millions of CFA francs. If that was not enough, these enterprising women took over the fishing industry: only they had the means to finance vessels and machinery. More so than African Church women in general, these Lomé ladies were able to support certain aspects of Church work, for instance costs in connection with the papal visit in 1988.

French-speaking Togo has a population of some 3 million while the western section of Togo in 1957 became part of Ghana as its Volta region, a process whereby the Churches were also partitioned in west and east. The Catholics number at least 800,000, or 30 per cent of the population and the Protestants – the 'Evangelical Church of Togo', the Methodists, Baptists, Pentecostals – number more than 142,000, or 5 per cent.

In its Catholic archbishop, Mgr Tonyui Messan Dosseh, Togo has a personality to match the situation. 'An archbishop is a prince of the Church' he would muse knowing that with his village Anyronkope he stood in a princely succession of chiefs. Archbishop at the early age of thirty-seven, he liked the idea of hierarchy and differentiated between a 'high' clergy – a privileged minority trained in Rome or holding university degrees – and a 'lower' clergy, 'forming the proletariat or rather the lumpenproletariat'.[10] The financial strength of the diocese is in accordance with the situation. Sources of many kinds are available: Rome, Germany, USA, Canada – and Togo itself, not least from the women resellers. At a time when the Churches for their worship preferably turn to African instruments – indigenous drums etc., – the repairs of the cathedral organ cost tens of millions of CFA francs.

The pressures for domination by an authoritarian president – by placing his *émissaires* into the evangelical Synod, or attempts to control elections for Church leadership – were continuously felt. Responsible Church leaders withstand the threats to democratic freedom, looking to the Church as 'the ultimate place for free opinion in our country'. The present incumbent of the Moderator's position reached this eminence by methods not always in accordance with the Church's constitution. Through it all the Church was thrown back upon essentials: a revival from 1964 and a new theology felt to be relevant to overwhelming needs: 'The whole Gospel for the whole man'.

Benin

Each of the countries along the West Coast has its own character, different from that of its neighbours. This is particularly true of Benin.

1. Nowhere else was the presence of traditional African religion as obtrusive and compact as here. Well over 60 per cent of the population in the north of the country subscribed – insofar as they were literate in a population with 90 per cent illiteracy – to a belief in ancient vodun deities.

2. Hardly anywhere else did modern Communism provoke such a response as here, with a president, Mathieu Kerekou, who for nearly twenty years proclaimed his Marxist–Leninist phrases to the masses.
3. Nowhere was the role of the Catholic 'Brazilian returnees' as conspicuous in public life as here.

On the coastline, with its cities of Cotonou and Porto Novo and the ancient Catholic centre of Whydah, the Beninese elite was strong, with influential Catholic families. It has assimilated French culture, in certain families they have been French-speaking for three to five generations. Besides this elite there is an intermediate class of artisans and clerks in administration and commerce. The Catholics honoured the memory of their remarkable Lyon (SMA) missionary, Fr Francis Aupiais, who in the first part of the century served Benin as an inspiring educationalist, promoting a numerous African elite, and a renowned ethnologist who placed Dahomean culture on the world map. Outstanding among the African clergy was Bernardin Gantin, consecrated bishop in 1957 at the exceptionally early age of thirty-four, then archbishop of Cotonou and promoted to cardinal in Rome in 1977, with responsibility for the Pontifical Commission for Justice and Peace. Since 1993 he has been Dean of the College of Cardinals.

To the Catholics and the Protestant Churches, the problem of the distant northern region of Benin presented a common challenge, tackled in different ways. The Catholics were able to recognize the presence in the north of an African initiative from the south: civil servants and traders who, on their own, had built their church for their worship. These Catholics in the north were to play a political role in spite of their being a minority in a Muslim *milieu*. The political leader of the country in the 1950s, Hubert Maga, was a man of the north. Bishop Gantin in 1960 established a Cistercian monastery in Parakou, soon to be followed by a Cistercian convent, both seen as a fortress against a Muslim majority in the north. A leprosarium was founded in Abomey.

There was a determined increase of Protestants in the north by the arrival of two American missions from the Assemblies of God and the Sudan Interior Mission. The SIM, faithful to its Bible translation tradition in other parts of Africa, undertook Bible translation work in four different languages: Pila-Pila, Dompago, Bariba and Boussa. The Catholic community in Benin now counts 1 million faithful and the Protestants number altogether about 25,000.

Things changed, even in a Marxist–Leninist state. Benin decided to form a 'High Council of the Republic' in order to promote a transfer from

Marxism–Leninism to democracy. The High Council met to elect a chairman. They needed a person whom they could trust. One name was proposed, that of the coadjutor bishop of Cotonou, Mgr Isidore de Souza, who was elected chairman, with 488 voting with seven abstentions. The new chairman was interviewed:

'What is your main preoccupation?'
'The poverty of our people.'
'What do you say about the Catholic Church in Benin?'
'In periods of crisis and trouble the people of God recover their intimate contact with God. We have experienced a hurricane of conversions to God.'[11]

The Countries of the Sahel

The whole region has a character of its own, marked by the harsh Sahelian landscape: sands, camels and old market towns. To be a Christian here is to be part of a tiny struggling minority. One 'follows the Jesus road' as they say in Niger, perhaps in some cases as the Little Sisters of Jesus are doing, in a tent with the nomads. To do mission work here is sowing a seed in the hope that there will be a harvest in a thousand years' time.

Mali

Here the Church is 'a Second Century Church', to use Fr Ela's phrase. The community is all. What about the priest? 'He fades away quite nicely.' (*Il s'efface tout doucement*.) It is a young community, marked by its youth and joy. 'The young find nothing foreign in Christianity.' In the Mali Catholic Church all are part of the community, nobody is excluded. 'In our community the people who are all polygamists have the faith but cannot receive the sacraments.'

The famous Dogon population, in their swallow-nest villages clinging to the walls of the mountain, at first offered determined resistance to the Christian message. However, there were some local 'sympathizers' and these met with virtual pogroms but the Fathers raised a huge wooden cross on the precipice as a signal for their determined attempt at proselytization: a mission station was founded in 1949. Three priests, twenty-three catechists and seven 'animators' were the staff, among them the 'flying cathechist', Marcel Douyon, who on his donkey or his moped seemed able to overcome any physical impediment. Over 100 'praying families' followed 'the road of the Christians'.

A striking example of Mali Catholicism is the national pilgrimage centre at Kita where the participants from near and far unite in torch processions by night followed by the Eucharist. In a population of some 7 million, 0.1 per cent are Christians, including seven Protestant groups, with the Evangelical Christian Church among the Dogon.[12]

Burkina Faso

Geography and ecology determine life, also Church life. The north of Burkina Faso was marked by the Sahel, while the south bordering on Ghana and the Ivory Coast was different, as well as because of the particular ethnic community, the Mossi, where the Church has the majority of its members. Population is growing fast with illiteracy a crushing problem. Of the nine Catholic dioceses, those in the south show comparatively large numbers while the dioceses in the north report much smaller communities. In the modern period in Ouagadougou and neighbouring dioceses, development also characterizes Church life. 'Development' is the watchword with some 250 different programmes, among which one must mention seventy-five centres for women's education and care. Here the Catholics have gathered 500,000 Christians and 500,000 catechumens, with 180 priests, 300 sisters and nine bishops of whom one is the cardinal, Paul Zoungrana.

The new period was heralded by the arrival in 1961 of a contemplative order, the Benedictines, from Toumliline in Morocco. The Koubri Benedictine monastery started under difficult conditions. Everything had to be brought to the place: water, wells and dams, electricity, roads, bridges, dispensaries and schools. With all this activity the centre grew: 'The more one does here the more the bush is populated.' Around the Benedictine monastery fourteen villages with some 10,000 people 'rely on us', the monks report. The staff of the monastery has seven White and five African professed, three of them priests, two with temporary promise and two novices. Here too Africanization is the rule with an African Prior. The monks use traditional Mossi music and musical instruments and dances in the Church. The monastery vibrates with a rich liturgical life, attractive festivals and daily Eucharist with the 'Kora' instrument, a guitar with twenty-one strings.

The Church in Burkina Faso provides a wide spectrum of enterprises. A centre for economic and social studies for West Africa was started there in 1960. In its first fourteen years 580 students from different countries in West Africa attended educational courses lasting from one to two years.[13]

Niger

Ninety-eight per cent of the population of 6.5 million are Muslims. There are 15,000 Christians, most of them foreigners, as well as thirty-five priests, ten brothers and seventy-five sisters, almost all Europeans. However, there also is 'Africanization', namely African sisters from Rwanda or Mauritius or from Burkina Faso. The missionaries are French Redemptorists or White Fathers, or the Little Brothers and Sisters of Jesus.

Among the Bororo nomads there are no huts: one's home place is in the shadow of a tree. Yet after years something happened. The missionary went so far in extravagance as to put up two thatched clay huts, 'one for the good God', and another for the sick, and in this dispensary one could rely on a new drug, penicillin.

The community is all and everything. The group decides on behalf of the individual, what to think and do. Even so an individual breakthrough was possible. In Easter Week 1983 the highly esteemed Muslim Imam and *marabout*, after ten years of preparation, was baptized, together with his wife. In 1970 walking through the market he had bought a little book, St John's Gospel, in Hausa with Arabic script. He began to read this little booklet on Jesus the Light and the Life. 'Then I said: "I am on the side of Jesus". When people saw me reading that book they warned me: "But you are becoming a Christian. You are utterly lost." I persevered.'

GHANA

Towards the new nation

In the late 1950s and early 1960s Ghana, led by the country's first leader Kwame Nkrumah, occupied an exalted position as the first sub-Saharan African country to gain independence from a European colonial power. The decolonization process between Britain and Ghana (then known as the Gold Coast), during the years 1951–57, was viewed as a great success and this reinforced Nkrumah's position as a Pan-African statesman.

Kwame Nkrumah was educated at a Catholic school in western Ghana and his first involvement with the Church was through the influence of a German Catholic priest, Fr George Fischer, who

> became almost my guardian during my early school days and so relieved my parents of most of the responsibility with regard to my primary education. My father was not at all religious but my mother was converted to the

> Catholic faith and it was through her and Father Fischer that I was also baptized into the Roman Catholic Church.[14]

While on a visit to the schools of western Ghana in 1926, the educationalist and churchman, the Revd A. G. Fraser, arranged for Nkrumah to attend the prestigious government college of Achimota in Accra. While at Achimota, Nkrumah came under the imaginative influence of James Kwegyir Aggrey, the famous Ghanaian Christian educationalist. A recent biographer of Nkrumah has suggested that 'Aggrey played a crucial role in Nkrumah's development by introducing him to the heady and exciting ideas of W. E. B. Du Bois and Marcus Garvey.'[15]

After attending Achimota, Nkrumah taught for three years at Catholic schools at Elmina and Axim before being appointed, in 1933, as a teacher at the Catholic Seminary at Amissano near Elmina.

This was a new institution and it was the first time that the Roman Catholic Church had established such a place in this country to train its own clergy. It was an honour to be the first teacher from the Gold Coast appointed to train these young men in their preliminary studies for this great vocation.[16]

In 1935 Nkrumah travelled to the United States and later gained two degrees from Lincoln University, the second was in Theology and his graduation address was entitled 'Ethiopia shall stretch forth her hand unto God'. While in America he preached in many Churches, particularly in Philadelphia and New York and 'the Presbyterian Church of Philadelphia invited him to undertake a sociological and economic survey of negro life in the city'. He later, described himself as a 'non-denominational Christian' rather than a devotional member of the Catholic Church.

Most of Nkrumah's cabinet members were southern Ghanaian, and almost all had attended Church schools. Most Church leaders and pastors, as well as the laity, were enthusiastic about independence. A number of clergymen joined Nkrumah's party, the Convention People's Party, or CPP. An Anglican priest, the Revd V. K. A. Saifah had been arrested in 1950 for his nationalist activity in support of Nkrumah.

During the 1950s all the main Protestant Churches had completed their own 'decolonization' or devolution from missionary authority. This achievement of local and national autonomy by the Churches had been pioneered by the Presbyterian and Methodist Churches, followed by the Evangelical Presbyterians and the Anglicans (who formed a Province of West Africa together with their Gambian, Sierra Leonean, Liberian and Nigerian brethren). In 1960 the country gained its first Ghanaian Catholic archbishop of Cape Coast, the Most Revd Francis Amissah.

The 1950s saw a large increase in Church membership. The situation was most marked in the Catholic Church: in 1950 there were 313,000 Catholics; in 1960: 594,000; by 1970 this number had increased to over 1 million. The rise in the number of Christians was closely linked to the expansion of educational work by the Churches. Catholic primary and secondary schools grew in number from 1,100 in 1953 to 1,554 in 1966, and the number of their secondary schools increased from five to sixteen over the same period. The Methodists had 665 primary schools in 1950, a number which rose to 1,130 by 1966. Teacher training facilities run by the Churches were also markedly expanded and this was combined with an improvement in the quality of teacher education.

Church and State 1957–72

Kwame Nkrumah ruled the country from independence in 1957 until his overthrow by a military *coup d'état* in 1966. The twin questions of ideology and authoritarianism in government and the ruling Convention People's Party (CPP) increasingly exercised the Churches as the Nkrumah period continued. The newly independent government wished to assert control of the country's resources. The first clash between the Churches and the government was over the control of schools and other educational facilities. In the eastern region of the country the government nationalized Church schools in 1959, 'because of the alleged anti-government attitude of some of the teachers'.[17]

The Churches were concerned over the growing personality cult surrounding Nkrumah and some churchmen felt that he encouraged the view that he was a messiah and a redeemer. In 1961 Nkrumah's birthplace was turned into a national shrine, paid for by public funds, an action which could be seen as an attempt by the CPP 'to accord Nkrumah the status of an object of worship and, therefore, divinity'.[18]

The Churches were also disquieted by the role and orientation of the 'Young Pioneers', the youth organization of the CPP, and by the movement's pledge of allegiance. The Anglican Bishop of Accra, the Rt Revd Roseveare, was expelled in August 1962 after criticizing the movement for ignoring 'the existence and claims of Almighty God. Moreover, it seems the Movement confuses the work and example of a great man with Divine Acts which are unique in history.'[19] This confrontation had already started in 1961 when the party and its youth movement announced the setting up of party branches or 'cells' in all organizations, including the Churches. The expelled Anglican bishop was, however, allowed to return a few months later.

This distrust by the Churches over the activities of the Young Pioneers led to an expansion in youth work by all the Churches. This was especially so of the Catholic Youth Organization (CYO), which again led to a clash between Church and State. In February 1963 a young priest active in the CYO was arrested with no explanation. In response, the Catholic Archbishop Amissah sat for three days outside the police station until his priest was released.

The creation of a one-party state in 1964 further accelerated the process of authoritarianism, until Nkrumah's government was brought down by Ghana's first coup d'état in 1966. The military leaders during the years 1966–69 sought the help of prominent Church leaders to rectify the mistakes of the Nkrumah period. Prominent among these was the leading Presbyterian churchman and scholar, the Revd Professor Christian Baëta, who represented the new government in discussion with France and West Germany. Baëta, with his long experience and ecumenical contacts, was a member of the constituent assembly which drew up plans for the return to civilian rule in 1969.

Professor Kofi Busia was elected prime minister in 1969. He was a leading lay Methodist and a lay adviser to the World Council of Churches. As part of his ecumenical concern he had undertaken a study of *Urban Churches in Britain*, commissioned by the WCC and published in 1966.

By the late 1960s Ghana was faced with an enormous problem of illegal immigration from other West African countries. One of Busia's first acts as prime minister was to announce the expulsion from the country of up to 1 million non-Ghanaian nationals, mostly Yoruba and Hausa Nigerians. About one third of the Nigerians were Christians, the rest Muslim. This expulsion order had a deleterious effect on the plurality of Christian and Muslim forms of worship in Ghana, especially in the towns and cities. A number of Yoruba and Igbo congregations in Accra, Cape Coast and Kumasi were long established and they had contributed to the substantial heritage of Christian culture in Ghana.

Church and State, 1972–92

The coup d'état that overthrew Prime Minister Busia in 1972 brought Colonel Achiempong to power. He stayed in office until a 'palace coup' removed him in 1978. Under Achiempong the economic and political conditions of the country rapidly deteriorated, compounded by the high price of oil on the world market and the relatively low price for cocoa. Under his government corruption increased to new levels and became widespread throughout the country. As Achiempong's military rule became more authoritarian and the economy worsened, many professional organizations together with the Churches demanded a return to civilian rule. Achiempong suggested himself as the ruler of a new joint military and civilian government in proposals known as 'Unigov' (a 'union' government of military and civilians). Teachers, doctors and lawyers all made known their opposition to such blatant attempts by the military to retain power. When this civilian protest was repressed, the Churches, through the Christian Council, tried to act as mediators between the military and the professionals. Achiempong tried to attain support from religious bodies for his 'Unigov' proposals and succeeded in gaining the backing of a number of Muslim leaders as well as some prophets from Independent and Spiritualist Churches. The colonel (by now, general) at this critical stage in his career came under the influence of an American spiritualist leader, Elizabeth Clare Prophet, known as the 'Mother Prophet of the Summit Lighthouse of the Keepers of the Flame Fraternity of South California'. Although born a Catholic, Achiempong invited the prophetess to Ghana in an attempt to gain spiritual support for his 'Unigov' proposals.

NIGERIA

Introduction

Nigeria achieved statehood in 1960 under a federal parliamentary constitution. The country embraced many hundreds of different peoples and languages. Each of the three regions was dominated politically by a particular ethnic community: in the west the Yoruba, in the east the Igbo and in the north the Hausa-Fulani (Fulbe). The first six years of civilian government under Prime Minister Abubakar Tafawa Balewa were marked by competitive regional politics and identities, which also had profound implications for both Muslim–Christian relations and for Christian attempts at unity. The assassination of political leaders in January 1966 heralded the arrival of Nigeria's first military government. A second military coup under the leadership of Yakubu Gowon, later in the year, failed to halt the growing regional suspicion and ethnic animosity that now paralyzed the federal unity of the country. A series of massacres of Igbos living in the north resulted in a mass exodus as people fled to the safety of their indigenous homes. This polarization of ethnic relations led to the outbreak of civil war in 1967. The Churches, especially the Catholics, were indivisibly caught up in the antagonisms and ramifications of the civil war. Bellicose propaganda – on both warring sides – often portrayed the conflict as a holy war between the forces of Christianity and Islam.

The end of the civil war and the maintenance of the integrity of the federal republic led to a remarkable period of reconciliation and reconstruction, under various military governments during the years 1970–79. Based on oil wealth, the federal and regional state governments initiated a series of ambitious development projects, including the programme for the introduction of Universal Primary Education (UPE) in 1976. Nigerian Churches played a leading role in the reconciliation between peoples after the devastating civil war, and Christian organizations worked harmoniously with government authorities in such areas as the reform and extension of the education system and the development of rural areas. After elections in 1979, Nigeria returned to civilian rule when Alhaji Shehu Shagari became president of the country. However, this experiment in democracy lasted little more than four years, when in 1983 the military again seized power. Since 1983 successive military rulers have sought to return Nigeria to democratic rule, and in December 1989 two political parties were legally established, and federal and state elections were held throughout 1992, in readiness for an expected return to civilian rule in 1993. The current constitution only allows two parties and there is a danger that there may be a division on religious lines, with the one Muslim-dominated, the other Christian.[20]

Nigeria has experienced the same difficulties as other African countries: a fast-growing and predominantly young population, a neglect of agriculture and a rapid increase in urbanization and urban poverty, political and economic corruption and mismanagement. Because of the country's enormous size, Nigeria has experienced these developmental difficulties on a vast scale. In 1963 the population was just under 56 million. By the year 2000 there may well be over 120 million Nigerians. This poses an enormous challenge to both Christians and Muslims to provide suitable and relevant spiritual support for these countless young people. In terms of religious demography, Islam has approximately accounted for a constant 45 per cent of the total population between the years 1950 and 1990. Christianity, on the other hand, has experienced a rapid expansion during recent decades. In 1952 just under 22 per cent of the total population described themselves as Christian; by 1963 this had increased to nearly 38 per cent; by the middle of the 1980s, the number of Christians had grown to 49 per cent of the total. It seems likely that before the year 2000, slightly more than half of all Nigerians will identify themselves as Christians.

The failure of Protestant attempts at Church union

Proposals for Church union amongst the main Protestant Churches emanated form Eastern Nigeria at the beginning of the twentieth century. In 1905 Anglican and Presbyterian leaders met in Calabar and agreed to co-ordinate their expanding work. By the end of the Second World War both of these Churches were anxious to unite but at the All-Nigerian Church Conference at Onitsha in 1947, they decided to delay union in order to include the predominantly Yoruba Methodist Church. The Church union committee, composed of Anglicans, Methodists and Presbyterians, issued a first draft of Church union in 1957, and in 1963 a third and final draft was sent to the participating Churches for approval. There was general agreement on the theological questions of union, over doctrine and ministry, worship and liturgy. Professor Ogbu Kalu, the historian of the Nigerian Church union movement, has written about the flexibility of the liturgical arrangement: 'firstly, it did not lay emphasis on uniformity but on unity in variety; secondly, it left a lot of room for liturgical reforms both at the congregational and national levels.'[21] However, theological unity was not enough: the drive towards Church union foundered and by November 1965 had collapsed.

There were many reasons why this attempt to create a united Church in Christ failed. On the surface, increasingly acrimonious disputes between leading Church personalities and contention over the distribution of dioceses led to the breakdown of moves towards union. 'The bargaining would amaze anyone with the least notion of what organic unity meant. It often sounded like a boundary dispute.'[22] Just beneath the surface, wider regional and ethnic rivalries militated against Church union. In eastern Nigeria, Protestant Churches had found it comparatively easy to co-operate, partly due to various agreements over separate spheres of mission work, but mainly because of the perceived necessity for evangelical collaboration in the face of a dramatic expansion of the Catholic Church in the region. In western Nigeria, where the Catholic Church is smaller than in the east, the dominant Churches were the Anglicans and the Methodists, 'who competed so seriously as to leave some Methodists threatened with the possibility of being swallowed up by Anglicans.'[23] This competitive spirit, a striking feature of the religious arena in Yoruba society, was hardly conducive to organic Church unity. A further factor was the growing regional and ethnic tension that had characterized Nigerian political life since independence in 1960. Growing distrust between Yoruba and Igbo meant that mutual 'suspicion was never lacking and since tribalism is the stuff from which

Nigerian politics was made, its effects in Church politics could always be assumed.'[24] Other, more localized, Church rivalries were between Ibibio and Efik in Calabar, and Egba and other Yoruba in Abeokuta.

There were other reasons, deeper and more intrinsic to the Church, that also accounted for the failure to create the largest Protestant Church in Africa. The vision of Nigerian Church union, in the form it took, was very much the creation of outsiders. Anglican, Methodist and Presbyterian missionaries, influenced by the growing ecumenical movement and supported by their home mission societies, played a leading role in launching the proposals for Nigerian Church union. Influenced by other Church unions such as the United Church of Canada in 1925, the Church of South India in 1947, and concurrent discussions in Zambia (leading to the United Church of Zambia in 1965), missionaries hoped the Nigerian Church would break out of its denominationalism. In terms of cross-Christian fertilization of ideas, the Nigerian unity proposals were widely influenced by the Church of South India scheme. 'In 1955 Bishop Sumitra, Moderator of the Church of South India, made an extensive tour of Nigeria. It has been suggested that the visit was deliberately arranged to combat the low degree of interest in Church union in Western Nigeria.'[25] Missionaries were chairmen or secretaries of important committees involved in planning Nigerian Church union. The Revd T. S. Garret, who chaired the committee on the proposed liturgy, had spent twenty-three years as a missionary in India and had been involved in the Church of South India unity negotiations. It might be said that the missionaries were more motivated by ecumenism than by the question of furthering an indigenous Church in Nigeria. 'The situation was full of irony, as missionaries wanted union while Nigerians clung tenaciously to denominations.'[26]

Proposals for Church union were very much a matter for the Church leaders, rather than for ordinary members in local congregations. Nigerian Church leaders were, perhaps, too concerned with discussions amongst themselves and were not sufficiently sensitive to the views and concerns expressed by their respective local congregations over proposals for Church union. Commenting after the collapse of the union initiative, the then president of the Nigeria Methodist Church, Dr Soremekum, blamed 'the failure of our leadership, ministerial and lay, to educate many of the rank and file of our membership as to the desirability of, and necessity for Church union.'[27] This lack of communication by the Church elite was manifestly part of the wider question of Church indigenization and ecclesiastical accountability in Nigeria. The vision of ecumenical unity was abstracted from local realities.

Civil war and the Churches

The unity of the country was torn apart when the eastern region seceded from the federation and declared itself independent, on 30 May, 1967, as the Republic of Biafra. Five weeks later the Nigerian civil war began, a terrible conflict that was to last until January 1970. Up to 1 million people died, including large numbers of children, mainly through starvation and disease. Nigerian Churches were inextricably involved – on both sides – in the conflict. At the international level, joint Church involvement was also a matter of considerable controversy. The outbreak of civil war was, to a large extent, provoked by the events of some six months before. Relations between the regions were convulsed by a series of massacres, in September/October 1966, of Igbos living in the predominantly Muslim northern region. This butchery has been described as 'the most traumatic experience in Igbo history'.[28] Migrant Igbos living in their *sabon garis* ('new towns') had formed a conspicuous Christian presence in the Muslim towns and cities of the north of the country. 'From all over Nigeria, a million or more Igbos poured back to their crowded homeland, abandoning jobs and property it had taken them a lifetime of struggle to acquire.'[29] For many, the massacres were seen as the beginning of a *jihad* (holy war) waged by Islam on Christianity, and this perception of events was adopted by Biafran secessionist propaganda.

Eastern Nigeria was the most solidly Christian of the three main regions of the country. In eastern Nigeria the Protestants were strongest amongst the ethnic minorities of the region, while the majority of the Igbo population were mostly Catholic (though there were also large Igbo Anglican and Methodist Churches). In the western region, amongst the Yoruba population, there were slightly more Christians than Muslims. In the west there were many independent, Aladura, Churches and the main Protestant Churches, such as the Anglicans and Methodists, were numerically larger than the Catholics. Yoruba society in the western region had experienced an intricate interaction between different faiths and religious groups, as well the greatest eclecticism in the formation of new religious assemblages and alignments. In the extensive northern region, nearly the entire population in the upper half of the region was Muslim; while in the lower half, the so-called Middle Belt, Christians accounted for about 35 per cent of the population in 1963, a proportion that later was to markedly increase. Professor Andrew Walls has written that for the Igbo

> a self-conscious Christian profession was part of the self-identity of Biafra. From the beginning the civil war was for the Biafrans a religious war . . . Few Biafrans had Muslim brothers-in-law. Biafra could claim a Christian identity

> as neither the Federation nor any state outside the former Eastern Region could do ... And, as Christianity gave self-identity to Biafra, so a Muslim identity was bestowed upon Federal Nigeria.[30]

Even though half or a majority of the Federal army were Christian, Biafran propaganda sought to portray the Federal forces as Muslim oppressors who were determined to Islamize the entire country.

The Biafrans saw the conflict in terms of religious symbolism and Christian identity. The Igbos were seen as God's own people, the chosen people who were at the vanguard of an anti-Islamic crusade. In his analysis of the Biafran press, Professor Walls has commented on the following themes: 'the identification of Biafra with Biblical Israel becomes a commonplace. The elect people are both resisting enslavement in Egypt and are destined to enter the promised land.'[31] At the beginning of the war, many Igbo felt God was behind the survival of Biafra. As the war progressed and advancing Federal forces encircled and compressed Biafra into a small enclave in central Igboland, many Igbo began to identify the suffering of their own people with that of Jesus Christ. One sermon published in the Biafran press gave 'as a cause of thanksgiving the privilege of suffering for the truth, and the friends God has given the nation in its suffering in an unfriendly world'.[32]

The Igbo people and their Biafran state had many friends and supporters in Churches throughout the world. Prominent among these were many Catholic Irish Holy Ghost Fathers and the Holy Rosary Sisters. Out of a total number of 1,050 Catholic missionaries in the Federation, over 600 – including 165 sisters – worked in the eastern region. Of the eight Catholic bishops in Biafra, three were Irish. The comparatively few Protestant missionaries, mostly British, in the east tended to work among the minority peoples of the region, who were not particularly sympathetic to the cause of Biafra. At the outbreak of civil war most missionaries decided to stay and continue their work. In minority areas 'they decided to stay at their missions and let the war roll over them on the basically sound assumption that their communities would do likewise.'[33] This was not the case in Igbo areas, where the predominantly Irish Holy Ghost Fathers and Holy Rosary Sisters moved with their Igbo congregations into Biafran territory as Federal military forces gained more territory. This meant that 'by the end of the first year of warfare, two of the orders – the Spiritans and the Holy Rosary Sisters – were concentrated almost exclusively inside the Biafran enclave while the other [Catholic] orders were basically outside it.'[34] These Catholic mission organizations provided one of the main conduits for reports on the war-induced civilian suffering to reach the outside world and the international media. These reports galvanized global Church organizations to respond to the deteriorating situation in the war-torn region. The international Christian response was initially concerned with attempts at peaceful mediation, but later was concentrated on the provision of relief and humanitarian aid to Biafra. In December 1967 a Vatican peace mission arrived in Lagos and in early 1968 visited Biafra. This visit gave Biafrans hope that they would gain international support. Pope Paul VI was personally committed to end the suffering caused by the civil war. In 1962, before becoming pope, he had been the first European cardinal to visit Nigeria and had been moved by the intensity of faith and 'spontaneity of devotion' of African Catholics.[35]

Protestant Church organizations were also involved in efforts to end the civil war. In March 1968 a British Council of Churches delegation under the Bishop of Birmingham flew to Biafra, and this visit was followed by a deputation from the WCC in conjunction with the All Africa Conference of Churches. The position of the WCC was complicated by the fact that one of its own vice presidents, Dr Sir Francis Ibiam, an eminent Igbo medical doctor and Presbyterian, was an outspoken supporter of Biafra. Soon after the outbreak of war he undertook an extensive tour of Europe and North America to gain support for the Biafran cause. At the Fourth Assembly of the WCC in July 1968 at Uppsala there was a confrontation between the official Nigerian delegation and an unofficial Biafran delegation led by Dr Ibiam.

After the fall of Port Harcourt in May 1968, the resultant isolation of Biafra was marked by widespread famine. Thirty-two Church agencies, both Catholic and Protestant, from twenty-eight countries participated in what was known as Joint Church Aid (JCA), a organization formed to airlift humanitarian and relief supplies to besieged Biafra. Throughout the course of the war JCA provided over 60,000 tons of food and medicines, airlifted in a total of 5,300 flights; the International Committee of the Red Cross (ICRC) also sent 41,000 tons of relief aid in 4,000 flights to Biafra. The Irish Holy Ghost Fathers also formed their own air relief organization, known as Africa Concern. Although the Federal Military Government sanctioned some relief flights by the ICRC, it was highly critical of the JCA airlift into Biafra. When the JCA and others refused to accept Nigerian supervision of the airlift, 'to prevent its abuse by the inclusion of arms and ammunition, a minor war of words developed between Gowon and the leaders of the humanitarian societies which continued on and off until the collapse of Biafra.'[36] The ecumenical co-operation and determination of international Christian NGOs (non-governmental organizations) in bringing relief to the

Igbo people is striking. It is a much harder question to assess the role that this aid played, by providing psychological and material support to Biafra, in lengthening the civil war. Somewhat harshly, it has been said that 'the sufferings of the people of Biafra were prolonged by such misguided charity.'[37]

Although the majority of the Federal government's troops were Christian, mainly from the so-called Middle Belt, Christian and Muslim soldiers fought together. 'Clergymen followed the troops to the front-line' and 'services were conducted whenever possible and baptism classes held' just behind the battle lines.[38] By the end of the civil war the total number of Federal soldiers stood at 250,000 and although this number was reduced in the years after the war, the army still totalled 180,000 at the time of the return to civilian rule in 1979. This massive expansion from 1967 in Nigerian military personnel entailed the building of new barracks and army encampments throughout the Federation, with the provision that all military bases were to have mosques and churches where soldiers could worship. In this way both Islam and Christianity gained a 'national' military presence throughout the country. Mosques were built in areas such as Eastern Nigeria where there had hardly been any Muslim presence prior to the civil war. Likewise, churches and chapels were built to denote a Christian presence in the Muslim savannas of the far north of the country.

The determination of the Nigerian government to maintain the integrity of the Federation was given steadfast expression by its military leader, General Yakubu Gowon. When the Biafran forces surrendered on 12 January 1970, 'General Gowon with characteristic humility ordered a Day of National Prayer instead of a "victory parade".'[39] His pursuance of a policy of reconciliation between the Igbo and other Nigerians was widely admired and has led one observer of the civil war to write: 'It may be that when history takes a longer view of Nigeria's war it will be shown that while the African has little to teach us about making a war, he has a real contribution to the making of peace.'[40] It perhaps can be said that Gowon felt it was his Christian duty to promote the politics of reconciliation in the aftermath of civil war.

Yakubu Gowon grew up in the CMS village of Wusasa just outside the city of Zaria, the capital of one of the larger Muslim emirates of northern Nigeria. His father, Yohanna Gowon, was one of the first Christians from among his own Angas people, who lived on the Bauchi Plateau. Born 'a member of a ruling family of the Angas, in due course he might well have become the chief of his people, an important person among all the Angas of the Plateau'.[41] Instead, he achieved renown by becoming an evangelist in the Anglican Church. When the CMS handed over its work on the Plateau to the Sudan United Mission, Yohanna Gowon wished to remain an Anglican and he moved with his family to the CMS mission at Wusasa, where he later became a pastor at St Bartholomew's, 'the oldest church in northern Nigeria built of red clay'.[42] His son, Yakubu, attended Anglican schools before going to Government College in Zaria, at that time the only government secondary school in northern Nigeria. Fluent in Hausa, the *lingua franca* of the north, Gowon learnt to appreciate the interrelationship of Islamic and Christian traditions at the Government College, where most of his peers were Muslim. After his removal as Nigeria's head of state, by a 'palace' coup d'état in 1975, General Gowon continued his father's tradition of loyalty to the Anglican Church. In exile in Britain, he became a church warden in his parish church, and later was appointed a lay selector of candidates recommended to bishops as suitable for the ministry in the Church of England.

Church expansion since the civil war

The years since the end of the civil war in 1970 have been characterized by renewed Church expansion and by vitality in Christian spiritually, both a result of the growth in the numbers of young people who achieved maturity in the 1970s and 1980s. The extension of primary education to all rural areas, the expansion of secondary education in urban areas and an increase in the number of universities have all had a profound effect on the multifarious expressions of Christian religiosity in the federal republic. The vivacious growth of charismatic movements, affecting all Churches since 1970, has been particularly striking.

Catholic work in eastern Nigeria after the civil war was initially affected by the expulsion of those missionaries who had favoured Biafra. Some 300 priests and 200 Sisters were expelled and, until the middle of the 1970s, no new expatriate priests were able to work in the country. This loss of expatriate support was, however, outweighed by the continuing strength of Igbo Catholicism. In 1973 there were eighty-four ordinations in Nigeria (out of a total of 200 for Africa) into the Catholic Church, of these, fifty-three came from the four Igbo dioceses. Out of a continental total of some 3,650 Africans training in 1974, as major seminarians, for the priesthood, over 800 were Nigerian and mostly from Igbo society.[43] Out of a total of over 6 million Catholics in 1975 in Nigeria, nearly 5 million came from eastern Nigeria.

In the former western and northern regions of the Federation,

Catholicism did not have the same relative dominance among Christian denominations as in the east of the country. Prior to the massacres of 1966, most Catholics in the upper half of the northern region came from Eastern Nigeria. 'The diocese of Sokoto in north-western Nigeria, which had 15,000 Ibo [Igbo] Catholics in 1965, had only 1,650 left in 1970.'[44] By 1975 the diocese was able to report that the numbers of Catholics in Sokoto had returned to 5,400, in what was the traditional seat of the caliphate of the northern emirates. This exodus of easterners weakened both the Catholic and Anglican Churches in the north but, as Peter Clarke has written, this had the effect

> that these Churches were now obliged to concern themselves increasingly with the creation of a 'local' Church, relying much more on local support and local initiative. In Borno State . . . the Catholic community was composed in the main of Ibos and with their departure the Church authorities had to extend their activities in a much more systematic way into the towns and rural areas of the state with a view to building a local Catholic community.[45]

In 1975 there were some 650,000 Catholics in the northern half of the country, with the dioceses of Kaduna, Jos and Makurdi the most numerous. 'From 1967 to 1973 the number of Nigerian bishops grew from 8 to 17 and local priests from 108 to 306 which represent one of the most rapid increases of any country in Africa or Asia.'[46]

21

CENTRAL AFRICA

CAMEROON

The north–south syndrome was an obvious factor also in Cameroon. On the political scene the 'UPC', 'Union of the Populations of Cameroon' seemed as a matter of course a southern idea and a Protestant idea, with an intellectual background in American Presbyterian Protestantism and a tradition of American liberalism and educational ambition. In the noisy *milieu* of the 1950s – African nationalism, 'pro-Independence' connections with the United Nations (Cameroon was a trustee territory) and internationalism – it was easy to suggest that Reuben Um Nyobe, the leader of Cameroonian nationalism, was an African Communist. He was portrayed as a West-Central African version of Mao and Ho Chi Minh, a highly inflammable comparison for French imperialists at a time when the French naturally felt that one Dien Bien Fu was more than enough. Not that all Protestants were 'UPC' or leftists by any means.

In Douala the vigorous Presbyterian Pastor Joseph Tjega would not admit Um Nyobe to the Lord's Table. In fact, he excommunicated the man who for a decade 'symbolized and embodied Cameroon nationalism' for being a communist and an atheist. The Catholic Ewondo, in Yaoundé region, would not fall for such hazardous temptations. Solid and conservative they followed Dr Aujoulat's 'Bloc democratic Camerounais' and could be trusted to subscribe to a French federal programme. So it was also with the Fulani Muslims further north. A new party Union Camerounaise was formed by Ahmadou Ahidjo.

Then in September 1958, altogether unforseen, Um Nyobe was shot dead and the whole political chessboard was toppled over and had to be reset. This time the northerners, with Ahidjo and his Union Camerounaise, were prepared. Half-Fulani and a Muslim, Ahidjo was nevertheless a pragmatist. He and his men pursued a 'policy of north–south equilibration', establishing bridges to the southerners wherever possible, a situation which was to last twenty-odd years.

When Ahidjo resigned, Paul Biya took over as president. Born 1933, hailing from the Yaoundé region, he was the son of a Yaoundé chief catechist and thus connected with a remarkable line of Cameroonian Church history. He had all the educational opportunities which the Catholic tradition could offer and for some time joined a junior seminary. In France he acquired degrees in law and political science. As president he showed, to the great delight of the western region of the country, that he spoke not only French but also the other official language, English. Biya's personality and competence made him an outstanding national leader of a country with immense natural riches (oil) and, even more, with immense resources of human talent.

The Catholics

Catholic history in independent Cameroon was introduced by a book by a young *abbé*, a penetrating study of the political situation, *Pour un nationalisme Chrétien*, published in 1960. The writer's name was Abbé Jean Zoa, and the following year he was appointed the Archbishop of Yaoundé, the leading post in Catholic Cameroon. In the next few years he became internationally well known by his role at Vatican II. With its fourteen dioceses it was necessary to establish a new archbishopric. Mgr Thomas Mongo had served as bishop of Douala from 1957–73 to be succeeded in 1973 by Mgr Simon Tonye. In 1982 the bishop of Douala was raised to be archbishop of the new province. Father Engelbert Mveng, S.J., of Yaoundé, a leading Cameroonian historian, published in 1963 his *Histoire de Cameroun*, comprising 500 pages. He has also written a doctoral thesis at the Sorbonne on a challenging theme: 'The Greek sources of Negro-African history from Homer to Strabon' (in French). He has become an interpreter of African art, organizing international conferences for the study of religion, the Church and African art, all this with a depth of understanding and personal involvement. In 1984 he was elected a member of the Acadamie des Sciences d'outre-mer, in Paris, being received on that occasion by Professor Robert Cornevin and responding with a memorable speech, an eloquent and impassioned *plaidoyer* for Africa and the importance of Human Rights in Africa.

No one has expressed 'the cry of the African' with as much prophetic pathos as Fr Jean-Marc Éla (born 1936). After studying at the Sorbonne and in Strasbourg – with a doctoral thesis on 'The Transcendence of God and human existence according to Luther' (1969), he published a number of books on the situation in rural and urban Africa.[1] In 1971 he left university life – at Yaoundé and in France – exchanging it for a pastoral task of the utmost simplicity and urgency, at Tocombere in northernmost Cameroon, 'in a cultural universe where, for the Kirdi of northern Cameroon, God has kept silent, abandoning man to misery, suffering and death'.[2] He thus followed the example of good old 'Baba Simon', a priest who a generation earlier had followed the same ascetic route.[3]

The Protestants

In the same way as the Kenyan, John Gatu of Nairobi, challenged the Church with a plea for 'Moratorium' in 1973, so did his Presbyterian co-denominationalist of Douala, Jean Kotto. As general secretary of the Evangelical Church of Cameroon, he challenged the total system of conventional missionary societies with their 'one-way traffic' from the West to the Third World, particularly in the case of the Paris Evangelical Missionary Society. Kotto highlighted the need for a 'two-way traffic' of evangelistic participation. Out of a Joint Apostolic Action conducted in 1971 by Churches associated with the Paris Mission, a Community for Evangelical Apostolic Action – CEVAA – was born. French-speaking Churches, seven in Africa, two in the Pacific and four in Europe pooled their resources in funds and personnel for the formation of this Community. On a shrinking globe with totally new opportunities for communication and fellowship, it was possible to attempt and achieve this.

In Western Cameroon the Presbyterian Church saw as the new head of the Nyasoso Theological College J. C. Kangsen, who came to the task after a decade of political activity including service as minister for education. 'The youth groups of Switzerland have helped me to wash me clean from politics', this devoted churchman suggested. One of his colleagues at the theological college was the well-known German missionary scholar Heinrich Balz, who served there for ten years combining teaching with research into the religious background of western Cameroon. This Presbyterian Church in western Cameroon felt the concern for missionary outreach. Aaron Su, the Church's imaginative and enterprising general secretary, led a tour of reconnaissance into the Mamfe Oberside region: a new mission was started there. Also here the multiplicity of languages was a problem for the Church but it was decided to use the Tiv language (also the language of Nigeria) with its literary resources. A number of schools and medical centres were started.[4]

CONGO

The three French-speaking countries, Congo, the Central African Republic and Chad had a common colonial history. After political independence the three countries developed along very different lines.

In Brazzaville young Abbé Foulbert Youlou was faced with a problem which many priests and pastors in contemporary Africa shared with him. Could a priest run for political office? Youlou insisted that this was possible and desirable, and against the express orders of his French bishop he allowed himself to stand as a candidate for mayor of Brazzaville, to which post he was elected in 1956. In 1960 he was elected president of the new Republic and attended to this office with unmistakable charisma and conviction. A Lari himself he even suggested that he carried André Matswa's spirit. After three years he was thrown out of office to be succeeded by another Lari, Massamba Débat, a Protestant teacher. As both Youlou and Débat were Lari the Churches felt assured that they had sympathetic support from those in power. However, in the meantime the ethnic communities in the north of the country gathered strength, with a radical Marxist–Leninist programme. Now it was the northerners' turn, and in the north the Catholic influence came to a standstill, another example of the north–south syndrome.

Whatever the policies of the Brazzaville government were, factors of wealth and poverty affected the nation and its fortunes. Off-shore finds of oil was an encouraging factor soon to represent 85 per cent of the income from exports. In the south the political pressures from the north induced a new sense of religious zeal. In fact church-going in the south took on an acute political dimension and intention. As the political leaders from the north enveloped the population in their never-ending Marxist–Leninist gibberish and jargon, the Christians in the south loved to participate in church worship – also as a means of defiant opposition to government.[5] This new life also had an ecumenical dimension and intention including contacts with the Evangelical Church and the Salvation Army. This was particularly strongly felt throughout the community when in 1976 Cardinal Emile Biayenda was murdered: all Christians felt that they had lost a good and great friend.

The Catholic Church in Brazzaville, more especially among the Lari in and around the capital, showed great vitality. From 1957, prior to Vatican II, a priest, later Archbishop Barthélemy Batanta inspired a liturgical break-through in the diocese, adapting Congo culture: hymns, music, rhythm and dance. Political independence in combination with the creative ideas of the second Vatican Council opened up new chapters for the Church in French-speaking Africa. The new freedom quickly found expressions in the world of sports. The Felix Eboué stadium in Brazzaville, on Church initiative and with the Church's blessing, became the ambitious, unrivalled centre for national and international competition in football.

The Brazzaville diocese was looking for 'a Congolese face to the Church', expressed in African art and rhythm. In an international city with no less than sixty different ethnic communities represented, one was necessarily looking for common African values. Brazzaville had become an artistic centre with a tradition to which the Church and its own art greatly contributed. It was stimulated by the well-known mark 'PPP', dignifying both painting and sculpture. It came as a revelation that African art, for too long looked down upon, in the Church too, could now hold its own: 'Our own art is now approved and is no longer regarded as fetish', as a faithful citizen observed.[6]

The cities, Brazzaville and Pointe Noire, grew at an alarming scale, attracting the rural population. Half of Pointe Noire's population was under twenty years of age and the city soon had 50,000 young people: 'The old rural world has lost its youth'. One was easily bewildered in these new enormous conglomerations. Young A. B. was told that his uncle lived in Pointe Noire, 'just next to the baobab tree'. When that tree was cut down, there was little left to serve as an orientation point.

A persistent Congolese custom here was that of the *Matanga*, celebrated in order 'to lift the sorrow' connected with death and funerals, a custom of infinite religious strength, with much drinking. This was now reformed, particularly by a new hymnological influence. A new generation of hymn writers gave fresh contributions towards the Christianization of the festival of funeral wakes. Baptism in the river also took on new significance, transmitting the Biblical message of Death and Resurrection to the individual and the group. In connection with the Apostles' Creed, the faithful would now kneel to the ground and make the sign of the Cross over the earth – the abode of the ancestors.

The new Church life could be seen in the capital, at Pointe Noire, and in the small local centres along the Zaïre and Ubangi rivers. The *Dibundu* (the Lari word for community) organization of parishes helped to vitalize the local Catholic groups in the expanding city. A new form of parish life was that of the Legion of Mary, introduced comparatively late, in 1954, in Brazzaville. In a matriarchal society this highly disciplined group had a stabilizing influence particularly on family life. 'The Legion is very structured and formalistic with its own ritual and flags. It gives an outlet for spiritual energy in visiting the sick and in its efforts to restore fidelity in family life. This gives the legion its strength – Africa is formalist after all.'

Along the 650 kilometres of the rivers Zaïre and Ubangi, Bishop Singha of Owondo organized canoe teams which would stay at lonely places for a fortnight each: 'we create an itinerant team on the river'. It was in places like these that the Assemblée Dominicale en Absence du Prêtre (ADAP) was active. The lay teams, only with difficulty reading a Bible text and then meditating on it felt themselves to be 'the Pygmies of God'.[7]

Religious orders that were given a promising field in southern Congo included the Holy Ghost Fathers, Marianists, Benedictines, Fathers of the Holy Sacraments and *Fidei Donum* priests. For the Christian Churches in Brazzaville and Pointe Noire, the school was of central importance. In Bishop Augouard's time, the 1920s, the bush school was arranged under a palm tree: one simply moved from one tree to another. Some children could pass two–three palm trees in a trimester, others had to spend years under the same palm tree, but this was old history. Now the emphasis was on secondary schools and higher seminaries. The Higher Seminary moved to Brazzaville in 1947, taking students from Congo, Gabon and Central African Republic (for a time Chad also sent its students to the Brazzaville seminary but this later changed; Chadians now attend the closer seminary at Maroua in northern Cameroon).

An expression of Lari spirituality was the *Croix-Koma* movement initiated in 1964 by a Roman Catholic layman, Ta (Father) Malanda (d. 1971). At his headquarters Malanda received great numbers of men and women anxious to surrender their *nkisi* (fetishes), one of the most important anti-witchcraft movements in modern Africa. At first some 30,000 persons a year spent some time at the headquarters, five years later 20 per cent of the entire Congo population had taken part, mainly among the Lari, Kongo and Sundi communities. After Ta Malanda's death the links with the Roman Catholic Church were severed and the movement took the form of an independent group.[8]

The Protestants

In 1961 the Evangelical Church of Congo declared itself independent *vis-à-vis* the missions, Swedish-Scandinavian *Missionsförbundet* organization which had helped and encouraged the work in various ways. In this Evangelical Church, irradiated by Revival, there was also a certain inherent ecclesiastical tendency in connection with the officious acts of the Church. An example of this tendency can be overheard in the formula used by the out-going president of the Church, the Revd Buana Kibongui solemnly addressing his successor in the office in the following terms: 'In the name of the Father and the Son and the Holy Spirit, I transmit unto you the blessing which Pastor Jaspard Kimpolo did transmit to me as the President of the Church', a succession clearly visible to the worshipping Church.

Government interest in the Protestant Churches followed the example given by President Mobutu, south of the Zaïre River. In 1978 a government decree stated that only six – or strictly speaking five – Churches were recognized by the State, namely the Roman Catholic Church, the Evangelical Church, the Salvation Army, the Kimbanguists, the Muslim community and the Seraphim movement. The rest, the 'thicket of sects', to quote the expression used, were officially unwanted, a consideration which did not hinder a number of enterprising prophets from carrying on their work. The pressures of Marxist government were felt in that all Church youth work was in principle forbidden so as not to compete with the Union of Socialist Youth. Fortunately the Sunday School, Bible study groups and choirs were permitted, and Churches could emphasize these activities more than ever.

The breakthrough of Revival (in 1947, see p. 761) was maintained in the Church through the decades although with characteristic variations, through occasional displays of the Gift of Tongues, the 'Gift of Writing' – in trance, a person would write pages of unreadable signs to be interpreted later by somebody able to understand such things – and the 'Gift of Climbing Trees' – thus demonstrating the power of Almighty God. There appeared 'therapeutic centres' where people with healing gifts and knowledge of healing plants could assist unfortunate fellow men; co-operation between these centres and the hospital were sometimes established.

The choir was the focus of the Congolese congregation. It dominated the lives of participants. Rehearsals required participation three evenings a week, followed by the final manifestation on Sunday in the chapel, and accompanied by accordion, guitar, drums and diverse other rhythmic instruments. The 'Kilombo' choir – or the Revival choir – was an intensified version. There most of the songs were created under the influence of visions or dreams by a participant, although such songs were subject to censure by a censoring committee to control its Biblical and theological contents. All this found liberating expression in a Church with a particular tradition of spiritual freedom and understanding. In historical perspective one thinks of leaders such as Nils Westlind, Karl Laman, Efraim Andersson, Joseph Samba, Buana Kibongui and Nkounkou Hilaire.

GABON, CENTRAL AFRICAN REPUBLIC AND CHAD

Since independence in 1960 Gabon has enjoyed a record of political, if authoritarian, stability and underpinned by a prosperous economy, based on substantial mineral resources of oil and manganese and extensive timber exports. With a population of between 600,000 and 1 million, the country's per capita income since independence has been about ten times that of most African countries. President Albert-Bernard Bongo became the republic's ruler after the death of Leon M'Ba, the country's first president. Soon after his succession the new president created the 'Parti Démocratique Gabonais' (PDG) and declared a one party state. Although the overwhelming majority of the population is Christian and there are very few Gabonese Muslims, the president in 1973 converted to Islam, renaming himself Omar Bongo. He took Gabon into the OIC (Organization of the Islamic Conference), which has given the country the distinction of being the least Islamized country in the Organization. By 1990 the appeal of rejuvenated democratic ideas and influences, that were currently sweeping Francophone Africa, reached Gabon and demonstrations in Libreville and Port Gentil shook President Bongo's rule. Elections were held in September 1990 and, amid the chaotic and contested results, the President declared himself the victor.[9]

The Catholic Church, organized into four dioceses, is by far the largest Church in Gabon, with close to 70 per cent of the population, with the remainder belonging to Protestant (20 per cent) and Independent (10 per cent) Churches. In Libreville the Catholics maintain a major seminary for clerical training, and there is a total of about forty Gabonese priests in the country together with some seventy expatriate clergy, mainly Spiritan and Salesian fathers. Apart from the work of the Legion of Mary, the Catholic Church in Gabon boasts one of the oldest indigenous women's orders in Africa, the Sisters of St Mary of Gabon (founded in 1917).

The main Protestant fellowship, the Evangelical Church of Gabon, founded by the American Board and American Presbyterians, had, since 1892, been run by the Paris Evangelical Missionary Society. The Church gained independence in 1961 and is overwhelmingly dominated by the Fang ethnic group (over 95 per cent) and particularly supported by Fang women (80 per cent of the congregations). There are currently about twenty-five Gabonese and five expatriate pastors, of which a previous missionary was Dr Albert Schweitzer, whose work at Lambarene became internationally known, until his death in 1965. As the Evangelical Church of Gabon was centred on the Fang population of western and northern Gabon, the southern half of the country was covered by a separate body, the Evangelical

Church of South Gabon, which had become an autonomous Church in 1956. The founding of this Church had originated from an initiative by Christian groups to the south in Congo.

The largest Independent group, the 'Church of the Initiates' emanates from the Bwiti movement and is thus dominated by the Fang population. The Church has over twenty churches in Libreville and it has been said that it 'aspires to be the national Church of Gabon'.[10]

Further north, in the Central African Republic, dramatic change took place, by Jean Bedel Bokassa's military revolt and take-over. Delusions of grandeur took on embarrassing forms with this self-styled Emperor whose regime came to an unlamented end in 1979.

The Catholic community in the Central African Republic is comparatively small with about half a million members in six dioceses. A relatively high number of foreigners, priests and nuns – Holy Ghost, Verona, Lyon and Oblates Capuchins – serve the dioceses. The Protestant community has been inspired by radical Protestant missions – the Sudan United, French Mennonites and the Worldwide Evangelization Crusade. In this part of the continent there are districts where the Protestant community is at least comparable in size with that of the Catholics. Swedish Baptists, (Örebro mission) were at work in Congo but were unfortunately omitted from the government decree of 1978 and therefore officially hindered from operating. The Evangelical Church in Congo came to their help. The Evangelicals expanded to the far north, to Ouesso, leaving the door open for Baptists from Bangui-Berberati to join their 'recognized' group on the other side of the frontier. Conservative Baptists have joined the international Protestant seminary in Bangui, a French-speaking replica of their English-speaking seminary in Nairobi.

The north–south syndrome to which we have had to refer in various contexts in this book is more clearly to be seen in Chad than elsewhere. The Churches – Catholic and Protestant – are localized in the far southern area of the country. The Catholics have some 300,000 members in four dioceses and the Protestant community is slightly larger than that of the Catholics.

ZAÏRE-CONGO

President and cardinal in conflict

In Zaïre a major conflict developed between president and cardinal with overtones which call to mind comparable conflicts in the early Church. Both men, President Mobutu and Cardinal Malula, were protagonists of 'Africanization' to replace the traumatic experience of colonial rule. President Mobutu gave Africanization a new name, 'Authenticity', soon to be changed to 'Mobutism'. The cardinal was no less eager for an authentic Africanization of Church life. This can be seen in his role for Zaïrean rite of the Mass, his emphasis on the role of Zaïrean lay leaders (*bakambi*) and his promotion of an order of African sisters, the Ba-Theresa.

However, this was not enough for the dictatorial President. As the economic and political problems of Zaïre increased so did the president's irritation at the 'foreignness' of the Catholic Church, its links with Rome and the West, while in his eyes Protestants and Kimbanguists were above such suspicion, as they appeared not to take orders from abroad. The president changed his name to Mobutu Sese Seko and insisted that authenticity implied the discarding of Biblical-ecclesiastical first names, to be replaced by 'genuine', African names.

The conflict between Mobutu and Malula flared up with surprising speed and vehemence and the effects of the confrontation soon threatened to demolish both Church and State. The Catholic Lovanium University was nationalized in 1971 and so were schools and hospitals, and an implantation of political youth representatives followed, to be enforced in schools and seminaries. Religion in schools was to be replaced by civic teaching and courses in political training. Christmas Day was no longer to be a holiday but a working day, crucifixes in schools and hospitals were to be replaced by the image of 'our Messiah', Mobutu himself. The ideology of the ruling party took sacral terms: 'our Church is the popular Revolutionary movement, its leader is Mobutu and we respect him as one respects the Pope. Our Gospel is Mobutism with Mobutu and his glorious mother, Mama Yemo.' The campaign was dramatized in 1972 as the Cardinal was temporarily expelled from the country.[11]

The battle could well have had devastating effects, had it not been for the maturity of judgement and the prudent strategy of the Church under intense provocation. The Bishops pronounced on the prolonged crisis:

> We believe in the strength of our common Bantu wisdom which can even out any family quarrels and we are profoundly convinced that as sons of the same country we are condemned to understand one another and to work hand in hand for the happiness of our people.

The President was temporarily appeased but the conflict could flare up again, as it did in 1982. At least six of the Zaïrean bishops, including the president of the bishops' conference, Mgr Kasebu of Kalémie (ex-Albertville) had spoken out against social injustice. This time the president, as a penalty, put a curfew on religious services between the hours of six and midnight, thereby hitting at the social fellowship of the Church. Through it all the Catholic Church in Zaïre continued its service to the people, not least through the dimension of 'development'. In the period 1969–80 the Church registered no less than 2,300 development projects of which 70 per cent were financed from Zaïre itself.[12]

Official regional administration and what had once been an infrastructure – such as roads – broke down and failed to function. Then the local population in certain areas took matters into their own hands. The most impressive example probably was that of the Nande in northern Kivu. Here the Catholic bishop – as a matter or course an African – enterprising and energetic, established himself as something of a modern chief. Under his leadership, the population built a hydroelectric dam and an airport – with the road system in disrepair, air transport becomes particularly important. Coffee, cattle and gold were the main items of local export and, paradoxically, these goods could be sold and could reach foreign markets. The secret of this surprising business success is a modern variation of age-old African co-operation and solidarity.

Zaïrean Society was falling to pieces while the president himself made himself one of the richest men in the world. The Archbishop of Kananga (ex-Luluabourg) wrote to his parishioners: 'We are witnessing an internal colonialism: a class of rich people are in the process of developing whose wealth rests on the misery of millions of citizens.'[13]

The Protestants

In Independent Zaïre, President Mobutu was faced with a great number of Protestant missions and Churches – more than eighty, most of them of a Baptist and Pentecostal type. There had been a Protestant Council of Congo from the colonial times, 1924–71, with a splendid succession of general secretaries, all expatriate: Emory Ross, American, Josef Öhrneman, Swedish, H. Wakelin Coxill, British, but the ecumenical idea of a Church union did not catch on. Here was obviously an ideal field for a forceful state president to achieve something unprecedented. Mobutu did not hesitate. On 31 December, 1971, he proclaimed a law with official recognition of three religious bodies in Zaïre, namely the Roman Catholic Church, the [Protestant] Church of Christ in Zaïre, and the [Kimbanguist] Church of Jesus Christ on Earth through the Prophet Simon Kimbangu. (The following year the Greek Orthodox Church was also given official recognition.)

With this act the Protestant Church bodies were reduced from eighty to –

one! The ex-missions and ex-Churches were now legally described as *communautés*, within the one common 'Eglise du Christ'. Some expatriate missions did not take this drastic change easily and decided to carry on as before but this was not popular with the state authorities and would-be obstructionists were advised to leave the country. Fortunately Dr Cecilia Irvine has with infinite tenacity managed to register all these groups in her *The Church of Christ in Zaïre: a Handbook of Protestant Churches, Missions and Communautés 1878–1978.*[14]

The Rt Revd Dr Itofo Bokeleale became the Protestant Church's 'President and Legal Representative'. By this election President Mobutu could feel assured of the Church's co-operation. The two men had been bosom friends since childhood and spoke the same language. As a further indication of a new ecclesiastical tendency in a generally non-conformist *milieu* it should be added that not only Dr Bokeleale adopted the Bishop's title but also some of the regional presidents and leaders of the *communautés*.

In the midst of the breakdown of the Zaïrean governmental administration, the Kimbanguist movement managed to establish itself as a well-organized body with a specialized secretariat and a ruling council of thirty-two pastors chosen by the Supreme Head, Diangienda, Simon Kimbangu's son. A significant change took place: the prophet movement was transformed into a well-organized Church, more particularly in connection with the admission in 1969 of the Kimbanguist group as a member Church of the World Council of Churches. This was a development induced by the efforts of the Swiss Society of Reconciliation and the Moravian Church. In the Geneva Secretariat of the World Council the move was engineered by the Revd Hank Crane, a former missionary in Zaïre of the American Presbyterian Church.

RWANDA AND BURUNDI

Independent Burundi had in the 1970s a population of some 3.5 million of whom 85 per cent were Hutu and the rest Tutsi. For Church and society in Burundi there was only a short step from triumph to tragedy. The triumph was for all to see, in the phenomenal growth of the Catholic Church, particularly from 1935, and on the Protestant side, too, there was rapid growth of Pentecostals. In the first years after independence, Burundi was the scene of clashes and collisions with prime ministers appointed and assassinated until in 1965 King Ntare V placed Micombero, a Tutsi, as prime minister. No sooner had Micombero taken office than he dethroned the king and proclaimed a republic with himself as president. The ever-repressed Hutu took the chance of a violent reaction and some Tutsi were killed. A bloody Tutsi revenge followed in which 131 Hutu parliamentarians were executed. This was only a dress rehearsal for an intense drama in 1972 with shocking violence. A cruel genocide was the result in which at least 120,000 Hutu were killed, including a whole generation of educated Hutu. The Catholic Church, by what it did and by what it did not do at the time, was deeply involved in this terrible drama. There was also a rapidly growing Pentecostal Church, most of them Hutu. Just as Rwandan Tutsi had fled east, into Tanzania, so Burundian Hutu now took the same direction and tens of thousands of them found a refuge within the Tanzanian borders (see pp. 910–12).

The Catholic Church had to bear the brunt of this turmoil. Its new policy inspired by Vatican II, transforming the local churches on the hills into 'basic communities' was felt by government as competing with its own 'restructuring policy' and made it nervous. Jean Baptise Bagaza, president of Burundi from 1976, felt that the Catholic Church had too much of an influence in finance, industry and education, having such feudal privileges as the Church had had in the Middle Ages in Europe, and decided to counteract this influence. He suggested, through his political actions and contact, that some Muslim influence – Libya or other Arab countries – might be more to his taste, in a country where the Muslims number less than 100,000. The Churches felt the great man's displeasure. Seminaries were nationalized. Three hundred missionaries, among them the Verona Fathers, were forced to leave the country. The Protestant radio station was silenced. 'These methods seek to humiliate the Church and its leaders.'[15]

Rwanda and Burundi were two nations which, in the first half of the century, showed distinct similarities in both Church and State, acquiring independence on the same date in 1962. After independence they turned away from each other, the one the inverse of the other, with increasing distance between Tutsi Burundi and Hutu Rwanda. For eleven years G. Kayibanda was president of Rwanda, to be succeeded by a military regime under General Habyelima. New political parties emerged: the UNAR which was pro-Tutsi and counted the aristocratic Bishop Bigirumwami as one of its own. On the other side was APROSOM, fighting for Hutu emancipation. For historical and other reasons the Anglican CMS seemed to veer towards a pro-Tutsi position. Other Protestants were Baptists, Free Methodists, Pentecostal and Adventists, together with Jehovah's Witnesses. Some of these groups, more particularly the Jehovah's Witnesses, caused the political administration worries. Saturday as a holy day for some of these groups could lead to endless problems.

With Rwandan independence approaching, the Catholics, under Bishop

Perraudin, switched from favouring the Tutsi to siding with the much more numerous Hutu. 'The fate of the little ones, the poor, the still numerous disinherited masses, must be the first priority of the Authorities' as a Catholic watchword said bearing Bishop Perraudin's imprint. This stand of the Belgian bishop made Tutsi clergy increasingly oppose the ecclesiastical regime laid down by the White Fathers. When the brilliant Abbé A. Kagame published his writings on Rwandan history he was thought to be a nationalist.

On both the Catholic and the Protestant side, Rwanda – the country 'where God passes His night' – saw remarkable expressions of an intense spirituality. The Catholic apparitions of 'the Mother of the Word' – or the Virgin Mary – attracted avid attention from November 1981 onwards (see below). The East African Revival, sometimes referred to as 'the Rwanda Revival', was particularly active among the Anglicans.[16]

Holy Mary in Rwanda

Church history is more than numbers and diagrams of 'Church growth', more than tensions between foreign influence and local reaction, more than the mechanics of power struggle between factions and interests. Ideally one is looking for the breakthrough of a new awareness and new dedication, one listens for the heartbeat of personal piety and spirituality. More particularly one looks for these matters in the young and neglected perhaps on the pages of Church history.

In the case of Kibeho, Rwanda, one meets with the very young and their identification with heavenly personalities. In the chapter on modern Egypt there is reference to the Virgin's visitation to Zaytooun, Cairo, in 1968. Fifteen years later it was Rwanda's turn to be favoured with holy apparitions by the Virgin and Jesus. The centre for these miracles was a little boarding school for girls at Kibeho in the impoverished southern part of the country, a school for 120 girls, with three European sisters and six lay teachers, of whom two were Protestants. These apparitions had been preceded in 1980–81 by iconoclastic hooliganism and destruction of statues of the Virgin. 'It was in this wave that the Virgin chose to visit us in Rwanda.'

On 29 November 1981, Alphonsine Mumureke had the first apparition. Mary said:

> My child, I am the Mother of the Word. I like that you and your friends have the faith, now they do not believe sufficiently.

On 5 August 1982, Anatolie Mukamazimpaka had her apparition:

> I speak to you but you do not hear. I wish to raise you up but you remain laying down. I call on you but you make your ear deaf. When will you do what I ask of you? When will you understand? I give many signs but you remain incredulous. For how long will you remain deaf to my appeals?

Together with four others Anatolie discovered that 'the world is sick, the world is bad, we must repent, we must be converted. We must return to God and turn away from what is bad.'

Four other girls received similar visions and auditions from 15 August 1982 to 2 May 1983. The themes conveyed on these occasions were the following:

i) The world will go under. Everything will burn, the trees and all other living things. Make haste to do good things. Satan will disappear from this world, he will remain only for a short while. Then you will no longer be tempted.
ii) Jesus will return. When you see wars of religion then you will know that I am on my way.
iii) The judgements of God. Every person will be judged according to the Book of Life.
iv) How to be prepared? Be vigilant: Repent.
v) My word will not disappear. Every word which has gone out of my mouth, let them be faithful as I have told you.

A special case was a young shepherd, fifteen years of age, who did not know the Kibeho girls schools. On 2 July 1982, on his way to his fields he heard a voice, 'My child, if you are given a task, will you do it?' Segatashya replied in the affirmative. 'At once Jesus gives me a message: "Tell them, Purify your hearts for the time is short." I asked him his name. "I am called Jesus. Carry my message to these people."' He was given a new name by Jesus: Emmanuel. 'I said thank you and went my way.' Young Emmanuel now went to the Mission and told them of the miracle. He was baptized at Whitsun 1983 and confirmed August 1983.

This took place in an ecclesiastical *milieu* dominated by the White Fathers' iron law according to which the catechumenate should take four years, no less. In this case these rules were waived. One sympathizes with the generosity of the responsible Father. Emmanuel knew that he had seen and heard Jesus. What catechumens' class could stand comparison with *that*![17]

ANGOLA

Protestants in Africa did on the whole contribute to the preparation of the populations for political independence. In their Bible African Christians read a message of liberation and equality and they wanted to see this translated into political reality. But nowhere was the bond between Protestant conviction and political awareness as unmistakable as in the case of Angola, a Portuguese and Roman Catholic colony (or as they said, 'an overseas province') where the term 'Protestant' was throughout the colonial period a word of abuse, and where any up-and-coming local political leader was, without much ado, placed under lock and key if he did not manage to flee into Zaïre, or deported into the middle of the Atlantic Ocean as a lighthouse keeper near Ascension island, in the case of the Revd Toco, a founder of an Independent Church.

In the 1960s there emerged three political parties in different regions of the country, at first closely linked together but eventually one of them, the MPLA (Popular Movement for the Liberation of Angola), became dominant while the other two, the FNLA (National Front for the Liberation of Angola) in the north and UNITA (National Union for the Total Independence of Angola) in the south, were forced either to retreat into Zaïre or to establish itself as a competing body. We are dealing with men of a certain standing in modern African politics and, moreover, the background and origin of the three show a similar or identical structure.

As shown in Chapter 15 the main body of Angolan Protestantism was in the past established in three areas, the Baptists in the north as an off-shoot from Zaïrean San Salvador, the Methodist Episcopal in the Mbundu country near the capital Luanda, and the Congregationalists in the south-central region, among the dynamic Ovimbundu, the 'American and Canadian Congregationalists'. The political leader in the north, Roberto Holden was son of Roberto Carcia, Baptist preacher in San Salvador, and both on the father's and mother's side other relatives were counted as pillars of faith in the Baptist Church with, consequently, a record of arrests. The son Roberto Holden was named after a British Baptist missionary Roberto Holden C. Graham and as a matter of course went to a Baptist mission school in Kinshasa (Léopoldville) in the 1940s. He was part of a Baptist refugee movement fleeing from the Portuguese police into what became Zaïre or else managed to hide in the bush country of northern Angola near Kibentele mission ('Kibentele' being a good Baptist name after the Baptist pioneer Holman Bentley).

Among the Kimbundu community near Luanda, the Methodists established themselves. One of the Methodist ministers in the area was Agostinho Petro Neto and his son Agostinho Neto was outstanding because, despite being a Protestant he managed, with his mission's encouragement, to complete a secondary education at the government school in Luanda. The

American Methodist mission gave Neto a scholarship for medical studies in Portugal and in spite of arrest and imprisonment he managed to complete his studies in medicine. Dr Neto became the leader of the MPLA party in 1962 and the country's first president between 1975 and 1979.

With regard to family background and opportunities the story in the south repeats the experiences of the other two areas. Among the Ovimbundu community near Lobito towards the south, American Congregationalists with their ambitious educational institutions saw among their first co-workers one Lote Malheiro Savimbi who had his chance of modernization on the Benguela railway. For a young Christian anxious to witness about his faith, a railway job was ideal: at every halt or siding he could find and win would-be converts. The mission made him a school inspector and then director of the Chilessa mission. He had a son, Jonas Savimbi, who studied at Protestant and Catholic schools in Angola until 1958. Then a mission scholarship gave him the chance to study in Lisbon but harassed there by the police he left Portugal for Switzerland in order to take a course in political science at the University of Lausanne. Parallel with these studies in the years 1962–64, he acted as foreign minister for the Revolutionary Council of Angola. It was felt by the southerners of the country that the two northern parties, the MPLA and FNLA neglected them and this was one reason for the formation of their own party, UNITA. In connection with the ambitious Ovimbundu in the south of the country it seems worthwhile to mention that the former general secretary of the Protestant AACC, of Nairobi, Jose Chipenda, comes from a pastor's family in Lobito and is himself known for distinguished service with the World Council of Churches in Geneva.[18]

22

SOUTHERN AFRICA

ZAMBIA

Zambia's freedom movement under Dr Kenneth Kaunda was an African response to the European-inspired and -dominated Central African Federation. Kaunda (b. 1925) began as a teacher and was the son of the Revd David Kaunda who, as we recall, built a solid Presbyterian Church in the north-western part of the country. Kenneth Kaunda himself had his experience of opposition and imprisonment – a 'prison graduate' – and became president of the country in 1964. 'Humanism' was his philosophy, humanism with a Christian theme:

> What we loosely call 'independence', 'freedom', 'uhuru' etc. will be meaningless unless MAN is put first ... If I overemphasize the importance of MAN it is because I fear that young countries are in danger of repeating the mistakes of older countries both of the East and the West where material development and plans to advance have become more important than MAN for whom these plans after all are made or supposedly made ... The forces and tools of progress are here – let us use them.[1]

The beginnings of the new nation were marred by the Lumpa rebellion, led by a prophetess Alice Lenshina. Coming from the same district as the president she had, like so many African prophets, both men and women, had a revelation of God. She had 'died' and 'been with Jesus' in heaven: He told her to proclaim God's message to the world. From 1963 there were violent clashes between her movement and and that of the governing United National Independence Party (UNIP), and virtual civil war broke out from July to October 1964: between 700 and 1,500 hundred people – most of them members of the Lumpa movment – were killed. Lenshina's faithful followers knew that the government's bullets could not harm them. If only one cried 'Jericho', one was safe. A reconciliation team led by Kaunda's devoted missionary friend, Colin Morris, attempted to settle the issue.

The relationship of Church and State was dominated by the personality of the president who represented a healthy Christian tradition and who through the years had demonstrated a keen interest in the affairs and plans of the Churches. An interested friend of the ecumenical movement, he addressed the 1968 World Council of Churches assembly in Uppsala, Sweden.

Like other African countries, Zambia was at first involved in the revolution of rising expectations. The copper industry provided wealth – at least for a few – and regular work for around 50,000 mine workers in 1970. Surrounded by eight countries, most of them potential sources of refugees, Zambia had to devote much concern to the refugee problem. The most formidable of these was that of the Jehovah's Witnesses, chased to and fro across frontiers and in one of the neighbouring countries, Malawi, exposed to callous, inhuman treatment. The United Church of Zambia and the Catholics co-operated in a Refugee committee. These Churches also shared common tasks with regard to modern evangelism. 'The Zambia Multi-Media' was made possible through Catholic–Protestant co-operation from 1971. Here they shared in a single organization to handle religious broadcasting, religious telecasts, a film unit, filmstrip and visual aids-library and press and publications.[2]

The Catholics

The Catholic Church struggled with problems of its own, inherent in the system. The preponderance of expatriate personnel and the scarcity of African religious personnel was obvious. Dr Frans J. Verstraelen who devoted research to *An African Church in Transition* reported that in 1973 there were in the Catholic archdiocese of Lusaka nine Zambian and sixty-five expatriate priests, three Zambian and forty-one expatriate brothers, thirty-five Zambian and 115 expatriate sisters.[3] Of the Zambian priests there were at the time of Dr Verstraelen's study only five actually involved in pastoral-missionary work (the African archbishop included), two of whom were studying abroad, one was serving in another diocese and one had left the priesthood. At the same time the choice for the Church between the rural areas and urban opportunities was difficult. 'Powerless the Catholic missionaries had to watch the constant flight from the countryside [into the cities].'[4] More dramatic was the fate of the highly popular archbishop himself. This deserves our attention.

Archbishop Milingo – an African Non-Conformist

It is difficult to think of any better example of the African Church's inculturation than involvement in healing through devoted personalities with charismatic gifts for such service. It so happens that the Catholic archdiocese of Lusaka had such a man, obviously endowed with gifts for healing and spiritual renewal, and this churchman was not just anybody but the Catholic archbishop himself, Emmanuel Milingo.

Africanization, indigenization and 'incarnation in a context' were the programme of Church and mission. But how to decide what was ultimately and genuinely African and yet fully acceptable in the Church? The Milingo crisis brought this question to the fore and the Milingo case will return, we think, in drama and song far into the next century.[5]

Emmanuel Milingo was one of the eleven bishops consecrated by Pope Paul VI in Kampala, Uganda. Born in 1930 and ordained in 1958 he was made bishop eleven years later to become archbishop of Lusaka. He had by then been secretary of the Commission on Communication for the Episcopate in Zambia and was thus, presumably, well-informed about modern techniques and developments. However, the African community and the Church had much to catch up with. He says drastically: 'I personally believe that the Church took us [Africans] as passive listeners and that we were in coma for five hundred years.'

Moving among the flock committed to his charge he discovered not only the economic misery of the African people and the jubilation of their worship but also illness, both physical and mental. Could anything be done about it? Could the bishop do anything about it? Everybody knew of course what a bishop should do: to preside at Mass, to bless catechumens and confirmands and to administer the affairs of a far-flung diocese. But here was something which could not be ignored.

In 1973 Milingo began to pray for people, first for a few individuals, then for a crowd and then again for hundreds, twice a week, at the archbishop's residence and at the cathedral. To his immense surprise he ascertained that his prayer was powerful and had a healing effect. But he knew how it came about: 'I say again, I am only a channel through which the healing powers flowed into my ailing brethren.'

In Zambian society the matter of healing through prayer was a problem. It was seen as misrepresented by the 'Zionists', of whom there were *legio* in any African township. For a Catholic bishop to be seen as a healer was therefore a serious matter. There were of course differences between the quiet and humble manner of the archbishop and the vociferous volume of sound associated with 'Zionist' healing. But this difference did not help.

This went on for nine years. In the midst of it all Archbishop Milingo found time for writing about his healing activity, admittedly not in an academic style but nonetheless well-informed and well-argued. There is, we think, no bishop in the Catholic Church, or any other Church in Africa in this century whom we can know so well and intimately as Archbishop Emmanuel Milingo, and the more one studies his writings the more one feels sympathy with this gifted, honest and straightforward churchman.[6]

In the end, however, the powers of ecclesiastical establishment were too strong for him. In 1982 Archbishop Milingo was recalled to Rome there being offered, as a kind of consolation prize, a task with the Papal Commission for Migration and Tourism in Rome. The irony of it is that the Archbishop can now devote himself to healing Europeans.

Protestant co-operation

The Mindolo Ecumenical Institute is unthinkable without Zambia's Copper Belt. Out in the bush there had suddenly arrived conglomerations of people and activity, of initiative and stimulation. Before too long half a million people congregated in the region. In this new *milieu* the Churches together took counsel for something exciting and creative. For twenty years, from 1932, the United Missions in the Copper Belt laboured at Mindolo in the fields of education, medicine and social work. In the early 1950s it was realized that these tasks had largely been taken over by government. Was there anything in particular that the Churches through Mindolo could do and must do, which nobody else did? Thus it was decided to make Mindolo a lay centre for training, consultation and research and in the field of training it was decided that priority should be given to the training of women. An international, interdenominational and interracial centre appeared. In 1963 Dr Donald Mthimkhulu, a South African educationalist, was made Mindolo's first principal. Other notable members of staff at this time included Peter Mathews, G. A. Krapf, Bengt Simonsson and F. Sillett.

This was a period of intense political debate in the country and the need was felt for a centre for political discussion, under sympathetic Christian auspices where African leaders could meet with European political leaders and heads of commercial and industrial organizations in order to envisage together the future of the nation. These were occasions of immense importance for Zambia and its Churches.

Very soon a spectrum of new activities was added to the programme: agriculture, community development 'national development', the study of urbanization problems, youth leadership, Church music. In 1959 an African Literature Centre was started, on the instigation of the International Missionary Council and the All Africa Council of Churches. More than 200 African writers, journalists and communicators from all over the continent came looking for ideas and skills. This Centre, together with the other activities of the Centre, are served by the Dag Hammarsjöld Library.

In Zambia, Church union negotiations showed that this concern at that time was mainly a 'Free Church' affair. Mindolo was wider. The involvement of the Anglican and other Churches in its work and witness was central. The outlook of the Centre was greatly widened through the presence, teaching and fellowship of Fr Adrian Hastings, WF, who spent fifteen months, 1969–70, as Liasion Officer for the Roman Catholic Church.

It was in the international councils of Mindolo that the idea of a move of the All Africa Church Conference from Mondolo to the city, to Nairobi, was first broached. West African theologians such as Samuel Amissah and James Lawson, resource persons for Mindolo, took up the matter with the principal, D. Mthimkhulu and with that trusted government official Henry Makhulu, and it was decided that the time had come to move the AACC as such to Nairobi, effectively supported by the World Council of Churches, while all other activities carried on with increasing strength at Mindolo.

MALAWI

In a modern Church history of Africa, the Malawian Churches occupy a special place thanks to their great gifts of initiative and communicability, reaching out with restless energy to neighbouring and far-off communities and countries. Independent Malawi no doubt retained some of these excellent qualities – but with a difference. For better or for worse new Malawi was marked, and perhaps subdued, by its first president, Dr Hastings Kamuzu Banda. He pursued a policy of his own, without too much co-operation with other presidential, more or less socialist, colleagues. Not that he or his government were inactive. The dream about his new capital, Lilongwe, was the President's great ambition and concern. If the great powers in the West did not support these plans or even neglected the idea, he would find support for the plan in unexpected quarters, in Pretoria, leading to economically favourable contacts with that city.

Another great concern were the destitute refugees streaming in from Mozambique. An unthinkable 850,000 refugees and perhaps another 150,000 unaccounted for, were welcomed on Malawian soil, given free range with rights to work, plough and to live anywhere. On behalf of the Malawian population itself important initiatives were taken for development in the districts, even if a recent Oxfam report shows an undue concentration of estate farming (in tobacco) owned by the few wealthy. President Banda, previously a medical doctor in Britain and Ghana, was by then an ageing African aristocrat, for many years an elder of the Presbyterian Church, but with a generous will to honour major functions of the other Churches with his presence.

In 1960 the Anglican community in Malawi could welcome a new bishop, Donald S. Arden (born 1916), who resigned in 1981 to make way for an African successor as archbishop: Walter Khotso Makhulu, archbishop of Central Africa since 1979 and president of the Anglican Consultative Council. From 1971 Arden became the archbishop of Central Africa (Botswana, Zimbabwe, Zambia and Malawi). Here was a bishop in tune with the times and with the new Africa. In co-operation with a young Scots layman, Albert Macadam, he developed a plan for the formation of an ecumenical institute for Malawi, a joint venture of Presbyterians, Anglicans, Roman Catholics and the Churches of Christ. In 1974 this led to the formation of the Chilema Institute.

This was comparable to Mindolo in Zambia. Mindolo is of course wider known, owing to its historic contacts with the AACC. Chilema's strength was to establish close contacts with the day-to-day life of the Malawian Christians, the grass roots of the Churches, creating thereby a centre for spiritual renewal and ecumenical co-operation. This centre of ecumenical dialogue coincided with Vatican II in Rome and with the activities of the World Council of Churches: while primarily concerned with local and national problems it took some of its inspiration from these sources.

The centre was concerned with the training of the clergy leading to a joint training with the Presbyterians, and to the TEEM – Theological Education by Extension, in Malawi. They invited Archbishop Patrick Kalilombe to take a clergy retreat. This remarkable Catholic archbishop was also a Bible translator: he translated the New Testament into the Chewa language. Chilema dealt with all kinds of Church training, from new bishops to old catechists. From the Presbyterian side Chilema invited as occasional lecturer Dr Silas Ncosana, able young general secretary of the Church of Central Africa Presbyterian.

The central role of Chilema within the Anglican communion is illustrated by the fact that CAPA (the Conference of Anglican Provinces in Africa) was formed at Chilema in 1979. This was the first time that the Anglican Church in Africa ever met together officially, apart from the bishops meeting together at Lambeth and at Canterbury. The new international world with increased air communication over the continent facilitated the meeting in the centre of Africa, heralding no doubt, for the new century, after AD 2000, comparable meetings on a continent-wide scale.

The Chilema centre had a broad outlook and was in a position to pursue development schemes for the regional areas of the country, sometimes with ecumenical funds from the West, more particularly the World Council of Churches. The Private Hospitals Association of Malawi (PHAM) was another great project leading to Church co-operation including, at first, ten training centres for nurses – Catholic, Anglican and Presbyterian. A new Anglican diocese, that of 'Lake Malawi', was formed with Josiah Mtekateka as the first bishop, being also the first Anglican African bishop in the country. The predicament of the Mozambican refugees placed the entire diocese before the great concerned of Africa at the time and widened the horizons of parish and individual.

As head of the Catholic Church, Bishop Patrick Kalilombe of Lilongwe took a refreshing view of Catholic problems.

> Many people seem to think that the basic problem for the future of the Church is shortage of priests. It definitely is not! The real issue at stake is rather: adequate ministry, understanding ministry in the wide sense to include all the functions and services needed to obtain a harmonious life and efficient work of the Church. Until such time as the laity have been fully involved, and a realistic redistribution of ministries, ordained and non-ordained, has been made, it is impossible to say whether we have too few priests or too many! There is plenty of room for a large number of non-ordained ministries which could be assumed by the laity![7]

A fuller understanding of present-day Churches in an historical perspective – from 1859 until now – is provided by a unique Africa study, *Magomero. Portrait of an African Village*, by Landeg White.[8] This account of a village in the southernmost area of Malawi finds room for a number of outstanding personalities including David Livingstone, Bishop Charles F. Mackenzie, John Chilembwe and Daniel Malekebu. Magomero has been

> a place of the utmost unimportance ... Yet this is the point of the book ... The record of these villagers, shut out of history or locked into their alternative history, is without charity or patronage fascinating in its own terms.[9]

How does such a community manage its affairs?

> In many ways the Churches have already supplanted the visage and the extended family as the centres of social groupings ... It is the Church leaders, for example, and not the village headmen who these days organize initiation ceremonies, whether of the orthodox Anglican, Catholic and Presbyterian varieties or of neo-traditional forms practised by the Ethiopian Churches.[10]

As to the question of land

the Churches give approval to inheritance through the male line. Reminded by me that this conflicts with Lomwe custom, spokesmen for the Anglican, Presbyterian and Ethiopian Churches all agreed: 'That is finished!'[11]

ZIMBABWE

The struggle for Zimbabwe

The Central African Federation never was a success. When Zambia and Malawi headed towards independence, developments in Zimbabwe were different. Ian Smith's illegal and unilateral declaration of independence 'to defend Christianity and Western Civilization in the midst of Africa' accelerated the eruption of civil war.

From 1965 onwards the Churches in Zimbabwe – Catholic, Protestant and Spirit Churches alike – were placed between the warring factions. When Ian Smith's minority regime issued its racialist legislation in the fields of land tenure and education there emerged a representative forum for criticism of government, this forum took the name 'Heads of Denominations'. In the mobilization against the proposed settlement of Southern Rhodesia's relations to Great Britain in the early 1970s, there appeared a new agency for ecumenical concern. The Methodist bishop Abel Muzorewa and the Wesleyan Methodist pastor Canaan Banana led the African National Council formed as a means for articulating the position of the African majority. On the Catholic side the effects of the Second Vatican Council were expressed in the formation of the Justice and Peace Committe of the Bishops Conference, highlighting atrocities perpetrated by the Rhodesian army and police.

From the middle of the 1970s the Zimbabwe African National Union (ZANU) under Robert Mugabe intensified operations from bases in Mozambique. In August 1978 there was time for the first official encounter between Church leaders and the leadership of the Zimbabwean liberation movements in Lusaka, Zambia. On behalf of the Church leaders there was an urgent plea for national unity and a constitutional settlement of the crisis.

When the war expanded the Protestant leadership likewise had to review its priorities. Loyalties with Bishop Muzorewa and his ANC continued to be strong, even after the widening split between the internal opposition of the ANC and its allies on the one hand and the liberation movements operating from Zambia or Mozambique on the other. At the constitutional conference in Geneva, December 1976, the Revd Canaan Banana decided to cross the floor and join the ZANU (PF) (Patriotic Front) delegation under Robert Mugabe.

At that time the Revd Banana did not manage to carry the Protestant majority with him. The Council of Churches did in fact give the so-called 'Internal Settlement' from 1978 a try. In the end Garfield Todd of the Dadaya Mission managed to qualify that position and facilitated the reconciliation mission of the Council at the time of the Lancaster House conference in 1979.

There were dramatic interactions at the local level of guerillas and parishioners in the rural areas. There also appeared emergency relief programmes operated by ecumenical agencies based in the cities such as the 'Christian Care'. From a more specialized Catholic agency we select the following illustration. Next to Chitungwiza, which is a town of almost half a million people, thirty kilometers from Harare, there was a refugee camp for about 18,000 people and next to it Chirambahuyo, a slum for another 18,000. Three Carmelite Fathers were in charge. They asked their Shona Jesuit colleague, Brother Canisius Chisiri, SJ, since 1975 engaged in a lay-persons training programme, to help the victims of war in Zimbabwe. He reports:

> This is how I started the Rehabilitation Retreats, using the methods of modern language, counselling retreats and psychological retreats ... We make them feel at home, assuring them that all their bodily needs during their stay with us at the weekend will be taken care of by us. What we want of them is to be themselves. It is a time to reflect about the past, present and future ... time to sing and time to cry for our loved ones who died a brutal death and who may even not be buried. Some had been forced to share the flesh of the victim before they could run for their lives ... consequently they became totally wrapped up in themselves without the ability to let their emotions out. All they could do was to run for their lives, leaving the victim unburied ... Among the Shona people, when someone dies ... each person goes to the close relative or the wife of the dead man and shakes hands, which is known as *kubata maoko* ... Then the people will begin to talk ... At this stage Scriptures suitable to the women's life experience (e.g., some sections of the book of Job, and Matthew 11, 28–30) are read ... They have deep wounds and need a dustbin to pour all their feeling into ... I and my team ... insist on forgiveness as one condition of peace between man and man as well as man and God. We ask each of them to forgive themselves, in particular those who had tried to commit suicide. Secondly, we ask them to forgive those who they thought were responsible for the killing of their loved ones ... Reconciliation must begin with your neighbour before considering reconciliation with God ... People who were wrapped up in their traumas are taught to face life once more with hope.[12]

After independence

The transition from Ian Smith's Rhodesia to Robert Mugabe's Zimbabwe was accompanied and informed by the latter's combination of 'Marxist–Leninist principles adjusted to Zimbabwean conditions' and a deliberate plea for national reconciliation. In terms of policy on religion Mugabe affirmed that his party has had good relations with the Church. 'We derive our backgrounds, all of us, from association with the Church, from having been brought up in Christian institutions.' He realized that 'the Churches, by and large, are the dominant influence among our people'. Thus he went on to affirm: 'We can never apply Marxist–Leninist principles in the same way that they have been applied in the Soviet Union or China or even in Mozambique.'[13]

As state president from 1980–88 the Revd Canaan Banana explored further the conditions for the unity of African socialism and Christian theology. He presented his *Theology of promise: the dynamics of self-reliance*.[14] On every page he demonstrates that he is well-informed about the debate in modern theology, referring to such authorities as Dr Frantz Fanon, Eric Fromm, James Cone and the Catholic bishops in Nicaragua and Brazil. The kind of Christianity he wishes to advocate is 'revolutionary Christianity' as 'the only possible form of Christianity'. The kingdom of God, he suggests is realized in Socialism. There is much more in Marxism than atheism. 'My vision', he goes on to say, 'is not based on theories and calculations but on real facts and observations. I can see that the "absent ones" are now present, those who make up the "Church of the people", the Proletarian Church', which he wishes to emerge in the new Zimbabwe.[15]

With different experiences from the war the Churches responded differently to the call for participation in nation-building issued by president and prime minister. Again Heads of Denominations emerged as a forum for ecumenical discussion with the national leadership. The Catholic Church expressed its position in Pastoral Letters, not least in the Letter of 1983 on the sensitive situation in Matabeleland, with the title 'Reconciliation is still Possible', together with Mugabe's sharp criticism. President Banana criticized the Christian Council for adopting a too passive attitude *vis-à-vis* the new political order. The contribution in 1987 of the Heads of Denominations to the question of national unity was a major achievement.

MOZAMBIQUE

Terror: Wiriyamu and elsewhere

The tight symbiosis between Portuguese colonial state – with its secret police, the PIDE-DGS – and the Catholic Church marked the Portuguese colony of Mozambique. For over four centuries the Portuguese had been the masters and they were resolved never to loose the grip. They could of course read the writing on the wall when, about 1960, African countries north of Mozambique became 'Independent'. This they thought could not happen in their own 'Overseas Province'. The colonial army was therefore strengthened and very soon the signs of its unhampered and violent activity were to be felt, particularly as the FRELIMO liberation movement began its activities from 1964. Terror was the lesson which the population could understand and terror of torture and death was meted out on thousands of defenceless communities.

This was particularly so in the Tete province in the north-west, where whole villages and communities were tortured, mowed down and burned. The Wiriyamu case was dramatically and widely noted as Fr Adrian Hastings published his *J'accuse* under the name *Wiriyamu* in 1974, bringing the Portuguese terror regime to the attention of world opinion.[16] After a concordat between Church and State in 1940 it had been possible for 'foreign', Catholic missions to serve in the country and the White Fathers and Italian Consolata Fathers came to Mozambique. In view of the impossible situation caused by the Portuguese army violence, these Catholic communities left Mozambique with a resounding bang of protest. These factors taken together with the decisive role of the FRELIMO liberation front helped to bring the Portuguese rule in Mozambique to an end, following upon the 1974 revolution in Portugal itself.

The non-Romans and FRELIMO

There were at this time leading non-Roman communities: the [Swiss] Presbyterian Church, the Episcopal Methodist and Free Methodist Churches from the USA, the Anglicans, and, after 1920, Scandinavian Baptists, International Holiness Mission, South Africa General Mission (expelled by the Portuguese in 1962) together with Seventh Day Adventists and two Pentecostal communities (the Pentecostal Assemblies of God being the largest Protestant community in Mozambique).

One realizes that this Protestant contribution had to be given in an atmosphere of intense suspicion from the Portuguese regime and constant police supervision. The present writer experienced this as early as 1953 in connection with the visit of the IMC Theological Commission to Africa during that year. My Presbyterian host took me to the airfield in Maputo (then called Lourenzo Marques). As we talked, an open PIDE car, of the Portuguese secret police, came close to us trying to register our words. I said to my host: 'As I leave you now, I wish you above all *donum perseverentiae*.' He retorted: 'Here it is not a question of *persévérer*, but of *durer*', a distinction indicating the special quality of this Swiss missionary staff at the Ricatla Seminary.

Recent books by African leaders show the role of these Swiss Presbyterian missionaries. The predominant problem for a Protestant mission in that situation was the educational one, how to provide elementary education and above all secondary education in a country where Protestants were effectively deprived of any opportunity to proceed beyond elementary education. Here it was the Swiss Presbyterian Mission who, with their American (with Swedish) Methodist colleagues, would try a far-sighted approach.

The fascinating *Life History of Raúl Honwana*, edited by Allen Isaacman, refers to the liberating role of that great missionary-cum-anthropologist, Henri Junod of Lausanne, at Ricatla, and together with Junod his younger colleagues, all gifted and devoted people: Paul Fatton, Maurice Schaller, Dr André-Daniel Clerc and the Revd Juillerat.[17] Honwana's mother sent her son to the Presbyterian Church and he remained a faithful member throughout his life. Honwana also devotes part of a chapter to a younger friend of his, a fellow student in the Presbyterian Church, by the name of Eduardo Mondlane, the son of a chief.

The Church helped Eduardo along for his elementary school and found a place for him in the Church's youth movement, 'Les Patrouilles', and in a secondary school in the Transvaal with which the Swiss mission had close contacts. Thanks to these connections, more particularly with Dr Clerc, the able Eduardo Mondlane was able to study at the University of the Witwatersrand (Johannesburg) and this provided another step for further doctoral studies at Northwestern University, Evanston, USA. At university Mondlane came into contact with African student organizations and had his first experience of political organization. At Dar es Salaam, in recently independent Tanzania, in 1962 he formed the FRELIMO – the Mozambiquean Liberation Front.

Eduardo Mondlane with his great and generous personality was singularly well-prepared for his role as a leader of the freedom movement; himself privileged, he cast lot with the oppressed and exploited.[18] There is a great chapter to be written on the noble company of African freedom heroes who set out to liberate their countries but whose lives were cut short and who were never permitted to complete the march. Eduardo Mondlane, it seems to us, was the greatest of them all.

Among all these Protestant communities the Anglicans puzzled the Portuguese. They were episcopal, yet not related to the bishop in Rome. They did enjoy certain advantages over most Protestant Churches and as British had 'some sort of respectability'.[19] The appointment in 1967 of a Lusitanian, Daniel de Pina Cabral, as the Bishop of Lebombo therefore at first seemed a brilliant stroke of Church politics. The new incumbent De Pina Cabral came from an aristocratic Portuguese family, being a distinguished lawyer and ordained priest and, in addition to all this a friend and pupil of Marcello Caetano, the prime minister of Portugal from 1968–74. When Caetano made a visit in 1969 to Lourenzo Marques (now Maputo) and was welcomed by the assembled dignitaries, he embraced the new Anglican bishop: a gesture which was not lost on the Portuguese, but perhaps rather less popular with the Africans. One year after Independence Bishop de Pina Cabral returned to Portugal.

Catholic adaptation

During the times of terror of the Portuguese army one of the Catholic bishops in the north, Pinto of Nampula, had publicly protested against his own government, an act which cost him dearly. His pious colleagues branded him as 'the Traitor of Nampula' and he was expelled from Mozambique. However, the revolutionary times worked for him: after a year he returned to a new Mozambique, now a socialist republic, and was welcomed with immense jubilation by his diocese.

In 1975 Cardinal Rossi consecrated the first two African bishops that Mozambique had ever had. At the same time many of the Portuguese staff of the Church found it best to return to Portugal: in 1974 almost two-thirds of the priests left. The change was felt most by the grass-roots, in the parishes. The number of priests declined from 1,513 in 1975 to 684 in 1977. But the Franciscans were, as always, mobile. A Portuguese Franciscan was installed as the new archbishop of Maputo. Excluding the exodus of more than 200,000 Portuguese, the proportion of Catholics among the African population 'had declined from about 17 per cent to a little more than 13 per cent' between the years 1970 and 1982.[20] The establishment of a new socialist regime was also a serious challenge to the Catholic Church.

Church and State after independence

With independence coming to Mozambique in 1975 things changed. 'Scientific Socialism' became the programme: schools and hospitals were nationalized. 'Down with Religion, Down with the Church' became a popular cry. 'Thousands of Church members opted for politics and the United Methodist Church lost 40 per cent of its membership between 1975 and 1979.'[21] The Anglican bishop, Diniz Sengulane and Bishop Almeida Penicela of the United Methodists initiated studies of 'Being Christian in a Socialist State'. The new general secretary of the Christian Council, Isaac Mahlalela, became a key figure in the relations between Church and State.

The new decade saw an improvement in the contacts between Church and State. In 1982 all the religious leaders – Catholic, Protestant, Muslim and Hindu – were invited to a conference with the president. The same year the Churches were gladdened by the announcement that December 25 – since Independence an ordinary workday – would be celebrated as a Public Holiday, called 'Family day'. Increasingly the Churches were recognized as beacons of hope. Under the new president, Joaquim Chissano, the Churches were entrusted with the responsible task of initiating negotiations with the rebel organization RENAMO (or MNR). This search for peace led to the first direct discussions between the government and the rebels, held in Rome in July 1990, and mediated by the Catholic archbishop of Beira, Mgr Jaime Goncalves, as well as by two members of the Saint Egidio community. In the same month of July 1990 President Chissano declared that Mozambique was to become a multi-party state and he invited the RENAMO rebel organization to become a political party in the country.

SOUTH AFRICA

Sharpeville and protest

The 1960s opened with the shock of Sharpeville, 21 March 1960. Sixty-nine African men, women and children were killed by South African police and nearly 200 wounded. The structural violence of apartheid society showed up in a glaring light.

The impact of the national tragedy brought the Churches together. Towards the end of the year, the English-speaking Churches and two of the Afrikaans-speaking Churches met at Cottesloe, Johannesburg, with prominent international Church leaders, including Dr Franklin C. Fry and Dr Vissert' Hooft of the World Council of Churches. Among African leaders present were Bishop Alpheus Zulu, Anglican, and the Revd E. E. Mahabane, Methodist. The demand for unity and equality of the various communities was emphasized by those present.

This ecumenical euphoria did not last long. The prime minister, Dr Hendrik Verwoerd reacted in characteristic manner with harsh reprimands, this time hitting at members of his own Church, the Dutch Reformed Church. They had, he insisted, been misled by international and liberal men from Geneva and had better recant, allowing the *laager* of apartheid to take over. No social control could be as tight-fisted as that of Afrikaaner national unity and so it was on this occasion. Most of the Dutch Reformed representatives who had signed the Cottesloe statement recanted while a few refused to do so, among them Dr Beyers Naudé. Naudé had been a moderator of the Southern Transvaal Synod of the DRC and, like his father, a member of the powerful *Broederbond*. He was now removed from this position and with a reverberating bang gave up the latter connection.

In 1963 Naudé started a protest and reform movement called the Christian Institute with an uncompromising stand against racialism and political and economic inequality. He also inspired another remarkable initiative through the African Independent Churches Association (AICA), an association of many smaller Independent African Churches – significantly the relatively influential and well-endowed among them preferred not to be aligned with the controversial Christian Institute. Here theological education adapted to the situation was provided by a group of devoted voluntary co-workers, White and Black. In an atmosphere of increasing polarization the Christian Institute remained a beacon of light until extinguished by state decree in 1976.

For a time the activities of the South African Council of Churches, the SACC, were overshadowed by Naudé's Christian Institute. This was a time of the 'Charismatics' in the Church, with local connections in South Africa, an altogether admirable movement, although in South Africa it tended to be pietistic and did not always face the wider political issues. When this ethos informed the SACC, the council lost some of its influence while Naudé's uncompromising programme, as long as it was permitted to function, appeared all the more attractive.

At about this time the Council of Churches got a new general secretary in the Methodist layman, John Rees, a brilliant administrator with a prophetic social concern, and had the Revd Habergaan, Moravian, as president. Together with E. A. Mahabane, they initiated a radical social programme. Special departments were formed, devoted to 'Justice and Reconciliation', labour problems, assistance for 'Dependents' – i.e., families of those in jail, sometimes serving life sentences. Archbishop Robert Selby Taylor has, over the years, given generous support to the 'Dependents' – challenging the government's 'Bantu Education' system, so-called.

In 1976 John Rees decided that it was time for an African general secretary and Bishop Desmond Tutu took over. Through Tutu's inspiring personality the South African Council of Churches, even more than before became a leading factor in the liberation struggle. A Christian Council in any country can be a soft, even innocuous affair, muffled by pressures from the high and mighty. When, in 1982–83, the SACC was brought to court to answer certain allegations resulting from the 'Eloff Commission', the spokesmen for the Council took a memorable stand. Both Bishop Tutu and the Revd Peter John Storey, Methodist, then president of the Council, came to the defence of the cause and did so with prophetic conviction, indignation and inspired eloquence unparalleled, we think, in the annals of the Christian Church on the continent anywhere after the Second World War. We quote:

> *Bishop Tutu*: Many in the black community ask why I still waste my time talking to whites and I tell them that our mandate is Biblical. Moses went to Pharaoh several times even if he knew that it was futile ... We in the SACC do many things that in more normal countries would be the responsibility of the State ... In other societies we would be lauded for this outstanding work. In our beloved country we are vilified, harassed and abused.
>
> *The Revd Storey*: Has it been forgotten that until the 1950s the Christian Church was responsible for virtually all the education there was for blacks in the land? Has it been forgotten that many of the proud institutions which produced the finest black leaders on the continent of Africa still stand as empty shells because of the deliberate policy of this Government? ... Thousands of night-schools run by the Churches across the land ... were summarily closed by the master architect of apartheid because they represented a threat to his theory of education ... Of course education has a role to play in liberation. We are committed to the freedom of the black people ... What in heaven's name is wrong with that?

The 'Bantustans' and the Churches

From the 1960s the Churches had to live with the fact of the eight 'Bantustans' or so-called 'Homelands'. These miserable little territories, masquerading as independent states, could, if the worst came to the worst, act as narrow encrustations for the Church. Thus Transkei's Kaiser Matanzima managed to divide his own Methodist Church, from which Church ministers had to flee as refugees into the Republic of South Africa.

Towards the end of the 1980s, with Matanzima dethroned from his presidency of Transkei, this conflict – lasting from 1978–87 – was settled and the whole of the Methodist Church in South Africa recognized Dr Stanley Moghoba as its leader. In the Venda republic any local police captain could try out his methods of terror and torture on pastors in the territory. Thus the Lutheran Dean Simon Farisani was repeatedly treated as an enemy of the state and eventually had to be invalided to the United States for psychiatric treatment.

Theology recognizes a Kairos

The debate over 'African Theology' versus 'Black Theology' had been continuing for years in South Africa, until a national state of emergency and the political crisis suddenly deepened into 'a Movement of Truth' and *a real Kairos*. The Churches, Catholic and non-Catholic, acted through the *Kairos Document*, September 1985.[22] This uncompromising document is the most powerful Church statement to appear on the continent of Africa, addressed to 'all who bear the name Christian'. It has a scathing critique of both 'State Theology' and of 'Church Theology' and pleads for a 'Prophetic Theology'.

State Theology is attacked because it provides theological justification for a *status quo*. The state makes use of the name of God and of 'Almighty God'. But that kind of god, the Kairos Document says, is an idol. 'The god of the South African state is not merely an idol or false god, it is the devil disguised as Almighty God – the antichrist.'[23] Neither does the Kairos Document spare what they call *Church Theology*: in a limited, guarded and cautious way this Church theology criticizes apartheid. The Churches speak of 'reconciliation' but any form of peace or reconciliation that allows the sin of injustice and oppression to continue is a false peace; it is not Christian reconciliation: it is sin. By avoiding a real 'social analysis' *Church Theology* has led to a spirituality which has dominated Church life for centuries and leaves Christians and Church leaders 'in a state of near paralysis'.[24]

Finally, *Prophetic Theology* has its point of departure in the Bible and in an understanding of the structural inequality (political, social and economic) expressed in discriminatory laws, institutions and practices which have led the people of South Africa 'into a virtual civil war' and rebellion against tyranny. The prophets of the Bible pointed to the message of hope. If the powerful message of hope has not been highlighted in Christian Theology, is this because they do not want to encourage the oppressed to be too hopeful for too much?[25] The Kairos rallying cry had a strong echo in South Africa and beyond its borders. 'The Evangelicals' produced their own statement in 1986 obviously aimed above all at disassociating themselves from a new wave of mission in South Africa, coming from Tulsa, Oklahoma, in the form of the state-approved Rhema Church.[26]

'How long will this last?' Together with a much concerned Western opinion the Black elite were asking the question: 'This cannot go on for ever. Apartheid must come to an end, but when?' In February 1990 the great leader of the Blacks, Nelson Mandela was freed, after twenty-seven years 'on the Island' and in jail. A decision taken by President F. W. de Klerk made this momentous change possible. The freeing of Mandela and the unbanning of the ANC opened up a new era for South Africa, worthy of its peoples, *and* all its peoples in the last decade of the twentieth century and for centuries to follow.

Our chapter on South Africa 1960–90 opened with 'Sharpeville 1960' and can now move to another note altogether, namely that of the National Initiative for Reconciliation at the Rustenburg meeting of November 1990. The conference opened with an incredibly moving exchange. On the first morning, Professor Willie Jonker rose to say:

> I confess before you and the Lord, not only my own sin and guilt, and my personal responsibility for the political, social, economical and structural wrongs that have been done to many of you and the results of which you and our whole country are still suffering from but vicariously I dare also to do that in the name of the NG Kerk (DRC) of which I am a member, and for the Afrikaans people as a whole. I have the liberty to do just that, because the NG Kerk (DRC) at its latest synod has declared apartheid a sin and confessed its own guilt of negligence in not warning against it and distancing itself from it long ago.[27]

Following Professor Jonker's confession, Archbishop Desmond Tutu rose to receive the confession and to offer forgiveness:

> I believe that I certainly stand under pressure of God's Holy Spirit to say that ... when confession is made, then those of us who have been wronged must say 'We forgive you.' And that altogether we may move to the reconstruction of our land. It [the confession] is not cheaply made and the response is not cheaply made.[28]

Prophetic voices were heard on that occasion. Nobody personified the momentous change that had come to the country as much as Beyers Naudé who said, 'No healing is possible without reconciliation and no reconciliation is possible without justice, and no justice is possible without some form of genuine restitution.' Such restitution, he went on to say, 'might best be made at Blood River or at the Voortrekker Monument' (Pretoria). From

Rustenburg the perspective opened towards the future, for the last few years of this century and towards a new South Africa, of immense importance for the Church in South Africa and, indeed, for the Church in all of Africa.

The Dutch Reformed Church

There is a tendency to describe the DRC as a monolithic system where, owing to extraordinary social pressures, no deviation from the official party programme is possible. This is not altogether true. There is even now, a tension within the DRC between what we have called an 'Evangelical influence' and the politicized 'nationalist' line. Three names show this.

The moderator of the Northern Transvaal Synod of the DRC from 1986 and elected for the following four years was Professor Johan Heyns, theological professor at the Pretoria university. He was aware of the fact that 80 per cent of all cabinet ministers and about 70 per cent of the members of parliament were members of the DRC. He said:

> The Church is the Church of Jesus Christ and not the Church of the African *volk*, of the white man. There is no such thing as white superiority or black inferiority. All people are equal before God. The policy of apartheid was wrong and the [DRC] Synod has acknowledged that. We are not going to give to apartheid a theological, ethical justification. That is completely wrong.

In 1986, a colleague at the theological faculty of Stellanbosch University, Professor Nico Smith, took the altogether unprecedented step of giving up his academic position in order, to live with his family, in and among the Black community of Mamelodi, near Pretoria, a social venture and adventure of symbolic value, called Koinonia.

Nobody represented the evangelical tradition in the DRC with greater theological awareness and more distinguished personal involvement than the late Professor David J. Bosch (1929–92, tragically killed in a car accident), Dean of the Theological Faculty at UNISA, Pretoria, general secretary of the Southern African Missiological Society (1968–92) and editor of the outstanding periodical *Missionalia*. David Bosch wrote internationally acclaimed missiological works and was altogether a remarkable Christian personality and faithful friend.

The Catholics

There was, perhaps, in Protestant South Africa an impression that the Roman Catholic Church was a foreign body led by foreign bishops. That impression now changed, not least due to the influence of Archbishop Dennis Hurley, of Durban, himself born in South Africa and a South African citizen. In the 1950s it was due to his leadership that the Roman Catholics refused to give up their mission schools and declined to have anything to do with 'Bantu Education' – even if, in 1973, the Catholic bishops 'not without extreme regret' found it impossible to continue financing their schools.

Increasingly the Catholic Church gave its support to the concerns of the Council of Churches and in 1975 there was a Joint Pastoral Letter from the Roman Catholic and Anglo-Catholic Bishops urging their people 'to co-operate in the work of restoring true unity in Christ between our two Churches'. The bishops appealed to the White community for a fundamental change: 'The White community of South Africa has the choice in its hands: a peaceful settlement or violence. History and world opinion are on the Black side ...' When the South African government warned against communism, the bishops retorted: 'The best antidote to Communism is not repression. It is justice.'

The Anglicans

The Africanization of the Churches can be seen not least with regard to the Anglicans and some of its bishops. In 1986 Bishop Desmond Tutu, Nobel Laureate for Peace, was elected Archbishop of Cape Town and head of the 'Church of the Province'.[29] Prior to this appointment he had on critical occasions been a spokesman for the Churches. As archbishop he could speak with great authority on behalf of his Church and of all the Churches in the country and, as president of the AACC, on behalf of the Churches in Africa as a whole. He had been trained by the Community of the Resurrection (CR), Rosettenville, Johannesburg. The twentieth-century Anglican contribution to the Church in South Africa has to a large extent been inspired by the CR.

Of great interest was the consecration of Bishop Sigqibo Dwane as bishop of the Order of Ethiopia, residing in Port Elizabeth. His name, Dwane, showed that he was related to, in fact the grandson of the Ethiopian leader at the beginning of the twentieth century. His grandfather, James M. Dwane, was head of the 'Order of Ethiopia', with limited independence within the Church of the Province. The ecclesiastical process had now been carried to a happy conclusion as the grandson, a well-known theologian and doctoral graduate from King's College, London, was consecrated bishop in the Anglican Communion. At the Lambeth Conference, at London and

Canterbury in 1988, Bishop Dwane stood forward as an authoritative theologian stressing the role of the Anglican community as a family.

A distinguished profile was that of Bishop Alphaeus H. Zulu, 1905–88, assistant Bishop of St John's in the Transkei and in 1968 Bishop of Zululand. It was characteristic of the malignant apartheid situation in the country that the South African government ruled that a Black bishop could not occupy the official residence of Bishophurst in 'White' Eshowe. Apparently unaffected by these racial barriers, Bishop Zulu remained Bishop of Zululand until his retirement in 1975. As a descendant of the royal Zulu clan he took a determined political stand for the affairs of the Zulu people.[30]

In the South African Church situation any attempt at intensifying the life of the mission-related Churches met with a reaction caused by the ever-present problem of the Independent Churches. Bishop Zulu experienced this. In 1948, together with his friend, later Canon Philip Mbatha, he formed a movement within the dioceses of Zululand and Durban called 'The Legion of Christ's Witnesses'. Both men had been influenced by the Community of the Resurrection, and the Legion rallied Zulu Christians to a life of personal dedication. This was expressed by the individual by subscribing to seven personal pledges and experiencing Baptism in the Holy Spirit, in a Church *milieu* generously open to the reality of visions and dreams, healing and exorcism in the name of Christ, driving out evil spirits. Friends of law and order in the clergy were frightened by this, suggesting that the new movement had deviated into Zionist ways. Fortunately a succession of Anglican bishops acknowledged the fact that the Church must be open to surprises from a creative God, and the Legion was permitted to grow. In 1956 sixty people came to the Legion conference, in 1984 approximately 2,000, all welcoming one another with the greeting of the Legionaries 'Christ is the Lord' and the answer 'He is reigning'. The conferences were lively occasions. One of the choruses was of a kind not always heard in Anglican circles:

We mzalwane	(Hey my friend,
Hey wena	Hey you,
	Why is it so silent
Kwathula kwathi du	When Jesus is coming)
Uyeza uJesu	

Just as important was the influence of this intense religious group life on an Anglican order of sisters, which had begun in the 1950s, 'The Community of the Holy Name'. In 1983 there were seventeen sisters in life vows, thirteen in temporary vows, ten novices and one postulant, all centred around prayer and participation in evangelism, teaching, healing, sewing and farming.[31]

The Lutherans

Bishop Manas Buthelezi was at first director of the Natal region of the Christian Institute, a fact which led the apartheid authorities to ban Dr Buthelezi for a decade. He became Bishop of the Lutheran Central diocese, that of the Rand, in 1986. Bishop Buthelezi emerged as 'the nestor of Black Theology in South Africa', while at the same time encouraging the parishes of his diocese.

The Pentecostals

The denominational map of South Africa was modified by the interrelationship of the various Pentecostal groups. There were the Apostolic Faith Mission, the Full Gospel Church and the Assemblies of God, all with both Black and White members, most often Afrikaans-speaking, while the Assemblies of God were English-speaking. Peter Watt's *From Africa's Soil: the Story of the Assemblies of God in Southern Africa*,[32] draws attention to the White leaders in the Assemblies movement, James Mullan, John Bond and others, and to the dissensions between personalities and between groups. In 1964 the American missionaries left the convention and formed their own International Assemblies of God in the country. Undefiled – though not unhurt – by these embarrassments, the great African leader Nicholas Bhengu continued his 'Back to God Crusade', with some useful practical assistance particularly from the American branch, the International Assemblies.

The country-wide charismatic revival in the 1970s showed the way forward towards co-operation and union but, towards the end of the decade, this attempt came to a halt, in a country where apartheid in Church and State was the decisive problem. We underline the role of Nicholas Bhengu (1909–85), great imaginative preacher to the masses – self-taught from his Bible except for a couple of years at the Dumisa Bible school – a great Church leader and a great personality.

Zion

It is not possible to follow in detail the developments which the South African Zion movement has gone through in the twentieth century. Fortunately Dr J. P. Kiernan of the University of Natal, who through decades with sympathetic and personal involvement, studied local Zionist groups at Kwa Mashu, Durban, can make a fundamental distinction alluding to trends of development. 'Christian Zionists' they called themselves, meaning by the term the local succession of Bible-true Zionists hailing from the very first Zulu Zion baptized on 24 May 1904 at Wakkerstroom and adhering strictly to visions and teachings in force then. Others who did not belong to this succession were contemptuously referred to as 'New Zionists', not being of the authentic sort.[33] This is one aspect of the characteristically South African Zion movement.

NAMIBIA

The Churches and the liberation struggle

For long decades Namibia, 'the last colony', seemed the most forgotten corner of the continent. From the end of the 1960s this view was to change drastically: the fate of Namibia was front page news, from the United Nations in New York to Pretoria. Thinly populated, only about 1 million, spread out over vast stretches of desert and savanna, 'South West Africa' was from 1920 a South African mandate territory and a settler colony with enormous riches: diamonds, uranium and karakul lamb: 'Abject poverty in Namibia is the result of policy and distribution, not of any absolute lack of resources or their exploitation.'[34]

The liberation struggle was eventually channelled into the efforts of the SWAPO, founded in 1960, with its leader Sam Nujoma. The struggle was fought both in Namibia and outside its borders. The role of the Churches was in this case particularly great. A prominent European diplomat, emissary of the secretary-general of the United Nations, expressed his view that a leadership of the various Churches 'could hardly be of any help in a development towards political freedom'.[35] Seldom has the proclamation of such an exalted personality been so mistaken as in this case. The role of the Churches in the 1970s and 1980s was indeed crucial.

The Churches' relative strength can be seen from the affiliation numbers: the Lutherans with some 320,000, the Catholics with 120,000, the Dutch Reformed some 50,000 and the Anglicans about 20,000. The Churches took a prominent part in the liberation struggle and had to pay for it: the Anglicans saw three of their English bishops, one after the other, expelled from the country. In 1981 James Hamupanda Kauluma was consecrated as the first African Bishop of Namibia for the Anglicans. The largest of the Churches, the Lutheran Ovambo-Kavango diocese had, more than the others, to shoulder the responsibility of involvement in the political struggle. The Lutheran bishop at this time was a leader of exceptional strength and wisdom, Leonard Auala (1908–83). His father was a king's councillor and his mother of royal descent. Bishop Auala started his career in life like most other Protestant Church leaders in Africa: as a teacher. At twenty-eight years old he found himself younger than most of his students in his class. The Church wanted him as a pastor but he objected: 'I have no calling for the clergy. I am a teacher.' Soon, however, he had to accept ordination and from 1933 was one of the young leaders of the Church. In 1960 he became moderator and in 1963 bishop. His consecration took place on 30 June, 1963. The consecrating bishop, Elis Gulin of Tampere, Finland, in his address made an ecumenical observation of a certain dimension: 'Look at the fellowship of the Church of Christ', this Finnish bishop exhorted. 'Precisely today, 30 June, 1963, in far-away Rome, a new Pope [Paul VI] is being consecrated, on the same day as here the first Bishop of the Ovambo-Kavango Church. The two of you enter your offices under the roof of the same Heavenly Tent. The fellowship of the Church of Christ is wonderful.'[36]

Soon Bishop Auala – a great man and a good man – was faced with unexpected tasks. In 1964 South Africa decided to extend its 'Homelands' policy to Namibia. The population was to be divided into ten little 'Bantustans'. More than anything else this policy was devised to aggravate apartheid and the pernicious migrant labour problem in the country. Bishop Auala faced the minister from Pretoria, de Wet Nel, warning against an enforced application of this plan while the Minister told him to mind his own business. The Plan had nothing to do with the Churches.

At this time the population was increasingly involved in political opposition through the SWAPO and other political parties. The majority of the members of the SWAPO were Ovambo, Bishop Auala's own people.

In June 1971, Namibian Radio announced that the International Law Court in the The Hague had decided that South Africa was in illegal occupation of Namibia, a piece of news which had an electrifying effect on the whole country. From this moment the liberation movement accelerated its efforts. Namibian refugees found their refuge beyond the borders, in Angola, Zambia and in Tanzania.

In 1971 there was a dramatic collision between the prime minister of South Africa, Ballthazar J. Vorster, and bishop Auala. Suddenly the Bishop stood out as the leading churchman in the struggle; the good old Pietist was drawn into a political controversy at the highest level. He told his young Finnish co-worker: 'My dear Mikko, when shall we ever again get time to preach the Gospel?' He said so mockingly for he was a good enough theologian to realize that on this occasion this political action was indeed the way of preaching the Gospel. Together with Bishop Gowaseb of the other Lutheran Church in the country, Bishop Auala published an Open Letter where they held that South Africa had violated a number of Articles in the United Nations Declarations of Human Rights (Articles No. 13, 18, 19, 20, 21, 22 and 25). Bishop Auala told the ministers from Pretoria: 'Your Government has made a mistake. It has despised the people.'

The struggle culminated in a solid, sometimes heated four-hour encounter between Bishop Auala and Prime Minister Vorster. The bishop attacked the apartheid policy, the migrant labour policy and various police methods of torture. 'The Government does not treat us as people but as something evil.'

Strangely, it was to take another twenty years until Namibia was free. In this brief chapter on the Church's role in the struggle, we have not mentioned pastors in the SWAPO, nor the changes in attitude to the Church on the part of successive generations of freedom fighters, all aspects of the Church history of Namibia. Bishop Auala was succeeded by Bishop Kleopas Dumeni.

Further south in the country there were the Churches related to the historically important Rhenish Mission. With increasing nationalism there were breakaways of various kinds from the 'Rhenish'. The Herero, victimized by the German colonial regime until 1920, found strength in their historical past and the memories of their heroes, mainly Chief Maherero and other 'living dead'. Since 1923 there has been an annual Maherero Day. In 1955 the Herero formed their own 'Oruuano' ('Fellowship') Church, a strength for the nationalist movement and oriented both to the people's past and their future. Here one recognizes from intimate expressions of prayer whether the praying person is a real Oruuano member or not: 'that one prays as a white man', one concludes about somebody who prays for other peoples and men and women of other nationalities; the real concern should be to pray for *Ehiretu* ('Our Land'), one's own Church, and for conversion and purification in and through 'Oruuano'.[37]

Another indication of the Churches' protest against South African occupation was the Catholic Church 'strike' on 11 October, 1987, when they closed their doors to the public as a protest against the destruction of the Omolulika Church.[38]

MADAGASCAR

The period between the Malagasy risings of 1947 until 1975 saw serious tension between expatriate missionary leadership and the Lutheran synod.

At the synod in 1950, the first two names for election to the presidency were those of expatriates; a Malagasy, Rakoto Andrianarijaona, only came in third place. There was a power struggle between the Malagasy Church and the missionaries. In 1976 there was tension between the two sections within the Protestant group of chiefs: on the one hand, consisting of the LMS, the Paris Evangelical Mission and the Quakers and, on the other, the Lutherans.

Also in the last quarter of the century the custom of *famadihana* – 'placing the dead' or perhaps better, 'renewed funeral service' – was still practised.[39] The Churches were struggling with the problem. There was a denominational difference in the attitude to this ancient religious custom. Protestants did not officially accept it, though in fact, only very few among them kept away from it. There was, however, a tendency to simplify or modify the feast; in any case it implied an economic tragedy for a poor country such as Madagascar. Psychological reasons made people adhere to it: in the case of women and their fertility it was supposed to be important. Bible reading and hymn singing were added to the actual ceremony and on the occasion there was the usual playing of horns, flutes and drums. Suddenly everything would be quiet. It was announced from the balcony that the dead person had in his lifetime been a Church catechist and had insisted against loud musical playing: his wish should be respected. In general, Protestant Church leaders would insist that one could not, in the long-run, participate in the custom without the Church suffering from it.

The president of the republic, Didier Ratsiraka, took a stand in the matter. On the occasion of a Bible Society meeting in 1985 he announced himself to be a personal Christian, intending to be a regular Bible reader. As such he could not, he said, be present at official ceremonies of *famadihana* with sacrifice of oxen.

The Malagasy Churches developed their special innate gifts, not least in the field of Malagasy music. Eilert Nielsen-Lund's music school at Ambato was immensely popular. The choir had 1,000 young singers with thirty violins and two organs, something of a record for Malagasy Church history. Protestant ecumenism developed not least in the field of music. Reformed and Lutheran Churches achieved a common hymn-book with some 800 hymns. One hundred and seventy bicycling evangelists found their way from the centres into the surroundings.[40]

23

EAST AFRICA

KENYA

Among African nationalist leaders who had studied in Europe or America in their youth, Jomo Kenyatta (1890s–1979) was unique. He took his doctorate at the London School of Economics and Political Science with a fascinating study called *Facing Mount Kenya: the tribal life of the Gikuyu.*[1] The war of liberation (Mau Mau) of 1952–58 made him the most famous 'prison graduate' of his generation. A towering personality with a pragmatic approach to politics he became president at Kenya's independence in 1963. Hailing from Kiambu in Kikuyu, he enhanced the role of the Kikuyu in Kenyan politics: most of his ministers came from the same district. He called his political programme 'Harambee socialism' ('Let's pull together'). Refusing to attach himself to any organized religion of the Church, he nevertheless 'believed in God' and his political speeches were studded with Biblical references.

His successor as president, Daniel arap Moi, grew up with that most fundamentalist of Kenya missions, the Africa Inland Mission and faithfully kept to that community, preaching in the chapel whenever invited to do so, taking for granted that any of his public meetings be opened with prayer to God. He found a Swahili term for his own political ideology, *Nyayo*, meaning 'footsteps', eventually defined as 'Peace, Love and Unity'. His *Nyayo*-ism, Moi claimed, is derived from three sources: African traditions of public affairs; Christian faith; and, pragmatism in governmental politics. As a devoted Christian he regarded the Church as part and parcel of the government. 'Church leaders are just leaders, all leaders must be part of the leadership corps, and *Nyayo* followers.' In his book *Kenya African Nationalism* he often referred to the role of the Christian faith, but never once mentions the institutional Church. 'The Church is not considered as an entity over against the State.'[2]

In Kenyatta's time and in that of his successor the climate of public opinion became increasingly discontented. Tension and violence were bound to appear because of the widening abyss between rich and poor in Kenyan society, 'between the twenty million poor and the twenty millionaires'. The political scene might have appeared strong and unshakeable in this increasingly capitalist country but was, in fact, fragile. 'Water is bitter – what do we drink?' – people would sing, with a strong political undertone. Three of the most brilliant of Kenyan politicians were assassinated: Tom Mboya in 1969, and Robert Ouko in 1990, both members of the Luo community, and J. M. Kariuki in 1975, co-worker and critic of Kenyatta.

The Catholics

In colonial times Kenya appeared as a thoroughly Anglican (CMS) and Protestant place with the Catholics – all the Catholic missionaries were non-British – more or less reduced to the background. In the period following independence the Roman Catholic Church was the most rapidly growing Church in Kenya. Father John Baur, '*Fidei Donum*' priest and Church history professor in East Africa interprets this growth in his *The Catholic Church in Kenya*.[3] He points to a 'post-Mau-Mau conversion boom'. Through the liberation war, traditional structures were disrupted and 'thus the Agikuyu found their *Ngai* in the Father of the suffering Christ, and the spiritual sacrifice of the Mass took the place of their old sacrifices.'[4] The harsh conditions in detention camps and 'transit camps' accentuated the need for a conversion boom. 'If a Gikuyu was on the list of the Christians, he knew that the priest would intervene for him if detained.'[5] The arrival of the Kiltegan Fathers from Ireland at the beginning of the 1950s meant a fresh start in many areas. In 1951 the first five Kiltegan Fathers arrived and by 1955 there were already twenty-two.

Kenya has twenty-three Catholic dioceses. The head of the church was Cardinal Maurice Otunga, Archbishop of Nairobi, who exercised his leadership with quiet strength. Called upon to mediate in matters related to the Catholic provinces further south on the continent, he approached delicate questions with that same strength. Nairobi has the headquarters of a number of Catholic institutions, such as the Kenya Catholic Secretariat, the AMECEA (the Association of Member Episcopal Conferences in Eastern Africa) and the Catholic Institute for East Africa (succeeding the Pastoral Institute, first in Gaba, Uganda and then moving in 1975 to Eldoret in Kenya, under the leadership of Father Aylward Shorter). The growth in Nairobi is striking, with seventeen parishes within the city. Of these, six are served by the Irish Holy Ghost Fathers, three by Maryknoll priests and two by diocesan priests.

This Catholic growth, with some 2.5 million Catholics, was sustained by a number of Western missionaries. There were 660 Western priests and 125 African priests, 973 Western Sisters and 738 African Sisters with 2,000 catechists. The Western missions included Mill Hill, Consolata, Capuchins, Spiritans, St Patrick, Trappists and, finally, the White Fathers – late-comers to Kenya – representing at the centre of the headquarters of East African Catholicism a group concerned with international relations, particularly those of the AMECEA. There are some forty sisters' congregations, of whom nine diocesan had only African Sisters. The Maria Legio which was started in Nairobi, has about 20,000 members. From this amazing concentration of activity and influence, ideas reached out in all directions.

In an Africa, where the Organization of African Unity is weakening and where the East African Community – Kenya, Tanzania and Uganda – has been ruptured, in that Africa, it seems, the only bond of unity that is valid is the communication and policy pursued by the Churches.[6]

Another concern is the pastoral care for the young in the slums, boys and girls, who having left school are unemployed. In 1973 Father Arnold Groll started the *Undugu* (Brotherhood) Society of Kenya. 'Facilities are created for games, drama and music. Craft skills in carpentry, masonry and mechanics are being taught. A small business loan scheme is operated.' About thirty miles outside Nairobi a farm is run where agricultural skills are taught. The whole programme is simply 'basic education in action'. There is also an *Udada* (Sisterhood) club for girls.

Special missionary concern was given to the nomad communities, especially the Pokot after 1977. The message of the New Testament was proclaimed there for the first time. At Christmas 1981 the head of the Pokot was faced with the strange Nativity story. His comment: 'Only the shepherds came, no one else came down to meet Him, nobody else.'

The Protestants

The role of the Anglican Church in Kenya has changed considerably. Earlier on it represented the Establishment – John Lonsdale and others have said: Nairobi's Anglican cathedral has been described, 'not inaccurately, as the colonial power at prayer.'[7] Following independence the congregations in the cathedral and other Anglican dioceses were still, presumably, 'at prayer', but with a difference. Increasingly, Anglican bishops, now all Africans, found themselves as leaders of an, at times, intense opposition. Accusations of ministerial land-grabbing and high-level corruption were levelled by more than one of these Anglican bishops. Some of them had a background in journalism through working on the radical Anglican paper, the *Target*, and as preachers in the Nairobi cathedral. One can hardly overrate the role of this journalistic experience for this generation of gifted, outspoken Anglican bishops.

A couple of names related to that of former Archbishop Manasses Kuria, in Nairobi, should be mentioned here. Bishop Henry Okullu (d. 1999) of Maseno South diocese was a *Target* man and as bishop produced thoughtful books on Church and State. He was the kind of bishop who knew that the Gospel message must be expressed in action. After consultations with the National Christian Council of Kenya he started a project intended to reach and uplift the small farmer in the diocese. Fifty rural development communities at parish level and about five hundred development committees at diocesan level were established in order to promote agriculture and health, and 'to start a movement ... of *conscientization*'.[8] After school education, Bishop Alexander Muge had six years of military training before joining theological schools first in East Africa and then in London. He too was a writer for the *Target*, a welcome place for his sharp criticism of tribalism, nepotism and graft in Church and State. As Bishop of Nakuru he excelled as a critic of corruption and bad government, always quoted at length in the Kenyan news magazine the *Weekly Review*, until he was killed in a car accident in August 1990, aged forty-two. His episcopal colleague, David Gitari had served as a Bible Society secretary before becoming Bishop of Mount Kenya East diocese and later Archbishop of the Province of Kenya.

The Presbyterians were 'almost entirely' a Kikuyu Church with close contacts with the high and mighty in the land. Through family ties the moderator, John Gatu had effective connections with President Kenyatta, sharing the President's views on political independence and on African land rights, a position which, of course, was held by most other Churches. In his youth Gathu joined the army and there spent seven formative years. Few could bring to the task of Church moderator as much authority, confidence and wisdom as did Gathu. Internationally he became renowned for his initiative over the so-called 'moratorium' for the Churches.

Gathu's successor as moderator, George Wanjau, had a preparation for his post which indicates some of the national and international connections of these Churches: Alliance High School (the 'Eton' of Protestant Kenya), teacher training college, Universities of London, Leeds and Lancaster, assistant pastor at the prestigious St Andrew's Church, Nairobi, study at Fuller Theological Seminary, California, USA. His wife was headmistress of St George's Primary School.[9]

With their concentration in the Meru area, the Methodists had at times seemed isolated in their corner of the country. All the more reason why the new Bishop Lawi Imathiu managed to place his Church centrally on the map of Kenya when in 1974 he was nominated by Kenyatta as a member of parliament 1974–79, thus carrying on a Methodist tradition in Britain and elsewhere, of political involvement.

The issue of Christian co-operation and Church unity has been a recurrent theme with the Kenyan Churches ever since the second decade of this century. In the Independent period the Churches were well served by studies of their work, notably the *Kenya Churches Handbook* and a thorough study by Agnes Chepkwony on the National Christian Council of Kenya (NCCK) 1963–78.[10] Dr Chepkwony highlights initiatives taken by the NCCK, on its own, and in co-operation with government. She even asks the question: 'The NCCK as the Agent of the Government?' She maintains:

> The rift in Church–State relations that had started between the NCCK and Churches at independence continued, although it was now reversed. At independence it was the NCCK that was critical of the colonial administration while the Churches played a more cautious game. After independence the NCCK became much closer to the state, while the Churches' relation with the state was at two levels: those congregations and some Church leaders that remained distant, and those Church leaders who joined the NCCK in its close co-operation with the state. Despite this rift, the NCCK effectively used its connections with overseas donor agencies and the Government to bring Churches, including the independent ones, under its umbrella for development while playing the role of an overseer and a co-ordinator.[11]

The NCCK initiated programmes for both rural and urban areas. A creative enterprise for rural areas was that of the 'Village Polytechnics'. In a situation where there was little opportunity for students after primary school, these Village Polytechnics provided two years of practical training, on the inspiration and with the support of the Danish Folk high schools and the Danish International Development Agency (DANIDA). In 1980, 250 such projects had been started with 25,000 trainees and 1,250 instructors.

The Kenya revival retained its characteristics developed over the decades by African leaders, most of them prominent laymen, all devoted to the local and East Africa-wide 'fellowship'. The annual Kenya 'conventions' attracted as many as 20,000 or 30,000 people. This was, however, changing to some extent. Western leaders – from South Africa and from the USA – brought new pressures to bear on the situation. On the scene there arrived the 'African Evangelistic Enterprise', led by Michael Cassidy of South Africa and inspired by the Billy Graham crusade. The big revival 'conventions' now had a number of overseas speakers – mainly North American – and participants were exposed to 'altar calls' and singing was of a different type.

Some revival leaders were engaged full-time in the new 'Enterprise'. Bishop Festo Kivengere, of Kabale, Uganda (d. 1988), travelled internationally for the Enterprise as much as he was in his Kabale diocese. In Tanzania the Anglican Bishop of Morogoro had throughout been an accepted revival leader. Bishop G. Chitemo of Morogoro was now engaged as a full-time worker with the Enterprise.

The number of Independent Churches in Kenya has increased rapidly, for the most part related to the ethnic factor, particularly in Nairobi and in the west of the country (Kisumu and surroundings). A new Pentecostal tradition established itself, above all in the new lease given to the African Independent Pentecostal Church of Africa. Formed in the 1930s, this Church was suppressed during the Mau Mau years. Political independence gave the Church a new opportunity: 'probably, the last example of what may be called the "separation" phenomenon – in this case the re-emergence in the era of political independence of a suppressed independent tradition . . . '[12]

The most striking new group was the 'Maria Legio', which emerged in 1963, the year of Kenya's independence. This was, exceptionally, a breakaway from the Roman Catholic Church, emerging among the Luo and the Kisii in western Kenya and soon comprising some 100,000 members. A survey from 1969 showed that 10 per cent of the members had formerly been Roman Catholics 'in good standing', 40 per cent lapsed, nominal or would-be Catholics, 10 per cent Protestants and about 40 per cent 'Traditional African', before becoming members of the new Church.[13] The Church had its roots in a revelation given to Gaudencia Aoko, a Luo woman. She saw Christ who directed her to found a new Church. About the same time a Roman Catholic catechist, Simeon Ondeto, was risen to heaven and told by Abraham, James and David to baptize all polygamists. Aoko and Ondeto joined forces, Gaudencia becoming a healer, while Ondeto – now appearing as a 'Pope' – appointed six cardinals, seventy-five bishops and a great number of priests. At precisely the same time as, through Vatican II, the Roman Catholics universally abandoned Latin for local languages, Pope Ondeto impressed his followers by retaining Latin phrases in the Mass.

Funerals are of great importance in African religious life. We mention here the most sensational legal case in East Africa in the last few years fought over a funeral in a prominent Christian family in Nairobi. In this book we necessarily deal mostly with poor people – together with kings and chiefs; for a change we shall now meet the wealthy. In December 1986 Mr S. Otieno, successful and wealthy lawyer in Nairobi, died aged fifty-five. His wife Virginia, no less prominent and obviously a personality of enormous strength, prepared for the funeral to take place where, according to Mrs

Otieno, the deceased had decided that he wished to be buried. This was, however, easier said than done. Kenya Radio sent two conflicting messages, the one from the widow inviting to Ngong on Saturday 3 January, 1987, the other from the deceased's brother, announcing that the funeral was to take place in the Siaya district, at the same hour on the same day, a place which the deceased's clan regarded as their very own. The legal struggle dragged on for more than four months – with the dead body meanwhile lying in the Nairobi mortuary. The legal case was fought before the High Court for 154 days and was concluded by a final judgment by the Court of Appeal, the highest legal authority in the land, settling for the deceased's clan and against the widow.

A number of issues were involved in the case: customary law *versus* general law, written law *versus* customary law; two African ethnic communities pitted against each other, Kikuyu (the widow's ethnic community) *versus* Luo (the deceased's ethnic community). The couple belonged to two different denominations: the deceased was Anglican, Mrs Otieno is a Presbyterian. There was also a question whether a woman and a wife had a right to hold a view in the matter. The Luo lawyer insisted that 'women are very migratory in nature . . . You do not leave burial matters in charge of a woman'. Mrs Otieno he continued, 'went out of her way to marry a Luo and having done that I submit that she walked out of her tribe and became a Luo'. The Bible was quoted by the lawyers in defence of the Luo position: 'Mrs Otieno should emulate the biblical Ruth . . . In accordance with the biblical Ruth, Mrs O. should stick to Magdalina A.' (her stepmother-in-law). No wonder that Mrs O. concluded, 'I have now discovered that women are discriminated against in Kenya'. A human, almost superhuman note, followed. Towards the end of the case, Mrs Otieno announced that she had been 'born again' and had found 'salvation in Jesus'. 'I will fight them [in court] with the assistance of Jesus'. In the courtroom she walked to her brother-in-law, shook hands with him and said 'May God save you. You should get saved and leave my husband alone'. There was no answer.

UGANDA

The Church's history in Uganda, 1970–85, is an object lesson in survival, how to steer through years of intimidation and terror and to keep the flock together in the face of an impossible situation, getting worse day by day. We recall the situation of the Churches before being hit by this disaster. For a number of countries along and above the equator one can discern, as we have already pointed out, a 'north–south syndrome', a tension in the country between a privileged south and a neglected north. Nowhere was this rift as frightening as in Uganda; ethnic tensions between Nilotic and Bantu, between a school-educated south and a military-trained north. These tensions had been there but contained throughout the colonial period, but in the period following independence they developed into violence, terror and sometimes war.

In the southern half of the country just prior to independence the political situation had developed into a struggle between two parties representing – basically – the two competing religious denominations: Uganda Peoples Congress for the Anglicans and the Democratic Party for the Catholics. In the last few years before independence, in the kingdom of Buganda, an extra political effort was made by members of both denominations: *Kabaka Yekka* (Kabaka Alone).

In 1962 Obote, a northerner, managed to achieve a fragile alliance between the Ugandan Peoples Congress and Buganda's *Kabaka Yekka* and defeated the Democratic Party in elections. This alliance did not last long, however. In 1967 Obote sent his troops under a hefty northerner, Colonel Amin against the *kabaka*'s palace at Mengo near Kampala. The king of Buganda fled to London, where he died in 1969. Soon it was Obote's own turn: when he left in 1971 for the Commonwealth conference in Singapore he was toppled by Amin who, in a coup, took over the post of President 'and in an almost literal sense all hell was then let loose'.

Amin and the others

With regard to the Churches Amin at first gave an impression of co-operation but soon showed his true face which was that of a terrorist in the president's chair. Amin's years, 1971–79, became an unmitigated disaster. Among the victims was the Anglican archbishop Janani Luwum, himself a northerner. A letter of protest signed by the Anglican bishops with the archbishop had been sent to Amin and there was no other response than murder in 1977. 'A joint letter with the Roman Catholics would perhaps have saved the Archbishop's life.'[14]

In 1979 Amin's misrule came to an end as the Tanzanian forces, through enormous effort, managed to defeat Amin. After various attempts by other short-lived rulers, Obote returned for a second term, 1980–85. In 1985 Yoweri Museveni's National Resistance Movement (NRM) 'seized power with a dramatic improvement in security'. Representing 'the left-leaning Bahima intelligentsia of post-independent Uganda', a son of Ankole, Museveni was the man for the moment and the future, representing the intelligentsia of East Africa – having studied at the University of Dar es Salaam. (Whether there might arise a competitor in Ronald Mutebi, the *kabaka*'s son, is another question to be answered by an as yet unknown future.) Museveni was not helped by Ma Lakwena, a charismatic prophetess who appeared to threaten his power for some time, supported as she claimed by 140,000 spirits and parts of animate and inanimate nature, bees, snakes, rivers, rocks and so on. A hundred years after the Uganda Martyrs of 1885 the 'Martyrs seminary' at Namugongo was attacked by an army and a large number of people including the principal were killed.

The dimension of loss in human life can only be guessed at. A document prepared in late 1986 for the new NRM government led by Yoweri Museveni stated that 'Obote and Amin must have by now killed over 800,000 Ugandans between them over the past twenty-two years of so called independence.'[15] This estimate does not include the immense loss to the country and to Africa as a whole, of those who in frustration left Uganda, splendid generations of an educated elite looking for a future elsewhere.

The Churches

The economy of a country basically fertile and potentially prosperous was in Obote's and Amin's time reduced to a rule of *magendo*, the modern Luganda term for any activity of black market and corruption. In the midst of it all, the Church was a bulwark and a sign of hope. Here also the Catholics were greatly inspired by Vatican II. Pope Paul VI visited Kampala in 1969 and brought encouragement and direction to the Church, incidentally also emphasizing ecumenical relationships with the Anglicans. A Church council for Anglicans, Catholics and Orthodox had been formed in 1964 but denominational tensions were sometimes aggravated by the political parties. Politically the Catholics moved cautiously. When several priests managed to win seats in the Ugandan parliament in the February 1989 general election – in itself a recognition of the local leadership which they exercised – Cardinal Em. Nsubuga told them to resign their positions. Priests were, according to Canon 285 of the Code of Canon Law, not allowed to play a part in party politics: 'their proper task was to serve God'.[16]

The Catholics

The Catholic Church had 520 diocesan priests most of them Africans and over 350 expatriate missionaries, while there were 1,760 expatriate sisters. For the Catholics in the 1960s the centre of gravity was still to be found in the south of the country, in the Masaka diocese, with its 428,000 Catholics and twenty-seven parishes, a diocese almost totally Africanized. Only four of the parishes were run by White missionaries, an exception which was allowed in order to demonstrate the universality of the Church. The diocese had monasteries of African orders, *Bannabikira* and *Bannakaroli*, with Cistercians of rigid observance in Butende, medical missionary sisters in Kitovu and White Sisters in Villa Maria. Led by Bishop Adrian K. Ddungu, they were seen as a 'conservative' diocese with a sense of tradition and history, deeper perhaps than in any other in Eastern Africa, a history ably interpreted by one of their own priests, the Revd Father John Waliggo in his doctoral thesis.[17]

Next to Masaka there was Mbarara which received its first Ankole bishop in 1969, consecrated by Pope Paul VI at the time of his visit to Kampala. The new bishop sometimes looked for advice from his old predecessor, Canadian Bishop F. X. Lacoursière W.F., who had arrived in 1914 and died in 1970, aged eighty-five. In 1934 he had been made 'Bishop of Ruwenzori', which then meant all of western Uganda. He ran it all, looking after schools, seminaries, development schemes, often hiking for five to six hours in the tropical sun. A practical man, he loved to repair broken Pentomax lamps in the missions, free of charge.[18] There were also African 'Sisters of the Lady of Good Advice'.

In the north of Uganda, Bishop Cesana (Verona Fathers) of Gulu had retired from his diocese and devoted the rest of his life to 240 leprosy patients at Morulom. At Moroto in 1970 a new missionary order was formed, 'the Apostles of Jesus', totally African in so far as initiative, leadership and support were concerned and creatively taken up in other parts of East Africa, Moshi, Nairobi etc.

Both Churches, Catholic and Anglican, had experienced and maintained the traditional abyss between them. Vatican II also brought a change in the ecumenical climate of Uganda. Just before Vatican II, Archbishop Cabana, French Canadian W.F., retired and went to Quebec. Before leaving he invited the Anglican archbishop to his residence. There he took out his *pallium* and placed it round the Anglican's shoulders, a unique gesture of appreciation.[19]

In spite of the appearance of an unchangeable Catholic citadel, changes were on the way, Toro being one example. Lay influence in the 1960s managed to form a Toro Catholic Council, composed of only laymen. This made the Bishop critical of the movement and in 1966 the council was officially disbanded. Dr Kassimir studied the role of the 'associations' related to the diocese. The role of the Legion of Mary, a highly structured organization, changed: educated people tended to abandon it and a 'Charismatic Renewal movement' attracted increased attention.

The Anglicans

When the Anglican Bishop Brown arrived in 1953 – after twenty-five years of distinguished service in South India – he was to discover things about the established place of the Anglican Church in Uganda society. As Anglican bishop he was, according to Ugandan protocol, placed in the third place, after governor and *kabaka*, 'often consulted by both of them'.[20] One could not make any mistakes about it: 'Every kind of social or political occasion – the *kabaka*'s birthday, Independence Day, the Queen's birthday – was marked by a State service in Namirembe Cathedral' and the Anglican bishop was supposed to preach each time as a matter of course. In 1961 the Anglican community was established as an independent Church province, with the Bishop of Kampala as archbishop. Until then there had been two Anglican dioceses; these were now divided into eight and soon into twenty-three. The shortage of priests was keenly felt: for forty or even ninety parishes there might be one priest. After the Service of Inauguration of Bishop Brown he greeted the jubilant crowds on the hills of Namirembe. As a good Evangelical he carried his mitre in his hand: 'The people shouted to me to put on my hat and I did so.' Traditions hallowed by the rules of Bishops Tucker and Willis were about to be changed, due to the pressures of African participation. In the Evangelical diocese it was taken for granted that when the bishop visited he always celebrated Holy Communion. 'No one had taught them this. It was felt instinctively by the Christians.'

This established order of things was to be shaken out of all recognition. It began with happenings up north. From now on one got used to the idea that most changes, and the traumatic ones at that, came from the north. One day in October 1965, the porter announced to Archbishop Brown that two men wanted to see him: they said they were bishops but, he added, 'they did not look like it'. They came from the north. They were assistant bishops Ngalamu and Dotiro, coming from the massacres of civilians in southern Sudan at Juba and Wau. They decided to see the archbishop and the journey had taken three months, so they could not appear as spruce as they might have wished to. 'Almost everything belonging to the Sudanese Christians had been destroyed except their faith.'[21] From the west, from Burundi, Tutsi refugees were streaming into the country, particularly the Kigezi in the south of the country.

With twenty dioceses spread over the country, the Anglican province, with some 4 million adherents, had 760 priests. The active revival movement within the Church had a total community of 450,000 members, particularly strong in the southern diocese of Kigezi, under the leadership of Bishop Festo Kivengere (d. 1988), an internationally renowned preacher. Now there were also ethnic tensions within the Church, shown sometimes in connection with the appointment of new bishops. The first African Anglican archbishop Erica Sabiti came not from Buganda but from the west of the country and he therefore found difficulties in being accepted in the archbishop's house on the Anglican hill of Namirembe, Kampala.

Busoga, in the south-east with its diocesan centre at Mbale, (population 40 per cent Anglican, 38 per cent Catholic and 7 per cent other denominations) is an example of the Development work with which the dioceses are concerned. In 1979 a Multi-Sectoral Rural Development Programme was launched. Dr Tom Tuma has played a leading role in guiding this programme at the same time acting as an inspiring factor in the co-operation of East African Theological colleges. Hundreds of wells and bore-holes have been dug and the people co-operate in order to improve health and agricultural production. The most encouraging aspect about the work, he felt, is that it is 'people-centred'.

TANZANIA

Certain dates stand out in the development of the country after Tanzania's independence in 1961. In 1964 Tanganyika was united with Zanzibar, expressed in the name of Tan*zan*ia. In 1967, through the Arusha Declaration, *ujamaa* became the socialist ideology of the TANU (later CCM) party and of the nation. Julius Nyerere did not, as did some other African leaders, align himself with any 'Marxist–Leninist' proclamation. In the local political propaganda, with not least Christian teachers supporting the regime, *ujamaa* socialism was recognized as a modern variation of 'our own age-old African collective solidarity'. In 1973 'villagization' was made compulsory, a measure which in some cases was carried through with a certain harshness. *Ujamaa* – a Swahili word for family relationship or brotherhood – was Tanzania's watchword under the guidance of Julius Nyerere, creating a united country from 120 ethnic communities. After 1974 Tanzania was to share to the full the economic lot of many African states – but through it all people and president carried the burden together, just as together they were to carry the burden of hundreds of thousands of refugees coming into their country across the frontiers.

Nyerere had himself started as a devoted teacher in a Catholic secondary school. As president he took a keen personal and ecumenical interest in the affairs of the Churches, ever ready to encourage and promote their activities, be it the consecration of a new cathedral, the opening of an agricultural show or the life of a hidden African sisterhood.

From the outset Tanzania decided on Swahili as its *lingua franca*, a decision of great democratic importance. In neighbouring countries the Western language, English, was the preference, with a resulting distance between a privileged elite and the members of a less fortunate mass of the people. In Swahili-speaking Tanzania any individual could find a ready hearing when turning to the authorities.

In 1983 the strict socialist programme was followed by a new agricultural policy of privatization of agriculture. Villagization was thus followed by 'a kind of de-villagization process reintroducing private large-scale farming and a liberalization process, initiated in 1984, enabling private business to participate fully in the revitalization process of the Tanzanian economy'.[22] Three adverse factors counteracted the country's socialist programme:

(i) the oil crisis in the 1970s;
(ii) Amin's war at the end of the 1970s which cost Tanzania 500 million dollars; and
(iii) the dramatic depreciation of the country's largest export commodity, coffee.

The value of the Tanzanian shilling dropped ominously. 'My monthly earnings of 2,790 shillings last only five days a month.' The peasants felt that they were 'uncaptured'[23] and the industrial workers and government servants had to find new ways and means.

Teachers were affected and with them the entire school system: a private educational system emerged within the public school system. Crucial was the woman's expanding economic role: her work in the continuous production of crops, selling of foodstuffs and other small-scale trading activities 'almost invariably exceeded the income of her employed husband or other employed family members'. An informal economy emerged, hesitatingly at first and then rapidly. In 1970 the self-employed accounted for 15 per cent of the population. By 1980 this figure had risen to 76 per cent.[24]

The Churches hold a relatively strong position in Tanzania. No aggressive proclamations, say, from the north of the continent could argue away or effectively order away this solid fact. After 1961 Church geography in Tanzania changed. Until 1961, the Church was largely to be found inland, related to different ethnic communities. After 1961 new generations found their way and their living in the capital, Dar es Salaam and along the coast and its hinterland, with rapidly growing parishes and institutions. The politics and the economy of the country may have experienced increasing problems, up until the present day. However, the Churches in Tanzania seem, humanly speaking, to be very much alive, offering to the educated and to the less educated, to the poor and to the desperately poor a haven, a 'place to feel at home'.

With the changing sociology of the country the role of the Churches also changed. Urbanization was a crucial factor, both with regard to the capital, Dar es Salaam, its parishes and the emerging network of smaller towns. Some of these towns increased rapidly, for example, Mbeya in the south, a railway junction on the new Chinese-constructed Tanzania–Zambia railway. Economic forces brought the younger generations, particularly the secondary school- and university-trained youth, to the capital and the new towns, there representing both a new bureaucracy and an impoverished jobless multitude.

Tanzania has an amazingly strong Roman Catholic Church with its twenty-seven dioceses, its imaginative Church strategy energetically followed up locally, its cardinal, Laurian Rugambwa, in Dar es Salaam (since 1963), its Orders for men and women, Africans and Westerners, and its impressive institutions. Fr Aylward Shorter in 1983–84 made a study of the 'pastoral anthropology' of the Catholic communities in the city and in the new towns. These centres required a 'specialized apostolate' for different categories of people such as university students, seafarers and fishermen, market women etc. For this work forty-five White Fathers were engaged. In the different towns this might imply forming 'small Christian communities' in the urban areas; smaller groups praying the rosary together; a student centre for seven schools (*Tabora*); sports clubs; a full-time hospital chaplain becoming a full member of the hospital staff; pastoral care of prisons and military barracks; or organizing an all-night vigil with Mass at dawn for between four and five hundred people.

The position of the Catholic Church in the *ujamaa* society of Tanzania was symbolically strengthened by the act of Bishop Christopher Mwoleka of Rulenge – beyond Lake Victoria – when he abandoned his episcopal residence in order to live with his flock in the *ujamaa* village itself. Vatican II also brought a new sense of liberation in Tanzania, exchanging the strict old uniform for a new outfit, not least with regard to some of the new foreign missionaries. They were searching for a more adequate approach, applied to the some of the hitherto neglected, forgotten communities. Father Vincent J. Donovan served among the Masai:

> Sitting facing me were several people. One was an illiterate elder; another a younger elder who could read and write. There was also a woman gifted in singing and in explaining the Christian message to non-Christians. And finally there was a preacher and a prayer ... I was preparing them to take over their Christian communities. I was training them for the priesthood ... The new song waiting to be sung ... is simply the song of creation. To move away from the theology of salvation to the theology of creation may be the task of our time.[25]

More daring than most in applying a Theology of Creation was Father Gerry Kohler, saying Mass in old cult places and with a baptism, often mass baptism, without much preparatory teaching.

The Anglican Church has its two sections, Evangelical in the centre of the country sustained by a lively revival movement with a very noticeable lay element and an Anglo-Catholic section along the coast, from the Usambaras to Masasi in the south, with Bishop Trevor Huddleston for some years at Masasi. The case of the Anglo-Catholic layman, Edmund John Sepeku, is revealing. He held a prominent position at Radio Tanzania but suddenly gave it up: on the night of 9 July 1967, he heard a voice:

> 'Be prepared to receive a guest, Jesus Christ'. I had been paid highly, £100 a month. I left all that. With a nice car, a Peugeot 403. I left all that. With a telephone in my house and in the office. I left all that. To accept Jesus' call.

He visited a man whose leg was swollen:

> I prayed for him. After three days of prayer that man was cured ... I was so terrified because I never expected it. I never expected it at all. I was only praying.
>
> I introduced prayers in my church – every Friday from 5 to 6. I started with people complaining of headaches, stomach aches, chest trouble. Gradually I prayed for women possessed by demons. The Holy Spirit was my wonderful teacher, not books about healing.

At Ilala he faced thousands of patients:

> I stayed there, fasting and praying; amongst them, there were crippled and blind people.

The Evangelical Lutheran Church had seven dioceses when officially formed in 1963 and now has sixteen dioceses, the result of concentration on linguistic communities. The greatest leader among the Lutherans was Bishop Josiah Kibira (1924–88), placed in Bukoba in the far west of the country and at the same time entrusted with the prestigious position of being president, 1977–84, of the Lutheran World Federation. His older brother, Emanuel Kibira was general secretary of the Bible Society of Tanzania. In the Tanganyika of the 1930s the Lutheran Teacher Training College at Marangu, Kilimanjaro, with its German and African staff, announced an essay competition in order to stimulate student writing. There was a generous prize offered for the winner, a trip to the United States. A bright young man named Stefano Moshi was the lucky winner. However, the pious organizers had second thoughts, far from realizing the urgency of the expectation of those who had engaged in the contest. 'One never knows what could happen to you in New York with all its temptations. You get your prize some other time, later on. Not yet. You just wait.' It took exactly twenty years until the Revd Stefano Moshi, one of the truly great leaders of the African Church and soon to become presiding bishop in the Evangelical Lutheran Church of Tanzania, was able to make that trip to the West, then to meet another time and another world altogether. As presiding bishop of the ELCT he was in the 1960s to go many times to the West, particularly to the United States.

The Moravians had significant traditions in the west and south and in co-operation with Anglicans and Lutherans. They have given special scope to women's initiative in the Church and formed the largest Moravian province in the world. The Mennonites in the far west, the Africa Inland Church in the west and the Baptists in the north found new centres for their activities. And the Pentecostals? Once we wrote to them asking how and where they defined their field (in connection with a Missionary Atlas which this author produced). They did not understand our question, 'Tanzania as a whole, of course, was their field', neither more nor less. Pentecostal Assemblies increased in number from sixty in 1967 to 160 in 1975. In independent Africa with its serious refugee problem the Pentecostals could also point to the fact that their numbers had largely increased by the hurried arrival of Pentecostals from Burundi, settling in their hundreds of thousands in south-central Tanzania and establishing, on the savannah, an intense Pentecostal community.

The Protestant Churches were stimulated by the move to town and city, liberating a new lay activity in the local parish through some of the following lay initiatives: Bible study groups; women's evangelization teams, particularly among the Nyakyusa and Bena Churches in the south; women's drama performances, not least among the Moravians in the Rungwe area (here following an old Moravian tradition in fostering the Moravian rule of collecting life histories of individual Church members); revival fellowship groups; and home visitation groups. Both the Bible study group and the church choir in the city had a social aspect in bringing lay members together in an active fellowship. The characteristic choir singing was often related to the local musical heritage, with words and tunes from the home district, thus serving to strengthen the links between local culture and city church.

Unique in East Africa was an ecumenical fellowship on the widest possible scale, including Islam in the Bukoba district of Tanzania. The name was *Liro*, a short term for *L*utherans, *I*slam, and *R*oman Catholics. It was formed in 1979 on a loose basis but none the less challenging: its concerns were common educational and social interests. In 1985 the group renamed itself *Umaka*.

Finally, we mention that army of anonymous actors in the Church during the period of Independence 1960–90, Catholic and Protestant, comprised of the women in the Church. We make this brief reference here for Tanzania while taking for granted that these lines also apply in various ways to women in other African countries. There is a new generation of women growing up in the cites, victims of a man's world. Consider 'Salome', of Pare. Her husband died early leaving her with nine children, the youngest two years old. Salome saw to it that they all had a good education – secondary school, university etc. – applying for this remarkable achievement the great African principle of financial solidarity of the extended family. 'The university-trained daughters are the first generation in public leadership, but it is only when the nature of their background is known that the sources of their creative work can be appreciated.'[26] In another part of Tanzania, 'Judith' together with her children managed, little by little, to put money aside, by selling bunches of bananas, so that she could buy her own plot of land; no one could now claim the land on the excuse of it being part of the male right to inheritance.

Leadership emerges with regard to two categories of women. First, they can take things into their own hands after becoming widows, divorcees or otherwise independent. Secondly, they can become leaders as primary school teachers in their own ethnic area. Great inspiration was given by the women's political organization UWT (*Umoja wa Wanawake wa Tanzania* – the Women's Union of Tanzania), related to the political party, CCM (previously, TANU). One of these anonymous women formulated it all in these words: 'Because of Nyerere I am free to speak'. It is often overlooked that the politically involved women are at the same time prominent in the women's groups of their Church. If this is not readily conceivable to a person thinking in secularized Western terms one must try to realize that in Tanzania, and in Africa as a whole, this is often a rule. Our best example is Thecla Mchauru of Dar es Salaam, for many years president of the Tanzanian women's political organization, UWT. Nobody could refer with greater affection to her Masasi bishops, 'Father Vincent' (Lucas) or 'Father

Trevor' (Huddleston) than this brave political lady. In Tanzania there must be thousands of women who combine leadership both in the political organizations and in some Church groups, such as their local organizations called 'Bethania'. In 1962 the Dar es Salaam women were the hosts for an All Africa Women's Congress, providing opportunities for meeting with African women leaders from all over the continent.

Apart from the country-wide and the continent-wide women's organization, another aspect was sometimes overlooked: local forms of associations. Professor Marja-Liisa Swantz mentions the following: women's credit associations on the coast, dance societies across tribal borders in Dar es Salaam; associations of instructresses of young girls; aspects of ritual cult groups; informal social and religious groups of mutual support; and age and neighbourhood groups, all aiding one another in work and in preparations for feasts and funerals.[27]

24

ECUMENICAL PERSPECTIVES

THE CATHOLICS AND VATICAN II

The Popes and Africa

The strength of the Roman Catholic Church had always been its solid foundations, its tradition, language, law and liturgy. Then the good Pope Johannes XXIII called the Church to an *aggiornamento*, and the Church was hit by the greatest spiritual change and challenge, yes, revolution, of the latter part of the twentieth century: Vatican II. To a degree which cannot be fathomed, at least not by a Protestant observer, the local dioceses of the Church in Africa, under African bishops, realized that they were now placed in a completely new situation, standing at the door to the future.

Pope Pius XII showed the way. His role cannot be referred to without mentioning his initiative in 1957, the encyclical *Fidei Donum*. In his Easter message of 1957 the Pope suggested that bishops in the 'First World' send some of their priests to Africa for a certain period. In fact these priests worked on average nine years in Africa, their average age being around fifty years old. In 1982 the following numbers were involved in the *Fidei Donum* programme: in North Africa thirty-seven, in Black Africa 124, and on Madagascar fourteen, devoted to the following tasks: pastoral service; Catholic Action; schools; and theological seminaries with catechetical training. Examples are known of priests who have served for over thirty years in this capacity, far beyond the retirement age.[1]

In 1969 Pope Paul VI visited Kampala, and consecrated twelve African bishops. He gave a challenging appeal to the bishops and the Church as a whole, in words which since then have been repeated over and over again: 'You can and you must have an African Christianity ... Now you Africans are your own missionaries, with an indigenous apostolate totally your own.' This visit of 1969 was followed by the visits of Pope John Paul II in 1980, 1982, 1985, 1988 and 1989 to East and West Africa, to Central Africa, to the South, and to Madagascar. These papal visits included the beatification of

Sister Anuarite in Kinshasa, murdered in 1964, Father Gérard, OMI, Roma, Lesotho, Jean Bernhard Rousseau, helper of the nineteenth-century slaves of Réunion, and Victoire Rasoamanrivo, devoted Malagasy Christian at the end of the nineteenth century.

These papal visits established a new and close personal relationship between the Pope and the Church in Africa. Nothing could to the same extent dramatize the Pope's concern for, and involvement in, the Church in Africa, sending happy reverberations throughout the villages and the cities and the slums. 'The Pope is coming to wash off our sins', cried some. Others again: 'Paul VI went to Uganda, and Uganda is a land of martyrs so nobody was surprised that a Pope went there on a pilgrimage. But John Paul is satisfied to come to Black Africa'.[2]

At Kampala Paul VI followed up the message of Vatican II underlining the necessity of ecumenical fellowship with the other Churches. As he visited Namugongo, the shrine of the Buganda martyrs, he was accompanied by, among others, the Anglican archbishop of Uganda, Leslie Brown. In the search for fellowship with other religious bodies Pope John Paul went out of his way to contact Muslim crowds in Nigeria, and he extended the 1985 visit by going to Morocco, on the invitation of King Hassan. At Casablanca he spoke to 80,000 Muslims of the common heritage in Abraham of old and of the common faith in one God, a message which opened vistas into the distant future of the continent of Africa.

From the point of view of long history, over the centuries and the millennia a most remarkable ecumenical meeting took place in Rome in 1973 between Egypt's Patriarch (Pope) Shenouda III – followed by nine bishops – and Pope Paul VI. Together they recalled the unhappy division following upon the Church Council in Chalcedon in 451. In a common declaration the two heads of Churches agreed on a declaration where they significantly referred to 'Apostolic traditions in agreement with the first *three* councils' (our italics), thus wisely avoiding any reference to Chalcedon. This time East and West were able to agree on a common creedal statement on the Sacraments, on the Blessed Virgin Mary and on the Saints, finding that the Catholic Church and the Coptic Church in wide measure held to the same understanding of the Church.[3]

African bishops at Vatican II

In and through its four lengthy sessions 1962–64 the Council went through dramatic changes, the most important being a new, Biblically oriented interpretation of the Church, seen no longer as primarily a static hierarchic institution but, dynamically, as the People of God in the world. All the other decisions of the Council were in fact derived from that central and fundamental insight, a fruit of the Biblical renaissance in Catholic scholarship in the decades preceding the Council.[4] A non-Catholic writer cannot entirely omit to mention a couple of other names: Oscar Cullmann and Nils Astrup Dahl. To the central results of the Council belonged the discovery of the Church as 'sacrament of salvation'. In the debates Cardinal Rugambwa of Tanzania, on behalf of the Africa bishops developed this idea: 'The Church is not a museum but a school of life. Priests must not be men of the past but should, from the inside, animate the emerging new world in order to save it.' Archbishop Tchidimbo from West Africa underlined: 'From Europe we have only use for the Gospel and nothing but the Gospel.' Their colleague Paul Zoungrana of Ouagadougou called out in moving words: 'Tell the world that Jesus Christ is the Revelation of God so that the world may believe and that the face of Jesus Christ may shine ever more over the earth.'

At the Council, Africa was represented by 260 prelates of whom at the time the majority were Westerners while sixty-one were Africans (one cardinal, thirteen archbishops and forty-seven bishops). The African bishops organized their own secretariat with Cardinal Rugambwa as chairman, Bishop J. B. Zoa as secretary for the French-speaking section and Bishop J. Blomjous as secretary for the English-speaking section. Among other leading bishops Zoungrana of Ouagadougou, Tchidimbo of Guinea and Rakatomalala of Madagascar, must be mentioned together with Coptic and Melkite bishops from Egypt.

The role of the African episcopate at the Council was summed up by Fr Congar, leading theologian at the Council, in saying that this was 'one of the revelations of the Council'.[5]

Pastoral concerns

Initiatives grew out of the Vatican II experience, with a new freedom of the spirit and of initiative following upon the Council: theologically, liturgically and sociologically. The Catholic Church had to struggle with the success of a rapid growth of Church numbers: enormous dioceses and Church provinces – but with alarmingly few African priests. How were these problems to be overcome? Some enterprising bishops discovered that they had to come to terms with new sociological facts of modern African Church life, the local quarter of the city or the hillside in the country. Here the idea of 'basic communities' emerged.

Nobody caught this new dimension as relevantly as the diocese in Kinshasa and Cardinal Malula. He responded to the challenges with enthusiasm and optimism: 'We have achieved something new', he referred then to the so-called *bakambi* of Kinshasa.[6] Kinshasa was not alone, as other dioceses in Pointe Noire, in Lilongwe, in Nairobi and elsewhere had the same idea and applied it, sometimes with new terms. The *bakambi* arrangement included selection of a certain number of laymen who, while continuing in their ordinary jobs, would receive some three years' training – weekends were the natural time for this. They became *bakambi*, animators for a parish in a certain part of the city, giving pastoral care and distributing the consecrated elements of the Eucharist.

Fr Tellkamp's warning of 1950 might have appeared unnecessarily alarming at the time, but it was going to be repeated with increasing concern in the following decades, more particularly when, in the 1970s and the 1980s, there appeared a serious decline in the numbers of the clergy in the West. After the independence of Africa the seriousness of the problem was increasingly felt. Two scholars have, more than others, considered the weight of Church statistics, Dr David Barrett and Professor Adrian Hastings. In considering in 1980 the rapid growth of the Churches Dr Barrett suggested that 'under the most favourable circumstances their growth could become catastrophic',[7] and Professor Hastings added: 'Such figures are frankly terrifying, at least when no one is doing the church planning that such an increase demands'.[8] Professor Hastings pointed out that while the great majority of Catholic bishops were Black the overwhelming majority of priests remained White – in some cases as much as 80 per cent. In Nigeria and in Tanzania a notable increase of African priests could be registered but not elsewhere. The total increase of secular African priests for the rest of the continent was only eighty per year, and the pastoral ratio, including only such priests as were actually engaged in pastoral work, was worsening. An example can be quoted from Tororo, Uganda, with 120 priests of whom only thirty were African and the rest, ninety, expatriate. The pastoral ratio was one priest to 8,642 faithful. In Rwanda-Burundi the pastoral ratio was one to 8,000. A consequence of all this is that the priest is being reduced to a travelling agent of the sacraments.

Yet, things change. While this was the situation even in the first years of the 1980s, it has changed to a remarkable degree in the last few years of the decade. This is related, we think, to the general social and political situation in African states, not very encouraging as this unfortunately is. With the loss of guidance from the side of the state, young people increasingly turn to the one power which seems to offer hope and a worthwhile future, the

Church. The *Camec* statistics – by the Catholic Missionary Education Centre in London – show a determined increase in the number of ordinations in the dioceses in Africa: 102 in 1967, 258 in 1977, 420 in 1987 and 518 in 1988. 'There is a real vocation explosion in Africa as well as in Asia and Latin America'.[9]

African liturgies

Africanization was the new motto and Vatican II caused a new expectation and liberated new powers of mobilization and creativity, stimulating the use of African language, rhythm, colour and happy participation, claiming 'Africa's right to be different'.[10] This can be seen in such liturgical acts as ordinarily perhaps might be written off as plain and unassuming, but were now given a new exciting form. The Mossi of Burkina Faso did this with their structure for 'Entrance into the Catechumenate'. Who ever thought of making this into something exciting. The Mossi did. There was now a special form of Welcoming the Strangers, preliminary interrogation, exorcism and signation, welcome drink (consisting of water and salt, prepared by godparents), naming ceremony and entrance procession into the family section of the church.[11]

For the Eucharist, new eucharistic prayers were formulated. Our example comes from Kenya:

Priest: O Father Great Elder,
we have no words to thank you
Congregation: Listen to us, aged God
Listen to us, ancient God
who has ears
Look at us, aged God
ancient God
who has eyes
Receive us, aged God
Ancient God
who has hands

Soon there was a whole series of new forms of the Mass, often with fascinating names, the Zaïrean rite, the Mass of the Lagunes, the Mass of the Savanna, the Ndzon-Melen Mass (the last mentioned in the diocese of Yaoundé). Uzukwu says of the Yaoundé Mass:

> The second part of the liturgy is dominated by joy – dancing and singing. This joy bursts out with the Offertory procession whose colour and brilliance

> lends itself ... to the image of a celestial liturgy. At the Sanctus, designated young maidens surround the altar to await the bridegroom; they are joined by the choir after the consecration and all sing the hymn of praise, Gloria, to welcome Emmanuel.[12]

For the Zaïre rite the local parish of St Alphonsus, Kinshasa, has nobles on either side of the celebrant carrying spears (honouring a dignitary). The celebrant wears a hat and each minister has his special vestment. The Zaïrean rite has been criticized for being too bold in its use of folklore, but says Uzukwu, it is 'rather the creation of a conducive atmosphere for the encounter between the community and God'.[13]

Or take the Church in Brazzaville at the time of the All Saints ritual, November 1, carried out in a supposedly Marxist–Leninist *milieu*. During his time as abbé, Cardinal Batantu of Brazzaville used traditional Laari waking ceremonies, Christianized with its all-night songs, and the dead member of the community speaks:

> E-e e weep over me my brothers,
> But be not contented only with weeping,
> Pray for me.
> I am (getting) ready to appear before God's throne,
> I do not know what is in store (for me) there.
> Do you understand brothers?
> Weep for me brothers. (E-e e ...)[14]

An African Council – chance or chimera?

Vatican II was taken very seriously by the Catholics in Africa and its visions were translated into the hope for an African Council. The idea had taken form in discussions throughout the 1970s and was first expressed by Alioune Diop. His circle round *Présence Africaine* organized and promoted cultural conferences of all sorts and sizes and it seemed logical to look towards an African Church Council, on African initiative while as a matter of course in close and necessary unity with the Bishop of Rome and the Holy See. In 1980 the bishops of Zaïre had the occasion to present the idea to Pope John Paul, at his visit in Zaïre: an African Council 'or at least an African Synod', as the bishops formulated their humble appeal. In 1983 the Pope referred to the proposal as 'a consultation necessary in one form or another',[15] and in the same year Bishop Tshibangu pressed the issue by underlining that the Council must take place in the course of the 1980s, 'that is, before 1990 so that it will respond to the necessity of the actual historic moment'.[16]

A number of prominent African churchmen and theologians have spoken to or written about these plans: Cardinals Malula and Zoungrana, Archbishop Zoa, Bishop Tshibangu, Professors Engelbert Mveng and E. J. Penoukou, Fr J. M. Ela and others. Themes for consideration by such a council are not lacking: new forms of the ministry, liturgies, spirituality, Church and society, political dependence and the promotion of justice, etc., all aiming at 'an African church for Africans'. Towards the end of the 1980s some of the original enthusiasm and determination was followed by cautious hesitation. The question of *place* – whether somewhere in Africa or in Rome – was still the problem when, at the beginning of 1989, the Pope declared that he was for a 'special synod for Africa', to meet perhaps in two or three years time, but precisely when and where was not known. Bishop Gabriel G. Ganaka of Jos, President of SECAM (Symposium of the Episcopal Conferences of Africa and Madagascar), underlined that meeting in Africa would be of special symbolic value. Nobody has expressed this with greater authority than the *maître* of them all, Professor Mveng. He noticed that in some of the meetings in Rome the bishops of Africa were not given sufficient time to express what the Spirit saith to the Churches in Africa. 'In such circumstances the African Council will be the privileged place where the Spirit in all liberty will be able to speak to the people of God which is in Africa and to reevaluate the message of Vatican II now compromised through the crisis in the West.'[17] *Finally* the decision from Rome followed: the African Synod was to take place in 1994 and in Rome. In April-May 1994 over 200 cardinals, archbishops, bishops and priests, from all over Africa, came to Rome to prepare the Catholic Church for the beginning of its third millennium on the continent.

A Catholic layman

Inevitably a chapter on the Catholic Church has to deal with cardinals and bishops and one or two theological professors. There must, however, also be some space for one or two laymen, at least for the greatest of them all: Alioune Diop. As a young Muslim from Senegal he arrived in Paris during the Second World War, a period of tension and despair in the French population. Under the influence of the Dominican Father Maydieu, he was led into the Christian faith and into the Catholic Church. Maydieu helped Diop to establish contacts with some of the creative men of French culture: Camus, Sartre, Malraux, Emmanuel Mounier (in 1947, the latter had visited West Africa and published a brilliant essay on his trip). Above all Diop gathered a whole generation of Black intellectuals from Africa, Madagascar and the West Indies. Greatly daring together with his friends he started a cultural review *Présence Africaine* in 1947.[18]

He looked frail but had a will of steel and was carried by a great vision of Africa, of Black Humanism, the dignity of the Black race, and loyalty to the Catholic Church. To these African intellectuals the post-war period seemed the dawn of a new era and *Présence Africaine* offered a centre for visions and plans: out of these deliberations there emerged a series of conferences and congresses on African culture. The First International Congress of Black Writers and Artists was held in Paris in 1956, the Second International Congress in Rome in 1959. In the Eternal City the group found a ready welcome from Pope John XXIII: as Nuntius Roncalli in Paris he had already met these young men and was attuned to their hopes and plans. This was the period of Bandung 1956, with its Asian predominance but Alioune Diop gave to the new movement of the Third World its own note of Africanness, of *négritude*. Two congresses on Black culture, at Dakar in 1971 and Lagos in 1977 gave voice to these expectations and insights.

THE PROTESTANTS, THE BIBLE AND ECUMENICAL CO-OPERATION

Protestant co-operation

The AACC and the others

The All Africa Conference of Churches, AACC, was founded in 1963 with headquarters, first at Mindolo, and then from the middle of the decade in Nairobi. In 1986 this continent-wide organization had 137 member Churches and national Christian councils. African Church leaders were at that time inspired by the urge for Christian unity. At the beginning of the 1960s, a prominent Lutheran Church leader, seeing the Western missionaries ready to leave for the West, said: 'When you missionaries leave our Churches will all unite into one body'. This was an optimistic forecast.

The AACC was a response to a vision for Christian unity for the whole continent. In 1963 Protestant leaders came together at Kampala. Among those who helped to kindle that vision there were Jean Kotto, Presbyterian from Cameroon, solid and unflappable leader; Gabriel Setiloane, Methodist from South Africa, brilliant, temperamental and with a fresh interpretation of what he called 'African theology'; and Dr Kofi Busia, Ghanaian sociologist, politician and devoted Methodist layman.

The AACC had its 'ups and downs', with both the 'ups' and the 'downs' clearly visible. Among the AACC general secretaries Canon Burgess Carr promoted the Moratorium idea. In the negotiations over the Sudan crisis in

1972 he took a leading constructive part. His successor, Maxime Rafransoa, from Madagascar, steered the organization for some time in the 1980s. Pressures from both outside and inside the Churches, unenviable for both of these men, eventually lifted both of them out of their eminent positions. Very fortunately the post was taken over in 1988 by a remarkable new incumbent, José Chipenda from Angola, with experience of ecumenical work in the World Council of Churches in Geneva.

Lutheran Church co-operation

At a time when the AACC showed signs of weakness and there was a feeling of vacuum in the centre of the federative body, it became especially important for local Churches to develop their own organizational and liturgical potentials and to cultivate relationships with their own denominational bodies. This was visible in the case of the Lutheran Church in Tanzania, especially the bishop in Bukoba, Josiah Kibira (1924–88), elected president of the Lutheran World Federation (LWF). This bishop was for ever commuting between his diocese on the equator and some other Church centres on the globe. As such he set a remarkable standard for any international Church leader: returning to his diocese from his world tours he would regularly give his diocese inspiring information on his experiences and acquaintances and present the home Church with an on-going ecumenical seminar.

For the 'two-way traffic' of ecumenical mutuality the Lutheran World Federation had a seminal role. In 1955 this Federation had already taken a far-reaching initiative in continent-wide fellowship, through its All Africa conference at Marangu, Tanzania. A generous LWF scholarship programme gave a generation of young men and women opportunities for studies in the West and thus prepared for the day of a take-over by African leaders.

'Inerrancy' vistas

The theological climate in Africa was exposed to new winds, which possibly might influence the future ecumenical *milieu*. Africa was informed that the interpretation of the Bible was endangered. 'Liberal' forces were supposed to discredit the trustworthiness of Holy Scriptures. *Afroscope*, the journal of the Association of Evangelicals (AEA) in Africa, which was founded in 1966, reported on 'inerrancy' conferences in the United States, 'inerrancy' being a 'kind of fundamental of fundamentals'.[19] A 'thorough-going biblicism' was recommended.

Tokunboh Adeyemo, general secretary of the Evangelicals' organization in Africa, found that the 'dream of a Graduate School of Theology' could now become a reality in Nairobi, while a French-speaking equivalent was developed in Bangui, Central African Republic.[20] Technical advance via satellites opened up infinite possibilities for conferences of this kind: 'new frontiers' for mission, on a world-wide Evangelical conference linking together half a million Christians from ninety locations, including ten locations in Africa was to be launched.[21] It is notoriously difficult to ascertain membership figures involved.[22]

Moratorium

After the Second World War the relationship between Western mission and Third World Church changed radically. This was particularly so with regard to the role of the expatriate missionary. Characteristically, the signal for change was first sounded by Kenyan Church leaders. Hardly any country in equatorial Africa had to such an extent been dominated by Westerners – whether as settlers, administrators or missionaries – as Kenya, and a reaction was not long in coming. We register here three African voices from Nairobi. In Kenya, the Presbyterian Church held a pivotal position on account of its history and its central influence in modern Kenya. When the president of the Church, John Gatu, in 1971 was invited to the sister Church in the United States, he felt that he had chosen the perfect time and place for a showdown.

In his address to the Reformed Church in America, at Milwaukee, Wisconsin he challenged the missions in the West and did so in words of prophetic seriousness.

> I am going to argue that the time has come for the withdrawal of foreign missionaries from many parts of the Third World, that the Churches of the Third World must be allowed to find their own identity and that the continuation of the present missionary movement is a hindrance to this selfhood of the Church.[23]

He summed up his impassioned appeal in these words:

> I started by saying that the missionaries should be withdrawn from the Third World for a period of at least five years. I will go further and say that missionaries should be withdrawn, period. The reason is that we must allow God the Holy Spirit to direct our next move without giving Him a timetable. The Gospel will then have a deeper and more far-reaching effect than our mission Christianity has provided so far.[24]

Gatu's Anglican counterpart in Nairobi, Bishop Henry Okullo, in his book *Church and Politics in East Africa*, supported the idea of a moratorium: 'My reply was, missionaries have got no future here. Of course it must be made clear that missionaries from overseas countries are still welcome, but they should be those who are willing to have no future.'[25]

The third voice from Nairobi was that of Canon Burgess Carr, at that time general secretary of the All Africa Conference of Churches. More than others he held the international perspective in view. Compared with the appeal of the two Kenyans, Canon Carr's analysis presents another note, a rhetoric and violent braggadocio with characteristic choice of words. 'The debate about a moratorium', he insisted, 'is not about individuals as such. It is a debate about structures of exploitation, spiritual exploitation at that. Why should someone save his soul at the expense of emasculating my humanity?'[26] This head of the All Africa Conference of Churches knew what to do with missions:

> Mission boards and missionary societies are perpetrators of structural violence at the deepest level of our humanity in the so-called Younger Churches, and they should be abolished in order that new relationships may evolve to internationalize the missionary task of the Churches.[27]

To some of his listeners, John Gatu's appeal may have come as a surprise. Yet warnings had been given decades earlier, and by the very best among Protestant mission thinkers. In 1931 the French Protestant, Maurice Leenhardt, said 'a missionary is not in his place in an organization where a Black could replace him there'.[28] And nobody had more incessantly warned missionaries against the danger of Western domination than the Anglican Roland Allen (1868–1947), who spent his last fifteen years in Kenya. A whole generation prior to the 'moratorium' debate he said:

> We still tacitly but effectually check any spontaneous expression on their part; we still bind catechists, teachers, evangelists, the whole Church in the bonds of our salaries ... Naturally they turned upon their foreign teachers: 'It is you who hold us down; it is your insistence upon your Western creeds which has crippled our thought; it is you who will not put us into positions of authority; it is you who will not trust us with money which you have taught us is necessary for any religious expansion.'[29]

Not a few African Churches had experienced what an *enforced* moratorium was all about, in that through two world wars they were deprived of missionaries and any financial support from abroad (see pp. 610–19). Suffice it to make the point that that experience, while bracing, was often an ecclesiastical 'blessing in disguise'.

However, it must not be taken for granted that the local African Churches were totally prepared to follow the signals from Nairobi. A problem in its own right was the discrepancy between these and the local reactions – or lack of reaction. The considered opinion of the Ethiopian Evangelical Church Mekane Yesus can serve as representing a majority of Churches and has a special interest, formulated as it was in 1975, by the then general secretary of the Church, the late Gudina Tumsa. He expressed as 'a firm conviction' that the Mekane Yesus Church, even with the continued presence of foreign personnel and funds, can assert its freedom from any and every kind of foreign dominance. Moratorium was rejected on theological grounds: the Church is one and should be interdependent. In fact, the Church in the new Ethiopia:

> should seek to find as many ways as possible to foster the well-being and development of the people. An important way of doing this is to secure the assistance of foreign personnel to aid in the development of the country. There is really no other answer, than *NO* in principle to the call for moratorium.[30]

On the whole the attitude of Catholic leaders in Africa to the moratorium issue in the 1970s was cautious and hesitant. Somehow one was given to understand that the matter was not really their concern. However, Catholic Yaoundé does not in any way lag behind Protestant utterance from Nairobi. Let Fr Fabien Eboussi Boulaga, SJ, speak for them all: 'What to do?' he asks in a conclusion. 'Let Europe and America as a priority evangelize themselves. Let them plan in good order the departure of the missionaries of Africa.' This is said in an article meaningfully headed 'La démission'.[31]

The Bible in Independent Africa

In Africa of the 1960s the use of the Bible saw a new day. The role and status of the Bible were greatly improved because of Vatican II and its 'Dogmatic Constitution on divine Revelation'. The Council broke with that strangely hesitant attitude towards the Bible (from the Council of Trent and Counter-Reformation until 1960) which had dominated the Roman Catholic Church, even in Africa. Now Vatican II formulated its concern that 'suitable and correct translations are made into different languages. And if, given the opportunity and the approval of Church authority, these translations are produced in co-operation with the separated brethren as well, all Christians will be able to use them.' It did not take long for a salutary co-operation to be established between Catholic and Protestant Bible translators throughout the continent, and African Cardinals (Malula and others) expressed their satisfaction at the Bible study and Bible reading in homes and parishes, and furthered this new Catholic concern with Bible translation. This applied not least to the Catholic Lingala translation of the 1980s, an immense achievement devoted as it was to one of the great languages of the future for Zaïre.

One looks with admiration at the efforts of Protestant missionaries who spent their lifetime at the task of Bible translation. There were sure to be linguistic limitations in the work, but a historian is bound to look at this work in terms of history. It is too easy to condemn by the standards of today's linguistics what had been done previously in this field. The team aspect of Bible translation work needs to be underlined and one thinks of the great fellowship experiences along the road, of Bishop Colenso and William Ngidi for the Zulu translation, George Pilkington and Henry Wright Duta for Luganda, and others. There was formed almost invariably a deep Christian fellowship between the foreigner and their African co-workers, the former always aware of his foreignness in this the most central of missionary tasks and therefore aware of his constant dependence on his local co-workers, the real experts. We have come across only one exception to this rule of team co-operation (the Bemba translation) but one exception cannot affect the total picture of enriching fellowship.

In independent Africa, after 1960, the whole Bible translation work was continued under new conditions necessarily directed by Africans. The United Bible Society, New York, wrote to us (1984) on this point:

> I think that the statement that many Bibles in Africa have become outmoded is absolutely true. There were two major reasons for this ... Most older translators were very concerned to retain the form of the original, both at the level of individual words and the discourse patterns. The second reason was that the non-native speaker translators, that is, the missionaries, had a sufficiently large input into the actual form of the translation that it was not natural. Today we lay great stress on the need for translators to be native speakers. Only if we need exegetical assistance do we turn to someone such as the missionary.[32]

The 'new day' of Bible translation can be seen through a new understanding of what is meant by translation, an insight inspired by modern linguistics and skilfully propagated by the United Bible Society and its Translations Research Co-ordinator, Dr Eugene A. Nida. This new approach has recently been called 'Dynamic Equivalent Interpretation' and, more recently, one refers to 'meaning-by-meaning translation'. Paul D. Fueter, for many years active in the United Bible Society, says: 'By discovering dynamic equivalent translation we have given twentieth-century Christians a real possibility of communicating the message to men and women today'. Briefly, 'translation has to make explicit what is implicit in the text, so that the culturally distant reader can understand with the minimum of obstacles'.[33]

The Bible is *the* book of Protestant Africa: to possess as one's very own, to read for inspiration and to carry with you, particularly to church services. The importance of 'carrying' the Bible to church as a visible badge of identification could strike the African Christian by comparison with other less manifest Church situations. One example among many: a pastor from Bukoba, Tanzania, spent some months in Sweden and its national Church. At the end of his experience in exotic Sweden he wrote a report, critical and frank. His first remark concerned the place of the Bible among ordinary Christians in Sweden. We quote:

> Firstly I was surprised by the meagre use of the Bible among Christians. The Hymn-book is more central in the life of the Church than the Bible. The people read mostly select passages according to the Church year and not the whole Bible. This is very serious and surely Lutherans should not behave like that.

Another observation about the use of the Bible in Africa is the surprising recollection by preacher and individual Christians of Bible passages and verses. Not all village preachers possess a Bible concordance of their own – in fact only very few do – but this lack is made up by remembering a bounty of precious Bible passages in the Old Testament and the New.

With expert advice from the United Bible Society, Bible translation in Africa has entered upon a new creative phase during the present time. The African 'translation consultants' – from Maseru and Mbabane to Nairobi and Kampala – stand out for the rare quality of these men and women, selected in order to promote this most central concern of the Church. Even this expertise, however, has to face discordant linguistic and vernacular problems. Any attempt at a language-embracing Bible version may turn out to be vilified as difficult and obnoxious. The most recent example is the uproar over the latest Igbo translation in eastern Nigeria, concerning a language representing some 20 million people. In the first decade of the century Archdeacon T. J. Dennis managed to achieve a *tour de force*, not only in producing a 'Union Igbo' translation but also spending one to two years travelling around Igbo country popularizing and promoting his new version. This time, in 1989, the situation appeared even more demanding. The Igbo language is supposed to comprise some 1,000 dialects and variants, and certain expressions acceptable in one dialect will be taboo in another. The recent *Baibulu Nso*, presumably a first class work, has met with excited opposition.[34]

Alexandria

An echo of these signals can be heard, or overheard, in the *Confession of Alexandria*, formulated by the General Committee of the All Africa Conference of Churches meeting in Alexandria, February 1976, representing 114 member Churches in thirty-three countries. This representative group could affirm that 'God through the continuing work of Christ, is charting His Highway of Freedom from Alexandria to the Cape of Good Hope', and rejoiced at meeting in Alexandria 'the holy city in which tradition places the martyrdom of St Mark the Evangelist'. They felt that this led to a deeper understanding of the heritage delivered to us by the Fathers of the early Church in North Africa. 'Our commitment to the struggle for human liberation ... evokes a response of love and joy that we are seeking to express and to share in language, modes of spirituality, liturgical forms, patterns of mission and structures of organization that belong uniquely to our cultural context.' This is what the Fathers of the early Church in North Africa did with the Gospel brought to them by St Mark. As a result they were able to develop a Christianity that was orthodox and catholic both in its outreach and in its cultural authenticity and a Church which, throughout the ages, has endured persecution and martyrdom and still survives, with renewed strength, until our day.

INDEPENDENT CHURCHES

In 1968 there were 5,000 African Independent Churches in Africa and a decade later that vast figure had climbed to about 10,000. With such a multitude, we are fortunately exempt from having to describe them all. In a rapidly developing Africa, the terminology in various fields is subject to a 'law of obsolescence'. Terms which once seemed helpful and even precise may after several decades prove to be unserviceable. The formula 'African Independent Churches' which was introduced in a book by B.Sr. from 1948 seemed good at a time when other writers unashamedly referred to them as 'the sects' or the 'Native Separatist Churches'. But now, with all of Africa independent north of the Limpopo, and with most of the mission-related Churches being independent as well, the question arises whether there is any reason for using this term 'African Independent Churches'.

What is perhaps even more surprising than the number of 'Independent' Churches is the number of studies devoted to these Churches – books, review articles, conference papers, all in many languages. A bibliography on the subject, published in 1977 by Harold W. Turner holds 1,906 titles, and since then no doubt some thousands more have been added to this bounty.[35] There is undeniably a certain tendency to romanticism in some of this literary activity. If Africa was to be 'the Christian Continent' at all it must be so, not in any recognizable Western form, but preferably dressed in as surprising a garment as possible.

A study of the African Indigenous (to use their term) Churches by John Padwick and David B. Barrett reveals that a fascinating *rapprochement* between the Coptic Orthodox Church of Egypt and certain African Indigenous Churches is taking place.[36] Pope Cyril VI and his successor Shenouda III have since the 1960s shown a keen interest in contacts with Black Independents. In 1965 the Pope and Patriarch added the term Pope of All Africa to his ecclesiastical title. A Coptic bishop named Antonious Markos was placed in Nairobi and established contacts with Independents all over the continent, in South Africa, in Zaïre with the Kimbanguists, etc. In 1978, twenty Independent leaders were invited to Cairo and an Organization of African Independent Churches was formed, with Bishop A. M. Ajouga of western Kenya as chairman and Bishop Antonius as organizing secretary. (It is well known that Bishop Ajouga was also a member of the so-called International Council of Christian Churches, USA, with its peculiar attitude in ecumenical matters.)

With the coming of political independence to African states the political and social conditions of 'Independent Churches' changed, sometimes dramatically. What had once been a despised prophet movement with the Prophet-Leader imprisoned for thirty years until his death – the Kimbanguists in Zaïre – now emerged as an honoured community in the land, with an administration that showed that in a society falling to pieces here was a body prepared, in a crisis, to take over leadership and with new ecumenical contacts on an international scale. The election of the Kimbanguist Church to the World Council of Churches in 1979 was an appreciated badge of acceptability, accentuating an incipient bureaucratization of a vast prophet movement.

In Nigeria the Aladura, once controversial and marginalized, now became of central importance in society, 'a force to reckon with'. Administratively they were 'increasingly tending towards the older Churches' and even the ecclesiastical wardrobe changed significantly: 'One can hardly distinguish between the robes of a C[herubim] & S[eraphim] Baba Aladura and an Anglican or Roman Catholic Bishop today'.[37] An observer, the Anglican Bishop Akin Omoyajowo, sometime Commissioner of the Public Service Commission, Ondo State, Nigeria, and lecturer in Religious Studies, University of Ibadan, had a special knowledge of the three leading Aladura

Churches – the Cherubim and Seraphim, the Christian Apostolic Church and the Church of the Lord, Aladura. He writes about the situation: 'Say what we may, the survival of the Christian Church in Nigeria today lies mainly in the direction of the Aladura Churches.'[38]

Only in South Africa were the Independent Churches still kept at arm's length, disapproved of by an established community whether White or Black. On the Rand, Ma Nku, incomparable prophetess, in a court case was relieved of her considerable bank account – possibly tens of thousands of pounds sterling – and at Ekuphakameni, near Durban, in embittered Natal, that most brilliant, promising young leader of part of the amaNazarethea Church, Londa Shembe – grandson of Isaiah Shembe, son of Johannes Galilee Shembe – was shot dead in his home, May 1989, an innocent victim of some vicious conspiracy.

Missionary attempts at assistance for the Independents

Quite a few mission Churches have attempted – while realizing the need for tact and sensitivity – to give African Independents assistance, advice and teaching. No Church has done this with anything like the involvement of the Mennonites of the USA. A radical Protestant Church, with Baptist practice, a Puritan message and high educational ambition, the Mennonites have been a considerable evangelistic force in various parts of Africa. With political Independence coming to African states, they decided to assist Independent Churches in the continent.

Pioneers among them were Edwin and Irene Weaver, a missionary couple who in 1959 started an entirely new and worthwhile ministry. They developed a pattern of Bible study among the Independents in Eastern Nigeria, involving a number of expatriate Mennonite workers in Bible teaching and in medical and educational work. Other Mennonites followed in their footsteps to Nigeria, Ghana and Zaïre and other countries in western Africa. In 1971 the Weavers started a Good News Training Institute in Ghana, with Theological Education by Extension (TEE) as the programme. In this context Wilbert Shenk and David Shank devoted themselves to the Harrists in the Ivory Coast. David A. Shank was to produce an extraordinarily thorough study of Harris' life. Soon the Mennonites turned to Southern Africa, establishing their work in the Union and related countries. Initiatives were taken on the invitation of the Independent Churches themselves.[39]

In South Africa a daring initiative was taken by the Christian Institute under the leadership of Dr Beyers Naudé. An African Independent Churches

Association (AICA) was formed in 1963 with hundreds of Independent Churches as members, at least the less prominent and the most needy among them, while the larger and strong among them decided that they had better avoid being associated with Dr Naudé's controversial enterprise. The AICA arranged an ambitious educational programme for leaders and members of the Independents. An elite of Western volunteers gave of their time and their concern to the AICA work under its African leadership until in the end there was a financial débâcle on a disturbing scale and AICA came to an end.

In Zimbabwe there was a highly successful initiative on behalf of the Shona-speaking Churches, both of an 'Ethiopian' and of a 'Zionist' type. Professor M. L. Daneel headed the effort and a 'Fambidzano' organization was formed for theological education. Senior tutors were for a time found among pastors of the 'main line' Churches and Ethiopian and Zionist pastors acted as junior tutors. Totally at home with these men and women – born and bred on a Zimbabwean mission station – Dr Daneel has managed to stimulate this movement on a surprising scale, himself withdrawing from the limelight while seeing to it that African leadership of this essentially theological movement was maintained. As if this was not enough, Dr Daneel has produced a series of informative volumes on the movement. After independence in 1980, 'Fambidzano' turned up as a modern movement with concerns for ecological conservation, on the way towards working out a viable theology of environment and thus also presenting a useful contact with an emerging association of traditional spirit mediums.[40]

ISLAM IN INDEPENDENT AFRICA

Decolonization and independence

The Bandung Conference of 1955 and the growth of the Non-Aligned Movement in the late 1950s and early 1960s provided a new political dimension for the newly independent African countries, whose nationalism had provided the momentum for the withdrawal of the European colonial powers. The Non-Aligned Movement, which most African countries were eager to join, was predominantly non-Christian, being overwhelmingly composed of Muslims, Hindus and Buddhists. This identification of Africa as part of the new political and ideological concept of the 'Third World' strengthened the gradual realization that African Muslims south of the Sahara were a essential part of the wider Islamic world.

The growing awareness of the powerful appeal of Pan-Islamism has been a vibrant feature of tropical Africa's religious politics and identity since the late 1950s. We can divide the years since independence into two chronological periods. During the first period, from the late 1950s until the early 1970s, Muslims in tropical Africa were keen to expand their political and social influence, especially in those countries where many of the nationalist leaders had arisen out of a Christian heritage. Muslims south of the Sahara, especially in West Africa, had extensive historical ties to the Muslim population of the Maghreb, Libya and Egypt. In addition, African Muslims had a long tradition of pilgrimage, or *hajj*, to the holy palaces of Islam in Arabia. In 1968 Professor Tareq Ismael wrote that 'approximately 50 per cent of Africa is Muslim and this accounts for about 20 per cent of world Muslims.'[41]

The second period, from the early 1970s to the present day, saw the beginnings of a more widespread and penetrative relationship between sub-Saharan African Muslims and the Islamic heartland of the Middle East and the Persian Gulf. The explosion of oil prices in 1973–74, resulting from the co-ordinated action of predominantly Middle Eastern petroleum producers, helped fuel a renaissance of Islamic thought and identity. This, in turn, has had a profound effect on African Muslims and their relations with the rest of the Islamic world. The Shiitic Islam revolution in Iran in the years after 1979 has also pervasively influenced African Muslims, particularly intellectuals and the urban poor.

Nasser and Islam in Africa

Arab concern for Muslims in sub-Saharan Africa during the 1950s and 1960s can be illustrated by reference to the interest shown by General Gamal Nasser (1918–70), the Egyptian president, between 1956–70, and Arab nationalist leader. Nasser dramatically expanded the centuries-old Egyptian tradition of providing Islamic education and training for many thousands of Black Africans in the great urban metropolis of Cairo. Modern Egypt not only promoted traditional Qur'anic scholarship and instruction in Islamic jurisprudence, but also now provided medical, scientific and technological education. Nasser also initiated the sending of many hundreds of Egyptian teachers and technical experts to the new independent African countries. Muslim students in tropical Africa did not now have to go to the Christian West for advanced modern education, as many other Arab and Asian countries followed Egypt's example and provided educational opportunities for African Muslims in sympathetic Islamic environments.

The University of Al-Azhar in Cairo was the intellectual and theological centre for the Islamic world. The university was host, in 1964 and 1965, to the first two Afro-Asian Islamic Conferences, and the then rector of Al-Azhar described the objectives of the university:

> The most prominent role of Al-Azhar is the international call to Islam, its propagation of the Holy Koran, the Arabic language, and religious jurisprudence among peoples who do not speak the language of the Holy Book.[42]

As well as opening a number of cultural centres in African countries, Al-Azhar sent hundreds of thousands of copies of the Qur'an to Africa as part of its missionary outreach. A meeting in 1965 of the World Council of Churches in Nigeria 'reported a sharp rise in the spread of Islam throughout Africa, which was partly credited to the increase of Islamic missionary work', thus testifying to the impressive contribution of Al-Azhar to the espousal of the Islamic faith.[43]

The Hajj

One of the five tenets of Islam is the enjoinment to Muslims to perform at least once in their life, a pilgrimage to the holy cities of the Hijaz and above all to Mecca. 'Whilst rites may be performed at any time of year, the majority of pilgrimages are made at the *Id al Hajj* (the Feast of the pilgrimage) which is the zenith of the Islamic year.'[44] For more than a millennium African Muslims have performed the rite of pilgrimage to the Hijaz.

In former years Africans would travel across the continent to Arabia by camel or by foot, often taking many years to perform this most pious and exacting of divine commands. Until recently most pilgrims would journey overland to Jeddah by motor vehicle and by boat. This tradition of migration is the greatest cyclical event in the history of human mobility inspired by religious devotion. Since the 1970s more and more pilgrims arrive in the holy cities by airplane and this fast, efficient means of transportation has allowed many more millions of Muslims to realize their dream of becoming an *al hajji*: 'one who has made the pilgrimage'. The numbers of Nigerians performing this sacred journey has increased enormously. 'Whereas in 1956 the figure was only 2,483, in 1973 an estimated 49,000 Nigerian pilgrims went to Mecca, and in 1977 about 106,000 Nigerians performed the *hajj*, making the number of pilgrims from Nigeria the second highest in the world.'[45]

25

EPILOGUE

1. Christianity is an Eastern faith, from Galilee and Judea, very soon reaching the Nile Delta and Egypt and from there speeding west along the coast and south to Nubia and Axum-Ethiopia. At the end of the fifteenth century the faith reached sub-Saharan Africa – Kongo, Mutapa and Mombasa. While Islam came by camel caravan – 'ships of the desert' – Christianity arrived by sailing ship: along the coastline and then, by way of canoe along the rivers and the lakes and from the south by ox-waggon, in each case mediated by groups of young African witnesses.
2. The Christian message as a power of motivation from 'Beyond the Seas' did not arrive alone. The proclamation of the Gospel was sabotaged by the powers of colonialism and race. The emerging Churches came to be seen as related to a political metropolis and to Western missionary societies. The identification of Western colonialism and Christian mission was even more accentuated by the concept of a 'national mission', representing the particular nationality of a colonial-imperial power, while other missions, from other countries and denominations were, presumably, beyond this privileged position.

   Another factor was that of race, particularly in South Africa and other territories with a dominating European minority. Relationships between the races, within the Churches as well, came to be decreed by anonymous segregation and by the legal enactments of apartheid. To the extent that the missions themselves were touched by these powers, they had to consider numbers of their Church members leaving the fellowship, founding thousands of 'Independent' Churches, a phenomenon which was to characterize developments in certain African countries more than on other continents.
3. The twentieth century has seen an increasing and even breathtaking growth in the numbers of membership of the Churches. This rapid growth is a fact of immense importance not only in itself but even more for political reasons related to sub-Saharan Africa as a whole, at present and for decades and centuries to come. There was a tendency with the

high and mighty in certain countries to underrate this statistical fact with a view to giving the impression that the Christian Church was rather a second-rate portent on the continent and insisting on this position to the extent that the publication of religious statistics was postponed or forbidden: without support of statistical fact one had to rely all the more on guess-work formed by blatant populist claims. This, however, can no longer succeed. The facts are there for everyone to see.

4. Over the decades and centuries the categories of Church affiliation changed. It has been suggested in this study that the nineteenth-century Church was a young men's Church while the twentieth-century Church was a women's Church. This generalization relies mainly on observations among Protestants but we have come to believe that it holds true for Catholics as well: this must be ascertained by local and regional research.
5. An embarrassing problem throughout the modern period has been the tension between Catholic and Protestant missions, a tension which the ecumenically inclined writer has perhaps tended to tone down. Vatican II brought new conditions and new hope. A spin-off of Catholic–Protestant competition was the increased scope for educational advance, in numbers of schools, and in educational quality.
6. Together with rapid growth one must emphasize the vitality of African Churches, individually and taken together, not least in the present upheaval of certain African states. When state machinery came to a halt, the Churches emerged as countervailing powers in the land, prepared by common effort and enthusiasm to overcome obstruction and frustration and disappointment, carried forward by faith, hope, love – and song.
7. The two latest centuries of Christian influence have made their decisive contribution to the Christian culture and life in sub-Saharan African. The north of the continent, of course, is mainly Muslim, with its increasing contacts with Mecca and other Islamic centres. The Christian Church, through its local congregations with fellowship and song, through its schools and colleges, its hospitals and development work have made sub-Saharan Africa – in west, east and southern Africa – the Christian part of the continent. No political argument and no ostentation can obliterate these facts or take away Christ's religion from the surface of Africa or from the hearts of African men, women and children.

Finally, at the end of this book one may ask what the Christian faith has meant to the men and women on the continent. It is a legitimate question to ask but impossible to answer in any one neat formula, covering all the complexities of a continent. Let us instead call upon three people to represent an answer all very different in culture and opportunity, but at one in their devotion to the One Lord and Saviour.

We have already referred to Alioune Diop, of Senegal and Paris, a great Catholic and international personality, a man of dignity and wisdom. After all his years in Paris he insisted: 'We [Africans] must avoid the desiccating rationalism – *rationalisme desséché* – of the West. We should develop our own personality and genius.' An international perspective helps: 'In order to discover Africa you have to be outside Africa. Negritude is something urgent for those who have been exposed to assimilationist influences, and the Christian Church must have self-confidence to convey its message.'[1]

We remember an old lady at Gera, Bukoba in Tanzania, from a population with a stratified, feudal, society and a harsh lot for women, both old and young. After the church service we spoke to this member of the congregation and asked her which hymn she liked best. There was no hesitation in her reply: 'That hymn with the words *Taliho atangwa*'.

> *Omunju yOmukama waitu*, No 150.
> In the house of our king
> there still is room
> He welcomes them all ...
> *Taliho atangwa*
> [Nobody is refused entry]

Finally we think of the Revd Michael Mzobe, on Easter morning, 1939. He was a Zulu pastor placed in a district in Natal, South Africa, one of the best preachers we ever heard, on any continent. A second-generation Christian, he had started as a teacher and then had four years of theological training at Rorke's Drift, Natal. In his humble little parsonage he transformed his new learning into a creative 'Christus-Victor' theology which would have gladdened the heart of St Irenaeus of old, relating the message to the martial tradition of his own great people.

For his Easter morning sermon he chose a text from the Old Testament, Ezekiel 37, the chapter on the resurrection of the dry bones: 'Come from the four winds, O breath, and breathe upon these slain that they may live'. In unforgettable terms the preacher showed how the First Adam, from his balcony in the heavens, surveyed the misfortunes of mankind, from Cain to King David, and all this as a punishment for his own original sin – until on the first Easter morning, the Second Adam, the Hero of Heaven – *iqhawe la seculwini* – entered the heavens approaching the Throne of Almighty God in order to carry report that from that great morning Sin and Sickness and Death were overcome by Him, the Second Adam. And the First Adam had peace ...

NOTES

INTRODUCTION

1 J. F. Ade Ajayi and E. A. Ayandele, 'Writing African Church history', in Peter Beyerhaus and Carl F. Hallencreutz (eds.), *The Church crossing frontiers: essays on the nature of mission* (Lund and Uppsala, 1969), p. 90.

2 *Ibid*., p. 94.

3 Lamin Sanneh, *West African Christianity: the religious impact* (London, 1983), p. xi.

CHAPTER I: THE BEGINNINGS

1 See Otto F. A. Meinardus, *Christian Egypt: ancient and modern* (2nd edn, Cairo, 1977) a chapter entitled 'Traditional sites associated with the flight of the Holy Family to Egypt', pp. 601–49.

2 Birger A. Pearson, 'Earliest Christianity in Egypt: some observations', in Birger A. Pearson and James E. Goehring (eds.), *The roots of Egyptian Christianity* (Philadelphia, 1986), p. 153.

3 Jean Daniélou, *Le mystère du salut des nations* (Paris, 1948), p. 52.

4 Efoé J. Penoukou, in *Concilium* (1977), p. 379.

5 Pearson, 'Earliest Christianity', pp. 144–45.

6 Maria Cramer, *Das Christlich-Koptische Ägypten Einst und Heute: Eine Orientierung* (Wiesbaden, 1959), p. 1.

7 Gustave Bardy, *La théologie de l'église de Saint Clément de Rome à Saint Irénée* (Paris, 1945), pp. 2, 245.

8 G. L. Prestige, *God in patristic thought* (2nd edn, London, 1952), p. 285.

9 See Ezra Gebremedhin, *Life-giving blessing: an inquiry into the Eucharistic doctrine of Cyril of Alexandria* (Uppsala, 1977).

10 Gerd Theissen, *Sociology of early Palestinian Christianity* (Philadelphia, 1978).

11 Fairy von Lilienfeld, *Spiritualität des frühen Wüstenmönchtums* (Erlangen, 1983), p. 98.

12 Palladius, *Historia Lausiaca* XXI, quoted in W. H. C. Frend, *The rise of the Monophysite movement: chapters in the history of the Church in the fifth and sixth centuries* (Cambridge, 1972), p. 73 n. 4.

13 Samuel Rubenson, *The letters of St Antony: Origenist theology, monastic tradition and the making of a saint* (Lund, 1990), pp. 96, 111, 186.

14 Philip Rousseau, *Ascetics, authority, and the Church in the age of Jerome and Cassian* (Oxford, 1978), p. 33.

15 Philip Rousseau, *Pachomius: the making of a community in fourth-century Egypt* (Berkeley, 1985), p. 159.

16 See Maria Cramer, *Das Altägyptische Lebenszeichen im christlichen (koptischen) Ägypten: Eine kultur- und religionsgeschictliche Studie auf Archäologischer Grundlage* (Wiesbaden, 1955).
17 Stephen Runciman, *A history of the crusades* (3 vols., Cambridge, 1954) vol. 3, p. 159.
18 Jean Daniélou and Henri Marrou, *Nouvelle histoire de l'Église, volume 1: des origines à Saint Grégoire le Grand* (Paris, 1963), p. 133.
19 See Charles Saumagne, *Saint Cyprien: Évêque de Carthage, 'Pape' d'Afrique (248–258): contribution à l'étude des 'persécutions' de Dèce et de Valérien* (Paris 1975).
20 Peter Brown, *Augustine of Hippo: a biography* (London, 1967), p. 168.
21 *Ibid.*, p. 206.
22 See Fréderic van der Meer, *Augustinus der Seelsorger* (Cologne, 1958).
23 See Elleck K. Mashingaidze, 'Christian missions in Mashonaland, 1890 to 1930', D.Phil. thesis, University of York, 1973.
24 Joseph Cuoq, *L'Église d'Afrique du Nord: du deuxième au douzième siécle* (Paris, 1984), p. 143.
25 W. H. C. Frend, *The Donatist Church: a movement of protest in Roman North Africa* (2nd edn, Oxford, 1971), p. 230.
26 Saint Augustine, *Confessions* (trans. Henry Chadwick, Oxford, 1991), pp. 49, 90.
27 Brown, *Augustine*, Communication from Professor Ragnar Holte, Uppsala and Lund, p. 118.
28 See van der Meer, *Augustinus*, pp. 25, 140.
29 William M. Green, 'Augustine's use of Punic', in Walter J. Fischel (ed.), *Semitic and Oriental studies: a volume presented to William Popper*, University of California publications in Semitic philology, vol. 11 (Berkeley and Los Angeles, 1951).
30 For St Augustine's thoughts about Christian fellowship, see Carolinne White, *Christian Friendship in the Fourth Century* (Cambridge, 1992), pp. 185–217.
31 W. H. C. Frend, *The rise of Christianity* (Philadelphia, 1984), p. 573.
32 C. P. Groves, *The planting of Christianity in Africa* (4 vols., London, 1948–58), vol. 1, pp. viii, 59, 83, 88–89.
33 Cecil Northcott, *Christianity in Africa* (London, 1963), p. 58.
34 Adolf von Harnack, *Die Mission und Ausbreitung des Christentums in den erster drei Jahrhunderten* (2 vols., 3rd edn, Leipzig, 1915), vol. 2, p. 315.
35 William Y. Adams, *Nubia: corridor to Africa* (London, 1977), p. 81.
36 Kazimierz Michalowski, 'The spread of Christianity in Nubia', in G. Mokhtar (ed.), *Unesco general history of Africa, vol. 2: ancient civilizations of Africa* (Paris, London and Berkeley, 1981), p. 329.
37 John Vantini, *The excavations at Faras: a contribution to the history of Christian Nubia* Museum Combonianum vol. 24 (Bologna, 1970), pp. 172–73.
38 Martin Krause (ed.), *Nubische Studien: Tagungsakten der 5: International konferenz der International Society for Nubian Studies* (Mainz am Rhein, 1986), p. 6.
39 P. L. Shinnie, 'Christian Nubia' in J. D. Fage (ed.), *Cambridge history of Africa: volume 2, from c. 500 BC to AD 1050* (Cambridge, 1978), p. 580.
40 Basil Davidson, *Old Africa rediscovered* (London, 1959), pp. 107–09; A. J. Arkell, *A history of the Sudan from the earliest times to 1821* (2nd edn, London, 1961), pp. 191–94.
41 Shinnie, 'Christian Nubia', pp. 574–77.
42 William Y. Adams, 'Three perspectives on the past: the historian, the art historian and the prehistorian', in Tomas Hägg (ed.), *Nubian culture: past and present* (Stockholm, 1987), p. 289.

43 J. M. Plumley, 'New evidence on Christian Nubia in the light of recent excavations', *Nubia Christiana*, 1 (1982), p. 20.

44 Joseph Cuoq, *Islamisation de la Nubie Chrétienne, VIIe-XVIe siècle* (Paris, 1986), pp. 91–102; Giovanni Vantini, *Christianity in the Sudan* (Bologna, 1981), pp. 206–7; Derek A. Welsby, 'A perspective of Nubia from Soba', in Hägg, *Nubian*, pp. 279–84.

45 Edward Ullendorff, *The Ethiopians: an introduction to country and people* (2nd edn, London, 1965), p. 69.

46 *Ibid*., p. 70.

47 See Steven Kaplan, *The monastic holy man and the Christianization of early Solomonic Ethiopia* (Wiesbaden, 1984).

CHAPTER 2: MARITIME CONNECTIONS

1 John Vogt, *Portuguese rule on the Gold Coast 1469–1682* (Athens, Ohio, 1979), p. 184.

2 *Ibid*., pp. 55–66.

3 Piere Lintingre, 'Le Vénérable Père Seraphin de Leon', *Collectanea Franciscana*, 41 (1971), 87–130. For the levitation phenomenon in Franciscan spirituality in Europe, see Carlo de Arembergh, *Flores Seraphici sive Icones* (Milan, 1648.)

4 Richard Gray, 'Christian traces and a Franciscan mission in the Central Sudan, 1700–1711', *Journal of African history*, 8 (1967), p. 387.

5 Alan F. C. Ryder, *Benin and the Europeans 1485–1897* (London, 1969), p. 46.

6 *Ibid*., p. 105.

7 *Ibid*., pp. 47, 102, 105, 118.

8 See Louis Jardin, 'Le Congo et la secte des Antoniens', in *Bulletin de l'Institut historique belge de Rome*, 33 (1961), 411–617, esp. pp. 430–40.

9 See François Bontinck (ed.), *Diaire Congolais (1690–1701) de Fra Luca da Caltanisetta* (Louvain and Paris, 1970).

10 See Richard Gray, '*Come Vero Prencipe Catolico*: the Capuchins and the rulers of Soyo in the late seventeenth century', *Africa*, 53 (1983), pp. 39–54.

11 *Ibid.*

12 Joseph C. Miller, 'The paradoxes of impoverishment in the Atlantic zone', in David Birmingham and Phyllis M. Martin (eds.), *History of Central Africa* (2 vols., London, 1983), vol. 1, p. 125.

13 Bontinck, *Diaire Congolais.*

14 *Ibid.*

15 Edoardo Pecoraio, 'Preambolo', in J. Metzler (ed.), *Sacrae Congregationis de Propaganda Fide Memoria Rerum: volume I/1: 1622–1700* (Rome, 1971), p. ix.

16 See Josef Metzler, 'Orientation, programme et premières décisions (1622–1649)', in *ibid*., p. 180.

17 Teobaldo Filesi, 'Cappucini italiani nel E Congo', in *Euntes Docete*, 21 (1968), p. 387.

18 See Sigbert Axelson, *Culture confrontation in the Lower Congo: from the old Congo Kingdom to the Congo Independent State with special reference to the Swedish missionaries in the 1880s and 1890s* (Uppsala, 1970).

19 C. R. Boxer, *Race relations in the Portuguese colonial empire, 1415–1825* (Oxford, 1963), pp. 38–39.

20 David Birmingham, 'Central Africa from Cameroun to the Zambezi', in Richard Gray (ed.), *Cambridge history of Africa, volume 4: from c. 1600 to c. 1790* (Cambridge 1975), p. 353.

21 António de Oliveira de Cadornega, *História geral das guerras Angolanas* (Ed. M. Delgado and A. da Cunha, 3 vols., Lisbon, 1940–2), vol. 3; and C. R. Boxer, *Race relations*, p. 37.

22 Boxer, *Portuguese society in the tropics* (Madison, 1965), p. 131.

23 See Teobaldo Filesi, 'L'epilogo della "Missio Antiqua" dei Cappuccini nel Regno del Congo (1800–1835)' *Euntes Docete*, 23 (1970); Teobaldo Filesi and Isidoro da Villapadrierna, *La 'Missio Antiqua' dei Cappuccini nel Congo 1645–1835: studio preliminare e guida delle fonti* (Rome, 1978).

24 Richard Elphick, *Kraal and castle: Khoikhoi and the founding of white South Africa* (New Haven and London, 1977), p. 96.

25 *Ibid.*, p. 108.

26 *Ibid.*, p. 207.

27 Shula Marks, 'Southern Africa and Madagascar', in Gray, *Cambridge history*, vol. 4, p. 452.

28 See Nigel Worden, *Slavery in Dutch South Africa* (Cambridge, 1985), p. 139.

29 Bernhard Krüger, *The pear tree blossoms: a history of the Moravian mission stations in South Africa 1737–1869* (Genadendal, 1966), p. 32.

30 B. M. Fagan, 'The Zambezi and Limpopo basins, 1100–1500', in D. T. Niane (ed.) *Unesco general history of Africa, vol. 4: Africa from the twelfth to the sixteenth century* (Paris, London and Berkeley, 1984), p. 540.

31 Paul Schebesta, *Portugals Konquistamission in Südost-Afrika: Missionsgeschichte Sambesiens und des Monomotapareiches (1560–1920)* (Steyl, 1966), p. 135.

32 *Ibid.*, pp. 243, 246.

33 Paul Schebesta mentions briefly this sung catechism, *ibid.*, p. 266.

34 *Ibid.*, p. 131.

35 Eric Axelson, *South-East Africa, 1488–1530* (London, 1940), p. 45.

36 G. S. P. Freeman-Grenville (ed.), *The Mombasa rising against the Portuguese, 1631: from sworn evidence* (London, 1980).

37 G. S. P. Freeman-Grenville, *Chronology of African history* (London, 1973), p. 105.

38 G. S. P. Freeman-Grenville, *The East African coast: select documents from the first to the earlier nineteenth century* (Oxford, 1962), p. 135.

39 *Ibid.*, p. 161.

40 G. Goyau, *La France Missionaire*, vol. II, 1948, pp. 29–64.; and *Petit Catechisme ... aux néophytes et Catechumènes de l'isle de Madagascar, le tout en Francais et en cette Langue* (Paris, 1658).

41 Joseph Cuoq, *L'Islam en Éthiopie des origines au XVIe siècle* (Paris, 1981), pp. 228, 233.

42 J. Spencer Trimingham, *Islam in Ethiopia* (Oxford, 1952), p. 99.

43 Sylvia Pankhurst, *Ethiopia: a cultural history* (Woodford Green, 1955), p. 386.

44 *Ibid.*, pp. 389–90.

45 J.-B. Coulbeaux, *Histoire politique et religieuse d'Abyssinie* (3 vols., Paris, 1929), vol. 2, p. 274.

46 M. Abir, 'Ethiopia and the Horn of Africa', in Gray, *Cambridge history*, vol. 4, p. 556.

CHAPTER 3: OVERVIEW TO THE NINETEENTH CENTURY

1 After C. P. Groves, *The planting of Christianity in Africa* (4 vols., London, 1948–58), vol. 2, p. 110.

2 Robert W. July, *A history of the African people* (3rd edn, New York, 1980), pp. 213–362.

3 *Ibid.*, p. 218.
4 Julian Cobbing, 'The mfecane as alibi: thoughts on Dithakong and Mbolompo', *Journal of African history*, 29 (1988), 518; John Wright, 'Political mythology and the making of Natal's mfecane', *Canadian journal of African studies*, 23 (1989), 272–91.
5 Roland Oliver, *The missionary factor in East Africa* (London, 1952), p. 15.
6 See Norman Etherington, *Preachers, peasants and politics in southeast Africa, 1835–1880: African Christian communities in Natal, Pondoland and Zululand* (London, 1978).
7 Bent Noack, *Matthæusevangeliets folkelighed* (Copenhagen, 1971), p. 143.
8 According to Pope Pius V Roman Catechism of 1566.
9 'Rapport de Maurice Leenhardt sur la Mission du Zambèze, et la Question de sa Cession' (1923), in the archives of the Paris Evangelical Mission Society.
10 Quoted in Benjamin Ray, *African religions: symbol, ritual, and community* (Englewood Cliffs, 1976), p. 50.
11 F. L. Bartels, *The roots of Ghana Methodism* (Cambridge, 1965), p. 55; Sidney George Williamson, *Akan religion and the Christian faith: a comparative study of the impact of two religions* (ed. Kwesi A. Dickson, Accra, 1965), p. 85.
12 Terence Ranger, 'Territorial cults in the history of Central Africa', *Journal of African history*, 14, 4 (1973), p. 582.
13 See M. L. Daneel, *The God of the Matopo Hills* (The Hague and Paris, 1970).
14 *Ibid.*, pp. 77–79.
15 *Ibid.*, p. 83.
16 J. Matthew Schoffeleers, *River of blood: the genesis of a martyr cult in southern Malawi, c. AD 1600* (Madison and London, 1992).
17 Matthew Schoffeleers, 'The history and political role of the M'Bona cult among the Mang'anja', in T. O. Ranger and I. N. Kimambo (eds.), *The historical study of African religion: with special reference to East and Central Africa* (London, 1972), pp. 73–94.
18 Matthew Schoffeleers, 'The interaction of the M'Bona cult and Christianity, 1859–1963', in T. O. Ranger and John Weller (eds.), *Themes in the Christian history of Central Africa* (London, 1975), p. 22.
19 J. M. Schoffeleers, 'Cult idioms and the dialectics of a region', in Richard P. Werbner (ed.), *Regional cults*, (London and New York, 1977), p. 237.
20 Monica Wilson, *Religion and the transformation of society: a study in social change in Africa* (Cambridge, 1971), p. 47.
21 Robin Horton, 'African conversion', *Africa*, 41 (1971), 85–108.
22 Robin Horton, 'On the rationality of conversion' (Parts 1 and 2), *Africa*, 45 (1975), 219–35, 373–99.
23 Horton, 'African conversion', p. 103.
24 Quoted by Richard Gray, 'Christianity and religious change in Africa', *African affairs*, 77 (1978), p. 97.
25 *Ibid.*
26 John Lonsdale, 'The European scramble and conquest in African history', in Roland Oliver and G. N. Sanderson (eds.), *Cambridge history of Africa, volume 6: from 1870 to 1905* (Cambridge, 1985), p. 722.
27 *Ibid.*, p. 747.
28 K. Onwuka Diker, *Trade and politics in the Niger Delta 1830–1885: an introduction to the economic and political history of Nigeria* (Oxford, 1956).
29 A comprehensive and penetrating book on Libermann has recently been published: Paul

Coulon and Paule Brasseur *et al.*, *Libermann 1802–1852: une pensée et une mystique missionnaires*, 1988, 940 pp., with a preface by Leopold Sedar Senghor. Furthermore, Fr Coulon is preparing a doctoral thesis on Libermann during the years 1839–49, to be published by the Institut Catholic de Paris and Paris IV, Sorbonne.

30 See Josef-Theodor Rath, 'Libermann, promoteur de clergé africain (1840–1849)', in Paul Coulon, Paule Brasseur *et al.*, *Libermann 1802–1852: une pensée et une mystique missionaires* (Paris, 1988), pp. 576–77.

31 In his timid Memorial for French Congo of 1892.

32 François Renault, *Cardinal Lavigerie: churchman, prophet and missionary*. Trans. John O'Donohue. London and Atlantic Highlands, NJ, 1994.

33 Charles Lavigerie, *Ecrits d'Afrique* (ed. A. Hamman, Paris, 1966), p. 65.

34 See Georges Goyau, *La France missionnaire dans les cinq parties du monde* (2 vols., Paris, 1948), vol. 2.

35 See W. E. Brown, *The Catholic Church in South Africa: from its origin to the present day* (London, 1960), and Herménégilde Charbonneau, *My name is Eugène de Mazenod: texts chosen from Bishop Charles Joseph Eugène de Mazenod* (trans. Francis D. Flanagan, Boston, 1976).

36 Edmund M. Hogan, 'The motivation of the modern Irish missionary movement 1912–1939', *Journal of religion in Africa*, 10 (1979), p. 158 (his italics).

37 See Clement Fusero, *Daniele Comboni* (Bologna, 1967); and Maria Caravaglios (ed.), *L'Africa ai tempi di Daniele Comboni* (Rome, 1981), a conference report, with contributions by P. Chichetta, R. Gray, G. M. Caravaglios, A. Gilli *et al.*).

38 Richard Gray, 'The significance of Comboni in the history of Africa', in Maria Caravaglios (ed.), *L'Africa a tempi di Daniele Comboni* (Rome, 1981), p. 18.

39 Fusero, *Daniele Comboni*, p. 298.

40 Richard Lovett, *The history of the London Missionary Society 1795–1895* (2 vols., London, 1899), vol. 1, p. 43.

41 W. Schlatter, *Geschichte der Basler Mission 1815–1915* (3 vols., Basel, 1916), vol. 1, p. 30.

42 *Ibid.*, vol. 1, p. 167.

43 Georg Haccius, *Hanoversche Missionsgeschichte* (Hermannsburg, 1910), vol. 2, pp. 215–37.

44 *Ibid.*, p. 245.

45 *Ibid.*, p. 280.

46 *Ibid.*, p. 230.

47 Werner Ustorf, *Die Missionsmethode Franz Michael Zahns und der Aufbau Kirchlicher Strukturen in West Afrika (1862–1900): Eine Missionsgeschichtliche Untersuchung* (Erlangen, 1989), pp. 31–38.

48 *Ibid.*

49 *Ibid.*

50 *Ibid.*

51 Hans-Werner Gensichen, 'The North German Missionary Society', in Stephen Neill and others (eds.), *Concise dictionary of the Christian world mission* (London, 1970), p. 451.

52 John Brown Myers (ed.), *The centenary volume of the Baptist Missionary Society 1792–1892* (London, 1892), p. 175.

53 John D. Hargreaves, *Aberdeenshire to Africa: northeast Scots and British overseas expansion.* (Aberdeen, 1981), pp. 20–39. See also Tim Jeal, *Livingstone* (London, 1973), pp. 30–31.

54 Leonard Bacon, *A plea for Africa* (New Haven, 1825), quoted by Clifton Jackson Phillips,

Protestant America and the pagan world: the first half century of the American Board of Commissioners for Foreign Missions, 1810–1860 (Cambridge, Mass., 1969), pp. 207–08.

55 Hampden C. DuBose, *Memoirs of Rev. John Leighton Wilson* (Richmond, VA, 1895), p. 100.

56 See Phillips, *Protestant America.*

57 St Clair Drake, *The redemption of Africa and Black religion* (Chicago 1970), p. 41. See also Walter L. Williams, *Black Americans and the evangelization of Africa 1897–1900* (Madison, 1982), pp. 6–7.

58 St Clair Drake, *The redemption of Africa and Black religion* (Chicago 1970), p. 51.

59 *Ibid.*, pp. 55–56.

60 Samuel B. Coles, *Preacher with a plow* (Cambridge, Mass., 1957), p. 216.

61 Leroy Fitts, *Lott Carey, first Black missionary to Africa* (Valley Forge, 1978), p. 21.

62 *Ibid.*, p. 11.

63 *Ibid.*, p. 89.

64 Sylvia M. Jacobs (ed.), *Black Americans and the missionary movement in Africa* (Westpoint and London, 1982), p. 161.

CHAPTER 4: NORTH AND NORTH-EASTERN AFRICA

1 Antoine Fattal, *Le statut légal des non-Musulmans en pays d'Islam* (Beyrouth, 1958).

2 Peter Grossmann, 'Zum Typ der "Breithauskirche" in Ägypten', *Oriens Christianus*, 59 (1975).

3 Otto F. A. Meinardus, *Christian Egypt: ancient and modern* (2nd edn, Cairo, 1977), p. 144.

4 Otto F. A. Meinardus, *Christian Egypt: faith and life* (Cairo, 1970), p. 20.

5 Eugene Stock, *The history of the Church Missionary Society* (4 vols., London, 1899–1916), vol. 1, p. 227.

6 Constance E. Padwick, *Temple Gairdner of Cairo*, (London, 1929), p. 276, emphasis in the original.

7 See Joseph Metzler, 'Werben um die koptische Kirche', in J. Metzler (ed.), *Sacrae Congregationis de Propaganda Fide Memoria Rerum, volume II: 1700–1815* (Rome, 1973), pp. 379–403.

8 Louis Baunard, *Le cardinal Lavigerie* (2 vols., Paris, 1898), vol. 1, p. 402.

9 See Revd Fr J. Lanfry, WF, *Notes sur les manuscrits du Père de Foucauld* (1972).

10 René Bazin, *Charles de Foucauld, explorateur du Maroc, ermite au Sahara* (Paris, 1921); Ronald W. C. Bodley, *The warrior saint* (London, 1954); correspondence with Revd Fr René Lamey, WF, Rome.

11 J. Richard Gray, *A history of the southern Sudan 1839–1889* (Oxford, 1961), p. 20.

12 *Ibid.*, p. 25.

13 Elias Toniolo and Richard Hill (eds.), *The opening of the Nile basin* (London, 1974), p. 5.

14 Gray, *History*, p. 32.

15 *Ibid.*, pp. 38–39.

16 Toniolo and Hill (eds.), *Opening*, p. 10.

17 *Ibid.*, p. 9.

18 Gray, *History*, p. 40.

19 Toniolo and Hill (eds.), *Opening*, pp. 13–14.

20 *Ibid.*, pp. 15–16.

21 Gray, *History*, p. 53.

22 *Ibid.*, p. 28.
23 Toniolo and Hill (eds.), *Opening*, p. 20.
24 *Ibid.*, p. 22.
25 *Ibid.*, pp. 23–24.
26 Douglas Johnson, 'Divinity abroad: Dinka missionaries in foreign lands', in Wendy James and Douglas Johnson (eds.), *Vernacular Christianity* (Oxford, 1988), p. 173.
27 *Ibid.*, p. 174.
28 *Ibid.*, p. 176.
29 *Ibid.*
30 Gordon Hewitt, *The problems of success: a history of the Church Missionary Society 1910–1942* (2 vols., London, 1971–7) vol. 1, p. 324.
31 J. Spencer Trimingham, *The Christian approach to Islam in the Sudan* (London, New York and Toronto, 1948), p. 20.
32 Mohamed Omer Beshir, *Educational development in the Sudan 1898–1956* (Oxford, 1969), p. 50.
33 Giovanni Vantini, *Christianity in the Sudan* (Bologna, 1981), p. 247.
34 Lilian Passmore Sanderson and Neville Sanderson, *Education, religion and politics in Southern Sudan 1899–1964* (London, 1981), p. 57.
35 *Ibid.*, p. 55.
36 D. N. Levine, *Wax and gold: tradition and innovation in Ethiopian culture* (Chicago and London, 1965), p. 27.
37 See Edward Ullendorf, *The Ethiopians: an introduction to country and people* (3rd edn, London, 1973), pp. 104–05.
38 *Ibid.*, p. 105.
39 Mordechai Abir, *Ethiopia: the era of the princes: the challenge of Islam and the re-unification of the Christian empire 1769–1855* (London, 1968), pp. 35–36.
40 Donald Crummey, *Priests and politicians: Protestant and Catholic missions in Orthodox Ethiopia 1830–1868* (Oxford, 1972), p. 31.
41 Sven Rubenson, 'Ethiopia and the Horn', in John E. Flint (ed.), *Cambridge History of Africa, volume 5: from c. 1790 to c. 1870* (Cambridge, 1976), p. 61.
42 Crummey, *Priests*, p. 26.
43 J. Spencer Trimingham, *Islam in Ethiopia* (Oxford, 1952), p. 112.
44 David Kessler, *The Falashas* (London, 1982), pp. 115, 126.
45 Crummey, *Priests*, p. 35.
46 *Ibid.*, p. 39.
47 *Ibid.*, p. 50.
48 Johann Ludwig Krapf, *An imperfect outline of the elements of the Galla language. Preceded by a few remarks concerning the nation of the Gallas, and an Evangelical Mission among them, by C. W. Isenberg* (London, 1840).
49 Crummey, *Priests*, p. 53.
50 Sven Rubenson, *The survival of Ethiopian independence* (London, 1976), p.150 ff.
51 Crummey, *Priests*, p. 55.
52 *Ibid.*, p. 63.
53 *Ibid.*, p. 66.
54 *Ibid.*, p. 77.
55 *Ibid.*, p. 78.
56 See Sven Rubenson, *King of kings, Tewodros of Ethiopia* (Addis Ababa, 1966).

57 *Ibid.*

58 See Rubenson, *Survival*, pp. 210–11 for the explanation.

59 Crummey, *Priests*, p. 26.

60 *Ibid.*, p. 123.

61 See Jean-Baptiste Coulbeaux, *Histoire politique et religieuse d'Abyssinie: depuis les temps les plus reculés jusqu'à l'avènement de Ménélick* II. (3 vols., Paris, 1929).

62 Crummey, *Priests*, pp. 81, 148.

63 Zewde Gabre-Sellassie, *Yohannes IV of Ethiopia: a political biography* (Oxford, 1975), p. 91; for the Boru-Meda Council, see Guébré Sellassie, *Chronique de regne de Ménélik II: roi des rois d'Ethiopie* (edited by Maurice de Coppet, 2 vols., Paris, 1930–32), chapter 27.

64 Correspondence, Crummey, 24 May, 1982, to B.Sr.

65 Gabre-Sellassie, *Yohannes*, p. 94.

66 Richard Pankhurst (ed.), *The Ethiopian royal chronicles* (Addis Ababa, 1967), p. 182.

67 Gustav Arén, *Evangelical pioneers in Ethiopia: origins of the Evangelical Church Mekane Yesus* (Stockholm and Addis Ababa, 1978), p. 167.

68 *Ibid.*, pp. 187.

69 *Ibid.*, pp. 189.

70 *Ibid.*, pp. 187, 326.

71 *Ibid.*, p. 363.

72 Crummey, *Priests*, p. 148.

CHAPTER 5: WESTERN AFRICA

1 *Encyclopédie des Gens du Monde* (22 vols., Paris, 1833–4), vol. 13, p. 293.

2 See H. Korern, *Les Spiritans: trois siècles d'histoire religieuse et missionaire*, (Paris, 1982).

3 See Paule Brasseur, 'A la recherche d'un absolu missionaire: Mgr Truffet, Vicaire Apostolique des Deux-Guinées (1812–1847)', in Paul Coulon, Paule Brasseur *et al.*, *Libermann 1802–1852: une pensée et une mystique missionaires* (Paris, 1988), pp. 457–87.

4 *Ibid.*

5 *Ibid.*

6 *Ibid.*

7 Bernard Noël, 'Aloÿs Kobès (1870–1872)', in Paul Coulon, Paule Brasseur *et al. op. cit.* pp. 649–57.

8 Paule Brasseur, 'Missions catholiques et administration française sur la côte d'Afrique de 1815 à 1870', *Revue française d'histoire d'Outre-Mer*, 62 (1975), p. 438; reprinted in Paul Coulon *et al.*, *Libermann 1802–1852: une pensée et une mystique misionnaires* (Paris, 1988), p. 873.

9 Christopher Fyfe, *Sierra Leone inheritance* (London, 1964), p. 120.

10 Christopher Fyfe, *A history of Sierra Leone* (London, 1962), p. 127.

11 *Ibid.*, p. 258.

12 Stiv. Jakobsson, *Am I not a man and a brother: British missions and the abolition of the slave trade and slavery in West Africa and the West Indies 1786–1838* (Lund, 1972), *passim*.

13 *Ibid.*, p. 633.

14 Eugene Stock, *The history of the Church Missionary Society* (4 vols., London, 1899–1916), vol. 1, p. 166.

15 Fyfe, *History*, p. 131.

16 *Ibid.*, p. 129.

17 *Ibid.*, p. 129.

18 Christopher Fyfe, 'The West African Methodists in the nineteenth century', *Sierra Leone bulletin of religion*, Vol. 3 (1961), p. 24.

19 Fyfe, *History*, pp. 233, 290.

20 *Ibid.*, p. 237.

21 Jakobsson, *Am I not a man*, p. 219.

22 Fyfe, *History*, p. 212.

23 J. F. Ade Ajayi, *Christian missions in Nigeria 1841–1891: the making of a new elite* (London, 1965), p. 27.

24 *Ibid.*, p. 23.

25 Arthur T. Porter, *Creoledom: a study of the development of Freetown society* (London, 1963), p. 51; it should be underlined that in Sierra Leone 'Krio' or 'Creole' does not imply 'half-caste'.

26 Ian F. Hancock, 'A provisional comparison of the English-derived Atlantic creoles'; and Allen D. Grimshaw, 'Some social forces and some social functions of pidgin and creole languages'; both chapters in Dell Hymes (ed.), *Pidginization and creolization of languages* (Cambridge, 1971), pp. 290, 438.

27 Fyfe, *Sierra Leone inheritance*, p. 211.

28 Fyfe, *History*, p. 350.

29 *Ibid.*, p. 306.

30 E. W. Fasholé-Luke, 'Religion in Freetown', in Christopher Fyfe and Eldred Jones (eds.), *Freetown: a symposium* (Freetown, 1968), p. 134.

31 Fyfe, *History*, p. 511.

32 *Ibid.*, p. 508.

33 Porter, *Creoledom*, p. 85.

34 Fyfe, *History*, p. 615.

35 K. Onwuka Dike, *Trade and politics in the Niger Delta 1830–1885* (Oxford, 1956), p. 114.

36 P. E. H. Hair, 'CMS "native clergy" in West Africa to 1900', *Sierra Leone bulletin of religion*, 4 (1962), pp. 71–72.

37 E. Francis White, 'Creole women traders in Sierra Leone: an economic and social history, 1792–1945', Ph.D. thesis, Boston University, 1978, p. 165. See also E. Francis White, *Sierra Leone's settler women traders: women on the Afro-European frontier* (Ann Arbor, 1987).

38 Ian F. Hancock, 'A survey of the pidgins and creoles of the world', in Hymes, *Pidginization*, p. 517.

39 J. C. Wold, *God's impatience in Liberia* (Grand Rapids, 1970), pp. 73–80.

40 Michel Bee, 'La christianisation de la basse Côte d'Ivoire', *Revue français d'histoire d'Outre-Mer*, 62 (1975), pp. 619–39.

41 David A. Shank, 'The prophet of modern times: the thought of William Waddy Harris', (2 vols., Xerox Reproductions No. 5, Centre for New Religious Movements, Selly Oak Colleges, Birmingham, 1985), vol. 1, pp. 327–28; originally a Ph.D. thesis, University of Aberdeen, 1981. See also David A. Shank, *Prophet Harris, the 'Black Elijah' of West Africa* (abr. Jocelyn Murray, Leiden, 1994).

42 *L'Echo*, February 1930.

43 Shank, 'The prophet' vol. 2, pp. 540–42.

44 *Ibid.*, vol. 1, p. 68.
45 Gordon MacKay Haliburton, *The Prophet Harris: a study of an African prophet and his mass-movement in the Ivory Coast and the Gold Coast 1913–1915* (London, 1971), pp. 49–50.
46 *Ibid.*, p. 50.
47 Shank, 'The prophet' vol. 2, pp. 647–48.
48 Sheila S. Walker, *The religious revolution in the Ivory Coast: the Prophet Harris and the Harrist Church* (Chapel Hill, 1983), p. 78.
49 Ivor Wilks, *Asante in the nineteenth century: the structure and evolution of a political order* (Cambridge, 1975), p. 26.
50 F. L. Bartels, *The roots of Ghana Methodism* (Cambridge, 1965), p. 6.
51 Philip Foster, *Education and social change in Ghana* (London, 1965), p. 104.
52 MMS archives, Biographical West Africa, Freeman, 'History of the rise and progress', cited in Bartels, *Roots*, p. 9.
53 Bartels, *Roots*, p. 13.
54 Allen Birtwhistle, *Thomas Birch Freeman: West African pioneer* (London, 1950), p. 32. See also *Thomas Birch Freeman: journal of various visits to the kingdoms of Ashanti, Aku, and Dahomi in western Africa* (1844. 3rd edn, London, 1968).
55 Foster, *Education*, p. 68.
56 Bartels, *Roots*, p. 86; David Kimble, *A political history of Ghana: the rise of Gold Coast nationalism 1850–1928* (Oxford, 1963), pp. 222ff.
57 Hans W. Debrunner, *A history of Christianity in Ghana* (Accra, 1967), p. 154.
58 *Ibid.*, p. 156.
59 Stanger, 2nd quarterly report, 1852, Basel Mission archives; Margaret J. Field, *Social organization of the Ga people* (Accra and London, 1940), p. 72.
60 Hans W. Debrunner, *A history of Christianity in Ghana* (Accra, 1967), p. 159.
61 Lodholtz, 28/4/1870 report, Basel Mission archives.
62 Zimmermann, quarterly report, 1853, Basel Mission archives.
63 Debrunner, *History*, p. 241.
64 Bartels, *Roots*, p. 213.
65 Wilhelm Schlatter, *Geschichte der Basler Mission 1815–1915* (3 vols., Basel, 1916), vol. 3, p. 103.
66 Debrunner, *History*, p. 195.
67 Paul Jenkins, 'A comment on M. P. Frempong's history of the Presbyterian Church at Bompata', *Ghana Notes and Queries*, 12 (1972), p. 25.
68 M. P. Frempong, 'A history of the Presbyterian Church at Bompata in Asante-Akyem' (trans. by E. A. Kyerematen), *Ghana Notes and Queries*, 12 (1972); and Paul Jenkins, 'Comment', *Ghana Notes and Queries*, 12 (1972).
69 Debrunner, *History*, p. 176.
70 *Ibid.*, p. 195.
71 *Ibid.*, p. 203.
72 Schlatter, *Geschichte*, vol. 1, p. 152.
73 F. L. Bartels, *The roots of Ghana Methodism* (Cambridge, 1965), p. 92.
74 *Ibid.*, p. 167.
75 *Ibid.*, pp. 130, 141.
76 James W. Brown, 'Kumasi, 1896–1923: urban Africa during the early colonial period', Ph.D. thesis, University of Wisconsin, 1972, p. 211.

77 Henry P. Thompson, *Into all lands: the history of the Society for the Propagation of the Gospel in Foreign Parts* (London, 1951), p. 584.

78 Werner Ustorf, *Die Missionsmethode Franz Michael Zahns und der Aufbau Kirchlicher Strukturen in West Afrika (1862–1900): Eine Missionsgeschichtliche Untersuchung* (Erlangen, 1989), pp. 191–13. See also Ustorf, Werner (ed.) *Mission im Kontext: Beiträge zur Sozialgeschichte der Norddeutschen Missionsgesellschaft im 19. Jahrhundert.* (Bremen, 1986).

79 *Ibid.*, pp. 194–205. See also Hans W. Debrunner, *A Church between colonial powers: a study of the Church in Togo* (London, 1965), pp. 127–30.

80 J. Schmidlin, *Katholische Missionsgeschichte*. Steyl, 1924.

81 John M. Todd, *African mission: a historical study of the Society of African Missions*, (London, 1962), pp. 52, 55.

82 *Ibid.*, see pp. 65–77.

83 Thomas Fowell Buxton, *The African slave trade and its remedy* (1839; reprinted, London, 1967), pp. 301–02, 511.

84 Felix Ekechi, *Missionary enterprise and rivalry in Igboland, 1857–1914* (London, 1972), p. 2.

85 See S. A. Adewale, 'The role of Ifa in the work of the nineteenth century missionaries', *Orita, Ibadan journal of religious studies*, 12 (1978).

86 See J. F. Ade Ajayi and Robert Smith, *Yoruba warfare in the nineteenth century* (2nd edn, Cambridge, 1971).

87 Stock, *History*, vol. 2, pp. 105, 111.

88 Ajayi, *Christian missions*, p. 79.

89 Stock, *History*, vol. 2, p. 441.

90 *Ibid.*, p. 438.

91 Communication from Professor J. D. Y. Peel, School of Oriental and African Studies, University of London.

92 Ajayi, *Christian missions*, p. 203.

93 James Bertin Webster, *The African Churches among the Yoruba 1888–1922* (Oxford, 1964), p. 66.

94 *Ibid.*, p. 68.

95 *Ibid.*, p. 69.

96 *Ibid.*, p. 89.

97 *Ibid.*, p. 105.

98 See E. A. Ayandele, *A visionary of the African Church: Mojola Agbebi (1860–1917)* (Nairobi, 1971).

99 E. A. Ayandele, *The missionary impact on modern Nigeria 1842–1914: a political and social analysis* (London, 1966), p. 14.

100 *Ibid.*, p. 53.

101 Robert Smith, 'Nigeria-Ijebu', in Michael Crowder (ed.), *West African resistance: the military response to colonial occupation* (2nd edn, London, 1978), p. 194.

102 See E. A. Ayandele, 'The ideological ferment in Ijebuland, 1892–1943', in his *Nigerian historical studies* (London, 1979), pp. 270–94; *idem*, *Holy Johnson: pioneer of African nationalism, 1836–1917* (London, 1970).

103 Ayandele, *Missionary impact*, p. 157.

104 Ajayi, *Christian missions*, p. 163.

105 *Ibid.*, pp. 153, 155.

106 Robert Smith, 'The Lagos consulate, 1851–1861: an outline', *Journal of African history*, 15 (1974), p. 401.

107 *Ibid.*

108 Elizabeth G. K. Hewat, *Vision and achievement 1796–1956: a history of the foreign missions of the Churches united in the Church of Scotland* (London and Edinburgh, 1960), p. 195.

109 See Dike, *Trade*.

110 See Peter C. Lloyd, 'The Itsekiri in the nineteenth century: an outline social history', *Journal of African history*, 4 (1963); Alan F. C. Ryder, *Benin and the Europeans 1485–1897* (London, 1969); and Samuel Erivwo, *The Urhobo, the Isoko and the Itsekiri* (Ibadan, 1979).

111 Buxton, *African slave trade*, pp. 492, 524.

112 Hewat, *Vision*, p. 193.

113 P. Amaury Talbot, *The peoples of Southern Nigeria: a sketch of their history, ethnology and languages with an abstract of the 1921 census* (4 vols., 1926; reprinted, London, 1969), vol. 1, p. 193.

114 Kannan K. Nair, *Politics and society in south eastern Nigeria 1841–1906: a study of power, diplomacy and commerce in old Calabar* (London, 1972), pp. 63–64.

115 Dike, *Trade*, p. 155.

116 A. J. H. Latham, *Old Calabar 1600–1891: the impact of the international economy upon a traditional society* (Oxford, 1973), p. 95.

117 Elizabeth Isichei, *The Ibo people and the Europeans: the genesis of a relationship – to 1906* (London, 1973), p. 87.

118 Latham, *Old Calabar*, p. 105.

119 Colman Cooke, 'The Roman Catholic mission in Calabar 1903–1960', Ph.D. thesis, University of London, 1977, p. 31.

120 Latham, *Old Calabar*, pp. 106, 109.

121 Ajayi, *Christian missions*, p. 118.

122 Nair, *Politics*, p. 61.

123 G. O. M. Tasie, *Christian missionary enterprise in the Niger Delta 1864–1918* (Leiden, 1978), p. 61.

124 Ekechi, *Missionary enterprise*, p. 8.

125 *Ibid.*, p. 15.

126 *Ibid.*

127 Peter Beyerhaus, *Die Selbständigkeit der jungen Kirchen als missionarische Problem* (Uppsala, 1956), pp. 142–43; P. R. McKenzie, *Inter-religious encounters in West Africa: Samuel Ajayi Crowther's attitude to African traditional religion and Islam*, (Leicester, 1976), p. 60.

128 Ekechi, *Missionary enterprise*, p. 16.

129 *Ibid.*, p. 19.

130 Ajayi, *Christian missions*, p. 222.

131 *Ibid.*, p. 223.

132 *Ibid.*, p. 224.

133 McKenzie, *Inter-religious*, p. 49.

134 *Ibid.*, p. 32n.

135 T. S. Johnson, *The story of a mission: the Sierra Leone Church: first daughter of CMS* (London, 1953), p. 62.
136 Jesse Page, *The Black Bishop: Samuel Adjai Crowther* (London, 1908), p. 385.
137 G. W. Brooke in Ayandele, *Missionary impact*, p. 213.
138 Ajayi, *Christian missions*, p. 253.
139 Ayandele, *Missionary impact*, p. vii.
140 Tasie, *Christian missionary*, pp. 14, 93–94, 172.
141 Ayandele, *Missionary impact*, p. 214; and CMS archives G3/A3/04.
142 Stock, *History*, vol. 2, p. 463.
143 Tasie, *Christian missionary*, p. 38.
144 Ekechi, *Missionary enterprise*, p. 119; Roland Oliver, *Sir Harry Johnston* (London, 1957), pp. 107–19.
145 C. P. Groves, *The planting of Christianity in Africa* (4 vols., London, 1948–58), vol. 3, p. 216.
146 Ekechi, *Missionary enterprise*, p. 73.
147 *Ibid.*, p. 180.
148 Ayandele, *Missionary impact*, p. 287.
149 Todd, *African mission*, pp. 121–22.
150 Ekechi, *Missionary enterprise*, p. 219.
151 Elizabeth Isichei, *A history of the Igbo people* (London, 1976), p. 128.
152 Ekechi, *Missionary enterprise*, p. 147.
153 *Ibid.*, p. 178.
154 *Ibid.*, p. 146.
155 Victor C. Uchendu, *The Igbo of southeast Nigeria* (New York, 1965), p. 19.
156 Vincent Monteil, *L'Islam noir: une religion à la conquête de l'Afrique* (Paris, 1980), pp. 105–10.
157 Thomas Hodgkin, *Nigerian perspectives: an historical anthology* (2nd edn, Oxford, 1975.), p. 284.
158 Ian Linden, 'Between two religions of the book: the Children of the Israelites (*c.*1846–*c.*1920)', in Elizabeth Isichei (ed.), *Varieties of Christian experience in Nigeria* (London, 1982), p. 95.
159 Michael Crowder, *The story of Nigeria* (4th edn, London, 1978), p. 196.
160 Sonia F. Graham, *Government and mission education in Northern Nigeria 1900–1919, with special reference to the work of Hanns Vischer* (Ibadan, 1966), p. 33.
161 G. O. Olusanya, 'The freed slaves' homes – an unknown aspect of Northern Nigerian social history', *Journal of the Historical Society of Nigeria*, 3 (1966), 538.
162 S. F. Nadel, *A Black Byzantium: the Kingdom of Nupe in Nigeria* (London, 1942), pp. 401–04.
163 E. N. Casaleggio, *"En die land sal sy vrug gee": Vyftig jaar van sendingwerk in die Soedan* (Cape Town, 1965), pp. 99–100.
164 See Akighirga S. Akiga, *Akiga's story: the Tiv tribe as seen by one of its members* (trans. and annot. Rupert East; 2nd edn, London, 1965).
165 Martin Lynn, 'Commerce, Christianity and the origins of the "Creoles" of Fernando Po', *Journal of African history*, 25 (1984), p. 260.
166 *Ibid.*
167 Jaap Van Slageren, *Les Origines de L'Église Évangélique du Cameroun* (Leiden, 1972), p. 19.

168 *Ibid.*, p. 22.

169 *Ibid.*, p. 32.

170 Brian Stanley, *The history of the Baptist Missionary Society 1792–1992* (Edinburgh, 1992), p. 108.

171 Erik Halldén, *The cultural policy of the Basel Mission in the Cameroons 1886–1905* (Uppsala, 1968), p. 109.

172 Julius Richter, *Allgemeine evangelische Missionsgeschichte*, vol. 3, *Geschichte der evangelischen Mission in Afrika* (Gütersloh, 1922), p. 174; B.Sr. correspondence with Church President Jean Kotto, 1984–87.

173 Van Slageren, *Les Origines*, p. 95.

174 *Ibid.*, p. 102.

175 See James W. Fernandez, 'Persuasion and performances of the beast in every body and the metaphors of Everyman', *Daedalus*, 101 (1972), pp. 39–60.

176 Engelbert Mveng, 'A la recherche d'un nouveau dialogue entre le christianisme, le génie culturel et les religions africaines actuelles', *Présence Africaine*, 96 (1975), 449.

177 Hermann Skolaster, *Die Pallottiner in Kamerun: 25 Jahre Missionsarbeit* (Limburg, 1924), p. 229.

178 *Ibid.*, pp. 230–33.

179 *Ibid.*, p. 238.

180 *Ibid.*, p. 239.

181 See Schlatter, *Geschichte*, vol. 3; Werner Keller, *Zur Freiheit berufen: Die Geschichte der Presbyterianischen Kirche in Kamerun* (Zurich, 1981); Philippe Laburthe-Tolra, *Mínlaaba: histoire et société traditionnelle chez les Bëti du Sud Cameroun* (3 vols., Lille, 1977).

182 Henry H. Bucher, 'The Mpongwe of the Gabon estuary: a history to 1860', Ph.D. thesis, University of Wisconsin, 1977.

183 Robert H. Nassau, *Fetishism in West Africa* (New York, 1904), p. 57.

184 See Bucher, 'Mpongwe'.

185 See Louis Roques, *Le Pionnier du Gabon: Jean-Rémi Bessieux* (Paris, 1971).

186 K. David Patterson, *The northern Gabon coast to 1875* (Oxford, 1975), p. 119.

187 See G. Lasserre, *Libreville, la ville et sa region* (Paris, 1958).

CHAPTER 6: WEST-CENTRAL AFRICA

1 Jan Vansina, *The Tio kingdom of the middle Congo 1880–1892* (London, 1973), p. 137.

2 *Ibid.*

3 *Les Missions Catholiques*, 1875, p. 142.

4 Jan Vansina, *L'Introduction à l'ethnographie du Congo* (Brussels, 1966), pp. 188–91.

5 Jan Vansina, *Kingdoms of the savanna* (Madison and London, 1966), p. 247. See *idem*, *Paths in the rainforests: toward a history of political tradition in equatorial Africa* (London, 1990).

6 See Wyatt MacGaffey, *Custom and government in the Lower Congo* (Berkeley, 1970), pp. 303–04.

7 Leopold Anckaer, *De evangelizatiemetode van de missionarissen van Scheut in Kongo (1888–1907)* (Brussels, 1970), p. 111.

8 Auguste Roeykens (ed.), *La politique religieuse de l'État Indépendant du Congo: documents: Léopold II, le saint-Siège et les Missions catholiques dans l'Afrique Equatoriale (1876–1885)* (Brussels, 1965), *passim*.

9 Pierre Savorgnan de Brazza, *Brazza explorateur: les traités Makolo 1880–1882* (ed. Henri Brunschwig, Paris 1972), p. 214.

10 *Ibid.*; Catherine Coquery-Vidrovitch, *Brazza et la prise de possession du Congo: la mission de l'Ouest Africain 1883–1885* (Paris, 1969).

11 See S. E. Crowe, *The Berlin West African Conference 1884–1885* (1942. Reprinted, Westport, 1970); Ruth Slade, *King Leopold's Congo: aspects of the development of race relations in the Congo Independent State* (London, 1962).

12 Neal Ascherson, *The king incorporated: Leopold II in the age of thrusts* (London, 1963), p. 203.

13 Catherine Coquery-Vidrovitch, *Le Congo au temps des grandes compagnies concessionnaires 1898–1930* (Paris, 1972), p. 183.

14 For Sjöblom, see David Lagergren, *Mission and state in the Congo: a study of the relations between Protestant missions and the Congo Independent State authorities with special reference to the Equator District, 1885–1903* (Lund, 1970); for Morrison, see T. C. Vinson, *William McCutchen Morrison: twenty years in Central Africa* (Richmond, 1921).

15 W. Holman Bentley, *Pioneering on the Congo* (2 vols., London, 1900; reprinted, New York, 1970), vol. 2, p. 425.

16 Anckaer, *De evangelizatiemetode*, p. 292.

17 See *Bulletin de l'Union missionnaire du Clergé*, 116 (October 1954).

18 See E. Parein, *L'enseignement au Congo: les réalisations*. n.d.

19 ex. P. Fredericksson, 5 May, 1892, to F. Merriman, ABFMS, and Bentley, *Pioneering*, vol. 2, p. 316 ff.

20 See Phyllis M. Martin, *The external trade of the Loango coast 1576–1870: the effects of changing commercial relations on the Vili kingdom of Loango* (Oxford, 1972).

21 *Les Missions Catholiques*, 1877–81.

22 *Ibid.*

23 Charles Duparquet, CSSp. Archive, Paris: Box 7:469.

24 Published at Loango, 1890.

25 See Auguste Roeykens (ed.), *La politique religieuse de l'Etat Indépendant du Congo: documents: Léopold II, le saint-Siège et les Missions catholiques dans l'Afrique Equatoriale (1876–1885)* (Brussels, 1965), p. 112.

26 See Mgr [Prosper-Philippe] Augouard, *Vingt-huit années au Congo: lettres de Mgr Augouard* (2 vols., Poitiers, 1905).

27 More of this French 'retreat', pp. 294–95.

28 Georges Mazenot, *La Likouala-Mossaka, histoire de la pénétration du Haut Congo 1878–1920* (Paris, 1970), p. 247.

29 Georges Goyau, *La France missionnaire dans les cinq parties du monde* (2 vols., Paris, 1948), vol. 2, p. 195.

30 Mazenot, *La Likouala-Mossaka*, p. 393.

31 Roeykens, *La politique* , p. 336.

32 Lagergren, *Mission*, p. 256.

33 Michaël Kratz, *La mission des rédemptoristes belges au Bas-Congo: la période des semailles (1899–1920)* (Brussels, 1970), *passim*.

34 Marcel Storme, *Het ontstaan van der Kasai-missie* (Brussels, 1961), p. 27; *idem.*, *Pater Cambier en de stichting van de Kasai-missie* (Brussels, 1964), p. 37; Letters to B.Sr. from Fr Dr M. Storme, 29 December, 1979, January and February 1980.

35 Storme, *Cambier*, p. 40.

36 Anckaer, *De evangelizatiemetode*, p. 154; Augouard, *Vingt-huit ans au Congo* (Poitiers, 1905); *idem*, *Physionomie documentaire ou Vie inconnue de Mgr Augouard* (Paris, 1938); Fr Remy, 'Vie de Mgr Augouard', typewritten *Annales Spiritains*, LXII, 1952; J. Derouet, *Le Séminaire de Mayumba* (Loango, 1912).
37 Bentley, *Pioneering*, vol. 1, p. 183.
38 *Ibid.*, vol. 2, p. 27.
39 Ruth M. Slade, *English-speaking missions in the Congo Independent State (1878–1908)* Académie Royale des Sciences Coloniales, Class des Sciences Morales et Politiques, Mémoires, N.S. 16, 1958–59 (Brussels, 1959), p. 97.
40 *Ibid.*, p. 102.
41 Quoted in *ibid.*, p. 133.
42 See Slade, *English-speaking missions*, p. 81; Brian Stanley, *The history of the Baptist Missionary Society 1792–1992* (Edinburgh, 1992), p. 124.
43 Harry H. Johnson, *George Grenfell and the Congo* (2 vols., London, 1908), vol. 1, p. 186.
44 C. P. Groves, *The planting of Christianity in Africa* (4 vols., London, 1948–58), vol. 3, p. 120.
45 Goyau, *La France*, vol. 2, p. 201.
46 *Ibid.*
47 Arvid Svärd, *I urskogens skugga: skildringar från Kongo* (Stockholm, 1922), p. 43.
48 Slade, *English-speaking missions*, p. 79.
49 Bentley, *Pioneering*, vol. 2, pp. 299–300.
50 See Lagergren, *Mission*, p. 83.
51 Bentley, *Pioneering* , vol. 2, p. 346.
52 Slade, *English-speaking missions*, p. 170.
53 MacGaffey, *Custom*, p. 251.
54 *Ibid.*
55 Wyatt MacGaffey, *Modern Kongo prophets: religion in a plural society* (Bloomington, 1983), p. 31.
56 *Ibid.*
57 MacGaffey, *Custom*, p. 252.
58 Quoted from Fanny E. Guinness, *The new world of Central Africa: with a history of the first Christian mission on the Congo* (London, 1890), pp. 431–2; see MacGaffey, *Modern Kongo prophets*, p. 29.
59 MacGaffey, *Custom*, p. 252.
60 Murdoch, 8 August, 1887 to Richards, ABFMS, cited in C. H. Stuart, 'The Lower Congo and the American Baptist Mission to 1910', Ph.D. thesis, Boston University, 1969.
61 Ruth Slade, *English-speaking missions*, p. 191.
62 See E. T. Wharton, *Led in triumph: sixty years of Southern Presbyterian missions in the Belgian Congo* (Nashville, 1952).
63 See George Hawker, *The life of George Grenfell: Congo missionary and explorer* (London, 1909).
64 *Ibid.*, p. 129.
65 See E. M. Braekman, *Histoire du Protestantisme au Congo* (Brussels, 1961), p. 178.
66 See T. C. Vinson, *William McCutchen Morrison: twenty years in Central Africa* (Richmond, 1921).
67 See Charles L. Crane, 'L'Église du Christ au Congo', in *Tamburam, Madras papers series* (vol. 2, London, 1939); Stanley Shaloff, *Reform in Leopold's Congo* (Richmond, Va., 1970), pp. 16–25.

68 Slade, *English-speaking missions*, p. 377.

69 Efraim Andersson, *Churches at the grass-roots: a study in Congo-Brazzaville* (London, 1968), p. 126.

70 Daniel Crawford, *Thinking Black: 22 years without a break in the long grass of Central Africa* (London, 1912).

71 Walter Rodney, *How Europe underdeveloped Africa* (London, 1972).

72 See René Pélissier, *Résistance et révoltes en Angola (1845–1961)* (3 vols., Paris, 1976)

73 See António Brasio, *Monumenta missionaria Africana* (15 vols., Lisbon, 1952–88).

74 W. G. Clarence-Smith, *Slaves, peasants and capitalists in southern Angola 1840–1926* (Cambridge, 1979), p. 90.

75 Louis A. Keiling, *Quarenta anos de Africa* (Braga, 1934).

76 Juel M. A. Nordby, 'The role of the Methodist class meeting in the growth of an African city Church: a historico-sociological study', Th.D. thesis, Boston University, 1967.

CHAPTER 7: SOUTHERN AFRICA

1 John D. Omer-Cooper, *The Zulu aftermath: a nineteenth-century revolution in Bantu Africa* (London, 1966), p. 168.

2 See Martin C. Legassick, 'The Griqua, the Sotho-Tswana and the missionaries, 1780–1840: the politics of a frontier zone', Ph.D. thesis, University of California at Los Angeles, 1970, p. 169.

3 See John D. Omer-Cooper, 'Colonial South Africa and its frontiers', in John E. Flint (ed.), *Cambridge history of Africa, volume 5: from c. 1790 to c. 1870* (Cambridge, 1976), pp. 353–92.

4 See Peter Hinchliff, *The Church in South Africa* (London, 1968), pp. 8–9; W. J. van der Merwe, *The development of missionary attitudes in the Dutch Reformed Church in South Africa* (Cape Town, 1934).

5 G. B. A. Gerdener, interview by B.Sr., 1942.

6 See Bernhard Kruger, *The pear tree blossoms: a history of the Moravian mission stations in South Africa, 1737–1869* (Genadendal, 1966).

7 *Ibid.*, pp. 86–87.

8 *Ibid.*, pp. 120, 185, 280.

9 See W. M. Macmillan, *The Cape colour question: a historical survey* (London, 1927), *passim.*

10 T. R. H. Davenport, 'The consolidation of a new society: the Cape Colony', in Monica Wilson and Leonard Thompson (eds.), *The Oxford history of South Africa* (2 vols., Oxford, 1969–71), vol. 1, p. 309.

11 Ido H. Enklaar, *De Levensgeschiedenis van Johannes Theodorus Van der Kemp: Stichter van het Nederlandsch Zendeling-Genootschap Pionier van de London Missionary Society onder Kaffers en Hottentotten in Zuid-Afrika, 1747–1811, tot zijn aankomst aan de Kaap in 1799* (Wageningen, 1972), pp. 38, 88, 97; for the English version, see *idem*, *Life and work of Dr J. Th. Van der Kemp 1747–1811: missionary pioneer and protagonist of racial equality in South Africa* (Cape Town and Rotterdam, 1988).

12 Jane Sales, *Mission stations and coloured communities of the eastern Cape 1800–1852* (Cape Town and Rotterdam, 1975), pp. 157–58.

13 *Ibid.*, p. 38.

14 Tony Kirk, 'Progress and decline in the Kat River settlement, 1829–54', *Journal of African history*, 14 (1973), p. 416.

15 Sales, *Mission stations*, p. 107.

16 William M. Macmillan, *The Cape colour question: a historical survey* (London, 1927), p. 266; Legassick, 'Griqua', p. 172.

17 Robert Ross, *Adam Kok's Griquas: a study in the development of stratification in South Africa* (Cambridge, 1976), pp. 16, 70.

18 Anderson and Janz, Report, Klaarwater (Griqua Town) 1/9/1808. South African Incoming Journals, LMS, Boxes l-4, 1798–1892, SOAS.

19 Ross, *Adam Kok's Griquas*, p. 46.

20 *Ibid.*, p. 78.

21 Legassick, 'The Griqua', p. 172.

22 *Ibid.*

23 Ross, *Adam Kok's Griquas*, p. 107.

24 *Ibid.*, p. 138; W. Keith Hancock, *Smuts, volume 1: the sanguine years 1870–1919* (Cambridge, 1962), p. 521.

25 See W. Gründler, *Hundert Jahre Berliner Mission* (Berlin, 1923), p. 51; Eduard Kratzenstein, *Kurze Geschichte der Berliner Mission in Süd- und Ostafrika* (3rd edn, Berlin, 1887), pp. 7ff.

26 C. and A. Albrecht, January–November 1809, Journal Account of C. Albrecht's journey in Kamiesberg, LMS archives, SOAS.

27 On Hugo Hahn, see Theo Sundermeier, *Mission, Bekenntnis und Kirche: Missionstheologische Probleme des 19. Jahrhunderts bei C. H. Hahn* (Wuppertal-Barmen, 1962), and on Knudsen, see [Otto] Emil Birkeli, *En økenvandrer: Norges første afrikamissionær H. C. Knudsen* (Oslo, 1925).

28 Lothar Engel, *Die Stellung der Rheinischen Missionsgesellschaft zu den politischen und gesellschaftlichen Verhältnissen Südwestafrikas und ihr Beitrag zur dortigen kirchlichen Entwicklung bis zum Nama-Herero-Aufstand 1904–1907* (Hamburg, 1972), pp. 59, 61, 63.

29 Heinrich Loth, *Die christliche Mission in Südwestafrika: zur destruktiven Rolle der Rheinischen Missionsgesellschaft beim Prozess der Staatsbildung in Südwestafrika (1842–1893)* (Berlin (GDR), 1963).

30 See Engel, *Die Stellung*; E. Strassberger, *The Rhenish Mission Society in South Africa 1830–1950* (Cape Town, 1969).

31 Sales, *Mission stations*, pp. 78, 95.

32 John Campbell, *Travels in South Africa: undertaken at the request of the missionary society* (London, 1815), p. 95.

33 LMS South Africa 1815–16, Bethany papers.

34 LMS Box 2, File 44, Africa 1814; Br. Messer's Journal, 12 and 20 December, 1814.

35 Br Messer's Journal, 20 December 1814.

36 Kruger, *Pear tree blossoms*, p. 108.

37 Robert Moffat, *Missionary labours and scenes in Southern Africa* (London, 1842), p. 185.

38 Sales, *Mission stations*, p. 37.

39 LMS, South Africa 1815–16, 20 Feb. 1816, at SOAS.

40 LMS, South Africa 1815–16, 20 Feb. 1816, Bethany, J. H. Schmelen, at SOAS.

41 C. F. Pascoe, *Two hundred years of the SPG: an historical account of the Society for the Propagation of the Gospel in Foreign Parts 1701–1900* (London, 1901) p. 287.

42 LMS, Box 2, File 44, Br. Messer's Journal, 2 Oct. & 13 Dec. 1814, at SOAS.

43 LMS *Quarterly Chronicle*, 1 (1815–20), p. 307.

44 Robert Moffat, *Apprenticeship at Kuruman: being the journals and letters of Robert and Mary Moffat 1820–1826* (ed. Isaac Schapera, London, 1951), p. 40.

45 Monica Hunter, *Reaction to conquest: effects of contact with Europeans on the Pondo of South Africa* (London, 1936), p. 561.
46 *Ibid.*
47 For the Buys clan among the Venda, Northern Transvaal, and the contribution of Coloureds in the evangelization north of the Limpopo, see Chapter 8.
48 J. Read, Report, LMS *Quarterly Chronicle*, 1 (1815–20), p. 19.
49 *Ibid.*
50 See A. Kropf, *Ntsikana, der Erstling aus den Kaffern und ein Prophet unter seinem Volk* (Berlin, 1891).
51 Jeffrey B. Peires, *The house of Phalo: a history of the Xhosa people in the days of their independence* (Berkeley, , 1982), p. 68.
52 Albert Kropf, *Ntsikana* (1891); Katesa Schlosser, *Prophetin in Afrika* (Braunschweig, 1949) p. 328.
53 See Janet Hodgson, *Ntsikana's great hymn: a Xhosa expression of Christianity in the early nineteenth century eastern Cape* (Cape Town, 1980).
54 *Ibid.*, p. 6.
55 *Ibid.*, p. 8.
56 *Ibid.*, p. 19.
57 *Ibid.*
58 See J. K. Bokwe, *Ntsikana: the story of an African hymn* (Lovedale, 1904).
59 William Shaw, *The story of my mission in south-eastern Africa* (1860; 2nd edn, London, 1872), p. 71.
60 Kratzenstein, *Kurze Geschichte*, pp. 104–15.
61 Roger B. Beck, 'Bibles and Beads: missionaries as traders in Southern Africa in the early nineteenth century', *Journal of African history*, 30 (1989), 211–12.
62 *Ibid.*, p. 219.
63 *Ibid.*, pp. 211–25.
64 Shaw, *Story*, pt. 2, pp. 102, 129.
65 See W. C. Holden, *British rule in South Africa, illustrated in the story of Kama and his tribe and of the war in Zululand* (1879; reprinted, Pretoria, 1969).
66 Archibald C. Jordan, *Towards an African literature: the emergence of literary form in Xhosa* (Berkeley, 1973), pp. 97–99.
67 Charles Buchner, *Acht Monate in Südafrika* (Gütersloh, 1894), p. 41.
68 Norman Etherington, *Preachers, peasants and politics in southeast Africa, 1835–1880: African Christian communities in Natal, Pondoland and Zululand* (London, 1978), p. 72.
69 *Ibid.*
70 William Beinart, *The political economy of Pondoland 1860–1930* (Cambridge, 1982), pp. 149ff.
71 John A. Chalmers, *Tiyo Soga: a page of South African mission work* (Edinburgh, 1877), p. 322; Wesleyan Methodist Missionary Society, *Report* 1838, pp. 61, 114.
72 James Stewart, 'The Lovedale Institution', in *Proceedings of the general conference on foreign missions held at the conference hall in Mildmay Park, London, in October, 1878* (London, 1879), p. 71.
73 Wesleyan Methodist Missionary Society, *Report*, June 1838, p. 53.
74 Quoted in Shaw, *Story*, pt. 2, p. 48.
75 Hinchliff, *Church*, p. 46.
76 Pascoe, *Two hundred years*, p. 784.

77 *Ibid.*, p. 287.

78 Robert Gray, *Journal of two visitations in 1848 and 1850* (London, 1851), pp. 31, 287.

79 Pascoe, *Two hundred years*, p. 309.

80 Shaw, *Story*, pt. 2, p. 164.

81 *Ibid.*, pp. 41–42.

82 Elizabeth G. K. Hewat, *Vision and achievement 1796–1956: a history of the foreign missions of the Churches united in the Church of Scotland* (London and Edinburgh, 1960), p. 179.

83 *African Papers* (Lovedale, 1878), No. 1, pp. 1–15.

84 See Chalmers, *Tiyo Soga*.

85 Donovan Williams, *Umfundisi: a biography of Tiyo Soga 1829–1871* (Lovedale, 1978), p. 31.

86 Chalmers, *Tiyo Soga*, pp. 133, 278, 358.

87 See Williams, *Umfundisi*.

88 William Taylor, *Christian adventures in South Africa* (London, 1868), p. 159.

89 Edwin W. Smith, *The life and times of Daniel Lindley (1801–80): missionary to the Zulus, pastor of the Voortrekkers, Ubebe Omhlope* (London, 1949), pp. 127, 132.

90 Edgar H. Brookes and Colin de B. Webb, *A history of Natal* (Pietermaritzburg, 1965), p. 60.

91 Norman A. Etherington, 'An American errand into the South African wilderness', *Church history*, 39 (1970), pp. 62–71.

92 Smith, *Daniel Lindley*, p. 396.

93 For a biography of Schreuder, see Olav G. Myklebust, *H. P. S. Schreuder: kirke og misjon* (Oslo, 1980).

94 Olav G. Myklebust, 'Sør-Afrika' in Olav G. Myklebust and others, *Det Norske Misjonsselskaps historia 1842–1942, vol. 3* (Stavanger, 1949), p. 27.

95 Etherington, *Preachers*, p. 34.

96 *Ibid.*, p. 60.

97 Kratzenstein, *Kurze Geschichte*, p. 157; Georg Haccius, *Hannoversche Missionsgeschichte*, vol. 2: *Insbesondere die Geschichte der Hermannsburger Mission von 1849 bis zu Louis Harm's Tode* (Hermannsburg, 1910), p. 312.

98 Etherington, *Preachers*, p. 102.

99 *Ibid.*, p. 33.

100 Sheila Hindson-Meintjies, 'The James Allison story', Ph.D. thesis, University of the Witwatersrand, 1980.

101 See Ezra Msimang to James Stuart, *The James Stuart Archive*, 4 (1986), p. 46.

102 Leslie A. Hewson, *An introduction to South Africa's Methodists* (Cape Town, 1950), p. 77.

103 George G. Findlay and William W. Holdsworth, *The history of the Wesleyan Methodist Missionary Society* (5 vols., London, 1921–4), vol. 4, p. 295; Absolom Vilakazi, *Zulu transformations: a study of the dynamics of social change* (Pietermaritzburg, 1962), p. 119.

104 Edgar H. Brookes, *The history of native policy in South Africa from 1830 to the present day* (1924; 2nd edn, Pretoria, 1927), p. 76.

105 Francis E. Colenso, *Colenso letters from Natal* (arr. Wyn Rees, Pietermaritzburg, 1958), p. 69.

106 Thomas T. Carter, *A memoir of John Armstrong DD, late Lord Bishop of Grahamstown* (Oxford, 1857), p. 265.

107 Etherington, *Preachers*, p. 52.

108 See Jeff Guy, *The heretic: a study of the life of John William Colenso, 1814–1883* (Pietermaritzburg and Johannesburg, 1983).

109 Gerhardus C. Oosthuizen, 'The Zanzibari Catholics and their contribution to the introduction of Catholicism to the Zulu people in Natal', *Neue Zeitschrift für Missionswissenschaft*, 46 (1990), pp. 188–99.

110 Shula Marks, *Reluctant rebellion: the 1906–08 disturbances in Natal* (Oxford, 1970).

111 Shula Marks, 'Christian African participation in the 1906 rebellion', *Bulletin of the Society for African Church History*, 2 (1965), p. 61.

112 See Shula Marks, *Reluctant rebellion.*

113 Colin Bundy, *The rise and fall of the South African peasantry* (London, 1979), p. 190.

114 Leonard Thompson, *Survival in two worlds: Moshoeshoe of Lesotho, 1786–1870* (Oxford, 1975), p. 216.

115 *Ibid.*, pp. 25, 70; L. B. J. Machobane, 'Mohlomi', in *Mohlomi, journal of Southern African historical studies*, 2 (1976), 5–27; and Omer-Cooper, *Zulu aftermath*, p. 104.

116 Casalis, correspondence, 21/11–1842, *Journal des missions évangéliques*, 1843, 163f.

117 Moffat, *Missionary labours*, p. 205; John Mackenzie, *Ten years north of the Orange River: a story of everyday life and work among the South African tribes from 1859–1869* (1871; 2nd edn, London, 1971), p. 58.

118 Thompson, *Survival*, p. 128.

119 *Journal des missions évangéliques* 20 (1845), p. 175.

120 Thompson, *Survival*, pp. 79, 94, 186; Claude H. Perrot, *Les Sotho et les missionnaires européens au 19e siècle* (Abidjan, 1970), p. 24.

121 Raoul S. Allier, *La Psychologie de la conversion chez less peuples non-civilisés* (2 vols., Paris, 1925) vol. 1, p. 157.

122 Thompson, *Survival*, pp. 91, 99; Perrot, *Sotho*, p. 41; James Backhouse, *A narrative of a visit to the Mauritius and South Africa* (London, 1844), p. 375.

123 Gabriel Setiloane, *The image of God among the Sotho-Tswana* (Rotterdam, 1976), p. 119.

124 Perrot, *Sotho*, p. 13.

125 Thompson, *Survival*, p. 102.

126 *Ibid.*, pp. 91–104, 199.

127 Letter, November 1848 to Robert Moffat, in David Livingstone, *Family Letters, 1841–56* (ed. Isaac Schapera, 2 vols., London, 1959), vol. 1, p. 260.

128 Thompson, *Survival*, p. 149.

129 Perrot, *Sotho*, p. 60.

130 Thompson, *Survival*, p. 150.

131 Perrot, *Sotho*, p. 73.

132 *Ibid.*, p. 117.

133 Thompson, *Survival*, p. 317.

134 Pascoe, *Two hundred years*, p. 325.

135 See Jean-Louis Richard, *L'experience de la conversion chez les Basotho* (Rome, 1977).

136 *Ibid.*, p. 48.

137 Thompson, *Survival*, p. 320.

138 *Ibid.*, p. 323.

139 See Judy Kimble, 'Labour Migration in Basutoland 1870–1885', in Shula Marks and Richard Rathbone (eds.), *Industrialization and Social Change in South Africa* (London, 1982).

140 Alexandre Berthoud, 'The birth of a Church: the Church of Basutoland', *International review of missions*, 38 (1949), pp. 156–64; Perrot, *Sotho*.

141 My thoughts for this section changed through discussions with the late Professor John Blacking of Queen's University, Belfast, and through the publication by Peter Delius, *This land belongs to us* (Cape Town, 1983, and Berkeley, 1984).

142 Alexander Merensky, *Erinnerungen aus dem Missionsleben in Transvaal, 1859–1882* (2nd edn, Berlin, 1889), p. 75.

143 See T. Wangerman, *Lebensbilder aus Südafrika* (Berlin, 1876) and Alexander Merensky, *Erinnerungen aus dem Missionsleben in Transvaal 1859–1882* (2nd edn, Berlin, 1899).

144 *Ibid.*

145 *Ibid.*

146 *Ibid.*

147 Findlay and Holdsworth, *History*, vol. 4, pp. 337ff., 367, 369; *Wesleyan missionary notices* (1883), p. 257.

148 Merensky, *Erinnerungen*, p. 123.

149 *Ibid.*, p. 97.

150 *Ibid.*

151 *Ibid.*, pp. 83, 97, 110, 114.

152 Kratzenstein, *Kurze Geschichte*, p. 208.

153 Merensky, *Erinnerungen*, p. 128.

154 Delius, *Land*, pp. 113–14.

155 Merensky, *Erinnerungen*, p. 88.

156 *Ibid.*, p. 173.

157 *Ibid.*, p. 190.

158 *Ibid.*, p. 193.

159 *Ibid.*, p. 205.

160 *Ibid.*

161 *Ibid.*; Delius, *Land*; Julius Richter, *Geschichte der Berliner Missionsgesellshaft* (Berlin, 1924).

162 Richter, *Geschichte*, p. 275; H. Theodor Wangemann, *Ein Zweites Reisejahr in Süd-Afrika* (Berlin, 1886), p. 170.

163 N. J. van Warmelo, letter to B.Sr. 24.9.79.

164 C. A. G. Hoffmann, *Der 'Meester' von Kratzenstein: Missionsgeschichte aus Nordtransvaal* (Berlin, n.d.[1920s]), p. 24.

165 W. Gründler, *Geschichte der Bawenda-mission in Nord-Transvaal* (Berlin, 1897), pp. 32–33, 36.

166 'Eine Art Conventikel', *Berliner Mission Bericht*, 1875, p. 401.

167 See C. Hoffmann, *Mphome* (Berlin, n.d.).

168 Kratzenstein, *Kurze Geschichte*, pp. 386–400.

169 Wangemann, *Ein Zweites Reisejahr*, p. 118.

170 Kratzenstein, *Kurze Geschichte*, p. 382.

171 E. J. Krige and J. D. Krige, *Realm of a rain-queen: a study of the pattern of Lovedu society* (London, 1943), p. 11.

172 Norman Goodall, *A history of the London Missionary Society 1895–1945* (Oxford, 1954), p. 290.

173 Francis Wilson, 'Farming, 1866–1966', in Wilson and Thompson, *Oxford history*, vol. 2, p. 104.

174 See Stanley Trapido, 'White conflict and non-White participation in the politics of the Cape of Good Hope', Ph.D. thesis, University of London, 1970; *idem*, 'African politics in the Cape colony, 1884–1900', *Journal of African history*, 9 (1968), 79–98.

175 See John A. Chalmers, *Tiyo Soga: a page of South African mission work* (Edinburgh, 1877) and Donovan Williams (ed.) *The journal and selected writings of the Reverend Tiyo Soga* (Cape Town, 1983).

176 *James Stuart Archive*, 1 (1976), 215, 223.

177 B.Sr. interview with A. W. G. Champion, 1953.

178 See *James Stuart Archive*, 1 (1976).

179 See Jarle Simensen *et al.*, 'Christian missions and socio-cultural change in Zululand 1850–1906: Norwegian strategy and African response', in J. Simensen (ed.) *Norwegian missions in African history*, I: *South Africa 1845–1906* (Oslo and London, 1986), p. 258.

180 R. Pierce Beaver, *Ecumenical beginnings in Protestant world mission: a history of comity* (New York, 1962), p. 193.

181 *Report, General Missionary Conference*, 1904–05, p. 45.

182 See L. F. Swanepoel, 'The origin and early history of the Seventh-day Adventist Church in the Union of South Africa, 1886–1920', MA thesis, University of South Africa (UNISA), 1972.

183 See Noreen Kagan, 'African settlements in the Johannesburg Area, 1903–1923', MA thesis, University of the Witwatersrand, 1978, p. 13.

184 Charles van Onselen, *Studies in the social and economic history of the Witwatersrand 1886–1914* (2 vols., Harlow, 1982), vol. 1, p. 5.

185 Findlay and Holdsworth, *History*, vol. 4, p. 341.

186 Pages 423–24.

187 Deborah L. Gaitskell, 'Female mission initiatives: Black and White women in three Witwatersrand Churches, 1903–1939' Ph.D. thesis, University of London, 1981; and Mia Brandel-Syrier, *Black women in search of God* (London, 1962).

188 Gaitskell, *ibid.*

189 *Ibid.*

190 See Edwin Farmer, *The Transvaal as a mission field* (London, 1900).

191 Pascoe, *Two hundred years*, p. 333.

192 *Ibid.*, p. 316.

193 Marks, *Reluctant rebellion*, p. 86.

194 *Ibid*; Pascoe, *Two hundred years*, pp. 340ff.

195 A. W. Lee, *Charles Johnson of Zululand* (London, 1930), pp. 184ff.

196 See O. J. Hogarth and R. L. White, *The life of William Marlborough Carter* (Paignton, 1952); Alan Wilkinson, *The Community of the Resurrection: a centenary history* (London, 1992), pp. 204–05.

197 Alf Helgesson, *Church, state and people in Mozambique: an historical study with special emphasis on Methodist developments in the Inhambane region* (Uppsala, 1994), pp. 132, 134; see Albert Weir Baker, *'Grace Triumphant': the life story of a carpenter, lawyer and missionary, in South Africa from 1856 to 1939* (Glasgow, 1939).

198 J. Richter, *Geschichte*, p. 416.

199 Georg Haccius, *Hannoversche Missionsgeschichte*, vol. 3, pt 2: *Insbesondere die Geschichte der Hermannsburger Mission von 1865 bis zu Gegenwart* (Hermannsburg, 1920), pp. 120, 224.

200 Adolf Schulze and Karl Müller, *200 Jahre Brüdermission* (Herrnhut, 1932), vol. 2, pp. 421, 439.

201 Francis Schimlek, *Mariannhill:a study in Bantu life and missionary effort* (Mariannhill, 1953), p. 16.

202 *Ibid.*, p. 142.

203 See William E. Brown, *The Catholic Church in South Africa: from its origins to the present day* (London, 1960); Walbert P. Bühlmann, *Die Christliche Terminologie als Missionsmethodisches Problem* (Schöneck-Beckenried, 1950); Lukas A. Mettler, *Christliche Terminologie und Katechismus Gestaltung in der Mariannhiller Mission 1910–1920* (Schöneck-Beckenried, 1967).

204 Erhard Kamphausen, *Anfänge der kirchlichen Unabhängigkeitsbewegung in Südafrika: Geschichte und Theologie der Äthiopischen Bewegung 1872–1912* (Berne, 1976), p. 117.

205 On the Ethiopians, until 1912, see Erhard Kamphausen's solid and rich study, *ibid*; also see Bengt Sundkler, *Zulu Zion and some Swazi Zionists* (Oxford and Lund, 1976); and the valuable study by Hans Jürgen Becken, *Theologie der Heilung: Das Heilen in den Afrikanischen Unabhängigen Kirchen in Südafrika* (Hermannsburg, 1972).

206 Moffat, *Missionary labours*, p. 230.

207 James Chapman, *Travels in the interior of South Africa* (2 vols., London, 1868), vol. 1, p. 132.

208 Mackenzie, *Ten years*, p. 80.

209 Robert Moffat, *The Matebele journals of Robert Moffat* (ed. J. P. R. Wallis, 2 vols., London, 1945), vol. 2, p. 205.

210 Moffat, *Missionary labours*, p. 490.

211 Moffat, *Matebele journals*, vol. 2, p. 128.

212 Moffat, *Apprenticeship*, p. 13.

213 Cecil Northcott, *Robert Moffat: pioneer of Africa* (London, 1961), p. 25.

214 Moffat, *Missionary labours*, p. 257.

215 David Livingstone, *South African papers, 1849–1853*, (ed. Isaac Schapera, Cape Town, 1974), p. 104.

216 *Ibid.*, pp. 99–111.

217 L. D. Ngcongco, *The career of Kgosi Gaseitswe* (Lesotho, 1977); Isaac Schapera, *Tribal innovators: Tswana chiefs and social change, 1795–1940* (London, 1970), p. 236.

218 Hewson, *Methodists*, p. 46.

219 See J. Mutero Chirenje, *Chief Kgama and his times, c.1835–1923: the story of a Southern African ruler* (London, 1978).

220 Jean Comaroff, *Body of powers, spirit of resistance: the culture and history of a South African people* (Chicago 1985), p. 153. In the book there follows a study of 'Alienation and the Kingdom of Zion'. Here we cannot, unfortunately, do justice to this brilliant study and limit ourselves to mentioning a unique contribution.

221 J. Mutero Chirenje, *A history of northern Botswana, 1850–1910* (Rutherford, 1977), p. 38.

222 Tim Jeal, *Livingstone* (London, Book Club Associates, 1973), p. 80.

223 *Ibid.*, pp. 94, 106; David Livingstone, *Missionary correspondence 1841–1856* (ed. Isaac Schapera, London, 1961), pp. 80, 104.

224 Livingstone, *Missionary correspondence*, p. 112.

225 Moffat, *Matabele journals*, vol. 1, p. 378.

226 Jeal, *Livingstone*, p. 84.

227 Livingstone, *Missionary correspondence*, p. 81.

228 *Ibid.*, p. 119.

229 Chirenje, *History*, p. 68.

230 R. Moffat, *Matabele journals*, vol. 1, pp. 156–57.

231 *Ibid.*, pp. 377–81.

232 Comaroff, *Body of power*, p. 30; see Isaac Schapera, 'Christianity and the Tswana', *Journal of the Royal Anthropological Institute*, 83 (1958), pp. 1–9.

233 Haccius, *Hannoversche*, vol. 2, pp. 321–9; Chirenje, *History*, p. 47.

234 Mackenzie, *Ten years*, p. 468.

235 Schapera, *Tribal innovators*, p. 44.

236 Gabriel M. Setiloane, *African theology: an introduction* (Johannesburg, 1986), p. 11.

237 Rauha Voipio, 'Contract work through Ovambo eyes', in Reginald H. Green, Kimmo Kiljunen and Marja-Liisa Kiljunen (eds.), *Namibia: the last colony* (Harlow, 1981), p. 112.

238 See Martti Eirola and others, *The cultural and social change in Ovamboland 1870–1915* (Joensuu, 1983).

239 Ensio Lehtonen, 'Finlands yttre mission', in K. B. Westman and others, *Nordisk missionshistoria* (Stockholm, 1949), p. 219.

240 Josef Metzler, 'Die Missionen in Südafrika und auf den ostafrikanischen Inseln', in Josef Metzler (ed.), *Sacrae Congregationis de Propaganda Fide Memoria Rerum, volume III/1: 1815–1972* (Rome, 1975), p. 322.

CHAPTER 8: SOUTH-CENTRAL AFRICA AND THE INDIAN OCEAN

1 See Elleck K. Mashingaidze, 'The forgotten frontiersmen in Christianity's northward outreach: the role of African evangelists in the extension of the mission's hinterland to the north of the Limpopo, 1869–1914' (paper presented at the CIHEC [Commission internationale d'histoire ecclésiastique Comparée] Conference in Uppsala, 1977; shorter version published in CIHEC, *The Church in a changing society: conflict, reconciliation or adjustment* (Uppsala, 1978), pp. 362–68.

2 See Eduard Kratzenstein, *Kurze Geschichte der Berliner Mission in Süd- und Ostafrika* (3rd edn, Berlin, 1887),

3 Philip Mason, *The birth of a dilemma: the conquest and settlement of Rhodesia* (London, 1958), p. 94; Kratzenstein, *Kurze Geschichte*, p. 380; Harold von Sicard, *Zvakaitika kare zveKereke yanaLuthere munyika yeRhodesia* (Chiedza Press, 1972), *idem*, *Föregångare i Rhodesia: missionförsök på 1800-talet* (Stockholm, 1944), pp. 20, 54.

4 Kratzenstein, *Kurze Geschichte*, p. 406.

5 Mason, *Birth of a dilemma*, pp. 105, 182, 194.

6 Andrew Roberts, *A history of Zambia* (London, 1976), p. 166.

7 Knight-Bruce, *Journal 1891–1892*, USPG archive, Rhodes House Library, Oxford; see C. E. Fripp and V. S. Hiller (eds), *Gold and the Gospel in Mashonaland* (London, 1949).

8 Knight-Bruce, *Journal 1891–1892.*

9 Michael Gelfand (ed.) *Gubulawayo and beyond: letters and journals of the early Jesuit missionaries to Zambesia 1879–1887* (London, 1968), pp. 65, 196. The Paraguay Reductions, or *reductiones*, refer to the series of vast and self-contained colonies, created during the seventeenth century. These *reductiones* were solely controlled by the Jesuit Order, and each encompassed up to 100,000 inhabitants and extended over thousands of square miles.

10 Terence O. Ranger, *Revolt in Southern Rhodesia 1896–7: a study in African resistance* (London, 1967), p. 314.

11 Elleck K. Mashingaidze, 'Christian missions in Mashonaland, 1890 to 1930', D.Phil. thesis, University of York, 1973, p. 135 *passim*.

12 George G. Findlay and William W. Holdsworth, *The history of the Wesleyan Methodist Missionary Society* (5 vols., London, 1921–4), vol. 4, p. 395.

13 See Jean Nicolson, *John Boyana Radasi: missionary to Zimbabwe* (Glasgow, 1996).

14 Letters to B.Sr. on the Mfengu in Zimbabwe, June 1979, by Archdeacon O. Somkence, Wilson M. Nyilika, and Ester Gwele; see Lewis H. Gann, *A history of Northern Rhodesia: early days to 1953* (London, 1964), p. 196.

15 Findlay and Holdsworth, *History*, vol. 4, pp. 384–94.

16 In C. F. Andrews, *John White of Mashonaland* (London, 1935), pp. 136–45, Chikala's name is spelt Chikara.

17 E. W. Nightingale and others, *The widening way* (London, 1952), p. 7, quoted in Peter Bolink, *Towards Church union in Zambia: a study of missionary co-operation and church-union efforts in Central Africa* (Franeker, 1967), p. 77.

18 Bolink, *Towards Church union*, pp. 77–8; see also S. D. Gray, *Frontiers of the kingdom: the story of Methodist missions in Rhodesia* (London, 1930).

19 Andrews, *John White*, p. 87–93; C. M. Brand, 'African nationalists and the missionaries in Rhodesia', in M. F. C. Bourdillon (ed.) *Christianity south of the Zambezi* (Gwelo, 1977), p. 70; Bengt Sundkler, 'The Churches' hinterland', in Michael G. Whisson and Martin West (eds.), *Religion and social change in Southern Africa: anthropological essays in honour of Monica Wilson* (Cape Town and London, 1975), p. 102.

20 See James Duffy, *Portuguese Africa* (Cambridge, Mass., 1959).

21 David Livingstone, *Missionary travels and researches in South Africa* (London, 1857), p. 435.

22 See P. E. H. Hair in *David Livingstone and Africa* (Edinburgh, 1973).

23 David Livingstone, *Livingstone's African Journal 1853–1856* (ed. Isaac Schapera, 2 vols., London, 1963), vol. 1, pp. 243–44.

24 J. W. Gregory, 'Livingstone as an explorer: an appreciation', *Scottish geographical magazine*, 29 (1913), 238–9, quoted by Isaac Schapera, 'Introduction', in David Livingstone, *Livingstone's African journal 1853–1856* (ed. Isaac Schapera, 2 vols., London, 1963), vol. 1, p. xii.

25 David Livingstone, *Some letters from Livingstone, 1840–1872* (ed. D. Chamberlain, London, 1940), pp. 249–50.

26 See Gwyn Prins, 'The battle for control of the camera in late nineteenth century western Zambia', *African affairs*, 97 (1990).

27 C. P. Groves, *The planting of Christianity in Africa* (4 vols., London, 1948–58), vol. 3, p. 139; Lewis H. Gann, *A history of Northern Rhodesia: early days to 1953* (London, 1964), p. 46.

28 François Coillard, *On the threshold of Central Africa: twenty years among the Barotsi* (trans. C. W. Mackintosh, London, 1897), p. 137.

29 *Ibid.*

30 *Ibid.*

31 *Ibid.*, p. 341.

32 *Ibid.*

33 *Ibid.*, pp. 448–49.

34 *Ibid.*, p. 335.

35 Jalla, report from Sesheke 2.12.1901, Paris Mission archives.

36 *Journal des missions évangéliques*, 1902.

37 Gwyn Prins, *The hidden hippopotamus: reappraisal in African history: the early colonial experience in western Zambia* (Cambridge, 1980, p. 203.

38 *Ibid.*, p. 220.

39 C. W. Mackintosh, *Coillard of the Zambezi: the lives of François and Christina Coillard* (London, 1907), p. 486.

40 Coillard, *Threshold*, p. 486.

41 Prins, *Hidden hippopotamus*, p. 164.

42 Gerald L. Caplan, *The elites of Barotseland 1878–1969: a political history of Zambia's western province* (Berkeley and Los Angeles, 1970), p. 78.

43 Bolink, *Towards Church union*, p. 74; Edwin W. Smith, *The way of the white fields in Rhodesia: a survey of Christian enterprise in Northern and Southern Rhodesia* (London, 1928), p. 82.

44 Andrew C. Ross, 'The origins and development of the Church of Scotland Mission, Blantyre, Nyasaland, 1875–1926', Ph.D. thesis, University of Edinburgh, 1968.

45 As stated by one the mission leaders, David Clement Scott; see Andrew C. Ross, 'The foundations of the Blantyre Mission, Nyasaland', *Religion in Africa* (Edinburgh, 1964).

46 John McCracken, *Politics and Christianity in Malawi 1875–1940: the impact of the Livingstonia Mission in the Northern Province* (Cambridge, 1977), p. 75.

47 J. Van Velsen, 'The missionary factor among the Lakeside Tonga of Nyasaland', *Human problems in British Central Africa*, 26 (1959), p. 17.

48 B. Pachai, *Malawi: the history of a nation* (London, 1973), p. 21.

49 McCracken, *Politics*, p. 80.

50 *Ibid.*, p. 84.

51 *Ibid.*, p. 132.

52 *Ibid.*, p. 131.

53 *World atlas of Christian missions* (New York, 1911), p. 95.

54 Quoted in McCracken, *Politics*, p. 99.

55 *Ibid.*

56 See T. Jack Thompson, *Christianity in northern Malawi: Donald Fraser's missionary methods and Ngoni culture* (Leiden, 1995).

57 Donald Fraser, *Winning a primitive people: sixteen years' work among the warlike tribe of the Ngoni and the Senga and Tumbuka peoples of Central Africa* (London, 1914), pp. 283–4.

58 Fergus Macpherson, interview with B.Sr., 1984.

59 Agnes R. Fraser, *Donald Fraser of Livingstonia* (London, 1934), p. 209.

60 Professor Monica Wilson, interview with B.Sr., February 1980.

61 McCracken, *Politics*, pp. 103–10.

62 J. L. Pretorius, 'Introduction to the history of the Dutch Reformed Church mission in Malawi 1889–1914', in Bridglal Pachai (ed.), *The early history of Malawi* (London, 1972), p. 365.

63 Ian Linden with Jane Linden, *Catholics, peasants, and Chewa resistance in Nyasaland 1889–1939* (London, 1974), p. 193.

64 George A. Shepperson and Thomas Price, *Independent Africa: John Chilembwe and the origins, setting and significance of the Nyasaland native rising of 1915* (Edinburgh, 1958), p. 146.

65 *Ibid.*, p. 223.

66 *Ibid.*, p. 435.

67 Translated from Joachim Mousinho d'Albuquerque, *Moçambique 1896–1898* (Lisbon, 1899).

68 António Barroso, *D. António Barroso, missionário, Cientista, missiólogo* (ed. António Brásio, Lisbon, 1961).

69 See Johannes Thauren, *Die Mission der Gesellschaft des göttl Wortes* (1931) vol. 2; and

Paul Schebesta, *Portugals Konquistamission in Südost-Afrika: Missionsgeschichte Sambesiens und des Monomotapareiches (1560–1920)* (Steyl, 1966).

70 Henri A. Junod, *Ernest Creux et Paul Berthoud, les fondateurs de la Mission Suisse en Afrique du Sud* (Lausanne, 1933), p. 144, quoted in Jan van Butselaar, *Africains, missionnaires et colonialistes: les origins de l'Église Presbytérienne du Mozambique (Mission Suisse), 1880–1896* (Leiden, 1984), p. 36.

71 Butselaar, *Africains*, p. 44–47.

72 *Ibid.*, pp. 48–50, *passim.*

73 *Ibid.*, pp. 52–53.

74 Junod, *Ernest Creux*, p. 145.

75 J. Beckmann, *Die Katholische Kirche im neuen Afrika* (1947); Alf Helgesson, *Church, state and people in Mozambique: an historical study with special emphasis on Methodist developments in the Inhambane region* (Uppsala, 1994); Allen and Barbara Isaacman, *Mozambique from colonialism to revolution, 1900–1982* (Boulder, 1983); Cecil Lewis and G. E. Edwards, *Historical records of the Church of the Province of South Africa* (London, 1934); W. Gordon A. Mears, *Methodist torchbearers* (Cape Town, 1955); Leroy Vail and Landeg White, *Capitalism and colonialism in Mozambique: a study of Quelimane district* (London, 1980).

76 Ludvig Munthe, *La Bible à Madagascar: les deux premières traductions du Nouveau Testament Malgache* (Oslo, 1969), p. 132.

77 Bonar A. Gow, *Madagascar and the Protestant impact: the work of the British missions, 1818–95* (London, 1979), p. 17.

78 J. Janine, *Le clergé colonial de 1815 à 1850* (Toulouse, 1935), p. 401.

79 See J. Fitzsimmons, *Father Laval: Jacques Désiré Laval: the 'Saint' of Mauritius* (Bootle, 1972).

80 Joseph Michel, *Le Père Jacques Laval: le 'saint' de l'Ile Maurice 1803–1864* (Paris, 1976), p. 145.

81 Adrien Boudou, *Les Jésuites à Madagascar au XIXe siècle* (2 vols., Paris, 1940–42), vol. 1, p. 136.

82 Gwyn Campbell, 'Madagascar in the context of the East African slave trade, 1861–95', *International journal of African historical studies*, 21, (1988).

83 See William Ellis, *Madagascar revisited: describing the events of a new reign and the revolution which followed* (London, 1967); *idem*, *The martyr Church: a narrative of the introduction, progress and triumph of Christianity in Madagascar* (London, 1870).

84 Françoise Raison-Jourde, 'Mission LMS et mission jésuite face aux communautés villageoises merina: fondation et fonctionnement des paroisses entre 1869 et 1876', *Africa* 53 (1983), 70.

85 Françoise Raison, 'La fondation des temples protestants à Tananarive entre 1861 et 1869', *Annales de l'Université de Madagascar, Série Lettres et Sciences humaines*, 11 (1970), 50.

86 Boudou, *Les Jésuites.*

87 Raison-Jourde, 'Mission LMS', p. 66.

88 Hubert Deschamps, 'Madagascar and France, 1870–1905', in Roland Oliver and G. N. Sanderson (eds.), *Cambridge History of Africa, VI: from 1870 to 1905* (Cambridge, 1985), p. 529.

89 See Jean Bauberot, 'L'antiprotestanisme politique à la fin du XIXe siècle: I, les débuts de 'antiprotestantisme et la question de Madagascar', *Revue d'histoire et de Philosophie religieuses*, 4 (1972), pp. 449–84.

59 Johanna Eggert, *Missionsschule und sozialer Wandel in Ostafrika. Der Beitrag der deutschen evangelischen Missionsgesellschaften zur Entwicklung des Schulwesens in Tanganyika 1891–1939* (Bielefeld, 1970), p. 183.

60 Stahl, *History*, pp. 203, 265, 351.

61 Fleisch, *Hundert Jahre*, p. 283.

62 See J. C. Winter, *Bruno Gutmann 1876–1966: a German approach to social anthropology* (Oxford, 1979); Bruno Gutmann, *Das Recht des Dschagga* (Munich, 1926); and *idem*, *Die Stammeslehren der Dschagga* (3 vols., Munich, 1932–38).

63 Anon., *Afrikanische Characterköpfe* (Leipzig Mission, 1921).

64 Eggert, *Missionsschule*, p. 170.

65 *Ibid.*, pp. 170–96; Kieran, 'Holy Ghost Fathers', p. 179; Fleisch, *Hundert Jahre*, p. 269. Siegfried Hertlein, *Wege christlicher Verkündigung: vol. 1: Christliche Verkündigung im Dienst der Grundlegung der Kirche (1860–1920)* (3 vols., Munsterschwarzach, 1976–83), vol. 1, pp. 64–65; Anza A.Lema, *The influence of Christian mission societies on education policies in Tanganyika 1868–1970.* Doctoral thesis, University of Geneva, 1979 (reprinted, Hong Kong, 1980).

66 Eugene Stock, *The history of the Church Missionary Society* (4 vols., London, 1899–1916) vol. 3, p. 73.

67 A. J. Temu, *British Protestant missions* (London, 1972), p. 64.

68 Simpson, *Dark companions*, p. 54.

69 Temu, *British*, p. 14.

70 Stock, *History*, vol. 3, p. 87.

71 A. Menzies, 'Frere Town', *Church missionary intelligencer*, 5 (1880), p. 305.

72 'The East African Mission', *Church missionary intelligencer*, 6 (1881), p. 37.

73 Robert W. Strayer, *The making of mission communities in East Africa: Anglicans and Africans in colonial Kenya, 1875–1935* (London, 1978), p. 28.

74 See Fred Morton, *Children of Ham: freed slaves and fugitive slaves on the Kenya coast, 1873 to 1907* (Boulder, 1990); Stock, *History*, vol. 3, p. 92; *Church missionary intelligencer*, 1884, p.167; Strayer, *Making*, p. 37.

75 V. Neckebrouck, *Le onzième commandement: étiologie d'une église indépendante au pied du mont Kenya* (Immensee, 1978), p. 105.

76 K. Jackson, in Bethwell Ogot (ed.), *Kenya before 1900* (Nairobi, 1976), p. 237.

77 Bernardo Bernardi, *The Mugwe, a failed prophet: a study of a religious and public dignitary of the Meru in Kenya* (London, 1959).

78 Neckebrouck, *Le onzième commandement*, p. 105.

79 Oginga Odinga, *Not yet Uhuru: the autobiography of Oginga Odinga* (London, 1967), p. 1.

80 See Jocelyn Murray, 'The Kikuyu female circumcision controversy: with special reference to the Church Missionary Society's sphere of influence', Ph.D. thesis, University of California, Los Angeles, 1974.

81 *Ibid.*, p. 59.

CHAPTER 10: EAST-CENTRAL AFRICA

1 Iris Berger, *Religion and resistance: East African kingdoms in the precolonial period* (Tervuren, 1981), p. 38; J. P. Crazzolara, *The Lwoo* (Verona, 1950).

2 See Michael Twaddle, 'The ending of slavery in Buganda', in Suzanne Miers and Richard Roberts (eds.), *The end of slavery in Africa* (Madison and London, 1988), p. 125.

3 J. Thoonen, *Black martyrs* (London, 1941), pp. 50–51.

4 Henry Morton Stanley, *Through the dark continent* (2 vols., London, 1878), vol. 1, p. 321.

5 Donald Simpson, *Dark companions: the African contribution to the European exploration of East Africa* (London, 1975), p. 121.

6 See Sir J. M. Gray, 'The correspondence of Dallington Maftaa', Uganda journal, 30 (1966), 13–24. In 1881 Maftaa was succeeded as secretary to Mutesa by another roving African from the coast, Jacob Wainwright, one of the Nasik (Bombay) Africans, and the one who accompanied David Livingstone's remains to Britain. See Donald Simpson, *Dark companions*.

7 See the biography by his sister, J. W. H[arrison], *A. M. Mackay: pioneer missionary of the CMS in Uganda* (London, 1890); also see John D. Hargreaves, *Aberdeenshire to Africa: northeast Scots and British overseas expansion* (Aberdeen, 1981), pp. 31–37.

8 Eugene Stock, *The history of the Church Missionary Society* (4 vols., London, 1899–1916), vol. 3, p. 109.

9 *Ibid.*, p. 411.

10 J. W. H[arrison], *A. M. Mackay*, p. 134.

11 See Cardinal Lavigerie, *Ecrits d'Afrique* (edited by A. Hamman, Paris, 1966), pp. 218, 180–232.

12 J. W. H[arrison], *A. M. Mackay: pioneer missionary of the CMS in Uganda* (London, 1890), pp. 138–40.

13 Yves Tourigny, *So abundant a harvest: the Catholic Church in Uganda 1879–1979* (London, 1979), pp. 33, 49.

14 Quoted by John V. Taylor, *The growth of the Church in Buganda: an attempt at understanding* (London, 1958), p. 46.

15 See Thoonen, *Black martyrs*.

16 Taylor, *Growth*, p. 48.

17 J. F. Faupel. *African holocaust: the story of the Uganda martyrs* (London, 1962), p. 47.

18 T. S. Eliot, *Little Gidding*.

19 John Rowe, 'The purge of Christians at Mwanga's court', *Journal of African history*, 5 (1964), 55–72.

20 J. W. H[arrison], *A. M. Mackay*, p. 383.

21 Faupel, *African holocaust*, p. 45ff.

22 'Letter from Sebwato', *Church missionary intelligencer*, 15 (1890), 34.

23 See D. Anthony Low and R. Cranford Pratt, *Buganda and British overrule 1900–1955: two studies* (Nairobi, 1970).

24 Richard Gray, 'Mission, Church and State in Colonial Africa', statement December 7th, 1984, at the public examination of Holger B. Hansen's doctoral thesis on Buganda. The problem is also discussed by F. B. Welbourn, *Religion and politics in Uganda 1952–1962* (Nairobi, 1965); D. Anthony Low, *Political parties in Uganda 1949–1962* (London, 1962); John M. Waliggo, 'The Catholic Church in the Buddu Province of Buganda, 1879–1925', Ph.D. thesis, University of Cambridge, 1976 and Michael Twaddle, *Kakungulu and the creation of Uganda* (London, 1993).

25 Roland Oliver, *The missionary factor in East Africa* (London, 1952), p. 75.

26 Stock, *History*, vol. 3, p. 440.

27 Taylor, *Growth*, p. 238.

28 Charles F. Harford-Battersby, *Pilkington of Uganda* (2nd edn, London, 1898), p. 192.

17 Margaret Nissen, *An African Church is born: the story of the Adamawa and central Sardauna provinces in Nigeria* (Dashen,1968), p. 184.

18 B.Sr. interview with the late Amos Lyimo, of Moshi, Tanzania, 1961.

19 Doig, 'Christian Church', 175–7.

20 Hollis R. Lynch, 'Pan-African responses in the United States to British colonial rule in Africa in the 1940s', in Prosser Gifford and Wm. Roger Louis (eds.), *The transfer of power in Africa: decolonization 1940–1960* (New Haven and London, 1982), p. 86.

21 Africa Committee of the Foreign Missions Conference of North America, *Abundant life in changing Africa: report of the West Central Africa regional conference held at Léopoldville, Congo Belge, July 13–24, 1946* (New York, 1946).

22 George L. S. Shackle, *Expectations in economics* (2nd edn, Cambridge, 1952).

23 See *Drumbeats from Kampala: report of the first assembly of the All Africa Conference of Churches, held at Kampala, April 20 to April 30, 1963* (London, 1963).

24 Françoise Raison-Jourde, 'Spiritualite et ecclsesiologie protestantes en Imerina sous la colonisation', *Revue d'histoire de la spiritualite*, 49 (1973), 165–97.

25 T. S. Eliot, *Little Gidding.*

26 See Church of Sweden Mission to Bukoba, Tanzania, 1953–5.

27 Colin Morris, *Church and challenge in a new Africa: political sermons* (London, 1964), p. 143.

28 Jaroslav Pelikan, *The vindication of tradition* (New Haven and London, 1986), p. 16.

29 J. N. D. Kelly, *The Oxford dictionary of Popes* (Oxford, 1986), p. 317.

30 See *inter alia*, Pierre Charles, *Études missiologiques* (Louvain, 1956).

31 Augustin Tellkamp, *Die Gefahr der Erstickung für die katholische Weltmission* (1950).

32 *Afer*, June 1934, p. 40.

33 Josef Metzler, 'Tätigkeit der Kongregation im Dienste der Glaubensverbreitung 1922–1972. Ein Überblick', Josef Metzler (ed.), *Sacrae Congregationis de Propaganda Fide Memoria Rerum, volume III/2: 1815–1972* (Rome, 1976), p. 520.

34 Bernard Jacqueline, 'L'organisation interne du dicastère missionnaire après 350 ans', in *ibid.*, p. 405.

35 Metzler, 'Tätigkeit', p. 521.

36 Author of *Winning a primitive people* (London, 1914), *African idylls* (4th edn, London, 1925), and *The new Africa* (London, 1927). See Agnes R. Fraser, *Donald Fraser of Livingstonia* (London, 1934.)

37 Diedrich Westermann, 'The value of the African's past', *International review of missions*, 15 (1926), 434–5; Edwin W. Smith, *The Christian mission in Africa* (London and New York, 1926), pp. 41–42.

38 W. C. Willoughby, 'Building the African Church', *International review of missions*, 15, (1926), 451.

39 Quoted in Smith, *Christian mission*, p. 38.

40 *Ibid.*, p. 52.

41 M. Searle Bates and others, *Survey of the training of the ministry in Africa, part II* (London and New York, 1954), p. 94.

42 F. B. Welbourn, *East African rebels: a study of some independent Churches* (London, 1961), p. 81–82.

43 L. Gray Cowan, in Don Piper and T. Cole (eds), *Post-primary education and political and economic development* (Cambridge, 1964), p. 182.

44 Roland Oliver, *The missionary factor in East Africa* (London, 1952), p. 270.

45 C. P. Groves, *The planting of Christianity in Africa: Vol. 4, 1914–1954* (London, 1958, p. 109ff.

46 F. Yao Boateng, 'The catechism and the rod, Presbyterian education in Ghana', in E. H. Berman (ed.), *African reactions to missionary education* (New York, 1975), p. 90.

47 Obafemi Awolowo, *Awo: the autobiography of Chief Obafemi Awolowo* (Cambridge, 1960), pp. 53, 98.

48 Roland Oliver, *The missionary factor in East Africa* (London, 1952), p. 275.

49 See Helen Kitchen (ed.), *The educated Africa: a country-by-country survey of educational development in Africa* (London, 1962), pp. 193, 335, esp. 167.

50 L. B. Greaves, *The Churches' educational task: address to the Methodist Church* (Accra, 1949), quoted in Bengt Sundkler, *The Christian Ministry in Africa* (Uppsala, 1960), p. 95.

51 Bengt Sundkler, *The Christian ministry in Africa* (Uppsala, 1960), p. 96.

52 John H. Harris, *Africa: slave or free* (London, 1919), p. 32.

53 B. G. Martin, *Muslim brotherhoods in nineteenth-century Africa* (Cambridge, 1976), p. 201.

54 *Ibid.*, p. 194.

55 I. M. Lewis, 'Introduction: Islam and the modern World', in I. M. Lewis (ed.), *Islam in Tropical Africa* (2nd edn, London, 1980), p. 82.

56 J. Spencer Trimingham, *The Christian Church and Islam in West Africa* (International Missionary Council Research Pamphlets, No. 3) (London, 1955), p. 10.

57 Nehemia Levtzion, 'Coastal West Africa', in James Kritzeck and William H. Lewis (eds.), *Islam in Africa* (New York, 1969), p. 309.

58 J. Spencer Trimingham, *The influence of Islam upon Africa* (London and Beirut, 1968), p. 104.

59 *Ibid.*, p. 109.

60 David S. Bone, 'Islam in Malawi', *Journal of religion in Africa*, 13 (1982), p. 136.

61 Adamu Mohammed Fika, *The Kano civil war and British over-rule 1882–1940* (Ibadan and Oxford, 1978), p. 237.

62 Peter B. Clarke, *West Africa and Islam: a study of religious development from the 8th to the 20th century* (London, 1982), p. 222.

63 Michael Crowder, *West Africa under colonial rule* (1st edn, London, 1968), p. 363.

64 Clarke, *West Africa*, p. 225.

65 *Ibid.*, p. 225.

66 Harm de Blij, 'South Africa', in Kritzeck and Lewis, *Islam*, p. 247.

67 Bone, 'Islam in Malawi', p. 136.

68 Crawford Young, 'The Congo', in Kritzeck and Lewis, *Islam*, p. 260.

69 Martin Lowenkopf, 'Uganda', in Kritzeck and Lewis, *Islam*, p. 218.

70 Quoted in Margaret Strobel, *Muslim women in Mombasa 1890–1975* (New Haven and London, 1979), p. 105.

71 T. G. O. Gbadamosi, *The growth of Islam among the Yoruba 1841–1908* (London, 1978), p. 137.

72 John Iliffe, *A modern history of Tanganyika* (Cambridge, 1979), p. 551.

73 Trimingham, *Influence*, p. 109.

74 Crowder, *West Africa*, p. 363.

75 Iliffe, *Modern history*, p. 211.

76 *Ibid.*, p. 212.

77 Donal C. Cruise O'Brien, *The Mourides of Senegal: the political and economic organization of an Islamic brotherhood* (Oxford, 1971), pp. 286–87.

situation', in Fasholé-Luke and others (eds.), *Christianity in independent Africa* (London, 1978).

49 *Pro Mundi Vita Dossiers*, May 1980, p. 6.

CHAPTER 13: NORTH AND NORTH-EASTERN AFRICA

1 David B. Barrett (ed.), *World Christian Encyclopaedia. A comparative study of Churches and religions in the modern world AD 1900–2000* (Oxford, 1982), p. 138.

2 Maurice Assad, 'Prägung der Koptischen Identität', in Paul Verghese (ed.), *Koptisches Christentum: die orthodoxen Kirchen Ägyptens und Äthiopiens* (Stuttgart, 1973), p. 93.

3 John R. Mott, 'The outlook in the Moslem world', *International review of missions*, 13 (1924), pp. 324–25.

4 Otto F. A. Meinardus, *Christian Egypt: ancient and modern* (2nd edn, Cairo, 1977), pp. 478–79.

5 Otto Meinardus, *Monk and monasteries of the Egyptian desert* (1st edn, Cairo, 1961), p. 152; *ibid.* (2nd edn, Cairo, 1989), p. 159.

6 Assad, 'Prägung' in Verghese, p. 94.

7 See Giovani Vantini, *Christianity in the Sudan* (Bologna, 1981), p. 264.

8 Gordon Hewitt, *The problems of success: a history of the Church Missionary Society 1910–1942* (2 vols., London, 1971–77), vol. 1, p. 324.

9 Lilian Sanderson, 'Educational development and administrative control in the Nuba Mountain region of the Sudan', *Journal of African history*, 4 (1963), 236–37.

10 Lilian Passmore Sanderson and Neville Sanderson, *Education, Religion and Politics in Southern Sudan 1899–1964* (London and Khartoum, 1981), p. 160.

11 *Ibid.*, pp. 238–40.

12 I refer to an recent study by three scholars, R. Ghiel, Y. Gezahegn and J. N. van Luik, *Faith Healing and Spirit Possession in Ghion, Ethiopia* (n.d.).

13 Friedrich Heyer, *Die Kirche Äthiopiens: eine Bestandsaufnahme* (Berlin, 1971), p. 181.

14 Olav Sæverås, *On Church mission relations in Ethiopia 1944–1969, with special reference to the Evangelical Church Mekane Yesus and the Lutheran missions* (Drammen, 1974), pp. 23–26.

15 Ger. van Winsen, 'L'Eglise Catholique en Ethiopie', *Neue Zeitschrift für Missionswissenschaft*, 21 (1965), p. 118.

CHAPTER 14: WEST AFRICA

1 Joseph-Roger de Benoist, *Église et pouvoir colonial au Soudan français. Les relations entre les administrateurs et les missionnaires catholiques dans la Boucle du Niger, de 1885 à 1945* (Paris, 1987).

2 *Ibid.*

3 *Ibid.*

4 *Ibid.*

5 Elliott P. Skinner, *African urban life: the transformation of Ouagadougou* (Princeton, 1974), p. 302.

6 Paul Baudu, *Vieil empire, jeune Eglise*, quote by Skinner, *ibid.*, p. 321.

7 Skinner, *African urban*, p. 324.

8 De Benoist, *Église et pouvoir*, p. 497.

9 See Robert Cornevin, *Le Togo, des origines à nos jours* (Paris, 1987); see also Pidalani Pignan, *Le mariage chrétien et le mariage traditionel Kabre* (1987).

10 Arthur T. Porter, *Creoledom: a study of the development of Freetown society* (London, 1963), p. 61.

11 John R. Cartwright, *Politics in Sierra Leone, 1947–1967* (Toronto, 1970), p. 16.

12 Gordon Hewitt, *The problems of success: a history of the Church Missionary Society 1910–1942* (2 vols., London, 1971–77), vol. 1, p. 9.

13 *Ibid.*, p. 9.

14 Christopher Fyfe, *A history of Sierra Leone* (London, 1962), p. 617.

15 Leo Spitzer, *The Creoles of Sierra Leone: responses to colonialism, 1870–1945* (Madison, 1974), p. 162.

16 Cartwright, *Politics*, p. 54.

17 See Akintola J. G. Wyse, *Dr Bankole-Bright and politics in colonial Sierra Leone, 1919–1958* (Cambridge, 1990).

18 E. Francis White, *Sierra Leone's settler women traders: women on the Afro-European frontier* (Ann Arbor, 1987), p. 95.

19 Filomina C. Steady, 'Protestant women's associations in Freetown, Sierra Leone', in Nancy J. Hafkin and Edna G. Bay (eds.), *Women in Africa* (Stanford, 1976), p. 218.

20 F. H. Hilliard, 'Fourah Bay College looks forward', in *East and west review* 16 (1950), p. 112.

21 T. S. Johnson, *The story of a mission: the Sierra Leone Church: first daughter of CMS* (London, 1953), p. 107.

22 *Ibid.*, p. 107.

23 Eldred D. Jones, 'Harry Sawyer', *West Africa*, 1 September, 1986, p. 1825.

24 *Ibid.*

25 Steady, 'Protestant', p. 221.

26 I. M. Ndanema, 'The Martha Davies Confidential Benevolent Association', in *Sierra Leone bulletin of religion*, 3 (1961), p. 65.

27 *Ibid.*, p. 66.

28 Arthur T. Porter, 'Religious affiliation in Freetown, Sierra Leone', *Africa*, 23 (1953), p. 10.

29 Adelaide M. Cromwell, *An African Victorian feminist: the life and times of Adelaide Smith Casely Hayford 1868–1960* (London, 1986), p. 91.

30 Quoted in Cromwell, *ibid.*, p. 137.

31 *Ibid.*, p. 195.

32 Cartwright, *Politics*, p. 27.

33 James Anquandah, *Together we sow and reap: the first fifty years of the Christian Council of Ghana 1929–1979* (Accra, 1979), p. 33.

34 *Tigare or Christ?* (Accra, [1948–9]).

35 James Anquandah, *Together we sow and reap – the first fifty years of the Christian Council of Ghana 1929–1979* (Accra, 1979), pp. 34–35.

36 Peter Baker, *Peter Dagadu – man of God* (Accra, 1983), p. 32.

37 Christian Council of the Gold Coast, *Christianity and African culture* (Accra, 1955).

38 F. L. Bartels, *The roots of Ghana Methodism* (Cambridge, 1965), p. 218.

39 Noel Smith, *The Presbyterian Church of Ghana, 1835–1960: a younger Church in a changing society* (Accra, 1966), p. 161.

40 Henry P. Thompson, *Into all lands: the history of the Society for the Propagation of the Gospel in Foreign Parts* (London, 1951), p. 584.

stigar: från Svenska Missionsförbundets arbete i Kongo åren 1881–1941 (Stockholm, 1941), p. 142.

14 Manne Lundgren, 'Ngouedi Seminarium', in *ibid.*, p. 296.

15 Andersson, *Churches*, pp. 37–39, 138, 199.

16 George Balandier, *Sociologie des Brazzaville Noires* (Paris, 1955), p. 164.

17 Michel de Schrevel, *Les forces politiques de la décolonisation congolaise jusq'à la veille de l'Indépendance* (Louvain, 1970), p. 63.

18 See Charles-André Gillis, *Kasa Vubu au coeur du drama Congolais* (Brussels, 1964).

19 Suzanne Comhaire-Sylvain, *Femmes de Kinshasa, hier et aujourd'hui* (Paris, 1968).

20 *Ibid.*, p. 305.

21 *Ibid.*, p. 319.

22 *Ibid.*, p. 321.

23 J. van Wing, S.J., 'Les missions Catholiques', in *Atlas général du Congo* (Brussels, 1961).

24 Bruce Fetter's term, see *The creation of Elizabethville, 1910–1940* (Stanford, 1976).

25 J. van Wing, *Études Bakongo* (2nd edn, Brussels, 1959), p. 236.

26 Premiére Conférence Plén. des Ordinaires des Missioné (1932); Troisième Conférence Plén. des Ordinaires (1945); Semaines Missionnaires Louvain 1930, with contributions by P. Mazé and Fr Pierre Charles and others; Fridolin Rauscher, *Die Mitarbeit der einheimischen Laien* (1935), pp. 230ff.

27 Fetter, *Creation*, p. 75.

28 *Ibid.*, p. 120.

29 Willy De Craemer, *The Jamaa and the Church: A Bantu Catholic movement in Zaïre* (Oxford, 1977), p. 18.

30 *Ibid.*, p. 22.

31 The book *Bantu Philosophy* was criticized also on methodological and ethnographic grounds. More importantly, members of the Roman Catholic hierarchy, such as Bishop de Hemptinne, thought the book was far too uncritical to traditional African beliefs, and that the book's thesis could lead to syncretism. In other words, criticism was founded on the issue of keeping Catholic doctrine 'pure' and thus 'uncontaminated by African elements'. (See De Craemer, *Jamaa*, p. 30.)

32 De Craemer, *Jamaa*, pp. 72, 74.

33 *Ibid.*; Johannes Fabian, *Jamaa: a charismatic movement in Katanga* (Evanston, 1971).

34 Cecilia Irvine, *The Church of Christ in Zaïre: a handbook of Protestant churches, missions and communities, 1878–1978* (Indianapolis, 1978).

35 Mumbauza mwa Bawele, in *Etudes d'histoire africaine*, 6 (1974), 255–74. Herbert Smith, *Fifty years in Congo: Disciples of Christ at the Equator* (Indianapolis, 1949); David Lagergren, *Mission and state in the Congo: a study of the relations between Protestant missions and the Congo Independent State authorities with special reference to the Equator District, 1885–1903* (Lund, 1970).

36 John M. Springer, *I love the trail: a sketch of the life of Helen Emily Springer* (Nashville, 1952), p. 136.

37 Marie-Louise Martin, *Kimbangu: an African prophet and his Church* (Oxford, 1975), p. 44.

38 John M. Janzen, *The quest for therapy in Lower Zaïre* (Berkeley, Los Angeles and London, 1978).

39 Schrevel, *Les forces*, p. 180.

40 See Charles-André Gillis, *Kimbangu, fondateur d'église* (Brussels, 1960).

41 *Ibid.*, p.108; P. Raymaekers and Henri Desroche, *L'administration et le sacré* (Brussel, 1983), p. 323.

42 Information from B.Sr.'s research notebooks, held at Uppsala University Library. See also Bengt Sundkler, *The Christian ministry in Africa* (Uppsala, 1960).

CHAPTER 16: SOUTHERN AFRICA

1 Lewis H. Gann, *A history of Northern Rhodesia: early days to 1953* (London, 1964), p. 204.

2 Fergus Macpherson, 'Note on Paul Mushindo', in Paul B. Mushindo, *The life of a Zambian evangelist: the reminiscences of the Reverend Paul Bwembya Mushindo* (ed. J. van Velsen and Fergus Macpherson, Lusaka, 1973), p. xxi.

3 *Ibid.*, p. 42.

4 *Ibid.*, p. xxiii.

5 A. J. Cross, in *World Dominion*, October, 1929.

6 A. G. Blood, *The history of the Universities' Mission to Central Africa*, vol. 3: *1933–1957* (London, 1962), p. 150.

7 See Rapport de Maurice Leenhardt sur la Mission du Zambeze, et la Question de sa Cession, unpublished report written in 1923. This report can be found in the Evangelical Mission Society archives in Paris. Also see James Clifford, Person and myth: Maurice Leenhardt in the Melanesian world (Durham NC and London, 1992), pp. 110–11.

8 Gerdien Verstraelen-Gilhuis, *From Dutch Mission Church to Reformed Church in Zambia: the scope for African leadership and initiative in the history of a Zambian mission Church* (Franeker, 1982).

9 David J. Cook, 'The influence of Livingstonia Mission upon the formation of welfare associations in Zambia, 1912–31', in Terence O. Ranger and John Weller (eds.), *Themes in the Christian history of Central Africa* (London, 1975), p. 108.

10 One could perhaps encircle the experience by use of the term *mentality*. My guess is that the idea of Death-Resurrection-Return of the prophet is an indication of a particular African mentality where the dream in these cases inspired by a crisis of illness (Khambule etc.) or, as in the case of Lenshina, of childbirth – plays an authoritative role as means of communication between the temporal and the supernatural. In the dream certain common stereotypes of white colour are by the Christianized dreamer identified as Jesus the Messiah. See the chapter on dreams in Bengt Sundkler, *Bantu prophets in South Africa* (2nd edn, London, 1961).

11 Tony Hodges, *Jehovah's Witnesses in Central Africa* (London: Minority Rights Group, 1976), p. 9.

12 J. Merle Davies (ed.), *Modern industry and the African* (London, 1933).

13 Peter Bolink, *Towards Church union in Zambia: a study of missionary co-operation and Church-union efforts in Central Africa* (Franeker, 1967), p. 327.

14 John V. Taylor and Dorothea Lehmann, *Christians of the Copperbelt: the growth of the church in Northern Rhodesia* (London, 1961), p. 3.

15 Dr Monica Fisher, correspondence with B.Sr.

16 See W. T. Stunt *et al.*, *Turning the world upside down: a century of missionary endeavour* (2nd edn, Bath, 1973), pp. 440, 452, 455.

77 Cottesloe Consultation, 1960.

78 Gustav B. A. Gerdener, *Recent developments in the South African mission field* (London and Edinburgh, 1958), p. 23.

79 Gustav B. A. Gerdener, *Studies in the evangelisation of South Africa* (London, 1911), p. 114.

80 D. Crafford, *Aan God die dank* (Pretoria, 1982), p. 223.

81 [The so-called Tomlinson Report] *Summary of the Report of the Commission for the Socio-Economic Development of the Bantu Areas within the Union of South Africa* (Pretoria, 1955), p. 22.

82 *Ibid.*, p. 23.

83 Gerdener, *Recent developments*, p. 18.

84 [The Tomlinson Report] *Summary of the Report*, p. 158.

85 See Alan Wilkinson, *The Community of the Resurrection: a centenary history* (London, 1992).

86 Trevor Huddleston, *Naught for Your Comfort* (London, 1956).

87 Michael Scott, *A time to speak* (London, 1958).

88 See Zachariah K. Matthews, *Freedom for my people: the autobiography of Z. K. Matthews: southern Africa 1901 to 1968.* Edited with a memoir by Monica Wilson. (London and Cape Town, 1981).

89 J. E. Brady, *'Princes of His people': the story of our bishops 1800–1951* (Johannesburg, 1951), p. 21.

90 See Francis Schimlek, *Against the stream: life of Father Bernard Huss, CMM* (Mariannhill, 1949), and *idem, Marianhill: a study in Bantu life and missionary effort* (Mariannhill, 1953).

91 Clement D. Doke and Benedict W. Vilakazi, *Zulu–English Dictionary* (Johannesburg, 1948).

92 See H. W. Florin, *Lutherans in South Africa* (2nd edn, Durban, 1967).

93 *Ibid.*, p. 51.

94 See Stanley M. Burgess and Gary B. McGee (eds), *Dictionary of Pentecostal and charismatic movements* (Grand Rapids, 1988), pp. 250–54.

95 G. C. Oosthuizen, *Pentecostal penetration into the Indian community in metropolitan Durban, South Africa* (Durban, 1975), p. 78.

96 *Ibid.*, p. 77, emphasis in original.

97 See *ibid.* and *idem, Moving to the waters: fifty years of Pentecostal revival in Bethesda, 1925–1975* (Durban, 1975).

98 Allie A. Dubb, *Community of the saved: an African revivalist Church in the East Cape* (Johannesburg, 1976), p. 120.

99 Walton Johnson, 'The Africanization of a mission Church: The African Methodist Episcopal Church in Zambia', in George Bond, Walton Johnson and Sheila S. Walker (eds.), *African Christianity; patterns of religious continuity* (New York, 1979), p. 101.

100 Theo Sundermeier, *Wir aber suchten Gemeinschaft, Kirchenwerdung und Kirchentrennung in Südwestafrika* (Erlangen, 1973), p. 89.

101 V. Thompson and R. Adloff, *The Malagasy Republic* (Stanford, 1965), p. 31.

102 *Ibid.*, p. 55.

103 *Ibid.*, p. 66.

104 Françoise Raison, 'Le catholicisme malgache: passé et présent', *Revue française d'études politiques africaines*, 53 (1970), p. 84.

CHAPTER 17: EASTERN AFRICA

1 John Iliffe, *A modern history of Tanganyika* (Cambridge, 1979), p. 321.

2 F. Rowling, 'The building of the Uganda Cathedral', *International review of missions*, 8 (1919), pp. 227–37.

3 John V. Taylor, *The growth of the Church in Buganda: an attempt at understanding* (London, 1958).

4 Holger Bernt Hansen, *Mission, Church and state in a colonial setting: Uganda 1890–1925* (London, 1984), p. 289.

5 *Ibid.*, p. 290.

6 *Ibid.*, pp. 291–92, 298–99.

7 See John M. Waliggo, 'The Catholic Church in the Buddu Province of Buganda, 1879–1925', Ph.D. thesis, University of Cambridge, 1976.

8 *Ibid.*

9 Sister Mary Louis, *Love is the answer* (Dublin, 1964), p. 116.

10 Sister Mary Louis, *Love is the answer* (Dublin 1964); Caroline Oliver, *Western women in colonial Africa* (London, 1982); John Mary Waliggo, 'Ganda traditional religion and Catholicism in Buganda, 1948–75', in Edward Fasholé-Luke and others, *Christianity in independent Africa* (London 1978).

11 Leslie Brown, *Three worlds, one word: account of a mission* (London, 1981), p. 160.

12 Waliggo, 'Catholic Church', p. 3.

13 D. Anthony Low, *Political parties in Uganda, 1949–62* (London, 1962), p. 35.

14 Adrian Hastings, *Church and mission in modern Africa* (London, 1967), p. 182.

15 Ian Linden, *Church and revolution in Rwanda* (Manchester, 1977), p. 202.

16 *Ibid.*, p. 154.

17 *Ibid.*, pp. 203–4; Gordon Hewitt, *The problem of success: a history of the Church Missionary Society 1910–1942* (2 vols., London, 1971–7), vol. 1, pp. 269, 274.

18 J. E. Church, *Quest for the highest: a diary of the East African Revival* (Exeter, 1981); Birgitta Larsson, *Conversion to greater freedom?: women, Church and social change in North-Western Tanzania under Colonial Rule* (Uppsala, 1991); Catherine Robins, 'Tukutendereza: a study of social change and withdrawal in the Balokole Revival of Uganda', Ph.D. thesis, Columbia University, 1975.

19 See Marcia Wright, 'The Catholic Church in East Central Africa: reflections on its receptivity to change', in CIHEC [Commission internationale d'histoire ecclésiastique Comparée], *The Church in a changing society: conflict, reconciliation or adjustment* (Uppsala, 1978), pp. 397–401.

20 Johanna Eggert, *Missionsschule und sozialer Wandel in Ostafrika. Der Beitrag der deutschen evangelischen Missionsgesellschaften zur Entwicklung des Schulwesens in Tanganyika 1891–1939* (Bielefeld, 1970), pp. 198–99.

21 J. Busse, *Junge Kirche im afrikanischen Gewand* (Stuttgart, 1966), p. 62.

22 Bengt Sundkler, *Bara Bukoba: Church and community in Tanzania* (London, 1980), pp. 27–29, 63.

23 Bengt Sundkler, *Ung kyrka i Tanganyika* (Stockholm, 1948), pp. 120–24.

24 Iliffe, *Modern history*, p. 408.

25 T. O. Ranger, 'Missionary adaptations of African religious institutions: the Masasi case', in T. O. Ranger and I. N. Kimambo (eds.), *The historical study of African religion: with special reference to East and Central Africa* (London, 1972), pp. 241, 247.

9 Maurice Assad, 'The Coptic Orthodox Church', *One World*, 24 (1977), 16.
10 Otto F. A Meinardus, *Christian Egypt: ancient and modern* (2nd edn, Cairo, 1977), pp. 49–50.
11 ACA, *The Copts*, September 1980.
12 Iris Habib al-Masri, *The story of the Copts, established by St Mark* (Cairo, 1978), p. 557.
13 Bishop Athanasius, *The Copts through the ages* (3rd edn, Cairo, 1973), p. 8.
14 al-Masri, *Story*, p. 558.
15 Bishop Kalilombe interview with B.Sr., November 1989.
16 We are indebted to Mr Jan Henningson, Uppsala, for sharing with us his knowledge about Coptic Egypt.
17 *Conference report*, 1965, p. 1.
18 See David Kessler and Tudor Parfitt, *The Falashas: the Jews of Ethiopia* (Minority Rights Group report, 67; London, 1982).
19 See Haile Mariam Larebo, 'The Ethiopian Orthodox Church and politics in the twentieth century: part 1', *Northeast African studies*, 9 (1987), 1–17; *idem*, 'The Ethiopian Orthodox Church and politics in the twentieth century: part 2', *Northeast African studies*, 10 (1988), 1–23.

CHAPTER 20: WEST AFRICA

1 Jacques Louis Hymans, *Léopold Sédar Senghor: an intellectual biography* (Edinburgh, 1971), p. 14.
2 *Ibid.*, p. 138.
3 Robert M. Baum, 'The emergence of a Diola Christianity', *Africa*, 60 (1990), p. 384.
4 *Ibid.*, p. 391.
5 *Ibid.*, p. 392.
6 *Ibid.*
7 Michael Crowder and Donal Cruise O'Brien, 'French West Africa, 1945–1960', in J. F. Ade Ajayi and Michael Crowder (eds.), *History of West Africa* (2 vols., London, 1971–4), vol. 2, p. 694.
8 Gustave Bienvenu, 'Les fruits de l'absence et le retour en Guinée Conakry', *Spiritus*, 28, No. 107 (1987), 192–96.
9 Sheila S. Walker, *The religious revolution in the Ivory Coast: the Prophet Harris and the Harrist Church* (Chapel Hill, 1983), p. 112.
10 Comi M. Toulabor, 'Mgr Dosseh, Archevêque de Lomé', *Politique Africaine*, 35 (1989), p. 69.
11 *Actualités religieuses*, 15.9.90.
12 'Niger', *Information für Informanten*, 68 (1988); 'Mali', *ibid.*, 70 (1988).
13 'Obervolta II', *Information für Informanten*, 32 (1975); 'Burkina Faso', *ibid.*, 66 (1986).
14 Kwame Nkrumah, *The autobiography of Kwame Nkrumah* (Edinburgh, 1957) p. 11.
15 David Rooney, *Kwame Nkrumah* (London, 1988), p. 9.
16 Nkrumah, *Autobiography*, p. 21.
17 Pro Mundi Vita, *The Church in Ghana* (Brussels, 1975), p. 9.
18 J. S. Pobee, 'Church and State in Ghana, 1949–1966', in J. S. Pobee (ed.), *Religion in a pluralistic society: essays presented to Professor C. G. Baëta* (Leiden, 1976), p. 140.
19 Roseveare's address to Anglican synod 1962, quoted from J. S. Pobee, *ibid.*
20 See *Africa confidential*, 29 (No. 24, 1988), p. 5.

21 Ogbu U. Kalu, 'The shattered cross: the Church union movement in Nigeria 1905–66', in Ogbu U. Kalu (ed.), *The history of Christianity in West Africa* (London, 1980), p. 349.
22 Ogbu U. Kalu, *Divided people of God: Church union movement in Nigeria: 1867–1966* (New York, 1978), p. 76.
23 *Ibid.*, p. 25.
24 *Ibid.*
25 Kalu, 'The shattered cross', p. 343.
26 Kalu, *Divided people*, p. 86.
27 *Ibid.*, p. 70.
28 Elizabeth Isichei, *A history of the Igbo people* (London, 1976), p. 245.
29 *Ibid.*, p. 246.
30 Andrew F. Walls, 'Religion and the press in "the Enclave" in the Nigerian Civil War', in Edward Fashole-Luke *et al.* (eds.), *Christianity in Independent Africa* (London, 1978), p. 209.
31 *Ibid.*, p. 213.
32 *Ibid.*, p. 214.
33 Laurie S. Wiseberg, 'Christian Churches and the Nigerian civil war', *Journal of African studies*, 2 (1975), p. 306.
34 *Ibid.*
35 Alden Hatch, *Pope Paul VI: apostle on the move* (London, 1967), p. 114.
36 John D. Clarke, *Yakubu Gowon: faith in a united Nigeria* (London, 1987), p. 109.
37 *Ibid.*
38 Edmund Patrick T. Crampton, *Christianity in Northern Nigeria* (Zaria, 1975), p. 174.
39 Clarke, *Gowon*, p. 134.
40 John de St Jorre, *The Nigerian civil war* (London, 1972), p. 407.
41 Clarke, *Gowon*, p. 4.
42 See 'Fire of Religion', *Newswatch*, 30/3/87, 15.
43 See Adrian Hastings, *A history of African Christianity 1950–1975* (Cambridge, 1979), p. 237.
44 David B. Barrett (ed.), *World Christian encyclopedia: a comparative study of Churches and religions in the modern world AD 1900–2000* (Oxford, 1982), p. 528.
45 Peter B. Clarke, *West Africa and Christianity* (London, 1986), p. 201.
46 Barrett, *World Christian*, p. 528.

CHAPTER 21: CENTRAL AFRICA

1 See Jean-Marc Éla, *My faith as an African* (trans. John P. Brown and Susan Perry, London, 1989)
2 Bénézst Bujo, *Herder Korrespondenz: Monatshefte für Gesellschaft und Religion*, 37 (February 1983), p. 50.
3 Jean-Marc Éla, *Le cri de l'homme africain* (Paris 1980).
4 Werner Keller, *Zur Freiheit berufen: die Geschichte der Presbyterianischen Kirche in Kamerun* (Zurich, 1981); Heinrich Balz, *Where the faith has to live: studies in Bakossi society and religion* (2 vols., Basel, 1984–85).
5 Interview with anonymous Congolese Church leader.
6 *Pentecoste sur le monde*, May–June 1975.

11 September, 1985. See also H. S. Dahle, *Madagaskar i Sikte* (Oslo, 1976) and Öj. Dahle, *Madagaskar: midt i brendningene* (Oslo, 1985)

CHAPTER 23: EAST AFRICA

1 Jomo Kenyatta, *Facing Mount Kenya: the tribal life of the Gikuyu* (London, 1938).

2 See G. P. Benson, 'Ideological politics versus biblical hermeneutics: Kenya's Protestant Churches and the *Nyayo* State', in Holger Bernt Hansen and Michael Twaddle (eds.) *Religion and politics in East Africa: the period since independence* (London, 1995), pp. 177–99.

3 John Baur, *The Catholic Church in Kenya: a centenary history* (Nairobi, 1990).

4 *Ibid.*, p. 49.

5 *Ibid.*, p. 136.

6 S. N. Clements, 'The Catholic Church in Kenya: a centre of hope', *Pro Mundi Vita Africa Dossier*, 22 (July 1982).

7 John Lonsdale with Stanley Booth-Clibborn and Andrew Hake, 'The emerging pattern of Church and State co-operation in Kenya', in Edward Fasholé-Luke and others (eds.), *Christianity in independent Africa* (London 1978), p. 269.

8 J. Henry Okullu, *Church and State in nation building and human development* (Nairobi, 1984), p. 105.

9 John Lonsdale and others, 'Emerging patterns', pp. 276, 282; *The Weekly review* (Nairobi), 3/5/85.

10 David B. Barrett *et al.* (eds), *Kenya Churches handbook: the development of Kenyan Christianity, 1498–1973* (Kisumu, 1973) and Agnes Chepkwony, *The role of non-governmental organizations in development: a study of the National Christian Council of Kenya (NCCK), 1963–1978*, (Uppsala, 1987).

11 Chepkwony, 'Non-governmental organizations', pp. 273–74.

12 Adrian Hastings, *A history of African Christianity 1950–1975* (Cambridge 1979), p. 252.

13 Barrett *et al.*, *Kenya Churches handbook*, p. 246.

14 Leslie Brown, *Three worlds, one word: account of a mission* (London, 1981), p. 234.

15 Quoted by Michael Twaddle, 'Museveni's Uganda: notes towards an analysis', in Holger Bernt Hansen and Michael Twaddle (eds.), *Uganda now: between decay and development* (London, 1988), p. 320.

16 *The Tablet*, 6 May, 1989.

17 John M. Waliggo, 'The Catholic Church in the Budda Province of Buganda, 1879–1925', Ph.D. thesis, University of Cambridge, 1976.

18 G. Völlinger, 'Das macht keine Schlagzeilen!!', *Information für Informanten*, 44 (1979), p. 29.

19 Brown, *Three worlds*, p. 162.

20 *Ibid.*, p. 100.

21 *Ibid.*, p. 159.

22 See C. K. Omari (ed.), *Toward rural development in Tanzania: some issues on policy implementation in the 1970s* (Arusha, 1984).

23 Goran Hyden, *Beyond ujamaa in Tanzania: underdevelopment and an uncaptured peasantry* (London, 1980), p. 33.

24 See Aili M. Tripp, 'Women and the changing urban household economy in Tanzania', *Journal of modern African studies*, 27 (1989), 601–23.

25 Vincent J. Donovan, *Christianity rediscovered: an epistle from the Masai* (2nd edn, London, 1982), pp. viii, 153.

26 Marja-Liisa Swantz, *Women in development: a creative role denied? The case of Tanzania* (London, 1985), p. 157.

27 *Ibid.*, pp. 122–52.

CHAPTER 24: ECUMENICAL PERSPECTIVES

1 *Spiritus*, June 1982: the whole issue is devoted to the *Fidei Donum*.

2 Jean-Marc Ela and René Luneau, *Voici le temps des héritiers: églises d'Afrique et voies nouvelles* (Paris, 1986), pp. 14, 152.

3 *Herder-Korrespondenz*, 27, No. 6 (1973).

4 See Augustin Bea, *The way to unity after the Council* (trans. Gerard Noel, London, 1967); Yves Congar, *Report from Rome: on the second session of the Vatican Council* (trans. Lancelot Sheppard), (London, 1964); *idem*, *Le concile de Vatican II: son église: peuple de Dieu et corps du Christ* (Paris, 1984).

5 Walter M. Abbott, *The documents of Vatican II* (New York, 1966); Georges Conus, *L'Église d'Afrique au Concile Vatican II* (Immensee, 1975),

6 *Herder-Korrespondenz*, 39 (1985), p. 563.

7 David B. Barrett, 'AD 2000: 350 million Christians in Africa', *International review of missions*, 59 (1970), p. 48.

8 See Adrian Hastings, *A history of African Christianity 1950–1975* (Cambridge, 1979), pp. 237–44.

9 Dr Omer Degrijse, the Euntes Institute, Louvain, 3 November, 1989 to B.Sr.

10 See E. Elochukwu Uzukwu, 'Africa's right to be different: Christian liturgical rites and African rites', *Bulletin of African theology*, 4 (January-June 1982), pp. 87–109.

11 See also Marie Le Roy Ladurie, *Pâques Africaines: de la communauté clanique àla communauté chrétienne* (Paris, 1965), pp. 198–200.

12 E. Elochukwu Uzukwu, 'Africa's right to be different, part 2: African rites in the making', *Bulletin of African theology*, 4 (July–December 1982), p. 269.

13 *Ibid.*, p. 272.

14 *Ibid.*, p. 249.

15 T. Tshibangu, 'Un Concile africain est-il opportun?', *Bulletin of African theology*, 5 (July–December 1983), p. 169.

16 *Ibid.*, p. 172.

17 Engelbert Mveng, *L'Afrique dans l'église: paroles d'un croyant* (Paris, 1985), p. 177.

18 See V. Y. Mudimbe (ed.), *The surreptitious speech: Présence Africaine and the politics of otherness 1947–1987* (Chicago, 1992).

19 Norman C. Geisler, in *Afroscope*, June 1979.

20 See *Afroscope*, August–October 1979.

21 See *Afroscope*, April–June 1985.

22 See *Evangelical ministries*, May–August 1986, p. 7.

23 John Gatu, Speech at the Mission Festival, Milwaukee, USA, 1971, published in the *Church Herald*.

24 *Ibid.*

25 See Henry Okullo, *Church and politics in East Africa* (Nairobi, 1974).

26 Burgess Carr, 'Internationalizing the mission', *IDOC Dossier*, 9 (1974), 72–74.

Ahanotu, Austin Metumara (ed.) *Religion, state and society in contemporary Africa: Nigeria, Sudan, South Africa, Zaïre and Mozambique*. New York, 1992.

Ajayi, J. F. Ade. *Christian missions in Nigeria, 1841–1891: the making of a new elite*. London, 1965.

al-Masry, Iris Habib. *The story of the Coptic Church of Egypt, established by St Mark*. Cairo, 1978.

Alays, Père. *Capucins missionaires en Afrique Orientale: pays Galla, en Ethiopie, Cote Française des Somalis*. Toulouse, 1931.

Aleme, Eshete. *Activités politiques de la mission Catholique (Lazariste) en Ethiopie (sous la règne de l'Emperor Johannes, 1869–1889)*. Paris, 1970.

La mission Catholique Lazariste en Ethiopie. Aix-en-Provence, 1972.

Allier, Raoul. *La psychologie de la conversion chex les peuples non-civilisés*. 2 vols. Paris, 1925.

Allison, Oliver. *A pilgrims Church's progress*. London, 1966.

Through fire and water: ten critical years in the life of the Church in the Southern Sudan, 1964–1974. London, 1976.

Travelling light: Bishop Oliver Allison of the Sudan remembers. Bexhill-on-Sea, 1983.

Alvares, Francisco. *The Prester John of the Indies: a true relation of the lands of the Prester John being the narrative of the Portuguese embassy to Ethiopia in 1520*. 2 vols. C. F. Beckingham and G. W. B. Huntingford (eds.) Cambridge, 1961.

Amanze, J. N. *Botswana handbook of Churches*. Gaborone, 1994.

Amissah, G. McLean. *Reminiscences of Adisadel: a short historical sketch of Adisadel College*. Accra, 1980.

Amucheazi, E. C. *Church and politics in Eastern Nigeria, 1945–1966: a study in pressure group politics*. Lagos, 1986.

Anckaer, Leopold. *De evangelizatiemetode van de missionarissen van Scheut in Kongo (1888–1907)*. Brussels, 1970.

Andersen, Knud Tage. *Ethiopiens Ortodokse Kirke*. Christiansfeld, 1971.

Fra mission til kirke. Christiansfeld, 1976.

Andersen, Knud Tage *et al. A brief history of the Mekane Yesus Church*. Christiansfeld, 1980.

Anderson, Dick. *We felt like grasshoppers: the story of Africa Inland Mission*. Nottingham, 1994.

Anderson, J. *The struggle for the school: the interaction of missionary, colonial government and nationalist enterprise in the development of formal education in Kenya*. London, 1970.

Anderson, William B. *Ambassadors by the Nile: the Church in North-East Africa*. London, 1963.

The Church in East Africa, 1840–1974. Dodoma, 1977.

Anderson-Morshead, A. E. M. *The history of the Universities' Mission to Central Africa: I: 1859–1909*. 6th edn, London, 1955. *III: 1933–1957*. London, 1962.

Andersson, Efraim. *Churches at the grass-roots: a study in Congo-Brazzaville*. London and New York, 1968.

Messianic popular movements in the Lower Congo. Uppsala, 1958.

Andrew, Veronica. *Ovamboland*. London, 1953.

Andrews, C. F. *John White of Mashonaland*. London, 1935.

Anglican Church in Ghana. *The Anglican Church in Ghana, 1752–1974: two hundred and twenty-second anniversary*. Accra, 1974.

Anquandah, James. *Together we sow and reap – the Christian Council of Ghana 1929–1979*. Accra, 1979.

Anstey, Roger. *King Leopold's legacy: the Congo under Belgian rule, 1908–1960*. London, 1966.

Antonius, Alberto. *The Apostolic Vicariate of the Galla (1846–1938): three of its vicars: Massaja, Cahagne, Jarosseau*. Rome, 1993.

Anyebe, Acheme Paul. *Ogboni (the birth and growth of the Reformed Ogboni Fraternity)*. Ikeja-Lagos, 1989.

Apostolischen Vikariat in Windhoek. *Geschichte der katholischen Mission in Südwestafrika 1896–1946: Festschrift zum fünfzigjährigen Bestehen der katholischen Mission in Südwestafrika*. Windhoek, 1946.

Appiah-Kubi, Kofi. *Man cures, God heals: religion and medical practice among the Akans of Ghana*. Totowa, 1981.

Arata, S. *Abuna Yakob, Apostolo dell'Abissinia (Mons. Giustino de Jacobis, CM) 1800–1860*. 2nd edn, Rome, 1934.

Arén, Gustav. *Evangelical pioneers in Ethiopia: origins of the Evangelical Church Mekane Yesus*. Stockholm and Addis Ababa, 1978.

Arkell, A. J. *A history of the Sudan from the earliest times to 1821*. 2nd edn, London, 1961.

Arnaud, D. *Les débuts de l'évangélisation du peuple Mossi-Nakomse*. Rome, 1979.

Arnot, Frederick Stanley. *Garenganze or, seven years pioneer mission work in Central Africa*. 1889. (2nd edn, London, 1969.)

Arnot, Frederick Stanley. *Missionary travels in Central Africa*. Bath, 1914.

Arnoux, (Père). *Histoire des missions en AOF*. Rome, 1950.

Arrowsmith-Brown, J. H. (ed. and trans.) *Prutky's travels in Ethiopia and other countries*. (Annot. Richard Pankhurst.) Hakluyt Society, second series, 174. London, 1991.

Arulefela, J. O. *Covenant in the Old Testament and in Yorubaland*. Ibadan, 1988.

Asabia, D. O. and Adegbesan. *Idoani past and present: the story of one Yoruba kingdom*. Ibadan, 1970.

Asante, S. K. B. *Pan-African protest: West Africa and the Italo-Ethiopian crisis, 1934–1941*. London, 1977.

Asch, Susan. *L'Eglise du Prophète Kimbangu: de ses origines à son rôle actuel au Zaïre, 1921–1981*. Paris, 1983.

Ashe, Robert Pickering. *Chronicles of Uganda*. 1894. 2nd edn, London, 1971.

Two kings of Uganda. London, 1890.

Assimeng, Max. *Religion and social change in West Africa*. Accra, 1989.

Saints and social structures. Tema, 1986.

Atanda, J. A. (ed.) *Baptist Churches in Nigeria, 1850–1950*. Ibadan, 1988.

Ashiwaju, Garba, and Abubakar, Yaya (eds.) *Nigeria since independence: IX: Religion*. Ibadan, 1989.

Athanasius, Bishop. *The Copts through the ages*. 3rd edn, Cairo, 1973.

Atiya, Aziz S. *A history of eastern Christianity*. London, 1968. (Repr. Millwood, NY, 1980.)

(ed.) *Coptic encyclopedia*. 8 vols. New York, 1991.

Attwater, Donald. *The White Fathers in Africa*. London, 1938.

Auala, Josef *et al.* (eds.) *Ongerki yomoWambokavango – Ambo Kavangon Kirkko – The Ovambo-Kavango Church*. Helsinki, 1970.

Auala, Leonard and Ihamäki, Kirsti. *Messlatte und Bischofsstab: ein Leben für Namibia*. (Trans. Marja Liisa Trillitzsch.) Wuppertal and Erlangen, 1988.

Augustine, Saint. *Confessions*. Trans. Henry Chadwick, Oxford, 1991.

Austen, Ralph A. *Northwest Tanzania under German and British rule: colonial policy and tribal politics, 1889–1939*. New Haven and London, 1968.

Axelson, Eric. *The Portuguese in south-east Africa 1600–1700*. Johannesburg, 1960.

The Portuguese in south-east Africa, 1488–1600. London, 1973.
Congo to Cape: early Portuguese explorers. London, 1973.

Axelson, Sigbert. *Culture confrontation in the Lower Congo: from the old Congo Kingdom to the Congo Independent State with special reference to the Swedish missionaries in the 1880s and 1890s*. Uppsala, 1970.

Ayandele, E. A. *The missionary impact on modern Nigeria 1842–1914: a political and social analysis*. London, 1966.
Holy Johnson: pioneer of African nationalism, 1836–1917. London, 1970.
A visionary of the African Church: Mojola Agbebi (1860–1917). Nairobi, 1971.

Babalola, E. O. *Christianity in West Africa (an historical analysis)*. Ibadan, 1988.

Baëta, C. G. *Prophetism in Ghana: a study of some 'spiritual' Churches*. London, 1962.
(ed.) *Christianity in tropical Africa*. London, 1968.

Bahendwa, L. Festo. *Christian religious education in the Lutheran dioceses of north-western Tanzania*. Helsinki, 1990.

Bakke, Johnny. *Christian ministry: patterns and functions within the Ethiopian Evangelical Church Mekane Yesus*. Oslo and New Jersey, 1987.

Balandier, Georges. *Daily life in the Kingdom of Kongo*. New York, 1968.

Balz, Heinrich. *Where the faith has to live: studies in Bakossi society and religion*. Basel, 1984.

Banana, Canaan Sodindo. *Come and share: an introduction to Christian theology*. Uppsala, 1991.
(ed.) *Turmoil and tenacity: Zimbabwe 1890–1990*. Harare, 1989.
(ed.) *A century of Methodism in Zimbabwe 1891–1991*. Harare, 1991.

Banda, Kelvin N. *A brief history of education in Malawi*. Blantyre, 1982.

Bane, Martin. *The Catholic story of Liberia*. New York, 1950.
Catholic pioneers in West Africa. Dublin, 1956.

Banton, Michael. *West African city: a study of tribal life in Freetown*. London, 1957.

Banville, Ghislain de. *Itinéraire d'un missionnaire: le Père Marc Pedron*. Bangui, 1989.
Saint Paul des Rapides: histoire d'une fondation 1893–1905. Bambari, 1989.

Baombolia, Bolamba *et al*. *L'Esprit et le Sel: recherches sur l'histoire de l'Eglise au Rwanda par un groupe de travail de l'Ecole de Théologie de Butare*. Butare, 1978.

Baptist Missionary Society, *1878–1978: one hundred years of Christian mission in Angola and Zaïre*. London, 1978.

Barker, Peter. *Peter Dagadu – man of God*. Accra, 1983.
(ed.) *Five hundred Churches: a brief survey of Christianity in Ghana*. Accra, 1978.

Barnes, Bertram Herbert. *Johnson of Nyasaland: a study of the life and work of William Percival Johnson, DD, Archdeacon of Nyasa, missionary pioneer 1876–1928*. London, 1933.

Barrett, David B. (ed.) *African initiatives in religion: twenty-one studies from eastern and Central Africa*. Nairobi, 1971.

Barret, David B. *et al*. (eds.) *Kenya Churches handbook: the development of Kenyan Christianity, 1498–1973*. Kisumu, 1973.

Bartels, F. L. *The roots of Ghana Methodism*. Cambridge and Accra, 1965.

Batsikama, R. *Ndona Béatrice: serait-elle témoin du Christ et de la foi du vieux Congo?* Kinshasa, 1970.

Batts, H. J. *The story of a hundred years, 1820–1920: being the history of the Baptist Church in South Africa*. Cape Town, n.d.

Baudu, Paul. *Vieil empire, jeune église: Mgr Johanny Thévenoud*. Paris, 1956.

Baumann, Franz (ed.) *No bird flies with just one wing: reflections on the history and identity of the Basel Mission*. Basel, 1990.

Baumann, Julius. *Mission und Ökumene in Südwestafrika: Dargestellt am Lebenswerk von Hermann Heinrich Vedder*. Leiden and Cologne, 1965.

(ed.) *Van sending tot kerk: 125 jaar Rynse sendingarbeid in Suidwes-Afrika, 1842–1967*. Karibib, 1967.

Baur, John. *The Catholic Church in Kenya: a centenary history*. Nairobi, 1990.

Baur, John. *Two thousand years of Christianity in Africa: an African history 62–1992*. Nairobi, 1994.

Bayly, J. *Congo crisis: a retrospect through the eyes of missionaries and Congolese Christians*. Grand Rapids, 1966.

Beach, D. N. *The Shona and Zimbabwe 900–1850: an outline of Shona history*. New York, 1980.

Beaver, R. Pierce. Ecumenical beginnings in Protestant world mission: a history of comity. New York, 1962.

Beaver, R. Pierce (ed.) *American missions in bicentennial perspective*. South Pasadena, 1977.

Becken, Hans Jürgen. *Theologie der Heilung: Das Heilen in den Afrikanischen Unabhängigen Kirchen in Südafrika*. Hermannsburg, 1972.

Beckmann, D. M. *Eden revival: spiritual Churches in Ghana*. St Louis, 1975.

Bedford, Francis John. *The Bible in East Africa*. London, 1954.

Bediako, Kwame. *Christianity in Africa: the renewal of a non-western religion*. Edinburgh and New York, 1995.

Bee, Michel. 'Les missions en Basse Côte d'Ivoire.' 2 vols. Thèse de 3ème cycle, University of Paris-Sorbonne, 1970.

Beeching, Jack. *An open path: Christian missionaries 1515–1914*. London, 1979.

Beetham, T. A. *Christianity and the new Africa*. London, 1967.

Behrens-Abouseif, Doris. *Die Kopten in der ägyptischen Gesellschaft von der Mitte 19 Jahrhunderts bis 1923*. Freiburg-im-Breisgau, 1972.

Beidelman, T. O. *Colonial evangelism: a socio-historical study of an East African mission at the grassroots*. Bloomington, 1982.

Bell, G. *Our Fernandian field*. London, 1926.

Bell, H. I. *Jews and Christians in Alexandria*. Oxford, 1924.

Bender, C. J. *Der Weltkrieg und die christlichen Missionen in Kamerun*. Kassel, 1921.

Bender, Gerald. *Angola under the Portuguese: the myth and the reality*. Berkeley, 1978.

Benedetto, Robert. (ed.) *Presbyterian reformers in Central Africa: a documentary account of the American Presbyterian Congo Mission and the human rights struggle in the Congo, 1890–1918*. (Trans. Winifried K. Vass.) Leiden, 1996.

Bening, R. Bagulo. *A history of education in northern Ghana 1907–1976*. Accra, 1990.

Bennett, Norman R. (ed.) *From Zanzibar to Ujiji: the journal of Arthur W. Dodgshun, 1877–1879*. Boston, 1969.

Bennett, Norman R. *Studies in East African history*. Boston, 1963.

Mirambo of Tanzania 1840?–1884. New York, 1971.

Benoist, Joseph-Roger de. *Docteur Lumière, quarante ans au service de l'homme en Haute-Volta*. Paris, 1975.

Église et pouvoir colonial au Soudan français: les relations entre les administrateurs et les missionnaires catholiques dans la Boucle du Niger, de 1885 à 1945. Paris, 1987.

Bentley, William Holman. *Pioneering on the Congo*. 2 vols., London, 1900; reprinted, New York, 1970.

Berger, Heinrich. *Mission und kolonial Politik: die katholische Mission in Kameroun während der deutschen Kolonialzeit*. Immersee, 1978.

Bergna, C. *La missione francescana in Libia*. Tripoli, 1924.

Berman, Edward H. (ed.) *African reactions to missionary education*. New York and London, 1975.

Bernander, Gustav. *Lutheran wartime assistance to Tanzanian Churches 1940–1945*. Uppsala and Lund, 1968.

Bernardi, B. *The Mugwe, a failing prophet: a study of a religious and public dignitary of the Meru of Kenya*. London, 1959

Bernier, C. *Plongée en Afrique*. Richelieu, 1969

Bernoville, G. *Monseigneur Jarosseau et la mission des Gallas: mission d'Ethiopie*. Paris, 1950.

Berry, Lewellyn L. *A century of missions of the African Methodist Episcopal Church, 1840–1940*. New York, 1942.

Berthelot, Lilian. *La prieure de Shembaganaur: une Carmélite mauricienne*. Port Louis, 1987.

Beshah, Girma and Aregay, Merid. *The question of the union of the Churches in Luso-Ethiopian relations*. Lisbon, 1964.

Beshir, Mohamed Omer. *Educational development in the Sudan, 1898 to 1956*. Oxford, 1969.

Beslier, C. G. *L'Apotre du Congo: Monseigneur Augouard*. Paris, 1946.

Bewes, T. F. C. *Kikuyu conflict: Mau Mau and the Christian witness*. London, 1953.

Bhebe, Ngwabi. *Christianity and traditional religion in western Zimbabwe 1859–1923*. London, 1979.

Bhebe, Ngwabi and Ranger, Terence O. (eds.) *Society in Zimbabwe's liberation war*. London, 1996.

Bhila, H. H. K. *Trade and politics in a Shona kingdom: the Manyika and their African and Portuguese neighbours 1575–1902*. Harlow, 1982.

Biermans, J. *A short history of the Vicariate of the Upper Nile, Uganda*. Kampala, 1920.

Billy, Edmond de. *En Côte d'Ivoire: mission Protestante d'AOF*. Paris, 1931.

Bingham, Rowland V. *Seven sevens of years and a jubilee*. Toronto, 1943.

Biobaku, Saburi O. *The Egba and their neighbours, 1842–1872*. London, 1965.

Birkeli, Fridtjov. *Politikk og mission: De politiske og interkonfesjonelle forhold på Madagaskar og deras betydning for den norske misjons grunnlegging 1861–1875*. (With a summary in English.) Oslo, 1952.

Birmingham, David. *Trade and conflict in Angola: the Mbundu and their neighbours under the influence of the Portuguese 1483–1700*. Oxford, 1966.

Birtwhistle, Allen. *Thomas Birch Freeman: West African pioneer*. London, 1950.

Blake, John W. *West Africa: quest for God and gold 1454–1578: a survey of the first century of White enterprise in West Africa, with particular reference to the achievement of the Portuguese and their rivalries with other European powers*. 2nd edn, London, 1977.

Blanc, R., Blocher, J. and Krüger, E. *Histoire des missions protestantes françaises*. Flavion, 1970.

Bloch, Maurice. *Placing the dead: tombs, ancestral villages and kinship organization in Madagascar*. London, 1971.

Blood, A. G. *The history of the Universities' Mission to Central Africa: II: 1907–1932*. London, 1957.

Blyden, Edward W. *Christianity, Islam and the Negro race*. 1888. Reprinted, Edinburgh, 1967.

Bockelman, W. and Bockelman, E. *Ethiopia: where Lutheran is spelled 'Mekane Yesus'*. Minneapolis, 1972.

Böckerman, G. *Etrangers en Algérie? Identité, motivations et attitudes des membres permanents des églises chrétiennes*. Algiers, 1979.

Boer, Harry R. *History of the Theological College of Northern Nigeria, 1950–1971*. Grand Rapids, 1983.

Boer, Jan Harm. *Missionary messengers of liberation in a colonial context: a case study of the Sudan United Mission*. Amsterdam, 1979.

Boesak, Allan. *Farewell to innocence: a social-ethical study of Black theology and Black power*. Johannesburg, 1977.

Boiteau, Pierre. *Contribution à l'histoire de la nation malgache*. Paris, 1958.

Bolink, P. *Towards Church union in Zambia: a study of missionary co-operation and Church union efforts in Central Africa*. Franeker, 1967.

Bond, G. C. *The politics of change in a Zambian community*. Chicago.

Bond, George, Johnson, Walton and Walker, Sheila S. (eds.) *African Christianity: patterns of religious continuity*. New York and London, 1979.

Bonhomme, Joseph. *Noir or: le Basutoland, mission noire, mission d'or*. Montréal, 1934.

Bonjour, Marius. *Le désert refleurira: un cri d'espoir face à la secheresse et à la famine*. 1987.

Bonn, A. *Ein Jahrhundert Rheinische Mission*. Barmen, 1928.

Bontinck, François. *L'évangélisation du Zaïre*. Kinshasa, 1980.

Bontinck, François (ed.) *Diaire Congolais (1690–1701) de Fr Luca da Caltanisetta*. Louvain and Paris, 1970.

Bontinck, François with Nsasi, D. Ndembe (ed.) *Le catéchisme Kikongo de 1624: réédition critique*. Brussels, 1978.

Booth, Bernard F. *Mill Hill Fathers in West Cameroon: education, health, and development, 1884–1970*. Bethesda, Md., 1995.

Bottignole, Silvana. *Kikuyu traditional culture and Christianity: self examination of an African Church*. Nairobi, 1984.

Bouchaud, Joseph. *L'Église en Afrique noire*. Paris and Geneva, 1958.

Bouche, Denise. *L'enseignement dans les territoires français de l'Afrique occidentale de 1817 à 1920: mission civilsatrice ou formation d'une élite?* Paris, 1975.

Boucher, A. *Au Congo français, les missions catholiques*. Paris, 1969.

Boucher, R. *A travers les missions du Togo et du Dahomey*. Paris, 1926.

Boudou, Adrien. *Les Jésuites à Madagascar au XIXe siècle*. 2 vols. Paris, 1940.

Bouniol, Joseph. *The White Fathers and their missions*. London, 1929.

Bourdillon, M. F. C. (ed.) *Christianity south of the Zambezi: II*. Gwelo, 1977.

Bowie, Fiona, Kirkwood, Deborah and Ardener, Shirley (eds.) *Women and missions: past and present: anthropological and historical perceptions*. Providence and Oxford, 1993.

Boxer, C. R. *Race relations in the Portuguese colonial empire, 1415–1825*. Oxford, 1963.

The Portuguese seaborne empire 1415–1825. London, 1969.

Mary and misogyny: women in Iberian expansion overseas 1415–1815: some fact, fancies and personalities. London, 1975.

The Church militant and Iberian expansion 1440–1770. Baltimore, 1978.

Boxer, C. R. and Azevedo, C. de. *Fort Jesus and the Portuguese in Mombasa 1593–1729*. London, 1960.

Brady, J. E. *'Princes of His people': the story of our bishops 1800–1951*. Johannesburg, 1951.

Trekking for souls. Cedara, Natal, 1952.

Braekman, E. M. *Histoire du Protestantisme au Congo*. Brussels, 1961.

Brain, J. B. *Catholics in Natal, 1886–1925*. Durban, 1982.

Christian Indians in Natal 1860–1911. Cape Town, 1983.

Brandel-Syrier, Mia. *Black women in search of God*. London, 1962.

Brásio, António (ed.) *Dom António Barroso: missionário, cientista, missiologo*. Lisbon, 1961.
História e missiologia: inéditos e esparsos. Luanda, 1973.
Monumenta missionaria Africana. 20 vols, first and second series, Lisbon, 1952–88.
Briggs, D. N. and Wing, J. *The harvest and the hope: the story of Congregationalism in Southern Africa*. Johannesburg, 1970.
Brokensha, David. *Social change at Larteh, Ghana*. London, 1966.
Broomfield, Gerald W. *Towards freedom*. London, 1957.
Brown, C. F. *The conversion experience in Axum during the fourth and fifth centuries*. Washington, 1973.
Brown, Godfrey N. and Hiskett, Mervyn (eds.) *Conflict and harmony in education in tropical Africa*. London, 1975.
Brown, Leslie. *Three worlds: one word: account of a mission*. London, 1981.
Brown, Mervyn. *A history of Madagascar*. London, 1995.
Brown, Peter. *Augustine of Hippo: a biography*. London, 1967.
Brown, W. E. *The Catholic Church in South Africa: from its origins to the present day*. London, 1960.
Browne, George D. *Ten years episcopacy: a reflection*. Sandpoint, 1980.
The Episcopal Church of Liberia under indigenous leadership. 1994.
Bureau, R. *Ethno-sociologie religieuse des Duala et apparentés*. Yaoundé, 1962.
Burman, Sandra. *Chiefdom politics and alien law: Basutoland under Cape rule, 1871–1884*. New York, 1981.
Burr, Elsie. *Kalene memories: annals of the old hill*. London, 1956.
Burton, G. F. *The waiting isle: Madagascar and its Church*. London, 1953.
Burton, Wm. F. P. *When God makes a missionary: the life story of Edgar Mahon*. 1936. Rev. edn, Minneapolis, 1961.
Butler, Alfred J. *The ancient Coptic Churches of Egypt*. Reprint, Oxford, 1970.
Butler, J. (ed.) *Boston University papers in African history: I*. Boston, 1964.
Butselaar, Jan van. *Africains, missionnaires et colonialistes: les origines de l'Église Presbytérienne du Mozambique (Mission Suisse), 1880–1896*. Leiden, 1984.
Buxton, Thomas Foxwell. *The African slave trade and its remedy*. 1839. Reprinted, London, 1967.
Byabazire, D. M. *The contribution of the Christian Churches to the development of western Uganda 1894–1974*. Frankfurt, 1979.
Byaruhanga-Akiiki, A. B. T. *Religion in Swaziland*. 2 vols. Kwaluseni, 1975.
Cairns, H. Alan C. *Prelude to imperialism: British reactions to Central African society 1840–1890*. London, 1965.
Campbell, Mavis C. *Back to Africa: George Ross and the Maroons: from Nova Scotia to Sierra Leone*. Trenton, 1993.
Campbell, Robert F. *Within the green wall: the story of Holy Cross Liberian Mission, 1922–1957*. West Park, NY, 1957.
Canton, William H. *A history of the British and Foreign Bible Society*. 5 vols. London, 1904–10.
Caplan, Gerald L. *The elites of Barotseland 1878–1969: a political history of Zambia's western province*. Berkeley and Los Angeles, 1970.
Caraman, Philip. *The lost empire: the story of the Jesuits in Ethiopia, 1555–1634*. London, 1985.
Caravaglios Maria (ed.) *L'Africa al tempi de Daniele Comboni*. Rome, 1981.

Carmody, Brendan P. *Conversion and Jesuit schooling in Zambia*. Leiden, 1992.

Carpenter, George Wayland. *Highways for God in Congo: commemorating seventy-five years of Protestant missions 1878–1953*. Léopoldville, 1952.

Carpenter, Joel A. and Shenk, Wilbert R. (eds.) *Earthen vessels: American evangelicals and foreign missions, 1880–1980*. Grand Rapids, 1990.

Carter, B. L. *The Copts in Egyptian politics*. London, 1986.

Casaleggio, E. N. *Die land sal sy vrug gee: fyftig jaar van sendingwerk in die Soedan*. Cape Town, 1965.

Cawood, Lesley. *The Churches and race relations in South Africa*. Johannesburg, 1964.

Cell, John W. (ed.) *By Kenya possessed: the correspondence of Norman Leys and J. H. Oldham, 1918–1926*. Chicago and London, 1976.

Cerulli, Enrico. *Etiopia in Palestine*. 2 vols., Rome, 1943–47.

(ed.) *Scritti teologici etiopici dei secoli* XVI–XVII. 2 vols. Rome, 1958–60.

Chadwick, Henry (ed.) *Alexandrian Christianity*. 2nd edn, London, 1982.

Augustine. Oxford, 1986.

Chadwick, Henry. *Early Christian thought and the classical tradition: studies in Justin, Clement, and Origen*. Oxford, 1966.

Chadwick, Owen. *Mackenzie's grave*. London, 1959.

Chaille, Y. *Les grandes missions français en Afrique occidentale*. Dakar, 1953.

Chamberlin, David (ed.) *Some letters from Livingstone 1840–1872*. London, 1940.

Charbonneau, Herménégilde. *My name is Eugène de Mazenod: texts chosen from Bishop Charles Joseph Eugène de Mazenod*. (Trans. Francis D. Flanagan.) Boston, 1976. [On the Oblates of Mary Immaculate.]

Charlton, Leslie. *Spark in the stubble: Colin Morris of Zambia*. London, 1969.

Chateaubriand, François René de. *Génie de christianisme ou Beauté de la religion chrétienne*. 5 vols. Paris, 1802.

Chatelain, Alida. *Héli Chatelain: l'ami de l'Angola, 1859–1908*. Lausanne, 1918.

Chater, Patricia. *Caught in the crossfire*. Harare, 1985.

Chepkwony, Agnes. *The role of non-governmental organizations in development: a study of the National Christian Council of Kenya (NCCK) 1963–1978*. Uppsala, 1987.

Chidester, David. *Religions of South Africa*. London and New York, 1992.

Chilcote, Ronald H. (ed.) *Protest and resistance in Angola and Brazil: comparative studies*. Berkeley, 1972.

Chirenje, J. Mutero. *A history of northern Botswana 1850–1910*. Cranbury, NJ, 1977.

Chief Kgama and his times: the story of a Southern African ruler. London, 1978.

Chomé, Jules. *La passion de Simon Kimbangu 1921–1951*. Paris, 1959.

Chopard-Lallier, Robert. *Chrétiens du Nord Dahomey*. Lomé, 1963.

Christensen, Torben and Hutchison, William R. (eds.) *Missionary ideologies in the imperialist era: 1880–1920*. Aarhus, 1982.

Christian Council of Ghana. *The rise of Independent Churches in Ghana*. Accra, 1990.

Christian Council of the Gold Coast. *Christianity and African culture*. Accra, 1955.

Chukwuma, Michael. Nigerian politics and the role of religion: an analysis of the role of religion in Nigerian politics at the early stages of national integration. Ph.D. thesis, University of Bonn, 1985.

Church, Joe. *Jesus satisfies: an account of revival in East Africa*. 2nd edn. Achimota, 1973.

Quest for the highest: an autobiographical account of the East African revival. Exeter, 1981.

'Church-state relations in Burundi', *Pro Mundi Vita*, African dossier, 39. Brussels, 1986.

Clapham, J. W. *John Olley, pioneer missionary to the Chad*. Glasgow, 1966.

Clarence-Smith, W. G. *Slaves, peasants and capitalists in southern Angola 1840–1926*. Cambridge, 1979.

Clarke, Peter B. *West Africa and Christianity: a study of religious development from the 15th to the 20th century*. London, 1986.

Clavier, Henri. *Thomas Arbousset: pionnier*. Paris, 1963.

Thomas Arbousset: recherche historique sur son milieu, sa personnalité, son œuvre, parallèle avec Livingstone. Paris, 1965.

Clinton, Iris. *'These vessels . . . ': the story of Inyati, 1859–1959*. Bulawayo, 1959.

Hope Fountain story. Gwelo, 1969.

Codere, Helen. *The biography of an African society: Rwanda 1900–1960: based on forty-eight Rwandan autobiographies*. Tervuren, 1973.

Cohen, Abner. *Custom and politics in urban Africa: a study of Hausa migrants in Yoruba towns*. Berkeley and Los Angeles: University of California Press, 1969.

The politics of elite culture: explorations in the dramaturgy of power in a modern African society. Berkeley, Los Angeles and London, 1981.

Cohen, David William and Odhiambo, E. S. Atieno. *Burying SM: the politics of knowledge and the sociology of power in Africa*. London and Portsmouth, NH, 1992.

Coillard, François. *On the threshold of Central Africa: twenty years among the Barotsi*. (Trans. C. W. Mackintosh.) London, 1897.

Cole, E. Keith. *The cross over Mount Kenya: a short history of the Anglican Church in the Diocese of Mount Kenya (1900–1970)*. Nairobi, 1970.

A history of the Church Missionary Society of Australia. Melbourne, 1971.

Cole, Robert Wellesley. *Kossoh town boy*. Cambridge, 1960.

Colenso, Francis E. *Letters from Natal*. Arr. with comments by Wyn Rees. Pietermaritzburg, 1958.

Collett, Martin. *Accra*. London, 1928.

Collins, Robert O. *Shadows in the grass: Britain in the Southern Sudan, 1918–1956*. New Haven, 1983.

Comaroff, Jean and Comaroff, John. *Of revelation and revolution: Christianity, colonialism and consciousness in South Africa*. Vol. 1. Chicago and London, 1991.

Comaroff, Jean. *Body of power, spirit of resistance: the culture and history of a South African People*. Chicago and London, 1985.

Comhaire-Sylvain, Suzanne. *Femmes de Kinshasa: hier et aujourd'hui*. Paris, 1968.

Commauche, F. *Le Père Edouard Epinette*. Paris, 1919.

Conacher, J. R. H. *General survey concerning Christian literature in Ethiopia*. Addis Ababa, 1970.

Conus, Georges. *L'Eglise d'Afrique au Concile Vatican II*. Immensee, 1975.

Conwell, Roy E. *Samwill of Sudan*. Brisbane, 1985.

Cook, Albert R. *Uganda memories (1897–1940)*. Kampala, 1945.

Cooke, Coleman. *Mary Charles Walker: the nun of Calabar*. Dublin, 1980.

Cooksey, J. J. *The land of the vanished Church*. London, 1926.

Cooksey, J. J. and McLeish, Alexander. *Religion and civilization in West Africa: a missionary survey of French, British, Spanish and Portuguese West Africa, with Liberia*. London, 1931.

Cooley, J. K. *Baal, Christ and Mohammed: religion and revolution in North Africa*. New York, 1965.

Cornet, Réne-Jules. *Medecine et explorations: premiers contacts de quelques explorateurs de l'Afrique centrale avec les maladies tropicales*. Brussels, 1970.

Cornevin, Robert. *Histoire du Dahomey*. Paris, 1962.

Histoire du Togo. 3rd edn, Paris, 1969.

Cotterell, F. Peter. *Born at midnight*. Chicago, 1973.

Coulbeaux, Jean-Baptiste. *Histoire politique et religieuse d'Abyssinie: depuis les temps les plus reculés jusqu'à l'avènement de Ménélick II*. 3 vols. Paris, 1929.

Coulon, Paul and Brasseur, Paule (eds.). *Libermann 1802–1852: une pensée et une mystique missionnaires*, Paris, 1988.

Coupland, Reginald. *Livingstone's last journey*. London, 1945.

Cowley, Roger W. *The traditional interpretation of the Apocalypse of St John in the Ethiopian Orthodox Church*. Cambridge, 1983.

Cox, E. D. *The Church of the United Brethren in Christ in Sierra Leone*. South Pasadena, 1970.

Cox, Peter. *The Amudat story*. London, 1967.

Cramer, Maria. *Das Altägyptische Lebenszeichen im christlichen (koptischen) Ägypten: Eine kultur- und religionsgeschictliche Studie auf Archäologischer Grundlage*. Wiesbaden, 1955.

Das Christlich-Koptische Ägypten Einst und Heute: Eine Orientierung. Wiesbaden, 1959.

Crampton, E. P. T. *Christianity in Northern Nigeria*. 3rd edn, London, 1975.

Crawford, Daniel. *Thinking Black: 22 years without a break in the long grass of Central Africa*. London, 1912.

Crawford, J. R. *Protestant missions in Congo, 1878–1969*. Kinshasa, 1970.

Cromwell, Adelaide M. *An African Victorian feminist: the life and times of Adelaide Smith Casely Hayford, 1868–1960*. London, 1986.

Crowther, Samuel and Taylor, John C. *The Gospel on the banks of the Niger: journals and notices of the native missionaries accompanying the Niger expedition of 1857–59*. Reprinted, London, 1968.

Crummey, Donald. *Priests and politicians: Protestant and Catholic missions in Orthodox Ethiopia 1830–1868*. Oxford, 1972.

Cunha, J. M. da Silva. *Aspectos dos movimentos associativos na Africa Negra*. 2 vols, Lisbon, 1958–9.

Cuoq, Joseph. *L'Islam en Ethiopie des origines au XVIe siècle*. Paris, 1981.

L'Église d'Afrique du Nord: du deuxième au douzième siècle. Paris, 1984.

Islamisation de la Nubie Chrétienne, VIIe–XVIe siècle. Paris, 1986.

Cushman, Mary Floyd. *Missionary doctor: the story of twenty years in Africa*. New York and London, 1944.

Cussac, J. *L'Apôtre de l'Ouganda, le Père Lourdel*. Paris, 1944.

Évêque et pionnier Monseigneur Streicher. Paris, 1955.

Cuvelier, J. (ed.) *Relations sur le Congo du Père Laurent de Lucques 1700–1717*. Brussels, 1953.

Da Costa, M. G. (ed.) *The Itinerário of Jerónimo Lobo*. (Trans. Donald M. Lockhart.) Annot. C. F. Beckingham. Hakluyt Society, second series, 162. London, 1984.

Dachs, A. J. (ed.) *Christianity south of the Zambezi: volume 1*. Gwelo, 1973.

Dachs, A. J. and Rea, W. F. *The Catholic Church and Zimbabwe 1879–1979*. Gwelo, 1979.

Dadié, Bernard. *Beatrice du Congo*. Paris, 1970.

Dah, Jonas N. *Missionary motivations and methods: a critical examination of the Basel Mission in Cameroon 1886–1914*. Basel, 1983.

(ed.) *Kangsen as they saw him*. Buea, [1989].

Presbyterian Church in Cameroon: history of the Theological College, Kumba (1952–1992). [1992].

Dalmalm, Åsa. *L'église á l'éprevue de la tradition: la Communauté Evangélique de Zaïre et le Kindoki*. Paris and Uppsala, 1986.

Daly, M. W. *Empire on the Nile: the Anglo-Egyptian Sudan, 1898–1934*. Cambridge, 1986.

Imperial Sudan: the Anglo-Egyptian Condominium, 1934–1956. Cambridge, 1991.

Damane, Mosebi. *Peace, the mother of nations: the 'saga' of the origin of the Protestant Church in Basutoland*. Morija, 1947.

Daneel, M. L. *The God of the Matopo Hills: an essay on the Mawri cult in Rhodesia*. The Hague and Paris, 1970.

Zionism and faith-healing in Rhodesia: aspects of African Independent Churches. (Trans, V. A. February.) The Hague and Paris, 1970.

Old and new in southern Shona Independent Churches, I: background and rise of the major movements. The Hague and Paris, 1971.

Old and new in southern Shona Independent Churches, II: Church growth – causative factors and recruitment techniques. The Hague and Paris, 1974.

Old and new in southern Shona Independent Churches, III: leadership and fission dynamics. Gweru, 1988.

Fambidzano: ecumenical movement of Zimbabwean independent Churches. Gweru, 1989.

Daniélou, Jean. *Les symbols chrétiens primitifs*. Paris, 1961.

Danielson, Elmer R. *Forty years with Christ in Tanzania 1928–1968*. New York, 1977.

Danquah, J. B. *The Akan doctrine of God: a fragment of ethics and religion*. London, 1944.

Davidson, Basil. *Old Africa rediscovered*. London, 1959.

Davies, Horton. *Great South African Christians*. Cape Town, 1951.

Davis, J. Merle. *Modern Industry and the Africa: an enquiry into the effect of the copper mines to Central Africa upon native society and the work of the Christian missions*. 2nd edn, London, 1967.

Davis, Raymond J. *Fire on the mountains: the story of a miracle – the Church in Ethiopia*. 1966. Reprinted, Scarborough, Ont, 1980.

The winds of God. Scarborough, Ont, 1984.

De Craemer, Willy. *The Jamaa and the Church: a Bantu Catholic movement in Zaïre*. Oxford, 1977.

De Grunchy, John W. *Theology and ministry in context and crisis: a South African perspective*. London, 1987.

Debenham, F. *The way to Ilala: David Livingstone's pilgrimage*. London, 1955.

Debrunner, Hans W. *Witchcraft in Ghana: a study on the belief in destructive witches and its effect on the Akan tribes*. Kumasi, 1959.

Owura Nico: the Rev. Nicholas Timothy Clerk, 1862–1961. Accra, 1965.

The story of Sampson Opong, the prophet. Accra, 1965.

A Church between colonial powers: a study of the Church in Togo. London, 1965.

A history of Christianity in Ghana. Accra, 1967.

Presence and prestige: Africans in Europe: a history of Africans in Europe before 1918. Basel, 1979.

Déjeux, Jean and Sanson, Henri. 'Algeria 1980: a Church in the midst of Islam', *Pro Mundi Vita*, Africa dossier, 13. Brussels, 1980.

Delacroix, S. *Histoire universelle des missions catholiques*. 4 vols. Paris, 1956–59.

Delavignette, Robert. *Christianisme et colonialisme*. Paris, 1960.

Delcourt, Jean. *Histoire religieuse du Sénégal*. Dakar, 1976.

Delval, Raymond. *Radama II: prince de la renaissance malgache 1861–1863*. Paris, 1972.

Dempsey, J. *Mission on the Nile*. London, 1955.

Deniel, Raymond. *Croyances religieuses et vie quotidienne: Islam et Christianisme à Ouagadougou*. Paris and Ouagadougou, 1970.

Religions dans la ville: croyances et changements sociaux à Abidjan. Abidjan, 1975.

Croyants dans le ville. Abidjan, 1982.

Denis, Leopold. *Les Jésuites belges au Kwango 1893–1943* (Brussels, 1943).

Deschamps, Hubert. *Histoire de Madagascar*. Paris, 1960.

Describes, Abbé. *L'Evangile au Dahomey – Missions de Lyon*. Lyon, n.d.

Dickson, Mora. *Beloved partner: Mary Moffat of Kuruman*. London, 1974. Reprinted Gaborone and Kuruman, 1989.

Dierks, Friedrich. *Evangelium im afrikanischen Kontext: Interkulturelle Kommunikation bei den Tswana*. Gütersloh, 1986.

Dieterlen, H. *Eugène casalis (1812–1891)*. Paris, 1930.

Adolphe Mabille (1836–1894). 2nd edn, Paris, 1933.

Dike, K. Onwuka. *Trade and politics in the Niger Delta 1830–1885: an introduction to the economic and political history of Nigeria*. Oxford, 1956.

Origins of the Niger Mission, 1841–1891. Ibadan, 1962.

Dillon-Malone, C. M. *The Korsten basketmakers: a study of the Masowe apostles, an indigenous African religious movement*. Manchester, 1978.

Dollen, Charles. *African triumph: life of Charles Lwanga*. Boston, 1967.

Doornbos, Martin R. *Not all the king's men: inequality as a political instrument in Ankole, Uganda*. The Hague, 1978.

Doresse, Jean. *Les livres secrets des Gnostiques d'Égypye: l'Évangile Selon Thomas ou les paroles secrètes de Jésus*. Paris, 1959.

Doti-Sanou, Bruno. *L'émancipation des femmes Madare: l'impact du projet administratif et missionnaire sur une société africaine, 1900–1960*. Leiden, New York and Cologne, 1994.

Dove, Reginald. *Anglican pioneers in Lesotho: some account of the Diocese of Lesotho, 1876–1930*. Mazenod, 1975.

Drake, St Clair. *The redemption of Africa and Black religion*. Chicago, 1970.

Drathschmidt, Ursula. *Portugiesischer Kulturimperialismus in Angola: ein halbes Jahrtausend 'christian Imperiums'*. Saarbrucken, 1982.

Driessler, H. *Die rheinische Mission in Südwestafrika*. Gutersloh, 1932.

Du Plessis, J. *A history of Christian missions in South Africa*. London, 1911.

Dubb, A. A. *Community of the saved: an African revivalist Church in the Eastern Cape*. Johannesburg, 1976.

Ducroz, Jean Marie. *Les actes des premières Chretiéns de Garoul*. Paris, 1976.

Dunn, D. Elwood. *A history of the Episcopal Church in Liberia, 1821–1980*. London and Metuchen, 1992.

Duval, Léon-Étienne with Ray, Marie-Christine. *Le cardinal Duval Evêque en Algérie: entretiens du cardinal Léon-Étienne Duval archevêque d'Alger avec Marie-Christine Ray*. Paris, 1984.

Eades, Jeremy Seymour. *Strangers and traders: Yoruba migrants, markets and the state in northern Ghana*. Edinburgh, 1993.

Eggert, Johanna. *Missionsschule und sozialer Wandel in Ostafrika: der Beitrag der deutschen evangelischen Missionsgesellschaften zur Entwicklung des Schulwesens in Tanganyika 1891–1939*. Bielefeld, 1970.

Eide, Øyvind M. *Revolution and religion in Ethiopia: a study of Church and politics with special reference to the Ethiopian Evangelical Church Mekane Yesus, 1974–1985*. Stavanger and Uppsala, 1996.

Eirola, Martti *et al. The cultural and social change in Ovamboland 1870–1915*. Joensuu, 1983.

Ekechi, F. K. *Missionary enterprise and rivalry in Igboland, 1857–1914*. London, 1971.

Tradition and transformation in eastern Nigeria: a sociological history of Owerri and its hinterland, 1902–1947. Kent, Ohio and London, 1989.

Eldredge, Elizabeth A. *A South African kingdom: the pursuit of security in nineteenth-century Lesotho*. Cambridge, 1993.

Elizabeth de la Trinité, Sœur. *Femme missionnaire en Afrique*. Paris, 1984.

Ellenberger, Victor F. *Landmarks in the story of the French Protestant Church in Basutoland during the first hundred years of its existence, 1833–1933*. Morija, 1933.

A century of mission work in Basutoland (1833–1933). Trans. Edmond M. Ellenberger. Morija, 1938.

Ellis, J. J. *Alexander Mackay: the Christian hero of Uganda*. London, n.d.

Frederick Stanley Arnot: missionary, explorer, benefactor. London, [1924].

Ellis, Kail C. (ed.) *The Vatican, Islam and the Middle East*. Syracuse, 1987.

Ellis, Stephen. *The rising of the red shawls: a revolt in Madagascar, 1895–1899*. Cambridge, 1985.

Elphick, Richard. *Kraal and castle: Khoikhoi and the founding of White South Africa*. New Haven and London, 1977.

Elphick, Richard and Giliomee, Hermann (eds.) *The shaping of South African society, 1652–1820*. Cape Town and London, 1979.

Emmanuel, Ghislain. *Diocese of Port-Louis, 1810–1973*. Port Louis, 1975.

Engel, Lothar. *Die Stellung der Rheinischen Missionsgesellschaft zu den politischen und gesellschaftlichen Verhältnissen Südwestafrikas und ihr Beitrag zur dortigen kirchlichen Entwicklung bis zum Nama-Herero-Aufstand 1904–1907*. Hamburg, 1972.

Kolonialismus und Nationalismus im deutschen Protestantismus in Namibia 1907 bis 1945. Berne, 1976.

Enklaar, Ido H. *Life and work of Dr J. Th. Van der Kemp 1747–1811: missionary pioneer and protagonist of racial equality in South Africa*. Cape Town and Rotterdam, 1988.

Ephraim, Isaac. *The Ethiopian Church*. Boston, 1968.

Erivwo, Samuel. *A history of Christianity in Nigeria: the Urhobo, the Isoko and the Itsekiri*. Ibadan, 1979.

Escande, E. *La Bible à Madagascar*. Paris, 1923.

Etherington, Norman. *Preachers peasants and politics in southeast Africa, 1835–1880: African Christian communities in Natal, Pondoland and Zululand*. London, 1978.

Ethiopian Orthodox Church. *The Church of Ethiopia: an introduction to the contemporary Church*. Addis Ababa, 1973.

Fabian, Johannes. *Jamaa: a charismatic movement in Katanga*. Northwestern University Press, 1971.

Language and colonial power: the appropriation of Swahili in the former Belgian Congo, 1880–1938. Cambridge, 1986.

Facélina, Raymond. *Théologie en situation: une communauté chrétienne dans le Tiers Monde (Algérie 1962–1974)*. Strasbourg, 1974.

Fafunwa, Aliu Babs. *History of education in Nigeria*. London, 1974.

Fage, J. D. (ed.) *Cambridge history of Africa: volume 2, from ca. 500 BC to AD 1050*. Cambridge, 1979.

Falk, Peter. *The growth of the Church in Africa*. Grand Rapids, 1979.

Familusi, M. M. *Methodism in Nigeria (1842–1992)*. Ibadan, 1992.

Fardon, Richard. *Between God, the dead and the wild: Chamba interpretations of religion and ritual*. Edinburgh, 1990.

Fargher, Brian L. *The origins of the new Churches' movement in southern Ethiopia, 1927–1944*. Leiden, 1996.

Farrant, Henry G. *Crescendo of the cross: answers the questions of the year 1904 – will the cross or the crescent prevail in the Sudan*. London, n.d.

Farrant, J. *Mashonaland martyr Bernard Mizeki and the pioneer Church*. Cape Town, 1966.

Fashole-Luke, Edward *et al.* (eds.) *Christianity in Independent Africa*. London, 1978.

Faupel, J. F. *African holocaust: the story of the Uganda martyrs*. London, 1962.

Fauré, Jean. *Togo, champ de missions*. Paris, 1948.

Histoire des missions et églises Protestantes en Afrique occidentale des origines à 1884. Yaoundé, 1978.

Feci, D. *Vie cachée et vie publique de Simon Kimbangu selon la littérature coloniale et missionnaire belge*. Brussels, 1972.

Ferguson, John. *Some Nigerian Church founders*. Ibadan, 1971.

Fernández, C. *Misiones y miseioneros en la Guinea Española*. Madrid, 1962.

Fernandez, James W. *Bwiti: an ethnography of the religious imagination*. Princeton, 1982.

Fiedler, Klaus. *The story of faith missions*. Oxford, 1994.

Christianity and African culture: conservative German Protestant missionaries in Tanzania, 1900–1940. Leiden, 1996.

Field, M. J. *Search for security: an ethno-psychiatric study of rural Ghana*. Evanston, 1960.

Fields, Karen E. *Revival and rebellion in colonial Central Africa*. Princeton, 1985.

Filesi, Teobaldo and Villapadierna, Isidoro de. *La 'Missio Antiqua' dei Cappuccini nel Congo (1645–1835): studio preliminare e guida delle fonti*. Rome, 1978.

Filesi, Teobaldo. *Nazionalismo e religione nel Congo all'inizio del 1700: la setta degli Antoniani*. Rome, 1972.

Findlay, George G. and Holdsworth, William W. *The history of the Wesleyan Methodist Missionary Society*. Volume 4. London, 1922.

Fischer, Friedrich Hermann. *Der Missionsarzt Rudolf Fisch und die Anfänge Medizinischer Arbeit der Basler Mission an der Gold Küste (Ghana)*. Herzogenrath, 1991.

Fisher, W. Singleton and Hoyte, Julyan. *Africa looks ahead: the life stories of Walter and Anna Fisher of Central Africa*. London, 1948.

Fitts, Leroy. *Lott Carey: first Black missionary to Africa*. Valley Forge, 1978.

Fitzsimmons, J. *Father Jacques Désiré Laval: the 'saint' of Mauritius*. Bootle, 1973.

Fleisch, Paul. *Hundert Jahre Lutherischer Mission*. Leipzig, 1936. [Leipzig Mission.]

Florin, Hans W. *Lutherans in South Africa*. 2nd edn. Durban, 1967.

Foray, C. P. *Sacred Heart Cathedral, Freetown: centenary 1887–1987: a brief history of the Cathedral and the Catholic Church in Sierra Leone*. Freetown, [1987].

Forristal, Desmond. *The second burial of Bishop Shanahan*. Dublin, 1990.

Forsberg, Malcolm. *Last days on the Nile*. Philadelphia, 1966.

Land beyond the Nile. Chicago, 1967.

Forslund, Eskil. *The word of God in Ethiopian tongues: rhetorical features in the preaching of the Ethiopian Evangelical Church Mekane Yesus*. Uppsala, 1993.

Forster, Peter G. *T. Cullen Young: missionary and anthropologist*. Hull, 1989.

Foskett, R. (ed.) *The Zambesi doctors: David Livingstone's letters to John Kirk 1858–1872*. Edinburgh, 1964.

Fosseus, Helge. *Mission blir kyrka: Lutherska kyrkobildning I södra Afrika 1957–1961*. Stockholm, 1974.

Foster, Philip. *Education and social change in Ghana*. London, 1965.

Foster, Raymond Samuel. *The Sierra Leone Church: an independent Anglican Church*. London, 1961.

Foster, W. D. *The early history of scientific medicine in Uganda*. Nairobi, Dar es Salaam and Kampala, 1970.

Fouquer, R. P. *Le docteur Adrien Atiman*. Paris, 1964.

Fraenkel, Merran. *Tribe and class in Monrovia*. London, 1964.

Frank, Cedric N. *The life of Bishop Steere: a Christian interpreter in East Africa*. Dar es Salaam, 1953.

Fraser, Agnes R. *Donald Fraser of Livingstonia*. London, 1934.

Fraser, Eileen. *The doctor comes to Lui*. London, 1938.

Freeman, Thomas Birch. *Journal of various visits to the kingdoms of Ashanti, Aku, and Dahomi in western Africa*. 1844. Reprinted, London, 1968.

Freeman-Grenville, G. S. P. *The East African coast: select documents from the first to the earlier nineteenth century*. Oxford, 1962.

The French at Kilwa island: an episode in eighteenth-century East African history. Oxford, 1965.

(ed.) *The Mombasa rising against the Portuguese, 1631: from sworn evidence*. London and Oxford, 1980.

The Swahili coast, 2nd to 19th centuries: Islam, Christianity and commerce in eastern Africa. London, 1988.

Frend, W. H. C. *Martyrdom and persecution in the early Church: a study of a conflict from the Maccabees to Donatus*. Oxford, 1965.

The rise of the Monophysite movement: chapters in the history of the Church in the fifth and sixth centuries. Cambridge, 1972.

The rise of Christianity. London and Philadelphia, 1984.

The Donatist Church: a movement of protest in Roman North Africa. Oxford, 1952. Reprinted, 1971.

Saints and sinners in the early Church: differing and conflicting traditions in the first six centuries. London, 1985.

Frost, Pamela Jean. *A bibliography of missions and missionaries in Natal*. Cape Town, 1969.

Fuglestad, Finn and Simensen, Jarle (ed.) *Norwegian missions in African history*. 2 vols., Oslo, 1986.

Furley, O. W. and Watson, T. *A history of education in East Africa*. New York, 1978.

Fusero, Clement. *Daniele Comboni*. Bologna, 1967.

Fwa, Luntadila Ndala Za. *Un rayon d'espoir: évangélisation dans les eglises africaines indépendantes*. Kinshasa, 1975.

Fyfe, Christopher. *A history of Sierra Leone*. London, 1962.

Sierra Leone inheritance. London, 1964.

Africanus Horton 1835–1883: West African scientist and patriot. New York, 1972.

Fyfe, Christopher (ed.) *'Our Children free and happy': letters from Black settlers in Africa in the 1790s.* Edinburgh, 1991.

Fyfe, Christopher and Jones, Eldred (eds.) *Freetown: a symposium.* Freetown and London, 1968.

Fyle, C. Magbaily. *The history of Sierra Leone.* London and Ibadan, 1981.

Gabre-Sellassie, Zewde. *Yohannes IV of Ethiopia: a political biography.* London, 1975.

Gabriel, Manuel Nunes. *Angola: Cinco séculos de Christianismo.* Queluz, 1978.

Padrões da Fé: Igrejas Antigas de Angola. Luanda, 1981.

Gahama, Joseph. *Le Burundi sous administration belge: la période du mandat 1919–1939.* Paris, 1983.

Gailey, Harry A. *A history of the Gambia.* London, 1964.

Gakobo, J. K. (comp.) *History of Christianity in Kenya 1844–1977: a select bibliography.* Nairobi, 1979.

Galbraith, John S. *Reluctant empire: British policy on the South African frontier 1834–1854.* Berkeley and Los Angeles, 1963.

Mackinnon and East Africa 1878–1895: a study in the 'new imperialism'. Cambridge, 1972.

Gale, H. P. *Uganda and the Mill Hill Fathers.* London, 1959.

Gale, W. Kendall. *Church planting in Madagascar.* London, 1937.

Gann, L. H. *The birth of a plural society: the development of Northern Rhodesia under the British South Africa Company 1894–1914.* Manchester, 1958.

Garcia, A. *Historia de Moçambique cristão.* Lourenço Marques, 1969.

Garfield, Robert. *A history of São Tomé island 1470–1655: the key to Guinea.* San Francisco, 1992.

Garvey, Brian. *Bembaland Church: religious and social change in south central Afica, 1891–1964.* Leiden, 1994.

Gatwa, Thracisse and Karamaga, André. *La présence protestante: les autres Chrétiens rwandais.* Kigali, 1990.

Gbagbo, Laurent. *Côte d'Ivoire: economie et société à la veille de l'indépendance, 1944–1960.* Paris, 1982.

Gebremedhin, Ezra. *Life-giving blessing: an inquiry into the Eucharistic doctrine of Cyril of Alexandria.* Uppsala, 1977.

Gehman, Richard J. *African traditional religion in biblical perspective.* 2nd edn, Nairobi, 1993.

Gelfand, Michael. *Livingstone the doctor: his life and travels: a study in medical history.* Oxford, 1957.

(ed.) *Gubulawayo and beyond: letters and journals of the early Jesuit missionaries to Zambesia (1879–1887).* London, 1968.

Gelsthorpe, A. M. *Introducing the Diocese of the Sudan.* London, 1946.

Gerard, Joseph. *Le Père Joseph nous parle.* Rome, 1969.

Gerdener, Gustav B. A. *Recent developments in the South African mission field.* London and Edinburgh, 1958.

Studies in the evangelization of South Africa. London, 1911.

Germond, Robert C. (ed. and trans.) *Chronicles of Basutoland: a running commentary on the events of the years 1830–1902 by the French Protestant missionaries in Southern Africa.* Morija, 1967.

Gerstner, Jonathan Neil. *The thousand generation covenant: Dutch Reformed covenant theology and group identity in colonial South Africa, 1652–1814*. Leiden, 1991.

Gifford, Paul. *Christianity and politics in Doe's Liberia*. Cambridge, 1993.

The Christian Churches and the democratisation of Africa Leiden, New York and Cologne, 1995.

Gilliland, Dean S. *African religion meets Islam: religious change in Northern Nigeria*. Lanham, New York and London, 1986.

Gillis, Charles-André. *Kimbangu, fondateur d'église*. Brussels, 1960.

Kasa Vuba au coeur du drama Congolais. Brussels, 1964.

Gingyera-Pinycwa, A. G. *Issues in pre-independence politics in Uganda: a case-study on the contribution of religion to political debate in Uganda in the decade 1952–62*. Kampala, 1976.

Girard, Jean. *Déima, I: prophétes paysans de l'environnement noir; II: les évangils selon le prophétesse Bagué Honoyo*. Grenoble, 1973–4.

Gobat, Samuel. *Journal of a three years' residence in Abyssinia, in furtherance of the objects of the Church Missionary Society*. 1834. Reprinted, Westpoint, 1969.

Goldthorpe, J. E. *Outlines of East African society*. Kampala, 1958.

Gonçalves, *Protestantismo em Africa: contribuição para o estudo do protestantismò na Africa Portuguesa*. 2 vols., Lisbon, 1960.

Goodall, Norman. *A history of the London Missionary Society 1895–1945*. London, 1954.

Gordon, Robert J. *The Bushmen myth: the making of a Namibian underclass*. Boulder, San Francisco and Oxford, 1992.

Gorju, Joseph. *La Côte d'Ivoire chrétienne*. Lyon, 1915.

Gottneid, Allan J. *Church and education in Tanzania*. Nairobi, 1976.

Gouellain, René. *Douala: ville et histoire*. Paris, 1975.

Gow, Bonar A. *Madagascar and the Protestant impact: the work of the British missions, 1818–95*. London, 1979.

Goyau, Georges. *Monseigneur Augouard*. Paris, 1926.

Graham, C. K. *The history of education in Ghana: from the earliest times to the declaration of independence*. London, 1971.

Graham, R. H. Carson. *Under seven Congo kings: for thirty-seven years a missionary in Portuguese Congo*. London, 1931.

Graham, Sonia F. *Government and mission education in Northern Nigeria 1900–1919: with special reference to the work of Hanns Vischer*. Ibadan, 1966.

Grandjean, A. *La race Thonga et la Suisse Romande: histoire abrégée de la Mission Suisse Romande*. Lausanne, 1921.

Grau, Eugene Emil. 'The Evangelical Presbyterian Church (Ghana and Togo) 1914–1946: a study in European mission relations affecting the beginnings of an indigenous Church', Ph.D. thesis, Hartford Seminary Foundation, 1964. Ann Arbor: University Microfilms International, 1964.

Gravrand, H. *Visage africain de l'église: une éxperience au Sénégal*. Paris, 1961.

Gray, J. Richard. *A history of the Southern Sudan, 1839–1889*. London, 1961.

Gray, John M. *A history of the Gambia*. 1940. Reprinted, London, 1966.

Gray, John. *Early Portuguese missionaries in East Africa*. Nairobi, 1958.

Gray, Richard. *Black Christians and White missionaries*. New Haven, 1990.

Gray, S. D. *Frontiers of the kingdom in Rhodesia: the story of Methodist missions in Rhodesia*. London, 1930.

Greaves, Leonard B. *Carey Francis of Kenya*. London, 1969.

Green, S. J. *Christian missions and their schools in Eastern Nigeria*. London, 1962.

Greenland, Jeremy. *Western education in Burundi 1916–1973: the consequences of instrumentalism*. Brussels, 1980.

Greenwood, John Ormerod. *Quaker encounters, volume 3: whispers of truth*. York, 1978.

Grenstedt, Steffan *Ambaricho: a remarkable venture in Ethiopian Christian solidarity*. Uppsala, 1995.

Griffith, Cyril E. *The African dream: Martin R. Delany and the emergence of pan-African thought*. Pennsylvania, and London, 1975.

Grimley, John B. and Robinson, Gordon E. *Church growth in Central and Southern Nigeria*. Grand Rapids, 1966.

Grob, Francis. *Témoins camerounaise de l'Evangile: les origines de l'Eglise Evangelique*. Yaoundé, 1967.

Grohs, Gerhard. *State and the Church in Angola, 1450–1980*. Geneva, 1983.

Groves, Charles P. *The planting of Christianity in Africa*. 4 vols. London, 1948–58.

Gründler, Horst. *Christliche Mission und deutscher Imperialismus: Eine politische Geschichte ihrer Beziehungen während der deutschen Kolonialzeit (1884–1914) unter besonderer Berücksichtigung Afrikas und Chinas*. Paderborn, 1982.

Gründer, Horst, Jenkins, Paul, and Njikam, Mary J. *Mission und Kolonialismus: Die Basler Mission und die Landfrage in Deutsch-Kamerun*. Basel, 1986.

Guillebaud, Lindesay. *A grain of mustard seed: the growth of the Ruanda Mission of CMS*. London, 1959.

Guinness, Fanny E. *The new world of Central Africa: with a history of the first Christian mission on the Congo*. London, 1890.

Gutmann, Bruno. *Das Recht der Dschagga*. Munich, 1926.

Gutsche, Thelma. *The bishop's lady*. Cape Town, 1970.

Guy, Jeff. *The heretic: a study of the life of John William Colenso, 1814–1883*. Pietermaritzburg and Johannesburg, 1983.

Haas, Waltraud and Jenkins, Paul. *Guide to the Basel Mission's Ghana archive*. Basel, 1979.

Haccius, Georg. *Hannoversche Missionsgeschichte*. 4 vols. Hermannsburg, 1905–1920.

Hackett, Rosalind I. *Religion in Calabar: the religious life and history of a Nigerian town*. Berlin and New York, 1989.

(ed.) *New religious movements in Nigeria*. Lewiston, Lampeter and Queenston, 1987.

Hägg, Tomas (ed.) *Nubian culture: past and present*. Sixth International Conference for Nubian Studies. Stockholm, 1987.

Hair, P. E. H. *The early study of Nigerian languages: essays and bibliographies*. Cambridge, 1967.

Hair, P. E. H. (Trans.) *Jesuit documents on the Guinea of Cape Verde and the Cape Verde islands 1585–1617*. Liverpool, 1989.

Haliburton, Gordon M. *The Prophet Harris: a study of an African prophet and his mass-movement in the Ivory Coast and the Gold Coast 1913–1915*. London, 1971.

Hall, L. B. *A brief history of the Lesotho training college*. Morija, 1969.

Halldén, Erik. *The culture policy of the Basel Mission in the Cameroons 1886–1905*. Uppsala, 1968.

Hallencreutz, Carl F. (ed.) *Missions from the north: Nordic Missionary Council fifty years*. Oslo, 1974.

(ed.) *On theological relevance: critical interactions with Canaan Sodindo Banana*. Uppsala, Gweru and Harare, 1992.

Hallencreutz, Carl F. and Moyo, Ambrose M. (eds.) *Church and state in Zimbabwe*. Gweru and Harare, 1988.

Hamelberg, E. (ed.) *Centenary souvenir of Holy Ghost Fathers in Sierra Leone, 1864–1964*. Freetown, 1965.

Hamilton, Jean. *The lonely lake: the Chad story*. 2nd edn, Sidcup, 1973.

Hammerschmidt, Ernst. *Äthiopien: Christliches Reich zwischen Gestern und Morgen*. Wiesbaden, 1967.

Hanna, A. J. *The beginnings of Nyasaland and north-eastern Rhodesia, 1859–95*. Oxford, 1956.

Hansen, Holger Bernt. *Mission, Church and State in a colonial setting: Uganda 1890–1925*. London, 1984.

Hansson, Gurli. *The rise of Vashandiri: the Ruwadzano movement in the Lutheran Church in Zimbabwe*. Uppsala, 1991.

Hardy, E. R. *Christian Egypt: Church and people*. New York, 1952.

Hardy, Georges. *Un apôtre d'aujourdhui: le Révérand Père Aupiais, Provincial des Missions Africaines de Lyon*. Paris, 1949.

Hardyman, J. T. *Madagascar on the move*. London, 1950.

Harford-Battersby, *Charles F. Pilkington of Uganda*. London, 1898.

Hargreaves, John D. *A life of Sir Samuel Lewis*. London, 1958.

Aberdeenshire to Africa: northeast Scots and British overseas expansion. Aberdeen, 1981.

Harlow, Vincent, Chilver, E. M. and Smith, Alison (eds.) *History of East Africa*, II. Oxford, 1965.

Harris, Joseph E. *The African presence in Asia: consequences of the East African slave trade*. Evanston, 1971.

Harris, W. T. and Sawyerr, Harry. *The springs of Mende belief and conduct*. Freetown, 1968.

Harrison, Christopher. *France and Islam in West Africa, 1860–1960*. Cambridge, 1988.

Hasselblatt, Gunnar. *Äthiopien: Menschen, Kirchen, Kulturen*. Stuttgart, 1979.

Nächstes Jahr im Oromoland: von der eklatanten Verletzung der Menschenrechte durch den abessinisch-amharischen Rassismus in Äthiopien. Stuttgart, 1982.

Hasselhorn, F. *Bauernmission in Südafrika: Die Hermansburger Mission in Spannungsfeld der Kolonialpolitik, 1890–1939*. Erlangen, 1988.

Hastings, Adrian. *Mission and ministry*. London and Sydney, 1971.

Wiriyamu: massacre in Mozambique. London, 1974.

African Christianity. London, 1976.

A history of African Christianity 1950–1975. Cambridge, 1979.

The Church in Africa 1450–1950. Oxford, 1994.

Hazlett, Ian (ed.) *Early Christianity: origins and evolution to AD 600. In honour of W. H. C. Frend*. London, 1991.

Hazoumé, Paul. *Cinquante ans d'apostolat*. Lyon, 1937.

Healey, Joseph G. *A fifth gospel: in search of Black Christian values*. London and New York, 1981.

Hebga, Meinrad P. *L'Eglise Catholique au Cameroun et les missions des prêtres du Sacré-Coeur de Saint Quentin*. Issy-les-Moulineaux, 1960.

Helgesson, Alf. *Church, state and people in Mozambique: an historical study with special emphasis on Methodist developments in the Inhambane region*. Uppsala, 1994.

Hellberg, Carl-Johan. *Missions on a colonial frontier west of Lake Victoria: Evangelical missions in north-west Tanganyika to 1932*. (Trans. Eric J. Sharpe.) Uppsala and Lund, 1965.

A voice of the voiceless: the involvement of the Lutheran World Federation in Southern Africa 1947–1977. Uppsala, 1979.

Henderson, Ian (ed.) *Man of Christian action: Canon John Collins – the man and his work*. Guildford and London, 1976.

Henderson, James. *Forerunners of modern Malawi*. Lovedale, 1968.

Henderson, Lawrence W. *A Igreja em Angola*. Lisbon, 1990.

Henkel, Reinhard. *Christian missions in Africa: a social geographical study of the impact of their activities in Zambia*. Berlin, 1989.

Henricson, Carl-Gustav. *The role of the hospital chaplain at Kilimanjaro Christian Medical Centre*. Åbo, 1985

Heremans, Roger. *Les établissements de l'Association Internationale Africaine au Lac Tanganyika et les Pères Blancs: Mpala et Karéma, 1877–1885*. Tervuren, 1966.

L'Éducation dans les missions des Pères Blancs en Afrique Centrale (1879–1914): objectifs et réalisations. Louvain-La-Neuve and Brussels, 1983.

Hertlein, Siegfried. *Die Kirche in Tansania: Ein kurzer Überblick über Geschichte und Gegenwart*. Münsterschwarzach, 1971.

Wege christlicher Verkündigung: Eine pastoralgeschichtliche Untersuchung aus dem Bereich der katholischen Kirche Tansanias. 3 vols. Münsterschwarzach, 1976–83.

Hertsens, L. 'Mozambique: a Church in a socialist state in a time of radical change', *Pro Mundi Vita*, African dossier, 33. Brussels, 1977.

Hetherwick, Alexander. *The building of the Blantyre Church, Nyasaland, 1888–1891*. Blantyre, 1940.

Hewat, Elizabeth G. K. *Vision and achievement 1796–1956: a history of the foreign missions of the Churches united in the Church of Scotland*. London, 1960.

Hewison, H. H. *Hedge of wild almonds: South Africa, the 'pro-Boers' and the Quaker conscience, 1890–1910*. London, 1989.

Hewitt, Gordon. *The problems of success: a history of the Church Missionary Society 1910–1942*. 2 vols., London, 1971–7.

Hewson, Leslie A. *An introduction to South Africa's Methodists*. Cape Town, 1950.

Hexham, Irving (ed.) *The scriptures of the Amanazaretha of Ekuphakameni: selected writings of the Zulu prophets Isaiah and Londa Shembe*. (Trans. Londa Shembe and Hans-Jürgen Becken.) Calgary, 1994.

Heyer, Friedrich. *Die Kirche Athiopiens*. Berlin, 1971.

Heyse, Théodore. *Associations religieuses au Congo belge et au Ruanda-Urundi*. Brussels, 1948.

Hickey, Raymond. *Heralds of Christ to Borno (the history of the Prefecture and Diocese of Maiduguri)*. Maiduguri, 1978.

A history of the Catholic Church in Northern Nigeria. Jos, 1981.

Christianity in Borno State and northern Gongola. Aachen, 1984.

Hildebrandt, Jonathan. *History of the Church in Africa: a survey*. 2nd edn, Achimota, Accra, 1987.

Hilton, Anne. *The kingdom of Kongo*. Oxford, 1985.

Hinchliff, Peter. *The Anglican Church in South Africa: an account of the history and development of the Church of the Province of South Africa*. London, 1963.

John William Colenso, Bishop of Natal. London, 1964.

Cyprian of Carthage and the unity of the Christian Church. London, 1974.

The Church in South Africa. London, 1968.

Hinfelaar, Hugo F. *Bemba-speaking women of Zambia in a century of religious change (1892–1992)*. Leiden, 1994.

Hodges, Tony. *Jehovah's Witnesses in Central Africa*. Minority Rights Group Report, 29. London, 1976.

Hodgson, Janet. *Ntsikana's great hymn*. Cape Town, 1980.

The God of the Xhosa: a study of the origins and development of the traditional concepts of the supreme being. Cape Town, 1982.

Hofmeyr, Isabel. *'We spend our years as a tale that is told': oral historical narrative in a South African chiefdom*. Johannesburg and London, 1993

Hofmeyr, J. W. and Cross, K. E. *History of the Church in Southern Africa, I: a select bibliography of published material to 1980*. Pretoria, 1986.

Hogan, Edmund M. *Catholic missionaries and Liberia: a study of Christian enterprise in West Africa, 1842–1950*. Cork, 1981.

Hohensee, D. *Church growth in Burundi*. South Pasadena, 1978.

Holas, B. *Le séparatisme religieux en Afrique noire: l'example de la Côte d'Ivoire*. Paris, 1965.

Holmberg, Åke. *African tribes and European agencies: colonialism and humanitarianism in Britsh South and East Africa 1870–1895*. Gothenburg, 1966.

Holmes, Brian (ed.) *Educational policy and the mission schools*. London, 1967.

Holmio, Armas Kustaa Ensio. *The Finnish Missionary Society, 1859–1950*. Hancock, Mich., 1950.

Honwana, Raúl. *The life history of Raúl Honwana: an inside view of Mozambique from colonialism to independence, 1905–1975*. Edit. Allen F. Isaacman. (Trans. Tamara Bender.) Boulder and London, 1988.

Hooton, W. S. and Wright, J. Stafford. *The first twenty-five years of the Bible Churchmen's Missionary Society (1922–47)*. London, 1947.

Horner, Norman A. *A guide to Christian Churches in the Middle East: present-day Christianity in the Middle East and North Africa*. Elkhart, 1989.

Horrell, Muriel. *The education of the Coloured community in South Africa, 1652 to 1970*. Johannesburg, 1970.

Hoskins, Irene E. *Friends in Africa*. Richmond, Ind.: American Friends Board of Missions, [c.1945].

Howell, A. E. *Bishop Dupont: king of the brigands*. Franklin, Pa., 1949.

Huddleston, Trevor. *Naught for your comfort*. London, 1956.

Hunter, J. H. *A flame of fire: the life and work of R. V. Bingham, DD*. Toronto, 1961.

Hunwick, John O. (ed.) *Religion and national integration in Africa: Islam, Christianity and politics in the Sudan and Nigeria*. Evanston, 1992.

Hutchison, William R. *Errand to the world: American Protestant thought and foreign missions*. Chicago and London, 1987.

Hyatt, Harry Middleton. *The Church of Abyssinia*. London, 1928.

Igwe, S. Okoronkwo. *Education in Eastern Nigeria 1847–1975: development and management: Church, State and community*. London and Ibadan, 1987.

Ijagbemi, E. Adeleye. *The role of M. J. P. Koledade (1902–73) in pioneering Nigerian education*. Lewiston, Queenston and Lampeter, 1992.

Iliffe, John. *Tanganyika under German rule 1905–1912*. Cambridge, 1969.

(ed.) *Modern Tanzanians: a volume of biographies*. Nairobi, 1973.

A modern history of Tanganyika. Cambridge, 1979.

Ilogu, Edmund. *Christianity and Igbo culture*. Leiden, 1974.

Igbo life and thought. N.p., 1985.

Indaru, Peter Albert. *Man with the lion heart: biography of Canon Ezekiel Apindi*. Accra, 1974.

Informationsstelee Südliches Afrika. *Die Kirche in Mosambik heute: zwischen Kolonialismus und Revolution*. Bonn, 1981.

Instituto de Estudios Politicos para America Latina y Africa. *La Iglesia en Mozambique Hoy: Entre el Colonialismo y la Revolucion*. Madrid, 1979.

International Missionary Council. *Conference of Christian workers among Moslems 1924: a brief account of the conferences together with their findings and lists of members*. New York, 1924.

International Review of Missions, double number, 1926.

Ipenburg, Arie N. *Lubwa: the Presbyterian mission and the eastern Bemba*. Lusaka, 1984.

'All good men': the development of Lubwa mission, Chinsali, Zambia, 1905–1967. Frankfurt am Main, 1992.

Irvine, Cecilia. *The Church of Christ in Zaïre: a handbook of Protestant Churches, missions and communities, 1878–1978*. Indianapolis, 1978.

Isaacman, Allen F. *Mozambique: the Africanization of a European institution: the Zambesi prazos, 1750–1902*. Madison, Milwaukee and London, 1972.

Isichei, Elizabeth. *The Ibo people and the Europeans: the genesis of a relationship – to 1906*. London, 1973.

A history of the Igbo people. London, 1976.

Entirely for God: the life of Michael Iwene Tansi. Ibadan, 1980.

(ed.) *Studies in the history of Plateau State, Nigeria*. London, 1982.

(ed.) *Varieties of Christian experience in Nigeria*. London, 1982.

A history of Christianity in Africa: from antiquity to the present. London, 1995.

Jackson, H. C. *Pastor on the Nile: a memoir of Bishop Llewellyn H. Gwynne*. London, 1960.

Jackson, S. *Catholic schools and their administration in the Old Calabar Province*. Calabar, 1961.

Jacobs, Sylvia M. *The African nexus: Black American perspectives on the European partition of Africa, 1880–1920*. Westport, 1981.

(ed.), *Black Americans and the missionary movement in Africa*. Westpoint and London, 1982.

Jadin, L. *L'Ancien Congo et l'Angola 1639–1655, d'après les archives romaines, portugaises, néerlandaises et espagnoles*. 3 vols. Brussels, 1975.

Jakobsson, Stiv. *Am I not a man and a brother? British missions and the abolition of the slave trade and slavery in West Africa and the West Indies 1786–1838*. Lund, 1972.

James, Wendy. *The listening ebony: moral knowledge, religion and power among the Uduk of Sudan*. Oxford, 1988.

Janzen, J. M. *The quest for therapy in Lower Zaïre*. Berkeley, Los Angeles and London, 1978.

Jasper, G. *Das Werden der Bethel-Mission*. Bethel, 1936.

Jeal, Tim. *Livingstone*. London, 1973.

Jedrej, M. C. and Shaw, Rosalind (eds.) *Dreaming, religion and society in Africa*. Leiden and New York, 1992.

Jenkins, David. *Black Zion: the return of Afro-Americans and West Indians to Africa*. London, 1975.

Jensen, Mogens. *To mænd og deras mission: Anton Marius Pedersen, Niels Høegh Brønnum og Dansk Forenet Sudan Mission 1905–1925*. Christiansfeld, 1992.

Johanson, B. (ed.) *The Church in South Africa – today and tomorrow*. Johannesburg, 1975.

Johanssen, Ernst. *Ruanda: Kleine Anfänge, grosse Aufgaben der evangelischen Mission in Zwischenseegebiet Deutsche-Ostafrikas*. Bethel, 1915.

Johansson, Erik and Söderström, Hugo. *Shona wisdom and Christian mission: the life and work of Jotham S. Hove*. Uppsala, 1990.

Johnson, James and Ellis, H. J. *Two missionary visits to the Ijebu country 1892: report on a missionary tour through a portion of Ijebu-Remo made between 3rd and 29th August, 1892.* Ibadan, 1974.

Johnson, T. S. *The story of a mission: the Sierra Leone Church: first daughter of CMS.* London: SPCK, 1953.

Johnson, V. E. *The Augustana Lutheran Mission of Tanganyika Territory, East Africa.* Rióck Island, Ill., 1939.

Johnson, W. R. *Worship and freedom: a Black American church in Zambia.* London, 1977.

Johnston, Geoffrey. *Of God and maxim guns: Presbyterianism in Nigeria 1846–1966.* Waterloo, Ont., 1988.

Joinet, Bernard. *Eglise et socialisme en Tanzanie.* Paris, 1976.

Jones, H. Gresford. *Uganda in transformation.* London, 1926.

Jones, Thomas Jesse (ed.) *Education in Africa: a study of West, South and equatorial Africa by the African Education Commission under the auspices of the Phelps-Stokes Fund and foreign mission societies of North America and Europe.* New York, 1922.

Education in East Africa: a study of East, Central and South Africa by the Second African Education Commission under the auspices of the Phelps-Stokes Fund, in co-operation with the International Education Board. New York and London, 1924.

Jordan, John P. *Bishop Shanahan of Southern Nigeria.* 2nd edn, Dublin, 1971.

Jørgensen, Torstein. *Contact and conflict: Norwegian missionaries, the Zulu kingdom and the Gospel 1850–1873.* Stavanger, 1987.

(ed.) *I tro och tjeneste: Det Norska Misjonsselskap 1842–1992.* 2 vols., Stavanger, 1992.

Joseph, Richard A. *Radical nationalism in Cameroun: social origins of the UPC rebellion.* Oxford, 1977.

Jules-Rosette, B. *African apostles: ritual and conversion in the Church of John Maranke.* Ithaca and London, 1975.

(ed.) *The new religions of Africa.* 1979.

Junod, H-Ph. *Henri-Alexandre Junod, missionnaire et savant.* Lausanne, 1934.

Le pasteur Calvin Mapopé. Lausanne, 1925.

Fünfzig Jahre Schweizer Mission in Südafrika. Zurich, 1928.

Ernest Creux et Paul Berthoud, les fondateurs de la Mission Suisse en Afrique du Sud. Lausanne, 1933.

Kabongo-Mbaya, P. *L'Eglise du Christ au Zaïre: formation et adaptation d'un Protestantisme en situation de dictature.* Paris, 1992.

Kake, Ibrahim Baba. *Dona Beatrice: la Jeanne d'Arc congolaise.* Paris, 1976.

Kalibwami, Justin. *Le catholicisme et la société rwandaise, 1900–1962.* Paris, 1991.

Kallaway, Peter (ed.) *Apartheid and education: the education of Black South Africans.* Johannesburg, 1984.

Kalu, O. U. *Divided people of God: Church union movement in Nigeria, 1867–1966.* New York and London, 1978.

(ed.) *Christianity in West Africa: the Nigerian story.* Ibadan, 1978.

(ed.) *The history of Christianity in West Africa.* London and New York, 1980.

(ed.) *African Church historiography: an ecumenical perspective.* Berne, 1988.

Kamphausen, Erhard. *Anfänge der kirchlichen Unabhängigkeitsbewegung in Südafrika: Geschichte und Theologie der Äthiopischen Bewegung 1872–1912.* Berne, 1976.

Kaplan, Steven. *The monastic holy man and the Christianization of early Solomonic Ethiopia.* Stuttgart and Wiesbaden, 1984.

Karl, Marilee (ed.) *Ujamaa and self-reliance: building socialism in Tanzania ... the Church within African socialism*. Rome, 1976.

Karugire, Samwiri Rubaraza. *A political history of Uganda*. Nairobi and London, 1980.

Kasozi, A. B. K., King, Noel and Oded, Ayre. *Islam and the confluence of religions in Uganda 1840–1966*. Florida, 1973.

Kast, Gertrude Elizabeth. *A missionary remembers*. Lansdowne, 1970.

Kastfelt, Niels. *Religion and politics in Nigeria: a study in Middle Belt Christianity*. London, 1994.

Katjavivi, Peter, Frostin Per and Mbuende, Kaire. *Church and liberation in Namibia*. London, 1989.

Kaunda, Kenneth D. *Zambia shall be free: an autobiography*. London, 1962.

Kaunda, Kenneth D. and Morris, Colin M. *A humanist in Africa: letters to Colin M. Morris from Kenneth D. Kaunda*. London, 1966.

Kavulu, D. *The Uganda martyrs*. Kampala, 1969.

Keiling, Louis Alfred. *Quarenta anos de Africa*. Braga, 1934.

Keller, Werner. *The history of the Presbyterian Church in West Cameroon*. Buea, 1969.

Zur Freiheit berufen: die Geschichte der Presbyterianischen Kirche in Kamerun. Zurich, 1981.

Kelly, John. *The Church in the town: re-thinking the African urban apostolate*. Eldoret, 1977.

Kendall, Elliott. *The end of an era: Africa and the missionary*. London, 1978.

Kenny, Joseph. *The Catholic Church in tropical Africa 1445–1850*. Ibadan, 1983.

Kenyatta, Jomo. *Facing Mount Kenya: the traditional life of the Gikuyu*. London, 1953

Kerharo, J. and Bouquet, A. *Sorciers, féticheurs et guérisseurs de la Côte d'Ivoire*. Paris, 1950.

Keteku, H. J. *The Reverends Theophilus Opoku and David Asante*. Accra, 1965.

Khambane, Chitlangou and Clerc, André-Daniel. *Chitlangou: fils de chef*. 2nd edn, Lausanne, 1946

Ki-Zerbo, Joseph. *Alfred Diban, premier chrétien de Haute-Volta*. Paris, 1983.

Kibira, Josiah M. *Church, clan, and the world*. Uppsala and Lund, 1974.

Kiernan, J. P. *Havens of health in a Zulu city: the production and management of therapeutic power in Zionist Churches*. Lewiston, Queenstown and Lampeter, 1990.

Kiggins, Thomas. *Maynooth mission to Africa: the story of St Patrick's, Kiltegan*. Dublin, 1991.

Kilaini, Method M. P. *The Catholic evangelization of Kagera in north-west Tanzania: the pioneer period 1892–1912*. Published doctoral thesis, Pontifical Gregorian University, Rome, 1990.

Kilgour, R. *The Bible throughout the world: a survey of scripture translations*. London, 1939.

Kimambo, I. N. and Temu, A. J. (eds.) *A history of Tanzania*. Nairobi, 1969.

Kimbembo, D. *Fétichisme et croyance de l'au-delà chez les Bacongo du Congo*. Brazzaville, 1964.

Kimble, David. *A political history of Ghana: the rise of Gold Coast nationalism 1850–1928*. London, 1963.

King, Kenneth James. *Pan-Africanism and education: a study of race philanthropy and education in the southern states of America and East Africa*. Oxford, 1971.

King, Noël. *Christian and Muslim in Africa*. London and New York, 1971.

King, Noël, Kasozi, Abdu and Oded, Arye. *Islam and the confluence of religions in Uganda, 1840–1966*. Tallahassee, 1973.

King, Paul S. (ed.) *Missions in Southern Rhodesia*. Bulawayo and Cape Town, 1959.

King, Willis J. *History of the Methodist Church mission in Liberia*. Monrovia, 1953.

Kirkman, J. S. *Fort Jesus*. Oxford, 1974.

Kirkwood, Dean R. (ed.) *Mission in mid-continent: Zaïre: one hundred years of American Baptist commitment in Zaïre, 1884–1984*. Valley Forge, [1984].

Kistner, Wolfram. *Outside the camp: a collection of writings*. Johannesburg, 1988.

Kitching, A. L. *On the backwaters of the Nile*. London, 1912.

From darkness to light. London, 1935.

Kittler, Glenn D. *The White Fathers*. London, 1957.

Kiwanuka, M. S. M. *A history of Buganda from the foundation of the kingdom to 1900*. London, 1971.

Klein, Carol M. *We went to Gabon*. Harrisburg, 1974.

Klintenberg, R. A. *Equatorial Guinea, Macias country: the forgotten refugees*. Geneva, 1978.

Koelle, Sigismund Wilhelm. *Polyglotta Africana*. London, 1854. 2nd edn. Graz, 1963.

Kopytoff, Jean Herskovits. *A preface to modern Nigeria: the 'Sierra Leonians' in Yoruba, 1830–1890*. Madison, Milwaukee and London, 1965.

Koren, Henry J. *To the ends of the earth: a general history of the Congregation of the Holy Ghost*. Pittsburgh, 1983.

Krabill, James R. *The hymnody of the Harrist Church among the Dida of south-central Ivory Coast (1913–1949): a historico-religious study*. Frankfurt am Main, 1995.

Krapf, Johann Ludwig. *An imperfect outline of the elements of the Galla language*. London, 1840.

Kratz, M. *La Mission des Rédemptoristes belges au Bas-Congo: la période de semailles*. Brussels, 1968.

Kruger, Bernhard. *The pear tree blossoms: a history of the Moravian mission stations in South Africa, 1737–1869*. Genadenal, 1966.

Kup, A. Peter. *A history of Sierra Leone 1400–1787*. Cambridge, 1961.

Kwamena-Poh, M. A. *The Reverend F. A. Ramseyer and the foundation of the Presbyterian Church in Kumasi*. Kumasi, n.d.

Kwast, Lloyd E. *The discipling of West Cameroon: a study of Baptist growth*. Grand Rapids, 1971.

Labouret, Henri and Rivet, Paul. *Le royaume d'Arda et son évangélisation au* XVIIe *siècle*. Paris, 1929.

Ladurie, Marie Le Roy. *Pâques africaines: de la communauté clanique à la communauté chrétienne*. Paris, 1965.

Lagergren, David. *Mission and state in the Congo: a study of the relations between Protestant missions and the Congo Independent State authorities with special reference to the Equator District, 1885–1903*. Lund, 1970.

Lagerwerf, Leny. *'They pray for you ... ': Independent Churches and women in Botswana*. Leiden and Utrecht, 1982.

Lagesse, L. *Le Père Laval: son oeuvre à l'île Maurice*. Port Louis, 1955.

Laing, George E. F. *Dom Bernard Clements in Africa*. London, 1944.

Laitin, David D. *Hegemony and culture: politics and religious change among the Yoruba*. Chicago and London, 1986.

Lamey, René X. *The holy martyrs of Uganda*. Rome, 1985.

Lamont, Donal. *Speech from the dock*. London, 1977.

Landau, Paul. S. *The realm of the word: language, gender, and Christianity in a Southern African kingdom*. London, 1995.

Larson, Mabel A. *Partners in education: Ilboru secondary school 1946–1969*. Arusha, 1977.

Larsson, Birgitta. *Conversion to greater freedom? Women, Church and social change in north-western Tanzania under colonial rule*. Uppsala, 1991.

Larsson, Per. *Bishop Josiah Kibira of Bukoba in an international perspective*. Nairobi and Dodoma, n.d.

Lautenschlager, Georg Max. *Die sozialen Ordnungen bei den Zulu und die Mariannhiller Mission, 1882–1909*. Reimlingen, 1963.

Lawuo, Z. E. *Education and social change in a rural community: a study of colonial education and local response among the Chagga between 1920 and 1945*. Dar es Salaam, n.d.

Le rôle de la femme dans les missions: rapports et compte rendu de la XXe *semaine de missiologie de Louvain*. Museum Lessianum, section missiologique, 29. Brussels and Paris, 1950.

Leflon, J. *Eugène de Mazenod, Evêque de Marseille, Fondateur des Missionaires Oblats de Marie Immaculée 1782–1861*. Paris, 1957. [Also in English.]

Lelong, M.-H. *N'Zérékoré: l'evangile dans la forêt*. Paris, 1949.

Lema, Anza Amen. *Partners in education in mainland Tanzania*. Arusha, 1972.

The influence of Christian mission societies on education policies in Tanganyika 1868–1970. Geneva, 1979; Hong Kong, 1980.

Lesourd, Paul. *L'œuvre civilisatrice et scientifique des missionnaires catholiques dans les colonies français*. Paris, 1931.

Levine, Donald N. *Wax and gold: tradition and innovation in Ethiopian culture*. Chicago, 1965.

Lewis, C. and Edwards, G. B. *Historical records of the Church of the Province of South Africa*. London, 1934.

Leys, Norman. *Kenya*. London, 1924.

Light, love, peace: one hundred years [of the] Catholic Church in Tanzania 1868–1968. Dar es Salaam, 1968.

Lilienfeld, Fairy von. *Spiritualität des frühen Wüstenmönchtums*. Erlangen, 1983.

Linden, Ian with Linden, Jane. *Church and revolution in Rwanda*. Manchester, 1977.

Linden, Ian. *Catholics, peasants and Chewa resistance in Nyasaland 1889–1939*. London, 1974.

Church and state in Rhodesia, 1959–1979. Munich and Mainz, 1979.

The Catholic Church and the struggle for Zimbabwe. London, 1979.

Lindqvist, Ingmar. *Partners in mission: a case-study of the missionary practice of the Lutheran foreign mission agency involvement in Tanzania since the early 1960s seen in a historical and theological perspective*. Åbo, 1982.

Lipisa, Abba Tito. *The cult of saints in the Ethiopian Church*. Rome, 1963.

Livingstone, David. *Missionary travels and researches in South Africa*. London, 1857.

Livingstone, W. P. *Laws of Livingstonia*. London, 1921.

Lloyd, M. (trans.) *Diaries of the Jesuits missionaries at Bulawayo, 1879–1881*. Salisbury, 1959.

Long, Norman. *Social change and the individual: a study of the social and religious responses to innovation in a Zambian rural community*. Manchester, 1968.

Lopes, Felix. *Missões Franciscanas em Moçambique, 1898–1870*. Braga, 1972.

Loth, Heinrich. *Die christliche Mission in Südwestafrika: zur destruktiven Rolle der Rheinischen Missionsgesellschaft beim Prozess der Staatsbildung in Südwestafrika (1842–1893)*. East Berlin, 1963.

Lovett, Richard. *The history of the London Missionary Society 1795–1895.* 2 vols., London, 1899.

Low, D. A. *Religion and society in Buganda 1875–1900.* Kampala, 1957.

Political parties in Uganda 1949–62. London, 1962.

The mind of Buganda: documents of the modern history of an African kingdom. London, 1971.

Buganda in modern history. London, 1971.

Low, D. A. and Smith, Alison (eds.) *History of East Africa, vol. III.* Oxford, 1976.

Low, D. Anthony and Pratt, R. Cranford. *Buganda and British overrule 1900–1955: two studies.* Nairobi and London, 1970.

Löytty, Seppo. *The Ovambo sermon: a study of the preaching of the Evangelical Lutheran Ovambo-Kavango Church in South West Africa.* Tampere, 1971.

Luck, Anne. *African saint: the story of Apolo Kivebulaya.* London, 1963.

Charles Stokes in Africa. Nairobi, 1972.

Ludwig, Charles. *Mama was a missionary.* Anderson, Ind., 1963.

Lundgren, Manfred. *Proclaiming Christ to His world: the experience of Radio Voice of the Gospel 1957–1977.* Geneva, 1984.

Lundström, Karl-Johan. *The Lotuho and the Verona Fathers: a case study of communication in development.* Uppsala, 1990.

Lupo, P. *Eglise et décolonisation a Madagascar.* Fianarantsoa, 1975.

Une église des laïcs à Madagascar: les Catholiques pendant la guerre coloniale de 1894–5. Paris, 1990.

Lutheran World Federation. *All Africa consultation on Christian theology and Christian education in the African context, Gaborone, Botswana, 5–14 October, 1978.* Geneva, 1979.

Lynch, Hollis R. *Edward Wilmot Blyden: pan-Negro patriot, 1832–1912.* London and New York, 1967.

M'Keown, Robert L. *Twenty-five years in Qua Iboe: the story of a missionary effort in Nigeria.* London and Belfast, 1912.

Mabelle, G. *L'appel du Soudanais.* Paris, n.d.

MacGaffey, Wyatt. *Custom and government in the lower Congo.* Berkeley, 1970.

Modern Kongo prophets: religion in a plural society. Bloomington, 1983.

Religion and society in Central Africa: the BaKongo of Lower Zaïre. Chicago and London, 1986.

MacIndoe, B. *Spotlight on Senegal.* London, n.d.

Mackintosh, C. W. *Some pioneer missions of Northern Rhodesia and Nyasaland.* Livingstone, 1950.

Macpherson, Fergus. *Kenneth Kaunda of Zambia: the times and the man.* Lusaka and London, 1974.

Macpherson, R. *The Presbyterian Church in Kenya: an account of the origins and growth of the Presbyterian Church of East Africa.* Nairobi, 1970.

Maindron, Gabriel. *Des apparitions à Kibeho: annonce de Marie au coeur de l'Afrique.* Paris, 1984.

Mair, Lucy P. *An African people in the twentieth century.* London, 1934.

Makozi, A. O. and Afolabi, G. J. *The history of the Catholic Church in Nigeria.* Lagos and Ibadan, 1982.

Malishi, Lukas. *Introduction to the history of Christianity in Africa.* Tabora and London, 1987.

Mamet, Joseph. *Le Diocèse de Port-Louis.* Port Louis, 1974.

Mara, Yolande. *The Church of Ethiopia: the national Church in the making.* Asmara, 1972.

Marcos Daoud. *The liturgy of the Ethiopian Church*. Addis Ababa, 1954.

Maree, W. L. *Uit Duisternis Geroep die Sendingwerk von die Nederduitse Gereformeerde Kerk onder die Bakgatla von Wes-Transvaal en Betsjoenaland*. Johannesburg, 1966.

Margeot, Jean. *L'Eglise aujourd'hui: foi et politique: tension et unité*. Port Louis, 1977.

Marie-Germaine, Sister. *Le Christ au Gabon*. Louvain, 1931.

Markowitz, Marvin D. *Cross and sword: the political role of Christian missions in the Belgian Congo, 1908–1960*. Stanford, 1973.

Marks, Shula. *Reluctant rebellion, the 1906–08 disturbances in Natal*. Oxford, 1970.

Marsden-Smedley, Philip. *Ethiopia and the holy land: a guide*. Jerusalem, 1991.

Martelli, George. *Livingstone's river*. London, 1970.

Martin, Marie-Louise. *Kimbangu: an African prophet and his Church*. (Trans. D. M. Moore.) Oxford, 1975.

Martin, Phyllis M. *The external trade of the Loango coast 1576–1870: the effects of changing commercial relations on the Vili kingdom of Loango*. Oxford, 1972.

Leisure and society in colonial Brazzaville. Cambridge, 1995.

Martin, V. *La chrétienté africaine de Dakar*. Dakar, 1964.

Mathieu, M. *Notes sur l'Islam et la Christianisme dans la subdivision centrale de Ouagadougou*. Paris, 1956.

Matthew, A. F. *The teaching of the Abyssinian Church, as set up by the doctors of the same*. London, 1936.

The Church of Ethiopia during the Italian occupation. Addis Ababa, 1943.

The Church of Ethiopia, 1941–1944. Addis Ababa, 1944.

Maurier, Henri. *Christianisme et croyances mossi*. Paris, 1960

Maxwell, J. Lowry. *Nigeria: the land, the people and Christian progress*. London [1928?].

Half a century of grace: a jubilee history of the Sudan United Mission. London [*c*. 1953].

Mbali, Zolile. *The Churches and racism: a Black South African perspective*. London, 1987.

Mbiti, John S. *New Testament eschatology in an African background: a study of the encounter between New Testament theology and African traditional concepts*. London, 1971.

Mbock, P. *La vie d'une Eglise au Cameroun*. Paris, 1931.

Mbugua, Judy (ed.) *Our time has come: African Christian women address the issues of today*. Carlisle and Grand Rapids, 1994.

McCracken, John. *Politics and Christianity in Malawi 1875–1940: the impact of the Livingstonia Mission in the northern province*. Cambridge, 1977.

McCulloch, Mary. *A time to remember: the story of the Diocese of Nyasaland*. London, 1959.

McCullum, Hugh. *The angels have left us: the Rwanda tragedy and the Churches*. Geneva, 1995.

McDonagh, Edna. *Church and politics: from theology to a case history of Zimbabwe*. Notre Dame, 1980.

McEwan, Dorethea. *A Catholic Sudan: dream, mission, reality*. Rome, 1987.

McGavran, Donald A. and Riddle, N. G. *Midday in missions:* Zaïre 1977. N.d.

McGregor, G. P. *King's College Budo: the first sixty years*. Nairobi and London, 1967.

McKenzie, Peter R. *Inter-religious encounters in West Africa: Samuel Ajayi Crowther's attitude to African traditional religion and Islam*. Leicester, 1976.

McLeish, Alex (ed.) *Light and darkness in East Africa*. London, 1927.

McPherson, Alexander. *James Fraser, 'the man who loved the people': a record of missionary endeavour in Rhodesia in the twentieth century*. London, 1967.

McWilliam, H. O. A. and Kwamena-Poh, M. A. *The development of education in Ghana: an outline*. London, 1975.

Mears, Gordon. *Methodism in Swaziland*. Rondebosch, 1955.

Meer, Frederik Gerben Louis van der. *Augustine the Bishop: the life and work of a Father of the Church*. Trans. Brian Battershaw and G. R. Lamb. London and New York, 1961.

Megill, Esther L. *Education in the African Church*. London, 1981.

Mehl, R. *Décolonisation et missions protestantes*. Paris, 1964.

Mein, J. D. *Five years in the life of the Christian Service Committee of the Churches in Malawi, 1968 to 1972*. Blantyre, 1972.

Meinardus, Otto F. A. *The Copts in Jerusalem*. Cairo, 1960.

Christian Egypt: faith and life. Cairo, 1970.

Christian Egypt: ancient and modern. 2nd edn, Cairo, 1977.

Monks and monasteries of the Egyptian deserts. 2nd edn, Cairo, 1989.

Melle, Scopas M. Elias. *Canon Ezra: my best friend in Sudan*. 1993.

Mellinghoff, G. and Kiwovele, J. (eds.) *Lutherische Kirche Tanzania: Ein Handbuch*. Erlangen, 1976.

Membe, J. L. C. *A short history of the AME Church in Central Africa*. Luanshya, 1969.

Menzel, Gustav. *Die Rheinische Mission: aus 150 Jahren Missionsgeschichte*. Wuppertal, 1978.

Die Bethel-Mission: aus 100 Jahren Missionsgeschichte. Neukirchen-Vluyn, Wuppertal and Bielefeld, 1986.

Merad, A. *Charles de Foucauld au regard de l'Islam*. Paris, 1976.

Mercer, Samuel A. B. *The Ethiopic liturgy: its sources, development, and present form*. London, 1915.

Mertens, F. and Singleton, M. *'Let my people go . . .': a survey of the Catholic Church in Western Nigeria*. Brussels, 1974.

Merwe, W. J. van der. *The development of missionary attitudes in the Dutch Reformed Church in South Africa*. Cape Town, 1934.

Metodio da Nembro, Padre. *La missione dei Cappuccini in Eritrea (1894–1952)*. Rome, 1953.

Vita missionaria in Eritrea. Rome, 1953.

Mettler, Lukas Anton. *Christliche Terminologie und Katechismus Gestaltung in der Mariannhiller Mission 1910–1920*. Sconeck-Beckenried, 1967.

Metuh, Emefie Ikenga. *God and man in African religion: a case study of the Igbo of Nigeria*. London, 1981.

Metzkes, J. *Otjimbingwe: aus alten Tagen einer rheinischen Missionsstation im Hererolande, Südwestafrika 1849–1890*. Windhoek, 1962.

Metzler, Josef (ed.) *Sacrae Congregationis de Propaganda Fide Memoria Rerum 1622–1972*. 5 vols. Rome, Freiburg i.B. and Vienna, 1971–76.

Mgadla, Part Themba. *Missionaries and western education in the Bechuanaland Protectorate 1859–1904: the case of the Bangwato*. Gaborone, 1989.

Mhlagazanhlansi [Jones, Neville]. *My friend Kumalo*. Reprinted, Bulawayo, 1972.

Michalowski, Kazimierz. *Faras: fouilles polonaises 1961–2*. Warsaw, 1965.

Faras: centre artistique de la Nubie Chrétienne. Leiden, 1966.

Faras: die Kathedrale aus dem Wüstensand. Zurich, 1967.

Faras: wall paintings in the collection of the National Museum in Warsaw. Warsaw, 1974.

Michel, Joseph. *Le Père Jacques Laval: le Saint de l'île Maurice, 1803–1864*. Paris, 1976.

Micklem, P. A. *Church and empire in Roman Africa*. St Leonards-on-Sea, 1964.

Mikhail, Kyriakos. *Copts and Moslems under British control*. 1911. Reprinted, Port Washington, 1971.

Miller, Joseph C. *Kings and kinsmen: early Mbundu states in Angola*. Oxford, 1976.

Way of death: merchant capitalism and the Angolan slave trade 1730–1830. London, 1988.

Mission catholique chinoise. *Les pratiques, rites et croyances de la religion populaire chinoise*. Port Louis, 1975.

Mobley, Harris W. *The Ghanaian's image of the missionary: an analysis of the published critiques of Christian missionaries by Ghanaians 1897–1965*. Leiden, 1970.

Moffat, Robert. *Apprenticeship at Kuruman: being the journals and letters of Robert and Mary Moffat 1820–1826*. Ed. Isaac Schapera. London, 1951.

Missionary labours and scenes in Southern Africa. 1842. Reprinted, New York, 1966.

Mojoli, Giuseppe *La Chiesa in Etiopia: note e ricordi di un nunzio*. Rome, 1973.

Molema, S. M. *Chief Moroka: his life, his times, his country and his people*. Cape Town, n.d.

Montshiwa, Barolong chief and patriot, 1815–1896. Cape Town, 1966.

Molina, A. J. *Historia da Igreja em Moçambique*. Lisbon, 1956.

Molnar, E. C. *The Ethiopian Orthodox Church: a contribution to the ecumenical study of less known Eastern Churches*. Pasadena, 1969.

Mondain, G. *Un siècle de mission à Madagascar*. Paris, 1948.

Montgomery, H. H. *Francis Balfour of Basutoland, evangelist and bishop*. London, 1925.

Moore, Basil (ed.) *Black theology: the South African voice*. London, 1973.

Moorhouse, Geoffrey. *The missionaries*. London, 1974.

Moreira, E. *Portuguese East Africa: a study of its religious needs*. London, 1936.

Morris, Colin. *The hour after midnight: a missionary's experiences of the racial and political struggle in Northern Rhodesia*. London, 1961.

Morton, Fred. *Children of Ham: freed slaves and fugitive slaves on the Kenya coast, 1873 to 1907*. Boulder, 1990.

Mosca, Liliana. *Il Madagascar nella vita di Raombana primo storico malgascio (1809–1855)*. Naples, 1980.

Mossolow, N. *Otjikango oder Gross Barmen: Ortsgeschichte der erster Rheinischen Herero-Missionsstation in Südwestafrika, 1844–1904*. Windhoek, 1968.

Mota, A. Teixeira da, and Hair, P. E. H. *East of Mina: Afro-European relations on the Gold Coast in the 1550s and 1560s: an essay with supporting documents*. Madison, 1988.

Moyangar, Bertin. 'Le rôle des missions catholiques dans l'histoire du Tchad de 1900 à 1970', Doctoral thesis, University of Paris, 1972.

Mudenge, S. I. G. *Christian education at the Mutapa court*. Harare, 1986.

A political history of Munhumutapa c. 1400–1902. London and Harare, 1988.

Mueller, Howard Ernest. 'Formation of a mission Church in an African culture: the United Brethren in Sierra Leone', Ph. D. thesis, Northwestern University. Ann Arbor: University Microfilms, 1973.

Mufuka, K. Nyamayaro. *Missions and politics in Malawi*. Kingston, Ont., 1977.

Muga, Erasto. *African responses to Western Christian religion: a sociological analysis of African separatist religious and political movements in East Africa*. Nairobi, 1975.

Mukonyora, I. Cox, J. L. and Verstraelen, F. J. (eds.) *'Rewriting' the Bible: the real issues: perspectives from within biblical and religious studies in Zimbabwe*. Gweru, 1993.

Muldoon, James. *Popes, lawyers, and infidels: the Church and the non-Christian world, 1250–1550*. University of Pennsylvania Press, 1979.

Müller, Karl. *Geschichte der katholischen Kirche in Togo*. Kaldenkirchen, 1958.

Histoire de l'église catholique au Togo (1892–1967). Lomé, 1968.

Müller, Reinhart (ed.) *Auftrag geht weiter: Beitrag zur Integration die Hermannsburger Mission in die lutherische Kirchen im südlichen Afrika und in Äthiopien: Festgabe für Hans Robert Wesenick*. Hermannsburg, 1979.

Mullings, Leith. *Therapy, ideology, and social change: mental healing in urban Ghana*. Berkeley, Los Angeles and London, 1984.

Munro, J. Forbes. *Colonial rule and the Kamba: social change in the Kenya highlands 1889–1939*. Oxford, 1975.

Munthe, Ludvig. *La Bible à Madagascar: les deux premières traductions du Nouveau Testament Malgache*. Oslo, 1969.

Murphree, Marshall W. *Christianity and the Shona*. London and New York, 1969.

Murray, A. Victor. *The school in the bush*. London, 1929.

Murray, Jocelyn. *Proclaim the good news: a short history of the Church Missionary Society*. London, 1985.

Murray-Brown, Jeremy. *Faith and the flag: the opening of Africa*. London, 1977.

Mushindo, Paul B. *The life of a Zambian evangelist: the reminiscences of the Reverend Paul Bwembya Mushindo*. Lusaka, 1973.

Musopole, Augustine C. *Being human in Africa: toward an African Christian anthropology*. New York, 1994.

Mutibwa, P. M. *The Malagasy and the Europeans: Madagascar's foreign relations 1861–1895*. London, 1974.

Mutua, Rosalind W. *Development of education in Kenya, 1846–1963*.

Mveng, Engelbert. *Histoire du Cameroun*. Paris, 1963.

Mwakabana, Hance. *The life and work of the Lutheran Church in urban Tanzania with special reference to Iringa*. Helsinki, 1982.

Myers, John Brown (ed.), *The centenary volume of the Baptist Missionary Society 1792–1892*. London, 1892.

Myklebust, Olav Guttorm. *H. P. S. Schreuder: kirke og misjon*. Oslo, 1980.

N'Deko, G. *Le kundu ou kindoki dans la société Lari*. Brazzaville, 1976.

Nagapen, Amédée. *L'Eglise à Maurice, 1810–1841*. Port Louis, 1984.

The Indo-Christian community in Mauritius. Port Louis, 1984.

Nair, Kannan K. *Politics and society in south eastern Nigeria, 1841–1906*. London, 1972.

Nasimiyu-Wasike, A. and Waruta, D. W. (eds.) *Mission in African Christianity: critical essays in missiology*. Nairobi, 1993.

Nassau, R. H. *Corisco days: the first thirty years of the West African mission*. Philadelphia, 1910.

National Catholic Welfare Conference. *African women speak: regional seminar of world union of Catholic women's organizations, Lomé, Togo, July 1958*. New York, 1960.

Ndiokwere, Nathaniel I. *Prophecy and revolution: the role of prophets in the Independent African Churches and in biblical tradition*. London, 1981.

Nduka, O. *Western education and the Nigerian cultural background*. Ibadan, 1964.

Neckebrouck, V. *Le Onzième Commandement: étiologie d'une église indépendante au pied du mont Kenya*. Immensee, 1978.

Negash, Tekeste. *Italian colonialism in Eritrea, 1882–1941: policies, praxis and impact*. Uppsala, 1987.

Neill, Stephen. *A history of Christian missions*. Harmondsworth, 1964.

Colonialism and Christian mission. London, 1966.

Nemer, Lawrence. *Anglican and Roman Catholic attitudes on missions: an historical study of two English missionary societies in the late nineteenth century (1865–1885)*. Steyl, 1981.

Neves, A. F. Santos. *Liturgia, Christianismo e sociedade em Angola*. Angola, 1968.

Newitt, M. D. *Portuguese settlement on the Zambezi*. London, 1973.

Newitt, Malyn. *A history of Mozambique*. London, 1995.

Ngcongco, L. D. *The career of Kgosi Gaseitswe of the Bangwaketse: a re-assessment*. 1977.

Ngongo, Louis. *Histoire des forces religieuses au Cameroun: de la Première Guerre Mondiale à l'independance (1916–1955)*. Paris, 1982.

Ngwoke, Ikem Bu Chukwu B. *Religion and religious liberty in Nigeria law (from the colonial days to 1983)*. Published doctoral thesis. Rome: Pontificia Università Lateranense, 1984.

Nicod, H. *Conquérants du Golfe de Guinée*. Lausanne, 1947.

Nicolson, Jean. *John Boyana Radasi: missionary to Zimbabwe*. Glasgow, 1996.

Niesel, Hans-Joachim. 'Kolonialverwaltung und Missionen in Deutsch Ostafrika 1890–1914', Ph.D. thesis, Free University of Berlin, 1971.

Nissen, Margaret. *An African Church is born: the story of the Adamawa and central Sardauna provinces in Nigeria*. Dashen, 1968.

Niwagila, Wilson B. *From the catacomb to a self-governing Church: a case study of the African initiative and the participation of the foreign missions in the mission history of the North-Western Diocese of the Evangelical Lutheran Church in Tanzania, 1890–1965*. Hamburg, 1988.

Njoku, Rose Adaure. *The advent of the Catholic Church in Nigeria: its growth in Owerri Diocese*. Owerri, 1980.

Nkulu Butombe, J. I. *La question du Zaïre et ses répercussions sur les juridictions ecclésiastiques (1865–1888)*. Kinshasa, 1982.

Nkwi, Paul Nchoji. *The Catholic Church in Kom: its foundation and growth, 1913–1977*. Yaoundé, 1977.

Nnabuife, Frederick Chukwudimma. *The history of the Catholic Church in Eastern Nigeria: the foundation period 1885–1905*. Published doctoral thesis. Rome: Pontificiae Universitatis Gregorianae, 1983.

Nock, Arthur Darby. *Conversion: the old and the new in religion from Alexander the Great to Augustine of Hippo*. 1993. Reprinted, London, 1963.

Nogueira, D. E. *Missão em Moçambique*. Vila Gabral, 1970.

Nolan, Francis. *Mission to the great lakes: the White Fathers in western Tanzania 1878–1978*. Tabora, 1978.

Norberg, Viveca Halldin. *Swedes in Haile Selassie's Ethiopia, 1924–1952: a study in early development co-operation*. Uppsala, 1977.

Northcott, Cecil. *Christianity in Africa*. London, 1963.

David Livingstone: his triumph, decline and fall. Guildford and London, 1973.

Robert Moffat: pioneer in Africa, 1817–1870. London, 1961.

Northcott, W. C. *Glorious company: one hundred and fifty years life and work of the London Missionary Society, 1795–1945*. London, 1945.

Nozière, A. *Algérie: les chrétiens dans la guerre*. Paris, 1979.

Nsumbu, Josef. *Culte et société: le culte Chrétien comme réflexion critique d'une société moderne africaine: cas du chant dans la Communauté Evangélique du Zaïre*. Uppsala, 1995.

Nthamburi, Zablon (ed.) *From mission to Church: a handbook of Christianity in East Africa*. Nairobi, 1991.

Nwoga, Donatus Ibe. *The Supreme God as stranger in Igbo religious thought*. Ahiazu Mbaise, 1984.

Nyansako-ni-Nku (ed.) *Journey in faith: the story of the Presbyterian Church in Cameroon*. Yaoundé, 1982.

Nyaundi, Nehemiah M. *Religion and social change: a sociological study of Seventh-day Adventism in Kenya*. Lund and Bromley, 1993.

Nzunda, Matembo S. and Ross, Kenneth R. (eds.) *Church, law and political transition in Malawi 1992–1994*. Gweru, 1995.

O'Donnell, John D. *Lavigerie in Tunisia: the interplay of imperialist and missionary*. Athens, Ga., 1979.

O'Hanlon, Douglas. *Features of the Abyssinian Church*. London, 1946.

O'Hara, Gerard. *Father Joseph Gerard, Oblate of Mary Immaculate*. Dublin, n.d.

O'Keefe, M. *One hundred villages: a study of Church medical work in Zambia today*. Lusaka, 1976.

O'Leary, D. E. *The Ethiopian Church*. London, 1936.

O'Meara, John. *The young Augustine*. Reprinted, London, 1980.

O'Neill, Patrick. *The Catholic faith in Ibadan Diocese, 1884–1974*. Ibadan, 1981.

O'Shea, Michael. *Missionaries and miners: a history of the beginnings of the Catholic Church in Zambia with particular reference to the Copperbelt*. Ndola, 1986.

O'Sullivan, O. *Zambezi mission: a history of the Capuchins in Zambia 1931–1981*. Lusaka, 1981.

Obafemi, Olu. *Pastor S. B. J. Oshoffa: God's 20th century gift to Africa*. Lagos, 1986.

Obeng, Pashington. *Asante Catholicism: religious and cultural reproduction among the Akan of Ghana*. Leiden, 1996.

Obi, C, A. *A hundred years of the Catholic Church in Eastern Nigeria*. Onitsha, 1985.

Obiechina, Emmanuel. *An African popular literature: a study of Onitsha market pamphlets*. Cambridge, 1973.

Odamtten, S. K. *The missionary factor in Ghana's development (1820–1880)*. Accra, 1978.

Odjidja, E. M. L. *Mustard seed: the growth of the Church in Kroboland*. Accra, 1973.

Oduyoye, Mercy Amba and Kanyoro, Musimbi (eds.) *The will to arise: women, tradition, and the Church in Africa*. New York, 1992.

Oduyoye, Modupe. *The planting of Christianity in Yorubaland*. Ibadan, n.d.

Oehler, W. *Geschichter der deutschen evangelischen Mission*. 2 vols. Baden-Baden, 1949–51.

Oeuvres Pontificales Missionnaires. *L'Eglise au Congo et au Ruanda-Urundi*. Edit. J. de Trannoy and others. Brussels, 1950.

Office International de l'Enseignement Catholique – Secretariat Regional pour l'Afrique et Madagascar. *L'enseignement catholique au service de l'Afrique: rapport de la conference panafricaine de l'enseignement catholique*. Belgium, 1966.

Ofori, Patrick E. *Black African traditional religions and philosophy: a select bibliographic survey of the sources from the earliest times to 1974*. Nendeln, 1975.

Ofosu-Appiah, L. H. *The life of Dr. J. E. K. Aggrey*. Accra, 1975.

Oger, J. M. *Where it all began*. Rome, 1991.

Ogot, B. A. and Kieran, J. A. (eds.) *Zamani: a survey of East African history*. Nairobi, 1968.

Oguntade, Joseph Oladipo. *Canon Josiah Jesse Ransome-Kuti (a short biography)*. Abeokuta, 1986.

Ohadike, Don C. *The Ekumeku movement: Western Igbo resistance to the British conquest of Nigeria, 1883–1914*. Athens, Ohio, 1991.

Okafor, Gabriel Maduka. *Christians and Muslims in Cameroon*. Würzburg and Altenberge, 1994.

Okafor-Omali, Dilim. *A Nigerian villager in two worlds*. London, 1965.

Okongwu, J. N. *History of education in Nigeria 1842–1942*. New York, 1946.

Okorocha, Cyril Chukwunonyerem. *The meaning of religious conversion in Africa: the case of the Igbo of Nigeria*. Aldershot, 1987.

Okullu, Henry. *Church and politics in East Africa*. Nairobi, 1975.

Church and marriage in East Africa. Nairobi, 1976.

Oliver, Roland and Mathew, Gervase (eds.) *History of East Africa*, vol. I. Oxford, 1963.

Oliver, Roland. *The missionary factor in East Africa*. London, 1952.

Olson, Gilbert W. *Church growth in Sierra Leone: a study of Church growth in Africa's oldest Protestant mission field*. Grand Rapids, 1969.

Olupona, Jacob K. (ed.) *Religion and peace in multi-faith Nigeria*. Ile-Ife, 1992.

Olusola, J. A. *Baba Mellor: frontline missionary in Nigeria*. Ibadan, 1973.

Omari, C. K. (ed.) *Essays on Church and society in Tanzania*. Arusha, 1976.

Omenka, Nicholas I. *The school in the service of evangelization: the Catholic educational impact in Eastern Nigeria 1886–1950*. Leiden and New York, 1989.

Omoyajowo, Akinyele J. *Cherubim and Seraphim: the history of an African Independent Church*. New York, London, Lagos and Enugu, 1982.

Diversity in unity: the development and expansion of the Cherubim and Seraphim Church in Nigeria. Lanham, New York and London, 1984.

(ed.) *Makers of the Church in Nigeria 1842–1947*. Lagos, 1995.

Onyehalu, Michael C. *Governments, Christianity and maskers: encounters in Eastern Nigeria*. Published doctoral thesis. Rome: Pontificia Università Lateranense, 1987.

Oosthuizen, Gerhardus C. *Moving to the waters: fifty years of Pentecostal revival in Bethesda, 1925–1975*. Durban, 1975.

Pentecostal penetration into the Indian community in metropolitan Durban, South Africa. Durban, 1975.

The healer-prophet in Afro-Christian Churches. Leiden and New York, 1992.

Oosthuizen, G. C., Edwards, S. D., Wessels, W. H. & Hexham, I. (eds.) *Afro-Christian religion and healing in Southern Africa*. Lewiston, 1989.

Oosthuizen, G. C. and Hexham, Irving (eds.) *Afro-Christian religion at the grassroots in Southern Africa*. Lewiston, 1991.

Orchard, Ronald K. *The High Commission Territories of Southern Africa*. London, 1951.

Osborn, H. H. *Fire in the hills*. Crowborough, 1991.

Oshatoba, Seth A. *SIM and ECWA in Nigeria: the story of the beginnings*. Ilorin, 1985.

Ozigi, Albert and Ocho, Lawrence. *Education in Northern Nigeria*. London, 1981.

Pachai, Bridglal (ed.) *Livingstone, man of Africa: memorial essays 1873–1973*. London, 1973.

Pachai, Bridglal. *Malawi: the history of the nation*. London, 1973.

Padwick, C. E. *Mackay of the great lake*. London, 1920.

Temple Gairdner of Cairo. London, 1929.

Palmaer, G. *Mästaren på Kongos stigar: från Svenska missionsförbundets arbete i Kongo åren 1881–1941*. Stockholm, 1941.

Parrinder, Geoffrey. *Religion in an African city*. London, 1953.

Parsons, Robert T. *The Churches and Ghana society 1918–1955: a survey of the work of three Protestant mission societies and the African Churches which they established in their assistance to societary development*. Leiden, 1963.

Pascoe, C. F. *Two hundred years of the SPG: an historical account of the Society for the Propagation of the Gospel in Foreign Parts, 1701–1900*. London, 1901.

Paternot, Marcel . *Lumière sur la Haute-Volta*. Lyon, 1946.

Patterson, K. David. *The northern Gabon coast to 1875*. London, 1975.

Paul, D. (ed.) *Die Leipziger Mission, daheim und draussen*. Leipzig, 1914

Paul, John. *Mozambique: memoirs of a revolution*. Harmondsworth, 1975.

Pauw, B. A. *Religion in a Tswana chiefdom*. London, 1960.

Christianity and Xhosa tradition: belief and ritual among Xhosa-speaking Christians. Cape Town and London, 1975.

Peaden, W. R. *Missionary attitudes to Shona culture, 1890–1923*. Salisbury, 1970.

Pearson, Birger A. and Goehring, James E. (eds.) *The roots of Egyptian Christianity*. Philadelphia, 1986.

Pedersen, K. *The history of the Ethiopian community in the Holy Land from the time of Emperor Tewodros II till 1974*. Israel, 1983.

Pedraza, Howard J. *Borrioboola-Gha: the story of Lokoja the first British settlement in Nigeria*. London, 1960.

Peel, J. D. Y. *Aladura: a religious movement among the Yoruba*. London, 1968.

Ijesha and Nigerians: the incorporation of a Yoruba kingdom, 1890s–1970s. Cambridge, 1983.

Pegard, Odette P. *Les Bissas du cercle de Garango à travers deux colonisations*. Paris, 1963.

Peires, J. B. *The house of Phalo: a history of the Xhosa people in the days of their independence*. Berkeley, Los Angeles and London, 1981.

The dead will arise: Nongqawuse and the great Xhosa cattle-killing movement of 1856–7. Johannesburg and London, 1989.

Pélissier, René. *Résistance et révoltes en Angola (1845–1961)*. 3 vols. Paris, 1976.

Perraudin, J. *Naissance d'une église: histoire du Burundi chrétien*. Usumbura, 1963.

Perrier, André. *Gabon, un reveil religieux, 1935–37*. Paris, 1988.

Perrin, Joseph. *Prêtre blanc en Afrique noire*. Paris, 1980.

Perrot, Claude H. *Les Sotho et les missionnaires européens au XIXe siècle*. Abidjan, 1970.

Peterson, John. *Province of freedom: a history of Sierra Leone 1787–1870*. London, 1969.

Pettifer, Julian and Bradley, Richard. *Missionaries*. London, 1990.

Pfann, Helene. *A short history of the Catholic Church in Ghana*. Cape Coast, 1965.

Philippe, A. *Missions des Pères Blancs en Tunisie, Algérie, Kabylie, Sahara*. Paris, 1931.

Phillips, Clifton Jackson. *Protestant America and the pagan world: the first half century of the American Board of Commissioners for Foreign Missions, 1810–1860*. Cambridge, Mass, 1969.

Philp, Horace R. A. *A new day in Kenya*. London, 1936.

Piault, Colette (ed.) *Prophétisme et thérapeutique: Albert Atcho et la communauté de Bregbo*. Paris, 1975.

Pigafetta, F. *A report of the Kingdom of Congo*. 1591. English trans. M Hutchinson. Reprinted, London, 1970.

Pirotte, Jean. *Périodiques missionnaires belges d'expression française reflets de cinquante années d'évolution d'une mentalité 1889–1940*. Louvain, 1973.

Pirouet, M. Louise *Black evangelists: the spread of Christianity in Uganda 1891–1914*. London, 1978.

Platt, William J. *An African prophet: the Ivory Coast movement and what came of it*. London, 1934.

Plessis, J. C. du. *A history of Christian missions in South Africa*. London, 1911.

Pobee, John S. *Kwame Nkrumah and the Church in Ghana 1949–1966*. Accra, 1988.

Religion and politics in Ghana. Accra, 1991.

(ed.) *Religion in a pluralistic society: essays presented to Professor C. G. Baëta*. Leiden, 1976.

Pobee, John S. and Kudadjie, J. N. (eds.) *Theological education in Africa: quo vadimus?* Geneva and Accra, 1990.

Pons, A. *La nouvelle Eglise d'Afrique ou le catholicisme en Algérie, en Tunisie et au Maroc depuis 1830*. Tunis, 1930.

Porter, Arthur T. *Creoledom: a study of the development of Freetown society*. London, 1963.

Prestige, G. L. *God in patristic thought*. 2nd edn, London, 1952.

Prickett, B. *Island base: a history of the Methodist Church in the Gambia, 1821–1969*. Bo, 1969.

Prins, Gwyn. *The hidden hippopotamus: reappraisal in African history: the early colonial experience in western Zambia*. Cambridge, 1980.

Prior, Andrew (ed.) *Catholics in apartheid society*. Cape Town and London, 1982.

Pritchard, Elizabeth. *For such a time as this: God's faithfulness through the Regions Beyond Missionary Union*. Eastbourne, 1973.

Pujadas, T. L. *La Iglesia en la Guinea Ecuatorial*. Madrid, 1968.

Ragsdale, John P. *Protestant mission education in Zambia 1880–1954*. London, 1986.

Raison-Jourde, Françoise. *Bible et pouvoir à Madagascar au XIXe siècle: invention d'une identité chrétienne et construction de l'État (1780–1880)*. Paris, 1991.

(ed.) *Les souverains de Madagascar: l'histoire royale et ses résurgences contemporaines*. Paris, 1983.

Ralaimihoatra, Edouard. *Histoire de Madagascar*. 2 vols., Tananarive, 1965–6.

Randall, M. W. *Profile for victory: new proposals for missions in Zambia*. South Pasadena, 1970.

Randles, W. G. L. *L'Ancien Royaume du Congo, des origines à la fin du XIXe siècle*. Paris, 1968.

The empire of Monomotapa from the fifteenth to the nineteenth century. Gwelo, 1981.

Randolph, B. W. *Arthur Douglas, missionary on Lake Nyasa: the story of his life*. London, 1912.

Ranger, Terence O. *State and Church in Southern Rhodesia, 1919–1939*. Salisbury, 1961.

Revolt in Southern Rhodesia 1896–7: a study in African resistance. London, 1967.

The African Churches of Tanzania. Nairobi, 1968.

The African voice in Southern Rhodesia 1898–1930. London and Nairobi, 1970.

Are we not also men? The Samkange family and African politics in Zimbabwe 1920–64. London, 1995.

Ransford, Oliver. *David Livingstone: the dark interior*. London, 1978.

Raponda-walker, A. and Sillans, R. *Rites et croyances des peuples du Gabon: essai sur les pratiques religieuses d'autrefois et d'aujourd'hui*. Paris, 1962.

Rasmussen, Ane Marie Bak. *A history of the Quaker movement in Africa*. London, 1995.

Rasmussen, Lissi. *Christian–Muslim relations in Africa: the cases of Northern Nigeria and Tanzania compared*. London, 1993.

Raven, Susan. *Rome in Africa*. 3rd edn, London and New York, 1993.

Ravenstein, Paul de Meester de. *L'Eglise d'Afrique hier et aujourd'hui*. Paris, 1980.

Raymaekers P. and Desroche, Henri. *L'administration et le sacré*. Brussels, 1983.

Rea, Kathleen. *The best is yet to be: fifty years in Zimbabwe with Fred and Kathleen Rea*. Harare, 1993.

Rea, W. *The economics of the Zambezi missions 1580–1759*. Rome, 1976.

Redkey, Edwin S. *Black exodus: Black nationalism and back-to-Africa movements, 1890–1910*. New Haven, 1969.

Reeck, Darrell. *Deep Mende: religious interaction in a changing African rural society*. Leiden, 1976.

Reeves, R. A. *Calvary now*. London, 1965.

Rego, A. De Silva and Santos, E. dos. *Atlas missionario português*. Lisbon, 1964.

Rego, A. De Silva. *Les missions Portugaises: aperçu général*. Lisbon, 1958.

Portuguese colonialism in the sixteenth century. Johannesburg, 1959.

Rein-Wuhrmann, Anna. *Fumban: die Stadt auf dem Schutte: Arbeit und Ernte im Missions dienst in Kamerun*. Basel, 1948.

Renault, François. *Cardinal Lavigerie: churchman, prophet and missionary*. Trans. John O'Donohue. London and Atlantic Highlands, 1994.

Renouard, G. *L'Ouest africain et les missions catholiques Congo et Oubangui*. Paris, 1956.

Repetici, P. *L'Algérie chrétienne, esquisse historique (1830–1930)*. Alger, 1930.

Richard, Jean-Louis. *L'experience de la conversion chez les Basotho*. Rome, 1977.

Richards, Elizabeth. *Fifty years in Nyanza 1906–1956: the history of the CMS and the Anglican Church in Nyanza province, Kenya*. Maseno, 1956.

Richardson, Kenneth. *Freedom in Congo*. London, 1962.

Garden of miracles: a history of the African Inland Mission. London and Eastbourne, 1968.

Richter, Julius. *Geschichte der evangelischen Mission in Africa*. Gütersloh, 1922.

Geschichte der Berliner Missiongesellschaft 1824–1924. Berlin, 1924.

Tanganyika and its future. London, 1934.

Riley, Grace. *No drums at dawn: a biography of the Reverend Canon A. B. H. Riley, pioneer missionary in the Sudan*. Melbourne, 1972.

Ripken, Peter (ed.) *Die Kirche in Mosambik heute: Zwischen Kolonialismus und Revolution*. Bonn, 1981.

Roberts, Andrew. *A history of the Bemba: political growth and change in north-eastern Zambia before 1900*. London, 1973.

A history of Zambia. London, 1976.

Roberts, George Arthur. *Let me tell you a story*. Bulawayo, 1964.

Roche, A. *'Clartés Australes': Joséph Gérard, OMI: le 'prêtre bien-aimé des Basotho', 1831–1914*. Lyon, 1951.

Rodney, Walter. *How Europe underdeveloped Africa*. London, 1972.

Roe, James M. *A history of the British and Foreign Bible Society 1905–1954*. London, 1965.

Roeykens Auguste (ed.) *La politique religieuse de l'état indépendant du Congo: documents: Léopold II, le saint-Siège et les Missions catholiques dan l'Afrique Equatoriale (1876–1885)*. Brussels, 1965.

Roman Catholic Mission, Swaziland. *Fifty years of missionary work, 1914–1964*. Mbabane, 1964.

Rondelez, V. *Scheut Congrégation Missionaire: ses origines – ses débuts*. Brussels, 1960.

Roome, W. J. *A great emancipation: a missionary survey of Nyasaland, Central Africa*. London, 1926.

Roques, L. *Le pionnier du Gabon: Jean-Rémi Bessieux*. Paris, 1971.

Roscoe, John. *Twenty-five years in East Africa*. Cambridge, 1921.

Ross, Andrew. *John Philip (1775–1851): missions, race and politics in South Africa*. Aberdeen, 1986.

Ross, Robert. *Adam Kok's Griquas: a study in the development of stratification in South Africa*. Cambridge, 1976.

Cape of torments: slavery and resistance in South Africa. London and Boston, 1983.

Rotberg, Robert I. *Christian missionaries and the creation of Northern Rhodesia 1880–1924*. Princeton, 1965.

Rousseau, Philip. *Ascetics, authority, and the Church in the age of Jerome and Cassian*. Oxford, 1978.

Pachomius: the making of a community in fourth-century Egypt. Berkeley, 1985.

Roux, André. *L'Evangile dans la forêt: naissance d'une Eglise en Afrique noire*. Paris, 1971.

Rowdon, Harold H. (ed.) *The Brethren contribution to the worldwide mission of the Church: International Brethren conference on missions held at the Anglo-Chinese School, Singapore, 9–15 June 1993*. Carlisle, 1994.

Rowe, John A. *Revolution in Buganda, 1885–1900*. Madison, 1966.

Rubenson, Samuel. *The letters of St Antony: Origenist theology, monastic tradition and the making of a saint*. Lund, 1990.

Rubenson, Sven. *The survival of Ethiopian independence*. London, Stockholm and Addis Ababa, 1976.

(ed.) *Proceedings of the seventh international conference of Ethiopian studies*. Addis Ababa, Uppsala and East Lancing, 1984.

Rubingh, Eugene. *Sons of Tiv: a study of the rise of the Church among the Tiv of central Nigeria*. Grand Rapids, 1969.

Rudin, Harry R. *Germans in the Cameroons: a case study in modern imperialism* New Haven, 1938.

Ruggieri, G. (ed.) *Eglise et histoire de l'Église en Afrique*. Paris, 1988.

Russell, Dorothea. *Medieval Cairo and the monasteries of Wadi Natrun*. London, 1962.

Russell, J. K. *Men without God? A study of the impact of the Christian message in the north of Uganda*. London, 1966.

Russell, Stanley Farrant. *Full fifty years: The BCMS story*. London: Patmos Press, 1972.

Rutayisire, Paul. *La christianisation du Rwanda (1900–1945): méthode missionnaire et politique selon Mgr Léon Classe*. Fribourg, 1987.

Ryan, Colleen. *Beyers Naudé: pilgrimage of faith*. Cape Town, Grand Rapids and Trenton, 1990.

Ryder, Alan F. C. *Benin and the Europeans 1485–1897*. London, 1969.

Saayman, Willem. *Christian mission in South Africa: political and ecumenical*. Pretoria, 1991.

Sachs, William L. *The transformation of Anglicanism: from State Church to global communion*. Cambridge, 1993.

Sæverås, Olav. *On Church-mission relations in Ethiopia 1944–1969 with special reference to the Evangelical Church Mekane Yesus and the Lutheran missions*. Oslo, 1974.

Sahlberg, Carl-Erik. *From Krapf to Rugambwa – a Church history of Tanzania*. Nairobi, 1986.

Sales, Jane M. *The planting of the Churches in South Africa*. Grand Rapids, 1971.

Mission stations and coloured communities of the eastern Cape 1800–1852. Cape Town and Rotterdam, 1975.

Salvadorini, Vittorio. *Le missioni a Benin e Warri nel* XVII *secolo*. Pisa, 1972.

Samuels, Michael A. *Education in Angola, 1878–1914: a history of culture transfer and administration*. New York, 1970.

Sanders, Peter. *Moshoeshoe: chief of the Sotho*. London, 1975.

Sanderson, Lilian Passmore and Sanderson, Neville. *Education, religion and politics in Southern Sudan 1899–1964*. London and Khartoum, 1981.

Sandgren, David P. *Christianity and the Kikuyu: religious divisions and social conflict*. New York, 1989.

Sangaré, Luc. *Paroles de nouvel an: témoignages de l'Eglise Catholique Malienne*. Bamako, 1988.

Sangree, Walter. *Age, prayer and politics in Tiriki, Kenya*. London, 1966.

Sanneh, Lamin. *West African Christianity: the religious impact*. London, 1983.

Sanson, Henri. *Christianisme au miroir de l'Islam: essai sur la rencontre des cultres en Algérie*. Paris, 1984.

Santi, Paul and Hill, Richard. *The Europeans in the Sudan, 1834–1878*. Oxford, 1980.

Santos, E. dos. *Religiões de Angola*. Lisbon, 1969.

Saumagne, Charles. *Saint Cyprien: Évêque de Carthage, 'Pape' d'Afrique (248–258): contribution à l'étude des 'persécutions' de Dèce et de Valérien*. Paris, 1975.

Saunders, A. C. de C. M. *A social history of Black slaves and freedmen in Portugal 1441–1555*. Cambridge, 1983.

Scanlon, David G. *Traditions of African education*. New York, 1964.

(ed.) *Church, State, and education in Africa*. New York, 1966.

Scarin, Antonio. *Chiesa locale incarnazione e missione: il principio di incarnazione nella evangelizzazione secondo il pensiero dell'episcopato Africano*. Bologna, 1981.

Schaaf, Ype. *On their way rejoicing: the history and role of the Bible in Africa*. Carlisle and Nairobi, 1994.

Schapera, I. (ed.) *David Livingstone: family letters 1841–1856*. 2 vols. London, 1959.

Livingstone's private journals 1851–1853. London, 1960.

Livingstone's missionary correspondence 1841–1856. London, 1961.

Livingstone's African journal 1853–1856. 2 vols. London, 1963.

Tribal innovators, Tswana chiefs and social change, 1875–1940. London, 1970.

David Livingstone: South African papers 1849–1853. Cape Town, 1974.

Schebesta, Paul. *Portugals Konquistamission in Südost-Afrika: Missionsgeschichte Sambesiens und des Monomotapareiches (1560–1920)*. Steyl, 1966.

Schick, Erick. *Vorboten und Bahnbtecher: Grundzüge der Evangelischen Missionsgeschichte bis zu den Anfängen der Basler Mission*. Basel, 1943.

Schimlek, Francis. *Mariannhill:a study in Bantu life and missionary effort*. Mariannhill, 1953.

Schlatter, W. *Geschichte der Basler Mission 1815–1915*. 3 vols., Basel, 1916.

Schlosser, Katesa. *Eingeborenenkirchen in Süd- und Südwestafrika, ihre Geschichte und Sozialstruktur*. Kiel, 1958.

Schlunk, Martin. *Die Norddeutsche Mission in Togo*. 2 vols. Bremen, 1910–12.

Schoeman, Karel (ed.) *The Wesleyan Mission in the Orange Free State, 1833–1854: as described in contemporary accounts*. Cape Town, 1991.

Schoffeleers, J. M. (ed.) *Guardians of the land: essays on central African territorial cults*. Gwelo, 1978.

River of blood: the genesis of a martyr cult in southern Malawi, c. AD 1600. Madison and London: University of Wisconsin, 1992.

Schulze, Adolf and Müller, Karl. *200 Jahre Brüdermission*. 2 vols. Herrnhut, 1932.

Scott, H. E. *A saint in Kenya: a life of Marion Scott Stevenson*. London, 1932.

Scott, Michael. *A time to speak*. London, 1958.

Sellassie, Sergew Hable. *Ancient and medieval Ethiopian history to 1270*. Addis Ababa, 1972.

Sellassie, Sergew Hable *et al*. *The Church of Ethiopia: a panorama of history and spiritual life*. Addis Ababa, 1970.

Setiloane, Gabriel. *The image of God among the Sotho-Tswana*. Rotterdam, 1976.

African theology, an introduction (1986)

Shaloff, Stanley. *Reform in Leopold's Congo*. Richmond, Va., 1970.

Shank, David A. *Prophet Harris, the 'Black Elijah' of West Africa*. Abr. by Jocelyn Murray. Leiden, 1994.

(ed.) *Ministry of missions to African Independent Churches*. Elkhart, 1987.

Shaw, Mabel. *God's candlelights: an educational venture in Northern Rhodesia*. London, 1941.
Shejavali, A. *The Ovambo-Kavango Church*. Helsinki, 1970.
Shenk, David. *Mennonite safari*. Scottdale, Pa., 1971.
Shenk, Wilbert R. *Henry Venn – missionary statesman*. New York and Ibadan, 1983.
Shepperson, George (ed.) *David Livingstone and the Rovuma*. Edinburgh, 1965.
Shepperson, George and Price, Thomas. *Independent African: John Chilembwe and the origins, setting and significance of the Nyasaland native rising of 1915*. Edinburgh, 1958.
Shewmaker, S. *Tonga Christianity*. South Pasadena, 1970.
Shick, Tom W. *Behold the promised land: a history of Afro-American settler society in nineteenth century Liberia*. Baltimore, 1980.
Shillito, Edward. *François Coillard: a wayfaring man*. London, 1923.
Shorten, Richard J. *The Legion of Christ's witnesses: change within the Anglican diocese of Zululand 1948–1984*. Cape Town, 1987.
Shorter, Aylward. *Chiefship in western Tanzania: a political history of the Kimbu*. Oxford, 1972.
East African societies. London and Boston, 1974.
The Church in the African city. London, 1991.
Sibree, James. *Fifty years in Madagascar: personal experiences of mission life and work*. London, 1924.
Sicard, Harald von. *Karangafolkets äldsta missionshistoria*. Stockholm, 1943.
Sicard, S. von. *The Lutheran Church on the coast of Tanzania 1887–1914 with special reference to the Evangelical Lutheran Church in Tanzania, synod of Uzaramo-Uluguru*. Lund, 1970.
Sidibe, S. P. M. *La rencontre de Jésus-Christ en milieu Bambara*. Leiden, 1978.
Silbermann, C. *La mission des Pères Blancs en Algérie de ses débuts jusqu'en 1936*. Published doctoral thesis, Rome, 1987.
Sillery, A. *John Mackenzie of Bechuanaland: a study in humanitarian imperialism, 1835–1899*. Cape Town, 1971.
Simensen, Jarle (ed.) *Norwegian missions in African history, vol. 1: South Africa 1845–1906* (Oslo and London, 1986) p. 258.
Simmons, J. *Livingstone and Africa*. London, 1955.
Simpson, Donald. *Dark companions: the African contribution to the European exploration of East Africa*. London, 1975.
Sinda, M. *Le Messianisme congolaise et ses incidences politiques*. Paris, 1972.
Le messianisme congolais et ses incidences politiques: Kimbanguisme, Matsouanisme, autres mouvements. Paris, 1972.
André Matsoua: fondateur du mouvement de liberation du Congo. Paris, 1977.
Sindima, Harvey J. *The legacy of Scottish missionaries in Malawi*. Lewiston, Lampeter and Queenstown, 1992.
Singleton, Michael. *Ethiopia Tikdem – Ethiopia first: the shades of things past and the shape of things to come for Roman Catholic Christianity in southern Ethiopia*. Brussels, 1977.
Siordet, J. E. *Adèle Mabille née Casalis (1840–1923)*. Paris, 1933.
Sivonen, Seppo. *White-collar or hoe handle: African education under British colonial policy 1920–1945*. Helsinki, 1995.
Skelton, Kenneth. *Bishop in Smith's Rhodesia: notes from a turbulent octave 1962–1970*. Gweru and Harare, 1985.
Skinner, Elliott P. *The Mossi of the Upper Volta: the political development of a Sudanese people*. Stanford, 1964.
African urban life: the transformation of Ouagadougou. Princeton, 1974.

Skolaster, Hermann. *Die Pallottiner in Kamerun: 25 Jahre Missionsarbeit*. Limburg, 1924.

Slade, Ruth M. *English-speaking missions in the Congo Independent State (1878–1908)*. Brussels, 1959.

Slageren, Jaap van. *L'Histoire de l'Eglise en Afrique*. Yaoundé, 1969.

Les origines de l'Église Évangélique du Cameroun: missions Européennes et christianisme autochtone. Leiden, 1972.

Smedjebacka, Henrik. *Lutheran Church autonomy in northern Tanzania 1940–1963*. Åbo, 1973.

Smidt, Olav. *Den Lutherske Kirke i Liberia*. Copenhagen, 1980.

Smith, Adrian B. *Interdenominational religious education in Africa: the emergence of common syllabuses*. Leiden and Utrecht, 1982.

Smith, Edgar H. *Tekas Fellowship of Churches: its origin and growth*. Jos, 1969.

Nigerian harvest. Grand Rapids, 1972.

Smith, Edwin W. *The Christian mission in Africa*. London and New York, 1926.

The golden stool. London, 1926.

The way of the white fields in Rhodesia: a survey of Christian enterprise in Northern and Southern Rhodesia. London, 1928.

Aggrey of Africa: a study in Black and White. London, 1929.

African beliefs and Christian faith. London, 1936.

The Mabilles of Basutoland. London, 1939.

The life and times of Daniel Lindley (1801–80): missionary to the Zulus, pastor of the Voortrekkers. London, 1949.

Great Lion of Bechuanaland: the life and times of Roger Price, missionary. London, 1957.

Smith, Gordon, Pachai, Bridglal and Tangri, Rodger (eds.) *Malawi past and present: selected papers from the University of Malawi history conference, 1967*. Blantyre, 1971.

Smith, Herbert. *Fifty years in Congo: Disciples of Christ at the Equator*. Indianapolis, 1949.

Smith, J. Stephen. *The history of the Alliance High School, 1927–1965*. Nairobi, 1973.

Smith, Maynard. *Frank, Bishop of Zanzibar*. London, 1926.

Smith, Noel. *The Presbyterian Church of Ghana, 1835–1960: a younger Church in a changing society*. Accra, 1966.

Smuck, Harold. *Friends in East Africa*. Richmond, Ind., 1987.

Snelson, P. D. *Educational development in Northern Rhodesia 1883–1945*. Lusaka, 1974.

Söderberg, Bertil. *Karl Edvard Laman: missionär, språkforskare, etnograf*. Stockholm, 1985.

Söderlund, Margit. *Pingstmission i Kongo och Ruanda-Urundi*. Stockholm, 1995.

Söderström, Hugo. *God gave growth: the history of the Lutheran Church in Zimbabwe, 1903–1980*. Uppsala, 1984.

Soldati, Gabriele. *The pioneer: the African adventure of Benedict Falda*. Trans. Michael Cunningham. Rome and Slough, 1990. [On the Consolata Fathers.]

Solihin, S. M. *Copts and Muslims in Egypt: a study in harmony and hostility*. Leicester, 1991.

Southon, Arthur E. *Gold Coast Methodism: the first hundred years, 1835–1935*. Cape Coast, 1934.

Spartalis, Peter J. *To the Nile and beyond: the birth and growth of the Sudanese Church of Christ*. Homebush West, 1981.

Karl Kumm: last of the Livingstones: pioneer missionary statesman. Bonn, 1994.

Spitzer, Leo. *The Creoles of Sierra Leone: their responses to colonialism, 1870–1945*. Madison, 1974.

St John, Patricia. *Breath of life: the story of the Ruanda Mission*. London, 1971.

Stakeman, Randolph. *The cultural politics of religious change: a study of the Sanoyea Kpelle in Liberia*. Lewiston, 1986.

Stanley, A. C. *Road to revival: the story of the Ruanda Mission*. London, 1946.

Stanley, Brian. *The Bible and the flag: Protestant missions and British imperialism in the nineteenth and twentieth centuries*. Leicester, 1990.

The history of the Baptist Missionary Society 1792–1992. Edinburgh, 1992.

Staudenraus, P. J. *The African colonization movement, 1816–1865*. New York, 1961.

Steere, Douglas V. *God's irregular: Arthur Shearly Cripps: a Rhodesian epic*. London, 1973.

Steinborn, Erwin. *Die Kirchenzucht in der Geschichte der deutschen evangelischen Mission*. Leipzig, 1928.

Stock, Eugene. *The history of the Church Missionary Society: its environment, its men, and its work*. 4 vols., London, 1899–1916.

Stoecklin, P. *et al. L'Eglise Evangélique du Gabon, 1842–1961*. Alençon, 1962.

Stonelake, Alfred R. *Congo, past and present*. London, 1937.

Storme, Marcel. *Het ontstaan van der Kasai-missie*. Brussels, 1961.

Pater Cambier en de Stichting van de Kasai-Missie. Brussels, 1964.

Stradling, Leslie E. *A bishop on safari*. London, 1960.

Strandes, Justus. *The Portuguese period in East Africa*. Trans. Jean F. Wallwork. Edit. J. S. Kirkman. Reprinted, Nairobi, 1961.

Strassberger, Elfriede J. *The Rhenish Mission Society in South Africa 1830–1950*. Cape Town, 1969.

Strayer, Robert W. *The making of mission communities in East Africa: Anglicans and Africans in colonial Kenya, 1875–1935*. London, 1978.

Stroup, Herbert. *Malawi: a report on the Churches and social development*. New York, 1967.

Stuart, Mary. *Land of promise: a story of the Church in Uganda*. London, 1957.

Stunt, W. T. *et al. Turning the world upside down: a century of missionary endeavour*. 2nd edn, Bath, 1973.

Sundermeier, Theo. *Mission, Bekenntnis und Kirche: Missionstheologische Probleme des 19. Jahrhunderts bei C. H. Hahn*. Wuppertal-Barmen, 1962.

Wir aber suchten Gemeinschaft, Kirchenwerdung und Kirchentrennung in Südwestafrika. Erlangen, 1973.

(ed.) *Church and nationalism in South Africa*. Johannesburg, 1975.

Sundkler, Bengt. *Ung kyrka i Tanganjika*. Stockholm, 1948.

The Christian ministry in Africa. Uppsala, 1960.

Bantu prophets in South Africa. 2nd edn. London, 1961

Zulu Zion and some Swazi Zionists. Lund and London, 1976.

Bara Bukoba: Church and community in Tanzania. London, 1980.

Svenska Kyrkans Missionsstyrelse. *Svenska Kyrkans Mission: sjuttiofem år*. Uppsala, 1949.

Swank, G. O. *Frontier peoples of central Nigeria and a strategy for outreach*. South Pasadena, 1977.

Taiwo, C. O. *Henry Carr: an African contribution to education*. Ibadan, 1975.

Takougang, Joseph. 'Victoria: an African township under British administration, 1916–1961', Ph.D. thesis, University of Illinois at Chicago. Ann Arbor and London: University Microfilms International, 1985.

Tamrat, Taddesse. *Church and state in Ethiopia 1270–1527*. Oxford, 1972.

Tanner, Ralph E. S. *Transition in African beliefs: traditional religion and Christian change – a study in Sukumaland, Tanzania, East Africa*. Maryknoll, 1967.

Tasie, G. O. M. *Christian missionary enterprise in the Niger Delta, 1864–1918*. Leiden, 1978.

Tatford, Fredk. A. *That the world may know, volume 6: light over the dark continent*. Bath, 1984.

Taylor, John V. *Processes of growth in an African Church*. London, 1958.

The growth of the Church in Buganda: an attempt at understanding. London, 1958.

The secret people. London, 1977.

Taylor, John V. and Lehmann, Dorothea. *Christians of the Copperbelt: the growth of the Church in Northern Rhodesia*. London, 1961.

Taylor, Prince A. *The life of my years*. Nashville, 1983.

Taylor, William H. *Mission to educate: a history of the educational work of the Scottish Presbyterian Mission in East Nigeria, 1846–1960*. Leiden, 1996.

Teissier, Henri. *Église en Islam: méditation sur l'existence chrétienne en Algérie*. Paris, 1984.

Temple, *Rain on the earth: scenes of the Church in Northern Rhodesia*. London, 1956.

Temu, A. J. *British Protestant missions*. London, 1972.

Ter Haar, Gerrie. *Faith of our fathers: studies on religious education in sub-Saharan Africa*. Utrecht, 1990.

Tett, Mollie E. *The road to freedom: Sudan United Mission 1904–1968*. Sidcup, n.d.

Teuwissen, Raymond W. 'Robert Hamill Nassau, 1835–1921: Presbyterian pioneer missionary to equatorial West Africa', Th.M. thesis, Louisville Theological Seminary, 1973.

Theal, G. M. *Records of south-eastern Africa*. 9 vols. 1898–1903. Reprinted, Cape Town, 1974.

Thévenoud, Johanny. *Dans la Boucle du Niger*. Namur, 1938.

Thiel, J. F. and Helf, Heinz. *Christliche Kunst in Afrika*. Berlin, 1984.

Thomas, D. G. *Councils in the ecumenical movement, South Africa, 1904–1975*. Johannesburg, 1979.

Thomas, H. B. and Scott, Robert. *Uganda*. London, 1935.

Thomas, W. T. and Faiman, E. B. *Africa and the United Presbyterians*. New York, 1959.

Thompson, H. P. *Into all lands: the history of the Society for the Propagation of the Gospel in Foreign parts 1701–1950*. London, 1951.

Thompson, Jack (ed.) *Into all the world: a history of 150 years of the overseas work of the Presbyterian Church in Ireland*. Belfast, 1990.

Thompson, Leonard M. *Survival in two worlds: Moshoeshoe of Lesotho 1786–1870*. Oxford, 1975.

Thompson, T. Jack. *Livingstonia 1875–1975*. Blantyre, 1975.

Christianity in northern Malawi: Donald Fraser's missionary methods and Ngoni culture. Leiden, 1995.

Thompson, Virginia and Adloff, Richard. *The Malagasy Republic: Madagascar today*. Stanford, 1965.

Thoonen, J. *Black martyrs*. London, 1941.

Thornton, John K. *The Kingdom of Kongo: civil war and transition 1641–1718*. Madison and London, 1983.

Thorogood, Bernard (ed.) *Gales of change: responding to a shifting missionary context: the story of the London Missionary Society 1945–1977*. Geneva, 1994.

Thorpe, Clarence. *Limpopo to Zimbabwe: sixty years of Methodism in Southern Rhodesia*. London, 1951.

Thuku, Harry. *An autobiography*. Nairobi and London, 1970.

Tiberondwa, Ado K. *Missionary teachers as agents of colonialism: a study of their activities in Uganda, 1877–1925*. Lusaka, 1978.

Tilsley, G. E. *Dan Crawford: missionary and pioneer in Central Africa*. London and Edinburgh, 1929.

Todd, John M. *African mission: a historical study of the Society of African Missions*. London, 1962.

Toews, John B. *The Mennonite Brethren Church in Zaïre*. Fresno, Calif., 1978.

Toniolo, Elias and Hill, Richard (eds.) *The opening of the Nile basin: writings by members of the Catholic Mission to Central Africa on the geography and ethnography of the Sudan 1842–1881*. London, 1974.

Tourigny, Yves. *Ancestors in the faith: the story of the first Catholic missionaries in Uganda*. Kisubi, 1974.

So abundant a harvest: the Catholic Church in Uganda 1879–1979. London, 1979.

Tournier, J. *La nouvelle Eglise de l'Afrique: la conquête religieuse de l'Algérie, 1830–1845*. Paris, 1930.

Trimingham, J. S. *The Christian approach to Islam in the Sudan*. London, 1948.

The Christian Church in post war Sudan. London, 1949.

The Christian Church and missions in Ethiopia (including Eritrea and the Somalilands). London, 1950.

Islam in Ethiopia. Oxford, 1952.

Tucker, A. R. *Eighteen years in Uganda and East Africa* 2nd edn, London, 1911.

Tucker, John T. *Angola: the land of the blacksmith prince*. London, 1933.

Tuma, A. D. T. *Building a Ugandan Church: African participation in Church growth and expansion in Busoga, 1891–1940*. Nairobi, 1980.

Tuma, Tom A. D. and Mutibwa, Phares (eds.) *A century of Christianity in Uganda, 1877–1977*. Nairobi, 1978.

Turner, Harold W. *Profile through preaching: a study of the sermon texts used in a West African Independent Church*. World Council of Churches Commission on World Mission and Evangelism research pamphlets, 13. London, 1965.

History of an African Independent Church. 2 vols. Oxford, 1967.

Turner, Jerry Michael. 'Les Bresiliens: the impact of former Brazilian slaves upon Dahomey', Ph.D. thesis, Boston University, 1975. Ann Arbor: University Microfilms, 1974.

Twaddle, Michael. *Kakungulu and the creation of Uganda 1868–1928*. London, Kampala, Nairobi and Athens, Ohio, 1993.

Twagirayesu, Michel and Butselaar, Jan van (eds.) *Ce don que nous avons reçu: histoire de l'Eglise Presbytérienne au Rwanda (1907–1982)*. Kigali, 1982.

Uka, E. M. *Missionaries go home? A sociological interpretation of an African response to Christian missions*. Berne, 1989.

Ullendorff, Edward. *The Ethiopians: an introduction to country and people*. 3rd edn, London, 1973.

Ethiopia and the Bible. 1968. Reprinted, Oxford, 1988.

Underhill, Edward Bean. *Alfred Saker, missionary to Africa: a biography*. 1884. Reprinted, London, 1958.

Uppsala University, Faculty of Theology. *Papers presented at the seminar 'Religion and war in Zimbabwe and Swedish relationships'*. Uppsala and Stockholm, 1992.

Urfer, S. *Socialisme et église en Tanzanie*. Paris, 1975.

Usman, Yusufu Bala. *The manipulation of religion in Nigeria 1977–1987*. Kaduna, 1987.

Ustorf, Werner. *Afrikanische Initiative: Das aktive Leiden des Prophet Simon Kimbangu*. Bern, 1975.

Die Missionsmethode Franz Michael Zahns und der Aufbau Kirchlicher Strukturen in West Afrika (1862–1900): Eine Missionsgeschichtliche Untersuchung. Erlangen, 1989.

(ed.) *Mission im Kontext: Beiträge zur Sozialgeschichte der Norddeutschen Missionsgesellschaft im 19. Jahrhundert*. Bremen, 1986.

Uya, Okon Edet (ed.) *Black brotherhood: Afro-Americans and Africa*. Lexington, 1971.

Uzukwu, E. Elochukwu. *Church and inculturation: a century of Roman Catholicism in Eastern Nigeria*. Uruowulu-Obosi, 1985.

Valentin, Peter. *Völkerkundliche auf Zeichnungen aus dem Notizbuch eines Kamerun-Missionärs 1890–1914*. Basel, 1978.

Van Binsbergen, Wim M. J. *Religious change in Zambia: exploratory studies*. London and Boston, 1981.

Van der Merwe, W. J. *Sendinggenade in Mashonaland*. Cape Town and Pretoria, 1952.

Van Rheenen, G. *Church planting in Uganda: a comparative study*. South Pasadena, 1976.

Vantini, Giovanni. *Christianity in the Sudan*. Bologna, 1981.

Vantini, John. *The excavations at Faras: a contribution to the history of Christian Nubia*. Bologna, 1970.

Veillette-Santerre, D. *Le catholicisme au Nord-Cameroun*. Québec, 1979.

Vernaud, G. *Etablissement d'une mission du plein Evangile au Gabon*. Pesseux, 1957.

Verryn, T. D. *A history of the Order of Ethiopia*. Cleveland, Transvaal, 1972.

Versteijnen, Frits. *The Catholic mission of Bagamoyo*. Bagamoyo, 1968.

Verstraelen, F. J. *An African Church in transition: from missionary dependence to mutuality in mission: a case-study on the Roman Catholic Church in Zambia*. 2 vols. Leiden, 1975.

Verstraelen-Gilhuis, Gerdien. *From Dutch Mission Church to Reformed Church in Zambia: the scope for African leadership and initiative in the history of a Zambian mission Church*. Franeker, 1982.

A new look at Christianity in Africa. Gweru, 1992.

Vezeau, R. *The Apostolic Vicariate of Nyasa: origins and first developments, 1889–1935*. Rome, 1989.

Vidal, Henri. *Le séparation des églises et de l'état à Madagascar (1861–1968)*. Paris, 1970.

Vilaldach, A. de V. *La secta del Bwiti en la Guinea Española*. Madrid, 1958.

Vogelsanger, Cornelia Monica Renate. *Pietismus und afrikanische Kultur an der Goldküste: Die Einstellung der Basler Mission zur Haussklaverei*. Published Ph.D. thesis, Zurich, 1977.

Vogt, John. *Portuguese rule on the Gold Coast 1469–1682*. Athens, Ohio, 1979.

Vos, K. *The church on the hill: St John's Parish, Wynberg*. Cape Town, 1972.

Vries, Johannes Lucas de. *Mission and colonialism in Namibia*. Johannesburg, 1978.

Namibia: Mission und Politik (1880–1918): der Einfluss des Deutschen Kolonialismus auf die Missionsarbeit der Rheinischen Missionsgesellschaft im fruheren Deutsch-Südwestafrika. Neukirchen-Vluyn, 1980.

Wahlström, Per Åke (ed.) *Svenska baptistsamfundets mission i Kongo 1914–1960*. Uppsala, 1966

Wakin, Edward. *A lonely minority: the modern story of Egypt's Copts*. New York, 1963.

Waliggo, J. M. *A history of African priests*. Masaka, Uganda, 1988.

Walker, André Raponda and Sillans, Roger. *Rites et croyances des peuples du Gabon: essai sur les pratiques religieuses d'autrefois et d'aujourd'hui*. Paris, 1962.

Walker, F. Deaville. *Thomas Birch Freeman: the son of an African*. London, 1929.

The romance of the black river: the story of the CMS Nigeria mission. London, 1930.

A hundred years in Nigeria: the story of the Methodist mission 1842–1942. London, 1943.

Walker, James W. St G. *The Black loyalists: the search for a promised land in Nova Scotia and Sierra Leone 1783–1870.* London, 1976.

Walker, Sheila S. *The religious revolution in the Ivory Coast: the Prophet Harris and the Harrist Church.* Chapel Hill, 1983.

Wallis, J. P. R. *The Zambesi expedition of David Livingstone 1858–1863.* 2 vols. London, 1956.

Walls, Andrew F. and Shenk, Wilbert R. K. (eds.) *Exploring new religious movements: essays in honour of Harold W. Turner.* Elkhart, 1990.

Walshe, Peter. *Church versus state in South Africa: the case of the Christian Institute.* London and Maryknoll, 1983.

Walters, C. C. *Christianity in Egypt: a cultural history to 1171 AD.* London, 1978.

Wambutda, Daniel N. *A study of conversion among the Angas of Plateau state of Nigeria with emphasis on Christianity.* Frankfurt am Main, 1991.

Wanyoike, E. N. *An African pastor: the life and work of the Rev. Wanyoike Kamawe, 1888–1970.* Nairobi, 1974.

Ward, W. E. F. *Fraser of Trinity and Achimota.* Accra, 1965.

Wassmann, Dietrich. *Der Durchbruch des Evangeliums im Gallaland: Ereignisse und Erlebnisse nach dem Italienisch-Abessinischen Kriege 1936–1941.* Hermannsburg, 1948.

Watt, Peter. *From Africa's soil: the story of the Assemblies of God in Southern Africa.* Cape Town, 1992.

Watts, C. C. *Dawn in Swaziland.* London, 1922.

Weber, Charles W. *International influences and Baptist mission in West Cameroon: German-American missionary endeavor under international mandate and British colonialism.* Leiden, 1993.

Webster, J. B. *The African Churches among the Yoruba, 1882–1922.* Oxford, 1964.

Welbourn, F. B. *East African rebels: a study of some Independent Churches.* London, 1961.

East African Christian. London, 1965.

Religion and politics in Uganda 1952–1962. Nairobi, 1965.

Welbourn, F. B. and Ogot, B. A. *A place to feel at home: a study of two Independent Churches in western Kenya.* Nairobi, 1966.

Welch, A. W. 'Colonial stepchildren: Catholic and Methodist missionaries in the Ivory Coast, 1845–1939', Ph.D. thesis, University of Birmingham, 1979.

Welch, F. G. *Training for the ministry in East Africa.* Limuru, 1963.

Weller, John and Linden, Jane. *Mainstream Christianity to 1980 in Malawi, Zambia and Zimbabwe.* Gweru and Harare, 1984.

Weller, John C. *The priest from the lakeside: the story of Leonard Kamungu of Malawi and Zambia, 1877–1913.* Blantyre, 1971.

Wendland, E. H. *A history of the Christian Church in Central Africa: the Lutheran Church of Central Africa 1953–1978.* Mequon, Wis., 1980.

Werbner, Richard. *Tears of the dead: the social biography of an African family.* Washington and Edinburgh, 1991.

West, M. *Bishops and prophets in a Black city: African Independent Churches in Soweto.* Johannesburg and Cape Town, 1975.

Westerlund, David. *Ujamaa na dini: a study of some aspects of society and religion in Tanzania, 1961–1977.* Stockholm, 1980.

Westlind, P. A. *Société de la mission suédoise au Congo*. Stockholm, 1982.

Westman, K. B. *et al. Nordisk missionshistoria*. Stockholm, 1949.

Wharton, E. T. *Led in triumph: sixty years of Southern Presbyterian missions in the Belgian Congo*. Nashville, 1952.

Wheeler, W. R. *The words of God in the African forest: the story of an American mission in West Africa*. New York, 1931.

Whetstone, Harold V. *Lutheran mission in Liberia*. Philadelphia, 1955.

White, E. Frances. *Sierra Leone's settler women traders: women on the Afro-European frontier*. Ann Arbor, 1987.

White, Landeg. *Magomero: portrait of an African village*. Cambridge, 1987.

White, W. M. *Friends in Madagascar, 1867–1967*. London, 1967.

Widman, Ragnar. *Trosföreställningar i Nedre Zaïre från 1880–talet*. Stockholm, 1979.

Wiley, Bell. I (ed.) *Slaves no more: letters from Liberia, 1833–1869*. Lexington, 1980.

Wilkinson, Alan. *The Community of the Resurrection: a centenary history*. London, 1992.

Williams, C. Kingsley. *Achimota: the early years, 1924–1948*. Accra and London, 1962.

Williams, Donovan. *Umfundisi, a biography of Tiyo Soga 1829–1871*. Lovedale, 1978.

Williams, Walter L. *Black Americans and the evangelization of Africa 1877–1900*. Madison and London, 1982.

Williamson, Sidney George. *Akan religion and the Christian faith: a comparative study of the impact of two religions*. Edited by Kwesi Dickson. Accra, 1965.

Willis, Roy. *A state in the making: myth, history, and social transformation in pre-colonial Ufipa*. Bloomington, 1981.

Willmott, Helen M. *The doors were opened: the remarkable advance of the Gospel in Ethiopia*. London, n.d.

Wills, David W. and Newman, Richard (eds.) *Black apostles at home and abroad: Afro-Americans and the Christian mission from the revolution to reconstruction*. Boston, Mass, 1982.

Wilson, Ellen Gibson. *John Clarkson and the African adventure*. London, 1980.

Wilson, Francis and Perrot, Dominique (eds.) *Outlook on a century: South Africa 1870–1970*. Bloemfontein, 1973.

Wilson, G. Herbert. *The history of the Universities' Mission to Central Africa*. London, 1936.

Wilson, Louis E. *The Krobo people of Ghana to 1892: a political and social history*. Athens, Ohio, 1991.

Wilson, Monica. *Communal rites of the Nyakyusa*. London, 1959.

For men and elders: change in the relations of generations and of men and women among the Nyakyusa-Ngonde people 1875–1971. New York, 1977.

Wiltgen, Ralph M. *Gold Coast mission history 1471–1880*. Techny, Ill., 1956.

Winninge, Ingrid and Winninge, Carol. *The international Church worker: investigations in Ethiopia*. Uppsala, 1976.

Winter, Colin O'Brien. *Namibia: the story of a Bishop in exile*. Guildford and London, 1977.

Winter, J. C. *Bruno Gutmann 1876–1966: a German approach to social anthropology*. Oxford, 1979.

Wipper, Audrey. *Rural rebels: a study of two protest movements in Kenya*. Nairobi and London, 1977.

Wishlade, R. L. *Sectarianism in southern Nyasaland*. London, 1965

Witschi, Hermann. *Geschichte der Basler Mission 1920–1940*. Basel, 1970.

Witte, C.-M. de. *Les Bulles pontificales et l'expansion portugaise au* XVe *siècle*. Louvain, 1958.

Witte, Jehan de. *Les deux Congo: 25 ans d'apostolat au Congo français*. Paris, 1913.

Monseigneur Augouard archeveque titulaire de Cassiopée, vicaire apostolique du Congo français. Paris, 1924.

Wold, Joseph C. *God's impatience in Liberia*. Grand Rapids, 1968.

Wolfe, E. M. *Beyond the thirst belt: the story of the Ovamboland Mission*. London, 1935.

Wondmagegnehu, Aymro and Motovu, Joachim (eds.) *The Ethiopian Orthodox Church*. Addis Ababa, 1970.

Wood, Joseph. *Methodism in South West Africa*. Rondebosch, 1956.

Wood-Lainé, Paul. *Le missionnaire Freeman et les débuts de la mission protestante au Dahomey-Togo*. Porto Novo, 1942.

Woodall, Ann. *Congo encounter: pages from the diary of Ann Woodall in Congo*. London, 1974.

Worden, Nigel. *Slavery in Dutch South Africa*. Cambridge, 1985.

Wright, Marcia. *German missions in Tanganyika 1891–1941: Lutherans and Moravians in the southern highlands*. Oxford, 1971.

Strategies of slaves and women: life-stories from East/Central Africa. London and New York, 1993.

Wright, Michael. *Buganda in the heroic age*. Nairobi and London, 1971.

Wyllie, Robert W. *Spiritism in Ghana: a study of new religious movements*. Missoula, 1980.

Wyse, Akintola J. G. *The Krio of Sierra Leone: an interpretive history*. London, 1989.

Yates, Walter Ladell. 'The history of the African Methodist Episcopal Zion Church in West Africa, Liberia, Gold Coast (Ghana) and Nigeria, 1900–1939', Ph.D. thesis, Hartford Seminary Foundation, 1967. Ann Arbor: University Microfilms International, 1967.

Youlou, Fulbert. *Le Matsouanisme*. Brazzaville, 1955.

Yrlid, Joel. *Den kristna missionen I Zaïre 1878–1990: utbredning och verksamhet*. Gothenburg, 1993.

Mission och kommunikation: Den kristna missionen och transportnätets utveckling I Belgiska Kongo/Zaïre 1787–1991. Gothenburg, 1994.

Ze-Meka, *L'Instauration du christianisme chez les populations Beti, Boulou, et Fang (1892–1957)*. Paris, 1980.

Zorn, Jean-François. *Une mission protestante à la Belle Epoque: l'action de la Société des missions évangeliques de Paris des origines à 1914*. Paris, 1993.

Zurcher, J. *111 years: Morija printing works*. Morija, 1972.

Zwemer, S. M., Wherry, E. M. and Barton, James L. (eds.) *The Mohammedan world of to-day: being papers read at the First Missionary Conference on behalf of the Mohammedan World held at Cairo April 4th-9th 1906*. New York, 1906.

NAME INDEX

SUBJECT INDEX